America's Top-Rated Cities: A Statistical Handbook

Volume 1

2004
Eleventh Edition

America's
Top-Rated Cities:
A Statistical Handbook

Volume 1: Southern Region

A UNIVERSAL REFERENCE BOOK

Grey House
Publishing

PUBLISHER:	Leslie Mackenzie
EDITORIAL DIRECTOR:	Laura Mars-Proietti
EDITOR:	David Garoogian
PRODUCTION MANAGER:	Karen Stevens
PRODUCTION ASSISTANT:	Alison Import
MARKETING DIRECTOR:	Jessica Moody
CONTRIBUTORS:	Philip Rich, Allison Blake

A Universal Reference Book
Grey House Publishing, Inc.
185 Millerton Road
Millerton, NY 12546
Phone: 518.789.8700 Fax: 518.789.0545
www.greyhouse.com
e-mail: books@greyhouse.com

Eleventh edition
10 9 8 7 6 5 4 3 2
Printed in the USA

Library of Congress Cataloging-in-Publication Data

America's top-rated cities. Vol. I, Southern region : a statistical handbook.. -- 1992 -

  v. : ill. ; cm.
  Annual, 1995-
  Irregular, 1992-1993
  ISSN: 1082-7102

1. Cities and towns--Ratings--Southern States--Statistics--Periodicals. 2. Cities and towns--Southern States--Statistics--Periodicals. 3. Social indicators--Southern States--Periodicals. 4. Quality of life--Southern States--Statistics--Periodicals. 5. Southern States--Social conditions--Statistics--Periodicals. I. Title: America's top rated cities. II. Title: Southern region

HT123.5.S6 A44
307.76/0973/05

95644648

4-Volume Set	ISBN	1-59237-038-1
Volume 1	**ISBN**	**1-59237-039-X**
Volume 2	ISBN	1-59237-040-3
Volume 3	ISBN	1-59237-041-1
Volume 4	ISBN	1-59237-042-X

Atlanta, Georgia

Austin, Texas

Baton Rouge, Louisiana

Birmingham, Alabama

Charleston, South Carolina

Columbia, South Carolina

Chattanooga, Tennessee

Dallas, Texas

El Paso, Texas

Fort Lauderdale, Florida

Fort Worth, Texas

Houston, Texas

Huntsville, Alabama

Jacksonville, Florida

Knoxville, Tennessee

Memphis, Tennessee

Miami, Florida

Nashville, Tennessee

New Orleans, Louisiana

Orlando, Florida

Tampa, Florida

Introduction

Welcome to the eleventh edition of *America's Top-Rated Cities (ATRC)*, a concise, statistical, 4-volume work identifying America's top-rated cities with populations of 100,000 or more. It covers 100 cities that have received high marks for their business and living environment from both long-running surveys, such as those appearing in *Money, Ladies Home Journal, Forbes, Men's Health, Entrepreneur, Conde Nast Traveler,* and *Expansion Management,* as well as first-hand visits, interviews and reports by our editors and research staff.

Each volume covers a different region of the country -- Southern, Western, Central and Eastern. Each includes a detailed Table of Contents, 25 city chapters, and four **Appendices**. Each city chapter incorporates information from hundreds of resources to create three major sections – **Background, Rankings**, and **Statistical Tables.**

NEW FOR 2004

This eleventh edition includes two **new topics – Gross Metropolitan Product (GMP) and House Price Index (HPI).** In addition, we've enhanced several tables, added dozens of new sources in the Rankings section, and updated over 70% of the data in the book. Here is a detailed look at each section:

BACKGROUND

Each of the 100 city chapters begins with an informative, page-long background that combines history with current events. Our revision process updates these narratives to reflect changes that have occurred in the city during the past year. They touch on the city's environment, politics, employment, cultural offerings, and usually include some interesting trivia. Research for this edition uncovered the following facts. Do you know. . . .(answers on next page)

1. What city's mayor has unveiled a program to make his city the nation's fittest?
2. What a funicular is, and who built one to connect its downtown with a newly built museum?
3. Where were the nation's first denim mills established?
4. What is "liquid sunshine" and where does it occur?
5. The name of the winning 9/11 memorial design and its designer?

RANKINGS

This section contains data from over 100 books, articles, and reports, and is presented in an easy-to-read, bulleted format. While most of these listings have been revised to reflect the most recent data, many totally new topics are included, for example: **Most Vegetarian-Friendly. . . Least Stressful . . .** and **Most Literate** are brand new, and added to favorites from last edition, like **America's Healthiest Cities** for People and Pets . . . **Most Creative Cities . . . Picture Perfect Cities . . . Most Fun Cities . . . Safest Cities . . . Most Alive Cities . . . Most Wired Cities . . . Best Cities to Save Money . . . Most Polite Cities . . . Top Arts Cities . . .** and overall **Best Cities** for Black Women, Singles, Men, Lesbians, Children, Sports Fans, Online Shoppers, Tourists, Job Seekers, and Entrepreneurs.

This edition also includes some rankings that are not all that flattering, such as **Fattest Cities . . . Asthma Hot Spots . . .** and **Most Dangerous for Pedestrians.** Top–rated doesn't necessarily mean perfect, and our goal is to provide an accurate portrayal of each featured city.

Sources for these rankings include both well-known magazines and other media, in including *Forbes, Nielson/Net Ratings, Yahoo!, Esquire, CNN/MoneyOnline, Ladies Home Journal, AARP, American Demographics,* and *Travel & Leisure,* as well as resources not as well known, such as *Center for Digital Government, The Wellness Councils of America, Association of Foreign Investors in Real Estate, Plant Sites & Parks,* and *Mercer Human Resources Consulting.*

STATISTICAL TABLES

Each city chapter in *ATRC 2004* includes 81 tables – 47 in the BUSINESS section and 34 in the LIVING section. **Business Environment** includes hard facts and figures on 13 topics, including City Finances, Demographics, Income, Employment, Taxes, Real Estate, and Transportation. **Living Environment** also includes 13 topics, such as Housing, Health Care, Education, Safety, Recreation, Media, and Climate.

To compile the Statistical Tables, our editors have again turned to a wide range of sources, some of which are obvious, such as the *U.S. Census Bureau, U.S. Environmental Protection Agency,* and *FBI* while some are more obscure, like *The Tax Foundation, Society of Industrial and Office Realtors,* and *Glenmary Research Center.*

> *"The only source of its kind . . ."*
>
> ARBA

> *" . . . excellent source to consult for information on relocation of a business or family.*
>
> Library Journal

> *"While this data exists elsewhere. . . Garoogian brings (it) together in one useful, handy source."*
>
> Choice

APPENDICES

Appendix A – Metropolitan Statistical Areas (MSA) and New England County Metropolitan Areas (NECMA): Includes counties that combine to form each city's metro area – defined as a "core area containing a large population nucleus, together with adjacent communities having a high degree of economic and social integration with the core."

Appendix B – Comparative Statistics: City-by-city comparison of 42 categories spread out over 70 tables that is both an overview of the city, and a broad profile of each geographical region of the country. All four volumes include all 100 cities, making for easy comparisons.

Appendix C – Chambers of Commerce and Economic Development Organizations: Addresses, phone numbers and fax numbers of these additional resources helps readers find more detailed information on each city.

Appendix D – State Departments of Labor and Employment: A source for additional, more specific economic and employment data, with address and phone number for easy access.

As in all previous editions, the material provided by public and private agencies and organizations was supplemented by original research, numerous library sources and Internet sites. *America's Top-Rated Cities, 2004,* is designed for a wide range of readers: private individuals considering relocating a residence or business; professionals considering expanding their businesses or changing careers; corporations considering relocation, opening up additional offices or creating new divisions; government agencies; general and market researchers; real estate consultants; human resource personnel; urban planners; investors; and urban government students.

(Answers – 1: Austin, TX; 2: Chattanooga, TN; 3: Durham, NC; 4: sun showers in Honolulu, HI; 5: Reflecting Absence by Michael Arad)

Atlanta, Georgia

Background

When you think of the South, you may imagine antebellum gentility. Atlanta, however, was borne of a rough-and-tumble past: first as a natural outgrowth of a thriving railroad network in the 1840s; and second, as a resilient go-getter that proudly rose again above the rubble of the Civil War.

Blanketed over the rolling hills of the Piedmont Plateau, at the foot of the Blue Ridge Mountains, Georgia's capital stands 1,000 feet above sea level. Atlanta is located in the northwest corner of Georgia where the terrain is rolling to hilly, and slopes downward to the east, west, and south.

Atlanta proper begins at the "terminus," or zero mile mark, of the now defunct Western and Atlantic Railroad Line. However its metropolitan area comprises 28 counties that include Fulton, DeKalb, Clayton and Gwinnet.

Atlanta's diversified economy allows for employment in a variety of sectors such as manufacturing, retail, and government. The city is headquarters to 24 Fortune 1,000 companies, including Cable News Network, Coca-Cola, BellSouth, Georgia-Pacific and Home Depot. In addition, the city is home to the federal Center for Disease Control.

These accomplishments are the result of an involved city government that seeks to work closely with its business community. This may be largely due to a change in its charter in 1974, when greater administrative powers were vested in the mayoral office, and when the city inaugurated its first black mayor.

As middle class residents, both white and black, continue to move to the suburbs separating themselves from Atlanta's old downtown, the city faces the complex issue of where it plans to move as an urban center in light of the conflict between the city and its surroundings.

While schools in the city remain predominantly black and schools in its suburbs predominantly white, Atlanta can still boast of a racially progressive climate. The Martin Luther King, Jr. Historic Site and Preservation District is located in the Sweet Auburn neighborhood, which includes King's birth home and the Ebenezer Baptist Church, where both he and his father preached. The city's consortium of black colleges that includes Morehouse College and the Interdenominational Theological Center testifies to the city's appreciation for a people who have always been one-third of Atlanta's population.

Indeed, King is one of Atlanta's two Nobel Peace Prize winners. Former President Jimmy Carter, famously of Plains, Georgia, also brings his name to Atlanta as namesake to the Carter Center. Devoted to human rights, the center is operated with neighboring Emory University, and sits adjacent to the Jimmy Carter Library and Museum on a hill overlooking the city.

Hatfield-Jackson Atlanta International Airport, the world's busiest passenger airport, is undergoing a significant expansion under its development program.

The Appalachian chain of mountains, the Gulf of Mexico, and the Atlantic Ocean influence Atlanta's climate. Temperatures are moderate throughout the year. Prolonged periods of hot weather are unusual and 100-degree heat is rarely experienced. Atlanta winters are mild with a few, short-lived cold spells. Summers can be humid.

Rankings

- Atlanta was ranked #7 out of 331 metro areas in *Cities Ranked & Rated*. Criteria: cost of living; climate; crime; transportation; economy and jobs; education; arts and culture; health and healthcare; leisure. *Cities Ranked & Rated, 1st Edition, 2004*

- *Ladies Home Journal* ranked America's 200 largest cities based on the qualities women surveyed care about most. Atlanta ranked #34 out of 57 in the big city category (population over 300,000). Criteria: crime; lifestyle; education; jobs; health; child care; politics; and the economy. *Ladies Home Journal Online, "The Best Cities for Women 2002"*

- The Atlanta metro area was selected as one of "America's Best Places to Live and Work 2003" by *Employment Review*. The area ranked #5 out of 20. Criteria: unemployment rate; projected job growth; cost of living; and industry specific data. *Employment Review, www.bestjobsusa.com*

- The Atlanta metro area was selected as one of America's "Best Places to Live and Work" by *Expansion Management* and rated as a "Four-Star Community." The annual "Quality of Life Quotient" measures nearly 50 indicators and compares them among the 329 metropolitan statistical areas in the United States. *Expansion Management, May 2003*

- Atlanta was selected as one of "America's Top Ten Vegetarian-Friendly Cities." The city was ranked #6. Criteria: number of vegetarian restaurants; number of health food stores; number of vegetarian groups. *www.peta.org, February 26, 2004*

- Atlanta was selected as one of "America's Pet Healthiest Cities" by Purina. The city ranked #16 out of 50. Criteria: veterinary services; environment; and legislation. *Purina Pet Institute, "America's Pet Healthiest Cities," August 14, 2001*

- Atlanta was selected as one of the "Best Cities for Black Families." The city ranked #17 out of 20. For six months, bet.com compiled data on African Americans in those U.S. cities with the largest Black populations. The data, for African Americans specifically, involved the following: infant mortality; high school graduation; median income; homeownership; unemployment; business ownership; poverty rates; AIDS infection rates; percentage of children in single parent, typically fatherless, households; teen pregnancy; economic segregation index; violent and property crime. *www.bet.com, October 1, 2002*

- Atlanta appeared on *Black Enterprise's* list of the "Top Ten Cities for African-Americans to Live, Work, and Play." The city was ranked #3, based on responses from 4,239 online survey respondents who ranked 21 quality-of-life factors. *Black Enterprise, July 2001*

- *Forbes* ranked the 40 most populous metro areas in the U.S. in terms of the best places to be single. The Atlanta metro area was ranked #5. Criteria: number of other singles; cost of living alone; nightlife; culture; job growth; coolness. *Forbes, June 5, 2003*

- *Forbes* ranked the 150 most populous metro areas in the U.S. in terms of the "Best Places for Business and Careers." The Atlanta metro area was ranked #4. Criteria: income and job growth; cost-of-doing-business; qualifications of the available pool of labor; crime rates; housing costs; net migration. *Forbes, May 9, 2003*

- Atlanta was selected as one of "America's Healthiest Cities" by *Natural Health* magazine. The city was ranked #4 out of the 50 largest urban areas in the U.S. Twenty-six criteria in the following four categories were examined: whether the city boasts natural offerings; how well the city promotes its resident's physical health; whether the city offers a healthy environment; how well the city fosters a sense of community. *Natural Health, April 2003*

- *Men's Health* ranked 101 U.S. cities in terms of the quality of their tap water. Atlanta received a grade of B. Criteria: levels of bacteria, arsenic, lead, trihalomethanes, and haloacetic acids were compared with the National Academy of Science's guidelines as well as with the EPA's more stringent maximum contaminant level goals. *Men's Health, March 2004*

- Sperling's BestPlaces ranked 331 metro areas and identified the most and least stressful U.S. cities. The Atlanta metro area ranked #43 out of the 100 largest metro areas (#1 = most stressful). Criteria: divorce rate; unemployment rate; violent and property crime; suicide rate; commute time; mental health; alcohol consumption; cloudy days. *www.BestPlaces.net, February 26, 2004*

- Sperling's BestPlaces in partnership with Pep Boys ranked 77 metro areas and identified "America's Most Drivable Cities." The Atlanta metro area ranked #20. Criteria: climate; road roughness; urban mobility; gas prices. *Pep Boys, "America's Most Drivable Cities," April 9, 2003*

- Atlanta was selected as a "Great College Town" by ePodunk. The city ranked #6 in the big city category. ePodunk.com looked at communities with four-year colleges and a total student enrollment of at least 1,500. Communities where the student ratio was too low or too high were ruled out, as were small cities with low rates of owner-occupied housing. Fifteen variables were then applied to assess arts and culture, recreation, intellectual activity, historic preservation, and cost of living. *www.ePodunk.com, April, 2002*

- Atlanta was ranked #158 out of America's 200 largest metro areas in *SELF Magazine's* ranking of "America's Healthiest Cities for Women." Criteria: safety; air/water quality; cancer rates; and 21 other factors relating to health. *SELF Magazine, November 2003*

- Atlanta was identified as one of the most dangerous large metro areas for pedestrians in the U.S. The area ranked #12 out of the nations 49 largest metro areas. Criteria: average yearly pedestrian fatalities per capita (for the years 2000 and 2001) adjusted for the number of walkers. *Surface Transportation Policy Project, "Mean Streets 2002"*

- Atlanta was selected as one of the 25 fattest cities in America by *Men's Fitness Online*. It ranked #7 out of America's 50 largest cities. Criteria: gyms/sporting goods; nutrition; exercise/sports; overweight/sedentary; junk food; alcohol; smoking; television; air and water quality; climate; geography; commute time; parks/open space; recreation facilities; and health care. *Men's Fitness Online, America's Fittest/Fattest Cities 2003*

- Atlanta was ranked #38 out of 100 cities surveyed in *Child* magazine's ranking of the "Best Cities for Families." Criteria: number of pediatricians per capita; proximity to a children's hospital; immunization rates; infant mortality rate; air quality; water quality; school spending; pupil-teacher ratio; availability of parks/green space; nearby recreational opportunities; average commute time; number of sunny days; average cost of a 3-bedroom home; unemployment rate; future job growth; crime rate; percentage of children under 5; mandated minimum child care ratios. *Child, April 2001*

- *Zero Population Growth* ranked 239 cities in terms of children's health, safety, and economic well-being. Atlanta was ranked #25 out of 25 major cities (main city in a metro area with population of greater than 2 million) and was given a grade of C-. Criteria: total population and population growth; percent of population under 18 years of age; number of children's museums; health improvement grade; percent of births to teens; percent of low birthweight infants; infant mortality rate; number of Title X-funded clinics; average SAT/ACT scores; average elementary and secondary class size; crime rate; unemployment rate; percent of affordable homes; number of bad air days; park acres per 1000 persons; library circulation per child; and children's program attendance counts. *Zero Population Growth, Kid Friendly Cities Report Card 2001*

- Mercer Human Resources Consulting ranked 215 cities worldwide in terms of overall quality of life. Atlanta ranked #63. Criteria: political, social, economic, and socio-cultural factors; medical and health considerations; schools and education; public services and transportation; recreation; consumer goods; housing; and natural environment. *Mercer Human Resources Consulting, March 3, 2003*

- *Ladies Home Journal* ranked America's 200 largest cities in terms of safety. Atlanta ranked #198 out of 200. Criteria: violent crimes; crimes against property; and rape. *Ladies Home Journal Online, "The Best Cities for Women 2002"*

- Atlanta was ranked #14 out of 268 metro areas in terms of its Creativity Index. The Creativity Index is a mix of four equally weighted factors: the Creative Class (scientists, engineers, architects, designers, writers, artists, musicians, or any profession where creativity is a key factor) share of the workforce; innovation, measured as patents per capita; high-tech industry, using the Milken Institute's Tech Pole Index; and diversity, measured by the Gay Index (a reasonable proxy for an areas' openness to different kinds of people and ideas). *The Rise of the Creative Class, 2002*

■ Atlanta was ranked #22 out of 125 regions worldwide in terms of its "Knowledge Competitiveness Index." The index attempts to measure the knowledge-based development taking place throughout the world and is based on 17 measures of economic performance that indicate a region's ability to translate its knowledge capacity into economic value. *Robert Huggins Associates, "2003-2004 World Knowledge Competitiveness Index"*

■ The Atlanta metro area was selected by *Yahoo! Internet Life* as one of "America's Most Wired Cities...and Towns." The area ranked #16 out of 87. Criteria: home and work net use; user sophistication; domain density; and available content. *Yahoo! Internet Life, April 2001*

■ The Atlanta metro area was selected by Cranium as one of the "Top 50 Fun Cities" in America. The area ranked #4. Criteria includes: number of sports teams, restaurants, and dance performances; number of toy stores; city budget spent on recreation. *Cranium, November 4, 2003*

■ Of the 25 largest U.S. markets, the Atlanta DMA (designated market area) ranked #10 in terms of online shopping. Criteria: telephone surveys of nearly 50,000 U.S. households between July 2000 and June 2001 conducted by market research firm Centris. *American Demographics, February 2002*

■ Atlanta was selected as one of the fastest-growing cities in the U.S. based on online user growth. The city ranked #1 out of 10. Criteria: online user growth (home use only) from June 2002 to June 2003. *Nielsen/NetRatings, July 21, 2003*

■ Atlanta was identified as one of the 100 "Most Unwired Cities" in the U.S. The area ranked #11. Criteria: number of public and commercial wireless access points; cell phone coverage offering wide area network Internet access; Internet penetration. *Intel, "Most Unwired Cities," March 4, 2003*

■ Scarborough Research measured the percentage of households who subscribe to cellular services among adults ages 18 and over in 75 U.S. markets. The Atlanta DMA (Designated Market Area) was ranked #1 out of 75. *Scarborough Research, Scarborough USA+ 2003 Release 1*

■ Atlanta was selected as one of "America's Most Literate Cities." The city ranked #4 out of the 64 largest U.S. cities. Criteria: booksellers; library support, holdings, and utilization; educational attainment; periodicals published; newspaper circulation. *University of Wisconsin-Whitewater, "America's Most Literate Cities," Summer 2003*

■ Atlanta was chosen as one of America's ten best cities for running. The city was ranked #7. Criteria: nominations from *Runner's World* readers; input from longtime runners and frequent travelers Jeff Galloway, John Bingham, Hal Higdon, Doug Rennie, and Burt Yasso; key statistical data concerning the cities' trail networks, weather, air quality, street safety, and the number of local running clubs and road races. *www.runnersworld.com, December 16, 2002*

■ Atlanta was ranked #105 in *Prevention* magazine's survey of the "Best Walking Cities in the U.S." The magazine, in conjunction with the American Podiatric Medical Association, surveyed 125 of the most populated cities and then tabulated and weighed 20 criteria of interest to pedestrians. *Prevention, April, 2004*

■ Atlanta was selected as one of "The Best Places to Start and Grow a Company." The area ranked #2 among large metro areas. Criteria: Significant Starts (firms started in the last 10 years that still employ at least 5 people) and Young Growers (firms 10 years old or less that grew significantly during the last 4 years). *Cognetics, "Entrepreneurial Hot Spots: The Best Places in America to Start and Grow a Company," 2001*

■ The Atlanta metro area was selected as one of "America's 50 Hottest Cities for Business Relocations and Expansions." The area ranked #1. Criteria: 70 of the industry's most prominent site selection consultants were asked which cities their clients found the most attractive when it came to selecting an expansion or relocation site in 2003. *Expansion Management, January 2004*

- The Atlanta metro area was selected as one of the "Top 60 CyberCities in America" by *Site Selection*. CyberCities are magnets for growing high-tech companies. Criteria: total employment; average wages; total payroll; number of companies; R&D spending and venture capital in the 45 Standard Industrial Classification (SIC) codes that define the high-technology industry. *Site Selection, March 2002*

- The Atlanta metro area was cited as one of America's "Top 50 Metros" in terms of the availability of highly skilled, highly educated workers. The area ranked #28 out of 50. Criteria: degree holders (bachelors, masters, professional, and Ph.D.) as a percent of the workforce; science and engineering workers as a percent of the workforce; number of patents issued; number and type of colleges in each metro area. *Expansion Management, March 2004*

- The Atlanta metro area was cited as one of "The Best Places in the U.S. to Locate a Company." The area ranked #50 out of 329. Criteria: education (with emphasis on college board test results and high school graduation rates); availability of quality healthcare services and the cost to employers; quality of life; logistics workforce and companies; transportation infrastructure; quality and quantity of highly educated technical workers; business climate. *Expansion Management, July 2003*

- Atlanta was cited as one of America's top 10 metro areas for new/expanded facilities in 2000. The area ranked #10 out of 10. *Site Selection, March 2002*

- Atlanta was cited as one of America's top 10 metro areas for new manufacturing plants in 2000. The area ranked #9 out of 10. *Site Selection, March 2002*

- The Atlanta metro area was cited as one of America's "Most Picture Perfect Metros" by *Plant Sites and Parks* magazine. Each year *PSP* readers rank the metro areas they consider best bets for their companies to relocate or expand to in the coming year. The area ranked #2 out of 10. *Plant Sites and Parks, March 2004*

- Atlanta was cited as a top metro area for European expansion. The area ranked #41 out of 50, based on European-based company expansions or relocations within the past two years that created at least 10 jobs and involved capital investment of at least $1 million. *Expansion Management, June 2003*

- The Atlanta metro area was selected as one of the "Top 40 Hottest Real Estate Markets" for expanding or relocating businesses." Criteria: rental costs; purchase prices; and vacancy rates of office and warehouse space. *Expansion Management, August 2003*

- The Atlanta metro area appeared on *Forbes/Milken Institute* list of "Best Places for Business and Career." Rank: #63 out of 200 metro areas. Criteria: salary growth; job growth; number of technology clusters; overall concentration of technology activity relative to national average; and technology output growth. *www.forbes.com, Forbes/Milken Institute Best Places 2002*

- The Atlanta metro area appeared on the "Milken Institute Best Performing Cities" index. Rank: #77 out of 200 large metro areas. Criteria: job growth; wage and salary growth; high-tech output growth. *Milken Institute, June 25, 2003*

- The Atlanta metro area appeared on *Entrepreneur* magazine's list of the "Best Cities for Entrepreneurs" in 2003. The area ranked #3 out of 61 in the large city category. Criteria: entrepreneurial activity; small-business growth; economic growth; and risk. *www.Entrepreneur.com*

- The Atlanta metro area was selected as one of the "Top 25 Cities for Doing Business in America." *Inc.* measured current-year employment growth in 277 regions as well as current trends in the annual average growth over the past three years, and compared employment expansion between the first and second halves of the last decade. Job growth factors account for two-thirds, and balance among industries accounts for one third of the final score for each city. The Atlanta metro area ranked #1 among large metro areas. *Inc. Magazine, March 2004*

- The Atlanta metro area was selected as one of "The Top 20 Boom Towns in America." *Business 2.0* magazine and econometric research firm Global Insight compared 319 metropolitan areas in the U.S. and ranked the 61 with populations over 1 million. Criteria: a weighted formula that includes forecast growth rates in sectors that contain the economy's 10 most skilled occupational clusters; the prevalence of college degrees in the local workforce; median salary. The area ranked #5 among large metro areas. *Business 2.0 Magazine, March 2004*

- The Atlanta metro area appeared on *IndustryWeek's* fourth annual World-Class Communities list. It ranked #15 out of 315 metro areas. Criteria: MSA Gross Metropolitan Product (GMP) per manufacturing employee; and MSA percent share of U.S. manufacturing Gross Domestic Product (GDP). *IndustryWeek, April 16, 2001*

- The Atlanta metro area was selected as a "2001 Choice City" by *Business Development Outlook* magazine. Twenty-five cities were selected, based on data from the Bureau of Labor Statistics, Census Bureau, Federal Reserve, The Conference Board, and the U.S. Conference of Mayors, as being the most desirable into which a business can relocate or expand. *Business Development Outlook, 2001 Choice Cities*

- ING Group ranked the 125 largest metro areas according to the general financial security of residents. The Atlanta metro area was ranked #26 out of 125. Criteria: Earnings and Wealth Potential (household income, education, net assets, cost of living); Safety Net (health insurance, retirement savings, life insurance, income support programs); Personal Threats (unemployment rate, low-income households, crime rate); Community Economic Vitality (cost of community services, job quality, job creation, housing costs). *ING Group, "The Best Cities to Earn and Save Money: A Ranking of the Largest 125 U.S. Cities," 2001 Edition*

Business Environment

CITY FINANCES

City Government Finances

Component	2000-2001 ($000)	2000-2001 ($ per capita)
Total Revenues	1,370,038	3,290
Total Expenditures	1,363,432	3,274
Debt Outstanding	3,024,341	7,262
Cash and Securities	3,632,640	8,722

Source: U.S Census Bureau, Government Finances 2000-2001, August 2003

City Government Revenue by Source

Source	2000-2001 ($000)	2000-2001 ($ per capita)
General Revenue		
From Federal Government	45,712	110
From State Government	17,649	42
From Local Governments	98,104	236
Taxes		
Property	119,463	287
Sales	110,313	265
Personal Income	0	0
License	0	0
Charges	519,318	1,247
Liquor Store	0	0
Utility	99,537	239
Employee Retirement	97,009	233
Other	262,933	631

Source: U.S Census Bureau, Government Finances 2000-2001, August 2003

City Government Expenditures by Function

Function	2000-2001 ($000)	2000-2001 ($ per capita)	2000-2001 (%)
General Expenditures			
Airports	238,697	573	17.5
Corrections	31,910	77	2.3
Education	0	0	0.0
Fire Protection	70,914	170	5.2
Governmental Administration	69,113	166	5.1
Health	0	0	0.0
Highways	47,374	114	3.5
Hospitals	0	0	0.0
Housing and Community Development	6,656	16	0.5
Interest on General Debt	79,440	191	5.8
Libraries	0	0	0.0
Parking	0	0	0.0
Parks and Recreation	44,344	106	3.3
Police Protection	119,585	287	8.8
Public Welfare	0	0	0.0
Sewerage	127,705	307	9.4
Solid Waste Management	37,831	91	2.8
Liquor Store	0	0	0.0
Utility	257,326	618	18.9
Employee Retirement	138,929	334	10.2
Other	93,608	225	6.9

Source: U.S Census Bureau, Government Finances 2000-2001, August 2003

Municipal Bond Ratings

Area	Moody's
City	Aaa

Source: Mergent Bond Record, February 2004

DEMOGRAPHICS

Population Growth

Area	1990 Census	2000 Census	2003 Estimate	2008 Projection	Population Growth (%) 1990-2000	Population Growth (%) 2000-2008
City	394,092	416,474	420,964	430,764	5.7	3.4
MSA[1]	2,959,936	4,112,198	4,456,928	5,019,805	38.9	22.1
U.S.	248,709,873	281,421,906	290,647,163	305,918,071	13.2	8.7

Note: (1) Metropolitan Statistical Area - see Appendix A for areas included
Source: Claritas, Inc.

Number of Households and Average Household Size

Area	1990 Census	2000 Census	2003 Estimate	2008 Projection	2003 Average Household Size
City	155,770	168,147	171,208	177,141	2.5
MSA[1]	1,102,573	1,504,871	1,625,870	1,822,027	2.7
U.S.	91,947,410	105,480,101	109,440,059	116,034,472	2.7

Note: (1) Metropolitan Statistical Area - see Appendix A for areas included
Source: Claritas, Inc.

Race and Ethnicity

Area	White Non-Hispanic	Black Non-Hispanic	Asian Non-Hispanic	Other Race Non-Hispanic	Hispanic
City	33.6	60.7	2.0	3.7	4.9
MSA[1]	62.4	29.1	3.5	5.1	7.0
U.S.	74.5	12.4	3.8	9.3	13.2

Note: Figures are 2003 estimates; (1) Metropolitan Statistical Area - see Appendix A for areas included
Source: Claritas, Inc.

Segregation

City		MSA[1]	
Index[2]	Rank[3]	Index[2]	Rank[4]
83.5	3	68.8	67

Note: Figures are based on an analysis of Census 2000 data; (1) Metropolitan Statistical Area - see Appendix A for areas included; (2) Dissimilarity Index—the most commonly used measure of segregation between two groups, reflecting their relative distributions across neighborhoods within a city or metropolitan area. It can range in value from 0, indicating complete integration, to 100, indicating complete segregation; (3) Ranges from 1 (most segregated) to 100 (least segregated) and includes all the cities in this book; (4) Ranges from 1 (most segregated) to 318 (least segregated) and includes 318 metropolitan areas.
Source: www.CensusScope.org

Ancestry

Area	German	Irish[2]	English	American	Italian	Polish	French[3]	Scottish
City	4.5	4.5	5.9	3.0	1.6	0.8	1.2	1.6
MSA[1]	8.3	8.5	8.8	10.4	2.7	1.4	1.8	2.0
U.S.	15.2	10.9	8.7	7.3	5.6	3.2	3.0	1.7

Note: Figures include multiple ancestry (e.g. if a person reported being Irish and Italian, they were included in both columns); (1) Metropolitan Statistical Area - see Appendix A for areas included; (2) Includes Celtic; (3) Includes Alsatian but excludes Basque
Source: Census 2000, Summary File 3

Foreign-Born Population

Area	Any Foreign Country	Percent of Population Born in: Europe	Asia	Africa	Oceania[2]	Canada	Mexico	Latin America[3]
City	6.6	0.9	1.4	0.7	0.0	0.2	2.1	1.1
MSA[1]	10.3	1.3	2.8	0.9	0.0	0.2	2.9	2.1
U.S.	11.1	1.7	2.9	0.3	0.1	0.3	3.3	2.5

Note: (1) Metropolitan Statistical Area - see Appendix A for areas included; (2) Includes Australia, New Zealand subregion, Melanesia, Micronesia, Polynesia, and Oceania n.e.c; (3) Includes Central America (excluding Mexico), South America, and the Caribbean.
Source: Census 2000, Summary File 3

Religion

Area	Catholic	Southern Baptist	United Methodist	ELCA[1]	LDS[2]	Presbyterian Church USA	Jewish Est.	Muslim Est.
County	8.8	10.0	9.2	0.8	0.3	3.7	8.1	2.7
U.S.	22.0	7.1	3.7	1.8	1.5	1.1	2.2	0.6

Note: Figures shown are the number of adherents as a percentage of the total population; Adherents are defined as all members, including full members, their children and the estimated number of other participants who are not considered members (e.g. the baptized, those not confirmed, those not eligible for communion, those regularly attending services, etc.); (1) Evangelical Lutheran Church in America; (2) The Church of Jesus Christ of Latter Day Saints
Source: Reprinted with permission from Religious Congregations and Membership in the United States 2000 (Nashville, Glenmary Research Center, 2002) Copyright Association of Statisticians of American Religious Bodies. All rights reserved.

Age Distribution

Area	Percent of Population						
	Under Age 5	Age 5 to 17	Age 18 to 34	Age 35 to 49	Age 50 to 64	Age 65 to 79	80 Years and Over
City	6.4	15.9	32.8	22.3	12.7	7.0	2.9
MSA[1]	7.5	19.1	27.0	25.4	13.5	5.8	1.8
U.S.	6.8	18.9	23.7	23.5	14.8	9.2	3.2

Note: (1) Metropolitan Statistical Area - see Appendix A for areas included
Source: Census 2000, Summary File 3

Marriage Status

Area	Never Married	Now Married Except Separated	Separated	Widowed	Divorced
City	45.5	31.4	4.1	7.7	11.3
MSA[1]	29.1	53.8	2.1	4.8	10.2
U.S.	27.1	54.4	2.2	6.6	9.7

Note: Figures cover population 15 years of age and older; (1) Metropolitan Statistical Area - see Appendix A for areas included
Source: Census 2000, Summary File 3

Male/Female Ratio

Area	Males	Females	Males per 100 Females
City	209,665	211,299	99.2
MSA[1]	2,200,527	2,256,401	97.5
U.S.	142,511,883	148,135,280	96.2

Note: Figures are 2003 estimates; (1) Metropolitan Statistical Area - see Appendix A for areas included
Source: Claritas, Inc.

ECONOMY

Gross Metropolitan Product

Area	1999	2000	2001	2002	2002 Rank[2]
MSA[1]	155.1	166.8	174.0	177.9	8

Note: Figures are in billions of dollars; (1) Metropolitan Statistical Area - see Appendix A for areas included; (2) Rank ranges from 1 to 319
Source: The U.S. Conference of Mayors, Metro Economies Report, July 2003

INCOME

Per Capita/Median/Average Income

Area	Per Capita ($)	Median Household ($)	Average Household ($)
City	28,822	40,606	69,545
MSA[1]	28,257	59,395	76,895
U.S.	24,078	46,868	63,207

Note: Figures are 2003 estimates; (1) Metropolitan Statistical Area - see Appendix A for areas included
Source: Claritas, Inc.

Household Income Distribution

Area	Percent of Households Earning							
	Under $15,000	$15,000 -24,999	$25,000 -34,999	$35,000 -49,999	$50,000 -74,999	$75,000 -99,000	$100,000 -149,999	$150,000 and up
City	21.6	12.3	11.2	13.3	14.4	8.6	9.1	9.7
MSA[1]	9.3	8.0	9.6	15.2	21.0	14.0	14.1	8.9
U.S.	14.1	11.5	11.7	16.0	19.2	11.3	10.2	6.0

Note: Figures are 2003 estimates; (1) Metropolitan Statistical Area - see Appendix A for areas included
Source: Claritas, Inc.

Poverty Rates by Age

Area	All Ages	Under 5 Years Old	5 to 17 Years Old	18 to 64 Years Old	65 Years and Over
City	24.4	2.7	6.4	13.2	2.1
MSA[1]	9.4	1.0	2.3	5.4	0.7
U.S.	12.4	1.2	3.0	6.9	1.2

Note: Figures are percent of population with income in 1999 below poverty level and only include population for whom poverty status is determined; (1) Metropolitan Statistical Area - see Appendix A for areas included
Source: Census 2000, Summary File 3

Personal Bankruptcy Filing Rate

Area	2002	2003
Fulton County	6.02	6.43
U.S.	5.34	5.58

Note: Numbers are per 1,000 population and include Chapter 7 and Chapter 13 filings
Source: Federal Deposit Insurance Corporation (FDIC), Regional Economic Conditions (RECON), 2/25/2004

EMPLOYMENT

Labor Force and Employment

Area	Civilian Labor Force			Workers Employed		
	Dec. 2002	Dec. 2003	% Chg.	Dec. 2002	Dec. 2003	% Chg.
City	241,484	245,196	1.5	221,503	229,519	3.6
MSA[1]	2,398,382	2,453,778	2.3	2,273,161	2,355,417	3.6
U.S.	144,807,000	146,501,000	1.2	136,599,000	138,556,000	1.4

Note: Data is not seasonally adjusted and covers workers 16 years of age and older;
(1) Metropolitan Statistical Area - see Appendix A for areas included
Source: Bureau of Labor Statistics, http://stats.bls.gov

Unemployment Rate

Area	2003											
	Jan.	Feb.	Mar.	Apr.	May	Jun.	Jul.	Aug.	Sep.	Oct.	Nov.	Dec.
City	7.4	7.4	7.4	7.1	7.6	8.9	8.4	7.9	7.8	7.2	6.6	6.4
MSA[1]	4.7	4.7	4.7	4.6	4.8	5.5	5.3	4.9	4.8	4.5	4.1	4.0
U.S.	6.5	6.4	6.2	5.8	5.8	6.5	6.3	6.0	5.8	5.6	5.6	5.4

Note: Data is not seasonally adjusted and covers workers 16 years of age and older; All figures are percentages; (1) Metropolitan Statistical Area - see Appendix A for areas included
Source: Bureau of Labor Statistics, http://stats.bls.gov

Employment by Occupation

Occupation Classification	City (%)	MSA[1] (%)	U.S. (%)
Sales and Office	25.6	28.7	26.7
Professional and Related	23.3	20.2	20.2
Service	16.4	12.1	14.9
Production, Transportation, and Material Moving	11.2	11.6	14.6
Management, Business, and Financial	17.2	17.3	13.5
Construction, Extraction, and Maintenance	6.0	10.0	9.4
Farming, Forestry, and Fishing	0.2	0.2	0.7

Note: Figures cover employed civilians 16 years of age and older;
(1) Metropolitan Statistical Area - see Appendix A for areas included
Source: Census 2000, Summary File 3

Employment by Industry

Sector	MSA[1]		U.S.
	Number of Employees	Percent of Total	Percent of Total
Government	293,100	13.4	16.7
Education and Health Services	214,800	9.9	12.9
Professional and Business Services	341,400	15.7	12.3
Retail Trade	250,000	11.5	11.8
Manufacturing	168,500	7.7	11.0
Leisure and Hospitality	202,100	9.3	9.1
Finance Activities	146,200	6.7	6.1
Construction	117,700	5.4	5.1
Wholesale Trade	136,800	6.3	4.3
Other Services	93,000	4.3	4.1
Transportation and Utilities	116,100	5.3	3.7
Information	97,700	4.5	2.4
Natural Resources and Mining	1,900	0.1	0.4

Note: Figures cover non-farm employment as of December 2003 and are not seasonally adjusted;
(1) Metropolitan Statistical Area - see Appendix A for areas included
Source: Bureau of Labor Statistics, http://stats.bls.gov

Average Wages

Occupation	$/Hr.	Occupation	$/Hr.
Accountants and Auditors	24.40	Maids and Housekeeping Cleaners	8.12
Automotive Mechanics	16.62	Maintenance and Repair Workers	14.35
Bookkeepers	13.69	Marketing Managers	40.45
Carpenters	15.12	Nuclear Medicine Technologists	21.71
Cashiers	8.00	Nurses, Licensed Practical	15.23
Clerks, General Office	12.31	Nurses, Registered	23.52
Clerks, Receptionists/Information	10.37	Nursing Aides/Orderlies/Attendants	9.82
Clerks, Shipping/Receiving	12.14	Packers and Packagers, Hand	8.77
Computer Programmers	28.85	Physical Therapists	29.38
Computer Support Specialists	19.86	Postal Service Mail Carriers	18.55
Computer Systems Analysts	35.36	Real Estate Brokers	41.12
Cooks, Restaurant	9.51	Retail Salespersons	10.90
Dentists	60.16	Sales Reps., Exc. Tech./Scientific	24.37
Electrical Engineers	31.80	Sales Reps., Tech./Scientific	31.29
Electricians	18.25	Secretaries, Exc. Legal/Med./Exec.	12.69
Financial Managers	42.89	Security Guards	9.43
First-Line Supervisors/Mgrs., Sales	15.68	Surgeons	88.61
Food Preparation Workers	8.33	Teacher Assistants	8.50
General and Operations Managers	40.54	Teachers, Elementary School	21.80
Hairdressers/Cosmetologists	12.36	Teachers, Secondary School	21.90
Internists	66.43	Telemarketers	12.11
Janitors and Cleaners	8.90	Truck Drivers, Heavy/Tractor-Trailer	18.58
Landscaping/Groundskeeping Workers	10.10	Truck Drivers, Light/Delivery Svcs.	12.72
Lawyers	45.94	Waiters and Waitresses	7.59

Note: Wage data is for 2002 and covers the Metropolitan Statistical Area (see Appendix A for areas included).
Hourly wages for elementary/secondary school teachers and teacher assistants were calculated by the editors
from annual wage data assuming a 40 hour work week; n/a not available.
Source: Bureau of Labor Statistics, 2002 Metro Area Occupational Employment and Wage Estimates

Occupational Employment Projections: 1996 - 2006

Occupations Expected to Have the Largest Job Growth (ranked by numerical growth)	Fast-Growing Occupations[1] (ranked by percent growth)
1. General managers & top executives	1. Medical assistants
2. Cashiers	2. Physical therapy assistants and aides
3. Salespersons, retail	3. Occupational therapists
4. Child care workers, private household	4. Home health aides
5. Truck drivers, light	5. Occupational therapy assistants
6. General office clerks	6. Personal and home care aides
7. Systems analysts	7. Paralegals
8. Registered nurses	8. Respiratory therapists
9. Marketing & sales, supervisors	9. Customer service representatives
10. Receptionists and information clerks	10. Child care workers, private household

Note: Projections cover Georgia; (1) Excludes occupations with total job growth less than 300
Source: U.S. Department of Labor, Employment and Training Administration, America's Labor Market Information System (ALMIS)

TAXES

State Corporate Income Tax Rates

State	Rate (%)	Number of Brackets	Low Bracket (Under $)	High Bracket (Over $)
Georgia	6.0	1	na	na

Note: Tax rates as of December 31, 2003; na not applicable
Source: Tax Foundation, www.taxfoundation.org

State Individual Income Tax Rates

State	Federal Deductibility	Marginal Rate (%)	Number of Brackets	Low Bracket (Under $)	High Bracket (Over $)
Georgia	No	1.0-6.0	6	0	7,000

Note: Tax rates as of December 31, 2003; Brackets apply to single taxpayers and married people filing separately; na not applicable
Source: Tax Foundation, www.taxfoundation.org

Various State and Local Tax Rates

State Sales and Use (%)	Total Sales and Use (%)	Gasoline (cents/gal.)	Cigarette (cents/pack)	Spirits ($/gal.)	Table Wine ($/gal.)	Beer ($/gal.)
4.0	7.0	7.5	12	3.79	1.51	0.48

Note: Tax rates as of December 31, 2003
Source: Tax Foundation, www.taxfoundation.org

State Tax Burdens

Area	Combined State and Local Tax Burden		Combined Federal, State and Local Tax Burden	
	Percent	Rank	Percent	Rank
Georgia	9.9	16	29.2	20
U.S. Average	9.7	-	30.0	-

Note: Figures are for 2003
Source: Tax Foundation, www.taxfoundation.org

Internal Revenue Service Tax Audits

IRS District	Percent of Returns Audited				
	1996	1997	1998	1999	2000
Georgia	0.78	0.64	0.48	0.31	0.11
U.S.	0.66	0.61	0.46	0.31	0.20

Note: Figures cover IRS district audits of federal income tax returns filed by individuals. Geographic data on district audits for 2001 and 2002 are being withheld by the IRS. TRAC is challenging this policy.
Source: Syracuse University, Transactional Records Access Clearinghouse (TRAC), "Odds of IRS District Tax Audit 2000"

RESIDENTIAL REAL ESTATE

Building Permits

Area	Single-Family			Multi-Family			Total		
	2001	2002	Pct. Chg.	2001	2002	Pct. Chg.	2001	2002	Pct. Chg.
City	781	759	-2.8	6,013	5,890	-2.0	6,794	6,649	-2.1
U.S.	1,235,600	1,332,600	7.9	401,100	415,100	3.5	1,636,700	1,747,700	6.8

Note: Figures represent new, privately-owned housing units authorized (unadjusted data)
Source: U.S. Census Bureau, Manufacturing, Mining, and Construction Statistics

Homeownership and Housing Vacancies

Area	Homeownership Rate[2] (%)			Rental Vacancy Rate[3] (%)			Homeowner Vacancy Rate[4] (%)		
	2001	2002[a]	2003	2001	2002[a]	2003	2001	2002[a]	2003
MSA[1]	66.6	69.0	67.9	11.9	15.0	16.8	2.0	1.9	3.4
U.S.	67.8	67.9	68.3	8.4	8.9	9.8	1.8	1.7	1.8

Note: (1) Metropolitan Statistical Area - see Appendix A for areas included; (2) The proportion of households that are owners; (3) The proportion of the rental inventory that is vacant for rent; (4) The proportion of the homeowner inventory that is vacant for sale; (a) 2002 figures have been revised; n/a not available
Source: U.S. Census Bureau, Housing Vacancies and Homeownership Annual Statistics: 2003

COMMERCIAL REAL ESTATE

Industrial/Office Markets

Type/Market Area	Inventory (sq. ft.)	Vacant (sq. ft.)	Vacancy Rate (%)	Under Construction (sq. ft.)	Net Absorption (sq. ft.)
Industrial Space					
Atlanta	430,480,625	82,123,917	19.08	795,703	3,968,825
Office Space					
Atlanta	149,902,091	32,905,544	21.95	881,136	-1,017,728

Note: Data as of 4th Quarter, 2003; n/a not available
Source: Society of Industrial and Office Realtors, 2004 Comparative Statistics of Industrial and Office Real Estate Markets

COMMERCIAL UTILITIES

Typical Monthly Electric Bills

Area	Commercial Service ($/month)		Industrial Service ($/month)	
	3 kW demand 1,000 kWh	40 kW demand 14,000 kWh	1,000 kW demand 200,000 kWh	50,000 kW demand 15,000,000 kWh
City	117	965	19,225	1,059,709
Average[1]	100	1,134	17,850	1,045,117

Note: Based on rates in effect July 1, 2003; (1) average based on 197 utilities
Source: Edison Electric Institute, Typical Bills and Average Rates Report, Summer 2003

TRANSPORTATION

Means of Transportation to Work

Area	Car/Truck/Van		Public Transportation			Bicycle	Walked	Other Means	Worked at Home
	Drove Alone	Car-pooled	Bus	Subway	Railroad				
City	64.0	12.4	11.5	3.0	0.2	0.3	3.5	1.3	3.8
MSA[1]	77.0	13.6	2.4	1.0	0.1	0.1	1.3	1.1	3.5
U.S.	75.7	12.2	2.5	1.5	0.5	0.4	2.9	1.0	3.3

Note: Figures shown are percentages and cover workers 16 years of age and older; (1) Metropolitan Statistical Area - see Appendix A for areas included
Source: Census 2000, Summary File 3

Travel Time to Work

Area	Less Than 15 Minutes	15 to 29 Minutes	30 to 44 Minutes	45 to 59 Minutes	60 Minutes or More
City	22.3	40.2	20.9	6.7	10.0
MSA[1]	18.3	32.4	25.1	12.4	11.8
U.S.	29.4	36.1	19.1	7.4	8.0

Note: Figures are percentages and include workers 16 years old and over; (1) Metropolitan Statistical Area - see Appendix A for areas included
Source: Census 2000, Summary File 3

Roadway Congestion Index

Area	1982	1990	1996	2000	2001
City	0.77	0.98	1.17	1.33	1.33
Average[1]	0.82	1.01	1.08	1.16	1.17

Note: Values greater than 1.00 indicate undesirable mobility levels; (1) average of 75 urban areas
Source: Texas Transportation Institute, The 2003 Annual Urban Mobility Report

Transportation Statistics

Interstate highways (2004)	I-20; I-75; I-85
Public transportation (2002)	Metropolitan Atlanta Rapid Transit Authority (MARTA)
Buses	
Average fleet age in years	7.6
No. operated in max. service	590
Heavy rail	
Average fleet age in years	16.2
No. operated in max. service	186
Demand response	
Average fleet age in years	2.7
No. operated in max. service	77
Passenger air service	
Airport	Hartsfield Atlanta International
Airlines (2003)	32
Boardings (2002)	37,720,556
Amtrak service (2004)	Yes
Major waterways/ports	None

Source: Federal Transit Administration, National Transit Database, 2002; Editor & Publisher Market Guide, 2004; Bureau of Transportation Statistics, Airport Enplanement Activity for CY2002; www.amtrak.com

BUSINESSES

Major Business Headquarters

Company Name	2003 Rankings	
	Fortune 500	Forbes 500
BellSouth	77	-
Coca-Cola	92	-
Coca-Cola Enterprises	108	-
Cox Communications	329	-
Cox Enterprises	-	27
Delta Air Lines	145	-
Genuine Parts	227	-
Georgia-Pacific	74	-
Home Depot	13	-
Mirant	259	-
National Distributing	-	149
Printpack	-	261
Southern	177	-
SunTrust Banks	248	-
United Parcel Service	43	-
Watkins Associated Industries	-	267

Note: Companies listed are located in the city; dashes indicate no ranking
Fortune 500: Companies that produce a 10-K are ranked 1 to 500 based on 2002 revenue
Forbes 500: Private companies are ranked 1 to 281 based on 2002 revenue
Source: Fortune, April 14, 2003; www.forbes.com, November 6, 2003

Best Companies to Work For

Alston & Bird; Barton Protective Svcs; HomeBanc Mortgage; Simmons, headquartered in Atlanta, are among the "100 Best Companies to Work for in 2004." Criteria: trust in management, pride in work/company, camaraderie, company responses to the Hewitt People Practices Inventory, and employee responses to their Great Place to Work survey. The companies also had to be at least 10 years old and have a minimum of 500 employees. *Fortune, January 12, 2004*

Manhattan Associates, headquartered in Atlanta, is among the "200 Best Small Companies in 2003." Criteria: 3,500 companies whose latest 12-month sales were $5 million to $600 million were screened. Those with a net margin or five-year average ROE below 5% were cut. Banks, utilities, real estate investment trusts and limited partnerships whose financial structures are too different from most operating companies were also excluded. Shares had to be trading above $5 by the end of September 2003. Financial statement footnotes were examined for major issues. For the final ranking, equal weight was given to growth in sales, earnings and ROE for the past five years and the latest 12 months. *www.forbes.com, October 27, 2003*

Bellsouth; Coca-Cola; United Parcel Service, headquartered in Atlanta, are among the "50 Best Companies for Minorities." Criteria: 1,200 of the largest U.S employers were surveyed—141 responded. Those companies were analyzed on 15 quantitative and qualitative measures—from how well minorities are paid to how many are in management. *Fortune, July 7, 2003*

Assurant Group; BellSouth Corp; EarthLink Inc, headquartered in Atlanta, are among the "100 Best Places to Work in IT 2003." Criteria: compensation, turnover and training. *www.computerworld.com, 3/15/2004*

Fast-Growing Businesses

According to *Inc.*, Atlanta is home to five of America's 500 fastest-growing private companies: **Afterburner; Digital Visual Display Technologies; Magnet Communications; Sigma Analytics and Consulting; The Access Group**. Criteria: must be an independent, privately-held, U.S. corporation, proprietorship or partnership; sales of at least $200,000 in 1998; five-year operating/sales history; increase in 2002 sales over 2001 sales; holding companies, regulated banks, and utilities were excluded. *Inc. 500, America's Fastest-Growing Private Companies, October 15, 2003*

Atlanta is home to one of *Business Week's* "hot growth" companies: **Rare Hospitality International**. Criteria: increase in sales and profits, return on capital and stock price. *Business Week, June 9, 2003*

According to *Fortune*, Atlanta is home to one of America's 100 fastest-growing companies: **Manhattan Associates**. Companies were ranked based on earnings-per-share growth, revenue growth and total return over the previous three years. Criteria for inclusion: public companies with sales of at least $50 million. Companies that lost money in the most recent quarter, or ended in the red for the past four quarters as a whole, were not eligible. Limited partnerships and REITs were also not considered. *Fortune, "America's Fastest-Growing Companies," September 1, 2003*

According to Deloitte & Touche LLP, Atlanta is home to five of North America's 500 fastest-growing high-technology companies: **EarthLink, Inc; InterNAP Network Services; Internet Security Systems, Inc; Magnet Communications; S1 Corporation**. Companies are ranked by percentage growth in revenue over a five-year period. Criteria for inclusion: must be a U.S. or Canadian company developing and/or providing technology products or services; company must have been in business for five years with 1998 operating revenues of at least $50,000 USD or $75,000 CD and 2002 operating revenues of at least $1 million USD/CD. *Deloitte & Touche LLP, 2003 Technology Fast 500*

Women-Owned Firms: Number, Employment and Sales

Area	Number of Firms	Employment	Sales ($000)	Rank[2]
MSA[1]	107,409	109,473	16,897,129	9

Note: (1) Metropolitan Statistical Area - see Appendix A for areas included;
(2) Calculated on an averaging of the number of businesses, employment, and sales
Source: The National Foundation for Women Business Owners, Women-Owned Businesses in the Top 50
Metropolitan Areas, 2002: A Fact Sheet

Women-Owned Firms: Growth

Area	Percent Change from 1997 to 2002			Rank[2]
	Number of Firms	Employment	Sales	
MSA[1]	23.3	n/a	n/a	36
Top 50 MSAs	14.0	31.4	42.6	-

Note: (1) Metropolitan Statistical Area - see Appendix A for areas included; (2) Calculated on an averaging of
the percent growth of number of businesses, employment, and sales
Source: The National Foundation for Women Business Owners, Women-Owned Businesses in the Top 50
Metropolitan Areas, 2002: A Fact Sheet

Minority and Women-Owned Businesses

Ownership	All Firms		Firms with Paid Employees			
	Firms	Sales ($000)	Firms	Sales ($000)	Employees	Payroll ($000)
Black	7,853	1,012,038	982	(a)	10,000-24,999	(a)
Hispanic	995	268,429	205	248,567	2,583	58,963
Women	10,686	3,098,935	1,928	2,830,228	25,136	730,665

Note: Figures cover firms located in the city; (a) Withheld to avoid disclosure
Source: 1997 Economic Census, Minority and Women-Owned Businesses

Minority Business Opportunity

Atlanta is home to two companies which are on the Black Enterprise Industrial/Service 100 list (100 largest companies based on gross sales): **H. J. Russell & Co.**; **The Gourmet Cos.**. Criteria: operational in previous calendar year; at least 51% black-owned and manufactures/owns the product it sells or provides industrial or consumer services. Brokerages, real estate firms and firms that provide professional services are not eligible. *Black Enterprise, www.blackenterprise.com, B.E. 100s, 2003 Report*

Atlanta is home to one company which is on the Black Enterprise Auto Dealer 100 list (100 largest dealers based on gross sales): **The Harrell Cos.**. Criteria: company must be operational in previous calendar year and at least 51% black-owned. *Black Enterprise, www.blackenterprise.com, B.E. 100s, 2003 Report*

Atlanta is home to two companies which are on the Black Enterprise Bank 25 list (25 largest banks based on total assets, capital, deposits and loans, including mortgage-backed securities for the calendar year): **Citizens Trust Bank**; **Capitol City Bank & Trust Company**. Criteria: commercial banks or savings and loans that are classified by the Federal Reserve as black institutions and have been fully operational for the previous calendar year. *Black Enterprise, www.blackenterprise.com, B.E. 100s, 2003 Report*

Four of the 500 largest Hispanic-owned companies in the U.S. are located in Atlanta. *Hispanic Business, June 2003*

Atlanta is home to one company which is on the Hispanic Business Fastest-Growing 100 list (greatest sales growth over the past five years): **Cape Environmental Management Inc.**. *Hispanic Business, July/August 2003*

HOTELS

Hotels/Motels

Area	Hotels/Motels	Average Minimum Rates ($)		
		Tourist	First-Class	Deluxe
City	179	71	127	175

Source: OAG Travel Planner Online, Spring 2004

Atlanta is home to one of the top 100 hotels in the U.S. and Canada according to *Travel & Leisure*: **Ritz-Carlton Buckhead** (#51). Criteria: value, rooms/ambience, location, facilities/activities and service. *Travel & Leisure, "The World's Best Hotels 2003"*

EVENT SITES

Major Event Sites, Meeting Places and Convention Centers

Name	Guest Rooms	Exhibit/ Meeting Space (sq. ft.)	Largest Meeting Room Capacity
America's Mart Atlanta	n/a	850,000	10,000
Atlanta Marriott Marquis	1,675	120,000	4,800
Cobb Galleria Centre	n/a	280,000	n/a
Georgia Dome	n/a	n/a	71,500
Georgia World Congress Center	n/a	1,400,000	n/a
Hilton Atlanta Hotel	1,224	104,500	2,200
Hyatt Regency Atlanta	1,264	180,000	3,243
Olympic Stadium	n/a	n/a	85,000
Omni Hotel at CNN Center	1,067	120,000	2,218
The Westin Peachtree Plaza	1,068	80,000	2,000

Note: n/a not available
Source: Original research

Living Environment

COST OF LIVING

Cost of Living Index

Year	Composite Index	Groceries	Housing	Utilities	Trans- portation	Health Care	Misc. Goods/ Services
2001	101.7	101.6	107.2	90.7	103.1	104.8	98.8
2002	98.8	102.2	97.5	91.7	103.0	103.6	98.1
2003	97.2	99.7	92.2	92.4	100.0	105.3	100.3

Note: U.S. = 100
Source: ACCRA, Cost of Living Index, 2001, 2002 and 2003 4-Quarter Averages

HOUSING

House Price Index (HPI)

Area	National Ranking[2]	Quarterly Change (%)	One-Year Change (%)	Five-Year Change (%)
MSA[1]	195	1.47	3.17	31.70
U.S.[3]	-	3.67	7.97	41.81

Note: The HPI is a weighted repeat sales index. It measures average price changes in repeat sales or refinancings on the same properties. This information is obtained by reviewing repeat mortgage transactions on single-family properties whose mortgages have been purchased or securitized by Fannie Mae of Freddie Mac in January 1975; (1) Metropolitan Statistical Area - see Appendix A for areas included; (2) Rankings are based on annual percentage change, for all MSAs containing at least 15,000 transactions over the last 10 years and ranges from 1 to 220; (3) figures based on a weighted division average; all figures are for the period ended December 31, 2003
Source: Office of Federal Housing Enterprise Oversight, House Price Index, March 1, 2004

Housing: Year Structure Built

Area	1990 -2000	1980 -1989	1970 -1979	1960 -1969	1950 -1959	1940 -1949	Before 1940	Median Year
City	11.2	9.2	13.8	20.6	17.8	10.7	16.8	1962
MSA[1]	30.8	24.6	18.0	12.0	7.1	3.2	4.2	1982
U.S.	17.0	15.8	18.5	13.7	12.7	7.3	15.0	1971

Note: Figures are percentages; (1) Metropolitan Statistical Area - see Appendix A for areas included
Source: Census 2000, Summary File 3

Average New Home Price

Area	2001	2002	2003
City	231,883	226,804	224,132
U.S.	212,643	236,567	248,193

Note: Figures, in dollars, are based on a new home with 2,400 sq. ft. of living area on an 8,000 sq. ft. lot.
Source: ACCRA, Cost of Living Index, 2001, 2002 and 2003 4-Quarter Averages

Average Apartment Rent

Area	2001	2002	2003
City	730	751	736
U.S.	674	708	721

Note: Figures, in dollars per month, are based on an unfurnished two bedroom, 1-1/2 or 2 bath apartment, approximately 950 sq. ft. in size, excluding all utilities except water
Source: ACCRA, Cost of Living Index, 2001, 2002 and 2003 4-Quarter Averages

RESIDENTIAL UTILITIES

Average Residential Utility Costs

Area	All Electric ($/mth)	Part Electric ($/mth)	Other Energy ($/mth)	Phone ($/mth)
City	105.80	–	–	24.90
U.S.	116.46	65.82	62.68	23.90

Source: ACCRA, Cost of Living Index, 2003 4-Quarter Average

HEALTH CARE

Average Health Care Costs

Area	Hospital ($/day)	Doctor ($/visit)	Dentist ($/visit)
City	560.69	75.15	93.04
U.S.	678.35	67.91	83.90

Note: Hospital—based on a semi-private room; Doctor—based on a general practitioner's routine exam of an established patient; Dentist—based on adult teeth cleaning and periodic oral exam.
Source: ACCRA, Cost of Living Index, 2003 4-Quarter Average

Distribution of Non-Federal, Office-Based Physicians

Area	Total	Family/ General Practice	Specialties Medical	Surgical	Other
MSA[1] (number)	6,993	629	2,647	1,814	1,903
MSA[1] (rate per 10,000 pop.)	17.0	1.5	6.4	4.4	4.6
Metro Average[2] (rate per 10,000 pop.)	33.1	2.2	7.7	4.8	5.6

Note: Data as of December 31, 2001; (1) Metropolitan Statistical Area - see Appendix A for areas included; (2) Average of 81 MSAs and CMSAs in this book
Source: American Medical Association, Physician Characteristics & Distribution in the U.S., 2003-2004

Hospitals

Atlanta has the following hospitals: 15 general medical and surgical; 2 psychiatric; 1 rehabilitation; 1 alcoholism and other chemical dependency; 1 long-term acute care; 2 other specialty; 1 children's general; 1 children's psychiatric.
AHA Guide to the Healthcare Field, 2003-2004

According to *U.S. News*, Atlanta has two of the best hospitals in the U.S.: **Emory University Hospital**; **Shepherd Center**; *U.S. News Online, "America's Best Hospitals 2003"*

PRESIDENTIAL ELECTION

2000 Presidential Election Results

Area	Gore	Bush	Nader	Buchanan	Other
Fulton County	58.0	40.0	0.0	0.2	1.7
U.S.	48.4	47.9	2.7	0.4	0.6

Note: Results are percentages and may not add to 100% due to rounding
Source: www.cbsnews.com; www.uselectionatlas.org

EDUCATION

Public School District Statistics

District Name	Schls.	Enroll-ment	Classroom Teachers	Pupil/ Teacher Ratio	Minority Pupils[1] (%)	Current Expend.[2] ($/pupil)
Atlanta City	97	56,586	3,742	15.1	93.2	8,623
Fulton County	77	69,841	4,638	15.1	51.5	7,118

Note: Data covers the 2001-02 school year unless otherwise noted; (1) Fall 2000; (2) FY2000; n/a not available
Source: U.S. Department of Education, National Center for Education Statistics, Common Core of Data, Local Education Agency (School District) Universe Survey: School Year 2001-2002; U.S. Department of Education, National Center for Education Statistics, Digest of Education Statistics 2002

Educational Quality

School District	Education Quotient[1]	Graduate Outcome[2]	Community Index[3]	Resource Index[4]
Atlanta City	8	2	32	72

Note: Scores are national percentile rankings and range from 1 (worst) to 99 (best); (1) Combination of the Graduate Outcome, Community and Resource indexes weighted to reflect the greater importance of the Graduate Outcome and Resource Index; (2) Based on graduation rates and college board scores (SAT/ACT); (3) Based on the surrounding community's level of affluence and adult education; (4) Based on teacher salaries, per-pupil expenditures and student-teacher ratios.
Source: Expansion Management, December 2003

Educational Attainment by Race

Area	High School Graduate (%)					Bachelor's Degree (%)				
	Total	White	Black	Asian	Hisp.[2]	Total	White	Black	Asian	Hisp.[2]
City	76.9	92.4	66.8	79.2	53.6	34.6	66.1	12.7	54.0	20.8
MSA[1]	84.0	86.8	81.0	80.0	51.7	32.0	36.1	21.9	46.4	16.1
U.S.	80.4	83.6	72.3	80.4	52.4	24.4	26.1	14.3	44.1	10.4

Note: Figures shown cover persons 25 years old and over; (1) Metropolitan Statistical Area - see Appendix A for areas included; (2) people of Hispanic origin can be of any race
Source: Census 2000, Summary File 3

School Enrollment by Type

Area	Grades KG to 8				Grades 9 to 12			
	Public		Private		Public		Private	
	Enrollment	%	Enrollment	%	Enrollment	%	Enrollment	%
City	44,189	90.4	4,700	9.6	18,138	88.8	2,282	11.2
MSA[1]	511,746	90.2	55,562	9.8	207,156	91.5	19,214	8.5
U.S.	33,526,011	88.7	4,285,121	11.3	14,848,628	90.6	1,532,323	9.4

Note: Figures shown cover persons 3 years old and over; (1) Metropolitan Statistical Area - see Appendix A for areas included
Source: Census 2000, Summary File 3

School Enrollment by Race

Area	Grades KG to 8 (%)				Grades 9 to 12 (%)			
	White	Black	Asian	Hisp.[1]	White	Black	Asian	Hisp.[1]
City	15.6	80.4	1.1	3.7	13.5	82.6	1.1	3.1
MSA[2]	56.5	35.2	3.0	6.2	56.3	35.5	3.6	5.3
U.S.	68.5	15.5	3.3	16.8	68.8	15.5	3.8	15.7

Note: Figures shown cover persons 3 years old and over; (1) people of Hispanic origin can be of any race; (2) Metropolitan Statistical Area - see Appendix A for areas included
Source: Census 2000, Summary File 3

Classroom Teacher Salaries in Public Schools

District	B.A. Degree		M.A. Degree		Maximum	
	Min. ($)	Rank[1]	Max. ($)	Rank[1]	Max. ($)	Rank[1]
Atlanta	35,090	19	56,206	28	69,250	10
DOD Average[2]	31,567	-	53,248	-	59,356	-

Note: Salaries are for 2001-2002; (1) Rank ranges from 1 to 100; (2) As per the U.S. Department of Defense Wage Fixing Authority
Source: American Federation of Teachers, Survey & Analysis of Teacher Salary Trends 2002

Higher Education

Four-Year Colleges			Two-Year Colleges			Medical Schools	Law Schools	Voc/ Tech
Public	Private Non-profit	Private For-profit	Public	Private Non-profit	Private For-profit			
2	18	7	3	0	6	2	3	17

Note: Figures cover institutions located within the city limits.
Source: National Center for Education Statistics, The Integrated Postsecondary Education System (IPEDS) Peer Analysis System, 2002; usnews.com, America's Best Graduate Schools 2004, Medical School Directory; The College Blue Book, Occupational Education, 2003; Barron's Guide to Law Schools, 2003; Medical School Admission Requirements U.S. & Canada, 2003-2004

**MAJOR
EMPLOYERS**

Major Employers

Company Name	Industry	Type
ADP	Data processing and preparation	Branch
Allied Automotive Group Inc	Trucking, except local	Headquarters
BellSouth	Telephone communication, except radio	Headquarters
Bristol Hotel Tenant Company	Hotels and motels	Headquarters
Childrens Healthcare Atlanta	Management services	Single
Clayton County Public Schools	Elementary and secondary schools	Headquarters
Coca-Cola	Flavoring extracts and syrups, nec	Headquarters
Cognisa Security Inc	Detective and armored car services	Single
Crestview Nursing Home	General medical and surgical hospitals	Headquarters
Delta Airlines	Air transportation, scheduled	Headquarters
Georgia Institute Technology	Colleges and universities	Branch
Georgia-Pacific	Timber tracts	Branch
Grady Health System The	General medical and surgical hospitals	Branch
Hagemeyer P P S North America	Durable goods, nec	Single
Lmaero	Repair services, nec	Single
Lockheed Martin	Aircraft	Branch
Musicland Group Inc	Musical instrument stores	Branch
Office of Intermodal Programs	Legislative bodies	Single
OLH LP	Hotels and motels	Branch
Springs Industries Inc	Broadwoven fabric mills, cotton	Single
USAG Fort McPherson	National security	Branch

Note: Companies shown are located in the metropolitan area and have 3,500 or more employees.
Source: www.zapdata.com, March 2004

PUBLIC SAFETY

Crime Rate

Area	All Crimes	Violent Crimes				Property Crimes		
		Murder	Forcible Rape	Robbery	Aggrav. Assault	Burglary	Larceny -Theft	Motor Vehicle Theft
City	11,355.2	34.9	63.4	957.1	1,233.8	1,964.2	5,443.5	1,658.3
Suburbs[1]	3,881.6	5.3	20.1	130.9	170.0	752.1	2,351.4	451.8
MSA[2]	4,638.5	8.3	24.5	214.6	277.7	874.9	2,664.6	574.0
U.S.	4,118.8	5.6	33.0	145.9	310.1	746.2	2,445.8	432.1

Note: Figures are crimes per 100,000 population; (1) All areas within the MSA that are located outside the city limits; (2) Metropolitan Statistical Area - see Appendix A for areas included
Source: FBI Uniform Crime Reports, 2002

RECREATION

Culture and Recreation

Museums	Orchestras	Opera Companies	Dance Companies	Professional Theatres	Zoos	Pro Sports Teams[1]
23	4	1	9	18	1	4

Note: (1) Covers the Metropolitan Statistical Area - see Appendix A for areas included.
Source: The Grey House Performing Arts Directory, 2002; Official Museum Directory, 2004; www.sportsvenues.com

Library System

The Atlanta-Fulton Public Library System has 30 branches, holdings of 1,970,278 volumes, and a budget of $29,826,397 (2002).
American Library Directory, 2003-2004

MEDIA

Newspapers

Name	Type	Freq.	Distribution	Circulation
Atlanta Daily World	Black	2x/wk	Local	45,000
The Atlanta Inquirer	Black	1x/wk	Area	61,082
The Atlanta Journal-Constitution	General	7x/wk	State	397,063
Atlanta Voice	Black	1x/wk	Area	133,000
The De Kalb Neighbor	General	1x/wk	Local	70,000
The Georgia Bulletin	Catholic	1x/wk	State	72,000
Mundo Hispanico	Hispanic	1x/wk	Local	30,000
The Northside Neighbor	General	1x/wk	Local	28,000
Rolling Out	General	1x/wk	United States	150,000
The Sandy Springs Neighbor	General	1x/wk	Local	28,061

Note: Includes newspapers whose offices are located in the city and whose circulations are 25,000 or more
Source: Burrelle's Media Directory, 2003

Television Stations

Name	Ch.	Affiliation	Type	Owner
WSB	2	ABCT	Commercial	Cox Enterprises Inc.
WAGA	5	FBC	Commercial	New World Communications
WGTV	8	PBS	Public	Georgia Public Broadcasting
WXIA	11	NBCT	Commercial	Gannett Broadcasting
WTBS	17	n/a	Commercial	Turner Broadcasting System Inc.
WDCO	29	n/a	Public	Georgia Public Broadcasting
WPBA	30	PBS	Public	Atlanta Board of Education
WUVG	34	n/a	Commercial	Univision Television Group
WATL	36	WB	Commercial	Tribune Broadcasting Company
WGCL	46	CBST	Commercial	Meredith Communications LLC
WATC	57	n/a	Non-comm.	Community Television of Southern California
WHSG	63	n/a	n/a	Trinity Broadcasting Network
WCI	67	TMUN	Commercial	James Sim
WUPA	69	UPN	Commercial	VSC Communications

Note: Stations included broadcast from the Atlanta metro area; n/a not available
Source: Burrelle's Media Directory, 2003

AM Radio Stations

Call Letters	Freq. (kHz)	Target Audience	Station Format	Music Format
WDWD	590	Children	Men	Women
WGST	640	General	M/N/S/T	Classic Rock
WCNN	680	General	M/N/S/T	Classical
WSB	750	General	M/N/S/T	Jazz
WQXI	790	General	M/S/T	Adult Standards
WAEC	860	Religious	M/T	Alternative
WAFS	920	Religious	M/T	Christian
WNIV	970	Senior	T	n/a
WGUN	1010	Religious	T	n/a
WMLB	1170	General	M/N/S/T	Adult Standards
WGKA	1190	General	M/T	Adult Standards
WFOM	1230	General	M/T	Classical
WTJH	1260	Religious	M	Gospel
WALR	1340	General	M/N/T	Alternative
WAOK	1380	Black	M/N/T	Adult Contemporary
WLTA	1400	General	M/T	Adult Standards
WYZE	1480	Religious	M	Gospel
WAZX	1550	Hispanic	M/N/S/T	Latin
WSSA	1570	R/W	M/N/S	Christian

Note: Stations included broadcast from the Atlanta metro area; n/a not available
The following abbreviations may be used:
Target Audience: A=Asian; B=Black; C=Christian; E=Ethnic; F=French; G=General; H=Hispanic;
M=Men; N=Native American; R=Religious; S=Senior Citizen; W=Women; Y=Young Adult; Z=Children
Station Format: E=Educational; M=Music; N=News; S=Sports; T=Talk
Source: Burrelle's Media Directory, 2003

FM Radio Stations

Call Letters	Freq. (mHz)	Target Audience	Station Format	Music Format
WJSP	88.1	General	M/N/T	Classical
WPPR	88.3	General	M/N/T	Classical
WRAS	88.5	General	M/N/S/T	Adult Standards
WRFG	89.3	Black	E/M/T	Jazz
WNGU	89.5	General	M/N	Classical
WDCO	89.7	General	M/N/T	Classical
WABE	90.1	M/W	M/N	Classical
WXVS	90.1	General	M/N/T	Classical
WJWV	90.9	General	M/N/T	Classical
WREK	91.1	General	E/M/N/S/T	Alternative
WABR	91.1	General	M/N/T	Classical
WWET	91.7	General	M/N/T	Classical
WUNV	91.7	General	M/N/T	Classical
WCLK	91.9	General	M/S/T	Jazz
WZGC	92.9	General	M/N/S	Classic Rock
WSTR	94.1	General	M/N/T	Top 40
WPCH	94.9	Women	M	Adult Contemporary
WBTS	95.5	General	M/N	Adult Contemporary
WKLS	96.1	General	M	AOR
WBZY	96.7	General	M	Alternative
WFOX	97.1	General	M	Oldies
WPZE	97.5	General	M/N/T	Gospel
WSB	98.5	General	M/N	Soft Rock
WNNX	99.7	General	M/N/S	Alternative
WWWQ	100.5	Women	M/N/T	Modern Rock
WKHX	101.5	General	M/N/T	Country
WVEE	103.3	General	M/N/S	Rhythm & Blues
WALR	104.1	General	M/N/T	Rhythm & Blues
WFSH	104.7	General	M/N/T	Christian
WMAX	105.3	General	M/N/T	80's
WMXV	105.7	General	M	Classic Rock
WYAY	106.7	General	M/N/T	Country
WJZZ	107.5	General	M/N	Jazz
WHTA	107.9	General	M/N	Adult Contemporary

Note: Stations included broadcast from the Atlanta metro area
The following abbreviations may be used:
Target Audience: A=Asian; B=Black; C=Christian; E=Ethnic; F=French; G=General; H=Hispanic; M=Men; N=Native American; R=Religious; S=Senior Citizen; W=Women; Y=Young Adult; Z=Children
Station Format: E=Educational; M=Music; N=News; S=Sports; T=Talk
Music Format: AOR=Album Oriented Rock; MOR=Middle of the Road
Source: Burrelle's Media Directory, 2003

CLIMATE

Average and Extreme Temperatures

Temperature	Jan	Feb	Mar	Apr	May	Jun	Jul	Aug	Sep	Oct	Nov	Dec	Yr.
Extreme High (°F)	79	80	85	93	95	101	105	102	98	95	84	77	105
Average High (°F)	52	56	64	73	80	86	88	88	82	73	63	54	72
Average Temp. (°F)	43	46	53	62	70	77	79	79	73	63	53	45	62
Average Low (°F)	33	36	42	51	59	66	70	69	64	52	42	35	52
Extreme Low (°F)	-8	5	10	26	37	46	53	55	36	28	3	0	-8

Note: Figures cover the years 1945-1990
Source: National Climatic Data Center, International Station Meteorological Climate Summary, 9/96

Average Precipitation/Snowfall/Humidity

Precip./Humidity	Jan	Feb	Mar	Apr	May	Jun	Jul	Aug	Sep	Oct	Nov	Dec	Yr.
Avg. Precip. (in.)	4.7	4.6	5.7	4.3	4.0	3.5	5.1	3.6	3.4	2.8	3.8	4.2	49.8
Avg. Snowfall (in.)	1	1	Tr	Tr	0	0	0	0	0	0	Tr	Tr	2
Avg. Rel. Hum. 7am (%)	79	77	78	78	82	83	88	89	88	84	81	79	82
Avg. Rel. Hum. 4pm (%)	56	50	48	45	49	52	57	56	56	51	52	55	52

Note: Figures cover the years 1945-1990; Tr = Trace amounts (<0.05 in. of rain; <0.5 in. of snow)
Source: National Climatic Data Center, International Station Meteorological Climate Summary, 9/96

Weather Conditions

Temperature			Daytime Sky			Precipitation		
10°F & below	32°F & below	90°F & above	Clear	Partly cloudy	Cloudy	0.01 inch or more precip.	0.1 inch or more snow/ice	Thunder-storms
1	49	38	98	147	120	116	3	48

Note: Figures are average number of days per year and covers the years 1945-1990
Source: National Climatic Data Center, International Station Meteorological Climate Summary, 9/96

HAZARDOUS WASTE

Superfund Sites

Atlanta has no sites on the EPA's Superfund National Priorities List.
U.S. Environmental Protection Agency, National Priorities List, March 15, 2004

AIR & WATER QUALITY

Maximum Pollutant Concentrations

	Particulate Matter (ug/m^3)	Carbon Monoxide (ppm)	Sulfur Dioxide (ppm)	Nitrogen Dioxide (ppm)	Ozone 1-hour (ppm)	Ozone 8-hour (ppm)	Lead (ug/m^3)
MSA[1] Level	52	4	0.018	0.019	0.14	0.1	0.04
NAAQS[2]	150	9	0.140	0.053	0.12	0.08	1.50
Met NAAQS[2]	Yes	Yes	Yes	Yes	No	No	Yes

Note: (1) Metropolitan Statistical Area - see Appendix A for areas included; (2) National Ambient Air Quality Standards; n/a not available
Units: ppm = parts per million; ug/m^3 = micrograms per cubic meter
Source: EPA, Latest Findings on National Air Quality: 2002 Status and Trends, August 2003

Air Quality Index

In the Atlanta MSA (see Appendix A for areas included), the Air Quality Index (AQI) exceeded 100 on 37 days in 2002. An AQI value greater than 100 indicates that air quality would have been in the unhealthful range on that day.
EPA, Latest Findings on National Air Quality: 2002 Status and Trends, August 2003

Watershed Health

The U.S. Environmental Protection Agency monitors the health of the aquatic resources for the nation's 2,000+ watersheds. **The Upper Ocmulgee watershed serves the Atlanta area and received an overall Index of Watershed Indicators (IWI) score of 3 (less serious problems - low vulnerability).** The IWI score is based on seven condition and nine vulnerability indicators. The overall IWI score ranges from 1 (best health) to 6 (worst health). The Condition Indicators include: designated use attainment, fish and wildlife consumption advisories, source water condition, contaminated sediments, ambient water quality, and wetlands loss index. The Vulnerability Indicators include: aquatic species at risk, conventional and toxic loads over permitted limits, urban and agricultural runoff potential, population change, hydrologic modification, estuarine pollution susceptibility, and air deposition. *EPA, Index of Watershed Indicators, October 26, 2001*

Drinking Water

Water System Name	Pop. Served	Primary Water Source Type	Number of Violations January 2002-February 2004		
			Health Based	Significant Monitoring	Monitoring
Atlanta	650,000	Surface	None	None	1

Note: Data as of February 19, 2004
Source: EPA, Office of Ground Water and Drinking Water, Safe Drinking Water Information System

Atlanta tap water is neutral, soft.
Editor & Publisher Market Guide, 2004

Austin, Texas

Background

Starting out in 1730 as a peaceful Spanish mission on the north bank of the Colorado River in south-central Texas, Austin soon engaged in an imbroglio of territorial wars, beginning when the "Father of Texas," Stephen F. Austin, annexed the territory from Mexico in 1833 as his own. Later, the Republic of Texas named the territory Austin in honor of the colonizer, and conferred upon it state capital status. Challenges to this decision ensued, ranging from an invasion by the Mexican government to reclaim its land, to Sam Houston's call that the capital ought to move from Austin to Houston.

During peaceful times, however, Austin has been called the "City of the Violet Crown." Coined by the short story writer, William Sydney Porter, or O. Henry, the name refers to the purple mist that circles the surrounding hills of the Colorado River Valley.

This city of technological innovation is home to a strong computer and electronics industry. Austin's high-tech focus has traditionally drawn numerous high-tech companies, including Solectron, Applied Materials, Tokyo Electron, and Dell Computer, the largest private employer in Central Texas. The 3M Electro Communications Market Center and Visual Systems Divisions are headquartered in Austin, as is Samsung Electronics Co. Ltd.'s major computer chip plant built in the late 1990s.

Alongside this growth has come the problem of increased traffic, especially on Interstate 35, the main highway linking the U.S. and Mexico. State transportation officials are developing plans for an 89-mile bypass that would take much of the traffic off I-35 in Central Texas and several miles east of downtown Austin.

In addition to its traditional business community, Austin is home to the main campus of the University of Texas. Perhaps this influx of young people has contributed to the city's growth as a thriving live music scene. It so important to the city that its local government maintains the Austin Music Commission to promote the local music industry.

Not only does the popular PBS series *Austin City Limits* hail from the city, but a notable industry conference takes place here each spring. The South by Southwest Conference (SXSW) showcases more than 1,000 musical acts at venues throughout the city. The growing film and interactive industries have been added to the conference in recent years.

The civic-minded city, whose mayor recently announced a drive to make Austin the nation's fittest in two years, also will see a new city hall which is scheduled to be completed in the fall of 2004. The building, at about 115,000 gross square feet in size, will also be home to a public plaza facing Town Lake.

The city sits at a desirable location along the Colorado River, and many recreational activities center on the water. For instance, Austin boasts three spring-fed swimming pools enjoyed by its residents.

The climate of Austin is subtropical with hot summers. Winters are mild, with below-freezing temperatures occurring on an average of 25 days a year. Cold spells are short, seldom lasting more than two days. Daytime temperatures in summer are hot, while summer nights are usually pleasant.

Rankings

- Austin was ranked #22 out of 331 metro areas in *Cities Ranked & Rated*. Criteria: cost of living; climate; crime; transportation; economy and jobs; education; arts and culture; health and healthcare; leisure. *Cities Ranked & Rated, 1st Edition, 2004*

- *Ladies Home Journal* ranked America's 200 largest cities based on the qualities women surveyed care about most. Austin ranked #4 out of 57 in the big city category (population over 300,000). Criteria: crime; lifestyle; education; jobs; health; child care; politics; and the economy. *Ladies Home Journal Online, "The Best Cities for Women 2002"*

- The Austin metro area was selected as one of "America's Best Places to Live and Work 2003" by *Employment Review*. The area ranked #3 out of 20. Criteria: unemployment rate; projected job growth; cost of living; and industry specific data. *Employment Review, www.bestjobsusa.com*

- Austin was selected as one of "America's Best Places to Live" by monstermoving.com. The top 10 cities were selected based the fact that they appear repeatedly on other publications "Top Cities" lists. *www.monstermoving.com, February 26, 2004*

- Austin was selected as one of "The 10 Best Cities in North America for Independent Moviemakers" in 2003. The city was ranked #4. *MovieMaker Magazine, Issue No. 49*

- Austin was selected as one of the "Top 10 Cities for Hispanics." The city was ranked #2. The cities were selected based on data from the following sources: *Forbes* magazine; CNN; *Money* magazine; local newspapers; U.S. Census; experts; natives and residents; www.bestplaces.net; www.findyourspot.com. *Hispanic Magazine, July/August 2002*

- *Forbes* ranked the 40 most populous metro areas in the U.S. in terms of the best places to be single. The Austin metro area was ranked #1. Criteria: number of other singles; cost of living alone; nightlife; culture; job growth; coolness. *Forbes, June 5, 2003*

- *Forbes* ranked the 150 most populous metro areas in the U.S. in terms of the "Best Places for Business and Careers." The Austin metro area was ranked #1. Criteria: income and job growth; cost-of-doing-business; qualifications of the available pool of labor; crime rates; housing costs; net migration. *Forbes, May 9, 2003*

- Austin was selected as one of "America's Healthiest Cities" by *Natural Health* magazine. The city was ranked #11 out of the 50 largest urban areas in the U.S. Twenty-six criteria in the following four categories were examined: whether the city boasts natural offerings; how well the city promotes its resident's physical health; whether the city offers a healthy environment; how well the city fosters a sense of community. *Natural Health, April 2003*

- *Men's Health* ranked 101 U.S. cities in terms of the quality of their tap water. Austin received a grade of B. Criteria: levels of bacteria, arsenic, lead, trihalomethanes, and haloacetic acids were compared with the National Academy of Science's guidelines as well as with the EPA's more stringent maximum contaminant level goals. *Men's Health, March 2004*

- Sperling's BestPlaces ranked 331 metro areas and identified the most and least stressful U.S. cities. The Austin metro area ranked #60 out of the 100 largest metro areas (#1 = most stressful). Criteria: divorce rate; unemployment rate; violent and property crime; suicide rate; commute time; mental health; alcohol consumption; cloudy days. *www.BestPlaces.net, February 26, 2004*

- Sperling's BestPlaces in partnership with Pep Boys ranked 77 metro areas and identified "America's Most Drivable Cities." The Austin metro area ranked #25. Criteria: climate; road roughness; urban mobility; gas prices. *Pep Boys, "America's Most Drivable Cities," April 9, 2003*

- Austin was selected as a "Great College Town" by ePodunk. The city ranked #7 in the big city category. ePodunk.com looked at communities with four-year colleges and a total student enrollment of at least 1,500. Communities where the student ratio was too low or too high were ruled out, as were small cities with low rates of owner-occupied housing. Fifteen variables were then applied to assess arts and culture, recreation, intellectual activity, historic preservation, and cost of living. *www.ePodunk.com, April, 2002*

- Austin was ranked #57 out of America's 200 largest metro areas in *SELF Magazine's* ranking of "America's Healthiest Cities for Women." Criteria: safety; air/water quality; cancer rates; and 21 other factors relating to health. *SELF Magazine, November 2003*

- Austin was identified as one of the most dangerous large metro areas for pedestrians in the U.S. The area ranked #25 out of the nations 49 largest metro areas. Criteria: average yearly pedestrian fatalities per capita (for the years 2000 and 2001) adjusted for the number of walkers. *Surface Transportation Policy Project, "Mean Streets 2002"*

- Austin was selected as one of the 25 fittest cities in America by *Men's Fitness Online*. It ranked #13 out of America's 50 largest cities. Criteria: gyms/sporting goods; nutrition; exercise/sports; overweight/sedentary; junk food; alcohol; smoking; television; air and water quality; climate; geography; commute time; parks/open space; recreation facilities; and health care. *Men's Fitness Online, America's Fittest/Fattest Cities 2003*

- Austin was ranked #27 out of 100 cities surveyed in *Child* magazine's ranking of the "Best Cities for Families." Criteria: number of pediatricians per capita; proximity to a children's hospital; immunization rates; infant mortality rate; air quality; water quality; school spending; pupil-teacher ratio; availability of parks/green space; nearby recreational opportunities; average commute time; number of sunny days; average cost of a 3-bedroom home; unemployment rate; future job growth; crime rate; percentage of children under 5; mandated minimum child care ratios. *Child, April 2001*

- Austin was cited as one of "25 Terrific Places to Bring Up a Family" in *Mothering* magazine. Criteria: physical beauty; clean air and water; good public transportation and bike trails; arts and cultural events; activities for teens; good public education and alternative schools; homeschooling network; farmers' markets; health food stores; natural birthing community; alternative healthcare practitioners; ethnic and cultural diversity; reasonable cost of living including affordable housing; laws and places of employment that respect the needs of families; legal philosophical vaccination exemption; recycling; sustainable energy resources; and cloth diaper services. *Mothering, July/August 2001*

- *Zero Population Growth* ranked 239 cities in terms of children's health, safety, and economic well-being. Austin was ranked #19 out of 140 independent cities (cities with populations greater than 100,000 which were neither major cities nor suburbs/outer cities) and was given a grade of A. Criteria: total population and population growth; percent of population under 18 years of age; number of children's museums; health improvement grade; percent of births to teens; percent of low birthweight infants; infant mortality rate; number of Title X-funded clinics; average SAT/ACT scores; average elementary and secondary class size; crime rate; unemployment rate; percent of affordable homes; number of bad air days; park acres per 1000 persons; library circulation per child; and children's program attendance counts. *Zero Population Growth, Kid Friendly Cities Report Card 2001*

- The Austin area was selected as one of "The 50 Most Alive Places to Live" in the U.S. Criteria: ethnic diversity; recreational options; cultural vitality; crime rate; opportunities for lifelong learning; quality of hospitals and restaurants; public transportation; walking accessibility; civic activities; and the kitsch factor. The area was ranked #1 out of 10 in the "College Town" category. *Modern Maturity, May-June 2000*

- Austin was selected as one of America's 32 most livable cities by the non-profit group, Partners for Livable Communities. Criteria: environmental quality; parkland; ability to train new workers; job market; education; and use of the arts for economic development. *www.Livable.com, March 3, 2003*

- Austin was identified as one of the safest large cities in America by Morgan Quitno. All cities with populations of 500,000 or more that reported crime rates in 2002 for murder, rape, robbery, aggravated assault, burglary, and motor vehicle thefts were ranked. The city ranked #4 out of the top 10. *www.morganquitno.com, 10th Annual America's Safest (and Most Dangerous) Cities Awards*

- *Ladies Home Journal* ranked America's 200 largest cities in terms of safety. Austin ranked #88 out of 200. Criteria: violent crimes; crimes against property; and rape. *Ladies Home Journal Online, "The Best Cities for Women 2002"*

- Austin was ranked #2 out of 268 metro areas in terms of its Creativity Index. The Creativity Index is a mix of four equally weighted factors: the Creative Class (scientists, engineers, architects, designers, writers, artists, musicians, or any profession where creativity is a key factor) share of the workforce; innovation, measured as patents per capita; high-tech industry, using the Milken Institute's Tech Pole Index; and diversity, measured by the Gay Index (a reasonable proxy for an areas' openness to different kinds of people and ideas). *The Rise of the Creative Class, 2002*

- Austin was ranked #2 out of 125 regions worldwide in terms of its "Knowledge Competitiveness Index." The index attempts to measure the knowledge-based development taking place throughout the world and is based on 17 measures of economic performance that indicate a region's ability to translate its knowledge capacity into economic value. *Robert Huggins Associates, "2003-2004 World Knowledge Competitiveness Index"*

- The Austin metro area was selected by *Yahoo! Internet Life* as one of "America's Most Wired Cities...and Towns." The area ranked #3 out of 87. Criteria: home and work net use; user sophistication; domain density; and available content. *Yahoo! Internet Life, April 2001*

- The Austin metro area was selected by Cranium as one of the "Top 50 Fun Cities" in America. The area ranked #44. Criteria includes: number of sports teams, restaurants, and dance performances; number of toy stores; city budget spent on recreation. *Cranium, November 4, 2003*

- Austin was identified as one of the 100 "Most Unwired Cities" in the U.S. The area ranked #3. Criteria: number of public and commercial wireless access points; cell phone coverage offering wide area network Internet access; Internet penetration. *Intel, "Most Unwired Cities," March 4, 2003*

- Scarborough Research measured the percentage of households who subscribe to cellular services among adults ages 18 and over in 75 U.S. markets. The Austin DMA (Designated Market Area) was ranked #3 out of 75. *Scarborough Research, Scarborough USA+ 2003 Release 1*

- Austin was selected as one of "America's Most Literate Cities." The city ranked #22 out of the 64 largest U.S. cities. Criteria: booksellers; library support, holdings, and utilization; educational attainment; periodicals published; newspaper circulation. *University of Wisconsin-Whitewater, "America's Most Literate Cities," Summer 2003*

- Austin was ranked #74 in *Prevention* magazine's survey of the "Best Walking Cities in the U.S." The magazine, in conjunction with the American Podiatric Medical Association, surveyed 125 of the most populated cities and then tabulated and weighed 20 criteria of interest to pedestrians. *Prevention, April, 2004*

- Austin was chosen as one of "The 10 Best Cities for Mountain Bikers." The city was ranked #3. The criteria for making the list was two-fold: 1) great trails within or very close to the city; 2) the city had to be a place where people could actually live—with good jobs, decent schools, afforable housing, arts and sports, and a sense of community. *Mountain Bike, June 2001*

- Austin was chosen as one of North America's best cities for bicycling. Rank: #2 (includes cities with populations of 500,000 to 1,000,000). Criteria: marked bike lanes; municipal bike racks; bicycle access to bridges and public transportation; a local government bicycle coordinator; area cycling advocacy efforts; bike-safety programs; budget for cycling programs; and local cycling culture. *Bicycling, November 2001*

- Austin was selected as one of "The Best Places to Start and Grow a Company." The area ranked #4 among small metro areas. Criteria: Significant Starts (firms started in the last 10 years that still employ at least 5 people) and Young Growers (firms 10 years old or less that grew significantly during the last 4 years). *Cognetics, "Entrepreneurial Hot Spots: The Best Places in America to Start and Grow a Company," 2001*

- The Austin metro area was selected as one of "America's 50 Hottest Cities for Business Relocations and Expansions." The area ranked #16. Criteria: 70 of the industry's most prominent site selection consultants were asked which cities their clients found the most attractive when it came to selecting an expansion or relocation site in 2003. *Expansion Management, January 2004*

- The Austin metro area was selected as one of the "Top 60 CyberCities in America" by *Site Selection*. CyberCities are magnets for growing high-tech companies. Criteria: total employment; average wages; total payroll; number of companies; R&D spending and venture capital in the 45 Standard Industrial Classification (SIC) codes that define the high-technology industry. *Site Selection, March 2002*

- The Austin metro area was cited as one of America's "Top 50 Metros" in terms of the availability of highly skilled, highly educated workers. The area ranked #10 out of 50. Criteria: degree holders (bachelors, masters, professional, and Ph.D.) as a percent of the workforce; science and engineering workers as a percent of the workforce; number of patents issued; number and type of colleges in each metro area. *Expansion Management, March 2004*

- The Austin metro area was cited as one of "The Best Places in the U.S. to Locate a Company." The area ranked #14 out of 329. Criteria: education (with emphasis on college board test results and high school graduation rates); availability of quality healthcare services and the cost to employers; quality of life; logistics workforce and companies; transportation infrastructure; quality and quantity of highly educated technical workers; business climate. *Expansion Management, July 2003*

- The Austin metro area was cited as one of America's "Most Picture Perfect Metros" by *Plant Sites and Parks* magazine. Each year *PSP* readers rank the metro areas they consider best bets for their companies to relocate or expand to in the coming year. The area ranked #10 out of 10. *Plant Sites and Parks, March 2004*

- The Austin metro area was selected as one of the "Top 40 Hottest Real Estate Markets" for expanding or relocating businesses." Criteria: rental costs; purchase prices; and vacancy rates of office and warehouse space. *Expansion Management, August 2003*

- The Austin metro area appeared on *Forbes/Milken Institute* list of "Best Places for Business and Career." Rank: #19 out of 200 metro areas. Criteria: salary growth; job growth; number of technology clusters; overall concentration of technology activity relative to national average; and technology output growth. *www.forbes.com, Forbes/Milken Institute Best Places 2002*

- The Austin metro area appeared on the "Milken Institute Best Performing Cities" index. Rank: #59 out of 200 large metro areas. Criteria: job growth; wage and salary growth; high-tech output growth. *Milken Institute, June 25, 2003*

- The Austin metro area appeared on *Entrepreneur* magazine's list of the "Best Cities for Entrepreneurs" in 2003. The area ranked #20 out of 61 in the large city category. Criteria: entrepreneurial activity; small-business growth; economic growth; and risk. *www.Entrepreneur.com*

- The Austin metro area was selected as one of the "Top 25 Cities for Doing Business in America." *Inc.* measured current-year employment growth in 277 regions as well as current trends in the annual average growth over the past three years, and compared employment expansion between the first and second halves of the last decade. Job growth factors account for two-thirds, and balance among industries accounts for one third of the final score for each city.The Austin metro area ranked #19 among large metro areas. *Inc. Magazine, March 2004*

- The Austin metro area was selected as one of "The Top 20 Boom Towns in America." *Business 2.0* magazine and econometric research firm Global Insight compared 319 metropolitan areas in the U.S. and ranked the 61 with populations over 1 million. Criteria: a weighted formula that includes forecast growth rates in sectors that contain the economy's 10 most skilled occupational clusters; the prevalence of college degrees in the local workforce; median salary. The area ranked #4 among large metro areas. *Business 2.0 Magazine, March 2004*

- The Austin metro area appeared on *IndustryWeek's* fourth annual World-Class Communities list. It ranked #11 out of 315 metro areas. Criteria: MSA Gross Metropolitan Product (GMP) per manufacturing employee; and MSA percent share of U.S. manufacturing Gross Domestic Product (GDP). *IndustryWeek, April 16, 2001*

- The Austin metro area was selected as a "2001 Choice City" by *Business Development Outlook* magazine. Twenty-five cities were selected, based on data from the Bureau of Labor Statistics, Census Bureau, Federal Reserve, The Conference Board, and the U.S. Conference of Mayors, as being the most desirable into which a business can relocate or expand. *Business Development Outlook, 2001 Choice Cities*

- The Austin metro area was highlighted as one of the ten fastest-growing metro areas in the U.S. between 1900 and 2000. The area ranked #5. *American Demographics, February 2003*

- ING Group ranked the 125 largest metro areas according to the general financial security of residents. The Austin metro area was ranked #81 out of 125. Criteria: Earnings and Wealth Potential (household income, education, net assets, cost of living); Safety Net (health insurance, retirement savings, life insurance, income support programs); Personal Threats (unemployment rate, low-income households, crime rate); Community Economic Vitality (cost of community services, job quality, job creation, housing costs). *ING Group, "The Best Cities to Earn and Save Money: A Ranking of the Largest 125 U.S. Cities," 2001 Edition*

Business Environment

CITY FINANCES

City Government Finances

Component	2000-2001 ($000)	2000-2001 ($ per capita)
Total Revenues	1,864,170	2,839
Total Expenditures	1,843,376	2,808
Debt Outstanding	4,295,039	6,542
Cash and Securities	3,120,347	4,753

Source: U.S Census Bureau, Government Finances 2000-2001, August 2003

City Government Revenue by Source

Source	2000-2001 ($000)	2000-2001 ($ per capita)
General Revenue		
From Federal Government	40,997	62
From State Government	16,800	26
From Local Governments	439	1
Taxes		
Property	180,289	275
Sales	164,614	251
Personal Income	0	0
License	0	0
Charges	313,608	478
Liquor Store	0	0
Utility	912,918	1,390
Employee Retirement	66,571	101
Other	167,934	256

Source: U.S Census Bureau, Government Finances 2000-2001, August 2003

City Government Expenditures by Function

Function	2000-2001 ($000)	2000-2001 ($ per capita)	2000-2001 (%)
General Expenditures			
Airports	68,456	104	3.7
Corrections	0	0	0.0
Education	0	0	0.0
Fire Protection	72,260	110	3.9
Governmental Administration	60,825	93	3.3
Health	80,150	122	4.3
Highways	39,268	60	2.1
Hospitals	1,487	2	0.1
Housing and Community Development	14,148	22	0.8
Interest on General Debt	96,729	147	5.2
Libraries	18,175	28	1.0
Parking	0	0	0.0
Parks and Recreation	81,399	124	4.4
Police Protection	110,469	168	6.0
Public Welfare	9,387	14	0.5
Sewerage	49,809	76	2.7
Solid Waste Management	41,536	63	2.3
Liquor Store	0	0	0.0
Utility	883,780	1,346	47.9
Employee Retirement	80,999	123	4.4
Other	134,499	205	7.3

Source: U.S Census Bureau, Government Finances 2000-2001, August 2003

Municipal Bond Ratings

Area	Moody's
City	Aaa

Source: Mergent Bond Record, February 2004

DEMOGRAPHICS

Population Growth

Area	1990 Census	2000 Census	2003 Estimate	2008 Projection	Population Growth (%) 1990-2000	Population Growth (%) 2000-2008
City	499,053	656,562	704,618	786,193	31.6	19.7
MSA[1]	846,217	1,249,763	1,398,133	1,638,145	47.7	31.1
U.S.	248,709,873	281,421,906	290,647,163	305,918,071	13.2	8.7

Note: (1) Metropolitan Statistical Area - see Appendix A for areas included
Source: Claritas, Inc.

Number of Households and Average Household Size

Area	1990 Census	2000 Census	2003 Estimate	2008 Projection	2003 Average Household Size
City	204,916	265,649	284,258	315,323	2.5
MSA[1]	325,992	471,855	525,004	609,817	2.7
U.S.	91,947,410	105,480,101	109,440,059	116,034,472	2.7

Note: (1) Metropolitan Statistical Area - see Appendix A for areas included
Source: Claritas, Inc.

Race and Ethnicity

Area	White Non-Hispanic	Black Non-Hispanic	Asian Non-Hispanic	Other Race Non-Hispanic	Hispanic
City	64.7	9.9	5.0	20.4	31.6
MSA[1]	72.4	7.8	3.7	16.1	26.6
U.S.	74.5	12.4	3.8	9.3	13.2

Note: Figures are 2003 estimates; (1) Metropolitan Statistical Area - see Appendix A for areas included
Source: Claritas, Inc.

Segregation

City Index[2]	City Rank[3]	MSA[1] Index[2]	MSA[1] Rank[4]
60.9	47	57.1	179

Note: Figures are based on an analysis of Census 2000 data; (1) Metropolitan Statistical Area - see Appendix A for areas included; (2) Dissimilarity Index—the most commonly used measure of segregation between two groups, reflecting their relative distributions across neighborhoods within a city or metropolitan area. It can range in value from 0, indicating complete integration, to 100, indicating complete segregation; (3) Ranges from 1 (most segregated) to 100 (least segregated) and includes all the cities in this book; (4) Ranges from 1 (most segregated) to 318 (least segregated) and includes 318 metropolitan areas.
Source: www.CensusScope.org

Ancestry

Area	German	Irish[2]	English	American	Italian	Polish	French[3]	Scottish
City	12.9	8.4	8.8	4.3	2.5	1.4	2.7	2.3
MSA[1]	15.3	9.3	9.7	5.3	2.5	1.5	2.9	2.4
U.S.	15.2	10.9	8.7	7.3	5.6	3.2	3.0	1.7

Note: Figures include multiple ancestry (e.g. if a person reported being Irish and Italian, they were included in both columns); (1) Metropolitan Statistical Area - see Appendix A for areas included; (2) Includes Celtic; (3) Includes Alsatian but excludes Basque
Source: Census 2000, Summary File 3

Foreign-Born Population

Area	Any Foreign Country	Percent of Population Born in: Europe	Asia	Africa	Oceania[2]	Canada	Mexico	Latin America[3]
City	16.6	1.1	3.8	0.3	0.1	0.3	9.4	1.6
MSA[1]	12.2	1.0	2.9	0.3	0.0	0.2	6.7	1.1
U.S.	11.1	1.7	2.9	0.3	0.1	0.3	3.3	2.5

Note: (1) Metropolitan Statistical Area - see Appendix A for areas included; (2) Includes Australia, New Zealand subregion, Melanesia, Micronesia, Polynesia, and Oceania n.e.c; (3) Includes Central America (excluding Mexico), South America, and the Caribbean.
Source: Census 2000, Summary File 3

Religion

Area	Catholic	Southern Baptist	United Methodist	ELCA[1]	LDS[2]	Presbyterian Church USA	Jewish Est.	Muslim Est.
County	20.4	9.5	2.7	1.5	0.6	1.3	1.7	0.4
U.S.	22.0	7.1	3.7	1.8	1.5	1.1	2.2	0.6

Note: Figures shown are the number of adherents as a percentage of the total population; Adherents are defined as all members, including full members, their children and the estimated number of other participants who are not considered members (e.g. the baptized, those not confirmed, those not eligible for communion, those regularly attending services, etc.); (1) Evangelical Lutheran Church in America; (2) The Church of Jesus Christ of Latter Day Saints
Source: Reprinted with permission from Religious Congregations and Membership in the United States 2000 (Nashville, Glenmary Research Center, 2002) Copyright Association of Statisticians of American Religious Bodies. All rights reserved.

Age Distribution

Area	Percent of Population						
	Under Age 5	Age 5 to 17	Age 18 to 34	Age 35 to 49	Age 50 to 64	Age 65 to 79	80 Years and Over
City	7.1	15.4	37.5	22.9	10.5	4.9	1.7
MSA[1]	7.4	17.9	31.5	24.4	11.7	5.4	1.8
U.S.	6.8	18.9	23.7	23.5	14.8	9.2	3.2

Note: (1) Metropolitan Statistical Area - see Appendix A for areas included
Source: Census 2000, Summary File 3

Marriage Status

Area	Never Married	Now Married Except Separated	Separated	Widowed	Divorced
City	39.4	43.9	2.0	3.7	11.0
MSA[1]	32.2	51.7	1.8	3.8	10.4
U.S.	27.1	54.4	2.2	6.6	9.7

Note: Figures cover population 15 years of age and older; (1) Metropolitan Statistical Area - see Appendix A for areas included
Source: Census 2000, Summary File 3

Male/Female Ratio

Area	Males	Females	Males per 100 Females
City	361,818	342,800	105.5
MSA[1]	708,670	689,463	102.8
U.S.	142,511,883	148,135,280	96.2

Note: Figures are 2003 estimates; (1) Metropolitan Statistical Area - see Appendix A for areas included
Source: Claritas, Inc.

ECONOMY

Gross Metropolitan Product

Area	1999	2000	2001	2002	2002 Rank[2]
MSA[1]	42.7	47.3	48.6	49.2	51

Note: Figures are in billions of dollars; (1) Metropolitan Statistical Area - see Appendix A for areas included; (2) Rank ranges from 1 to 319
Source: The U.S. Conference of Mayors, Metro Economies Report, July 2003

INCOME

Per Capita/Median/Average Income

Area	Per Capita ($)	Median Household ($)	Average Household ($)
City	27,963	49,984	68,594
MSA[1]	28,467	58,013	75,230
U.S.	24,078	46,868	63,207

Note: Figures are 2003 estimates; (1) Metropolitan Statistical Area - see Appendix A for areas included
Source: Claritas, Inc.

Household Income Distribution

Area	Percent of Households Earning							
	Under $15,000	$15,000 -24,999	$25,000 -34,999	$35,000 -49,999	$50,000 -74,999	$75,000 -99,000	$100,000 -149,999	$150,000 and up
City	12.4	9.9	11.5	16.1	19.3	11.7	11.5	7.4
MSA[1]	10.2	8.4	9.9	15.1	20.2	13.7	14.0	8.6
U.S.	14.1	11.5	11.7	16.0	19.2	11.3	10.2	6.0

Note: Figures are 2003 estimates; (1) Metropolitan Statistical Area - see Appendix A for areas included
Source: Claritas, Inc.

Poverty Rates by Age

Area	All Ages	Under 5 Years Old	5 to 17 Years Old	18 to 64 Years Old	65 Years and Over
City	14.4	1.3	2.6	10.0	0.6
MSA[1]	11.1	1.0	2.1	7.4	0.6
U.S.	12.4	1.2	3.0	6.9	1.2

Note: Figures are percent of population with income in 1999 below poverty level and only include population for whom poverty status is determined; (1) Metropolitan Statistical Area - see Appendix A for areas included
Source: Census 2000, Summary File 3

Personal Bankruptcy Filing Rate

Area	2002	2003
Travis County	3.23	3.86
U.S.	5.34	5.58

Note: Numbers are per 1,000 population and include Chapter 7 and Chapter 13 filings
Source: Federal Deposit Insurance Corporation (FDIC), Regional Economic Conditions (RECON), 2/25/2004

EMPLOYMENT

Labor Force and Employment

Area	Civilian Labor Force			Workers Employed		
	Dec. 2002	Dec. 2003	% Chg.	Dec. 2002	Dec. 2003	% Chg.
City	410,034	420,005	2.4	387,900	399,355	3.0
MSA[1]	772,810	792,089	2.5	734,363	756,049	3.0
U.S.	144,807,000	146,501,000	1.2	136,599,000	138,556,000	1.4

Note: Data is not seasonally adjusted and covers workers 16 years of age and older;
(1) Metropolitan Statistical Area - see Appendix A for areas included
Source: Bureau of Labor Statistics, http://stats.bls.gov

Unemployment Rate

Area	2003											
	Jan.	Feb.	Mar.	Apr.	May	Jun.	Jul.	Aug.	Sep.	Oct.	Nov.	Dec.
City	6.2	6.0	6.2	5.7	6.0	6.8	6.4	6.1	6.0	5.4	5.3	4.9
MSA[1]	5.7	5.6	5.7	5.3	5.5	6.3	5.9	5.7	5.6	5.0	4.9	4.5
U.S.	6.5	6.4	6.2	5.8	5.8	6.5	6.3	6.0	5.8	5.6	5.6	5.4

Note: Data is not seasonally adjusted and covers workers 16 years of age and older; All figures are percentages; (1) Metropolitan Statistical Area - see Appendix A for areas included
Source: Bureau of Labor Statistics, http://stats.bls.gov

Employment by Occupation

Occupation Classification	City (%)	MSA[1] (%)	U.S. (%)
Sales and Office	26.0	26.7	26.7
Professional and Related	27.7	25.7	20.2
Service	13.2	12.4	14.9
Production, Transportation, and Material Moving	8.6	9.3	14.6
Management, Business, and Financial	15.4	16.2	13.5
Construction, Extraction, and Maintenance	9.0	9.5	9.4
Farming, Forestry, and Fishing	0.1	0.2	0.7

Note: Figures cover employed civilians 16 years of age and older;
(1) Metropolitan Statistical Area - see Appendix A for areas included
Source: Census 2000, Summary File 3

Employment by Industry

| Sector | MSA[1] | | U.S. |
	Number of Employees	Percent of Total	Percent of Total
Government	145,500	22.2	16.7
Education and Health Services	66,500	10.1	12.9
Professional and Business Services	85,000	13.0	12.3
Retail Trade	71,700	10.9	11.8
Manufacturing	57,100	8.7	11.0
Leisure and Hospitality	63,500	9.7	9.1
Finance Activities	40,300	6.1	6.1
Construction	35,100	5.3	5.1
Wholesale Trade	34,300	5.2	4.3
Other Services	24,700	3.8	4.1
Transportation and Utilities	10,700	1.6	3.7
Information	20,200	3.1	2.4
Natural Resources and Mining	1,500	0.2	0.4

Note: Figures cover non-farm employment as of December 2003 and are not seasonally adjusted;
(1) Metropolitan Statistical Area - see Appendix A for areas included
Source: Bureau of Labor Statistics, http://stats.bls.gov

Average Wages

Occupation	$/Hr.	Occupation	$/Hr.
Accountants and Auditors	24.15	Maids and Housekeeping Cleaners	7.83
Automotive Mechanics	17.47	Maintenance and Repair Workers	12.80
Bookkeepers	14.09	Marketing Managers	38.42
Carpenters	14.34	Nuclear Medicine Technologists	24.21
Cashiers	8.24	Nurses, Licensed Practical	15.92
Clerks, General Office	11.78	Nurses, Registered	22.06
Clerks, Receptionists/Information	11.42	Nursing Aides/Orderlies/Attendants	9.35
Clerks, Shipping/Receiving	12.14	Packers and Packagers, Hand	8.07
Computer Programmers	34.02	Physical Therapists	26.37
Computer Support Specialists	22.79	Postal Service Mail Carriers	18.80
Computer Systems Analysts	28.91	Real Estate Brokers	42.40
Cooks, Restaurant	9.19	Retail Salespersons	11.46
Dentists	82.17	Sales Reps., Exc. Tech./Scientific	21.39
Electrical Engineers	38.45	Sales Reps., Tech./Scientific	32.20
Electricians	18.17	Secretaries, Exc. Legal/Med./Exec.	12.32
Financial Managers	39.86	Security Guards	10.01
First-Line Supervisors/Mgrs., Sales	15.39	Surgeons	97.57
Food Preparation Workers	7.88	Teacher Assistants	9.60
General and Operations Managers	38.74	Teachers, Elementary School	19.50
Hairdressers/Cosmetologists	10.92	Teachers, Secondary School	20.20
Internists	n/a	Telemarketers	11.44
Janitors and Cleaners	8.40	Truck Drivers, Heavy/Tractor-Trailer	14.72
Landscaping/Groundskeeping Workers	8.86	Truck Drivers, Light/Delivery Svcs.	13.19
Lawyers	46.12	Waiters and Waitresses	7.61

Note: Wage data is for 2002 and covers the Metropolitan Statistical Area (see Appendix A for areas included).
Hourly wages for elementary/secondary school teachers and teacher assistants were calculated by the editors
from annual wage data assuming a 40 hour work week; n/a not available.
Source: Bureau of Labor Statistics, 2002 Metro Area Occupational Employment and Wage Estimates

Occupational Employment Projections: 1996 - 2006

Occupations Expected to Have the Largest Job Growth (ranked by numerical growth)	Fast-Growing Occupations[1] (ranked by percent growth)
1. Cashiers	1. Desktop publishers
2. Salespersons, retail	2. Systems analysts
3. General managers & top executives	3. Customer service representatives
4. Truck drivers, light	4. Physical therapy assistants and aides
5. Child care workers, private household	5. Computer engineers
6. General office clerks	6. Emergency medical technicians
7. Systems analysts	7. Medical assistants
8. Food preparation workers	8. Respiratory therapists
9. Food service workers	9. Telephone & cable TV line install & repair
10. Registered nurses	10. Physical therapists

Note: Projections cover Texas; (1) Excludes occupations with total job growth less than 300
Source: U.S. Department of Labor, Employment and Training Administration, America's Labor Market Information System (ALMIS)

TAXES

State Corporate Income Tax Rates

State	Rate (%)	Number of Brackets	Low Bracket (Under $)	High Bracket (Over $)
Texas	None	na	na	na

Note: Tax rates as of December 31, 2003; na not applicable
Source: Tax Foundation, www.taxfoundation.org

State Individual Income Tax Rates

State	Federal Deductibility	Marginal Rate (%)	Number of Brackets	Low Bracket (Under $)	High Bracket (Over $)
Texas	No	None	na	na	na

Note: Tax rates as of December 31, 2003; Brackets apply to single taxpayers and married people filing separately; na not applicable
Source: Tax Foundation, www.taxfoundation.org

Various State and Local Tax Rates

State Sales and Use (%)	Total Sales and Use (%)	Gasoline (cents/gal.)	Cigarette (cents/pack)	Spirits ($/gal.)	Table Wine ($/gal.)	Beer ($/gal.)
6.25	8.25	20	41	2.40	0.20	0.20

Note: Tax rates as of December 31, 2003
Source: Tax Foundation, www.taxfoundation.org

State Tax Burdens

Area	Combined State and Local Tax Burden		Combined Federal, State and Local Tax Burden	
	Percent	Rank	Percent	Rank
Texas	8.3	47	28.4	31
U.S. Average	9.7	-	30.0	-

Note: Figures are for 2003
Source: Tax Foundation, www.taxfoundation.org

Internal Revenue Service Tax Audits

IRS District	Percent of Returns Audited				
	1996	1997	1998	1999	2000
South Texas	0.55	0.50	0.50	0.31	0.17
U.S.	0.66	0.61	0.46	0.31	0.20

Note: Figures cover IRS district audits of federal income tax returns filed by individuals. Geographic data on district audits for 2001 and 2002 are being withheld by the IRS. TRAC is challenging this policy.
Source: Syracuse University, Transactional Records Access Clearinghouse (TRAC), "Odds of IRS District Tax Audit 2000"

**RESIDENTIAL
REAL ESTATE**

Building Permits

Area	Single-Family			Multi-Family			Total		
	2001	2002	Pct. Chg.	2001	2002	Pct. Chg.	2001	2002	Pct. Chg.
City	2,119	2,431	14.7	4,603	3,943	-14.3	6,722	6,374	-5.2
U.S.	1,235,600	1,332,600	7.9	401,100	415,100	3.5	1,636,700	1,747,700	6.8

Note: Figures represent new, privately-owned housing units authorized (unadjusted data)
Source: U.S. Census Bureau, Manufacturing, Mining, and Construction Statistics

Homeownership and Housing Vacancies

Area	Homeownership Rate[2] (%)			Rental Vacancy Rate[3] (%)			Homeowner Vacancy Rate[4] (%)		
	2001	2002[a]	2003	2001	2002[a]	2003	2001	2002[a]	2003
MSA[1]	57.7	56.0	59.1	8.8	12.0	14.8	1.1	1.9	1.4
U.S.	67.8	67.9	68.3	8.4	8.9	9.8	1.8	1.7	1.8

Note: (1) Metropolitan Statistical Area - see Appendix A for areas included; (2) The proportion of households that are owners; (3) The proportion of the rental inventory that is vacant for rent; (4) The proportion of the homeowner inventory that is vacant for sale; (a) 2002 figures have been revised; n/a not available
Source: U.S. Census Bureau, Housing Vacancies and Homeownership Annual Statistics: 2003

**COMMERCIAL
REAL ESTATE**

Industrial/Office Markets

Type/Market Area	Inventory (sq. ft.)	Vacant (sq. ft.)	Vacancy Rate (%)	Under Construction (sq. ft.)	Net Absorption (sq. ft.)
Industrial Space					
Austin	32,267,907	6,686,476	20.72	0	-629,372
Office Space					
Austin	33,547,929	6,466,917	19.28	525,000	220,619

Note: Data as of 4th Quarter, 2003; n/a not available
Source: Society of Industrial and Office Realtors, 2004 Comparative Statistics of Industrial and Office Real Estate Markets

**COMMERCIAL
UTILITIES**

Typical Monthly Electric Bills

Area	Commercial Service ($/month)		Industrial Service ($/month)	
	12 kW demand 1,500 kWh	120 kW demand 30,000 kWh	1,000 kW demand 400,000 kWh	20,000 kW demand 10,000,000 kWh
City	116	2,673	27,636	566,200

Note: Based on rates in effect January 1, 2003
Source: Memphis Light, Gas and Water, 2003 Utility Bill Comparisons for Selected U.S. Cities

TRANSPORTATION

Means of Transportation to Work

Area	Car/Truck/Van		Public Transportation			Bicycle	Walked	Other Means	Worked at Home
	Drove Alone	Car-pooled	Bus	Subway	Railroad				
City	73.6	13.9	4.3	0.0	0.0	0.9	2.5	1.3	3.4
MSA[1]	76.5	13.7	2.5	0.0	0.0	0.6	2.1	1.1	3.6
U.S.	75.7	12.2	2.5	1.5	0.5	0.4	2.9	1.0	3.3

Note: Figures shown are percentages and cover workers 16 years of age and older;
(1) Metropolitan Statistical Area - see Appendix A for areas included
Source: Census 2000, Summary File 3

Travel Time to Work

Area	Less Than 15 Minutes	15 to 29 Minutes	30 to 44 Minutes	45 to 59 Minutes	60 Minutes or More
City	27.0	45.2	19.1	4.5	4.2
MSA[1]	24.5	38.6	22.5	8.3	6.1
U.S.	29.4	36.1	19.1	7.4	8.0

Note: Figures are percentages and include workers 16 years old and over; (1) Metropolitan Statistical Area - see Appendix A for areas included
Source: Census 2000, Summary File 3

Roadway Congestion Index

Area	1982	1990	1996	2000	2001
City	0.73	0.90	0.97	1.12	1.17
Average[1]	0.82	1.01	1.08	1.16	1.17

Note: Values greater than 1.00 indicate undesirable mobility levels; (1) average of 75 urban areas
Source: Texas Transportation Institute, The 2003 Annual Urban Mobility Report

Transportation Statistics

Interstate highways (2004)	I-35
Public transportation (2002)	Capital Metropolitan Transportation Authority (CMTA)
Buses	
Average fleet age in years	6.2
No. operated in max. service	407
Demand response	
Average fleet age in years	1.2
No. operated in max. service	105
Passenger air service	
Airport	Austin-Bergstrom International
Airlines (2003)	11
Boardings (2002)	3,186,381
Amtrak service (2004)	Yes
Major waterways/ports	None

Source: Federal Transit Administration, National Transit Database, 2002; Editor & Publisher Market Guide, 2004; Bureau of Transportation Statistics, Airport Enplanement Activity for CY2002; www.amtrak.com

BUSINESSES

Major Business Headquarters

Company Name	2003 Rankings	
	Fortune 500	Forbes 500
Temple-Inland	353	-

Note: Companies listed are located in the city; dashes indicate no ranking
Fortune 500: Companies that produce a 10-K are ranked 1 to 500 based on 2002 revenue
Forbes 500: Private companies are ranked 1 to 281 based on 2002 revenue
Source: Fortune, April 14, 2003; www.forbes.com, November 6, 2003

Best Companies to Work For

National Instruments; Whole Foods Market, headquartered in Austin, are among the "100 Best Companies to Work for in 2004." Criteria: trust in management, pride in work/company, camaraderie, company responses to the Hewitt People Practices Inventory, and employee responses to their Great Place to Work survey. The companies also had to be at least 10 years old and have a minimum of 500 employees. *Fortune, January 12, 2004*

National Instruments, headquartered in Austin, is among the "200 Best Small Companies in 2003." Criteria: 3,500 companies whose latest 12-month sales were $5 million to $600 million were screened. Those with a net margin or five-year average ROE below 5% were cut. Banks, utilities, real estate investment trusts and limited partnerships whose financial structures are too different from most operating companies were also excluded. Shares had to be trading above $5 by the end of September 2003. Financial statement footnotes were examined for major issues. For the final ranking, equal weight was given to growth in sales, earnings and ROE for the past five years and the latest 12 months. *www.forbes.com, October 27, 2003*

Fast-Growing Businesses

According to *Inc.*, Austin is home to four of America's 500 fastest-growing private companies: **Four Hands; Motive Communications; National Bankcard Systems; Obsidian Software.** Criteria: must be an independent, privately-held, U.S. corporation, proprietorship or partnership; sales of at least $200,000 in 1998; five-year operating/sales history; increase in 2002 sales over 2001 sales; holding companies, regulated banks, and utilities were excluded. *Inc. 500, America's Fastest-Growing Private Companies, October 15, 2003*

According to Deloitte & Touche LLP, Austin is home to seven of North America's 500 fastest-growing high-technology companies: **Active Power, Inc; Crossroads Systems, Inc; Luminex Corporation; Motive Communications, Inc; Perficient, Inc; Silicon Laboratories; Vignette Corporation.** Companies are ranked by percentage growth in revenue over a five-year period. Criteria for inclusion: must be a U.S. or Canadian company developing and/or providing technology products or services; company must have been in business for five years with 1998 operating revenues of at least $50,000 USD or $75,000 CD and 2002 operating revenues of at least $1 million USD/CD. *Deloitte & Touche LLP, 2003 Technology Fast 500*

Women-Owned Firms: Number, Employment and Sales

Area	Number of Firms	Employ-ment	Sales ($000)	Rank[2]
MSA[1]	29,407	62,727	8,659,282	36

Note: (1) Metropolitan Statistical Area - see Appendix A for areas included;
(2) Calculated on an averaging of the number of businesses, employment, and sales
Source: The National Foundation for Women Business Owners, Women-Owned Businesses in the Top 50 Metropolitan Areas, 2002: A Fact Sheet

Women-Owned Firms: Growth

Area	Percent Change from 1997 to 2002			Rank[2]
	Number of Firms	Employ-ment	Sales	
MSA[1]	13.8	43.7	62.5	8
Top 50 MSAs	14.0	31.4	42.6	-

Note: (1) Metropolitan Statistical Area - see Appendix A for areas included; (2) Calculated on an averaging of the percent growth of number of businesses, employment, and sales
Source: The National Foundation for Women Business Owners, Women-Owned Businesses in the Top 50 Metropolitan Areas, 2002: A Fact Sheet

Minority and Women-Owned Businesses

Ownership	All Firms		Firms with Paid Employees			
	Firms	Sales ($000)	Firms	Sales ($000)	Employees	Payroll ($000)
Black	1,737	150,641	259	129,270	1,254	23,653
Hispanic	7,172	1,010,088	1,317	872,508	5,764	137,111
Women	14,387	4,121,478	2,710	3,824,095	32,263	710,156

Note: Figures cover firms located in the city
Source: 1997 Economic Census, Minority and Women-Owned Businesses

Minority Business Opportunity

Austin is home to one company which is on the Black Enterprise Auto Dealer 100 list (100 largest dealers based on gross sales): **JMC Auto Group.** Criteria: company must be operational in previous calendar year and at least 51% black-owned. *Black Enterprise, www.blackenterprise.com, B.E. 100s, 2003 Report*

Two of the 500 largest Hispanic-owned companies in the U.S. are located in Austin. *Hispanic Business, June 2003*

HOTELS

Hotels/Motels

Area	Hotels/Motels	Average Minimum Rates ($)		
		Tourist	First-Class	Deluxe
City	141	62	112	230

Source: OAG Travel Planner Online, Spring 2004

Austin is home to one of the top 100 hotels in the U.S. and Canada according to *Travel & Leisure*: **Four Seasons Hotel** (#98). Criteria: value, rooms/ambience, location, facilities/activities and service. *Travel & Leisure, "The World's Best Hotels 2003"*

EVENT SITES

Major Event Sites, Meeting Places and Convention Centers

Name	Guest Rooms	Exhibit/ Meeting Space (sq. ft.)	Largest Meeting Room Capacity
Austin Convention Center	n/a	881,400	4,348
Austin North Hilton and Towers	237	27,000	900
Doubletree Hotel Austin North	350	27,000	1,400
F.C. Erwin Jr. Special Events Center	n/a	n/a	17,844
Hyatt Regency - Austin	447	23,000	1,400
Omni Austin Hotel Downtown	372	20,000	400
Renaissance Austin Hotel	478	60,000	3,500

Note: n/a not available
Source: Original research

Living Environment

COST OF LIVING

Cost of Living Index

Year	Composite Index	Groceries	Housing	Utilities	Trans-portation	Health Care	Misc. Goods/ Services
2001	105.4	98.2	116.5	96.5	98.7	107.3	103.2
2002	103.1	93.3	108.4	100.7	101.2	102.5	104.7
2003	102.2	89.8	107.8	105.4	96.7	106.2	102.6

Note: U.S. = 100
Source: ACCRA, Cost of Living Index, 2001, 2002 and 2003 4-Quarter Averages

HOUSING

House Price Index (HPI)

Area	National Ranking[2]	Quarterly Change (%)	One-Year Change (%)	Five-Year Change (%)
MSA[1]	220	1.23	0.78	34.94
U.S.[3]	-	3.67	7.97	41.81

Note: The HPI is a weighted repeat sales index. It measures average price changes in repeat sales or refinancings on the same properties. This information is obtained by reviewing repeat mortgage transactions on single-family properties whose mortgages have been purchased or securitized by Fannie Mae of Freddie Mac in January 1975; (1) Metropolitan Statistical Area - see Appendix A for areas included; (2) Rankings are based on annual percentage change, for all MSAs containing at least 15,000 transactions over the last 10 years and ranges from 1 to 220; (3) figures based on a weighted division average; all figures are for the period ended December 31, 2003
Source: Office of Federal Housing Enterprise Oversight, House Price Index, March 1, 2004

Housing: Year Structure Built

Area	1990 -2000	1980 -1989	1970 -1979	1960 -1969	1950 -1959	1940 -1949	Before 1940	Median Year
City	21.4	26.4	23.9	12.0	8.4	4.1	3.8	1979
MSA[1]	30.2	27.4	20.2	8.8	6.2	3.3	3.9	1983
U.S.	17.0	15.8	18.5	13.7	12.7	7.3	15.0	1971

Note: Figures are percentages; (1) Metropolitan Statistical Area - see Appendix A for areas included
Source: Census 2000, Summary File 3

Average New Home Price

Area	2001	2002	2003
City	233,877	241,924	255,261
U.S.	212,643	236,567	248,193

Note: Figures, in dollars, are based on a new home with 2,400 sq. ft. of living area on an 8,000 sq. ft. lot.
Source: ACCRA, Cost of Living Index, 2001, 2002 and 2003 4-Quarter Averages

Average Apartment Rent

Area	2001	2002	2003
City	997	1,004	931
U.S.	674	708	721

Note: Figures, in dollars per month, are based on an unfurnished two bedroom, 1-1/2 or 2 bath apartment, approximately 950 sq. ft. in size, excluding all utilities except water
Source: ACCRA, Cost of Living Index, 2001, 2002 and 2003 4-Quarter Averages

RESIDENTIAL UTILITIES

Average Residential Utility Costs

Area	All Electric ($/mth)	Part Electric ($/mth)	Other Energy ($/mth)	Phone ($/mth)
City	–	94.75	39.47	24.14
U.S.	116.46	65.82	62.68	23.90

Source: ACCRA, Cost of Living Index, 2003 4-Quarter Average

HEALTH CARE

Average Health Care Costs

Area	Hospital ($/day)	Doctor ($/visit)	Dentist ($/visit)
City	568.81	80.87	91.53
U.S.	678.35	67.91	83.90

Note: Hospital—based on a semi-private room; Doctor—based on a general practitioner's routine exam of an established patient; Dentist—based on adult teeth cleaning and periodic oral exam.
Source: ACCRA, Cost of Living Index, 2003 4-Quarter Average

Distribution of Non-Federal, Office-Based Physicians

Area	Total	Family/ General Practice	Specialties Medical	Specialties Surgical	Specialties Other
MSA[1] (number)	2,173	353	674	534	612
MSA[1] (rate per 10,000 pop.)	17.4	2.8	5.4	4.3	4.9
Metro Average[2] (rate per 10,000 pop.)	33.1	2.2	7.7	4.8	5.6

Note: Data as of December 31, 2001; (1) Metropolitan Statistical Area - see Appendix A for areas included; (2) Average of 81 MSAs and CMSAs in this book
Source: American Medical Association, Physician Characteristics & Distribution in the U.S., 2003-2004

Hospitals

Austin has the following hospitals: 5 general medical and surgical; 3 psychiatric; 3 rehabilitation; 1 long-term acute care; 1 other specialty.
AHA Guide to the Healthcare Field, 2003-2004

PRESIDENTIAL ELECTION

2000 Presidential Election Results

Area	Gore	Bush	Nader	Buchanan	Other
Travis County	41.7	46.9	10.4	0.2	0.9
U.S.	48.4	47.9	2.7	0.4	0.6

Note: Results are percentages and may not add to 100% due to rounding
Source: www.cbsnews.com; www.uselectionatlas.org

EDUCATION

Public School District Statistics

District Name	Schls.	Enroll-ment	Classroom Teachers	Pupil/ Teacher Ratio	Minority Pupils[1] (%)	Current Expend.[2] ($/pupil)
Austin ISD	111	77,684	5,303	14.6	66.3	6,314
Eanes ISD	11	7,260	557	13.0	n/a	n/a
Lake Travis ISD	7	4,376	336	13.0	n/a	n/a

Note: Data covers the 2001-02 school year unless otherwise noted; (1) Fall 2000; (2) FY2000; n/a not available
Source: U.S. Department of Education, National Center for Education Statistics, Common Core of Data, Local Education Agency (School District) Universe Survey: School Year 2001-2002; U.S. Department of Education, National Center for Education Statistics, Digest of Education Statistics 2002

Educational Quality

School District	Education Quotient[1]	Graduate Outcome[2]	Community Index[3]	Resource Index[4]
Austin ISD	73	75	27	54

Note: Scores are national percentile rankings and range from 1 (worst) to 99 (best); (1) Combination of the Graduate Outcome, Community and Resource indexes weighted to reflect the greater importance of the Graduate Outcome and Resource Index; (2) Based on graduation rates and college board scores (SAT/ACT); (3) Based on the surrounding community's level of affluence and adult education; (4) Based on teacher salaries, per-pupil expenditures and student-teacher ratios.
Source: Expansion Management, December 2003

Educational Attainment by Race

Area	High School Graduate (%)					Bachelor's Degree (%)				
	Total	White	Black	Asian	Hisp.[2]	Total	White	Black	Asian	Hisp.[2]
City	83.4	90.2	79.1	90.7	55.7	40.4	47.6	19.0	67.0	15.5
MSA[1]	84.8	89.7	80.0	88.5	58.6	36.7	41.1	20.1	62.2	14.7
U.S.	80.4	83.6	72.3	80.4	52.4	24.4	26.1	14.3	44.1	10.4

Note: Figures shown cover persons 25 years old and over; (1) Metropolitan Statistical Area - see Appendix A for areas included; (2) people of Hispanic origin can be of any race
Source: Census 2000, Summary File 3

School Enrollment by Type

Area	Grades KG to 8				Grades 9 to 12			
	Public		Private		Public		Private	
	Enrollment	%	Enrollment	%	Enrollment	%	Enrollment	%
City	66,530	92.0	5,793	8.0	26,233	93.4	1,863	6.6
MSA[1]	147,604	92.3	12,299	7.7	60,104	94.4	3,576	5.6
U.S.	33,526,011	88.7	4,285,121	11.3	14,848,628	90.6	1,532,323	9.4

Note: Figures shown cover persons 3 years old and over; (1) Metropolitan Statistical Area - see Appendix A for areas included
Source: Census 2000, Summary File 3

School Enrollment by Race

Area	Grades KG to 8 (%)				Grades 9 to 12 (%)			
	White	Black	Asian	Hisp.[1]	White	Black	Asian	Hisp.[1]
City	54.5	13.6	3.5	42.7	55.5	14.5	3.1	39.1
MSA[2]	66.6	9.5	2.7	34.2	67.3	10.3	2.5	31.0
U.S.	68.5	15.5	3.3	16.8	68.8	15.5	3.8	15.7

Note: Figures shown cover persons 3 years old and over; (1) people of Hispanic origin can be of any race; (2) Metropolitan Statistical Area - see Appendix A for areas included
Source: Census 2000, Summary File 3

Classroom Teacher Salaries in Public Schools

District	B.A. Degree		M.A. Degree		Maximum	
	Min. ($)	Rank[1]	Max. ($)	Rank[1]	Max. ($)	Rank[1]
Austin	32,000	37	50,820	62	50,820	83
DOD Average[2]	31,567	-	53,248	-	59,356	-

Note: Salaries are for 2001-2002; (1) Rank ranges from 1 to 100; (2) As per the U.S. Department of Defense Wage Fixing Authority
Source: American Federation of Teachers, Survey & Analysis of Teacher Salary Trends 2002

Higher Education

Four-Year Colleges			Two-Year Colleges			Medical Schools	Law Schools	Voc/ Tech
Public	Private Non-profit	Private For-profit	Public	Private Non-profit	Private For-profit			
1	6	2	1	1	3	0	1	8

Note: Figures cover institutions located within the city limits.
Source: National Center for Education Statistics, The Integrated Postsecondary Education System (IPEDS) Peer Analysis System, 2002; usnews.com, America's Best Graduate Schools 2004, Medical School Directory; The College Blue Book, Occupational Education, 2003; Barron's Guide to Law Schools, 2003; Medical School Admission Requirements U.S. & Canada, 2003-2004

MAJOR EMPLOYERS

Major Employers

Company Name	Industry	Type
3M	Paper; coated and laminated, nec	Branch
Applied Materials	Special industry machinery, nec	Branch
Attorney General	Legal counsel and prosecution	Headquarters
Austin Community College Dist	Junior colleges	Headquarters
Dell	Electronic computers	Headquarters
Department Mechanical Engrg	Colleges and universities	Branch
Dept of Health Texas	Administration of public health programs	Headquarters
Executive Office State of TX	Legal counsel and prosecution	Branch
FPK LLC	Plastics foam products	Single
Hospital Housekeeping Systems	Building maintenance services, nec	Single
Information Release Dept	Regulation, miscellaneous commercial sectors	Branch
Nextel	Radiotelephone communication	Single
Northport V A Medical Center	Administration of veterans' affairs	Branch
State Farm Insurance	Fire, marine, and casualty insurance	Branch
Texas Dept of Public Safety	Police protection	Headquarters
Texas Legislative Office	Legislative bodies	Headquarters
Tivoli Systems	Custom computer programming services	Headquarters
TNRCC	Air, water, and solid waste management	Headquarters
University Book Store	Colleges and universities	Headquarters
Workforce Commission Texas	Regulation, miscellaneous commercial sectors	Headquarters

Note: Companies shown are located in the metropolitan area and have 1,500 or more employees.
Source: www.zapdata.com, March 2004

PUBLIC SAFETY

Crime Rate

Area	All Crimes	Violent Crimes				Property Crimes		
		Murder	Forcible Rape	Robbery	Aggrav. Assault	Burglary	Larceny -Theft	Motor Vehicle Theft
City	6,267.1	3.6	37.3	171.2	254.9	1,008.5	4,334.5	457.1
Suburbs[1]	3,095.4	2.3	39.5	37.0	185.1	656.7	2,019.4	155.4
MSA[2]	4,761.6	3.0	38.4	107.5	221.8	841.5	3,235.6	313.9
U.S.	4,118.8	5.6	33.0	145.9	310.1	746.2	2,445.8	432.1

Note: Figures are crimes per 100,000 population; (1) All areas within the MSA that are located outside the city limits; (2) Metropolitan Statistical Area - see Appendix A for areas included
Source: FBI Uniform Crime Reports, 2002

RECREATION

Culture and Recreation

Museums	Orchestras	Opera Companies	Dance Companies	Professional Theatres	Zoos	Pro Sports Teams[1]
15	1	1	6	5	0	0

Note: (1) Covers the Metropolitan Statistical Area - see Appendix A for areas included.
Source: The Grey House Performing Arts Directory, 2002; Official Museum Directory, 2004; www.sportsvenues.com

Library System

The Austin Public Library has 21 branches and holdings of 1,420,818 volumes.
American Library Directory, 2003-2004

MEDIA

Newspapers

Name	Type	Freq.	Distribution	Circulation
Austin American-Statesman	General	7x/wk	Area	175,000
Austin Chronicle	Alternative	1x/wk	Local	80,000
Austin Sun	Black	1x/wk	Local	15,000
The Catholic Spirit	Cath/Relig	1x/mth	Regional	32,000
El Mundo	Hispanic	1x/wk	Area	20,000
Lake and Country Living	General	1x/mth	Local	15,000
La Prensa-Austin	Hispanic	1x/wk	Local	10,000
Texas Observer	Alternative	2x/mth	Regional	12,000

Note: Includes newspapers whose offices are located in the city and whose circulations are 10,000 or more
Source: Burrelle's Media Directory, 2003

Television Stations

Name	Ch.	Affiliation	Type	Owner
KTBC	7	FBC	Commercial	Fox Television Stations Inc.
KVC	13	FBC	Commercial	n/a
KXAM	14	NBCT	Commercial	n/a
KLRU	18	PBS	Public	Capital of Texas Public Telecommunications
KVUE	24	ABCT	Commercial	Belo Corporation
KXAN	36	NBCT	Commercial	Lin Broadcasting
KEYE	42	CBST	Commercial	CBS Broadcasting Company
KNVA	54	WB	Commercial	54 Broadcasting Inc.

Note: Stations included broadcast from the Austin metro area; n/a not available
Source: Burrelle's Media Directory, 2003

AM Radio Stations

Call Letters	Freq. (kHz)	Target Audience	Station Format	Music Format
KLBJ	590	General	N/S/T	n/a
KIXL	970	Religious	T	n/a
KFIT	1060	B/H	M/N/T	Christian
KTAE	1260	Hispanic	M/N/S/T	Latin
KVET	1300	General	S	n/a
KJCE	1370	General	N/S/T	n/a
KELG	1440	Hispanic	M	Latin
KFON	1490	General	M	Latin
KTXZ	1560	Hispanic	M/N/S	Latin

Note: Stations included broadcast from the Austin metro area; n/a not available
The following abbreviations may be used:
Target Audience: A=Asian; B=Black; C=Christian; E=Ethnic; F=French; G=General; H=Hispanic;
M=Men; N=Native American; R=Religious; S=Senior Citizen; W=Women; Y=Young Adult; Z=Children
Station Format: E=Educational; M=Music; N=News; S=Sports; T=Talk
Source: Burrelle's Media Directory, 2003

FM Radio Stations

Call Letters	Freq. (mHz)	Target Audience	Station Format	Music Format
KNLE	88.1	General	M	Adult Contemporary
KAZI	88.7	B/R	E/M/N/S/T	Blues
KMFA	89.5	General	E/M	Classical
KUTX	90.1	General	E/M/N/T	Classical
KUT	90.5	General	E/M/N	Blues
KOOP	91.7	Hispanic	E/M/N/T	Latin
KVRX	91.7	Hispanic	E/M/N/S/T	Alternative
KKLB	92.5	Hispanic	M	Latin
KXMG	93.3	General	M	Rhythm & Blues
KLBJ	93.7	General	M/N/S	AOR
KAMX	94.7	General	M/N/T	Adult Contemporary
KKMJ	95.5	General	M	Adult Contemporary
KHFI	96.7	General	M/N/T	Top 40
KVET	98.1	General	M/N/S	Country
KHHL	98.9	Hispanic	M	Latin
KASE	100.7	General	M/N/T	Country
KROX	101.5	Young Adult	M/T	Alternative
KPEZ	102.3	General	M/S	Classic Rock
KEYI	103.5	General	M	Oldies
KQBT	104.3	General	M/N/S/T	Adult Top 40
KFMK	105.9	General	M	Oldies
KGSR	107.1	General	M	Alternative

Note: Stations included broadcast from the Austin metro area
The following abbreviations may be used:
Target Audience: A=Asian; B=Black; C=Christian; E=Ethnic; F=French; G=General; H=Hispanic;
M=Men; N=Native American; R=Religious; S=Senior Citizen; W=Women; Y=Young Adult; Z=Children
Station Format: E=Educational; M=Music; N=News; S=Sports; T=Talk
Music Format: AOR=Album Oriented Rock; MOR=Middle of the Road
Source: Burrelle's Media Directory, 2003

CLIMATE

Average and Extreme Temperatures

Temperature	Jan	Feb	Mar	Apr	May	Jun	Jul	Aug	Sep	Oct	Nov	Dec	Yr.
Extreme High (°F)	90	97	98	98	100	105	109	106	104	98	91	90	109
Average High (°F)	60	64	72	79	85	91	95	96	90	81	70	63	79
Average Temp. (°F)	50	53	61	69	75	82	85	85	80	70	60	52	69
Average Low (°F)	39	43	50	58	65	72	74	74	69	59	49	41	58
Extreme Low (°F)	-2	7	18	35	43	53	64	61	47	32	20	4	-2

Note: Figures cover the years 1948-1990
Source: National Climatic Data Center, International Station Meteorological Climate Summary, 9/96

Average Precipitation/Snowfall/Humidity

Precip./Humidity	Jan	Feb	Mar	Apr	May	Jun	Jul	Aug	Sep	Oct	Nov	Dec	Yr.
Avg. Precip. (in.)	1.6	2.3	1.8	2.9	4.3	3.5	1.9	1.9	3.3	3.5	2.1	1.9	31.1
Avg. Snowfall (in.)	1	Tr	Tr	0	0	0	0	0	0	0	Tr	Tr	1
Avg. Rel. Hum. 6am (%)	79	80	79	83	88	89	88	87	86	84	81	79	84
Avg. Rel. Hum. 3pm (%)	53	51	47	50	53	49	43	42	47	47	49	51	48

Note: Figures cover the years 1948-1990; Tr = Trace amounts (<0.05 in. of rain; <0.5 in. of snow)
Source: National Climatic Data Center, International Station Meteorological Climate Summary, 9/96

Weather Conditions

Temperature			Daytime Sky			Precipitation		
10°F & below	32°F & below	90°F & above	Clear	Partly cloudy	Cloudy	0.01 inch or more precip.	0.1 inch or more snow/ice	Thunder-storms
< 1	20	111	105	148	112	83	1	41

Note: Figures are average number of days per year and covers the years 1948-1990
Source: National Climatic Data Center, International Station Meteorological Climate Summary, 9/96

HAZARDOUS WASTE

Superfund Sites

Austin has no sites on the EPA's Superfund National Priorities List.
U.S. Environmental Protection Agency, National Priorities List, March 15, 2004

AIR & WATER QUALITY

Maximum Pollutant Concentrations

	Particulate Matter (ug/m^3)	Carbon Monoxide (ppm)	Sulfur Dioxide (ppm)	Nitrogen Dioxide (ppm)	Ozone 1-hour (ppm)	Ozone 8-hour (ppm)	Lead (ug/m^3)
MSA[1] Level	43	1	n/a	0.004	0.1	0.09	n/a
NAAQS[2]	150	9	0.140	0.053	0.12	0.08	1.50
Met NAAQS[2]	Yes	Yes	n/a	Yes	Yes	No	n/a

Note: (1) Metropolitan Statistical Area - see Appendix A for areas included; (2) National Ambient Air Quality Standards; n/a not available
Units: ppm = parts per million; ug/m^3 = micrograms per cubic meter
Source: EPA, Latest Findings on National Air Quality: 2002 Status and Trends, August 2003

Air Quality Index

In the Austin MSA (see Appendix A for areas included), the Air Quality Index (AQI) exceeded 100 on 5 days in 2002. An AQI value greater than 100 indicates that air quality would have been in the unhealthful range on that day.
EPA, Latest Findings on National Air Quality: 2002 Status and Trends, August 2003

Watershed Health

The U.S. Environmental Protection Agency monitors the health of the aquatic resources for the nation's 2,000+ watersheds. **The Austin-Travis Lakes watershed serves the Austin area and received an overall Index of Watershed Indicators (IWI) score of 3 (less serious problems - low vulnerability).** The IWI score is based on seven condition and nine vulnerability indicators. The overall IWI score ranges from 1 (best health) to 6 (worst health). The Condition Indicators include: designated use attainment, fish and wildlife consumption advisories, source water condition, contaminated sediments, ambient water quality, and wetlands loss index. The Vulnerability Indicators include: aquatic species at risk, conventional and toxic loads over permitted limits, urban and agricultural runoff potential, population change, hydrologic modification, estuarine pollution susceptibility, and air deposition. *EPA, Index of Watershed Indicators, October 26, 2001*

Drinking Water

Water System Name	Pop. Served	Primary Water Source Type	Number of Violations January 2002-February 2004		
			Health Based	Significant Monitoring	Monitoring
Austin Water & Wastewater	718,612	Surface	None	None	3

Note: Data as of February 19, 2004
Source: EPA, Office of Ground Water and Drinking Water, Safe Drinking Water Information System

Austin tap water is alkaline, soft and fluoridated.
Editor & Publisher Market Guide, 2004

Baton Rouge, Louisiana

Background

Baton Rouge, the capital of Louisiana, stretches along the Istrouma Bluff on the east bank of the Mississippi River, and is the key industrial city in the area, at the center of an immense industrial and shipping complex. The seat of government for East Baton Rouge Parish, the city's greater metropolitan area, includes Baton Rouge itself, Baker, and Zachary. The metropolitan area is the second-largest in the state, next to New Orleans.

Originally the site of an Indian village, and an important trade center since 1699 when a French expedition first explored the area, Baton Rouge was incorporated in 1817 and made the state capital in 1882.

Baton Rouge, or "Red Stick," is so-named because of a distinctive boundary marker—a 30-foot pole that marked the boundary between the Oumas and Bayagoula tribes. The pole was used in earlier times as a point of reference by the many missionaries, traders, and settlers who traveled this way on the Mississippi River.

The historical complexity of Baton Rouge is hinted at by the various elements that appear on the official city flag, which is laid out on a field of crimson, and features, of course, the red, white, and blue of the United States. The flag also displays the fleur-de-lis of France, the Castile of Spain, and the union jack of Great Britain. This portrait, though, only begins to do justice to Baton Rouge's rich history. The city has lived under seven distinct governments in its 300-year development from trading post to modern metropolis: French, English, Spanish, West Floridian, Louisiana, Confederate, and American.

As many cities in the country have enlarged their convention centers, so has Baton Rouge. The city's Riverside Centroplex Convention Center is undergoing a major expansion, adding 100,000 square feet of convention space, 20,000 square feet of state-of-the-art meeting space and a ballroom. The project is slated for completion in 2004.

In addition, Baton Rouge recently unveiled the Irene W. Pennington Planetarium at the Louisiana Arts and Science Museum. Among its featured attractions is the multimedia ExxonMobil Space Theater.

Louisiana State University, a traditional leader among the nation's institutions, is located here. In early 2004, the university's Pennington Biomedical Research Center, which specializes in nutrition research, opened a 180,000 square foot, $42 million research building. Southern University and A&M College, the largest predominantly African-American institution in the nation, is another of the area's main institutions of higher learning.

The state capitol building in Baton Rouge is one of America's most notable buildings. Completed in 1932, the 34-story building is located on the old campus of Louisiana State University, and surrounded by 27 acres of landscaped grounds. Ten miles of walks and drives are bordered by a collection of trees, flowering shrubs, bulbs, and flower beds, which are tended to yield maximal color in every season. From the capitol's observation tower, one can see for 30 miles in every direction. Louisiana's legendary Governor and Senator Huey P. Long, under whose administration the building was constructed, was assassinated in a corridor here in 1935 and is buried in the front grounds. A 12-foot bronze statue by Charles Keck memorializes The Kingfish, as Long was nicknamed.

Baton Rouge has a subtropical climate free of extreme temperatures. Winters are mild with only occasional cold spells.

Rankings

- Baton Rouge was ranked #295 out of 331 metro areas in *Cities Ranked & Rated*. Criteria: cost of living; climate; crime; transportation; economy and jobs; education; arts and culture; health and healthcare; leisure. *Cities Ranked & Rated, 1st Edition, 2004*

- *Ladies Home Journal* ranked America's 200 largest cities based on the qualities women surveyed care about most. Baton Rouge ranked #137 out of 143 in the smaller city category (population under 300,000). Criteria: crime; lifestyle; education; jobs; health; child care; politics; and the economy. *Ladies Home Journal Online, "The Best Cities for Women 2002"*

- *Forbes* ranked the 150 most populous metro areas in the U.S. in terms of the "Best Places for Business and Careers." The Baton Rouge metro area was ranked #70. Criteria: income and job growth; cost-of-doing-business; qualifications of the available pool of labor; crime rates; housing costs; net migration. *Forbes, May 9, 2003*

- *Men's Health* ranked 101 U.S. cities in terms of the quality of their tap water. Baton Rouge received a grade of A. Criteria: levels of bacteria, arsenic, lead, trihalomethanes, and haloacetic acids were compared with the National Academy of Science's guidelines as well as with the EPA's more stringent maximum contaminant level goals. *Men's Health, March 2004*

- Sperling's BestPlaces ranked 331 metro areas and identified the most and least stressful U.S. cities. The Baton Rouge metro area ranked #33 out of the 100 largest metro areas (#1 = most stressful). Criteria: divorce rate; unemployment rate; violent and property crime; suicide rate; commute time; mental health; alcohol consumption; cloudy days. *www.BestPlaces.net, February 26, 2004*

- Baton Rouge was ranked #156 out of America's 200 largest metro areas in *SELF Magazine's* ranking of "America's Healthiest Cities for Women." Criteria: safety; air/water quality; cancer rates; and 21 other factors relating to health. *SELF Magazine, November 2003*

- Baton Rouge was ranked #81 out of 100 cities surveyed in *Child* magazine's ranking of the "Best Cities for Families." Criteria: number of pediatricians per capita; proximity to a children's hospital; immunization rates; infant mortality rate; air quality; water quality; school spending; pupil-teacher ratio; availability of parks/green space; nearby recreational opportunities; average commute time; number of sunny days; average cost of a 3-bedroom home; unemployment rate; future job growth; crime rate; percentage of children under 5; mandated minimum child care ratios. *Child, April 2001*

- *Zero Population Growth* ranked 239 cities in terms of children's health, safety, and economic well-being. Baton Rouge was ranked #110 out of 140 independent cities (cities with populations greater than 100,000 which were neither major cities nor suburbs/outer cities) and was given a grade of C. Criteria: total population and population growth; percent of population under 18 years of age; number of children's museums; health improvement grade; percent of births to teens; percent of low birthweight infants; infant mortality rate; number of Title X-funded clinics; average SAT/ACT scores; average elementary and secondary class size; crime rate; unemployment rate; percent of affordable homes; number of bad air days; park acres per 1000 persons; library circulation per child; and children's program attendance counts. *Zero Population Growth, Kid Friendly Cities Report Card 2001*

- *Ladies Home Journal* ranked America's 200 largest cities in terms of safety. Baton Rouge ranked #179 out of 200. Criteria: violent crimes; crimes against property; and rape. *Ladies Home Journal Online, "The Best Cities for Women 2002"*

- The Baton Rouge metro area was selected by *Yahoo! Internet Life* as one of "America's Most Wired Cities...and Towns." The area ranked #62 out of 87. Criteria: home and work net use; user sophistication; domain density; and available content. *Yahoo! Internet Life, April 2001*

- Baton Rouge was identified as one of the 100 "Most Unwired Cities" in the U.S. The area ranked #83. Criteria: number of public and commercial wireless access points; cell phone coverage offering wide area network Internet access; Internet penetration. *Intel, "Most Unwired Cities," March 4, 2003*

- Baton Rouge was ranked #120 in *Prevention* magazine's survey of the "Best Walking Cities in the U.S." The magazine, in conjunction with the American Podiatric Medical Association, surveyed 125 of the most populated cities and then tabulated and weighed 20 criteria of interest to pedestrians. *Prevention, April, 2004*

- The Baton Rouge metro area was cited as one of "The Best Places in the U.S. to Locate a Company." The area ranked #146 out of 329. Criteria: education (with emphasis on college board test results and high school graduation rates); availability of quality healthcare services and the cost to employers; quality of life; logistics workforce and companies; transportation infrastructure; quality and quantity of highly educated technical workers; business climate. *Expansion Management, July 2003*

- The Baton Rouge metro area appeared on *Forbes/Milken Institute* list of "Best Places for Business and Career." Rank: #110 out of 200 metro areas. Criteria: salary growth; job growth; number of technology clusters; overall concentration of technology activity relative to national average; and technology output growth. *www.forbes.com, Forbes/Milken Institute Best Places 2002*

- The Baton Rouge metro area appeared on the "Milken Institute Best Performing Cities" index. Rank: #86 out of 200 large metro areas. Criteria: job growth; wage and salary growth; high-tech output growth. *Milken Institute, June 25, 2003*

- The Baton Rouge metro area was selected as one of the "Top 25 Cities for Doing Business in America." *Inc.* measured current-year employment growth in 277 regions as well as current trends in the annual average growth over the past three years, and compared employment expansion between the first and second halves of the last decade. Job growth factors account for two-thirds, and balance among industries accounts for one third of the final score for each city. The Baton Rouge metro area ranked #19 among medium metro areas. *Inc. Magazine, March 2004*

- The Baton Rouge metro area appeared on *IndustryWeek's* fourth annual World-Class Communities list. It ranked #73 out of 315 metro areas. Criteria: MSA Gross Metropolitan Product (GMP) per manufacturing employee; and MSA percent share of U.S. manufacturing Gross Domestic Product (GDP). *IndustryWeek, April 16, 2001*

- ING Group ranked the 125 largest metro areas according to the general financial security of residents. The Baton Rouge metro area was ranked #110 out of 125. Criteria: Earnings and Wealth Potential (household income, education, net assets, cost of living); Safety Net (health insurance, retirement savings, life insurance, income support programs); Personal Threats (unemployment rate, low-income households, crime rate); Community Economic Vitality (cost of community services, job quality, job creation, housing costs). *ING Group, "The Best Cities to Earn and Save Money: A Ranking of the Largest 125 U.S. Cities," 2001 Edition*

Business Environment

CITY FINANCES

City Government Finances

Component	2000-2001 ($000)	2000-2001 ($ per capita)
Total Revenues	642,696	1,657
Total Expenditures	621,976	1,604
Debt Outstanding	880,681	2,271
Cash and Securities	1,329,868	3,429

Source: U.S Census Bureau, Government Finances 2000-2001, August 2003

City Government Revenue by Source

Source	2000-2001 ($000)	2000-2001 ($ per capita)
General Revenue		
From Federal Government	26,125	67
From State Government	58,419	151
From Local Governments	1,304	3
Taxes		
Property	92,077	237
Sales	202,007	521
Personal Income	0	0
License	0	0
Charges	138,719	358
Liquor Store	0	0
Utility	11,949	31
Employee Retirement	26,183	68
Other	85,913	222

Source: U.S Census Bureau, Government Finances 2000-2001, August 2003

City Government Expenditures by Function

Function	2000-2001 ($000)	2000-2001 ($ per capita)	2000-2001 (%)
General Expenditures			
Airports	8,700	22	1.4
Corrections	9,419	24	1.5
Education	0	0	0.0
Fire Protection	46,077	119	7.4
Governmental Administration	93,100	240	15.0
Health	12,612	33	2.0
Highways	49,188	127	7.9
Hospitals	40,146	104	6.5
Housing and Community Development	34,153	88	5.5
Interest on General Debt	57,918	149	9.3
Libraries	17,114	44	2.8
Parking	736	2	0.1
Parks and Recreation	29,986	77	4.8
Police Protection	56,461	146	9.1
Public Welfare	2,234	6	0.4
Sewerage	52,220	135	8.4
Solid Waste Management	32,915	85	5.3
Liquor Store	0	0	0.0
Utility	17,611	45	2.8
Employee Retirement	46,276	119	7.4
Other	15,110	39	2.4

Source: U.S Census Bureau, Government Finances 2000-2001, August 2003

Municipal Bond Ratings

Area	Moody's
City	Aaa

Source: Mergent Bond Record, February 2004

DEMOGRAPHICS

Population Growth

Area	1990 Census	2000 Census	2003 Estimate	2008 Projection	Population Growth (%) 1990-2000	Population Growth (%) 2000-2008
City	223,299	227,818	225,958	223,972	2.0	-1.7
MSA[1]	528,264	602,894	616,014	639,011	14.1	6.0
U.S.	248,709,873	281,421,906	290,647,163	305,918,071	13.2	8.7

Note: (1) Metropolitan Statistical Area - see Appendix A for areas included
Source: Claritas, Inc.

Number of Households and Average Household Size

Area	1990 Census	2000 Census	2003 Estimate	2008 Projection	2003 Average Household Size
City	84,586	88,973	89,185	89,990	2.5
MSA[1]	188,377	223,349	231,137	245,072	2.7
U.S.	91,947,410	105,480,101	109,440,059	116,034,472	2.7

Note: (1) Metropolitan Statistical Area - see Appendix A for areas included
Source: Claritas, Inc.

Race and Ethnicity

Area	White Non-Hispanic	Black Non-Hispanic	Asian Non-Hispanic	Other Race Non-Hispanic	Hispanic
City	44.8	50.6	2.8	1.7	1.8
MSA[1]	64.8	31.9	1.6	1.7	1.8
U.S.	74.5	12.4	3.8	9.3	13.2

Note: Figures are 2003 estimates; (1) Metropolitan Statistical Area - see Appendix A for areas included
Source: Claritas, Inc.

Segregation

City		MSA[1]	
Index[2]	Rank[3]	Index[2]	Rank[4]
75.1	13	73.1	33

Note: Figures are based on an analysis of Census 2000 data; (1) Metropolitan Statistical Area - see Appendix A for areas included; (2) Dissimilarity Index—the most commonly used measure of segregation between two groups, reflecting their relative distributions across neighborhoods within a city or metropolitan area. It can range in value from 0, indicating complete integration, to 100, indicating complete segregation; (3) Ranges from 1 (most segregated) to 100 (least segregated) and includes all the cities in this book; (4) Ranges from 1 (most segregated) to 318 (least segregated) and includes 318 metropolitan areas.
Source: www.CensusScope.org

Ancestry

Area	German	Irish[2]	English	American	Italian	Polish	French[3]	Scottish
City	6.2	5.7	6.3	4.2	3.9	0.5	8.9	1.1
MSA[1]	7.1	7.8	6.6	8.9	4.7	0.5	13.0	1.1
U.S.	15.2	10.9	8.7	7.3	5.6	3.2	3.0	1.7

Note: Figures include multiple ancestry (e.g. if a person reported being Irish and Italian, they were included in both columns); (1) Metropolitan Statistical Area - see Appendix A for areas included; (2) Includes Celtic; (3) Includes Alsatian but excludes Basque
Source: Census 2000, Summary File 3

Foreign-Born Population

Area	Any Foreign Country	Percent of Population Born in: Europe	Asia	Africa	Oceania[2]	Canada	Mexico	Latin America[3]
City	4.4	0.7	2.2	0.4	0.0	0.1	0.2	0.8
MSA[1]	3.0	0.5	1.3	0.2	0.0	0.1	0.3	0.6
U.S.	11.1	1.7	2.9	0.3	0.1	0.3	3.3	2.5

Note: (1) Metropolitan Statistical Area - see Appendix A for areas included; (2) Includes Australia, New Zealand subregion, Melanesia, Micronesia, Polynesia, and Oceania n.e.c; (3) Includes Central America (excluding Mexico), South America, and the Caribbean.
Source: Census 2000, Summary File 3

Religion

Area	Catholic	Southern Baptist	United Methodist	ELCA[1]	LDS[2]	Presbyterian Church USA	Jewish Est.	Muslim Est.
County	23.2	13.7	5.7	0.2	0.4	1.0	0.2	0.4
U.S.	22.0	7.1	3.7	1.8	1.5	1.1	2.2	0.6

Note: Figures shown are the number of adherents as a percentage of the total population; Adherents are defined as all members, including full members, their children and the estimated number of other participants who are not considered members (e.g. the baptized, those not confirmed, those not eligible for communion, those regularly attending services, etc.); (1) Evangelical Lutheran Church in America; (2) The Church of Jesus Christ of Latter Day Saints
Source: Reprinted with permission from Religious Congregations and Membership in the United States 2000 (Nashville, Glenmary Research Center, 2002) Copyright Association of Statisticians of American Religious Bodies. All rights reserved.

Age Distribution

Area	Percent of Population						
	Under Age 5	Age 5 to 17	Age 18 to 34	Age 35 to 49	Age 50 to 64	Age 65 to 79	80 Years and Over
City	6.8	17.6	31.1	20.2	12.8	8.5	3.0
MSA[1]	7.2	20.0	26.9	22.9	13.6	7.3	2.2
U.S.	6.8	18.9	23.7	23.5	14.8	9.2	3.2

Note: (1) Metropolitan Statistical Area - see Appendix A for areas included
Source: Census 2000, Summary File 3

Marriage Status

Area	Never Married	Now Married Except Separated	Separated	Widowed	Divorced
City	39.3	40.6	2.8	7.2	10.1
MSA[1]	30.8	51.1	2.2	6.0	10.0
U.S.	27.1	54.4	2.2	6.6	9.7

Note: Figures cover population 15 years of age and older; (1) Metropolitan Statistical Area - see Appendix A for areas included
Source: Census 2000, Summary File 3

Male/Female Ratio

Area	Males	Females	Males per 100 Females
City	107,551	118,407	90.8
MSA[1]	298,537	317,477	94.0
U.S.	142,511,883	148,135,280	96.2

Note: Figures are 2003 estimates; (1) Metropolitan Statistical Area - see Appendix A for areas included
Source: Claritas, Inc.

ECONOMY

Gross Metropolitan Product

Area	1999	2000	2001	2002	2002 Rank[2]
MSA[1]	18.3	19.5	20.0	20.7	92

Note: Figures are in billions of dollars; (1) Metropolitan Statistical Area - see Appendix A for areas included; (2) Rank ranges from 1 to 319
Source: The U.S. Conference of Mayors, Metro Economies Report, July 2003

INCOME

Per Capita/Median/Average Income

Area	Per Capita ($)	Median Household ($)	Average Household ($)
City	20,671	33,715	51,759
MSA[1]	21,500	43,167	56,892
U.S.	24,078	46,868	63,207

Note: Figures are 2003 estimates; (1) Metropolitan Statistical Area - see Appendix A for areas included
Source: Claritas, Inc.

Household Income Distribution

Area	Percent of Households Earning							
	Under $15,000	$15,000 -24,999	$25,000 -34,999	$35,000 -49,999	$50,000 -74,999	$75,000 -99,000	$100,000 -149,999	$150,000 and up
City	24.2	14.9	12.6	14.3	14.0	8.2	7.1	4.7
MSA[1]	17.3	12.4	11.8	15.6	18.1	11.2	9.3	4.2
U.S.	14.1	11.5	11.7	16.0	19.2	11.3	10.2	6.0

Note: Figures are 2003 estimates; (1) Metropolitan Statistical Area - see Appendix A for areas included
Source: Claritas, Inc.

Poverty Rates by Age

Area	All Ages	Under 5 Years Old	5 to 17 Years Old	18 to 64 Years Old	65 Years and Over
City	24.0	2.5	5.5	14.3	1.6
MSA[1]	16.2	1.6	3.9	9.5	1.2
U.S.	12.4	1.2	3.0	6.9	1.2

Note: Figures are percent of population with income in 1999 below poverty level and only include population for whom poverty status is determined; (1) Metropolitan Statistical Area - see Appendix A for areas included
Source: Census 2000, Summary File 3

Personal Bankruptcy Filing Rate

Area	2002	2003
East Baton Rouge Parish	5.26	5.66
U.S.	5.34	5.58

Note: Numbers are per 1,000 population and include Chapter 7 and Chapter 13 filings
Source: Federal Deposit Insurance Corporation (FDIC), Regional Economic Conditions (RECON), 2/25/2004

EMPLOYMENT

Labor Force and Employment

Area	Civilian Labor Force			Workers Employed		
	Dec. 2002	Dec. 2003	% Chg.	Dec. 2002	Dec. 2003	% Chg.
City	115,576	119,821	3.7	108,658	112,854	3.9
MSA[1]	297,985	309,240	3.8	281,068	291,921	3.9
U.S.	144,807,000	146,501,000	1.2	136,599,000	138,556,000	1.4

Note: Data is not seasonally adjusted and covers workers 16 years of age and older;
(1) Metropolitan Statistical Area - see Appendix A for areas included
Source: Bureau of Labor Statistics, http://stats.bls.gov

Unemployment Rate

Area	2003											
	Jan.	Feb.	Mar.	Apr.	May	Jun.	Jul.	Aug.	Sep.	Oct.	Nov.	Dec.
City	6.2	5.5	5.7	5.3	5.7	7.9	7.7	7.4	6.3	5.7	5.6	5.8
MSA[1]	5.9	5.2	5.5	5.1	5.5	7.5	7.4	7.1	5.9	5.3	5.4	5.6
U.S.	6.5	6.4	6.2	5.8	5.8	6.5	6.3	6.0	5.8	5.6	5.6	5.4

Note: Data is not seasonally adjusted and covers workers 16 years of age and older; All figures are percentages; (1) Metropolitan Statistical Area - see Appendix A for areas included
Source: Bureau of Labor Statistics, http://stats.bls.gov

Employment by Occupation

Occupation Classification	City (%)	MSA[1] (%)	U.S. (%)
Sales and Office	28.4	28.6	26.7
Professional and Related	24.6	21.1	20.2
Service	17.2	14.3	14.9
Production, Transportation, and Material Moving	10.3	12.4	14.6
Management, Business, and Financial	12.1	12.1	13.5
Construction, Extraction, and Maintenance	7.2	11.4	9.4
Farming, Forestry, and Fishing	0.1	0.2	0.7

Note: Figures cover employed civilians 16 years of age and older;
(1) Metropolitan Statistical Area - see Appendix A for areas included
Source: Census 2000, Summary File 3

Employment by Industry

Sector	MSA[1]		U.S.
	Number of Employees	Percent of Total	Percent of Total
Government	60,200	19.5	16.7
Education and Health Services	34,700	11.2	12.9
Professional and Business Services	35,800	11.6	12.3
Retail Trade	36,300	11.8	11.8
Manufacturing	21,400	6.9	11.0
Leisure and Hospitality	28,800	9.3	9.1
Finance Activities	17,100	5.5	6.1
Construction	32,500	10.5	5.1
Wholesale Trade	12,800	4.1	4.3
Other Services	11,200	3.6	4.1
Transportation and Utilities	11,000	3.6	3.7
Information	5,600	1.8	2.4
Natural Resources and Mining	1,200	0.4	0.4

Note: Figures cover non-farm employment as of December 2003 and are not seasonally adjusted;
(1) Metropolitan Statistical Area - see Appendix A for areas included
Source: Bureau of Labor Statistics, http://stats.bls.gov

Average Wages

Occupation	$/Hr.	Occupation	$/Hr.
Accountants and Auditors	22.18	Maids and Housekeeping Cleaners	6.76
Automotive Mechanics	13.29	Maintenance and Repair Workers	14.63
Bookkeepers	12.06	Marketing Managers	31.04
Carpenters	15.25	Nuclear Medicine Technologists	n/a
Cashiers	7.05	Nurses, Licensed Practical	13.10
Clerks, General Office	9.28	Nurses, Registered	20.27
Clerks, Receptionists/Information	9.08	Nursing Aides/Orderlies/Attendants	7.19
Clerks, Shipping/Receiving	11.40	Packers and Packagers, Hand	7.80
Computer Programmers	24.18	Physical Therapists	32.79
Computer Support Specialists	18.95	Postal Service Mail Carriers	18.43
Computer Systems Analysts	25.34	Real Estate Brokers	n/a
Cooks, Restaurant	8.22	Retail Salespersons	9.51
Dentists	64.43	Sales Reps., Exc. Tech./Scientific	20.56
Electrical Engineers	36.74	Sales Reps., Tech./Scientific	28.64
Electricians	15.24	Secretaries, Exc. Legal/Med./Exec.	10.94
Financial Managers	28.41	Security Guards	9.41
First-Line Supervisors/Mgrs., Sales	15.16	Surgeons	99.42
Food Preparation Workers	6.64	Teacher Assistants	7.80
General and Operations Managers	33.47	Teachers, Elementary School	17.10
Hairdressers/Cosmetologists	9.38	Teachers, Secondary School	n/a
Internists	93.20	Telemarketers	n/a
Janitors and Cleaners	7.75	Truck Drivers, Heavy/Tractor-Trailer	15.12
Landscaping/Groundskeeping Workers	8.63	Truck Drivers, Light/Delivery Svcs.	12.26
Lawyers	49.05	Waiters and Waitresses	6.35

Note: Wage data is for 2002 and covers the Metropolitan Statistical Area (see Appendix A for areas included).
Hourly wages for elementary/secondary school teachers and teacher assistants were calculated by the editors
from annual wage data assuming a 40 hour work week; n/a not available.
Source: Bureau of Labor Statistics, 2002 Metro Area Occupational Employment and Wage Estimates

Occupational Employment Projections: 1996 - 2006

Occupations Expected to Have the Largest Job Growth (ranked by numerical growth)	Fast-Growing Occupations[1] (ranked by percent growth)
1. Cashiers	1. Database administrators
2. Salespersons, retail	2. Systems analysts
3. Registered nurses	3. Physical therapy assistants and aides
4. Truck drivers, light	4. Home health aides
5. General managers & top executives	5. Emergency medical technicians
6. Cooks, fast food and short order	6. Computer engineers
7. Home health aides	7. Medical assistants
8. Marketing & sales, supervisors	8. Engineering/science/computer sys. mgrs.
9. Maintenance repairers, general utility	9. Data processing equipment repairers
10. Nursing aides/orderlies/attendants	10. Physical therapists

Note: Projections cover Louisiana; (1) Excludes occupations with total job growth less than 300
Source: U.S. Department of Labor, Employment and Training Administration, America's Labor Market Information System (ALMIS)

TAXES

State Corporate Income Tax Rates

State	Rate (%)	Number of Brackets	Low Bracket (Under $)	High Bracket (Over $)
Louisiana	4.0-8.0	5	0	200,000

Note: Tax rates as of December 31, 2003; na not applicable; Federal deductability.
Source: Tax Foundation, www.taxfoundation.org

State Individual Income Tax Rates

State	Federal Deductibility	Marginal Rate (%)	Number of Brackets	Low Bracket (Under $)	High Bracket (Over $)
Louisiana	Yes	2.0-6.0	3	0	50,000

Note: Tax rates as of December 31, 2003; Brackets apply to single taxpayers and married people filing separately; na not applicable
Source: Tax Foundation, www.taxfoundation.org

Various State and Local Tax Rates

State Sales and Use (%)	Total Sales and Use (%)	Gasoline (cents/gal.)	Cigarette (cents/pack)	Spirits ($/gal.)	Table Wine ($/gal.)	Beer ($/gal.)
4.0	9.0	20	36	2.50	0.11	0.32

Note: Tax rates as of December 31, 2003
Source: Tax Foundation, www.taxfoundation.org

State Tax Burdens

Area	Combined State and Local Tax Burden		Combined Federal, State and Local Tax Burden	
	Percent	Rank	Percent	Rank
Louisiana	9.5	29	26.7	45
U.S. Average	9.7	-	30.0	-

Note: Figures are for 2003
Source: Tax Foundation, www.taxfoundation.org

Internal Revenue Service Tax Audits

IRS District	Percent of Returns Audited				
	1996	1997	1998	1999	2000
Gulf Coast	0.83	0.74	0.50	0.41	0.20
U.S.	0.66	0.61	0.46	0.31	0.20

Note: Figures cover IRS district audits of federal income tax returns filed by individuals. Geographic data on district audits for 2001 and 2002 are being withheld by the IRS. TRAC is challenging this policy.
Source: Syracuse University, Transactional Records Access Clearinghouse (TRAC), "Odds of IRS District Tax Audit 2000"

**RESIDENTIAL
REAL ESTATE**

Building Permits

Area	Single-Family			Multi-Family			Total		
	2001	2002	Pct. Chg.	2001	2002	Pct. Chg.	2001	2002	Pct. Chg.
City	215	260	20.9	134	445	232.1	349	705	102.0
U.S.	1,235,600	1,332,600	7.9	401,100	415,100	3.5	1,636,700	1,747,700	6.8

Note: Figures represent new, privately-owned housing units authorized (unadjusted data)
Source: U.S. Census Bureau, Manufacturing, Mining, and Construction Statistics

Homeownership and Housing Vacancies

Area	Homeownership Rate[2] (%)			Rental Vacancy Rate[3] (%)			Homeowner Vacancy Rate[4] (%)		
	2001	2002[a]	2003	2001	2002[a]	2003	2001	2002[a]	2003
MSA[1]	n/a	n/a	n/a	n/a	n/a	n/a	n/a	n/a	n/a
U.S.	67.8	67.9	68.3	8.4	8.9	9.8	1.8	1.7	1.8

Note: (1) Metropolitan Statistical Area - see Appendix A for areas included; (2) The proportion of households that are owners; (3) The proportion of the rental inventory that is vacant for rent; (4) The proportion of the homeowner inventory that is vacant for sale; (a) 2002 figures have been revised; n/a not available
Source: U.S. Census Bureau, Housing Vacancies and Homeownership Annual Statistics: 2003

**COMMERCIAL
REAL ESTATE**

Industrial/Office Markets

Type/Market Area	Inventory (sq. ft.)	Vacant (sq. ft.)	Vacancy Rate (%)	Under Construction (sq. ft.)	Net Absorption (sq. ft.)
Industrial Space					
Baton Rouge	19,456,602	1,961,891	10.08	682,789	544,829
Office Space					
Baton Rouge	4,203,113	444,065	10.57	0	-10,139

Note: Data as of 4th Quarter, 2003; n/a not available
Source: Society of Industrial and Office Realtors, 2004 Comparative Statistics of Industrial and Office Real Estate Markets

**COMMERCIAL
UTILITIES**

Typical Monthly Electric Bills

Area	Commercial Service ($/month)		Industrial Service ($/month)	
	3 kW demand 1,000 kWh	40 kW demand 14,000 kWh	1,000 kW demand 200,000 kWh	50,000 kW demand 15,000,000 kWh
City	116	1,149	17,318	1,121,251
Average[1]	100	1,134	17,850	1,045,117

Note: Based on rates in effect July 1, 2003; (1) average based on 197 utilities
Source: Edison Electric Institute, Typical Bills and Average Rates Report, Summer 2003

TRANSPORTATION

Means of Transportation to Work

Area	Car/Truck/Van		Public Transportation			Bicycle	Walked	Other Means	Worked at Home
	Drove Alone	Car-pooled	Bus	Subway	Railroad				
City	77.6	12.4	2.2	0.0	0.0	0.8	3.8	0.8	2.4
MSA[1]	82.0	11.7	1.0	0.0	0.0	0.3	2.0	0.8	2.2
U.S.	75.7	12.2	2.5	1.5	0.5	0.4	2.9	1.0	3.3

Note: Figures shown are percentages and cover workers 16 years of age and older;
(1) Metropolitan Statistical Area - see Appendix A for areas included
Source: Census 2000, Summary File 3

Travel Time to Work

Area	Less Than 15 Minutes	15 to 29 Minutes	30 to 44 Minutes	45 to 59 Minutes	60 Minutes or More
City	32.7	46.4	13.6	3.2	4.1
MSA[1]	24.9	41.2	21.2	7.0	5.7
U.S.	29.4	36.1	19.1	7.4	8.0

Note: Figures are percentages and include workers 16 years old and over; (1) Metropolitan Statistical Area - see Appendix A for areas included
Source: Census 2000, Summary File 3

Transportation Statistics

Interstate highways (2004)	I-10; I-12
Public transportation (2002)	Capital Transportation Corp. (CTC)
Buses	
Average fleet age in years	8.3
No. operated in max. service	59
Demand response	
Average fleet age in years	3.2
No. operated in max. service	7
Passenger air service	
Airport	Baton Rouge Metropolitan
Airlines (2003)	5
Boardings (2002)	367,557
Amtrak service (2004)	Bus connection
Major waterways/ports	Mississippi River

Source: Federal Transit Administration, National Transit Database, 2002; Editor & Publisher Market Guide, 2004; Bureau of Transportation Statistics, Airport Enplanement Activity for CY2002; www.amtrak.com

BUSINESSES

Major Business Headquarters

Company Name	2003 Rankings	
	Fortune 500	Forbes 500
Shaw Group	479	-

Note: Companies listed are located in the city; dashes indicate no ranking
Fortune 500: Companies that produce a 10-K are ranked 1 to 500 based on 2002 revenue
Forbes 500: Private companies are ranked 1 to 281 based on 2002 revenue
Source: Fortune, April 14, 2003; www.forbes.com, November 6, 2003

Minority and Women-Owned Businesses

Ownership	All Firms		Firms with Paid Employees			
	Firms	Sales ($000)	Firms	Sales ($000)	Employees	Payroll ($000)
Black	2,480	180,323	281	122,333	1,837	34,402
Hispanic	393	(a)	57	(a)	250 - 499	(a)
Women	4,367	820,152	902	739,598	7,953	169,858

Note: Figures cover firms located in the city; (a) Withheld to avoid disclosure
Source: 1997 Economic Census, Minority and Women-Owned Businesses

HOTELS

Hotels/Motels

Area	Hotels/Motels	Average Minimum Rates ($)		
		Tourist	First-Class	Deluxe
City	46	62	81	n/a

Note: n/a not available
Source: OAG Travel Planner Online, Spring 2004

EVENT SITES

Major Event Sites, Meeting Places and Convention Centers

Name	Guest Rooms	Exhibit/ Meeting Space (sq. ft.)	Largest Meeting Room Capacity
Baton Rouge Hilton	297	16,900	900
Baton Rouge Riverside Centroplex	n/a	72,000	n/a
E.G. Clark Activity Center Southern University	n/a	n/a	8,000
Maravich Assembly Center	n/a	n/a	14,236
Radisson Hotel & Conference Center	294	32,000	2,100

Note: n/a not available
Source: Original research

Living Environment

COST OF LIVING

Cost of Living Index

Year	Composite Index	Groceries	Housing	Utilities	Trans-portation	Health Care	Misc. Goods/Services
2001	105.5	108.9	100.3	128.7	103.6	96.3	104.6
2002	102.8	109.0	95.8	107.2	99.1	105.3	105.3
2003	100.9	110.4	94.4	110.5	99.4	110.1	99.1

Note: U.S. = 100
Source: ACCRA, Cost of Living Index, 2001, 2002 and 2003 4-Quarter Averages

HOUSING

House Price Index (HPI)

Area	National Ranking[2]	Quarterly Change (%)	One-Year Change (%)	Five-Year Change (%)
MSA[1]	191	1.12	3.30	20.71
U.S.[3]	-	3.67	7.97	41.81

Note: The HPI is a weighted repeat sales index. It measures average price changes in repeat sales or refinancings on the same properties. This information is obtained by reviewing repeat mortgage transactions on single-family properties whose mortgages have been purchased or securitized by Fannie Mae of Freddie Mac in January 1975; (1) Metropolitan Statistical Area - see Appendix A for areas included; (2) Rankings are based on annual percentage change, for all MSAs containing at least 15,000 transactions over the last 10 years and ranges from 1 to 220; (3) figures based on a weighted division average; all figures are for the period ended December 31, 2003
Source: Office of Federal Housing Enterprise Oversight, House Price Index, March 1, 2004

Housing: Year Structure Built

Area	1990-2000	1980-1989	1970-1979	1960-1969	1950-1959	1940-1949	Before 1940	Median Year
City	7.3	14.9	25.5	20.1	16.6	9.4	6.2	1969
MSA[1]	19.2	21.5	24.5	14.9	10.6	5.3	4.0	1976
U.S.	17.0	15.8	18.5	13.7	12.7	7.3	15.0	1971

Note: Figures are percentages; (1) Metropolitan Statistical Area - see Appendix A for areas included
Source: Census 2000, Summary File 3

Average New Home Price

Area	2001	2002	2003
City	222,783	239,729	241,149
U.S.	212,643	236,567	248,193

Note: Figures, in dollars, are based on a new home with 2,400 sq. ft. of living area on an 8,000 sq. ft. lot.
Source: ACCRA, Cost of Living Index, 2001, 2002 and 2003 4-Quarter Averages

Average Apartment Rent

Area	2001	2002	2003
City	572	583	610
U.S.	674	708	721

Note: Figures, in dollars per month, are based on an unfurnished two bedroom, 1-1/2 or 2 bath apartment, approximately 950 sq. ft. in size, excluding all utilities except water
Source: ACCRA, Cost of Living Index, 2001, 2002 and 2003 4-Quarter Averages

RESIDENTIAL UTILITIES

Average Residential Utility Costs

Area	All Electric ($/mth)	Part Electric ($/mth)	Other Energy ($/mth)	Phone ($/mth)
City	149.41	–	–	23.19
U.S.	116.46	65.82	62.68	23.90

Source: ACCRA, Cost of Living Index, 2003 4-Quarter Average

HEALTH CARE

Average Health Care Costs

Area	Hospital ($/day)	Doctor ($/visit)	Dentist ($/visit)
City	434.41	80.63	98.02
U.S.	678.35	67.91	83.90

Note: Hospital—based on a semi-private room; Doctor—based on a general practitioner's routine exam of an established patient; Dentist—based on adult teeth cleaning and periodic oral exam.
Source: ACCRA, Cost of Living Index, 2003 4-Quarter Average

Distribution of Non-Federal, Office-Based Physicians

Area	Total	Family/ General Practice	Specialties		
			Medical	Surgical	Other
MSA[1] (number)	1,028	139	359	280	250
MSA[1] (rate per 10,000 pop.)	17.1	2.3	6.0	4.6	4.1
Metro Average[2] (rate per 10,000 pop.)	33.1	2.2	7.7	4.8	5.6

Note: Data as of December 31, 2001; (1) Metropolitan Statistical Area - see Appendix A for areas included; (2) Average of 81 MSAs and CMSAs in this book
Source: American Medical Association, Physician Characteristics & Distribution in the U.S., 2003-2004

Hospitals

Baton Rouge has the following hospitals: 4 general medical and surgical; 1 psychiatric; 1 obstetrics and gynecology; 1 rehabilitation.
AHA Guide to the Healthcare Field, 2003-2004

PRESIDENTIAL ELECTION

2000 Presidential Election Results

Area	Gore	Bush	Nader	Buchanan	Other
East Baton Rouge Parish	45.3	52.7	1.2	0.4	0.3
U.S.	48.4	47.9	2.7	0.4	0.6

Note: Results are percentages and may not add to 100% due to rounding
Source: www.cbsnews.com; www.uselectionatlas.org

EDUCATION

Public School District Statistics

District Name	Schls.	Enroll- ment	Classroom Teachers	Pupil/ Teacher Ratio	Minority Pupils[1] (%)	Current Expend.[2] ($/pupil)
East Baton Rouge Parish	106	52,350	3,567	14.7	72.0	6,383
LSU Laboratory School	1	811	61	13.2	n/a	n/a
La Department of Corrections	7	1,076	110	9.8	n/a	n/a
Southern University Lab School	1	496	34	14.6	n/a	n/a

Note: Data covers the 2001-02 school year unless otherwise noted; (1) Fall 2000; (2) FY2000; n/a not available
Source: U.S. Department of Education, National Center for Education Statistics, Common Core of Data, Local Education Agency (School District) Universe Survey: School Year 2001-2002; U.S. Department of Education, National Center for Education Statistics, Digest of Education Statistics 2002

Educational Quality

School District	Education Quotient[1]	Graduate Outcome[2]	Community Index[3]	Resource Index[4]
East Baton Rouge Parish	21	19	46	50

Note: Scores are national percentile rankings and range from 1 (worst) to 99 (best); (1) Combination of the Graduate Outcome, Community and Resource indexes weighted to reflect the greater importance of the Graduate Outcome and Resource Index; (2) Based on graduation rates and college board scores (SAT/ACT); (3) Based on the surrounding community's level of affluence and adult education; (4) Based on teacher salaries, per-pupil expenditures and student-teacher ratios.
Source: Expansion Management, December 2003

Educational Attainment by Race

Area	High School Graduate (%)					Bachelor's Degree (%)				
	Total	White	Black	Asian	Hisp.[2]	Total	White	Black	Asian	Hisp.[2]
City	80.1	91.9	67.2	74.1	77.6	31.7	45.1	15.6	47.8	34.5
MSA[1]	81.9	87.1	69.6	75.9	77.9	24.9	27.9	16.4	50.0	30.0
U.S.	80.4	83.6	72.3	80.4	52.4	24.4	26.1	14.3	44.1	10.4

Note: Figures shown cover persons 25 years old and over; (1) Metropolitan Statistical Area - see Appendix A for areas included; (2) people of Hispanic origin can be of any race
Source: Census 2000, Summary File 3

School Enrollment by Type

Area	Grades KG to 8				Grades 9 to 12			
	Public		Private		Public		Private	
	Enrollment	%	Enrollment	%	Enrollment	%	Enrollment	%
City	22,342	77.9	6,338	22.1	10,183	81.1	2,369	18.9
MSA[1]	66,397	78.6	18,036	21.4	31,093	82.9	6,425	17.1
U.S.	33,526,011	88.7	4,285,121	11.3	14,848,628	90.6	1,532,323	9.4

Note: Figures shown cover persons 3 years old and over; (1) Metropolitan Statistical Area - see Appendix A for areas included
Source: Census 2000, Summary File 3

School Enrollment by Race

Area	Grades KG to 8 (%)				Grades 9 to 12 (%)			
	White	Black	Asian	Hisp.[1]	White	Black	Asian	Hisp.[1]
City	29.5	66.4	1.9	1.8	33.2	62.2	3.0	1.0
MSA[2]	56.8	40.0	1.2	1.8	58.4	38.0	1.9	1.6
U.S.	68.5	15.5	3.3	16.8	68.8	15.5	3.8	15.7

Note: Figures shown cover persons 3 years old and over; (1) people of Hispanic origin can be of any race; (2) Metropolitan Statistical Area - see Appendix A for areas included
Source: Census 2000, Summary File 3

Classroom Teacher Salaries in Public Schools

District	B.A. Degree		M.A. Degree		Maximum	
	Min. ($)	Rank[1]	Max. ($)	Rank[1]	Max. ($)	Rank[1]
Baton Rouge	25,716	99	39,853	98	44,287	97
DOD Average[2]	31,567	-	53,248	-	59,356	-

Note: Salaries are for 2001-2002; (1) Rank ranges from 1 to 100; (2) As per the U.S. Department of Defense Wage Fixing Authority
Source: American Federation of Teachers, Survey & Analysis of Teacher Salary Trends 2002

Higher Education

Four-Year Colleges			Two-Year Colleges			Medical Schools	Law Schools	Voc/ Tech
Public	Private Non-profit	Private For-profit	Public	Private Non-profit	Private For-profit			
2	2	0	2	2	6	0	2	6

Note: Figures cover institutions located within the city limits.
Source: National Center for Education Statistics, The Integrated Postsecondary Education System (IPEDS) Peer Analysis System, 2002; usnews.com, America's Best Graduate Schools 2004, Medical School Directory; The College Blue Book, Occupational Education, 2003; Barron's Guide to Law Schools, 2003; Medical School Admission Requirements U.S. & Canada, 2003-2004

MAJOR EMPLOYERS

Major Employers

Company Name	Industry	Type
Aegis Lending	Loan brokers	Single
AG Center Business Office	Commercial physical research	Branch
Baton Rouge General Med Ctr	Medical laboratories	Branch
Bilingual Education	Administration of educational programs	Branch
Blue Cross and Blue Shield	Hospital and medical service plans	Headquarters
City Parish Government	Executive offices	Headquarters
Ecolab Inc	Soap and other detergents	Branch
Exxon	Petroleum refining	Branch
Harmony LLC	Industrial buildings and warehouses	Headquarters
Health and Hospitals Dept	Administration of public health programs	Headquarters
Honeywell	Electrical equipment and supplies, nec	Branch
Mid City Medical Center	General medical and surgical hospitals	Single
Newtron Group Inc	Electrical work	Headquarters
Ochsner Clinic Foundation	Offices and clinics of medical doctors	Branch
Our Lady Lake Regional Med Ctr	General medical and surgical hospitals	Headquarters
Public Utility Commission	Regulation, administration of utilities	Branch
Southern University Book Store	Colleges and universities	Headquarters
University of Louisiana	Colleges and universities	Branch
Womans Hospital	General medical and surgical hospitals	Headquarters

Note: Companies shown are located in the metropolitan area and have 1,000 or more employees.
Source: www.zapdata.com, March 2004

PUBLIC SAFETY

Crime Rate

Area	All Crimes	Violent Crimes				Property Crimes		
		Murder	Forcible Rape	Robbery	Aggrav. Assault	Burglary	Larceny -Theft	Motor Vehicle Theft
City	8,292.2	25.8	58.2	484.4	600.0	1,781.1	4,710.0	632.8
Suburbs[1]	5,701.9	7.2	34.0	80.0	332.8	1,145.9	3,819.5	282.5
MSA[2]	6,680.7	14.2	43.2	232.8	433.7	1,385.9	4,156.0	414.9
U.S.	4,118.8	5.6	33.0	145.9	310.1	746.2	2,445.8	432.1

Note: Figures are crimes per 100,000 population; (1) All areas within the MSA that are located outside the city limits; (2) Metropolitan Statistical Area - see Appendix A for areas included
Source: FBI Uniform Crime Reports, 2002

RECREATION

Culture and Recreation

Museums	Orchestras	Opera Companies	Dance Companies	Professional Theatres	Zoos	Pro Sports Teams[1]
8	1	1	1	0	1	0

Note: (1) Covers the Metropolitan Statistical Area - see Appendix A for areas included.
Source: The Grey House Performing Arts Directory, 2002; Official Museum Directory, 2004; www.sportsvenues.com

Library System

The East Baton Rouge Parish Library has 11 branches, holdings of 1,226,346 volumes, and a budget of $13,290,737 (2001).
American Library Directory, 2003-2004

MEDIA

Newspapers

Name	Type	Freq.	Distribution	Circulation
The Advocate	General	7x/wk	State	118,000
Baton Rouge Weekly Press	General	1x/wk	State	7,500

Note: Includes newspapers whose offices are located in the city and whose circulations are 1,000 or more
Source: Burrelle's Media Directory, 2003

Television Stations

Name	Ch.	Affiliation	Type	Owner
WBRZ	2	ABCT	Commercial	Louisiana Television Broadcasting Corp.
WAFB	9	CBST	Commercial	Raycom Media Inc.
KLTM	13	PBS	Public	Louisiana Educational Television Authority
KLTL	18	PBS	Public	Louisiana Educational Television Authority
WBTR	19	n/a	Commercial	n/a
WTCN	21	n/a	Non-comm.	n/a
KLPB	24	PBS	Public	Louisiana Educational Television Authority
KLTS	24	PBS	Public	Louisiana Educational Television Authority
WLPB	27	PBS	Public	Louisiana Educational Television Authority
WVLA	33	NBCT	Commercial	White Knight Broadcasting
WGMB	44	FBC	Commercial	Communications Corporation Inc.

Note: Stations included broadcast from the Baton Rouge metro area; n/a not available
Source: Burrelle's Media Directory, 2003

AM Radio Stations

Call Letters	Freq. (kHz)	Target Audience	Station Format	Music Format
WNDC	910	Religious	M	Christian
WJBO	1150	General	N/S/T	n/a
WSKR	1210	G/M	S	n/a
KBRH	1260	General	M	Alternative
WIBR	1300	General	S	n/a
WYNK	1380	Children	M	Oldies
WXOK	1460	B/R	M	Gospel
WPFC	1550	B/R	E/M/N/S/T	Christian

Note: Stations included broadcast from the Baton Rouge metro area; n/a not available
The following abbreviations may be used:
Target Audience: A=Asian; B=Black; C=Christian; E=Ethnic; F=French; G=General; H=Hispanic;
M=Men; N=Native American; R=Religious; S=Senior Citizen; W=Women; Y=Young Adult; Z=Children
Station Format: E=Educational; M=Music; N=News; S=Sports; T=Talk
Source: Burrelle's Media Directory, 2003

FM Radio Stations

Call Letters	Freq. (mHz)	Target Audience	Station Format	Music Format
WJFM	88.5	Religious	E/M/N/T	Christian
WRKF	89.3	General	M/N/T	Classical
WBRH	90.3	General	E/M	Jazz
KLSU	91.1	General	M/N/S	Alternative
WQCK	92.7	Religious	M	Adult Contemporary
KOOJ	93.7	General	M	Oldies
WEMX	94.1	General	M	Urban Contemporary
KRVE	96.1	General	M	Adult Contemporary
WDGL	98.1	General	M/N/S/T	Classic Rock
WXCT	100.7	General	M/N	Country
WYNK	101.5	General	M/N/T	Country
WFMF	102.5	General	M/N/T	Top 40
WBBE	103.3	Women	M/N/S	Adult Contemporary
KQXL	106.5	Black	M	Urban Contemporary
WJNH	107.3	General	M	Urban Contemporary

Note: Stations included broadcast from the Baton Rouge metro area
The following abbreviations may be used:
Target Audience: A=Asian; B=Black; C=Christian; E=Ethnic; F=French; G=General; H=Hispanic;
M=Men; N=Native American; R=Religious; S=Senior Citizen; W=Women; Y=Young Adult; Z=Children
Station Format: E=Educational; M=Music; N=News; S=Sports; T=Talk
Source: Burrelle's Media Directory, 2003

CLIMATE

Average and Extreme Temperatures

Temperature	Jan	Feb	Mar	Apr	May	Jun	Jul	Aug	Sep	Oct	Nov	Dec	Yr.
Extreme High (°F)	82	85	91	92	98	103	101	102	99	94	87	85	103
Average High (°F)	61	65	71	79	85	90	91	91	87	80	70	64	78
Average Temp. (°F)	51	54	61	68	75	81	82	82	78	69	59	53	68
Average Low (°F)	41	44	50	57	64	70	73	72	68	57	48	43	57
Extreme Low (°F)	9	13	20	32	44	53	58	59	43	30	21	8	8

Note: Figures cover the years 1948-1995
Source: National Climatic Data Center, International Station Meteorological Climate Summary, 9/96

Average Precipitation/Snowfall/Humidity

Precip./Humidity	Jan	Feb	Mar	Apr	May	Jun	Jul	Aug	Sep	Oct	Nov	Dec	Yr.
Avg. Precip. (in.)	4.9	5.1	4.8	5.5	5.0	4.4	6.6	5.4	4.1	3.1	4.2	5.3	58.5
Avg. Snowfall (in.)	Tr	Tr	Tr	0	0	0	0	0	0	0	Tr	Tr	Tr
Avg. Rel. Hum. 6am (%)	85	85	86	89	91	91	92	93	91	89	88	86	89
Avg. Rel. Hum. 3pm (%)	59	55	52	52	54	57	62	61	59	51	53	57	56

Note: Figures cover the years 1948-1995; Tr = Trace amounts (<0.05 in. of rain; <0.5 in. of snow)
Source: National Climatic Data Center, International Station Meteorological Climate Summary, 9/96

Weather Conditions

Temperature			Daytime Sky			Precipitation		
10°F & below	32°F & below	90°F & above	Clear	Partly cloudy	Cloudy	0.01 inch or more precip.	0.1 inch or more snow/ice	Thunder-storms
< 1	21	86	99	150	116	113	< 1	73

Note: Figures are average number of days per year and covers the years 1948-1995
Source: National Climatic Data Center, International Station Meteorological Climate Summary, 9/96

HAZARDOUS WASTE

Superfund Sites

Baton Rouge has no sites on the EPA's Superfund National Priorities List.
U.S. Environmental Protection Agency, National Priorities List, March 15, 2004

AIR & WATER QUALITY

Maximum Pollutant Concentrations

	Particulate Matter (ug/m³)	Carbon Monoxide (ppm)	Sulfur Dioxide (ppm)	Nitrogen Dioxide (ppm)	Ozone 1-hour (ppm)	Ozone 8-hour (ppm)	Lead (ug/m³)
MSA[1] Level	69	4	0.036	0.018	0.13	0.08	n/a
NAAQS[2]	150	9	0.140	0.053	0.12	0.08	1.50
Met NAAQS[2]	Yes	Yes	Yes	Yes	No	Yes	n/a

Note: (1) Metropolitan Statistical Area - see Appendix A for areas included; (2) National Ambient Air Quality Standards; n/a not available
Units: ppm = parts per million; ug/m³ = micrograms per cubic meter
Source: EPA, Latest Findings on National Air Quality: 2002 Status and Trends, August 2003

Air Quality Index

In the Baton Rouge MSA (see Appendix A for areas included), the Air Quality Index (AQI) exceeded 100 on 7 days in 2002. An AQI value greater than 100 indicates that air quality would have been in the unhealthful range on that day.
EPA, Latest Findings on National Air Quality: 2002 Status and Trends, August 2003

Watershed Health

The U.S. Environmental Protection Agency monitors the health of the aquatic resources for the nation's 2,000+ watersheds. **The Amite watershed serves the Baton Rouge area and received an overall Index of Watershed Indicators (IWI) score of 6 (more serious problems - high vulnerability).** The IWI score is based on seven condition and nine vulnerability indicators. The overall IWI score ranges from 1 (best health) to 6 (worst health). The Condition Indicators include: designated use attainment, fish and wildlife consumption advisories, source water condition, contaminated sediments, ambient water quality, and wetlands loss index. The Vulnerability Indicators include: aquatic species at risk, conventional and toxic loads over permitted limits, urban and agricultural runoff potential, population change, hydrologic modification, estuarine pollution susceptibility, and air deposition. *EPA, Index of Watershed Indicators, October 26, 2001*

Drinking Water

Water System Name	Pop. Served	Primary Water Source Type	Number of Violations January 2002-February 2004		
			Health Based	Significant Monitoring	Monitoring
Baton Rouge Water Company	425,732	Ground	None	None	None

Note: Data as of February 19, 2004
Source: EPA, Office of Ground Water and Drinking Water, Safe Drinking Water Information System

Baton Rouge tap water is neutral, very soft and not fluoridated.
Editor & Publisher Market Guide, 2004

Birmingham, Alabama

Background

Lying in the South's Appalachian Ridge and Valley, Birmingham's founding reaches back to 1813, and was later named after the industrial city of England. During the Civil War, a small iron factory was developed. Realizing the potential of an area rich in iron ore and coal, businessmen in later years founded the city in 1871. Birmingham expanded, but tragedy struck when a cholera epidemic and the economic depression of 1873 simultaneously hit the area. The city nearly collapsed.

A change in fortunes occurred in 1880 when railroads crisscrossed the area and the state's first blast furnace began spewing out iron. The decade of the 1880s saw great demands for iron, which helped expand the city's manufacturing base. The population rose so miraculously, from a few thousand in 1880 to over 100,000 in 1910, that Birmingham earned the sobriquet, the Magic City. In the early 1960s the city was the scene of dramatic developments in the civil rights movement.

Race relations have improved markedly since then, as the city's electorate in 1979 chose Richard Arrington, Jr., as its first African-American mayor, and the black middle class has expanded in recent years. The Birmingham Civil Rights Institute, a research library and exhibition center, opened in 1992, further helping to bind the city's racial wounds.

Due to its location in the mineral-rich Jones Valley, Birmingham became the most important steel and iron manufacturing site in the South in the late nineteenth century and through much of the twentieth. Atop Red Mountain to the south, as a dedication to the importance of the industry, stands a cast-iron statue, the largest in the world, of the Roman deity Vulcan, patron of ironsmiths. After a six-year closure, the rehabilitated Vulcan Park opened in 2004.

Now 85 percent of employees work in businesses other than manufacturing. The third-largest employer in Birmingham is the telecommunications industry; South Central Bell and Bell South have located their headquarters there. The remaining employees are in 850 factories, producing such items as chemicals, transportation equipment, and pipe—all this in addition to the still-important manufacture of steel and iron.

The city's economy also features a large financial sector, with four of the nation's top fifty banks located here, helping to rank the city as the second largest U.S. banking center by the number of top 50 banks headquartered within the metro area, according to Economic Development Partnership of Alabama report.

Honda Corporation chose a site 45 minutes east of Birmingham's city limits, in Lincoln, for its factory that produces the Odyssey mini-van. The first Odyssey rolled off the assembly line in November, 2001. In 2002, the company announced plans to invest an additional $425 million and double the plant's size.

The state of Alabama also offers newcomers a tax credit for long-term capital investment.

There are many opportunities for higher education, principal of which is the local campus of the University of Alabama at Birmingham, the city's largest employer. In 1945, the university opened its Medical Center, which experienced great expansion in the late 1970s and early 1980s. Also located here is Samford University, Alabama's largest privately supported institution for higher learning and closely aligned with the Southern Baptist Convention.

Furthering the city's cultural life are the Birmingham Botanical Gardens, and the Birmingham Museum of Art with a wide-ranging collection of pieces from 5,000 BC to the present.

The metropolitan area possesses a mild climate, enduring less rain than do some other parts of the state, although it is still relatively abundant. Summers tend to be hot and humid, as is expected in the Deep South. Because of its location on the edge of the Appalachian Range, however, Birmingham's winters are cooler than one would expect in a subtropical region, with temperatures ranging from freezing to moderate.

Rankings

- Birmingham was ranked #218 out of 331 metro areas in *Cities Ranked & Rated*. Criteria: cost of living; climate; crime; transportation; economy and jobs; education; arts and culture; health and healthcare; leisure. *Cities Ranked & Rated, 1st Edition, 2004*

- *Ladies Home Journal* ranked America's 200 largest cities based on the qualities women surveyed care about most. Birmingham ranked #133 out of 143 in the smaller city category (population under 300,000). Criteria: crime; lifestyle; education; jobs; health; child care; politics; and the economy. *Ladies Home Journal Online, "The Best Cities for Women 2002"*

- *Forbes* ranked the 150 most populous metro areas in the U.S. in terms of the "Best Places for Business and Careers." The Birmingham metro area was ranked #87. Criteria: income and job growth; cost-of-doing-business; qualifications of the available pool of labor; crime rates; housing costs; net migration. *Forbes, May 9, 2003*

- *Men's Health* ranked 101 U.S. cities in terms of the quality of their tap water. Birmingham received a grade of A. Criteria: levels of bacteria, arsenic, lead, trihalomethanes, and haloacetic acids were compared with the National Academy of Science's guidelines as well as with the EPA's more stringent maximum contaminant level goals. *Men's Health, March 2004*

- Sperling's BestPlaces ranked 331 metro areas and identified the most and least stressful U.S. cities. The Birmingham metro area ranked #40 out of the 100 largest metro areas (#1 = most stressful). Criteria: divorce rate; unemployment rate; violent and property crime; suicide rate; commute time; mental health; alcohol consumption; cloudy days. *www.BestPlaces.net, February 26, 2004*

- Sperling's BestPlaces in partnership with Pep Boys ranked 77 metro areas and identified "America's Most Drivable Cities." The Birmingham metro area ranked #7. Criteria: climate; road roughness; urban mobility; gas prices. *Pep Boys, "America's Most Drivable Cities," April 9, 2003*

- Birmingham was ranked #133 out of America's 200 largest metro areas in *SELF Magazine's* ranking of "America's Healthiest Cities for Women." Criteria: safety; air/water quality; cancer rates; and 21 other factors relating to health. *SELF Magazine, November 2003*

- Birmingham was identified as an asthma "hot spot" where high prevalence makes the condition a key issue and environmental "triggers" and other factors can make living with asthma a particular challenge. The area ranked #23 out of the nations 100 largest metro areas. Criteria: local asthma prevalence and mortality data; pollen scores; air pollution; asthma prescriptions; smoking laws; number of asthma specialists. *GlaxoSmithKline, October 29, 2002*

- Birmingham was ranked #88 out of 100 cities surveyed in *Child* magazine's ranking of the "Best Cities for Families." Criteria: number of pediatricians per capita; proximity to a children's hospital; immunization rates; infant mortality rate; air quality; water quality; school spending; pupil-teacher ratio; availability of parks/green space; nearby recreational opportunities; average commute time; number of sunny days; average cost of a 3-bedroom home; unemployment rate; future job growth; crime rate; percentage of children under 5; mandated minimum child care ratios. *Child, April 2001*

- *Zero Population Growth* ranked 239 cities in terms of children's health, safety, and economic well-being. Birmingham was ranked #104 out of 140 independent cities (cities with populations greater than 100,000 which were neither major cities nor suburbs/outer cities) and was given a grade of C+. Criteria: total population and population growth; percent of population under 18 years of age; number of children's museums; health improvement grade; percent of births to teens; percent of low birthweight infants; infant mortality rate; number of Title X-funded clinics; average SAT/ACT scores; average elementary and secondary class size; crime rate; unemployment rate; percent of affordable homes; number of bad air days; park acres per 1000 persons; library circulation per child; and children's program attendance counts. *Zero Population Growth, Kid Friendly Cities Report Card 2001*

- *Ladies Home Journal* ranked America's 200 largest cities in terms of safety. Birmingham ranked #177 out of 200. Criteria: violent crimes; crimes against property; and rape. *Ladies Home Journal Online, "The Best Cities for Women 2002"*

- The Birmingham metro area was selected by *Yahoo! Internet Life* as one of "America's Most Wired Cities...and Towns." The area ranked #72 out of 87. Criteria: home and work net use; user sophistication; domain density; and available content. *Yahoo! Internet Life, April 2001*

- Birmingham was identified as one of the 100 "Most Unwired Cities" in the U.S. The area ranked #87. Criteria: number of public and commercial wireless access points; cell phone coverage offering wide area network Internet access; Internet penetration. *Intel, "Most Unwired Cities," March 4, 2003*

- Scarborough Research measured the percentage of households who subscribe to cellular services among adults ages 18 and over in 75 U.S. markets. The Birmingham DMA (Designated Market Area) was ranked #17 out of 75. *Scarborough Research, Scarborough USA+ 2003 Release 1*

- Birmingham was selected as one of "America's Most Literate Cities." The city ranked #19 out of the 64 largest U.S. cities. Criteria: booksellers; library support, holdings, and utilization; educational attainment; periodicals published; newspaper circulation. *University of Wisconsin-Whitewater, "America's Most Literate Cities," Summer 2003*

- Birmingham was ranked #116 in *Prevention* magazine's survey of the "Best Walking Cities in the U.S." The magazine, in conjunction with the American Podiatric Medical Association, surveyed 125 of the most populated cities and then tabulated and weighed 20 criteria of interest to pedestrians. *Prevention, April, 2004*

- Birmingham was selected as one of "The Best Places to Start and Grow a Company." The area ranked #8 among large metro areas. Criteria: Significant Starts (firms started in the last 10 years that still employ at least 5 people) and Young Growers (firms 10 years old or less that grew significantly during the last 4 years). *Cognetics, "Entrepreneurial Hot Spots: The Best Places in America to Start and Grow a Company," 2001*

- The Birmingham metro area was selected as one of "America's 50 Hottest Cities for Business Relocations and Expansions." The area ranked #25. Criteria: 70 of the industry's most prominent site selection consultants were asked which cities their clients found the most attractive when it came to selecting an expansion or relocation site in 2003. *Expansion Management, January 2004*

- The Birmingham metro area was cited as one of "The Best Places in the U.S. to Locate a Company." The area ranked #18 out of 329. Criteria: education (with emphasis on college board test results and high school graduation rates); availability of quality healthcare services and the cost to employers; quality of life; logistics workforce and companies; transportation infrastructure; quality and quantity of highly educated technical workers; business climate. *Expansion Management, July 2003*

- Birmingham was cited as a top metro area for European expansion. The area ranked #4 out of 50, based on European-based company expansions or relocations within the past two years that created at least 10 jobs and involved capital investment of at least $1 million. *Expansion Management, June 2003*

- The Birmingham metro area was selected as one of the "Top 40 Hottest Real Estate Markets" for expanding or relocating businesses." Criteria: rental costs; purchase prices; and vacancy rates of office and warehouse space. *Expansion Management, August 2003*

- The Birmingham metro area appeared on *Forbes/Milken Institute* list of "Best Places for Business and Career." Rank: #129 out of 200 metro areas. Criteria: salary growth; job growth; number of technology clusters; overall concentration of technology activity relative to national average; and technology output growth. *www.forbes.com, Forbes/Milken Institute Best Places 2002*

- The Birmingham metro area appeared on the "Milken Institute Best Performing Cities" index. Rank: #95 out of 200 large metro areas. Criteria: job growth; wage and salary growth; high-tech output growth. *Milken Institute, June 25, 2003*

- The Birmingham metro area appeared on *IndustryWeek's* fourth annual World-Class Communities list. It ranked #236 out of 315 metro areas. Criteria: MSA Gross Metropolitan Product (GMP) per manufacturing employee; and MSA percent share of U.S. manufacturing Gross Domestic Product (GDP). *IndustryWeek, April 16, 2001*

- ING Group ranked the 125 largest metro areas according to the general financial security of residents. The Birmingham metro area was ranked #47 out of 125. Criteria: Earnings and Wealth Potential (household income, education, net assets, cost of living); Safety Net (health insurance, retirement savings, life insurance, income support programs); Personal Threats (unemployment rate, low-income households, crime rate); Community Economic Vitality (cost of community services, job quality, job creation, housing costs). *ING Group, "The Best Cities to Earn and Save Money: A Ranking of the Largest 125 U.S. Cities," 2001 Edition*

Business Environment

CITY FINANCES

City Government Finances

Component	2000-2001 ($000)	2000-2001 ($ per capita)
Total Revenues	524,372	2,160
Total Expenditures	560,393	2,308
Debt Outstanding	997,435	4,108
Cash and Securities	1,538,102	6,334

Source: U.S Census Bureau, Government Finances 2000-2001, August 2003

City Government Revenue by Source

Source	2000-2001 ($000)	2000-2001 ($ per capita)
General Revenue		
From Federal Government	15,952	66
From State Government	20,561	85
From Local Governments	11,191	46
Taxes		
Property	38,725	159
Sales	106,341	438
Personal Income	62,091	256
License	0	0
Charges	29,104	120
Liquor Store	0	0
Utility	65,735	271
Employee Retirement	73,155	301
Other	101,517	418

Source: U.S Census Bureau, Government Finances 2000-2001, August 2003

City Government Expenditures by Function

Function	2000-2001 ($000)	2000-2001 ($ per capita)	2000-2001 (%)
General Expenditures			
Airports	0	0	0.0
Corrections	570	2	0.1
Education	11,535	48	2.1
Fire Protection	36,571	151	6.5
Governmental Administration	37,494	154	6.7
Health	5,451	22	1.0
Highways	17,018	70	3.0
Hospitals	0	0	0.0
Housing and Community Development	11,870	49	2.1
Interest on General Debt	37,108	153	6.6
Libraries	12,629	52	2.3
Parking	27,888	115	5.0
Parks and Recreation	27,236	112	4.9
Police Protection	64,960	268	11.6
Public Welfare	0	0	0.0
Sewerage	2,370	10	0.4
Solid Waste Management	38,850	160	6.9
Liquor Store	0	0	0.0
Utility	81,438	335	14.5
Employee Retirement	37,794	156	6.7
Other	109,611	451	19.6

Source: U.S Census Bureau, Government Finances 2000-2001, August 2003

Municipal Bond Ratings

Area	Moody's
City	Aaa

Source: Mergent Bond Record, February 2004

DEMOGRAPHICS

Population Growth

Area	1990 Census	2000 Census	2003 Estimate	2008 Projection	Population Growth (%) 1990-2000	2000-2008
City	266,532	242,820	234,546	221,211	-8.9	-8.9
MSA[1]	840,140	921,106	933,112	952,310	9.6	3.4
U.S.	248,709,873	281,421,906	290,647,163	305,918,071	13.2	8.7

Note: (1) Metropolitan Statistical Area - see Appendix A for areas included
Source: Claritas, Inc.

Number of Households and Average Household Size

Area	1990 Census	2000 Census	2003 Estimate	2008 Projection	2003 Average Household Size
City	105,634	98,782	96,180	91,882	2.4
MSA[1]	319,774	361,304	369,866	384,282	2.5
U.S.	91,947,410	105,480,101	109,440,059	116,034,472	2.7

Note: (1) Metropolitan Statistical Area - see Appendix A for areas included
Source: Claritas, Inc.

Race and Ethnicity

Area	White Non-Hispanic	Black Non-Hispanic	Asian Non-Hispanic	Other Race Non-Hispanic	Hispanic
City	23.0	74.3	0.8	1.8	1.8
MSA[1]	67.4	29.8	0.9	1.9	2.0
U.S.	74.5	12.4	3.8	9.3	13.2

Note: Figures are 2003 estimates; (1) Metropolitan Statistical Area - see Appendix A for areas included
Source: Claritas, Inc.

Segregation

City Index[2]	Rank[3]	MSA[1] Index[2]	Rank[4]
66.3	32	77.4	15

Note: Figures are based on an analysis of Census 2000 data; (1) Metropolitan Statistical Area - see Appendix A for areas included; (2) Dissimilarity Index—the most commonly used measure of segregation between two groups, reflecting their relative distributions across neighborhoods within a city or metropolitan area. It can range in value from 0, indicating complete integration, to 100, indicating complete segregation; (3) Ranges from 1 (most segregated) to 100 (least segregated) and includes all the cities in this book; (4) Ranges from 1 (most segregated) to 318 (least segregated) and includes 318 metropolitan areas.
Source: www.CensusScope.org

Ancestry

Area	German	Irish[2]	English	American	Italian	Polish	French[3]	Scottish
City	2.3	2.8	3.2	3.9	0.8	0.3	0.6	0.8
MSA[1]	6.0	7.7	9.0	12.8	1.9	0.6	1.5	2.0
U.S.	15.2	10.9	8.7	7.3	5.6	3.2	3.0	1.7

Note: Figures include multiple ancestry (e.g. if a person reported being Irish and Italian, they were included in both columns); (1) Metropolitan Statistical Area - see Appendix A for areas included; (2) Includes Celtic; (3) Includes Alsatian but excludes Basque
Source: Census 2000, Summary File 3

Foreign-Born Population

Area	Any Foreign Country	Europe	Asia	Africa	Oceania[2]	Canada	Mexico	Latin America[3]
City	2.1	0.3	0.6	0.2	0.0	0.1	0.7	0.3
MSA[1]	2.3	0.4	0.7	0.1	0.0	0.1	0.7	0.3
U.S.	11.1	1.7	2.9	0.3	0.1	0.3	3.3	2.5

Note: (1) Metropolitan Statistical Area - see Appendix A for areas included; (2) Includes Australia, New Zealand subregion, Melanesia, Micronesia, Polynesia, and Oceania n.e.c; (3) Includes Central America (excluding Mexico), South America, and the Caribbean.
Source: Census 2000, Summary File 3

Religion

Area	Catholic	Southern Baptist	United Methodist	ELCA[1]	LDS[2]	Presbyterian Church USA	Jewish Est.	Muslim Est.
County	6.7	29.7	8.0	0.2	0.3	1.5	0.8	0.3
U.S.	22.0	7.1	3.7	1.8	1.5	1.1	2.2	0.6

Note: Figures shown are the number of adherents as a percentage of the total population; Adherents are defined as all members, including full members, their children and the estimated number of other participants who are not considered members (e.g. the baptized, those not confirmed, those not eligible for communion, those regularly attending services, etc.); (1) Evangelical Lutheran Church in America; (2) The Church of Jesus Christ of Latter Day Saints
Source: Reprinted with permission from Religious Congregations and Membership in the United States 2000 (Nashville, Glenmary Research Center, 2002) Copyright Association of Statisticians of American Religious Bodies. All rights reserved.

Age Distribution

Area	Percent of Population						
	Under Age 5	Age 5 to 17	Age 18 to 34	Age 35 to 49	Age 50 to 64	Age 65 to 79	80 Years and Over
City	6.8	18.3	25.9	22.6	12.9	9.9	3.7
MSA[1]	6.7	18.4	23.5	23.7	15.0	9.5	3.2
U.S.	6.8	18.9	23.7	23.5	14.8	9.2	3.2

Note: (1) Metropolitan Statistical Area - see Appendix A for areas included
Source: Census 2000, Summary File 3

Marriage Status

Area	Never Married	Now Married Except Separated	Separated	Widowed	Divorced
City	35.2	38.0	4.0	9.5	13.3
MSA[1]	25.1	54.5	2.1	7.6	10.8
U.S.	27.1	54.4	2.2	6.6	9.7

Note: Figures cover population 15 years of age and older; (1) Metropolitan Statistical Area - see Appendix A for areas included
Source: Census 2000, Summary File 3

Male/Female Ratio

Area	Males	Females	Males per 100 Females
City	108,682	125,864	86.3
MSA[1]	447,063	486,049	92.0
U.S.	142,511,883	148,135,280	96.2

Note: Figures are 2003 estimates; (1) Metropolitan Statistical Area - see Appendix A for areas included
Source: Claritas, Inc.

ECONOMY

Gross Metropolitan Product

Area	1999	2000	2001	2002	2002 Rank[2]
MSA[1]	30.5	31.9	33.1	34.3	65

Note: Figures are in billions of dollars; (1) Metropolitan Statistical Area - see Appendix A for areas included; (2) Rank ranges from 1 to 319
Source: The U.S. Conference of Mayors, Metro Economies Report, July 2003

INCOME

Per Capita/Median/Average Income

Area	Per Capita ($)	Median Household ($)	Average Household ($)
City	17,107	29,968	40,519
MSA[1]	24,503	44,759	61,272
U.S.	24,078	46,868	63,207

Note: Figures are 2003 estimates; (1) Metropolitan Statistical Area - see Appendix A for areas included
Source: Claritas, Inc.

Household Income Distribution

Area	Percent of Households Earning							
	Under $15,000	$15,000 -24,999	$25,000 -34,999	$35,000 -49,999	$50,000 -74,999	$75,000 -99,000	$100,000 -149,999	$150,000 and up
City	26.8	16.1	14.2	16.6	14.1	6.1	4.1	2.0
MSA[1]	16.0	11.7	11.8	16.2	18.4	10.8	9.5	5.7
U.S.	14.1	11.5	11.7	16.0	19.2	11.3	10.2	6.0

Note: Figures are 2003 estimates; (1) Metropolitan Statistical Area - see Appendix A for areas included
Source: Claritas, Inc.

Poverty Rates by Age

Area	All Ages	Under 5 Years Old	5 to 17 Years Old	18 to 64 Years Old	65 Years and Over
City	24.7	2.6	6.4	13.3	2.4
MSA[1]	13.1	1.3	3.2	7.1	1.6
U.S.	12.4	1.2	3.0	6.9	1.2

Note: Figures are percent of population with income in 1999 below poverty level and only include population
for whom poverty status is determined; (1) Metropolitan Statistical Area - see Appendix A for areas included
Source: Census 2000, Summary File 3

Personal Bankruptcy Filing Rate

Area	2002	2003
Jefferson County	12.48	13.47
U.S.	5.34	5.58

Note: Numbers are per 1,000 population and include Chapter 7 and Chapter 13 filings
Source: Federal Deposit Insurance Corporation (FDIC), Regional Economic Conditions (RECON), 2/25/2004

EMPLOYMENT

Labor Force and Employment

Area	Civilian Labor Force			Workers Employed		
	Dec. 2002	Dec. 2003	% Chg.	Dec. 2002	Dec. 2003	% Chg.
City	128,078	133,278	4.1	119,550	124,258	3.9
MSA[1]	470,689	488,736	3.8	450,674	468,420	3.9
U.S.	144,807,000	146,501,000	1.2	136,599,000	138,556,000	1.4

Note: Data is not seasonally adjusted and covers workers 16 years of age and older;
(1) Metropolitan Statistical Area - see Appendix A for areas included
Source: Bureau of Labor Statistics, http://stats.bls.gov

Unemployment Rate

Area	2003											
	Jan.	Feb.	Mar.	Apr.	May	Jun.	Jul.	Aug.	Sep.	Oct.	Nov.	Dec.
City	6.7	6.7	6.5	6.5	6.5	7.7	7.0	7.4	6.9	7.3	7.2	6.8
MSA[1]	4.3	4.3	4.1	4.1	4.1	4.8	4.4	4.5	4.3	4.5	4.4	4.2
U.S.	6.5	6.4	6.2	5.8	5.8	6.5	6.3	6.0	5.8	5.6	5.6	5.4

Note: Data is not seasonally adjusted and covers workers 16 years of age and older; All figures are
percentages; (1) Metropolitan Statistical Area - see Appendix A for areas included
Source: Bureau of Labor Statistics, http://stats.bls.gov

Employment by Occupation

Occupation Classification	City (%)	MSA[1] (%)	U.S. (%)
Sales and Office	29.8	29.8	26.7
Professional and Related	18.6	20.6	20.2
Service	19.3	12.7	14.9
Production, Transportation, and Material Moving	15.4	12.9	14.6
Management, Business, and Financial	9.4	13.8	13.5
Construction, Extraction, and Maintenance	7.4	9.9	9.4
Farming, Forestry, and Fishing	0.1	0.2	0.7

Note: Figures cover employed civilians 16 years of age and older;
(1) Metropolitan Statistical Area - see Appendix A for areas included
Source: Census 2000, Summary File 3

Employment by Industry

Sector	MSA[1]		U.S.
	Number of Employees	Percent of Total	Percent of Total
Government	74,400	15.5	16.7
Education and Health Services	54,100	11.3	12.9
Professional and Business Services	60,200	12.5	12.3
Retail Trade	59,700	12.4	11.8
Manufacturing	39,400	8.2	11.0
Leisure and Hospitality	38,600	8.0	9.1
Finance Activities	39,400	8.2	6.1
Construction	n/a	n/a	5.1
Wholesale Trade	28,600	6.0	4.3
Other Services	22,800	4.7	4.1
Transportation and Utilities	17,200	3.6	3.7
Information	13,700	2.9	2.4
Natural Resources and Mining	n/a	n/a	0.4

Note: Figures cover non-farm employment as of December 2003 and are not seasonally adjusted;
(1) Metropolitan Statistical Area - see Appendix A for areas included; n/a not available
Source: Bureau of Labor Statistics, http://stats.bls.gov

Average Wages

Occupation	$/Hr.	Occupation	$/Hr.
Accountants and Auditors	24.11	Maids and Housekeeping Cleaners	6.97
Automotive Mechanics	14.67	Maintenance and Repair Workers	14.29
Bookkeepers	13.33	Marketing Managers	35.39
Carpenters	14.38	Nuclear Medicine Technologists	20.75
Cashiers	7.13	Nurses, Licensed Practical	14.01
Clerks, General Office	10.57	Nurses, Registered	22.54
Clerks, Receptionists/Information	10.05	Nursing Aides/Orderlies/Attendants	8.99
Clerks, Shipping/Receiving	11.24	Packers and Packagers, Hand	7.76
Computer Programmers	27.63	Physical Therapists	29.88
Computer Support Specialists	20.24	Postal Service Mail Carriers	18.44
Computer Systems Analysts	28.62	Real Estate Brokers	21.14
Cooks, Restaurant	8.20	Retail Salespersons	10.91
Dentists	86.46	Sales Reps., Exc. Tech./Scientific	25.16
Electrical Engineers	30.86	Sales Reps., Tech./Scientific	32.20
Electricians	16.12	Secretaries, Exc. Legal/Med./Exec.	11.49
Financial Managers	33.90	Security Guards	8.82
First-Line Supervisors/Mgrs., Sales	15.23	Surgeons	101.06
Food Preparation Workers	8.38	Teacher Assistants	7.80
General and Operations Managers	40.99	Teachers, Elementary School	18.70
Hairdressers/Cosmetologists	9.95	Teachers, Secondary School	20.60
Internists	91.60	Telemarketers	8.49
Janitors and Cleaners	7.87	Truck Drivers, Heavy/Tractor-Trailer	17.00
Landscaping/Groundskeeping Workers	9.36	Truck Drivers, Light/Delivery Svcs.	12.76
Lawyers	50.02	Waiters and Waitresses	6.57

Note: Wage data is for 2002 and covers the Metropolitan Statistical Area (see Appendix A for areas included).
Hourly wages for elementary/secondary school teachers and teacher assistants were calculated by the editors
from annual wage data assuming a 40 hour work week; n/a not available.
Source: Bureau of Labor Statistics, 2002 Metro Area Occupational Employment and Wage Estimates

Occupational Employment Projections: 1996 - 2006

Occupations Expected to Have the Largest Job Growth (ranked by numerical growth)	Fast-Growing Occupations[1] (ranked by percent growth)
1. Cashiers	1. Computer engineers
2. Teachers, secondary school	2. Personal and home care aides
3. Truck drivers, light	3. Database administrators
4. General managers & top executives	4. Occupational therapists
5. Nursing aides/orderlies/attendants	5. Systems analysts
6. Janitors/cleaners/maids, ex. priv. hshld.	6. Home health aides
7. Registered nurses	7. Physical therapy assistants and aides
8. Home health aides	8. Medical assistants
9. Marketing & sales, supervisors	9. Teachers, special education
10. Systems analysts	10. Physical therapists

Note: Projections cover Alabama; (1) Excludes occupations with total job growth less than 300
Source: U.S. Department of Labor, Employment and Training Administration, America's Labor Market Information System (ALMIS)

TAXES

State Corporate Income Tax Rates

State	Rate (%)	Number of Brackets	Low Bracket (Under $)	High Bracket (Over $)
Alabama	6.5	1	na	na

Note: Tax rates as of December 31, 2003; na not applicable; Federal deductibility.
Source: Tax Foundation, www.taxfoundation.org

State Individual Income Tax Rates

State	Federal Deductibility	Marginal Rate (%)	Number of Brackets	Low Bracket (Under $)	High Bracket (Over $)
Alabama	Yes (z)	2.0-5.0	3	0	3,000

Note: Tax rates as of December 31, 2003; Brackets apply to single taxpayers and married people filing separately; na not applicable; (z) Residents should deduct the federal income tax liability as shown on their 2003 federal income tax return, less any federal Advance Child Tax Credit for 2003.
Source: Tax Foundation, www.taxfoundation.org

Various State and Local Tax Rates

State Sales and Use (%)	Total Sales and Use (%)	Gasoline (cents/gal.)	Cigarette (cents/pack)	Spirits ($/gal.)	Table Wine ($/gal.)	Beer ($/gal.)
4.0	8.0	16	16.5	(b)	1.70	0.52

Note: Tax rates as of December 31, 2003.(b) States where the state government controls all sales.
Source: Tax Foundation, www.taxfoundation.org

State Tax Burdens

Area	Combined State and Local Tax Burden		Combined Federal, State and Local Tax Burden	
	Percent	Rank	Percent	Rank
Alabama	8.4	46	26.3	49
U.S. Average	9.7	-	30.0	-

Note: Figures are for 2003
Source: Tax Foundation, www.taxfoundation.org

Internal Revenue Service Tax Audits

IRS District	Percent of Returns Audited				
	1996	1997	1998	1999	2000
Gulf Coast	0.83	0.74	0.50	0.41	0.20
U.S.	0.66	0.61	0.46	0.31	0.20

Note: Figures cover IRS district audits of federal income tax returns filed by individuals. Geographic data on district audits for 2001 and 2002 are being withheld by the IRS. TRAC is challenging this policy.
Source: Syracuse University, Transactional Records Access Clearinghouse (TRAC), "Odds of IRS District Tax Audit 2000"

**RESIDENTIAL
REAL ESTATE**

Building Permits

Area	Single-Family			Multi-Family			Total		
	2001	2002	Pct. Chg.	2001	2002	Pct. Chg.	2001	2002	Pct. Chg.
City	108	188	74.1	24	76	216.7	132	264	100.0
U.S.	1,235,600	1,332,600	7.9	401,100	415,100	3.5	1,636,700	1,747,700	6.8

Note: Figures represent new, privately-owned housing units authorized (unadjusted data)
Source: U.S. Census Bureau, Manufacturing, Mining, and Construction Statistics

Homeownership and Housing Vacancies

Area	Homeownership Rate[2] (%)			Rental Vacancy Rate[3] (%)			Homeowner Vacancy Rate[4] (%)		
	2001	2002[a]	2003	2001	2002[a]	2003	2001	2002[a]	2003
MSA[1]	70.8	68.7	71.3	17.6	12.3	15.4	2.3	2.2	1.4
U.S.	67.8	67.9	68.3	8.4	8.9	9.8	1.8	1.7	1.8

Note: (1) Metropolitan Statistical Area - see Appendix A for areas included; (2) The proportion of households
that are owners; (3) The proportion of the rental inventory that is vacant for rent; (4) The proportion of the
homeowner inventory that is vacant for sale; (a) 2002 figures have been revised; n/a not available
Source: U.S. Census Bureau, Housing Vacancies and Homeownership Annual Statistics: 2003

**COMMERCIAL
REAL ESTATE**

Industrial/Office Markets

Type/Market Area	Inventory (sq. ft.)	Vacant (sq. ft.)	Vacancy Rate (%)	Under Construction (sq. ft.)	Net Absorption (sq. ft.)
Industrial Space					
Birmingham	96,389,516	9,090,822	9.43	1,200,000	3,418,679
Office Space					
Birmingham	21,033,000	2,362,002	11.23	0	-148,780

Note: Data as of 4th Quarter, 2003; n/a not available
Source: Society of Industrial and Office Realtors, 2004 Comparative Statistics of Industrial and Office Real
Estate Markets

**COMMERCIAL
UTILITIES**

Typical Monthly Electric Bills

Area	Commercial Service ($/month)		Industrial Service ($/month)	
	3 kW demand 1,000 kWh	40 kW demand 14,000 kWh	1,000 kW demand 200,000 kWh	50,000 kW demand 15,000,000 kWh
City	93	1,048	13,447	833,079
Average[1]	100	1,134	17,850	1,045,117

Note: Based on rates in effect July 1, 2003; (1) average based on 197 utilities
Source: Edison Electric Institute, Typical Bills and Average Rates Report, Summer 2003

TRANSPORTATION

Means of Transportation to Work

Area	Car/Truck/Van		Public Transportation			Bicycle	Walked	Other Means	Worked at Home
	Drove Alone	Car-pooled	Bus	Subway	Railroad				
City	76.9	15.8	2.4	0.0	0.0	0.1	2.4	1.1	1.2
MSA[1]	83.5	11.7	0.7	0.0	0.0	0.1	1.2	0.7	2.2
U.S.	75.7	12.2	2.5	1.5	0.5	0.4	2.9	1.0	3.3

Note: Figures shown are percentages and cover workers 16 years of age and older;
(1) Metropolitan Statistical Area - see Appendix A for areas included
Source: Census 2000, Summary File 3

Travel Time to Work

Area	Less Than 15 Minutes	15 to 29 Minutes	30 to 44 Minutes	45 to 59 Minutes	60 Minutes or More
City	23.7	48.1	19.8	3.7	4.6
MSA[1]	21.4	40.4	24.4	8.1	5.6
U.S.	29.4	36.1	19.1	7.4	8.0

Note: Figures are percentages and include workers 16 years old and over; (1) Metropolitan Statistical Area - see Appendix A for areas included
Source: Census 2000, Summary File 3

Roadway Congestion Index

Area	1982	1990	1996	2000	2001
City	0.69	0.78	0.90	0.99	1.00
Average[1]	0.82	1.01	1.08	1.16	1.17

Note: Values greater than 1.00 indicate undesirable mobility levels; (1) average of 75 urban areas
Source: Texas Transportation Institute, The 2003 Annual Urban Mobility Report

Transportation Statistics

Interstate highways (2004)	I-65; I-59; I-20
Public transportation (2002)	Birminghan-Jefferson Co. Transit Authority (MAX)
Buses	
Average fleet age in years	4.1
No. operated in max. service	80
Demand response	
Average fleet age in years	1.0
No. operated in max. service	22
Passenger air service	
Airport	Birmingham International
Airlines (2003)	8
Boardings (2002)	1,405,395
Amtrak service (2004)	Yes
Major waterways/ports	None

Source: Federal Transit Administration, National Transit Database, 2002; Editor & Publisher Market Guide, 2004; Bureau of Transportation Statistics, Airport Enplanement Activity for CY2002; www.amtrak.com

BUSINESSES

Major Business Headquarters

Company Name	2003 Rankings	
	Fortune 500	Forbes 500
AmSouth Bancorp.	492	-
BE & K	-	249
Brasfield & Gorrie	-	276
Caremark Rx	267	-
Ebsco Industries	-	176
HealthSouth	379	-
McWane	-	158
Regions Financial	420	-
Saks	294	-
SouthTrust Corp.	460	-

Note: Companies listed are located in the city; dashes indicate no ranking
Fortune 500: Companies that produce a 10-K are ranked 1 to 500 based on 2002 revenue
Forbes 500: Private companies are ranked 1 to 281 based on 2002 revenue
Source: Fortune, April 14, 2003; www.forbes.com, November 6, 2003

Best Companies to Work For

American Cast Iron Pipe, headquartered in Birmingham, is among the "100 Best Companies to Work for in 2004." Criteria: trust in management, pride in work/company, camaraderie, company responses to the Hewitt People Practices Inventory, and employee responses to their Great Place to Work survey. The companies also had to be at least 10 years old and have a minimum of 500 employees. *Fortune, January 12, 2004*

Hibbett Sporting Goods, headquartered in Birmingham, is among the "200 Best Small Companies in 2003." Criteria: 3,500 companies whose latest 12-month sales were $5 million to $600 million were screened. Those with a net margin or five-year average ROE below 5% were cut. Banks, utilities, real estate investment trusts and limited partnerships whose financial structures are too different from most operating companies were also excluded. Shares had to be trading above $5 by the end of September 2003. Financial statement footnotes were examined for major issues. For the final ranking, equal weight was given to growth in sales, earnings and ROE for the past five years and the latest 12 months. *www.forbes.com, October 27, 2003*

Fast-Growing Businesses

According to *Inc.*, Birmingham is home to two of America's 500 fastest-growing private companies: **ComFrame Software; Savela & Associates**. Criteria: must be an independent, privately-held, U.S. corporation, proprietorship or partnership; sales of at least $200,000 in 1998; five-year operating/sales history; increase in 2002 sales over 2001 sales; holding companies, regulated banks, and utilities were excluded. *Inc. 500, America's Fastest-Growing Private Companies, October 15, 2003*

Birmingham is home to one of *Business Week's* "hot growth" companies: **Hibbett Sporting Goods**. Criteria: increase in sales and profits, return on capital and stock price. *Business Week, June 9, 2003*

Minority and Women-Owned Businesses

Ownership	All Firms		Firms with Paid Employees			
	Firms	Sales ($000)	Firms	Sales ($000)	Employees	Payroll ($000)
Black	3,477	157,951	463	118,253	2,715	50,950
Hispanic	n/a	n/a	n/a	n/a	n/a	n/a
Women	3,712	954,702	826	822,530	8,384	221,913

Note: Figures cover firms located in the city; n/a not available
Source: 1997 Economic Census, Minority and Women-Owned Businesses

Minority Business Opportunity

Birmingham is home to one company which is on the Black Enterprise Auto Dealer 100 list (100 largest dealers based on gross sales): **Midfield Dodge Inc.**. Criteria: company must be operational in previous calendar year and at least 51% black-owned. *Black Enterprise, www.blackenterprise.com, B.E. 100s, 2003 Report*

Birmingham is home to one company which is on the Black Enterprise Bank 25 list (25 largest banks based on total assets, capital, deposits and loans, including mortgage-backed securities for the calendar year): **CFS Bancshares Inc.**. Criteria: commercial banks or savings and loans that are classified by the Federal Reserve as black institutions and have been fully operational for the previous calendar year. *Black Enterprise, www.blackenterprise.com, B.E. 100s, 2003 Report*

One of the 500 largest Hispanic-owned companies in the U.S. are located in Birmingham. *Hispanic Business, June 2003*

HOTELS

Hotels/Motels

Area	Hotels/Motels	Average Minimum Rates ($)		
		Tourist	First-Class	Deluxe
City	58	60	101	155

Source: OAG Travel Planner Online, Spring 2004

EVENT SITES

Major Event Sites, Meeting Places and Convention Centers

Name	Guest Rooms	Exhibit/ Meeting Space (sq. ft.)	Largest Meeting Room Capacity
Birmingham Jefferson Convention Complex	n/a	220,000	19,000
Boutwell Municipal Auditorium	n/a	29,350	5,700
The Chamber Conference Center	n/a	4,500	150
Harbert Center	n/a	n/a	1,000
Park West Business Conference & Meeting Center	n/a	2,400	105
Pickwick Conference Center	n/a	10,000	300

Note: n/a not available
Source: Original research

Living Environment

COST OF LIVING

Cost of Living Index

Year	Composite Index	Groceries	Housing	Utilities	Trans-portation	Health Care	Misc. Goods/Services
2001	97.5	95.0	92.4	109.5	98.2	90.4	101.0
2002	96.7	104.0	85.2	100.4	101.9	90.1	101.4
2003	96.5	100.4	84.2	104.3	95.6	84.2	105.0

Note: U.S. = 100; Figures are for the Metropolitan Statistical Area - see Appendix A for areas included
Source: ACCRA, Cost of Living Index, 2001, 2002 and 2003 4-Quarter Averages

HOUSING

House Price Index (HPI)

Area	National Ranking[2]	Quarterly Change (%)	One-Year Change (%)	Five-Year Change (%)
MSA[1]	155	1.11	4.32	22.64
U.S.[3]	-	3.67	7.97	41.81

Note: The HPI is a weighted repeat sales index. It measures average price changes in repeat sales or refinancings on the same properties. This information is obtained by reviewing repeat mortgage transactions on single-family properties whose mortgages have been purchased or securitized by Fannie Mae of Freddie Mac in January 1975; (1) Metropolitan Statistical Area - see Appendix A for areas included; (2) Rankings are based on annual percentage change, for all MSAs containing at least 15,000 transactions over the last 10 years and ranges from 1 to 220; (3) figures based on a weighted division average; all figures are for the period ended December 31, 2003
Source: Office of Federal Housing Enterprise Oversight, House Price Index, March 1, 2004

Housing: Year Structure Built

Area	1990 -2000	1980 -1989	1970 -1979	1960 -1969	1950 -1959	1940 -1949	Before 1940	Median Year
City	5.4	9.2	16.6	19.7	21.6	12.8	14.7	1960
MSA[1]	20.3	15.4	19.6	15.3	13.3	7.7	8.4	1973
U.S.	17.0	15.8	18.5	13.7	12.7	7.3	15.0	1971

Note: Figures are percentages; (1) Metropolitan Statistical Area - see Appendix A for areas included
Source: Census 2000, Summary File 3

Average New Home Price

Area	2001	2002	2003
MSA[1]	198,427	204,083	206,856
U.S.	212,643	236,567	248,193

Note: Figures, in dollars, are based on a new home with 2,400 sq. ft. of living area on an 8,000 sq. ft. lot; (1) Metropolitan Statistical Area - see Appendix A for areas included
Source: ACCRA, Cost of Living Index, 2001, 2002 and 2003 4-Quarter Averages

Average Apartment Rent

Area	2001	2002	2003
MSA[1]	623	623	650
U.S.	674	708	721

Note: Figures, in dollars per month, are based on an unfurnished two bedroom, 1-1/2 or 2 bath apartment, approximately 950 sq. ft., excluding utilities except water; (1) Metropolitan Statistical Area - see Appendix A for areas included
Source: ACCRA, Cost of Living Index, 2001, 2002 and 2003 4-Quarter Averages

RESIDENTIAL UTILITIES

Average Residential Utility Costs

Area	All Electric ($/mth)	Part Electric ($/mth)	Other Energy ($/mth)	Phone ($/mth)
MSA[1]	–	67.63	63.91	24.62
U.S.	116.46	65.82	62.68	23.90

Note: (1) Metropolitan Statistical Area - see Appendix A for areas included
Source: ACCRA, Cost of Living Index, 2003 4-Quarter Average

HEALTH CARE

Average Health Care Costs

Area	Hospital ($/day)	Doctor ($/visit)	Dentist ($/visit)
MSA[1]	574.30	59.84	66.22
U.S.	678.35	67.91	83.90

Note: Hospital—based on a semi-private room; Doctor—based on a general practitioner's routine exam of an established patient; Dentist—based on adult teeth cleaning and periodic oral exam;
(1) Metropolitan Statistical Area - see Appendix A for areas included
Source: ACCRA, Cost of Living Index, 2003 4-Quarter Average

Distribution of Non-Federal, Office-Based Physicians

Area	Total	Family/ General Practice	Specialties Medical	Specialties Surgical	Specialties Other
MSA[1] (number)	2,230	180	856	596	598
MSA[1] (rate per 10,000 pop.)	24.2	2.0	9.3	6.5	6.5
Metro Average[2] (rate per 10,000 pop.)	33.1	2.2	7.7	4.8	5.6

Note: Data as of December 31, 2001; (1) Metropolitan Statistical Area - see Appendix A for areas included; (2) Average of 81 MSAs and CMSAs in this book
Source: American Medical Association, Physician Characteristics & Distribution in the U.S., 2003-2004

Hospitals

Birmingham has the following hospitals: 10 general medical and surgical; 1 psychiatric; 1 eye, ear, nose and throat; 1 rehabilitation; 1 children's general.
AHA Guide to the Healthcare Field, 2003-2004

According to *U.S. News*, Birmingham has one of the best hospitals in the U.S.: **University of Alabama Hospital at Birmingham**; *U.S. News Online, "America's Best Hospitals 2003"*

PRESIDENTIAL ELECTION

2000 Presidential Election Results

Area	Gore	Bush	Nader	Buchanan	Other
Jefferson County	47.5	50.6	1.2	0.2	0.4
U.S.	48.4	47.9	2.7	0.4	0.6

Note: Results are percentages and may not add to 100% due to rounding
Source: www.cbsnews.com; www.uselectionatlas.org

EDUCATION

Public School District Statistics

District Name	Schls.	Enroll- ment	Classroom Teachers	Pupil/ Teacher Ratio	Minority Pupils[1] (%)	Current Expend.[2] ($/pupil)
Birmingham City SD	92	37,154	2,307	16.1	n/a	6,392
Jefferson County SD	62	40,396	2,477	16.3	n/a	5,548
Vestavia Hills City SD	6	4,544	303	15.0	n/a	n/a

Note: Data covers the 2001-02 school year unless otherwise noted; (1) Fall 2000; (2) FY2000; n/a not available
Source: U.S. Department of Education, National Center for Education Statistics, Common Core of Data, Local Education Agency (School District) Universe Survey: School Year 2001-2002; U.S. Department of Education, National Center for Education Statistics, Digest of Education Statistics 2002

Educational Quality

School District	Education Quotient[1]	Graduate Outcome[2]	Community Index[3]	Resource Index[4]
Birmingham City	12	16	15	25

Note: Scores are national percentile rankings and range from 1 (worst) to 99 (best); (1) Combination of the Graduate Outcome, Community and Resource indexes weighted to reflect the greater importance of the Graduate Outcome and Resource Index; (2) Based on graduation rates and college board scores (SAT/ACT); (3) Based on the surrounding community's level of affluence and adult education; (4) Based on teacher salaries, per-pupil expenditures and student-teacher ratios.
Source: Expansion Management, December 2003

Educational Attainment by Race

Area	High School Graduate (%)					Bachelor's Degree (%)				
	Total	White	Black	Asian	Hisp.[2]	Total	White	Black	Asian	Hisp.[2]
City	75.5	81.0	73.1	88.3	56.2	18.5	30.7	12.8	66.8	15.7
MSA[1]	80.6	83.2	74.2	87.6	57.9	24.7	28.3	14.6	65.5	17.3
U.S.	80.4	83.6	72.3	80.4	52.4	24.4	26.1	14.3	44.1	10.4

Note: Figures shown cover persons 25 years old and over; (1) Metropolitan Statistical Area - see Appendix A for areas included; (2) people of Hispanic origin can be of any race
Source: Census 2000, Summary File 3

School Enrollment by Type

Area	Grades KG to 8				Grades 9 to 12			
	Public		Private		Public		Private	
	Enrollment	%	Enrollment	%	Enrollment	%	Enrollment	%
City	29,131	89.8	3,301	10.2	12,815	92.3	1,073	7.7
MSA[1]	108,002	88.8	13,686	11.2	46,620	91.2	4,503	8.8
U.S.	33,526,011	88.7	4,285,121	11.3	14,848,628	90.6	1,532,323	9.4

Note: Figures shown cover persons 3 years old and over; (1) Metropolitan Statistical Area - see Appendix A for areas included
Source: Census 2000, Summary File 3

School Enrollment by Race

Area	Grades KG to 8 (%)				Grades 9 to 12 (%)			
	White	Black	Asian	Hisp.[1]	White	Black	Asian	Hisp.[1]
City	8.9	89.3	0.3	1.2	9.5	88.5	0.4	1.1
MSA[2]	60.1	37.1	0.6	2.0	59.8	38.0	0.6	1.3
U.S.	68.5	15.5	3.3	16.8	68.8	15.5	3.8	15.7

Note: Figures shown cover persons 3 years old and over; (1) people of Hispanic origin can be of any race; (2) Metropolitan Statistical Area - see Appendix A for areas included
Source: Census 2000, Summary File 3

Classroom Teacher Salaries in Public Schools

District	B.A. Degree		M.A. Degree		Maximum	
	Min. ($)	Rank[1]	Max. ($)	Rank[1]	Max. ($)	Rank[1]
Birmingham	29,502	61	42,542	93	49.217	89
DOD Average[2]	31,567	-	53,248	-	59,356	-

Note: Salaries are for 2001-2002; (1) Rank ranges from 1 to 100; (2) As per the U.S. Department of Defense Wage Fixing Authority
Source: American Federation of Teachers, Survey & Analysis of Teacher Salary Trends 2002

Higher Education

Four-Year Colleges			Two-Year Colleges			Medical Schools	Law Schools	Voc/ Tech
Public	Private Non-profit	Private For-profit	Public	Private Non-profit	Private For-profit			
1	6	4	2	2	0	1	1	2

Note: Figures cover institutions located within the city limits.
Source: National Center for Education Statistics, The Integrated Postsecondary Education System (IPEDS) Peer Analysis System, 2002; usnews.com, America's Best Graduate Schools 2004, Medical School Directory; The College Blue Book, Occupational Education, 2003; Barron's Guide to Law Schools, 2003; Medical School Admission Requirements U.S. & Canada, 2003-2004

MAJOR EMPLOYERS

Major Employers

Company Name	Industry	Type
Accenture	Computer related services, nec	Branch
Acipco	Gray and ductile iron foundries	Headquarters
Alabama Power Company	Electric services	Headquarters
Birmingham V A Medical Center	Administration of veterans' affairs	Branch
Blue Cross	Hospital and medical service plans	Headquarters
Carraway Methodist Medical Ctr	General medical and surgical hospitals	Headquarters
Childrens Hospital	Specialty hospitals, except psychiatric	Headquarters
Commissioners Office	Legislative bodies	Branch
County of Jefferson	Executive offices	Headquarters
HealthSouth	Specialty outpatient clinics, nec	Headquarters
Marathon Oil Company	Petroleum refining	Branch
Medical Center East Inc	General medical and surgical hospitals	Headquarters
Pemco Aeroplex Inc	Airports, flying fields, and services	Headquarters
Procurement & Supply	U.s. postal service	Branch
Protective Life Corporation	Life insurance	Headquarters
Samford University	Colleges and universities	Single
Social Security Administration	Administration of social and manpower programs	Branch
Southtrust Bank	State commercial banks	Headquarters
St Vincents Hospital	General medical and surgical hospitals	Headquarters
Tyson	Poultry slaughtering and processing	Branch
U S Steel	Blast furnaces and steel mills	Branch
UAB	Colleges and universities	Headquarters

Note: Companies shown are located in the metropolitan area and have 1,000 or more employees.
Source: www.zapdata.com, March 2004

PUBLIC SAFETY

Crime Rate

Area	All Crimes	Violent Crimes				Property Crimes		
		Murder	Forcible Rape	Robbery	Aggrav. Assault	Burglary	Larceny -Theft	Motor Vehicle Theft
City	8,680.6	26.5	97.6	484.1	692.7	1,791.6	4,751.6	836.4
Suburbs[1]	3,261.0	2.9	24.3	95.7	139.6	620.1	2,128.3	250.2
MSA[2]	4,689.7	9.1	43.6	198.1	285.4	928.9	2,819.8	404.7
U.S.	4,118.8	5.6	33.0	145.9	310.1	746.2	2,445.8	432.1

Note: Figures are crimes per 100,000 population; (1) All areas within the MSA that are located outside the city limits; (2) Metropolitan Statistical Area - see Appendix A for areas included
Source: FBI Uniform Crime Reports, 2002

RECREATION

Culture and Recreation

Museums	Orchestras	Opera Companies	Dance Companies	Professional Theatres	Zoos	Pro Sports Teams[1]
6	2	1	1	1	1	0

Note: (1) Covers the Metropolitan Statistical Area - see Appendix A for areas included.
Source: The Grey House Performing Arts Directory, 2002; Official Museum Directory, 2004; www.sportsvenues.com

Library System

The Birmingham Public Library has 20 branches, holdings of 893,500 volumes, and a budget of $13,787,322 (2000-2001).
American Library Directory, 2003-2004

MEDIA

Newspapers

Name	Type	Freq.	Distribution	Circulation
Alabama Messenger	General	1x/wk	Local	2,500
The Birmingham News	General	7x/wk	Area	178,132
Birmingham Post-Herald	General	6x/wk	Area	24,910
Birmingham Times	Black/Christ	1x/wk	Area	16,500
Community Shopper	General	1x/mth	Local	20,000
The Deep South Jewish Voice	Jewish	1x/mth	Regional	3,500
Jewish Star	Religious	4x/yr	Area	8,000
One Voice	Religious	1x/wk	Area	19,400
Over the Mountain Journal	General	2x/mth	Local	42,000

Note: Includes newspapers whose offices are located in the city and whose circulations are 1,000 or more
Source: Burrelle's Media Directory, 2003

Television Stations

Name	Ch.	Affiliation	Type	Owner
WDIQ	2	PBS	Public	Alabama ETV Commission
WBRC	6	FBC	Commercial	Fox Television Stations Inc.
WCIQ	7	PBS	Public	Alabama ETV Commission
WBIQ	10	PBS	Public	Alabama ETV Commission
WVTM	13	NBCT	Commercial	General Electric Corporation
WTTO	21	FBC/WB	Commercial	Sinclair Broadcast Group
WHIQ	25	PBS	Public	Alabama ETV Commission
WAIQ	26	PBS	Public	Alabama ETV Commission
WFIQ	36	PBS	Public	Alabama ETV Commission
WJSU	40	ABCT	Commercial	Osborn Communications; LMA by Allbritton Communications
WIIQ	41	PBS	Public	Alabama ETV Commission
WEIQ	42	PBS	Public	Alabama ETV Commission
WIAT	42	CBST	Commercial	Media General Inc.
WGIQ	43	PBS	Public	Alabama ETV Commission
WPXH	44	PAXTV	Commercial	Paxson Communications Corporation
WABM	68	UPN	Commercial	Sinclair Broadcast Group

Note: Stations included broadcast from the Birmingham metro area; n/a not available
Source: Burrelle's Media Directory, 2003

AM Radio Stations

Call Letters	Freq. (kHz)	Target Audience	Station Format	Music Format
WAGG	610	Religious	M/N/T	Gospel
WJOX	690	G/M	M/S	Oldies
WYDE	850	Children	M/S/T	Urban Contemporary
WATV	900	General	M/N/T	Gospel
WERC	960	General	M/N/T	Oldies
WAPI	1070	General	M/N/T	Gospel
WAYE	1220	B/R	M/N	Gospel
WLGS	1260	General	M	Oldies
WRJS	1320	G/H	M/N/S	Latin
WJLD	1400	General	M/T	Gospel
WSMQ	1450	General	S/T	n/a
WLPH	1480	Religious	M/N	Christian

Note: Stations included broadcast from the Birmingham metro area; n/a not available
The following abbreviations may be used:
Target Audience: A=Asian; B=Black; C=Christian; E=Ethnic; F=French; G=General; H=Hispanic;
M=Men; N=Native American; R=Religious; S=Senior Citizen; W=Women; Y=Young Adult; Z=Children
Station Format: E=Educational; M=Music; N=News; S=Sports; T=Talk
Source: Burrelle's Media Directory, 2003

FM Radio Stations

Call Letters	Freq. (mHz)	Target Audience	Station Format	Music Format
WLJR	88.5	Christian	M/T	Christian
WBFR	89.5	C/G	E/M/N/T	Christian
WBHM	90.3	General	M/N	Classical
WVSU	91.1	General	M	Adult Standards
WGIB	91.9	Religious	M/T	Christian
WQOP	92.5	Religious	M/T	Christian
WDJC	93.7	Christian	General	Religious
WYSF	94.5	General	M	Adult Contemporary
WBHJ	95.7	Young Adult	M	Urban Contemporary
WMJJ	96.5	General	M	Adult Contemporary
WODL	97.3	General	M/T	Oldies
WBHK	98.7	General	M/N/T	Rhythm & Blues
WZRR	99.5	General	M	Classic Rock
WRRS	101.1	General	M/N/T	Adult Contemporary
WQEM	101.5	General	M	Adult Top 40
WDXB	102.5	General	M	Country
WQEN	103.7	General	M/N/T	Adult Contemporary
WZZK	104.7	General	M/N/S	Country
WENN	105.9	General	M	Urban Contemporary
WBPT	106.9	General	M/N/S	80's
WRAX	107.7	General	M	Alternative

Note: Stations included broadcast from the Birmingham metro area
The following abbreviations may be used:
Target Audience: A=Asian; B=Black; C=Christian; E=Ethnic; F=French; G=General; H=Hispanic;
M=Men; N=Native American; R=Religious; S=Senior Citizen; W=Women; Y=Young Adult; Z=Children
Station Format: E=Educational; M=Music; N=News; S=Sports; T=Talk
Source: Burrelle's Media Directory, 2003

CLIMATE

Average and Extreme Temperatures

Temperature	Jan	Feb	Mar	Apr	May	Jun	Jul	Aug	Sep	Oct	Nov	Dec	Yr.
Extreme High (°F)	81	83	89	92	99	102	106	103	100	94	84	80	106
Average High (°F)	53	58	66	75	82	88	90	90	84	75	64	56	74
Average Temp. (°F)	43	47	54	63	70	77	80	80	74	63	53	46	63
Average Low (°F)	33	36	42	50	58	66	70	69	63	51	41	35	51
Extreme Low (°F)	-6	3	2	26	36	42	51	52	37	27	5	1	-6

Note: Figures cover the years 1948-1995
Source: National Climatic Data Center, International Station Meteorological Climate Summary, 9/96

Average Precipitation/Snowfall/Humidity

Precip./Humidity	Jan	Feb	Mar	Apr	May	Jun	Jul	Aug	Sep	Oct	Nov	Dec	Yr.
Avg. Precip. (in.)	5.0	4.8	5.9	4.6	4.4	3.8	5.1	3.8	4.1	2.9	4.3	4.8	53.5
Avg. Snowfall (in.)	1	Tr	Tr	Tr	0	0	0	0	0	Tr	Tr	Tr	2
Avg. Rel. Hum. 7am (%)	82	81	78	76	76	78	81	82	81	82	82	82	80
Avg. Rel. Hum. 4pm (%)	57	53	48	46	51	54	58	55	54	50	52	58	53

Note: Figures cover the years 1948-1995; Tr = Trace amounts (<0.05 in. of rain; <0.5 in. of snow)
Source: National Climatic Data Center, International Station Meteorological Climate Summary, 9/96

Weather Conditions

Temperature			Daytime Sky			Precipitation		
10°F & below	32°F & below	90°F & above	Clear	Partly cloudy	Cloudy	0.01 inch or more precip.	0.1 inch or more snow/ice	Thunder-storms
1	57	59	91	161	113	119	1	57

Note: Figures are average number of days per year and covers the years 1948-1995
Source: National Climatic Data Center, International Station Meteorological Climate Summary, 9/96

**HAZARDOUS
WASTE**

Superfund Sites

Birmingham has no sites on the EPA's Superfund National Priorities List.
U.S. Environmental Protection Agency, National Priorities List, March 15, 2004

**AIR & WATER
QUALITY**

Maximum Pollutant Concentrations

	Particulate Matter (ug/m^3)	Carbon Monoxide (ppm)	Sulfur Dioxide (ppm)	Nitrogen Dioxide (ppm)	Ozone 1-hour (ppm)	Ozone 8-hour (ppm)	Lead (ug/m^3)
MSA[1] Level	160	12	0.015	n/a	0.11	0.09	n/a
NAAQS[2]	150	9	0.140	0.053	0.12	0.08	1.50
Met NAAQS[2]	No	No	Yes	n/a	Yes	No	n/a

Note: (1) Metropolitan Statistical Area - see Appendix A for areas included; (2) National Ambient Air Quality Standards; n/a not available
Units: ppm = parts per million; ug/m^3 = micrograms per cubic meter
Source: EPA, Latest Findings on National Air Quality: 2002 Status and Trends, August 2003

Air Quality Index

In the Birmingham MSA (see Appendix A for areas included), the Air Quality Index (AQI) exceeded 100 on 23 days in 2002. An AQI value greater than 100 indicates that air quality would have been in the unhealthful range on that day.
EPA, Latest Findings on National Air Quality: 2002 Status and Trends, August 2003

Watershed Health

The U.S. Environmental Protection Agency monitors the health of the aquatic resources for the nation's 2,000+ watersheds. **The Locust watershed serves the Birmingham area and received an overall Index of Watershed Indicators (IWI) score of 3 (less serious problems - low vulnerability).** The IWI score is based on seven condition and nine vulnerability indicators. The overall IWI score ranges from 1 (best health) to 6 (worst health). The Condition Indicators include: designated use attainment, fish and wildlife consumption advisories, source water condition, contaminated sediments, ambient water quality, and wetlands loss index. The Vulnerability Indicators include: aquatic species at risk, conventional and toxic loads over permitted limits, urban and agricultural runoff potential, population change, hydrologic modification, estuarine pollution susceptibility, and air deposition. *EPA, Index of Watershed Indicators, October 26, 2001*

Drinking Water

Water System Name	Pop. Served	Primary Water Source Type	Number of Violations January 2002-February 2004		
			Health Based	Significant Monitoring	Monitoring
Birmingham Water Board	585,000	Surface	None	None	None

Note: Data as of February 19, 2004
Source: EPA, Office of Ground Water and Drinking Water, Safe Drinking Water Information System

Birmingham tap water is alkaline, soft.
Editor & Publisher Market Guide, 2004

Charleston, South Carolina

Background

Charleston, South Carolina is located on the state's Atlantic coastline, 110 miles southeast of Columbia and 100 miles north of Savannah, Georgia. The city, named for King Charles II of England, is the county seat of Charleston County. Charleston is located on a bay at the end of a peninsula between the Ashley and Cooper rivers. The terrain is low-lying and coastal with nearby islands and inlets.

In 1670, English colonists established a nearby settlement, and subsequently moved to Charleston's present site. Charleston became an early trading center for rice, indigo, cotton and other goods. As the plantation economy grew, Charleston became a slave-trading center. In 1861, the Confederacy fired the cannon shot that launched the Civil War from the city's Battery, aimed at the Union's Fort Sumter in Charleston Harbor. Charleston was under siege during the Civil War, and experienced many difficulties during Reconstruction. Manufacturing industries including mills and foundries became important in the nineteenth century.

Charleston is part of a larger metropolitan area that includes North Charleston and Mount Pleasant and covers Charleston, Berkley and Dorchester counties. This area is a regional commercial and cultural center and a southern transportation hub whose port is among the nation's busiest shipping facilities. Charleston's other contemporary economic sectors include manufacturing, health care, business and professional services, defense activity, retail and wholesale trade, tourism, education and construction.

Charleston is a popular tourist area, based on its scenery, history and recreation. The city's center is well-known for its historic neighborhoods with distinctive early southern architecture and ambiance. As one of the first American cities in the early twentieth century to actively encourage historic restoration and preservation, Charleston has more recently undertaken numerous revitalization initiatives, including the Charleston Place hotel and retail complex and Waterfront Park. North Charleston and other communities are also growing with industry and suburban development.

The founding of the Charleston Naval Shipyard stimulated a military-based economy after 1901. Numerous other defense facilities were later established, including the Charleston Air Force Base, located in North Charleston. Several military facilities were closed in the 1990s, including the shipyard, although other defense-related operations have remained.

In 2000, the Confederate submarine the *HL Hunley,* which sank in 1864, was raised, and brought to a conversation laboratory at the old Charleston Naval Base. A museum to house the submarine is currently in the planning stages. The museum is expected to cost as much as $40 million and will be located in North Charleston.

Charleston is a center for health care and medical research. The Medical University of South Carolina, founded in 1824, is the region's largest single employer with approximately 8,000 employees. Other area educational institutions include The College of Charleston, The Citadel Military College, Trident Technical College, Charleston Southern University, and a campus of Johnson and Wales University offering culinary and hospitality education.

The Charleston area has numerous parks—including one with a skateboard center—and public waterfront areas. Coastal recreation activities such as boating, swimming, fishing and beaches are popular, as are golf and other land sports.

The Charleston Museum is the nation's oldest, founded in 1773. Other attractions include the South Carolina Aquarium with its IMAX® theater, the American Military Museum, the Drayton Hall plantation museum, the Gibbes Museum of Art and the Karpeles Manuscript Museum. A North Charleston Convention Center and Performing Arts Center complex opened in 1999. Cultural organizations include the Spoleto Festival USA annual summer arts festival.

The nearby Atlantic Ocean moderates the climate, especially in winter when it helps to lower temperatures from inland sites. This also keeps summer a bit cooler—relatively speaking—because Charleston expects warmth and humidity during this time of year. Expect Indian summers in fall—and a possible hurricane—while spring sharply turns from the cold winds of March to lovely May. Severe storms are possible.

Rankings

- Charleston was ranked #63 out of 331 metro areas in *Cities Ranked & Rated*. Criteria: cost of living; climate; crime; transportation; economy and jobs; education; arts and culture; health and healthcare; leisure. *Cities Ranked & Rated, 1st Edition, 2004*

- *Forbes* ranked the 150 most populous metro areas in the U.S. in terms of the "Best Places for Business and Careers." The Charleston metro area was ranked #33. Criteria: income and job growth; cost-of-doing-business; qualifications of the available pool of labor; crime rates; housing costs; net migration. *Forbes, May 9, 2003*

- *Men's Health* ranked 101 U.S. cities in terms of the quality of their tap water. Charleston received a grade of. Criteria: levels of bacteria, arsenic, lead, trihalomethanes, and haloacetic acids were compared with the National Academy of Science's guidelines as well as with the EPA's more stringent maximum contaminant level goals. *Men's Health, March 2004*

- Sperling's BestPlaces ranked 331 metro areas and identified the most and least stressful U.S. cities. The Charleston metro area ranked #71 out of the 100 largest metro areas (#1 = most stressful). Criteria: divorce rate; unemployment rate; violent and property crime; suicide rate; commute time; mental health; alcohol consumption; cloudy days. *www.BestPlaces.net, February 26, 2004*

- Sperling's BestPlaces in partnership with Pep Boys ranked 77 metro areas and identified "America's Most Drivable Cities." The Charleston metro area ranked #15. Criteria: climate; road roughness; urban mobility; gas prices. *Pep Boys, "America's Most Drivable Cities," April 9, 2003*

- Charleston was ranked #68 out of America's 200 largest metro areas in *SELF Magazine's* ranking of "America's Healthiest Cities for Women." Criteria: safety; air/water quality; cancer rates; and 21 other factors relating to health. *SELF Magazine, November 2003*

- Charleston was selected as one of "The 15 Best Places to Live the Good Life." Criteria: availability of jobs; affordable housing; culture and entertainment; access to outdoor recreation; safety; colleges and universities; sense of community; proximity to comprehensive, well-regarded health care facilities; good public high schools; ease of getting around. *AARP The Magazine, May/June 2003*

- Charleston was selected as one of America's 32 most livable cities by the non-profit group, Partners for Livable Communities. Criteria: environmental quality; parkland; ability to train new workers; job market; education; and use of the arts for economic development. *www.Livable.com, March 3, 2003*

- Charleston appeared on *Travel & Leisure's* list of the ten best cities in the U.S. and Canada. The city was ranked #8. Criteria: activities/attractions; culture/arts; restaurants/food; people; and value. *Travel & Leisure, "The World's Best Awards 2003"*

- *Condé Nast Traveler* polled over 32,000 readers for travel satisfaction. American cities were ranked based on the following criteria: friendliness; ambiance; culture/sites; restaurants; lodging and shopping. Charleston appeared in the top 10, ranking #3. *Condé Nast Traveler, Readers' Choice Awards 2003*

- The Charleston metro area was selected by *Yahoo! Internet Life* as one of "America's Most Wired Cities...and Towns." The area ranked #63 out of 87. Criteria: home and work net use; user sophistication; domain density; and available content. *Yahoo! Internet Life, April 2001*

- Charleston was identified as one of the 100 "Most Unwired Cities" in the U.S. The area ranked #88. Criteria: number of public and commercial wireless access points; cell phone coverage offering wide area network Internet access; Internet penetration. *Intel, "Most Unwired Cities," March 4, 2003*

- Charleston was ranked #63 in *Prevention* magazine's survey of the "Best Walking Cities in the U.S." The magazine, in conjunction with the American Podiatric Medical Association, surveyed 125 of the most populated cities and then tabulated and weighed 20 criteria of interest to pedestrians. *Prevention, April, 2004*

- Charleston was selected as one of America's best-mannered cities. The area ranked in the top 10 at #1. The list is based on thousands of letters and faxes received by etiquette expert Marjabelle Young Stewart. *The Associated Press, January 17, 2004*

- Charleston was selected as one of "The Best Places to Start and Grow a Company." The area ranked #3 among small metro areas. Criteria: Significant Starts (firms started in the last 10 years that still employ at least 5 people) and Young Growers (firms 10 years old or less that grew significantly during the last 4 years). *Cognetics, "Entrepreneurial Hot Spots: The Best Places in America to Start and Grow a Company," 2001*

- The Charleston metro area was selected as one of "America's 50 Hottest Cities for Business Relocations and Expansions." The area ranked #43. Criteria: 70 of the industry's most prominent site selection consultants were asked which cities their clients found the most attractive when it came to selecting an expansion or relocation site in 2003. *Expansion Management, January 2004*

- The Charleston metro area was cited as one of "The Best Places in the U.S. to Locate a Company." The area ranked #76 out of 329. Criteria: education (with emphasis on college board test results and high school graduation rates); availability of quality healthcare services and the cost to employers; quality of life; logistics workforce and companies; transportation infrastructure; quality and quantity of highly educated technical workers; business climate. *Expansion Management, July 2003*

- Charleston was cited as a top metro area for European expansion. The area ranked #17 out of 50, based on European-based company expansions or relocations within the past two years that created at least 10 jobs and involved capital investment of at least $1 million. *Expansion Management, June 2003*

- The Charleston metro area appeared on *Forbes/Milken Institute* list of "Best Places for Business and Career." Rank: #87 out of 200 metro areas. Criteria: salary growth; job growth; number of technology clusters; overall concentration of technology activity relative to national average; and technology output growth. *www.forbes.com, Forbes/Milken Institute Best Places 2002*

- The Charleston metro area appeared on the "Milken Institute Best Performing Cities" index. Rank: #35 out of 200 large metro areas. Criteria: job growth; wage and salary growth; high-tech output growth. *Milken Institute, June 25, 2003*

- The Charleston metro area appeared on *IndustryWeek's* fourth annual World-Class Communities list. It ranked #151 out of 315 metro areas. Criteria: MSA Gross Metropolitan Product (GMP) per manufacturing employee; and MSA percent share of U.S. manufacturing Gross Domestic Product (GDP). *IndustryWeek, April 16, 2001*

- The Charleston metro area was selected as a "2001 Choice City" by *Business Development Outlook* magazine. Twenty-five cities were selected, based on data from the Bureau of Labor Statistics, Census Bureau, Federal Reserve, The Conference Board, and the U.S. Conference of Mayors, as being the most desirable into which a business can relocate or expand. *Business Development Outlook, 2001 Choice Cities*

- ING Group ranked the 125 largest metro areas according to the general financial security of residents. The Charleston metro area was ranked #88 out of 125. Criteria: Earnings and Wealth Potential (household income, education, net assets, cost of living); Safety Net (health insurance, retirement savings, life insurance, income support programs); Personal Threats (unemployment rate, low-income households, crime rate); Community Economic Vitality (cost of community services, job quality, job creation, housing costs). *ING Group, "The Best Cities to Earn and Save Money: A Ranking of the Largest 125 U.S. Cities," 2001 Edition*

Business Environment

CITY FINANCES

City Government Finances

Component	2000-2001 ($000)	2000-2001 ($ per capita)
Total Revenues	n/a	n/a
Total Expenditures	n/a	n/a
Debt Outstanding	n/a	n/a
Cash and Securities	n/a	n/a

Source: U.S Census Bureau, Government Finances 2000-2001, August 2003

City Government Revenue by Source

Source	2000-2001 ($000)	2000-2001 ($ per capita)
General Revenue		
From Federal Government	n/a	n/a
From State Government	n/a	n/a
From Local Governments	n/a	n/a
Taxes		
Property	n/a	n/a
Sales	n/a	n/a
Personal Income	n/a	n/a
License	n/a	n/a
Charges	n/a	n/a
Liquor Store	n/a	n/a
Utility	n/a	n/a
Employee Retirement	n/a	n/a
Other	n/a	n/a

Source: U.S Census Bureau, Government Finances 2000-2001, August 2003

City Government Expenditures by Function

Function	2000-2001 ($000)	2000-2001 ($ per capita)	2000-2001 (%)
General Expenditures			
Airports	n/a	n/a	n/a
Corrections	n/a	n/a	n/a
Education	n/a	n/a	n/a
Fire Protection	n/a	n/a	n/a
Governmental Administration	n/a	n/a	n/a
Health	n/a	n/a	n/a
Highways	n/a	n/a	n/a
Hospitals	n/a	n/a	n/a
Housing and Community Development	n/a	n/a	n/a
Interest on General Debt	n/a	n/a	n/a
Libraries	n/a	n/a	n/a
Parking	n/a	n/a	n/a
Parks and Recreation	n/a	n/a	n/a
Police Protection	n/a	n/a	n/a
Public Welfare	n/a	n/a	n/a
Sewerage	n/a	n/a	n/a
Solid Waste Management	n/a	n/a	n/a
Liquor Store	n/a	n/a	n/a
Utility	n/a	n/a	n/a
Employee Retirement	n/a	n/a	n/a
Other	n/a	n/a	n/a

Source: U.S Census Bureau, Government Finances 2000-2001, August 2003

Municipal Bond Ratings

Area	Moody's
City	Aa2

Source: Mergent Bond Record, February 2004

DEMOGRAPHICS

Population Growth

Area	1990 Census	2000 Census	2003 Estimate	2008 Projection	Population Growth (%) 1990-2000	Population Growth (%) 2000-2008
City	96,102	96,650	97,153	97,990	0.6	1.4
MSA[1]	506,875	549,033	564,037	587,443	8.3	7.0
U.S.	248,709,873	281,421,906	290,647,163	305,918,071	13.2	8.7

Note: (1) Metropolitan Statistical Area - see Appendix A for areas included
Source: Claritas, Inc.

Number of Households and Average Household Size

Area	1990 Census	2000 Census	2003 Estimate	2008 Projection	2003 Average Household Size
City	36,669	40,791	41,888	43,637	2.3
MSA[1]	177,668	207,957	217,790	233,540	2.6
U.S.	91,947,410	105,480,101	109,440,059	116,034,472	2.7

Note: (1) Metropolitan Statistical Area - see Appendix A for areas included
Source: Claritas, Inc.

Race and Ethnicity

Area	White Non-Hispanic	Black Non-Hispanic	Asian Non-Hispanic	Other Race Non-Hispanic	Hispanic
City	63.9	33.0	1.3	1.8	1.7
MSA[1]	64.8	30.9	1.4	2.9	2.6
U.S.	74.5	12.4	3.8	9.3	13.2

Note: Figures are 2003 estimates; (1) Metropolitan Statistical Area - see Appendix A for areas included
Source: Claritas, Inc.

Segregation

City Index[2]	City Rank[3]	MSA[1] Index[2]	MSA[1] Rank[4]
63.8	35	54.1	205

Note: Figures are based on an analysis of Census 2000 data; (1) Metropolitan Statistical Area - see Appendix A for areas included; (2) Dissimilarity Index—the most commonly used measure of segregation between two groups, reflecting their relative distributions across neighborhoods within a city or metropolitan area. It can range in value from 0, indicating complete integration, to 100, indicating complete segregation; (3) Ranges from 1 (most segregated) to 100 (least segregated) and includes all the cities in this book; (4) Ranges from 1 (most segregated) to 318 (least segregated) and includes 318 metropolitan areas.
Source: www.CensusScope.org

Ancestry

Area	German	Irish[2]	English	American	Italian	Polish	French[3]	Scottish
City	10.7	9.2	10.9	6.2	3.2	1.6	2.8	3.3
MSA[1]	10.7	9.0	9.5	9.4	3.1	1.3	2.7	2.4
U.S.	15.2	10.9	8.7	7.3	5.6	3.2	3.0	1.7

Note: Figures include multiple ancestry (e.g. if a person reported being Irish and Italian, they were included in both columns); (1) Metropolitan Statistical Area - see Appendix A for areas included; (2) Includes Celtic; (3) Includes Alsatian but excludes Basque
Source: Census 2000, Summary File 3

Foreign-Born Population

Area	Any Foreign Country	Percent of Population Born in: Europe	Asia	Africa	Oceania[2]	Canada	Mexico	Latin America[3]
City	3.6	1.4	1.1	0.2	0.0	0.2	0.2	0.4
MSA[1]	3.3	1.0	1.0	0.1	0.1	0.2	0.6	0.4
U.S.	11.1	1.7	2.9	0.3	0.1	0.3	3.3	2.5

Note: (1) Metropolitan Statistical Area - see Appendix A for areas included; (2) Includes Australia, New Zealand subregion, Melanesia, Micronesia, Polynesia, and Oceania n.e.c; (3) Includes Central America (excluding Mexico), South America, and the Caribbean.
Source: Census 2000, Summary File 3

Religion

Area	Catholic	Southern Baptist	United Methodist	ELCA[1]	LDS[2]	Presbyterian Church USA	Jewish Est.	Muslim Est.
County	7.7	11.6	5.7	1.9	0.5	3.9	1.6	0.7
U.S.	22.0	7.1	3.7	1.8	1.5	1.1	2.2	0.6

Note: Figures shown are the number of adherents as a percentage of the total population; Adherents are defined as all members, including full members, their children and the estimated number of other participants who are not considered members (e.g. the baptized, those not confirmed, those not eligible for communion, those regularly attending services, etc.); (1) Evangelical Lutheran Church in America; (2) The Church of Jesus Christ of Latter Day Saints
Source: Reprinted with permission from Religious Congregations and Membership in the United States 2000 (Nashville, Glenmary Research Center, 2002) Copyright Association of Statisticians of American Religious Bodies. All rights reserved.

Age Distribution

Area	Percent of Population						
	Under Age 5	Age 5 to 17	Age 18 to 34	Age 35 to 49	Age 50 to 64	Age 65 to 79	80 Years and Over
City	5.6	14.4	32.1	20.4	13.8	9.6	4.1
MSA[1]	6.7	19.0	25.6	23.6	14.8	8.0	2.4
U.S.	6.8	18.9	23.7	23.5	14.8	9.2	3.2

Note: (1) Metropolitan Statistical Area - see Appendix A for areas included
Source: Census 2000, Summary File 3

Marriage Status

Area	Never Married	Now Married Except Separated	Separated	Widowed	Divorced
City	40.2	40.0	3.2	7.9	8.8
MSA[1]	29.5	51.6	3.3	6.3	9.3
U.S.	27.1	54.4	2.2	6.6	9.7

Note: Figures cover population 15 years of age and older; (1) Metropolitan Statistical Area - see Appendix A for areas included
Source: Census 2000, Summary File 3

Male/Female Ratio

Area	Males	Females	Males per 100 Females
City	46,016	51,137	90.0
MSA[1]	276,599	287,438	96.2
U.S.	142,511,883	148,135,280	96.2

Note: Figures are 2003 estimates; (1) Metropolitan Statistical Area - see Appendix A for areas included
Source: Claritas, Inc.

ECONOMY

Gross Metropolitan Product

Area	1999	2000	2001	2002	2002 Rank[2]
MSA[1]	13.8	14.8	15.8	16.3	112

Note: Figures are in billions of dollars; (1) Metropolitan Statistical Area - see Appendix A for areas included; (2) Rank ranges from 1 to 319
Source: The U.S. Conference of Mayors, Metro Economies Report, July 2003

INCOME

Per Capita/Median/Average Income

Area	Per Capita ($)	Median Household ($)	Average Household ($)
City	25,538	39,766	58,373
MSA[1]	22,786	44,364	58,219
U.S.	24,078	46,868	63,207

Note: Figures are 2003 estimates; (1) Metropolitan Statistical Area - see Appendix A for areas included
Source: Claritas, Inc.

Household Income Distribution

Area	Percent of Households Earning							
	Under $15,000	$15,000 -24,999	$25,000 -34,999	$35,000 -49,999	$50,000 -74,999	$75,000 -99,000	$100,000 -149,999	$150,000 and up
City	20.6	12.5	12.1	15.0	16.3	9.1	8.4	5.9
MSA[1]	15.2	11.9	12.4	16.9	19.5	10.8	8.9	4.4
U.S.	14.1	11.5	11.7	16.0	19.2	11.3	10.2	6.0

Note: Figures are 2003 estimates; (1) Metropolitan Statistical Area - see Appendix A for areas included
Source: Claritas, Inc.

Poverty Rates by Age

Area	All Ages	Under 5 Years Old	5 to 17 Years Old	18 to 64 Years Old	65 Years and Over
City	19.1	1.6	3.5	12.1	1.9
MSA[1]	14.0	1.4	3.6	7.7	1.3
U.S.	12.4	1.2	3.0	6.9	1.2

Note: Figures are percent of population with income in 1999 below poverty level and only include population for whom poverty status is determined; (1) Metropolitan Statistical Area - see Appendix A for areas included
Source: Census 2000, Summary File 3

Personal Bankruptcy Filing Rate

Area	2002	2003
Charleston County	2.82	2.89
U.S.	5.34	5.58

Note: Numbers are per 1,000 population and include Chapter 7 and Chapter 13 filings
Source: Federal Deposit Insurance Corporation (FDIC), Regional Economic Conditions (RECON), 2/25/2004

EMPLOYMENT

Labor Force and Employment

Area	Civilian Labor Force			Workers Employed		
	Dec. 2002	Dec. 2003	% Chg.	Dec. 2002	Dec. 2003	% Chg.
City	44,952	53,409	18.8	43,130	51,443	19.3
MSA[1]	277,025	329,336	18.9	266,379	317,722	19.3
U.S.	144,807,000	146,501,000	1.2	136,599,000	138,556,000	1.4

Note: Data is not seasonally adjusted and covers workers 16 years of age and older;
(1) Metropolitan Statistical Area - see Appendix A for areas included
Source: Bureau of Labor Statistics, http://stats.bls.gov

Unemployment Rate

Area	2003											
	Jan.	Feb.	Mar.	Apr.	May	Jun.	Jul.	Aug.	Sep.	Oct.	Nov.	Dec.
City	4.5	4.5	3.7	3.7	4.1	5.0	5.3	4.7	4.3	4.8	4.4	3.7
MSA[1]	4.4	4.4	3.6	3.7	4.2	4.9	5.1	4.6	4.3	4.7	4.3	3.5
U.S.	6.5	6.4	6.2	5.8	5.8	6.5	6.3	6.0	5.8	5.6	5.6	5.4

Note: Data is not seasonally adjusted and covers workers 16 years of age and older; All figures are percentages; (1) Metropolitan Statistical Area - see Appendix A for areas included
Source: Bureau of Labor Statistics, http://stats.bls.gov

Employment by Occupation

Occupation Classification	City (%)	MSA[1] (%)	U.S. (%)
Sales and Office	25.9	26.3	26.7
Professional and Related	27.1	20.4	20.2
Service	19.1	16.2	14.9
Production, Transportation, and Material Moving	7.3	13.1	14.6
Management, Business, and Financial	13.4	12.1	13.5
Construction, Extraction, and Maintenance	6.8	11.5	9.4
Farming, Forestry, and Fishing	0.4	0.5	0.7

Note: Figures cover employed civilians 16 years of age and older;
(1) Metropolitan Statistical Area - see Appendix A for areas included
Source: Census 2000, Summary File 3

Employment by Industry

Sector	MSA[1]		U.S.
	Number of Employees	Percent of Total	Percent of Total
Government	51,700	19.9	16.7
Education and Health Services	28,900	11.1	12.9
Professional and Business Services	33,300	12.8	12.3
Retail Trade	33,400	12.8	11.8
Manufacturing	20,600	7.9	11.0
Leisure and Hospitality	30,100	11.6	9.1
Finance Activities	11,000	4.2	6.1
Construction	n/a	n/a	5.1
Wholesale Trade	8,100	3.1	4.3
Other Services	7,600	2.9	4.1
Transportation and Utilities	11,900	4.6	3.7
Information	3,500	1.3	2.4
Natural Resources and Mining	n/a	n/a	0.4

Note: Figures cover non-farm employment as of December 2003 and are not seasonally adjusted;
(1) Metropolitan Statistical Area - see Appendix A for areas included; n/a not available
Source: Bureau of Labor Statistics, http://stats.bls.gov

Average Wages

Occupation	$/Hr.	Occupation	$/Hr.
Accountants and Auditors	21.26	Maids and Housekeeping Cleaners	7.30
Automotive Mechanics	14.91	Maintenance and Repair Workers	14.00
Bookkeepers	12.20	Marketing Managers	25.63
Carpenters	14.23	Nuclear Medicine Technologists	n/a
Cashiers	7.06	Nurses, Licensed Practical	13.98
Clerks, General Office	10.49	Nurses, Registered	24.64
Clerks, Receptionists/Information	9.59	Nursing Aides/Orderlies/Attendants	8.49
Clerks, Shipping/Receiving	10.66	Packers and Packagers, Hand	8.10
Computer Programmers	22.36	Physical Therapists	26.37
Computer Support Specialists	16.46	Postal Service Mail Carriers	18.63
Computer Systems Analysts	22.35	Real Estate Brokers	48.01
Cooks, Restaurant	9.23	Retail Salespersons	10.23
Dentists	77.41	Sales Reps., Exc. Tech./Scientific	18.49
Electrical Engineers	25.59	Sales Reps., Tech./Scientific	25.84
Electricians	16.28	Secretaries, Exc. Legal/Med./Exec.	11.38
Financial Managers	29.96	Security Guards	8.77
First-Line Supervisors/Mgrs., Sales	16.53	Surgeons	82.95
Food Preparation Workers	7.79	Teacher Assistants	7.70
General and Operations Managers	31.19	Teachers, Elementary School	17.60
Hairdressers/Cosmetologists	13.45	Teachers, Secondary School	16.80
Internists	63.82	Telemarketers	9.68
Janitors and Cleaners	7.90	Truck Drivers, Heavy/Tractor-Trailer	15.96
Landscaping/Groundskeeping Workers	8.83	Truck Drivers, Light/Delivery Svcs.	11.18
Lawyers	52.48	Waiters and Waitresses	6.43

Note: Wage data is for 2002 and covers the Metropolitan Statistical Area (see Appendix A for areas included).
Hourly wages for elementary/secondary school teachers and teacher assistants were calculated by the editors
from annual wage data assuming a 40 hour work week; n/a not available.
Source: Bureau of Labor Statistics, 2002 Metro Area Occupational Employment and Wage Estimates

Occupational Employment Projections: 1996 - 2006

Occupations Expected to Have the Largest Job Growth (ranked by numerical growth)	Fast-Growing Occupations[1] (ranked by percent growth)
1. Cashiers	1. Desktop publishers
2. Salespersons, retail	2. Database administrators
3. General managers & top executives	3. Computer engineers
4. Marketing & sales, supervisors	4. Paralegals
5. Food preparation workers	5. Systems analysts
6. Truck drivers, light	6. Personal and home care aides
7. Cooks, fast food and short order	7. Medical assistants
8. Food service workers	8. Physical therapy assistants and aides
9. Waiters & waitresses	9. Respiratory therapists
10. Food service and lodging managers	10. Data processing equipment repairers

Note: Projections cover South Carolina; (1) Excludes occupations with total job growth less than 300
Source: U.S. Department of Labor, Employment and Training Administration, America's Labor Market Information System (ALMIS)

TAXES

State Corporate Income Tax Rates

State	Rate (%)	Number of Brackets	Low Bracket (Under $)	High Bracket (Over $)
South Carolina	5.0	1	na	na

Note: Tax rates as of December 31, 2003; na not applicable; 4.5% for banks; 6% for savings and loans.
Source: Tax Foundation, www.taxfoundation.org

State Individual Income Tax Rates

State	Federal Deductibility	Marginal Rate (%)	Number of Brackets	Low Bracket (Under $)	High Bracket (Over $)
South Carolina	No	2.5-7.0	6	0	12,000

Note: Tax rates as of December 31, 2003; Brackets apply to single taxpayers and married people filing separately; na not applicable
Source: Tax Foundation, www.taxfoundation.org

Various State and Local Tax Rates

State Sales and Use (%)	Total Sales and Use (%)	Gasoline (cents/gal.)	Cigarette (cents/pack)	Spirits ($/gal.)	Table Wine ($/gal.)	Beer ($/gal.)
5.0	6.0	16	7	2.72	1.08 (d)	0.77

Note: Tax rates as of December 31, 2003.(d) South Carolina's rate of $1.08 includes 18 cents additional tax.
Source: Tax Foundation, www.taxfoundation.org

State Tax Burdens

Area	Combined State and Local Tax Burden		Combined Federal, State and Local Tax Burden	
	Percent	Rank	Percent	Rank
South Carolina	9.0	39	27.1	42
U.S. Average	9.7	-	30.0	-

Note: Figures are for 2003
Source: Tax Foundation, www.taxfoundation.org

Internal Revenue Service Tax Audits

IRS District	Percent of Returns Audited				
	1996	1997	1998	1999	2000
North-South Carolina	0.48	0.34	0.28	0.21	0.16
U.S.	0.66	0.61	0.46	0.31	0.20

Note: Figures cover IRS district audits of federal income tax returns filed by individuals. Geographic data on district audits for 2001 and 2002 are being withheld by the IRS. TRAC is challenging this policy.
Source: Syracuse University, Transactional Records Access Clearinghouse (TRAC), "Odds of IRS District Tax Audit 2000"

RESIDENTIAL REAL ESTATE

Building Permits

Area	Single-Family			Multi-Family			Total		
	2001	2002	Pct. Chg.	2001	2002	Pct. Chg.	2001	2002	Pct. Chg.
City	782	1,053	34.7	144	380	163.9	926	1,433	54.8
U.S.	1,235,600	1,332,600	7.9	401,100	415,100	3.5	1,636,700	1,747,700	6.8

Note: Figures represent new, privately-owned housing units authorized (unadjusted data)
Source: U.S. Census Bureau, Manufacturing, Mining, and Construction Statistics

Homeownership and Housing Vacancies

Area	Homeownership Rate[2] (%)			Rental Vacancy Rate[3] (%)			Homeowner Vacancy Rate[4] (%)		
	2001	2002[a]	2003	2001	2002[a]	2003	2001	2002[a]	2003
MSA[1]	n/a	n/a	n/a	n/a	n/a	n/a	n/a	n/a	n/a
U.S.	67.8	67.9	68.3	8.4	8.9	9.8	1.8	1.7	1.8

Note: (1) Metropolitan Statistical Area - see Appendix A for areas included; (2) The proportion of households that are owners; (3) The proportion of the rental inventory that is vacant for rent; (4) The proportion of the homeowner inventory that is vacant for sale; (a) 2002 figures have been revised; n/a not available
Source: U.S. Census Bureau, Housing Vacancies and Homeownership Annual Statistics: 2003

COMMERCIAL REAL ESTATE

Industrial/Office Markets

Type/Market Area	Inventory (sq. ft.)	Vacant (sq. ft.)	Vacancy Rate (%)	Under Construction (sq. ft.)	Net Absorption (sq. ft.)
Industrial Space					
Charleston	20,000,000	3,040,000	15.20	100,000	510,000
Office Space					
Charleston	5,405,428	773,370	14.31	408,600	119,632

Note: Data as of 4th Quarter, 2003; n/a not available
Source: Society of Industrial and Office Realtors, 2004 Comparative Statistics of Industrial and Office Real Estate Markets

COMMERCIAL UTILITIES

Typical Monthly Electric Bills

Area	Commercial Service ($/month)		Industrial Service ($/month)	
	3 kW demand 1,000 kWh	40 kW demand 14,000 kWh	1,000 kW demand 200,000 kWh	50,000 kW demand 15,000,000 kWh
City	103	1,211	17,456	935,150
Average[1]	100	1,134	17,850	1,045,117

Note: Based on rates in effect July 1, 2003; (1) average based on 197 utilities
Source: Edison Electric Institute, Typical Bills and Average Rates Report, Summer 2003

TRANSPORTATION

Means of Transportation to Work

Area	Car/Truck/Van		Public Transportation			Bicycle	Walked	Other Means	Worked at Home
	Drove Alone	Car-pooled	Bus	Subway	Railroad				
City	73.5	11.6	2.7	0.0	0.0	1.2	6.6	1.6	2.7
MSA[1]	78.1	13.0	1.1	0.0	0.0	0.5	3.5	1.6	2.2
U.S.	75.7	12.2	2.5	1.5	0.5	0.4	2.9	1.0	3.3

Note: Figures shown are percentages and cover workers 16 years of age and older;
(1) Metropolitan Statistical Area - see Appendix A for areas included
Source: Census 2000, Summary File 3

Travel Time to Work

Area	Less Than 15 Minutes	15 to 29 Minutes	30 to 44 Minutes	45 to 59 Minutes	60 Minutes or More
City	34.8	44.1	14.7	3.2	3.2
MSA[1]	26.7	39.6	21.5	6.9	5.2
U.S.	29.4	36.1	19.1	7.4	8.0

*Note: Figures are percentages and include workers 16 years old and over; (1) Metropolitan Statistical Area -
see Appendix A for areas included*
Source: Census 2000, Summary File 3

Roadway Congestion Index

Area	1982	1990	1996	2000	2001
City	0.85	0.96	0.92	0.98	0.95
Average[1]	0.82	1.01	1.08	1.16	1.17

Note: Values greater than 1.00 indicate undesirable mobility levels; (1) average of 75 urban areas
Source: Texas Transportation Institute, The 2003 Annual Urban Mobility Report

Transportation Statistics

Interstate highways (2004)	I-26; I-95
Public transportation (2002)	Charleston Area Regional Transportation (CARTA)
Buses	
Average fleet age in years	5.5
No. operated in max. service	43
Demand response	
Average fleet age in years	3.7
No. operated in max. service	15
Passenger air service	
Airport	Charleston International Airport
Airlines (2003)	n/a
Boardings (2002)	788,811
Amtrak service (2004)	Yes (station is located in North Charleston)
Major waterways/ports	Atlantic Ocean

*Source: Federal Transit Administration, National Transit Database, 2002; Editor & Publisher Market Guide,
2004; Bureau of Transportation Statistics, Airport Enplanement Activity for CY2002; www.amtrak.com*

BUSINESSES

Major Business Headquarters

Company Name	2003 Rankings	
	Fortune 500	Forbes 500
No companies listed	-	-

Note: Companies listed are located in the city; dashes indicate no ranking
Fortune 500: Companies that produce a 10-K are ranked 1 to 500 based on 2002 revenue
Forbes 500: Private companies are ranked 1 to 281 based on 2002 revenue
Source: Fortune, April 14, 2003; www.forbes.com, November 6, 2003

Minority and Women-Owned Businesses

Ownership	All Firms		Firms with Paid Employees			
	Firms	Sales ($000)	Firms	Sales ($000)	Employees	Payroll ($000)
Black	863	40,609	127	28,118	700	8,775
Hispanic	n/a	n/a	n/a	n/a	n/a	n/a
Women	2,294	303,405	523	256,250	3,075	49,192

Note: Figures cover firms located in the city; n/a not available
Source: 1997 Economic Census, Minority and Women-Owned Businesses

Minority Business Opportunity

One of the 500 largest Hispanic-owned companies in the U.S. are located in Charleston.
Hispanic Business, June 2003

HOTELS

Hotels/Motels

Area	Hotels/Motels	Average Minimum Rates ($)		
		Tourist	First-Class	Deluxe
City	61	73	129	207

Source: OAG Travel Planner Online, Spring 2004

Charleston is home to two of the top 100 hotels in the U.S. and Canada according to *Travel & Leisure*: **Charleston Place Hotel** (#29); **Planters Inn** (#39). Criteria: value, rooms/ambience, location, facilities/activities and service. *Travel & Leisure, "The World's Best Hotels 2003"*

EVENT SITES

Major Event Sites, Meeting Places and Convention Centers

Name	Guest Rooms	Exhibit/ Meeting Space (sq. ft.)	Largest Meeting Room Capacity
Charleston Area Convention Center Complex	n/a	150,000	n/a
Embassy Suites Airport Convention Center	255	40,250	n/a

Note: n/a not available
Source: Original research

Living Environment

COST OF LIVING

Cost of Living Index

Year	Composite Index	Groceries	Housing	Utilities	Trans-portation	Health Care	Misc. Goods/ Services
2001	102.2	102.2	104.9	99.7	94.9	99.9	102.9
2002	101.7	100.8	102.2	99.5	98.3	101.3	103.3
2003	98.4	99.0	94.2	101.4	97.2	102.4	100.8

Note: U.S. = 100; Figures are for the Metropolitan Statistical Area - see Appendix A for areas included
Source: ACCRA, Cost of Living Index, 2001, 2002 and 2003 4-Quarter Averages

HOUSING

House Price Index (HPI)

Area	National Ranking[2]	Quarterly Change (%)	One-Year Change (%)	Five-Year Change (%)
MSA[1]	169	0.94	3.98	44.46
U.S.[3]	-	3.67	7.97	41.81

Note: The HPI is a weighted repeat sales index. It measures average price changes in repeat sales or refinancings on the same properties. This information is obtained by reviewing repeat mortgage transactions on single-family properties whose mortgages have been purchased or securitized by Fannie Mae of Freddie Mac in January 1975; (1) Metropolitan Statistical Area - see Appendix A for areas included; (2) Rankings are based on annual percentage change, for all MSAs containing at least 15,000 transactions over the last 10 years and ranges from 1 to 220; (3) figures based on a weighted division average; all figures are for the period ended December 31, 2003
Source: Office of Federal Housing Enterprise Oversight, House Price Index, March 1, 2004

Housing: Year Structure Built

Area	1990 -2000	1980 -1989	1970 -1979	1960 -1969	1950 -1959	1940 -1949	Before 1940	Median Year
City	16.3	17.3	15.9	14.7	10.3	7.6	17.9	1970
MSA[1]	22.0	23.9	21.3	14.0	8.4	4.7	5.9	1978
U.S.	17.0	15.8	18.5	13.7	12.7	7.3	15.0	1971

Note: Figures are percentages; (1) Metropolitan Statistical Area - see Appendix A for areas included
Source: Census 2000, Summary File 3

Average New Home Price

Area	2001	2002	2003
MSA[1]	226,584	242,888	233,846
U.S.	212,643	236,567	248,193

Note: Figures, in dollars, are based on a new home with 2,400 sq. ft. of living area on an 8,000 sq. ft. lot; (1) Metropolitan Statistical Area - see Appendix A for areas included
Source: ACCRA, Cost of Living Index, 2001, 2002 and 2003 4-Quarter Averages

Average Apartment Rent

Area	2001	2002	2003
MSA[1]	718	725	722
U.S.	674	708	721

Note: Figures, in dollars per month, are based on an unfurnished two bedroom, 1-1/2 or 2 bath apartment, approximately 950 sq. ft., excluding utilities except water; (1) Metropolitan Statistical Area - see Appendix A for areas included
Source: ACCRA, Cost of Living Index, 2001, 2002 and 2003 4-Quarter Averages

RESIDENTIAL UTILITIES

Average Residential Utility Costs

Area	All Electric ($/mth)	Part Electric ($/mth)	Other Energy ($/mth)	Phone ($/mth)
MSA[1]	134.18	–	–	22.17
U.S.	116.46	65.82	62.68	23.90

Note: (1) Metropolitan Statistical Area - see Appendix A for areas included
Source: ACCRA, Cost of Living Index, 2003 4-Quarter Average

HEALTH CARE

Average Health Care Costs

Area	Hospital ($/day)	Doctor ($/visit)	Dentist ($/visit)
MSA[1]	614.92	77.36	83.69
U.S.	678.35	67.91	83.90

Note: Hospital—based on a semi-private room; Doctor—based on a general practitioner's routine exam of an established patient; Dentist—based on adult teeth cleaning and periodic oral exam;
(1) Metropolitan Statistical Area - see Appendix A for areas included
Source: ACCRA, Cost of Living Index, 2003 4-Quarter Average

Distribution of Non-Federal, Office-Based Physicians

Area	Total	Family/ General Practice	Specialties		
			Medical	Surgical	Other
MSA[1] (number)	1,397	145	460	350	442
MSA[1] (rate per 10,000 pop.)	25.4	2.6	8.4	6.4	8.1
Metro Average[2] (rate per 10,000 pop.)	33.1	2.2	7.7	4.8	5.6

Note: Data as of December 31, 2001; (1) Metropolitan Statistical Area - see Appendix A for areas included;
(2) Average of 81 MSAs and CMSAs in this book
Source: American Medical Association, Physician Characteristics & Distribution in the U.S., 2003-2004

Hospitals

Charleston has the following hospitals: 6 general medical and surgical; 1 psychiatric.
AHA Guide to the Healthcare Field, 2003-2004

According to *U.S. News*, Charleston has one of the best hospitals in the U.S.: **Medical University of South Carolina**; *U.S. News Online, "America's Best Hospitals 2003"*

PRESIDENTIAL ELECTION

2000 Presidential Election Results

Area	Gore	Bush	Nader	Buchanan	Other
Charleston County	44.4	52.2	2.4	0.1	0.8
U.S.	48.4	47.9	2.7	0.4	0.6

Note: Results are percentages and may not add to 100% due to rounding
Source: www.cbsnews.com; www.uselectionatlas.org

EDUCATION

Public School District Statistics

District Name	Schls.	Enroll-ment	Classroom Teachers	Pupil/ Teacher Ratio	Minority Pupils[1] (%)	Current Expend.[2] ($/pupil)
Charleston County SD	75	43,516	3,045	14.3	n/a	5,803

Note: Data covers the 2001-02 school year unless otherwise noted; (1) Fall 2000; (2) FY2000; n/a not available
Source: U.S. Department of Education, National Center for Education Statistics, Common Core of Data, Local Education Agency (School District) Universe Survey: School Year 2001-2002; U.S. Department of Education, National Center for Education Statistics, Digest of Education Statistics 2002

Educational Quality

School District	Education Quotient[1]	Graduate Outcome[2]	Community Index[3]	Resource Index[4]
Charleston County	28	25	45	54

Note: Scores are national percentile rankings and range from 1 (worst) to 99 (best); (1) Combination of the Graduate Outcome, Community and Resource indexes weighted to reflect the greater importance of the Graduate Outcome and Resource Index; (2) Based on graduation rates and college board scores (SAT/ACT); (3) Based on the surrounding community's level of affluence and adult education; (4) Based on teacher salaries, per-pupil expenditures and student-teacher ratios.
Source: Expansion Management, December 2003

Educational Attainment by Race

Area	High School Graduate (%)					Bachelor's Degree (%)				
	Total	White	Black	Asian	Hisp.[2]	Total	White	Black	Asian	Hisp.[2]
City	83.7	93.3	64.5	86.3	77.3	37.5	48.8	14.7	57.2	26.3
MSA[1]	81.3	87.4	67.3	79.3	67.5	25.0	30.9	10.7	38.0	16.5
U.S.	80.4	83.6	72.3	80.4	52.4	24.4	26.1	14.3	44.1	10.4

Note: Figures shown cover persons 25 years old and over; (1) Metropolitan Statistical Area - see Appendix A for areas included; (2) people of Hispanic origin can be of any race
Source: Census 2000, Summary File 3

School Enrollment by Type

Area	Grades KG to 8				Grades 9 to 12			
	Public		Private		Public		Private	
	Enrollment	%	Enrollment	%	Enrollment	%	Enrollment	%
City	8,108	80.5	1,962	19.5	3,422	79.0	908	21.0
MSA[1]	65,879	86.6	10,174	13.4	27,841	87.9	3,845	12.1
U.S.	33,526,011	88.7	4,285,121	11.3	14,848,628	90.6	1,532,323	9.4

Note: Figures shown cover persons 3 years old and over; (1) Metropolitan Statistical Area - see Appendix A for areas included
Source: Census 2000, Summary File 3

School Enrollment by Race

Area	Grades KG to 8 (%)				Grades 9 to 12 (%)			
	White	Black	Asian	Hisp.[1]	White	Black	Asian	Hisp.[1]
City	43.6	52.9	1.6	1.3	47.2	50.6	0.8	0.9
MSA[2]	54.5	40.7	1.0	2.6	53.4	42.0	1.5	2.5
U.S.	68.5	15.5	3.3	16.8	68.8	15.5	3.8	15.7

Note: Figures shown cover persons 3 years old and over; (1) people of Hispanic origin can be of any race; (2) Metropolitan Statistical Area - see Appendix A for areas included
Source: Census 2000, Summary File 3

Classroom Teacher Salaries in Public Schools

District	B.A. Degree		M.A. Degree		Maximum	
	Min. ($)	Rank[1]	Max. ($)	Rank[1]	Max. ($)	Rank[1]
City	n/a	n/a	n/a	n/a	n/a	n/a
DOD Average[2]	31,567	-	53,248	-	59,356	-

Note: Salaries are for 2001-2002; (1) Rank ranges from 1 to 100; (2) As per the U.S. Department of Defense Wage Fixing Authority
Source: American Federation of Teachers, Survey & Analysis of Teacher Salary Trends 2002

Higher Education

Four-Year Colleges			Two-Year Colleges			Medical Schools	Law Schools	Voc/ Tech
Public	Private Non-profit	Private For-profit	Public	Private Non-profit	Private For-profit			
3	2	0	1	0	0	1	0	4

Note: Figures cover institutions located within the city limits.
Source: National Center for Education Statistics, The Integrated Postsecondary Education System (IPEDS) Peer Analysis System, 2002; usnews.com, America's Best Graduate Schools 2004, Medical School Directory; The College Blue Book, Occupational Education, 2003; Barron's Guide to Law Schools, 2003; Medical School Admission Requirements U.S. & Canada, 2003-2004

MAJOR EMPLOYERS

Major Employers

Company Name	Industry	Type
Abel Leasing	Help supply services	Single
AGFA Corporation	Photographic equipment and supplies	Branch
Bayer Corporation	Chemicals and allied products, nec	Branch
Bon-Scurs St Frncis Xvier Hosp	General medical and surgical hospitals	Branch
Charleston Kraft Mill	Paperboard mills	Branch
Cummins	Internal combustion engines, nec	Branch
Medical University SC	Colleges and universities	Headquarters
Naval Nuclear Pwr Training Unit	National security	Branch
Nucor Steel	Blast furnaces and steel mills	Branch
PGI	Nonwoven fabrics	Headquarters
Ralph H Johnson V A Med Ctr	Administration of veterans' affairs	Branch
Roper Hospital Inc	General medical and surgical hospitals	Headquarters
Space & Naval Warfare Systems	National security	Branch
Talbots Inc	Catalog and mail-order houses	Branch
Trident Medical Center LLC	General medical and surgical hospitals	Headquarters
University of Charleston	Colleges and universities	Headquarters
Westvaco Corporation	Paperboard mills	Branch
Williams Technologies Inc	Motor vehicle parts and accessories	Headquarters

Note: Companies shown are located in the metropolitan area and have 750 or more employees.
Source: www.zapdata.com, March 2004

PUBLIC SAFETY

Crime Rate

Area	All Crimes	Violent Crimes				Property Crimes		
		Murder	Forcible Rape	Robbery	Aggrav. Assault	Burglary	Larceny -Theft	Motor Vehicle Theft
City	7,071.8	13.1	37.4	261.8	546.8	1,031.9	4,299.5	881.3
Suburbs[1]	5,532.1	8.4	52.3	175.3	600.5	976.0	3,108.5	611.1
MSA[2]	5,803.1	9.3	49.6	190.6	591.0	985.8	3,318.2	658.7
U.S.	4,118.8	5.6	33.0	145.9	310.1	746.2	2,445.8	432.1

Note: Figures are crimes per 100,000 population; (1) All areas within the MSA that are located outside the city limits; (2) Metropolitan Statistical Area - see Appendix A for areas included
Source: FBI Uniform Crime Reports, 2002

RECREATION

Culture and Recreation

Museums	Orchestras	Opera Companies	Dance Companies	Professional Theatres	Zoos	Pro Sports Teams[1]
12	1	2	3	1	0	0

Note: (1) Covers the Metropolitan Statistical Area - see Appendix A for areas included.
Source: The Grey House Performing Arts Directory, 2002; Official Museum Directory, 2004; www.sportsvenues.com

Library System

The Charleston County Public Library has 14 branches, holdings of 1,084,483 volumes, and a budget of $11,125,597 (2001-2002).
American Library Directory, 2003-2004

MEDIA

Newspapers

Name	Type	Freq.	Distribution	Circulation
The Charleston Chronicle	Black	1x/wk	Local	6,000
Charleston Jewish Voice	Religious	1x/mth	Local	2,600
The New Catholic Miscellany	Religious	1x/wk	State	27,000
The Post and Courier	General	7x/wk	Area	106,000

Note: Includes newspapers whose offices are located in the city and whose circulations are 500 or more
Source: Burrelle's Media Directory, 2003

Television Stations

Name	Ch.	Affiliation	Type	Owner
WCBD	2	NBCT	Commercial	Media General Inc.
WCIV	4	ABCT	Commercial	Allbritton Communications Company
WCSC	5	n/a	Commercial	Jefferson-Pilot Communications Company
WTAT	24	FBC	Commercial	Sinclair Broadcast Group
WMMP	36	UPN	Commercial	Sinclair Broadcast Group

Note: Stations included broadcast from the Charleston metro area; n/a not available
Source: Burrelle's Media Directory, 2003

AM Radio Stations

Call Letters	Freq. (kHz)	Target Audience	Station Format	Music Format
WPAL	730	Hispanic	M	Gospel
WTMZ	910	General	N/S	n/a
WTMA	1250	General	N/T	n/a
WQSC	1340	General	S	n/a
WXTC	1390	General	M	Gospel
WQNT	1450	General	N	n/a

Note: Stations included broadcast from the Charleston metro area; n/a not available
The following abbreviations may be used:
Target Audience: A=Asian; B=Black; C=Christian; E=Ethnic; F=French; G=General; H=Hispanic;
M=Men; N=Native American; R=Religious; S=Senior Citizen; W=Women; Y=Young Adult; Z=Children
Station Format: E=Educational; M=Music; N=News; S=Sports; T=Talk
Source: Burrelle's Media Directory, 2003

FM Radio Stations

Call Letters	Freq. (mHz)	Target Audience	Station Format	Music Format
WWWZ	93.3	General	M	Urban Contemporary
WSSP	94.3	General	M/N/S	Urban Contemporary
WSSX	95.1	General	M/N/T	Top 40
WAVF	96.1	General	M/N/T	Alternative
WSUY	96.9	General	M	Adult Contemporary
WYBB	98.1	General	M	AOR
WALC	100.5	General	M	Adult Top 40
WPAL	100.9	General	M/N/S/T	Rhythm & Blues
WMGL	101.7	General	M	Adult Contemporary
WXLY	102.5	General	M/N/T	Oldies
WEZL	103.5	General	M/N/T	Country
WRFQ	104.5	General	M/N/T	Classic Rock
WCOO	105.3	General	M/N/T	Oldies
WNKT	107.5	General	M/N/S	Country

Note: Stations included broadcast from the Charleston metro area
The following abbreviations may be used:
Target Audience: A=Asian; B=Black; C=Christian; E=Ethnic; F=French; G=General; H=Hispanic;
M=Men; N=Native American; R=Religious; S=Senior Citizen; W=Women; Y=Young Adult; Z=Children
Station Format: E=Educational; M=Music; N=News; S=Sports; T=Talk
Music Format: AOR=Album Oriented Rock; MOR=Middle of the Road
Source: Burrelle's Media Directory, 2003

CLIMATE

Average and Extreme Temperatures

Temperature	Jan	Feb	Mar	Apr	May	Jun	Jul	Aug	Sep	Oct	Nov	Dec	Yr.
Extreme High (°F)	83	87	90	94	98	101	104	102	97	94	88	83	104
Average High (°F)	59	62	68	76	83	88	90	89	85	77	69	61	76
Average Temp. (°F)	49	51	57	65	73	78	81	81	76	67	58	51	66
Average Low (°F)	38	40	46	53	62	69	72	72	67	56	46	39	55
Extreme Low (°F)	6	12	15	30	36	50	58	56	42	27	15	8	6

Note: Figures cover the years 1945-1995
Source: National Climatic Data Center, International Station Meteorological Climate Summary, 9/96

Average Precipitation/Snowfall/Humidity

Precip./Humidity	Jan	Feb	Mar	Apr	May	Jun	Jul	Aug	Sep	Oct	Nov	Dec	Yr.
Avg. Precip. (in.)	3.5	3.1	4.4	2.8	4.1	6.0	7.2	6.9	5.6	3.1	2.5	3.1	52.1
Avg. Snowfall (in.)	Tr	Tr	Tr	0	0	0	0	0	0	0	Tr	Tr	1
Avg. Rel. Hum. 7am (%)	83	81	83	84	85	86	88	90	91	89	86	83	86
Avg. Rel. Hum. 4pm (%)	55	52	51	51	56	62	66	66	65	58	56	55	58

Note: Figures cover the years 1945-1995; Tr = Trace amounts (<0.05 in. of rain; <0.5 in. of snow)
Source: National Climatic Data Center, International Station Meteorological Climate Summary, 9/96

Weather Conditions

Temperature			Daytime Sky			Precipitation		
10°F & below	32°F & below	90°F & above	Clear	Partly cloudy	Cloudy	0.01 inch or more precip.	0.1 inch or more snow/ice	Thunder-storms
< 1	33	53	89	162	114	114	1	59

Note: Figures are average number of days per year and covers the years 1945-1995
Source: National Climatic Data Center, International Station Meteorological Climate Summary, 9/96

HAZARDOUS WASTE

Superfund Sites

Charleston has one hazardous waste site on the EPA's Superfund National Priorities List: **Koppers Co. Inc. (Charleston Plant)**. *U.S. Environmental Protection Agency, National Priorities List, March 15, 2004*

AIR & WATER QUALITY

Maximum Pollutant Concentrations

	Particulate Matter (ug/m³)	Carbon Monoxide (ppm)	Sulfur Dioxide (ppm)	Nitrogen Dioxide (ppm)	Ozone 1-hour (ppm)	Ozone 8-hour (ppm)	Lead (ug/m³)
MSA[1] Level	40	3	0.01	0.01	0.1	0.07	0.01
NAAQS[2]	150	9	0.140	0.053	0.12	0.08	1.50
Met NAAQS[2]	Yes	Yes	Yes	Yes	Yes	Yes	Yes

Note: (1) Metropolitan Statistical Area - see Appendix A for areas included; (2) National Ambient Air Quality Standards; n/a not available
Units: ppm = parts per million; ug/m³ = micrograms per cubic meter
Source: EPA, Latest Findings on National Air Quality: 2002 Status and Trends, August 2003

Air Quality Index

In the Charleston MSA (see Appendix A for areas included), the Air Quality Index (AQI) exceeded 100 on 3 days in 2002. An AQI value greater than 100 indicates that air quality would have been in the unhealthful range on that day.
EPA, Latest Findings on National Air Quality: 2002 Status and Trends, August 2003

Watershed Health

The U.S. Environmental Protection Agency monitors the health of the aquatic resources for the nation's 2,000+ watersheds. **The watershed serves the area and received an overall Index of Watershed Indicators (IWI) score of 0 (insufficient data).** The IWI score is based on seven condition and nine vulnerability indicators. The overall IWI score ranges from 1 (best health) to 6 (worst health). The Condition Indicators include: designated use attainment, fish and wildlife consumption advisories, source water condition, contaminated sediments, ambient water quality, and wetlands loss index. The Vulnerability Indicators include: aquatic species at risk, conventional and toxic loads over permitted limits, urban and agricultural runoff potential, population change, hydrologic modification, estuarine pollution susceptibility, and air deposition. *EPA, Index of Watershed Indicators, October 26, 2001*

Drinking Water

Water System Name	Pop. Served	Primary Water Source Type	Number of Violations January 2002-February 2004		
			Health Based	Significant Monitoring	Monitoring
Charleston CPW	327,620	Surface	None	None	None

Note: Data as of February 19, 2004
Source: EPA, Office of Ground Water and Drinking Water, Safe Drinking Water Information System

Charleston tap water is alkaline, very soft and fluoridated.
Editor & Publisher Market Guide, 2004

Chattanooga, Tennessee

Background

Chattanooga is located on the Tennessee River near the Georgia border. Its name derives from a Cherokee word meaning "rock rising to a point," which refers to nearby Lookout Mountain. The city rests in a valley ringed by Lookout and Signal mountains, and by Missionary Ridge. Chattanooga is a dynamic tourist, financial, services, and manufacturing center, with unique features to interest anyone who wants to explore a prosperous and innovative community.

In 1803, John Brown, a half-Cherokee, set up a ferry which became an important crossroads between Southern and Eastern markets, and Chattanooga soon established itself as a modest but important salt-trading center. The city was incorporated in 1839 and, with the construction in 1849 of a Western and Atlantic Railroad link to other cities, Chattanooga became a major rail hub, distributing many Southern products—bacon, flour, iron, whiskey, and, increasingly, cotton—throughout the South Atlantic Eastern seaboard.

During the Civil War, Union troops took the city, and it was from here that General Sherman began his march to the sea. The major battles of Chickamauga and Chattanooga were fought nearby, and the nation's first national military park commemorating these battles is close by. Chattanooga's postwar economy was revived first by coal and iron, and later by the building of the Tennessee Valley Authority dams and associated projects, which resulted in considerable industrial expansion.

Chattanooga has been dubbed one of America's most "Enlightened Towns" by the *Utne Reader,* and is often held up as a model of sustainable community development. One of the most pedestrian-friendly cities in the Southeast, Chattanooga has developed a Green Space Master Plan, including tree-lined boulevards, parks and a network of walking and biking paths.

One key to the city's renaissance has been the revitalization of its historic theaters and inns, and the construction of Riverwalk, a waterfront park lined by once-abandoned factories. The Riverwalk is part of a planned 75-mile circuit of greenways. Efforts are underway to further improve the Tennessee River waterfront. Fruits of this effort are already being seen. For instance, the Tennessee Aquarium, which attracted 1.5 million visitors during its first year of operation in 1992, is undergoing a $30 million expansion slated for a spring of 2005 opening. The new building will extend the aquarium's story of the Tennessee River and further explore the Gulf of Mexico, into which the river flows.

Also in 2005, a $19.5 million expansion to the Hunter Museum of American Art will open, and include a pedestrian bridge across the Riverfront Parkway and a funicular to help visitors traverse the steep grade to the museum, all designed to better connect the facility with downtown.

The city is also home to The Houston Museum of Decorative Art—the legacy of Anna Safley Houston—which displays rare antique glass and ceramic pieces.

On the sports front, Chattanooga has been home to the U.S. women's Olympic rowing team, a professional soccer team, and sports teams from the University of Tennessee at Chattanooga. In addition to a campus of the University of Tennessee at Chattanooga, established in 1886, Tennessee Temple University and a thriving community college are also here.

No description of Chattanooga would be complete without mention of the Chattanooga Choo Choo Complex, an old station, now part of a hotel, which features the world's largest HO gauge model railroad layout.

Chattanooga's nearby mountains tend to moderate the winters, by retarding the flow of cold air from the north and west. As a result, winters, though cool, are slightly warmer than nearby locations of similar elevation. Snowfall tends to melt fairly quickly and ice storms are not uncommon. Summers are warm to hot, with afternoon thunderstorms. Annual precipitation is fairly heavy.

Rankings

- Chattanooga was ranked #210 out of 331 metro areas in *Cities Ranked & Rated*. Criteria: cost of living; climate; crime; transportation; economy and jobs; education; arts and culture; health and healthcare; leisure. *Cities Ranked & Rated, 1st Edition, 2004*

- *Ladies Home Journal* ranked America's 200 largest cities based on the qualities women surveyed care about most. Chattanooga ranked #126 out of 143 in the smaller city category (population under 300,000). Criteria: crime; lifestyle; education; jobs; health; child care; politics; and the economy. *Ladies Home Journal Online, "The Best Cities for Women 2002"*

- *Forbes* ranked the 150 most populous metro areas in the U.S. in terms of the "Best Places for Business and Careers." The Chattanooga metro area was ranked #104. Criteria: income and job growth; cost-of-doing-business; qualifications of the available pool of labor; crime rates; housing costs; net migration. *Forbes, May 9, 2003*

- *Men's Health* ranked 101 U.S. cities in terms of the quality of their tap water. Chattanooga received a grade of. Criteria: levels of bacteria, arsenic, lead, trihalomethanes, and haloacetic acids were compared with the National Academy of Science's guidelines as well as with the EPA's more stringent maximum contaminant level goals. *Men's Health, March 2004*

- Sperling's BestPlaces ranked 331 metro areas and identified the most and least stressful U.S. cities. The Chattanooga metro area ranked #47 out of 114 mid-size metro areas (#1 = most stressful). Criteria: divorce rate; unemployment rate; violent and property crime; suicide rate; commute time; mental health; alcohol consumption; cloudy days. *www.BestPlaces.net, February 26, 2004*

- Chattanooga was ranked #125 out of America's 200 largest metro areas in *SELF Magazine's* ranking of "America's Healthiest Cities for Women." Criteria: safety; air/water quality; cancer rates; and 21 other factors relating to health. *SELF Magazine, November 2003*

- *Zero Population Growth* ranked 239 cities in terms of children's health, safety, and economic well-being. Chattanooga was ranked #131 out of 140 independent cities (cities with populations greater than 100,000 which were neither major cities nor suburbs/outer cities) and was given a grade of C-. Criteria: total population and population growth; percent of population under 18 years of age; number of children's museums; health improvement grade; percent of births to teens; percent of low birthweight infants; infant mortality rate; number of Title X-funded clinics; average SAT/ACT scores; average elementary and secondary class size; crime rate; unemployment rate; percent of affordable homes; number of bad air days; park acres per 1000 persons; library circulation per child; and children's program attendance counts. *Zero Population Growth, Kid Friendly Cities Report Card 2001*

- Chattanooga was selected as one of America's 32 most livable cities by the non-profit group, Partners for Livable Communities. Criteria: environmental quality; parkland; ability to train new workers; job market; education; and use of the arts for economic development. *www.Livable.com, March 3, 2003*

- Chattanooga was given "Well City USA" status by The Wellness Councils of America, whose objective is to engage entire business communities in building healthy workforces. Criteria: 20% of a community's working population must be employed by either Bronze, Silver, Gold or Platinum designated Well Workplace Award winning companies. To date, six communities have achieved Well City USA status and five communities have Well City projects in progress. *The Wellness Councils of America, Well City USA 2004*

- *Ladies Home Journal* ranked America's 200 largest cities in terms of safety. Chattanooga ranked #193 out of 200. Criteria: violent crimes; crimes against property; and rape. *Ladies Home Journal Online, "The Best Cities for Women 2002"*

- Chattanooga was ranked #122 in *Prevention* magazine's survey of the "Best Walking Cities in the U.S." The magazine, in conjunction with the American Podiatric Medical Association, surveyed 125 of the most populated cities and then tabulated and weighed 20 criteria of interest to pedestrians. *Prevention, April, 2004*

- The Chattanooga metro area was cited as one of "The Best Places in the U.S. to Locate a Company." The area ranked #157 out of 329. Criteria: education (with emphasis on college board test results and high school graduation rates); availability of quality healthcare services and the cost to employers; quality of life; logistics workforce and companies; transportation infrastructure; quality and quantity of highly educated technical workers; business climate. *Expansion Management, July 2003*

- The Chattanooga metro area appeared on *Forbes/Milken Institute* list of "Best Places for Business and Career." Rank: #140 out of 200 metro areas. Criteria: salary growth; job growth; number of technology clusters; overall concentration of technology activity relative to national average; and technology output growth. *www.forbes.com, Forbes/Milken Institute Best Places 2002*

- The Chattanooga metro area appeared on the "Milken Institute Best Performing Cities" index. Rank: #139 out of 200 large metro areas. Criteria: job growth; wage and salary growth; high-tech output growth. *Milken Institute, June 25, 2003*

- The Chattanooga metro area appeared on *IndustryWeek's* fourth annual World-Class Communities list. It ranked #166 out of 315 metro areas. Criteria: MSA Gross Metropolitan Product (GMP) per manufacturing employee; and MSA percent share of U.S. manufacturing Gross Domestic Product (GDP). *IndustryWeek, April 16, 2001*

- ING Group ranked the 125 largest metro areas according to the general financial security of residents. The Chattanooga metro area was ranked #106 out of 125. Criteria: Earnings and Wealth Potential (household income, education, net assets, cost of living); Safety Net (health insurance, retirement savings, life insurance, income support programs); Personal Threats (unemployment rate, low-income households, crime rate); Community Economic Vitality (cost of community services, job quality, job creation, housing costs). *ING Group, "The Best Cities to Earn and Save Money: A Ranking of the Largest 125 U.S. Cities," 2001 Edition*

Business Environment

CITY FINANCES

City Government Finances

Component	2000-2001 ($000)	2000-2001 ($ per capita)
Total Revenues	611,282	3,930
Total Expenditures	606,114	3,896
Debt Outstanding	505,256	3,248
Cash and Securities	734,376	4,721

Source: U.S Census Bureau, Government Finances 2000-2001, August 2003

City Government Revenue by Source

Source	2000-2001 ($000)	2000-2001 ($ per capita)
General Revenue		
From Federal Government	14,447	93
From State Government	26,536	171
From Local Governments	29,347	189
Taxes		
Property	66,416	427
Sales	27,117	174
Personal Income	0	0
License	411	3
Charges	46,893	301
Liquor Store	0	0
Utility	360,815	2,320
Employee Retirement	15,295	98
Other	24,005	154

Source: U.S Census Bureau, Government Finances 2000-2001, August 2003

City Government Expenditures by Function

Function	2000-2001 ($000)	2000-2001 ($ per capita)	2000-2001 (%)
General Expenditures			
Airports	5,956	38	1.0
Corrections	0	0	0.0
Education	0	0	0.0
Fire Protection	23,500	151	3.9
Governmental Administration	20,205	130	3.3
Health	1,593	10	0.3
Highways	19,089	123	3.1
Hospitals	0	0	0.0
Housing and Community Development	9,856	63	1.6
Interest on General Debt	17,307	111	2.9
Libraries	4,917	32	0.8
Parking	2,532	16	0.4
Parks and Recreation	22,570	145	3.7
Police Protection	34,579	222	5.7
Public Welfare	12,813	82	2.1
Sewerage	20,516	132	3.4
Solid Waste Management	13,980	90	2.3
Liquor Store	0	0	0.0
Utility	344,276	2,213	56.8
Employee Retirement	12,093	78	2.0
Other	40,332	259	6.7

Source: U.S Census Bureau, Government Finances 2000-2001, August 2003

Municipal Bond Ratings

Area	Moody's
City	Aaa

Source: Mergent Bond Record, February 2004

DEMOGRAPHICS

Population Growth

Area	1990 Census	2000 Census	2003 Estimate	2008 Projection	Population Growth (%) 1990-2000	Population Growth (%) 2000-2008
City	152,695	155,554	154,883	153,872	1.9	-1.1
MSA[1]	424,303	465,161	472,948	485,306	9.6	4.3
U.S.	248,709,873	281,421,906	290,647,163	305,918,071	13.2	8.7

Note: (1) Metropolitan Statistical Area - see Appendix A for areas included
Source: Claritas, Inc.

Number of Households and Average Household Size

Area	1990 Census	2000 Census	2003 Estimate	2008 Projection	2003 Average Household Size
City	62,275	65,499	65,880	66,594	2.4
MSA[1]	163,101	185,144	190,378	199,089	2.5
U.S.	91,947,410	105,480,101	109,440,059	116,034,472	2.7

Note: (1) Metropolitan Statistical Area - see Appendix A for areas included
Source: Claritas, Inc.

Race and Ethnicity

Area	White Non-Hispanic	Black Non-Hispanic	Asian Non-Hispanic	Other Race Non-Hispanic	Hispanic
City	59.1	36.3	1.6	2.9	2.4
MSA[1]	82.6	14.3	1.0	2.1	1.7
U.S.	74.5	12.4	3.8	9.3	13.2

Note: Figures are 2003 estimates; (1) Metropolitan Statistical Area - see Appendix A for areas included
Source: Claritas, Inc.

Segregation

City Index[2]	City Rank[3]	MSA[1] Index[2]	MSA[1] Rank[4]
66.9	31	73.1	34

Note: Figures are based on an analysis of Census 2000 data; (1) Metropolitan Statistical Area - see Appendix A for areas included; (2) Dissimilarity Index—the most commonly used measure of segregation between two groups, reflecting their relative distributions across neighborhoods within a city or metropolitan area. It can range in value from 0, indicating complete integration, to 100, indicating complete segregation; (3) Ranges from 1 (most segregated) to 100 (least segregated) and includes all the cities in this book; (4) Ranges from 1 (most segregated) to 318 (least segregated) and includes 318 metropolitan areas.
Source: www.CensusScope.org

Ancestry

Area	German	Irish[2]	English	American	Italian	Polish	French[3]	Scottish
City	6.4	7.5	7.9	12.3	1.1	0.5	1.5	1.9
MSA[1]	8.0	9.8	9.6	18.7	1.3	0.6	1.6	2.0
U.S.	15.2	10.9	8.7	7.3	5.6	3.2	3.0	1.7

Note: Figures include multiple ancestry (e.g. if a person reported being Irish and Italian, they were included in both columns); (1) Metropolitan Statistical Area - see Appendix A for areas included; (2) Includes Celtic; (3) Includes Alsatian but excludes Basque
Source: Census 2000, Summary File 3

Foreign-Born Population

Area	Any Foreign Country	Percent of Population Born in: Europe	Asia	Africa	Oceania[2]	Canada	Mexico	Latin America[3]
City	3.4	0.6	1.5	0.1	0.0	0.1	0.5	0.6
MSA[1]	2.4	0.6	0.9	0.1	0.0	0.1	0.3	0.4
U.S.	11.1	1.7	2.9	0.3	0.1	0.3	3.3	2.5

Note: (1) Metropolitan Statistical Area - see Appendix A for areas included; (2) Includes Australia, New Zealand subregion, Melanesia, Micronesia, Polynesia, and Oceania n.e.c; (3) Includes Central America (excluding Mexico), South America, and the Caribbean.
Source: Census 2000, Summary File 3

Religion

Area	Catholic	Southern Baptist	United Methodist	ELCA[1]	LDS[2]	Presbyterian Church USA	Jewish Est.	Muslim Est.
County	3.2	21.6	8.0	0.3	0.2	1.3	0.5	0.7
U.S.	22.0	7.1	3.7	1.8	1.5	1.1	2.2	0.6

Note: Figures shown are the number of adherents as a percentage of the total population; Adherents are defined as all members, including full members, their children and the estimated number of other participants who are not considered members (e.g. the baptized, those not confirmed, those not eligible for communion, those regularly attending services, etc.); (1) Evangelical Lutheran Church in America; (2) The Church of Jesus Christ of Latter Day Saints
Source: Reprinted with permission from Religious Congregations and Membership in the United States 2000 (Nashville, Glenmary Research Center, 2002) Copyright Association of Statisticians of American Religious Bodies. All rights reserved.

Age Distribution

Area	Percent of Population						
	Under Age 5	Age 5 to 17	Age 18 to 34	Age 35 to 49	Age 50 to 64	Age 65 to 79	80 Years and Over
City	5.9	16.4	24.8	21.9	15.7	11.2	4.1
MSA[1]	6.1	17.6	22.8	23.3	16.7	10.2	3.3
U.S.	6.8	18.9	23.7	23.5	14.8	9.2	3.2

Note: (1) Metropolitan Statistical Area - see Appendix A for areas included
Source: Census 2000, Summary File 3

Marriage Status

Area	Never Married	Now Married Except Separated	Separated	Widowed	Divorced
City	28.3	46.1	2.6	9.4	13.6
MSA[1]	22.0	57.0	1.7	7.7	11.7
U.S.	27.1	54.4	2.2	6.6	9.7

Note: Figures cover population 15 years of age and older; (1) Metropolitan Statistical Area - see Appendix A for areas included
Source: Census 2000, Summary File 3

Male/Female Ratio

Area	Males	Females	Males per 100 Females
City	73,226	81,657	89.7
MSA[1]	227,718	245,230	92.9
U.S.	142,511,883	148,135,280	96.2

Note: Figures are 2003 estimates; (1) Metropolitan Statistical Area - see Appendix A for areas included
Source: Claritas, Inc.

ECONOMY

Gross Metropolitan Product

Area	1999	2000	2001	2002	2002 Rank[2]
MSA[1]	16.7	17.7	18.2	19.1	100

Note: Figures are in billions of dollars; (1) Metropolitan Statistical Area - see Appendix A for areas included; (2) Rank ranges from 1 to 319
Source: The U.S. Conference of Mayors, Metro Economies Report, July 2003

INCOME

Per Capita/Median/Average Income

Area	Per Capita ($)	Median Household ($)	Average Household ($)
City	21,983	36,560	50,990
MSA[1]	22,626	42,449	55,764
U.S.	24,078	46,868	63,207

Note: Figures are 2003 estimates; (1) Metropolitan Statistical Area - see Appendix A for areas included
Source: Claritas, Inc.

Household Income Distribution

Area	Percent of Households Earning							
	Under $15,000	$15,000 -24,999	$25,000 -34,999	$35,000 -49,999	$50,000 -74,999	$75,000 -99,000	$100,000 -149,999	$150,000 and up
City	20.3	14.6	13.3	16.5	16.7	8.3	6.1	4.1
MSA[1]	15.8	12.7	12.9	17.2	19.6	10.0	7.7	4.1
U.S.	14.1	11.5	11.7	16.0	19.2	11.3	10.2	6.0

Note: Figures are 2003 estimates; (1) Metropolitan Statistical Area - see Appendix A for areas included
Source: Claritas, Inc.

Poverty Rates by Age

Area	All Ages	Under 5 Years Old	5 to 17 Years Old	18 to 64 Years Old	65 Years and Over
City	17.9	1.8	4.4	9.6	2.1
MSA[1]	11.9	1.1	2.8	6.4	1.5
U.S.	12.4	1.2	3.0	6.9	1.2

Note: Figures are percent of population with income in 1999 below poverty level and only include population for whom poverty status is determined; (1) Metropolitan Statistical Area - see Appendix A for areas included
Source: Census 2000, Summary File 3

Personal Bankruptcy Filing Rate

Area	2002	2003
Hamilton County	10.34	9.94
U.S.	5.34	5.58

Note: Numbers are per 1,000 population and include Chapter 7 and Chapter 13 filings
Source: Federal Deposit Insurance Corporation (FDIC), Regional Economic Conditions (RECON), 2/25/2004

EMPLOYMENT

Labor Force and Employment

Area	Civilian Labor Force			Workers Employed		
	Dec. 2002	Dec. 2003	% Chg.	Dec. 2002	Dec. 2003	% Chg.
City	80,303	79,318	-1.2	77,085	75,831	-1.6
MSA[1]	239,084	236,945	-0.9	230,578	228,677	-0.8
U.S.	144,807,000	146,501,000	1.2	136,599,000	138,556,000	1.4

Note: Data is not seasonally adjusted and covers workers 16 years of age and older;
(1) Metropolitan Statistical Area - see Appendix A for areas included
Source: Bureau of Labor Statistics, http://stats.bls.gov

Unemployment Rate

Area	2003											
	Jan.	Feb.	Mar.	Apr.	May	Jun.	Jul.	Aug.	Sep.	Oct.	Nov.	Dec.
City	4.4	4.2	4.0	4.2	3.9	4.9	4.6	4.7	4.4	4.5	4.8	4.4
MSA[1]	3.5	3.5	3.4	3.3	3.3	4.0	3.8	3.7	3.5	3.7	3.7	3.5
U.S.	6.5	6.4	6.2	5.8	5.8	6.5	6.3	6.0	5.8	5.6	5.6	5.4

Note: Data is not seasonally adjusted and covers workers 16 years of age and older; All figures are percentages; (1) Metropolitan Statistical Area - see Appendix A for areas included
Source: Bureau of Labor Statistics, http://stats.bls.gov

Employment by Occupation

Occupation Classification	City (%)	MSA[1] (%)	U.S. (%)
Sales and Office	27.1	26.8	26.7
Professional and Related	19.6	17.7	20.2
Service	16.6	13.5	14.9
Production, Transportation, and Material Moving	18.1	19.8	14.6
Management, Business, and Financial	11.8	12.2	13.5
Construction, Extraction, and Maintenance	6.7	9.8	9.4
Farming, Forestry, and Fishing	0.1	0.2	0.7

Note: Figures cover employed civilians 16 years of age and older;
(1) Metropolitan Statistical Area - see Appendix A for areas included
Source: Census 2000, Summary File 3

Employment by Industry

Sector	MSA[1]		U.S.
	Number of Employees	Percent of Total	Percent of Total
Government	36,200	15.3	16.7
Education and Health Services	23,200	9.8	12.9
Professional and Business Services	25,800	10.9	12.3
Retail Trade	27,400	11.6	11.8
Manufacturing	35,000	14.8	11.0
Leisure and Hospitality	19,200	8.1	9.1
Finance Activities	18,100	7.6	6.1
Construction	n/a	n/a	5.1
Wholesale Trade	9,100	3.8	4.3
Other Services	10,600	4.5	4.1
Transportation and Utilities	20,500	8.7	3.7
Information	2,800	1.2	2.4
Natural Resources and Mining	n/a	n/a	0.4

Note: Figures cover non-farm employment as of December 2003 and are not seasonally adjusted;
(1) Metropolitan Statistical Area - see Appendix A for areas included; n/a not available
Source: Bureau of Labor Statistics, http://stats.bls.gov

Average Wages

Occupation	$/Hr.	Occupation	$/Hr.
Accountants and Auditors	21.30	Maids and Housekeeping Cleaners	7.62
Automotive Mechanics	13.23	Maintenance and Repair Workers	14.79
Bookkeepers	12.73	Marketing Managers	31.72
Carpenters	15.53	Nuclear Medicine Technologists	n/a
Cashiers	7.50	Nurses, Licensed Practical	14.35
Clerks, General Office	9.98	Nurses, Registered	20.90
Clerks, Receptionists/Information	9.80	Nursing Aides/Orderlies/Attendants	9.13
Clerks, Shipping/Receiving	12.35	Packers and Packagers, Hand	8.63
Computer Programmers	25.65	Physical Therapists	29.34
Computer Support Specialists	17.78	Postal Service Mail Carriers	18.58
Computer Systems Analysts	26.71	Real Estate Brokers	n/a
Cooks, Restaurant	9.40	Retail Salespersons	10.74
Dentists	92.86	Sales Reps., Exc. Tech./Scientific	21.05
Electrical Engineers	33.67	Sales Reps., Tech./Scientific	26.24
Electricians	19.74	Secretaries, Exc. Legal/Med./Exec.	10.85
Financial Managers	27.32	Security Guards	9.42
First-Line Supervisors/Mgrs., Sales	15.34	Surgeons	93.09
Food Preparation Workers	7.99	Teacher Assistants	8.10
General and Operations Managers	33.05	Teachers, Elementary School	18.20
Hairdressers/Cosmetologists	10.84	Teachers, Secondary School	19.50
Internists	99.33	Telemarketers	7.88
Janitors and Cleaners	8.77	Truck Drivers, Heavy/Tractor-Trailer	18.33
Landscaping/Groundskeeping Workers	9.88	Truck Drivers, Light/Delivery Svcs.	12.70
Lawyers	48.26	Waiters and Waitresses	7.41

Note: Wage data is for 2002 and covers the Metropolitan Statistical Area (see Appendix A for areas included).
Hourly wages for elementary/secondary school teachers and teacher assistants were calculated by the editors
from annual wage data assuming a 40 hour work week; n/a not available.
Source: Bureau of Labor Statistics, 2002 Metro Area Occupational Employment and Wage Estimates

Occupational Employment Projections: 1996 - 2006

Occupations Expected to Have the Largest Job Growth (ranked by numerical growth)	Fast-Growing Occupations[1] (ranked by percent growth)
1. Salespersons, retail	1. Personal and home care aides
2. Truck drivers, light	2. Systems analysts
3. Cashiers	3. Paralegals
4. General managers & top executives	4. Respiratory therapists
5. Janitors/cleaners/maids, ex. priv. hshld.	5. Home health aides
6. Food service workers	6. Directors, religious activities & educ.
7. Child care workers, private household	7. Computer engineers
8. Cooks, fast food and short order	8. Child care workers, private household
9. Registered nurses	9. Corrections officers & jailers
10. Waiters & waitresses	10. Emergency medical technicians

Note: Projections cover Tennessee; (1) Excludes occupations with total job growth less than 300
Source: U.S. Department of Labor, Employment and Training Administration, America's Labor Market Information System (ALMIS)

TAXES

State Corporate Income Tax Rates

State	Rate (%)	Number of Brackets	Low Bracket (Under $)	High Bracket (Over $)
Tennessee	6.5	1	na	na

Note: Tax rates as of December 31, 2003; na not applicable
Source: Tax Foundation, www.taxfoundation.org

State Individual Income Tax Rates

State	Federal Deductibility	Marginal Rate (%)	Number of Brackets	Low Bracket (Under $)	High Bracket (Over $)
Tennessee	No	6.0 (h)	na	na	na

Note: Tax rates as of December 31, 2003; Brackets apply to single taxpayers and married people filing separately; na not applicable; (h) Applies to interest and dividend income only.
Source: Tax Foundation, www.taxfoundation.org

Various State and Local Tax Rates

State Sales and Use (%)	Total Sales and Use (%)	Gasoline (cents/gal.)	Cigarette (cents/pack)	Spirits ($/gal.)	Table Wine ($/gal.)	Beer ($/gal.)
7.0 (l)	9.25	20	20	4.40	1.21	0.14

Note: Tax rates as of December 31, 2003.(l) Rate rose from 6% to 7% on July 1, 2002, but the rate on food remained 6%.
Source: Tax Foundation, www.taxfoundation.org

State Tax Burdens

Area	Combined State and Local Tax Burden		Combined Federal, State and Local Tax Burden	
	Percent	Rank	Percent	Rank
Tennessee	7.7	48	26.3	48
U.S. Average	9.7	-	30.0	-

Note: Figures are for 2003
Source: Tax Foundation, www.taxfoundation.org

Internal Revenue Service Tax Audits

IRS District	Percent of Returns Audited				
	1996	1997	1998	1999	2000
Kentucky-Tennessee	0.40	0.48	0.36	0.22	0.13
U.S.	0.66	0.61	0.46	0.31	0.20

Note: Figures cover IRS district audits of federal income tax returns filed by individuals. Geographic data on district audits for 2001 and 2002 are being withheld by the IRS. TRAC is challenging this policy.
Source: Syracuse University, Transactional Records Access Clearinghouse (TRAC), "Odds of IRS District Tax Audit 2000"

**RESIDENTIAL
REAL ESTATE**

Building Permits

Area	Single-Family 2001	Single-Family 2002	Single-Family Pct. Chg.	Multi-Family 2001	Multi-Family 2002	Multi-Family Pct. Chg.	Total 2001	Total 2002	Total Pct. Chg.
City	533	549	3.0	360	159	-55.8	893	708	-20.7
U.S.	1,235,600	1,332,600	7.9	401,100	415,100	3.5	1,636,700	1,747,700	6.8

Note: Figures represent new, privately-owned housing units authorized (unadjusted data)
Source: U.S. Census Bureau, Manufacturing, Mining, and Construction Statistics

Homeownership and Housing Vacancies

Area	Homeownership Rate[2] (%) 2001	2002[a]	2003	Rental Vacancy Rate[3] (%) 2001	2002[a]	2003	Homeowner Vacancy Rate[4] (%) 2001	2002[a]	2003
MSA[1]	n/a	n/a	n/a	n/a	n/a	n/a	n/a	n/a	n/a
U.S.	67.8	67.9	68.3	8.4	8.9	9.8	1.8	1.7	1.8

Note: (1) Metropolitan Statistical Area - see Appendix A for areas included; (2) The proportion of households that are owners; (3) The proportion of the rental inventory that is vacant for rent; (4) The proportion of the homeowner inventory that is vacant for sale; (a) 2002 figures have been revised; n/a not available
Source: U.S. Census Bureau, Housing Vacancies and Homeownership Annual Statistics: 2003

**COMMERCIAL
REAL ESTATE**

Industrial/Office Markets

Type/Market Area	Inventory (sq. ft.)	Vacant (sq. ft.)	Vacancy Rate (%)	Under Construction (sq. ft.)	Net Absorption (sq. ft.)
Industrial Space					
Chattanooga	35,050,000	3,580,000	10.21	0	-410,000
Office Space					
Chattanooga	4,607,650	175,000	3.80	180,000	219,424

Note: Data as of 4th Quarter, 2003; n/a not available
Source: Society of Industrial and Office Realtors, 2004 Comparative Statistics of Industrial and Office Real Estate Markets

**COMMERCIAL
UTILITIES**

Typical Monthly Electric Bills

Area	Commercial Service ($/month) 3 kW demand 1,000 kWh	40 kW demand 14,000 kWh	Industrial Service ($/month) 1,000 kW demand 200,000 kWh	50,000 kW demand 15,000,000 kWh
City	n/a	n/a	n/a	n/a
Average[1]	100	1,134	17,850	1,045,117

Note: Based on rates in effect July 1, 2003; (1) average based on 197 utilities; n/a not available
Source: Edison Electric Institute, Typical Bills and Average Rates Report, Summer 2003

TRANSPORTATION

Means of Transportation to Work

Area	Car/Truck/Van Drove Alone	Car-pooled	Public Transportation Bus	Subway	Railroad	Bicycle	Walked	Other Means	Worked at Home
City	79.5	13.3	1.6	0.0	0.0	0.2	2.2	1.2	2.1
MSA[1]	82.7	12.2	0.6	0.0	0.0	0.1	1.5	0.8	2.1
U.S.	75.7	12.2	2.5	1.5	0.5	0.4	2.9	1.0	3.3

Note: Figures shown are percentages and cover workers 16 years of age and older;
(1) Metropolitan Statistical Area - see Appendix A for areas included
Source: Census 2000, Summary File 3

Travel Time to Work

Area	Less Than 15 Minutes	15 to 29 Minutes	30 to 44 Minutes	45 to 59 Minutes	60 Minutes or More
City	33.4	48.0	13.1	2.4	3.2
MSA[1]	25.4	44.3	20.6	5.6	4.1
U.S.	29.4	36.1	19.1	7.4	8.0

Note: Figures are percentages and include workers 16 years old and over; (1) Metropolitan Statistical Area - see Appendix A for areas included
Source: Census 2000, Summary File 3

Transportation Statistics

Interstate highways (2004)	I-24; I-59; I-75
Public transportation (2002)	Chattanooga Area Regional Transportation Authority (CARTA)
Buses	
Average fleet age in years	6.6
No. operated in max. service	51
Light rail	
Average fleet age in years	15.0 (inclined plane)
No. operated in max. service	2 (inclined plane)
Demand response	
Average fleet age in years	4.8
No. operated in max. service	9
Passenger air service	
Airport	Chattanooga Metropolitan (Lovell Field)
Airlines (2003)	4
Boardings (2002)	248,512
Amtrak service (2004)	Bus connection
Major waterways/ports	Tennessee River

Source: Federal Transit Administration, National Transit Database, 2002; Editor & Publisher Market Guide, 2004; Bureau of Transportation Statistics, Airport Enplanement Activity for CY2002; www.amtrak.com

BUSINESSES

Major Business Headquarters

Company Name	2003 Rankings	
	Fortune 500	Forbes 500
UnumProvident	192	-

Note: Companies listed are located in the city; dashes indicate no ranking
Fortune 500: Companies that produce a 10-K are ranked 1 to 500 based on 2002 revenue
Forbes 500: Private companies are ranked 1 to 281 based on 2002 revenue
Source: Fortune, April 14, 2003; www.forbes.com, November 6, 2003

Minority and Women-Owned Businesses

Ownership	All Firms		Firms with Paid Employees			
	Firms	Sales ($000)	Firms	Sales ($000)	Employees	Payroll ($000)
Black	712	69,796	154	61,778	1,237	23,620
Hispanic	193	19,131	34	(a)	250 - 499	(a)
Women	3,080	1,140,116	852	1,071,760	10,961	235,944

Note: Figures cover firms located in the city; (a) Withheld to avoid disclosure
Source: 1997 Economic Census, Minority and Women-Owned Businesses

HOTELS

Hotels/Motels

Area	Hotels/Motels	Average Minimum Rates ($)		
		Tourist	First-Class	Deluxe
City	70	53	95	n/a

Note: n/a not available
Source: OAG Travel Planner Online, Spring 2004

EVENT SITES

Major Event Sites, Meeting Places and Convention Centers

Name	Guest Rooms	Exhibit/ Meeting Space (sq. ft.)	Largest Meeting Room Capacity
Chattanooga Marriott	343	7,500	450
Chattanooga/Hamilton Co. Convention Ctr.	n/a	60,000	6,000
Clarion Hotel River Plaza	201	19,700	640
Holiday Inn Chattanooga	350	44,000	1,200
Radisson Read House Hotel	238	16,488	500
UTC Arena	n/a	n/a	12,000

Note: n/a not available
Source: Original research

Living Environment

COST OF LIVING

Cost of Living Index

Year	Composite Index	Groceries	Housing	Utilities	Trans-portation	Health Care	Misc. Goods/ Services
2001	96.3	99.0	93.8	88.7	97.0	85.7	100.5
2002	93.1	96.8	84.0	91.7	97.9	92.7	97.8
2003	93.0	94.3	83.9	89.6	100.6	101.6	98.3

Note: U.S. = 100
Source: ACCRA, Cost of Living Index, 2001, 2002 and 2003 4-Quarter Averages

HOUSING

House Price Index (HPI)

Area	National Ranking[2]	Quarterly Change (%)	One-Year Change (%)	Five-Year Change (%)
MSA[1]	137	1.95	4.93	24.92
U.S.[3]	-	3.67	7.97	41.81

Note: The HPI is a weighted repeat sales index. It measures average price changes in repeat sales or refinancings on the same properties. This information is obtained by reviewing repeat mortgage transactions on single-family properties whose mortgages have been purchased or securitized by Fannie Mae of Freddie Mac in January 1975; (1) Metropolitan Statistical Area - see Appendix A for areas included; (2) Rankings are based on annual percentage change, for all MSAs containing at least 15,000 transactions over the last 10 years and ranges from 1 to 220; (3) figures based on a weighted division average; all figures are for the period ended December 31, 2003
Source: Office of Federal Housing Enterprise Oversight, House Price Index, March 1, 2004

Housing: Year Structure Built

Area	1990 -2000	1980 -1989	1970 -1979	1960 -1969	1950 -1959	1940 -1949	Before 1940	Median Year
City	10.4	12.5	17.3	19.3	16.9	10.2	13.4	1965
MSA[1]	18.1	15.8	20.0	15.9	13.4	8.0	8.9	1972
U.S.	17.0	15.8	18.5	13.7	12.7	7.3	15.0	1971

Note: Figures are percentages; (1) Metropolitan Statistical Area - see Appendix A for areas included
Source: Census 2000, Summary File 3

Average New Home Price

Area	2001	2002	2003
City	202,949	196,294	206,085
U.S.	212,643	236,567	248,193

Note: Figures, in dollars, are based on a new home with 2,400 sq. ft. of living area on an 8,000 sq. ft. lot.
Source: ACCRA, Cost of Living Index, 2001, 2002 and 2003 4-Quarter Averages

Average Apartment Rent

Area	2001	2002	2003
City	620	630	654
U.S.	674	708	721

Note: Figures, in dollars per month, are based on an unfurnished two bedroom, 1-1/2 or 2 bath apartment, approximately 950 sq. ft. in size, excluding all utilities except water
Source: ACCRA, Cost of Living Index, 2001, 2002 and 2003 4-Quarter Averages

RESIDENTIAL UTILITIES

Average Residential Utility Costs

Area	All Electric ($/mth)	Part Electric ($/mth)	Other Energy ($/mth)	Phone ($/mth)
City	–	48.85	66.85	20.37
U.S.	116.46	65.82	62.68	23.90

Source: ACCRA, Cost of Living Index, 2003 4-Quarter Average

HEALTH CARE

Average Health Care Costs

Area	Hospital ($/day)	Doctor ($/visit)	Dentist ($/visit)
City	599.15	91.30	75.51
U.S.	678.35	67.91	83.90

Note: Hospital—based on a semi-private room; Doctor—based on a general practitioner's routine exam of an established patient; Dentist—based on adult teeth cleaning and periodic oral exam.
Source: ACCRA, Cost of Living Index, 2003 4-Quarter Average

Distribution of Non-Federal, Office-Based Physicians

Area	Total	Family/ General Practice	Specialties Medical	Specialties Surgical	Specialties Other
MSA[1] (number)	875	96	298	240	241
MSA[1] (rate per 10,000 pop.)	18.8	2.1	6.4	5.2	5.2
Metro Average[2] (rate per 10,000 pop.)	33.1	2.2	7.7	4.8	5.6

Note: Data as of December 31, 2001; (1) Metropolitan Statistical Area - see Appendix A for areas included; (2) Average of 81 MSAs and CMSAs in this book
Source: American Medical Association, Physician Characteristics & Distribution in the U.S., 2003-2004

Hospitals

Chattanooga has the following hospitals: 3 general medical and surgical; 1 psychiatric; 2 rehabilitation; 1 other specialty.
AHA Guide to the Healthcare Field, 2003-2004

PRESIDENTIAL ELECTION

2000 Presidential Election Results

Area	Gore	Bush	Nader	Buchanan	Other
Hamilton County	43.0	55.4	1.1	0.2	0.4
U.S.	48.4	47.9	2.7	0.4	0.6

Note: Results are percentages and may not add to 100% due to rounding
Source: www.cbsnews.com; www.uselectionatlas.org

EDUCATION

Public School District Statistics

District Name	Schls.	Enroll-ment	Classroom Teachers	Pupil/ Teacher Ratio	Minority Pupils[1] (%)	Current Expend.[2] ($/pupil)
Hamilton County SD	80	40,514	2,669	15.2	n/a	5,895

Note: Data covers the 2001-02 school year unless otherwise noted; (1) Fall 2000; (2) FY2000; n/a not available
Source: U.S. Department of Education, National Center for Education Statistics, Common Core of Data, Local Education Agency (School District) Universe Survey: School Year 2001-2002; U.S. Department of Education, National Center for Education Statistics, Digest of Education Statistics 2002

Educational Quality

School District	Education Quotient[1]	Graduate Outcome[2]	Community Index[3]	Resource Index[4]
Hamilton County	17	16	45	41

Note: Scores are national percentile rankings and range from 1 (worst) to 99 (best); (1) Combination of the Graduate Outcome, Community and Resource indexes weighted to reflect the greater importance of the Graduate Outcome and Resource Index; (2) Based on graduation rates and college board scores (SAT/ACT); (3) Based on the surrounding community's level of affluence and adult education; (4) Based on teacher salaries, per-pupil expenditures and student-teacher ratios.
Source: Expansion Management, December 2003

Educational Attainment by Race

Area	High School Graduate (%)					Bachelor's Degree (%)				
	Total	White	Black	Asian	Hisp.[2]	Total	White	Black	Asian	Hisp.[2]
City	77.6	81.7	69.9	86.7	58.9	21.5	27.0	9.3	51.1	16.3
MSA[1]	77.0	78.0	70.8	83.7	64.3	19.7	20.9	10.3	46.1	17.3
U.S.	80.4	83.6	72.3	80.4	52.4	24.4	26.1	14.3	44.1	10.4

Note: Figures shown cover persons 25 years old and over; (1) Metropolitan Statistical Area - see Appendix A for areas included; (2) people of Hispanic origin can be of any race
Source: Census 2000, Summary File 3

School Enrollment by Type

Area	Grades KG to 8				Grades 9 to 12			
	Public		Private		Public		Private	
	Enrollment	%	Enrollment	%	Enrollment	%	Enrollment	%
City	15,709	84.9	2,790	15.1	6,176	85.0	1,091	15.0
MSA[1]	50,400	86.5	7,842	13.5	19,835	83.3	3,969	16.7
U.S.	33,526,011	88.7	4,285,121	11.3	14,848,628	90.6	1,532,323	9.4

Note: Figures shown cover persons 3 years old and over; (1) Metropolitan Statistical Area - see Appendix A for areas included
Source: Census 2000, Summary File 3

School Enrollment by Race

Area	Grades KG to 8 (%)				Grades 9 to 12 (%)			
	White	Black	Asian	Hisp.[1]	White	Black	Asian	Hisp.[1]
City	43.3	51.4	1.5	2.3	42.8	52.5	2.2	1.0
MSA[2]	77.2	19.3	0.9	1.8	77.6	18.9	1.4	1.3
U.S.	68.5	15.5	3.3	16.8	68.8	15.5	3.8	15.7

Note: Figures shown cover persons 3 years old and over; (1) people of Hispanic origin can be of any race; (2) Metropolitan Statistical Area - see Appendix A for areas included
Source: Census 2000, Summary File 3

Classroom Teacher Salaries in Public Schools

District	B.A. Degree		M.A. Degree		Maximum	
	Min. ($)	Rank[1]	Max. ($)	Rank[1]	Max. ($)	Rank[1]
City	n/a	n/a	n/a	n/a	n/a	n/a
DOD Average[2]	31,567	-	53,248	-	59,356	-

Note: Salaries are for 2001-2002; (1) Rank ranges from 1 to 100; (2) As per the U.S. Department of Defense Wage Fixing Authority
Source: American Federation of Teachers, Survey & Analysis of Teacher Salary Trends 2002

Higher Education

Four-Year Colleges			Two-Year Colleges			Medical Schools	Law Schools	Voc/Tech
Public	Private Non-profit	Private For-profit	Public	Private Non-profit	Private For-profit			
1	2	0	1	0	1	0	0	2

Note: Figures cover institutions located within the city limits.
Source: National Center for Education Statistics, The Integrated Postsecondary Education System (IPEDS) Peer Analysis System, 2002; usnews.com, America's Best Graduate Schools 2004, Medical School Directory; The College Blue Book, Occupational Education, 2003; Barron's Guide to Law Schools, 2003; Medical School Admission Requirements U.S. & Canada, 2003-2004

MAJOR EMPLOYERS

Major Employers

Company Name	Industry	Type
Advantage Personnel Cons	Management consulting services	Single
Blue Cross and Blue Shield	Hospital and medical service plans	Headquarters
Chattanooga Paperboard Corp	Converted paper products, nec	Single
County of Hamilton	Executive offices	Headquarters
Covenant Transport Inc (tn)	Trucking, except local	Headquarters
Dupont Sabanci International	Yarn spinning mills	Branch
GE Appliances	Household cooking equipment	Headquarters
Hutcheson Medical Center	General medical and surgical hospitals	Headquarters
Kindred Healthcare Inc	General medical and surgical hospitals	Branch
McKee Foods Corporation	Bread, cake, and related products	Headquarters
Parkridge Medical Center	General medical and surgical hospitals	Headquarters
Provident Insurance	Accident and health insurance	Headquarters
Seaboard Farms of Chattanooga	Poultry slaughtering and processing	Branch
Sheriff	Police protection	Branch
Si Corporation	Broadwoven fabric mills, manmade	Headquarters
Stellar Management Group Inc	Electrical appliances, television and radio	Branch
U S Xpress Inc	Trucking, except local	Headquarters
University Tenn At Chattanooga	Colleges and universities	Branch
Wheland Foundry	Gray and ductile iron foundries	Branch

Note: Companies shown are located in the metropolitan area and have 750 or more employees.
Source: www.zapdata.com, March 2004

PUBLIC SAFETY

Crime Rate

Area	All Crimes	Violent Crimes				Property Crimes		
		Murder	Forcible Rape	Robbery	Aggrav. Assault	Burglary	Larceny -Theft	Motor Vehicle Theft
City	10,010.3	15.1	70.7	394.3	1,033.4	1,623.9	5,969.5	903.4
Suburbs[1]	3,264.3	4.4	17.6	32.0	256.2	685.1	2,050.9	218.2
MSA[2]	5,503.9	8.0	35.2	152.3	514.2	996.8	3,351.8	445.7
U.S.	4,118.8	5.6	33.0	145.9	310.1	746.2	2,445.8	432.1

Note: Figures are crimes per 100,000 population; (1) All areas within the MSA that are located outside the city limits; (2) Metropolitan Statistical Area - see Appendix A for areas included
Source: FBI Uniform Crime Reports, 2002

RECREATION

Culture and Recreation

Museums	Orchestras	Opera Companies	Dance Companies	Professional Theatres	Zoos	Pro Sports Teams[1]
8	1	1	2	0	1	0

Note: (1) Covers the Metropolitan Statistical Area - see Appendix A for areas included.
Source: The Grey House Performing Arts Directory, 2002; Official Museum Directory, 2004; www.sportsvenues.com

Library System

The Chattanooga-Hamilton County Bicentennial Library has four branches, holdings of 499,351 volumes, and a budget of $5,279,011 (2001-2002).
American Library Directory, 2003-2004

MEDIA

Newspapers

Name	Type	Freq.	Distribution	Circulation
Chattanooga Shofar	Religious	10x/yr	Local	1,100
The Chattanooga Times & The Chattanooga Free Press	General	7x/wk	Area	76,945

Note: Includes newspapers whose offices are located in the city and whose circulations are 1,000 or more
Source: Burrelle's Media Directory, 2003

Television Stations

Name	Ch.	Affiliation	Type	Owner
WRCB	3	NBCT	Commercial	Sarkes Tarzian Inc.
WTVC	9	ABCT	Commercial	Freedom Communications Inc.
WDEF	12	CBST	Commercial	Media General Inc.
WTCI	45	PBS	Public	Greater Chattanooga Public TV Corp.
WFLI	53	WB	Commercial	n/a
WDSI	61	FBC	Commercial	Pegasus Communications Corporation

Note: Stations included broadcast from the Chattanooga metro area; n/a not available
Source: Burrelle's Media Directory, 2003

AM Radio Stations

Call Letters	Freq. (kHz)	Target Audience	Station Format	Music Format
WUUS	980	Christian	M/N/T	Adult Contemporary
WFLI	1070	Religious	M/N/S/T	Gospel
WGOW	1150	General	N/S/T	n/a
WDST	1240	General	M	AOR
WNOO	1260	Black	Children	General
WDOD	1310	General	M	Adult Standards
WDEF	1370	General	S	n/a
WLMR	1450	Christian	Religious	M/N/S

Note: Stations included broadcast from the Chattanooga metro area; n/a not available
The following abbreviations may be used:
Target Audience: A=Asian; B=Black; C=Christian; E=Ethnic; F=French; G=General; H=Hispanic; M=Men; N=Native American; R=Religious; S=Senior Citizen; W=Women; Y=Young Adult; Z=Children
Station Format: E=Educational; M=Music; N=News; S=Sports; T=Talk
Music Format: AOR=Album Oriented Rock; MOR=Middle of the Road
Source: Burrelle's Media Directory, 2003

FM Radio Stations

Call Letters	Freq. (mHz)	Target Audience	Station Format	Music Format
WUTC	88.1	General	M/N	Adult Contemporary
WMBW	88.9	Religious	E/M/N/T	Christian
WDYN	89.7	Religious	E/M/T	Christian
WSMC	90.5	General	M/N	Classical
WDEF	92.3	General	M	Adult Contemporary
WMPZ	93.7	General	M/N/S	Adult Contemporary
WJTT	94.3	General	E/M/N/S/T	Urban Contemporary
WDOD	96.5	General	M	AOR
WLOV	97.3	General	M	Oldies
WKXJ	98.1	General	M	Top 40
WUSY	100.7	General	M/N/T	Country
WSGC	101.9	General	M	Rhythm & Blues
WRXR	105.5	General	M/N/T	Adult Contemporary
WSKZ	106.5	General	M/N/S	Classic Rock
WOGT	107.9	General	M/N/T	Oldies

Note: Stations included broadcast from the Chattanooga metro area
The following abbreviations may be used:
Target Audience: A=Asian; B=Black; C=Christian; E=Ethnic; F=French; G=General; H=Hispanic; M=Men; N=Native American; R=Religious; S=Senior Citizen; W=Women; Y=Young Adult; Z=Children
Station Format: E=Educational; M=Music; N=News; S=Sports; T=Talk
Music Format: AOR=Album Oriented Rock; MOR=Middle of the Road
Source: Burrelle's Media Directory, 2003

CLIMATE

Average and Extreme Temperatures

Temperature	Jan	Feb	Mar	Apr	May	Jun	Jul	Aug	Sep	Oct	Nov	Dec	Yr.
Extreme High (°F)	78	79	87	92	97	104	106	104	102	94	84	78	106
Average High (°F)	49	53	62	72	80	87	90	89	83	72	61	51	71
Average Temp. (°F)	39	43	51	60	68	76	79	78	72	61	50	42	60
Average Low (°F)	29	32	39	47	56	64	68	68	61	48	38	32	49
Extreme Low (°F)	-10	1	8	26	34	41	51	53	36	22	4	-2	-10

Note: Figures cover the years 1948-1990
Source: National Climatic Data Center, International Station Meteorological Climate Summary, 9/96

Average Precipitation/Snowfall/Humidity

Precip./Humidity	Jan	Feb	Mar	Apr	May	Jun	Jul	Aug	Sep	Oct	Nov	Dec	Yr.
Avg. Precip. (in.)	5.3	5.0	5.9	4.3	4.1	3.6	4.8	3.5	4.2	3.2	4.5	5.1	53.3
Avg. Snowfall (in.)	2	1	Tr	Tr	0	0	0	0	0	Tr	Tr	1	4
Avg. Rel. Hum. 7am (%)	81	81	81	83	88	89	90	92	92	91	86	83	86
Avg. Rel. Hum. 4pm (%)	58	53	48	44	50	52	55	55	55	50	52	57	52

Note: Figures cover the years 1948-1990; Tr = Trace amounts (<0.05 in. of rain; <0.5 in. of snow)
Source: National Climatic Data Center, International Station Meteorological Climate Summary, 9/96

Weather Conditions

Temperature			Daytime Sky			Precipitation		
10°F & below	32°F & below	90°F & above	Clear	Partly cloudy	Cloudy	0.01 inch or more precip.	0.1 inch or more snow/ice	Thunder-storms
2	73	48	88	141	136	120	3	55

Note: Figures are average number of days per year and covers the years 1948-1990
Source: National Climatic Data Center, International Station Meteorological Climate Summary, 9/96

HAZARDOUS WASTE

Superfund Sites

Chattanooga has one hazardous waste site on the EPA's Superfund National Priorities List: **Tennessee Products.** *U.S. Environmental Protection Agency, National Priorities List, March 15, 2004*

AIR & WATER QUALITY

Maximum Pollutant Concentrations

	Particulate Matter (ug/m³)	Carbon Monoxide (ppm)	Sulfur Dioxide (ppm)	Nitrogen Dioxide (ppm)	Ozone 1-hour (ppm)	Ozone 8-hour (ppm)	Lead (ug/m³)
MSA[1] Level	50	n/a	n/a	n/a	0.11	0.1	n/a
NAAQS[2]	150	9	0.140	0.053	0.12	0.08	1.50
Met NAAQS[2]	Yes	n/a	n/a	n/a	Yes	No	n/a

Note: (1) Metropolitan Statistical Area - see Appendix A for areas included; (2) National Ambient Air Quality Standards; n/a not available
Units: ppm = parts per million; ug/m³ = micrograms per cubic meter
Source: EPA, Latest Findings on National Air Quality: 2002 Status and Trends, August 2003

Air Quality Index

Data not available.

Watershed Health

The U.S. Environmental Protection Agency monitors the health of the aquatic resources for the nation's 2,000+ watersheds. **The Middle Tennessee-Chickamauga watershed serves the Chattanooga area and received an overall Index of Watershed Indicators (IWI) score of 3 (less serious problems - low vulnerability).** The IWI score is based on seven condition and nine vulnerability indicators. The overall IWI score ranges from 1 (best health) to 6 (worst health). The Condition Indicators include: designated use attainment, fish and wildlife consumption advisories, source water condition, contaminated sediments, ambient water quality, and wetlands loss index. The Vulnerability Indicators include: aquatic species at risk, conventional and toxic loads over permitted limits, urban and agricultural runoff potential, population change, hydrologic modification, estuarine pollution susceptibility, and air deposition. *EPA, Index of Watershed Indicators, October 26, 2001*

Drinking Water

Water System Name	Pop. Served	Primary Water Source Type	Number of Violations January 2002-February 2004		
			Health Based	Significant Monitoring	Monitoring
Tenn.-American Water Co.	169,389	Surface	None	None	None

Note: Data as of February 19, 2004
Source: EPA, Office of Ground Water and Drinking Water, Safe Drinking Water Information System

Chattanooga tap water is slightly alkaline, moderately hard and fluoridated.
Editor & Publisher Market Guide, 2004

Columbia, South Carolina

Background

Columbia, on the Congaree River, is South Carolina's capital and largest city, and the seat of Richland County. It is a center for local and state government, and an important financial, insurance, and medical center.

The region has been a trade center from at least 1718, when a trading post was established just to the south of the present-day city. In 1754, a ferry was established by the colonial government to facilitate contact with the surrounding settlements, and in 1786, when the new state government introduced a bill to create a state capital, Columbia was chosen. Located at almost the dead center of the state, Columbia represented a compromise between South Carolinians on the coast and those in the interior.

The city was planned from the ground up and was originally designed to rest along the river in 400 blocks, which were then divided into half-acre lots. Buyers were required to build houses at least 30 feet long and 18 feet wide within three years, or face penalties. The main thoroughfares were 150 feet wide, and the other streets were also designed generously. Most of this spacious layout still survives, lending an expansive feel to the city as a whole. Columbia, only the second planned city in the United States, achieved a population of nearly 1,000 just after 1800. It was chartered as a town in 1805, and first governed by a mayor, or "intendent," John Taylor, who later served in the state general assembly, in the U.S. Congress, and, finally, as governor of the state.

By 1854, Columbia was a full-fledged chartered city with an elected mayor and six aldermen, a full-time police force, one schoolteacher who was also the city's attorney, and a waterworks, which pumped water via steam engine to a wooden tank and thence by iron and lead pipes to homes and businesses in the area.

Columbia was staunchly Confederate during the Civil War, and in 1865 it was attacked by General Sherman's troops and burned by fires set by both Union attackers and Confederate evacuees. After the war and Reconstruction, Columbia saw a revitalization as South Carolina's main industrial and farm products hub.

The *State,* the local newspaper, recently ranked Blue Cross and Blue Shield of S.C. as the area's largest private employer. Following close behind is Palmetto Health, with its two hospitals, Palmetto Richland and Palmetto Baptist. Rounding out the top five are SCANA Corp., the area's electricity and natural gas utility; Gold Kist, Inc, a poultry operation in nearby Sumter.and Lexington Medical Center.

Columbia is the area's cultural center, hosting theaters, galleries, dance companies, and an orchestra. The Columbia Museum of Art is a major regional museum, and the Koger Center for the Arts at the University of South Carolina holds year-round theater, music, and dance productions.

The South Carolina State Museum offers exhibits in natural history, art, science, and technology. On the drawing board is multi-million dollar observatory/planetarium and large-format theater projected to open in 2005 called the OPT Project. This includes a 55-foot domed theater in the planetarium and a 3-D theater.

Major historic architecture in Columbia includes the City Hall, designed by President Ulysses S. Grant's federal architect, Alfred Bult Mullet, and the Lutheran Survey Print Building. The city also offers 500 acres of park lands.

The main campus of the University of South Carolina is in Columbia, as are Lutheran Theological Seminary, Columbia College, Benedict College, Allen University, and Columbia Bible College and Seminary.

Located about 150 miles southeast of the Appalachian Mountains, Columbia has a relatively temperate climate. Summers are long and often hot and humid with summer thunderstorms, thanks to the Bermuda High. Winters are mild with little snow, while spring is changeable and can include infrequent tornadoes or hail. Fall is considered the most pleasant season.

Rankings

- Columbia was ranked #50 out of 331 metro areas in *Cities Ranked & Rated*. Criteria: cost of living; climate; crime; transportation; economy and jobs; education; arts and culture; health and healthcare; leisure. *Cities Ranked & Rated, 1st Edition, 2004*

- *Ladies Home Journal* ranked America's 200 largest cities based on the qualities women surveyed care about most. Columbia ranked #60 out of 143 in the smaller city category (population under 300,000). Criteria: crime; lifestyle; education; jobs; health; child care; politics; and the economy. *Ladies Home Journal Online, "The Best Cities for Women 2002"*

- The Columbia metro area was selected as one of America's "Best Places to Live and Work" by *Expansion Management* and rated as a "Four-Star Community." The annual "Quality of Life Quotient" measures nearly 50 indicators and compares them among the 329 metropolitan statistical areas in the United States. *Expansion Management, May 2003*

- *Forbes* ranked the 150 most populous metro areas in the U.S. in terms of the "Best Places for Business and Careers." The Columbia metro area was ranked #17. Criteria: income and job growth; cost-of-doing-business; qualifications of the available pool of labor; crime rates; housing costs; net migration. *Forbes, May 9, 2003*

- *Men's Health* ranked 101 U.S. cities in terms of the quality of their tap water. Columbia received a grade of. Criteria: levels of bacteria, arsenic, lead, trihalomethanes, and haloacetic acids were compared with the National Academy of Science's guidelines as well as with the EPA's more stringent maximum contaminant level goals. *Men's Health, March 2004*

- Sperling's BestPlaces ranked 331 metro areas and identified the most and least stressful U.S. cities. The Columbia metro area ranked #79 out of the 100 largest metro areas (#1 = most stressful). Criteria: divorce rate; unemployment rate; violent and property crime; suicide rate; commute time; mental health; alcohol consumption; cloudy days. *www.BestPlaces.net, February 26, 2004*

- Columbia was selected as a "Great College Town" by ePodunk. The city ranked #1 in the medium-sized city category. ePodunk.com looked at communities with four-year colleges and a total student enrollment of at least 1,500. Communities where the student ratio was too low or too high were ruled out, as were small cities with low rates of owner-occupied housing. Fifteen variables were then applied to assess arts and culture, recreation, intellectual activity, historic preservation, and cost of living. *www.ePodunk.com, April, 2002*

- Columbia was ranked #100 out of America's 200 largest metro areas in *SELF Magazine's* ranking of "America's Healthiest Cities for Women." Criteria: safety; air/water quality; cancer rates; and 21 other factors relating to health. *SELF Magazine, November 2003*

- *Zero Population Growth* ranked 239 cities in terms of children's health, safety, and economic well-being. Columbia was ranked #93 out of 140 independent cities (cities with populations greater than 100,000 which were neither major cities nor suburbs/outer cities) and was given a grade of B-. Criteria: total population and population growth; percent of population under 18 years of age; number of children's museums; health improvement grade; percent of births to teens; percent of low birthweight infants; infant mortality rate; number of Title X-funded clinics; average SAT/ACT scores; average elementary and secondary class size; crime rate; unemployment rate; percent of affordable homes; number of bad air days; park acres per 1000 persons; library circulation per child; and children's program attendance counts. *Zero Population Growth, Kid Friendly Cities Report Card 2001*

- *Ladies Home Journal* ranked America's 200 largest cities in terms of safety. Columbia ranked #127 out of 200. Criteria: violent crimes; crimes against property; and rape. *Ladies Home Journal Online, "The Best Cities for Women 2002"*

- Columbia was identified as one of the 100 "Most Unwired Cities" in the U.S. The area ranked #72. Criteria: number of public and commercial wireless access points; cell phone coverage offering wide area network Internet access; Internet penetration. *Intel, "Most Unwired Cities," March 4, 2003*

- Columbia was ranked #57 in *Prevention* magazine's survey of the "Best Walking Cities in the U.S." The magazine, in conjunction with the American Podiatric Medical Association, surveyed 125 of the most populated cities and then tabulated and weighed 20 criteria of interest to pedestrians. *Prevention, April, 2004*

- The Columbia metro area was selected as one of "America's 50 Hottest Cities for Business Relocations and Expansions." The area ranked #49. Criteria: 70 of the industry's most prominent site selection consultants were asked which cities their clients found the most attractive when it came to selecting an expansion or relocation site in 2003. *Expansion Management, January 2004*

- The Columbia metro area was cited as one of "The Best Places in the U.S. to Locate a Company." The area ranked #9 out of 329. Criteria: education (with emphasis on college board test results and high school graduation rates); availability of quality healthcare services and the cost to employers; quality of life; logistics workforce and companies; transportation infrastructure; quality and quantity of highly educated technical workers; business climate. *Expansion Management, July 2003*

- Columbia was cited as a top metro area for European expansion. The area ranked #7 out of 50, based on European-based company expansions or relocations within the past two years that created at least 10 jobs and involved capital investment of at least $1 million. *Expansion Management, June 2003*

- The Columbia metro area appeared on *Forbes/Milken Institute* list of "Best Places for Business and Career." Rank: #158 out of 200 metro areas. Criteria: salary growth; job growth; number of technology clusters; overall concentration of technology activity relative to national average; and technology output growth. *www.forbes.com, Forbes/Milken Institute Best Places 2002*

- The Columbia metro area appeared on the "Milken Institute Best Performing Cities" index. Rank: #142 out of 200 large metro areas. Criteria: job growth; wage and salary growth; high-tech output growth. *Milken Institute, June 25, 2003*

- The Columbia metro area appeared on *IndustryWeek's* fourth annual World-Class Communities list. It ranked #244 out of 315 metro areas. Criteria: MSA Gross Metropolitan Product (GMP) per manufacturing employee; and MSA percent share of U.S. manufacturing Gross Domestic Product (GDP). *IndustryWeek, April 16, 2001*

- ING Group ranked the 125 largest metro areas according to the general financial security of residents. The Columbia metro area was ranked #54 out of 125. Criteria: Earnings and Wealth Potential (household income, education, net assets, cost of living); Safety Net (health insurance, retirement savings, life insurance, income support programs); Personal Threats (unemployment rate, low-income households, crime rate); Community Economic Vitality (cost of community services, job quality, job creation, housing costs). *ING Group, "The Best Cities to Earn and Save Money: A Ranking of the Largest 125 U.S. Cities," 2001 Edition*

Business Environment

CITY FINANCES

City Government Finances

Component	2000-2001 ($000)	2000-2001 ($ per capita)
Total Revenues	176,892	1,521
Total Expenditures	168,535	1,449
Debt Outstanding	177,725	1,528
Cash and Securities	182,642	1,571

Source: U.S Census Bureau, Government Finances 2000-2001, August 2003

City Government Revenue by Source

Source	2000-2001 ($000)	2000-2001 ($ per capita)
General Revenue		
From Federal Government	5,002	43
From State Government	5,810	50
From Local Governments	6,623	57
Taxes		
Property	25,931	223
Sales	7,280	63
Personal Income	0	0
License	0	0
Charges	49,546	426
Liquor Store	0	0
Utility	37,016	318
Employee Retirement	0	0
Other	39,684	341

Source: U.S Census Bureau, Government Finances 2000-2001, August 2003

City Government Expenditures by Function

Function	2000-2001 ($000)	2000-2001 ($ per capita)	2000-2001 (%)
General Expenditures			
Airports	0	0	0.0
Corrections	0	0	0.0
Education	0	0	0.0
Fire Protection	19,157	165	11.4
Governmental Administration	30,995	267	18.4
Health	918	8	0.5
Highways	5,143	44	3.1
Hospitals	0	0	0.0
Housing and Community Development	3,668	32	2.2
Interest on General Debt	817	7	0.5
Libraries	0	0	0.0
Parking	2,044	18	1.2
Parks and Recreation	9,369	81	5.6
Police Protection	20,525	177	12.2
Public Welfare	0	0	0.0
Sewerage	11,590	100	6.9
Solid Waste Management	8,056	69	4.8
Liquor Store	0	0	0.0
Utility	48,083	414	28.5
Employee Retirement	0	0	0.0
Other	8,170	70	4.8

Source: U.S Census Bureau, Government Finances 2000-2001, August 2003

Municipal Bond Ratings

Area	Moody's
City	Aa2

Source: Mergent Bond Record, February 2004

DEMOGRAPHICS

Population Growth

Area	1990 Census	2000 Census	2003 Estimate	2008 Projection	Population Growth (%) 1990-2000	Population Growth (%) 2000-2008
City	115,475	116,278	115,539	114,575	0.7	-1.5
MSA[1]	453,181	536,691	553,888	583,847	18.4	8.8
U.S.	248,709,873	281,421,906	290,647,163	305,918,071	13.2	8.7

Note: (1) Metropolitan Statistical Area - see Appendix A for areas included
Source: Claritas, Inc.

Number of Households and Average Household Size

Area	1990 Census	2000 Census	2003 Estimate	2008 Projection	2003 Average Household Size
City	40,144	42,245	42,781	43,789	2.7
MSA[1]	163,167	203,341	213,375	231,271	2.6
U.S.	91,947,410	105,480,101	109,440,059	116,034,472	2.7

Note: (1) Metropolitan Statistical Area - see Appendix A for areas included
Source: Claritas, Inc.

Race and Ethnicity

Area	White Non-Hispanic	Black Non-Hispanic	Asian Non-Hispanic	Other Race Non-Hispanic	Hispanic
City	49.5	45.5	1.7	3.2	3.3
MSA[1]	63.7	32.1	1.5	2.7	2.6
U.S.	74.5	12.4	3.8	9.3	13.2

Note: Figures are 2003 estimates; (1) Metropolitan Statistical Area - see Appendix A for areas included
Source: Claritas, Inc.

Segregation

City Index[2]	City Rank[3]	MSA[1] Index[2]	MSA[1] Rank[4]
63.8	36	58.9	160

Note: Figures are based on an analysis of Census 2000 data; (1) Metropolitan Statistical Area - see Appendix A for areas included; (2) Dissimilarity Index—the most commonly used measure of segregation between two groups, reflecting their relative distributions across neighborhoods within a city or metropolitan area. It can range in value from 0, indicating complete integration, to 100, indicating complete segregation; (3) Ranges from 1 (most segregated) to 100 (least segregated) and includes all the cities in this book; (4) Ranges from 1 (most segregated) to 318 (least segregated) and includes 318 metropolitan areas.
Source: www.CensusScope.org

Ancestry

Area	German	Irish[2]	English	American	Italian	Polish	French[3]	Scottish
City	8.3	6.2	7.7	5.2	2.1	0.9	1.9	2.2
MSA[1]	11.2	7.7	8.5	10.7	2.1	1.0	1.8	2.0
U.S.	15.2	10.9	8.7	7.3	5.6	3.2	3.0	1.7

Note: Figures include multiple ancestry (e.g. if a person reported being Irish and Italian, they were included in both columns); (1) Metropolitan Statistical Area - see Appendix A for areas included; (2) Includes Celtic; (3) Includes Alsatian but excludes Basque
Source: Census 2000, Summary File 3

Foreign-Born Population

Area	Any Foreign Country	Percent of Population Born in: Europe	Asia	Africa	Oceania[2]	Canada	Mexico	Latin America[3]
City	4.1	0.9	1.5	0.2	0.0	0.2	0.6	0.7
MSA[1]	3.5	0.9	1.2	0.1	0.0	0.2	0.6	0.6
U.S.	11.1	1.7	2.9	0.3	0.1	0.3	3.3	2.5

Note: (1) Metropolitan Statistical Area - see Appendix A for areas included; (2) Includes Australia, New Zealand subregion, Melanesia, Micronesia, Polynesia, and Oceania n.e.c; (3) Includes Central America (excluding Mexico), South America, and the Caribbean.
Source: Census 2000, Summary File 3

Religion

Area	Catholic	Southern Baptist	United Meth-odist	ELCA[1]	LDS[2]	Presby-terian Church USA	Jewish Est.	Muslim Est.
County	4.0	13.5	7.0	2.7	0.3	3.1	0.9	0.4
U.S.	22.0	7.1	3.7	1.8	1.5	1.1	2.2	0.6

Note: Figures shown are the number of adherents as a percentage of the total population; Adherents are defined as all members, including full members, their children and the estimated number of other participants who are not considered members (e.g. the baptized, those not confirmed, those not eligible for communion, those regularly attending services, etc.); (1) Evangelical Lutheran Church in America; (2) The Church of Jesus Christ of Latter Day Saints
Source: Reprinted with permission from Religious Congregations and Membership in the United States 2000 (Nashville, Glenmary Research Center, 2002) Copyright Association of Statisticians of American Religious Bodies. All rights reserved.

Age Distribution

Area	Percent of Population						
	Under Age 5	Age 5 to 17	Age 18 to 34	Age 35 to 49	Age 50 to 64	Age 65 to 79	80 Years and Over
City	5.4	14.7	39.3	19.5	10.8	7.4	2.8
MSA[1]	6.5	18.5	26.5	24.2	14.5	7.6	2.3
U.S.	6.8	18.9	23.7	23.5	14.8	9.2	3.2

Note: (1) Metropolitan Statistical Area - see Appendix A for areas included
Source: Census 2000, Summary File 3

Marriage Status

Area	Never Married	Now Married Except Separated	Separated	Widowed	Divorced
City	41.6	40.5	3.3	6.5	8.2
MSA[1]	28.7	53.3	2.9	5.9	9.3
U.S.	27.1	54.4	2.2	6.6	9.7

Note: Figures cover population 15 years of age and older; (1) Metropolitan Statistical Area - see Appendix A for areas included
Source: Census 2000, Summary File 3

Male/Female Ratio

Area	Males	Females	Males per 100 Females
City	56,728	58,811	96.5
MSA[1]	267,919	285,969	93.7
U.S.	142,511,883	148,135,280	96.2

Note: Figures are 2003 estimates; (1) Metropolitan Statistical Area - see Appendix A for areas included
Source: Claritas, Inc.

ECONOMY

Gross Metropolitan Product

Area	1999	2000	2001	2002	2002 Rank[2]
MSA[1]	18.5	19.2	21.1	21.4	90

Note: Figures are in billions of dollars; (1) Metropolitan Statistical Area - see Appendix A for areas included; (2) Rank ranges from 1 to 319
Source: The U.S. Conference of Mayors, Metro Economies Report, July 2003

INCOME

Per Capita/Median/Average Income

Area	Per Capita ($)	Median Household ($)	Average Household ($)
City	21,306	34,829	53,702
MSA[1]	23,834	46,665	60,761
U.S.	24,078	46,868	63,207

Note: Figures are 2003 estimates; (1) Metropolitan Statistical Area - see Appendix A for areas included
Source: Claritas, Inc.

Household Income Distribution

Area	Percent of Households Earning							
	Under $15,000	$15,000 -24,999	$25,000 -34,999	$35,000 -49,999	$50,000 -74,999	$75,000 -99,000	$100,000 -149,999	$150,000 and up
City	22.6	14.6	13.0	15.9	14.7	7.2	6.5	5.6
MSA[1]	13.2	11.5	12.2	16.9	20.1	11.7	9.6	4.8
U.S.	14.1	11.5	11.7	16.0	19.2	11.3	10.2	6.0

Note: Figures are 2003 estimates; (1) Metropolitan Statistical Area - see Appendix A for areas included
Source: Claritas, Inc.

Poverty Rates by Age

Area	All Ages	Under 5 Years Old	5 to 17 Years Old	18 to 64 Years Old	65 Years and Over
City	22.1	2.1	4.9	13.0	2.0
MSA[1]	11.7	1.1	2.7	6.8	1.1
U.S.	12.4	1.2	3.0	6.9	1.2

Note: Figures are percent of population with income in 1999 below poverty level and only include population for whom poverty status is determined; (1) Metropolitan Statistical Area - see Appendix A for areas included
Source: Census 2000, Summary File 3

Personal Bankruptcy Filing Rate

Area	2002	2003
Richland County	4.44	4.85
U.S.	5.34	5.58

Note: Numbers are per 1,000 population and include Chapter 7 and Chapter 13 filings
Source: Federal Deposit Insurance Corporation (FDIC), Regional Economic Conditions (RECON), 2/25/2004

EMPLOYMENT

Labor Force and Employment

Area	Civilian Labor Force			Workers Employed		
	Dec. 2002	Dec. 2003	% Chg.	Dec. 2002	Dec. 2003	% Chg.
City	48,589	48,196	-0.8	46,060	45,461	-1.3
MSA[1]	283,060	280,004	-1.1	273,357	269,802	-1.3
U.S.	144,807,000	146,501,000	1.2	136,599,000	138,556,000	1.4

Note: Data is not seasonally adjusted and covers workers 16 years of age and older;
(1) Metropolitan Statistical Area - see Appendix A for areas included
Source: Bureau of Labor Statistics, http://stats.bls.gov

Unemployment Rate

Area	2003											
	Jan.	Feb.	Mar.	Apr.	May	Jun.	Jul.	Aug.	Sep.	Oct.	Nov.	Dec.
City	6.1	6.0	5.5	5.2	6.1	6.3	6.4	6.0	6.0	6.5	5.8	5.7
MSA[1]	3.9	3.9	3.4	3.4	3.9	4.1	4.2	3.9	3.9	4.2	3.8	3.6
U.S.	6.5	6.4	6.2	5.8	5.8	6.5	6.3	6.0	5.8	5.6	5.6	5.4

Note: Data is not seasonally adjusted and covers workers 16 years of age and older; All figures are percentages; (1) Metropolitan Statistical Area - see Appendix A for areas included
Source: Bureau of Labor Statistics, http://stats.bls.gov

Employment by Occupation

Occupation Classification	City (%)	MSA[1] (%)	U.S. (%)
Sales and Office	26.3	28.0	26.7
Professional and Related	28.2	22.6	20.2
Service	17.7	14.1	14.9
Production, Transportation, and Material Moving	8.8	11.2	14.6
Management, Business, and Financial	12.8	14.6	13.5
Construction, Extraction, and Maintenance	5.9	9.1	9.4
Farming, Forestry, and Fishing	0.3	0.3	0.7

Note: Figures cover employed civilians 16 years of age and older;
(1) Metropolitan Statistical Area - see Appendix A for areas included
Source: Census 2000, Summary File 3

Employment by Industry

Sector	MSA[1] Number of Employees	MSA[1] Percent of Total	U.S. Percent of Total
Government	73,700	24.5	16.7
Education and Health Services	33,500	11.1	12.9
Professional and Business Services	33,000	11.0	12.3
Retail Trade	35,800	11.9	11.8
Manufacturing	23,200	7.7	11.0
Leisure and Hospitality	26,800	8.9	9.1
Finance Activities	25,300	8.4	6.1
Construction	n/a	n/a	5.1
Wholesale Trade	11,600	3.9	4.3
Other Services	9,000	3.0	4.1
Transportation and Utilities	7,100	2.4	3.7
Information	5,600	1.9	2.4
Natural Resources and Mining	n/a	n/a	0.4

Note: Figures cover non-farm employment as of December 2003 and are not seasonally adjusted; (1) Metropolitan Statistical Area - see Appendix A for areas included; n/a not available
Source: Bureau of Labor Statistics, http://stats.bls.gov

Average Wages

Occupation	$/Hr.	Occupation	$/Hr.
Accountants and Auditors	19.47	Maids and Housekeeping Cleaners	7.52
Automotive Mechanics	16.29	Maintenance and Repair Workers	13.60
Bookkeepers	11.38	Marketing Managers	33.00
Carpenters	13.22	Nuclear Medicine Technologists	23.13
Cashiers	7.31	Nurses, Licensed Practical	14.83
Clerks, General Office	10.51	Nurses, Registered	22.17
Clerks, Receptionists/Information	10.64	Nursing Aides/Orderlies/Attendants	9.78
Clerks, Shipping/Receiving	11.28	Packers and Packagers, Hand	8.36
Computer Programmers	24.78	Physical Therapists	27.42
Computer Support Specialists	16.26	Postal Service Mail Carriers	n/a
Computer Systems Analysts	24.12	Real Estate Brokers	41.20
Cooks, Restaurant	8.28	Retail Salespersons	10.49
Dentists	60.17	Sales Reps., Exc. Tech./Scientific	22.23
Electrical Engineers	29.30	Sales Reps., Tech./Scientific	24.32
Electricians	17.49	Secretaries, Exc. Legal/Med./Exec.	11.36
Financial Managers	29.94	Security Guards	8.70
First-Line Supervisors/Mgrs., Sales	15.83	Surgeons	n/a
Food Preparation Workers	n/a	Teacher Assistants	7.50
General and Operations Managers	31.84	Teachers, Elementary School	17.30
Hairdressers/Cosmetologists	10.17	Teachers, Secondary School	19.20
Internists	64.24	Telemarketers	n/a
Janitors and Cleaners	7.84	Truck Drivers, Heavy/Tractor-Trailer	16.57
Landscaping/Groundskeeping Workers	9.35	Truck Drivers, Light/Delivery Svcs.	12.10
Lawyers	40.87	Waiters and Waitresses	6.91

Note: Wage data is for 2002 and covers the Metropolitan Statistical Area (see Appendix A for areas included). Hourly wages for elementary/secondary school teachers and teacher assistants were calculated by the editors from annual wage data assuming a 40 hour work week; n/a not available.
Source: Bureau of Labor Statistics, 2002 Metro Area Occupational Employment and Wage Estimates

Occupational Employment Projections: 1996 - 2006

Occupations Expected to Have the Largest Job Growth (ranked by numerical growth)	Fast-Growing Occupations[1] (ranked by percent growth)
1. Cashiers	1. Desktop publishers
2. Salespersons, retail	2. Database administrators
3. General managers & top executives	3. Computer engineers
4. Marketing & sales, supervisors	4. Paralegals
5. Food preparation workers	5. Systems analysts
6. Truck drivers, light	6. Personal and home care aides
7. Cooks, fast food and short order	7. Medical assistants
8. Food service workers	8. Physical therapy assistants and aides
9. Waiters & waitresses	9. Respiratory therapists
10. Food service and lodging managers	10. Data processing equipment repairers

Note: Projections cover South Carolina; (1) Excludes occupations with total job growth less than 300
Source: U.S. Department of Labor, Employment and Training Administration, America's Labor Market Information System (ALMIS)

TAXES

State Corporate Income Tax Rates

State	Rate (%)	Number of Brackets	Low Bracket (Under $)	High Bracket (Over $)
South Carolina	5.0	1	na	na

Note: Tax rates as of December 31, 2003; na not applicable; 4.5% for banks; 6% for savings and loans.
Source: Tax Foundation, www.taxfoundation.org

State Individual Income Tax Rates

State	Federal Deductibility	Marginal Rate (%)	Number of Brackets	Low Bracket (Under $)	High Bracket (Over $)
South Carolina	No	2.5-7.0	6	0	12,000

Note: Tax rates as of December 31, 2003; Brackets apply to single taxpayers and married people filing separately; na not applicable
Source: Tax Foundation, www.taxfoundation.org

Various State and Local Tax Rates

State Sales and Use (%)	Total Sales and Use (%)	Gasoline (cents/gal.)	Cigarette (cents/pack)	Spirits ($/gal.)	Table Wine ($/gal.)	Beer ($/gal.)
5.0	5.0	16	7	2.72	1.08 (d)	0.77

Note: Tax rates as of December 31, 2003.(d) South Carolina's rate of $1.08 includes 18 cents additional tax.
Source: Tax Foundation, www.taxfoundation.org

State Tax Burdens

Area	Combined State and Local Tax Burden		Combined Federal, State and Local Tax Burden	
	Percent	Rank	Percent	Rank
South Carolina	9.0	39	27.1	42
U.S. Average	9.7	-	30.0	-

Note: Figures are for 2003
Source: Tax Foundation, www.taxfoundation.org

Internal Revenue Service Tax Audits

IRS District	Percent of Returns Audited				
	1996	1997	1998	1999	2000
North-South Carolina	0.48	0.34	0.28	0.21	0.16
U.S.	0.66	0.61	0.46	0.31	0.20

Note: Figures cover IRS district audits of federal income tax returns filed by individuals. Geographic data on district audits for 2001 and 2002 are being withheld by the IRS. TRAC is challenging this policy.
Source: Syracuse University, Transactional Records Access Clearinghouse (TRAC), "Odds of IRS District Tax Audit 2000"

**RESIDENTIAL
REAL ESTATE**

Building Permits

Area	Single-Family			Multi-Family			Total		
	2001	2002	Pct. Chg.	2001	2002	Pct. Chg.	2001	2002	Pct. Chg.
City	443	398	-10.2	0	258	-	443	656	48.1
U.S.	1,235,600	1,332,600	7.9	401,100	415,100	3.5	1,636,700	1,747,700	6.8

Note: Figures represent new, privately-owned housing units authorized (unadjusted data)
Source: U.S. Census Bureau, Manufacturing, Mining, and Construction Statistics

Homeownership and Housing Vacancies

Area	Homeownership Rate[2] (%)			Rental Vacancy Rate[3] (%)			Homeowner Vacancy Rate[4] (%)		
	2001	2002[a]	2003	2001	2002[a]	2003	2001	2002[a]	2003
MSA[1]	n/a	n/a	n/a	n/a	n/a	n/a	n/a	n/a	n/a
U.S.	67.8	67.9	68.3	8.4	8.9	9.8	1.8	1.7	1.8

Note: (1) Metropolitan Statistical Area - see Appendix A for areas included; (2) The proportion of households that are owners; (3) The proportion of the rental inventory that is vacant for rent; (4) The proportion of the homeowner inventory that is vacant for sale; (a) 2002 figures have been revised; n/a not available
Source: U.S. Census Bureau, Housing Vacancies and Homeownership Annual Statistics: 2003

**COMMERCIAL
REAL ESTATE**

Industrial/Office Markets

Type/Market Area	Inventory (sq. ft.)	Vacant (sq. ft.)	Vacancy Rate (%)	Under Construction (sq. ft.)	Net Absorption (sq. ft.)
Industrial Space					
Columbia	30,309,814	4,646,493	15.33	0	-542,544
Office Space					
Columbia	5,400,009	749,227	13.87	360,000	120,781

Note: Data as of 4th Quarter, 2003; n/a not available
Source: Society of Industrial and Office Realtors, 2004 Comparative Statistics of Industrial and Office Real Estate Markets

**COMMERCIAL
UTILITIES**

Typical Monthly Electric Bills

Area	Commercial Service ($/month)		Industrial Service ($/month)	
	3 kW demand 1,000 kWh	40 kW demand 14,000 kWh	1,000 kW demand 200,000 kWh	50,000 kW demand 15,000,000 kWh
City	n/a	n/a	n/a	n/a
Average[1]	100	1,134	17,850	1,045,117

Note: Based on rates in effect July 1, 2003; (1) average based on 197 utilities; n/a not available
Source: Edison Electric Institute, Typical Bills and Average Rates Report, Summer 2003

TRANSPORTATION

Means of Transportation to Work

Area	Car/Truck/Van		Public Transportation			Bicycle	Walked	Other Means	Worked at Home
	Drove Alone	Car-pooled	Bus	Subway	Railroad				
City	65.4	11.3	3.7	0.0	0.0	0.4	13.4	3.1	2.7
MSA[1]	79.3	11.9	1.1	0.0	0.0	0.1	3.7	1.3	2.5
U.S.	75.7	12.2	2.5	1.5	0.5	0.4	2.9	1.0	3.3

Note: Figures shown are percentages and cover workers 16 years of age and older;
(1) Metropolitan Statistical Area - see Appendix A for areas included
Source: Census 2000, Summary File 3

Travel Time to Work

Area	Less Than 15 Minutes	15 to 29 Minutes	30 to 44 Minutes	45 to 59 Minutes	60 Minutes or More
City	45.1	39.6	9.8	2.0	3.5
MSA[1]	27.7	42.5	20.2	5.0	4.6
U.S.	29.4	36.1	19.1	7.4	8.0

Note: Figures are percentages and include workers 16 years old and over; (1) Metropolitan Statistical Area - see Appendix A for areas included
Source: Census 2000, Summary File 3

Transportation Statistics

Interstate highways (2004)	I-20; I-26; I-77
Public transportation (2002)	South Carolina Electric & Gas Company-Columbia (SCE&G Transit)
Buses	
Average fleet age in years	21.7
No. operated in max. service	34
Demand response	
Average fleet age in years	2.4
No. operated in max. service	11
Passenger air service	
Airport	Columbia Metropolitan
Airlines (2003)	5
Boardings (2002)	513,307
Amtrak service (2004)	Yes
Major waterways/ports	Congaree River

Source: Federal Transit Administration, National Transit Database, 2002; Editor & Publisher Market Guide, 2004; Bureau of Transportation Statistics, Airport Enplanement Activity for CY2002; www.amtrak.com

BUSINESSES

Major Business Headquarters

Company Name	2003 Rankings Fortune 500	Forbes 500
SCANA	499	-

Note: Companies listed are located in the city; dashes indicate no ranking
Fortune 500: Companies that produce a 10-K are ranked 1 to 500 based on 2002 revenue
Forbes 500: Private companies are ranked 1 to 281 based on 2002 revenue
Source: Fortune, April 14, 2003; www.forbes.com, November 6, 2003

Minority and Women-Owned Businesses

Ownership	All Firms Firms	Sales ($000)	Firms with Paid Employees Firms	Sales ($000)	Employees	Payroll ($000)
Black	1,484	140,150	242	113,218	1,397	22,408
Hispanic	n/a	n/a	n/a	n/a	n/a	n/a
Women	2,547	399,305	523	342,319	3,806	69,552

Note: Figures cover firms located in the city; n/a not available
Source: 1997 Economic Census, Minority and Women-Owned Businesses

HOTELS

Hotels/Motels

Area	Hotels/Motels	Tourist	First-Class	Deluxe
City	78	54	93	n/a

Note: n/a not available
Source: OAG Travel Planner Online, Spring 2004

EVENT SITES

Major Event Sites, Meeting Places and Convention Centers

Name	Guest Rooms	Exhibit/ Meeting Space (sq. ft.)	Largest Meeting Room Capacity
Adam's Mark Columbia	301	26,000	700
Carolina Coliseum	n/a	n/a	72,000
Embassy Suites Columbia	214	15,000	1,000
Sheraton Columbia Hotel	237	20,000	1,300
William-Brice Stadium	n/a	n/a	72,400

Note: n/a not available
Source: Original research

Living Environment

COST OF LIVING

Cost of Living Index

Year	Composite Index	Groceries	Housing	Utilities	Trans-portation	Health Care	Misc. Goods/ Services
2001	94.2	100.2	90.5	104.1	86.9	92.1	94.5
2002	95.3	98.7	91.6	110.6	86.9	92.9	96.1
2003	96.1	97.4	90.3	110.3	92.0	97.2	97.3

Note: U.S. = 100
Source: ACCRA, Cost of Living Index, 2001, 2002 and 2003 4-Quarter Averages

HOUSING

House Price Index (HPI)

Area	National Ranking[2]	Quarterly Change (%)	One-Year Change (%)	Five-Year Change (%)
MSA[1]	157	1.90	4.26	23.67
U.S.[3]	-	3.67	7.97	41.81

Note: The HPI is a weighted repeat sales index. It measures average price changes in repeat sales or refinancings on the same properties. This information is obtained by reviewing repeat mortgage transactions on single-family properties whose mortgages have been purchased or securitized by Fannie Mae of Freddie Mac in January 1975; (1) Metropolitan Statistical Area - see Appendix A for areas included; (2) Rankings are based on annual percentage change, for all MSAs containing at least 15,000 transactions over the last 10 years and ranges from 1 to 220; (3) figures based on a weighted division average; all figures are for the period ended December 31, 2003
Source: Office of Federal Housing Enterprise Oversight, House Price Index, March 1, 2004

Housing: Year Structure Built

Area	1990 -2000	1980 -1989	1970 -1979	1960 -1969	1950 -1959	1940 -1949	Before 1940	Median Year
City	13.5	10.5	15.1	18.3	19.3	11.0	12.3	1964
MSA[1]	24.8	20.1	22.1	14.4	9.9	4.2	4.6	1978
U.S.	17.0	15.8	18.5	13.7	12.7	7.3	15.0	1971

Note: Figures are percentages; (1) Metropolitan Statistical Area - see Appendix A for areas included
Source: Census 2000, Summary File 3

Average New Home Price

Area	2001	2002	2003
City	191,497	211,177	217,136
U.S.	212,643	236,567	248,193

Note: Figures, in dollars, are based on a new home with 2,400 sq. ft. of living area on an 8,000 sq. ft. lot.
Source: ACCRA, Cost of Living Index, 2001, 2002 and 2003 4-Quarter Averages

Average Apartment Rent

Area	2001	2002	2003
City	662	721	752
U.S.	674	708	721

Note: Figures, in dollars per month, are based on an unfurnished two bedroom, 1-1/2 or 2 bath apartment, approximately 950 sq. ft. in size, excluding all utilities except water
Source: ACCRA, Cost of Living Index, 2001, 2002 and 2003 4-Quarter Averages

RESIDENTIAL UTILITIES

Average Residential Utility Costs

Area	All Electric ($/mth)	Part Electric ($/mth)	Other Energy ($/mth)	Phone ($/mth)
City	146.19	–	–	24.03
U.S.	116.46	65.82	62.68	23.90

Source: ACCRA, Cost of Living Index, 2003 4-Quarter Average

HEALTH CARE

Average Health Care Costs

Area	Hospital ($/day)	Doctor ($/visit)	Dentist ($/visit)
City	445.44	67.50	87.50
U.S.	678.35	67.91	83.90

Note: Hospital—based on a semi-private room; Doctor—based on a general practitioner's routine exam of an established patient; Dentist—based on adult teeth cleaning and periodic oral exam.
Source: ACCRA, Cost of Living Index, 2003 4-Quarter Average

Distribution of Non-Federal, Office-Based Physicians

Area	Total	Family/ General Practice	Specialties		
			Medical	Surgical	Other
MSA[1] (number)	1,167	163	349	296	359
MSA[1] (rate per 10,000 pop.)	21.7	3.0	6.5	5.5	6.7
Metro Average[2] (rate per 10,000 pop.)	33.1	2.2	7.7	4.8	5.6

Note: Data as of December 31, 2001; (1) Metropolitan Statistical Area - see Appendix A for areas included; (2) Average of 81 MSAs and CMSAs in this book
Source: American Medical Association, Physician Characteristics & Distribution in the U.S., 2003-2004

Hospitals

Columbia has the following hospitals: 4 general medical and surgical; 2 psychiatric; 1 rehabilitation; 1 other specialty.
AHA Guide to the Healthcare Field, 2003-2004

PRESIDENTIAL ELECTION

2000 Presidential Election Results

Area	Gore	Bush	Nader	Buchanan	Other
Richland County	54.3	43.1	1.9	0.1	0.5
U.S.	48.4	47.9	2.7	0.4	0.6

Note: Results are percentages and may not add to 100% due to rounding
Source: www.cbsnews.com; www.uselectionatlas.org

EDUCATION

Public School District Statistics

District Name	Schls.	Enroll-ment	Classroom Teachers	Pupil/ Teacher Ratio	Minority Pupils[1] (%)	Current Expend.[2] ($/pupil)
Fort Jackson District	3	983	72	13.7	n/a	n/a
Juvenile Justice	4	n/a	107	n/a	n/a	n/a
Palmetto Unified SD	16	n/a	43	n/a	n/a	n/a
Richland County SD 01	48	26,408	2,090	12.6	n/a	7,277
Richland County SD 02	21	18,213	1,230	14.8	n/a	6,389

Note: Data covers the 2001-02 school year unless otherwise noted; (1) Fall 2000; (2) FY2000; n/a not available
Source: U.S. Department of Education, National Center for Education Statistics, Common Core of Data, Local Education Agency (School District) Universe Survey: School Year 2001-2002; U.S. Department of Education, National Center for Education Statistics, Digest of Education Statistics 2002

Educational Quality

School District	Education Quotient[1]	Graduate Outcome[2]	Community Index[3]	Resource Index[4]
Richland School District 01	25	19	39	72

Note: Scores are national percentile rankings and range from 1 (worst) to 99 (best); (1) Combination of the Graduate Outcome, Community and Resource indexes weighted to reflect the greater importance of the Graduate Outcome and Resource Index; (2) Based on graduation rates and college board scores (SAT/ACT); (3) Based on the surrounding community's level of affluence and adult education; (4) Based on teacher salaries, per-pupil expenditures and student-teacher ratios.
Source: Expansion Management, December 2003

Educational Attainment by Race

Area	High School Graduate (%)					Bachelor's Degree (%)				
	Total	White	Black	Asian	Hisp.[2]	Total	White	Black	Asian	Hisp.[2]
City	82.3	91.5	70.5	96.6	77.9	35.7	52.8	13.9	63.6	25.2
MSA[1]	84.3	87.6	77.2	84.6	70.2	29.2	34.1	17.3	50.7	21.1
U.S.	80.4	83.6	72.3	80.4	52.4	24.4	26.1	14.3	44.1	10.4

Note: Figures shown cover persons 25 years old and over; (1) Metropolitan Statistical Area - see Appendix A for areas included; (2) people of Hispanic origin can be of any race
Source: Census 2000, Summary File 3

School Enrollment by Type

Area	Grades KG to 8				Grades 9 to 12			
	Public		Private		Public		Private	
	Enrollment	%	Enrollment	%	Enrollment	%	Enrollment	%
City	10,338	87.7	1,454	12.3	4,994	87.1	741	12.9
MSA[1]	64,099	91.7	5,837	8.3	28,539	92.5	2,319	7.5
U.S.	33,526,011	88.7	4,285,121	11.3	14,848,628	90.6	1,532,323	9.4

Note: Figures shown cover persons 3 years old and over; (1) Metropolitan Statistical Area - see Appendix A for areas included
Source: Census 2000, Summary File 3

School Enrollment by Race

Area	Grades KG to 8 (%)				Grades 9 to 12 (%)			
	White	Black	Asian	Hisp.[1]	White	Black	Asian	Hisp.[1]
City	30.5	64.3	0.9	2.7	30.6	65.9	0.6	2.7
MSA[2]	56.0	40.0	1.0	2.7	54.2	41.6	1.4	2.2
U.S.	68.5	15.5	3.3	16.8	68.8	15.5	3.8	15.7

Note: Figures shown cover persons 3 years old and over; (1) people of Hispanic origin can be of any race; (2) Metropolitan Statistical Area - see Appendix A for areas included
Source: Census 2000, Summary File 3

Classroom Teacher Salaries in Public Schools

District	B.A. Degree		M.A. Degree		Maximum	
	Min. ($)	Rank[1]	Max. ($)	Rank[1]	Max. ($)	Rank[1]
City	n/a	n/a	n/a	n/a	n/a	n/a
DOD Average[2]	31,567	-	53,248	-	59,356	-

Note: Salaries are for 2001-2002; (1) Rank ranges from 1 to 100; (2) As per the U.S. Department of Defense Wage Fixing Authority
Source: American Federation of Teachers, Survey & Analysis of Teacher Salary Trends 2002

Higher Education

Four-Year Colleges			Two-Year Colleges			Medical Schools	Law Schools	Voc/ Tech
Public	Private Non-profit	Private For-profit	Public	Private Non-profit	Private For-profit			
1	6	0	1	0	1	1	1	4

Note: Figures cover institutions located within the city limits.
Source: National Center for Education Statistics, The Integrated Postsecondary Education System (IPEDS) Peer Analysis System, 2002; usnews.com, America's Best Graduate Schools 2004, Medical School Directory; The College Blue Book, Occupational Education, 2003; Barron's Guide to Law Schools, 2003; Medical School Admission Requirements U.S. & Canada, 2003-2004

MAJOR EMPLOYERS

Major Employers

Company Name	Industry	Type
Air National Guard	Executive offices	Branch
APAC Customer Services Inc	Business services, nec	Branch
BLUE CROSS	Hospital and medical service plans	Headquarters
CBS	Television broadcasting stations	Branch
County of Richland	Executive offices	Headquarters
Department Transporation SC	Highway and street construction	Headquarters
Health and Envmtl Ctrl Dept	Administration of public health programs	Headquarters
Lexington County Hlth Svc Dst	General medical and surgical hospitals	Headquarters
Mental Health Department SC	Administration of public health programs	Branch
NCR	Calculating and accounting equipment	Branch
Signum LLC	Help supply services	Single
Solectron Corporation	Printed circuit boards	Headquarters
South Carolina Dept Trnsp	Regulation, administration of transportation	Branch
South Carolina Elec & Gas Co	Electric services	Headquarters
Transportation Department SC	Regulation, administration of transportation	Headquarters
University of South Carolina	Colleges and universities	Headquarters
US Army Training Center	National security	Branch
William Jennings Bryan Dorn	Administration of veterans' affairs	Branch

Note: Companies shown are located in the metropolitan area and have 1,000 or more employees.
Source: www.zapdata.com, March 2004

PUBLIC SAFETY

Crime Rate

Area	All Crimes	Violent Crimes				Property Crimes		
		Murder	Forcible Rape	Robbery	Aggrav. Assault	Burglary	Larceny -Theft	Motor Vehicle Theft
City	8,658.7	8.4	69.7	417.5	797.2	1,376.9	5,219.4	769.5
Suburbs[1]	5,212.5	7.2	43.9	153.1	560.2	1,068.8	2,929.0	450.3
MSA[2]	5,959.2	7.5	49.5	210.4	611.6	1,135.6	3,425.2	519.5
U.S.	4,118.8	5.6	33.0	145.9	310.1	746.2	2,445.8	432.1

Note: Figures are crimes per 100,000 population; (1) All areas within the MSA that are located outside the city limits; (2) Metropolitan Statistical Area - see Appendix A for areas included
Source: FBI Uniform Crime Reports, 2002

RECREATION

Culture and Recreation

Museums	Orchestras	Opera Companies	Dance Companies	Professional Theatres	Zoos	Pro Sports Teams[1]
8	0	0	2	1	1	0

Note: (1) Covers the Metropolitan Statistical Area - see Appendix A for areas included.
Source: The Grey House Performing Arts Directory, 2002; Official Museum Directory, 2004; www.sportsvenues.com

Library System

The Richland County Public Library has nine branches, holdings of 1,059,806 volumes, and a budget of $12,813,651 (2000-2001).
American Library Directory, 2003-2004

MEDIA

Newspapers

Name	Type	Freq.	Distribution	Circulation
Carolina Panorama	General	1x/wk	n/a	16,000
Charleston Black Times	Black	1x/wk	Local	11,261
Columbia Black News	Black	1x/wk	Local	30,536
The Columbia Star	General	1x/wk	Local	10,000
Florence Black Sun	Black	1x/wk	Local	6,792
Greenville Black Star	Black	1x/wk	Local	9,381
Orangeburg Black Voice	Black	1x/wk	Local	7,596
Point	Alternative	1x/mth	Local	20,000
Rock Hill Black Views	Black/Gen	1x/wk	Local	5,266
The State	General	7x/wk	State	120,458
Sumter Black Post	Black	1x/wk	Local	6,146

Note: Includes newspapers whose offices are located in the city and whose circulations are 500 or more; n/a not available
Source: Burrelle's Media Directory, 2003

Television Stations

Name	Ch.	Affiliation	Type	Owner
WITV	7	PBS	Public	South Carolina Educational Television Commission
WIS	10	NBCT	Commercial	Cosmos Broadcasting Corporation
WEBA	14	PBS	Public	South Carolina Educational Television Commission
WJWJ	16	PBS	Public	South Carolina Educational Television Commission
WLTX	19	CBST	Commercial	Gannett Broadcasting
WJPM	21	PBS	Public	South Carolina Educational Television Commission
WRJA	21	PBS	Public	South Carolina Educational Television Commission
WHMC	23	PBS	Public	South Carolina Educational Television Commission
WOLO	25	ABCT	Commercial	Bahakel Communications Inc.
WNTV	29	PBS	Public	South Carolina Educational Television Commission
WRLK	35	PBS	Public	South Carolina Educational Television Commission
WNEH	38	PBS	Public	South Carolina Educational Television Commission
WACH	57	FBC	Commercial	Raycom Media Inc.

Note: Stations included broadcast from the Columbia metro area; n/a not available
Source: Burrelle's Media Directory, 2003

AM Radio Stations

Call Letters	Freq. (kHz)	Target Audience	Station Format	Music Format
WVOC	560	General	N/S/T	n/a
WOIC	1230	General	S/T	n/a
WISW	1320	General	N/T	n/a
WCOS	1400	General	S/T	n/a
WQXL	1470	Religious	M/N/S/T	Christian

Note: Stations included broadcast from the Columbia metro area; n/a not available
The following abbreviations may be used:
Target Audience: A=Asian; B=Black; C=Christian; E=Ethnic; F=French; G=General; H=Hispanic; M=Men; N=Native American; R=Religious; S=Senior Citizen; W=Women; Y=Young Adult; Z=Children
Station Format: E=Educational; M=Music; N=News; S=Sports; T=Talk
Source: Burrelle's Media Directory, 2003

FM Radio Stations

Call Letters	Freq. (mHz)	Target Audience	Station Format	Music Format
WJWJ	81.9	General	E/M/N	Jazz
WRJA	88.1	General	N	n/a
WNSC	88.9	General	M	Jazz
WLJK	89.1	General	M/N	Classical
WSCI	89.3	General	E/M	Classical
WMHK	89.7	Religious	E/M/N/S	Adult Contemporary
WEPR	90.1	General	M/N/S	Classical
WHMC	90.1	General	M/N	Big Band
WUSC	90.5	General	M/N/T	Alternative
WLTR	91.3	General	M/N	Classical
WZMJ	93.1	General	M/N/T	Oldies
WARQ	93.5	General	M	Alternative
WQKI	93.9	B/G	M/N/S	Urban Contemporary
WLTY	96.7	General	M/N	Soft Rock
WCOS	97.5	General	M/N/T	Country
WSCQ	100.1	General	M/N/T	Oldies
WWDM	101.3	General	M	Urban Contemporary
WMFX	102.3	G/M	M	AOR
WOMG	103.1	General	M	Oldies
WHXT	103.9	Black	M	Urban Contemporary
WNOK	104.7	General	M	Adult Top 40
WTCB	106.7	General	M/N/T	Adult Contemporary

Note: Stations included broadcast from the Columbia metro area; n/a not available
The following abbreviations may be used:
Target Audience: A=Asian; B=Black; C=Christian; E=Ethnic; F=French; G=General; H=Hispanic;
M=Men; N=Native American; R=Religious; S=Senior Citizen; W=Women; Y=Young Adult; Z=Children
Station Format: E=Educational; M=Music; N=News; S=Sports; T=Talk
Music Format: AOR=Album Oriented Rock; MOR=Middle of the Road
Source: Burrelle's Media Directory, 2003

CLIMATE

Average and Extreme Temperatures

Temperature	Jan	Feb	Mar	Apr	May	Jun	Jul	Aug	Sep	Oct	Nov	Dec	Yr.
Extreme High (°F)	84	84	91	94	101	107	107	107	101	101	90	83	107
Average High (°F)	56	60	67	77	84	90	92	91	85	77	67	59	75
Average Temp. (°F)	45	48	55	64	72	78	82	80	75	64	54	47	64
Average Low (°F)	33	35	42	50	59	66	70	69	64	51	41	35	51
Extreme Low (°F)	-1	5	4	26	34	44	54	53	40	23	12	4	-1

Note: Figures cover the years 1948-1990
Source: National Climatic Data Center, International Station Meteorological Climate Summary, 9/96

Average Precipitation/Snowfall/Humidity

Precip./Humidity	Jan	Feb	Mar	Apr	May	Jun	Jul	Aug	Sep	Oct	Nov	Dec	Yr.
Avg. Precip. (in.)	4.0	4.0	4.7	3.4	3.6	4.2	5.5	5.9	4.0	2.9	2.7	3.4	48.3
Avg. Snowfall (in.)	1	1	Tr	0	0	0	0	0	0	0	Tr	Tr	2
Avg. Rel. Hum. 7am (%)	83	83	84	82	84	85	88	91	91	90	88	84	86
Avg. Rel. Hum. 4pm (%)	51	47	44	41	46	50	54	56	54	49	48	51	49

Note: Figures cover the years 1948-1990; Tr = Trace amounts (<0.05 in. of rain; <0.5 in. of snow)
Source: National Climatic Data Center, International Station Meteorological Climate Summary, 9/96

Weather Conditions

Temperature			Daytime Sky			Precipitation		
10°F & below	32°F & below	90°F & above	Clear	Partly cloudy	Cloudy	0.01 inch or more precip.	0.1 inch or more snow/ice	Thunder-storms
< 1	58	77	97	149	119	110	1	53

Note: Figures are average number of days per year and covers the years 1948-1990
Source: National Climatic Data Center, International Station Meteorological Climate Summary, 9/96

**HAZARDOUS
WASTE**

Superfund Sites

Columbia has one hazardous waste site on the EPA's Superfund National Priorities List: **Scrdi Bluff Road**. *U.S. Environmental Protection Agency, National Priorities List, March 15, 2004*

**AIR & WATER
QUALITY**

Maximum Pollutant Concentrations

	Particulate Matter (ug/m³)	Carbon Monoxide (ppm)	Sulfur Dioxide (ppm)	Nitrogen Dioxide (ppm)	Ozone 1-hour (ppm)	Ozone 8-hour (ppm)	Lead (ug/m³)
MSA[1] Level	111	3	0.018	0.012	0.12	0.09	0.01
NAAQS[2]	150	9	0.140	0.053	0.12	0.08	1.50
Met NAAQS[2]	Yes	Yes	Yes	Yes	Yes	No	Yes

Note: (1) Metropolitan Statistical Area - see Appendix A for areas included; (2) National Ambient Air Quality Standards; n/a not available
Units: ppm = parts per million; ug/m³ = micrograms per cubic meter
Source: EPA, Latest Findings on National Air Quality: 2002 Status and Trends, August 2003

Air Quality Index

Data not available.

Watershed Health

The U.S. Environmental Protection Agency monitors the health of the aquatic resources for the nation's 2,000+ watersheds. **The Congaree watershed serves the Columbia area and received an overall Index of Watershed Indicators (IWI) score of 3 (less serious problems - low vulnerability).** The IWI score is based on seven condition and nine vulnerability indicators. The overall IWI score ranges from 1 (best health) to 6 (worst health). The Condition Indicators include: designated use attainment, fish and wildlife consumption advisories, source water condition, contaminated sediments, ambient water quality, and wetlands loss index. The Vulnerability Indicators include: aquatic species at risk, conventional and toxic loads over permitted limits, urban and agricultural runoff potential, population change, hydrologic modification, estuarine pollution susceptibility, and air deposition. *EPA, Index of Watershed Indicators, October 26, 2001*

Drinking Water

Water System Name	Pop. Served	Primary Water Source Type	Number of Violations January 2002-February 2004		
			Health Based	Significant Monitoring	Monitoring
City of Columbia	223,660	Surface	None	None	None

Note: Data as of February 19, 2004
Source: EPA, Office of Ground Water and Drinking Water, Safe Drinking Water Information System

Columbia tap water is alkaline, very soft and fluoridated.
Editor & Publisher Market Guide, 2004

Dallas, Texas

Background

Dallas is one of those cities that offers everything. Founded in 1841 by Tennessee lawyer and trader, John Neely Bryan, Dallas has come to symbolize in modern times all that is big, exciting, and affluent.

Originally one of the largest markets for cotton in the U.S., Dallas moved on to become one of the largest markets for oil in the country. In the 1930s, oil was struck on the eastern fields of Texas. As a result, oil companies were founded and millionaires were made. The face we now associate with Dallas and the state of Texas had emerged.

Today, oil still plays a dominant role in the Dallas economy. Outside of Alaska, Texas holds most of the U.S. oil reserves. For that reason, many oil companies choose to headquarter in the silver skyscrapers of Dallas.

In addition to employment opportunities in the oil industry, the Dallas branch of the Federal Reserve Bank, and a host of other banks and investment firms clustering around the Federal Reserve hub employ thousands. Other opportunities are offered in the aircraft, advertising, motion picture, and publishing industries.

The North Central Texas Council of Governments reports the following as the major employers in the Dallas area for 2003: American Airlines (Dallas-Fort Worth Airport); Lockheed Martin (in nearby Fort Worth); University of North Texas in Denton; Parkland Memorial Hospital; and Baylor University Medical center.

Also early in 2004, Vought Aircraft Industries unrolled plans to consolidate its manufacturing operations at its Dallas location, which is estimated to nearly double its local workforce by adding employees to its existing 3,200 by 2009.

The Dallas Convention Center, with more than two million square feet of space, is the largest convention center in Texas with more than 1 million square feet of exhibit area, including nearly 800,000 square feet of same level, contiguous prime exhibit space. More than 3.8 million people attended more than 3,600 conventions in Dallas in 2002.

Dallas also offers a busy cultural calendar. A host of independent theater groups is sponsored by Southern Methodist University. The Museum of Fine Arts houses an excellent collection of modern art, especially American paintings, and the Dallas Opera has showcased Maria Callas, Joan Sutherland, and Monserrat Caballe. The city also contains many historical districts such as the Swiss Avenue District, and elegant buildings such as the City Hall Building designed by I.M. Pei.

Colleges and universities in the Dallas area include: Southern Methodist University, University of North Texas, University of Dallas, and University of Texas at Dallas.

The climate of Dallas is generally temperate. Occasional periods of extreme cold are short-lived, and extremely high temperatures that sometimes occur in summer usually do not last for extended periods.

Rankings

- Dallas was ranked #95 out of 331 metro areas in *Cities Ranked & Rated*. Criteria: cost of living; climate; crime; transportation; economy and jobs; education; arts and culture; health and healthcare; leisure. *Cities Ranked & Rated, 1st Edition, 2004*

- *Ladies Home Journal* ranked America's 200 largest cities based on the qualities women surveyed care about most. Dallas ranked #44 out of 57 in the big city category (population over 300,000). Criteria: crime; lifestyle; education; jobs; health; child care; politics; and the economy. *Ladies Home Journal Online, "The Best Cities for Women 2002"*

- Dallas was selected as one of "America's Pet Healthiest Cities" by Purina. The city ranked #36 out of 50. Criteria: veterinary services; environment; and legislation. *Purina Pet Institute, "America's Pet Healthiest Cities," August 14, 2001*

- Dallas was selected as one of the "Best Cities for Black Families." The city ranked #11 out of 20. For six months, bet.com compiled data on African Americans in those U.S. cities with the largest Black populations. The data, for African Americans specifically, involved the following: infant mortality; high school graduation; median income; homeownership; unemployment; business ownership; poverty rates; AIDS infection rates; percentage of children in single parent, typically fatherless, households; teen pregnancy; economic segregation index; violent and property crime. *www.bet.com, October 1, 2002*

- Dallas appeared on *Black Enterprise's* list of the "Top Ten Cities for African-Americans to Live, Work, and Play." The city was ranked #8, based on responses from 4,239 online survey respondents who ranked 21 quality-of-life factors. *Black Enterprise, July 2001*

- *Forbes* ranked the 40 most populous metro areas in the U.S. in terms of the best places to be single. The Dallas metro area was ranked #10. Criteria: number of other singles; cost of living alone; nightlife; culture; job growth; coolness. *Forbes, June 5, 2003*

- *Forbes* ranked the 150 most populous metro areas in the U.S. in terms of the "Best Places for Business and Careers." The Dallas metro area was ranked #9. Criteria: income and job growth; cost-of-doing-business; qualifications of the available pool of labor; crime rates; housing costs; net migration. *Forbes, May 9, 2003*

- Dallas was selected as one of "America's Healthiest Cities" by *Natural Health* magazine. The city was ranked #26 out of the 50 largest urban areas in the U.S. Twenty-six criteria in the following four categories were examined: whether the city boasts natural offerings; how well the city promotes its resident's physical health; whether the city offers a healthy environment; how well the city fosters a sense of community. *Natural Health, April 2003*

- *Men's Health* ranked 101 U.S. cities in terms of the quality of their tap water. Dallas received a grade of B. Criteria: levels of bacteria, arsenic, lead, trihalomethanes, and haloacetic acids were compared with the National Academy of Science's guidelines as well as with the EPA's more stringent maximum contaminant level goals. *Men's Health, March 2004*

- Sperling's BestPlaces ranked 331 metro areas and identified the most and least stressful U.S. cities. The Dallas metro area ranked #10 out of the 100 largest metro areas (#1 = most stressful). Criteria: divorce rate; unemployment rate; violent and property crime; suicide rate; commute time; mental health; alcohol consumption; cloudy days. *www.BestPlaces.net, February 26, 2004*

- Sperling's BestPlaces in partnership with Pep Boys ranked 77 metro areas and identified "America's Most Drivable Cities." The Dallas metro area ranked #40. Criteria: climate; road roughness; urban mobility; gas prices. *Pep Boys, "America's Most Drivable Cities," April 9, 2003*

- Dallas was ranked #173 out of America's 200 largest metro areas in *SELF Magazine's* ranking of "America's Healthiest Cities for Women." Criteria: safety; air/water quality; cancer rates; and 21 other factors relating to health. *SELF Magazine, November 2003*

■ Dallas was identified as an asthma "hot spot" where high prevalence makes the condition a key issue and environmental "triggers" and other factors can make living with asthma a particular challenge. The area ranked #17 out of the nations 100 largest metro areas. Criteria: local asthma prevalence and mortality data; pollen scores; air pollution; asthma prescriptions; smoking laws; number of asthma specialists. *GlaxoSmithKline, October 29, 2002*

■ Dallas was identified as one of the most dangerous large metro areas for pedestrians in the U.S. The area ranked #9 out of the nations 49 largest metro areas. Criteria: average yearly pedestrian fatalities per capita (for the years 2000 and 2001) adjusted for the number of walkers. *Surface Transportation Policy Project, "Mean Streets 2002"*

■ Dallas was selected as one of the 25 fattest cities in America by *Men's Fitness Online*. It ranked #9 out of America's 50 largest cities. Criteria: gyms/sporting goods; nutrition; exercise/sports; overweight/sedentary; junk food; alcohol; smoking; television; air and water quality; climate; geography; commute time; parks/open space; recreation facilities; and health care. *Men's Fitness Online, America's Fittest/Fattest Cities 2003*

■ Dallas was ranked #45 out of 100 cities surveyed in *Child* magazine's ranking of the "Best Cities for Families." Criteria: number of pediatricians per capita; proximity to a children's hospital; immunization rates; infant mortality rate; air quality; water quality; school spending; pupil-teacher ratio; availability of parks/green space; nearby recreational opportunities; average commute time; number of sunny days; average cost of a 3-bedroom home; unemployment rate; future job growth; crime rate; percentage of children under 5; mandated minimum child care ratios. *Child, April 2001*

■ *Zero Population Growth* ranked 239 cities in terms of children's health, safety, and economic well-being. Dallas was ranked #12 out of 25 major cities (main city in a metro area with population of greater than 2 million) and was given a grade of B. Criteria: total population and population growth; percent of population under 18 years of age; number of children's museums; health improvement grade; percent of births to teens; percent of low birthweight infants; infant mortality rate; number of Title X-funded clinics; average SAT/ACT scores; average elementary and secondary class size; crime rate; unemployment rate; percent of affordable homes; number of bad air days; park acres per 1000 persons; library circulation per child; and children's program attendance counts. *Zero Population Growth, Kid Friendly Cities Report Card 2001*

■ *Ladies Home Journal* ranked America's 200 largest cities in terms of safety. Dallas ranked #172 out of 200. Criteria: violent crimes; crimes against property; and rape. *Ladies Home Journal Online, "The Best Cities for Women 2002"*

■ Dallas was ranked #11 out of 268 metro areas in terms of its Creativity Index. The Creativity Index is a mix of four equally weighted factors: the Creative Class (scientists, engineers, architects, designers, writers, artists, musicians, or any profession where creativity is a key factor) share of the workforce; innovation, measured as patents per capita; high-tech industry, using the Milken Institute's Tech Pole Index; and diversity, measured by the Gay Index (a reasonable proxy for an areas' openness to different kinds of people and ideas). *The Rise of the Creative Class, 2002*

■ Dallas was ranked #13 out of 125 regions worldwide in terms of its "Knowledge Competitiveness Index." The index attempts to measure the knowledge-based development taking place throughout the world and is based on 17 measures of economic performance that indicate a region's ability to translate its knowledge capacity into economic value. *Robert Huggins Associates, "2003-2004 World Knowledge Competitiveness Index"*

■ The Dallas metro area was selected by *Yahoo! Internet Life* as one of "America's Most Wired Cities...and Towns." The area ranked #17 out of 87. Criteria: home and work net use; user sophistication; domain density; and available content. *Yahoo! Internet Life, April 2001*

■ The Dallas metro area was selected by Cranium as one of the "Top 50 Fun Cities" in America. The area ranked #34. Criteria includes: number of sports teams, restaurants, and dance performances; number of toy stores; city budget spent on recreation. *Cranium, November 4, 2003*

- Of the 25 largest U.S. markets, the Dallas DMA (designated market area) ranked #5 in terms of online shopping. Criteria: telephone surveys of nearly 50,000 U.S. households between July 2000 and June 2001 conducted by market research firm Centris. *American Demographics, February 2002*

- Dallas was selected as one of the fastest-growing cities in the U.S. based on online user growth. The city ranked #6 out of 10. Criteria: online user growth (home use only) from June 2002 to June 2003. *Nielsen/NetRatings, July 21, 2003*

- Dallas was identified as one of the 100 "Most Unwired Cities" in the U.S. The area ranked #16. Criteria: number of public and commercial wireless access points; cell phone coverage offering wide area network Internet access; Internet penetration. *Intel, "Most Unwired Cities," March 4, 2003*

- Scarborough Research measured the percentage of households who subscribe to cellular services among adults ages 18 and over in 75 U.S. markets. The Dallas DMA (Designated Market Area) was ranked #6 out of 75. *Scarborough Research, Scarborough USA+ 2003 Release 1*

- Dallas was selected as one of "America's Most Literate Cities." The city ranked #36 out of the 64 largest U.S. cities. Criteria: booksellers; library support, holdings, and utilization; educational attainment; periodicals published; newspaper circulation. *University of Wisconsin-Whitewater, "America's Most Literate Cities," Summer 2003*

- Dallas was ranked #98 in *Prevention* magazine's survey of the "Best Walking Cities in the U.S." The magazine, in conjunction with the American Podiatric Medical Association, surveyed 125 of the most populated cities and then tabulated and weighed 20 criteria of interest to pedestrians. *Prevention, April, 2004*

- Dallas was selected as one of the nation's greatest sports cities. The city ranked #9 out of 13. The cities were selected by Randy Hill based on his sports-writing experiences in various cities along with the buzz generated through newspaper hysteria, radio talk-show paranoia and frequency of crucial, sports-related street chatter. *The Sporting News Online, "Best Sports Cities 2001"*

- *The Sporting News* selected the best sports cities for seven different sports. Dallas was selected as the best city for professional basketball (NBA). *The Sporting News Online, "Best Cities, Sport by Sport," August 13, 2003*

- The Dallas metro area was selected as one of "America's 50 Hottest Cities for Business Relocations and Expansions." The area ranked #17. Criteria: 70 of the industry's most prominent site selection consultants were asked which cities their clients found the most attractive when it came to selecting an expansion or relocation site in 2003. *Expansion Management, January 2004*

- The Dallas metro area was selected as one of the "Top 60 CyberCities in America" by *Site Selection*. CyberCities are magnets for growing high-tech companies. Criteria: total employment; average wages; total payroll; number of companies; R&D spending and venture capital in the 45 Standard Industrial Classification (SIC) codes that define the high-technology industry. *Site Selection, March 2002*

- The Dallas metro area was cited as one of America's "Top 50 Metros" in terms of the availability of highly skilled, highly educated workers. The area ranked #36 out of 50. Criteria: degree holders (bachelors, masters, professional, and Ph.D.) as a percent of the workforce; science and engineering workers as a percent of the workforce; number of patents issued; number and type of colleges in each metro area. *Expansion Management, March 2004*

- The Dallas metro area was cited as one of "The Best Places in the U.S. to Locate a Company." The area ranked #12 out of 329. Criteria: education (with emphasis on college board test results and high school graduation rates); availability of quality healthcare services and the cost to employers; quality of life; logistics workforce and companies; transportation infrastructure; quality and quantity of highly educated technical workers; business climate. *Expansion Management, July 2003*

- The Dallas metro area was cited as one of America's "Most Picture Perfect Metros" by *Plant Sites and Parks* magazine. Each year *PSP* readers rank the metro areas they consider best bets for their companies to relocate or expand to in the coming year. The area ranked #1 out of 10. *Plant Sites and Parks, March 2004*

- The Dallas metro area was selected as one of the "Top 40 Hottest Real Estate Markets" for expanding or relocating businesses." Criteria: rental costs; purchase prices; and vacancy rates of office and warehouse space. *Expansion Management, August 2003*

- The Dallas metro area appeared on *Forbes/Milken Institute* list of "Best Places for Business and Career." Rank: #14 out of 200 metro areas. Criteria: salary growth; job growth; number of technology clusters; overall concentration of technology activity relative to national average; and technology output growth. *www.forbes.com, Forbes/Milken Institute Best Places 2002*

- The Dallas metro area appeared on the "Milken Institute Best Performing Cities" index. Rank: #78 out of 200 large metro areas. Criteria: job growth; wage and salary growth; high-tech output growth. *Milken Institute, June 25, 2003*

- The Dallas metro area appeared on *Entrepreneur* magazine's list of the "Best Cities for Entrepreneurs" in 2003. The area ranked #24 out of 61 in the large city category. Criteria: entrepreneurial activity; small-business growth; economic growth; and risk. *www.Entrepreneur.com*

- The Dallas metro area was selected as one of "The Top 20 Boom Towns in America." *Business 2.0* magazine and econometric research firm Global Insight compared 319 metropolitan areas in the U.S. and ranked the 61 with populations over 1 million. Criteria: a weighted formula that includes forecast growth rates in sectors that contain the economy's 10 most skilled occupational clusters; the prevalence of college degrees in the local workforce; median salary. The area ranked #18 among large metro areas. *Business 2.0 Magazine, March 2004*

- The Dallas metro area appeared on *IndustryWeek's* fourth annual World-Class Communities list. It ranked #5 out of 315 metro areas. Criteria: MSA Gross Metropolitan Product (GMP) per manufacturing employee; and MSA percent share of U.S. manufacturing Gross Domestic Product (GDP). *IndustryWeek, April 16, 2001*

- ING Group ranked the 125 largest metro areas according to the general financial security of residents. The Dallas metro area was ranked #35 out of 125. Criteria: Earnings and Wealth Potential (household income, education, net assets, cost of living); Safety Net (health insurance, retirement savings, life insurance, income support programs); Personal Threats (unemployment rate, low-income households, crime rate); Community Economic Vitality (cost of community services, job quality, job creation, housing costs). *ING Group, "The Best Cities to Earn and Save Money: A Ranking of the Largest 125 U.S. Cities," 2001 Edition*

Business Environment

CITY FINANCES

City Government Finances

Component	2000-2001 ($000)	2000-2001 ($ per capita)
Total Revenues	2,307,858	1,942
Total Expenditures	2,072,615	1,744
Debt Outstanding	4,766,411	4,010
Cash and Securities	5,002,074	4,208

Source: U.S Census Bureau, Government Finances 2000-2001, August 2003

City Government Revenue by Source

Source	2000-2001 ($000)	2000-2001 ($ per capita)
General Revenue		
From Federal Government	62,700	53
From State Government	49,646	42
From Local Governments	1,392	1
Taxes		
Property	375,378	316
Sales	335,697	282
Personal Income	0	0
License	0	0
Charges	638,917	538
Liquor Store	0	0
Utility	199,543	168
Employee Retirement	421,019	354
Other	223,566	188

Source: U.S Census Bureau, Government Finances 2000-2001, August 2003

City Government Expenditures by Function

Function	2000-2001 ($000)	2000-2001 ($ per capita)	2000-2001 (%)
General Expenditures			
Airports	411,582	346	19.9
Corrections	5,557	5	0.3
Education	0	0	0.0
Fire Protection	112,013	94	5.4
Governmental Administration	111,155	94	5.4
Health	23,341	20	1.1
Highways	93,532	79	4.5
Hospitals	0	0	0.0
Housing and Community Development	33,674	28	1.6
Interest on General Debt	236,951	199	11.4
Libraries	20,142	17	1.0
Parking	1,915	2	0.1
Parks and Recreation	173,901	146	8.4
Police Protection	207,520	175	10.0
Public Welfare	2,879	2	0.1
Sewerage	131,849	111	6.4
Solid Waste Management	46,102	39	2.2
Liquor Store	0	0	0.0
Utility	181,910	153	8.8
Employee Retirement	163,862	138	7.9
Other	114,730	97	5.5

Source: U.S Census Bureau, Government Finances 2000-2001, August 2003

Municipal Bond Ratings

Area	Moody's
City	Aaa

Source: Mergent Bond Record, February 2004

DEMOGRAPHICS

Population Growth

Area	1990 Census	2000 Census	2003 Estimate	2008 Projection	Population Growth (%) 1990-2000	Population Growth (%) 2000-2008
City	1,006,971	1,188,580	1,235,129	1,317,220	18.0	10.8
MSA[1]	2,676,248	3,519,176	3,800,863	4,265,338	31.5	21.2
U.S.	248,709,873	281,421,906	290,647,163	305,918,071	13.2	8.7

Note: (1) Metropolitan Statistical Area - see Appendix A for areas included
Source: Claritas, Inc.

Number of Households and Average Household Size

Area	1990 Census	2000 Census	2003 Estimate	2008 Projection	2003 Average Household Size
City	402,081	451,833	465,725	490,883	2.7
MSA[1]	1,001,750	1,281,957	1,376,504	1,531,019	2.8
U.S.	91,947,410	105,480,101	109,440,059	116,034,472	2.7

Note: (1) Metropolitan Statistical Area - see Appendix A for areas included
Source: Claritas, Inc.

Race and Ethnicity

Area	White Non-Hispanic	Black Non-Hispanic	Asian Non-Hispanic	Other Race Non-Hispanic	Hispanic
City	50.5	25.4	2.9	21.3	37.4
MSA[1]	66.9	14.8	4.3	14.0	23.8
U.S.	74.5	12.4	3.8	9.3	13.2

Note: Figures are 2003 estimates; (1) Metropolitan Statistical Area - see Appendix A for areas included
Source: Claritas, Inc.

Segregation

City Index[2]	City Rank[3]	MSA[1] Index[2]	MSA[1] Rank[4]
71.5	19	64.4	110

Note: Figures are based on an analysis of Census 2000 data; (1) Metropolitan Statistical Area - see Appendix A for areas included; (2) Dissimilarity Index—the most commonly used measure of segregation between two groups, reflecting their relative distributions across neighborhoods within a city or metropolitan area. It can range in value from 0, indicating complete integration, to 100, indicating complete segregation; (3) Ranges from 1 (most segregated) to 100 (least segregated) and includes all the cities in this book; (4) Ranges from 1 (most segregated) to 318 (least segregated) and includes 318 metropolitan areas.
Source: www.CensusScope.org

Ancestry

Area	German	Irish[2]	English	American	Italian	Polish	French[3]	Scottish
City	6.1	5.0	5.8	4.1	1.4	0.8	1.5	1.2
MSA[1]	10.0	8.1	8.2	7.8	2.1	1.2	2.1	1.7
U.S.	15.2	10.9	8.7	7.3	5.6	3.2	3.0	1.7

Note: Figures include multiple ancestry (e.g. if a person reported being Irish and Italian, they were included in both columns); (1) Metropolitan Statistical Area - see Appendix A for areas included; (2) Includes Celtic; (3) Includes Alsatian but excludes Basque
Source: Census 2000, Summary File 3

Foreign-Born Population

Area	Any Foreign Country	Percent of Population Born in: Europe	Asia	Africa	Oceania[2]	Canada	Mexico	Latin America[3]
City	24.4	0.9	2.6	0.9	0.0	0.2	17.6	2.3
MSA[1]	16.8	0.9	3.4	0.6	0.0	0.3	9.8	1.8
U.S.	11.1	1.7	2.9	0.3	0.1	0.3	3.3	2.5

Note: (1) Metropolitan Statistical Area - see Appendix A for areas included; (2) Includes Australia, New Zealand subregion, Melanesia, Micronesia, Polynesia, and Oceania n.e.c; (3) Includes Central America (excluding Mexico), South America, and the Caribbean.
Source: Census 2000, Summary File 3

Religion

Area	Catholic	Southern Baptist	United Methodist	ELCA[1]	LDS[2]	Presbyterian Church USA	Jewish Est.	Muslim Est.
County	21.7	12.7	4.8	0.5	0.5	1.3	1.7	1.0
U.S.	22.0	7.1	3.7	1.8	1.5	1.1	2.2	0.6

Note: Figures shown are the number of adherents as a percentage of the total population; Adherents are defined as all members, including full members, their children and the estimated number of other participants who are not considered members (e.g. the baptized, those not confirmed, those not eligible for communion, those regularly attending services, etc.); (1) Evangelical Lutheran Church in America; (2) The Church of Jesus Christ of Latter Day Saints
Source: Reprinted with permission from Religious Congregations and Membership in the United States 2000 (Nashville, Glenmary Research Center, 2002) Copyright Association of Statisticians of American Religious Bodies. All rights reserved.

Age Distribution

Area	Percent of Population						
	Under Age 5	Age 5 to 17	Age 18 to 34	Age 35 to 49	Age 50 to 64	Age 65 to 79	80 Years and Over
City	8.3	18.2	31.5	22.0	11.4	6.3	2.3
MSA[1]	8.1	19.9	27.3	24.4	12.7	5.8	1.8
U.S.	6.8	18.9	23.7	23.5	14.8	9.2	3.2

Note: (1) Metropolitan Statistical Area - see Appendix A for areas included
Source: Census 2000, Summary File 3

Marriage Status

Area	Never Married	Now Married Except Separated	Separated	Widowed	Divorced
City	34.4	45.8	3.5	5.4	10.8
MSA[1]	27.2	55.6	2.5	4.6	10.1
U.S.	27.1	54.4	2.2	6.6	9.7

Note: Figures cover population 15 years of age and older; (1) Metropolitan Statistical Area - see Appendix A for areas included
Source: Census 2000, Summary File 3

Male/Female Ratio

Area	Males	Females	Males per 100 Females
City	622,614	612,515	101.6
MSA[1]	1,894,408	1,906,455	99.4
U.S.	142,511,883	148,135,280	96.2

Note: Figures are 2003 estimates; (1) Metropolitan Statistical Area - see Appendix A for areas included
Source: Claritas, Inc.

ECONOMY

Gross Metropolitan Product

Area	1999	2000	2001	2002	2002 Rank[2]
MSA[1]	148.3	159.9	164.7	166.9	9

Note: Figures are in billions of dollars; (1) Metropolitan Statistical Area - see Appendix A for areas included; (2) Rank ranges from 1 to 319
Source: The U.S. Conference of Mayors, Metro Economies Report, July 2003

INCOME

Per Capita/Median/Average Income

Area	Per Capita ($)	Median Household ($)	Average Household ($)
City	23,942	42,295	62,952
MSA[1]	27,294	55,076	74,939
U.S.	24,078	46,868	63,207

Note: Figures are 2003 estimates; (1) Metropolitan Statistical Area - see Appendix A for areas included
Source: Claritas, Inc.

Household Income Distribution

Area	Percent of Households Earning							
	Under $15,000	$15,000 -24,999	$25,000 -34,999	$35,000 -49,999	$50,000 -74,999	$75,000 -99,000	$100,000 -149,999	$150,000 and up
City	14.9	12.7	13.8	17.7	16.9	8.9	8.1	6.9
MSA[1]	10.2	9.2	10.9	15.8	19.4	12.7	13.0	8.9
U.S.	14.1	11.5	11.7	16.0	19.2	11.3	10.2	6.0

Note: Figures are 2003 estimates; (1) Metropolitan Statistical Area - see Appendix A for areas included
Source: Claritas, Inc.

Poverty Rates by Age

Area	All Ages	Under 5 Years Old	5 to 17 Years Old	18 to 64 Years Old	65 Years and Over
City	17.8	2.2	4.6	9.9	1.1
MSA[1]	11.1	1.3	2.8	6.3	0.7
U.S.	12.4	1.2	3.0	6.9	1.2

Note: Figures are percent of population with income in 1999 below poverty level and only include population for whom poverty status is determined; (1) Metropolitan Statistical Area - see Appendix A for areas included
Source: Census 2000, Summary File 3

Personal Bankruptcy Filing Rate

Area	2002	2003
Dallas County	4.12	4.53
U.S.	5.34	5.58

Note: Numbers are per 1,000 population and include Chapter 7 and Chapter 13 filings
Source: Federal Deposit Insurance Corporation (FDIC), Regional Economic Conditions (RECON), 2/25/2004

EMPLOYMENT

Labor Force and Employment

Area	Civilian Labor Force			Workers Employed		
	Dec. 2002	Dec. 2003	% Chg.	Dec. 2002	Dec. 2003	% Chg.
City	697,119	703,480	0.9	640,249	649,853	1.5
MSA[1]	2,030,240	2,051,670	1.1	1,900,545	1,929,052	1.5
U.S.	144,807,000	146,501,000	1.2	136,599,000	138,556,000	1.4

Note: Data is not seasonally adjusted and covers workers 16 years of age and older;
(1) Metropolitan Statistical Area - see Appendix A for areas included
Source: Bureau of Labor Statistics, http://stats.bls.gov

Unemployment Rate

Area	2003											
	Jan.	Feb.	Mar.	Apr.	May	Jun.	Jul.	Aug.	Sep.	Oct.	Nov.	Dec.
City	9.3	9.1	8.8	8.4	8.9	10.0	9.3	9.0	8.8	8.2	8.0	7.6
MSA[1]	7.3	7.2	7.0	6.7	7.1	8.0	7.4	7.1	7.0	6.4	6.3	6.0
U.S.	6.5	6.4	6.2	5.8	5.8	6.5	6.3	6.0	5.8	5.6	5.6	5.4

Note: Data is not seasonally adjusted and covers workers 16 years of age and older; All figures are percentages; (1) Metropolitan Statistical Area - see Appendix A for areas included
Source: Bureau of Labor Statistics, http://stats.bls.gov

Employment by Occupation

Occupation Classification	City (%)	MSA[1] (%)	U.S. (%)
Sales and Office	27.7	28.7	26.7
Professional and Related	18.2	20.4	20.2
Service	14.8	12.3	14.9
Production, Transportation, and Material Moving	13.1	11.8	14.6
Management, Business, and Financial	14.8	16.8	13.5
Construction, Extraction, and Maintenance	11.2	9.9	9.4
Farming, Forestry, and Fishing	0.1	0.2	0.7

Note: Figures cover employed civilians 16 years of age and older;
(1) Metropolitan Statistical Area - see Appendix A for areas included
Source: Census 2000, Summary File 3

Employment by Industry

Sector	MSA[1]		U.S.
	Number of Employees	Percent of Total	Percent of Total
Government	241,000	12.6	16.7
Education and Health Services	191,600	10.0	12.9
Professional and Business Services	271,700	14.2	12.3
Retail Trade	222,800	11.6	11.8
Manufacturing	198,400	10.3	11.0
Leisure and Hospitality	170,700	8.9	9.1
Finance Activities	170,000	8.9	6.1
Construction	95,700	5.0	5.1
Wholesale Trade	123,400	6.4	4.3
Other Services	72,400	3.8	4.1
Transportation and Utilities	75,700	3.9	3.7
Information	77,800	4.1	2.4
Natural Resources and Mining	6,500	0.3	0.4

Note: Figures cover non-farm employment as of December 2003 and are not seasonally adjusted;
(1) Metropolitan Statistical Area - see Appendix A for areas included
Source: Bureau of Labor Statistics, http://stats.bls.gov

Average Wages

Occupation	$/Hr.	Occupation	$/Hr.
Accountants and Auditors	27.10	Maids and Housekeeping Cleaners	7.77
Automotive Mechanics	15.52	Maintenance and Repair Workers	13.28
Bookkeepers	14.98	Marketing Managers	42.93
Carpenters	13.66	Nuclear Medicine Technologists	26.90
Cashiers	8.22	Nurses, Licensed Practical	18.26
Clerks, General Office	11.70	Nurses, Registered	23.12
Clerks, Receptionists/Information	11.39	Nursing Aides/Orderlies/Attendants	9.16
Clerks, Shipping/Receiving	11.68	Packers and Packagers, Hand	8.85
Computer Programmers	35.10	Physical Therapists	31.68
Computer Support Specialists	23.53	Postal Service Mail Carriers	18.77
Computer Systems Analysts	31.49	Real Estate Brokers	29.72
Cooks, Restaurant	8.59	Retail Salespersons	10.86
Dentists	61.06	Sales Reps., Exc. Tech./Scientific	25.29
Electrical Engineers	38.29	Sales Reps., Tech./Scientific	30.77
Electricians	17.75	Secretaries, Exc. Legal/Med./Exec.	13.02
Financial Managers	43.37	Security Guards	10.18
First-Line Supervisors/Mgrs., Sales	18.46	Surgeons	71.39
Food Preparation Workers	7.92	Teacher Assistants	8.40
General and Operations Managers	41.74	Teachers, Elementary School	20.40
Hairdressers/Cosmetologists	11.04	Teachers, Secondary School	21.60
Internists	n/a	Telemarketers	11.82
Janitors and Cleaners	8.67	Truck Drivers, Heavy/Tractor-Trailer	16.40
Landscaping/Groundskeeping Workers	9.36	Truck Drivers, Light/Delivery Svcs.	13.50
Lawyers	56.67	Waiters and Waitresses	7.53

Note: Wage data is for 2002 and covers the Metropolitan Statistical Area (see Appendix A for areas included).
Hourly wages for elementary/secondary school teachers and teacher assistants were calculated by the editors
from annual wage data assuming a 40 hour work week; n/a not available.
Source: Bureau of Labor Statistics, 2002 Metro Area Occupational Employment and Wage Estimates

Occupational Employment Projections: 1996 - 2006

Occupations Expected to Have the Largest Job Growth (ranked by numerical growth)	Fast-Growing Occupations[1] (ranked by percent growth)
1. Cashiers	1. Desktop publishers
2. Salespersons, retail	2. Systems analysts
3. General managers & top executives	3. Customer service representatives
4. Truck drivers, light	4. Physical therapy assistants and aides
5. Child care workers, private household	5. Computer engineers
6. General office clerks	6. Emergency medical technicians
7. Systems analysts	7. Medical assistants
8. Food preparation workers	8. Respiratory therapists
9. Food service workers	9. Telephone & cable TV line install & repair
10. Registered nurses	10. Physical therapists

Note: Projections cover Texas; (1) Excludes occupations with total job growth less than 300
Source: U.S. Department of Labor, Employment and Training Administration, America's Labor Market
Information System (ALMIS)

TAXES

State Corporate Income Tax Rates

State	Rate (%)	Number of Brackets	Low Bracket (Under $)	High Bracket (Over $)
Texas	None	na	na	na

Note: Tax rates as of December 31, 2003; na not applicable
Source: Tax Foundation, www.taxfoundation.org

State Individual Income Tax Rates

State	Federal Deductibility	Marginal Rate (%)	Number of Brackets	Low Bracket (Under $)	High Bracket (Over $)
Texas	No	None	na	na	na

Note: Tax rates as of December 31, 2003; Brackets apply to single taxpayers and married people filing
separately; na not applicable
Source: Tax Foundation, www.taxfoundation.org

Various State and Local Tax Rates

State Sales and Use (%)	Total Sales and Use (%)	Gasoline (cents/gal.)	Cigarette (cents/pack)	Spirits ($/gal.)	Table Wine ($/gal.)	Beer ($/gal.)
6.25	8.25	20	41	2.40	0.20	0.20

Note: Tax rates as of December 31, 2003
Source: Tax Foundation, www.taxfoundation.org

State Tax Burdens

Area	Combined State and Local Tax Burden		Combined Federal, State and Local Tax Burden	
	Percent	Rank	Percent	Rank
Texas	8.3	47	28.4	31
U.S. Average	9.7	-	30.0	-

Note: Figures are for 2003
Source: Tax Foundation, www.taxfoundation.org

Internal Revenue Service Tax Audits

IRS District	Percent of Returns Audited				
	1996	1997	1998	1999	2000
North Texas	0.95	0.82	0.50	0.35	0.19
U.S.	0.66	0.61	0.46	0.31	0.20

Note: Figures cover IRS district audits of federal income tax returns filed by individuals. Geographic data on
district audits for 2001 and 2002 are being withheld by the IRS. TRAC is challenging this policy.
Source: Syracuse University, Transactional Records Access Clearinghouse (TRAC), "Odds of IRS District Tax
Audit 2000"

RESIDENTIAL REAL ESTATE

Building Permits

Area	Single-Family			Multi-Family			Total		
	2001	2002	Pct. Chg.	2001	2002	Pct. Chg.	2001	2002	Pct. Chg.
City	1,913	2,024	5.8	3,237	4,054	25.2	5,150	6,078	18.0
U.S.	1,235,600	1,332,600	7.9	401,100	415,100	3.5	1,636,700	1,747,700	6.8

Note: Figures represent new, privately-owned housing units authorized (unadjusted data)
Source: U.S. Census Bureau, Manufacturing, Mining, and Construction Statistics

Homeownership and Housing Vacancies

Area	Homeownership Rate[2] (%)			Rental Vacancy Rate[3] (%)			Homeowner Vacancy Rate[4] (%)		
	2001	2002[a]	2003	2001	2002[a]	2003	2001	2002[a]	2003
MSA[1]	62.8	61.1	63.1	6.5	11.6	12.4	2.0	1.4	2.0
U.S.	67.8	67.9	68.3	8.4	8.9	9.8	1.8	1.7	1.8

Note: (1) Metropolitan Statistical Area - see Appendix A for areas included; (2) The proportion of households that are owners; (3) The proportion of the rental inventory that is vacant for rent; (4) The proportion of the homeowner inventory that is vacant for sale; (a) 2002 figures have been revised; n/a not available
Source: U.S. Census Bureau, Housing Vacancies and Homeownership Annual Statistics: 2003

COMMERCIAL REAL ESTATE

Industrial/Office Markets

Type/Market Area	Inventory (sq. ft.)	Vacant (sq. ft.)	Vacancy Rate (%)	Under Construction (sq. ft.)	Net Absorption (sq. ft.)
Industrial Space					
Dallas	467,000,000	56,040,000	12.00	5,250,000	-1,455,000
Office Space					
Dallas	208,546,421	45,696,679	21.91	2,047,328	-3,916,225

Note: Data as of 4th Quarter, 2003; n/a not available
Source: Society of Industrial and Office Realtors, 2004 Comparative Statistics of Industrial and Office Real Estate Markets

COMMERCIAL UTILITIES

Typical Monthly Electric Bills

Area	Commercial Service ($/month)		Industrial Service ($/month)	
	3 kW demand 1,000 kWh	40 kW demand 14,000 kWh	1,000 kW demand 200,000 kWh	50,000 kW demand 15,000,000 kWh
City	114	1,271	n/a	n/a
Average[1]	100	1,134	17,850	1,045,117

Note: Based on rates in effect July 1, 2003; (1) average based on 197 utilities; n/a not available
Source: Edison Electric Institute, Typical Bills and Average Rates Report, Summer 2003

TRANSPORTATION

Means of Transportation to Work

Area	Car/Truck/Van		Public Transportation			Bicycle	Walked	Other Means	Worked at Home
	Drove Alone	Car-pooled	Bus	Subway	Railroad				
City	70.8	17.8	5.0	0.2	0.2	0.1	1.9	1.2	2.8
MSA[1]	77.6	14.3	2.1	0.1	0.1	0.1	1.5	1.0	3.1
U.S.	75.7	12.2	2.5	1.5	0.5	0.4	2.9	1.0	3.3

Note: Figures shown are percentages and cover workers 16 years of age and older;
(1) Metropolitan Statistical Area - see Appendix A for areas included
Source: Census 2000, Summary File 3

Travel Time to Work

Area	Less Than 15 Minutes	15 to 29 Minutes	30 to 44 Minutes	45 to 59 Minutes	60 Minutes or More
City	20.3	39.7	25.4	7.8	6.8
MSA[1]	22.0	35.0	24.7	10.4	7.9
U.S.	29.4	36.1	19.1	7.4	8.0

Note: Figures are percentages and include workers 16 years old and over; (1) Metropolitan Statistical Area - see Appendix A for areas included
Source: Census 2000, Summary File 3

Roadway Congestion Index

Area	1982	1990	1996	2000	2001
City	0.73	0.96	0.98	1.11	1.12
Average[1]	0.82	1.01	1.08	1.16	1.17

Note: Values greater than 1.00 indicate undesirable mobility levels; (1) average of 75 urban areas
Source: Texas Transportation Institute, The 2003 Annual Urban Mobility Report

Transportation Statistics

Interstate highways (2004)	I-20; I-30; I-35E; I-45
Public transportation (2002)	Dallas Area Rapid Transit Authority (DART); First Transit Inc; Vancom
Buses	
Average fleet age in years	4.8; 7.2
No. operated in max. service	452; 265
Light rail	
Average fleet age in years	4.6; 13.9 (commuter rail)
No. operated in max. service	56; 17 (commuter rail)
Demand response	
Average fleet age in years	2.8 (2001)
No. operated in max. service	255 (2001)
Passenger air service	
Airport	Dallas-Fort Worth International; Love Field
Airlines (2003)	37 (both airports)
Boardings (2002)	24,761,105; 2,815,907
Amtrak service (2004)	Yes
Major waterways/ports	None

Source: Federal Transit Administration, National Transit Database, 2002; Editor & Publisher Market Guide, 2004; Bureau of Transportation Statistics, Airport Enplanement Activity for CY2002; www.amtrak.com

BUSINESSES

Major Business Headquarters

Company Name	2003 Rankings	
	Fortune 500	Forbes 500
Affiliated Computer Svcs.	488	-
Austin Industries	-	260
Builders FirstSource	-	155
Centex	241	-
Dean Foods	201	-
Dr Pepper/7 Up Bottling Group	-	118
Glazer's Wholesale Drug	-	143
Hunt Consolidated/Hunt Oil	-	105
Kinko's	-	98
Mary Kay	-	148
Neiman Marcus	500	-
Sammons Enterprises	-	104
Southwest Airlines	306	-
TXU	134	-
Texas Instruments	223	-
Triad Hospitals	442	-
VarTec Telecom	-	197
Vought Aircraft Industries	-	218

Note: Companies listed are located in the city; dashes indicate no ranking
Fortune 500: Companies that produce a 10-K are ranked 1 to 500 based on 2002 revenue
Forbes 500: Private companies are ranked 1 to 281 based on 2002 revenue
Source: Fortune, April 14, 2003; www.forbes.com, November 6, 2003

Best Companies to Work For

Container Store; TDIndustries; Texas Instruments, headquartered in Dallas, are among the "100 Best Companies to Work for in 2004." Criteria: trust in management, pride in work/company, camaraderie, company responses to the Hewitt People Practices Inventory, and employee responses to their Great Place to Work survey. The companies also had to be at least 10 years old and have a minimum of 500 employees. *Fortune, January 12, 2004*

Texas Instruments Inc, headquartered in Dallas, is among the "100 Best Companies for Working Mothers." Criteria: fair wages, opportunities for women to advance, support for child care, flexible work schedules, family-friendly benefits, and work/life supports. *Working Mother, October 2003*

Wyndham International, headquartered in Dallas, is among the "50 Best Companies for Minorities." Criteria: 1,200 of the largest U.S employers were surveyed—141 responded. Those companies were analyzed on 15 quantitative and qualitative measures—from how well minorities are paid to how many are in management. *Fortune, July 7, 2003*

J.C. Penney Co, headquartered in Dallas, is among the "100 Best Places to Work in IT 2003." Criteria: compensation, turnover and training. *www.computerworld.com, 3/15/2004*

Fast-Growing Businesses

According to *Inc.*, Dallas is home to 10 of America's 500 fastest-growing private companies: **Adea Solutions; Capstone; Career Control Group; Foremark; MapFrame; Monitronics International; Quorum Business Solutions; Resulte Universal; Texas Residential Mortgage/Bankers Alliance; The Diamond Group**. Criteria: must be an independent, privately-held, U.S. corporation, proprietorship or partnership; sales of at least $200,000 in 1998; five-year operating/sales history; increase in 2002 sales over 2001 sales; holding companies, regulated banks, and utilities were excluded. *Inc. 500, America's Fastest-Growing Private Companies, October 15, 2003*

Dallas is home to one of *Business Week's* "hot growth" companies: **Odyssey Healthcare**. Criteria: increase in sales and profits, return on capital and stock price. *Business Week, June 9, 2003*

According to *Fortune*, Dallas is home to one of America's 100 fastest-growing companies: **ENSCO International**. Companies were ranked based on earnings-per-share growth, revenue growth and total return over the previous three years. Criteria for inclusion: public companies with sales of at least $50 million. Companies that lost money in the most recent quarter, or ended in the red for the past four quarters as a whole, were not eligible. Limited partnerships and REITs were also not considered. *Fortune, "America's Fastest-Growing Companies," September 1, 2003*

According to Deloitte & Touche LLP, Dallas is home to nine of North America's 500 fastest-growing high-technology companies: **Allegiance Telecom, Inc; Claimsnet.com; Global HealthNet, Inc; MapFrame Corporation; MarketNet, Inc; Pegasus Solutions, Inc; The Planet Internet Services, Inc; Tyler Technologies, Inc; WorldQuest Networks, Inc**. Companies are ranked by percentage growth in revenue over a five-year period. Criteria for inclusion: must be a U.S. or Canadian company developing and/or providing technology products or services; company must have been in business for five years with 1998 operating revenues of at least $50,000 USD or $75,000 CD and 2002 operating revenues of at least $1 million USD/CD. *Deloitte & Touche LLP, 2003 Technology Fast 500*

Women-Owned Firms: Number, Employment and Sales

Area	Number of Firms	Employ-ment	Sales ($000)	Rank[2]
MSA[1]	86,918	144,458	19,932,483	8

Note: (1) Metropolitan Statistical Area - see Appendix A for areas included;
(2) Calculated on an averaging of the number of businesses, employment, and sales
Source: The National Foundation for Women Business Owners, Women-Owned Businesses in the Top 50 Metropolitan Areas, 2002: A Fact Sheet

Women-Owned Firms: Growth

Area	Percent Change from 1997 to 2002			Rank[2]
	Number of Firms	Employ-ment	Sales	
MSA[1]	13.8	43.7	62.5	8
Top 50 MSAs	14.0	31.4	42.6	-

Note: (1) Metropolitan Statistical Area - see Appendix A for areas included; (2) Calculated on an averaging of the percent growth of number of businesses, employment, and sales
Source: The National Foundation for Women Business Owners, Women-Owned Businesses in the Top 50 Metropolitan Areas, 2002: A Fact Sheet

Minority and Women-Owned Businesses

Ownership	All Firms		Firms with Paid Employees			
	Firms	Sales ($000)	Firms	Sales ($000)	Employees	Payroll ($000)
Black	7,661	1,546,748	1,326	1,407,849	10,649	218,589
Hispanic	11,451	1,184,782	2,384	808,134	9,009	203,450
Women	26,136	6,024,613	6,019	5,457,664	52,548	1,311,125

Note: Figures cover firms located in the city
Source: 1997 Economic Census, Minority and Women-Owned Businesses

Minority Business Opportunity

Dallas is home to two companies which are on the Black Enterprise Industrial/Service 100 list (100 largest companies based on gross sales): **Facility Interiors Inc.; PrimeSource Food Service Equipment Inc.**. Criteria: operational in previous calendar year; at least 51% black-owned and manufactures/owns the product it sells or provides industrial or consumer services. Brokerages, real estate firms and firms that provide professional services are not eligible. *Black Enterprise, www.blackenterprise.com, B.E. 100s, 2003 Report*

Dallas is home to one company which is on the Black Enterprise Auto Dealer 100 list (100 largest dealers based on gross sales): **Powell Chevrolet**. Criteria: company must be operational in previous calendar year and at least 51% black-owned. *Black Enterprise, www.blackenterprise.com, B.E. 100s, 2003 Report*

Seven of the 500 largest Hispanic-owned companies in the U.S. are located in Dallas. *Hispanic Business, June 2003*

Dallas is home to four companies which are on the Hispanic Business Fastest-Growing 100 list (greatest sales growth over the past five years): **Trevino Mechanical Contractors**;

Paragon Project Resources Inc.; Phillips/May Corp.; Couriers On Demand Inc..
Hispanic Business, July/August 2003

HOTELS

Hotels/Motels

Area	Hotels/Motels	Average Minimum Rates ($)		
		Tourist	First-Class	Deluxe
City	140	74	110	351

Source: OAG Travel Planner Online, Spring 2004

Dallas is home to one of the top 100 hotels in the U.S. and Canada according to *Travel & Leisure*: **Mansion on Turtle Creek** (#28). Criteria: value, rooms/ambience, location, facilities/activities and service. *Travel & Leisure, "The World's Best Hotels 2003"*

EVENT SITES

Major Event Sites, Meeting Places and Convention Centers

Name	Guest Rooms	Exhibit/ Meeting Space (sq. ft.)	Largest Meeting Room Capacity
Adams Mark Dallas	1,842	230,000	5,000
Dallas Convention Center	n/a	n/a	9,500
Fair Park	n/a	n/a	72,000
Hotel Inter-Continental Dallas	528	100,000	3,000
Hyatt Regency DFW	1,369	130,000	6,885
Reunion Arena	n/a	n/a	19,000
Starplex Amphitheater	n/a	n/a	20,111
Wyndham Anatole Hotel	1,620	315,000	5,250

Note: n/a not available
Source: Original research

Living Environment

COST OF LIVING

Cost of Living Index

Year	Composite Index	Groceries	Housing	Utilities	Trans-portation	Health Care	Misc. Goods/ Services
2001	98.4	98.4	94.9	95.7	102.2	99.3	100.6
2002	98.7	96.5	94.0	100.9	98.3	99.6	103.3
2003	96.7	95.3	92.1	91.3	100.1	100.6	101.4

Note: U.S. = 100; Figures are for the Metropolitan Statistical Area - see Appendix A for areas included
Source: ACCRA, Cost of Living Index, 2001, 2002 and 2003 4-Quarter Averages

HOUSING

House Price Index (HPI)

Area	National Ranking[2]	Quarterly Change (%)	One-Year Change (%)	Five-Year Change (%)
MSA[1]	212	0.67	2.10	26.76
U.S.[3]	-	3.67	7.97	41.81

Note: The HPI is a weighted repeat sales index. It measures average price changes in repeat sales or refinancings on the same properties. This information is obtained by reviewing repeat mortgage transactions on single-family properties whose mortgages have been purchased or securitized by Fannie Mae of Freddie Mac in January 1975; (1) Metropolitan Statistical Area - see Appendix A for areas included; (2) Rankings are based on annual percentage change, for all MSAs containing at least 15,000 transactions over the last 10 years and ranges from 1 to 220; (3) figures based on a weighted division average; all figures are for the period ended December 31, 2003
Source: Office of Federal Housing Enterprise Oversight, House Price Index, March 1, 2004

Housing: Year Structure Built

Area	1990 -2000	1980 -1989	1970 -1979	1960 -1969	1950 -1959	1940 -1949	Before 1940	Median Year
City	12.5	20.2	20.1	18.5	16.0	7.0	5.7	1971
MSA[1]	23.9	24.7	20.2	13.7	9.8	4.0	3.7	1979
U.S.	17.0	15.8	18.5	13.7	12.7	7.3	15.0	1971

Note: Figures are percentages; (1) Metropolitan Statistical Area - see Appendix A for areas included
Source: Census 2000, Summary File 3

Average New Home Price

Area	2001	2002	2003
MSA[1]	189,327	203,220	209,222
U.S.	212,643	236,567	248,193

Note: Figures, in dollars, are based on a new home with 2,400 sq. ft. of living area on an 8,000 sq. ft. lot; (1) Metropolitan Statistical Area - see Appendix A for areas included
Source: ACCRA, Cost of Living Index, 2001, 2002 and 2003 4-Quarter Averages

Average Apartment Rent

Area	2001	2002	2003
MSA[1]	851	902	902
U.S.	674	708	721

Note: Figures, in dollars per month, are based on an unfurnished two bedroom, 1-1/2 or 2 bath apartment, approximately 950 sq. ft., excluding utilities except water; (1) Metropolitan Statistical Area - see Appendix A for areas included
Source: ACCRA, Cost of Living Index, 2001, 2002 and 2003 4-Quarter Averages

RESIDENTIAL UTILITIES

Average Residential Utility Costs

Area	All Electric ($/mth)	Part Electric ($/mth)	Other Energy ($/mth)	Phone ($/mth)
MSA[1]	–	92.80	29.63	19.46
U.S.	116.46	65.82	62.68	23.90

Note: (1) Metropolitan Statistical Area - see Appendix A for areas included
Source: ACCRA, Cost of Living Index, 2003 4-Quarter Average

HEALTH CARE

Average Health Care Costs

Area	Hospital ($/day)	Doctor ($/visit)	Dentist ($/visit)
MSA[1]	679.73	72.63	79.66
U.S.	678.35	67.91	83.90

Note: Hospital—based on a semi-private room; Doctor—based on a general practitioner's routine exam of an established patient; Dentist—based on adult teeth cleaning and periodic oral exam;
(1) Metropolitan Statistical Area - see Appendix A for areas included
Source: ACCRA, Cost of Living Index, 2003 4-Quarter Average

Distribution of Non-Federal, Office-Based Physicians

Area	Total	Family/ General Practice	Specialties		
			Medical	Surgical	Other
CMSA[3] (number)	7,867	989	2,601	2,050	2,227
CMSA[3] (rate per 10,000 pop.)	15.1	1.9	5.0	3.9	4.3
Metro Average[2] (rate per 10,000 pop.)	33.1	2.2	7.7	4.8	5.6

Note: Data as of December 31, 2001; (1) Metropolitan Statistical Area - see Appendix A for areas included; (2) Average of 81 MSAs and CMSAs in this book; (3) Dallas-Fort Worth, TX Consolidated Metropolitan Statistical Area includes the following counties: Collin; Dallas; Denton; Ellis; Henderson; Hood; Hunt; Johnson; Kaufman; Parker; Rockwall; Tarrant
Source: American Medical Association, Physician Characteristics & Distribution in the U.S., 2003-2004

Hospitals

Dallas has the following hospitals: 13 general medical and surgical; 2 psychiatric; 3 rehabilitation; 1 chronic disease; 3 long-term acute care; 1 other specialty; 1 children's general; 1 children's other specialty; 1 children's long-term acute care.
AHA Guide to the Healthcare Field, 2003-2004

According to *U.S. News,* Dallas has two of the best hospitals in the U.S.: **Baylor University Medical Center**; **Parkland Memorial Hospital**; *U.S. News Online, "America's Best Hospitals 2003"*

PRESIDENTIAL ELECTION

2000 Presidential Election Results

Area	Gore	Bush	Nader	Buchanan	Other
Dallas County	44.9	52.6	1.9	0.1	0.4
U.S.	48.4	47.9	2.7	0.4	0.6

Note: Results are percentages and may not add to 100% due to rounding
Source: www.cbsnews.com; www.uselectionatlas.org

EDUCATION

Public School District Statistics

District Name	Schls.	Enroll- ment	Classroom Teachers	Pupil/ Teacher Ratio	Minority Pupils[1] (%)	Current Expend.[2] ($/pupil)
Dallas Can Academy Charter	2	849	38	22.3	n/a	n/a
Dallas ISD	226	163,562	10,562	15.5	92.2	5,950
Faith Family Academy	1	844	60	13.9	n/a	n/a
Highland Park ISD	7	5,893	416	14.2	n/a	n/a
Honors Academy	12	2,018	131	15.4	n/a	n/a
Life Charter School	1	794	42	18.9	n/a	n/a
Oak Cliff Academy	1	674	34	19.8	n/a	n/a
Rylie Faith Family Academy	1	783	50	15.7	n/a	n/a
Wilmer-Hutchins ISD	7	3,025	198	15.3	n/a	n/a

Note: Data covers the 2001-02 school year unless otherwise noted; (1) Fall 2000; (2) FY2000; n/a not available
Source: U.S. Department of Education, National Center for Education Statistics, Common Core of Data, Local Education Agency (School District) Universe Survey: School Year 2001-2002; U.S. Department of Education, National Center for Education Statistics, Digest of Education Statistics 2002

Educational Quality

School District	Education Quotient[1]	Graduate Outcome[2]	Community Index[3]	Resource Index[4]
Dallas ISD	28	25	69	45

Note: Scores are national percentile rankings and range from 1 (worst) to 99 (best); (1) Combination of the Graduate Outcome, Community and Resource indexes weighted to reflect the greater importance of the Graduate Outcome and Resource Index; (2) Based on graduation rates and college board scores (SAT/ACT); (3) Based on the surrounding community's level of affluence and adult education; (4) Based on teacher salaries, per-pupil expenditures and student-teacher ratios.
Source: Expansion Management, December 2003

Educational Attainment by Race

Area	High School Graduate (%)					Bachelor's Degree (%)				
	Total	White	Black	Asian	Hisp.[2]	Total	White	Black	Asian	Hisp.[2]
City	70.4	78.3	73.9	78.5	33.4	27.7	38.5	13.5	50.5	6.5
MSA[1]	79.4	84.4	78.9	83.4	41.5	30.0	34.0	18.5	52.2	8.7
U.S.	80.4	83.6	72.3	80.4	52.4	24.4	26.1	14.3	44.1	10.4

Note: Figures shown cover persons 25 years old and over; (1) Metropolitan Statistical Area - see Appendix A for areas included; (2) people of Hispanic origin can be of any race
Source: Census 2000, Summary File 3

School Enrollment by Type

Area	Grades KG to 8				Grades 9 to 12			
	Public		Private		Public		Private	
	Enrollment	%	Enrollment	%	Enrollment	%	Enrollment	%
City	141,212	89.6	16,443	10.4	54,733	89.9	6,166	10.1
MSA[1]	456,971	90.7	46,953	9.3	181,249	92.2	15,405	7.8
U.S.	33,526,011	88.7	4,285,121	11.3	14,848,628	90.6	1,532,323	9.4

Note: Figures shown cover persons 3 years old and over; (1) Metropolitan Statistical Area - see Appendix A for areas included
Source: Census 2000, Summary File 3

School Enrollment by Race

Area	Grades KG to 8 (%)				Grades 9 to 12 (%)			
	White	Black	Asian	Hisp.[1]	White	Black	Asian	Hisp.[1]
City	38.8	31.5	2.0	46.8	36.8	34.6	2.6	41.8
MSA[2]	60.7	18.0	3.6	28.9	61.2	18.7	4.0	25.8
U.S.	68.5	15.5	3.3	16.8	68.8	15.5	3.8	15.7

Note: Figures shown cover persons 3 years old and over; (1) people of Hispanic origin can be of any race; (2) Metropolitan Statistical Area - see Appendix A for areas included
Source: Census 2000, Summary File 3

Classroom Teacher Salaries in Public Schools

District	B.A. Degree		M.A. Degree		Maximum	
	Min. ($)	Rank[1]	Max. ($)	Rank[1]	Max. ($)	Rank[1]
Dallas	34,100	26	55,821[e]	29	57,821[e]	55
DOD Average[2]	31,567	-	53,248	-	59,356	-

Note: Salaries are for 2001-2002; (1) Rank ranges from 1 to 100; (2) As per the U.S. Department of Defense Wage Fixing Authority
Source: American Federation of Teachers, Survey & Analysis of Teacher Salary Trends 2002

Higher Education

Four-Year Colleges			Two-Year Colleges			Medical Schools	Law Schools	Voc/ Tech
Public	Private Non-profit	Private For-profit	Public	Private Non-profit	Private For-profit			
1	7	3	3	3	6	1	1	17

Note: Figures cover institutions located within the city limits.
Source: National Center for Education Statistics, The Integrated Postsecondary Education System (IPEDS) Peer Analysis System, 2002; usnews.com, America's Best Graduate Schools 2004, Medical School Directory; The College Blue Book, Occupational Education, 2003; Barron's Guide to Law Schools, 2003; Medical School Admission Requirements U.S. & Canada, 2003-2004

MAJOR EMPLOYERS

Major Employers

Company Name	Industry	Type
A M R Corporation	Air transportation, scheduled	Headquarters
Accountemps	Employment agencies	Branch
Alcatel USA Inc	Telephone and telegraph apparatus	Branch
Bank of America	National commercial banks	Branch
Baylor University Medical Ctr	General medical and surgical hospitals	Headquarters
EDS	Data processing and preparation	Headquarters
GTE	Business services, nec	Single
JCP Publications Corp	Miscellaneous publishing	Headquarters
National Elec Contrs Assn	Insurance agents, brokers, and service	Headquarters
Nortel Networks Inc	General warehousing and storage	Branch
Parkland Health & Hospital Sys	General medical and surgical hospitals	Headquarters
PCJ Realty Two Inc	Real estate agents and managers	Single
Raytheon	Search and navigation equipment	Branch
Southwestern Medical School	Colleges and universities	Headquarters
Texas A & M Univ - Commerce	Public relations services	Branch
Texas Instruments	Semiconductors and related devices	Headquarters
UT Sothwstern Mdcal- Trnsplnts	Offices and clinics of medical doctors	Branch
Worldcom	Telephone communication, except radio	Branch

Note: Companies shown are located in the metropolitan area and have 3,500 or more employees.
Source: www.zapdata.com, March 2004

PUBLIC SAFETY

Crime Rate

Area	All Crimes	Violent Crimes				Property Crimes		
		Murder	Forcible Rape	Robbery	Aggrav. Assault	Burglary	Larceny -Theft	Motor Vehicle Theft
City	9,024.7	15.8	52.8	647.7	654.5	1,639.3	4,535.4	1,479.3
Suburbs[1]	4,275.2	3.7	29.5	81.4	216.9	815.7	2,747.2	380.9
MSA[2]	5,879.3	7.8	37.4	272.6	364.7	1,093.9	3,351.1	751.9
U.S.	4,118.8	5.6	33.0	145.9	310.1	746.2	2,445.8	432.1

Note: Figures are crimes per 100,000 population; (1) All areas within the MSA that are located outside the city limits; (2) Metropolitan Statistical Area - see Appendix A for areas included
Source: FBI Uniform Crime Reports, 2002

RECREATION

Culture and Recreation

Museums	Orchestras	Opera Companies	Dance Companies	Professional Theatres	Zoos	Pro Sports Teams[1]
16	3	1	2	12	1	3

Note: (1) Covers the Metropolitan Statistical Area - see Appendix A for areas included.
Source: The Grey House Performing Arts Directory, 2002; Official Museum Directory, 2004; www.sportsvenues.com

Library System

The Dallas Public Library has 22 branches and holdings of 2,248,107 volumes.
American Library Directory, 2003-2004

MEDIA

Newspapers

Name	Type	Freq.	Distribution	Circulation
The Dallas Morning News	General	7x/wk	Regional	511,159
Dallas Observer	Alternative	1x/wk	Local	115,000
Dallas Post Tribune	Black	1x/wk	Local	45,000
El Extra	Hispanic	1x/wk	Area	27,000
El Hispano News	Hispanic	1x/wk	Local	35,000
Novedades News	Hispanic	1x/wk	Local	32,000
Texas Catholic	Religious	2x/mth	Local	50,199
United Methodist Reporter	Religious	1x/wk	U.S./Int'l	110,000
United Methodist Review	Religious	2x/mth	United States	140,000

Note: Includes newspapers whose offices are located in the city and whose circulations are 25,000 or more
Source: Burrelle's Media Directory, 2003

Television Stations

Name	Ch.	Affiliation	Type	Owner
KDTN	2	PBS	Non-comm.	North Texas Public Broadcasting Inc.
KDFW	4	FBC	Commercial	Fox Television Stations Inc.
WFAA	8	ABCT	Commercial	Belo Corporation
KTVT	11	CBST	Commercial	CBS
KERA	13	PBS	Public	North Texas Public Broadcasting Inc.
KTXA	21	UPN	Commercial	CBS
KUVN	23	UNIN	Commercial	Perenchio Television Inc.
KDFI	27	FBC	Commercial	Fox Television Stations Inc.
KDAF	33	WB	Commercial	Tribune Broadcasting Company
KXTX	39	TMUN	Commercial	Telemundo Group Inc.
KSTR	49	UNIN	Commercial	Univision Television Group
KFWD	52	n/a	Commercial	n/a
KDTX	58	n/a	Non-comm.	Trinity Broadcasting Network

Note: Stations included broadcast from the Dallas metro area; n/a not available
Source: Burrelle's Media Directory, 2003

AM Radio Stations

Call Letters	Freq. (kHz)	Target Audience	Station Format	Music Format
KLIF	570	Men	N/T	n/a
KSKY	660	H/R	M/S/T	Christian
KKDA	730	General	M	Rhythm & Blues
KAAM	770	General	M	Big Band
KKLF	950	General	N/T	n/a
KHVN	970	Christian	M	Christian
KGGR	1040	B/R	M/T	Christian
KRLD	1080	General	N/T	n/a
KBIS	1150	Hispanic	M/N/T	Latin
KTRA	1190	General	S/T	n/a
KESS	1270	Hispanic	M/N/T	Latin
KTCK	1310	General	M/S/T	Top 40
KAHZ	1360	Hispanic	E/M/N/S/T	80's
KGVL	1400	General	M/N/S	Country
KDXX	1480	Hispanic	M/N/T	Latin
KZMP	1540	Hispanic	M	Adult Contemporary
KEGG	1560	Religious	M/N/T	Christian
KRVA	1600	Hispanic	M/N/T	Latin
KTBK	1700	General	M/S	Classic Rock

Note: Stations included broadcast from the Dallas metro area; n/a not available
The following abbreviations may be used:
Target Audience: A=Asian; B=Black; C=Christian; E=Ethnic; F=French; G=General; H=Hispanic;
M=Men; N=Native American; R=Religious; S=Senior Citizen; W=Women; Y=Young Adult; Z=Children
Station Format: E=Educational; M=Music; N=News; S=Sports; T=Talk
Source: Burrelle's Media Directory, 2003

FM Radio Stations

Call Letters	Freq. (mHz)	Target Audience	Station Format	Music Format
KEOM	88.5	General	E/M/N/S	Oldies
KMQX	89.1	General	E/M/T	Christian
KNON	89.3	B/H	E/M/N/T	Adult Standards
KTPW	89.7	Christian	M	Christian
KERA	90.1	General	M/N/T	Alternative
KCBI	90.9	Religious	M/N/S	Christian
KVTT	91.7	Religious	E/M/T	Christian
KZPS	92.5	General	M/N/T	Classic Rock
KDBN	93.3	General	M/N/T	Classic Rock
KIKT	93.5	General	M	Country
KLNO	94.1	Hispanic	M	Latin
KSOC	94.5	General	M/N/T	Adult Contemporary
KLTY	94.9	Religious	M/N/T	Adult Contemporary
KEGL	97.1	General	M/N/S/T	Modern Rock
KBFB	97.9	General	M	Rhythm & Blues
KLUV	98.7	General	M/N/T	Oldies
KHCK	99.1	Hispanic	M	Latin
KPLX	99.5	General	M	Country
KRBV	100.3	General	M	Top 40
WRR	101.1	General	M/N/T	Classical
KZMP	101.7	Hispanic	M	Adult Contemporary
KDGE	102.1	Young Adult	M/N/T	Alternative
KDMX	102.9	Women	M/N/T	Adult Contemporary
KVIL	103.7	General	M	Adult Contemporary
KKDA	104.5	Black	M	Urban Contemporary
KTCY	104.9	H/R	M/N/T	Christian
KYNG	105.3	General	M/T	80's
KRNB	105.7	General	M/N/S	Rhythm & Blues
KHKS	106.1	General	M/N/T	Top 40
KDXT	106.7	Hispanic	M/N	Latin
KRVA	106.9	Hispanic	M/N/T	Latin
KRVF	107.1	Hispanic	M/N/S	Latin
KOAI	107.5	General	M/T	Adult Standards
KDXX	107.9	Hispanic	M/N/T	Latin

Note: Stations included broadcast from the Dallas metro area
The following abbreviations may be used:
Target Audience: A=Asian; B=Black; C=Christian; E=Ethnic; F=French; G=General; H=Hispanic;
M=Men; N=Native American; R=Religious; S=Senior Citizen; W=Women; Y=Young Adult; Z=Children
Station Format: E=Educational; M=Music; N=News; S=Sports; T=Talk
Music Format: AOR=Album Oriented Rock; MOR=Middle of the Road
Source: Burrelle's Media Directory, 2003

CLIMATE

Average and Extreme Temperatures

Temperature	Jan	Feb	Mar	Apr	May	Jun	Jul	Aug	Sep	Oct	Nov	Dec	Yr.
Extreme High (°F)	85	90	100	100	101	112	111	109	107	101	91	87	112
Average High (°F)	55	60	68	76	84	92	96	96	89	79	67	58	77
Average Temp. (°F)	45	50	57	66	74	82	86	86	79	68	56	48	67
Average Low (°F)	35	39	47	56	64	72	76	75	68	57	46	38	56
Extreme Low (°F)	-2	9	12	30	39	53	58	58	42	24	16	0	-2

Note: Figures cover the years 1945-1993
Source: National Climatic Data Center, International Station Meteorological Climate Summary, 9/96

Average Precipitation/Snowfall/Humidity

Precip./Humidity	Jan	Feb	Mar	Apr	May	Jun	Jul	Aug	Sep	Oct	Nov	Dec	Yr.
Avg. Precip. (in.)	1.9	2.3	2.6	3.8	4.9	3.4	2.1	2.3	2.9	3.3	2.3	2.1	33.9
Avg. Snowfall (in.)	1	1	Tr	Tr	0	0	0	0	0	Tr	Tr	Tr	3
Avg. Rel. Hum. 6am (%)	78	77	75	77	82	81	77	76	80	79	78	77	78
Avg. Rel. Hum. 3pm (%)	53	51	47	49	51	48	43	41	46	46	48	51	48

Note: Figures cover the years 1945-1993; Tr = Trace amounts (<0.05 in. of rain; <0.5 in. of snow)
Source: National Climatic Data Center, International Station Meteorological Climate Summary, 9/96

Weather Conditions

Temperature			Daytime Sky			Precipitation		
10°F & below	32°F & below	90°F & above	Clear	Partly cloudy	Cloudy	0.01 inch or more precip.	0.1 inch or more snow/ice	Thunder-storms
1	34	102	108	160	97	78	2	49

Note: Figures are average number of days per year and covers the years 1945-1993
Source: National Climatic Data Center, International Station Meteorological Climate Summary, 9/96

HAZARDOUS WASTE

Superfund Sites

Dallas has one hazardous waste site on the EPA's Superfund National Priorities List: **RSR Corporation**. *U.S. Environmental Protection Agency, National Priorities List, March 15, 2004*

AIR & WATER QUALITY

Maximum Pollutant Concentrations

	Particulate Matter (ug/m³)	Carbon Monoxide (ppm)	Sulfur Dioxide (ppm)	Nitrogen Dioxide (ppm)	Ozone 1-hour (ppm)	Ozone 8-hour (ppm)	Lead (ug/m³)
MSA[1] Level	62	2	0.016	0.018	0.13	0.1	0.48a
NAAQS[2]	150	9	0.140	0.053	0.12	0.08	1.50
Met NAAQS[2]	Yes	Yes	Yes	Yes	No	No	Yes

Note: (1) Metropolitan Statistical Area - see Appendix A for areas included; (2) National Ambient Air Quality Standards; n/a not available; (a) Localized impact from an industrial source in Dallas. Concentration from highest nonpoint source site is 0.11 ug/m³ in Collin County)
Units: ppm = parts per million; ug/m³ = micrograms per cubic meter
Source: EPA, Latest Findings on National Air Quality: 2002 Status and Trends, August 2003

Air Quality Index

In the Dallas MSA (see Appendix A for areas included), the Air Quality Index (AQI) exceeded 100 on 22 days in 2002. An AQI value greater than 100 indicates that air quality would have been in the unhealthful range on that day.
EPA, Latest Findings on National Air Quality: 2002 Status and Trends, August 2003

Watershed Health

The U.S. Environmental Protection Agency monitors the health of the aquatic resources for the nation's 2,000+ watersheds. **The Upper Trinity watershed serves the Dallas area and received an overall Index of Watershed Indicators (IWI) score of 5 (more serious problems - low vulnerability).** The IWI score is based on seven condition and nine vulnerability indicators. The overall IWI score ranges from 1 (best health) to 6 (worst health). The Condition Indicators include: designated use attainment, fish and wildlife consumption advisories, source water condition, contaminated sediments, ambient water quality, and wetlands loss index. The Vulnerability Indicators include: aquatic species at risk, conventional and toxic loads over permitted limits, urban and agricultural runoff potential, population change, hydrologic modification, estuarine pollution susceptibility, and air deposition. *EPA, Index of Watershed Indicators, October 26, 2001*

Drinking Water

Water System Name	Pop. Served	Primary Water Source Type	Number of Violations January 2002-February 2004		
			Health Based	Significant Monitoring	Monitoring
Dallas Water Utility	1,188,580	Surface	None	None	2

Note: Data as of February 19, 2004
Source: EPA, Office of Ground Water and Drinking Water, Safe Drinking Water Information System

Dallas tap water is moderately hard and fluoridated.
Editor & Publisher Market Guide, 2004

El Paso, Texas

Background

El Paso is so named because it sits in a spectacular pass through the Franklin Mountains, at an average elevation of 3,700 feet and in direct view of peaks that rise to 7,200 feet. El Paso is the fourth-largest city in Texas. It lies just south of New Mexico on the Rio Grande and just north of Juarez, Mexico.

The early Spanish explorer Alvar Nunez Cabeza de Vaca (circa 1530) probably passed through this area, but the city was named in 1598 by Juan de Onante, who dubbed it El Paso del Rio del Norte, or The Pass at the River of the North. It was also Onante who declared the area Spanish, on the authority of King Philip II, but a mission was not established until 1649. For some time, El Paso del Norte was the seat of government for northern Mexico, but settlement in and around the present-day city was sparse for many years.

This had changed considerably by 1807, when Zebulon A. Pike, a United States Army officer, was interned in El Paso after being convicted of trespassing on Spanish territory. He found the area pleasant and well-tended, with many irrigated fields and vineyards and a thriving trade in brandy and wine. In spite of Pike's stay there, though, El Paso remained for many years a largely Mexican region, escaping most of the military action connected to the Texas Revolution.

In the wake of the Mexican War (1846-1848) and in response to the California gold rush in 1849, El Paso emerged as a significant way station on the road West. A federal garrison, Fort Bliss, was established there in 1849, and was briefly occupied by Confederate sympathizers in 1862. Federal forces quickly reoccupied the fort, however, and the area was firmly controlled by Union armies. El Paso was incorporated in 1873, and after 1881, growth accelerated considerably with the building of rail links through the city, giving rise to ironworks, mills, and breweries.

During the Mexican Revolution (1911), El Paso was an important and disputed city, with Pancho Villa himself a frequent visitor, and many of his followers residents of the town. Mexico's national history, in fact, continued to affect El Paso until 1967 when, by way of settling a historic border dispute, a small portion of the city was ceded to Mexico.

One of the major points of entry to the U.S. from Mexico, El Paso is a vitally important international city and a burgeoning center of rail, road, and air transportation. During the 1990s, the city's economy shifted more toward a service-oriented economy and away from a manufacturing base, according to a 2002 report from the Federal Reserve Bank of Dallas. Transportation services and motor freight transportation and warehousing increased. In addition, tourism is becoming a growing segment of the economy. Government and military are also sources of employment.

The city hosts the University of Texas at El Paso, and a community college. Cultural amenities include the Tigua Indian Cultural Center, a Wilderness Park Museum, a symphony orchestra, a ballet company, and many theaters.

The weather in El Paso is of the mountain-desert type, with very little precipitation. Summers are hot, humidity is low and winters are mild. However, temperatures in the flat Rio Grande Valley nearby are notably cooler at night year-round. There is plenty of sunshine and clear skies 202 days of the year.

Rankings

- El Paso was ranked #225 out of 331 metro areas in *Cities Ranked & Rated*. Criteria: cost of living; climate; crime; transportation; economy and jobs; education; arts and culture; health and healthcare; leisure. *Cities Ranked & Rated, 1st Edition, 2004*

- *Ladies Home Journal* ranked America's 200 largest cities based on the qualities women surveyed care about most. El Paso ranked #45 out of 57 in the big city category (population over 300,000). Criteria: crime; lifestyle; education; jobs; health; child care; politics; and the economy. *Ladies Home Journal Online, "The Best Cities for Women 2002"*

- El Paso was selected as one of the "Top 10 Cities for Hispanics." The city was ranked #5. The cities were selected based on data from the following sources: *Forbes* magazine; CNN; *Money* magazine; local newspapers; U.S. Census; experts; natives and residents; www.bestplaces.net; www.findyourspot.com. *Hispanic Magazine, July/August 2002*

- *Forbes* ranked the 150 most populous metro areas in the U.S. in terms of the "Best Places for Business and Careers." The El Paso metro area was ranked #144. Criteria: income and job growth; cost-of-doing-business; qualifications of the available pool of labor; crime rates; housing costs; net migration. *Forbes, May 9, 2003*

- El Paso was selected as one of "America's Healthiest Cities" by *Natural Health* magazine. The city was ranked #41 out of the 50 largest urban areas in the U.S. Twenty-six criteria in the following four categories were examined: whether the city boasts natural offerings; how well the city promotes its resident's physical health; whether the city offers a healthy environment; how well the city fosters a sense of community. *Natural Health, April 2003*

- *Men's Health* ranked 101 U.S. cities in terms of the quality of their tap water. El Paso received a grade of D. Criteria: levels of bacteria, arsenic, lead, trihalomethanes, and haloacetic acids were compared with the National Academy of Science's guidelines as well as with the EPA's more stringent maximum contaminant level goals. *Men's Health, March 2004*

- Sperling's BestPlaces ranked 331 metro areas and identified the most and least stressful U.S. cities. The El Paso metro area ranked #59 out of the 100 largest metro areas (#1 = most stressful). Criteria: divorce rate; unemployment rate; violent and property crime; suicide rate; commute time; mental health; alcohol consumption; cloudy days. *www.BestPlaces.net, February 26, 2004*

- Sperling's BestPlaces in partnership with Pep Boys ranked 77 metro areas and identified "America's Most Drivable Cities." The El Paso metro area ranked #8. Criteria: climate; road roughness; urban mobility; gas prices. *Pep Boys, "America's Most Drivable Cities," April 9, 2003*

- El Paso was ranked #116 out of America's 200 largest metro areas in *SELF Magazine's* ranking of "America's Healthiest Cities for Women." Criteria: safety; air/water quality; cancer rates; and 21 other factors relating to health. *SELF Magazine, November 2003*

- El Paso was identified as an asthma "hot spot" where high prevalence makes the condition a key issue and environmental "triggers" and other factors can make living with asthma a particular challenge. The area ranked #6 out of the nations 100 largest metro areas. Criteria: local asthma prevalence and mortality data; pollen scores; air pollution; asthma prescriptions; smoking laws; number of asthma specialists. *GlaxoSmithKline, October 29, 2002*

- El Paso was selected as one of the 25 fattest cities in America by *Men's Fitness Online*. It ranked #17 out of America's 50 largest cities. Criteria: gyms/sporting goods; nutrition; exercise/sports; overweight/sedentary; junk food; alcohol; smoking; television; air and water quality; climate; geography; commute time; parks/open space; recreation facilities; and health care. *Men's Fitness Online, America's Fittest/Fattest Cities 2003*

■ El Paso was ranked #35 out of 100 cities surveyed in *Child* magazine's ranking of the "Best Cities for Families." Criteria: number of pediatricians per capita; proximity to a children's hospital; immunization rates; infant mortality rate; air quality; water quality; school spending; pupil-teacher ratio; availability of parks/green space; nearby recreational opportunities; average commute time; number of sunny days; average cost of a 3-bedroom home; unemployment rate; future job growth; crime rate; percentage of children under 5; mandated minimum child care ratios. *Child, April 2001*

■ *Zero Population Growth* ranked 239 cities in terms of children's health, safety, and economic well-being. El Paso was ranked #66 out of 140 independent cities (cities with populations greater than 100,000 which were neither major cities nor suburbs/outer cities) and was given a grade of B. Criteria: total population and population growth; percent of population under 18 years of age; number of children's museums; health improvement grade; percent of births to teens; percent of low birthweight infants; infant mortality rate; number of Title X-funded clinics; average SAT/ACT scores; average elementary and secondary class size; crime rate; unemployment rate; percent of affordable homes; number of bad air days; park acres per 1000 persons; library circulation per child; and children's program attendance counts. *Zero Population Growth, Kid Friendly Cities Report Card 2001*

■ El Paso was identified as one of the safest large cities in America by Morgan Quitno. All cities with populations of 500,000 or more that reported crime rates in 2002 for murder, rape, robbery, aggravated assault, burglary, and motor vehicle thefts were ranked. The city ranked #2 out of the top 10. *www.morganquitno.com, 10th Annual America's Safest (and Most Dangerous) Cities Awards*

■ *Ladies Home Journal* ranked America's 200 largest cities in terms of safety. El Paso ranked #59 out of 200. Criteria: violent crimes; crimes against property; and rape. *Ladies Home Journal Online, "The Best Cities for Women 2002"*

■ The El Paso metro area was selected by *Yahoo! Internet Life* as one of "America's Most Wired Cities...and Towns." The area ranked #83 out of 87. Criteria: home and work net use; user sophistication; domain density; and available content. *Yahoo! Internet Life, April 2001*

■ El Paso was identified as one of the 100 "Most Unwired Cities" in the U.S. The area ranked #68. Criteria: number of public and commercial wireless access points; cell phone coverage offering wide area network Internet access; Internet penetration. *Intel, "Most Unwired Cities," March 4, 2003*

■ Scarborough Research measured the percentage of households who subscribe to cellular services among adults ages 18 and over in 75 U.S. markets. The El Paso DMA (Designated Market Area) was ranked #59 out of 75. *Scarborough Research, Scarborough USA+ 2003 Release 1*

■ El Paso was selected as one of "America's Most Literate Cities." The city ranked #64 out of the 64 largest U.S. cities. Criteria: booksellers; library support, holdings, and utilization; educational attainment; periodicals published; newspaper circulation. *University of Wisconsin-Whitewater, "America's Most Literate Cities," Summer 2003*

■ El Paso was ranked #21 in *Prevention* magazine's survey of the "Best Walking Cities in the U.S." The magazine, in conjunction with the American Podiatric Medical Association, surveyed 125 of the most populated cities and then tabulated and weighed 20 criteria of interest to pedestrians. *Prevention, April, 2004*

■ The El Paso metro area was cited as one of "The Best Places in the U.S. to Locate a Company." The area ranked #248 out of 329. Criteria: education (with emphasis on college board test results and high school graduation rates); availability of quality healthcare services and the cost to employers; quality of life; logistics workforce and companies; transportation infrastructure; quality and quantity of highly educated technical workers; business climate. *Expansion Management, July 2003*

■ The El Paso metro area was selected as one of the "Top 40 Hottest Real Estate Markets" for expanding or relocating businesses." Criteria: rental costs; purchase prices; and vacancy rates of office and warehouse space. *Expansion Management, August 2003*

- The El Paso metro area appeared on *Forbes/Milken Institute* list of "Best Places for Business and Career." Rank: #136 out of 200 metro areas. Criteria: salary growth; job growth; number of technology clusters; overall concentration of technology activity relative to national average; and technology output growth. *www.forbes.com, Forbes/Milken Institute Best Places 2002*

- The El Paso metro area appeared on the "Milken Institute Best Performing Cities" index. Rank: #174 out of 200 large metro areas. Criteria: job growth; wage and salary growth; high-tech output growth. *Milken Institute, June 25, 2003*

- The El Paso metro area appeared on *IndustryWeek's* fourth annual World-Class Communities list. It ranked #267 out of 315 metro areas. Criteria: MSA Gross Metropolitan Product (GMP) per manufacturing employee; and MSA percent share of U.S. manufacturing Gross Domestic Product (GDP). *IndustryWeek, April 16, 2001*

- ING Group ranked the 125 largest metro areas according to the general financial security of residents. The El Paso metro area was ranked #121 out of 125. Criteria: Earnings and Wealth Potential (household income, education, net assets, cost of living); Safety Net (health insurance, retirement savings, life insurance, income support programs); Personal Threats (unemployment rate, low-income households, crime rate); Community Economic Vitality (cost of community services, job quality, job creation, housing costs). *ING Group, "The Best Cities to Earn and Save Money: A Ranking of the Largest 125 U.S. Cities," 2001 Edition*

Business Environment

CITY FINANCES

City Government Finances

Component	2000-2001 ($000)	2000-2001 ($ per capita)
Total Revenues	550,347	976
Total Expenditures	547,455	971
Debt Outstanding	700,796	1,243
Cash and Securities	1,256,304	2,229

Source: U.S Census Bureau, Government Finances 2000-2001, August 2003

City Government Revenue by Source

Source	2000-2001 ($000)	2000-2001 ($ per capita)
General Revenue		
From Federal Government	45,890	81
From State Government	11,428	20
From Local Governments	7,794	14
Taxes		
Property	106,829	190
Sales	92,610	164
Personal Income	0	0
License	0	0
Charges	109,272	194
Liquor Store	0	0
Utility	62,385	111
Employee Retirement	47,428	84
Other	66,711	118

Source: U.S Census Bureau, Government Finances 2000-2001, August 2003

City Government Expenditures by Function

Function	2000-2001 ($000)	2000-2001 ($ per capita)	2000-2001 (%)
General Expenditures			
Airports	24,465	43	4.5
Corrections	0	0	0.0
Education	0	0	0.0
Fire Protection	39,867	71	7.3
Governmental Administration	27,557	49	5.0
Health	22,381	40	4.1
Highways	24,543	44	4.5
Hospitals	0	0	0.0
Housing and Community Development	22,052	39	4.0
Interest on General Debt	25,617	45	4.7
Libraries	10,074	18	1.8
Parking	120	< 1	< 0.1
Parks and Recreation	19,684	35	3.6
Police Protection	76,749	136	14.0
Public Welfare	0	0	0.0
Sewerage	57,132	101	10.4
Solid Waste Management	14,352	25	2.6
Liquor Store	0	0	0.0
Utility	106,167	188	19.4
Employee Retirement	38,530	68	7.0
Other	38,165	68	7.0

Source: U.S Census Bureau, Government Finances 2000-2001, August 2003

Municipal Bond Ratings

Area	Moody's
City	Aaa

Source: Mergent Bond Record, February 2004

DEMOGRAPHICS

Population Growth

Area	1990 Census	2000 Census	2003 Estimate	2008 Projection	Population Growth (%) 1990-2000	Population Growth (%) 2000-2008
City	515,541	563,662	581,541	611,827	9.3	8.5
MSA[1]	591,610	679,622	707,569	754,535	14.9	11.0
U.S.	248,709,873	281,421,906	290,647,163	305,918,071	13.2	8.7

Note: (1) Metropolitan Statistical Area - see Appendix A for areas included
Source: Claritas, Inc.

Number of Households and Average Household Size

Area	1990 Census	2000 Census	2003 Estimate	2008 Projection	2003 Average Household Size
City	160,622	182,063	189,640	202,639	3.1
MSA[1]	178,366	210,022	220,367	238,064	3.2
U.S.	91,947,410	105,480,101	109,440,059	116,034,472	2.7

Note: (1) Metropolitan Statistical Area - see Appendix A for areas included
Source: Claritas, Inc.

Race and Ethnicity

Area	White Non-Hispanic	Black Non-Hispanic	Asian Non-Hispanic	Other Race Non-Hispanic	Hispanic
City	72.8	3.2	1.2	22.8	77.8
MSA[1]	73.6	3.1	1.0	22.3	79.4
U.S.	74.5	12.4	3.8	9.3	13.2

Note: Figures are 2003 estimates; (1) Metropolitan Statistical Area - see Appendix A for areas included
Source: Claritas, Inc.

Segregation

City Index[2]	City Rank[3]	MSA[1] Index[2]	MSA[1] Rank[4]
39.5	85	41.1	296

Note: Figures are based on an analysis of Census 2000 data; (1) Metropolitan Statistical Area - see Appendix A for areas included; (2) Dissimilarity Index—the most commonly used measure of segregation between two groups, reflecting their relative distributions across neighborhoods within a city or metropolitan area. It can range in value from 0, indicating complete integration, to 100, indicating complete segregation; (3) Ranges from 1 (most segregated) to 100 (least segregated) and includes all the cities in this book; (4) Ranges from 1 (most segregated) to 318 (least segregated) and includes 318 metropolitan areas.
Source: www.CensusScope.org

Ancestry

Area	German	Irish[2]	English	American	Italian	Polish	French[3]	Scottish
City	4.6	2.9	2.8	2.7	1.2	0.5	1.0	0.6
MSA[1]	4.2	2.7	2.5	2.6	1.1	0.5	0.9	0.5
U.S.	15.2	10.9	8.7	7.3	5.6	3.2	3.0	1.7

Note: Figures include multiple ancestry (e.g. if a person reported being Irish and Italian, they were included in both columns); (1) Metropolitan Statistical Area - see Appendix A for areas included; (2) Includes Celtic; (3) Includes Alsatian but excludes Basque
Source: Census 2000, Summary File 3

Foreign-Born Population

Area	Any Foreign Country	Percent of Population Born in: Europe	Asia	Africa	Oceania[2]	Canada	Mexico	Latin America[3]
City	26.1	1.0	1.0	0.1	0.0	0.1	23.4	0.5
MSA[1]	27.4	0.9	0.9	0.1	0.0	0.1	25.0	0.5
U.S.	11.1	1.7	2.9	0.3	0.1	0.3	3.3	2.5

Note: (1) Metropolitan Statistical Area - see Appendix A for areas included; (2) Includes Australia, New Zealand subregion, Melanesia, Micronesia, Polynesia, and Oceania n.e.c; (3) Includes Central America (excluding Mexico), South America, and the Caribbean.
Source: Census 2000, Summary File 3

Religion

Area	Catholic	Southern Baptist	United Methodist	ELCA[1]	LDS[2]	Presbyterian Church USA	Jewish Est.	Muslim Est.
County	51.5	3.6	1.3	0.2	0.8	0.4	0.7	0.1
U.S.	22.0	7.1	3.7	1.8	1.5	1.1	2.2	0.6

Note: Figures shown are the number of adherents as a percentage of the total population; Adherents are defined as all members, including full members, their children and the estimated number of other participants who are not considered members (e.g. the baptized, those not confirmed, those not eligible for communion, those regularly attending services, etc.); (1) Evangelical Lutheran Church in America; (2) The Church of Jesus Christ of Latter Day Saints
Source: Reprinted with permission from Religious Congregations and Membership in the United States 2000 (Nashville, Glenmary Research Center, 2002) Copyright Association of Statisticians of American Religious Bodies. All rights reserved.

Age Distribution

Area	Percent of Population						
	Under Age 5	Age 5 to 17	Age 18 to 34	Age 35 to 49	Age 50 to 64	Age 65 to 79	80 Years and Over
City	8.3	22.6	24.1	21.6	12.7	8.5	2.2
MSA[1]	8.6	23.3	24.8	21.4	12.1	7.8	2.0
U.S.	6.8	18.9	23.7	23.5	14.8	9.2	3.2

Note: (1) Metropolitan Statistical Area - see Appendix A for areas included
Source: Census 2000, Summary File 3

Marriage Status

Area	Never Married	Now Married Except Separated	Separated	Widowed	Divorced
City	26.8	54.3	3.2	6.1	9.7
MSA[1]	26.8	55.3	3.1	5.7	9.1
U.S.	27.1	54.4	2.2	6.6	9.7

Note: Figures cover population 15 years of age and older; (1) Metropolitan Statistical Area - see Appendix A for areas included
Source: Census 2000, Summary File 3

Male/Female Ratio

Area	Males	Females	Males per 100 Females
City	276,321	305,220	90.5
MSA[1]	341,357	366,212	93.2
U.S.	142,511,883	148,135,280	96.2

Note: Figures are 2003 estimates; (1) Metropolitan Statistical Area - see Appendix A for areas included
Source: Claritas, Inc.

ECONOMY

Gross Metropolitan Product

Area	1999	2000	2001	2002	2002 Rank[2]
MSA[1]	17.7	18.7	19.1	19.9	95

Note: Figures are in billions of dollars; (1) Metropolitan Statistical Area - see Appendix A for areas included; (2) Rank ranges from 1 to 319
Source: The U.S. Conference of Mayors, Metro Economies Report, July 2003

INCOME

Per Capita/Median/Average Income

Area	Per Capita ($)	Median Household ($)	Average Household ($)
City	16,122	36,076	49,108
MSA[1]	14,907	34,389	47,147
U.S.	24,078	46,868	63,207

Note: Figures are 2003 estimates; (1) Metropolitan Statistical Area - see Appendix A for areas included
Source: Claritas, Inc.

Household Income Distribution

Area	Percent of Households Earning							
	Under $15,000	$15,000 -24,999	$25,000 -34,999	$35,000 -49,999	$50,000 -74,999	$75,000 -99,000	$100,000 -149,999	$150,000 and up
City	19.9	14.9	13.9	16.8	16.9	8.1	6.3	3.1
MSA[1]	20.4	16.1	14.4	16.8	16.1	7.6	5.7	2.8
U.S.	14.1	11.5	11.7	16.0	19.2	11.3	10.2	6.0

Note: Figures are 2003 estimates; (1) Metropolitan Statistical Area - see Appendix A for areas included
Source: Claritas, Inc.

Poverty Rates by Age

Area	All Ages	Under 5 Years Old	5 to 17 Years Old	18 to 64 Years Old	65 Years and Over
City	22.2	2.6	6.7	11.1	1.9
MSA[1]	23.8	2.8	7.4	11.8	1.8
U.S.	12.4	1.2	3.0	6.9	1.2

Note: Figures are percent of population with income in 1999 below poverty level and only include population
for whom poverty status is determined; (1) Metropolitan Statistical Area - see Appendix A for areas included
Source: Census 2000, Summary File 3

Personal Bankruptcy Filing Rate

Area	2002	2003
El Paso County	4.28	4.52
U.S.	5.34	5.58

Note: Numbers are per 1,000 population and include Chapter 7 and Chapter 13 filings
Source: Federal Deposit Insurance Corporation (FDIC), Regional Economic Conditions (RECON), 2/25/2004

EMPLOYMENT

Labor Force and Employment

Area	Civilian Labor Force			Workers Employed		
	Dec. 2002	Dec. 2003	% Chg.	Dec. 2002	Dec. 2003	% Chg.
City	266,666	272,278	2.1	245,780	251,167	2.2
MSA[1]	296,759	302,993	2.1	272,516	278,489	2.2
U.S.	144,807,000	146,501,000	1.2	136,599,000	138,556,000	1.4

Note: Data is not seasonally adjusted and covers workers 16 years of age and older;
(1) Metropolitan Statistical Area - see Appendix A for areas included
Source: Bureau of Labor Statistics, http://stats.bls.gov

Unemployment Rate

Area	2003											
	Jan.	Feb.	Mar.	Apr.	May	Jun.	Jul.	Aug.	Sep.	Oct.	Nov.	Dec.
City	9.4	9.0	8.6	8.0	8.8	10.2	9.5	9.5	9.4	8.6	8.2	7.8
MSA[1]	9.8	9.4	8.9	8.3	9.2	10.6	9.9	9.9	9.8	9.0	8.6	8.1
U.S.	6.5	6.4	6.2	5.8	5.8	6.5	6.3	6.0	5.8	5.6	5.6	5.4

Note: Data is not seasonally adjusted and covers workers 16 years of age and older; All figures are
percentages; (1) Metropolitan Statistical Area - see Appendix A for areas included
Source: Bureau of Labor Statistics, http://stats.bls.gov

Employment by Occupation

Occupation Classification	City (%)	MSA[1] (%)	U.S. (%)
Sales and Office	29.1	28.1	26.7
Professional and Related	19.7	18.4	20.2
Service	16.9	16.9	14.9
Production, Transportation, and Material Moving	14.9	16.8	14.6
Management, Business, and Financial	11.6	10.8	13.5
Construction, Extraction, and Maintenance	7.6	8.7	9.4
Farming, Forestry, and Fishing	0.2	0.4	0.7

Note: Figures cover employed civilians 16 years of age and older;
(1) Metropolitan Statistical Area - see Appendix A for areas included
Source: Census 2000, Summary File 3

Employment by Industry

Sector	MSA[1]		U.S.
	Number of Employees	Percent of Total	Percent of Total
Government	61,400	23.8	16.7
Education and Health Services	28,900	11.2	12.9
Professional and Business Services	25,300	9.8	12.3
Retail Trade	34,700	13.4	11.8
Manufacturing	25,500	9.9	11.0
Leisure and Hospitality	23,600	9.1	9.1
Finance Activities	12,000	4.6	6.1
Construction	n/a	n/a	5.1
Wholesale Trade	9,700	3.8	4.3
Other Services	7,300	2.8	4.1
Transportation and Utilities	12,400	4.8	3.7
Information	5,400	2.1	2.4
Natural Resources and Mining	n/a	n/a	0.4

Note: Figures cover non-farm employment as of December 2003 and are not seasonally adjusted; (1) Metropolitan Statistical Area - see Appendix A for areas included; n/a not available
Source: Bureau of Labor Statistics, http://stats.bls.gov

Average Wages

Occupation	$/Hr.	Occupation	$/Hr.
Accountants and Auditors	23.42	Maids and Housekeeping Cleaners	6.60
Automotive Mechanics	12.33	Maintenance and Repair Workers	11.67
Bookkeepers	11.61	Marketing Managers	32.09
Carpenters	9.59	Nuclear Medicine Technologists	n/a
Cashiers	6.93	Nurses, Licensed Practical	15.96
Clerks, General Office	8.88	Nurses, Registered	21.14
Clerks, Receptionists/Information	8.30	Nursing Aides/Orderlies/Attendants	8.03
Clerks, Shipping/Receiving	9.61	Packers and Packagers, Hand	7.32
Computer Programmers	n/a	Physical Therapists	27.71
Computer Support Specialists	16.15	Postal Service Mail Carriers	n/a
Computer Systems Analysts	25.23	Real Estate Brokers	n/a
Cooks, Restaurant	7.46	Retail Salespersons	9.39
Dentists	96.87	Sales Reps., Exc. Tech./Scientific	19.45
Electrical Engineers	28.30	Sales Reps., Tech./Scientific	36.55
Electricians	16.36	Secretaries, Exc. Legal/Med./Exec.	9.77
Financial Managers	33.79	Security Guards	8.27
First-Line Supervisors/Mgrs., Sales	14.84	Surgeons	n/a
Food Preparation Workers	6.91	Teacher Assistants	7.50
General and Operations Managers	31.96	Teachers, Elementary School	19.00
Hairdressers/Cosmetologists	7.58	Teachers, Secondary School	19.40
Internists	n/a	Telemarketers	n/a
Janitors and Cleaners	7.41	Truck Drivers, Heavy/Tractor-Trailer	12.84
Landscaping/Groundskeeping Workers	8.28	Truck Drivers, Light/Delivery Svcs.	11.29
Lawyers	57.37	Waiters and Waitresses	6.68

Note: Wage data is for 2002 and covers the Metropolitan Statistical Area (see Appendix A for areas included). Hourly wages for elementary/secondary school teachers and teacher assistants were calculated by the editors from annual wage data assuming a 40 hour work week; n/a not available.
Source: Bureau of Labor Statistics, 2002 Metro Area Occupational Employment and Wage Estimates

Occupational Employment Projections: 1996 - 2006

Occupations Expected to Have the Largest Job Growth (ranked by numerical growth)	Fast-Growing Occupations[1] (ranked by percent growth)
1. Cashiers	1. Desktop publishers
2. Salespersons, retail	2. Systems analysts
3. General managers & top executives	3. Customer service representatives
4. Truck drivers, light	4. Physical therapy assistants and aides
5. Child care workers, private household	5. Computer engineers
6. General office clerks	6. Emergency medical technicians
7. Systems analysts	7. Medical assistants
8. Food preparation workers	8. Respiratory therapists
9. Food service workers	9. Telephone & cable TV line install & repair
10. Registered nurses	10. Physical therapists

Note: Projections cover Texas; (1) Excludes occupations with total job growth less than 300
Source: U.S. Department of Labor, Employment and Training Administration, America's Labor Market Information System (ALMIS)

TAXES

State Corporate Income Tax Rates

State	Rate (%)	Number of Brackets	Low Bracket (Under $)	High Bracket (Over $)
Texas	None	na	na	na

Note: Tax rates as of December 31, 2003; na not applicable
Source: Tax Foundation, www.taxfoundation.org

State Individual Income Tax Rates

State	Federal Deductibility	Marginal Rate (%)	Number of Brackets	Low Bracket (Under $)	High Bracket (Over $)
Texas	No	None	na	na	na

Note: Tax rates as of December 31, 2003; Brackets apply to single taxpayers and married people filing separately; na not applicable
Source: Tax Foundation, www.taxfoundation.org

Various State and Local Tax Rates

State Sales and Use (%)	Total Sales and Use (%)	Gasoline (cents/gal.)	Cigarette (cents/pack)	Spirits ($/gal.)	Table Wine ($/gal.)	Beer ($/gal.)
6.25	8.25	20	41	2.40	0.20	0.20

Note: Tax rates as of December 31, 2003
Source: Tax Foundation, www.taxfoundation.org

State Tax Burdens

Area	Combined State and Local Tax Burden		Combined Federal, State and Local Tax Burden	
	Percent	Rank	Percent	Rank
Texas	8.3	47	28.4	31
U.S. Average	9.7	-	30.0	-

Note: Figures are for 2003
Source: Tax Foundation, www.taxfoundation.org

Internal Revenue Service Tax Audits

IRS District	Percent of Returns Audited				
	1996	1997	1998	1999	2000
South Texas	0.55	0.50	0.50	0.31	0.17
U.S.	0.66	0.61	0.46	0.31	0.20

Note: Figures cover IRS district audits of federal income tax returns filed by individuals. Geographic data on district audits for 2001 and 2002 are being withheld by the IRS. TRAC is challenging this policy.
Source: Syracuse University, Transactional Records Access Clearinghouse (TRAC), "Odds of IRS District Tax Audit 2000"

RESIDENTIAL REAL ESTATE

Building Permits

Area	Single-Family			Multi-Family			Total		
	2001	2002	Pct. Chg.	2001	2002	Pct. Chg.	2001	2002	Pct. Chg.
City	2,964	3,180	7.3	121	171	41.3	3,085	3,351	8.6
U.S.	1,235,600	1,332,600	7.9	401,100	415,100	3.5	1,636,700	1,747,700	6.8

Note: Figures represent new, privately-owned housing units authorized (unadjusted data)
Source: U.S. Census Bureau, Manufacturing, Mining, and Construction Statistics

Homeownership and Housing Vacancies

Area	Homeownership Rate[2] (%)			Rental Vacancy Rate[3] (%)			Homeowner Vacancy Rate[4] (%)		
	2001	2002[a]	2003	2001	2002[a]	2003	2001	2002[a]	2003
MSA[1]	n/a	n/a	n/a	n/a	n/a	n/a	n/a	n/a	n/a
U.S.	67.8	67.9	68.3	8.4	8.9	9.8	1.8	1.7	1.8

Note: (1) Metropolitan Statistical Area - see Appendix A for areas included; (2) The proportion of households that are owners; (3) The proportion of the rental inventory that is vacant for rent; (4) The proportion of the homeowner inventory that is vacant for sale; (a) 2002 figures have been revised; n/a not available
Source: U.S. Census Bureau, Housing Vacancies and Homeownership Annual Statistics: 2003

COMMERCIAL REAL ESTATE

Industrial/Office Markets

Type/Market Area	Inventory (sq. ft.)	Vacant (sq. ft.)	Vacancy Rate (%)	Under Construction (sq. ft.)	Net Absorption (sq. ft.)
Industrial Space					
El Paso	54,306,550	8,381,022	15.43	0	254,916
Office Space					
El Paso	8,090,327	1,999,285	24.71	0	-140,156

Note: Data as of 4th Quarter, 2003; n/a not available
Source: Society of Industrial and Office Realtors, 2004 Comparative Statistics of Industrial and Office Real Estate Markets

COMMERCIAL UTILITIES

Typical Monthly Electric Bills

Area	Commercial Service ($/month)		Industrial Service ($/month)	
	3 kW demand 1,000 kWh	40 kW demand 14,000 kWh	1,000 kW demand 200,000 kWh	50,000 kW demand 15,000,000 kWh
City	146	1,149	29,538	1,517,450
Average[1]	100	1,134	17,850	1,045,117

Note: Based on rates in effect July 1, 2003; (1) average based on 197 utilities
Source: Edison Electric Institute, Typical Bills and Average Rates Report, Summer 2003

TRANSPORTATION

Means of Transportation to Work

Area	Car/Truck/Van		Public Transportation			Bicycle	Walked	Other Means	Worked at Home
	Drove Alone	Car-pooled	Bus	Subway	Railroad				
City	76.5	15.8	2.2	0.0	0.0	0.1	2.0	1.1	2.2
MSA[1]	75.9	16.2	2.2	0.0	0.0	0.1	2.2	1.3	2.1
U.S.	75.7	12.2	2.5	1.5	0.5	0.4	2.9	1.0	3.3

Note: Figures shown are percentages and cover workers 16 years of age and older;
(1) Metropolitan Statistical Area - see Appendix A for areas included
Source: Census 2000, Summary File 3

Travel Time to Work

Area	Less Than 15 Minutes	15 to 29 Minutes	30 to 44 Minutes	45 to 59 Minutes	60 Minutes or More
City	25.4	47.9	19.5	3.7	3.4
MSA[1]	25.7	45.9	20.5	4.3	3.5
U.S.	29.4	36.1	19.1	7.4	8.0

Note: Figures are percentages and include workers 16 years old and over; (1) Metropolitan Statistical Area - see Appendix A for areas included
Source: Census 2000, Summary File 3

Roadway Congestion Index

Area	1982	1990	1996	2000	2001
City	0.62	0.73	0.84	0.98	0.99
Average[1]	0.82	1.01	1.08	1.16	1.17

Note: Values greater than 1.00 indicate undesirable mobility levels; (1) average of 75 urban areas
Source: Texas Transportation Institute, The 2003 Annual Urban Mobility Report

Transportation Statistics

Interstate highways (2004)	I-10
Public transportation (2002)	Mass Transit Department-City of El Paso (Sun Metro)
Buses	
Average fleet age in years	9.3
No. operated in max. service	121
Demand response	
Average fleet age in years	3.2
No. operated in max. service	64
Passenger air service	
Airport	El Paso International
Airlines (2003)	8
Boardings (2002)	1,452,631
Amtrak service (2004)	Yes
Major waterways/ports	Rio Grande

Source: Federal Transit Administration, National Transit Database, 2002; Editor & Publisher Market Guide, 2004; Bureau of Transportation Statistics, Airport Enplanement Activity for CY2002; www.amtrak.com

BUSINESSES

Major Business Headquarters

Company Name	2003 Rankings	
	Fortune 500	Forbes 500
El Paso	152	-

Note: Companies listed are located in the city; dashes indicate no ranking
Fortune 500: Companies that produce a 10-K are ranked 1 to 500 based on 2002 revenue
Forbes 500: Private companies are ranked 1 to 281 based on 2002 revenue
Source: Fortune, April 14, 2003; www.forbes.com, November 6, 2003

Minority and Women-Owned Businesses

Ownership	All Firms		Firms with Paid Employees			
	Firms	Sales ($000)	Firms	Sales ($000)	Employees	Payroll ($000)
Black	n/a	n/a	n/a	n/a	n/a	n/a
Hispanic	16,925	3,525,409	4,887	3,191,597	41,500	541,007
Women	7,867	1,939,390	1,866	1,824,579	36,447	520,700

Note: Figures cover firms located in the city; n/a not available
Source: 1997 Economic Census, Minority and Women-Owned Businesses

Minority Business Opportunity

Seven of the 500 largest Hispanic-owned companies in the U.S. are located in El Paso.
Hispanic Business, June 2003

El Paso is home to four companies which are on the Hispanic Business Fastest-Growing 100 list (greatest sales growth over the past five years): **JC General Contractors Inc.; Biotech**

Pharmacy Inc.; NLR Builders Inc.; Fred Loya Insurance. *Hispanic Business, July/August 2003*

HOTELS

Hotels/Motels

Area	Hotels/Motels	Average Minimum Rates ($)		
		Tourist	First-Class	Deluxe
City	53	54	83	89

Source: OAG Travel Planner Online, Spring 2004

EVENT SITES

Major Event Sites, Meeting Places and Convention Centers

Name	Guest Rooms	Exhibit/ Meeting Space (sq. ft.)	Largest Meeting Room Capacity
Camino Real Hotel	337	13,000	800
El Paso Convention Center	n/a	60,000	6,000
El Paso County Coliseum	n/a	19,360	8,500
El Paso Marriott	296	10,000	1,200
Hilton El Paso Airport	272	22,000	1,020
Magoffin Auditorium	n/a	n/a	52,000

Note: n/a not available
Source: Original research

Living Environment

COST OF LIVING

Cost of Living Index

Year	Composite Index	Groceries	Housing	Utilities	Trans-portation	Health Care	Misc. Goods/ Services
2001	94.1	102.8	79.5	106.8	103.8	89.5	96.8
2002	95.8	104.1	82.9	90.8	100.5	112.7	100.1
2003	92.9	104.2	83.3	93.3	95.8	112.5	93.3

Note: U.S. = 100
Source: ACCRA, Cost of Living Index, 2001, 2002 and 2003 4-Quarter Averages

HOUSING

House Price Index (HPI)

Area	National Ranking[2]	Quarterly Change (%)	One-Year Change (%)	Five-Year Change (%)
MSA[1]	158	0.97	4.21	16.96
U.S.[3]	-	3.67	7.97	41.81

Note: The HPI is a weighted repeat sales index. It measures average price changes in repeat sales or refinancings on the same properties. This information is obtained by reviewing repeat mortgage transactions on single-family properties whose mortgages have been purchased or securitized by Fannie Mae of Freddie Mac in January 1975; (1) Metropolitan Statistical Area - see Appendix A for areas included; (2) Rankings are based on annual percentage change, for all MSAs containing at least 15,000 transactions over the last 10 years and ranges from 1 to 220; (3) figures based on a weighted division average; all figures are for the period ended December 31, 2003
Source: Office of Federal Housing Enterprise Oversight, House Price Index, March 1, 2004

Housing: Year Structure Built

Area	1990 -2000	1980 -1989	1970 -1979	1960 -1969	1950 -1959	1940 -1949	Before 1940	Median Year
City	17.7	18.7	22.5	15.7	14.2	5.1	6.0	1974
MSA[1]	20.6	19.7	22.0	14.4	12.9	4.8	5.6	1976
U.S.	17.0	15.8	18.5	13.7	12.7	7.3	15.0	1971

Note: Figures are percentages; (1) Metropolitan Statistical Area - see Appendix A for areas included
Source: Census 2000, Summary File 3

Average New Home Price

Area	2001	2002	2003
City	165,690	189,050	201,646
U.S.	212,643	236,567	248,193

Note: Figures, in dollars, are based on a new home with 2,400 sq. ft. of living area on an 8,000 sq. ft. lot.
Source: ACCRA, Cost of Living Index, 2001, 2002 and 2003 4-Quarter Averages

Average Apartment Rent

Area	2001	2002	2003
City	581	658	660
U.S.	674	708	721

Note: Figures, in dollars per month, are based on an unfurnished two bedroom, 1-1/2 or 2 bath apartment, approximately 950 sq. ft. in size, excluding all utilities except water
Source: ACCRA, Cost of Living Index, 2001, 2002 and 2003 4-Quarter Averages

RESIDENTIAL UTILITIES

Average Residential Utility Costs

Area	All Electric ($/mth)	Part Electric ($/mth)	Other Energy ($/mth)	Phone ($/mth)
City	–	76.51	34.98	23.80
U.S.	116.46	65.82	62.68	23.90

Source: ACCRA, Cost of Living Index, 2003 4-Quarter Average

HEALTH CARE

Average Health Care Costs

Area	Hospital ($/day)	Doctor ($/visit)	Dentist ($/visit)
City	923.31	71.39	91.44
U.S.	678.35	67.91	83.90

Note: Hospital—based on a semi-private room; Doctor—based on a general practitioner's routine exam of an established patient; Dentist—based on adult teeth cleaning and periodic oral exam.
Source: ACCRA, Cost of Living Index, 2003 4-Quarter Average

Distribution of Non-Federal, Office-Based Physicians

Area	Total	Family/ General Practice	Specialties		
			Medical	Surgical	Other
MSA[1] (number)	814	83	282	211	238
MSA[1] (rate per 10,000 pop.)	12.0	1.2	4.1	3.1	3.5
Metro Average[2] (rate per 10,000 pop.)	33.1	2.2	7.7	4.8	5.6

Note: Data as of December 31, 2001; (1) Metropolitan Statistical Area - see Appendix A for areas included; (2) Average of 81 MSAs and CMSAs in this book
Source: American Medical Association, Physician Characteristics & Distribution in the U.S., 2003-2004

Hospitals

El Paso has the following hospitals: 7 general medical and surgical; 1 psychiatric; 2 rehabilitation.
AHA Guide to the Healthcare Field, 2003-2004

PRESIDENTIAL ELECTION

2000 Presidential Election Results

Area	Gore	Bush	Nader	Buchanan	Other
El Paso County	57.8	39.7	2.0	0.2	0.4
U.S.	48.4	47.9	2.7	0.4	0.6

Note: Results are percentages and may not add to 100% due to rounding
Source: www.cbsnews.com; www.uselectionatlas.org

EDUCATION

Public School District Statistics

District Name	Schls.	Enroll-ment	Classroom Teachers	Pupil/ Teacher Ratio	Minority Pupils[1] (%)	Current Expend.[2] ($/pupil)
El Paso ISD	88	62,844	4,163	15.1	84.8	5,961
Socorro ISD	29	28,268	1,650	17.1	n/a	5,245
Ysleta ISD	59	46,811	2,986	15.7	91.4	6,101

Note: Data covers the 2001-02 school year unless otherwise noted; (1) Fall 2000; (2) FY2000; n/a not available
Source: U.S. Department of Education, National Center for Education Statistics, Common Core of Data, Local Education Agency (School District) Universe Survey: School Year 2001-2002; U.S. Department of Education, National Center for Education Statistics, Digest of Education Statistics 2002

Educational Quality

School District	Education Quotient[1]	Graduate Outcome[2]	Community Index[3]	Resource Index[4]
El Paso ISD	49	52	13	44

Note: Scores are national percentile rankings and range from 1 (worst) to 99 (best); (1) Combination of the Graduate Outcome, Community and Resource indexes weighted to reflect the greater importance of the Graduate Outcome and Resource Index; (2) Based on graduation rates and college board scores (SAT/ACT); (3) Based on the surrounding community's level of affluence and adult education; (4) Based on teacher salaries, per-pupil expenditures and student-teacher ratios.
Source: Expansion Management, December 2003

Educational Attainment by Race

Area	High School Graduate (%)					Bachelor's Degree (%)				
	Total	White	Black	Asian	Hisp.[2]	Total	White	Black	Asian	Hisp.[2]
City	68.6	69.6	89.6	83.4	59.9	18.3	20.0	21.7	42.7	12.0
MSA[1]	65.8	66.5	88.1	83.2	57.0	16.6	18.0	21.1	42.7	10.6
U.S.	80.4	83.6	72.3	80.4	52.4	24.4	26.1	14.3	44.1	10.4

Note: Figures shown cover persons 25 years old and over; (1) Metropolitan Statistical Area - see Appendix A for areas included; (2) people of Hispanic origin can be of any race
Source: Census 2000, Summary File 3

School Enrollment by Type

Area	Grades KG to 8				Grades 9 to 12			
	Public		Private		Public		Private	
	Enrollment	%	Enrollment	%	Enrollment	%	Enrollment	%
City	86,000	93.3	6,128	6.7	39,565	94.1	2,469	5.9
MSA[1]	107,817	94.1	6,804	5.9	49,887	94.5	2,915	5.5
U.S.	33,526,011	88.7	4,285,121	11.3	14,848,628	90.6	1,532,323	9.4

Note: Figures shown cover persons 3 years old and over; (1) Metropolitan Statistical Area - see Appendix A for areas included
Source: Census 2000, Summary File 3

School Enrollment by Race

Area	Grades KG to 8 (%)				Grades 9 to 12 (%)			
	White	Black	Asian	Hisp.[1]	White	Black	Asian	Hisp.[1]
City	71.0	3.1	0.8	83.3	71.2	3.0	1.1	82.1
MSA[2]	72.4	2.8	0.7	85.0	71.9	2.8	1.0	83.9
U.S.	68.5	15.5	3.3	16.8	68.8	15.5	3.8	15.7

Note: Figures shown cover persons 3 years old and over; (1) people of Hispanic origin can be of any race; (2) Metropolitan Statistical Area - see Appendix A for areas included
Source: Census 2000, Summary File 3

Classroom Teacher Salaries in Public Schools

District	B.A. Degree		M.A. Degree		Maximum	
	Min. ($)	Rank[1]	Max. ($)	Rank[1]	Max. ($)	Rank[1]
El Paso	30,000	58	52,217	53	53,217	77
DOD Average[2]	31,567	-	53,248	-	59,356	-

Note: Salaries are for 2001-2002; (1) Rank ranges from 1 to 100; (2) As per the U.S. Department of Defense Wage Fixing Authority
Source: American Federation of Teachers, Survey & Analysis of Teacher Salary Trends 2002

Higher Education

Four-Year Colleges			Two-Year Colleges			Medical Schools	Law Schools	Voc/ Tech
Public	Private Non-profit	Private For-profit	Public	Private Non-profit	Private For-profit			
1	0	0	1	0	4	0	0	7

Note: Figures cover institutions located within the city limits.
Source: National Center for Education Statistics, The Integrated Postsecondary Education System (IPEDS) Peer Analysis System, 2002; usnews.com, America's Best Graduate Schools 2004, Medical School Directory; The College Blue Book, Occupational Education, 2003; Barron's Guide to Law Schools, 2003; Medical School Admission Requirements U.S. & Canada, 2003-2004

MAJOR EMPLOYERS

Major Employers

Company Name	Industry	Type
GE	Motors and generators	Branch
Gecis Americas	Data processing and preparation	Headquarters
Las Palmas Medical Center	General medical and surgical hospitals	Branch
National Ctr/Employ Disabled	Corrugated and solid fiber boxes	Single
NCED/Sahara	Employment agencies	Single
Parks & Recreation Dept	Land, mineral, and wildlife conservation	Branch
Philips Monitors De Juares	Computer terminals	Branch
Police Dept	Police protection	Branch
Providence Memorial Hospital	Offices and clinics of medical doctors	Branch
R E Thomason General Hospital	General medical and surgical hospitals	Headquarters
Sierra Medical Center	General medical and surgical hospitals	Branch
T&T	Employment agencies	Single
Union Pacific Railroad Company	Railroads, line-haul operating	Branch
University of Texas System	Colleges and universities	Branch
University Texas At El Paso	Colleges and universities	Headquarters
US Post Office	U.s. postal service	Branch
VF	Girl's and children's outerwear, nec	Branch

Note: Companies shown are located in the metropolitan area and have 1,100 or more employees.
Source: www.zapdata.com, March 2004

PUBLIC SAFETY

Crime Rate

Area	All Crimes	Violent Crimes				Property Crimes		
		Murder	Forcible Rape	Robbery	Aggrav. Assault	Burglary	Larceny -Theft	Motor Vehicle Theft
City	4,585.6	2.4	37.5	97.7	523.5	377.2	3,208.0	339.4
Suburbs[1]	2,488.4	2.5	42.1	21.5	270.8	404.6	1,541.4	205.6
MSA[2]	4,227.8	2.4	38.3	84.7	480.4	381.9	2,923.6	316.5
U.S.	4,118.8	5.6	33.0	145.9	310.1	746.2	2,445.8	432.1

Note: Figures are crimes per 100,000 population; (1) All areas within the MSA that are located outside the city limits; (2) Metropolitan Statistical Area - see Appendix A for areas included
Source: FBI Uniform Crime Reports, 2002

RECREATION

Culture and Recreation

Museums	Orchestras	Opera Companies	Dance Companies	Professional Theatres	Zoos	Pro Sports Teams[1]
8	1	0	0	0	1	0

Note: (1) Covers the Metropolitan Statistical Area - see Appendix A for areas included.
Source: The Grey House Performing Arts Directory, 2002; Official Museum Directory, 2004; www.sportsvenues.com

Library System

The El Paso Public Library has nine branches, holdings of 699,957 volumes, and a budget of $6,103,665 (2002-2003).
American Library Directory, 2003-2004

MEDIA

Newspapers

Name	Type	Freq.	Distribution	Circulation
El Paso Shopping Guide	Hispanic	1x/wk	Local	290,000
El Paso Times	General	7x/wk	Local	47,000
The Fort Bliss Monitor	General	1x/wk	Local	20,000
The Rio Grande Catholic	Cath/Relig	1x/mth	Area	30,000

Note: Includes newspapers whose offices are located in the city and whose circulations are 1,000 or more
Source: Burrelle's Media Directory, 2003

Television Stations

Name	Ch.	Affiliation	Type	Owner
KDBC	4	n/a	Commercial	Imes Communications Group
KVIA	7	ABCT	Commercial	Saint Joseph News-Press
KTSM	9	NBCT	Commercial	Comcorp
KCOS	13	PBS	Public	El Paso TV Foundation
KFOX	14	FBC	Commercial	Cox Enterprises Inc.
KINT	26	UNIN	Commercial	Univision Communications Inc.
KSCE	38	n/a	Non-comm.	Channel 38 Christian Television
KTYO	48	TMUN	Commercial	Lee Enterprises Inc.

Note: Stations included broadcast from the El Paso metro area; n/a not available
Source: Burrelle's Media Directory, 2003

AM Radio Stations

Call Letters	Freq. (kHz)	Target Audience	Station Format	Music Format
KROD	600	General	N/S/T	n/a
KTSM	690	General	N/T	n/a
KAMA	750	Hispanic	M	Latin
KBNA	920	Hispanic	M/N/S	Adult Contemporary
KXPL	1060	Hispanic	M	n/a
KVIV	1340	H/R	M	Christian
KHEY	1380	General	S/T	n/a
KELP	1590	Religious	M/T	Christian

Note: Stations included broadcast from the El Paso metro area; n/a not available
The following abbreviations may be used:
Target Audience: A=Asian; B=Black; C=Christian; E=Ethnic; F=French; G=General; H=Hispanic;
M=Men; N=Native American; R=Religious; S=Senior Citizen; W=Women; Y=Young Adult; Z=Children
Station Format: E=Educational; M=Music; N=News; S=Sports; T=Talk
Source: Burrelle's Media Directory, 2003

FM Radio Stations

Call Letters	Freq. (mHz)	Target Audience	Station Format	Music Format
KTEP	88.5	General	M/N	Classical
KXCR	89.5	General	M	Adult Contemporary
KVER	91.1	H/R	M	Gospel
KOFX	92.3	General	M	Oldies
KSII	93.1	General	M	Adult Contemporary
KHRO	94.7	General	M	Classic Rock
KLAQ	95.5	General	M	AOR
KHEY	96.3	General	M/N/S	Country
KBNA	97.5	Hispanic	M/N/S	Adult Contemporary
KTSM	99.9	General	M	Adult Contemporary
KPRR	102.1	General	M/N	Adult Contemporary
KPAS	103.1	H/R	M/N/S	Christian

Note: Stations included broadcast from the El Paso metro area
The following abbreviations may be used:
Target Audience: A=Asian; B=Black; C=Christian; E=Ethnic; F=French; G=General; H=Hispanic;
M=Men; N=Native American; R=Religious; S=Senior Citizen; W=Women; Y=Young Adult; Z=Children
Station Format: E=Educational; M=Music; N=News; S=Sports; T=Talk
Music Format: AOR=Album Oriented Rock; MOR=Middle of the Road
Source: Burrelle's Media Directory, 2003

CLIMATE

Average and Extreme Temperatures

Temperature	Jan	Feb	Mar	Apr	May	Jun	Jul	Aug	Sep	Oct	Nov	Dec	Yr.
Extreme High (°F)	80	83	89	98	104	114	112	108	104	96	87	80	114
Average High (°F)	57	63	70	79	87	96	95	93	88	79	66	58	78
Average Temp. (°F)	44	49	56	64	73	81	83	81	75	65	52	45	64
Average Low (°F)	31	35	41	49	58	66	70	68	62	50	38	32	50
Extreme Low (°F)	-8	8	14	23	31	46	57	56	42	25	1	5	-8

Note: Figures cover the years 1948-1995
Source: National Climatic Data Center, International Station Meteorological Climate Summary, 9/96

Average Precipitation/Snowfall/Humidity

Precip./Humidity	Jan	Feb	Mar	Apr	May	Jun	Jul	Aug	Sep	Oct	Nov	Dec	Yr.
Avg. Precip. (in.)	0.4	0.4	0.3	0.2	0.3	0.7	1.6	1.5	1.4	0.7	0.3	0.6	8.6
Avg. Snowfall (in.)	1	1	Tr	Tr	0	0	0	0	0	Tr	1	2	6
Avg. Rel. Hum. 6am (%)	68	60	50	43	44	46	63	69	72	66	63	68	59
Avg. Rel. Hum. 3pm (%)	34	27	21	17	17	17	28	30	32	29	30	36	26

Note: Figures cover the years 1948-1995; Tr = Trace amounts (<0.05 in. of rain; <0.5 in. of snow)
Source: National Climatic Data Center, International Station Meteorological Climate Summary, 9/96

Weather Conditions

Temperature			Daytime Sky			Precipitation		
10°F & below	32°F & below	90°F & above	Clear	Partly cloudy	Cloudy	0.01 inch or more precip.	0.1 inch or more snow/ice	Thunder-storms
1	59	106	147	164	54	49	3	35

Note: Figures are average number of days per year and covers the years 1948-1995
Source: National Climatic Data Center, International Station Meteorological Climate Summary, 9/96

HAZARDOUS WASTE

Superfund Sites

El Paso has no sites on the EPA's Superfund National Priorities List.
U.S. Environmental Protection Agency, National Priorities List, March 15, 2004

AIR & WATER QUALITY

Maximum Pollutant Concentrations

	Particulate Matter (ug/m^3)	Carbon Monoxide (ppm)	Sulfur Dioxide (ppm)	Nitrogen Dioxide (ppm)	Ozone 1-hour (ppm)	Ozone 8-hour (ppm)	Lead (ug/m^3)
MSA[1] Level	534	7	0.006	0.021	0.13	0.09	1.02
NAAQS[2]	150	9	0.140	0.053	0.12	0.08	1.50
Met NAAQS[2]	No	Yes	Yes	Yes	No	No	Yes

Note: (1) Metropolitan Statistical Area - see Appendix A for areas included; (2) National Ambient Air Quality Standards; n/a not available
Units: ppm = parts per million; ug/m^3 = micrograms per cubic meter
Source: EPA, Latest Findings on National Air Quality: 2002 Status and Trends, August 2003

Air Quality Index

In the El Paso MSA (see Appendix A for areas included), the Air Quality Index (AQI) exceeded 100 on 18 days in 2002. An AQI value greater than 100 indicates that air quality would have been in the unhealthful range on that day.
EPA, Latest Findings on National Air Quality: 2002 Status and Trends, August 2003

Watershed Health

The U.S. Environmental Protection Agency monitors the health of the aquatic resources for the nation's 2,000+ watersheds. **The Rio Grande-Fort Quitman watershed serves the El Paso area and received an overall Index of Watershed Indicators (IWI) score of 1 (better quality - low vulnerability).** The IWI score is based on seven condition and nine vulnerability indicators. The overall IWI score ranges from 1 (best health) to 6 (worst health). The Condition Indicators include: designated use attainment, fish and wildlife consumption advisories, source water condition, contaminated sediments, ambient water quality, and wetlands loss index. The Vulnerability Indicators include: aquatic species at risk, conventional and toxic loads over permitted limits, urban and agricultural runoff potential, population change, hydrologic modification, estuarine pollution susceptibility, and air deposition. *EPA, Index of Watershed Indicators, October 26, 2001*

Drinking Water

Water System Name	Pop. Served	Primary Water Source Type	Number of Violations January 2002-February 2004		
			Health Based	Significant Monitoring	Monitoring
El Paso Water Utilities	620,000	Surface	None	None	2

Note: Data as of February 19, 2004
Source: EPA, Office of Ground Water and Drinking Water, Safe Drinking Water Information System

El Paso tap water is soft and fluoridated.
Editor & Publisher Market Guide, 2004

Fort Lauderdale, Florida

Background

Located on the Atlantic Ocean in southeast Florida, Fort Lauderdale is a city of tiny residential islands, canals, and yacht basins, and is called the "Venice of America."

Originally built as a fortification in 1837 for the Seminole War, Fort Lauderdale eased into more peaceful times as a top tourist spot. Photos of students on spring break, cars cruising "The Strip," and tan young men and women on the beach stimulated the imagination of people around the world.

Today, Fort Lauderdale remains a popular tourist spot, hosting many attractions. More than 8.5 million visitors traveled to the Greater Fort Lauderdale area in 2003. Three new hotels are slated to open in 2004 (including the Seminole Hard Rock Hotel & Casino Hollywood, developed for Florida's Seminole Tribe), followed by the St. Regis Hotel and Residences in 2005 and the West Fort Lauderdale Hotel and Residences in 2006.

Nearby Port Everglades is the winter homeport for the Queen Elizabeth II—Cunard Line's new $800 million flagship launched in 2004.

Fashionable Las Olas Boulevard, the main artery of downtown, is full of shops and restaurants and a quaint street on which to stroll. The Museum of Art is a handsome modern edifice that showcases nineteenth- and twentieth-century paintings and Japanese objects d'art, and is noted as having the largest U.S. collection of artwork from Copenhagen, Brussels, and Amsterdam. The Museum of Discovery and Science includes the Blockbuster IMAX® Theater, compliments of the multi-corporation mogul

Wayne Huizenga, and is fascinating to children of all ages. And the Broward Center for Performing Arts hosts Broadway plays and other major cultural events.

The busy Fort Lauderdale-Hollywood International Airport is growing faster than any other major airport in the country, according to the Greater Fort Lauderdale Convention & Visitors Bureau.

As home to one of the biggest yacht basins in the country, Fort Lauderdale's boating products industry stays busy. And, because of its largely residential character, the home improvement industry—concrete, air conditioning, and roofing—lays a large claim to the economy as well.

Fort Lauderdale's climate is primarily subtropical marine which produces a long, warm summer with abundant rainfall, followed by a mild, dry winter. Hurricanes occasionally affect the area, with most occurring in September and October. Funnel clouds and waterspouts are sometimes sighted during the summer months, but neither causes significant damage. Strong and sometimes spectacular lightning storms occur most often during June, July, and August.

Rankings

- Fort Lauderdale was ranked #57 out of 331 metro areas in *Cities Ranked & Rated*. Criteria: cost of living; climate; crime; transportation; economy and jobs; education; arts and culture; health and healthcare; leisure. *Cities Ranked & Rated, 1st Edition, 2004*

- *Ladies Home Journal* ranked America's 200 largest cities based on the qualities women surveyed care about most. Fort Lauderdale ranked #131 out of 143 in the smaller city category (population under 300,000). Criteria: crime; lifestyle; education; jobs; health; child care; politics; and the economy. *Ladies Home Journal Online, "The Best Cities for Women 2002"*

- Fort Lauderdale was selected as one of "America's Pet Healthiest Cities" by Purina. The city ranked #47 out of 50. Criteria: veterinary services; environment; and legislation. *Purina Pet Institute, "America's Pet Healthiest Cities," August 14, 2001*

- *Forbes* ranked the 150 most populous metro areas in the U.S. in terms of the "Best Places for Business and Careers." The Fort Lauderdale metro area was ranked #47. Criteria: income and job growth; cost-of-doing-business; qualifications of the available pool of labor; crime rates; housing costs; net migration. *Forbes, May 9, 2003*

- *Men's Health* ranked 101 U.S. cities in terms of the quality of their tap water. Fort Lauderdale received a grade of. Criteria: levels of bacteria, arsenic, lead, trihalomethanes, and haloacetic acids were compared with the National Academy of Science's guidelines as well as with the EPA's more stringent maximum contaminant level goals. *Men's Health, March 2004*

- Sperling's BestPlaces ranked 331 metro areas and identified the most and least stressful U.S. cities. The Fort Lauderdale metro area ranked #14 out of the 100 largest metro areas (#1 = most stressful). Criteria: divorce rate; unemployment rate; violent and property crime; suicide rate; commute time; mental health; alcohol consumption; cloudy days. *www.BestPlaces.net, February 26, 2004*

- Sperling's BestPlaces in partnership with Pep Boys ranked 77 metro areas and identified "America's Most Drivable Cities." The Fort Lauderdale metro area ranked #28. Criteria: climate; road roughness; urban mobility; gas prices. *Pep Boys, "America's Most Drivable Cities," April 9, 2003*

- Fort Lauderdale was ranked #102 out of America's 200 largest metro areas in *SELF Magazine's* ranking of "America's Healthiest Cities for Women." Criteria: safety; air/water quality; cancer rates; and 21 other factors relating to health. *SELF Magazine, November 2003*

- Fort Lauderdale was identified as one of the most dangerous large metro areas for pedestrians in the U.S. The area ranked #5 out of the nations 49 largest metro areas. Criteria: average yearly pedestrian fatalities per capita (for the years 2000 and 2001) adjusted for the number of walkers. *Surface Transportation Policy Project, "Mean Streets 2002"*

- Fort Lauderdale was ranked #64 out of 100 cities surveyed in *Child* magazine's ranking of the "Best Cities for Families." Criteria: number of pediatricians per capita; proximity to a children's hospital; immunization rates; infant mortality rate; air quality; water quality; school spending; pupil-teacher ratio; availability of parks/green space; nearby recreational opportunities; average commute time; number of sunny days; average cost of a 3-bedroom home; unemployment rate; future job growth; crime rate; percentage of children under 5; mandated minimum child care ratios. *Child, April 2001*

- *Zero Population Growth* ranked 239 cities in terms of children's health, safety, and economic well-being. Fort Lauderdale was ranked #120 out of 140 independent cities (cities with populations greater than 100,000 which were neither major cities nor suburbs/outer cities) and was given a grade of C. Criteria: total population and population growth; percent of population under 18 years of age; number of children's museums; health improvement grade; percent of births to teens; percent of low birthweight infants; infant mortality rate; number of Title X-funded clinics; average SAT/ACT scores; average elementary and secondary class size; crime rate; unemployment rate; percent of affordable homes; number of bad air days; park acres per 1000 persons; library circulation per child; and children's program attendance counts. *Zero Population Growth, Kid Friendly Cities Report Card 2001*

■ Fort Lauderdale was selected as one of America's best places to retire. Criteria: safety; climate; access to shopping, fun, games and entertainment; community; health care; and transportation. *America's 100 Best Places to Retire, 2000*

■ *Ladies Home Journal* ranked America's 200 largest cities in terms of safety. Fort Lauderdale ranked #133 out of 200. Criteria: violent crimes; crimes against property; and rape. *Ladies Home Journal Online, "The Best Cities for Women 2002"*

■ Fort Lauderdale was ranked #62 out of 125 regions worldwide in terms of its "Knowledge Competitiveness Index." The index attempts to measure the knowledge-based development taking place throughout the world and is based on 17 measures of economic performance that indicate a region's ability to translate its knowledge capacity into economic value. *Robert Huggins Associates, "2003-2004 World Knowledge Competitiveness Index"*

■ The Fort Lauderdale metro area was selected by *Yahoo! Internet Life* as one of "America's Most Wired Cities...and Towns." The area ranked #25 out of 87. Criteria: home and work net use; user sophistication; domain density; and available content. *Yahoo! Internet Life, April 2001*

■ The Fort Lauderdale metro area was selected by Cranium as one of the "Top 50 Fun Cities" in America. The area ranked #48. Criteria includes: number of sports teams, restaurants, and dance performances; number of toy stores; city budget spent on recreation. *Cranium, November 4, 2003*

■ Fort Lauderdale was identified as one of the 100 "Most Unwired Cities" in the U.S. The area ranked #43. Criteria: number of public and commercial wireless access points; cell phone coverage offering wide area network Internet access; Internet penetration. *Intel, "Most Unwired Cities," March 4, 2003*

■ Scarborough Research measured the percentage of households who subscribe to cellular services among adults ages 18 and over in 75 U.S. markets. The Fort Lauderdale DMA (Designated Market Area) was ranked #5 out of 75. *Scarborough Research, Scarborough USA+ 2003 Release 1*

■ Fort Lauderdale was ranked #37 in *Prevention* magazine's survey of the "Best Walking Cities in the U.S." The magazine, in conjunction with the American Podiatric Medical Association, surveyed 125 of the most populated cities and then tabulated and weighed 20 criteria of interest to pedestrians. *Prevention, April, 2004*

■ The Fort Lauderdale metro area was selected as one of the "Top 60 CyberCities in America" by *Site Selection*. CyberCities are magnets for growing high-tech companies. Criteria: total employment; average wages; total payroll; number of companies; R&D spending and venture capital in the 45 Standard Industrial Classification (SIC) codes that define the high-technology industry. *Site Selection, March 2002*

■ The Fort Lauderdale metro area was cited as one of "The Best Places in the U.S. to Locate a Company." The area ranked #264 out of 329. Criteria: education (with emphasis on college board test results and high school graduation rates); availability of quality healthcare services and the cost to employers; quality of life; logistics workforce and companies; transportation infrastructure; quality and quantity of highly educated technical workers; business climate. *Expansion Management, July 2003*

■ The Fort Lauderdale metro area was selected as one of the "Top 40 Hottest Real Estate Markets" for expanding or relocating businesses." Criteria: rental costs; purchase prices; and vacancy rates of office and warehouse space. *Expansion Management, August 2003*

■ Fort Lauderdale was selected as one of the five best places to buy real estate in 2003. Criteria: projected median home price appreciation. *www.Forbes.com, January 10, 2003*

■ The Fort Lauderdale metro area was selected as one of the "10 Hottest Housing Markets" in the U.S. The area ranked #7 out of 120 markets tracked by the National Association of Realtors. Criteria: year-over-year change of median home prices between Q4 of 2001 and Q4 of 2002. *CNN/Money Online, February 12, 2003*

- The Fort Lauderdale metro area appeared on *Forbes/Milken Institute* list of "Best Places for Business and Career." Rank: #30 out of 200 metro areas. Criteria: salary growth; job growth; number of technology clusters; overall concentration of technology activity relative to national average; and technology output growth. *www.forbes.com, Forbes/Milken Institute Best Places 2002*

- The Fort Lauderdale metro area appeared on the "Milken Institute Best Performing Cities" index. Rank: #29 out of 200 large metro areas. Criteria: job growth; wage and salary growth; high-tech output growth. *Milken Institute, June 25, 2003*

- The Fort Lauderdale metro area appeared on *Entrepreneur* magazine's list of the "Best Cities for Entrepreneurs" in 2003. The area ranked #4 out of 61 in the large city category. Criteria: entrepreneurial activity; small-business growth; economic growth; and risk. *www.Entrepreneur.com*

- The Fort Lauderdale metro area was selected as one of the "Top 25 Cities for Doing Business in America." *Inc.* measured current-year employment growth in 277 regions as well as current trends in the annual average growth over the past three years, and compared employment expansion between the first and second halves of the last decade. Job growth factors account for two-thirds, and balance among industries accounts for one third of the final score for each city. The Fort Lauderdale metro area ranked #7 among large metro areas. *Inc. Magazine, March 2004*

- The Fort Lauderdale metro area appeared on *IndustryWeek's* fourth annual World-Class Communities list. It ranked #290 out of 315 metro areas. Criteria: MSA Gross Metropolitan Product (GMP) per manufacturing employee; and MSA percent share of U.S. manufacturing Gross Domestic Product (GDP). *IndustryWeek, April 16, 2001*

- ING Group ranked the 125 largest metro areas according to the general financial security of residents. The Fort Lauderdale metro area was ranked #95 out of 125. Criteria: Earnings and Wealth Potential (household income, education, net assets, cost of living); Safety Net (health insurance, retirement savings, life insurance, income support programs); Personal Threats (unemployment rate, low-income households, crime rate); Community Economic Vitality (cost of community services, job quality, job creation, housing costs). *ING Group, "The Best Cities to Earn and Save Money: A Ranking of the Largest 125 U.S. Cities," 2001 Edition*

Business Environment

CITY FINANCES

City Government Finances

Component	2000-2001 ($000)	2000-2001 ($ per capita)
Total Revenues	343,561	2,254
Total Expenditures	298,947	1,962
Debt Outstanding	80,688	529
Cash and Securities	814,130	5,342

Source: U.S Census Bureau, Government Finances 2000-2001, August 2003

City Government Revenue by Source

Source	2000-2001 ($000)	2000-2001 ($ per capita)
General Revenue		
From Federal Government	9,850	65
From State Government	14,491	95
From Local Governments	3,768	25
Taxes		
Property	62,551	410
Sales	41,175	270
Personal Income	0	0
License	0	0
Charges	46,536	305
Liquor Store	0	0
Utility	61,935	406
Employee Retirement	60,768	399
Other	42,487	279

Source: U.S Census Bureau, Government Finances 2000-2001, August 2003

City Government Expenditures by Function

Function	2000-2001 ($000)	2000-2001 ($ per capita)	2000-2001 (%)
General Expenditures			
Airports	5,555	36	1.9
Corrections	0	0	0.0
Education	0	0	0.0
Fire Protection	30,466	200	10.2
Governmental Administration	22,596	148	7.6
Health	0	0	0.0
Highways	4,626	30	1.5
Hospitals	0	0	0.0
Housing and Community Development	8,559	56	2.9
Interest on General Debt	5,941	39	2.0
Libraries	0	0	0.0
Parking	5,093	33	1.7
Parks and Recreation	31,346	206	10.5
Police Protection	70,150	460	23.5
Public Welfare	0	0	0.0
Sewerage	0	0	0.0
Solid Waste Management	17,560	115	5.9
Liquor Store	0	0	0.0
Utility	45,281	297	15.1
Employee Retirement	30,043	197	10.0
Other	21,731	143	7.3

Source: U.S Census Bureau, Government Finances 2000-2001, August 2003

Municipal Bond Ratings

Area	Moody's
City	Aa3

Source: Mergent Bond Record, February 2004

DEMOGRAPHICS

Population Growth

Area	1990 Census	2000 Census	2003 Estimate	2008 Projection	Population Growth (%) 1990-2000	Population Growth (%) 2000-2008
City	149,908	152,397	154,143	158,586	1.7	4.1
MSA[1]	1,255,488	1,623,018	1,710,917	1,869,055	29.3	15.2
U.S.	248,709,873	281,421,906	290,647,163	305,918,071	13.2	8.7

Note: (1) Metropolitan Statistical Area - see Appendix A for areas included
Source: Claritas, Inc.

Number of Households and Average Household Size

Area	1990 Census	2000 Census	2003 Estimate	2008 Projection	2003 Average Household Size
City	66,672	68,468	69,305	71,085	2.2
MSA[1]	528,442	654,445	681,636	730,063	2.5
U.S.	91,947,410	105,480,101	109,440,059	116,034,472	2.7

Note: (1) Metropolitan Statistical Area - see Appendix A for areas included
Source: Claritas, Inc.

Race and Ethnicity

Area	White Non-Hispanic	Black Non-Hispanic	Asian Non-Hispanic	Other Race Non-Hispanic	Hispanic
City	63.6	29.1	1.1	6.2	9.9
MSA[1]	69.4	21.1	2.4	7.1	17.9
U.S.	74.5	12.4	3.8	9.3	13.2

Note: Figures are 2003 estimates; (1) Metropolitan Statistical Area - see Appendix A for areas included
Source: Claritas, Inc.

Segregation

City Index[2]	City Rank[3]	MSA[1] Index[2]	MSA[1] Rank[4]
80.5	6	64.8	101

Note: Figures are based on an analysis of Census 2000 data; (1) Metropolitan Statistical Area - see Appendix A for areas included; (2) Dissimilarity Index—the most commonly used measure of segregation between two groups, reflecting their relative distributions across neighborhoods within a city or metropolitan area. It can range in value from 0, indicating complete integration, to 100, indicating complete segregation; (3) Ranges from 1 (most segregated) to 100 (least segregated) and includes all the cities in this book; (4) Ranges from 1 (most segregated) to 318 (least segregated) and includes 318 metropolitan areas.
Source: www.CensusScope.org

Ancestry

Area	German	Irish[2]	English	American	Italian	Polish	French[3]	Scottish
City	10.4	10.3	8.2	5.9	7.6	2.9	2.7	1.8
MSA[1]	9.1	9.0	5.7	6.5	9.5	3.7	2.2	1.2
U.S.	15.2	10.9	8.7	7.3	5.6	3.2	3.0	1.7

Note: Figures include multiple ancestry (e.g. if a person reported being Irish and Italian, they were included in both columns); (1) Metropolitan Statistical Area - see Appendix A for areas included; (2) Includes Celtic; (3) Includes Alsatian but excludes Basque
Source: Census 2000, Summary File 3

Foreign-Born Population

Area	Any Foreign Country	Percent of Population Born in: Europe	Asia	Africa	Oceania[2]	Canada	Mexico	Latin America[3]
City	21.7	3.8	1.3	0.4	0.1	1.1	0.5	14.5
MSA[1]	25.3	3.6	1.9	0.4	0.0	1.3	0.7	17.5
U.S.	11.1	1.7	2.9	0.3	0.1	0.3	3.3	2.5

Note: (1) Metropolitan Statistical Area - see Appendix A for areas included; (2) Includes Australia, New Zealand subregion, Melanesia, Micronesia, Polynesia, and Oceania n.e.c; (3) Includes Central America (excluding Mexico), South America, and the Caribbean.
Source: Census 2000, Summary File 3

Religion

Area	Catholic	Southern Baptist	United Meth-odist	ELCA[1]	LDS[2]	Presby-terian Church USA	Jewish Est.	Muslim Est.
County	21.1	3.6	1.2	0.3	0.3	0.4	13.1	0.4
U.S.	22.0	7.1	3.7	1.8	1.5	1.1	2.2	0.6

Note: Figures shown are the number of adherents as a percentage of the total population; Adherents are defined as all members, including full members, their children and the estimated number of other participants who are not considered members (e.g. the baptized, those not confirmed, those not eligible for communion, those regularly attending services, etc.); (1) Evangelical Lutheran Church in America; (2) The Church of Jesus Christ of Latter Day Saints
Source: Reprinted with permission from Religious Congregations and Membership in the United States 2000 (Nashville, Glenmary Research Center, 2002) Copyright Association of Statisticians of American Religious Bodies. All rights reserved.

Age Distribution

Area	Percent of Population						
	Under Age 5	Age 5 to 17	Age 18 to 34	Age 35 to 49	Age 50 to 64	Age 65 to 79	80 Years and Over
City	5.1	14.1	22.6	26.1	16.7	11.1	4.3
MSA[1]	6.3	17.2	21.3	24.8	14.4	10.7	5.4
U.S.	6.8	18.9	23.7	23.5	14.8	9.2	3.2

Note: (1) Metropolitan Statistical Area - see Appendix A for areas included
Source: Census 2000, Summary File 3

Marriage Status

Area	Never Married	Now Married Except Separated	Separated	Widowed	Divorced
City	35.3	40.0	3.3	7.3	14.0
MSA[1]	25.9	51.3	2.6	8.4	11.8
U.S.	27.1	54.4	2.2	6.6	9.7

Note: Figures cover population 15 years of age and older; (1) Metropolitan Statistical Area - see Appendix A for areas included
Source: Census 2000, Summary File 3

Male/Female Ratio

Area	Males	Females	Males per 100 Females
City	80,556	73,587	109.5
MSA[1]	824,485	886,432	93.0
U.S.	142,511,883	148,135,280	96.2

Note: Figures are 2003 estimates; (1) Metropolitan Statistical Area - see Appendix A for areas included
Source: Claritas, Inc.

ECONOMY

Gross Metropolitan Product

Area	1999	2000	2001	2002	2002 Rank[2]
MSA[1]	42.4	45.8	48.6	50.7	49

Note: Figures are in billions of dollars; (1) Metropolitan Statistical Area - see Appendix A for areas included; (2) Rank ranges from 1 to 319
Source: The U.S. Conference of Mayors, Metro Economies Report, July 2003

INCOME

Per Capita/Median/Average Income

Area	Per Capita ($)	Median Household ($)	Average Household ($)
City	30,206	42,335	66,164
MSA[1]	25,557	46,403	63,742
U.S.	24,078	46,868	63,207

Note: Figures are 2003 estimates; (1) Metropolitan Statistical Area - see Appendix A for areas included
Source: Claritas, Inc.

Household Income Distribution

Area	Percent of Households Earning							
	Under $15,000	$15,000 -24,999	$25,000 -34,999	$35,000 -49,999	$50,000 -74,999	$75,000 -99,000	$100,000 -149,999	$150,000 and up
City	16.9	13.0	12.3	15.8	16.7	8.6	8.2	8.4
MSA[1]	13.8	11.9	12.0	16.2	18.6	11.1	10.3	6.2
U.S.	14.1	11.5	11.7	16.0	19.2	11.3	10.2	6.0

Note: Figures are 2003 estimates; (1) Metropolitan Statistical Area - see Appendix A for areas included
Source: Claritas, Inc.

Poverty Rates by Age

Area	All Ages	Under 5 Years Old	5 to 17 Years Old	18 to 64 Years Old	65 Years and Over
City	17.7	1.6	4.1	10.3	1.7
MSA[1]	11.5	1.0	2.7	6.2	1.6
U.S.	12.4	1.2	3.0	6.9	1.2

Note: Figures are percent of population with income in 1999 below poverty level and only include population
for whom poverty status is determined; (1) Metropolitan Statistical Area - see Appendix A for areas included
Source: Census 2000, Summary File 3

Personal Bankruptcy Filing Rate

Area	2002	2003
Broward County	5.91	5.56
U.S.	5.34	5.58

Note: Numbers are per 1,000 population and include Chapter 7 and Chapter 13 filings
Source: Federal Deposit Insurance Corporation (FDIC), Regional Economic Conditions (RECON), 2/25/2004

EMPLOYMENT

Labor Force and Employment

Area	Civilian Labor Force			Workers Employed		
	Dec. 2002	Dec. 2003	% Chg.	Dec. 2002	Dec. 2003	% Chg.
City	105,616	104,678	-0.9	98,392	98,523	0.1
MSA[1]	858,512	852,633	-0.7	811,482	812,562	0.1
U.S.	144,807,000	146,501,000	1.2	136,599,000	138,556,000	1.4

Note: Data is not seasonally adjusted and covers workers 16 years of age and older;
(1) Metropolitan Statistical Area - see Appendix A for areas included
Source: Bureau of Labor Statistics, http://stats.bls.gov

Unemployment Rate

Area	2003											
	Jan.	Feb.	Mar.	Apr.	May	Jun.	Jul.	Aug.	Sep.	Oct.	Nov.	Dec.
City	7.7	7.2	7.0	7.2	7.0	7.6	7.3	7.5	7.3	6.8	6.6	5.9
MSA[1]	6.1	5.8	5.6	5.8	5.6	6.1	5.8	6.0	5.9	5.4	5.3	4.7
U.S.	6.5	6.4	6.2	5.8	5.8	6.5	6.3	6.0	5.8	5.6	5.6	5.4

Note: Data is not seasonally adjusted and covers workers 16 years of age and older; All figures are
percentages; (1) Metropolitan Statistical Area - see Appendix A for areas included
Source: Bureau of Labor Statistics, http://stats.bls.gov

Employment by Occupation

Occupation Classification	City (%)	MSA[1] (%)	U.S. (%)
Sales and Office	27.4	31.0	26.7
Professional and Related	17.9	18.4	20.2
Service	20.1	16.3	14.9
Production, Transportation, and Material Moving	9.8	9.3	14.6
Management, Business, and Financial	15.5	14.9	13.5
Construction, Extraction, and Maintenance	9.1	9.8	9.4
Farming, Forestry, and Fishing	0.3	0.2	0.7

Note: Figures cover employed civilians 16 years of age and older;
(1) Metropolitan Statistical Area - see Appendix A for areas included
Source: Census 2000, Summary File 3

Employment by Industry

Sector	MSA[1]		U.S.
	Number of Employees	Percent of Total	Percent of Total
Government	100,700	13.7	16.7
Education and Health Services	81,800	11.1	12.9
Professional and Business Services	131,300	17.9	12.3
Retail Trade	101,600	13.8	11.8
Manufacturing	30,700	4.2	11.0
Leisure and Hospitality	75,500	10.3	9.1
Finance Activities	58,300	7.9	6.1
Construction	n/a	n/a	5.1
Wholesale Trade	39,300	5.4	4.3
Other Services	30,800	4.2	4.1
Transportation and Utilities	19,400	2.6	3.7
Information	19,300	2.6	2.4
Natural Resources and Mining	n/a	n/a	0.4

Note: Figures cover non-farm employment as of December 2003 and are not seasonally adjusted;
(1) Metropolitan Statistical Area - see Appendix A for areas included; n/a not available
Source: Bureau of Labor Statistics, http://stats.bls.gov

Average Wages

Occupation	$/Hr.	Occupation	$/Hr.
Accountants and Auditors	22.76	Maids and Housekeeping Cleaners	7.64
Automotive Mechanics	16.27	Maintenance and Repair Workers	12.97
Bookkeepers	13.80	Marketing Managers	38.99
Carpenters	15.53	Nuclear Medicine Technologists	24.04
Cashiers	7.81	Nurses, Licensed Practical	16.25
Clerks, General Office	10.18	Nurses, Registered	23.19
Clerks, Receptionists/Information	10.50	Nursing Aides/Orderlies/Attendants	9.25
Clerks, Shipping/Receiving	11.23	Packers and Packagers, Hand	7.25
Computer Programmers	30.14	Physical Therapists	28.32
Computer Support Specialists	18.06	Postal Service Mail Carriers	n/a
Computer Systems Analysts	30.40	Real Estate Brokers	56.66
Cooks, Restaurant	9.36	Retail Salespersons	10.66
Dentists	75.78	Sales Reps., Exc. Tech./Scientific	26.73
Electrical Engineers	31.20	Sales Reps., Tech./Scientific	25.60
Electricians	16.69	Secretaries, Exc. Legal/Med./Exec.	12.00
Financial Managers	40.21	Security Guards	9.49
First-Line Supervisors/Mgrs., Sales	18.88	Surgeons	63.11
Food Preparation Workers	7.99	Teacher Assistants	n/a
General and Operations Managers	42.05	Teachers, Elementary School	n/a
Hairdressers/Cosmetologists	9.17	Teachers, Secondary School	n/a
Internists	81.87	Telemarketers	10.22
Janitors and Cleaners	8.64	Truck Drivers, Heavy/Tractor-Trailer	14.07
Landscaping/Groundskeeping Workers	10.00	Truck Drivers, Light/Delivery Svcs.	11.57
Lawyers	57.76	Waiters and Waitresses	7.65

Note: Wage data is for 2002 and covers the Metropolitan Statistical Area (see Appendix A for areas included).
Hourly wages for elementary/secondary school teachers and teacher assistants were calculated by the editors
from annual wage data assuming a 40 hour work week; n/a not available.
Source: Bureau of Labor Statistics, 2002 Metro Area Occupational Employment and Wage Estimates

Occupational Employment Projections: 1996 - 2006

Occupations Expected to Have the Largest Job Growth (ranked by numerical growth)	Fast-Growing Occupations[1] (ranked by percent growth)
1. Cashiers	1. Systems analysts
2. Salespersons, retail	2. Physical therapy assistants and aides
3. General managers & top executives	3. Desktop publishers
4. Registered nurses	4. Home health aides
5. Waiters & waitresses	5. Computer engineers
6. Marketing & sales, supervisors	6. Medical assistants
7. Janitors/cleaners/maids, ex. priv. hshld.	7. Physical therapists
8. General office clerks	8. Paralegals
9. Food preparation workers	9. Emergency medical technicians
10. Hand packers & packagers	10. Occupational therapists

Note: Projections cover Florida; (1) Excludes occupations with total job growth less than 300
Source: U.S. Department of Labor, Employment and Training Administration, America's Labor Market Information System (ALMIS)

TAXES

State Corporate Income Tax Rates

State	Rate (%)	Number of Brackets	Low Bracket (Under $)	High Bracket (Over $)
Florida	5.5	1	na	na

Note: Tax rates as of December 31, 2003; na not applicable; 3.3% alternative minimum rate.
Source: Tax Foundation, www.taxfoundation.org

State Individual Income Tax Rates

State	Federal Deductibility	Marginal Rate (%)	Number of Brackets	Low Bracket (Under $)	High Bracket (Over $)
Florida	No	None	na	na	na

Note: Tax rates as of December 31, 2003; Brackets apply to single taxpayers and married people filing separately; na not applicable
Source: Tax Foundation, www.taxfoundation.org

Various State and Local Tax Rates

State Sales and Use (%)	Total Sales and Use (%)	Gasoline (cents/gal.)	Cigarette (cents/pack)	Spirits ($/gal.)	Table Wine ($/gal.)	Beer ($/gal.)
6.0	6.0	13.9	33.9	6.50	2.25	0.48

Note: Tax rates as of December 31, 2003
Source: Tax Foundation, www.taxfoundation.org

State Tax Burdens

Area	Combined State and Local Tax Burden Percent	Rank	Combined Federal, State and Local Tax Burden Percent	Rank
Florida	8.4	45	29.0	23
U.S. Average	9.7	-	30.0	-

Note: Figures are for 2003
Source: Tax Foundation, www.taxfoundation.org

Internal Revenue Service Tax Audits

IRS District	Percent of Returns Audited 1996	1997	1998	1999	2000
South Florida	0.71	0.68	0.50	0.42	0.23
U.S.	0.66	0.61	0.46	0.31	0.20

Note: Figures cover IRS district audits of federal income tax returns filed by individuals. Geographic data on district audits for 2001 and 2002 are being withheld by the IRS. TRAC is challenging this policy.
Source: Syracuse University, Transactional Records Access Clearinghouse (TRAC), "Odds of IRS District Tax Audit 2000"

RESIDENTIAL REAL ESTATE

Building Permits

Area	Single-Family			Multi-Family			Total		
	2001	2002	Pct. Chg.	2001	2002	Pct. Chg.	2001	2002	Pct. Chg.
City	189	232	22.8	286	2,691	840.9	475	2,923	515.4
U.S.	1,235,600	1,332,600	7.9	401,100	415,100	3.5	1,636,700	1,747,700	6.8

Note: Figures represent new, privately-owned housing units authorized (unadjusted data)
Source: U.S. Census Bureau, Manufacturing, Mining, and Construction Statistics

Homeownership and Housing Vacancies

Area	Homeownership Rate[2] (%)			Rental Vacancy Rate[3] (%)			Homeowner Vacancy Rate[4] (%)		
	2001	2002[a]	2003	2001	2002[a]	2003	2001	2002[a]	2003
MSA[1]	76.1	73.7	74.0	7.1	6.0	8.1	2.4	2.4	1.5
U.S.	67.8	67.9	68.3	8.4	8.9	9.8	1.8	1.7	1.8

Note: (1) Metropolitan Statistical Area - see Appendix A for areas included; (2) The proportion of households that are owners; (3) The proportion of the rental inventory that is vacant for rent; (4) The proportion of the homeowner inventory that is vacant for sale; (a) 2002 figures have been revised; n/a not available
Source: U.S. Census Bureau, Housing Vacancies and Homeownership Annual Statistics: 2003

COMMERCIAL UTILITIES

Typical Monthly Electric Bills

Area	Commercial Service ($/month)		Industrial Service ($/month)	
	3 kW demand 1,000 kWh	40 kW demand 14,000 kWh	1,000 kW demand 200,000 kWh	50,000 kW demand 15,000,000 kWh
City	88	952	17,273	1,081,336
Average[1]	100	1,134	17,850	1,045,117

Note: Based on rates in effect July 1, 2003; (1) average based on 197 utilities
Source: Edison Electric Institute, Typical Bills and Average Rates Report, Summer 2003

TRANSPORTATION

Means of Transportation to Work

Area	Car/Truck/Van		Public Transportation			Bicycle	Walked	Other Means	Worked at Home
	Drove Alone	Car-pooled	Bus	Subway	Railroad				
City	75.2	11.3	4.4	0.0	0.2	1.1	2.4	1.7	3.8
MSA[1]	80.0	12.0	1.9	0.0	0.1	0.5	1.3	1.1	2.9
U.S.	75.7	12.2	2.5	1.5	0.5	0.4	2.9	1.0	3.3

Note: Figures shown are percentages and cover workers 16 years of age and older;
(1) Metropolitan Statistical Area - see Appendix A for areas included
Source: Census 2000, Summary File 3

Travel Time to Work

Area	Less Than 15 Minutes	15 to 29 Minutes	30 to 44 Minutes	45 to 59 Minutes	60 Minutes or More
City	29.7	38.5	19.7	5.8	6.4
MSA[1]	20.9	36.5	26.0	9.5	7.1
U.S.	29.4	36.1	19.1	7.4	8.0

Note: Figures are percentages and include workers 16 years old and over; (1) Metropolitan Statistical Area - see Appendix A for areas included
Source: Census 2000, Summary File 3

Roadway Congestion Index

Area	1982	1990	1996	2000	2001
City	0.69	0.90	1.07	1.23	1.28
Average[1]	0.82	1.01	1.08	1.16	1.17

Note: Values greater than 1.00 indicate undesirable mobility levels; (1) average of 75 urban areas
Source: Texas Transportation Institute, The 2003 Annual Urban Mobility Report

Transportation Statistics

Interstate highways (2004)	I-95
Public transportation (2002)	Broward County Commission (BCT); Tri-County Commuter Rail Authority
Buses	
Average fleet age in years	4.8
No. operated in max. service	275
Light rail	
Average fleet age in years	12.7 (Tri-Rail)
No. operated in max. service	20 (Tri-Rail)
Demand response	
Average fleet age in years	2.6
No. operated in max. service	258
Passenger air service	
Airport	Ft. Lauderdale-Hollywood International
Airlines (2003)	25
Boardings (2002)	8,266,788
Amtrak service (2004)	Yes
Major waterways/ports	Intracoastal Waterway; Port Everglades

Source: Federal Transit Administration, National Transit Database, 2002; Editor & Publisher Market Guide, 2004; Bureau of Transportation Statistics, Airport Enplanement Activity for CY2002; www.amtrak.com

BUSINESSES

Major Business Headquarters

Company Name	2003 Rankings	
	Fortune 500	Forbes 500
AutoNation	93	-

Note: Companies listed are located in the city; dashes indicate no ranking
Fortune 500: Companies that produce a 10-K are ranked 1 to 500 based on 2002 revenue
Forbes 500: Private companies are ranked 1 to 281 based on 2002 revenue
Source: Fortune, April 14, 2003; www.forbes.com, November 6, 2003

Best Companies to Work For

Citrix Systems, headquartered in Fort Lauderdale, is among the "200 Best Small Companies in 2003." Criteria: 3,500 companies whose latest 12-month sales were $5 million to $600 million were screened. Those with a net margin or five-year average ROE below 5% were cut. Banks, utilities, real estate investment trusts and limited partnerships whose financial structures are too different from most operating companies were also excluded. Shares had to be trading above $5 by the end of September 2003. Financial statement footnotes were examined for major issues. For the final ranking, equal weight was given to growth in sales, earnings and ROE for the past five years and the latest 12 months. *www.forbes.com, October 27, 2003*

Fast-Growing Businesses

According to *Inc.*, Fort Lauderdale is home to two of America's 500 fastest-growing private companies: **A.M.E.'s Uniforms; Starmark International**. Criteria: must be an independent, privately-held, U.S. corporation, proprietorship or partnership; sales of at least $200,000 in 1998; five-year operating/sales history; increase in 2002 sales over 2001 sales; holding companies, regulated banks, and utilities were excluded. *Inc. 500, America's Fastest-Growing Private Companies, October 15, 2003*

Women-Owned Firms: Number, Employment and Sales

Area	Number of Firms	Employ-ment	Sales ($000)	Rank[2]
MSA[1]	45,909	40,718	6,255,583	40

Note: (1) Metropolitan Statistical Area - see Appendix A for areas included;
(2) Calculated on an averaging of the number of businesses, employment, and sales
Source: The National Foundation for Women Business Owners, Women-Owned Businesses in the Top 50 Metropolitan Areas, 2002: A Fact Sheet

Women-Owned Firms: Growth

| Area | Percent Change from 1997 to 2002 | | | Rank[2] |
	Number of Firms	Employ-ment	Sales	
MSA[1]	22.7	26.6	55.4	13
Top 50 MSAs	14.0	31.4	42.6	-

Note: (1) Metropolitan Statistical Area - see Appendix A for areas included; (2) Calculated on an averaging of the percent growth of number of businesses, employment, and sales
Source: The National Foundation for Women Business Owners, Women-Owned Businesses in the Top 50 Metropolitan Areas, 2002: A Fact Sheet

Minority and Women-Owned Businesses

| Ownership | All Firms | | Firms with Paid Employees | | | |
	Firms	Sales ($000)	Firms	Sales ($000)	Employees	Payroll ($000)
Black	1,283	42,603	97	23,633	509	8,632
Hispanic	1,601	269,378	490	207,907	1,480	37,350
Women	4,273	754,235	940	636,022	3,980	108,811

Note: Figures cover firms located in the city
Source: 1997 Economic Census, Minority and Women-Owned Businesses

Minority Business Opportunity

One of the 500 largest Hispanic-owned companies in the U.S. are located in Fort Lauderdale.
Hispanic Business, June 2003

HOTELS

Hotels/Motels

| Area | Hotels/Motels | Average Minimum Rates ($) | | |
		Tourist	First-Class	Deluxe
City	95	69	118	199

Source: OAG Travel Planner Online, Spring 2004

EVENT SITES

Major Event Sites, Meeting Places and Convention Centers

Name	Guest Rooms	Exhibit/ Meeting Space (sq. ft.)	Largest Meeting Room Capacity
Broward Center for the Performing Arts	n/a	n/a	2,700
Broward County Convention Center	n/a	600,000	5,000
Fort Lauderdale Stadium	n/a	n/a	8,340
Marriott's Harbor Beach Resort	637	30,000	2,000
War Memorial Auditorium	n/a	20,000	4,000
Westin Diplomat Resort and Spa	1,000	209,000	5,555

Note: n/a not available
Source: Original research

Living Environment

COST OF LIVING

Cost of Living Index

Year	Composite Index	Groceries	Housing	Utilities	Trans-portation	Health Care	Misc. Goods/ Services
2001	n/a	n/a	n/a	n/a	n/a	n/a	n/a
2002	n/a	n/a	n/a	n/a	n/a	n/a	n/a
2003	121.3	103.2	157.3	104.8	104.1	123.0	107.3

Note: U.S. = 100; n/a not available
Source: ACCRA, Cost of Living Index, 2001, 2002 and 2003 4-Quarter Averages

HOUSING

House Price Index (HPI)

Area	National Ranking[2]	Quarterly Change (%)	One-Year Change (%)	Five-Year Change (%)
MSA[1]	20	5.89	14.10	69.29
U.S.[3]	-	3.67	7.97	41.81

Note: The HPI is a weighted repeat sales index. It measures average price changes in repeat sales or refinancings on the same properties. This information is obtained by reviewing repeat mortgage transactions on single-family properties whose mortgages have been purchased or securitized by Fannie Mae of Freddie Mac in January 1975; (1) Metropolitan Statistical Area - see Appendix A for areas included; (2) Rankings are based on annual percentage change, for all MSAs containing at least 15,000 transactions over the last 10 years and ranges from 1 to 220; (3) figures based on a weighted division average; all figures are for the period ended December 31, 2003
Source: Office of Federal Housing Enterprise Oversight, House Price Index, March 1, 2004

Housing: Year Structure Built

Area	1990 -2000	1980 -1989	1970 -1979	1960 -1969	1950 -1959	1940 -1949	Before 1940	Median Year
City	4.6	6.9	24.9	29.0	25.1	6.2	3.2	1965
MSA[1]	19.5	21.2	29.8	17.2	9.5	1.7	1.0	1977
U.S.	17.0	15.8	18.5	13.7	12.7	7.3	15.0	1971

Note: Figures are percentages; (1) Metropolitan Statistical Area - see Appendix A for areas included
Source: Census 2000, Summary File 3

Average New Home Price

Area	2001	2002	2003
City	n/a	n/a	387,300
U.S.	212,643	236,567	248,193

Note: Figures, in dollars, are based on a new home with 2,400 sq. ft. of living area on an 8,000 sq. ft. lot.
Source: ACCRA, Cost of Living Index, 2001, 2002 and 2003 4-Quarter Averages

Average Apartment Rent

Area	2001	2002	2003
City	n/a	n/a	1,178
U.S.	674	708	721

Note: Figures, in dollars per month, are based on an unfurnished two bedroom, 1-1/2 or 2 bath apartment, approximately 950 sq. ft. in size, excluding all utilities except water
Source: ACCRA, Cost of Living Index, 2001, 2002 and 2003 4-Quarter Averages

RESIDENTIAL UTILITIES

Average Residential Utility Costs

Area	All Electric ($/mth)	Part Electric ($/mth)	Other Energy ($/mth)	Phone ($/mth)
City	144.82	–	–	21.44
U.S.	116.46	65.82	62.68	23.90

Source: ACCRA, Cost of Living Index, 2003 4-Quarter Average

HEALTH CARE

Average Health Care Costs

Area	Hospital ($/day)	Doctor ($/visit)	Dentist ($/visit)
City	625.40	91.74	108.68
U.S.	678.35	67.91	83.90

Note: Hospital—based on a semi-private room; Doctor—based on a general practitioner's routine exam of an established patient; Dentist—based on adult teeth cleaning and periodic oral exam.
Source: ACCRA, Cost of Living Index, 2003 4-Quarter Average

Distribution of Non-Federal, Office-Based Physicians

Area	Total	Family/ General Practice	Specialties		
			Medical	Surgical	Other
CMSA[3] (number)	8,384	965	3,380	1,963	2,076
CMSA[3] (rate per 10,000 pop.)	21.6	2.5	8.7	5.1	5.4
Metro Average[2] (rate per 10,000 pop.)	33.1	2.2	7.7	4.8	5.6

Note: Data as of December 31, 2001; (1) Metropolitan Statistical Area - see Appendix A for areas included; (2) Average of 81 MSAs and CMSAs in this book; (3) Miami-Fort Lauderdale, FL Consolidated Metropolitan Statistical Area includes the following counties: Broward; Miami-Dade
Source: American Medical Association, Physician Characteristics & Distribution in the U.S., 2003-2004

Hospitals

Fort Lauderdale has the following hospitals: 5 general medical and surgical; 2 psychiatric; 1 orthopedic; 1 other specialty.
AHA Guide to the Healthcare Field, 2003-2004

PRESIDENTIAL ELECTION

2000 Presidential Election Results

Area	Gore	Bush	Nader	Buchanan	Other
Broward County	67.4	30.9	1.2	0.1	0.3
U.S.	48.4	47.9	2.7	0.4	0.6

Note: Results are percentages and may not add to 100% due to rounding
Source: www.cbsnews.com; www.uselectionatlas.org

EDUCATION

Public School District Statistics

District Name	Schls.	Enroll-ment	Classroom Teachers	Pupil/ Teacher Ratio	Minority Pupils[1] (%)	Current Expend.[2] ($/pupil)
Broward County SD	244	262,055	12,763	20.5	58.8	5,630

Note: Data covers the 2001-02 school year unless otherwise noted; (1) Fall 2000; (2) FY2000; n/a not available
Source: U.S. Department of Education, National Center for Education Statistics, Common Core of Data, Local Education Agency (School District) Universe Survey: School Year 2001-2002; U.S. Department of Education, National Center for Education Statistics, Digest of Education Statistics 2002

Educational Quality

School District	Education Quotient[1]	Graduate Outcome[2]	Community Index[3]	Resource Index[4]
Broward County	13	14	50	27

Note: Scores are national percentile rankings and range from 1 (worst) to 99 (best); (1) Combination of the Graduate Outcome, Community and Resource indexes weighted to reflect the greater importance of the Graduate Outcome and Resource Index; (2) Based on graduation rates and college board scores (SAT/ACT); (3) Based on the surrounding community's level of affluence and adult education; (4) Based on teacher salaries, per-pupil expenditures and student-teacher ratios.
Source: Expansion Management, December 2003

Educational Attainment by Race

Area	High School Graduate (%)					Bachelor's Degree (%)				
	Total	White	Black	Asian	Hisp.[2]	Total	White	Black	Asian	Hisp.[2]
City	79.0	88.9	50.3	72.9	68.3	27.9	35.4	5.2	30.3	22.7
MSA[1]	82.0	85.5	69.2	81.0	75.7	24.5	26.8	14.7	38.8	23.0
U.S.	80.4	83.6	72.3	80.4	52.4	24.4	26.1	14.3	44.1	10.4

Note: Figures shown cover persons 25 years old and over; (1) Metropolitan Statistical Area - see Appendix A for areas included; (2) people of Hispanic origin can be of any race
Source: Census 2000, Summary File 3

School Enrollment by Type

Area	Grades KG to 8				Grades 9 to 12			
	Public		Private		Public		Private	
	Enrollment	%	Enrollment	%	Enrollment	%	Enrollment	%
City	12,934	82.4	2,769	17.6	6,278	84.6	1,141	15.4
MSA[1]	175,895	86.9	26,604	13.1	77,084	87.7	10,767	12.3
U.S.	33,526,011	88.7	4,285,121	11.3	14,848,628	90.6	1,532,323	9.4

Note: Figures shown cover persons 3 years old and over; (1) Metropolitan Statistical Area - see Appendix A for areas included
Source: Census 2000, Summary File 3

School Enrollment by Race

Area	Grades KG to 8 (%)				Grades 9 to 12 (%)			
	White	Black	Asian	Hisp.[1]	White	Black	Asian	Hisp.[1]
City	40.8	50.4	1.0	8.8	35.5	52.6	1.5	10.2
MSA[2]	59.2	30.1	2.2	19.3	55.9	32.4	2.4	19.4
U.S.	68.5	15.5	3.3	16.8	68.8	15.5	3.8	15.7

Note: Figures shown cover persons 3 years old and over; (1) people of Hispanic origin can be of any race; (2) Metropolitan Statistical Area - see Appendix A for areas included
Source: Census 2000, Summary File 3

Classroom Teacher Salaries in Public Schools

District	B.A. Degree		M.A. Degree		Maximum	
	Min. ($)	Rank[1]	Max. ($)	Rank[1]	Max. ($)	Rank[1]
City	n/a	n/a	n/a	n/a	n/a	n/a
DOD Average[2]	31,567	-	53,248	-	59,356	-

Note: Salaries are for 2001-2002; (1) Rank ranges from 1 to 100; (2) As per the U.S. Department of Defense Wage Fixing Authority
Source: American Federation of Teachers, Survey & Analysis of Teacher Salary Trends 2002

Higher Education

Four-Year Colleges			Two-Year Colleges			Medical Schools	Law Schools	Voc/ Tech
Public	Private Non-profit	Private For-profit	Public	Private Non-profit	Private For-profit			
0	2	4	1	1	3	1	1	4

Note: Figures cover institutions located within the city limits.
Source: National Center for Education Statistics, The Integrated Postsecondary Education System (IPEDS) Peer Analysis System, 2002; usnews.com, America's Best Graduate Schools 2004, Medical School Directory; The College Blue Book, Occupational Education, 2003; Barron's Guide to Law Schools, 2003; Medical School Admission Requirements U.S. & Canada, 2003-2004

**MAJOR
EMPLOYERS**

Major Employers

Company Name	Industry	Type
American Express	Short-term business credit	Branch
Answer Group Inc	Custom computer programming services	Single
Central Business Office	General medical and surgical hospitals	Branch
City of Fort Lauderdale	Executive offices	Headquarters
City of Hollywood	Executive offices	Headquarters
Energy Lighting & Chem Fla	Industrial supplies	Single
Fort Lauderdale Main PO	U.s. postal service	Branch
Holy Cross Hospital Inc	General medical and surgical hospitals	Branch
Holy Cross Medical Group	General medical and surgical hospitals	Headquarters
Joe Dimaggio Childrens Hospital	Specialty hospitals, except psychiatric	Branch
Main Post Office	U.s. postal service	Branch
Memorial Hospital West	General medical and surgical hospitals	Branch
Memorial Regional Hospital	General medical and surgical hospitals	Single
Motorola	Radio and t.v. communications equipment	Branch
Nova Southeastern University	Colleges and universities	Headquarters
Planning & Economic Dev Dept	Executive offices	Branch
Spherion ATL Workforce LLC	Help supply services	Single
Trauma Center	General medical and surgical hospitals	Single

Note: Companies shown are located in the metropolitan area and have 1,500 or more employees.
Source: www.zapdata.com, March 2004

PUBLIC SAFETY

Crime Rate

Area	All Crimes	Violent Crimes				Property Crimes		
		Murder	Forcible Rape	Robbery	Aggrav. Assault	Burglary	Larceny -Theft	Motor Vehicle Theft
City	7,329.7	7.5	24.5	419.8	431.1	1,557.4	4,027.2	862.2
Suburbs[1]	3,993.5	5.1	27.9	150.2	326.6	665.5	2,367.2	451.0
MSA[2]	4,306.8	5.3	27.6	175.5	336.4	749.3	2,523.1	489.6
U.S.	4,118.8	5.6	33.0	145.9	310.1	746.2	2,445.8	432.1

Note: Figures are crimes per 100,000 population; (1) All areas within the MSA that are located outside the city limits; (2) Metropolitan Statistical Area - see Appendix A for areas included
Source: FBI Uniform Crime Reports, 2002

RECREATION

Culture and Recreation

Museums	Orchestras	Opera Companies	Dance Companies	Professional Theatres	Zoos	Pro Sports Teams[1]
6	2	2	0	1	0	1

Note: (1) Covers the Metropolitan Statistical Area - see Appendix A for areas included.
Source: The Grey House Performing Arts Directory, 2002; Official Museum Directory, 2004; www.sportsvenues.com

Library System

The Broward County Division of Libraries has 39 branches, holdings of 2,879,237 volumes, and a budget of $40,010,820 (2000-2001).
American Library Directory, 2003-2004

MEDIA

Newspapers

Name	Type	Freq.	Distribution	Circulation
Broward Daily Business Review	General	5x/wk	n/a	10,000
City Link	Alter/Gen	1x/wk	Regional	56,000
El Heraldo de Broward	Hispanic	1x/wk	Local	22,000
Miramar Community News	General	1x/wk	Local	100,000
New Times - Broward/Palm Beach	Alternative	1x/wk	State	70,000
Pembroke Pines Community News	General	1x/wk	Local	27,000
Plantation Community News	General	1x/wk	Local	23,000
South Florida Sun-Sentinel	General	7x/wk	Area	251,970
Weston Community News	General	1x/wk	Local	18,000
Westside Gazette	General	1x/wk	Area	65,000

Note: Includes newspapers whose offices are located in the city and whose circulations are 500 or more; n/a not available
Source: Burrelle's Media Directory, 2003

Television Stations

Name	Ch.	Affiliation	Type	Owner
WTVJ	6	NBCT	Commercial	General Electric Corporation
WPXM	35	PAXTV	Commercial	Paxson Communications Corporation
WBZL	39	WB	Commercial	Tribune Broadcasting Company
WHFT	45	n/a	Non-comm.	Trinity Broadcasting Network
WSCV	51	TMUN	Commercial	Telemundo Group Inc.

Note: Stations included broadcast from the Fort Lauderdale metro area; n/a not available
Source: Burrelle's Media Directory, 2003

AM Radio Stations

Call Letters	Freq. (kHz)	Target Audience	Station Format	Music Format
WINZ	940	General	S/T	n/a
WAVS	1170	Black	E/M/N/S/T	Reggae
WEXY	1520	Religious	M	Gospel
WSRF	1580	General	M/N/S/T	Christian

Note: Stations included broadcast from the Fort Lauderdale metro area; n/a not available
The following abbreviations may be used:
Target Audience: A=Asian; B=Black; C=Christian; E=Ethnic; F=French; G=General; H=Hispanic; M=Men; N=Native American; R=Religious; S=Senior Citizen; W=Women; Y=Young Adult; Z=Children
Station Format: E=Educational; M=Music; N=News; S=Sports; T=Talk
Source: Burrelle's Media Directory, 2003

FM Radio Stations

Call Letters	Freq. (mHz)	Target Audience	Station Format	Music Format
WKPX	88.5	General	E/M/N/S	Alternative
WAFG	90.3	Religious	E/M/T	Christian
WPYM	93.1	General	M	Top 40
WLVE	93.9	General	M/N/T	Jazz
WZTA	94.9	General	M/N/S	Alternative
WFLC	97.3	General	M/N	Adult Top 40
WHYI	100.7	General	M/N/T	Alternative
WMGE	103.5	General	M/N/T	Rhythm & Blues
WHQT	105.1	General	M/N/T	Adult Contemporary
WBGG	105.9	General	M/S	Classic Rock

Note: Stations included broadcast from the Fort Lauderdale metro area
The following abbreviations may be used:
Target Audience: A=Asian; B=Black; C=Christian; E=Ethnic; F=French; G=General; H=Hispanic; M=Men; N=Native American; R=Religious; S=Senior Citizen; W=Women; Y=Young Adult; Z=Children
Station Format: E=Educational; M=Music; N=News; S=Sports; T=Talk
Source: Burrelle's Media Directory, 2003

CLIMATE

Average and Extreme Temperatures

Temperature	Jan	Feb	Mar	Apr	May	Jun	Jul	Aug	Sep	Oct	Nov	Dec	Yr.
Extreme High (°F)	88	89	92	96	95	98	98	98	97	95	89	87	98
Average High (°F)	75	77	79	82	85	88	89	90	88	85	80	77	83
Average Temp. (°F)	68	69	72	75	79	82	83	83	82	78	73	69	76
Average Low (°F)	59	60	64	68	72	75	76	76	76	72	66	61	69
Extreme Low (°F)	30	35	32	42	55	60	69	68	68	53	39	30	30

Note: Figures cover the years 1948-1990
Source: National Climatic Data Center, International Station Meteorological Climate Summary, 9/96

Average Precipitation/Snowfall/Humidity

Precip./Humidity	Jan	Feb	Mar	Apr	May	Jun	Jul	Aug	Sep	Oct	Nov	Dec	Yr.
Avg. Precip. (in.)	1.9	2.0	2.3	3.0	6.2	8.7	6.1	7.5	8.2	6.6	2.7	1.8	57.1
Avg. Snowfall (in.)	0	0	0	0	0	0	0	0	0	0	0	0	0
Avg. Rel. Hum. 7am (%)	84	84	82	80	81	84	84	86	88	87	85	84	84
Avg. Rel. Hum. 4pm (%)	59	57	57	57	62	68	66	67	69	65	63	60	63

Note: Figures cover the years 1948-1990; Tr = Trace amounts (<0.05 in. of rain; <0.5 in. of snow)
Source: National Climatic Data Center, International Station Meteorological Climate Summary, 9/96

Weather Conditions

Temperature			Daytime Sky			Precipitation		
32°F & below	45°F & below	90°F & above	Clear	Partly cloudy	Cloudy	0.01 inch or more precip.	0.1 inch or more snow/ice	Thunder-storms
< 1	7	55	48	263	54	128	0	74

Note: Figures are average number of days per year and covers the years 1948-1990
Source: National Climatic Data Center, International Station Meteorological Climate Summary, 9/96

HAZARDOUS WASTE

Superfund Sites

Fort Lauderdale has three hazardous waste sites on the EPA's Superfund National Priorities List: **Florida Petroleum Reprocessors; Hollingsworth Solderless Terminal; Wingate Road Municipal Incinerator Dump.** *U.S. Environmental Protection Agency, National Priorities List, March 15, 2004*

AIR & WATER QUALITY

Maximum Pollutant Concentrations

	Particulate Matter (ug/m³)	Carbon Monoxide (ppm)	Sulfur Dioxide (ppm)	Nitrogen Dioxide (ppm)	Ozone 1-hour (ppm)	Ozone 8-hour (ppm)	Lead (ug/m³)
MSA[1] Level	35	4	0.011	0.009	0.1	0.07	n/a
NAAQS[2]	150	9	0.140	0.053	0.12	0.08	1.50
Met NAAQS[2]	Yes	Yes	Yes	Yes	Yes	Yes	n/a

Note: (1) Metropolitan Statistical Area - see Appendix A for areas included; (2) National Ambient Air Quality Standards; n/a not available
Units: ppm = parts per million; ug/m³ = micrograms per cubic meter
Source: EPA, Latest Findings on National Air Quality: 2002 Status and Trends, August 2003

Air Quality Index

In the Fort Lauderdale MSA (see Appendix A for areas included), the Air Quality Index (AQI) exceeded 100 on 3 days in 2002. An AQI value greater than 100 indicates that air quality would have been in the unhealthful range on that day.
EPA, Latest Findings on National Air Quality: 2002 Status and Trends, August 2003

Watershed Health

The U.S. Environmental Protection Agency monitors the health of the aquatic resources for the nation's 2,000+ watersheds. **The Everglades watershed serves the Fort Lauderdale area and received an overall Index of Watershed Indicators (IWI) score of 4 (less serious problems - high vulnerability).** The IWI score is based on seven condition and nine vulnerability indicators. The overall IWI score ranges from 1 (best health) to 6 (worst health). The Condition Indicators include: designated use attainment, fish and wildlife consumption advisories, source water condition, contaminated sediments, ambient water quality, and wetlands loss index. The Vulnerability Indicators include: aquatic species at risk, conventional and toxic loads over permitted limits, urban and agricultural runoff potential, population change, hydrologic modification, estuarine pollution susceptibility, and air deposition. *EPA, Index of Watershed Indicators, October 26, 2001*

Drinking Water

Water System Name	Pop. Served	Primary Water Source Type	Number of Violations January 2002-February 2004		
			Health Based	Significant Monitoring	Monitoring
City of Fort Lauderdale	172,680	Ground	None	None	None

Note: Data as of February 19, 2004
Source: EPA, Office of Ground Water and Drinking Water, Safe Drinking Water Information System

Fort Lauderdale tap water is alkaline, very soft and fluoridated.
Editor & Publisher Market Guide, 2004

Fort Worth, Texas

Background

Fort Worth lies in north central Texas near the headwaters of the Trinity River. Despite its modern skyscrapers, multiple freeways, shopping malls, and extensive industry, the city is known for its easygoing, Western atmosphere.

The area has seen many travelers. Nomadic Native Americans of the plains rode through on horses bred from those brought by Spanish explorers. The 1840s saw American-Anglos settle in the region. On June 6, 1849, Major Ripley A. Arnold and his U.S. Cavalry troop established an outpost on the Trinity River to protect settlers moving westward. The fort was named for General William J. Worth, Commander of the U.S. Army's Texas department. When the fort was abandoned in 1853, settlers moved in and converted the vacant barracks into trading establishments and homes, stealing the county seat from Birdville (an act made legal in the 1860 election).

In the 1860s, Fort Worth, which was close to the Chisholm Trail, became an oasis for cowboys traveling to and from Kansas. Although the town's growth virtually stopped during the Civil War, Fort Worth was incorporated as a city in 1873. In a race against time, the final 26 miles of the Texas & Pacific Line were completed and Fort Worth survived to be a part of the West Texas oil boom in 1917.

Real prosperity followed at the end of World War II, when the city became a center for a number of military installations. Aviation has been the city's principal source of economic growth. Among the city's leading industries are the manufacture of aircraft, automobiles, machinery, and containers, as well as food processing and brewing.

Major corporations here include Pier 1 Imports, American Airlines, RadioShack, Textron, Bell Helicopter, and Lockheed Martin.

Local developers are planning a $300 million redevelopment project in the historic Samuels Avenue neighborhood northeast to downtown, further extending the areas' revitalization. And in early 2004, the *Fort Worth Star-Telegram* carried a report of plans at the so-called Walsh Ranch, west of town, which would be developed to eventually accommodate 40,000 residents.

Winter temperatures and rainfall are both modified by the northeast-northwest mountain barrier which prevents shallow cold air masses from crossing over from the west. Summer temperatures vary with cloud and shower activity, but are generally mild. Summer precipitation is largely from local thunderstorms and varies from year to year. Damaging rains are infrequent. Hurricanes have produced heavy rainfall, but are usually not accompanied by destructive winds.

Rankings

- Fort Worth was ranked #36 out of 331 metro areas in *Cities Ranked & Rated*. Criteria: cost of living; climate; crime; transportation; economy and jobs; education; arts and culture; health and healthcare; leisure. *Cities Ranked & Rated, 1st Edition, 2004*

- *Ladies Home Journal* ranked America's 200 largest cities based on the qualities women surveyed care about most. Fort Worth ranked #22 out of 57 in the big city category (population over 300,000). Criteria: crime; lifestyle; education; jobs; health; child care; politics; and the economy. *Ladies Home Journal Online, "The Best Cities for Women 2002"*

- The Fort Worth metro area was selected as one of America's "Best Places to Live and Work" by *Expansion Management* and rated as a "Four-Star Community." The annual "Quality of Life Quotient" measures nearly 50 indicators and compares them among the 329 metropolitan statistical areas in the United States. *Expansion Management, May 2003*

- Fort Worth was selected as one of "America's Pet Healthiest Cities" by Purina. The city ranked #43 out of 50. Criteria: veterinary services; environment; and legislation. *Purina Pet Institute, "America's Pet Healthiest Cities," August 14, 2001*

- *Forbes* ranked the 40 most populous metro areas in the U.S. in terms of the best places to be single. The Fort Worth metro area was ranked #10. Criteria: number of other singles; cost of living alone; nightlife; culture; job growth; coolness. *Forbes, June 5, 2003*

- *Forbes* ranked the 150 most populous metro areas in the U.S. in terms of the "Best Places for Business and Careers." The Fort Worth metro area was ranked #16. Criteria: income and job growth; cost-of-doing-business; qualifications of the available pool of labor; crime rates; housing costs; net migration. *Forbes, May 9, 2003*

- Fort Worth was selected as one of "America's Healthiest Cities" by *Natural Health* magazine. The city was ranked #25 out of the 50 largest urban areas in the U.S. Twenty-six criteria in the following four categories were examined: whether the city boasts natural offerings; how well the city promotes its resident's physical health; whether the city offers a healthy environment; how well the city fosters a sense of community. *Natural Health, April 2003*

- *Men's Health* ranked 101 U.S. cities in terms of the quality of their tap water. Fort Worth received a grade of B. Criteria: levels of bacteria, arsenic, lead, trihalomethanes, and haloacetic acids were compared with the National Academy of Science's guidelines as well as with the EPA's more stringent maximum contaminant level goals. *Men's Health, March 2004*

- Sperling's BestPlaces ranked 331 metro areas and identified the most and least stressful U.S. cities. The Fort Worth metro area ranked #23 out of the 100 largest metro areas (#1 = most stressful). Criteria: divorce rate; unemployment rate; violent and property crime; suicide rate; commute time; mental health; alcohol consumption; cloudy days. *www.BestPlaces.net, February 26, 2004*

- Sperling's BestPlaces in partnership with Pep Boys ranked 77 metro areas and identified "America's Most Drivable Cities." The Fort Worth metro area ranked #35. Criteria: climate; road roughness; urban mobility; gas prices. *Pep Boys, "America's Most Drivable Cities," April 9, 2003*

- Fort Worth was ranked #192 out of America's 200 largest metro areas in *SELF Magazine's* ranking of "America's Healthiest Cities for Women." Criteria: safety; air/water quality; cancer rates; and 21 other factors relating to health. *SELF Magazine, November 2003*

- Fort Worth was identified as an asthma "hot spot" where high prevalence makes the condition a key issue and environmental "triggers" and other factors can make living with asthma a particular challenge. The area ranked #12 out of the nations 100 largest metro areas. Criteria: local asthma prevalence and mortality data; pollen scores; air pollution; asthma prescriptions; smoking laws; number of asthma specialists. *GlaxoSmithKline, October 29, 2002*

- Fort Worth was identified as one of the most dangerous large metro areas for pedestrians in the U.S. The area ranked #9 out of the nations 49 largest metro areas. Criteria: average yearly pedestrian fatalities per capita (for the years 2000 and 2001) adjusted for the number of walkers. *Surface Transportation Policy Project, "Mean Streets 2002"*

- Fort Worth was selected as one of the 25 fattest cities in America by *Men's Fitness Online*. It ranked #16 out of America's 50 largest cities. Criteria: gyms/sporting goods; nutrition; exercise/sports; overweight/sedentary; junk food; alcohol; smoking; television; air and water quality; climate; geography; commute time; parks/open space; recreation facilities; and health care. *Men's Fitness Online, America's Fittest/Fattest Cities 2003*

- Fort Worth was ranked #63 out of 100 cities surveyed in *Child* magazine's ranking of the "Best Cities for Families." Criteria: number of pediatricians per capita; proximity to a children's hospital; immunization rates; infant mortality rate; air quality; water quality; school spending; pupil-teacher ratio; availability of parks/green space; nearby recreational opportunities; average commute time; number of sunny days; average cost of a 3-bedroom home; unemployment rate; future job growth; crime rate; percentage of children under 5; mandated minimum child care ratios. *Child, April 2001*

- *Zero Population Growth* ranked 239 cities in terms of children's health, safety, and economic well-being. Fort Worth was ranked #8 out of 25 major cities (main city in a metro area with population of greater than 2 million) and was given a grade of B+. Criteria: total population and population growth; percent of population under 18 years of age; number of children's museums; health improvement grade; percent of births to teens; percent of low birthweight infants; infant mortality rate; number of Title X-funded clinics; average SAT/ACT scores; average elementary and secondary class size; crime rate; unemployment rate; percent of affordable homes; number of bad air days; park acres per 1000 persons; library circulation per child; and children's program attendance counts. *Zero Population Growth, Kid Friendly Cities Report Card 2001*

- *Ladies Home Journal* ranked America's 200 largest cities in terms of safety. Fort Worth ranked #125 out of 200. Criteria: violent crimes; crimes against property; and rape. *Ladies Home Journal Online, "The Best Cities for Women 2002"*

- Fort Worth was ranked #13 out of 125 regions worldwide in terms of its "Knowledge Competitiveness Index." The index attempts to measure the knowledge-based development taking place throughout the world and is based on 17 measures of economic performance that indicate a region's ability to translate its knowledge capacity into economic value. *Robert Huggins Associates, "2003-2004 World Knowledge Competitiveness Index"*

- The Fort Worth metro area was selected by *Yahoo! Internet Life* as one of "America's Most Wired Cities...and Towns." The area ranked #47 out of 87. Criteria: home and work net use; user sophistication; domain density; and available content. *Yahoo! Internet Life, April 2001*

- The Fort Worth metro area was selected by Cranium as one of the "Top 50 Fun Cities" in America. The area ranked #38. Criteria includes: number of sports teams, restaurants, and dance performances; number of toy stores; city budget spent on recreation. *Cranium, November 4, 2003*

- Of the 25 largest U.S. markets, the Fort Worth DMA (designated market area) ranked #5 in terms of online shopping. Criteria: telephone surveys of nearly 50,000 U.S. households between July 2000 and June 2001 conducted by market research firm Centris. *American Demographics, February 2002*

- Fort Worth was identified as one of the 100 "Most Unwired Cities" in the U.S. The area ranked #16. Criteria: number of public and commercial wireless access points; cell phone coverage offering wide area network Internet access; Internet penetration. *Intel, "Most Unwired Cities," March 4, 2003*

- Scarborough Research measured the percentage of households who subscribe to cellular services among adults ages 18 and over in 75 U.S. markets. The Fort Worth DMA (Designated Market Area) was ranked #6 out of 75. *Scarborough Research, Scarborough USA+ 2003 Release 1*

- Fort Worth was selected as one of "America's Most Literate Cities." The city ranked #35 out of the 64 largest U.S. cities. Criteria: booksellers; library support, holdings, and utilization; educational attainment; periodicals published; newspaper circulation. *University of Wisconsin-Whitewater, "America's Most Literate Cities," Summer 2003*

■ Fort Worth was ranked #86 in *Prevention* magazine's survey of the "Best Walking Cities in the U.S." The magazine, in conjunction with the American Podiatric Medical Association, surveyed 125 of the most populated cities and then tabulated and weighed 20 criteria of interest to pedestrians. *Prevention, April, 2004*

■ The Fort Worth metro area was selected as one of "America's 50 Hottest Cities for Business Relocations and Expansions." The area ranked #34. Criteria: 70 of the industry's most prominent site selection consultants were asked which cities their clients found the most attractive when it came to selecting an expansion or relocation site in 2003. *Expansion Management, January 2004*

■ The Fort Worth metro area was selected as one of the "Top 60 CyberCities in America" by *Site Selection.* CyberCities are magnets for growing high-tech companies. Criteria: total employment; average wages; total payroll; number of companies; R&D spending and venture capital in the 45 Standard Industrial Classification (SIC) codes that define the high-technology industry. *Site Selection, March 2002*

■ The Fort Worth metro area was cited as one of "The Best Places in the U.S. to Locate a Company." The area ranked #19 out of 329. Criteria: education (with emphasis on college board test results and high school graduation rates); availability of quality healthcare services and the cost to employers; quality of life; logistics workforce and companies; transportation infrastructure; quality and quantity of highly educated technical workers; business climate. *Expansion Management, July 2003*

■ The Fort Worth metro area was selected as one of the "Top 40 Hottest Real Estate Markets" for expanding or relocating businesses." Criteria: rental costs; purchase prices; and vacancy rates of office and warehouse space. *Expansion Management, August 2003*

■ The Fort Worth metro area appeared on *Forbes/Milken Institute* list of "Best Places for Business and Career." Rank: #26 out of 200 metro areas. Criteria: salary growth; job growth; number of technology clusters; overall concentration of technology activity relative to national average; and technology output growth. *www.forbes.com, Forbes/Milken Institute Best Places 2002*

■ The Fort Worth metro area appeared on the "Milken Institute Best Performing Cities" index. Rank: #33 out of 200 large metro areas. Criteria: job growth; wage and salary growth; high-tech output growth. *Milken Institute, June 25, 2003*

■ The Fort Worth metro area appeared on *Entrepreneur* magazine's list of the "Best Cities for Entrepreneurs" in 2003. The area ranked #36 out of 61 in the large city category. Criteria: entrepreneurial activity; small-business growth; economic growth; and risk. *www.Entrepreneur.com*

■ The Fort Worth metro area appeared on *IndustryWeek's* fourth annual World-Class Communities list. It ranked #81 out of 315 metro areas. Criteria: MSA Gross Metropolitan Product (GMP) per manufacturing employee; and MSA percent share of U.S. manufacturing Gross Domestic Product (GDP). *IndustryWeek, April 16, 2001*

■ The Fort Worth metro area was selected as a "2001 Choice City" by *Business Development Outlook* magazine. Twenty-five cities were selected, based on data from the Bureau of Labor Statistics, Census Bureau, Federal Reserve, The Conference Board, and the U.S. Conference of Mayors, as being the most desirable into which a business can relocate or expand. *Business Development Outlook, 2001 Choice Cities*

■ ING Group ranked the 125 largest metro areas according to the general financial security of residents. The Fort Worth metro area was ranked #46 out of 125. Criteria: Earnings and Wealth Potential (household income, education, net assets, cost of living); Safety Net (health insurance, retirement savings, life insurance, income support programs); Personal Threats (unemployment rate, low-income households, crime rate); Community Economic Vitality (cost of community services, job quality, job creation, housing costs). *ING Group, "The Best Cities to Earn and Save Money: A Ranking of the Largest 125 U.S. Cities," 2001 Edition*

Business Environment

CITY FINANCES

City Government Finances

Component	2000-2001 ($000)	2000-2001 ($ per capita)
Total Revenues	841,636	1,574
Total Expenditures	811,293	1,517
Debt Outstanding	1,094,557	2,047
Cash and Securities	1,851,659	3,463

Source: U.S Census Bureau, Government Finances 2000-2001, August 2003

City Government Revenue by Source

Source	2000-2001 ($000)	2000-2001 ($ per capita)
General Revenue		
From Federal Government	0	0
From State Government	32,598	61
From Local Governments	0	0
Taxes		
Property	157,430	294
Sales	124,834	233
Personal Income	0	0
License	0	0
Charges	99,977	187
Liquor Store	0	0
Utility	129,093	241
Employee Retirement	171,873	321
Other	125,831	235

Source: U.S Census Bureau, Government Finances 2000-2001, August 2003

City Government Expenditures by Function

Function	2000-2001 ($000)	2000-2001 ($ per capita)	2000-2001 (%)
General Expenditures			
Airports	7,034	13	0.9
Corrections	0	0	0.0
Education	0	0	0.0
Fire Protection	56,842	106	7.0
Governmental Administration	36,944	69	4.6
Health	5,769	11	0.7
Highways	72,960	136	9.0
Hospitals	0	0	0.0
Housing and Community Development	9,968	19	1.2
Interest on General Debt	32,419	61	4.0
Libraries	14,000	26	1.7
Parking	245	< 1	< 0.1
Parks and Recreation	53,133	99	6.5
Police Protection	111,343	208	13.7
Public Welfare	0	0	0.0
Sewerage	77,154	144	9.5
Solid Waste Management	23,068	43	2.8
Liquor Store	0	0	0.0
Utility	206,245	386	25.4
Employee Retirement	58,974	110	7.3
Other	45,195	85	5.6

Source: U.S Census Bureau, Government Finances 2000-2001, August 2003

Municipal Bond Ratings

Area	Moody's
City	n/a

Source: Mergent Bond Record, February 2004

DEMOGRAPHICS

Population Growth

Area	1990 Census	2000 Census	2003 Estimate	2008 Projection	Population Growth (%) 1990-2000	Population Growth (%) 2000-2008
City	448,311	534,694	564,479	614,113	19.3	14.9
MSA[1]	1,361,034	1,702,625	1,820,026	2,012,839	25.1	18.2
U.S.	248,709,873	281,421,906	290,647,163	305,918,071	13.2	8.7

Note: (1) Metropolitan Statistical Area - see Appendix A for areas included
Source: Claritas, Inc.

Number of Households and Average Household Size

Area	1990 Census	2000 Census	2003 Estimate	2008 Projection	2003 Average Household Size
City	168,516	195,078	204,867	221,001	2.8
MSA[1]	506,281	624,807	666,045	733,150	2.7
U.S.	91,947,410	105,480,101	109,440,059	116,034,472	2.7

Note: (1) Metropolitan Statistical Area - see Appendix A for areas included
Source: Claritas, Inc.

Race and Ethnicity

Area	White Non-Hispanic	Black Non-Hispanic	Asian Non-Hispanic	Other Race Non-Hispanic	Hispanic
City	59.4	20.1	2.8	17.7	30.9
MSA[1]	73.7	11.3	3.3	11.7	19.0
U.S.	74.5	12.4	3.8	9.3	13.2

Note: Figures are 2003 estimates; (1) Metropolitan Statistical Area - see Appendix A for areas included
Source: Claritas, Inc.

Segregation

City Index[2]	City Rank[3]	MSA[1] Index[2]	MSA[1] Rank[4]
62.5	41	64.5	106

Note: Figures are based on an analysis of Census 2000 data; (1) Metropolitan Statistical Area - see Appendix A for areas included; (2) Dissimilarity Index—the most commonly used measure of segregation between two groups, reflecting their relative distributions across neighborhoods within a city or metropolitan area. It can range in value from 0, indicating complete integration, to 100, indicating complete segregation; (3) Ranges from 1 (most segregated) to 100 (least segregated) and includes all the cities in this book; (4) Ranges from 1 (most segregated) to 318 (least segregated) and includes 318 metropolitan areas.
Source: www.CensusScope.org

Ancestry

Area	German	Irish[2]	English	American	Italian	Polish	French[3]	Scottish
City	7.4	6.2	6.5	6.5	1.4	0.8	1.8	1.5
MSA[1]	11.4	9.2	9.1	9.7	2.0	1.2	2.4	1.9
U.S.	15.2	10.9	8.7	7.3	5.6	3.2	3.0	1.7

Note: Figures include multiple ancestry (e.g. if a person reported being Irish and Italian, they were included in both columns); (1) Metropolitan Statistical Area - see Appendix A for areas included; (2) Includes Celtic; (3) Includes Alsatian but excludes Basque
Source: Census 2000, Summary File 3

Foreign-Born Population

Area	Any Foreign Country	Percent of Population Born in: Europe	Asia	Africa	Oceania[2]	Canada	Mexico	Latin America[3]
City	16.3	0.8	2.2	0.2	0.1	0.1	12.0	0.9
MSA[1]	11.4	0.8	2.6	0.4	0.1	0.2	6.5	0.8
U.S.	11.1	1.7	2.9	0.3	0.1	0.3	3.3	2.5

Note: (1) Metropolitan Statistical Area - see Appendix A for areas included; (2) Includes Australia, New Zealand subregion, Melanesia, Micronesia, Polynesia, and Oceania n.e.c; (3) Includes Central America (excluding Mexico), South America, and the Caribbean.
Source: Census 2000, Summary File 3

Religion

Area	Catholic	Southern Baptist	United Methodist	ELCA[1]	LDS[2]	Presbyterian Church USA	Jewish Est.	Muslim Est.
County	11.5	18.7	6.8	0.6	0.8	0.8	0.4	1.0
U.S.	22.0	7.1	3.7	1.8	1.5	1.1	2.2	0.6

Note: Figures shown are the number of adherents as a percentage of the total population; Adherents are defined as all members, including full members, their children and the estimated number of other participants who are not considered members (e.g. the baptized, those not confirmed, those not eligible for communion, those regularly attending services, etc.); (1) Evangelical Lutheran Church in America; (2) The Church of Jesus Christ of Latter Day Saints
Source: Reprinted with permission from Religious Congregations and Membership in the United States 2000 (Nashville, Glenmary Research Center, 2002) Copyright Association of Statisticians of American Religious Bodies. All rights reserved.

Age Distribution

Area	Percent of Population						
	Under Age 5	Age 5 to 17	Age 18 to 34	Age 35 to 49	Age 50 to 64	Age 65 to 79	80 Years and Over
City	8.4	19.7	28.1	22.4	11.8	7.0	2.6
MSA[1]	7.7	20.2	25.2	24.6	13.5	6.7	2.0
U.S.	6.8	18.9	23.7	23.5	14.8	9.2	3.2

Note: (1) Metropolitan Statistical Area - see Appendix A for areas included
Source: Census 2000, Summary File 3

Marriage Status

Area	Never Married	Now Married Except Separated	Separated	Widowed	Divorced
City	28.5	50.8	3.1	5.9	11.8
MSA[1]	24.3	57.5	2.3	4.9	11.0
U.S.	27.1	54.4	2.2	6.6	9.7

Note: Figures cover population 15 years of age and older; (1) Metropolitan Statistical Area - see Appendix A for areas included
Source: Census 2000, Summary File 3

Male/Female Ratio

Area	Males	Females	Males per 100 Females
City	278,756	285,723	97.6
MSA[1]	902,285	917,741	98.3
U.S.	142,511,883	148,135,280	96.2

Note: Figures are 2003 estimates; (1) Metropolitan Statistical Area - see Appendix A for areas included
Source: Claritas, Inc.

ECONOMY

Gross Metropolitan Product

Area	1999	2000	2001	2002	2002 Rank[2]
MSA[1]	56.8	61.7	64.1	66.2	36

Note: Figures are in billions of dollars; (1) Metropolitan Statistical Area - see Appendix A for areas included; (2) Rank ranges from 1 to 319
Source: The U.S. Conference of Mayors, Metro Economies Report, July 2003

INCOME

Per Capita/Median/Average Income

Area	Per Capita ($)	Median Household ($)	Average Household ($)
City	20,396	41,811	55,090
MSA[1]	24,731	51,391	66,968
U.S.	24,078	46,868	63,207

Note: Figures are 2003 estimates; (1) Metropolitan Statistical Area - see Appendix A for areas included
Source: Claritas, Inc.

Household Income Distribution

Area	Percent of Households Earning							
	Under $15,000	$15,000 -24,999	$25,000 -34,999	$35,000 -49,999	$50,000 -74,999	$75,000 -99,000	$100,000 -149,999	$150,000 and up
City	15.4	13.1	13.4	17.8	18.4	10.0	8.0	3.9
MSA[1]	10.6	10.0	11.5	16.8	20.5	12.7	11.8	6.1
U.S.	14.1	11.5	11.7	16.0	19.2	11.3	10.2	6.0

Note: Figures are 2003 estimates; (1) Metropolitan Statistical Area - see Appendix A for areas included
Source: Claritas, Inc.

Poverty Rates by Age

Area	All Ages	Under 5 Years Old	5 to 17 Years Old	18 to 64 Years Old	65 Years and Over
City	15.9	2.0	4.2	8.6	1.1
MSA[1]	10.3	1.2	2.6	5.7	0.8
U.S.	12.4	1.2	3.0	6.9	1.2

Note: Figures are percent of population with income in 1999 below poverty level and only include population
for whom poverty status is determined; (1) Metropolitan Statistical Area - see Appendix A for areas included
Source: Census 2000, Summary File 3

Personal Bankruptcy Filing Rate

Area	2002	2003
Tarrant County	4.99	6.28
U.S.	5.34	5.58

Note: Numbers are per 1,000 population and include Chapter 7 and Chapter 13 filings
Source: Federal Deposit Insurance Corporation (FDIC), Regional Economic Conditions (RECON), 2/25/2004

EMPLOYMENT

Labor Force and Employment

Area	Civilian Labor Force			Workers Employed		
	Dec. 2002	Dec. 2003	% Chg.	Dec. 2002	Dec. 2003	% Chg.
City	291,840	294,724	1.0	270,240	273,911	1.4
MSA[1]	960,267	970,256	1.0	906,339	918,653	1.4
U.S.	144,807,000	146,501,000	1.2	136,599,000	138,556,000	1.4

Note: Data is not seasonally adjusted and covers workers 16 years of age and older;
(1) Metropolitan Statistical Area - see Appendix A for areas included
Source: Bureau of Labor Statistics, http://stats.bls.gov

Unemployment Rate

Area	2003											
	Jan.	Feb.	Mar.	Apr.	May	Jun.	Jul.	Aug.	Sep.	Oct.	Nov.	Dec.
City	8.4	8.2	8.1	7.9	8.3	9.4	8.9	8.5	8.3	7.6	7.4	7.1
MSA[1]	6.4	6.2	6.2	5.9	6.3	7.1	6.7	6.4	6.3	5.7	5.6	5.3
U.S.	6.5	6.4	6.2	5.8	5.8	6.5	6.3	6.0	5.8	5.6	5.6	5.4

Note: Data is not seasonally adjusted and covers workers 16 years of age and older; All figures are
percentages; (1) Metropolitan Statistical Area - see Appendix A for areas included
Source: Bureau of Labor Statistics, http://stats.bls.gov

Employment by Occupation

Occupation Classification	City (%)	MSA[1] (%)	U.S. (%)
Sales and Office	27.2	29.3	26.7
Professional and Related	18.3	19.0	20.2
Service	14.8	12.8	14.9
Production, Transportation, and Material Moving	16.1	13.8	14.6
Management, Business, and Financial	11.9	14.6	13.5
Construction, Extraction, and Maintenance	11.5	10.3	9.4
Farming, Forestry, and Fishing	0.1	0.1	0.7

Note: Figures cover employed civilians 16 years of age and older;
(1) Metropolitan Statistical Area - see Appendix A for areas included
Source: Census 2000, Summary File 3

Employment by Industry

Sector	MSA[1] Number of Employees	MSA[1] Percent of Total	U.S. Percent of Total
Government	110,400	14.1	16.7
Education and Health Services	84,800	10.8	12.9
Professional and Business Services	83,700	10.7	12.3
Retail Trade	95,400	12.2	11.8
Manufacturing	96,300	12.3	11.0
Leisure and Hospitality	75,000	9.6	9.1
Finance Activities	45,700	5.8	6.1
Construction	42,200	5.4	5.1
Wholesale Trade	36,400	4.7	4.3
Other Services	31,800	4.1	4.1
Transportation and Utilities	58,100	7.4	3.7
Information	18,000	2.3	2.4
Natural Resources and Mining	3,800	0.5	0.4

Note: Figures cover non-farm employment as of December 2003 and are not seasonally adjusted; (1) Metropolitan Statistical Area - see Appendix A for areas included
Source: Bureau of Labor Statistics, http://stats.bls.gov

Average Wages

Occupation	$/Hr.	Occupation	$/Hr.
Accountants and Auditors	25.79	Maids and Housekeeping Cleaners	7.74
Automotive Mechanics	16.23	Maintenance and Repair Workers	14.00
Bookkeepers	13.56	Marketing Managers	38.86
Carpenters	13.91	Nuclear Medicine Technologists	24.56
Cashiers	7.93	Nurses, Licensed Practical	15.95
Clerks, General Office	11.27	Nurses, Registered	23.96
Clerks, Receptionists/Information	11.06	Nursing Aides/Orderlies/Attendants	9.38
Clerks, Shipping/Receiving	11.90	Packers and Packagers, Hand	8.13
Computer Programmers	30.86	Physical Therapists	29.92
Computer Support Specialists	16.71	Postal Service Mail Carriers	18.77
Computer Systems Analysts	31.34	Real Estate Brokers	n/a
Cooks, Restaurant	9.20	Retail Salespersons	10.75
Dentists	n/a	Sales Reps., Exc. Tech./Scientific	22.41
Electrical Engineers	33.93	Sales Reps., Tech./Scientific	27.06
Electricians	17.76	Secretaries, Exc. Legal/Med./Exec.	12.88
Financial Managers	37.48	Security Guards	10.41
First-Line Supervisors/Mgrs., Sales	17.06	Surgeons	77.46
Food Preparation Workers	8.05	Teacher Assistants	7.80
General and Operations Managers	35.45	Teachers, Elementary School	19.50
Hairdressers/Cosmetologists	10.30	Teachers, Secondary School	22.20
Internists	81.24	Telemarketers	9.42
Janitors and Cleaners	9.44	Truck Drivers, Heavy/Tractor-Trailer	16.18
Landscaping/Groundskeeping Workers	9.21	Truck Drivers, Light/Delivery Svcs.	12.59
Lawyers	44.07	Waiters and Waitresses	8.43

Note: Wage data is for 2002 and covers the Metropolitan Statistical Area (see Appendix A for areas included). Hourly wages for elementary/secondary school teachers and teacher assistants were calculated by the editors from annual wage data assuming a 40 hour work week; n/a not available.
Source: Bureau of Labor Statistics, 2002 Metro Area Occupational Employment and Wage Estimates

Occupational Employment Projections: 1996 - 2006

Occupations Expected to Have the Largest Job Growth (ranked by numerical growth)	Fast-Growing Occupations[1] (ranked by percent growth)
1. Cashiers	1. Desktop publishers
2. Salespersons, retail	2. Systems analysts
3. General managers & top executives	3. Customer service representatives
4. Truck drivers, light	4. Physical therapy assistants and aides
5. Child care workers, private household	5. Computer engineers
6. General office clerks	6. Emergency medical technicians
7. Systems analysts	7. Medical assistants
8. Food preparation workers	8. Respiratory therapists
9. Food service workers	9. Telephone & cable TV line install & repair
10. Registered nurses	10. Physical therapists

Note: Projections cover Texas; (1) Excludes occupations with total job growth less than 300
Source: U.S. Department of Labor, Employment and Training Administration, America's Labor Market Information System (ALMIS)

TAXES

State Corporate Income Tax Rates

State	Rate (%)	Number of Brackets	Low Bracket (Under $)	High Bracket (Over $)
Texas	None	na	na	na

Note: Tax rates as of December 31, 2003; na not applicable
Source: Tax Foundation, www.taxfoundation.org

State Individual Income Tax Rates

State	Federal Deductibility	Marginal Rate (%)	Number of Brackets	Low Bracket (Under $)	High Bracket (Over $)
Texas	No	None	na	na	na

Note: Tax rates as of December 31, 2003; Brackets apply to single taxpayers and married people filing separately; na not applicable
Source: Tax Foundation, www.taxfoundation.org

Various State and Local Tax Rates

State Sales and Use (%)	Total Sales and Use (%)	Gasoline (cents/gal.)	Cigarette (cents/pack)	Spirits ($/gal.)	Table Wine ($/gal.)	Beer ($/gal.)
6.25	8.25	20	41	2.40	0.20	0.20

Note: Tax rates as of December 31, 2003
Source: Tax Foundation, www.taxfoundation.org

State Tax Burdens

Area	Combined State and Local Tax Burden		Combined Federal, State and Local Tax Burden	
	Percent	Rank	Percent	Rank
Texas	8.3	47	28.4	31
U.S. Average	9.7	-	30.0	-

Note: Figures are for 2003
Source: Tax Foundation, www.taxfoundation.org

Internal Revenue Service Tax Audits

IRS District	Percent of Returns Audited				
	1996	1997	1998	1999	2000
North Texas	0.95	0.82	0.50	0.35	0.19
U.S.	0.66	0.61	0.46	0.31	0.20

Note: Figures cover IRS district audits of federal income tax returns filed by individuals. Geographic data on district audits for 2001 and 2002 are being withheld by the IRS. TRAC is challenging this policy.
Source: Syracuse University, Transactional Records Access Clearinghouse (TRAC), "Odds of IRS District Tax Audit 2000"

RESIDENTIAL REAL ESTATE

Building Permits

Area	Single-Family			Multi-Family			Total		
	2001	2002	Pct. Chg.	2001	2002	Pct. Chg.	2001	2002	Pct. Chg.
City	5,026	6,649	32.3	832	1,460	75.5	5,858	8,109	38.4
U.S.	1,235,600	1,332,600	7.9	401,100	415,100	3.5	1,636,700	1,747,700	6.8

Note: Figures represent new, privately-owned housing units authorized (unadjusted data)
Source: U.S. Census Bureau, Manufacturing, Mining, and Construction Statistics

Homeownership and Housing Vacancies

Area	Homeownership Rate[2] (%)			Rental Vacancy Rate[3] (%)			Homeowner Vacancy Rate[4] (%)		
	2001	2002[a]	2003	2001	2002[a]	2003	2001	2002[a]	2003
MSA[1]	62.3	61.3	65.1	8.1	11.2	14.0	0.7	1.5	1.4
U.S.	67.8	67.9	68.3	8.4	8.9	9.8	1.8	1.7	1.8

Note: (1) Metropolitan Statistical Area - see Appendix A for areas included; (2) The proportion of households that are owners; (3) The proportion of the rental inventory that is vacant for rent; (4) The proportion of the homeowner inventory that is vacant for sale; (a) 2002 figures have been revised; n/a not available
Source: U.S. Census Bureau, Housing Vacancies and Homeownership Annual Statistics: 2003

COMMERCIAL REAL ESTATE

Industrial/Office Markets

Type/Market Area	Inventory (sq. ft.)	Vacant (sq. ft.)	Vacancy Rate (%)	Under Construction (sq. ft.)	Net Absorption (sq. ft.)
Industrial Space					
Fort Worth	191,441,968	23,850,876	12.46	2,609,661	-1,395,627
Office Space					
Fort Worth	20,237,293	3,835,627	18.95	0	-1,268,169

Note: Data as of 4th Quarter, 2003; n/a not available
Source: Society of Industrial and Office Realtors, 2004 Comparative Statistics of Industrial and Office Real Estate Markets

COMMERCIAL UTILITIES

Typical Monthly Electric Bills

Area	Commercial Service ($/month)		Industrial Service ($/month)	
	3 kW demand 1,000 kWh	40 kW demand 14,000 kWh	1,000 kW demand 200,000 kWh	50,000 kW demand 15,000,000 kWh
City	114	1,271	n/a	n/a
Average[1]	100	1,134	17,850	1,045,117

Note: Based on rates in effect July 1, 2003; (1) average based on 197 utilities; n/a not available
Source: Edison Electric Institute, Typical Bills and Average Rates Report, Summer 2003

TRANSPORTATION

Means of Transportation to Work

Area	Car/Truck/Van		Public Transportation			Bicycle	Walked	Other Means	Worked at Home
	Drove Alone	Car-pooled	Bus	Subway	Railroad				
City	77.0	16.7	1.3	0.0	0.0	0.1	1.7	1.0	2.1
MSA[1]	81.2	13.3	0.4	0.0	0.0	0.1	1.4	0.9	2.7
U.S.	75.7	12.2	2.5	1.5	0.5	0.4	2.9	1.0	3.3

Note: Figures shown are percentages and cover workers 16 years of age and older;
(1) Metropolitan Statistical Area - see Appendix A for areas included
Source: Census 2000, Summary File 3

Travel Time to Work

Area	Less Than 15 Minutes	15 to 29 Minutes	30 to 44 Minutes	45 to 59 Minutes	60 Minutes or More
City	24.6	42.7	19.9	6.5	6.2
MSA[1]	23.4	37.8	22.6	8.8	7.5
U.S.	29.4	36.1	19.1	7.4	8.0

Note: Figures are percentages and include workers 16 years old and over; (1) Metropolitan Statistical Area - see Appendix A for areas included
Source: Census 2000, Summary File 3

Roadway Congestion Index

Area	1982	1990	1996	2000	2001
City	0.73	0.96	0.98	1.11	1.12
Average[1]	0.82	1.01	1.08	1.16	1.17

Note: Values greater than 1.00 indicate undesirable mobility levels; (1) average of 75 urban areas
Source: Texas Transportation Institute, The 2003 Annual Urban Mobility Report

Transportation Statistics

Interstate highways (2004)	I-20; I-35W; I-30
Public transportation (2002)	Fort Worth Transportation Authority (The T)
Buses	
Average fleet age in years	6.8
No. operated in max. service	139
Light rail	
Average fleet age in years	18.8 (commuter rail)
No. operated in max. service	14 (commuter rail)
Demand response	
Average fleet age in years	4.1
No. operated in max. service	101
Passenger air service	
Airport	Dallas-Fort Worth International; Dallas Love Field
Airlines (2003)	37 (both airports)
Boardings (2002)	24,761,105; 2,815,907
Amtrak service (2004)	Yes
Major waterways/ports	None

Source: Federal Transit Administration, National Transit Database, 2002; Editor & Publisher Market Guide, 2004; Bureau of Transportation Statistics, Airport Enplanement Activity for CY2002; www.amtrak.com

BUSINESSES

Major Business Headquarters

Company Name	2003 Rankings	
	Fortune 500	Forbes 500
AMR	104	-
Ben E Keith	-	190
Burlington No. Santa Fe	205	-
RadioShack	358	-

Note: Companies listed are located in the city; dashes indicate no ranking
Fortune 500: Companies that produce a 10-K are ranked 1 to 500 based on 2002 revenue
Forbes 500: Private companies are ranked 1 to 281 based on 2002 revenue
Source: Fortune, April 14, 2003; www.forbes.com, November 6, 2003

Best Companies to Work For

Alcon Laboratories, headquartered in Fort Worth, is among the "100 Best Companies to Work for in 2004." Criteria: trust in management, pride in work/company, camaraderie, company responses to the Hewitt People Practices Inventory, and employee responses to their Great Place to Work survey. The companies also had to be at least 10 years old and have a minimum of 500 employees. *Fortune, January 12, 2004*

RadioShack Corp, headquartered in Fort Worth, is among the "100 Best Places to Work in IT 2003." Criteria: compensation, turnover and training. *www.computerworld.com, 3/15/2004*

Fast-Growing Businesses

According to *Inc.*, Fort Worth is home to one of America's 500 fastest-growing private companies: **American Ironhorse Motorcycle**. Criteria: must be an independent, privately-held, U.S. corporation, proprietorship or partnership; sales of at least $200,000 in 1998; five-year operating/sales history; increase in 2002 sales over 2001 sales; holding companies, regulated banks, and utilities were excluded. *Inc. 500, America's Fastest-Growing Private Companies, October 15, 2003*

According to *Fortune*, Fort Worth is home to three of America's 100 fastest-growing companies: **AmeriCredit; Quicksilver Resources; XTO Energy**. Companies were ranked based on earnings-per-share growth, revenue growth and total return over the previous three years. Criteria for inclusion: public companies with sales of at least $50 million. Companies that lost money in the most recent quarter, or ended in the red for the past four quarters as a whole, were not eligible. Limited partnerships and REITs were also not considered. *Fortune, "America's Fastest-Growing Companies," September 1, 2003*

Women-Owned Firms: Number, Employment and Sales

Area	Number of Firms	Employ-ment	Sales ($000)	Rank[2]
MSA[1]	38,434	79,248	9,103,728	26

Note: (1) Metropolitan Statistical Area - see Appendix A for areas included;
(2) Calculated on an averaging of the number of businesses, employment, and sales
Source: The National Foundation for Women Business Owners, Women-Owned Businesses in the Top 50 Metropolitan Areas, 2002: A Fact Sheet

Women-Owned Firms: Growth

| Area | Percent Change from 1997 to 2002 | | | Rank[2] |
	Number of Firms	Employ-ment	Sales	
MSA[1]	13.8	43.7	62.5	8
Top 50 MSAs	14.0	31.4	42.6	-

Note: (1) Metropolitan Statistical Area - see Appendix A for areas included; (2) Calculated on an averaging of the percent growth of number of businesses, employment, and sales
Source: The National Foundation for Women Business Owners, Women-Owned Businesses in the Top 50 Metropolitan Areas, 2002: A Fact Sheet

Minority and Women-Owned Businesses

| Ownership | All Firms | | Firms with Paid Employees | | | |
	Firms	Sales ($000)	Firms	Sales ($000)	Employees	Payroll ($000)
Black	1,442	143,594	203	121,982	1,356	39,069
Hispanic	2,294	271,257	361	235,130	2,734	54,075
Women	9,182	1,792,880	1,458	1,611,446	11,948	264,209

Note: Figures cover firms located in the city
Source: 1997 Economic Census, Minority and Women-Owned Businesses

Minority Business Opportunity

Fort Worth is home to one company which is on the Black Enterprise Auto Dealer 100 list (100 largest dealers based on gross sales): **Alan Young Pontiac-Buick-GMC Trucks**. Criteria: company must be operational in previous calendar year and at least 51% black-owned. *Black Enterprise, www.blackenterprise.com, B.E. 100s, 2003 Report*

One of the 500 largest Hispanic-owned companies in the U.S. are located in Fort Worth. *Hispanic Business, June 2003*

Fort Worth is home to one company which is on the Hispanic Business Fastest-Growing 100 list (greatest sales growth over the past five years): **Elite Temporary Services Inc.**. *Hispanic Business, July/August 2003*

HOTELS

Hotels/Motels

Area	Hotels/Motels	Average Minimum Rates ($)		
		Tourist	First-Class	Deluxe
City	75	57	108	139

Source: OAG Travel Planner Online, Spring 2004

EVENT SITES

Major Event Sites, Meeting Places and Convention Centers

Name	Guest Rooms	Exhibit/ Meeting Space (sq. ft.)	Largest Meeting Room Capacity

None listed in city

Source: Original research

Living Environment

COST OF LIVING

Cost of Living Index

Year	Composite Index	Groceries	Housing	Utilities	Trans-portation	Health Care	Misc. Goods/ Services
2001	95.8	95.1	93.9	91.3	106.3	90.4	96.4
2002	93.9	92.2	88.7	103.8	93.4	94.3	96.7
2003	93.7	97.2	86.2	95.6	94.8	98.3	97.3

Note: U.S. = 100
Source: ACCRA, Cost of Living Index, 2001, 2002 and 2003 4-Quarter Averages

HOUSING

House Price Index (HPI)

Area	National Ranking[2]	Quarterly Change (%)	One-Year Change (%)	Five-Year Change (%)
MSA[1]	197	0.79	2.99	25.12
U.S.[3]	-	3.67	7.97	41.81

Note: The HPI is a weighted repeat sales index. It measures average price changes in repeat sales or refinancings on the same properties. This information is obtained by reviewing repeat mortgage transactions on single-family properties whose mortgages have been purchased or securitized by Fannie Mae of Freddie Mac in January 1975; (1) Metropolitan Statistical Area - see Appendix A for areas included; (2) Rankings are based on annual percentage change, for all MSAs containing at least 15,000 transactions over the last 10 years and ranges from 1 to 220; (3) figures based on a weighted division average; all figures are for the period ended December 31, 2003
Source: Office of Federal Housing Enterprise Oversight, House Price Index, March 1, 2004

Housing: Year Structure Built

Area	1990 -2000	1980 -1989	1970 -1979	1960 -1969	1950 -1959	1940 -1949	Before 1940	Median Year
City	16.0	19.9	13.8	13.9	17.5	10.1	8.8	1970
MSA[1]	21.4	26.8	19.2	12.5	11.1	4.9	4.1	1979
U.S.	17.0	15.8	18.5	13.7	12.7	7.3	15.0	1971

Note: Figures are percentages; (1) Metropolitan Statistical Area - see Appendix A for areas included
Source: Census 2000, Summary File 3

Average New Home Price

Area	2001	2002	2003
City	197,100	203,996	205,387
U.S.	212,643	236,567	248,193

Note: Figures, in dollars, are based on a new home with 2,400 sq. ft. of living area on an 8,000 sq. ft. lot.
Source: ACCRA, Cost of Living Index, 2001, 2002 and 2003 4-Quarter Averages

Average Apartment Rent

Area	2001	2002	2003
City	743	719	748
U.S.	674	708	721

Note: Figures, in dollars per month, are based on an unfurnished two bedroom, 1-1/2 or 2 bath apartment, approximately 950 sq. ft. in size, excluding all utilities except water
Source: ACCRA, Cost of Living Index, 2001, 2002 and 2003 4-Quarter Averages

RESIDENTIAL UTILITIES

Average Residential Utility Costs

Area	All Electric ($/mth)	Part Electric ($/mth)	Other Energy ($/mth)	Phone ($/mth)
City	–	93.25	33.43	20.67
U.S.	116.46	65.82	62.68	23.90

Source: ACCRA, Cost of Living Index, 2003 4-Quarter Average

HEALTH CARE

Average Health Care Costs

Area	Hospital ($/day)	Doctor ($/visit)	Dentist ($/visit)
City	568.40	65.81	87.45
U.S.	678.35	67.91	83.90

Note: Hospital—based on a semi-private room; Doctor—based on a general practitioner's routine exam of an established patient; Dentist—based on adult teeth cleaning and periodic oral exam.
Source: ACCRA, Cost of Living Index, 2003 4-Quarter Average

Distribution of Non-Federal, Office-Based Physicians

Area	Total	Family/ General Practice	Specialties		
			Medical	Surgical	Other
CMSA[3] (number)	7,867	989	2,601	2,050	2,227
CMSA[3] (rate per 10,000 pop.)	15.1	1.9	5.0	3.9	4.3
Metro Average[2] (rate per 10,000 pop.)	33.1	2.2	7.7	4.8	5.6

Note: Data as of December 31, 2001; (1) Metropolitan Statistical Area - see Appendix A for areas included; (2) Average of 81 MSAs and CMSAs in this book; (3) Dallas-Fort Worth, TX Consolidated Metropolitan Statistical Area includes the following counties: Collin; Dallas; Denton; Ellis; Henderson; Hood; Hunt; Johnson; Kaufman; Parker; Rockwall; Tarrant
Source: American Medical Association, Physician Characteristics & Distribution in the U.S., 2003-2004

Hospitals

Fort Worth has the following hospitals: 7 general medical and surgical; 2 rehabilitation; 3 long-term acute care; 1 children's general; 1 children's psychiatric.
AHA Guide to the Healthcare Field, 2003-2004

PRESIDENTIAL ELECTION

2000 Presidential Election Results

Area	Gore	Bush	Nader	Buchanan	Other
Tarrant County	36.8	60.7	1.9	0.2	0.4
U.S.	48.4	47.9	2.7	0.4	0.6

Note: Results are percentages and may not add to 100% due to rounding
Source: www.cbsnews.com; www.uselectionatlas.org

EDUCATION

Public School District Statistics

District Name	Schls.	Enroll-ment	Classroom Teachers	Pupil/ Teacher Ratio	Minority Pupils[1] (%)	Current Expend.[2] ($/pupil)
Castleberry ISD	8	3,232	218	14.8	n/a	n/a
Eagle Mt-Saginaw ISD	12	7,185	426	16.9	n/a	n/a
Fort Worth ISD	143	80,597	5,024	16.0	78.6	5,990

Note: Data covers the 2001-02 school year unless otherwise noted; (1) Fall 2000; (2) FY2000; n/a not available
Source: U.S. Department of Education, National Center for Education Statistics, Common Core of Data, Local Education Agency (School District) Universe Survey: School Year 2001-2002; U.S. Department of Education, National Center for Education Statistics, Digest of Education Statistics 2002

Educational Quality

School District	Education Quotient[1]	Graduate Outcome[2]	Community Index[3]	Resource Index[4]
Fort Worth ISD	19	16	66	47

Note: Scores are national percentile rankings and range from 1 (worst) to 99 (best); (1) Combination of the Graduate Outcome, Community and Resource indexes weighted to reflect the greater importance of the Graduate Outcome and Resource Index; (2) Based on graduation rates and college board scores (SAT/ACT); (3) Based on the surrounding community's level of affluence and adult education; (4) Based on teacher salaries, per-pupil expenditures and student-teacher ratios.
Source: Expansion Management, December 2003

Educational Attainment by Race

Area	High School Graduate (%)					Bachelor's Degree (%)				
	Total	White	Black	Asian	Hisp.[2]	Total	White	Black	Asian	Hisp.[2]
City	72.8	79.2	74.8	71.8	37.3	22.3	28.2	11.4	36.3	6.7
MSA[1]	81.0	84.9	80.2	72.4	46.6	25.1	27.3	16.8	36.3	9.2
U.S.	80.4	83.6	72.3	80.4	52.4	24.4	26.1	14.3	44.1	10.4

Note: Figures shown cover persons 25 years old and over; (1) Metropolitan Statistical Area - see Appendix A for areas included; (2) people of Hispanic origin can be of any race
Source: Census 2000, Summary File 3

School Enrollment by Type

Area	Grades KG to 8				Grades 9 to 12			
	Public		Private		Public		Private	
	Enrollment	%	Enrollment	%	Enrollment	%	Enrollment	%
City	69,958	91.1	6,845	8.9	27,222	91.5	2,543	8.5
MSA[1]	224,258	91.0	22,110	9.0	91,305	92.3	7,600	7.7
U.S.	33,526,011	88.7	4,285,121	11.3	14,848,628	90.6	1,532,323	9.4

Note: Figures shown cover persons 3 years old and over; (1) Metropolitan Statistical Area - see Appendix A for areas included
Source: Census 2000, Summary File 3

School Enrollment by Race

Area	Grades KG to 8 (%)				Grades 9 to 12 (%)			
	White	Black	Asian	Hisp.[1]	White	Black	Asian	Hisp.[1]
City	51.1	23.2	2.3	39.7	47.8	27.5	2.8	35.1
MSA[2]	69.1	12.9	2.8	23.7	69.0	14.1	3.6	19.9
U.S.	68.5	15.5	3.3	16.8	68.8	15.5	3.8	15.7

Note: Figures shown cover persons 3 years old and over; (1) people of Hispanic origin can be of any race; (2) Metropolitan Statistical Area - see Appendix A for areas included
Source: Census 2000, Summary File 3

Classroom Teacher Salaries in Public Schools

District	B.A. Degree		M.A. Degree		Maximum	
	Min. ($)	Rank[1]	Max. ($)	Rank[1]	Max. ($)	Rank[1]
Fort Worth	36,250	14	56,421	26	59,541	45
DOD Average[2]	31,567	-	53,248	-	59,356	-

Note: Salaries are for 2001-2002; (1) Rank ranges from 1 to 100; (2) As per the U.S. Department of Defense Wage Fixing Authority
Source: American Federation of Teachers, Survey & Analysis of Teacher Salary Trends 2002

Higher Education

Four-Year Colleges			Two-Year Colleges			Medical Schools	Law Schools	Voc/ Tech
Public	Private Non-profit	Private For-profit	Public	Private Non-profit	Private For-profit			
1	5	0	2	0	1	1	1	10

Note: Figures cover institutions located within the city limits.
Source: National Center for Education Statistics, The Integrated Postsecondary Education System (IPEDS) Peer Analysis System, 2002; usnews.com, America's Best Graduate Schools 2004, Medical School Directory; The College Blue Book, Occupational Education, 2003; Barron's Guide to Law Schools, 2003; Medical School Admission Requirements U.S. & Canada, 2003-2004

**MAJOR
EMPLOYERS**

Major Employers

Company Name	Industry	Type
Alcon Laboratories Inc	Pharmaceutical preparations	Headquarters
AMR Eagle	Business services, nec	Branch
Bell Helicopter Textron Inc	Aircraft	Headquarters
Con-Way Southern Express Inc	Trucking, except local	Headquarters
General Motors	Motor vehicles and car bodies	Branch
Huguley Memorial Medical Ctr	General medical and surgical hospitals	Branch
John Peter Smith Hospital	General medical and surgical hospitals	Headquarters
John Peter Smith Hospital	Accounting, auditing, and bookkeeping	Branch
Mrs Bairds Bakeries	Bread, cake, and related products	Headquarters
Odyssey Resource Management	Help supply services	Headquarters
Presbyterian Hospital Dallas	Management services	Headquarters
Psychological/Deaf Svcs Dept	Elementary and secondary schools	Branch
Radio Shack	Radio, television, and electronic stores	Headquarters
Sabre Travel Info Network	Business services, nec	Branch
Sabre Travel Info Network	Information retrieval services	Headquarters
Sprint P C S	Telephone communication, except radio	Branch
Texas Pacific Group Inc	Investors, nec	Headquarters
United States Postal Service	U.s. postal service	Branch
University Book Store	Colleges and universities	Headquarters

Note: Companies shown are located in the metropolitan area and have 2,000 or more employees.
Source: www.zapdata.com, March 2004

PUBLIC SAFETY

Crime Rate

Area	All Crimes	Violent Crimes				Property Crimes		
		Murder	Forcible Rape	Robbery	Aggrav. Assault	Burglary	Larceny -Theft	Motor Vehicle Theft
City	8,021.7	9.5	57.5	295.1	397.7	1,743.4	4,813.5	705.0
Suburbs[1]	4,729.9	3.0	32.1	99.3	223.5	825.7	3,188.8	357.6
MSA[2]	5,763.6	5.0	40.1	160.8	278.2	1,113.9	3,699.0	466.7
U.S.	4,118.8	5.6	33.0	145.9	310.1	746.2	2,445.8	432.1

Note: Figures are crimes per 100,000 population; (1) All areas within the MSA that are located outside the city limits; (2) Metropolitan Statistical Area - see Appendix A for areas included
Source: FBI Uniform Crime Reports, 2002

RECREATION

Culture and Recreation

Museums	Orchestras	Opera Companies	Dance Companies	Professional Theatres	Zoos	Pro Sports Teams[1]
9	2	1	2	6	1	1

Note: (1) Covers the Metropolitan Statistical Area - see Appendix A for areas included.
Source: The Grey House Performing Arts Directory, 2002; Official Museum Directory, 2004; www.sportsvenues.com

Library System

The Ft. Worth Public Library has 14 branches, holdings of 2,200,000 volumes, and a budget of $12,858,807 (2001-2002).
American Library Directory, 2003-2004

MEDIA

Newspapers

Name	Type	Freq.	Distribution	Circulation
Benbrook News	General	1x/wk	Local	7,500
El Informador Hispano	Gener/Hisp	1x/wk	Local	25,000
Fort Worth Star-Telegram	General	7x/wk	Area	235,622
FW Weekly	General	1x/wk	Area	85,000
North Texas Catholic	Catholic	2x/mth	Local	26,500
River Oaks News	General	1x/wk	Local	4,500
Texas Jewish Post	Religious	1x/wk	Local	10,000
White Settlement Bomber News	General	1x/wk	Local	7,000

Note: Includes newspapers whose offices are located in the city and whose circulations are 1,000 or more
Source: Burrelle's Media Directory, 2003

Television Stations

Name	Ch.	Affiliation	Type	Owner
KXAS	5	NBCT	Commercial	General Electric Corporation
KTXA	21	UPN	Commercial	CBS
KMPX	29	n/a	Non-comm.	n/a
KFWD	52	n/a	Commercial	n/a
KPXD	68	PAXTV	Commercial	Paxson Communications Corporation

Note: Stations included broadcast from the Fort Worth metro area; n/a not available
Source: Burrelle's Media Directory, 2003

AM Radio Stations

Call Letters	Freq. (kHz)	Target Audience	Station Format	Music Format
KMKI	620	General	M	Oldies
WBAP	820	General	E/N/S/T	n/a
KFJZ	870	Hispanic	M/S/T	Latin
KRLD	1080	General	N/T	n/a
KTNO	1440	H/R	M/T	Gospel

Note: Stations included broadcast from the Fort Worth metro area; n/a not available
The following abbreviations may be used:
Target Audience: A=Asian; B=Black; C=Christian; E=Ethnic; F=French; G=General; H=Hispanic; M=Men; N=Native American; R=Religious; S=Senior Citizen; W=Women; Y=Young Adult; Z=Children
Station Format: E=Educational; M=Music; N=News; S=Sports; T=Talk
Source: Burrelle's Media Directory, 2003

FM Radio Stations

Call Letters	Freq. (mHz)	Target Audience	Station Format	Music Format
KTCU	88.7	General	M/N/S	Adult Standards
KCBI	90.9	Religious	M/N/S	Christian
KDKR	91.3	General	E/M	Gospel
KSCS	96.3	General	M/N/T	Country
KMEO	96.7	General	M/N/T	Adult Contemporary
KESN	103.3	General	S/T	n/a

Note: Stations included broadcast from the Fort Worth metro area; n/a not available
The following abbreviations may be used:
Target Audience: A=Asian; B=Black; C=Christian; E=Ethnic; F=French; G=General; H=Hispanic; M=Men; N=Native American; R=Religious; S=Senior Citizen; W=Women; Y=Young Adult; Z=Children
Station Format: E=Educational; M=Music; N=News; S=Sports; T=Talk
Source: Burrelle's Media Directory, 2003

CLIMATE

Average and Extreme Temperatures

Temperature	Jan	Feb	Mar	Apr	May	Jun	Jul	Aug	Sep	Oct	Nov	Dec	Yr.
Extreme High (°F)	88	88	96	98	103	113	110	108	107	106	89	90	113
Average High (°F)	54	59	67	76	83	92	96	96	88	79	67	58	76
Average Temp. (°F)	44	49	57	66	73	81	85	85	78	68	56	47	66
Average Low (°F)	33	38	45	54	63	71	75	74	67	56	45	37	55
Extreme Low (°F)	4	6	11	29	41	51	59	56	43	29	19	-1	-1

Note: Figures cover the years 1953-1990
Source: National Climatic Data Center, International Station Meteorological Climate Summary, 9/96

Average Precipitation/Snowfall/Humidity

Precip./Humidity	Jan	Feb	Mar	Apr	May	Jun	Jul	Aug	Sep	Oct	Nov	Dec	Yr.
Avg. Precip. (in.)	1.8	2.2	2.6	3.7	4.9	2.8	2.1	1.9	3.0	3.3	2.1	1.7	32.3
Avg. Snowfall (in.)	1	1	Tr	0	0	0	0	0	0	0	Tr	Tr	3
Avg. Rel. Hum. 6am (%)	79	79	79	81	86	85	80	79	83	82	80	79	81
Avg. Rel. Hum. 3pm (%)	52	51	48	50	53	47	42	41	46	47	49	51	48

Note: Figures cover the years 1953-1990; Tr = Trace amounts (<0.05 in. of rain; <0.5 in. of snow)
Source: National Climatic Data Center, International Station Meteorological Climate Summary, 9/96

Weather Conditions

Temperature			Daytime Sky			Precipitation		
10°F & below	32°F & below	90°F & above	Clear	Partly cloudy	Cloudy	0.01 inch or more precip.	0.1 inch or more snow/ice	Thunder-storms
1	40	100	123	136	106	79	3	47

Note: Figures are average number of days per year and covers the years 1953-1990
Source: National Climatic Data Center, International Station Meteorological Climate Summary, 9/96

HAZARDOUS WASTE

Superfund Sites

Fort Worth has one hazardous waste site on the EPA's Superfund National Priorities List: **Air Force Plant #4 (General Dynamics)**. *U.S. Environmental Protection Agency, National Priorities List, March 15, 2004*

AIR & WATER QUALITY

Maximum Pollutant Concentrations

	Particulate Matter (ug/m³)	Carbon Monoxide (ppm)	Sulfur Dioxide (ppm)	Nitrogen Dioxide (ppm)	Ozone 1-hour (ppm)	Ozone 8-hour (ppm)	Lead (ug/m³)
MSA[1] Level	50	2	n/a	0.013	0.14	0.11	n/a
NAAQS[2]	150	9	0.140	0.053	0.12	0.08	1.50
Met NAAQS[2]	Yes	Yes	n/a	Yes	No	No	n/a

Note: (1) Metropolitan Statistical Area - see Appendix A for areas included; (2) National Ambient Air Quality Standards; n/a not available
Units: ppm = parts per million; ug/m³ = micrograms per cubic meter
Source: EPA, Latest Findings on National Air Quality: 2002 Status and Trends, August 2003

Air Quality Index

In the Fort Worth MSA (see Appendix A for areas included), the Air Quality Index (AQI) exceeded 100 on 33 days in 2002. An AQI value greater than 100 indicates that air quality would have been in the unhealthful range on that day.
EPA, Latest Findings on National Air Quality: 2002 Status and Trends, August 2003

Watershed Health

The U.S. Environmental Protection Agency monitors the health of the aquatic resources for the nation's 2,000+ watersheds. **The Lower West Fork Trinity watershed serves the Fort Worth area and received an overall Index of Watershed Indicators (IWI) score of 1 (better quality - low vulnerability).** The IWI score is based on seven condition and nine vulnerability indicators. The overall IWI score ranges from 1 (best health) to 6 (worst health).

The Condition Indicators include: designated use attainment, fish and wildlife consumption advisories, source water condition, contaminated sediments, ambient water quality, and wetlands loss index. The Vulnerability Indicators include: aquatic species at risk, conventional and toxic loads over permitted limits, urban and agricultural runoff potential, population change, hydrologic modification, estuarine pollution susceptibility, and air deposition. *EPA, Index of Watershed Indicators, October 26, 2001*

Drinking Water

Water System Name	Pop. Served	Primary Water Source Type	Number of Violations January 2002-February 2004		
			Health Based	Significant Monitoring	Monitoring
City of Fort Worth	534,695	Surface	None	None	1

Note: Data as of February 19, 2004
Source: EPA, Office of Ground Water and Drinking Water, Safe Drinking Water Information System

Fort Worth tap water is alkaline, hard and fluoridated.
Editor & Publisher Market Guide, 2004

Houston, Texas

Background

Back in 1836, two brothers—John K. and Augustus C. Allen—bought a 6,642-acre tract of marshy, mosquito-infested land 56 miles north of the Gulf of Mexico and named it Houston, after the hero of San Jacinto. From that moment on, Houston has experienced nothing but impressive economic and population growth.

By the end of its first year in the Republic of Texas, Houston claimed 1,500 residents, one theater, and interestingly, no churches. The first churches came three years later. By the end of its second year, Houston saw its first steamship, establishing its position as one of the top-ranking ports in the country.

Certainly, Houston owes much to the Houston ship channel, the "golden strip" on which oil refineries, chemical plants, cement factories, and grain elevators conduct their bustling economic activity. The diversity of these industries is a testament to Houston's economy in general.

Tonnage through the Port of Houston has grown to the point that the Port says it is number one in the nation for foreign tonnage. Plus, the Norwegian Cruise Line launched from the port in 2003.

As Texas' biggest city, Houston is also enjoying new manufacturing expansion in its diversified economy. A revitalized downtown recently became Continental Airlines' relocated worldwide headquarters, bringing in over 3,000 jobs from the suburbs. Landing at Houston's three airports are F-16s, jumbo jets, luxurious corporate jets, home-built aircraft, crop dusters and every model of airplane in between.

Not limited to being a manufacturing center, Houston boasts of being one of the major scientific research areas in the world. The presence of the Lyndon B. Johnson Space Center has spawned a number of related industries in medical and technological research. The Texas Medical Center oversees a network of medical institutions, including St. Luke's Episcopal Hospital, the Texas Children's Hospital, and the Methodist Hospital.

As a city whose reputation rests upon advanced research, Houston is also devoted to education and the arts. Rice University, for example, whose admission standards rank as one of the highest in the nation, is located in Houston, as are Dominican College and the University of St. Thomas.

Houston also is patron to the Museum of Fine Arts, the Contemporary Arts Museum, and the Houston Ballet and Grand Opera. A host of smaller cultural institutions, such as the Gilbert and Sullivan Society, the Virtuoso Quartet, and the Houston Harpsichord Society enliven the scene. Two privately funded museums, the Holocaust Museum Houston and the Houston Museum of Natural Science, are historical and educational attractions, and a new baseball stadium was completed in April 1999 in the city's downtown.

Houstonians are eagerly embracing a revitalized downtown. This urban comeback has resulted in a virtual explosion of dining and entertainment options in the heart of the city. The opening of the Bayou Place complex has especially generated excitement, providing a variety of restaurants and entertainment options in one facility.

Located in the flat coastal plains, Houston's climate is predominantly marine. The terrain includes many small streams and bayous which, together with the nearness to Galveston Bay, favor the development of fog. Temperatures are moderated by the influence of winds from the Gulf of Mexico, which is 50 miles away. Mild winters are the norm, as is abundant rainfall. Polar air penetrates the area frequently enough to provide variability in the weather.

Rankings

- Houston was ranked #158 out of 331 metro areas in *Cities Ranked & Rated*. Criteria: cost of living; climate; crime; transportation; economy and jobs; education; arts and culture; health and healthcare; leisure. *Cities Ranked & Rated, 1st Edition, 2004*

- *Ladies Home Journal* ranked America's 200 largest cities based on the qualities women surveyed care about most. Houston ranked #48 out of 57 in the big city category (population over 300,000). Criteria: crime; lifestyle; education; jobs; health; child care; politics; and the economy. *Ladies Home Journal Online, "The Best Cities for Women 2002"*

- Houston was selected as one of "America's Top Ten Vegetarian-Friendly Cities." The city was ranked #10. Criteria: number of vegetarian restaurants; number of health food stores; number of vegetarian groups. *www.peta.org, February 26, 2004*

- Houston was selected as one of "America's Pet Healthiest Cities" by Purina. The city ranked #33 out of 50. Criteria: veterinary services; environment; and legislation. *Purina Pet Institute, "America's Pet Healthiest Cities," August 14, 2001*

- Houston was selected as one of the "Best Cities for Black Families." The city ranked #2 out of 20. For six months, bet.com compiled data on African Americans in those U.S. cities with the largest Black populations. The data, for African Americans specifically, involved the following: infant mortality; high school graduation; median income; homeownership; unemployment; business ownership; poverty rates; AIDS infection rates; percentage of children in single parent, typically fatherless, households; teen pregnancy; economic segregation index; violent and property crime. *www.bet.com, October 1, 2002*

- Houston appeared on *Black Enterprise's* list of the "Top Ten Cities for African-Americans to Live, Work, and Play." The city was ranked #1, based on responses from 4,239 online survey respondents who ranked 21 quality-of-life factors. *Black Enterprise, July 2001*

- *Forbes* ranked the 40 most populous metro areas in the U.S. in terms of the best places to be single. The Houston metro area was ranked #18. Criteria: number of other singles; cost of living alone; nightlife; culture; job growth; coolness. *Forbes, June 5, 2003*

- *Forbes* ranked the 150 most populous metro areas in the U.S. in terms of the "Best Places for Business and Careers." The Houston metro area was ranked #15. Criteria: income and job growth; cost-of-doing-business; qualifications of the available pool of labor; crime rates; housing costs; net migration. *Forbes, May 9, 2003*

- Houston was selected as one of "America's Healthiest Cities" by *Natural Health* magazine. The city was ranked #46 out of the 50 largest urban areas in the U.S. Twenty-six criteria in the following four categories were examined: whether the city boasts natural offerings; how well the city promotes its resident's physical health; whether the city offers a healthy environment; how well the city fosters a sense of community. *Natural Health, April 2003*

- *Men's Health* ranked 101 U.S. cities in terms of the quality of their tap water. Houston received a grade of F. Criteria: levels of bacteria, arsenic, lead, trihalomethanes, and haloacetic acids were compared with the National Academy of Science's guidelines as well as with the EPA's more stringent maximum contaminant level goals. *Men's Health, March 2004*

- Sperling's BestPlaces ranked 331 metro areas and identified the most and least stressful U.S. cities. The Houston metro area ranked #13 out of the 100 largest metro areas (#1 = most stressful). Criteria: divorce rate; unemployment rate; violent and property crime; suicide rate; commute time; mental health; alcohol consumption; cloudy days. *www.BestPlaces.net, February 26, 2004*

- Sperling's BestPlaces in partnership with Pep Boys ranked 77 metro areas and identified "America's Most Drivable Cities." The Houston metro area ranked #34. Criteria: climate; road roughness; urban mobility; gas prices. *Pep Boys, "America's Most Drivable Cities," April 9, 2003*

- Houston was ranked #160 out of America's 200 largest metro areas in *SELF Magazine's* ranking of "America's Healthiest Cities for Women." Criteria: safety; air/water quality; cancer rates; and 21 other factors relating to health. *SELF Magazine, November 2003*

- Houston was identified as one of the most dangerous large metro areas for pedestrians in the U.S. The area ranked #7 out of the nations 49 largest metro areas. Criteria: average yearly pedestrian fatalities per capita (for the years 2000 and 2001) adjusted for the number of walkers. *Surface Transportation Policy Project, "Mean Streets 2002"*

- Houston was selected as one of the 25 fattest cities in America by *Men's Fitness Online*. It ranked #1 out of America's 50 largest cities. Criteria: gyms/sporting goods; nutrition; exercise/sports; overweight/sedentary; junk food; alcohol; smoking; television; air and water quality; climate; geography; commute time; parks/open space; recreation facilities; and health care. *Men's Fitness Online, America's Fittest/Fattest Cities 2003*

- Houston was ranked #55 out of 100 cities surveyed in *Child* magazine's ranking of the "Best Cities for Families." Criteria: number of pediatricians per capita; proximity to a children's hospital; immunization rates; infant mortality rate; air quality; water quality; school spending; pupil-teacher ratio; availability of parks/green space; nearby recreational opportunities; average commute time; number of sunny days; average cost of a 3-bedroom home; unemployment rate; future job growth; crime rate; percentage of children under 5; mandated minimum child care ratios. *Child, April 2001*

- *Zero Population Growth* ranked 239 cities in terms of children's health, safety, and economic well-being. Houston was ranked #9 out of 25 major cities (main city in a metro area with population of greater than 2 million) and was given a grade of B+. Criteria: total population and population growth; percent of population under 18 years of age; number of children's museums; health improvement grade; percent of births to teens; percent of low birthweight infants; infant mortality rate; number of Title X-funded clinics; average SAT/ACT scores; average elementary and secondary class size; crime rate; unemployment rate; percent of affordable homes; number of bad air days; park acres per 1000 persons; library circulation per child; and children's program attendance counts. *Zero Population Growth, Kid Friendly Cities Report Card 2001*

- Mercer Human Resources Consulting ranked 215 cities worldwide in terms of overall quality of life. Houston ranked #55. Criteria: political, social, economic, and socio-cultural factors; medical and health considerations; schools and education; public services and transportation; recreation; consumer goods; housing; and natural environment. *Mercer Human Resources Consulting, March 3, 2003*

- The U.S. Conference of Mayors and Waste Management sponsors the City Livability Awards Program. The awards recognize and honor mayors for exemplary leadership in developing and implementing programs that improve the quality of life in America's cities. Houston received Top Honors for its its efforts to bridge the digital divide. SimHouston, a web-enabled virtual software application, allows all city residents with a public library card to access through the Internet, word processing, email and other software. *U.S Conference of Mayors, "2003 City Livability Awards"*

- *Ladies Home Journal* ranked America's 200 largest cities in terms of safety. Houston ranked #136 out of 200. Criteria: violent crimes; crimes against property; and rape. *Ladies Home Journal Online, "The Best Cities for Women 2002"*

- Houston was ranked #7 out of 268 metro areas in terms of its Creativity Index. The Creativity Index is a mix of four equally weighted factors: the Creative Class (scientists, engineers, architects, designers, writers, artists, musicians, or any profession where creativity is a key factor) share of the workforce; innovation, measured as patents per capita; high-tech industry, using the Milken Institute's Tech Pole Index; and diversity, measured by the Gay Index (a reasonable proxy for an areas' openness to different kinds of people and ideas). *The Rise of the Creative Class, 2002*

- Houston was ranked #32 out of 125 regions worldwide in terms of its "Knowledge Competitiveness Index." The index attempts to measure the knowledge-based development taking place throughout the world and is based on 17 measures of economic performance that indicate a region's ability to translate its knowledge capacity into economic value. *Robert Huggins Associates, "2003-2004 World Knowledge Competitiveness Index"*

- The Houston metro area was selected by *Yahoo! Internet Life* as one of "America's Most Wired Cities...and Towns." The area ranked #31 out of 87. Criteria: home and work net use; user sophistication; domain density; and available content. *Yahoo! Internet Life, April 2001*

- The Houston metro area was selected by Cranium as one of the "Top 50 Fun Cities" in America. The area ranked #32. Criteria includes: number of sports teams, restaurants, and dance performances; number of toy stores; city budget spent on recreation. *Cranium, November 4, 2003*

- Of the 25 largest U.S. markets, the Houston DMA (designated market area) ranked #7 in terms of online shopping. Criteria: telephone surveys of nearly 50,000 U.S. households between July 2000 and June 2001 conducted by market research firm Centris. *American Demographics, February 2002*

- Houston was identified as one of the 100 "Most Unwired Cities" in the U.S. The area ranked #14. Criteria: number of public and commercial wireless access points; cell phone coverage offering wide area network Internet access; Internet penetration. *Intel, "Most Unwired Cities," March 4, 2003*

- Scarborough Research measured the percentage of households who subscribe to cellular services among adults ages 18 and over in 75 U.S. markets. The Houston DMA (Designated Market Area) was ranked #14 out of 75. *Scarborough Research, Scarborough USA+ 2003 Release 1*

- Houston was selected as one of "America's Most Literate Cities." The city ranked #49 out of the 64 largest U.S. cities. Criteria: booksellers; library support, holdings, and utilization; educational attainment; periodicals published; newspaper circulation. *University of Wisconsin-Whitewater, "America's Most Literate Cities," Summer 2003*

- Houston was ranked #73 in *Prevention* magazine's survey of the "Best Walking Cities in the U.S." The magazine, in conjunction with the American Podiatric Medical Association, surveyed 125 of the most populated cities and then tabulated and weighed 20 criteria of interest to pedestrians. *Prevention, April, 2004*

- The Houston metro area was selected as one of "America's 50 Hottest Cities for Business Relocations and Expansions." The area ranked #41. Criteria: 70 of the industry's most prominent site selection consultants were asked which cities their clients found the most attractive when it came to selecting an expansion or relocation site in 2003. *Expansion Management, January 2004*

- The Houston metro area was selected as one of the "Top 60 CyberCities in America" by *Site Selection*. CyberCities are magnets for growing high-tech companies. Criteria: total employment; average wages; total payroll; number of companies; R&D spending and venture capital in the 45 Standard Industrial Classification (SIC) codes that define the high-technology industry. *Site Selection, March 2002*

- The Houston metro area was cited as one of America's "Top 50 Metros" in terms of the availability of highly skilled, highly educated workers. The area ranked #32 out of 50. Criteria: degree holders (bachelors, masters, professional, and Ph.D.) as a percent of the workforce; science and engineering workers as a percent of the workforce; number of patents issued; number and type of colleges in each metro area. *Expansion Management, March 2004*

- The Houston metro area was cited as one of "The Best Places in the U.S. to Locate a Company." The area ranked #46 out of 329. Criteria: education (with emphasis on college board test results and high school graduation rates); availability of quality healthcare services and the cost to employers; quality of life; logistics workforce and companies; transportation infrastructure; quality and quantity of highly educated technical workers; business climate. *Expansion Management, July 2003*

- Houston was cited as one of America's top 10 metro areas for new/expanded facilities in 2000. The area ranked #6 out of 10. *Site Selection, March 2002*

- Houston was cited as one of America's top 10 metro areas for new manufacturing plants in 2000. The area ranked #7 out of 10. *Site Selection, March 2002*

- Houston was cited as a top metro area for European expansion. The area ranked #44 out of 50, based on European-based company expansions or relocations within the past two years that created at least 10 jobs and involved capital investment of at least $1 million. *Expansion Management, June 2003*

- The Houston metro area was selected as one of the "Top 40 Hottest Real Estate Markets" for expanding or relocating businesses." Criteria: rental costs; purchase prices; and vacancy rates of office and warehouse space. *Expansion Management, August 2003*

- The Houston metro area appeared on *Forbes/Milken Institute* list of "Best Places for Business and Career." Rank: #21 out of 200 metro areas. Criteria: salary growth; job growth; number of technology clusters; overall concentration of technology activity relative to national average; and technology output growth. *www.forbes.com, Forbes/Milken Institute Best Places 2002*

- The Houston metro area appeared on the "Milken Institute Best Performing Cities" index. Rank: #25 out of 200 large metro areas. Criteria: job growth; wage and salary growth; high-tech output growth. *Milken Institute, June 25, 2003*

- The Houston metro area appeared on *Entrepreneur* magazine's list of the "Best Cities for Entrepreneurs" in 2003. The area ranked #21 out of 61 in the large city category. Criteria: entrepreneurial activity; small-business growth; economic growth; and risk. *www.Entrepreneur.com*

- The Houston metro area appeared on *IndustryWeek's* fourth annual World-Class Communities list. It ranked #4 out of 315 metro areas. Criteria: MSA Gross Metropolitan Product (GMP) per manufacturing employee; and MSA percent share of U.S. manufacturing Gross Domestic Product (GDP). *IndustryWeek, April 16, 2001*

- ING Group ranked the 125 largest metro areas according to the general financial security of residents. The Houston metro area was ranked #75 out of 125. Criteria: Earnings and Wealth Potential (household income, education, net assets, cost of living); Safety Net (health insurance, retirement savings, life insurance, income support programs); Personal Threats (unemployment rate, low-income households, crime rate); Community Economic Vitality (cost of community services, job quality, job creation, housing costs). *ING Group, "The Best Cities to Earn and Save Money: A Ranking of the Largest 125 U.S. Cities," 2001 Edition*

Business Environment

CITY FINANCES

City Government Finances

Component	2000-2001 ($000)	2000-2001 ($ per capita)
Total Revenues	2,569,047	1,315
Total Expenditures	2,871,329	1,470
Debt Outstanding	7,887,363	4,037
Cash and Securities	7,738,589	3,961

Source: U.S Census Bureau, Government Finances 2000-2001, August 2003

City Government Revenue by Source

Source	2000-2001 ($000)	2000-2001 ($ per capita)
General Revenue		
From Federal Government	121,374	62
From State Government	37,682	19
From Local Governments	3,989	2
Taxes		
Property	567,116	290
Sales	551,948	283
Personal Income	0	0
License	0	0
Charges	592,206	303
Liquor Store	0	0
Utility	281,183	144
Employee Retirement	123,855	63
Other	289,694	148

Source: U.S Census Bureau, Government Finances 2000-2001, August 2003

City Government Expenditures by Function

Function	2000-2001 ($000)	2000-2001 ($ per capita)	2000-2001 (%)
General Expenditures			
Airports	448,189	229	15.6
Corrections	13,876	7	0.5
Education	0	0	0.0
Fire Protection	226,651	116	7.9
Governmental Administration	106,717	55	3.7
Health	97,812	50	3.4
Highways	193,914	99	6.8
Hospitals	0	0	0.0
Housing and Community Development	61,647	32	2.1
Interest on General Debt	244,209	125	8.5
Libraries	39,741	20	1.4
Parking	0	0	0.0
Parks and Recreation	138,884	71	4.8
Police Protection	421,915	216	14.7
Public Welfare	0	0	0.0
Sewerage	251,878	129	8.8
Solid Waste Management	70,478	36	2.5
Liquor Store	0	0	0.0
Utility	277,515	142	9.7
Employee Retirement	167,990	86	5.9
Other	109,913	56	3.8

Source: U.S Census Bureau, Government Finances 2000-2001, August 2003

Municipal Bond Ratings

Area	Moody's
City	Aaa

Source: Mergent Bond Record, February 2004

DEMOGRAPHICS

Population Growth

Area	1990 Census	2000 Census	2003 Estimate	2008 Projection	Population Growth (%)	
					1990-2000	2000-2008
City	1,697,610	1,953,631	2,026,976	2,154,705	15.1	10.3
MSA[1]	3,322,025	4,177,646	4,440,137	4,880,084	25.8	16.8
U.S.	248,709,873	281,421,906	290,647,163	305,918,071	13.2	8.7

Note: (1) Metropolitan Statistical Area - see Appendix A for areas included
Source: Claritas, Inc.

Number of Households and Average Household Size

Area	1990 Census	2000 Census	2003 Estimate	2008 Projection	2003 Average Household Size
City	641,561	717,945	740,360	779,391	2.7
MSA[1]	1,193,305	1,462,665	1,545,709	1,683,473	2.9
U.S.	91,947,410	105,480,101	109,440,059	116,034,472	2.7

Note: (1) Metropolitan Statistical Area - see Appendix A for areas included
Source: Claritas, Inc.

Race and Ethnicity

Area	White Non-Hispanic	Black Non-Hispanic	Asian Non-Hispanic	Other Race Non-Hispanic	Hispanic
City	48.8	25.0	5.5	20.6	38.9
MSA[1]	60.7	17.3	5.5	16.5	30.9
U.S.	74.5	12.4	3.8	9.3	13.2

Note: Figures are 2003 estimates; (1) Metropolitan Statistical Area - see Appendix A for areas included
Source: Claritas, Inc.

Segregation

City		MSA[1]	
Index[2]	Rank[3]	Index[2]	Rank[4]
75.5	11	71.8	45

Note: Figures are based on an analysis of Census 2000 data; (1) Metropolitan Statistical Area - see Appendix A for areas included; (2) Dissimilarity Index—the most commonly used measure of segregation between two groups, reflecting their relative distributions across neighborhoods within a city or metropolitan area. It can range in value from 0, indicating complete integration, to 100, indicating complete segregation; (3) Ranges from 1 (most segregated) to 100 (least segregated) and includes all the cities in this book; (4) Ranges from 1 (most segregated) to 318 (least segregated) and includes 318 metropolitan areas.
Source: www.CensusScope.org

Ancestry

Area	German	Irish[2]	English	American	Italian	Polish	French[3]	Scottish
City	6.1	4.3	5.0	3.7	1.6	1.0	1.9	1.0
MSA[1]	9.2	6.6	6.6	5.9	2.2	1.4	2.6	1.3
U.S.	15.2	10.9	8.7	7.3	5.6	3.2	3.0	1.7

Note: Figures include multiple ancestry (e.g. if a person reported being Irish and Italian, they were included in both columns); (1) Metropolitan Statistical Area - see Appendix A for areas included; (2) Includes Celtic; (3) Includes Alsatian but excludes Basque
Source: Census 2000, Summary File 3

Foreign-Born Population

Area	Percent of Population Born in:							
	Any Foreign Country	Europe	Asia	Africa	Oceania[2]	Canada	Mexico	Latin America[3]
City	26.4	1.2	4.7	0.9	0.1	0.2	14.0	5.4
MSA[1]	20.5	1.1	4.3	0.6	0.0	0.2	10.4	3.8
U.S.	11.1	1.7	2.9	0.3	0.1	0.3	3.3	2.5

Note: (1) Metropolitan Statistical Area - see Appendix A for areas included; (2) Includes Australia, New Zealand subregion, Melanesia, Micronesia, Polynesia, and Oceania n.e.c; (3) Includes Central America (excluding Mexico), South America, and the Caribbean.
Source: Census 2000, Summary File 3

Religion

Area	Catholic	Southern Baptist	United Methodist	ELCA[1]	LDS[2]	Presbyterian Church USA	Jewish Est.	Muslim Est.
County	18.2	14.3	5.0	0.5	0.7	1.1	1.1	1.4
U.S.	22.0	7.1	3.7	1.8	1.5	1.1	2.2	0.6

Note: Figures shown are the number of adherents as a percentage of the total population; Adherents are defined as all members, including full members, their children and the estimated number of other participants who are not considered members (e.g. the baptized, those not confirmed, those not eligible for communion, those regularly attending services, etc.); (1) Evangelical Lutheran Church in America; (2) The Church of Jesus Christ of Latter Day Saints
Source: Reprinted with permission from Religious Congregations and Membership in the United States 2000 (Nashville, Glenmary Research Center, 2002) Copyright Association of Statisticians of American Religious Bodies. All rights reserved.

Age Distribution

Area	Percent of Population						
	Under Age 5	Age 5 to 17	Age 18 to 34	Age 35 to 49	Age 50 to 64	Age 65 to 79	80 Years and Over
City	8.2	19.2	29.2	22.7	12.4	6.4	1.9
MSA[1]	8.1	21.1	26.0	24.6	12.9	5.8	1.6
U.S.	6.8	18.9	23.7	23.5	14.8	9.2	3.2

Note: (1) Metropolitan Statistical Area - see Appendix A for areas included
Source: Census 2000, Summary File 3

Marriage Status

Area	Never Married	Now Married Except Separated	Separated	Widowed	Divorced
City	32.2	48.9	3.6	5.4	10.0
MSA[1]	27.4	55.6	2.8	4.8	9.5
U.S.	27.1	54.4	2.2	6.6	9.7

Note: Figures cover population 15 years of age and older; (1) Metropolitan Statistical Area - see Appendix A for areas included
Source: Census 2000, Summary File 3

Male/Female Ratio

Area	Males	Females	Males per 100 Females
City	1,012,395	1,014,581	99.8
MSA[1]	2,208,890	2,231,247	99.0
U.S.	142,511,883	148,135,280	96.2

Note: Figures are 2003 estimates; (1) Metropolitan Statistical Area - see Appendix A for areas included
Source: Claritas, Inc.

ECONOMY

Gross Metropolitan Product

Area	1999	2000	2001	2002	2002 Rank[2]
MSA[1]	156.8	170.5	179.4	185.4	7

Note: Figures are in billions of dollars; (1) Metropolitan Statistical Area - see Appendix A for areas included; (2) Rank ranges from 1 to 319
Source: The U.S. Conference of Mayors, Metro Economies Report, July 2003

INCOME

Per Capita/Median/Average Income

Area	Per Capita ($)	Median Household ($)	Average Household ($)
City	21,792	40,970	59,131
MSA[1]	24,199	49,676	69,099
U.S.	24,078	46,868	63,207

Note: Figures are 2003 estimates; (1) Metropolitan Statistical Area - see Appendix A for areas included
Source: Claritas, Inc.

Household Income Distribution

Area	Percent of Households Earning							
	Under $15,000	$15,000 -24,999	$25,000 -34,999	$35,000 -49,999	$50,000 -74,999	$75,000 -99,000	$100,000 -149,999	$150,000 and up
City	16.6	13.1	13.5	17.0	16.6	8.9	8.4	5.9
MSA[1]	12.6	10.5	11.4	15.8	18.4	11.7	11.9	7.6
U.S.	14.1	11.5	11.7	16.0	19.2	11.3	10.2	6.0

Note: Figures are 2003 estimates; (1) Metropolitan Statistical Area - see Appendix A for areas included
Source: Claritas, Inc.

Poverty Rates by Age

Area	All Ages	Under 5 Years Old	5 to 17 Years Old	18 to 64 Years Old	65 Years and Over
City	19.2	2.3	5.0	10.8	1.2
MSA[1]	13.9	1.6	3.7	7.7	0.9
U.S.	12.4	1.2	3.0	6.9	1.2

Note: Figures are percent of population with income in 1999 below poverty level and only include population for whom poverty status is determined; (1) Metropolitan Statistical Area - see Appendix A for areas included
Source: Census 2000, Summary File 3

Personal Bankruptcy Filing Rate

Area	2002	2003
Harris County	3.06	3.67
U.S.	5.34	5.58

Note: Numbers are per 1,000 population and include Chapter 7 and Chapter 13 filings
Source: Federal Deposit Insurance Corporation (FDIC), Regional Economic Conditions (RECON), 2/25/2004

EMPLOYMENT

Labor Force and Employment

Area	Civilian Labor Force			Workers Employed		
	Dec. 2002	Dec. 2003	% Chg.	Dec. 2002	Dec. 2003	% Chg.
City	1,081,601	1,114,017	3.0	1,008,041	1,033,619	2.5
MSA[1]	2,279,494	2,347,043	3.0	2,152,882	2,207,509	2.5
U.S.	144,807,000	146,501,000	1.2	136,599,000	138,556,000	1.4

Note: Data is not seasonally adjusted and covers workers 16 years of age and older;
(1) Metropolitan Statistical Area - see Appendix A for areas included
Source: Bureau of Labor Statistics, http://stats.bls.gov

Unemployment Rate

Area	2003											
	Jan.	Feb.	Mar.	Apr.	May	Jun.	Jul.	Aug.	Sep.	Oct.	Nov.	Dec.
City	7.9	7.8	7.7	7.7	8.2	9.3	8.8	8.5	8.4	7.7	7.7	7.2
MSA[1]	6.5	6.4	6.4	6.3	6.7	7.7	7.2	7.0	6.9	6.3	6.3	5.9
U.S.	6.5	6.4	6.2	5.8	5.8	6.5	6.3	6.0	5.8	5.6	5.6	5.4

Note: Data is not seasonally adjusted and covers workers 16 years of age and older; All figures are percentages; (1) Metropolitan Statistical Area - see Appendix A for areas included
Source: Bureau of Labor Statistics, http://stats.bls.gov

Employment by Occupation

Occupation Classification	City (%)	MSA[1] (%)	U.S. (%)
Sales and Office	26.4	27.6	26.7
Professional and Related	20.6	20.5	20.2
Service	15.7	13.6	14.9
Production, Transportation, and Material Moving	12.9	12.5	14.6
Management, Business, and Financial	13.3	14.8	13.5
Construction, Extraction, and Maintenance	11.0	10.9	9.4
Farming, Forestry, and Fishing	0.1	0.2	0.7

Note: Figures cover employed civilians 16 years of age and older;
(1) Metropolitan Statistical Area - see Appendix A for areas included
Source: Census 2000, Summary File 3

Employment by Industry

Sector	MSA[1]		U.S.
	Number of Employees	Percent of Total	Percent of Total
Government	300,400	14.2	16.7
Education and Health Services	238,300	11.3	12.9
Professional and Business Services	289,100	13.7	12.3
Retail Trade	230,600	10.9	11.8
Manufacturing	187,200	8.9	11.0
Leisure and Hospitality	176,600	8.4	9.1
Finance Activities	125,600	6.0	6.1
Construction	156,000	7.4	5.1
Wholesale Trade	113,100	5.4	4.3
Other Services	84,700	4.0	4.1
Transportation and Utilities	106,500	5.0	3.7
Information	36,700	1.7	2.4
Natural Resources and Mining	64,200	3.0	0.4

Note: Figures cover non-farm employment as of December 2003 and are not seasonally adjusted; (1) Metropolitan Statistical Area - see Appendix A for areas included
Source: Bureau of Labor Statistics, http://stats.bls.gov

Average Wages

Occupation	$/Hr.	Occupation	$/Hr.
Accountants and Auditors	25.39	Maids and Housekeeping Cleaners	7.35
Automotive Mechanics	16.59	Maintenance and Repair Workers	13.60
Bookkeepers	14.60	Marketing Managers	39.67
Carpenters	14.42	Nuclear Medicine Technologists	24.82
Cashiers	7.51	Nurses, Licensed Practical	17.57
Clerks, General Office	10.77	Nurses, Registered	24.60
Clerks, Receptionists/Information	10.87	Nursing Aides/Orderlies/Attendants	8.59
Clerks, Shipping/Receiving	12.12	Packers and Packagers, Hand	7.99
Computer Programmers	37.78	Physical Therapists	30.64
Computer Support Specialists	20.95	Postal Service Mail Carriers	19.12
Computer Systems Analysts	30.95	Real Estate Brokers	25.98
Cooks, Restaurant	8.92	Retail Salespersons	10.53
Dentists	64.20	Sales Reps., Exc. Tech./Scientific	25.16
Electrical Engineers	36.99	Sales Reps., Tech./Scientific	28.39
Electricians	18.16	Secretaries, Exc. Legal/Med./Exec.	12.15
Financial Managers	42.03	Security Guards	9.31
First-Line Supervisors/Mgrs., Sales	16.94	Surgeons	n/a
Food Preparation Workers	7.86	Teacher Assistants	7.90
General and Operations Managers	39.11	Teachers, Elementary School	20.00
Hairdressers/Cosmetologists	12.11	Teachers, Secondary School	21.30
Internists	n/a	Telemarketers	10.09
Janitors and Cleaners	7.65	Truck Drivers, Heavy/Tractor-Trailer	15.73
Landscaping/Groundskeeping Workers	8.86	Truck Drivers, Light/Delivery Svcs.	12.50
Lawyers	65.87	Waiters and Waitresses	8.34

Note: Wage data is for 2002 and covers the Metropolitan Statistical Area (see Appendix A for areas included). Hourly wages for elementary/secondary school teachers and teacher assistants were calculated by the editors from annual wage data assuming a 40 hour work week; n/a not available.
Source: Bureau of Labor Statistics, 2002 Metro Area Occupational Employment and Wage Estimates

Occupational Employment Projections: 1996 - 2006

Occupations Expected to Have the Largest Job Growth (ranked by numerical growth)	Fast-Growing Occupations[1] (ranked by percent growth)
1. Cashiers	1. Desktop publishers
2. Salespersons, retail	2. Systems analysts
3. General managers & top executives	3. Customer service representatives
4. Truck drivers, light	4. Physical therapy assistants and aides
5. Child care workers, private household	5. Computer engineers
6. General office clerks	6. Emergency medical technicians
7. Systems analysts	7. Medical assistants
8. Food preparation workers	8. Respiratory therapists
9. Food service workers	9. Telephone & cable TV line install & repair
10. Registered nurses	10. Physical therapists

Note: Projections cover Texas; (1) Excludes occupations with total job growth less than 300
Source: U.S. Department of Labor, Employment and Training Administration, America's Labor Market Information System (ALMIS)

TAXES

State Corporate Income Tax Rates

State	Rate (%)	Number of Brackets	Low Bracket (Under $)	High Bracket (Over $)
Texas	None	na	na	na

Note: Tax rates as of December 31, 2003; na not applicable
Source: Tax Foundation, www.taxfoundation.org

State Individual Income Tax Rates

State	Federal Deductibility	Marginal Rate (%)	Number of Brackets	Low Bracket (Under $)	High Bracket (Over $)
Texas	No	None	na	na	na

Note: Tax rates as of December 31, 2003; Brackets apply to single taxpayers and married people filing separately; na not applicable
Source: Tax Foundation, www.taxfoundation.org

Various State and Local Tax Rates

State Sales and Use (%)	Total Sales and Use (%)	Gasoline (cents/gal.)	Cigarette (cents/pack)	Spirits ($/gal.)	Table Wine ($/gal.)	Beer ($/gal.)
6.25	8.25	20	41	2.40	0.20	0.20

Note: Tax rates as of December 31, 2003
Source: Tax Foundation, www.taxfoundation.org

State Tax Burdens

Area	Combined State and Local Tax Burden		Combined Federal, State and Local Tax Burden	
	Percent	Rank	Percent	Rank
Texas	8.3	47	28.4	31
U.S. Average	9.7	-	30.0	-

Note: Figures are for 2003
Source: Tax Foundation, www.taxfoundation.org

Internal Revenue Service Tax Audits

IRS District	Percent of Returns Audited				
	1996	1997	1998	1999	2000
Houston	0.76	0.64	0.53	0.44	0.22
U.S.	0.66	0.61	0.46	0.31	0.20

Note: Figures cover IRS district audits of federal income tax returns filed by individuals. Geographic data on district audits for 2001 and 2002 are being withheld by the IRS. TRAC is challenging this policy.
Source: Syracuse University, Transactional Records Access Clearinghouse (TRAC), "Odds of IRS District Tax Audit 2000"

RESIDENTIAL REAL ESTATE

Building Permits

Area	Single-Family			Multi-Family			Total		
	2001	2002	Pct. Chg.	2001	2002	Pct. Chg.	2001	2002	Pct. Chg.
City	4,366	4,547	4.1	5,521	6,673	20.9	9,887	11,220	13.5
U.S.	1,235,600	1,332,600	7.9	401,100	415,100	3.5	1,636,700	1,747,700	6.8

Note: Figures represent new, privately-owned housing units authorized (unadjusted data)
Source: U.S. Census Bureau, Manufacturing, Mining, and Construction Statistics

Homeownership and Housing Vacancies

Area	Homeownership Rate[2] (%)			Rental Vacancy Rate[3] (%)			Homeowner Vacancy Rate[4] (%)		
	2001	2002[a]	2003	2001	2002[a]	2003	2001	2002[a]	2003
MSA[1]	55.9	56.5	56.6	11.1	12.9	15.8	1.3	1.1	1.9
U.S.	67.8	67.9	68.3	8.4	8.9	9.8	1.8	1.7	1.8

Note: (1) Metropolitan Statistical Area - see Appendix A for areas included; (2) The proportion of households that are owners; (3) The proportion of the rental inventory that is vacant for rent; (4) The proportion of the homeowner inventory that is vacant for sale; (a) 2002 figures have been revised; n/a not available
Source: U.S. Census Bureau, Housing Vacancies and Homeownership Annual Statistics: 2003

COMMERCIAL REAL ESTATE

Industrial/Office Markets

Type/Market Area	Inventory (sq. ft.)	Vacant (sq. ft.)	Vacancy Rate (%)	Under Construction (sq. ft.)	Net Absorption (sq. ft.)
Industrial Space Houston	365,115,727	35,245,078	9.65	1,058,154	-761,985
Office Space Houston	173,407,479	22,510,838	12.98	1,652,090	4,729,564

Note: Data as of 4th Quarter, 2003; n/a not available
Source: Society of Industrial and Office Realtors, 2004 Comparative Statistics of Industrial and Office Real Estate Markets

COMMERCIAL UTILITIES

Typical Monthly Electric Bills

Area	Commercial Service ($/month)		Industrial Service ($/month)	
	3 kW demand 1,000 kWh	40 kW demand 14,000 kWh	1,000 kW demand 200,000 kWh	50,000 kW demand 15,000,000 kWh
City	n/a	n/a	n/a	n/a
Average[1]	100	1,134	17,850	1,045,117

Note: Based on rates in effect July 1, 2003; (1) average based on 197 utilities; n/a not available
Source: Edison Electric Institute, Typical Bills and Average Rates Report, Summer 2003

TRANSPORTATION

Means of Transportation to Work

Area	Car/Truck/Van		Public Transportation			Bicycle	Walked	Other Means	Worked at Home
	Drove Alone	Car-pooled	Bus	Subway	Railroad				
City	71.8	15.9	5.7	0.0	0.0	0.5	2.3	1.4	2.3
MSA[1]	76.6	14.4	3.4	0.0	0.0	0.3	1.6	1.2	2.5
U.S.	75.7	12.2	2.5	1.5	0.5	0.4	2.9	1.0	3.3

Note: Figures shown are percentages and cover workers 16 years of age and older;
(1) Metropolitan Statistical Area - see Appendix A for areas included
Source: Census 2000, Summary File 3

Travel Time to Work

Area	Less Than 15 Minutes	15 to 29 Minutes	30 to 44 Minutes	45 to 59 Minutes	60 Minutes or More
City	20.8	37.3	26.1	8.3	7.5
MSA[1]	20.3	33.8	25.5	11.1	9.3
U.S.	29.4	36.1	19.1	7.4	8.0

Note: Figures are percentages and include workers 16 years old and over; (1) Metropolitan Statistical Area - see Appendix A for areas included
Source: Census 2000, Summary File 3

Roadway Congestion Index

Area	1982	1990	1996	2000	2001
City	1.03	1.04	1.02	1.17	1.19
Average[1]	0.82	1.01	1.08	1.16	1.17

Note: Values greater than 1.00 indicate undesirable mobility levels; (1) average of 75 urban areas
Source: Texas Transportation Institute, The 2003 Annual Urban Mobility Report

Transportation Statistics

Interstate highways (2004)	I-10; I-45
Public transportation (2002)	Metropolitan Transit Authority of Harris County (METRO)
Buses	
Average fleet age in years	4.1
No. operated in max. service	1,053
Demand response	
Average fleet age in years	0.0
No. operated in max. service	552
Passenger air service	
Airport	George Bush Intercontinental; William P. Hobby
Airlines (2003)	27 (both airports)
Boardings (2002)	15,865,479; 3,819,306
Amtrak service (2004)	Yes
Major waterways/ports	Gulf of Mexico; Port of Houston

Source: Federal Transit Administration, National Transit Database, 2002; Editor & Publisher Market Guide, 2004; Bureau of Transportation Statistics, Airport Enplanement Activity for CY2002; www.amtrak.com

BUSINESSES

Major Business Headquarters

Company Name	2003 Rankings	
	Fortune 500	Forbes 500
Baker Hughes	320	-
Burlington Resources	497	-
CenterPoint Energy	236	-
ConocoPhillips	12	-
Continental Airlines	220	-
Dynegy	336	-
Encompass Services	449	-
Enterprise Products	438	-
Fiesta Mart	-	264
Goodman Manufacturing	-	235
Grocers Supply	-	157
Group 1 Automotive	383	-
Gulf States Toyota	-	37
Halliburton	153	-
Lyondell Chemical	467	-
Marathon Oil	52	-
Plains All Amer. Pipeline	221	-
Reliant Resources	164	-
Smith International	480	-
Sysco	73	-
Waste Management	171	-

Note: Companies listed are located in the city; dashes indicate no ranking
Fortune 500: Companies that produce a 10-K are ranked 1 to 500 based on 2002 revenue
Forbes 500: Private companies are ranked 1 to 281 based on 2002 revenue
Source: Fortune, April 14, 2003; www.forbes.com, November 6, 2003

Best Companies to Work For

Continental Airlines; Saint Luke's; Sterling Bank, headquartered in Houston, are among the "100 Best Companies to Work for in 2004." Criteria: trust in management, pride in work/company, camaraderie, company responses to the Hewitt People Practices Inventory, and employee responses to their Great Place to Work survey. The companies also had to be at least 10 years old and have a minimum of 500 employees. *Fortune, January 12, 2004*

Kirby; Oceaneering International; Riviana Foods; US Physical Therapy, headquartered in Houston, are among the "200 Best Small Companies in 2003." Criteria: 3,500 companies whose latest 12-month sales were $5 million to $600 million were screened. Those with a net margin or five-year average ROE below 5% were cut. Banks, utilities, real estate investment trusts and limited partnerships whose financial structures are too different from most operating companies were also excluded. Shares had to be trading above $5 by the end of September 2003. Financial statement footnotes were examined for major issues. For the final ranking, equal weight was given to growth in sales, earnings and ROE for the past five years and the latest 12 months. *www.forbes.com, October 27, 2003*

Fast-Growing Businesses

According to *Inc.*, Houston is home to 10 of America's 500 fastest-growing private companies: **Advanced Health Education Center; Amerisource Funding; Bridgeway Capital Management; Cardtronics; Court Reporter's Clearinghouse; Grant Harrison Advertising; MRE Consulting; No Brainer Enterprises; Republic State Mortgage; Synhrgy HR Technologies**. Criteria: must be an independent, privately-held, U.S. corporation, proprietorship or partnership; sales of at least $200,000 in 1998; five-year operating/sales history; increase in 2002 sales over 2001 sales; holding companies, regulated banks, and utilities were excluded. *Inc. 500, America's Fastest-Growing Private Companies, October 15, 2003*

Houston is home to two of *Business Week's* "hot growth" companies: **Hydril; Pogo Producing**. Criteria: increase in sales and profits, return on capital and stock price. *Business Week, June 9, 2003*

According to *Fortune*, Houston is home to eight of America's 100 fastest-growing companies: **Dynacq International; GulfTerra Energy Partners; Houston Exploration; Landry's Restaurants; National-Oilwell; Pogo Producing; Prosperity Bancshares; Spinnaker Exploration**. Companies were ranked based on earnings-per-share growth, revenue growth and total return over the previous three years. Criteria for inclusion: public companies with sales of at least $50 million. Companies that lost money in the most recent quarter, or ended in the red for the past four quarters as a whole, were not eligible. Limited partnerships and REITs were also not considered. *Fortune, "America's Fastest-Growing Companies," September 1, 2003*

According to Deloitte & Touche LLP, Houston is home to three of North America's 500 fastest-growing high-technology companies: **Crown Castle International Corp; DataCert, Inc; Synhrgy HR Technologies, Inc**. Companies are ranked by percentage growth in revenue over a five-year period. Criteria for inclusion: must be a U.S. or Canadian company developing and/or providing technology products or services; company must have been in business for five years with 1998 operating revenues of at least $50,000 USD or $75,000 CD and 2002 operating revenues of at least $1 million USD/CD. *Deloitte & Touche LLP, 2003 Technology Fast 500*

Women-Owned Firms: Number, Employment and Sales

Area	Number of Firms	Employ-ment	Sales ($000)	Rank[2]
MSA[1]	89,907	169,014	27,639,753	5

Note: (1) Metropolitan Statistical Area - see Appendix A for areas included;
(2) Calculated on an averaging of the number of businesses, employment, and sales
Source: The National Foundation for Women Business Owners, Women-Owned Businesses in the Top 50 Metropolitan Areas, 2002: A Fact Sheet

Women-Owned Firms: Growth

Area	Percent Change from 1997 to 2002			Rank[2]
	Number of Firms	Employ-ment	Sales	
MSA[1]	13.8	43.7	62.5	8
Top 50 MSAs	14.0	31.4	42.6	-

Note: (1) Metropolitan Statistical Area - see Appendix A for areas included; (2) Calculated on an averaging of the percent growth of number of businesses, employment, and sales
Source: The National Foundation for Women Business Owners, Women-Owned Businesses in the Top 50 Metropolitan Areas, 2002: A Fact Sheet

Minority and Women-Owned Businesses

Ownership	All Firms		Firms with Paid Employees			
	Firms	Sales ($000)	Firms	Sales ($000)	Employees	Payroll ($000)
Black	16,855	1,418,893	2,216	1,120,166	22,409	426,757
Hispanic	23,661	10,023,546	4,087	9,205,177	31,444	826,062
Women	41,094	11,144,538	8,554	10,191,000	89,114	2,462,193

Note: Figures cover firms located in the city
Source: 1997 Economic Census, Minority and Women-Owned Businesses

Minority Business Opportunity

Houston is home to two companies which are on the Black Enterprise Industrial/Service 100 list (100 largest companies based on gross sales): **CAMAC; Total Premier Services Inc.**. Criteria: operational in previous calendar year; at least 51% black-owned and manufactures/owns the product it sells or provides industrial or consumer services. Brokerages, real estate firms and firms that provide professional services are not eligible. *Black Enterprise, www.blackenterprise.com, B.E. 100s, 2003 Report*

20 of the 500 largest Hispanic-owned companies in the U.S. are located in Houston. *Hispanic Business, June 2003*

Houston is home to five companies which are on the Hispanic Business Fastest-Growing 100 list (greatest sales growth over the past five years): **Reytec Construction Resources Inc.; G&A OutSourcing Inc.; Sunland Group; Muniz Engineering Inc.; WalkerCom Inc.**. *Hispanic Business, July/August 2003*

HOTELS

Hotels/Motels

Area	Hotels/Motels	Average Minimum Rates ($)		
		Tourist	First-Class	Deluxe
City	307	63	108	321

Source: OAG Travel Planner Online, Spring 2004

Houston is home to two of the top 100 hotels in the U.S. and Canada according to *Travel & Leisure*: **Four Seasons Hotel** (#36); **St. Regis** (#100). Criteria: value, rooms/ambience, location, facilities/activities and service. *Travel & Leisure, "The World's Best Hotels 2003"*

EVENT SITES

Major Event Sites, Meeting Places and Convention Centers

Name	Guest Rooms	Exhibit/ Meeting Space (sq. ft.)	Largest Meeting Room Capacity
Astrodome USA	n/a	62,640	75,000
George R. Brown Convention Center	n/a	n/a	4,000
Houston Livestock Show & Rodeo Inc.	n/a	n/a	56,000
Hyatt Regency Houston	963	66,000	8,035
Majestic Theatre	n/a	n/a	2,311
Music Hall	n/a	n/a	3,000
Radisson Astrodome Hotel & Convention Center	630	55,000	2,500

Note: n/a not available
Source: Original research

Living Environment

COST OF LIVING

Cost of Living Index

Year	Composite Index	Groceries	Housing	Utilities	Trans-portation	Health Care	Misc. Goods/ Services
2001	95.3	92.8	83.9	110.4	105.7	107.9	97.7
2002	91.8	87.2	80.4	97.8	106.3	103.0	96.2
2003	91.2	85.8	79.4	100.3	104.3	102.6	95.7

Note: U.S. = 100; Figures are for the Metropolitan Statistical Area - see Appendix A for areas included
Source: ACCRA, Cost of Living Index, 2001, 2002 and 2003 4-Quarter Averages

HOUSING

House Price Index (HPI)

Area	National Ranking[2]	Quarterly Change (%)	One-Year Change (%)	Five-Year Change (%)
MSA[1]	186	1.54	3.53	32.00
U.S.[3]	-	3.67	7.97	41.81

Note: The HPI is a weighted repeat sales index. It measures average price changes in repeat sales or refinancings on the same properties. This information is obtained by reviewing repeat mortgage transactions on single-family properties whose mortgages have been purchased or securitized by Fannie Mae of Freddie Mac in January 1975; (1) Metropolitan Statistical Area - see Appendix A for areas included; (2) Rankings are based on annual percentage change, for all MSAs containing at least 15,000 transactions over the last 10 years and ranges from 1 to 220; (3) figures based on a weighted division average; all figures are for the period ended December 31, 2003
Source: Office of Federal Housing Enterprise Oversight, House Price Index, March 1, 2004

Housing: Year Structure Built

Area	1990 -2000	1980 -1989	1970 -1979	1960 -1969	1950 -1959	1940 -1949	Before 1940	Median Year
City	11.1	17.8	27.8	18.6	13.4	6.1	5.2	1972
MSA[1]	19.8	23.0	26.6	13.6	9.4	4.3	3.4	1977
U.S.	17.0	15.8	18.5	13.7	12.7	7.3	15.0	1971

Note: Figures are percentages; (1) Metropolitan Statistical Area - see Appendix A for areas included
Source: Census 2000, Summary File 3

Average New Home Price

Area	2001	2002	2003
MSA[1]	171,028	178,851	184,831
U.S.	212,643	236,567	248,193

Note: Figures, in dollars, are based on a new home with 2,400 sq. ft. of living area on an 8,000 sq. ft. lot; (1) Metropolitan Statistical Area - see Appendix A for areas included
Source: ACCRA, Cost of Living Index, 2001, 2002 and 2003 4-Quarter Averages

Average Apartment Rent

Area	2001	2002	2003
MSA[1]	724	749	767
U.S.	674	708	721

Note: Figures, in dollars per month, are based on an unfurnished two bedroom, 1-1/2 or 2 bath apartment, approximately 950 sq. ft., excluding utilities except water; (1) Metropolitan Statistical Area - see Appendix A for areas included
Source: ACCRA, Cost of Living Index, 2001, 2002 and 2003 4-Quarter Averages

RESIDENTIAL UTILITIES

Average Residential Utility Costs

Area	All Electric ($/mth)	Part Electric ($/mth)	Other Energy ($/mth)	Phone ($/mth)
MSA[1]	-	98.55	35.03	21.67
U.S.	116.46	65.82	62.68	23.90

Note: (1) Metropolitan Statistical Area - see Appendix A for areas included
Source: ACCRA, Cost of Living Index, 2003 4-Quarter Average

HEALTH CARE

Average Health Care Costs

Area	Hospital ($/day)	Doctor ($/visit)	Dentist ($/visit)
MSA[1]	617.69	72.75	87.08
U.S.	678.35	67.91	83.90

Note: Hospital—based on a semi-private room; Doctor—based on a general practitioner's routine exam of an established patient; Dentist—based on adult teeth cleaning and periodic oral exam;
(1) Metropolitan Statistical Area - see Appendix A for areas included
Source: ACCRA, Cost of Living Index, 2003 4-Quarter Average

Distribution of Non-Federal, Office-Based Physicians

Area	Total	Family/ General Practice	Specialties		
			Medical	Surgical	Other
CMSA[3] (number)	8,383	1,065	2,860	2,012	2,446
CMSA[3] (rate per 10,000 pop.)	18.0	2.3	6.1	4.3	5.2
Metro Average[2] (rate per 10,000 pop.)	33.1	2.2	7.7	4.8	5.6

Note: Data as of December 31, 2001; (1) Metropolitan Statistical Area - see Appendix A for areas included; (2) Average of 81 MSAs and CMSAs in this book; (3) Houston-Galveston-Brazoria, TX Consolidated Metropolitan Statistical Area includes the following counties: Brazoria; Chambers; Fort Bend; Galveston; Harris; Liberty; Montgomery; Waller
Source: American Medical Association, Physician Characteristics & Distribution in the U.S., 2003-2004

Hospitals

Houston has the following hospitals: 21 general medical and surgical; 6 psychiatric; 1 obstetrics and gynecology; 2 rehabilitation; 1 orthopedic; 1 cancer; 7 long-term acute care; 2 other specialty; 1 children's general; 1 children's orthopedic.
AHA Guide to the Healthcare Field, 2003-2004

According to *U.S. News,* Houston has seven of the best hospitals in the U.S.: **Memorial Hermann Hospital**; **Methodist Hospital**; **The Menninger Clinic**; **TIRR-The Institute for Rehabilitation and Research**; **Texas Children's Hospital**; **Texas Heart Institute-St. Luke's Episcopal Hospital**; **University of Texas (M. D. Anderson Cancer Center)**; *U.S. News Online, "America's Best Hospitals 2003"*

PRESIDENTIAL ELECTION

2000 Presidential Election Results

Area	Gore	Bush	Nader	Buchanan	Other
Harris County	42.9	54.3	2.4	0.2	0.3
U.S.	48.4	47.9	2.7	0.4	0.6

Note: Results are percentages and may not add to 100% due to rounding
Source: www.cbsnews.com; www.uselectionatlas.org

EDUCATION

Public School District Statistics

District Name	Schls.	Enroll-ment	Classroom Teachers	Pupil/ Teacher Ratio	Minority Pupils[1] (%)	Current Expend.[2] ($/pupil)
Academy of Houston	1	479	33	14.1	n/a	n/a
Aldine ISD	65	53,332	3,574	14.9	89.8	6,519
Alief ISD	40	43,697	2,692	16.2	n/a	5,695
Alphonso Crutch's	1	1,235	43	28.3	n/a	n/a
Cypress-Fairbanks ISD	57	67,562	4,452	15.2	41.5	6,109
Gulf Shores Academy	3	46	45	1.0	n/a	n/a
Harris County Juvenile	6	686	62	10.9	n/a	n/a
Houston Advantage Charter	1	632	29	21.8	n/a	n/a
Houston ISD	299	210,950	12,097	17.4	90.0	6,196
North Forest ISD	16	11,716	697	16.8	n/a	n/a
Prepared Table	3	1,287	n/a	n/a	n/a	n/a
Raul Yzaguirre School	1	645	37	17.2	n/a	n/a
Sheldon ISD	7	4,069	287	14.1	n/a	n/a
Southwest High School	4	447	31	14.2	n/a	n/a
Spring Branch ISD	49	32,578	2,149	15.2	n/a	6,338
Spring ISD	26	24,529	1,619	15.1	n/a	5,940
Varnett Charter School	1	720	41	17.6	n/a	n/a

Note: Data covers the 2001-02 school year unless otherwise noted; (1) Fall 2000; (2) FY2000; n/a not available
Source: U.S. Department of Education, National Center for Education Statistics, Common Core of Data, Local Education Agency (School District) Universe Survey: School Year 2001-2002; U.S. Department of Education, National Center for Education Statistics, Digest of Education Statistics 2002

Educational Quality

School District	Education Quotient[1]	Graduate Outcome[2]	Community Index[3]	Resource Index[4]
Houston ISD	31	32	26	44

Note: Scores are national percentile rankings and range from 1 (worst) to 99 (best); (1) Combination of the Graduate Outcome, Community and Resource indexes weighted to reflect the greater importance of the Graduate Outcome and Resource Index; (2) Based on graduation rates and college board scores (SAT/ACT); (3) Based on the surrounding community's level of affluence and adult education; (4) Based on teacher salaries, per-pupil expenditures and student-teacher ratios.
Source: Expansion Management, December 2003

Educational Attainment by Race

Area	High School Graduate (%)					Bachelor's Degree (%)				
	Total	White	Black	Asian	Hisp.[2]	Total	White	Black	Asian	Hisp.[2]
City	70.4	77.0	74.7	78.7	38.8	27.0	35.5	15.9	47.4	7.9
MSA[1]	75.9	81.4	77.5	80.1	43.6	27.2	31.4	18.4	47.7	8.5
U.S.	80.4	83.6	72.3	80.4	52.4	24.4	26.1	14.3	44.1	10.4

Note: Figures shown cover persons 25 years old and over; (1) Metropolitan Statistical Area - see Appendix A for areas included; (2) people of Hispanic origin can be of any race
Source: Census 2000, Summary File 3

School Enrollment by Type

Area	Grades KG to 8				Grades 9 to 12			
	Public		Private		Public		Private	
	Enrollment	%	Enrollment	%	Enrollment	%	Enrollment	%
City	256,005	92.3	21,375	7.7	101,938	92.5	8,210	7.5
MSA[1]	589,699	92.3	49,169	7.7	244,239	93.2	17,795	6.8
U.S.	33,526,011	88.7	4,285,121	11.3	14,848,628	90.6	1,532,323	9.4

Note: Figures shown cover persons 3 years old and over; (1) Metropolitan Statistical Area - see Appendix A for areas included
Source: Census 2000, Summary File 3

School Enrollment by Race

Area	Grades KG to 8 (%)				Grades 9 to 12 (%)			
	White	Black	Asian	Hisp.[1]	White	Black	Asian	Hisp.[1]
City	41.3	29.3	3.9	46.6	40.3	29.7	5.3	43.3
MSA[2]	56.0	19.6	4.3	36.5	56.0	19.8	5.4	32.8
U.S.	68.5	15.5	3.3	16.8	68.8	15.5	3.8	15.7

Note: Figures shown cover persons 3 years old and over; (1) people of Hispanic origin can be of any race; (2) Metropolitan Statistical Area - see Appendix A for areas included
Source: Census 2000, Summary File 3

Classroom Teacher Salaries in Public Schools

District	B.A. Degree		M.A. Degree		Maximum	
	Min. ($)	Rank[1]	Max. ($)	Rank[1]	Max. ($)	Rank[1]
Houston	34,588	22	55,729	31	58,578	49
DOD Average[2]	31,567	-	53,248	-	59,356	-

Note: Salaries are for 2001-2002; (1) Rank ranges from 1 to 100; (2) As per the U.S. Department of Defense Wage Fixing Authority
Source: American Federation of Teachers, Survey & Analysis of Teacher Salary Trends 2002

Higher Education

Four-Year Colleges			Two-Year Colleges			Medical Schools	Law Schools	Voc/ Tech
Public	Private Non-profit	Private For-profit	Public	Private Non-profit	Private For-profit			
6	11	2	4	4	12	2	3	41

Note: Figures cover institutions located within the city limits.
Source: National Center for Education Statistics, The Integrated Postsecondary Education System (IPEDS) Peer Analysis System, 2002; usnews.com, America's Best Graduate Schools 2004, Medical School Directory; The College Blue Book, Occupational Education, 2003; Barron's Guide to Law Schools, 2003; Medical School Admission Requirements U.S. & Canada, 2003-2004

MAJOR EMPLOYERS

Major Employers

Company Name	Industry	Type
B P Corporation North America	Petroleum refining	Branch
Baylor College of Medicine	Colleges and universities	Headquarters
Compaq	Electronic computers	Headquarters
Conoco-Downstream Admin	Management services	Branch
County of Harris	Executive offices	Headquarters
Eagle Global Logistics LP	Freight transportation arrangement	Single
Equistar 1 Houston Ctr	Industrial organic chemicals	nec
Exxon	Petroleum refining	Branch
Halliburton Energy Services	Oil and gas field services	nec
Houston V A Medical Center	Administration of veterans' affairs	Branch
Kellogg Brown & Root Inc	Heavy construction	nec
Kosa	Plastics materials and resins	Headquarters
M D Anderson Hospital	Noncommercial research organizations	Headquarters
Marshall Middle School	Elementary and secondary schools	Branch
MD Anderson Cancer Center	Offices and clinics of medical doctors	Branch
Methodist Hospital	General medical and surgical hospitals	Headquarters
Schlumberger Well Completions	Oil and gas field services	nec
St Lukes Episcopal Hospital	General medical and surgical hospitals	Headquarters
Stewart & Stevenson Uk Inc	Industrial machinery and equipment	Single

Note: Companies shown are located in the metropolitan area and have 3,500 or more employees.
Source: www.zapdata.com, March 2004

PUBLIC SAFETY

Crime Rate

Area	All Crimes	Violent Crimes				Property Crimes		
		Murder	Forcible Rape	Robbery	Aggrav. Assault	Burglary	Larceny -Theft	Motor Vehicle Theft
City	7,313.9	12.5	43.7	549.5	617.4	1,318.5	3,599.2	1,173.1
Suburbs[1]	3,916.7	4.7	29.8	122.3	298.3	799.6	2,280.2	381.9
MSA[2]	5,505.4	8.4	36.3	322.1	447.5	1,042.2	2,897.0	751.9
U.S.	4,118.8	5.6	33.0	145.9	310.1	746.2	2,445.8	432.1

Note: Figures are crimes per 100,000 population; (1) All areas within the MSA that are located outside the city limits; (2) Metropolitan Statistical Area - see Appendix A for areas included
Source: FBI Uniform Crime Reports, 2002

RECREATION

Culture and Recreation

Museums	Orchestras	Opera Companies	Dance Companies	Professional Theatres	Zoos	Pro Sports Teams[1]
15	2	1	7	8	1	3

Note: (1) Covers the Metropolitan Statistical Area - see Appendix A for areas included.
Source: The Grey House Performing Arts Directory, 2002; Official Museum Directory, 2004; www.sportsvenues.com

Library System

The Houston Public Library has 48 branches, holdings of 4,474,297 volumes and a budget of $36,540,000 (2000-2001). The Harris County Public Library has 25 branches, holdings of 1,885,146 volumes and a budget of $14,741,597 (2000-2001).
American Library Directory, 2003-2004

MEDIA

Newspapers

Name	Type	Freq.	Distribution	Circulation
African-American News & Issues	Black	1x/wk	State	350,000
African Community News Digest	General	1x/wk	n/a	85,000
The Citizen	General	1x/wk	Local	27,000
El Dia	Hispanic	6x/wk	Area	26,000
El Mexica	Hispanic	1x/wk	Local	55,000
Houston Chronicle	General	7x/wk	Area	545,727
Houston Defender	Black	1x/wk	Local	40,000
Houston Forward Times	Black	1x/wk	Local	64,580
The Houston Press	Alternative	1x/wk	Local	120,000
Houston Sun	Black	1x/wk	Local	80,000
The Informer and Texas Freeman	Black	1x/wk	Local	40,000
La Buena Suerte	Hispanic	1x/wk	Area	100,000
La Informacion	Hispanic	1x/wk	Local	85,000
La Subasta	Hispanic	3x/wk	State	185,000
La Voz de Houston Newspaper	Hispanic	1x/wk	Local	80,000
The Leader	General	1x/wk	Local	77,160
Metro Weekender	Black	1x/wk	Local	75,000
Northeast News	General	1x/wk	Local	32,000
The 1960 Sun	General	1x/wk	Area	76,000
Semana News	Hispanic	1x/wk	Local	115,000
Southern Chinese News	Asian	7x/wk	Local	25,000

Note: Includes newspapers whose offices are located in the city and whose circulations are 25,000 or more; n/a not available
Source: Burrelle's Media Directory, 2003

Television Stations

Name	Ch.	Affiliation	Type	Owner
KPRC	2	NBCT	Commercial	Post-Newsweek Business Information Inc.
KUHT	8	PBS	Commercial	University of Houston
KHOU	11	CBST	Commercial	Belo Corporation
KTRK	13	ABCT	Commercial	ABC Inc.
KTXH	20	UPN	Commercial	United Paramount Network
KRIV	26	FBC	Commercial	Fox Television Stations Inc.
KHWB	39	WB	Commercial	Tribune Broadcasting Company
KXLN	45	UNIN	Commercial	Univision Television Group
KTMD	48	TMUN	Commercial	Telemundo Group Inc.
KPXB	49	PAXTV	Commercial	Paxson Communications Corporation
KNWS	51	n/a	Public	Johnson Broadcasting Corporation
KTBU	55	n/a	Commercial	n/a
KAZH	57	n/a	Non-comm.	Pappas Telecasting Companies
KZJL	61	n/a	Commercial	Liberman Broadcasting

Note: Stations included broadcast from the Houston metro area; n/a not available
Source: Burrelle's Media Directory, 2003

AM Radio Stations

Call Letters	Freq. (kHz)	Target Audience	Station Format	Music Format
KILT	610	General	M/S/T	Jazz
KIKK	650	General	E/N/T	n/a
KSEV	700	General	M/N/T	Alternative
KTRH	740	General	M/N/S	Christian
KBME	790	General	M/N	Adult Standards
KEYH	850	Hispanic	M	Latin
KJOJ	880	Hispanic	M/N/S/T	Latin
KYST	920	Hispanic	M/S/T	Alternative
KPRC	950	General	M/T	Alternative
KLAT	1010	Hispanic	M	Latin
KKHT	1070	Religious	M/T	Adult Contemporary
KTEK	1110	Ethnic	M/T	Christian
KTMR	1130	H/R	M	Christian
KGOL	1180	Asian	E/M/N/T	World Music
KXYZ	1320	Hispanic	N/T	n/a
KHCB	1400	H/R	M/N/T	Christian
KHCH	1400	Religious	M/N/T	Christian
KCUL	1410	General	M/N/S/T	Oldies
KCOH	1430	Black	E/M/N/S/T	Rhythm & Blues
KYND	1520	General	N/T	n/a

Note: Stations included broadcast from the Houston metro area; n/a not available
The following abbreviations may be used:
Target Audience: A=Asian; B=Black; C=Christian; E=Ethnic; F=French; G=General; H=Hispanic;
M=Men; N=Native American; R=Religious; S=Senior Citizen; W=Women; Y=Young Adult; Z=Children
Station Format: E=Educational; M=Music; N=News; S=Sports; T=Talk
Source: Burrelle's Media Directory, 2003

FM Radio Stations

Call Letters	Freq. (mHz)	Target Audience	Station Format	Music Format
KUHF	88.7	General	M/N	Classical
KSBJ	89.3	Religious	E/M/N/S	Christian
KPFT	90.1	General	M	Adult Standards
KTSU	90.9	General	M	Jazz
KBWC	91.1	General	E/M	Christian
KRTS	92.1	General	M	Classical
KCUL	92.3	General	M/N/S	Oldies
KKBQ	92.9	General	M	Country
KKRW	93.7	General	M	Classic Rock
KTBZ	94.5	General	M/N/T	Alternative
KIKK	95.7	General	M	Alternative
KHMX	96.5	General	M/N/S	Adult Contemporary
KTHT	97.1	General	M/T	Top 40
KBXX	97.9	Black	Hispanic	Men
KTJM	98.5	General	M/N/T	Latin
KODA	99.1	General	M	Adult Contemporary
KILT	100.3	General	M/N/T	Country
KRTX	100.7	Hispanic	M	Latin
KLOL	101.1	G/M	M/N/S/T	AOR
KMJQ	102.1	General	M	Urban Contemporary
KLTN	102.9	Hispanic	M	Latin
KZEY	103.9	B/R/W	M	Adult Contemporary
KRBE	104.1	General	M/N/T	Adult Contemporary
KHCB	105.7	Religious	M/N/T	Christian
KHPT	106.9	General	M/N/T	80's
KLDE	107.5	General	M	Oldies
KQQK	107.9	Hispanic	M	Latin

Note: Stations included broadcast from the Houston metro area
The following abbreviations may be used:
Target Audience: A=Asian; B=Black; C=Christian; E=Ethnic; F=French; G=General; H=Hispanic;
M=Men; N=Native American; R=Religious; S=Senior Citizen; W=Women; Y=Young Adult; Z=Children
Station Format: E=Educational; M=Music; N=News; S=Sports; T=Talk
Music Format: AOR=Album Oriented Rock; MOR=Middle of the Road
Source: Burrelle's Media Directory, 2003

CLIMATE

Average and Extreme Temperatures

Temperature	Jan	Feb	Mar	Apr	May	Jun	Jul	Aug	Sep	Oct	Nov	Dec	Yr.
Extreme High (°F)	84	91	91	95	97	103	104	107	102	94	89	83	107
Average High (°F)	61	65	73	79	85	91	93	93	89	81	72	65	79
Average Temp. (°F)	51	54	62	69	75	81	83	83	79	70	61	54	69
Average Low (°F)	41	43	51	58	65	71	73	73	68	58	50	43	58
Extreme Low (°F)	12	20	22	31	44	52	62	62	48	32	19	7	7

Note: Figures cover the years 1969-1990
Source: National Climatic Data Center, International Station Meteorological Climate Summary, 9/96

Average Precipitation/Snowfall/Humidity

Precip./Humidity	Jan	Feb	Mar	Apr	May	Jun	Jul	Aug	Sep	Oct	Nov	Dec	Yr.
Avg. Precip. (in.)	3.3	2.7	3.3	3.3	5.6	4.9	3.7	3.7	4.8	4.7	3.7	3.3	46.9
Avg. Snowfall (in.)	Tr	Tr	0	0	0	0	0	0	0	0	Tr	Tr	Tr
Avg. Rel. Hum. 6am (%)	85	86	87	89	91	92	93	93	93	91	89	86	90
Avg. Rel. Hum. 3pm (%)	58	55	54	54	57	56	55	55	57	53	55	57	55

Note: Figures cover the years 1969-1990; Tr = Trace amounts (<0.05 in. of rain; <0.5 in. of snow)
Source: National Climatic Data Center, International Station Meteorological Climate Summary, 9/96

Weather Conditions

Temperature			Daytime Sky			Precipitation		
32°F & below	45°F & below	90°F & above	Clear	Partly cloudy	Cloudy	0.01 inch or more precip.	0.1 inch or more snow/ice	Thunder-storms
21	87	96	83	168	114	101	1	62

Note: Figures are average number of days per year and covers the years 1969-1990
Source: National Climatic Data Center, International Station Meteorological Climate Summary, 9/96

HAZARDOUS WASTE

Superfund Sites

Houston has seven hazardous waste sites on the EPA's Superfund National Priorities List: **Crystal Chemical Co.; Geneva Industries/Fuhrmann Energy; Many Diversified Interests, Inc.; North Cavalcade Street; Sol Lynn/Industrial Transformers; South Cavalcade Street; Jones Road Ground Water Plume**. *U.S. Environmental Protection Agency, National Priorities List, March 15, 2004*

AIR & WATER QUALITY

Maximum Pollutant Concentrations

	Particulate Matter (ug/m³)	Carbon Monoxide (ppm)	Sulfur Dioxide (ppm)	Nitrogen Dioxide (ppm)	Ozone 1-hour (ppm)	Ozone 8-hour (ppm)	Lead (ug/m³)
MSA[1] Level	95	3	0.022	0.019	0.17	0.1	0.01
NAAQS[2]	150	9	0.140	0.053	0.12	0.08	1.50
Met NAAQS[2]	Yes	Yes	Yes	Yes	No	No	Yes

Note: (1) Metropolitan Statistical Area - see Appendix A for areas included; (2) National Ambient Air Quality Standards; n/a not available
Units: ppm = parts per million; ug/m³ = micrograms per cubic meter
Source: EPA, Latest Findings on National Air Quality: 2002 Status and Trends, August 2003

Air Quality Index

In the Houston MSA (see Appendix A for areas included), the Air Quality Index (AQI) exceeded 100 on 30 days in 2002. An AQI value greater than 100 indicates that air quality would have been in the unhealthful range on that day.
EPA, Latest Findings on National Air Quality: 2002 Status and Trends, August 2003

Watershed Health

The U.S. Environmental Protection Agency monitors the health of the aquatic resources for the nation's 2,000+ watersheds. **The Buffalo-San Jacinto watershed serves the Houston area and received an overall Index of Watershed Indicators (IWI) score of 5 (more serious problems - low vulnerability)**. The IWI score is based on seven condition and nine vulnerability indicators. The overall IWI score ranges from 1 (best health) to 6 (worst health). The Condition Indicators include: designated use attainment, fish and wildlife consumption advisories, source water condition, contaminated sediments, ambient water quality, and wetlands loss index. The Vulnerability Indicators include: aquatic species at risk, conventional and toxic loads over permitted limits, urban and agricultural runoff potential, population change, hydrologic modification, estuarine pollution susceptibility, and air deposition. *EPA, Index of Watershed Indicators, October 26, 2001*

Drinking Water

Water System Name	Pop. Served	Primary Water Source Type	Number of Violations January 2002-February 2004		
			Health Based	Significant Monitoring	Monitoring
Houston Public Works Dept.	2,700,000	Surface	None	None	1

Note: Data as of February 19, 2004
Source: EPA, Office of Ground Water and Drinking Water, Safe Drinking Water Information System

Houston tap water is alkaline, hard.
Editor & Publisher Market Guide, 2004

Huntsville, Alabama

Background

The seat of Madison County, Huntsville is richly evocative of the antebellum Deep South. It is also a uniquely cosmopolitan town that remains one of the South's fastest-growing, with the highest per capita income in the Southeast.

Huntsville became the seat of Madison County—named for President James Madison—when that jurisdiction was created in 1808. Originally home to Cherokee and Chickasaw Indians, the Huntsville area was rich in forests and game animals. The town itself is named for John Hunt, a Virginia Revolutionary War veteran who built a cabin in 1805 on what is now the corner of Bank Street and Oak Avenue.

The fertility of the valley began to attract both smaller farmers and wealthy plantation investors. Leroy Pope, having donated land to the embryonic municipality, wished to rename it Twickenham, after a London suburb that was home to his relative, the poet Alexander Pope. However, resentment against all things British, which surged following the War of 1812, was sufficient to reestablish Huntsville under its original moniker.

Huntsville was the largest town in the Alabama Territory by 1819, the same year Alabama received statehood. The town was the site of the state's first constitutional convention and briefly served as the state capital. It quickly became a major hub for the sale and processing of corn, tobacco, and cotton, with the last crop becoming the economic mainstay. The establishment of textile mills allowed the town to take wealth from both primary production and finished products. In 1852, the last leg of the Memphis and Charleston Railway was completed, establishing Huntsville as a major center in a larger regional marketplace. By the middle of the nineteenth century, the region's planters, merchants, and shippers had transformed Huntsville into one of the main commercial cities in the South.

Because many wealthy residents had remained loyal to the Union at the outset of the Civil War, the town was largely undamaged by occupying forces and, as a result, Huntsville boasts one of the largest collections of undamaged antebellum houses in the South. Walking tours of the Twickenham historic district offer the charms of the 1819 Weeden House Museum and the 1860 Huntsville Depot Museum. Restored nineteenth-century cabins and farm buildings are displayed at the mountaintop Burritt Museum and Park.

Huntsville's U.S. Space and Rocket Center—the state's largest tourist attraction—showcases space technology. The Huntsville Botanical Garden, features year-long floral and aquatic gardens, and the Huntsville Museum of Art features both contemporary and classical exhibits.

The city's modern Von Braun Center hosts national and international trade shows and conventions and local sports teams; it also has a concert hall and playhouse. The city also has an outstanding symphony orchestra.

Institutions of higher learning include the University of Alabama in Huntsville (established 1950), and Oakwood College (1896), while Alabama Agricultural and Mechanical University (1875) is in nearby Normal, Alabama.

Redstone Arsenal is the main engine that propelled Huntsville into the high-tech hub it is today, and is the United States' most crucial strategic and research site for the development and implementation of rocketry, aviation, and related programs. In 1950, German rocket scientists, most notably the famous Wernher von Braun, came to the Redstone Arsenal to develop rockets for the U.S. Army. Within the decade, the Redstone complex had developed the rocket that launched America's first satellite into space, and in subsequent years the rockets that put astronauts into space and eventually landed them on the moon.

The movement into the area of scientists, technicians, and managers from throughout the country and the world has made Huntsville a surprisingly cosmopolitan community in its region.

Despite the economic downturn of the early 1990s, Huntsville has seen progress on the manufacturing front. In 2003, Toyota opened a $220 million plant, in which the company's first V8 engines outside of Japan will be made. Target, the big-box retailer, also recently opened a Target Department Store Distribution Center.

Huntsville enjoys a mild, temperate climate. Only four to five weeks during the middle of winter see temperatures below freezing, and snow falls rarely. Rainfall is fairly abundant.

Rankings

- Huntsville was ranked #226 out of 331 metro areas in *Cities Ranked & Rated*. Criteria: cost of living; climate; crime; transportation; economy and jobs; education; arts and culture; health and healthcare; leisure. *Cities Ranked & Rated, 1st Edition, 2004*

- *Ladies Home Journal* ranked America's 200 largest cities based on the qualities women surveyed care about most. Huntsville ranked #104 out of 143 in the smaller city category (population under 300,000). Criteria: crime; lifestyle; education; jobs; health; child care; politics; and the economy. *Ladies Home Journal Online, "The Best Cities for Women 2002"*

- The Huntsville metro area was selected as one of "America's Best Places to Live and Work 2003" by *Employment Review*. The area ranked #4 out of 20. Criteria: unemployment rate; projected job growth; cost of living; and industry specific data. *Employment Review, www.bestjobsusa.com*

- *Forbes* ranked the 150 most populous metro areas in the U.S. in terms of the "Best Places for Business and Careers." The Huntsville metro area was ranked #11. Criteria: income and job growth; cost-of-doing-business; qualifications of the available pool of labor; crime rates; housing costs; net migration. *Forbes, May 9, 2003*

- *Men's Health* ranked 101 U.S. cities in terms of the quality of their tap water. Huntsville received a grade of. Criteria: levels of bacteria, arsenic, lead, trihalomethanes, and haloacetic acids were compared with the National Academy of Science's guidelines as well as with the EPA's more stringent maximum contaminant level goals. *Men's Health, March 2004*

- Sperling's BestPlaces ranked 331 metro areas and identified the most and least stressful U.S. cities. The Huntsville metro area ranked #79 out of 114 mid-size metro areas (#1 = most stressful). Criteria: divorce rate; unemployment rate; violent and property crime; suicide rate; commute time; mental health; alcohol consumption; cloudy days. *www.BestPlaces.net, February 26, 2004*

- Huntsville was ranked #130 out of America's 200 largest metro areas in *SELF Magazine's* ranking of "America's Healthiest Cities for Women." Criteria: safety; air/water quality; cancer rates; and 21 other factors relating to health. *SELF Magazine, November 2003*

- Huntsville was ranked #56 out of 100 cities surveyed in *Child* magazine's ranking of the "Best Cities for Families." Criteria: number of pediatricians per capita; proximity to a children's hospital; immunization rates; infant mortality rate; air quality; water quality; school spending; pupil-teacher ratio; availability of parks/green space; nearby recreational opportunities; average commute time; number of sunny days; average cost of a 3-bedroom home; unemployment rate; future job growth; crime rate; percentage of children under 5; mandated minimum child care ratios. *Child, April 2001*

- *Zero Population Growth* ranked 239 cities in terms of children's health, safety, and economic well-being. Huntsville was ranked #54 out of 140 independent cities (cities with populations greater than 100,000 which were neither major cities nor suburbs/outer cities) and was given a grade of B+. Criteria: total population and population growth; percent of population under 18 years of age; number of children's museums; health improvement grade; percent of births to teens; percent of low birthweight infants; infant mortality rate; number of Title X-funded clinics; average SAT/ACT scores; average elementary and secondary class size; crime rate; unemployment rate; percent of affordable homes; number of bad air days; park acres per 1000 persons; library circulation per child; and children's program attendance counts. *Zero Population Growth, Kid Friendly Cities Report Card 2001*

- *Ladies Home Journal* ranked America's 200 largest cities in terms of safety. Huntsville ranked #87 out of 200. Criteria: violent crimes; crimes against property; and rape. *Ladies Home Journal Online, "The Best Cities for Women 2002"*

- Huntsville was selected as one of "The Best Places to Start and Grow a Company." The area ranked #9 among small metro areas. Criteria: Significant Starts (firms started in the last 10 years that still employ at least 5 people) and Young Growers (firms 10 years old or less that grew significantly during the last 4 years). *Cognetics, "Entrepreneurial Hot Spots: The Best Places in America to Start and Grow a Company," 2001*

- The Huntsville metro area was selected as one of "America's 50 Hottest Cities for Business Relocations and Expansions." The area ranked #44. Criteria: 70 of the industry's most prominent site selection consultants were asked which cities their clients found the most attractive when it came to selecting an expansion or relocation site in 2003. *Expansion Management, January 2004*

- Huntsville was selected as a "High-Tech Market to Watch" by *Site Selection*. Five emerging U.S. markets which show corporate growth developing in technology clusters were highlighted. *Site Selection, July 2001*

- The Huntsville metro area was selected as one of the "Top 60 CyberCities in America" by *Site Selection*. CyberCities are magnets for growing high-tech companies. Criteria: total employment; average wages; total payroll; number of companies; R&D spending and venture capital in the 45 Standard Industrial Classification (SIC) codes that define the high-technology industry. *Site Selection, March 2002*

- The Huntsville metro area was cited as one of "The Best Places in the U.S. to Locate a Company." The area ranked #28 out of 329. Criteria: education (with emphasis on college board test results and high school graduation rates); availability of quality healthcare services and the cost to employers; quality of life; logistics workforce and companies; transportation infrastructure; quality and quantity of highly educated technical workers; business climate. *Expansion Management, July 2003*

- The Huntsville metro area appeared on *Forbes/Milken Institute* list of "Best Places for Business and Career." Rank: #71 out of 200 metro areas. Criteria: salary growth; job growth; number of technology clusters; overall concentration of technology activity relative to national average; and technology output growth. *www.forbes.com, Forbes/Milken Institute Best Places 2002*

- The Huntsville metro area appeared on the "Milken Institute Best Performing Cities" index. Rank: #117 out of 200 large metro areas. Criteria: job growth; wage and salary growth; high-tech output growth. *Milken Institute, June 25, 2003*

- The Huntsville metro area appeared on *IndustryWeek's* fourth annual World-Class Communities list. It ranked #104 out of 315 metro areas. Criteria: MSA Gross Metropolitan Product (GMP) per manufacturing employee; and MSA percent share of U.S. manufacturing Gross Domestic Product (GDP). *IndustryWeek, April 16, 2001*

Business Environment

CITY FINANCES

City Government Finances

Component	2000-2001 ($000)	2000-2001 ($ per capita)
Total Revenues	501,314	3,169
Total Expenditures	526,336	3,327
Debt Outstanding	517,482	3,271
Cash and Securities	287,219	1,815

Source: U.S Census Bureau, Government Finances 2000-2001, August 2003

City Government Revenue by Source

Source	2000-2001 ($000)	2000-2001 ($ per capita)
General Revenue		
From Federal Government	5,576	35
From State Government	21,498	136
From Local Governments	0	0
Taxes		
Property	16,688	105
Sales	86,584	547
Personal Income	0	0
License	0	0
Charges	35,495	224
Liquor Store	0	0
Utility	287,822	1,819
Employee Retirement	0	0
Other	47,651	301

Source: U.S Census Bureau, Government Finances 2000-2001, August 2003

City Government Expenditures by Function

Function	2000-2001 ($000)	2000-2001 ($ per capita)	2000-2001 (%)
General Expenditures			
Airports	0	0	0.0
Corrections	0	0	0.0
Education	9	< 1	< 0.1
Fire Protection	16,221	103	3.1
Governmental Administration	14,952	95	2.8
Health	3,323	21	0.6
Highways	8,637	55	1.6
Hospitals	0	0	0.0
Housing and Community Development	9,493	60	1.8
Interest on General Debt	33,100	209	6.3
Libraries	4,581	29	0.9
Parking	5,218	33	1.0
Parks and Recreation	22,623	143	4.3
Police Protection	27,000	171	5.1
Public Welfare	348	2	0.1
Sewerage	14,918	94	2.8
Solid Waste Management	12,875	81	2.4
Liquor Store	0	0	0.0
Utility	316,668	2,001	60.2
Employee Retirement	0	0	0.0
Other	36,370	230	6.9

Source: U.S Census Bureau, Government Finances 2000-2001, August 2003

Municipal Bond Ratings

Area	Moody's
City	Aaa

Source: Mergent Bond Record, February 2004

DEMOGRAPHICS

Population Growth

Area	1990 Census	2000 Census	2003 Estimate	2008 Projection	Population Growth (%) 1990-2000	Population Growth (%) 2000-2008
City	161,842	158,216	156,323	153,460	-2.2	-3.0
MSA[1]	293,047	342,376	350,652	364,618	16.8	6.5
U.S.	248,709,873	281,421,906	290,647,163	305,918,071	13.2	8.7

Note: (1) Metropolitan Statistical Area - see Appendix A for areas included
Source: Claritas, Inc.

Number of Households and Average Household Size

Area	1990 Census	2000 Census	2003 Estimate	2008 Projection	2003 Average Household Size
City	63,838	66,742	67,373	68,611	2.3
MSA[1]	110,893	134,643	139,782	148,726	2.5
U.S.	91,947,410	105,480,101	109,440,059	116,034,472	2.7

Note: (1) Metropolitan Statistical Area - see Appendix A for areas included
Source: Claritas, Inc.

Race and Ethnicity

Area	White Non-Hispanic	Black Non-Hispanic	Asian Non-Hispanic	Other Race Non-Hispanic	Hispanic
City	62.8	31.7	2.3	3.3	2.2
MSA[1]	73.5	21.6	1.6	3.3	2.2
U.S.	74.5	12.4	3.8	9.3	13.2

Note: Figures are 2003 estimates; (1) Metropolitan Statistical Area - see Appendix A for areas included
Source: Claritas, Inc.

Segregation

City Index[2]	City Rank[3]	MSA[1] Index[2]	MSA[1] Rank[4]
67.9	28	60.5	141

Note: Figures are based on an analysis of Census 2000 data; (1) Metropolitan Statistical Area - see Appendix A for areas included; (2) Dissimilarity Index—the most commonly used measure of segregation between two groups, reflecting their relative distributions across neighborhoods within a city or metropolitan area. It can range in value from 0, indicating complete integration, to 100, indicating complete segregation; (3) Ranges from 1 (most segregated) to 100 (least segregated) and includes all the cities in this book; (4) Ranges from 1 (most segregated) to 318 (least segregated) and includes 318 metropolitan areas.
Source: www.CensusScope.org

Ancestry

Area	German	Irish[2]	English	American	Italian	Polish	French[3]	Scottish
City	9.0	8.2	10.8	11.5	1.8	1.1	1.9	2.1
MSA[1]	9.0	9.3	10.1	15.8	1.7	1.0	1.9	2.0
U.S.	15.2	10.9	8.7	7.3	5.6	3.2	3.0	1.7

Note: Figures include multiple ancestry (e.g. if a person reported being Irish and Italian, they were included in both columns); (1) Metropolitan Statistical Area - see Appendix A for areas included; (2) Includes Celtic; (3) Includes Alsatian but excludes Basque
Source: Census 2000, Summary File 3

Foreign-Born Population

Area	Any Foreign Country	Percent of Population Born in: Europe	Asia	Africa	Oceania[2]	Canada	Mexico	Latin America[3]
City	4.9	1.3	1.7	0.4	0.0	0.3	0.5	0.8
MSA[1]	3.5	0.8	1.3	0.2	0.0	0.2	0.5	0.5
U.S.	11.1	1.7	2.9	0.3	0.1	0.3	3.3	2.5

Note: (1) Metropolitan Statistical Area - see Appendix A for areas included; (2) Includes Australia, New Zealand subregion, Melanesia, Micronesia, Polynesia, and Oceania n.e.c; (3) Includes Central America (excluding Mexico), South America, and the Caribbean.
Source: Census 2000, Summary File 3

Religion

Area	Catholic	Southern Baptist	United Methodist	ELCA[1]	LDS[2]	Presbyterian Church USA	Jewish Est.	Muslim Est.
County	5.8	22.4	7.7	0.7	0.8	1.6	0.3	0.4
U.S.	22.0	7.1	3.7	1.8	1.5	1.1	2.2	0.6

Note: Figures shown are the number of adherents as a percentage of the total population; Adherents are defined as all members, including full members, their children and the estimated number of other participants who are not considered members (e.g. the baptized, those not confirmed, those not eligible for communion, those regularly attending services, etc.); (1) Evangelical Lutheran Church in America; (2) The Church of Jesus Christ of Latter Day Saints
Source: Reprinted with permission from Religious Congregations and Membership in the United States 2000 (Nashville, Glenmary Research Center, 2002) Copyright Association of Statisticians of American Religious Bodies. All rights reserved.

Age Distribution

Area	Percent of Population						
	Under Age 5	Age 5 to 17	Age 18 to 34	Age 35 to 49	Age 50 to 64	Age 65 to 79	80 Years and Over
City	6.1	17.0	23.9	23.2	16.6	10.3	3.0
MSA[1]	6.8	18.6	23.1	25.0	15.6	8.6	2.3
U.S.	6.8	18.9	23.7	23.5	14.8	9.2	3.2

Note: (1) Metropolitan Statistical Area - see Appendix A for areas included
Source: Census 2000, Summary File 3

Marriage Status

Area	Never Married	Now Married Except Separated	Separated	Widowed	Divorced
City	26.5	52.4	2.4	6.7	12.0
MSA[1]	22.6	58.7	1.9	5.9	10.9
U.S.	27.1	54.4	2.2	6.6	9.7

Note: Figures cover population 15 years of age and older; (1) Metropolitan Statistical Area - see Appendix A for areas included
Source: Census 2000, Summary File 3

Male/Female Ratio

Area	Males	Females	Males per 100 Females
City	75,124	81,199	92.5
MSA[1]	172,258	178,394	96.6
U.S.	142,511,883	148,135,280	96.2

Note: Figures are 2003 estimates; (1) Metropolitan Statistical Area - see Appendix A for areas included
Source: Claritas, Inc.

ECONOMY

Gross Metropolitan Product

Area	1999	2000	2001	2002	2002 Rank[2]
MSA[1]	10.4	10.9	11.3	11.8	148

Note: Figures are in billions of dollars; (1) Metropolitan Statistical Area - see Appendix A for areas included; (2) Rank ranges from 1 to 319
Source: The U.S. Conference of Mayors, Metro Economies Report, July 2003

INCOME

Per Capita/Median/Average Income

Area	Per Capita ($)	Median Household ($)	Average Household ($)
City	27,117	45,391	62,235
MSA[1]	24,935	47,917	62,008
U.S.	24,078	46,868	63,207

Note: Figures are 2003 estimates; (1) Metropolitan Statistical Area - see Appendix A for areas included
Source: Claritas, Inc.

Household Income Distribution

Area	Percent of Households Earning							
	Under $15,000	$15,000 -24,999	$25,000 -34,999	$35,000 -49,999	$50,000 -74,999	$75,000 -99,000	$100,000 -149,999	$150,000 and up
City	15.6	12.3	11.7	15.0	18.0	10.8	10.4	6.2
MSA[1]	13.7	11.5	11.4	15.6	19.3	12.1	11.2	5.2
U.S.	14.1	11.5	11.7	16.0	19.2	11.3	10.2	6.0

Note: Figures are 2003 estimates; (1) Metropolitan Statistical Area - see Appendix A for areas included
Source: Claritas, Inc.

Poverty Rates by Age

Area	All Ages	Under 5 Years Old	5 to 17 Years Old	18 to 64 Years Old	65 Years and Over
City	12.8	1.4	3.0	7.2	1.2
MSA[1]	10.9	1.2	2.6	5.9	1.2
U.S.	12.4	1.2	3.0	6.9	1.2

Note: Figures are percent of population with income in 1999 below poverty level and only include population for whom poverty status is determined; (1) Metropolitan Statistical Area - see Appendix A for areas included
Source: Census 2000, Summary File 3

Personal Bankruptcy Filing Rate

Area	2002	2003
Madison County	6.68	6.92
U.S.	5.34	5.58

Note: Numbers are per 1,000 population and include Chapter 7 and Chapter 13 filings
Source: Federal Deposit Insurance Corporation (FDIC), Regional Economic Conditions (RECON), 2/25/2004

EMPLOYMENT

Labor Force and Employment

Area	Civilian Labor Force			Workers Employed		
	Dec. 2002	Dec. 2003	% Chg.	Dec. 2002	Dec. 2003	% Chg.
City	98,254	100,001	1.8	94,296	94,939	0.7
MSA[1]	175,600	178,231	1.5	168,389	169,537	0.7
U.S.	144,807,000	146,501,000	1.2	136,599,000	138,556,000	1.4

Note: Data is not seasonally adjusted and covers workers 16 years of age and older;
(1) Metropolitan Statistical Area - see Appendix A for areas included
Source: Bureau of Labor Statistics, http://stats.bls.gov

Unemployment Rate

Area	2003											
	Jan.	Feb.	Mar.	Apr.	May	Jun.	Jul.	Aug.	Sep.	Oct.	Nov.	Dec.
City	4.3	4.2	4.0	4.0	4.0	4.7	4.8	4.7	4.6	4.9	4.9	5.1
MSA[1]	4.4	4.3	4.3	4.5	4.0	4.7	4.9	4.6	4.6	4.8	4.9	4.9
U.S.	6.5	6.4	6.2	5.8	5.8	6.5	6.3	6.0	5.8	5.6	5.6	5.4

Note: Data is not seasonally adjusted and covers workers 16 years of age and older; All figures are percentages; (1) Metropolitan Statistical Area - see Appendix A for areas included
Source: Bureau of Labor Statistics, http://stats.bls.gov

Employment by Occupation

Occupation Classification	City (%)	MSA[1] (%)	U.S. (%)
Sales and Office	23.9	23.5	26.7
Professional and Related	30.1	26.6	20.2
Service	13.7	12.4	14.9
Production, Transportation, and Material Moving	11.9	14.8	14.6
Management, Business, and Financial	14.3	13.8	13.5
Construction, Extraction, and Maintenance	6.0	8.6	9.4
Farming, Forestry, and Fishing	0.2	0.3	0.7

Note: Figures cover employed civilians 16 years of age and older;
(1) Metropolitan Statistical Area - see Appendix A for areas included
Source: Census 2000, Summary File 3

Employment by Industry

Sector	MSA[1]		U.S.
	Number of Employees	Percent of Total	Percent of Total
Government	41,400	21.8	16.7
Education and Health Services	12,500	6.6	12.9
Professional and Business Services	36,700	19.3	12.3
Retail Trade	22,700	11.9	11.8
Manufacturing	30,200	15.9	11.0
Leisure and Hospitality	15,700	8.3	9.1
Finance Activities	5,800	3.0	6.1
Construction	n/a	n/a	5.1
Wholesale Trade	5,400	2.8	4.3
Other Services	7,400	3.9	4.1
Transportation and Utilities	2,700	1.4	3.7
Information	2,200	1.2	2.4
Natural Resources and Mining	n/a	n/a	0.4

Note: Figures cover non-farm employment as of December 2003 and are not seasonally adjusted;
(1) Metropolitan Statistical Area - see Appendix A for areas included; n/a not available
Source: Bureau of Labor Statistics, http://stats.bls.gov

Average Wages

Occupation	$/Hr.	Occupation	$/Hr.
Accountants and Auditors	22.61	Maids and Housekeeping Cleaners	6.92
Automotive Mechanics	14.09	Maintenance and Repair Workers	15.24
Bookkeepers	12.21	Marketing Managers	39.10
Carpenters	13.79	Nuclear Medicine Technologists	n/a
Cashiers	7.10	Nurses, Licensed Practical	12.18
Clerks, General Office	10.39	Nurses, Registered	n/a
Clerks, Receptionists/Information	9.83	Nursing Aides/Orderlies/Attendants	7.95
Clerks, Shipping/Receiving	10.88	Packers and Packagers, Hand	n/a
Computer Programmers	n/a	Physical Therapists	22.70
Computer Support Specialists	19.49	Postal Service Mail Carriers	n/a
Computer Systems Analysts	29.97	Real Estate Brokers	n/a
Cooks, Restaurant	7.08	Retail Salespersons	9.79
Dentists	82.44	Sales Reps., Exc. Tech./Scientific	24.13
Electrical Engineers	32.86	Sales Reps., Tech./Scientific	28.65
Electricians	19.69	Secretaries, Exc. Legal/Med./Exec.	11.86
Financial Managers	30.67	Security Guards	9.95
First-Line Supervisors/Mgrs., Sales	14.86	Surgeons	n/a
Food Preparation Workers	7.99	Teacher Assistants	6.90
General and Operations Managers	36.73	Teachers, Elementary School	19.50
Hairdressers/Cosmetologists	8.70	Teachers, Secondary School	19.90
Internists	74.00	Telemarketers	8.18
Janitors and Cleaners	8.18	Truck Drivers, Heavy/Tractor-Trailer	14.37
Landscaping/Groundskeeping Workers	10.00	Truck Drivers, Light/Delivery Svcs.	11.67
Lawyers	45.45	Waiters and Waitresses	6.30

Note: Wage data is for 2002 and covers the Metropolitan Statistical Area (see Appendix A for areas included).
Hourly wages for elementary/secondary school teachers and teacher assistants were calculated by the editors
from annual wage data assuming a 40 hour work week; n/a not available.
Source: Bureau of Labor Statistics, 2002 Metro Area Occupational Employment and Wage Estimates

Occupational Employment Projections: 1996 - 2006

Occupations Expected to Have the Largest Job Growth (ranked by numerical growth)	Fast-Growing Occupations[1] (ranked by percent growth)
1. Cashiers	1. Computer engineers
2. Teachers, secondary school	2. Personal and home care aides
3. Truck drivers, light	3. Database administrators
4. General managers & top executives	4. Occupational therapists
5. Nursing aides/orderlies/attendants	5. Systems analysts
6. Janitors/cleaners/maids, ex. priv. hshld.	6. Home health aides
7. Registered nurses	7. Physical therapy assistants and aides
8. Home health aides	8. Medical assistants
9. Marketing & sales, supervisors	9. Teachers, special education
10. Systems analysts	10. Physical therapists

Note: Projections cover Alabama; (1) Excludes occupations with total job growth less than 300
Source: U.S. Department of Labor, Employment and Training Administration, America's Labor Market Information System (ALMIS)

TAXES

State Corporate Income Tax Rates

State	Rate (%)	Number of Brackets	Low Bracket (Under $)	High Bracket (Over $)
Alabama	6.5	1	na	na

Note: Tax rates as of December 31, 2003; na not applicable; Federal deductibility.
Source: Tax Foundation, www.taxfoundation.org

State Individual Income Tax Rates

State	Federal Deductibility	Marginal Rate (%)	Number of Brackets	Low Bracket (Under $)	High Bracket (Over $)
Alabama	Yes (z)	2.0-5.0	3	0	3,000

Note: Tax rates as of December 31, 2003; Brackets apply to single taxpayers and married people filing separately; na not applicable; (z) Residents should deduct the federal income tax liability as shown on their 2003 federal income tax return, less any federal Advance Child Tax Credit for 2003.
Source: Tax Foundation, www.taxfoundation.org

Various State and Local Tax Rates

State Sales and Use (%)	Total Sales and Use (%)	Gasoline (cents/gal.)	Cigarette (cents/pack)	Spirits ($/gal.)	Table Wine ($/gal.)	Beer ($/gal.)
4.0	8.0	16	16.5	(b)	1.70	0.52

Note: Tax rates as of December 31, 2003.(b) States where the state government controls all sales.
Source: Tax Foundation, www.taxfoundation.org

State Tax Burdens

Area	Combined State and Local Tax Burden		Combined Federal, State and Local Tax Burden	
	Percent	Rank	Percent	Rank
Alabama	8.4	46	26.3	49
U.S. Average	9.7	-	30.0	-

Note: Figures are for 2003
Source: Tax Foundation, www.taxfoundation.org

Internal Revenue Service Tax Audits

IRS District	Percent of Returns Audited				
	1996	1997	1998	1999	2000
Gulf Coast	0.83	0.74	0.50	0.41	0.20
U.S.	0.66	0.61	0.46	0.31	0.20

Note: Figures cover IRS district audits of federal income tax returns filed by individuals. Geographic data on district audits for 2001 and 2002 are being withheld by the IRS. TRAC is challenging this policy.
Source: Syracuse University, Transactional Records Access Clearinghouse (TRAC), "Odds of IRS District Tax Audit 2000"

**RESIDENTIAL
REAL ESTATE**

Building Permits

Area	Single-Family			Multi-Family			Total		
	2001	2002	Pct. Chg.	2001	2002	Pct. Chg.	2001	2002	Pct. Chg.
City	400	514	28.5	558	172	-69.2	958	686	-28.4
U.S.	1,235,600	1,332,600	7.9	401,100	415,100	3.5	1,636,700	1,747,700	6.8

Note: Figures represent new, privately-owned housing units authorized (unadjusted data)
Source: U.S. Census Bureau, Manufacturing, Mining, and Construction Statistics

Homeownership and Housing Vacancies

Area	Homeownership Rate[2] (%)			Rental Vacancy Rate[3] (%)			Homeowner Vacancy Rate[4] (%)		
	2001	2002[a]	2003	2001	2002[a]	2003	2001	2002[a]	2003
MSA[1]	n/a	n/a	n/a	n/a	n/a	n/a	n/a	n/a	n/a
U.S.	67.8	67.9	68.3	8.4	8.9	9.8	1.8	1.7	1.8

Note: (1) Metropolitan Statistical Area - see Appendix A for areas included; (2) The proportion of households that are owners; (3) The proportion of the rental inventory that is vacant for rent; (4) The proportion of the homeowner inventory that is vacant for sale; (a) 2002 figures have been revised; n/a not available
Source: U.S. Census Bureau, Housing Vacancies and Homeownership Annual Statistics: 2003

**COMMERCIAL
REAL ESTATE**

Industrial/Office Markets

Type/Market Area	Inventory (sq. ft.)	Vacant (sq. ft.)	Vacancy Rate (%)	Under Construction (sq. ft.)	Net Absorption (sq. ft.)
Industrial Space					
Huntsville	13,209,690	1,141,270	8.64	0	-146,000
Office Space					
Huntsville	4,193,341	290,911	6.94	0	140,499

Note: Data as of 4th Quarter, 2003; n/a not available
Source: Society of Industrial and Office Realtors, 2004 Comparative Statistics of Industrial and Office Real Estate Markets

**COMMERCIAL
UTILITIES**

Typical Monthly Electric Bills

Area	Commercial Service ($/month)		Industrial Service ($/month)	
	3 kW demand 1,000 kWh	40 kW demand 14,000 kWh	1,000 kW demand 200,000 kWh	50,000 kW demand 15,000,000 kWh
City	n/a	n/a	n/a	n/a
Average[1]	100	1,134	17,850	1,045,117

Note: Based on rates in effect July 1, 2003; (1) average based on 197 utilities; n/a not available
Source: Edison Electric Institute, Typical Bills and Average Rates Report, Summer 2003

TRANSPORTATION

Means of Transportation to Work

Area	Car/Truck/Van		Public Transportation			Bicycle	Walked	Other Means	Worked at Home
	Drove Alone	Car-pooled	Bus	Subway	Railroad				
City	83.8	11.2	0.3	0.0	0.0	0.2	1.5	0.7	2.4
MSA[1]	83.9	11.5	0.2	0.0	0.0	0.1	1.3	0.7	2.3
U.S.	75.7	12.2	2.5	1.5	0.5	0.4	2.9	1.0	3.3

Note: Figures shown are percentages and cover workers 16 years of age and older;
(1) Metropolitan Statistical Area - see Appendix A for areas included
Source: Census 2000, Summary File 3

Travel Time to Work

Area	Less Than 15 Minutes	15 to 29 Minutes	30 to 44 Minutes	45 to 59 Minutes	60 Minutes or More
City	38.0	47.4	10.4	1.9	2.3
MSA[1]	28.7	44.5	19.1	4.6	3.0
U.S.	29.4	36.1	19.1	7.4	8.0

Note: Figures are percentages and include workers 16 years old and over; (1) Metropolitan Statistical Area - see Appendix A for areas included
Source: Census 2000, Summary File 3

Transportation Statistics

Interstate highways (2004)	I-65
Public transportation (2002)	City of Huntsville, Alabama Dept. of Parking & Public Transit
Buses	
Average fleet age in years	4.4
No. operated in max. service	11
Demand response	
Average fleet age in years	3.3
No. operated in max. service	20
Passenger air service	
Airport	Huntsville International
Airlines (2003)	5
Boardings (2002)	481,374
Amtrak service (2004)	No
Major waterways/ports	Near the Tennessee River (12 miles)

Source: Federal Transit Administration, National Transit Database, 2002; Editor & Publisher Market Guide, 2004; Bureau of Transportation Statistics, Airport Enplanement Activity for CY2002; www.amtrak.com

BUSINESSES

Major Business Headquarters

Company Name	2003 Rankings	
	Fortune 500	Forbes 500
No companies listed	-	-

Note: Companies listed are located in the city; dashes indicate no ranking
Fortune 500: Companies that produce a 10-K are ranked 1 to 500 based on 2002 revenue
Forbes 500: Private companies are ranked 1 to 281 based on 2002 revenue
Source: Fortune, April 14, 2003; www.forbes.com, November 6, 2003

Best Companies to Work For

Adtran, headquartered in Huntsville, is among the "200 Best Small Companies in 2003." Criteria: 3,500 companies whose latest 12-month sales were $5 million to $600 million were screened. Those with a net margin or five-year average ROE below 5% were cut. Banks, utilities, real estate investment trusts and limited partnerships whose financial structures are too different from most operating companies were also excluded. Shares had to be trading above $5 by the end of September 2003. Financial statement footnotes were examined for major issues. For the final ranking, equal weight was given to growth in sales, earnings and ROE for the past five years and the latest 12 months. *www.forbes.com, October 27, 2003*

Fast-Growing Businesses

According to *Inc.*, Huntsville is home to two of America's 500 fastest-growing private companies: **Belzon; Morgan Research**. Criteria: must be an independent, privately-held, U.S. corporation, proprietorship or partnership; sales of at least $200,000 in 1998; five-year operating/sales history; increase in 2002 sales over 2001 sales; holding companies, regulated banks, and utilities were excluded. *Inc. 500, America's Fastest-Growing Private Companies, October 15, 2003*

According to Deloitte & Touche LLP, Huntsville is home to one of North America's 500 fastest-growing high-technology companies: **Integrated Defense Technologies, Inc**. Companies are ranked by percentage growth in revenue over a five-year period. Criteria for inclusion: must be a U.S. or Canadian company developing and/or providing technology products or services; company must have been in business for five years with 1998 operating revenues of at least $50,000 USD or $75,000 CD and 2002 operating revenues of at least $1 million USD/CD. *Deloitte & Touche LLP, 2003 Technology Fast 500*

Minority and Women-Owned Businesses

Ownership	All Firms		Firms with Paid Employees			
	Firms	Sales ($000)	Firms	Sales ($000)	Employees	Payroll ($000)
Black	1,121	175,346	133	161,702	1,888	56,500
Hispanic	116	94,327	36	93,624	1,057	48,502
Women	3,304	500,284	745	(a)	5,000 - 9,999	(a)

Note: Figures cover firms located in the city; (a) Withheld to avoid disclosure
Source: 1997 Economic Census, Minority and Women-Owned Businesses

Minority Business Opportunity

Huntsville is home to one company which is on the Black Enterprise Industrial/Service 100 list (100 largest companies based on gross sales): **Madison Research Corp.**. Criteria: operational in previous calendar year; at least 51% black-owned and manufactures/owns the product it sells or provides industrial or consumer services. Brokerages, real estate firms and firms that provide professional services are not eligible. *Black Enterprise, www.blackenterprise.com, B.E. 100s, 2003 Report*

Huntsville is home to one company which is on the Black Enterprise Auto Dealer 100 list (100 largest dealers based on gross sales): **Huntsville Autoplex**. Criteria: company must be operational in previous calendar year and at least 51% black-owned. *Black Enterprise, www.blackenterprise.com, B.E. 100s, 2003 Report*

Two of the 500 largest Hispanic-owned companies in the U.S. are located in Huntsville. *Hispanic Business, June 2003*

Huntsville is home to two companies which are on the Hispanic Business Fastest-Growing 100 list (greatest sales growth over the past five years): **SEI Group Inc.**; **Analytical Services Inc.**. *Hispanic Business, July/August 2003*

HOTELS

Hotels/Motels

Area	Hotels/Motels	Average Minimum Rates ($)		
		Tourist	First-Class	Deluxe
City	32	69	72	n/a

Note: n/a not available
Source: OAG Travel Planner Online, Spring 2004

EVENT SITES

Major Event Sites, Meeting Places and Convention Centers

Name	Guest Rooms	Exhibit/ Meeting Space (sq. ft.)	Largest Meeting Room Capacity
Sheraton Four Points	148	n/a	n/a
Bevill Center	100	20,000	n/a
Huntsville Hilton	277	14,000	600
Huntsville Marriott	290	11,000	800
Von Braun Civic Center	n/a	180,000	9,150

Note: n/a not available
Source: Original research

Living Environment

COST OF LIVING

Cost of Living Index

Year	Composite Index	Groceries	Housing	Utilities	Trans-portation	Health Care	Misc. Goods/Services
2001	95.2	97.7	85.1	80.4	103.3	97.1	103.4
2002	92.4	95.8	80.1	82.7	102.6	90.8	100.7
2003	93.0	99.8	76.3	92.6	103.0	89.5	102.4

Note: U.S. = 100
Source: ACCRA, Cost of Living Index, 2001, 2002 and 2003 4-Quarter Averages

HOUSING

House Price Index (HPI)

Area	National Ranking[2]	Quarterly Change (%)	One-Year Change (%)	Five-Year Change (%)
MSA[1]	203	0.42	2.73	16.45
U.S.[3]	-	3.67	7.97	41.81

Note: The HPI is a weighted repeat sales index. It measures average price changes in repeat sales or refinancings on the same properties. This information is obtained by reviewing repeat mortgage transactions on single-family properties whose mortgages have been purchased or securitized by Fannie Mae of Freddie Mac in January 1975; (1) Metropolitan Statistical Area - see Appendix A for areas included; (2) Rankings are based on annual percentage change, for all MSAs containing at least 15,000 transactions over the last 10 years and ranges from 1 to 220; (3) figures based on a weighted division average; all figures are for the period ended December 31, 2003
Source: Office of Federal Housing Enterprise Oversight, House Price Index, March 1, 2004

Housing: Year Structure Built

Area	1990 -2000	1980 -1989	1970 -1979	1960 -1969	1950 -1959	1940 -1949	Before 1940	Median Year
City	14.0	19.7	20.1	28.0	11.7	3.1	3.4	1972
MSA[1]	26.1	22.7	16.9	19.2	8.6	3.0	3.4	1979
U.S.	17.0	15.8	18.5	13.7	12.7	7.3	15.0	1971

Note: Figures are percentages; (1) Metropolitan Statistical Area - see Appendix A for areas included
Source: Census 2000, Summary File 3

Average New Home Price

Area	2001	2002	2003
City	184,077	188,756	187,354
U.S.	212,643	236,567	248,193

Note: Figures, in dollars, are based on a new home with 2,400 sq. ft. of living area on an 8,000 sq. ft. lot.
Source: ACCRA, Cost of Living Index, 2001, 2002 and 2003 4-Quarter Averages

Average Apartment Rent

Area	2001	2002	2003
City	574	587	585
U.S.	674	708	721

Note: Figures, in dollars per month, are based on an unfurnished two bedroom, 1-1/2 or 2 bath apartment, approximately 950 sq. ft. in size, excluding all utilities except water
Source: ACCRA, Cost of Living Index, 2001, 2002 and 2003 4-Quarter Averages

RESIDENTIAL UTILITIES

Average Residential Utility Costs

Area	All Electric ($/mth)	Part Electric ($/mth)	Other Energy ($/mth)	Phone ($/mth)
City	96.98	–	–	27.58
U.S.	116.46	65.82	62.68	23.90

Source: ACCRA, Cost of Living Index, 2003 4-Quarter Average

HEALTH CARE

Average Health Care Costs

Area	Hospital ($/day)	Doctor ($/visit)	Dentist ($/visit)
City	645.13	57.70	73.55
U.S.	678.35	67.91	83.90

Note: Hospital—based on a semi-private room; Doctor—based on a general practitioner's routine exam of an established patient; Dentist—based on adult teeth cleaning and periodic oral exam.
Source: ACCRA, Cost of Living Index, 2003 4-Quarter Average

Distribution of Non-Federal, Office-Based Physicians

Area	Total	Family/ General Practice	Specialties Medical	Specialties Surgical	Specialties Other
MSA[1] (number)	583	109	180	156	138
MSA[1] (rate per 10,000 pop.)	17.0	3.2	5.3	4.6	4.0
Metro Average[2] (rate per 10,000 pop.)	33.1	2.2	7.7	4.8	5.6

Note: Data as of December 31, 2001; (1) Metropolitan Statistical Area - see Appendix A for areas included; (2) Average of 81 MSAs and CMSAs in this book
Source: American Medical Association, Physician Characteristics & Distribution in the U.S., 2003-2004

Hospitals

Huntsville has the following hospitals: 2 general medical and surgical; 1 rehabilitation.
AHA Guide to the Healthcare Field, 2003-2004

PRESIDENTIAL ELECTION

2000 Presidential Election Results

Area	Gore	Bush	Nader	Buchanan	Other
Madison County	42.6	55.0	1.5	0.3	0.6
U.S.	48.4	47.9	2.7	0.4	0.6

Note: Results are percentages and may not add to 100% due to rounding
Source: www.cbsnews.com; www.uselectionatlas.org

EDUCATION

Public School District Statistics

District Name	Schls.	Enroll- ment	Classroom Teachers	Pupil/ Teacher Ratio	Minority Pupils[1] (%)	Current Expend.[2] ($/pupil)
Huntsville City SD	48	22,762	1,541	14.8	n/a	6,560
Madison County SD	24	16,075	937	17.2	n/a	5,356

Note: Data covers the 2001-02 school year unless otherwise noted; (1) Fall 2000; (2) FY2000; n/a not available
Source: U.S. Department of Education, National Center for Education Statistics, Common Core of Data, Local Education Agency (School District) Universe Survey: School Year 2001-2002; U.S. Department of Education, National Center for Education Statistics, Digest of Education Statistics 2002

Educational Quality

School District	Education Quotient[1]	Graduate Outcome[2]	Community Index[3]	Resource Index[4]
Huntsville City	38	40	57	29

Note: Scores are national percentile rankings and range from 1 (worst) to 99 (best); (1) Combination of the Graduate Outcome, Community and Resource indexes weighted to reflect the greater importance of the Graduate Outcome and Resource Index; (2) Based on graduation rates and college board scores (SAT/ACT); (3) Based on the surrounding community's level of affluence and adult education; (4) Based on teacher salaries, per-pupil expenditures and student-teacher ratios.
Source: Expansion Management, December 2003

Educational Attainment by Race

Area	High School Graduate (%)					Bachelor's Degree (%)				
	Total	White	Black	Asian	Hisp.[2]	Total	White	Black	Asian	Hisp.[2]
City	85.7	89.2	76.0	84.3	69.8	36.1	41.2	20.5	54.9	28.4
MSA[1]	83.3	84.9	76.4	85.1	68.7	30.9	32.8	21.8	53.4	22.4
U.S.	80.4	83.6	72.3	80.4	52.4	24.4	26.1	14.3	44.1	10.4

Note: Figures shown cover persons 25 years old and over; (1) Metropolitan Statistical Area - see Appendix A for areas included; (2) people of Hispanic origin can be of any race
Source: Census 2000, Summary File 3

School Enrollment by Type

Area	Grades KG to 8				Grades 9 to 12			
	Public		Private		Public		Private	
	Enrollment	%	Enrollment	%	Enrollment	%	Enrollment	%
City	16,163	87.1	2,404	12.9	7,179	87.7	1,010	12.3
MSA[1]	39,989	87.7	5,601	12.3	16,226	89.1	1,975	10.9
U.S.	33,526,011	88.7	4,285,121	11.3	14,848,628	90.6	1,532,323	9.4

Note: Figures shown cover persons 3 years old and over; (1) Metropolitan Statistical Area - see Appendix A for areas included
Source: Census 2000, Summary File 3

School Enrollment by Race

Area	Grades KG to 8 (%)				Grades 9 to 12 (%)			
	White	Black	Asian	Hisp.[1]	White	Black	Asian	Hisp.[1]
City	55.6	37.8	1.2	2.8	57.1	34.8	2.7	3.1
MSA[2]	70.7	23.3	1.3	2.8	68.7	25.2	1.6	2.8
U.S.	68.5	15.5	3.3	16.8	68.8	15.5	3.8	15.7

Note: Figures shown cover persons 3 years old and over; (1) people of Hispanic origin can be of any race; (2) Metropolitan Statistical Area - see Appendix A for areas included
Source: Census 2000, Summary File 3

Classroom Teacher Salaries in Public Schools

District	B.A. Degree		M.A. Degree		Maximum	
	Min. ($)	Rank[1]	Max. ($)	Rank[1]	Max. ($)	Rank[1]
City	n/a	n/a	n/a	n/a	n/a	n/a
DOD Average[2]	31,567	-	53,248	-	59,356	-

Note: Salaries are for 2001-2002; (1) Rank ranges from 1 to 100; (2) As per the U.S. Department of Defense Wage Fixing Authority
Source: American Federation of Teachers, Survey & Analysis of Teacher Salary Trends 2002

Higher Education

Four-Year Colleges			Two-Year Colleges			Medical Schools	Law Schools	Voc/Tech
Public	Private Non-profit	Private For-profit	Public	Private Non-profit	Private For-profit			
1	2	0	1	2	2	0	0	5

Note: Figures cover institutions located within the city limits.
Source: National Center for Education Statistics, The Integrated Postsecondary Education System (IPEDS) Peer Analysis System, 2002; usnews.com, America's Best Graduate Schools 2004, Medical School Directory; The College Blue Book, Occupational Education, 2003; Barron's Guide to Law Schools, 2003; Medical School Admission Requirements U.S. & Canada, 2003-2004

MAJOR EMPLOYERS

Major Employers

Company Name	Industry	Type
Adtran Inc	Telephone and telegraph apparatus	Headquarters
Alabama A & M University	Colleges and universities	Headquarters
AMSMI-RD-BA	National security	Branch
Commander	National security	Branch
Commissioners Dept	Executive offices	Headquarters
Conagra Poultry Company	Poultry slaughtering and processing	Branch
Contracting Dept	National security	Branch
Corporate Information Ctr	National security	Branch
Daimlerchrysler Corporation	Motor vehicle parts and accessories	Branch
Huntsville Hospital	General medical and surgical hospitals	Headquarters
Huntsville Hospital East	General medical and surgical hospitals	Branch
Intergraph Government Solution	Computer integrated systems design	Headquarters
ITC Deltacom Corp Office	Business consulting, nec	Single
Kwajalein Range Services LLC	Facilities support services	Headquarters
NASA	Space research and technology	Branch
Pratt & Whitney	Space propulsion units and parts	Branch
SAIC	Commercial physical research	Branch
SCI Systems Inc	Electronic components, nec	Branch
SCI Systems Inc	Printed circuit boards	Branch
Science Applications Intl Corp	Computer integrated systems design	Branch
Teledyne Brown Engineering	Commercial physical research	Headquarters

Note: Companies shown are located in the metropolitan area and have 750 or more employees.
Source: www.zapdata.com, March 2004

PUBLIC SAFETY

Crime Rate

Area	All Crimes	Violent Crimes				Property Crimes		
		Murder	Forcible Rape	Robbery	Aggrav. Assault	Burglary	Larceny -Theft	Motor Vehicle Theft
City	6,369.6	3.1	51.4	197.3	350.2	1,073.8	4,208.8	484.9
Suburbs[1]	2,417.8	4.8	18.8	37.1	97.4	544.2	1,545.8	169.5
MSA[2]	4,243.9	4.1	33.9	111.2	214.2	788.9	2,776.4	315.3
U.S.	4,118.8	5.6	33.0	145.9	310.1	746.2	2,445.8	432.1

Note: Figures are crimes per 100,000 population; (1) All areas within the MSA that are located outside the city limits; (2) Metropolitan Statistical Area - see Appendix A for areas included
Source: FBI Uniform Crime Reports, 2002

RECREATION

Culture and Recreation

Museums	Orchestras	Opera Companies	Dance Companies	Professional Theatres	Zoos	Pro Sports Teams[1]
4	2	1	1	0	0	0

Note: (1) Covers the Metropolitan Statistical Area - see Appendix A for areas included.
Source: The Grey House Performing Arts Directory, 2002; Official Museum Directory, 2004; www.sportsvenues.com

Library System

The Huntsville-Madison County Public Library has 13 branches and holdings of 542,677 volumes.
American Library Directory, 2003-2004

MEDIA

Newspapers

Name	Type	Freq.	Distribution	Circulation
The Huntsville Times	General	7x/wk	Area	62,000
Speakin' Out News	Black	1x/wk	Local	25,600

Note: Includes newspapers whose offices are located in the city and whose circulations are 1,000 or more
Source: Burrelle's Media Directory, 2003

Television Stations

Name	Ch.	Affiliation	Type	Owner
WHNT	19	CBST	Commercial	New York Times Company
WAAY	31	ABCT	Commercial	Gocom Communications
WAFF	48	NBCT	Commercial	Raycom Media Inc.
WZDX	54	FBC	Commercial	Huntsville Television Acquisition Corporation

Note: Stations included broadcast from the Huntsville metro area; n/a not available
Source: Burrelle's Media Directory, 2003

AM Radio Stations

Call Letters	Freq. (kHz)	Target Audience	Station Format	Music Format
WUMP	730	General	N/S/T	n/a
WVNN	770	Men	N/T	n/a
WDJL	1000	General	M	Christian
WBHP	1230	General	N/T	n/a
WTKI	1450	General	M/N/T	Country
WLOR	1550	B/R	M/N/T	Oldies
WEUP	1600	B/R	M/N/T	Gospel
WEUV	1750	Religious	M	Gospel

Note: Stations included broadcast from the Huntsville metro area; n/a not available
The following abbreviations may be used:
Target Audience: A=Asian; B=Black; C=Christian; E=Ethnic; F=French; G=General; H=Hispanic;
M=Men; N=Native American; R=Religious; S=Senior Citizen; W=Women; Y=Young Adult; Z=Children
Station Format: E=Educational; M=Music; N=News; S=Sports; T=Talk
Source: Burrelle's Media Directory, 2003

FM Radio Stations

Call Letters	Freq. (mHz)	Target Audience	Station Format	Music Format
WLRH	89.3	General	M/N	Classical
WOCG	90.1	Religious	E/M/N/S/T	Christian
WJAB	90.9	General	E/M/N/S	Gospel
WYFD	91.7	Religious	E/M/N	Christian
WEUZ	92.1	General	M	Rhythm & Blues
WXQW	94.1	General	M/N	Oldies
WRTT	95.1	Religious	M/N/S	Classic Rock
WAHR	99.1	Women	M/N/T	Adult Contemporary
WEUP	103.1	Black	M/N/S	Urban Contemporary

Note: Stations included broadcast from the Huntsville metro area
The following abbreviations may be used:
Target Audience: A=Asian; B=Black; C=Christian; E=Ethnic; F=French; G=General; H=Hispanic;
M=Men; N=Native American; R=Religious; S=Senior Citizen; W=Women; Y=Young Adult; Z=Children
Station Format: E=Educational; M=Music; N=News; S=Sports; T=Talk
Source: Burrelle's Media Directory, 2003

CLIMATE

Average and Extreme Temperatures

Temperature	Jan	Feb	Mar	Apr	May	Jun	Jul	Aug	Sep	Oct	Nov	Dec	Yr.
Extreme High (°F)	76	82	88	92	96	101	104	103	101	91	84	77	104
Average High (°F)	49	54	63	73	80	87	90	89	83	73	62	52	71
Average Temp. (°F)	39	44	52	61	69	76	80	79	73	62	51	43	61
Average Low (°F)	30	33	41	49	58	65	69	68	62	50	40	33	50
Extreme Low (°F)	-11	5	6	26	36	45	53	52	37	28	15	-3	-11

Note: Figures cover the years 1958-1995
Source: National Climatic Data Center, International Station Meteorological Climate Summary, 9/96

Average Precipitation/Snowfall/Humidity

Precip./Humidity	Jan	Feb	Mar	Apr	May	Jun	Jul	Aug	Sep	Oct	Nov	Dec	Yr.
Avg. Precip. (in.)	5.0	5.0	6.6	4.8	5.1	4.3	4.6	3.5	4.1	3.3	4.7	5.7	56.8
Avg. Snowfall (in.)	2	1	1	Tr	0	0	0	0	0	Tr	Tr	1	4
Avg. Rel. Hum. 7am (%)	82	81	79	78	79	81	84	86	85	86	84	81	82
Avg. Rel. Hum. 4pm (%)	60	56	51	46	51	53	56	55	54	51	55	60	54

Note: Figures cover the years 1958-1995; Tr = Trace amounts (<0.05 in. of rain; <0.5 in. of snow)
Source: National Climatic Data Center, International Station Meteorological Climate Summary, 9/96

Weather Conditions

Temperature			Daytime Sky			Precipitation		
10°F & below	32°F & below	90°F & above	Clear	Partly cloudy	Cloudy	0.01 inch or more precip.	0.1 inch or more snow/ice	Thunder-storms
2	66	49	70	118	177	116	2	54

Note: Figures are average number of days per year and covers the years 1958-1995
Source: National Climatic Data Center, International Station Meteorological Climate Summary, 9/96

HAZARDOUS WASTE

Superfund Sites

Huntsville has one hazardous waste site on the EPA's Superfund National Priorities List: **Redstone Arsenal (USARMY/NASA)**. *U.S. Environmental Protection Agency, National Priorities List, March 15, 2004*

AIR & WATER QUALITY

Maximum Pollutant Concentrations

	Particulate Matter (ug/m³)	Carbon Monoxide (ppm)	Sulfur Dioxide (ppm)	Nitrogen Dioxide (ppm)	Ozone 1-hour (ppm)	Ozone 8-hour (ppm)	Lead (ug/m³)
MSA[1] Level	47	n/a	n/a	n/a	0.1	0.08	n/a
NAAQS[2]	150	9	0.140	0.053	0.12	0.08	1.50
Met NAAQS[2]	Yes	n/a	n/a	n/a	Yes	Yes	n/a

Note: (1) Metropolitan Statistical Area - see Appendix A for areas included; (2) National Ambient Air Quality Standards; n/a not available
Units: ppm = parts per million; ug/m³ = micrograms per cubic meter
Source: EPA, Latest Findings on National Air Quality: 2002 Status and Trends, August 2003

Air Quality Index

Data not available.

Watershed Health

The U.S. Environmental Protection Agency monitors the health of the aquatic resources for the nation's 2,000+ watersheds. **The Wheeler Lake watershed serves the Huntsville area and received an overall Index of Watershed Indicators (IWI) score of 6 (more serious problems - high vulnerability)**. The IWI score is based on seven condition and nine vulnerability indicators. The overall IWI score ranges from 1 (best health) to 6 (worst health). The Condition Indicators include: designated use attainment, fish and wildlife consumption advisories, source water condition, contaminated sediments, ambient water quality, and wetlands loss index. The Vulnerability Indicators include: aquatic species at risk, conventional and toxic loads over permitted limits, urban and agricultural runoff potential, population change, hydrologic modification, estuarine pollution susceptibility, and air deposition. *EPA, Index of Watershed Indicators, October 26, 2001*

Drinking Water

Water System Name	Pop. Served	Primary Water Source Type	Number of Violations January 2002-February 2004		
			Health Based	Significant Monitoring	Monitoring
Huntsville Utilities	208,548	Surface	None	None	None

Note: Data as of February 19, 2004
Source: EPA, Office of Ground Water and Drinking Water, Safe Drinking Water Information System

Huntsville tap water is Neutral, hard and fluoridated.
Editor & Publisher Market Guide, 2004

Jacksonville, Florida

Background

The Jacksonville we see today is largely a product of the reconstruction that occurred during the 1940s after a fire had razed 147 city blocks a few decades earlier. Lying under the modern structures, however, is a history that dates back earlier than the settlement of Plymouth by the Pilgrims.

Located in the northeast part of Florida, on the St. John's River, Jacksonville was settled by English, Spanish, and French explorers from the sixteenth through the eighteenth centuries. Sites commemorating their presence include: the Fort Caroline National Monument, marking the French settlement led by Rene de Goulaine Laudonniere in 1564; Spanish Pond one-quarter of a mile east of Fort Caroline, where Spanish forces led by Pedro Menendez captured the Fort; and Fort George Island, from which General James Oglethorpe led English attacks against the Spanish during the eighteenth century.

Jacksonville was attractive to these early settlers because of its easy access to the Atlantic Ocean, which meant a favorable port.

Today, Jacksonville remains an advantageous port and is home to Naval Air Station Jacksonville, a major employer in the area. In addition, this is the financial hub of Florida. Companies recently expanding or relocating in the city include Flightstar Aircraft Services, Cingular Wireless, and Citi Cards. Fidelity National Financial launched a move of its financial services headquarters to the city in 2003.

Other significant employers include the Winn-Dixie corporate headquarters, Blue Cross/Blue Shield of Florida, and Bank of America, which also has a regional banking system headquarters in Jacksonville. The East Coast's largest rail network, CSX Transportion, also maintains its headquarters here.

On the cultural front, Jacksonville boasts a range of options, including the Children's Museum, the Jacksonville Symphony Orchestra, the Gator Bowl, and beach facilities. In 2007, the city will welcome Super Bowl XXXIX to ALLTEL Stadium, home of the Jacksonville Jaguars NFL team.

Summers are long, warm, and relatively humid. Winters are generally mild, although periodic invasions of cold northern air bring the temperature down. Temperatures along the beaches rarely rise above 90 degrees. Summer thunderstorms usually occur before noon along the beaches, and inland in the afternoons. The greatest rainfall, as localized thunder showers, occurs during the summer months. Although the area is in the hurricane Belt, this section of the coast has been very fortunate in escaping hurricane-force winds.

Rankings

- Jacksonville was ranked #82 out of 331 metro areas in *Cities Ranked & Rated*. Criteria: cost of living; climate; crime; transportation; economy and jobs; education; arts and culture; health and healthcare; leisure. *Cities Ranked & Rated, 1st Edition, 2004*

- *Ladies Home Journal* ranked America's 200 largest cities based on the qualities women surveyed care about most. Jacksonville ranked #35 out of 57 in the big city category (population over 300,000). Criteria: crime; lifestyle; education; jobs; health; child care; politics; and the economy. *Ladies Home Journal Online, "The Best Cities for Women 2002"*

- The Jacksonville metro area was selected as one of America's "Best Places to Live and Work" by *Expansion Management* and rated as a "Four-Star Community." The annual "Quality of Life Quotient" measures nearly 50 indicators and compares them among the 329 metropolitan statistical areas in the United States. *Expansion Management, May 2003*

- Jacksonville was selected as one of the "Best Cities for Black Families." The city ranked #10 out of 20. For six months, bet.com compiled data on African Americans in those U.S. cities with the largest Black populations. The data, for African Americans specifically, involved the following: infant mortality; high school graduation; median income; homeownership; unemployment; business ownership; poverty rates; AIDS infection rates; percentage of children in single parent, typically fatherless, households; teen pregnancy; economic segregation index; violent and property crime. *www.bet.com, October 1, 2002*

- *Forbes* ranked the 150 most populous metro areas in the U.S. in terms of the "Best Places for Business and Careers." The Jacksonville metro area was ranked #48. Criteria: income and job growth; cost-of-doing-business; qualifications of the available pool of labor; crime rates; housing costs; net migration. *Forbes, May 9, 2003*

- Jacksonville was selected as one of "America's Healthiest Cities" by *Natural Health* magazine. The city was ranked #36 out of the 50 largest urban areas in the U.S. Twenty-six criteria in the following four categories were examined: whether the city boasts natural offerings; how well the city promotes its resident's physical health; whether the city offers a healthy environment; how well the city fosters a sense of community. *Natural Health, April 2003*

- *Men's Health* ranked 101 U.S. cities in terms of the quality of their tap water. Jacksonville received a grade of B. Criteria: levels of bacteria, arsenic, lead, trihalomethanes, and haloacetic acids were compared with the National Academy of Science's guidelines as well as with the EPA's more stringent maximum contaminant level goals. *Men's Health, March 2004*

- Sperling's BestPlaces ranked 331 metro areas and identified the most and least stressful U.S. cities. The Jacksonville metro area ranked #18 out of the 100 largest metro areas (#1 = most stressful). Criteria: divorce rate; unemployment rate; violent and property crime; suicide rate; commute time; mental health; alcohol consumption; cloudy days. *www.BestPlaces.net, February 26, 2004*

- Sperling's BestPlaces in partnership with Pep Boys ranked 77 metro areas and identified "America's Most Drivable Cities." The Jacksonville metro area ranked #11. Criteria: climate; road roughness; urban mobility; gas prices. *Pep Boys, "America's Most Drivable Cities," April 9, 2003*

- Jacksonville was selected as a 2003 Digital Cities Survey winner. The city ranked #9 in the large city category. The survey examined and assessed how city governments are utilizing information technology to operate and deliver quality service to their customers and citizens. *Center for Digital Government, "2003 Digital Cities Survey"*

- Jacksonville was ranked #157 out of America's 200 largest metro areas in *SELF Magazine's* ranking of "America's Healthiest Cities for Women." Criteria: safety; air/water quality; cancer rates; and 21 other factors relating to health. *SELF Magazine, November 2003*

- Jacksonville was identified as one of the most dangerous large metro areas for pedestrians in the U.S. The area ranked #6 out of the nations 49 largest metro areas. Criteria: average yearly pedestrian fatalities per capita (for the years 2000 and 2001) adjusted for the number of walkers. *Surface Transportation Policy Project, "Mean Streets 2002"*

- Jacksonville was selected as one of the 25 fittest cities in America by *Men's Fitness Online*. It ranked #18 out of America's 50 largest cities. Criteria: gyms/sporting goods; nutrition; exercise/sports; overweight/sedentary; junk food; alcohol; smoking; television; air and water quality; climate; geography; commute time; parks/open space; recreation facilities; and health care. *Men's Fitness Online, America's Fittest/Fattest Cities 2003*

- Jacksonville was ranked #21 out of 100 cities surveyed in *Child* magazine's ranking of the "Best Cities for Families." Criteria: number of pediatricians per capita; proximity to a children's hospital; immunization rates; infant mortality rate; air quality; water quality; school spending; pupil-teacher ratio; availability of parks/green space; nearby recreational opportunities; average commute time; number of sunny days; average cost of a 3-bedroom home; unemployment rate; future job growth; crime rate; percentage of children under 5; mandated minimum child care ratios. *Child, April 2001*

- *Zero Population Growth* ranked 239 cities in terms of children's health, safety, and economic well-being. Jacksonville was ranked #107 out of 140 independent cities (cities with populations greater than 100,000 which were neither major cities nor suburbs/outer cities) and was given a grade of C+. Criteria: total population and population growth; percent of population under 18 years of age; number of children's museums; health improvement grade; percent of births to teens; percent of low birthweight infants; infant mortality rate; number of Title X-funded clinics; average SAT/ACT scores; average elementary and secondary class size; crime rate; unemployment rate; percent of affordable homes; number of bad air days; park acres per 1000 persons; library circulation per child; and children's program attendance counts. *Zero Population Growth, Kid Friendly Cities Report Card 2001*

- Jacksonville was given "Well City USA" status by The Wellness Councils of America, whose objective is to engage entire business communities in building healthy workforces. Criteria: 20% of a community's working population must be employed by either Bronze, Silver, Gold or Platinum designated Well Workplace Award winning companies. To date, six communities have achieved Well City USA status and five communities have Well City projects in progress. *The Wellness Councils of America, Well City USA 2004*

- *Ladies Home Journal* ranked America's 200 largest cities in terms of safety. Jacksonville ranked #160 out of 200. Criteria: violent crimes; crimes against property; and rape. *Ladies Home Journal Online, "The Best Cities for Women 2002"*

- Jacksonville was ranked #64 out of 268 metro areas in terms of its Creativity Index. The Creativity Index is a mix of four equally weighted factors: the Creative Class (scientists, engineers, architects, designers, writers, artists, musicians, or any profession where creativity is a key factor) share of the workforce; innovation, measured as patents per capita; high-tech industry, using the Milken Institute's Tech Pole Index; and diversity, measured by the Gay Index (a reasonable proxy for an areas' openness to different kinds of people and ideas). *The Rise of the Creative Class, 2002*

- Jacksonville was ranked #47 out of 125 regions worldwide in terms of its "Knowledge Competitiveness Index." The index attempts to measure the knowledge-based development taking place throughout the world and is based on 17 measures of economic performance that indicate a region's ability to translate its knowledge capacity into economic value. *Robert Huggins Associates, "2003-2004 World Knowledge Competitiveness Index"*

- The Jacksonville metro area was selected by *Yahoo! Internet Life* as one of "America's Most Wired Cities...and Towns." The area ranked #41 out of 87. Criteria: home and work net use; user sophistication; domain density; and available content. *Yahoo! Internet Life, April 2001*

- Jacksonville was identified as one of the 100 "Most Unwired Cities" in the U.S. The area ranked #49. Criteria: number of public and commercial wireless access points; cell phone coverage offering wide area network Internet access; Internet penetration. *Intel, "Most Unwired Cities," March 4, 2003*

- Scarborough Research measured the percentage of households who subscribe to cellular services among adults ages 18 and over in 75 U.S. markets. The Jacksonville DMA (Designated Market Area) was ranked #29 out of 75. *Scarborough Research, Scarborough USA+ 2003 Release 1*

■ Jacksonville was selected as one of "America's Most Literate Cities." The city ranked #57 out of the 64 largest U.S. cities. Criteria: booksellers; library support, holdings, and utilization; educational attainment; periodicals published; newspaper circulation. *University of Wisconsin-Whitewater, "America's Most Literate Cities," Summer 2003*

■ Jacksonville was chosen as one of America's ten best cities for running. The city was ranked #5. Criteria: nominations from *Runner's World* readers; input from longtime runners and frequent travelers Jeff Galloway, John Bingham, Hal Higdon, Doug Rennie, and Burt Yasso; key statistical data concerning the cities' trail networks, weather, air quality, street safety, and the number of local running clubs and road races. *www.runnersworld.com, December 16, 2002*

■ Jacksonville was ranked #104 in *Prevention* magazine's survey of the "Best Walking Cities in the U.S." The magazine, in conjunction with the American Podiatric Medical Association, surveyed 125 of the most populated cities and then tabulated and weighed 20 criteria of interest to pedestrians. *Prevention, April, 2004*

■ The Jacksonville metro area was selected as one of "America's 50 Hottest Cities for Business Relocations and Expansions." The area ranked #3. Criteria: 70 of the industry's most prominent site selection consultants were asked which cities their clients found the most attractive when it came to selecting an expansion or relocation site in 2003. *Expansion Management, January 2004*

■ The Jacksonville metro area was cited as one of "The Best Places in the U.S. to Locate a Company." The area ranked #126 out of 329. Criteria: education (with emphasis on college board test results and high school graduation rates); availability of quality healthcare services and the cost to employers; quality of life; logistics workforce and companies; transportation infrastructure; quality and quantity of highly educated technical workers; business climate. *Expansion Management, July 2003*

■ Jacksonville was cited as a top metro area for European expansion. The area ranked #33 out of 50, based on European-based company expansions or relocations within the past two years that created at least 10 jobs and involved capital investment of at least $1 million. *Expansion Management, June 2003*

■ The Jacksonville metro area was selected as one of the "Top 40 Hottest Real Estate Markets" for expanding or relocating businesses." Criteria: rental costs; purchase prices; and vacancy rates of office and warehouse space. *Expansion Management, August 2003*

■ The Jacksonville metro area appeared on *Forbes/Milken Institute* list of "Best Places for Business and Career." Rank: #44 out of 200 metro areas. Criteria: salary growth; job growth; number of technology clusters; overall concentration of technology activity relative to national average; and technology output growth. *www.forbes.com, Forbes/Milken Institute Best Places 2002*

■ The Jacksonville metro area appeared on the "Milken Institute Best Performing Cities" index. Rank: #47 out of 200 large metro areas. Criteria: job growth; wage and salary growth; high-tech output growth. *Milken Institute, June 25, 2003*

■ The Jacksonville metro area appeared on *Entrepreneur* magazine's list of the "Best Cities for Entrepreneurs" in 2003. The area ranked #19 out of 61 in the large city category. Criteria: entrepreneurial activity; small-business growth; economic growth; and risk. *www.Entrepreneur.com*

■ The Jacksonville metro area was selected as one of the "Top 25 Cities for Doing Business in America." *Inc.* measured current-year employment growth in 277 regions as well as current trends in the annual average growth over the past three years, and compared employment expansion between the first and second halves of the last decade. Job growth factors account for two-thirds, and balance among industries accounts for one third of the final score for each city.The Jacksonville metro area ranked #8 among large metro areas. *Inc. Magazine, March 2004*

■ The Jacksonville metro area appeared on *IndustryWeek's* fourth annual World-Class Communities list. It ranked #169 out of 315 metro areas. Criteria: MSA Gross Metropolitan Product (GMP) per manufacturing employee; and MSA percent share of U.S. manufacturing Gross Domestic Product (GDP). *IndustryWeek, April 16, 2001*

■ The Jacksonville metro area was selected as a "2001 Choice City" by *Business Development Outlook* magazine. Twenty-five cities were selected, based on data from the Bureau of Labor Statistics, Census Bureau, Federal Reserve, The Conference Board, and the U.S. Conference of Mayors, as being the most desirable into which a business can relocate or expand. *Business Development Outlook, 2001 Choice Cities*

■ ING Group ranked the 125 largest metro areas according to the general financial security of residents. The Jacksonville metro area was ranked #93 out of 125. Criteria: Earnings and Wealth Potential (household income, education, net assets, cost of living); Safety Net (health insurance, retirement savings, life insurance, income support programs); Personal Threats (unemployment rate, low-income households, crime rate); Community Economic Vitality (cost of community services, job quality, job creation, housing costs). *ING Group, "The Best Cities to Earn and Save Money: A Ranking of the Largest 125 U.S. Cities," 2001 Edition*

Business Environment

CITY FINANCES

City Government Finances

Component	2000-2001 ($000)	2000-2001 ($ per capita)
Total Revenues	2,230,090	3,032
Total Expenditures	2,280,006	3,099
Debt Outstanding	5,705,860	7,757
Cash and Securities	4,685,919	6,370

Source: U.S Census Bureau, Government Finances 2000-2001, August 2003

City Government Revenue by Source

Source	2000-2001 ($000)	2000-2001 ($ per capita)
General Revenue		
From Federal Government	130,291	177
From State Government	123,367	168
From Local Governments	0	0
Taxes		
Property	283,427	385
Sales	214,498	292
Personal Income	0	0
License	542	1
Charges	234,650	319
Liquor Store	0	0
Utility	887,318	1,206
Employee Retirement	125,446	171
Other	230,551	313

Source: U.S Census Bureau, Government Finances 2000-2001, August 2003

City Government Expenditures by Function

Function	2000-2001 ($000)	2000-2001 ($ per capita)	2000-2001 (%)
General Expenditures			
Airports	53,060	72	2.3
Corrections	46,164	63	2.0
Education	0	0	0.0
Fire Protection	88,937	121	3.9
Governmental Administration	88,392	120	3.9
Health	19,973	27	0.9
Highways	64,276	87	2.8
Hospitals	20,540	28	0.9
Housing and Community Development	11,968	16	0.5
Interest on General Debt	168,300	229	7.4
Libraries	16,443	22	0.7
Parking	2,529	3	0.1
Parks and Recreation	44,737	61	2.0
Police Protection	142,106	193	6.2
Public Welfare	31,120	42	1.4
Sewerage	189,907	258	8.3
Solid Waste Management	59,654	81	2.6
Liquor Store	0	0	0.0
Utility	890,674	1,211	39.1
Employee Retirement	98,538	134	4.3
Other	242,688	330	10.6

Source: U.S Census Bureau, Government Finances 2000-2001, August 2003

Municipal Bond Ratings

Area	Moody's
City	Aa2

Source: Mergent Bond Record, February 2004

DEMOGRAPHICS

Population Growth

Area	1990 Census	2000 Census	2003 Estimate	2008 Projection	Population Growth (%) 1990-2000	Population Growth (%) 2000-2008
City	635,221	735,617	776,321	843,311	15.8	14.6
MSA[1]	906,727	1,100,491	1,170,545	1,287,102	21.4	17.0
U.S.	248,709,873	281,421,906	290,647,163	305,918,071	13.2	8.7

Note: (1) Metropolitan Statistical Area - see Appendix A for areas included
Source: Claritas, Inc.

Number of Households and Average Household Size

Area	1990 Census	2000 Census	2003 Estimate	2008 Projection	2003 Average Household Size
City	241,379	284,499	301,422	329,500	2.6
MSA[1]	343,526	425,584	455,145	504,849	2.6
U.S.	91,947,410	105,480,101	109,440,059	116,034,472	2.7

Note: (1) Metropolitan Statistical Area - see Appendix A for areas included
Source: Claritas, Inc.

Race and Ethnicity

Area	White Non-Hispanic	Black Non-Hispanic	Asian Non-Hispanic	Other Race Non-Hispanic	Hispanic
City	63.4	29.8	2.9	3.9	4.4
MSA[1]	72.0	22.1	2.4	3.5	4.0
U.S.	74.5	12.4	3.8	9.3	13.2

Note: Figures are 2003 estimates; (1) Metropolitan Statistical Area - see Appendix A for areas included
Source: Claritas, Inc.

Segregation

City Index[2]	City Rank[3]	MSA[1] Index[2]	MSA[1] Rank[4]
55.8	62	59.3	154

Note: Figures are based on an analysis of Census 2000 data; (1) Metropolitan Statistical Area - see Appendix A for areas included; (2) Dissimilarity Index—the most commonly used measure of segregation between two groups, reflecting their relative distributions across neighborhoods within a city or metropolitan area. It can range in value from 0, indicating complete integration, to 100, indicating complete segregation; (3) Ranges from 1 (most segregated) to 100 (least segregated) and includes all the cities in this book; (4) Ranges from 1 (most segregated) to 318 (least segregated) and includes 318 metropolitan areas.
Source: www.CensusScope.org

Ancestry

Area	German	Irish[2]	English	American	Italian	Polish	French[3]	Scottish
City	9.6	9.0	8.5	9.3	3.5	1.4	2.2	1.8
MSA[1]	11.0	10.5	10.2	10.3	4.1	1.8	2.7	2.1
U.S.	15.2	10.9	8.7	7.3	5.6	3.2	3.0	1.7

Note: Figures include multiple ancestry (e.g. if a person reported being Irish and Italian, they were included in both columns); (1) Metropolitan Statistical Area - see Appendix A for areas included; (2) Includes Celtic; (3) Includes Alsatian but excludes Basque
Source: Census 2000, Summary File 3

Foreign-Born Population

Area	Any Foreign Country	Percent of Population Born in: Europe	Asia	Africa	Oceania[2]	Canada	Mexico	Latin America[3]
City	5.9	1.5	2.4	0.2	0.0	0.2	0.2	1.5
MSA[1]	5.4	1.5	2.0	0.2	0.0	0.3	0.2	1.3
U.S.	11.1	1.7	2.9	0.3	0.1	0.3	3.3	2.5

Note: (1) Metropolitan Statistical Area - see Appendix A for areas included; (2) Includes Australia, New Zealand subregion, Melanesia, Micronesia, Polynesia, and Oceania n.e.c; (3) Includes Central America (excluding Mexico), South America, and the Caribbean.
Source: Census 2000, Summary File 3

Religion

Area	Catholic	Southern Baptist	United Meth-odist	ELCA[1]	LDS[2]	Presby-terian Church USA	Jewish Est.	Muslim Est.
County	8.3	18.4	3.7	0.5	0.7	1.7	0.8	0.3
U.S.	22.0	7.1	3.7	1.8	1.5	1.1	2.2	0.6

Note: Figures shown are the number of adherents as a percentage of the total population; Adherents are defined as all members, including full members, their children and the estimated number of other participants who are not considered members (e.g. the baptized, those not confirmed, those not eligible for communion, those regularly attending services, etc.); (1) Evangelical Lutheran Church in America; (2) The Church of Jesus Christ of Latter Day Saints
Source: Reprinted with permission from Religious Congregations and Membership in the United States 2000 (Nashville, Glenmary Research Center, 2002) Copyright Association of Statisticians of American Religious Bodies. All rights reserved.

Age Distribution

Area	Percent of Population						
	Under Age 5	Age 5 to 17	Age 18 to 34	Age 35 to 49	Age 50 to 64	Age 65 to 79	80 Years and Over
City	7.3	19.4	25.1	24.2	13.8	7.8	2.4
MSA[1]	6.8	19.3	23.3	24.6	15.0	8.5	2.6
U.S.	6.8	18.9	23.7	23.5	14.8	9.2	3.2

Note: (1) Metropolitan Statistical Area - see Appendix A for areas included
Source: Census 2000, Summary File 3

Marriage Status

Area	Never Married	Now Married Except Separated	Separated	Widowed	Divorced
City	26.5	50.9	3.0	6.3	13.3
MSA[1]	24.4	54.1	2.5	6.2	12.6
U.S.	27.1	54.4	2.2	6.6	9.7

Note: Figures cover population 15 years of age and older; (1) Metropolitan Statistical Area - see Appendix A for areas included
Source: Census 2000, Summary File 3

Male/Female Ratio

Area	Males	Females	Males per 100 Females
City	376,017	400,304	93.9
MSA[1]	569,303	601,242	94.7
U.S.	142,511,883	148,135,280	96.2

Note: Figures are 2003 estimates; (1) Metropolitan Statistical Area - see Appendix A for areas included
Source: Claritas, Inc.

ECONOMY

Gross Metropolitan Product

Area	1999	2000	2001	2002	2002 Rank[2]
MSA[1]	40.2	42.9	44.4	45.9	55

Note: Figures are in billions of dollars; (1) Metropolitan Statistical Area - see Appendix A for areas included; (2) Rank ranges from 1 to 319
Source: The U.S. Conference of Mayors, Metro Economies Report, July 2003

INCOME

Per Capita/Median/Average Income

Area	Per Capita ($)	Median Household ($)	Average Household ($)
City	22,858	44,875	58,231
MSA[1]	24,688	47,784	62,889
U.S.	24,078	46,868	63,207

Note: Figures are 2003 estimates; (1) Metropolitan Statistical Area - see Appendix A for areas included
Source: Claritas, Inc.

Household Income Distribution

Area	Percent of Households Earning							
	Under $15,000	$15,000 -24,999	$25,000 -34,999	$35,000 -49,999	$50,000 -74,999	$75,000 -99,000	$100,000 -149,999	$150,000 and up
City	13.7	11.7	12.8	17.9	20.2	10.8	8.6	4.2
MSA[1]	12.2	11.0	12.2	17.2	20.7	11.6	9.9	5.3
U.S.	14.1	11.5	11.7	16.0	19.2	11.3	10.2	6.0

Note: Figures are 2003 estimates; (1) Metropolitan Statistical Area - see Appendix A for areas included
Source: Claritas, Inc.

Poverty Rates by Age

Area	All Ages	Under 5 Years Old	5 to 17 Years Old	18 to 64 Years Old	65 Years and Over
City	12.2	1.3	3.2	6.4	1.2
MSA[1]	10.7	1.1	2.8	5.7	1.1
U.S.	12.4	1.2	3.0	6.9	1.2

Note: Figures are percent of population with income in 1999 below poverty level and only include population for whom poverty status is determined; (1) Metropolitan Statistical Area - see Appendix A for areas included
Source: Census 2000, Summary File 3

Personal Bankruptcy Filing Rate

Area	2002	2003
Duval County	6.90	7.19
U.S.	5.34	5.58

Note: Numbers are per 1,000 population and include Chapter 7 and Chapter 13 filings
Source: Federal Deposit Insurance Corporation (FDIC), Regional Economic Conditions (RECON), 2/25/2004

EMPLOYMENT

Labor Force and Employment

Area	Civilian Labor Force			Workers Employed		
	Dec. 2002	Dec. 2003	% Chg.	Dec. 2002	Dec. 2003	% Chg.
City	385,615	385,451	0.0	365,490	365,658	0.0
MSA[1]	582,804	582,231	-0.1	555,153	555,410	0.0
U.S.	144,807,000	146,501,000	1.2	136,599,000	138,556,000	1.4

Note: Data is not seasonally adjusted and covers workers 16 years of age and older;
(1) Metropolitan Statistical Area - see Appendix A for areas included
Source: Bureau of Labor Statistics, http://stats.bls.gov

Unemployment Rate

Area	2003											
	Jan.	Feb.	Mar.	Apr.	May	Jun.	Jul.	Aug.	Sep.	Oct.	Nov.	Dec.
City	5.9	5.5	5.4	5.6	5.5	6.8	6.4	6.1	6.1	5.7	5.6	5.1
MSA[1]	5.4	5.1	5.0	5.1	5.0	6.1	5.7	5.5	5.5	5.1	5.1	4.6
U.S.	6.5	6.4	6.2	5.8	5.8	6.5	6.3	6.0	5.8	5.6	5.6	5.4

Note: Data is not seasonally adjusted and covers workers 16 years of age and older; All figures are percentages; (1) Metropolitan Statistical Area - see Appendix A for areas included
Source: Bureau of Labor Statistics, http://stats.bls.gov

Employment by Occupation

Occupation Classification	City (%)	MSA[1] (%)	U.S. (%)
Sales and Office	32.6	31.4	26.7
Professional and Related	17.6	17.9	20.2
Service	14.0	14.4	14.9
Production, Transportation, and Material Moving	12.4	11.8	14.6
Management, Business, and Financial	13.6	14.1	13.5
Construction, Extraction, and Maintenance	9.5	10.1	9.4
Farming, Forestry, and Fishing	0.2	0.3	0.7

Note: Figures cover employed civilians 16 years of age and older;
(1) Metropolitan Statistical Area - see Appendix A for areas included
Source: Census 2000, Summary File 3

Employment by Industry

| Sector | MSA[1] | | U.S. |
	Number of Employees	Percent of Total	Percent of Total
Government	72,600	12.7	16.7
Education and Health Services	65,300	11.4	12.9
Professional and Business Services	84,600	14.8	12.3
Retail Trade	72,500	12.7	11.8
Manufacturing	32,300	5.7	11.0
Leisure and Hospitality	52,300	9.2	9.1
Finance Activities	58,100	10.2	6.1
Construction	36,500	6.4	5.1
Wholesale Trade	28,100	4.9	4.3
Other Services	26,200	4.6	4.1
Transportation and Utilities	29,200	5.1	3.7
Information	12,800	2.2	2.4
Natural Resources and Mining	500	0.1	0.4

Note: Figures cover non-farm employment as of December 2003 and are not seasonally adjusted;
(1) Metropolitan Statistical Area - see Appendix A for areas included
Source: Bureau of Labor Statistics, http://stats.bls.gov

Average Wages

Occupation	$/Hr.	Occupation	$/Hr.
Accountants and Auditors	23.50	Maids and Housekeeping Cleaners	7.63
Automotive Mechanics	16.86	Maintenance and Repair Workers	13.79
Bookkeepers	12.42	Marketing Managers	38.96
Carpenters	13.67	Nuclear Medicine Technologists	22.58
Cashiers	7.56	Nurses, Licensed Practical	16.01
Clerks, General Office	10.18	Nurses, Registered	22.48
Clerks, Receptionists/Information	9.87	Nursing Aides/Orderlies/Attendants	9.66
Clerks, Shipping/Receiving	11.52	Packers and Packagers, Hand	7.41
Computer Programmers	42.08	Physical Therapists	25.74
Computer Support Specialists	19.10	Postal Service Mail Carriers	18.88
Computer Systems Analysts	30.68	Real Estate Brokers	40.39
Cooks, Restaurant	9.64	Retail Salespersons	10.25
Dentists	80.07	Sales Reps., Exc. Tech./Scientific	21.95
Electrical Engineers	32.28	Sales Reps., Tech./Scientific	21.42
Electricians	17.81	Secretaries, Exc. Legal/Med./Exec.	11.77
Financial Managers	40.36	Security Guards	8.95
First-Line Supervisors/Mgrs., Sales	17.66	Surgeons	93.54
Food Preparation Workers	7.57	Teacher Assistants	9.80
General and Operations Managers	39.15	Teachers, Elementary School	20.60
Hairdressers/Cosmetologists	10.20	Teachers, Secondary School	20.70
Internists	83.14	Telemarketers	11.06
Janitors and Cleaners	8.67	Truck Drivers, Heavy/Tractor-Trailer	16.90
Landscaping/Groundskeeping Workers	10.20	Truck Drivers, Light/Delivery Svcs.	14.10
Lawyers	61.09	Waiters and Waitresses	7.45

Note: Wage data is for 2002 and covers the Metropolitan Statistical Area (see Appendix A for areas included).
Hourly wages for elementary/secondary school teachers and teacher assistants were calculated by the editors
from annual wage data assuming a 40 hour work week; n/a not available.
Source: Bureau of Labor Statistics, 2002 Metro Area Occupational Employment and Wage Estimates

Occupational Employment Projections: 1996 - 2006

Occupations Expected to Have the Largest Job Growth (ranked by numerical growth)	Fast-Growing Occupations[1] (ranked by percent growth)
1. Cashiers	1. Systems analysts
2. Salespersons, retail	2. Physical therapy assistants and aides
3. General managers & top executives	3. Desktop publishers
4. Registered nurses	4. Home health aides
5. Waiters & waitresses	5. Computer engineers
6. Marketing & sales, supervisors	6. Medical assistants
7. Janitors/cleaners/maids, ex. priv. hshld.	7. Physical therapists
8. General office clerks	8. Paralegals
9. Food preparation workers	9. Emergency medical technicians
10. Hand packers & packagers	10. Occupational therapists

Note: Projections cover Florida; (1) Excludes occupations with total job growth less than 300
Source: U.S. Department of Labor, Employment and Training Administration, America's Labor Market Information System (ALMIS)

TAXES

State Corporate Income Tax Rates

State	Rate (%)	Number of Brackets	Low Bracket (Under $)	High Bracket (Over $)
Florida	5.5	1	na	na

Note: Tax rates as of December 31, 2003; na not applicable; 3.3% alternative minimum rate.
Source: Tax Foundation, www.taxfoundation.org

State Individual Income Tax Rates

State	Federal Deductibility	Marginal Rate (%)	Number of Brackets	Low Bracket (Under $)	High Bracket (Over $)
Florida	No	None	na	na	na

Note: Tax rates as of December 31, 2003; Brackets apply to single taxpayers and married people filing separately; na not applicable
Source: Tax Foundation, www.taxfoundation.org

Various State and Local Tax Rates

State Sales and Use (%)	Total Sales and Use (%)	Gasoline (cents/gal.)	Cigarette (cents/pack)	Spirits ($/gal.)	Table Wine ($/gal.)	Beer ($/gal.)
6.0	7.0	13.9	33.9	6.50	2.25	0.48

Note: Tax rates as of December 31, 2003
Source: Tax Foundation, www.taxfoundation.org

State Tax Burdens

Area	Combined State and Local Tax Burden		Combined Federal, State and Local Tax Burden	
	Percent	Rank	Percent	Rank
Florida	8.4	45	29.0	23
U.S. Average	9.7	-	30.0	-

Note: Figures are for 2003
Source: Tax Foundation, www.taxfoundation.org

Internal Revenue Service Tax Audits

IRS District	Percent of Returns Audited				
	1996	1997	1998	1999	2000
North Florida	0.52	0.45	0.29	0.24	0.14
U.S.	0.66	0.61	0.46	0.31	0.20

Note: Figures cover IRS district audits of federal income tax returns filed by individuals. Geographic data on district audits for 2001 and 2002 are being withheld by the IRS. TRAC is challenging this policy.
Source: Syracuse University, Transactional Records Access Clearinghouse (TRAC), "Odds of IRS District Tax Audit 2000"

RESIDENTIAL REAL ESTATE

Building Permits

Area	Single-Family			Multi-Family			Total		
	2001	2002	Pct. Chg.	2001	2002	Pct. Chg.	2001	2002	Pct. Chg.
City	4,832	5,397	11.7	1,765	2,612	48.0	6,597	8,009	21.4
U.S.	1,235,600	1,332,600	7.9	401,100	415,100	3.5	1,636,700	1,747,700	6.8

Note: Figures represent new, privately-owned housing units authorized (unadjusted data)
Source: U.S. Census Bureau, Manufacturing, Mining, and Construction Statistics

Homeownership and Housing Vacancies

Area	Homeownership Rate[2] (%)			Rental Vacancy Rate[3] (%)			Homeowner Vacancy Rate[4] (%)		
	2001	2002[a]	2003	2001	2002[a]	2003	2001	2002[a]	2003
MSA[1]	68.4	66.1	67.2	4.6	7.3	9.7	0.6	0.8	4.8
U.S.	67.8	67.9	68.3	8.4	8.9	9.8	1.8	1.7	1.8

Note: (1) Metropolitan Statistical Area - see Appendix A for areas included; (2) The proportion of households that are owners; (3) The proportion of the rental inventory that is vacant for rent; (4) The proportion of the homeowner inventory that is vacant for sale; (a) 2002 figures have been revised; n/a not available
Source: U.S. Census Bureau, Housing Vacancies and Homeownership Annual Statistics: 2003

COMMERCIAL REAL ESTATE

Industrial/Office Markets

Type/Market Area	Inventory (sq. ft.)	Vacant (sq. ft.)	Vacancy Rate (%)	Under Construction (sq. ft.)	Net Absorption (sq. ft.)
Industrial Space Jacksonville	82,990,736	8,232,681	9.92	1,245,500	1,202,300

Note: Data as of 4th Quarter, 2003; n/a not available
Source: Society of Industrial and Office Realtors, 2004 Comparative Statistics of Industrial and Office Real Estate Markets

COMMERCIAL UTILITIES

Typical Monthly Electric Bills

Area	Commercial Service ($/month)		Industrial Service ($/month)	
	12 kW demand 1,500 kWh	120 kW demand 30,000 kWh	1,000 kW demand 400,000 kWh	20,000 kW demand 10,000,000 kWh
City	98	1,870	20,974	461,743

Note: Based on rates in effect January 1, 2003
Source: Memphis Light, Gas and Water, 2003 Utility Bill Comparisons for Selected U.S. Cities

TRANSPORTATION

Means of Transportation to Work

Area	Car/Truck/Van		Public Transportation			Bicycle	Walked	Other Means	Worked at Home
	Drove Alone	Car-pooled	Bus	Subway	Railroad				
City	79.2	13.4	1.7	0.0	0.0	0.4	1.8	1.5	1.9
MSA[1]	80.3	12.6	1.3	0.0	0.0	0.5	1.7	1.4	2.3
U.S.	75.7	12.2	2.5	1.5	0.5	0.4	2.9	1.0	3.3

Note: Figures shown are percentages and cover workers 16 years of age and older;
(1) Metropolitan Statistical Area - see Appendix A for areas included
Source: Census 2000, Summary File 3

Travel Time to Work

Area	Less Than 15 Minutes	15 to 29 Minutes	30 to 44 Minutes	45 to 59 Minutes	60 Minutes or More
City	21.2	43.7	24.1	6.4	4.6
MSA[1]	22.2	38.8	24.4	8.7	5.9
U.S.	29.4	36.1	19.1	7.4	8.0

Note: Figures are percentages and include workers 16 years old and over; (1) Metropolitan Statistical Area - see Appendix A for areas included
Source: Census 2000, Summary File 3

Roadway Congestion Index

Area	1982	1990	1996	2000	2001
City	0.75	0.94	1.02	1.03	1.02
Average[1]	0.82	1.01	1.08	1.16	1.17

Note: Values greater than 1.00 indicate undesirable mobility levels; (1) average of 75 urban areas
Source: Texas Transportation Institute, The 2003 Annual Urban Mobility Report

Transportation Statistics

Interstate highways (2004)	I-10; I-95
Public transportation (2002)	Jacksonville Transportation Authority (JTA)
Buses	
Average fleet age in years	7.1
No. operated in max. service	139
Light rail	
Average fleet age in years	4.6 (automated guideway)
No. operated in max. service	6 (automated guideway)
Demand response	
Average fleet age in years	2.1
No. operated in max. service	105
Passenger air service	
Airport	Jacksonville International
Airlines (2003)	11
Boardings (2002)	2,462,399
Amtrak service (2004)	Yes
Major waterways/ports	St. Johns River

Source: Federal Transit Administration, National Transit Database, 2002; Editor & Publisher Market Guide, 2004; Bureau of Transportation Statistics, Airport Enplanement Activity for CY2002; www.amtrak.com

BUSINESSES

Major Business Headquarters

Company Name	2003 Rankings	
	Fortune 500	Forbes 500
Winn-Dixie Stores	149	-

Note: Companies listed are located in the city; dashes indicate no ranking
Fortune 500: Companies that produce a 10-K are ranked 1 to 500 based on 2002 revenue
Forbes 500: Private companies are ranked 1 to 281 based on 2002 revenue
Source: Fortune, April 14, 2003; www.forbes.com, November 6, 2003

Minority and Women-Owned Businesses

Ownership	All Firms		Firms with Paid Employees			
	Firms	Sales ($000)	Firms	Sales ($000)	Employees	Payroll ($000)
Black	3,220	158,486	497	(a)	1,000 - 2,499	(a)
Hispanic	739	195,321	230	182,503	1,211	34,554
Women	12,014	2,868,768	2,874	2,648,409	21,077	432,645

Note: Figures cover firms located in the city; (a) Withheld to avoid disclosure
Source: 1997 Economic Census, Minority and Women-Owned Businesses

Minority Business Opportunity

Two of the 500 largest Hispanic-owned companies in the U.S. are located in Jacksonville.
Hispanic Business, June 2003

Jacksonville is home to one company which is on the Hispanic Business Fastest-Growing 100 list (greatest sales growth over the past five years): **N.P. Construction of North Florida Inc.**.
Hispanic Business, July/August 2003

HOTELS

Hotels/Motels

Area	Hotels/Motels	Average Minimum Rates ($)		
		Tourist	First-Class	Deluxe
City	89	67	92	n/a

Note: n/a not available
Source: OAG Travel Planner Online, Spring 2004

Jacksonville is home to one of the top 100 hotels in the U.S. and Canada according to *Travel & Leisure*: **Ritz-Carlton (Amelia Island)** (#31). Criteria: value, rooms/ambience, location, facilities/activities and service. *Travel & Leisure, "The World's Best Hotels 2003"*

EVENT SITES

Major Event Sites, Meeting Places and Convention Centers

Name	Guest Rooms	Exhibit/ Meeting Space (sq. ft.)	Largest Meeting Room Capacity
ALLTEL Stadium	n/a	n/a	76,000
Adam's Mark Jacksonville	966	110,000	4,300
Florida Theatre	n/a	n/a	1,930
Jacksonville Veteran's Memorial Arena	n/a	n/a	16,000
Omni Jacksonville Hotel	354	14,000	700
Prime F. Osborn III Convention Center	n/a	78,500	5,500
Radisson Riverwalk Hotel Jacksonville	322	25,000	1,400
Morocco Shrine Auditorium	n/a	24,320	2,700
Times-Union Center for the Performing Arts	n/a	n/a	2,979

Note: n/a not available
Source: Original research

Living Environment

COST OF LIVING

Cost of Living Index

Year	Composite Index	Groceries	Housing	Utilities	Trans-portation	Health Care	Misc. Goods/Services
2001	91.7	101.7	86.3	84.1	93.9	88.3	93.2
2002	94.7	104.8	86.6	86.2	95.5	86.9	99.6
2003	91.2	102.9	82.3	89.3	95.1	79.9	94.8

Note: U.S. = 100
Source: ACCRA, Cost of Living Index, 2001, 2002 and 2003 4-Quarter Averages

HOUSING

House Price Index (HPI)

Area	National Ranking[2]	Quarterly Change (%)	One-Year Change (%)	Five-Year Change (%)
MSA[1]	75	4.32	9.18	48.48
U.S.[3]	-	3.67	7.97	41.81

Note: The HPI is a weighted repeat sales index. It measures average price changes in repeat sales or refinancings on the same properties. This information is obtained by reviewing repeat mortgage transactions on single-family properties whose mortgages have been purchased or securitized by Fannie Mae of Freddie Mac in January 1975; (1) Metropolitan Statistical Area - see Appendix A for areas included; (2) Rankings are based on annual percentage change, for all MSAs containing at least 15,000 transactions over the last 10 years and ranges from 1 to 220; (3) figures based on a weighted division average; all figures are for the period ended December 31, 2003
Source: Office of Federal Housing Enterprise Oversight, House Price Index, March 1, 2004

Housing: Year Structure Built

Area	1990 -2000	1980 -1989	1970 -1979	1960 -1969	1950 -1959	1940 -1949	Before 1940	Median Year
City	20.3	20.9	17.0	15.1	14.2	7.0	5.4	1975
MSA[1]	24.1	23.9	17.6	12.7	11.5	5.5	4.8	1979
U.S.	17.0	15.8	18.5	13.7	12.7	7.3	15.0	1971

Note: Figures are percentages; (1) Metropolitan Statistical Area - see Appendix A for areas included
Source: Census 2000, Summary File 3

Average New Home Price

Area	2001	2002	2003
City	174,853	191,044	193,957
U.S.	212,643	236,567	248,193

Note: Figures, in dollars, are based on a new home with 2,400 sq. ft. of living area on an 8,000 sq. ft. lot.
Source: ACCRA, Cost of Living Index, 2001, 2002 and 2003 4-Quarter Averages

Average Apartment Rent

Area	2001	2002	2003
City	696	780	700
U.S.	674	708	721

Note: Figures, in dollars per month, are based on an unfurnished two bedroom, 1-1/2 or 2 bath apartment, approximately 950 sq. ft. in size, excluding all utilities except water
Source: ACCRA, Cost of Living Index, 2001, 2002 and 2003 4-Quarter Averages

RESIDENTIAL UTILITIES

Average Residential Utility Costs

Area	All Electric ($/mth)	Part Electric ($/mth)	Other Energy ($/mth)	Phone ($/mth)
City	98.66	–	–	25.12
U.S.	116.46	65.82	62.68	23.90

Source: ACCRA, Cost of Living Index, 2003 4-Quarter Average

HEALTH CARE

Average Health Care Costs

Area	Hospital ($/day)	Doctor ($/visit)	Dentist ($/visit)
City	495.50	62.50	59.50
U.S.	678.35	67.91	83.90

Note: Hospital—based on a semi-private room; Doctor—based on a general practitioner's routine exam of an established patient; Dentist—based on adult teeth cleaning and periodic oral exam.
Source: ACCRA, Cost of Living Index, 2003 4-Quarter Average

Distribution of Non-Federal, Office-Based Physicians

Area	Total	Family/ General Practice	Specialties		
			Medical	Surgical	Other
MSA[1] (number)	2,054	303	691	501	559
MSA[1] (rate per 10,000 pop.)	18.7	2.8	6.3	4.6	5.1
Metro Average[2] (rate per 10,000 pop.)	33.1	2.2	7.7	4.8	5.6

Note: Data as of December 31, 2001; (1) Metropolitan Statistical Area - see Appendix A for areas included; (2) Average of 81 MSAs and CMSAs in this book
Source: American Medical Association, Physician Characteristics & Distribution in the U.S., 2003-2004

Hospitals

Jacksonville has the following hospitals: 6 general medical and surgical; 1 psychiatric; 1 rehabilitation; 1 long-term acute care.
AHA Guide to the Healthcare Field, 2003-2004

According to *U.S. News,* Jacksonville has two of the best hospitals in the U.S.: **Mayo Clinic**; **St. Vincent's Medical Center**; *U.S. News Online, "America's Best Hospitals 2003"*

PRESIDENTIAL ELECTION

2000 Presidential Election Results

Area	Gore	Bush	Nader	Buchanan	Other
Duval County	40.7	57.5	1.0	0.2	0.5
U.S.	48.4	47.9	2.7	0.4	0.6

Note: Results are percentages and may not add to 100% due to rounding
Source: www.cbsnews.com; www.uselectionatlas.org

EDUCATION

Public School District Statistics

District Name	Schls.	Enroll-ment	Classroom Teachers	Pupil/ Teacher Ratio	Minority Pupils[1] (%)	Current Expend.[2] ($/pupil)
Duval County SD	178	127,392	6,478	19.7	49.8	5,354

Note: Data covers the 2001-02 school year unless otherwise noted; (1) Fall 2000; (2) FY2000; n/a not available
Source: U.S. Department of Education, National Center for Education Statistics, Common Core of Data, Local Education Agency (School District) Universe Survey: School Year 2001-2002; U.S. Department of Education, National Center for Education Statistics, Digest of Education Statistics 2002

Educational Quality

School District	Education Quotient[1]	Graduate Outcome[2]	Community Index[3]	Resource Index[4]
Duval County	31	34	47	22

Note: Scores are national percentile rankings and range from 1 (worst) to 99 (best); (1) Combination of the Graduate Outcome, Community and Resource indexes weighted to reflect the greater importance of the Graduate Outcome and Resource Index; (2) Based on graduation rates and college board scores (SAT/ACT); (3) Based on the surrounding community's level of affluence and adult education; (4) Based on teacher salaries, per-pupil expenditures and student-teacher ratios.
Source: Expansion Management, December 2003

Educational Attainment by Race

Area	High School Graduate (%)					Bachelor's Degree (%)				
	Total	White	Black	Asian	Hisp.[2]	Total	White	Black	Asian	Hisp.[2]
City	82.3	85.4	74.2	81.5	79.0	21.1	23.7	13.2	34.7	21.9
MSA[1]	83.6	86.2	74.0	81.5	79.5	22.9	25.0	13.2	35.2	21.4
U.S.	80.4	83.6	72.3	80.4	52.4	24.4	26.1	14.3	44.1	10.4

Note: Figures shown cover persons 25 years old and over; (1) Metropolitan Statistical Area - see Appendix A for areas included; (2) people of Hispanic origin can be of any race
Source: Census 2000, Summary File 3

School Enrollment by Type

Area	Grades KG to 8				Grades 9 to 12			
	Public		Private		Public		Private	
	Enrollment	%	Enrollment	%	Enrollment	%	Enrollment	%
City	88,145	85.4	15,094	14.6	35,819	86.6	5,563	13.4
MSA[1]	131,666	86.5	20,471	13.5	55,375	88.2	7,379	11.8
U.S.	33,526,011	88.7	4,285,121	11.3	14,848,628	90.6	1,532,323	9.4

Note: Figures shown cover persons 3 years old and over; (1) Metropolitan Statistical Area - see Appendix A for areas included
Source: Census 2000, Summary File 3

School Enrollment by Race

Area	Grades KG to 8 (%)				Grades 9 to 12 (%)			
	White	Black	Asian	Hisp.[1]	White	Black	Asian	Hisp.[1]
City	54.5	38.4	2.3	4.5	54.0	38.8	2.9	4.9
MSA[2]	64.6	29.0	1.9	4.4	64.2	28.7	2.5	5.0
U.S.	68.5	15.5	3.3	16.8	68.8	15.5	3.8	15.7

Note: Figures shown cover persons 3 years old and over; (1) people of Hispanic origin can be of any race; (2) Metropolitan Statistical Area - see Appendix A for areas included
Source: Census 2000, Summary File 3

Classroom Teacher Salaries in Public Schools

District	B.A. Degree		M.A. Degree		Maximum	
	Min. ($)	Rank[1]	Max. ($)	Rank[1]	Max. ($)	Rank[1]
Jacksonville	28,155	82	51,600	57	54,647	70
DOD Average[2]	31,567	-	53,248	-	59,356	-

Note: Salaries are for 2001-2002; (1) Rank ranges from 1 to 100; (2) As per the U.S. Department of Defense Wage Fixing Authority
Source: American Federation of Teachers, Survey & Analysis of Teacher Salary Trends 2002

Higher Education

Four-Year Colleges			Two-Year Colleges			Medical Schools	Law Schools	Voc/Tech
Public	Private Non-profit	Private For-profit	Public	Private Non-profit	Private For-profit			
1	8	4	1	0	3	0	1	11

Note: Figures cover institutions located within the city limits.
Source: National Center for Education Statistics, The Integrated Postsecondary Education System (IPEDS) Peer Analysis System, 2002; usnews.com, America's Best Graduate Schools 2004, Medical School Directory; The College Blue Book, Occupational Education, 2003; Barron's Guide to Law Schools, 2003; Medical School Admission Requirements U.S. & Canada, 2003-2004

MAJOR EMPLOYERS

Major Employers

Company Name	Industry	Type
Alltel Mortgage Info Svcs	Data processing and preparation	Single
Amelia Island Plantation	Hotels and motels	Headquarters
Baptist Medical Center	General medical and surgical hospitals	Headquarters
BellSouth	Telephone communication, except radio	Branch
Blue Cross/Blue Shield of Fla	Hospital and medical service plans	Branch
Chase Manhattan	Mortgage bankers and correspondents	Branch
City of JaxCommunications Office	Finance, taxation, and monetary policy	Branch
Convergys	Business services, nec	Branch
Florida Times Union The	Newspapers	Branch
Kelley-Clarke Inc	Business services, nec	Single
Marketplace	Grocery stores	Headquarters
Mayo Clinic Jacksonville Inc	Offices and clinics of medical doctors	Headquarters
Memorial Hospital Jacksonville	General medical and surgical hospitals	Single
Naval Regional Medical Center	General medical and surgical hospitals	Branch
Northrop Grumman Systems Corp	Aircraft	Branch
Personnel Department	Air, water, and solid waste management	Branch
Saint Johns County School Dist	Elementary and secondary schools	Headquarters
Saint Vincents Medical Center	General medical and surgical hospitals	Headquarters
St Johns County/Summary Court	Courts	Branch
St Lukes Hospital	General medical and surgical hospitals	Headquarters
University Health Groups	Real estate agents and managers	Headquarters
Vistakon	Ophthalmic goods	Headquarters

Note: Companies shown are located in the metropolitan area and have 1,000 or more employees.
Source: www.zapdata.com, March 2004

PUBLIC SAFETY

Crime Rate

Area	All Crimes	Violent Crimes				Property Crimes		
		Murder	Forcible Rape	Robbery	Aggrav. Assault	Burglary	Larceny -Theft	Motor Vehicle Theft
City	6,632.5	11.7	36.0	262.1	605.8	1,192.5	3,820.7	703.8
Suburbs[1]	4,186.5	3.1	34.9	90.9	549.9	792.8	2,414.6	300.3
MSA[2]	5,821.5	8.9	35.6	205.3	587.2	1,059.9	3,354.5	570.0
U.S.	4,118.8	5.6	33.0	145.9	310.1	746.2	2,445.8	432.1

Note: Figures are crimes per 100,000 population; (1) All areas within the MSA that are located outside the city limits; (2) Metropolitan Statistical Area - see Appendix A for areas included
Source: FBI Uniform Crime Reports, 2002

RECREATION

Culture and Recreation

Museums	Orchestras	Opera Companies	Dance Companies	Professional Theatres	Zoos	Pro Sports Teams[1]
8	1	0	2	1	1	1

Note: (1) Covers the Metropolitan Statistical Area - see Appendix A for areas included.
Source: The Grey House Performing Arts Directory, 2002; Official Museum Directory, 2004; www.sportsvenues.com

Library System

The Jacksonville Public Library has 15 branches, holdings of 2,349,482 volumes, and a budget of $22,596,598 (2002-2003).
American Library Directory, 2003-2004

MEDIA

Newspapers

Name	Type	Freq.	Distribution	Circulation
The Florida Times-Union	General	7x/wk	Regional	197,706
Jacksonville Advocate	Black	1x/wk	Area	36,000
Jacksonville Free Press	Black	1x/wk	U.S./Int'l	36,230
Northeast Florida Advocate	Black	1x/wk	United States	35,017
The Veteran Voice	General	1x/mth	Regional	10,000

Note: Includes newspapers whose offices are located in the city and whose circulations are 10,000 or more
Source: Burrelle's Media Directory, 2003

Television Stations

Name	Ch.	Affiliation	Type	Owner
WJXT	3	n/a	Commercial	Post-Newsweek Stations Inc.
WJCT	7	PBS	Commercial	WJCT Inc.
WTLV	12	NBCT	Commercial	Gannett Broadcasting
WJWB	17	WB	Commercial	Media General Inc.
WJXX	25	ABCT	Commercial	Gannett Broadcasting
WAWS	30	FBC	Commercial	Clear Channel Communications Inc.
WTEV	47	CBST	Commercial	n/a
WJEB	59	n/a	Non-comm.	Jacksonville Educators Broadcasting Corp.

Note: Stations included broadcast from the Jacksonville metro area; n/a not available
Source: Burrelle's Media Directory, 2003

AM Radio Stations

Call Letters	Freq. (kHz)	Target Audience	Station Format	Music Format
WOKV	690	General	N/T	n/a
WFXJ	930	General	M/N	n/a
WNZS	930	General	S	n/a
WIOJ	1010	Religious	M/T	Christian
WROS	1050	Christian	General	Religious
WJAX	1220	General	M	Easy Listening
WJGR	1320	General	N/S/T	n/a
WCGL	1360	B/R	M/T	Christian
WZAZ	1400	Religious	M	Christian
WZNZ	1460	General	N/S/T	n/a
WOBS	1530	Religious	E/M/N/T	Christian
WQOP	1600	General	T	n/a

Note: Stations included broadcast from the Jacksonville metro area; n/a not available
The following abbreviations may be used:
Target Audience: A=Asian; B=Black; C=Christian; E=Ethnic; F=French; G=General; H=Hispanic; M=Men; N=Native American; R=Religious; S=Senior Citizen; W=Women; Y=Young Adult; Z=Children
Station Format: E=Educational; M=Music; N=News; S=Sports; T=Talk
Source: Burrelle's Media Directory, 2003

FM Radio Stations

Call Letters	Freq. (mHz)	Target Audience	Station Format	Music Format
WJFR	88.7	Religious	E/M/N	Christian
WJCT	89.9	General	M/N/T	Classical
WKTZ	90.9	General	M	Easy Listening
WNLE	91.7	Religious	E/M/N	Christian
WJBT	92.7	B/G	M/N/T	Rhythm & Blues
WPLA	93.3	General	M/N	Alternative
WAPE	95.1	General	M/N/T	Top 40
WEJZ	96.1	General	M	Adult Contemporary
WKQL	96.9	General	M	Oldies
WFKS	97.9	General	M/N/T	Rhythm & Blues
WQIK	99.1	General	M/N	Country
WSOL	101.5	Black	M/N/S	Adult Contemporary
WMXQ	102.9	General	M/N/S	Adult Contemporary
WFYV	104.5	General	M	AOR
WBGB	106.5	Christian	M/N/T	Christian
WROO	107.3	General	E/M/N/S	Country

Note: Stations included broadcast from the Jacksonville metro area
The following abbreviations may be used:
Target Audience: A=Asian; B=Black; C=Christian; E=Ethnic; F=French; G=General; H=Hispanic;
M=Men; N=Native American; R=Religious; S=Senior Citizen; W=Women; Y=Young Adult; Z=Children
Station Format: E=Educational; M=Music; N=News; S=Sports; T=Talk
Music Format: AOR=Album Oriented Rock; MOR=Middle of the Road
Source: Burrelle's Media Directory, 2003

CLIMATE

Average and Extreme Temperatures

Temperature	Jan	Feb	Mar	Apr	May	Jun	Jul	Aug	Sep	Oct	Nov	Dec	Yr.
Extreme High (°F)	84	88	91	95	100	103	103	102	98	96	88	84	103
Average High (°F)	65	68	74	80	86	90	92	91	87	80	73	67	79
Average Temp. (°F)	54	57	62	69	75	80	83	82	79	71	62	56	69
Average Low (°F)	43	45	51	57	64	70	73	73	70	61	51	44	58
Extreme Low (°F)	7	22	23	34	45	47	61	63	48	36	21	11	7

Note: Figures cover the years 1948-1990
Source: National Climatic Data Center, International Station Meteorological Climate Summary, 9/96

Average Precipitation/Snowfall/Humidity

Precip./Humidity	Jan	Feb	Mar	Apr	May	Jun	Jul	Aug	Sep	Oct	Nov	Dec	Yr.
Avg. Precip. (in.)	3.0	3.7	3.8	3.0	3.6	5.3	6.2	7.4	7.8	3.7	2.0	2.6	52.0
Avg. Snowfall (in.)	Tr	Tr	Tr	0	0	0	0	0	0	0	0	Tr	0
Avg. Rel. Hum. 7am (%)	86	86	87	86	86	88	89	91	92	91	89	88	88
Avg. Rel. Hum. 4pm (%)	56	53	50	49	54	61	64	65	66	62	58	58	58

Note: Figures cover the years 1948-1990; Tr = Trace amounts (<0.05 in. of rain; <0.5 in. of snow)
Source: National Climatic Data Center, International Station Meteorological Climate Summary, 9/96

Weather Conditions

Temperature			Daytime Sky			Precipitation		
10°F & below	32°F & below	90°F & above	Clear	Partly cloudy	Cloudy	0.01 inch or more precip.	0.1 inch or more snow/ice	Thunder-storms
< 1	16	83	86	181	98	114	1	65

Note: Figures are average number of days per year and covers the years 1948-1990
Source: National Climatic Data Center, International Station Meteorological Climate Summary, 9/96

HAZARDOUS WASTE

Superfund Sites

Jacksonville has three hazardous waste sites on the EPA's Superfund National Priorities List: **Cecil Field Naval Air Station; Jacksonville Naval Air Station; Pickettville Road Landfill.**
U.S. Environmental Protection Agency, National Priorities List, March 15, 2004

AIR & WATER QUALITY

Maximum Pollutant Concentrations

	Particulate Matter (ug/m³)	Carbon Monoxide (ppm)	Sulfur Dioxide (ppm)	Nitrogen Dioxide (ppm)	Ozone 1-hour (ppm)	Ozone 8-hour (ppm)	Lead (ug/m³)
MSA[1] Level	119	3	0.054	0.015	0.09	0.07	0.01
NAAQS[2]	150	9	0.140	0.053	0.12	0.08	1.50
Met NAAQS[2]	Yes	Yes	Yes	Yes	Yes	Yes	Yes

Note: (1) Metropolitan Statistical Area - see Appendix A for areas included; (2) National Ambient Air Quality Standards; n/a not available
Units: ppm = parts per million; ug/m³ = micrograms per cubic meter
Source: EPA, Latest Findings on National Air Quality: 2002 Status and Trends, August 2003

Air Quality Index

In the Jacksonville MSA (see Appendix A for areas included), the Air Quality Index (AQI) exceeded 100 on 1 day in 2002. An AQI value greater than 100 indicates that air quality would have been in the unhealthful range on that day.
EPA, Latest Findings on National Air Quality: 2002 Status and Trends, August 2003

Watershed Health

The U.S. Environmental Protection Agency monitors the health of the aquatic resources for the nation's 2,000+ watersheds. **The Lower St. Johns watershed serves the Jacksonville area and received an overall Index of Watershed Indicators (IWI) score of 6 (more serious problems - high vulnerability).** The IWI score is based on seven condition and nine vulnerability indicators. The overall IWI score ranges from 1 (best health) to 6 (worst health). The Condition Indicators include: designated use attainment, fish and wildlife consumption advisories, source water condition, contaminated sediments, ambient water quality, and wetlands loss index. The Vulnerability Indicators include: aquatic species at risk, conventional and toxic loads over permitted limits, urban and agricultural runoff potential, population change, hydrologic modification, estuarine pollution susceptibility, and air deposition. *EPA, Index of Watershed Indicators, October 26, 2001*

Drinking Water

Water System Name	Pop. Served	Primary Water Source Type	Number of Violations January 2002-February 2004		
			Health Based	Significant Monitoring	Monitoring
JEA-North Grid	420,989	Ground	None	None	None
JEA-South Grid	396,461	Ground	None	None	2

Note: Data as of February 19, 2004
Source: EPA, Office of Ground Water and Drinking Water, Safe Drinking Water Information System

Jacksonville tap water is alkaline, very hard and naturally fluoridated.
Editor & Publisher Market Guide, 2004

Knoxville, Tennessee

Background

Home of the Tennessee Valley Authority, "Bleak House" (Confederate Memorial Hall), and the 1982 World's Fair, Knoxville's central business district reflects every period of its history. Knoxville was settled at the end of the eighteenth century when a flood of pioneers migrated to Tennessee. It soon established itself as the gateway to the West. In 1791, William Blount, its first territorial governor, chose James White's Fort as the capital of the territory, subsequently renaming it for Secretary of War, James Knox.

The city played an important part in the Civil War and was occupied by both the Confederate and Union armies. Knoxville rapidly recovered during Reconstruction and became the business center of the east Tennessee Valley.

Metropolitan Knoxville is home to many widely diversified industries. Aluminum and clothing constitute the primary manufactured products. Automobile parts and pre-fabricated homes, fiberglass boats, and health-care products are some of its other products.

The U.S. Department of Energy facility at Oak Ridge, which is close by, was built during World War II to develop the atomic bomb. The facility is the area's largest employer, with more than 12,000 people working there. The second- and third-largest employers are educational in nature: the University of Tennessee, Knoxville, and Knox County Public School System employ more than 17,000 area residents.

Through the years, Knoxville has played host to numerous sports championships: the 1988 National Chess Championship for elementary school children; the 1993 A.A.U. Junior Olympic Games; the 1996 National Gymnastics Championship; and the 1997 Super National Scholastic Chess Championships—the largest ever held in the United States and possibly the world. Pulitzer Prize-winner James Agee is Knoxville's native son. The author fondly depicts his background in a number of his works.

The city is located where the Holston and French Broad rivers meet to create the Tennessee River, about 110 miles northeast of Chattanooga. It lies in a broad valley between the Cumberland Mountains to the northwest and the Great Smoky Mountains to the southeast. The Cumberland Mountains weaken the force of cold winter air, which frequently moves south of Knoxville, and modifies the hot summer winds common to the plains to the west. The topography also creates winds that are generally light and discourages tornadoes.

Rankings

- Knoxville was ranked #103 out of 331 metro areas in *Cities Ranked & Rated*. Criteria: cost of living; climate; crime; transportation; economy and jobs; education; arts and culture; health and healthcare; leisure. *Cities Ranked & Rated, 1st Edition, 2004*

- *Ladies Home Journal* ranked America's 200 largest cities based on the qualities women surveyed care about most. Knoxville ranked #113 out of 143 in the smaller city category (population under 300,000). Criteria: crime; lifestyle; education; jobs; health; child care; politics; and the economy. *Ladies Home Journal Online, "The Best Cities for Women 2002"*

- The Knoxville metro area was selected as one of America's "Best Places to Live and Work" by *Expansion Management* and rated as a "Four-Star Community." The annual "Quality of Life Quotient" measures nearly 50 indicators and compares them among the 329 metropolitan statistical areas in the United States. *Expansion Management, May 2003*

- *Forbes* ranked the 150 most populous metro areas in the U.S. in terms of the "Best Places for Business and Careers." The Knoxville metro area was ranked #22. Criteria: income and job growth; cost-of-doing-business; qualifications of the available pool of labor; crime rates; housing costs; net migration. *Forbes, May 9, 2003*

- *Men's Health* ranked 101 U.S. cities in terms of the quality of their tap water. Knoxville received a grade of. Criteria: levels of bacteria, arsenic, lead, trihalomethanes, and haloacetic acids were compared with the National Academy of Science's guidelines as well as with the EPA's more stringent maximum contaminant level goals. *Men's Health, March 2004*

- Sperling's BestPlaces ranked 331 metro areas and identified the most and least stressful U.S. cities. The Knoxville metro area ranked #76 out of the 100 largest metro areas (#1 = most stressful). Criteria: divorce rate; unemployment rate; violent and property crime; suicide rate; commute time; mental health; alcohol consumption; cloudy days. *www.BestPlaces.net, February 26, 2004*

- Knoxville was ranked #141 out of America's 200 largest metro areas in *SELF Magazine's* ranking of "America's Healthiest Cities for Women." Criteria: safety; air/water quality; cancer rates; and 21 other factors relating to health. *SELF Magazine, November 2003*

- Knoxville was ranked #71 out of 100 cities surveyed in *Child* magazine's ranking of the "Best Cities for Families." Criteria: number of pediatricians per capita; proximity to a children's hospital; immunization rates; infant mortality rate; air quality; water quality; school spending; pupil-teacher ratio; availability of parks/green space; nearby recreational opportunities; average commute time; number of sunny days; average cost of a 3-bedroom home; unemployment rate; future job growth; crime rate; percentage of children under 5; mandated minimum child care ratios. *Child, April 2001*

- *Zero Population Growth* ranked 239 cities in terms of children's health, safety, and economic well-being. Knoxville was ranked #63 out of 140 independent cities (cities with populations greater than 100,000 which were neither major cities nor suburbs/outer cities) and was given a grade of B. Criteria: total population and population growth; percent of population under 18 years of age; number of children's museums; health improvement grade; percent of births to teens; percent of low birthweight infants; infant mortality rate; number of Title X-funded clinics; average SAT/ACT scores; average elementary and secondary class size; crime rate; unemployment rate; percent of affordable homes; number of bad air days; park acres per 1000 persons; library circulation per child; and children's program attendance counts. *Zero Population Growth, Kid Friendly Cities Report Card 2001*

- *Ladies Home Journal* ranked America's 200 largest cities in terms of safety. Knoxville ranked #119 out of 200. Criteria: violent crimes; crimes against property; and rape. *Ladies Home Journal Online, "The Best Cities for Women 2002"*

- The Knoxville metro area was selected by *Yahoo! Internet Life* as one of "America's Most Wired Cities...and Towns." The area ranked #60 out of 87. Criteria: home and work net use; user sophistication; domain density; and available content. *Yahoo! Internet Life, April 2001*

- Knoxville was identified as one of the 100 "Most Unwired Cities" in the U.S. The area ranked #90. Criteria: number of public and commercial wireless access points; cell phone coverage offering wide area network Internet access; Internet penetration. *Intel, "Most Unwired Cities," March 4, 2003*

- Scarborough Research measured the percentage of households who subscribe to cellular services among adults ages 18 and over in 75 U.S. markets. The Knoxville DMA (Designated Market Area) was ranked #57 out of 75. *Scarborough Research, Scarborough USA+ 2003 Release 1*

- Knoxville was ranked #118 in *Prevention* magazine's survey of the "Best Walking Cities in the U.S." The magazine, in conjunction with the American Podiatric Medical Association, surveyed 125 of the most populated cities and then tabulated and weighed 20 criteria of interest to pedestrians. *Prevention, April, 2004*

- The Knoxville metro area was cited as one of "The Best Places in the U.S. to Locate a Company." The area ranked #60 out of 329. Criteria: education (with emphasis on college board test results and high school graduation rates); availability of quality healthcare services and the cost to employers; quality of life; logistics workforce and companies; transportation infrastructure; quality and quantity of highly educated technical workers; business climate. *Expansion Management, July 2003*

- The Knoxville metro area appeared on *Forbes/Milken Institute* list of "Best Places for Business and Career." Rank: #107 out of 200 metro areas. Criteria: salary growth; job growth; number of technology clusters; overall concentration of technology activity relative to national average; and technology output growth. *www.forbes.com, Forbes/Milken Institute Best Places 2002*

- The Knoxville metro area appeared on the "Milken Institute Best Performing Cities" index. Rank: #48 out of 200 large metro areas. Criteria: job growth; wage and salary growth; high-tech output growth. *Milken Institute, June 25, 2003*

- The Knoxville metro area appeared on *IndustryWeek's* fourth annual World-Class Communities list. It ranked #195 out of 315 metro areas. Criteria: MSA Gross Metropolitan Product (GMP) per manufacturing employee; and MSA percent share of U.S. manufacturing Gross Domestic Product (GDP). *IndustryWeek, April 16, 2001*

- ING Group ranked the 125 largest metro areas according to the general financial security of residents. The Knoxville metro area was ranked #75 out of 125. Criteria: Earnings and Wealth Potential (household income, education, net assets, cost of living); Safety Net (health insurance, retirement savings, life insurance, income support programs); Personal Threats (unemployment rate, low-income households, crime rate); Community Economic Vitality (cost of community services, job quality, job creation, housing costs). *ING Group, "The Best Cities to Earn and Save Money: A Ranking of the Largest 125 U.S. Cities," 2001 Edition*

Business Environment

CITY FINANCES

City Government Finances

Component	2000-2001 ($000)	2000-2001 ($ per capita)
Total Revenues	761,799	4,381
Total Expenditures	834,511	4,799
Debt Outstanding	394,241	2,267
Cash and Securities	641,022	3,686

Source: U.S Census Bureau, Government Finances 2000-2001, August 2003

City Government Revenue by Source

Source	2000-2001 ($000)	2000-2001 ($ per capita)
General Revenue		
From Federal Government	19,510	112
From State Government	39,002	224
From Local Governments	15,556	89
Taxes		
Property	74,123	426
Sales	55,101	317
Personal Income	0	0
License	0	0
Charges	32,920	189
Liquor Store	0	0
Utility	456,114	2,623
Employee Retirement	27,884	160
Other	41,589	239

Source: U.S Census Bureau, Government Finances 2000-2001, August 2003

City Government Expenditures by Function

Function	2000-2001 ($000)	2000-2001 ($ per capita)	2000-2001 (%)
General Expenditures			
Airports	0	0	0.0
Corrections	0	0	0.0
Education	115	1	0.0
Fire Protection	26,432	152	3.2
Governmental Administration	119,369	686	14.3
Health	0	0	0.0
Highways	53,269	306	6.4
Hospitals	0	0	0.0
Housing and Community Development	14,336	82	1.7
Interest on General Debt	10,705	62	1.3
Libraries	0	0	0.0
Parking	785	5	0.1
Parks and Recreation	20,189	116	2.4
Police Protection	37,536	216	4.5
Public Welfare	8,307	48	1.0
Sewerage	26,875	155	3.2
Solid Waste Management	7,787	45	0.9
Liquor Store	0	0	0.0
Utility	445,446	2,562	53.4
Employee Retirement	20,781	120	2.5
Other	42,579	245	5.1

Source: U.S Census Bureau, Government Finances 2000-2001, August 2003

Municipal Bond Ratings

Area	Moody's
City	Aaa

Source: Mergent Bond Record, February 2004

DEMOGRAPHICS

Population Growth

Area	1990 Census	2000 Census	2003 Estimate	2008 Projection	Population Growth (%)	
					1990-2000	2000-2008
City	173,288	173,890	172,155	169,563	0.3	-2.5
MSA[1]	585,970	687,249	704,383	733,195	17.3	6.7
U.S.	248,709,873	281,421,906	290,647,163	305,918,071	13.2	8.7

Note: (1) Metropolitan Statistical Area - see Appendix A for areas included
Source: Claritas, Inc.

Number of Households and Average Household Size

Area	1990 Census	2000 Census	2003 Estimate	2008 Projection	2003 Average Household Size
City	73,148	76,650	76,870	77,354	2.2
MSA[1]	231,258	281,472	291,800	309,677	2.4
U.S.	91,947,410	105,480,101	109,440,059	116,034,472	2.7

Note: (1) Metropolitan Statistical Area - see Appendix A for areas included
Source: Claritas, Inc.

Race and Ethnicity

Area	White Non-Hispanic	Black Non-Hispanic	Asian Non-Hispanic	Other Race Non-Hispanic	Hispanic
City	78.9	16.8	1.5	2.8	1.7
MSA[1]	91.1	5.8	1.0	2.0	1.4
U.S.	74.5	12.4	3.8	9.3	13.2

Note: Figures are 2003 estimates; (1) Metropolitan Statistical Area - see Appendix A for areas included
Source: Claritas, Inc.

Segregation

City		MSA[1]	
Index[2]	Rank[3]	Index[2]	Rank[4]
59.6	50	63.2	119

Note: Figures are based on an analysis of Census 2000 data; (1) Metropolitan Statistical Area - see Appendix A for areas included; (2) Dissimilarity Index—the most commonly used measure of segregation between two groups, reflecting their relative distributions across neighborhoods within a city or metropolitan area. It can range in value from 0, indicating complete integration, to 100, indicating complete segregation; (3) Ranges from 1 (most segregated) to 100 (least segregated) and includes all the cities in this book; (4) Ranges from 1 (most segregated) to 318 (least segregated) and includes 318 metropolitan areas.
Source: www.CensusScope.org

Ancestry

Area	German	Irish[2]	English	American	Italian	Polish	French[3]	Scottish
City	10.0	9.9	10.2	13.3	1.9	0.9	1.7	2.5
MSA[1]	11.2	10.9	11.4	17.4	1.8	1.0	2.0	2.5
U.S.	15.2	10.9	8.7	7.3	5.6	3.2	3.0	1.7

Note: Figures include multiple ancestry (e.g. if a person reported being Irish and Italian, they were included in both columns); (1) Metropolitan Statistical Area - see Appendix A for areas included; (2) Includes Celtic; (3) Includes Alsatian but excludes Basque
Source: Census 2000, Summary File 3

Foreign-Born Population

Area	Percent of Population Born in:							
	Any Foreign Country	Europe	Asia	Africa	Oceania[2]	Canada	Mexico	Latin America[3]
City	3.0	0.9	1.2	0.1	0.0	0.1	0.4	0.3
MSA[1]	2.1	0.6	0.8	0.1	0.0	0.1	0.3	0.2
U.S.	11.1	1.7	2.9	0.3	0.1	0.3	3.3	2.5

Note: (1) Metropolitan Statistical Area - see Appendix A for areas included; (2) Includes Australia, New Zealand subregion, Melanesia, Micronesia, Polynesia, and Oceania n.e.c; (3) Includes Central America (excluding Mexico), South America, and the Caribbean.
Source: Census 2000, Summary File 3

Religion

Area	Catholic	Southern Baptist	United Methodist	ELCA[1]	LDS[2]	Presbyterian Church USA	Jewish Est.	Muslim Est.
County	4.0	31.5	8.4	0.7	0.4	2.6	0.5	0.9
U.S.	22.0	7.1	3.7	1.8	1.5	1.1	2.2	0.6

Note: Figures shown are the number of adherents as a percentage of the total population; Adherents are defined as all members, including full members, their children and the estimated number of other participants who are not considered members (e.g. the baptized, those not confirmed, those not eligible for communion, those regularly attending services, etc.); (1) Evangelical Lutheran Church in America; (2) The Church of Jesus Christ of Latter Day Saints
Source: Reprinted with permission from Religious Congregations and Membership in the United States 2000 (Nashville, Glenmary Research Center, 2002) Copyright Association of Statisticians of American Religious Bodies. All rights reserved.

Age Distribution

Area	Percent of Population						
	Under Age 5	Age 5 to 17	Age 18 to 34	Age 35 to 49	Age 50 to 64	Age 65 to 79	80 Years and Over
City	5.8	13.8	32.4	20.4	13.2	10.3	4.1
MSA[1]	6.0	16.6	23.8	23.5	16.7	10.2	3.3
U.S.	6.8	18.9	23.7	23.5	14.8	9.2	3.2

Note: (1) Metropolitan Statistical Area - see Appendix A for areas included
Source: Census 2000, Summary File 3

Marriage Status

Area	Never Married	Now Married Except Separated	Separated	Widowed	Divorced
City	34.6	41.6	2.2	8.4	13.3
MSA[1]	22.7	57.5	1.5	7.0	11.4
U.S.	27.1	54.4	2.2	6.6	9.7

Note: Figures cover population 15 years of age and older; (1) Metropolitan Statistical Area - see Appendix A for areas included
Source: Census 2000, Summary File 3

Male/Female Ratio

Area	Males	Females	Males per 100 Females
City	81,851	90,304	90.6
MSA[1]	340,800	363,583	93.7
U.S.	142,511,883	148,135,280	96.2

Note: Figures are 2003 estimates; (1) Metropolitan Statistical Area - see Appendix A for areas included
Source: Claritas, Inc.

ECONOMY

Gross Metropolitan Product

Area	1999	2000	2001	2002	2002 Rank[2]
MSA[1]	20.1	21.1	22.0	23.5	80

Note: Figures are in billions of dollars; (1) Metropolitan Statistical Area - see Appendix A for areas included; (2) Rank ranges from 1 to 319
Source: The U.S. Conference of Mayors, Metro Economies Report, July 2003

INCOME

Per Capita/Median/Average Income

Area	Per Capita ($)	Median Household ($)	Average Household ($)
City	19,971	30,976	43,541
MSA[1]	23,235	41,624	55,515
U.S.	24,078	46,868	63,207

Note: Figures are 2003 estimates; (1) Metropolitan Statistical Area - see Appendix A for areas included
Source: Claritas, Inc.

Household Income Distribution

Area	Percent of Households Earning							
	Under $15,000	$15,000 -24,999	$25,000 -34,999	$35,000 -49,999	$50,000 -74,999	$75,000 -99,000	$100,000 -149,999	$150,000 and up
City	25.3	16.4	14.0	16.1	14.2	6.6	4.9	2.7
MSA[1]	16.4	13.1	13.0	16.8	18.6	9.8	8.0	4.2
U.S.	14.1	11.5	11.7	16.0	19.2	11.3	10.2	6.0

Note: Figures are 2003 estimates; (1) Metropolitan Statistical Area - see Appendix A for areas included
Source: Claritas, Inc.

Poverty Rates by Age

Area	All Ages	Under 5 Years Old	5 to 17 Years Old	18 to 64 Years Old	65 Years and Over
City	20.8	1.9	3.5	13.7	1.7
MSA[1]	12.0	1.1	2.4	7.3	1.3
U.S.	12.4	1.2	3.0	6.9	1.2

Note: Figures are percent of population with income in 1999 below poverty level and only include population for whom poverty status is determined; (1) Metropolitan Statistical Area - see Appendix A for areas included
Source: Census 2000, Summary File 3

Personal Bankruptcy Filing Rate

Area	2002	2003
Knox County	6.48	6.71
U.S.	5.34	5.58

Note: Numbers are per 1,000 population and include Chapter 7 and Chapter 13 filings
Source: Federal Deposit Insurance Corporation (FDIC), Regional Economic Conditions (RECON), 2/25/2004

EMPLOYMENT

Labor Force and Employment

Area	Civilian Labor Force			Workers Employed		
	Dec. 2002	Dec. 2003	% Chg.	Dec. 2002	Dec. 2003	% Chg.
City	99,236	98,441	-0.8	96,228	94,921	-1.4
MSA[1]	379,630	376,118	-0.9	368,178	363,179	-1.4
U.S.	144,807,000	146,501,000	1.2	136,599,000	138,556,000	1.4

Note: Data is not seasonally adjusted and covers workers 16 years of age and older;
(1) Metropolitan Statistical Area - see Appendix A for areas included
Source: Bureau of Labor Statistics, http://stats.bls.gov

Unemployment Rate

Area	2003											
	Jan.	Feb.	Mar.	Apr.	May	Jun.	Jul.	Aug.	Sep.	Oct.	Nov.	Dec.
City	3.5	3.5	3.2	3.2	3.4	4.1	3.8	3.8	3.6	3.8	4.0	3.6
MSA[1]	4.3	4.1	3.7	3.2	3.0	3.5	3.3	3.2	3.1	3.2	3.6	3.4
U.S.	6.5	6.4	6.2	5.8	5.8	6.5	6.3	6.0	5.8	5.6	5.6	5.4

Note: Data is not seasonally adjusted and covers workers 16 years of age and older; All figures are percentages; (1) Metropolitan Statistical Area - see Appendix A for areas included
Source: Bureau of Labor Statistics, http://stats.bls.gov

Employment by Occupation

Occupation Classification	City (%)	MSA[1] (%)	U.S. (%)
Sales and Office	29.1	27.9	26.7
Professional and Related	22.4	20.4	20.2
Service	17.9	15.0	14.9
Production, Transportation, and Material Moving	12.4	14.5	14.6
Management, Business, and Financial	10.2	12.1	13.5
Construction, Extraction, and Maintenance	7.8	9.9	9.4
Farming, Forestry, and Fishing	0.2	0.3	0.7

Note: Figures cover employed civilians 16 years of age and older;
(1) Metropolitan Statistical Area - see Appendix A for areas included
Source: Census 2000, Summary File 3

Employment by Industry

Sector	MSA[1]		U.S.
	Number of Employees	Percent of Total	Percent of Total
Government	60,000	16.7	16.7
Education and Health Services	38,500	10.7	12.9
Professional and Business Services	39,700	11.0	12.3
Retail Trade	50,900	14.1	11.8
Manufacturing	41,700	11.6	11.0
Leisure and Hospitality	45,000	12.5	9.1
Finance Activities	18,200	5.1	6.1
Construction	n/a	n/a	5.1
Wholesale Trade	16,100	4.5	4.3
Other Services	15,300	4.2	4.1
Transportation and Utilities	10,900	3.0	3.7
Information	6,300	1.7	2.4
Natural Resources and Mining	n/a	n/a	0.4

Note: Figures cover non-farm employment as of December 2003 and are not seasonally adjusted;
(1) Metropolitan Statistical Area - see Appendix A for areas included; n/a not available
Source: Bureau of Labor Statistics, http://stats.bls.gov

Average Wages

Occupation	$/Hr.	Occupation	$/Hr.
Accountants and Auditors	22.30	Maids and Housekeeping Cleaners	7.75
Automotive Mechanics	13.73	Maintenance and Repair Workers	13.38
Bookkeepers	12.24	Marketing Managers	29.21
Carpenters	13.11	Nuclear Medicine Technologists	20.65
Cashiers	7.85	Nurses, Licensed Practical	13.14
Clerks, General Office	10.53	Nurses, Registered	20.33
Clerks, Receptionists/Information	9.67	Nursing Aides/Orderlies/Attendants	8.65
Clerks, Shipping/Receiving	11.36	Packers and Packagers, Hand	8.86
Computer Programmers	25.89	Physical Therapists	27.04
Computer Support Specialists	16.49	Postal Service Mail Carriers	18.65
Computer Systems Analysts	27.16	Real Estate Brokers	27.46
Cooks, Restaurant	9.34	Retail Salespersons	10.75
Dentists	72.33	Sales Reps., Exc. Tech./Scientific	23.76
Electrical Engineers	32.04	Sales Reps., Tech./Scientific	21.99
Electricians	17.43	Secretaries, Exc. Legal/Med./Exec.	10.37
Financial Managers	27.63	Security Guards	9.25
First-Line Supervisors/Mgrs., Sales	14.21	Surgeons	95.08
Food Preparation Workers	8.38	Teacher Assistants	7.10
General and Operations Managers	33.53	Teachers, Elementary School	18.80
Hairdressers/Cosmetologists	11.78	Teachers, Secondary School	19.80
Internists	81.46	Telemarketers	n/a
Janitors and Cleaners	8.45	Truck Drivers, Heavy/Tractor-Trailer	16.94
Landscaping/Groundskeeping Workers	9.38	Truck Drivers, Light/Delivery Svcs.	10.84
Lawyers	41.03	Waiters and Waitresses	6.59

Note: Wage data is for 2002 and covers the Metropolitan Statistical Area (see Appendix A for areas included).
Hourly wages for elementary/secondary school teachers and teacher assistants were calculated by the editors
from annual wage data assuming a 40 hour work week; n/a not available.
Source: Bureau of Labor Statistics, 2002 Metro Area Occupational Employment and Wage Estimates

Occupational Employment Projections: 1996 - 2006

Occupations Expected to Have the Largest Job Growth (ranked by numerical growth)	Fast-Growing Occupations[1] (ranked by percent growth)
1. Salespersons, retail	1. Personal and home care aides
2. Truck drivers, light	2. Systems analysts
3. Cashiers	3. Paralegals
4. General managers & top executives	4. Respiratory therapists
5. Janitors/cleaners/maids, ex. priv. hshld.	5. Home health aides
6. Food service workers	6. Directors, religious activities & educ.
7. Child care workers, private household	7. Computer engineers
8. Cooks, fast food and short order	8. Child care workers, private household
9. Registered nurses	9. Corrections officers & jailers
10. Waiters & waitresses	10. Emergency medical technicians

Note: Projections cover Tennessee; (1) Excludes occupations with total job growth less than 300
Source: U.S. Department of Labor, Employment and Training Administration, America's Labor Market Information System (ALMIS)

TAXES

State Corporate Income Tax Rates

State	Rate (%)	Number of Brackets	Low Bracket (Under $)	High Bracket (Over $)
Tennessee	6.5	1	na	na

Note: Tax rates as of December 31, 2003; na not applicable
Source: Tax Foundation, www.taxfoundation.org

State Individual Income Tax Rates

State	Federal Deductibility	Marginal Rate (%)	Number of Brackets	Low Bracket (Under $)	High Bracket (Over $)
Tennessee	No	6.0 (h)	na	na	na

Note: Tax rates as of December 31, 2003; Brackets apply to single taxpayers and married people filing separately; na not applicable; (h) Applies to interest and dividend income only.
Source: Tax Foundation, www.taxfoundation.org

Various State and Local Tax Rates

State Sales and Use (%)	Total Sales and Use (%)	Gasoline (cents/gal.)	Cigarette (cents/pack)	Spirits ($/gal.)	Table Wine ($/gal.)	Beer ($/gal.)
7.0 (l)	9.25	20	20	4.40	1.21	0.14

Note: Tax rates as of December 31, 2003.(l) Rate rose from 6% to 7% on July 1, 2002, but the rate on food remained 6%.
Source: Tax Foundation, www.taxfoundation.org

State Tax Burdens

Area	Combined State and Local Tax Burden		Combined Federal, State and Local Tax Burden	
	Percent	Rank	Percent	Rank
Tennessee	7.7	48	26.3	48
U.S. Average	9.7	-	30.0	-

Note: Figures are for 2003
Source: Tax Foundation, www.taxfoundation.org

Internal Revenue Service Tax Audits

IRS District	Percent of Returns Audited				
	1996	1997	1998	1999	2000
Kentucky-Tennessee	0.40	0.48	0.36	0.22	0.13
U.S.	0.66	0.61	0.46	0.31	0.20

Note: Figures cover IRS district audits of federal income tax returns filed by individuals. Geographic data on district audits for 2001 and 2002 are being withheld by the IRS. TRAC is challenging this policy.
Source: Syracuse University, Transactional Records Access Clearinghouse (TRAC), "Odds of IRS District Tax Audit 2000"

**RESIDENTIAL
REAL ESTATE**

Building Permits

Area	Single-Family			Multi-Family			Total		
	2001	2002	Pct. Chg.	2001	2002	Pct. Chg.	2001	2002	Pct. Chg.
City	336	327	-2.7	208	337	62.0	544	664	22.1
U.S.	1,235,600	1,332,600	7.9	401,100	415,100	3.5	1,636,700	1,747,700	6.8

Note: Figures represent new, privately-owned housing units authorized (unadjusted data)
Source: U.S. Census Bureau, Manufacturing, Mining, and Construction Statistics

Homeownership and Housing Vacancies

Area	Homeownership Rate[2] (%)			Rental Vacancy Rate[3] (%)			Homeowner Vacancy Rate[4] (%)		
	2001	2002[a]	2003	2001	2002[a]	2003	2001	2002[a]	2003
MSA[1]	n/a	n/a	n/a	n/a	n/a	n/a	n/a	n/a	n/a
U.S.	67.8	67.9	68.3	8.4	8.9	9.8	1.8	1.7	1.8

Note: (1) Metropolitan Statistical Area - see Appendix A for areas included; (2) The proportion of households that are owners; (3) The proportion of the rental inventory that is vacant for rent; (4) The proportion of the homeowner inventory that is vacant for sale; (a) 2002 figures have been revised; n/a not available
Source: U.S. Census Bureau, Housing Vacancies and Homeownership Annual Statistics: 2003

**COMMERCIAL
REAL ESTATE**

Industrial/Office Markets

Type/Market Area	Inventory (sq. ft.)	Vacant (sq. ft.)	Vacancy Rate (%)	Under Construction (sq. ft.)	Net Absorption (sq. ft.)
Industrial Space					
Knoxville	34,900,000	2,100,000	6.02	0	245,000

Note: Data as of 4th Quarter, 2003; n/a not available
Source: Society of Industrial and Office Realtors, 2004 Comparative Statistics of Industrial and Office Real Estate Markets

**COMMERCIAL
UTILITIES**

Typical Monthly Electric Bills

Area	Commercial Service ($/month)		Industrial Service ($/month)	
	3 kW demand 1,000 kWh	40 kW demand 14,000 kWh	1,000 kW demand 200,000 kWh	50,000 kW demand 15,000,000 kWh
City	n/a	n/a	n/a	n/a
Average[1]	100	1,134	17,850	1,045,117

Note: Based on rates in effect July 1, 2003; (1) average based on 197 utilities; n/a not available
Source: Edison Electric Institute, Typical Bills and Average Rates Report, Summer 2003

TRANSPORTATION

Means of Transportation to Work

Area	Car/Truck/Van		Public Transportation			Bicycle	Walked	Other Means	Worked at Home
	Drove Alone	Car-pooled	Bus	Subway	Railroad				
City	80.5	10.5	1.3	0.0	0.0	0.3	4.2	0.8	2.3
MSA[1]	84.2	10.0	0.4	0.0	0.0	0.1	1.9	0.6	2.7
U.S.	75.7	12.2	2.5	1.5	0.5	0.4	2.9	1.0	3.3

Note: Figures shown are percentages and cover workers 16 years of age and older;
(1) Metropolitan Statistical Area - see Appendix A for areas included
Source: Census 2000, Summary File 3

Travel Time to Work

Area	Less Than 15 Minutes	15 to 29 Minutes	30 to 44 Minutes	45 to 59 Minutes	60 Minutes or More
City	33.2	46.8	13.8	3.2	3.1
MSA[1]	26.6	43.0	21.0	5.5	3.9
U.S.	29.4	36.1	19.1	7.4	8.0

Note: Figures are percentages and include workers 16 years old and over; (1) Metropolitan Statistical Area - see Appendix A for areas included
Source: Census 2000, Summary File 3

Transportation Statistics

Interstate highways (2004)	I-40; I-75
Public transportation (2002)	Knoxville Transporation Authority (KAT)
Buses	
Average fleet age in years	9.5
No. operated in max. service	68
Demand response	
Average fleet age in years	3.9
No. operated in max. service	11
Passenger air service	
Airport	McGhee-Tyson Airport
Airlines (2003)	8
Boardings (2002)	693,351
Amtrak service (2004)	No
Major waterways/ports	Tennessee River; Port of Knoxville

Source: Federal Transit Administration, National Transit Database, 2002; Editor & Publisher Market Guide, 2004; Bureau of Transportation Statistics, Airport Enplanement Activity for CY2002; www.amtrak.com

BUSINESSES

Major Business Headquarters

Company Name	2003 Rankings	
	Fortune 500	Forbes 500
Anderson News	-	236
HT Hackney	-	61

Note: Companies listed are located in the city; dashes indicate no ranking
Fortune 500: Companies that produce a 10-K are ranked 1 to 500 based on 2002 revenue
Forbes 500: Private companies are ranked 1 to 281 based on 2002 revenue
Source: Fortune, April 14, 2003; www.forbes.com, November 6, 2003

Minority and Women-Owned Businesses

Ownership	All Firms		Firms with Paid Employees			
	Firms	Sales ($000)	Firms	Sales ($000)	Employees	Payroll ($000)
Black	590	32,231	123	24,646	500	6,367
Hispanic	175	40,633	55	39,566	655	11,243
Women	3,985	990,683	906	940,618	9,256	167,244

Note: Figures cover firms located in the city
Source: 1997 Economic Census, Minority and Women-Owned Businesses

HOTELS

Hotels/Motels

Area	Hotels/Motels	Average Minimum Rates ($)		
		Tourist	First-Class	Deluxe
City	76	51	78	n/a

Note: n/a not available
Source: OAG Travel Planner Online, Spring 2004

EVENT SITES

Major Event Sites, Meeting Places and Convention Centers

Name	Guest Rooms	Exhibit/ Meeting Space (sq. ft.)	Largest Meeting Room Capacity
Hyatt Regency Knoxville	385	39,575	3,211
Knoxville Civic Auditorium Coliseum	n/a	n/a	10,000
Knoxville Convention/Exhibition Center	n/a	n/a	7,000
Merchants Town Square	n/a	120,000	n/a
Thompson-Boling Assembly Center	n/a	n/a	24,451
World's Fair Park & Festival Center	n/a	n/a	50,000

Note: n/a not available
Source: Original research

Living Environment

COST OF LIVING

Cost of Living Index

Year	Composite Index	Groceries	Housing	Utilities	Trans-portation	Health Care	Misc. Goods/ Services
2001	91.9	95.5	85.4	92.2	88.6	90.4	96.9
2002	89.3	94.4	80.8	90.4	88.8	89.2	93.8
2003	89.6	93.6	78.8	95.0	88.3	88.9	96.2

Note: U.S. = 100
Source: ACCRA, Cost of Living Index, 2001, 2002 and 2003 4-Quarter Averages

HOUSING

House Price Index (HPI)

Area	National Ranking[2]	Quarterly Change (%)	One-Year Change (%)	Five-Year Change (%)
MSA[1]	128	1.64	5.17	22.02
U.S.[3]	-	3.67	7.97	41.81

Note: The HPI is a weighted repeat sales index. It measures average price changes in repeat sales or refinancings on the same properties. This information is obtained by reviewing repeat mortgage transactions on single-family properties whose mortgages have been purchased or securitized by Fannie Mae of Freddie Mac in January 1975; (1) Metropolitan Statistical Area - see Appendix A for areas included; (2) Rankings are based on annual percentage change, for all MSAs containing at least 15,000 transactions over the last 10 years and ranges from 1 to 220; (3) figures based on a weighted division average; all figures are for the period ended December 31, 2003
Source: Office of Federal Housing Enterprise Oversight, House Price Index, March 1, 2004

Housing: Year Structure Built

Area	1990 -2000	1980 -1989	1970 -1979	1960 -1969	1950 -1959	1940 -1949	Before 1940	Median Year
City	11.2	11.1	17.8	17.4	18.6	11.0	12.9	1964
MSA[1]	25.5	16.9	18.4	12.7	11.2	7.8	7.5	1976
U.S.	17.0	15.8	18.5	13.7	12.7	7.3	15.0	1971

Note: Figures are percentages; (1) Metropolitan Statistical Area - see Appendix A for areas included
Source: Census 2000, Summary File 3

Average New Home Price

Area	2001	2002	2003
City	183,288	190,361	194,357
U.S.	212,643	236,567	248,193

Note: Figures, in dollars, are based on a new home with 2,400 sq. ft. of living area on an 8,000 sq. ft. lot.
Source: ACCRA, Cost of Living Index, 2001, 2002 and 2003 4-Quarter Averages

Average Apartment Rent

Area	2001	2002	2003
City	582	588	593
U.S.	674	708	721

Note: Figures, in dollars per month, are based on an unfurnished two bedroom, 1-1/2 or 2 bath apartment, approximately 950 sq. ft. in size, excluding all utilities except water
Source: ACCRA, Cost of Living Index, 2001, 2002 and 2003 4-Quarter Averages

RESIDENTIAL UTILITIES

Average Residential Utility Costs

Area	All Electric ($/mth)	Part Electric ($/mth)	Other Energy ($/mth)	Phone ($/mth)
City	–	52.60	64.51	23.20
U.S.	116.46	65.82	62.68	23.90

Source: ACCRA, Cost of Living Index, 2003 4-Quarter Average

HEALTH CARE

Average Health Care Costs

Area	Hospital ($/day)	Doctor ($/visit)	Dentist ($/visit)
City	555.93	66.25	73.15
U.S.	678.35	67.91	83.90

Note: Hospital—based on a semi-private room; Doctor—based on a general practitioner's routine exam of an established patient; Dentist—based on adult teeth cleaning and periodic oral exam.
Source: ACCRA, Cost of Living Index, 2003 4-Quarter Average

Distribution of Non-Federal, Office-Based Physicians

Area	Total	Family/ General Practice	Specialties		
			Medical	Surgical	Other
MSA[1] (number)	1,591	236	551	395	409
MSA[1] (rate per 10,000 pop.)	23.2	3.4	8.0	5.7	6.0
Metro Average[2] (rate per 10,000 pop.)	33.1	2.2	7.7	4.8	5.6

Note: Data as of December 31, 2001; (1) Metropolitan Statistical Area - see Appendix A for areas included; (2) Average of 81 MSAs and CMSAs in this book
Source: American Medical Association, Physician Characteristics & Distribution in the U.S., 2003-2004

Hospitals

Knoxville has the following hospitals: 5 general medical and surgical; 1 psychiatric; 1 children's general.
AHA Guide to the Healthcare Field, 2003-2004

PRESIDENTIAL ELECTION

2000 Presidential Election Results

Area	Gore	Bush	Nader	Buchanan	Other
Knox County	40.5	57.7	1.2	0.2	0.5
U.S.	48.4	47.9	2.7	0.4	0.6

Note: Results are percentages and may not add to 100% due to rounding
Source: www.cbsnews.com; www.uselectionatlas.org

EDUCATION

Public School District Statistics

District Name	Schls.	Enroll-ment	Classroom Teachers	Pupil/ Teacher Ratio	Minority Pupils[1] (%)	Current Expend.[2] ($/pupil)
Knox County SD	89	51,866	3,587	14.5	n/a	5,670

Note: Data covers the 2001-02 school year unless otherwise noted; (1) Fall 2000; (2) FY2000; n/a not available
Source: U.S. Department of Education, National Center for Education Statistics, Common Core of Data, Local Education Agency (School District) Universe Survey: School Year 2001-2002; U.S. Department of Education, National Center for Education Statistics, Digest of Education Statistics 2002

Educational Quality

School District	Education Quotient[1]	Graduate Outcome[2]	Community Index[3]	Resource Index[4]
Knox County	24	24	50	38

Note: Scores are national percentile rankings and range from 1 (worst) to 99 (best); (1) Combination of the Graduate Outcome, Community and Resource indexes weighted to reflect the greater importance of the Graduate Outcome and Resource Index; (2) Based on graduation rates and college board scores (SAT/ACT); (3) Based on the surrounding community's level of affluence and adult education; (4) Based on teacher salaries, per-pupil expenditures and student-teacher ratios.
Source: Expansion Management, December 2003

Educational Attainment by Race

Area	High School Graduate (%)					Bachelor's Degree (%)				
	Total	White	Black	Asian	Hisp.[2]	Total	White	Black	Asian	Hisp.[2]
City	78.4	79.4	73.3	88.1	69.6	24.6	26.0	13.5	63.2	26.4
MSA[1]	79.6	79.8	76.0	88.9	71.4	23.5	23.6	15.6	60.9	23.6
U.S.	80.4	83.6	72.3	80.4	52.4	24.4	26.1	14.3	44.1	10.4

Note: Figures shown cover persons 25 years old and over; (1) Metropolitan Statistical Area - see Appendix A for areas included; (2) people of Hispanic origin can be of any race
Source: Census 2000, Summary File 3

School Enrollment by Type

Area	Grades KG to 8				Grades 9 to 12			
	Public		Private		Public		Private	
	Enrollment	%	Enrollment	%	Enrollment	%	Enrollment	%
City	15,184	88.4	1,990	11.6	6,409	89.2	776	10.8
MSA[1]	72,586	90.0	8,074	10.0	31,473	91.8	2,809	8.2
U.S.	33,526,011	88.7	4,285,121	11.3	14,848,628	90.6	1,532,323	9.4

Note: Figures shown cover persons 3 years old and over; (1) Metropolitan Statistical Area - see Appendix A for areas included
Source: Census 2000, Summary File 3

School Enrollment by Race

Area	Grades KG to 8 (%)				Grades 9 to 12 (%)			
	White	Black	Asian	Hisp.[1]	White	Black	Asian	Hisp.[1]
City	68.2	26.4	1.0	2.0	66.5	28.6	1.6	1.0
MSA[2]	88.4	8.0	0.9	1.3	88.5	8.2	1.0	1.1
U.S.	68.5	15.5	3.3	16.8	68.8	15.5	3.8	15.7

Note: Figures shown cover persons 3 years old and over; (1) people of Hispanic origin can be of any race; (2) Metropolitan Statistical Area - see Appendix A for areas included
Source: Census 2000, Summary File 3

Classroom Teacher Salaries in Public Schools

District	B.A. Degree		M.A. Degree		Maximum	
	Min. ($)	Rank[1]	Max. ($)	Rank[1]	Max. ($)	Rank[1]
City	n/a	n/a	n/a	n/a	n/a	n/a
DOD Average[2]	31,567	-	53,248	-	59,356	-

Note: Salaries are for 2001-2002; (1) Rank ranges from 1 to 100; (2) As per the U.S. Department of Defense Wage Fixing Authority
Source: American Federation of Teachers, Survey & Analysis of Teacher Salary Trends 2002

Higher Education

Four-Year Colleges			Two-Year Colleges			Medical Schools	Law Schools	Voc/Tech
Public	Private Non-profit	Private For-profit	Public	Private Non-profit	Private For-profit			
1	2	2	1	1	3	0	1	5

Note: Figures cover institutions located within the city limits.
Source: National Center for Education Statistics, The Integrated Postsecondary Education System (IPEDS) Peer Analysis System, 2002; usnews.com, America's Best Graduate Schools 2004, Medical School Directory; The College Blue Book, Occupational Education, 2003; Barron's Guide to Law Schools, 2003; Medical School Admission Requirements U.S. & Canada, 2003-2004

MAJOR EMPLOYERS

Major Employers

Company Name	Industry	Type
Accounting Dept	General medical and surgical hospitals	Single
ACN	Catalog and mail-order houses	Single
Alcoa	Secondary nonferrous metals	Branch
Baptist Health System	Management services	Headquarters
Baptist Hospital West	General medical and surgical hospitals	Single
Blount County School District	Elementary and secondary schools	Branch
Blount Memorial Hospital	General medical and surgical hospitals	Headquarters
BWXT Y-12 LLC	Ammunition, except for small arms, nec	Single
C A S A Anderson Cnty Fax Line	Executive offices	Headquarters
Fort Sanders Regional Med Ctr	General medical and surgical hospitals	Headquarters
Fort Sanders-Parkwest Med Ctr	General medical and surgical hospitals	Headquarters
Honeywell	Fabricated textile products, nec	Branch
Methodist Hospital Foundation	General medical and surgical hospitals	Headquarters
Saint Marys Corp Health Svcs	Management services	Headquarters
SCG Inc	Security systems services	Single
Sea Ray Boats Florida Corp	Boatbuilding and repairing	Headquarters
Tennessee Denso Manufacturing	Engine electrical equipment	Single
TVA	Electric services	Headquarters
University of Tennessee	Colleges and universities	Headquarters
UT Memorial Hospital	General medical and surgical hospitals	Headquarters
UT-Battelle LLC	Commercial physical research	Headquarters

Note: Companies shown are located in the metropolitan area and have 1,000 or more employees.
Source: www.zapdata.com, March 2004

PUBLIC SAFETY

Crime Rate

Area	All Crimes	Violent Crimes				Property Crimes		
		Murder	Forcible Rape	Robbery	Aggrav. Assault	Burglary	Larceny -Theft	Motor Vehicle Theft
City	6,762.8	11.9	41.8	312.1	738.2	1,204.9	3,769.9	684.0
Suburbs[1]	3,653.2	2.7	27.3	40.7	269.2	880.1	2,180.1	253.1
MSA[2]	4,440.0	5.0	31.0	109.4	387.8	962.3	2,582.3	362.1
U.S.	4,118.8	5.6	33.0	145.9	310.1	746.2	2,445.8	432.1

Note: Figures are crimes per 100,000 population; (1) All areas within the MSA that are located outside the city limits; (2) Metropolitan Statistical Area - see Appendix A for areas included
Source: FBI Uniform Crime Reports, 2002

RECREATION

Culture and Recreation

Museums	Orchestras	Opera Companies	Dance Companies	Professional Theatres	Zoos	Pro Sports Teams[1]
9	1	1	2	3	1	0

Note: (1) Covers the Metropolitan Statistical Area - see Appendix A for areas included.
Source: The Grey House Performing Arts Directory, 2002; Official Museum Directory, 2004; www.sportsvenues.com

Library System

The Knox County Public Library System has 17 branches, holdings of 980,903 volumes, and a budget of $8,582,744 (2001-2002).
American Library Directory, 2003-2004

MEDIA

Newspapers

Name	Type	Freq.	Distribution	Circulation
The East Tennessee Catholic	Catholic	2x/mth	Regional	16,000
The Knoxville News-Sentinel	General	7x/wk	Area	119,529
Metro Pulse	Alternative	1x/wk	Regional	31,000
Press Enterprise	General	1x/wk	Local	15,000

Note: Includes newspapers whose offices are located in the city and whose circulations are 1,000 or more
Source: Burrelle's Media Directory, 2003

Television Stations

Name	Ch.	Affiliation	Type	Owner
WSJK	2	PBS	Public	East Tennessee Public Communications Corp.
WATE	6	n/a	Commercial	Young Broadcasting Inc.
WVLT	8	CBST	Commercial	Gray Communications Inc.
WBIR	10	NBCT	Commercial	Gannett Broadcasting
WKOP	15	PBS	Public	East Tennessee Public Communications Corp.
WBXX	20	WB	Commercial	Acme Broadcasting Inc.
WTNZ	43	FBC/UPN	Commercial	Raycom Media Inc.
WPXK	54	PAXTV	Commercial	Paxson Communications Corporation

Note: Stations included broadcast from the Knoxville metro area; n/a not available
Source: Burrelle's Media Directory, 2003

AM Radio Stations

Call Letters	Freq. (kHz)	Target Audience	Station Format	Music Format
WRJZ	620	Religious	E/M/N/T	Christian
WMEN	760	General	T	n/a
WKXV	900	Religious	M/T	Gospel
WNOX	990	General	N/T	n/a
WQBB	1040	General	M/N	Adult Standards
WLOD	1140	General	T	n/a
WHJM	1180	Religious	M	Adult Contemporary
WIMZ	1240	General	S	n/a
WATO	1290	General	S/T	n/a
WKGN	1340	General	M/N/T	Urban Contemporary
WITA	1490	G/R	M/N/T	Christian

Note: Stations included broadcast from the Knoxville metro area; n/a not available
The following abbreviations may be used:
Target Audience: A=Asian; B=Black; C=Christian; E=Ethnic; F=French; G=General; H=Hispanic; M=Men; N=Native American; R=Religious; S=Senior Citizen; W=Women; Y=Young Adult; Z=Children
Station Format: E=Educational; M=Music; N=News; S=Sports; T=Talk
Source: Burrelle's Media Directory, 2003

FM Radio Stations

Call Letters	Freq. (mHz)	Target Audience	Station Format	Music Format
WUTK	90.3	General	M/N/S	Alternative
WKCS	91.1	General	M	Adult Contemporary
WUOT	91.9	General	M/N/T	Classical
WMYU	93.1	General	M	Oldies
WNFZ	94.3	General	M/N/T	Modern Rock
WYFC	95.3	General	E/M	Christian
WTXM	95.7	General	S/T	n/a
WJXB	97.5	General	M	Adult Contemporary
WSMJ	98.7	General	M/N/T	Jazz
WNOX	99.1	General	N/S/T	n/a
WOKI	100.3	General	M/N	Modern Rock
WWST	102.1	General	M	Top 40
WIMZ	103.5	General	M/N/S	Classic Rock
WBON	104.5	General	M/N	Classic Rock
WIVK	107.7	General	M/N/S	Country

Note: Stations included broadcast from the Knoxville metro area; n/a not available
The following abbreviations may be used:
Target Audience: A=Asian; B=Black; C=Christian; E=Ethnic; F=French; G=General; H=Hispanic;
M=Men; N=Native American; R=Religious; S=Senior Citizen; W=Women; Y=Young Adult; Z=Children
Station Format: E=Educational; M=Music; N=News; S=Sports; T=Talk
Source: Burrelle's Media Directory, 2003

CLIMATE

Average and Extreme Temperatures

Temperature	Jan	Feb	Mar	Apr	May	Jun	Jul	Aug	Sep	Oct	Nov	Dec	Yr.
Extreme High (°F)	77	83	86	91	94	102	103	102	103	91	84	80	103
Average High (°F)	47	52	61	71	78	85	88	87	82	71	59	50	69
Average Temp. (°F)	38	42	50	59	67	75	78	77	71	60	49	41	59
Average Low (°F)	29	32	39	47	56	64	68	67	61	48	38	32	48
Extreme Low (°F)	-24	-2	1	22	32	43	49	53	36	25	5	-6	-24

Note: Figures cover the years 1948-1990
Source: National Climatic Data Center, International Station Meteorological Climate Summary, 9/96

Average Precipitation/Snowfall/Humidity

Precip./Humidity	Jan	Feb	Mar	Apr	May	Jun	Jul	Aug	Sep	Oct	Nov	Dec	Yr.
Avg. Precip. (in.)	4.5	4.3	5.0	3.6	3.9	3.8	4.5	3.1	2.9	2.8	3.8	4.5	46.7
Avg. Snowfall (in.)	5	4	2	1	0	0	0	0	0	Tr	1	2	13
Avg. Rel. Hum. 7am (%)	81	80	79	80	85	86	89	91	91	89	84	82	85
Avg. Rel. Hum. 4pm (%)	60	54	50	46	52	54	56	55	54	51	54	59	54

Note: Figures cover the years 1948-1990; Tr = Trace amounts (<0.05 in. of rain; <0.5 in. of snow)
Source: National Climatic Data Center, International Station Meteorological Climate Summary, 9/96

Weather Conditions

Temperature			Daytime Sky			Precipitation		
10°F & below	32°F & below	90°F & above	Clear	Partly cloudy	Cloudy	0.01 inch or more precip.	0.1 inch or more snow/ice	Thunder- storms
3	73	33	85	142	138	125	8	47

Note: Figures are average number of days per year and covers the years 1948-1990
Source: National Climatic Data Center, International Station Meteorological Climate Summary, 9/96

HAZARDOUS WASTE

Superfund Sites

Knoxville has no sites on the EPA's Superfund National Priorities List.
U.S. Environmental Protection Agency, National Priorities List, March 15, 2004

**AIR & WATER
QUALITY**

Maximum Pollutant Concentrations

	Particulate Matter (ug/m^3)	Carbon Monoxide (ppm)	Sulfur Dioxide (ppm)	Nitrogen Dioxide (ppm)	Ozone 1-hour (ppm)	Ozone 8-hour (ppm)	Lead (ug/m^3)
MSA[1] Level	135	2	0.07	n/a	0.12	0.1	n/a
NAAQS[2]	150	9	0.140	0.053	0.12	0.08	1.50
Met NAAQS[2]	Yes	Yes	Yes	n/a	Yes	No	n/a

Note: (1) Metropolitan Statistical Area - see Appendix A for areas included; (2) National Ambient Air Quality Standards; n/a not available
Units: ppm = parts per million; ug/m^3 = micrograms per cubic meter
Source: EPA, Latest Findings on National Air Quality: 2002 Status and Trends, August 2003

Air Quality Index

In the Knoxville MSA (see Appendix A for areas included), the Air Quality Index (AQI) exceeded 100 on 45 days in 2002. An AQI value greater than 100 indicates that air quality would have been in the unhealthful range on that day.
EPA, Latest Findings on National Air Quality: 2002 Status and Trends, August 2003

Watershed Health

The U.S. Environmental Protection Agency monitors the health of the aquatic resources for the nation's 2,000+ watersheds. **The Watts Bar Lake watershed serves the Knoxville area and received an overall Index of Watershed Indicators (IWI) score of 5 (more serious problems - low vulnerability).** The IWI score is based on seven condition and nine vulnerability indicators. The overall IWI score ranges from 1 (best health) to 6 (worst health). The Condition Indicators include: designated use attainment, fish and wildlife consumption advisories, source water condition, contaminated sediments, ambient water quality, and wetlands loss index. The Vulnerability Indicators include: aquatic species at risk, conventional and toxic loads over permitted limits, urban and agricultural runoff potential, population change, hydrologic modification, estuarine pollution susceptibility, and air deposition. *EPA, Index of Watershed Indicators, October 26, 2001*

Drinking Water

Water System Name	Pop. Served	Primary Water Source Type	Number of Violations January 2002-February 2004		
			Health Based	Significant Monitoring	Monitoring
Knoxville UB#1 Whitaker Plant	195,474	Surface	None	None	None

Note: Data as of February 19, 2004
Source: EPA, Office of Ground Water and Drinking Water, Safe Drinking Water Information System

Knoxville tap water is alkaline, hard and fluoridated.
Editor & Publisher Market Guide, 2004

Memphis, Tennessee

Background

Memphis, named after the ancient city in Egypt, has had a long and illustrious history. Inhabited for centuries by the Chickasaws, it came to the attention of early white explorers, and was visited by Hernando de Soto in 1541. French explorers followed. By the Treaty of Paris of 1783 the western lands up to the Mississippi claimed by the British crown passed to the newly independent United States, and the Chickasaws gave up their claim to the area of Memphis in 1818. The next year a trio of American citizens, James Winchester, John Overton, and General Andrew Jackson, the last fresh from his victory at the Battle of New Orleans, in 1815, organized a settlement.

In the years before the Civil War, Memphis flourished, serving as a natural inland port because of its advantageous location on the Mississippi. At the opening of the Civil War, it was a prize of both Northern and Southern armies. As the war lengthened and the North drew a cordon around its Southern foes, Memphis fell. But the city survived, and by the end of the nineteenth century, was clearly flourishing. In the next century Memphis took its place as the virtual economic capital of Tennessee and the state's largest city. The driving forces in the early expansion of Memphis were cotton, and, by the end of the nineteenth century, the rapidly expanding lumber trade. After World War II the city's industry saw a rapid expansion, including foodstuffs, chemicals, and electrical goods.

Livestock and meatpacking have proved highly profitable, and the city has attracted such agricultural products from across the Upper South, earning the sobriquet America's Distribution Center. Medical care has been a principal occupation of many residents, with a large hospital complex, the Memphis Medical Center, including the famous St. Jude Children's Research Hospital, located in the city. FedEx, the shipping company, has its corporate headquarters here.

The recording industry, too, has flourished in Memphis, for music has long been important. The composer W.C. Handy developed the blues in Memphis, and, of course, the late rock-and-roll idol Elvis Presley and his home Graceland had brought renown to the city.

For a while the city seemed to be decaying at its core, in that buildings were being vacated or even razed. But in the late 1970s the city fathers undertook to revive the core area, and launched a project that, by the 1990s, had spent three-quarters of a billion dollars in reviving buildings and in new construction. A convention center and a theme park (Mud Island Park) have been built, the latter connected by monorail to the downtown area. In the course of renovation the Orpheum Theater and the Peabody Hotel, both early landmarks, have been restored to their previous grandeur.

Fabled Beale Street, with its history as a place to hear the blues, fell into decay in the mid-20th century; it has seen a major comeback as a center for blues and music over the last 20 years and is now a major tourist draw.

By 2002, development projects were slated for, or begun in, the Medical District, including the UT/Baptist Bio Tech Research Park, UT Cancer Institute medical research facility, the formation of the Methodist University Hospital, and the MATA trolley rail expansion.

The $250 million NBA FedEx Forum, the catalyst for new growth and development in the Sports and Entertainment District and home to the Memphis Grizzlies basketball team, opens in the fall of 2004.

The year 2004 also marks the grand opening of the newly expanded and renovated Memphis Cook Convention Center, including the state-of-the-art Cannon Center for the Performing Arts.

The climate of Memphis is mild. Most precipitation occurs during winter and spring, with a secondary surge in rainfall due to thunderstorm activity. Severe storms are relatively infrequent.

Rankings

- Memphis was ranked #109 out of 331 metro areas in *Cities Ranked & Rated*. Criteria: cost of living; climate; crime; transportation; economy and jobs; education; arts and culture; health and healthcare; leisure. *Cities Ranked & Rated, 1st Edition, 2004*

- *Ladies Home Journal* ranked America's 200 largest cities based on the qualities women surveyed care about most. Memphis ranked #55 out of 57 in the big city category (population over 300,000). Criteria: crime; lifestyle; education; jobs; health; child care; politics; and the economy. *Ladies Home Journal Online, "The Best Cities for Women 2002"*

- Memphis was selected as one of the "Best Cities for Black Families." The city ranked #14 out of 20. For six months, bet.com compiled data on African Americans in those U.S. cities with the largest Black populations. The data, for African Americans specifically, involved the following: infant mortality; high school graduation; median income; homeownership; unemployment; business ownership; poverty rates; AIDS infection rates; percentage of children in single parent, typically fatherless, households; teen pregnancy; economic segregation index; violent and property crime. *www.bet.com, October 1, 2002*

- Memphis appeared on *Black Enterprise's* list of the "Top Ten Cities for African-Americans to Live, Work, and Play." The city was ranked #5, based on responses from 4,239 online survey respondents who ranked 21 quality-of-life factors. *Black Enterprise, July 2001*

- *Forbes* ranked the 150 most populous metro areas in the U.S. in terms of the "Best Places for Business and Careers." The Memphis metro area was ranked #106. Criteria: income and job growth; cost-of-doing-business; qualifications of the available pool of labor; crime rates; housing costs; net migration. *Forbes, May 9, 2003*

- Memphis was selected as one of "America's Healthiest Cities" by *Natural Health* magazine. The city was ranked #29 out of the 50 largest urban areas in the U.S. Twenty-six criteria in the following four categories were examined: whether the city boasts natural offerings; how well the city promotes its resident's physical health; whether the city offers a healthy environment; how well the city fosters a sense of community. *Natural Health, April 2003*

- *Men's Health* ranked 101 U.S. cities in terms of the quality of their tap water. Memphis received a grade of A. Criteria: levels of bacteria, arsenic, lead, trihalomethanes, and haloacetic acids were compared with the National Academy of Science's guidelines as well as with the EPA's more stringent maximum contaminant level goals. *Men's Health, March 2004*

- Sperling's BestPlaces ranked 331 metro areas and identified the most and least stressful U.S. cities. The Memphis metro area ranked #38 out of the 100 largest metro areas (#1 = most stressful). Criteria: divorce rate; unemployment rate; violent and property crime; suicide rate; commute time; mental health; alcohol consumption; cloudy days. *www.BestPlaces.net, February 26, 2004*

- Sperling's BestPlaces in partnership with Pep Boys ranked 77 metro areas and identified "America's Most Drivable Cities." The Memphis metro area ranked #9. Criteria: climate; road roughness; urban mobility; gas prices. *Pep Boys, "America's Most Drivable Cities," April 9, 2003*

- Memphis was ranked #168 out of America's 200 largest metro areas in *SELF Magazine's* ranking of "America's Healthiest Cities for Women." Criteria: safety; air/water quality; cancer rates; and 21 other factors relating to health. *SELF Magazine, November 2003*

- Memphis was identified as one of the most dangerous large metro areas for pedestrians in the U.S. The area ranked #4 out of the nations 49 largest metro areas. Criteria: average yearly pedestrian fatalities per capita (for the years 2000 and 2001) adjusted for the number of walkers. *Surface Transportation Policy Project, "Mean Streets 2002"*

- Memphis was selected as one of the 25 fittest cities in America by *Men's Fitness Online*. It ranked #21 out of America's 50 largest cities. Criteria: gyms/sporting goods; nutrition; exercise/sports; overweight/sedentary; junk food; alcohol; smoking; television; air and water quality; climate; geography; commute time; parks/open space; recreation facilities; and health care. *Men's Fitness Online, America's Fittest/Fattest Cities 2003*

■ Memphis was ranked #95 out of 100 cities surveyed in *Child* magazine's ranking of the "Best Cities for Families." Criteria: number of pediatricians per capita; proximity to a children's hospital; immunization rates; infant mortality rate; air quality; water quality; school spending; pupil-teacher ratio; availability of parks/green space; nearby recreational opportunities; average commute time; number of sunny days; average cost of a 3-bedroom home; unemployment rate; future job growth; crime rate; percentage of children under 5; mandated minimum child care ratios. *Child, April 2001*

■ *Zero Population Growth* ranked 239 cities in terms of children's health, safety, and economic well-being. Memphis was ranked #128 out of 140 independent cities (cities with populations greater than 100,000 which were neither major cities nor suburbs/outer cities) and was given a grade of C-. Criteria: total population and population growth; percent of population under 18 years of age; number of children's museums; health improvement grade; percent of births to teens; percent of low birthweight infants; infant mortality rate; number of Title X-funded clinics; average SAT/ACT scores; average elementary and secondary class size; crime rate; unemployment rate; percent of affordable homes; number of bad air days; park acres per 1000 persons; library circulation per child; and children's program attendance counts. *Zero Population Growth, Kid Friendly Cities Report Card 2001*

■ Memphis was selected as one of America's 32 most livable cities by the non-profit group, Partners for Livable Communities. Criteria: environmental quality; parkland; ability to train new workers; job market; education; and use of the arts for economic development. *www.Livable.com, March 3, 2003*

■ *Ladies Home Journal* ranked America's 200 largest cities in terms of safety. Memphis ranked #194 out of 200. Criteria: violent crimes; crimes against property; and rape. *Ladies Home Journal Online, "The Best Cities for Women 2002"*

■ Memphis was ranked #132 out of 268 metro areas in terms of its Creativity Index. The Creativity Index is a mix of four equally weighted factors: the Creative Class (scientists, engineers, architects, designers, writers, artists, musicians, or any profession where creativity is a key factor) share of the workforce; innovation, measured as patents per capita; high-tech industry, using the Milken Institute's Tech Pole Index; and diversity, measured by the Gay Index (a reasonable proxy for an areas' openness to different kinds of people and ideas). *The Rise of the Creative Class, 2002*

■ Memphis was ranked #52 out of 125 regions worldwide in terms of its "Knowledge Competitiveness Index." The index attempts to measure the knowledge-based development taking place throughout the world and is based on 17 measures of economic performance that indicate a region's ability to translate its knowledge capacity into economic value. *Robert Huggins Associates, "2003-2004 World Knowledge Competitiveness Index"*

■ The Memphis metro area was selected by *Yahoo! Internet Life* as one of "America's Most Wired Cities...and Towns." The area ranked #77 out of 87. Criteria: home and work net use; user sophistication; domain density; and available content. *Yahoo! Internet Life, April 2001*

■ The Memphis metro area was selected by Cranium as one of the "Top 50 Fun Cities" in America. The area ranked #35. Criteria includes: number of sports teams, restaurants, and dance performances; number of toy stores; city budget spent on recreation. *Cranium, November 4, 2003*

■ Memphis was identified as one of the 100 "Most Unwired Cities" in the U.S. The area ranked #85. Criteria: number of public and commercial wireless access points; cell phone coverage offering wide area network Internet access; Internet penetration. *Intel, "Most Unwired Cities," March 4, 2003*

■ Scarborough Research measured the percentage of households who subscribe to cellular services among adults ages 18 and over in 75 U.S. markets. The Memphis DMA (Designated Market Area) was ranked #7 out of 75. *Scarborough Research, Scarborough USA+ 2003 Release 1*

■ Memphis was selected as one of "America's Most Literate Cities." The city ranked #58 out of the 64 largest U.S. cities. Criteria: booksellers; library support, holdings, and utilization; educational attainment; periodicals published; newspaper circulation. *University of Wisconsin-Whitewater, "America's Most Literate Cities," Summer 2003*

- Memphis was ranked #107 in *Prevention* magazine's survey of the "Best Walking Cities in the U.S." The magazine, in conjunction with the American Podiatric Medical Association, surveyed 125 of the most populated cities and then tabulated and weighed 20 criteria of interest to pedestrians. *Prevention, April, 2004*

- Memphis was selected as one of "The Best Places to Start and Grow a Company." The area ranked #10 among large metro areas. Criteria: Significant Starts (firms started in the last 10 years that still employ at least 5 people) and Young Growers (firms 10 years old or less that grew significantly during the last 4 years). *Cognetics, "Entrepreneurial Hot Spots: The Best Places in America to Start and Grow a Company," 2001*

- The Memphis metro area was selected as one of "America's 50 Hottest Cities for Business Relocations and Expansions." The area ranked #5. Criteria: 70 of the industry's most prominent site selection consultants were asked which cities their clients found the most attractive when it came to selecting an expansion or relocation site in 2003. *Expansion Management, January 2004*

- The Memphis metro area was cited as one of "The Best Places in the U.S. to Locate a Company." The area ranked #156 out of 329. Criteria: education (with emphasis on college board test results and high school graduation rates); availability of quality healthcare services and the cost to employers; quality of life; logistics workforce and companies; transportation infrastructure; quality and quantity of highly educated technical workers; business climate. *Expansion Management, July 2003*

- The Memphis metro area was selected as one of the "Top 40 Hottest Real Estate Markets" for expanding or relocating businesses." Criteria: rental costs; purchase prices; and vacancy rates of office and warehouse space. *Expansion Management, August 2003*

- The Memphis metro area appeared on *Forbes/Milken Institute* list of "Best Places for Business and Career." Rank: #150 out of 200 metro areas. Criteria: salary growth; job growth; number of technology clusters; overall concentration of technology activity relative to national average; and technology output growth. *www.forbes.com, Forbes/Milken Institute Best Places 2002*

- The Memphis metro area appeared on the "Milken Institute Best Performing Cities" index. Rank: #159 out of 200 large metro areas. Criteria: job growth; wage and salary growth; high-tech output growth. *Milken Institute, June 25, 2003*

- The Memphis metro area appeared on *Entrepreneur* magazine's list of the "Best Cities for Entrepreneurs" in 2003. The area ranked #35 out of 61 in the large city category. Criteria: entrepreneurial activity; small-business growth; economic growth; and risk. *www.Entrepreneur.com*

- The Memphis metro area appeared on *IndustryWeek's* fourth annual World-Class Communities list. It ranked #181 out of 315 metro areas. Criteria: MSA Gross Metropolitan Product (GMP) per manufacturing employee; and MSA percent share of U.S. manufacturing Gross Domestic Product (GDP). *IndustryWeek, April 16, 2001*

- ING Group ranked the 125 largest metro areas according to the general financial security of residents. The Memphis metro area was ranked #102 out of 125. Criteria: Earnings and Wealth Potential (household income, education, net assets, cost of living); Safety Net (health insurance, retirement savings, life insurance, income support programs); Personal Threats (unemployment rate, low-income households, crime rate); Community Economic Vitality (cost of community services, job quality, job creation, housing costs). *ING Group, "The Best Cities to Earn and Save Money: A Ranking of the Largest 125 U.S. Cities," 2001 Edition*

Business Environment

CITY FINANCES

City Government Finances

Component	2000-2001 ($000)	2000-2001 ($ per capita)
Total Revenues	2,940,786	4,524
Total Expenditures	3,007,275	4,626
Debt Outstanding	1,010,883	1,555
Cash and Securities	3,129,176	4,813

Source: U.S Census Bureau, Government Finances 2000-2001, August 2003

City Government Revenue by Source

Source	2000-2001 ($000)	2000-2001 ($ per capita)
General Revenue		
From Federal Government	19,525	30
From State Government	495,912	763
From Local Governments	479,105	737
Taxes		
Property	274,915	423
Sales	43,598	67
Personal Income	0	0
License	10,465	16
Charges	132,964	205
Liquor Store	0	0
Utility	1,180,052	1,815
Employee Retirement	228,835	352
Other	75,415	116

Source: U.S Census Bureau, Government Finances 2000-2001, August 2003

City Government Expenditures by Function

Function	2000-2001 ($000)	2000-2001 ($ per capita)	2000-2001 (%)
General Expenditures			
Airports	0	0	0.0
Corrections	0	0	0.0
Education	945,535	1,454	31.4
Fire Protection	103,695	160	3.4
Governmental Administration	32,842	51	1.1
Health	2,919	4	0.1
Highways	57,942	89	1.9
Hospitals	0	0	0.0
Housing and Community Development	18,124	28	0.6
Interest on General Debt	47,908	74	1.6
Libraries	33,990	52	1.1
Parking	215	< 1	< 0.1
Parks and Recreation	77,539	119	2.6
Police Protection	186,443	287	6.2
Public Welfare	0	0	0.0
Sewerage	34,419	53	1.1
Solid Waste Management	43,046	66	1.4
Liquor Store	0	0	0.0
Utility	1,196,046	1,840	39.8
Employee Retirement	158,777	244	5.3
Other	67,835	104	2.3

Source: U.S Census Bureau, Government Finances 2000-2001, August 2003

Municipal Bond Ratings

Area	Moody's
City	Aa2

Source: Mergent Bond Record, February 2004

DEMOGRAPHICS

Population Growth

Area	1990 Census	2000 Census	2003 Estimate	2008 Projection	Population Growth (%)	
					1990-2000	2000-2008
City	660,536	650,100	640,811	627,176	-1.6	-3.5
MSA[1]	1,007,306	1,135,614	1,160,656	1,201,191	12.7	5.8
U.S.	248,709,873	281,421,906	290,647,163	305,918,071	13.2	8.7

Note: (1) Metropolitan Statistical Area - see Appendix A for areas included
Source: Claritas, Inc.

Number of Households and Average Household Size

Area	1990 Census	2000 Census	2003 Estimate	2008 Projection	2003 Average Household Size
City	251,013	250,721	248,203	244,576	2.6
MSA[1]	365,450	424,202	436,859	457,995	2.7
U.S.	91,947,410	105,480,101	109,440,059	116,034,472	2.7

Note: (1) Metropolitan Statistical Area - see Appendix A for areas included
Source: Claritas, Inc.

Race and Ethnicity

Area	White Non-Hispanic	Black Non-Hispanic	Asian Non-Hispanic	Other Race Non-Hispanic	Hispanic
City	32.9	62.6	1.6	3.0	3.4
MSA[1]	52.9	43.1	1.5	2.5	2.7
U.S.	74.5	12.4	3.8	9.3	13.2

Note: Figures are 2003 estimates; (1) Metropolitan Statistical Area - see Appendix A for areas included
Source: Claritas, Inc.

Segregation

City		MSA[1]	
Index[2]	Rank[3]	Index[2]	Rank[4]
68.6	26	72.2	40

Note: Figures are based on an analysis of Census 2000 data; (1) Metropolitan Statistical Area - see Appendix A for areas included; (2) Dissimilarity Index—the most commonly used measure of segregation between two groups, reflecting their relative distributions across neighborhoods within a city or metropolitan area. It can range in value from 0, indicating complete integration, to 100, indicating complete segregation; (3) Ranges from 1 (most segregated) to 100 (least segregated) and includes all the cities in this book; (4) Ranges from 1 (most segregated) to 318 (least segregated) and includes 318 metropolitan areas.
Source: www.CensusScope.org

Ancestry

Area	German	Irish[2]	English	American	Italian	Polish	French[3]	Scottish
City	4.2	4.9	5.2	4.5	1.6	0.5	1.1	1.2
MSA[1]	6.3	7.5	7.2	8.6	2.2	0.7	1.6	1.5
U.S.	15.2	10.9	8.7	7.3	5.6	3.2	3.0	1.7

Note: Figures include multiple ancestry (e.g. if a person reported being Irish and Italian, they were included in both columns); (1) Metropolitan Statistical Area - see Appendix A for areas included; (2) Includes Celtic; (3) Includes Alsatian but excludes Basque
Source: Census 2000, Summary File 3

Foreign-Born Population

Area	Percent of Population Born in:							
	Any Foreign Country	Europe	Asia	Africa	Oceania[2]	Canada	Mexico	Latin America[3]
City	4.0	0.4	1.4	0.3	0.0	0.1	1.5	0.4
MSA[1]	3.3	0.5	1.2	0.2	0.0	0.1	1.0	0.3
U.S.	11.1	1.7	2.9	0.3	0.1	0.3	3.3	2.5

Note: (1) Metropolitan Statistical Area - see Appendix A for areas included; (2) Includes Australia, New Zealand subregion, Melanesia, Micronesia, Polynesia, and Oceania n.e.c; (3) Includes Central America (excluding Mexico), South America, and the Caribbean.
Source: Census 2000, Summary File 3

Religion

Area	Catholic	Southern Baptist	United Methodist	ELCA[1]	LDS[2]	Presbyterian Church USA	Jewish Est.	Muslim Est.
County	5.7	16.9	5.4	0.2	0.3	1.2	1.0	0.4
U.S.	22.0	7.1	3.7	1.8	1.5	1.1	2.2	0.6

Note: Figures shown are the number of adherents as a percentage of the total population; Adherents are defined as all members, including full members, their children and the estimated number of other participants who are not considered members (e.g. the baptized, those not confirmed, those not eligible for communion, those regularly attending services, etc.); (1) Evangelical Lutheran Church in America; (2) The Church of Jesus Christ of Latter Day Saints
Source: Reprinted with permission from Religious Congregations and Membership in the United States 2000 (Nashville, Glenmary Research Center, 2002) Copyright Association of Statisticians of American Religious Bodies. All rights reserved.

Age Distribution

Area	Percent of Population						
	Under Age 5	Age 5 to 17	Age 18 to 34	Age 35 to 49	Age 50 to 64	Age 65 to 79	80 Years and Over
City	7.7	20.1	26.4	22.1	12.7	8.1	2.8
MSA[1]	7.6	20.7	24.1	23.7	13.9	7.6	2.4
U.S.	6.8	18.9	23.7	23.5	14.8	9.2	3.2

Note: (1) Metropolitan Statistical Area - see Appendix A for areas included
Source: Census 2000, Summary File 3

Marriage Status

Area	Never Married	Now Married Except Separated	Separated	Widowed	Divorced
City	36.1	39.2	4.8	7.9	12.0
MSA[1]	29.8	49.1	3.6	6.7	10.7
U.S.	27.1	54.4	2.2	6.6	9.7

Note: Figures cover population 15 years of age and older; (1) Metropolitan Statistical Area - see Appendix A for areas included
Source: Census 2000, Summary File 3

Male/Female Ratio

Area	Males	Females	Males per 100 Females
City	304,021	336,790	90.3
MSA[1]	558,663	601,993	92.8
U.S.	142,511,883	148,135,280	96.2

Note: Figures are 2003 estimates; (1) Metropolitan Statistical Area - see Appendix A for areas included
Source: Claritas, Inc.

ECONOMY

Gross Metropolitan Product

Area	1999	2000	2001	2002	2002 Rank[2]
MSA[1]	37.6	39.2	40.4	41.8	58

Note: Figures are in billions of dollars; (1) Metropolitan Statistical Area - see Appendix A for areas included; (2) Rank ranges from 1 to 319
Source: The U.S. Conference of Mayors, Metro Economies Report, July 2003

INCOME

Per Capita/Median/Average Income

Area	Per Capita ($)	Median Household ($)	Average Household ($)
City	19,770	36,771	50,342
MSA[1]	23,258	45,698	61,289
U.S.	24,078	46,868	63,207

Note: Figures are 2003 estimates; (1) Metropolitan Statistical Area - see Appendix A for areas included
Source: Claritas, Inc.

Household Income Distribution

Area	Percent of Households Earning							
	Under $15,000	$15,000 -24,999	$25,000 -34,999	$35,000 -49,999	$50,000 -74,999	$75,000 -99,000	$100,000 -149,999	$150,000 and up
City	20.1	14.0	13.9	17.1	17.1	8.1	6.2	3.5
MSA[1]	15.5	11.3	11.7	16.1	19.1	11.3	9.6	5.3
U.S.	14.1	11.5	11.7	16.0	19.2	11.3	10.2	6.0

Note: Figures are 2003 estimates; (1) Metropolitan Statistical Area - see Appendix A for areas included
Source: Claritas, Inc.

Poverty Rates by Age

Area	All Ages	Under 5 Years Old	5 to 17 Years Old	18 to 64 Years Old	65 Years and Over
City	20.6	2.7	5.8	10.4	1.6
MSA[1]	15.3	1.9	4.3	7.7	1.3
U.S.	12.4	1.2	3.0	6.9	1.2

Note: Figures are percent of population with income in 1999 below poverty level and only include population
for whom poverty status is determined; (1) Metropolitan Statistical Area - see Appendix A for areas included
Source: Census 2000, Summary File 3

Personal Bankruptcy Filing Rate

Area	2002	2003
Shelby County	19.99	20.22
U.S.	5.34	5.58

Note: Numbers are per 1,000 population and include Chapter 7 and Chapter 13 filings
Source: Federal Deposit Insurance Corporation (FDIC), Regional Economic Conditions (RECON), 2/25/2004

EMPLOYMENT

Labor Force and Employment

Area	Civilian Labor Force			Workers Employed		
	Dec. 2002	Dec. 2003	% Chg.	Dec. 2002	Dec. 2003	% Chg.
City	325,454	324,558	-0.3	306,656	301,316	-1.7
MSA[1]	577,101	576,375	-0.1	549,381	543,521	-1.1
U.S.	144,807,000	146,501,000	1.2	136,599,000	138,556,000	1.4

Note: Data is not seasonally adjusted and covers workers 16 years of age and older;
(1) Metropolitan Statistical Area - see Appendix A for areas included
Source: Bureau of Labor Statistics, http://stats.bls.gov

Unemployment Rate

Area	2003											
	Jan.	Feb.	Mar.	Apr.	May	Jun.	Jul.	Aug.	Sep.	Oct.	Nov.	Dec.
City	6.5	6.1	6.1	6.0	6.2	7.8	7.1	7.1	7.1	7.6	8.1	7.2
MSA[1]	5.4	5.1	5.0	4.9	5.1	6.3	5.7	5.7	5.6	6.1	6.4	5.7
U.S.	6.5	6.4	6.2	5.8	5.8	6.5	6.3	6.0	5.8	5.6	5.6	5.4

Note: Data is not seasonally adjusted and covers workers 16 years of age and older; All figures are
percentages; (1) Metropolitan Statistical Area - see Appendix A for areas included
Source: Bureau of Labor Statistics, http://stats.bls.gov

Employment by Occupation

Occupation Classification	City (%)	MSA[1] (%)	U.S. (%)
Sales and Office	29.7	29.7	26.7
Professional and Related	18.5	18.5	20.2
Service	16.1	14.1	14.9
Production, Transportation, and Material Moving	16.6	15.4	14.6
Management, Business, and Financial	11.0	13.2	13.5
Construction, Extraction, and Maintenance	7.9	8.9	9.4
Farming, Forestry, and Fishing	0.1	0.2	0.7

Note: Figures cover employed civilians 16 years of age and older;
(1) Metropolitan Statistical Area - see Appendix A for areas included
Source: Census 2000, Summary File 3

Employment by Industry

Sector	MSA[1]		U.S.
	Number of Employees	Percent of Total	Percent of Total
Government	88,000	14.8	16.7
Education and Health Services	69,200	11.6	12.9
Professional and Business Services	73,400	12.3	12.3
Retail Trade	70,700	11.9	11.8
Manufacturing	50,200	8.4	11.0
Leisure and Hospitality	52,000	8.7	9.1
Finance Activities	32,300	5.4	6.1
Construction	n/a	n/a	5.1
Wholesale Trade	37,600	6.3	4.3
Other Services	24,000	4.0	4.1
Transportation and Utilities	63,000	10.6	3.7
Information	9,600	1.6	2.4
Natural Resources and Mining	n/a	n/a	0.4

Note: Figures cover non-farm employment as of December 2003 and are not seasonally adjusted;
(1) Metropolitan Statistical Area - see Appendix A for areas included; n/a not available
Source: Bureau of Labor Statistics, http://stats.bls.gov

Average Wages

Occupation	$/Hr.	Occupation	$/Hr.
Accountants and Auditors	22.40	Maids and Housekeeping Cleaners	7.36
Automotive Mechanics	15.82	Maintenance and Repair Workers	14.86
Bookkeepers	13.66	Marketing Managers	37.19
Carpenters	15.80	Nuclear Medicine Technologists	20.16
Cashiers	7.56	Nurses, Licensed Practical	14.39
Clerks, General Office	11.16	Nurses, Registered	20.97
Clerks, Receptionists/Information	10.23	Nursing Aides/Orderlies/Attendants	9.54
Clerks, Shipping/Receiving	11.25	Packers and Packagers, Hand	9.09
Computer Programmers	29.21	Physical Therapists	27.77
Computer Support Specialists	16.96	Postal Service Mail Carriers	18.87
Computer Systems Analysts	27.53	Real Estate Brokers	46.83
Cooks, Restaurant	8.43	Retail Salespersons	11.39
Dentists	84.77	Sales Reps., Exc. Tech./Scientific	21.53
Electrical Engineers	31.12	Sales Reps., Tech./Scientific	37.20
Electricians	18.04	Secretaries, Exc. Legal/Med./Exec.	11.79
Financial Managers	31.85	Security Guards	9.63
First-Line Supervisors/Mgrs., Sales	15.20	Surgeons	100.39
Food Preparation Workers	7.66	Teacher Assistants	6.80
General and Operations Managers	38.30	Teachers, Elementary School	20.00
Hairdressers/Cosmetologists	12.54	Teachers, Secondary School	18.90
Internists	89.16	Telemarketers	11.66
Janitors and Cleaners	8.15	Truck Drivers, Heavy/Tractor-Trailer	17.38
Landscaping/Groundskeeping Workers	10.13	Truck Drivers, Light/Delivery Svcs.	12.27
Lawyers	42.15	Waiters and Waitresses	7.44

Note: Wage data is for 2002 and covers the Metropolitan Statistical Area (see Appendix A for areas included).
Hourly wages for elementary/secondary school teachers and teacher assistants were calculated by the editors
from annual wage data assuming a 40 hour work week; n/a not available.
Source: Bureau of Labor Statistics, 2002 Metro Area Occupational Employment and Wage Estimates

Occupational Employment Projections: 1996 - 2006

Occupations Expected to Have the Largest Job Growth (ranked by numerical growth)	Fast-Growing Occupations[1] (ranked by percent growth)
1. Salespersons, retail	1. Personal and home care aides
2. Truck drivers, light	2. Systems analysts
3. Cashiers	3. Paralegals
4. General managers & top executives	4. Respiratory therapists
5. Janitors/cleaners/maids, ex. priv. hshld.	5. Home health aides
6. Food service workers	6. Directors, religious activities & educ.
7. Child care workers, private household	7. Computer engineers
8. Cooks, fast food and short order	8. Child care workers, private household
9. Registered nurses	9. Corrections officers & jailers
10. Waiters & waitresses	10. Emergency medical technicians

Note: Projections cover Tennessee; (1) Excludes occupations with total job growth less than 300
Source: U.S. Department of Labor, Employment and Training Administration, America's Labor Market Information System (ALMIS)

TAXES

State Corporate Income Tax Rates

State	Rate (%)	Number of Brackets	Low Bracket (Under $)	High Bracket (Over $)
Tennessee	6.5	1	na	na

Note: Tax rates as of December 31, 2003; na not applicable
Source: Tax Foundation, www.taxfoundation.org

State Individual Income Tax Rates

State	Federal Deductibility	Marginal Rate (%)	Number of Brackets	Low Bracket (Under $)	High Bracket (Over $)
Tennessee	No	6.0 (h)	na	na	na

Note: Tax rates as of December 31, 2003; Brackets apply to single taxpayers and married people filing separately; na not applicable; (h) Applies to interest and dividend income only.
Source: Tax Foundation, www.taxfoundation.org

Various State and Local Tax Rates

State Sales and Use (%)	Total Sales and Use (%)	Gasoline (cents/gal.)	Cigarette (cents/pack)	Spirits ($/gal.)	Table Wine ($/gal.)	Beer ($/gal.)
7.0 (l)	9.25	20	20	4.40	1.21	0.14

Note: Tax rates as of December 31, 2003.(l) Rate rose from 6% to 7% on July 1, 2002, but the rate on food remained 6%.
Source: Tax Foundation, www.taxfoundation.org

State Tax Burdens

Area	Combined State and Local Tax Burden		Combined Federal, State and Local Tax Burden	
	Percent	Rank	Percent	Rank
Tennessee	7.7	48	26.3	48
U.S. Average	9.7	-	30.0	-

Note: Figures are for 2003
Source: Tax Foundation, www.taxfoundation.org

Internal Revenue Service Tax Audits

IRS District	Percent of Returns Audited				
	1996	1997	1998	1999	2000
Kentucky-Tennessee	0.40	0.48	0.36	0.22	0.13
U.S.	0.66	0.61	0.46	0.31	0.20

Note: Figures cover IRS district audits of federal income tax returns filed by individuals. Geographic data on district audits for 2001 and 2002 are being withheld by the IRS. TRAC is challenging this policy.
Source: Syracuse University, Transactional Records Access Clearinghouse (TRAC), "Odds of IRS District Tax Audit 2000"

RESIDENTIAL REAL ESTATE

Building Permits

Area	Single-Family 2001	2002	Pct. Chg.	Multi-Family 2001	2002	Pct. Chg.	Total 2001	2002	Pct. Chg.
Co.[1]	3,450	4,147	20.2	1,310	1,189	-9.2	4,760	5,336	12.1
U.S.	1,235,600	1,332,600	7.9	401,100	415,100	3.5	1,636,700	1,747,700	6.8

Note: Figures cover Shelby County and represent new, privately-owned housing units authorized (unadjusted data)
Source: U.S. Census Bureau, Manufacturing, Mining, and Construction Statistics

Homeownership and Housing Vacancies

Area	Homeownership Rate[2] (%) 2001	2002[a]	2003	Rental Vacancy Rate[3] (%) 2001	2002[a]	2003	Homeowner Vacancy Rate[4] (%) 2001	2002[a]	2003
MSA[1]	66.4	66.1	65.8	8.8	12.2	12.2	2.6	2.1	1.5
U.S.	67.8	67.9	68.3	8.4	8.9	9.8	1.8	1.7	1.8

Note: (1) Metropolitan Statistical Area - see Appendix A for areas included; (2) The proportion of households that are owners; (3) The proportion of the rental inventory that is vacant for rent; (4) The proportion of the homeowner inventory that is vacant for sale; (a) 2002 figures have been revised; n/a not available
Source: U.S. Census Bureau, Housing Vacancies and Homeownership Annual Statistics: 2003

COMMERCIAL REAL ESTATE

Industrial/Office Markets

Type/Market Area	Inventory (sq. ft.)	Vacant (sq. ft.)	Vacancy Rate (%)	Under Construction (sq. ft.)	Net Absorption (sq. ft.)
Industrial Space					
Memphis	163,828,309	22,814,350	13.93	2,740,440	14,944
Office Space					
Memphis	24,333,959	3,295,124	13.54	489,000	538,631

Note: Data as of 4th Quarter, 2003; n/a not available
Source: Society of Industrial and Office Realtors, 2004 Comparative Statistics of Industrial and Office Real Estate Markets

COMMERCIAL UTILITIES

Typical Monthly Electric Bills

Area	Commercial Service ($/month) 12 kW demand 1,500 kWh	120 kW demand 30,000 kWh	Industrial Service ($/month) 1,000 kW demand 400,000 kWh	20,000 kW demand 10,000,000 kWh
City	109	2,197	23,204	485,500

Note: Based on rates in effect January 1, 2003
Source: Memphis Light, Gas and Water, 2003 Utility Bill Comparisons for Selected U.S. Cities

TRANSPORTATION

Means of Transportation to Work

Area	Car/Truck/Van Drove Alone	Car-pooled	Public Transportation Bus	Subway	Railroad	Bicycle	Walked	Other Means	Worked at Home
City	76.6	15.7	2.8	0.0	0.0	0.1	1.9	1.1	1.7
MSA[1]	80.9	13.0	1.6	0.0	0.0	0.1	1.3	0.9	2.2
U.S.	75.7	12.2	2.5	1.5	0.5	0.4	2.9	1.0	3.3

Note: Figures shown are percentages and cover workers 16 years of age and older;
(1) Metropolitan Statistical Area - see Appendix A for areas included
Source: Census 2000, Summary File 3

Travel Time to Work

Area	Less Than 15 Minutes	15 to 29 Minutes	30 to 44 Minutes	45 to 59 Minutes	60 Minutes or More
City	24.0	48.2	20.0	3.9	3.9
MSA[1]	22.9	43.4	23.2	6.1	4.4
U.S.	29.4	36.1	19.1	7.4	8.0

Note: Figures are percentages and include workers 16 years old and over; (1) Metropolitan Statistical Area - see Appendix A for areas included
Source: Census 2000, Summary File 3

Roadway Congestion Index

Area	1982	1990	1996	2000	2001
City	0.71	0.88	0.98	1.00	1.03
Average[1]	0.82	1.01	1.08	1.16	1.17

Note: Values greater than 1.00 indicate undesirable mobility levels; (1) average of 75 urban areas
Source: Texas Transportation Institute, The 2003 Annual Urban Mobility Report

Transportation Statistics

Interstate highways (2004)	I-40; I-55
Public transportation (2002)	Memphia Area Transit Authority (MATA)
Buses	
Average fleet age in years	8.9
No. operated in max. service	164
Light rail	
Average fleet age in years	6.9
No. operated in max. service	10
Demand response	
Average fleet age in years	3.0
No. operated in max. service	44
Passenger air service	
Airport	Memphis International
Airlines (2003)	10
Boardings (2002)	5,231,998
Amtrak service (2004)	Yes
Major waterways/ports	Mississippi River

Source: Federal Transit Administration, National Transit Database, 2002; Editor & Publisher Market Guide, 2004; Bureau of Transportation Statistics, Airport Enplanement Activity for CY2002; www.amtrak.com

BUSINESSES

Major Business Headquarters

Company Name	2003 Rankings	
	Fortune 500	Forbes 500
AutoZone	314	-
Dunavant Enterprises	-	248
FedEx	83	-

Note: Companies listed are located in the city; dashes indicate no ranking
Fortune 500: Companies that produce a 10-K are ranked 1 to 500 based on 2002 revenue
Forbes 500: Private companies are ranked 1 to 281 based on 2002 revenue
Source: Fortune, April 14, 2003; www.forbes.com, November 6, 2003

Best Companies to Work For

FedEx; First Tennessee, headquartered in Memphis, are among the "100 Best Companies to Work for in 2004." Criteria: trust in management, pride in work/company, camaraderie, company responses to the Hewitt People Practices Inventory, and employee responses to their Great Place to Work survey. The companies also had to be at least 10 years old and have a minimum of 500 employees. *Fortune, January 12, 2004*

First Tennessee Ntl. Corp, headquartered in Memphis, is among the "100 Best Companies for Working Mothers." Criteria: fair wages, opportunities for women to advance, support for child care, flexible work schedules, family-friendly benefits, and work/life supports. *Working Mother, October 2003*

Fedex, headquartered in Memphis, is among the "50 Best Companies for Minorities." Criteria: 1,200 of the largest U.S employers were surveyed—141 responded. Those companies were analyzed on 15 quantitative and qualitative measures—from how well minorities are paid to how many are in management. *Fortune, July 7, 2003*

Harrah's Entertainment Inc, headquartered in Memphis, is among the "100 Best Places to Work in IT 2003." Criteria: compensation, turnover and training. *www.computerworld.com, 3/15/2004*

Fast-Growing Businesses

According to *Inc.*, Memphis is home to two of America's 500 fastest-growing private companies: **BCS Industries; Interactive Solutions**. Criteria: must be an independent, privately-held, U.S. corporation, proprietorship or partnership; sales of at least $200,000 in 1998; five-year operating/sales history; increase in 2002 sales over 2001 sales; holding companies, regulated banks, and utilities were excluded. *Inc. 500, America's Fastest-Growing Private Companies, October 15, 2003*

Memphis is home to one of *Business Week's* "hot growth" companies: **Fred's**. Criteria: increase in sales and profits, return on capital and stock price. *Business Week, June 9, 2003*

Minority and Women-Owned Businesses

Ownership	All Firms		Firms with Paid Employees			
	Firms	Sales ($000)	Firms	Sales ($000)	Employees	Payroll ($000)
Black	8,080	573,370	1,074	408,495	7,667	127,324
Hispanic	365	130,665	58	117,370	434	13,715
Women	8,924	2,099,116	1,872	1,936,249	16,170	363,775

Note: Figures cover firms located in the city
Source: 1997 Economic Census, Minority and Women-Owned Businesses

Minority Business Opportunity

Memphis is home to one company which is on the Black Enterprise Auto Dealer 100 list (100 largest dealers based on gross sales): **Lexus of Memphis**. Criteria: company must be operational in previous calendar year and at least 51% black-owned. *Black Enterprise, www.blackenterprise.com, B.E. 100s, 2003 Report*

Memphis is home to one company which is on the Black Enterprise Bank 25 list (25 largest banks based on total assets, capital, deposits and loans, including mortgage-backed securities for the calendar year): **Tri-State Bank of Memphis**. Criteria: commercial banks or savings and loans that are classified by the Federal Reserve as black institutions and have been fully operational for the previous calendar year. *Black Enterprise, www.blackenterprise.com, B.E. 100s, 2003 Report*

HOTELS

Hotels/Motels

Area	Hotels/Motels	Average Minimum Rates ($)		
		Tourist	First-Class	Deluxe
City	114	68	87	n/a

Note: n/a not available
Source: OAG Travel Planner Online, Spring 2004

EVENT SITES

Major Event Sites, Meeting Places and Convention Centers

Name	Guest Rooms	Exhibit/ Meeting Space (sq. ft.)	Largest Meeting Room Capacity
Adam's Mark Memphis	408	25,000	1,250
Four Points Hotel	380	31,000	1,400
Memphis Cook Convention Center	n/a	n/a	10,000
Mid-South Coliseum	n/a	n/a	12,000
The Peabody	468	74,000	1,600

Note: n/a not available
Source: Original research

Living Environment

COST OF LIVING

Cost of Living Index

Year	Composite Index	Groceries	Housing	Utilities	Trans- portation	Health Care	Misc. Goods/ Services
2001	89.0	92.9	83.1	82.0	98.2	87.2	91.2
2002	89.9	95.4	80.1	79.7	97.0	90.9	95.7
2003	90.3	92.0	79.4	86.9	95.8	95.5	97.7

Note: U.S. = 100
Source: ACCRA, Cost of Living Index, 2001, 2002 and 2003 4-Quarter Averages

HOUSING

House Price Index (HPI)

Area	National Ranking[2]	Quarterly Change (%)	One-Year Change (%)	Five-Year Change (%)
MSA[1]	205	1.32	2.66	16.68
U.S.[3]	-	3.67	7.97	41.81

Note: The HPI is a weighted repeat sales index. It measures average price changes in repeat sales or refinancings on the same properties. This information is obtained by reviewing repeat mortgage transactions on single-family properties whose mortgages have been purchased or securitized by Fannie Mae of Freddie Mac in January 1975; (1) Metropolitan Statistical Area - see Appendix A for areas included; (2) Rankings are based on annual percentage change, for all MSAs containing at least 15,000 transactions over the last 10 years and ranges from 1 to 220; (3) figures based on a weighted division average; all figures are for the period ended December 31, 2003
Source: Office of Federal Housing Enterprise Oversight, House Price Index, March 1, 2004

Housing: Year Structure Built

Area	1990 -2000	1980 -1989	1970 -1979	1960 -1969	1950 -1959	1940 -1949	Before 1940	Median Year
City	7.6	12.8	20.4	21.2	19.4	9.4	9.0	1966
MSA[1]	21.3	16.3	20.1	16.1	13.2	6.6	6.4	1974
U.S.	17.0	15.8	18.5	13.7	12.7	7.3	15.0	1971

Note: Figures are percentages; (1) Metropolitan Statistical Area - see Appendix A for areas included
Source: Census 2000, Summary File 3

Average New Home Price

Area	2001	2002	2003
City	170,840	183,095	188,690
U.S.	212,643	236,567	248,193

Note: Figures, in dollars, are based on a new home with 2,400 sq. ft. of living area on an 8,000 sq. ft. lot.
Source: ACCRA, Cost of Living Index, 2001, 2002 and 2003 4-Quarter Averages

Average Apartment Rent

Area	2001	2002	2003
City	639	638	678
U.S.	674	708	721

Note: Figures, in dollars per month, are based on an unfurnished two bedroom, 1-1/2 or 2 bath apartment, approximately 950 sq. ft. in size, excluding all utilities except water
Source: ACCRA, Cost of Living Index, 2001, 2002 and 2003 4-Quarter Averages

RESIDENTIAL UTILITIES

Average Residential Utility Costs

Area	All Electric ($/mth)	Part Electric ($/mth)	Other Energy ($/mth)	Phone ($/mth)
City	–	55.47	42.66	23.85
U.S.	116.46	65.82	62.68	23.90

Source: ACCRA, Cost of Living Index, 2003 4-Quarter Average

HEALTH CARE

Average Health Care Costs

Area	Hospital ($/day)	Doctor ($/visit)	Dentist ($/visit)
City	492.00	71.25	82.75
U.S.	678.35	67.91	83.90

Note: Hospital—based on a semi-private room; Doctor—based on a general practitioner's routine exam of an established patient; Dentist—based on adult teeth cleaning and periodic oral exam.
Source: ACCRA, Cost of Living Index, 2003 4-Quarter Average

Distribution of Non-Federal, Office-Based Physicians

Area	Total	Family/ General Practice	Specialties		
			Medical	Surgical	Other
MSA[1] (number)	2,082	200	798	540	544
MSA[1] (rate per 10,000 pop.)	18.3	1.8	7.0	4.8	4.8
Metro Average[2] (rate per 10,000 pop.)	33.1	2.2	7.7	4.8	5.6

Note: Data as of December 31, 2001; (1) Metropolitan Statistical Area - see Appendix A for areas included; (2) Average of 81 MSAs and CMSAs in this book
Source: American Medical Association, Physician Characteristics & Distribution in the U.S., 2003-2004

Hospitals

Memphis has the following hospitals: 8 general medical and surgical; 2 psychiatric; 2 rehabilitation; 1 children's other specialty.
AHA Guide to the Healthcare Field, 2003-2004

According to *U.S. News*, Memphis has two of the best hospitals in the U.S.: **St. Jude Children's Research Hospital**; **University of Tennessee Medical Center**; *U.S. News Online, "America's Best Hospitals 2003"*

PRESIDENTIAL ELECTION

2000 Presidential Election Results

Area	Gore	Bush	Nader	Buchanan	Other
Shelby County	56.6	42.1	0.8	0.1	0.4
U.S.	48.4	47.9	2.7	0.4	0.6

Note: Results are percentages and may not add to 100% due to rounding
Source: www.cbsnews.com; www.uselectionatlas.org

EDUCATION

Public School District Statistics

District Name	Schls.	Enroll- ment	Classroom Teachers	Pupil/ Teacher Ratio	Minority Pupils[1] (%)	Current Expend.[2] ($/pupil)
Memphis City SD	174	115,992	7,154	16.2	n/a	6,188
Shelby County SD	46	44,547	2,517	17.7	n/a	4,578

Note: Data covers the 2001-02 school year unless otherwise noted; (1) Fall 2000; (2) FY2000; n/a not available
Source: U.S. Department of Education, National Center for Education Statistics, Common Core of Data, Local Education Agency (School District) Universe Survey: School Year 2001-2002; U.S. Department of Education, National Center for Education Statistics, Digest of Education Statistics 2002

Educational Quality

School District	Education Quotient[1]	Graduate Outcome[2]	Community Index[3]	Resource Index[4]
Memphis City	2	1	24	41

Note: Scores are national percentile rankings and range from 1 (worst) to 99 (best); (1) Combination of the Graduate Outcome, Community and Resource indexes weighted to reflect the greater importance of the Graduate Outcome and Resource Index; (2) Based on graduation rates and college board scores (SAT/ACT); (3) Based on the surrounding community's level of affluence and adult education; (4) Based on teacher salaries, per-pupil expenditures and student-teacher ratios.
Source: Expansion Management, December 2003

Educational Attainment by Race

Area	High School Graduate (%)					Bachelor's Degree (%)				
	Total	White	Black	Asian	Hisp.[2]	Total	White	Black	Asian	Hisp.[2]
City	76.4	86.1	69.8	75.8	46.1	20.9	32.9	11.3	49.5	12.6
MSA[1]	79.8	87.1	69.6	78.7	52.4	22.7	29.2	12.1	48.4	14.1
U.S.	80.4	83.6	72.3	80.4	52.4	24.4	26.1	14.3	44.1	10.4

Note: Figures shown cover persons 25 years old and over; (1) Metropolitan Statistical Area - see Appendix A for areas included; (2) people of Hispanic origin can be of any race
Source: Census 2000, Summary File 3

School Enrollment by Type

Area	Grades KG to 8				Grades 9 to 12			
	Public		Private		Public		Private	
	Enrollment	%	Enrollment	%	Enrollment	%	Enrollment	%
City	85,881	90.2	9,354	9.8	35,249	89.5	4,154	10.5
MSA[1]	149,569	88.4	19,693	11.6	61,138	87.4	8,828	12.6
U.S.	33,526,011	88.7	4,285,121	11.3	14,848,628	90.6	1,532,323	9.4

Note: Figures shown cover persons 3 years old and over; (1) Metropolitan Statistical Area - see Appendix A for areas included
Source: Census 2000, Summary File 3

School Enrollment by Race

Area	Grades KG to 8 (%)				Grades 9 to 12 (%)			
	White	Black	Asian	Hisp.[1]	White	Black	Asian	Hisp.[1]
City	20.0	76.1	1.1	2.6	21.6	74.8	1.1	2.1
MSA[2]	43.1	53.1	1.2	2.2	44.0	52.4	1.3	1.9
U.S.	68.5	15.5	3.3	16.8	68.8	15.5	3.8	15.7

Note: Figures shown cover persons 3 years old and over; (1) people of Hispanic origin can be of any race; (2) Metropolitan Statistical Area - see Appendix A for areas included
Source: Census 2000, Summary File 3

Classroom Teacher Salaries in Public Schools

District	B.A. Degree		M.A. Degree		Maximum	
	Min. ($)	Rank[1]	Max. ($)	Rank[1]	Max. ($)	Rank[1]
Memphis	33,306	33	50,505	67	57,707	56
DOD Average[2]	31,567	-	53,248	-	59,356	-

Note: Salaries are for 2001-2002; (1) Rank ranges from 1 to 100; (2) As per the U.S. Department of Defense Wage Fixing Authority
Source: American Federation of Teachers, Survey & Analysis of Teacher Salary Trends 2002

Higher Education

Four-Year Colleges			Two-Year Colleges			Medical Schools	Law Schools	Voc/Tech
Public	Private Non-profit	Private For-profit	Public	Private Non-profit	Private For-profit			
2	10	1	2	3	2	1	1	17

Note: Figures cover institutions located within the city limits.
Source: National Center for Education Statistics, The Integrated Postsecondary Education System (IPEDS) Peer Analysis System, 2002; usnews.com, America's Best Graduate Schools 2004, Medical School Directory; The College Blue Book, Occupational Education, 2003; Barron's Guide to Law Schools, 2003; Medical School Admission Requirements U.S. & Canada, 2003-2004

MAJOR EMPLOYERS

Major Employers

Company Name	Industry	Type
Autozone	Auto and home supply stores	Headquarters
Baptist Mem Hosptial-Memphis	General medical and surgical hospitals	Headquarters
Carrier Air Cond Co	Refrigeration and heating equipment	Branch
City of Memphis	Combination utilities, nec	Branch
Defense Depot Memphis	National security	Branch
Fedex	Air courier services	Branch
Fedex	Air transportation, scheduled	Branch
Le Bonheur Childrens Med Ctr	Specialty hospitals, except psychiatric	Branch
Memphis Methodist	General medical and surgical hospitals	Headquarters
Memphis VAMC	Administration of veterans' affairs	Branch
Northwest Airlines	Air transportation, scheduled	Branch
Regional Medical Ctr Tenessee	General medical and surgical hospitals	Branch
ServiceMaster Company	Lawn and garden services	Branch
Sheriffs Dept	Police protection	Branch
St Francis Hospital	General medical and surgical hospitals	Headquarters
St Judes Children RES Hosp	Membership organizations, nec	Single
Tennessee National Guard	National security	Branch
University of Memphis	Colleges and universities	Headquarters
US Naval Hospital	Offices and clinics of dentists	Branch
US Post Office	U.s. postal service	Branch

Note: Companies shown are located in the metropolitan area and have 1,500 or more employees.
Source: www.zapdata.com, March 2004

PUBLIC SAFETY

Crime Rate

Area	All Crimes	Violent Crimes				Property Crimes		
		Murder	Forcible Rape	Robbery	Aggrav. Assault	Burglary	Larceny -Theft	Motor Vehicle Theft
City	9,939.9	22.8	78.0	640.1	836.0	2,466.6	4,504.7	1,391.7
Suburbs[1]	n/a	n/a	n/a	n/a	n/a	n/a	n/a	n/a
MSA[2]	n/a	n/a	n/a	n/a	n/a	n/a	n/a	n/a
U.S.	4,118.8	5.6	33.0	145.9	310.1	746.2	2,445.8	432.1

Note: Figures are crimes per 100,000 population; (1) All areas within the MSA that are located outside the city limits; (2) Metropolitan Statistical Area - see Appendix A for areas included; n/a not available
Source: FBI Uniform Crime Reports, 2002

RECREATION

Culture and Recreation

Museums	Orchestras	Opera Companies	Dance Companies	Professional Theatres	Zoos	Pro Sports Teams[1]
12	1	0	0	1	1	0

Note: (1) Covers the Metropolitan Statistical Area - see Appendix A for areas included.
Source: The Grey House Performing Arts Directory, 2002; Official Museum Directory, 2004; www.sportsvenues.com

Library System

The Memphis-Shelby County Public Library has 26 branches, holdings of 1,758,592 volumes, and a budget of $19,278,582 (2001-2002).
American Library Directory, 2003-2004

MEDIA

Newspapers

Name	Type	Freq.	Distribution	Circulation
The Commercial Appeal	General	7x/wk	Area	210,000
Daily News	General	5x/wk	State	50,000
East Memphis Shoppers News	General	1x/wk	Local	193,000
Hebrew Watchman	Jewish	1x/wk	Local	3,000
The Mid South Tribune	Hispanic	1x/wk	State	26,300
North Shelby Times	General	1x/wk	Local	63,000
Silver Star News	Black	1x/wk	Local	28,000
Tri-State Defender	Black/Eth	1x/wk	Regional	31,975
West Tennessee Catholic	Cath/Relig	1x/wk	Regional	17,100

Note: Includes newspapers whose offices are located in the city and whose circulations are 1,000 or more
Source: Burrelle's Media Directory, 2003

Television Stations

Name	Ch.	Affiliation	Type	Owner
WREG	3	CBST	Commercial	New York Times Company
WMC	5	NBCT	Commercial	Raycom Media Inc.
WKNO	10	PBS	n/a	n/a
WHBQ	13	FBC	Commercial	Fox Television Stations Inc.
WPTY	24	ABCT	Commercial	Clear Channel Communications Inc.
WLMT	30	UPN	Commercial	Clear Channel Communications Inc.
WBUY	40	n/a	Non-comm.	Trinity Broadcasting Network
WPXX	50	PAXTV	n/a	Paxson Communications Corporation

Note: Stations included broadcast from the Memphis metro area; n/a not available
Source: Burrelle's Media Directory, 2003

AM Radio Stations

Call Letters	Freq. (kHz)	Target Audience	Station Format	Music Format
WHBQ	560	General	S/T	n/a
WREC	600	General	M/N/S/T	Gospel
WCRV	640	Religious	M/T	Adult Contemporary
WJCE	680	General	M/N/S	Easy Listening
WMC	790	General	M/N/S/T	Classic Rock
KWAM	990	General	M/N	Gospel
WGSF	1030	Christian	General	Hispanic
WDIA	1070	B/G	M	Adult Contemporary
WLOK	1340	General	M	Gospel
WZNG	1400	General	M/N/S/T	Classic Rock
WBBP	1480	Religious	M/N/S	Christian
WLIJ	1580	General	M/N/S	Country

Note: Stations included broadcast from the Memphis metro area; n/a not available
The following abbreviations may be used:
Target Audience: A=Asian; B=Black; C=Christian; E=Ethnic; F=French; G=General; H=Hispanic;
M=Men; N=Native American; R=Religious; S=Senior Citizen; W=Women; Y=Young Adult; Z=Children
Station Format: E=Educational; M=Music; N=News; S=Sports; T=Talk
Source: Burrelle's Media Directory, 2003

FM Radio Stations

Call Letters	Freq. (mHz)	Target Audience	Station Format	Music Format
WKNA	88.9	General	E/M/N/T	Classical
WEVL	89.9	General	E/M	Adult Standards
WKNP	90.1	General	M/N/T	Classical
WKNQ	90.7	General	M/N	Classical
WKNO	91.1	General	M/N/T	Classical
WUMR	91.7	General	E/M/N/S/T	Jazz
WMFS	92.9	General	M/T	Alternative
WMBZ	94.1	General	M	Adult Contemporary
WOTO	95.7	General	M/N/T	Oldies
WYYL	96.1	General	M	Country
WHRK	97.1	General	M	Urban Contemporary
WSRR	98.1	General	M	Classic Rock
WMC	99.7	General	M	Adult Contemporary
KJMS	101.1	General	M	Adult Contemporary
WEGR	102.7	General	M/N/S/T	Classic Rock
WRBO	103.5	General	M	Oldies
WRVR	104.5	General	M	Adult Contemporary
WGKX	105.9	General	M	Country
KXHT	107.1	B/Y	M/N/S	Urban Contemporary
WMPS	107.5	General	M	Adult Contemporary

Note: Stations included broadcast from the Memphis metro area
The following abbreviations may be used:
Target Audience: A=Asian; B=Black; C=Christian; E=Ethnic; F=French; G=General; H=Hispanic;
M=Men; N=Native American; R=Religious; S=Senior Citizen; W=Women; Y=Young Adult; Z=Children
Station Format: E=Educational; M=Music; N=News; S=Sports; T=Talk
Source: Burrelle's Media Directory, 2003

CLIMATE

Average and Extreme Temperatures

Temperature	Jan	Feb	Mar	Apr	May	Jun	Jul	Aug	Sep	Oct	Nov	Dec	Yr.
Extreme High (°F)	83	85	90	95	99	104	107	104	105	97	86	82	107
Average High (°F)	57	62	69	78	84	90	92	92	87	78	68	60	77
Average Temp. (°F)	46	50	57	65	72	79	81	81	76	65	55	48	65
Average Low (°F)	34	37	44	51	59	67	70	69	64	51	42	36	52
Extreme Low (°F)	0	8	15	28	38	42	55	53	34	24	16	2	0

Note: Figures cover the years 1948-1990
Source: National Climatic Data Center, International Station Meteorological Climate Summary, 9/96

Average Precipitation/Snowfall/Humidity

Precip./Humidity	Jan	Feb	Mar	Apr	May	Jun	Jul	Aug	Sep	Oct	Nov	Dec	Yr.
Avg. Precip. (in.)	4.9	5.1	6.6	5.2	4.3	3.7	5.3	3.5	3.6	2.7	4.2	5.6	54.8
Avg. Snowfall (in.)	1	Tr	Tr	Tr	0	0	0	0	0	0	Tr	Tr	1
Avg. Rel. Hum. 6am (%)	87	86	87	90	91	91	93	93	92	91	88	87	90
Avg. Rel. Hum. 3pm (%)	56	51	47	46	50	52	57	54	54	48	49	54	51

Note: Figures cover the years 1948-1990; Tr = Trace amounts (<0.05 in. of rain; <0.5 in. of snow)
Source: National Climatic Data Center, International Station Meteorological Climate Summary, 9/96

Weather Conditions

Temperature			Daytime Sky			Precipitation		
10°F & below	32°F & below	90°F & above	Clear	Partly cloudy	Cloudy	0.01 inch or more precip.	0.1 inch or more snow/ice	Thunder- storms
1	53	86	101	152	112	104	2	59

Note: Figures are average number of days per year and covers the years 1948-1990
Source: National Climatic Data Center, International Station Meteorological Climate Summary, 9/96

**HAZARDOUS
WASTE**

Superfund Sites

Memphis has one hazardous waste site on the EPA's Superfund National Priorities List: **Memphis Defense Depot (DLA)**. *U.S. Environmental Protection Agency, National Priorities List, March 15, 2004*

**AIR & WATER
QUALITY**

Maximum Pollutant Concentrations

	Particulate Matter (ug/m³)	Carbon Monoxide (ppm)	Sulfur Dioxide (ppm)	Nitrogen Dioxide (ppm)	Ozone 1-hour (ppm)	Ozone 8-hour (ppm)	Lead (ug/m³)
MSA[1] Level	56	4	0.03	0.022	0.13	0.1	0.01a
NAAQS[2]	150	9	0.140	0.053	0.12	0.08	1.50
Met NAAQS[2]	Yes	Yes	Yes	Yes	No	No	Yes

Note: (1) Metropolitan Statistical Area - see Appendix A for areas included; (2) National Ambient Air Quality Standards; n/a not available; (a) Localized impact from an industrial source in Memphis
Units: ppm = parts per million; ug/m³ = micrograms per cubic meter
Source: EPA, Latest Findings on National Air Quality: 2002 Status and Trends, August 2003

Air Quality Index

In the Memphis MSA (see Appendix A for areas included), the Air Quality Index (AQI) exceeded 100 on 17 days in 2002. An AQI value greater than 100 indicates that air quality would have been in the unhealthful range on that day.
EPA, Latest Findings on National Air Quality: 2002 Status and Trends, August 2003

Watershed Health

The U.S. Environmental Protection Agency monitors the health of the aquatic resources for the nation's 2,000+ watersheds. **The Lower Mississippi-Memphis watershed serves the Memphis area and received an overall Index of Watershed Indicators (IWI) score of 1 (better quality - low vulnerability).** The IWI score is based on seven condition and nine vulnerability indicators. The overall IWI score ranges from 1 (best health) to 6 (worst health). The Condition Indicators include: designated use attainment, fish and wildlife consumption advisories, source water condition, contaminated sediments, ambient water quality, and wetlands loss index. The Vulnerability Indicators include: aquatic species at risk, conventional and toxic loads over permitted limits, urban and agricultural runoff potential, population change, hydrologic modification, estuarine pollution susceptibility, and air deposition. *EPA, Index of Watershed Indicators, October 26, 2001*

Drinking Water

Water System Name	Pop. Served	Primary Water Source Type	Number of Violations January 2002-February 2004		
			Health Based	Significant Monitoring	Monitoring
MLG&W	654,267	Ground	None	None	None

Note: Data as of February 19, 2004
Source: EPA, Office of Ground Water and Drinking Water, Safe Drinking Water Information System

Memphis tap water is neutral, hardness 46ppm and fluoridated.
Editor & Publisher Market Guide, 2004

Miami, Florida

Background

While the majority of Miami's residents are Caucasian of European descent, there is a growing number of Cubans, Puerto Ricans, and Haitians. Given this flavorful mix, Miami is a hot international setting with a Latin-American accent.

Thanks to early pioneer Julia Tuttle, railroad magnate Henry Flagler extended the East Coast Railroad beyond Palm Beach. Within 15 years of that decision, Miami became known as the "Gold Coast." The land boom of the 1920s brought wealthy socialites, as well as African-Americans in search of work. Pink- and aquamarine-hued art deco hotels were squeezed onto a tiny tract of land called Miami Beach, and the population of the Miami metro area swelled.

Given Miami's origins in a tourist-oriented economy, many of the activities in which residents engage are "leisurely," including swimming, scuba diving, golf, tennis, and boating. For those who enjoy professional sports, the city is host to the following teams: the Miami Dolphins, football; the Florida Marlins, baseball; the Miami Heat, basketball; and the Florida Panthers, hockey. Cultural activities range from the Miami City Ballet and the Coconut Grove Playhouse to numerous art galleries and museums, including the Bass Museum of Art. Visits to the Villa Vizcaya, a gorgeous palazzo built by industrialist James Deering in the Italian Renaissance style, and to the Miami MetroZoo are popular pastimes.

Miami's prime location on Biscayne Bay in the southeastern United States makes it a perfect nexus for travel and trade. The Port of Miami is a bustling center for many cruise and cargo ships. The Port is also a base for the National Oceanic and Atmospheric Administration. The Miami International Airport is a busy destination point to and from many Latin-American and Caribbean countries.

Miami is still at the trading crossroads of the Western Hemisphere as the chief shipment point for exports and imports with Latin America and the Caribbean. And one out of every three North American cruise passengers sails from Miami.

The sultry, subtropical climate against a backdrop of Spanish, art deco, and modern architecture makes Miami a uniquely cosmopolitan city. The Art Deco Historic District, known as South Beach and located on the tip of Miami Beach, has recently developed an international reputation in the fashion, film, and music industries. Greater Miami is now a center for film, television, and print production in the country.

Long, warm summers are typical, as are mild, dry winters. The marine influence is evidenced by the narrow daily range of temperature and the rapid warming of cold air masses. During the summer months, rainfall occurs in early morning near the ocean and in early afternoon further inland. Hurricanes occasionally affect the Miami area, usually in September and October, while destructive tornadoes are quite rare. Funnel clouds are occasionally sighted and a few touch the ground briefly, but significant destruction is unusual. Waterspouts are visible from the beaches during the summer months but seldom cause any damage. During June, July, and August, there are numerous beautiful, but dangerous, lightning events.

Rankings

- Miami was ranked #125 out of 331 metro areas in *Cities Ranked & Rated*. Criteria: cost of living; climate; crime; transportation; economy and jobs; education; arts and culture; health and healthcare; leisure. *Cities Ranked & Rated, 1st Edition, 2004*

- *Ladies Home Journal* ranked America's 200 largest cities based on the qualities women surveyed care about most. Miami ranked #53 out of 57 in the big city category (population over 300,000). Criteria: crime; lifestyle; education; jobs; health; child care; politics; and the economy. *Ladies Home Journal Online, "The Best Cities for Women 2002"*

- Miami was selected as one of "America's Pet Healthiest Cities" by Purina. The city ranked #50 out of 50. Criteria: veterinary services; environment; and legislation. *Purina Pet Institute, "America's Pet Healthiest Cities," August 14, 2001*

- Miami was selected as one of the "Top 10 Cities for Hispanics." The city was ranked #3. The cities were selected based on data from the following sources: *Forbes* magazine; CNN; *Money* magazine; local newspapers; U.S. Census; experts; natives and residents; www.bestplaces.net; www.findyourspot.com. *Hispanic Magazine, July/August 2002*

- *Forbes* ranked the 40 most populous metro areas in the U.S. in terms of the best places to be single. The Miami metro area was ranked #12. Criteria: number of other singles; cost of living alone; nightlife; culture; job growth; coolness. *Forbes, June 5, 2003*

- *Forbes* ranked the 150 most populous metro areas in the U.S. in terms of the "Best Places for Business and Careers." The Miami metro area was ranked #130. Criteria: income and job growth; cost-of-doing-business; qualifications of the available pool of labor; crime rates; housing costs; net migration. *Forbes, May 9, 2003*

- Miami was selected as one of "America's Healthiest Cities" by *Natural Health* magazine. The city was ranked #14 out of the 50 largest urban areas in the U.S. Twenty-six criteria in the following four categories were examined: whether the city boasts natural offerings; how well the city promotes its resident's physical health; whether the city offers a healthy environment; how well the city fosters a sense of community. *Natural Health, April 2003*

- *Men's Health* ranked 101 U.S. cities in terms of the quality of their tap water. Miami received a grade of D. Criteria: levels of bacteria, arsenic, lead, trihalomethanes, and haloacetic acids were compared with the National Academy of Science's guidelines as well as with the EPA's more stringent maximum contaminant level goals. *Men's Health, March 2004*

- Sperling's BestPlaces ranked 331 metro areas and identified the most and least stressful U.S. cities. The Miami metro area ranked #2 out of the 100 largest metro areas (#1 = most stressful). Criteria: divorce rate; unemployment rate; violent and property crime; suicide rate; commute time; mental health; alcohol consumption; cloudy days. *www.BestPlaces.net, February 26, 2004*

- Sperling's BestPlaces in partnership with Pep Boys ranked 77 metro areas and identified "America's Most Drivable Cities." The Miami metro area ranked #49. Criteria: climate; road roughness; urban mobility; gas prices. *Pep Boys, "America's Most Drivable Cities," April 9, 2003*

- Miami was ranked #84 out of America's 200 largest metro areas in *SELF Magazine's* ranking of "America's Healthiest Cities for Women." Criteria: safety; air/water quality; cancer rates; and 21 other factors relating to health. *SELF Magazine, November 2003*

- Miami was identified as one of the most dangerous large metro areas for pedestrians in the U.S. The area ranked #5 out of the nations 49 largest metro areas. Criteria: average yearly pedestrian fatalities per capita (for the years 2000 and 2001) adjusted for the number of walkers. *Surface Transportation Policy Project, "Mean Streets 2002"*

- Miami was selected as one of the 25 fattest cities in America by *Men's Fitness Online*. It ranked #24 out of America's 50 largest cities. Criteria: gyms/sporting goods; nutrition; exercise/sports; overweight/sedentary; junk food; alcohol; smoking; television; air and water quality; climate; geography; commute time; parks/open space; recreation facilities; and health care. *Men's Fitness Online, America's Fittest/Fattest Cities 2003*

- Miami was selected as one of "The 10 Best Cities for Families" by *Child* magazine. It ranked #4 out of 100 cities surveyed. Criteria: number of pediatricians per capita; proximity to a children's hospital; immunization rates; infant mortality rate; air quality; water quality; school spending; pupil-teacher ratio; availability of parks/green space; nearby recreational opportunities; average commute time; number of sunny days; average cost of a 3-bedroom home; unemployment rate; future job growth; crime rate; percentage of children under 5; mandated minimum child care ratios. *Child, April 2001*

- *Zero Population Growth* ranked 239 cities in terms of children's health, safety, and economic well-being. Miami was ranked #20 out of 25 major cities (main city in a metro area with population of greater than 2 million) and was given a grade of C. Criteria: total population and population growth; percent of population under 18 years of age; number of children's museums; health improvement grade; percent of births to teens; percent of low birthweight infants; infant mortality rate; number of Title X-funded clinics; average SAT/ACT scores; average elementary and secondary class size; crime rate; unemployment rate; percent of affordable homes; number of bad air days; park acres per 1000 persons; library circulation per child; and children's program attendance counts. *Zero Population Growth, Kid Friendly Cities Report Card 2001*

- Mercer Human Resources Consulting ranked 215 cities worldwide in terms of overall quality of life. Miami ranked #63. Criteria: political, social, economic, and socio-cultural factors; medical and health considerations; schools and education; public services and transportation; recreation; consumer goods; housing; and natural environment. *Mercer Human Resources Consulting, March 3, 2003*

- Mercer Human Resources Consulting ranked 144 urban areas worldwide in terms of cost-of-living. Miami ranked #27 (the lower the ranking, the higher the cost-of-living). The survey measured the comparative cost of over 200 items (i.e. housing, food, clothing, household goods, transportation, and entertainment) in each location. *Mercer Human Resources Consulting, June 16, 2003*

- *Ladies Home Journal* ranked America's 200 largest cities in terms of safety. Miami ranked #145 out of 200. Criteria: violent crimes; crimes against property; and rape. *Ladies Home Journal Online, "The Best Cities for Women 2002"*

- Miami was ranked #43 out of 268 metro areas in terms of its Creativity Index. The Creativity Index is a mix of four equally weighted factors: the Creative Class (scientists, engineers, architects, designers, writers, artists, musicians, or any profession where creativity is a key factor) share of the workforce; innovation, measured as patents per capita; high-tech industry, using the Milken Institute's Tech Pole Index; and diversity, measured by the Gay Index (a reasonable proxy for an areas' openness to different kinds of people and ideas). *The Rise of the Creative Class, 2002*

- Miami was ranked #62 out of 125 regions worldwide in terms of its "Knowledge Competitiveness Index." The index attempts to measure the knowledge-based development taking place throughout the world and is based on 17 measures of economic performance that indicate a region's ability to translate its knowledge capacity into economic value. *Robert Huggins Associates, "2003-2004 World Knowledge Competitiveness Index"*

- The Miami metro area was selected by *Yahoo! Internet Life* as one of "America's Most Wired Cities...and Towns." The area ranked #39 out of 87. Criteria: home and work net use; user sophistication; domain density; and available content. *Yahoo! Internet Life, April 2001*

- The Miami metro area was selected by Cranium as one of the "Top 50 Fun Cities" in America. The area ranked #46. Criteria includes: number of sports teams, restaurants, and dance performances; number of toy stores; city budget spent on recreation. *Cranium, November 4, 2003*

- Miami was identified as one of the 100 "Most Unwired Cities" in the U.S. The area ranked #43. Criteria: number of public and commercial wireless access points; cell phone coverage offering wide area network Internet access; Internet penetration. *Intel, "Most Unwired Cities," March 4, 2003*

■ Scarborough Research measured the percentage of households who subscribe to cellular services among adults ages 18 and over in 75 U.S. markets. The Miami DMA (Designated Market Area) was ranked #5 out of 75. *Scarborough Research, Scarborough USA+ 2003 Release 1*

■ Miami was selected as one of "America's Most Literate Cities." The city ranked #12 out of the 64 largest U.S. cities. Criteria: booksellers; library support, holdings, and utilization; educational attainment; periodicals published; newspaper circulation. *University of Wisconsin-Whitewater, "America's Most Literate Cities," Summer 2003*

■ Miami was ranked #30 in *Prevention* magazine's survey of the "Best Walking Cities in the U.S." The magazine, in conjunction with the American Podiatric Medical Association, surveyed 125 of the most populated cities and then tabulated and weighed 20 criteria of interest to pedestrians. *Prevention, April, 2004*

■ Miami was selected as one of "America's Top 25 Arts Destinations." The area ranked #18 out of 25. Criteria: readers' top choices for arts travel destinations based on the richness and variety of visual arts sites, activities and events. *American Style, Winter 2002-2003*

■ The Miami metro area was selected as one of the "Top 60 CyberCities in America" by *Site Selection*. CyberCities are magnets for growing high-tech companies. Criteria: total employment; average wages; total payroll; number of companies; R&D spending and venture capital in the 45 Standard Industrial Classification (SIC) codes that define the high-technology industry. *Site Selection, March 2002*

■ The Miami metro area was cited as one of "The Best Places in the U.S. to Locate a Company." The area ranked #272 out of 329. Criteria: education (with emphasis on college board test results and high school graduation rates); availability of quality healthcare services and the cost to employers; quality of life; logistics workforce and companies; transportation infrastructure; quality and quantity of highly educated technical workers; business climate. *Expansion Management, July 2003*

■ The Miami metro area appeared on *Forbes/Milken Institute* list of "Best Places for Business and Career." Rank: #85 out of 200 metro areas. Criteria: salary growth; job growth; number of technology clusters; overall concentration of technology activity relative to national average; and technology output growth. *www.forbes.com, Forbes/Milken Institute Best Places 2002*

■ The Miami metro area appeared on the "Milken Institute Best Performing Cities" index. Rank: #55 out of 200 large metro areas. Criteria: job growth; wage and salary growth; high-tech output growth. *Milken Institute, June 25, 2003*

■ The Miami metro area appeared on *Entrepreneur* magazine's list of the "Best Cities for Entrepreneurs" in 2003. The area ranked #8 out of 61 in the large city category. Criteria: entrepreneurial activity; small-business growth; economic growth; and risk. *www.Entrepreneur.com*

■ The Miami metro area was selected as one of the "Top 25 Cities for Doing Business in America." *Inc.* measured current-year employment growth in 277 regions as well as current trends in the annual average growth over the past three years, and compared employment expansion between the first and second halves of the last decade. Job growth factors account for two-thirds, and balance among industries accounts for one third of the final score for each city.The Miami metro area ranked #22 among large metro areas. *Inc. Magazine, March 2004*

■ The Miami metro area appeared on *IndustryWeek's* fourth annual World-Class Communities list. It ranked #292 out of 315 metro areas. Criteria: MSA Gross Metropolitan Product (GMP) per manufacturing employee; and MSA percent share of U.S. manufacturing Gross Domestic Product (GDP). *IndustryWeek, April 16, 2001*

■ ING Group ranked the 125 largest metro areas according to the general financial security of residents. The Miami metro area was ranked #123 out of 125. Criteria: Earnings and Wealth Potential (household income, education, net assets, cost of living); Safety Net (health insurance, retirement savings, life insurance, income support programs); Personal Threats (unemployment rate, low-income households, crime rate); Community Economic Vitality (cost of community services, job quality, job creation, housing costs). *ING Group, "The Best Cities to Earn and Save Money: A Ranking of the Largest 125 U.S. Cities," 2001 Edition*

Business Environment

CITY FINANCES

City Government Finances

Component	2000-2001 ($000)	2000-2001 ($ per capita)
Total Revenues	682,259	1,882
Total Expenditures	481,417	1,328
Debt Outstanding	508,455	1,403
Cash and Securities	1,967,765	5,429

Source: U.S Census Bureau, Government Finances 2000-2001, August 2003

City Government Revenue by Source

Source	2000-2001 ($000)	2000-2001 ($ per capita)
General Revenue		
From Federal Government	31,777	88
From State Government	25,975	72
From Local Governments	4,481	12
Taxes		
Property	162,109	447
Sales	76,508	211
Personal Income	0	0
License	0	0
Charges	72,093	199
Liquor Store	0	0
Utility	0	0
Employee Retirement	243,475	672
Other	65,841	182

Source: U.S Census Bureau, Government Finances 2000-2001, August 2003

City Government Expenditures by Function

Function	2000-2001 ($000)	2000-2001 ($ per capita)	2000-2001 (%)
General Expenditures			
Airports	0	0	0.0
Corrections	0	0	0.0
Education	0	0	0.0
Fire Protection	50,373	139	10.5
Governmental Administration	34,276	95	7.1
Health	0	0	0.0
Highways	8,927	25	1.9
Hospitals	0	0	0.0
Housing and Community Development	29,198	81	6.1
Interest on General Debt	33,018	91	6.9
Libraries	0	0	0.0
Parking	7,393	20	1.5
Parks and Recreation	27,160	75	5.6
Police Protection	107,988	298	22.4
Public Welfare	0	0	0.0
Sewerage	14,595	40	3.0
Solid Waste Management	19,564	54	4.1
Liquor Store	0	0	0.0
Utility	0	0	0.0
Employee Retirement	74,639	206	15.5
Other	74,286	205	15.4

Source: U.S Census Bureau, Government Finances 2000-2001, August 2003

Municipal Bond Ratings

Area	Moody's
City	Aaa

Source: Mergent Bond Record, February 2004

DEMOGRAPHICS

Population Growth

Area	1990 Census	2000 Census	2003 Estimate	2008 Projection	Population Growth (%)	
					1990-2000	2000-2008
City	358,843	362,470	367,581	377,654	1.0	4.2
MSA[1]	1,937,094	2,253,362	2,354,447	2,526,221	16.3	12.1
U.S.	248,709,873	281,421,906	290,647,163	305,918,071	13.2	8.7

Note: (1) Metropolitan Statistical Area - see Appendix A for areas included
Source: Claritas, Inc.

Number of Households and Average Household Size

Area	1990 Census	2000 Census	2003 Estimate	2008 Projection	2003 Average Household Size
City	130,371	134,198	136,783	141,107	2.7
MSA[1]	692,355	776,774	804,566	850,859	2.9
U.S.	91,947,410	105,480,101	109,440,059	116,034,472	2.7

Note: (1) Metropolitan Statistical Area - see Appendix A for areas included
Source: Claritas, Inc.

Race and Ethnicity

Area	White Non-Hispanic	Black Non-Hispanic	Asian Non-Hispanic	Other Race Non-Hispanic	Hispanic
City	67.3	21.4	0.7	10.6	66.3
MSA[1]	69.6	20.2	1.5	8.8	58.6
U.S.	74.5	12.4	3.8	9.3	13.2

Note: Figures are 2003 estimates; (1) Metropolitan Statistical Area - see Appendix A for areas included
Source: Claritas, Inc.

Segregation

City		MSA[1]	
Index[2]	Rank[3]	Index[2]	Rank[4]
80.3	7	75.8	22

Note: Figures are based on an analysis of Census 2000 data; (1) Metropolitan Statistical Area - see Appendix A for areas included; (2) Dissimilarity Index—the most commonly used measure of segregation between two groups, reflecting their relative distributions across neighborhoods within a city or metropolitan area. It can range in value from 0, indicating complete integration, to 100, indicating complete segregation; (3) Ranges from 1 (most segregated) to 100 (least segregated) and includes all the cities in this book; (4) Ranges from 1 (most segregated) to 318 (least segregated) and includes 318 metropolitan areas.
Source: www.CensusScope.org

Ancestry

Area	German	Irish[2]	English	American	Italian	Polish	French[3]	Scottish
City	1.2	1.0	1.1	3.1	1.4	0.4	0.8	0.3
MSA[1]	2.6	2.3	2.0	4.0	2.3	1.0	1.0	0.4
U.S.	15.2	10.9	8.7	7.3	5.6	3.2	3.0	1.7

Note: Figures include multiple ancestry (e.g. if a person reported being Irish and Italian, they were included in both columns); (1) Metropolitan Statistical Area - see Appendix A for areas included; (2) Includes Celtic; (3) Includes Alsatian but excludes Basque
Source: Census 2000, Summary File 3

Foreign-Born Population

Area	Percent of Population Born in:							
	Any Foreign Country	Europe	Asia	Africa	Oceania[2]	Canada	Mexico	Latin America[3]
City	59.5	1.2	0.6	0.1	0.0	0.1	0.6	56.8
MSA[1]	50.9	2.0	1.3	0.2	0.0	0.2	0.9	46.3
U.S.	11.1	1.7	2.9	0.3	0.1	0.3	3.3	2.5

Note: (1) Metropolitan Statistical Area - see Appendix A for areas included; (2) Includes Australia, New Zealand subregion, Melanesia, Micronesia, Polynesia, and Oceania n.e.c; (3) Includes Central America (excluding Mexico), South America, and the Caribbean.
Source: Census 2000, Summary File 3

Religion

Area	Catholic	Southern Baptist	United Methodist	ELCA[1]	LDS[2]	Presbyterian Church USA	Jewish Est.	Muslim Est.
County	24.1	3.6	0.8	0.3	0.3	0.2	5.5	0.3
U.S.	22.0	7.1	3.7	1.8	1.5	1.1	2.2	0.6

Note: Figures shown are the number of adherents as a percentage of the total population; Adherents are defined as all members, including full members, their children and the estimated number of other participants who are not considered members (e.g. the baptized, those not confirmed, those not eligible for communion, those regularly attending services, etc.); (1) Evangelical Lutheran Church in America; (2) The Church of Jesus Christ of Latter Day Saints
Source: Reprinted with permission from Religious Congregations and Membership in the United States 2000 (Nashville, Glenmary Research Center, 2002) Copyright Association of Statisticians of American Religious Bodies. All rights reserved.

Age Distribution

Area	Percent of Population						
	Under Age 5	Age 5 to 17	Age 18 to 34	Age 35 to 49	Age 50 to 64	Age 65 to 79	80 Years and Over
City	5.9	15.8	23.6	22.3	15.3	12.4	4.6
MSA[1]	6.4	18.3	23.9	23.2	14.9	9.9	3.4
U.S.	6.8	18.9	23.7	23.5	14.8	9.2	3.2

Note: (1) Metropolitan Statistical Area - see Appendix A for areas included
Source: Census 2000, Summary File 3

Marriage Status

Area	Never Married	Now Married Except Separated	Separated	Widowed	Divorced
City	32.2	42.0	4.7	8.3	12.8
MSA[1]	28.7	49.2	3.6	6.9	11.5
U.S.	27.1	54.4	2.2	6.6	9.7

Note: Figures cover population 15 years of age and older; (1) Metropolitan Statistical Area - see Appendix A for areas included
Source: Census 2000, Summary File 3

Male/Female Ratio

Area	Males	Females	Males per 100 Females
City	182,308	185,273	98.4
MSA[1]	1,136,735	1,217,712	93.4
U.S.	142,511,883	148,135,280	96.2

Note: Figures are 2003 estimates; (1) Metropolitan Statistical Area - see Appendix A for areas included
Source: Claritas, Inc.

ECONOMY

Gross Metropolitan Product

Area	1999	2000	2001	2002	2002 Rank[2]
MSA[1]	66.6	70.6	73.5	75.7	30

Note: Figures are in billions of dollars; (1) Metropolitan Statistical Area - see Appendix A for areas included; (2) Rank ranges from 1 to 319
Source: The U.S. Conference of Mayors, Metro Economies Report, July 2003

INCOME

Per Capita/Median/Average Income

Area	Per Capita ($)	Median Household ($)	Average Household ($)
City	16,584	25,824	43,367
MSA[1]	20,063	39,947	58,022
U.S.	24,078	46,868	63,207

Note: Figures are 2003 estimates; (1) Metropolitan Statistical Area - see Appendix A for areas included
Source: Claritas, Inc.

Household Income Distribution

Area	Percent of Households Earning							
	Under $15,000	$15,000 -24,999	$25,000 -34,999	$35,000 -49,999	$50,000 -74,999	$75,000 -99,000	$100,000 -149,999	$150,000 and up
City	32.6	16.4	12.6	13.2	11.4	5.4	4.7	3.8
MSA[1]	19.5	13.1	12.3	15.6	16.7	9.1	8.0	5.7
U.S.	14.1	11.5	11.7	16.0	19.2	11.3	10.2	6.0

Note: Figures are 2003 estimates; (1) Metropolitan Statistical Area - see Appendix A for areas included
Source: Claritas, Inc.

Poverty Rates by Age

Area	All Ages	Under 5 Years Old	5 to 17 Years Old	18 to 64 Years Old	65 Years and Over
City	28.5	2.2	6.2	15.0	5.0
MSA[1]	18.0	1.5	4.3	9.7	2.5
U.S.	12.4	1.2	3.0	6.9	1.2

*Note: Figures are percent of population with income in 1999 below poverty level and only include population
for whom poverty status is determined; (1) Metropolitan Statistical Area - see Appendix A for areas included*
Source: Census 2000, Summary File 3

Personal Bankruptcy Filing Rate

Area	2002	2003
Miami-Dade County	6.53	6.42
U.S.	5.34	5.58

Note: Numbers are per 1,000 population and include Chapter 7 and Chapter 13 filings
Source: Federal Deposit Insurance Corporation (FDIC), Regional Economic Conditions (RECON), 2/25/2004

EMPLOYMENT

Labor Force and Employment

Area	Civilian Labor Force			Workers Employed		
	Dec. 2002	Dec. 2003	% Chg.	Dec. 2002	Dec. 2003	% Chg.
City	193,371	189,850	-1.8	173,873	173,194	-0.4
MSA[1]	1,113,155	1,097,776	-1.4	1,035,374	1,031,331	-0.4
U.S.	144,807,000	146,501,000	1.2	136,599,000	138,556,000	1.4

*Note: Data is not seasonally adjusted and covers workers 16 years of age and older;
(1) Metropolitan Statistical Area - see Appendix A for areas included*
Source: Bureau of Labor Statistics, http://stats.bls.gov

Unemployment Rate

Area	2003											
	Jan.	Feb.	Mar.	Apr.	May	Jun.	Jul.	Aug.	Sep.	Oct.	Nov.	Dec.
City	11.2	10.7	10.3	10.7	10.3	11.2	10.7	10.9	10.5	9.9	9.7	8.8
MSA[1]	7.8	7.4	7.2	7.4	7.2	7.8	7.4	7.6	7.3	6.8	6.7	6.1
U.S.	6.5	6.4	6.2	5.8	5.8	6.5	6.3	6.0	5.8	5.6	5.6	5.4

*Note: Data is not seasonally adjusted and covers workers 16 years of age and older; All figures are
percentages; (1) Metropolitan Statistical Area - see Appendix A for areas included*
Source: Bureau of Labor Statistics, http://stats.bls.gov

Employment by Occupation

Occupation Classification	City (%)	MSA[1] (%)	U.S. (%)
Sales and Office	26.2	31.0	26.7
Professional and Related	13.4	16.9	20.2
Service	22.1	16.9	14.9
Production, Transportation, and Material Moving	13.8	11.9	14.6
Management, Business, and Financial	10.4	13.3	13.5
Construction, Extraction, and Maintenance	13.6	9.5	9.4
Farming, Forestry, and Fishing	0.5	0.6	0.7

*Note: Figures cover employed civilians 16 years of age and older;
(1) Metropolitan Statistical Area - see Appendix A for areas included*
Source: Census 2000, Summary File 3

Employment by Industry

| Sector | MSA[1] | | U.S. |
	Number of Employees	Percent of Total	Percent of Total
Government	153,400	15.1	16.7
Education and Health Services	132,800	13.0	12.9
Professional and Business Services	147,000	14.4	12.3
Retail Trade	122,100	12.0	11.8
Manufacturing	52,300	5.1	11.0
Leisure and Hospitality	93,700	9.2	9.1
Finance Activities	68,100	6.7	6.1
Construction	42,100	4.1	5.1
Wholesale Trade	70,600	6.9	4.3
Other Services	42,600	4.2	4.1
Transportation and Utilities	65,000	6.4	3.7
Information	27,900	2.7	2.4
Natural Resources and Mining	500	<0.1	0.4

Note: Figures cover non-farm employment as of December 2003 and are not seasonally adjusted;
(1) Metropolitan Statistical Area - see Appendix A for areas included
Source: Bureau of Labor Statistics, http://stats.bls.gov

Average Wages

Occupation	$/Hr.	Occupation	$/Hr.
Accountants and Auditors	27.03	Maids and Housekeeping Cleaners	7.32
Automotive Mechanics	14.56	Maintenance and Repair Workers	11.97
Bookkeepers	13.21	Marketing Managers	39.54
Carpenters	13.52	Nuclear Medicine Technologists	25.59
Cashiers	7.78	Nurses, Licensed Practical	15.25
Clerks, General Office	10.70	Nurses, Registered	24.94
Clerks, Receptionists/Information	9.21	Nursing Aides/Orderlies/Attendants	8.85
Clerks, Shipping/Receiving	10.56	Packers and Packagers, Hand	7.50
Computer Programmers	27.14	Physical Therapists	30.53
Computer Support Specialists	18.98	Postal Service Mail Carriers	n/a
Computer Systems Analysts	28.93	Real Estate Brokers	60.54
Cooks, Restaurant	9.45	Retail Salespersons	10.23
Dentists	85.76	Sales Reps., Exc. Tech./Scientific	21.44
Electrical Engineers	35.13	Sales Reps., Tech./Scientific	27.99
Electricians	15.66	Secretaries, Exc. Legal/Med./Exec.	11.46
Financial Managers	40.01	Security Guards	8.53
First-Line Supervisors/Mgrs., Sales	19.56	Surgeons	98.53
Food Preparation Workers	8.07	Teacher Assistants	7.50
General and Operations Managers	39.80	Teachers, Elementary School	n/a
Hairdressers/Cosmetologists	10.32	Teachers, Secondary School	n/a
Internists	66.08	Telemarketers	12.56
Janitors and Cleaners	8.09	Truck Drivers, Heavy/Tractor-Trailer	14.97
Landscaping/Groundskeeping Workers	9.32	Truck Drivers, Light/Delivery Svcs.	12.12
Lawyers	51.54	Waiters and Waitresses	7.33

Note: Wage data is for 2002 and covers the Metropolitan Statistical Area (see Appendix A for areas included).
Hourly wages for elementary/secondary school teachers and teacher assistants were calculated by the editors
from annual wage data assuming a 40 hour work week; n/a not available.
Source: Bureau of Labor Statistics, 2002 Metro Area Occupational Employment and Wage Estimates

Occupational Employment Projections: 1996 - 2006

Occupations Expected to Have the Largest Job Growth (ranked by numerical growth)	Fast-Growing Occupations[1] (ranked by percent growth)
1. Cashiers	1. Systems analysts
2. Salespersons, retail	2. Physical therapy assistants and aides
3. General managers & top executives	3. Desktop publishers
4. Registered nurses	4. Home health aides
5. Waiters & waitresses	5. Computer engineers
6. Marketing & sales, supervisors	6. Medical assistants
7. Janitors/cleaners/maids, ex. priv. hshld.	7. Physical therapists
8. General office clerks	8. Paralegals
9. Food preparation workers	9. Emergency medical technicians
10. Hand packers & packagers	10. Occupational therapists

Note: Projections cover Florida; (1) Excludes occupations with total job growth less than 300
Source: U.S. Department of Labor, Employment and Training Administration, America's Labor Market Information System (ALMIS)

TAXES

State Corporate Income Tax Rates

State	Rate (%)	Number of Brackets	Low Bracket (Under $)	High Bracket (Over $)
Florida	5.5	1	na	na

Note: Tax rates as of December 31, 2003; na not applicable; 3.3% alternative minimum rate.
Source: Tax Foundation, www.taxfoundation.org

State Individual Income Tax Rates

State	Federal Deductibility	Marginal Rate (%)	Number of Brackets	Low Bracket (Under $)	High Bracket (Over $)
Florida	No	None	na	na	na

Note: Tax rates as of December 31, 2003; Brackets apply to single taxpayers and married people filing separately; na not applicable
Source: Tax Foundation, www.taxfoundation.org

Various State and Local Tax Rates

State Sales and Use (%)	Total Sales and Use (%)	Gasoline (cents/gal.)	Cigarette (cents/pack)	Spirits ($/gal.)	Table Wine ($/gal.)	Beer ($/gal.)
6.0	7.0	13.9	33.9	6.50	2.25	0.48

Note: Tax rates as of December 31, 2003
Source: Tax Foundation, www.taxfoundation.org

State Tax Burdens

Area	Combined State and Local Tax Burden		Combined Federal, State and Local Tax Burden	
	Percent	Rank	Percent	Rank
Florida	8.4	45	29.0	23
U.S. Average	9.7	-	30.0	-

Note: Figures are for 2003
Source: Tax Foundation, www.taxfoundation.org

Internal Revenue Service Tax Audits

IRS District	Percent of Returns Audited				
	1996	1997	1998	1999	2000
South Florida	0.71	0.68	0.50	0.42	0.23
U.S.	0.66	0.61	0.46	0.31	0.20

Note: Figures cover IRS district audits of federal income tax returns filed by individuals. Geographic data on district audits for 2001 and 2002 are being withheld by the IRS. TRAC is challenging this policy.
Source: Syracuse University, Transactional Records Access Clearinghouse (TRAC), "Odds of IRS District Tax Audit 2000"

**RESIDENTIAL
REAL ESTATE**

Building Permits

Area	Single-Family			Multi-Family			Total		
	2001	2002	Pct. Chg.	2001	2002	Pct. Chg.	2001	2002	Pct. Chg.
City	79	112	41.8	2,754	2,962	7.6	2,833	3,074	8.5
U.S.	1,235,600	1,332,600	7.9	401,100	415,100	3.5	1,636,700	1,747,700	6.8

Note: Figures represent new, privately-owned housing units authorized (unadjusted data)
Source: U.S. Census Bureau, Manufacturing, Mining, and Construction Statistics

Homeownership and Housing Vacancies

Area	Homeownership Rate[2] (%)			Rental Vacancy Rate[3] (%)			Homeowner Vacancy Rate[4] (%)		
	2001	2002[a]	2003	2001	2002[a]	2003	2001	2002[a]	2003
MSA[1]	58.8	55.1	55.9	8.3	7.9	8.8	1.6	1.5	1.9
U.S.	67.8	67.9	68.3	8.4	8.9	9.8	1.8	1.7	1.8

Note: (1) Metropolitan Statistical Area - see Appendix A for areas included; (2) The proportion of households that are owners; (3) The proportion of the rental inventory that is vacant for rent; (4) The proportion of the homeowner inventory that is vacant for sale; (a) 2002 figures have been revised; n/a not available
Source: U.S. Census Bureau, Housing Vacancies and Homeownership Annual Statistics: 2003

**COMMERCIAL
REAL ESTATE**

Industrial/Office Markets

Type/Market Area	Inventory (sq. ft.)	Vacant (sq. ft.)	Vacancy Rate (%)	Under Construction (sq. ft.)	Net Absorption (sq. ft.)
Industrial Space					
Miami	162,000,000	12,600,000	7.78	400,000	-1,219,000
Office Space					
Miami	45,022,095	5,855,815	13.01	1,173,569	14,300,571

Note: Data as of 4th Quarter, 2003; n/a not available
Source: Society of Industrial and Office Realtors, 2004 Comparative Statistics of Industrial and Office Real Estate Markets

**COMMERCIAL
UTILITIES**

Typical Monthly Electric Bills

Area	Commercial Service ($/month)		Industrial Service ($/month)	
	3 kW demand 1,000 kWh	40 kW demand 14,000 kWh	1,000 kW demand 200,000 kWh	50,000 kW demand 15,000,000 kWh
City	88	952	17,273	1,081,336
Average[1]	100	1,134	17,850	1,045,117

Note: Based on rates in effect July 1, 2003; (1) average based on 197 utilities
Source: Edison Electric Institute, Typical Bills and Average Rates Report, Summer 2003

TRANSPORTATION

Means of Transportation to Work

Area	Car/Truck/Van		Public Transportation			Bicycle	Walked	Other Means	Worked at Home
	Drove Alone	Car-pooled	Bus	Subway	Railroad				
City	64.5	16.3	10.0	0.7	0.3	0.6	3.7	1.9	2.1
MSA[1]	73.8	14.6	4.3	0.6	0.2	0.5	2.2	1.2	2.7
U.S.	75.7	12.2	2.5	1.5	0.5	0.4	2.9	1.0	3.3

Note: Figures shown are percentages and cover workers 16 years of age and older;
(1) Metropolitan Statistical Area - see Appendix A for areas included
Source: Census 2000, Summary File 3

Travel Time to Work

Area	Less Than 15 Minutes	15 to 29 Minutes	30 to 44 Minutes	45 to 59 Minutes	60 Minutes or More
City	20.0	38.9	24.8	6.6	9.6
MSA[1]	17.4	34.2	27.2	10.9	10.3
U.S.	29.4	36.1	19.1	7.4	8.0

Note: Figures are percentages and include workers 16 years old and over; (1) Metropolitan Statistical Area - see Appendix A for areas included
Source: Census 2000, Summary File 3

Roadway Congestion Index

Area	1982	1990	1996	2000	2001
City	0.95	1.20	1.23	1.31	1.29
Average[1]	0.82	1.01	1.08	1.16	1.17

Note: Values greater than 1.00 indicate undesirable mobility levels; (1) average of 75 urban areas
Source: Texas Transportation Institute, The 2003 Annual Urban Mobility Report

Transportation Statistics

Interstate highways (2004)	I-95
Public transportation (2002)	Miami-Dade Transit Agency; Tri-County Commuter Rail Authority (Tri-Rail)
Buses	
Average fleet age in years	6.6
No. operated in max. service	564
Heavy rail	
Average fleet age in years	20.0
No. operated in max. service	90
Light rail	
Average fleet age in years	11.9 (automated guideway); 12.7 (Tri-Rail)
No. operated in max. service	18 (automated guideway); 20 (Tri-Rail)
Passenger air service	
Airport	Miami International
Airlines (2003)	50+
Boardings (2002)	14,020,686
Amtrak service (2004)	Yes
Major waterways/ports	Port of Miami; Atlantic Intracoastal Waterway

Source: Federal Transit Administration, National Transit Database, 2002; Editor & Publisher Market Guide, 2004; Bureau of Transportation Statistics, Airport Enplanement Activity for CY2002; www.amtrak.com

BUSINESSES

Major Business Headquarters

Company Name	2003 Rankings	
	Fortune 500	Forbes 500
Burger King	-	239
Lennar	256	-
Ryder System	345	-
Southern Wine & Spirits	-	28

Note: Companies listed are located in the city; dashes indicate no ranking
Fortune 500: Companies that produce a 10-K are ranked 1 to 500 based on 2002 revenue
Forbes 500: Private companies are ranked 1 to 281 based on 2002 revenue
Source: Fortune, April 14, 2003; www.forbes.com, November 6, 2003

Best Companies to Work For

SFBC International, headquartered in Miami, is among the "200 Best Small Companies in 2003." Criteria: 3,500 companies whose latest 12-month sales were $5 million to $600 million were screened. Those with a net margin or five-year average ROE below 5% were cut. Banks, utilities, real estate investment trusts and limited partnerships whose financial structures are too different from most operating companies were also excluded. Shares had to be trading above $5 by the end of September 2003. Financial statement footnotes were examined for major issues. For the final ranking, equal weight was given to growth in sales, earnings and ROE for the past five years and the latest 12 months. *www.forbes.com, October 27, 2003*

Royal Caribbean Cruises Ltd, headquartered in Miami, is among the "100 Best Places to Work in IT 2003." Criteria: compensation, turnover and training. *www.computerworld.com, 3/15/2004*

Fast-Growing Businesses

According to *Inc.*, Miami is home to three of America's 500 fastest-growing private companies: **Blue Star Food Products; Brightstar; Governor's Distributors**. Criteria: must be an independent, privately-held, U.S. corporation, proprietorship or partnership; sales of at least $200,000 in 1998; five-year operating/sales history; increase in 2002 sales over 2001 sales; holding companies, regulated banks, and utilities were excluded. *Inc. 500, America's Fastest-Growing Private Companies, October 15, 2003*

According to *Fortune*, Miami is home to one of America's 100 fastest-growing companies: **Lennar**. Companies were ranked based on earnings-per-share growth, revenue growth and total return over the previous three years. Criteria for inclusion: public companies with sales of at least $50 million. Companies that lost money in the most recent quarter, or ended in the red for the past four quarters as a whole, were not eligible. Limited partnerships and REITs were also not considered. *Fortune, "America's Fastest-Growing Companies," September 1, 2003*

According to Deloitte & Touche LLP, Miami is home to four of North America's 500 fastest-growing high-technology companies: **Global Entertainment Holdings/Equities, Inc; GlobeTel Communications Corp; KOS Pharmaceuticals, Inc; SFBC International, Inc**. Companies are ranked by percentage growth in revenue over a five-year period. Criteria for inclusion: must be a U.S. or Canadian company developing and/or providing technology products or services; company must have been in business for five years with 1998 operating revenues of at least $50,000 USD or $75,000 CD and 2002 operating revenues of at least $1 million USD/CD. *Deloitte & Touche LLP, 2003 Technology Fast 500*

Women-Owned Firms: Number, Employment and Sales

Area	Number of Firms	Employ-ment	Sales ($000)	Rank[2]
MSA[1]	68,998	70,574	12,639,716	22

Note: (1) Metropolitan Statistical Area - see Appendix A for areas included;
(2) Calculated on an averaging of the number of businesses, employment, and sales
Source: The National Foundation for Women Business Owners, Women-Owned Businesses in the Top 50 Metropolitan Areas, 2002: A Fact Sheet

Women-Owned Firms: Growth

Area	Percent Change from 1997 to 2002			Rank[2]
	Number of Firms	Employ-ment	Sales	
MSA[1]	22.7	26.6	55.4	13
Top 50 MSAs	14.0	31.4	42.6	-

Note: (1) Metropolitan Statistical Area - see Appendix A for areas included; (2) Calculated on an averaging of the percent growth of number of businesses, employment, and sales
Source: The National Foundation for Women Business Owners, Women-Owned Businesses in the Top 50 Metropolitan Areas, 2002: A Fact Sheet

Minority and Women-Owned Businesses

Ownership	All Firms		Firms with Paid Employees			
	Firms	Sales ($000)	Firms	Sales ($000)	Employees	Payroll ($000)
Black	2,954	194,620	468	156,457	2,718	45,129
Hispanic	26,225	5,711,614	5,601	5,196,957	28,391	668,633
Women	12,953	2,818,554	2,402	2,567,146	19,792	403,765

Note: Figures cover firms located in the city
Source: 1997 Economic Census, Minority and Women-Owned Businesses

Minority Business Opportunity

72 of the 500 largest Hispanic-owned companies in the U.S. are located in Miami. *Hispanic Business, June 2003*

Miami is home to nine companies which are on the Hispanic Business Fastest-Growing 100 list (greatest sales growth over the past five years): **Brightstar Corp.; Alienware Corp.; Pharmed Group Corp.; John Keeler & Co. Inc.; GEC Associates Inc.; Professional Casualty Insurance; Wendium of Florida Inc. (Wendys); Rowland Coffee Roasters Inc.; Central Concrete Supermix Inc.**. *Hispanic Business, July/August 2003*

HOTELS

Hotels/Motels

Area	Hotels/Motels	Average Minimum Rates ($)		
		Tourist	First-Class	Deluxe
City	97	92	118	249

Source: OAG Travel Planner Online, Spring 2004

Miami is home to two of the top 100 hotels in the U.S. and Canada according to *Travel & Leisure*: **Ritz-Carlton (Key Biscayne)** (#74); **Mandarin Oriental** (#83). Criteria: value, rooms/ambience, location, facilities/activities and service. *Travel & Leisure, "The World's Best Hotels 2003"*

EVENT SITES

Major Event Sites, Meeting Places and Convention Centers

Name	Guest Rooms	Exhibit/ Meeting Space (sq. ft.)	Largest Meeting Room Capacity
AT&T Amphitheatre at Bayfront	n/a	n/a	12,000
Coconut Grove Convention Center	750	150,000	6,500
Doral Golf Resort & Spa	694	100,000	1,000
Golden Panther Arena	n/a	n/a	5,000
Hyatt Regency Miami	612	100,000	3,110
James L. Knight Center	n/a	n/a	5,000
Joe Robbie Stadium	n/a	n/a	74,916
Miami Arena	n/a	n/a	16,000
Radisson Mart Plaza Hotel & Convention Center	334	138,064	7,500

Note: n/a not available
Source: Original research

Living Environment

COST OF LIVING

Cost of Living Index

Year	Composite Index	Groceries	Housing	Utilities	Trans-portation	Health Care	Misc. Goods/ Services
2001	105.6	105.5	101.5	109.2	111.0	124.7	103.7
2002	n/a	n/a	n/a	n/a	n/a	n/a	n/a
2003	113.8	104.5	130.9	104.6	108.5	107.5	108.0

Note: U.S. = 100; n/a not available
Source: ACCRA, Cost of Living Index, 2001, 2002 and 2003 4-Quarter Averages

HOUSING

House Price Index (HPI)

Area	National Ranking[2]	Quarterly Change (%)	One-Year Change (%)	Five-Year Change (%)
MSA[1]	18	5.72	14.25	64.07
U.S.[3]	-	3.67	7.97	41.81

Note: The HPI is a weighted repeat sales index. It measures average price changes in repeat sales or refinancings on the same properties. This information is obtained by reviewing repeat mortgage transactions on single-family properties whose mortgages have been purchased or securitized by Fannie Mae of Freddie Mac in January 1975; (1) Metropolitan Statistical Area - see Appendix A for areas included; (2) Rankings are based on annual percentage change, for all MSAs containing at least 15,000 transactions over the last 10 years and ranges from 1 to 220; (3) figures based on a weighted division average; all figures are for the period ended December 31, 2003
Source: Office of Federal Housing Enterprise Oversight, House Price Index, March 1, 2004

Housing: Year Structure Built

Area	1990 -2000	1980 -1989	1970 -1979	1960 -1969	1950 -1959	1940 -1949	Before 1940	Median Year
City	7.7	11.3	19.0	17.9	19.2	14.2	10.6	1963
MSA[1]	15.2	18.2	22.5	16.8	16.5	6.7	4.2	1973
U.S.	17.0	15.8	18.5	13.7	12.7	7.3	15.0	1971

Note: Figures are percentages; (1) Metropolitan Statistical Area - see Appendix A for areas included
Source: Census 2000, Summary File 3

Average New Home Price

Area	2001	2002	2003
City[1]	207,381	n/a	308,295
U.S.	212,643	236,567	248,193

Note: Figures, in dollars, are based on a new home with 2,400 sq. ft. of living area on an 8,000 sq. ft. lot; (1) Miami/Dade County
Source: ACCRA, Cost of Living Index, 2001, 2002 and 2003 4-Quarter Averages

Average Apartment Rent

Area	2001	2002	2003
City[1]	841	n/a	1,163
U.S.	674	708	721

Note: Figures, in dollars per month, are based on an unfurnished two bedroom, 1-1/2 or 2 bath apartment, approximately 950 sq. ft. in size, excluding all utilities except water; (1) Miami/Dade County
Source: ACCRA, Cost of Living Index, 2001, 2002 and 2003 4-Quarter Averages

RESIDENTIAL UTILITIES

Average Residential Utility Costs

Area	All Electric ($/mth)	Part Electric ($/mth)	Other Energy ($/mth)	Phone ($/mth)
City[1]	144.82	–	–	21.31
U.S.	116.46	65.82	62.68	23.90

Note: (1) Miami/Dade County
Source: ACCRA, Cost of Living Index, 2003 4-Quarter Average

HEALTH CARE

Average Health Care Costs

Area	Hospital ($/day)	Doctor ($/visit)	Dentist ($/visit)
City[1]	911.21	78.18	81.48
U.S.	678.35	67.91	83.90

Note: Hospital—based on a semi-private room; Doctor—based on a general practitioner's routine exam of an established patient; Dentist—based on adult teeth cleaning and periodic oral exam;
(1) Miami/Dade County
Source: ACCRA, Cost of Living Index, 2003 4-Quarter Average

Distribution of Non-Federal, Office-Based Physicians

Area	Total	Family/ General Practice	Specialties Medical	Specialties Surgical	Specialties Other
CMSA[3] (number)	8,384	965	3,380	1,963	2,076
CMSA[3] (rate per 10,000 pop.)	21.6	2.5	8.7	5.1	5.4
Metro Average[2] (rate per 10,000 pop.)	33.1	2.2	7.7	4.8	5.6

Note: Data as of December 31, 2001; (1) Metropolitan Statistical Area - see Appendix A for areas included; (2) Average of 81 MSAs and CMSAs in this book; (3) Miami-Fort Lauderdale, FL Consolidated Metropolitan Statistical Area includes the following counties: Broward; Miami-Dade
Source: American Medical Association, Physician Characteristics & Distribution in the U.S., 2003-2004

Hospitals

Miami has the following hospitals: 13 general medical and surgical; 1 psychiatric; 1 eye, ear, nose and throat; 1 rehabilitation; 1 other specialty; 1 children's general.
AHA Guide to the Healthcare Field, 2003-2004

According to *U.S. News*, Miami has two of the best hospitals in the U.S.: **Miami Children's Hospital**; **University of Miami (Jackson Memorial Hospital)**; *U.S. News Online, "America's Best Hospitals 2003"*

PRESIDENTIAL ELECTION

2000 Presidential Election Results

Area	Gore	Bush	Nader	Buchanan	Other
Dade County	52.6	46.3	0.9	0.1	0.2
U.S.	48.4	47.9	2.7	0.4	0.6

Note: Results are percentages and may not add to 100% due to rounding
Source: www.cbsnews.com; www.uselectionatlas.org

EDUCATION

Public School District Statistics

District Name	Schls.	Enroll-ment	Classroom Teachers	Pupil/ Teacher Ratio	Minority Pupils[1] (%)	Current Expend.[2] ($/pupil)
Dade County SD	363	375,836	19,043	19.7	88.7	6,202

Note: Data covers the 2001-02 school year unless otherwise noted; (1) Fall 2000; (2) FY2000; n/a not available
Source: U.S. Department of Education, National Center for Education Statistics, Common Core of Data, Local Education Agency (School District) Universe Survey: School Year 2001-2002; U.S. Department of Education, National Center for Education Statistics, Digest of Education Statistics 2002

Educational Quality

School District	Education Quotient[1]	Graduate Outcome[2]	Community Index[3]	Resource Index[4]
Dade County	4	5	22	38

Note: Scores are national percentile rankings and range from 1 (worst) to 99 (best); (1) Combination of the Graduate Outcome, Community and Resource indexes weighted to reflect the greater importance of the Graduate Outcome and Resource Index; (2) Based on graduation rates and college board scores (SAT/ACT); (3) Based on the surrounding community's level of affluence and adult education; (4) Based on teacher salaries, per-pupil expenditures and student-teacher ratios.
Source: Expansion Management, December 2003

Educational Attainment by Race

Area	High School Graduate (%)					Bachelor's Degree (%)				
	Total	White	Black	Asian	Hisp.[2]	Total	White	Black	Asian	Hisp.[2]
City	52.7	54.4	49.6	81.4	47.2	16.2	19.5	6.5	44.6	13.4
MSA[1]	67.9	69.4	63.3	80.5	61.2	21.7	24.3	11.5	45.1	18.1
U.S.	80.4	83.6	72.3	80.4	52.4	24.4	26.1	14.3	44.1	10.4

Note: Figures shown cover persons 25 years old and over; (1) Metropolitan Statistical Area - see Appendix A for areas included; (2) people of Hispanic origin can be of any race
Source: Census 2000, Summary File 3

School Enrollment by Type

Area	Grades KG to 8				Grades 9 to 12			
	Public		Private		Public		Private	
	Enrollment	%	Enrollment	%	Enrollment	%	Enrollment	%
City	38,677	92.7	3,053	7.3	21,451	92.1	1,842	7.9
MSA[1]	257,812	87.1	38,141	12.9	130,916	88.5	16,983	11.5
U.S.	33,526,011	88.7	4,285,121	11.3	14,848,628	90.6	1,532,323	9.4

Note: Figures shown cover persons 3 years old and over; (1) Metropolitan Statistical Area - see Appendix A for areas included
Source: Census 2000, Summary File 3

School Enrollment by Race

Area	Grades KG to 8 (%)				Grades 9 to 12 (%)			
	White	Black	Asian	Hisp.[1]	White	Black	Asian	Hisp.[1]
City	56.2	32.0	0.3	54.1	52.1	33.2	0.4	57.2
MSA[2]	62.1	27.4	1.1	49.4	57.8	29.7	1.2	52.5
U.S.	68.5	15.5	3.3	16.8	68.8	15.5	3.8	15.7

Note: Figures shown cover persons 3 years old and over; (1) people of Hispanic origin can be of any race; (2) Metropolitan Statistical Area - see Appendix A for areas included
Source: Census 2000, Summary File 3

Classroom Teacher Salaries in Public Schools

District	B.A. Degree		M.A. Degree		Maximum	
	Min. ($)	Rank[1]	Max. ($)	Rank[1]	Max. ($)	Rank[1]
Miami	32,425	36	60,775	14	64,755	24
DOD Average[2]	31,567	-	53,248	-	59,356	-

Note: Salaries are for 2001-2002; (1) Rank ranges from 1 to 100; (2) As per the U.S. Department of Defense Wage Fixing Authority
Source: American Federation of Teachers, Survey & Analysis of Teacher Salary Trends 2002

Higher Education

Four-Year Colleges			Two-Year Colleges			Medical Schools	Law Schools	Voc/Tech
Public	Private Non-profit	Private For-profit	Public	Private Non-profit	Private For-profit			
1	8	2	6	1	7	1	1	22

Note: Figures cover institutions located within the city limits.
Source: National Center for Education Statistics, The Integrated Postsecondary Education System (IPEDS) Peer Analysis System, 2002; usnews.com, America's Best Graduate Schools 2004, Medical School Directory; The College Blue Book, Occupational Education, 2003; Barron's Guide to Law Schools, 2003; Medical School Admission Requirements U.S. & Canada, 2003-2004

MAJOR EMPLOYERS

Major Employers

Company Name	Industry	Type
Aluma Craft Products	Sheet metalwork	Single
Baptist Health South Florida	General medical and surgical hospitals	Headquarters
Baptist Hospital of Miami Inc	General medical and surgical hospitals	Headquarters
Bursars Office	Colleges and universities	Branch
Chevron Texaco Latin America	Petroleum refining	Single
Dade County	Executive and legislative combined	Headquarters
Florida International Univ	Colleges and universities	Headquarters
Health Services	Administration of public health programs	Branch
Ivax Baker Norton	Pharmaceutical preparations	Single
Miami Childrens Hospital	Specialty hospitals, except psychiatric	Headquarters
Miami VAMC	Administration of veterans' affairs	Branch
Mount Sinai & Miami Heart	General medical and surgical hospitals	Headquarters
Pizza Hut	Eating places	Headquarters
Precision Response Corporation	Management consulting services	Branch
Royal Caribbean Cruises Ltd	Business services, nec	Branch
Royal Caribbean International	Deep sea passenger transport, except ferry	Headquarters
Ryder Automotive Operations	Truck rental and leasing, without drivers	Headquarters
South Miami Hospital Inc	General medical and surgical hospitals	Headquarters
The Sunrise Group	Residential care	Single
Unity International Trading	Electrical apparatus and equipment	Single
University of Miami	Colleges and universities	Branch
Water & Sewer	Air, water, and solid waste management	Branch

Note: Companies shown are located in the metropolitan area and have 2,000 or more employees.
Source: www.zapdata.com, March 2004

PUBLIC SAFETY

Crime Rate

Area	All Crimes	Violent Crimes				Property Crimes		
		Murder	Forcible Rape	Robbery	Aggrav. Assault	Burglary	Larceny -Theft	Motor Vehicle Theft
City	8,957.3	17.1	25.3	713.9	1,150.5	1,572.9	4,191.1	1,286.4
Suburbs[1]	6,828.1	7.0	37.5	289.7	630.4	1,019.4	4,018.2	825.8
MSA[2]	7,170.6	8.7	35.5	358.0	714.1	1,108.5	4,046.0	899.9
U.S.	4,118.8	5.6	33.0	145.9	310.1	746.2	2,445.8	432.1

Note: Figures are crimes per 100,000 population; (1) All areas within the MSA that are located outside the city limits; (2) Metropolitan Statistical Area - see Appendix A for areas included
Source: FBI Uniform Crime Reports, 2002

RECREATION

Culture and Recreation

Museums	Orchestras	Opera Companies	Dance Companies	Professional Theatres	Zoos	Pro Sports Teams[1]
10	2	1	3	3	1	3

Note: (1) Covers the Metropolitan Statistical Area - see Appendix A for areas included.
Source: The Grey House Performing Arts Directory, 2002; Official Museum Directory, 2004; www.sportsvenues.com

Library System

The Miami-Dade Public Library System has 33 branches and holdings of 4,000,000 volumes.
American Library Directory, 2003-2004

MEDIA

Newspapers

Name	Type	Freq.	Distribution	Circulation
Diario las Americas	Hispanic	6x/wk	Local	69,100
El Especial	Hispanic	Senior Citizen	1x/wk	Local
El Nuevo Herald	Hispanic	7x/wk	Area	88,329
El Nuevo Patria	Hispanic	1x/wk	Local	28,000
Florida Review Newspaper	General	2x/mth	U.S./Int'l	45,000
The Flyer	Hispanic	1x/wk	Area	1,121,000
Miami Daily Business Review	General	5x/wk	Area	10,000
The Miami Herald	General	7x/wk	Area	314,592
Miami New Times	Alternative	1x/wk	Local	105,000
The Miami Times	Black	1x/wk	Local	28,170
Prensa Grafica	Hispanic	1x/wk	Area	31,000
River Cities Gazette	General	1x/wk	Local	12,000
Sabor Magazine	Hispanic	1x/wk	Local	28,000
The Weekly News - TWN	Gay/Lesbian	1x/wk	Area	22,500

Note: Includes newspapers whose offices are located in the city and whose circulations are 1,000 or more
Source: Burrelle's Media Directory, 2003

Television Stations

Name	Ch.	Affiliation	Type	Owner
WPBT	2	PBS	Public	Community TV Foundation of South Florida Inc.
WFOR	4	CBST	Commercial	CBS
WSVN	7	FBC	Commercial	Edmund N. Ansin
WWTU	8	n/a	Commercial	Hispanic Keys Broadcasting
WPLG	10	ABCT	Commercial	Post-Newsweek Business Information Inc.
WLRN	17	PBS	Public	School Board of Dade County
WVIB	21	n/a	Commercial	Hispanic Keys Broadcasting
WLTV	23	UNIN	Commercial	Univision Communications Inc.
WBFS	33	UPN	Commercial	United Paramount Network
WAMI	69	n/a	Commercial	Univision Communications Inc.

Note: Stations included broadcast from the Miami metro area; n/a not available
Source: Burrelle's Media Directory, 2003

AM Radio Stations

Call Letters	Freq. (kHz)	Target Audience	Station Format	Music Format
WQAM	560	G/M	S/T	n/a
WIOD	610	General	M/N/S/T	Big Band
WWFE	670	Hispanic	M/N/S/T	Classical
WAQI	710	Hispanic	N/T	n/a
WAXY	790	General	M/S/T	Oldies
WVCG	1080	Hispanic	M/N/T	Christian
WQBA	1140	Hispanic	N/S/T	n/a
WNMA	1210	Hispanic	N/S/T	n/a
WSUA	1260	G/H	M/N/S/T	Adult Contemporary
WKAT	1360	Hispanic	M/N/S/T	Classical
WOCN	1450	Hispanic	M/N/S/T	Big Band
WMBM	1490	Christian	E/M/N/S/T	Christian
WRHC	1560	Hispanic	M/N/T	Big Band

Note: Stations included broadcast from the Miami metro area; n/a not available
The following abbreviations may be used:
Target Audience: A=Asian; B=Black; C=Christian; E=Ethnic; F=French; G=General; H=Hispanic; M=Men; N=Native American; R=Religious; S=Senior Citizen; W=Women; Y=Young Adult; Z=Children
Station Format: E=Educational; M=Music; N=News; S=Sports; T=Talk
Source: Burrelle's Media Directory, 2003

FM Radio Stations

Call Letters	Freq. (mHz)	Target Audience	Station Format	Music Format
WRGP	88.1	General	M/N/T	International
WDNA	88.9	Hispanic	M/N	Big Band
WMCU	89.7	Religious	M/N	Adult Contemporary
WVUM	90.5	General	M/N/S	Alternative
WLRN	91.3	General	M/N/T	Big Band
WCMQ	92.3	Hispanic	M/N	Adult Top 40
WPYM	93.1	General	M	Top 40
WXDJ	95.7	Hispanic	M	Latin
WPOW	96.5	General	M	Top 40
WFLC	97.3	General	M/N	Adult Top 40
WRTO	98.3	Hispanic	M	Latin
WEDR	99.1	Black	M	Rhythm & Blues
WKIS	99.9	General	M/N/S	Country
WLYF	101.5	G/W	M	Adult Contemporary
WMXJ	102.7	General	M	Oldies
WHQT	105.1	General	M/N/T	Adult Contemporary
WZMQ	106.3	Hispanic	M	Latin
WRMA	106.7	Hispanic	M	Adult Contemporary
WAMR	107.5	Hispanic	M	Latin
WVMQ	107.9	Hispanic	M	Latin

Note: Stations included broadcast from the Miami metro area
The following abbreviations may be used:
Target Audience: A=Asian; B=Black; C=Christian; E=Ethnic; F=French; G=General; H=Hispanic; M=Men; N=Native American; R=Religious; S=Senior Citizen; W=Women; Y=Young Adult; Z=Children
Station Format: E=Educational; M=Music; N=News; S=Sports; T=Talk
Source: Burrelle's Media Directory, 2003

CLIMATE

Average and Extreme Temperatures

Temperature	Jan	Feb	Mar	Apr	May	Jun	Jul	Aug	Sep	Oct	Nov	Dec	Yr.
Extreme High (°F)	88	89	92	96	95	98	98	98	97	95	89	87	98
Average High (°F)	75	77	79	82	85	88	89	90	88	85	80	77	83
Average Temp. (°F)	68	69	72	75	79	82	83	83	82	78	73	69	76
Average Low (°F)	59	60	64	68	72	75	76	76	76	72	66	61	69
Extreme Low (°F)	30	35	32	42	55	60	69	68	68	53	39	30	30

Note: Figures cover the years 1948-1990
Source: National Climatic Data Center, International Station Meteorological Climate Summary, 9/96

Average Precipitation/Snowfall/Humidity

Precip./Humidity	Jan	Feb	Mar	Apr	May	Jun	Jul	Aug	Sep	Oct	Nov	Dec	Yr.
Avg. Precip. (in.)	1.9	2.0	2.3	3.0	6.2	8.7	6.1	7.5	8.2	6.6	2.7	1.8	57.1
Avg. Snowfall (in.)	0	0	0	0	0	0	0	0	0	0	0	0	0
Avg. Rel. Hum. 7am (%)	84	84	82	80	81	84	84	86	88	87	85	84	84
Avg. Rel. Hum. 4pm (%)	59	57	57	57	62	68	66	67	69	65	63	60	63

Note: Figures cover the years 1948-1990; Tr = Trace amounts (<0.05 in. of rain; <0.5 in. of snow)
Source: National Climatic Data Center, International Station Meteorological Climate Summary, 9/96

Weather Conditions

Temperature			Daytime Sky			Precipitation		
32°F & below	45°F & below	90°F & above	Clear	Partly cloudy	Cloudy	0.01 inch or more precip.	0.1 inch or more snow/ice	Thunder-storms
< 1	7	55	48	263	54	128	0	74

Note: Figures are average number of days per year and covers the years 1948-1990
Source: National Climatic Data Center, International Station Meteorological Climate Summary, 9/96

**HAZARDOUS
WASTE**

Superfund Sites

Miami has two hazardous waste sites on the EPA's Superfund National Priorities List: **Airco Plating Co.**; **Miami Drum Services**. *U.S. Environmental Protection Agency, National Priorities List, March 15, 2004*

**AIR & WATER
QUALITY**

Maximum Pollutant Concentrations

	Particulate Matter (ug/m³)	Carbon Monoxide (ppm)	Sulfur Dioxide (ppm)	Nitrogen Dioxide (ppm)	Ozone 1-hour (ppm)	Ozone 8-hour (ppm)	Lead (ug/m³)
MSA[1] Level	43	3	0.004	0.014	0.09	0.07	n/a
NAAQS[2]	150	9	0.140	0.053	0.12	0.08	1.50
Met NAAQS[2]	Yes	Yes	Yes	Yes	Yes	Yes	n/a

Note: (1) Metropolitan Statistical Area - see Appendix A for areas included; (2) National Ambient Air Quality Standards; n/a not available
Units: ppm = parts per million; ug/m³ = micrograms per cubic meter
Source: EPA, Latest Findings on National Air Quality: 2002 Status and Trends, August 2003

Air Quality Index

In the Miami MSA (see Appendix A for areas included), the Air Quality Index (AQI) exceeded 100 on 1 day in 2002. An AQI value greater than 100 indicates that air quality would have been in the unhealthful range on that day.
EPA, Latest Findings on National Air Quality: 2002 Status and Trends, August 2003

Watershed Health

The U.S. Environmental Protection Agency monitors the health of the aquatic resources for the nation's 2,000+ watersheds. **The Everglades watershed serves the Miami area and received an overall Index of Watershed Indicators (IWI) score of 4 (less serious problems - high vulnerability)**. The IWI score is based on seven condition and nine vulnerability indicators. The overall IWI score ranges from 1 (best health) to 6 (worst health). The Condition Indicators include: designated use attainment, fish and wildlife consumption advisories, source water condition, contaminated sediments, ambient water quality, and wetlands loss index. The Vulnerability Indicators include: aquatic species at risk, conventional and toxic loads over permitted limits, urban and agricultural runoff potential, population change, hydrologic modification, estuarine pollution susceptibility, and air deposition. *EPA, Index of Watershed Indicators, October 26, 2001*

Drinking Water

Water System Name	Pop. Served	Primary Water Source Type	Number of Violations January 2002-February 2004		
			Health Based	Significant Monitoring	Monitoring
MDWASA - Main System	1,705,156	Ground	None	None	None

Note: Data as of February 19, 2004
Source: EPA, Office of Ground Water and Drinking Water, Safe Drinking Water Information System

Miami tap water is alkaline, soft and fluoridated.
Editor & Publisher Market Guide, 2004

Nashville, Tennessee

Background

Nashville, the capital of Tennessee, was founded on Christmas Day in 1779 by James Robertson and John Donelson, and sits in the minds of millions as the country music capital of the world. This is the place to record if you want to make it into the country music industry, and where the Grand Ole Opry—the longest-running radio show in the country—still captures the hearts of millions of devoted listeners. It is no wonder, given how profoundly this industry has touched people, names like Dolly, Chet, Loretta, Hank, and Johnny are more familiar than the city's true native sons: Andrew, James, and Sam. Jackson, Polk, and Houston, that is.

Among the latest to discover Nashville's musical charms is the USA Network. It has unveiled "Nashville Star," a country-style "American Idol" that left its 2003 winner, Buddy Jewell, with a Clint Black-produced album that debuted at No. 1 on the Billboard Country music charts, according to the Country Music Association.

The magnitude of Nashville's recording industry is impressive, but other industries are important to the city, such as health care management, automobile production, and printing and publishing.

Nashville is also a devoted patron of education. The Davidson Academy, forerunner of the George Peabody College for Teachers, was founded in Nashville, as were Vanderbilt and Fisk universities, the latter being the first private black university in the United States. Vanderbilt University and Medical Center is the region's largest non-governmental employer.

Nashville citizens take pride in their numerous museums, including the Cumberland Science Museum, with its 40-foot Sudekum Planetarium; the Aaron Douglas Gallery at Fisk University, which features a remarkable collection of African-American art; and the Carl Van Vechten Gallery, also at Fisk University, home to works by Alfred Stieglitz, Picasso, Cezanne, and Georgia O'Keefe. Also, the Cheekwood Botanical Garden and Museum of Art includes 55 acres of gardens and contemporary art galleries.

Gracing the city are majestic mansions and plantations that testify to the mid-nineteenth-century splendor for which the South came to be famous. Known as the "Queen of the Tennessee Plantations," the Belle Meade Plantation is an 1853 Greek Revival mansion crowning a 5,400-acre thoroughbred stud farm and nursery. The Belmont Mansion, built in 1850 by Adelicia Acklen, one of the wealthiest women in America, is constructed in the style of an Italian villa and was originally intended to be the summer home of the Acklens. Travelers' Rest Plantation served as a haven for weary travelers, past and present, and is Nashville's oldest plantation home open to the public. It features docents dressed in period costume who explain and demonstrate life in the plantations' heyday. Carnton Plantation was the site of the Civil War's Battle of Franklin, and The Hermitage was the home of Andrew Jackson, the seventh president of the United States. Tennessee's historic State Capitol Building, completed in 1859, has had much of its interior restored to its nineteenth-century appearance.

The Nashville area comprises many urban, suburban, rural, and historic districts, which can differ immensely from each other. Most of the best restaurants, clubs, and shops are on the west side of the Cumberland River; however, the east side encompasses fine neighborhoods, interesting homes, plenty of shopping, and good food, as well. Outdoor activities include camping, fishing, hiking, and biking at the many scenic and accessible lakes in the region.

Located on the Cumberland River in central Tennessee, Nashville's average relative humidity is moderate, as is its weather, with great temperature extremes a rarity. The city is not in the most common path of storms that cross the country, but is in a zone of moderate frequency for thunderstorms.

Rankings

- Nashville was ranked #206 out of 331 metro areas in *Cities Ranked & Rated*. Criteria: cost of living; climate; crime; transportation; economy and jobs; education; arts and culture; health and healthcare; leisure. *Cities Ranked & Rated, 1st Edition, 2004*

- *Ladies Home Journal* ranked America's 200 largest cities based on the qualities women surveyed care about most. Nashville ranked #46 out of 57 in the big city category (population over 300,000). Criteria: crime; lifestyle; education; jobs; health; child care; politics; and the economy. *Ladies Home Journal Online, "The Best Cities for Women 2002"*

- The Nashville metro area was selected as one of "America's Best Places to Live and Work 2003" by *Employment Review*. The area ranked #6 out of 20. Criteria: unemployment rate; projected job growth; cost of living; and industry specific data. *Employment Review, www.bestjobsusa.com*

- The Nashville metro area was selected as one of America's "Best Places to Live and Work" by *Expansion Management* and rated as a "Four-Star Community." The annual "Quality of Life Quotient" measures nearly 50 indicators and compares them among the 329 metropolitan statistical areas in the United States. *Expansion Management, May 2003*

- Nashville was selected as one of "America's Pet Healthiest Cities" by Purina. The city ranked #44 out of 50. Criteria: veterinary services; environment; and legislation. *Purina Pet Institute, "America's Pet Healthiest Cities," August 14, 2001*

- Nashville was selected as one of the "Best Cities for Black Families." The city ranked #10 out of 20. For six months, bet.com compiled data on African Americans in those U.S. cities with the largest Black populations. The data, for African Americans specifically, involved the following: infant mortality; high school graduation; median income; homeownership; unemployment; business ownership; poverty rates; AIDS infection rates; percentage of children in single parent, typically fatherless, households; teen pregnancy; economic segregation index; violent and property crime. *www.bet.com, October 1, 2002*

- *Forbes* ranked the 40 most populous metro areas in the U.S. in terms of the best places to be single. The Nashville metro area was ranked #24. Criteria: number of other singles; cost of living alone; nightlife; culture; job growth; coolness. *Forbes, June 5, 2003*

- *Forbes* ranked the 150 most populous metro areas in the U.S. in terms of the "Best Places for Business and Careers." The Nashville metro area was ranked #25. Criteria: income and job growth; cost-of-doing-business; qualifications of the available pool of labor; crime rates; housing costs; net migration. *Forbes, May 9, 2003*

- Nashville was selected as one of "America's Healthiest Cities" by *Natural Health* magazine. The city was ranked #24 out of the 50 largest urban areas in the U.S. Twenty-six criteria in the following four categories were examined: whether the city boasts natural offerings; how well the city promotes its resident's physical health; whether the city offers a healthy environment; how well the city fosters a sense of community. *Natural Health, April 2003*

- *Men's Health* ranked 101 U.S. cities in terms of the quality of their tap water. Nashville received a grade of B. Criteria: levels of bacteria, arsenic, lead, trihalomethanes, and haloacetic acids were compared with the National Academy of Science's guidelines as well as with the EPA's more stringent maximum contaminant level goals. *Men's Health, March 2004*

- Sperling's BestPlaces ranked 331 metro areas and identified the most and least stressful U.S. cities. The Nashville metro area ranked #39 out of the 100 largest metro areas (#1 = most stressful). Criteria: divorce rate; unemployment rate; violent and property crime; suicide rate; commute time; mental health; alcohol consumption; cloudy days. *www.BestPlaces.net, February 26, 2004*

- Sperling's BestPlaces in partnership with Pep Boys ranked 77 metro areas and identified "America's Most Drivable Cities." The Nashville metro area ranked #16. Criteria: climate; road roughness; urban mobility; gas prices. *Pep Boys, "America's Most Drivable Cities," April 9, 2003*

- Nashville was selected as a 2003 Digital Cities Survey winner. The city ranked #6 in the large city category. The survey examined and assessed how city governments are utilizing information technology to operate and deliver quality service to their customers and citizens. *Center for Digital Government, "2003 Digital Cities Survey"*

- Nashville was ranked #132 out of America's 200 largest metro areas in *SELF Magazine's* ranking of "America's Healthiest Cities for Women." Criteria: safety; air/water quality; cancer rates; and 21 other factors relating to health. *SELF Magazine, November 2003*

- Nashville was identified as one of the most dangerous large metro areas for pedestrians in the U.S. The area ranked #10 out of the nations 49 largest metro areas. Criteria: average yearly pedestrian fatalities per capita (for the years 2000 and 2001) adjusted for the number of walkers. *Surface Transportation Policy Project, "Mean Streets 2002"*

- Nashville was selected as one of the 25 fittest cities in America by *Men's Fitness Online*. It ranked #23 out of America's 50 largest cities. Criteria: gyms/sporting goods; nutrition; exercise/sports; overweight/sedentary; junk food; alcohol; smoking; television; air and water quality; climate; geography; commute time; parks/open space; recreation facilities; and health care. *Men's Fitness Online, America's Fittest/Fattest Cities 2003*

- Nashville was ranked #82 out of 100 cities surveyed in *Child* magazine's ranking of the "Best Cities for Families." Criteria: number of pediatricians per capita; proximity to a children's hospital; immunization rates; infant mortality rate; air quality; water quality; school spending; pupil-teacher ratio; availability of parks/green space; nearby recreational opportunities; average commute time; number of sunny days; average cost of a 3-bedroom home; unemployment rate; future job growth; crime rate; percentage of children under 5; mandated minimum child care ratios. *Child, April 2001*

- *Zero Population Growth* ranked 239 cities in terms of children's health, safety, and economic well-being. Nashville was ranked #91 out of 140 independent cities (cities with populations greater than 100,000 which were neither major cities nor suburbs/outer cities) and was given a grade of B-. Criteria: total population and population growth; percent of population under 18 years of age; number of children's museums; health improvement grade; percent of births to teens; percent of low birthweight infants; infant mortality rate; number of Title X-funded clinics; average SAT/ACT scores; average elementary and secondary class size; crime rate; unemployment rate; percent of affordable homes; number of bad air days; park acres per 1000 persons; library circulation per child; and children's program attendance counts. *Zero Population Growth, Kid Friendly Cities Report Card 2001*

- *Ladies Home Journal* ranked America's 200 largest cities in terms of safety. Nashville ranked #188 out of 200. Criteria: violent crimes; crimes against property; and rape. *Ladies Home Journal Online, "The Best Cities for Women 2002"*

- Nashville was ranked #67 out of 268 metro areas in terms of its Creativity Index. The Creativity Index is a mix of four equally weighted factors: the Creative Class (scientists, engineers, architects, designers, writers, artists, musicians, or any profession where creativity is a key factor) share of the workforce; innovation, measured as patents per capita; high-tech industry, using the Milken Institute's Tech Pole Index; and diversity, measured by the Gay Index (a reasonable proxy for an areas' openness to different kinds of people and ideas). *The Rise of the Creative Class, 2002*

- Nashville was ranked #42 out of 125 regions worldwide in terms of its "Knowledge Competitiveness Index." The index attempts to measure the knowledge-based development taking place throughout the world and is based on 17 measures of economic performance that indicate a region's ability to translate its knowledge capacity into economic value. *Robert Huggins Associates, "2003-2004 World Knowledge Competitiveness Index"*

- The Nashville metro area was selected by *Yahoo! Internet Life* as one of "America's Most Wired Cities...and Towns." The area ranked #44 out of 87. Criteria: home and work net use; user sophistication; domain density; and available content. *Yahoo! Internet Life, April 2001*

- The Nashville metro area was selected by Cranium as one of the "Top 50 Fun Cities" in America. The area ranked #24. Criteria includes: number of sports teams, restaurants, and dance performances; number of toy stores; city budget spent on recreation. *Cranium, November 4, 2003*

- Nashville was identified as one of the 100 "Most Unwired Cities" in the U.S. The area ranked #42. Criteria: number of public and commercial wireless access points; cell phone coverage offering wide area network Internet access; Internet penetration. *Intel, "Most Unwired Cities," March 4, 2003*

- Scarborough Research measured the percentage of households who subscribe to cellular services among adults ages 18 and over in 75 U.S. markets. The Nashville DMA (Designated Market Area) was ranked #38 out of 75. *Scarborough Research, Scarborough USA+ 2003 Release 1*

- Nashville was selected as one of "America's Most Literate Cities." The city ranked #21 out of the 64 largest U.S. cities. Criteria: booksellers; library support, holdings, and utilization; educational attainment; periodicals published; newspaper circulation. *University of Wisconsin-Whitewater, "America's Most Literate Cities," Summer 2003*

- Nashville was ranked #115 in *Prevention* magazine's survey of the "Best Walking Cities in the U.S." The magazine, in conjunction with the American Podiatric Medical Association, surveyed 125 of the most populated cities and then tabulated and weighed 20 criteria of interest to pedestrians. *Prevention, April, 2004*

- Nashville was selected as one of America's best-mannered cities. The area ranked in the top 10 at #6. The list is based on thousands of letters and faxes received by etiquette expert Marjabelle Young Stewart. *The Associated Press, January 17, 2004*

- The Nashville metro area was selected as one of "America's 50 Hottest Cities for Business Relocations and Expansions." The area ranked #2. Criteria: 70 of the industry's most prominent site selection consultants were asked which cities their clients found the most attractive when it came to selecting an expansion or relocation site in 2003. *Expansion Management, January 2004*

- The Nashville metro area was cited as one of "The Best Places in the U.S. to Locate a Company." The area ranked #44 out of 329. Criteria: education (with emphasis on college board test results and high school graduation rates); availability of quality healthcare services and the cost to employers; quality of life; logistics workforce and companies; transportation infrastructure; quality and quantity of highly educated technical workers; business climate. *Expansion Management, July 2003*

- The Nashville metro area was selected as one of the "Top 40 Hottest Real Estate Markets" for expanding or relocating businesses." Criteria: rental costs; purchase prices; and vacancy rates of office and warehouse space. *Expansion Management, August 2003*

- The Nashville metro area appeared on *Forbes/Milken Institute* list of "Best Places for Business and Career." Rank: #76 out of 200 metro areas. Criteria: salary growth; job growth; number of technology clusters; overall concentration of technology activity relative to national average; and technology output growth. *www.forbes.com, Forbes/Milken Institute Best Places 2002*

- The Nashville metro area appeared on the "Milken Institute Best Performing Cities" index. Rank: #53 out of 200 large metro areas. Criteria: job growth; wage and salary growth; high-tech output growth. *Milken Institute, June 25, 2003*

- The Nashville metro area appeared on *Entrepreneur* magazine's list of the "Best Cities for Entrepreneurs" in 2003. The area ranked #45 out of 61 in the large city category. Criteria: entrepreneurial activity; small-business growth; economic growth; and risk. *www.Entrepreneur.com*

- The Nashville metro area appeared on *IndustryWeek's* fourth annual World-Class Communities list. It ranked #235 out of 315 metro areas. Criteria: MSA Gross Metropolitan Product (GMP) per manufacturing employee; and MSA percent share of U.S. manufacturing Gross Domestic Product (GDP). *IndustryWeek, April 16, 2001*

- The Nashville metro area was selected as a "2001 Choice City" by *Business Development Outlook* magazine. Twenty-five cities were selected, based on data from the Bureau of Labor Statistics, Census Bureau, Federal Reserve, The Conference Board, and the U.S. Conference of Mayors, as being the most desirable into which a business can relocate or expand. *Business Development Outlook, 2001 Choice Cities*

■ ING Group ranked the 125 largest metro areas according to the general financial security of residents. The Nashville metro area was ranked #38 out of 125. Criteria: Earnings and Wealth Potential (household income, education, net assets, cost of living); Safety Net (health insurance, retirement savings, life insurance, income support programs); Personal Threats (unemployment rate, low-income households, crime rate); Community Economic Vitality (cost of community services, job quality, job creation, housing costs). *ING Group, "The Best Cities to Earn and Save Money: A Ranking of the Largest 125 U.S. Cities," 2001 Edition*

Business Environment

CITY FINANCES

City Government Finances

Component	2000-2001 ($000)	2000-2001 ($ per capita)
Total Revenues	2,409,129	4,227
Total Expenditures	2,457,542	4,312
Debt Outstanding	3,643,011	6,392
Cash and Securities	4,341,965	7,619

Source: U.S Census Bureau, Government Finances 2000-2001, August 2003

City Government Revenue by Source

Source	2000-2001 ($000)	2000-2001 ($ per capita)
General Revenue		
From Federal Government	7,423	13
From State Government	299,773	526
From Local Governments	2,894	5
Taxes		
Property	474,863	833
Sales	270,638	475
Personal Income	0	0
License	10,952	19
Charges	233,544	410
Liquor Store	0	0
Utility	800,210	1,404
Employee Retirement	88,972	156
Other	219,860	386

Source: U.S Census Bureau, Government Finances 2000-2001, August 2003

City Government Expenditures by Function

Function	2000-2001 ($000)	2000-2001 ($ per capita)	2000-2001 (%)
General Expenditures			
Airports	0	0	0.0
Corrections	43,476	76	1.8
Education	521,256	915	21.2
Fire Protection	67,146	118	2.7
Governmental Administration	82,486	145	3.4
Health	29,015	51	1.2
Highways	30,877	54	1.3
Hospitals	109,614	192	4.5
Housing and Community Development	0	0	0.0
Interest on General Debt	130,264	229	5.3
Libraries	12,747	22	0.5
Parking	0	0	0.0
Parks and Recreation	47,299	83	1.9
Police Protection	104,738	184	4.3
Public Welfare	16,308	29	0.7
Sewerage	53,789	94	2.2
Solid Waste Management	35,231	62	1.4
Liquor Store	0	0	0.0
Utility	858,537	1,506	34.9
Employee Retirement	102,007	179	4.2
Other	212,752	373	8.7

Source: U.S Census Bureau, Government Finances 2000-2001, August 2003

Municipal Bond Ratings

Area	Moody's
City	Aaa

Source: Mergent Bond Record, February 2004

DEMOGRAPHICS

Population Growth

Area	1990 Census	2000 Census	2003 Estimate	2008 Projection	Population Growth (%)	
					1990-2000	2000-2008
City	488,364	545,524	550,914	560,627	11.7	2.8
MSA[1]	985,028	1,231,311	1,281,020	1,363,394	25.0	10.7
U.S.	248,709,873	281,421,906	290,647,163	305,918,071	13.2	8.7

Note: (1) Metropolitan Statistical Area - see Appendix A for areas included
Source: Claritas, Inc.

Number of Households and Average Household Size

Area	1990 Census	2000 Census	2003 Estimate	2008 Projection	2003 Average Household Size
City	198,581	227,403	231,568	238,993	2.4
MSA[1]	375,832	479,569	502,533	541,519	2.5
U.S.	91,947,410	105,480,101	109,440,059	116,034,472	2.7

Note: (1) Metropolitan Statistical Area - see Appendix A for areas included
Source: Claritas, Inc.

Race and Ethnicity

Area	White Non-Hispanic	Black Non-Hispanic	Asian Non-Hispanic	Other Race Non-Hispanic	Hispanic
City	64.9	27.2	2.5	5.4	5.3
MSA[1]	79.2	15.5	1.7	3.6	3.6
U.S.	74.5	12.4	3.8	9.3	13.2

Note: Figures are 2003 estimates; (1) Metropolitan Statistical Area - see Appendix A for areas included
Source: Claritas, Inc.

Segregation

City		MSA[1]	
Index[2]	Rank[3]	Index[2]	Rank[4]
57.6	58	61.7	128

Note: Figures are based on an analysis of Census 2000 data; (1) Metropolitan Statistical Area - see Appendix A for areas included; (2) Dissimilarity Index—the most commonly used measure of segregation between two groups, reflecting their relative distributions across neighborhoods within a city or metropolitan area. It can range in value from 0, indicating complete integration, to 100, indicating complete segregation; (3) Ranges from 1 (most segregated) to 100 (least segregated) and includes all the cities in this book; (4) Ranges from 1 (most segregated) to 318 (least segregated) and includes 318 metropolitan areas.
Source: www.CensusScope.org

Ancestry

Area	German	Irish[2]	English	American	Italian	Polish	French[3]	Scottish
City	8.8	8.9	9.0	10.9	1.9	0.9	1.8	2.0
MSA[1]	9.8	10.2	10.4	15.4	2.1	1.1	2.1	2.2
U.S.	15.2	10.9	8.7	7.3	5.6	3.2	3.0	1.7

Note: Figures include multiple ancestry (e.g. if a person reported being Irish and Italian, they were included in both columns); (1) Metropolitan Statistical Area - see Appendix A for areas included; (2) Includes Celtic; (3) Includes Alsatian but excludes Basque
Source: Census 2000, Summary File 3

Foreign-Born Population

Area	Percent of Population Born in:							
	Any Foreign Country	Europe	Asia	Africa	Oceania[2]	Canada	Mexico	Latin America[3]
City	7.1	0.9	2.3	0.8	0.0	0.2	1.9	1.0
MSA[1]	4.7	0.7	1.5	0.4	0.0	0.2	1.3	0.6
U.S.	11.1	1.7	2.9	0.3	0.1	0.3	3.3	2.5

Note: (1) Metropolitan Statistical Area - see Appendix A for areas included; (2) Includes Australia, New Zealand subregion, Melanesia, Micronesia, Polynesia, and Oceania n.e.c.; (3) Includes Central America (excluding Mexico), South America, and the Caribbean.
Source: Census 2000, Summary File 3

Religion

Area	Catholic	Southern Baptist	United Methodist	ELCA[1]	LDS[2]	Presbyterian Church USA	Jewish Est.	Muslim Est.
County	0.0	0.0	0.0	0.0	0.0	0.0	0.0	0.0
U.S.	22.0	7.1	3.7	1.8	1.5	1.1	2.2	0.6

Note: Figures shown are the number of adherents as a percentage of the total population; Adherents are defined as all members, including full members, their children and the estimated number of other participants who are not considered members (e.g. the baptized, those not confirmed, those not eligible for communion, those regularly attending services, etc.); (1) Evangelical Lutheran Church in America; (2) The Church of Jesus Christ of Latter Day Saints
Source: Reprinted with permission from Religious Congregations and Membership in the United States 2000 (Nashville, Glenmary Research Center, 2002) Copyright Association of Statisticians of American Religious Bodies. All rights reserved.

Age Distribution

Area	Percent of Population						
	Under Age 5	Age 5 to 17	Age 18 to 34	Age 35 to 49	Age 50 to 64	Age 65 to 79	80 Years and Over
City	6.6	15.5	29.6	23.8	13.6	8.1	2.9
MSA[1]	6.9	17.9	25.9	24.8	14.5	7.6	2.5
U.S.	6.8	18.9	23.7	23.5	14.8	9.2	3.2

Note: (1) Metropolitan Statistical Area - see Appendix A for areas included
Source: Census 2000, Summary File 3

Marriage Status

Area	Never Married	Now Married Except Separated	Separated	Widowed	Divorced
City	32.6	45.5	2.3	6.4	13.2
MSA[1]	26.3	54.8	1.8	5.6	11.5
U.S.	27.1	54.4	2.2	6.6	9.7

Note: Figures cover population 15 years of age and older; (1) Metropolitan Statistical Area - see Appendix A for areas included
Source: Census 2000, Summary File 3

Male/Female Ratio

Area	Males	Females	Males per 100 Females
City	267,034	283,880	94.1
MSA[1]	627,564	653,456	96.0
U.S.	142,511,883	148,135,280	96.2

Note: Figures are 2003 estimates; (1) Metropolitan Statistical Area - see Appendix A for areas included
Source: Claritas, Inc.

ECONOMY

Gross Metropolitan Product

Area	1999	2000	2001	2002	2002 Rank[2]
MSA[1]	42.7	44.6	45.9	48.0	53

Note: Figures are in billions of dollars; (1) Metropolitan Statistical Area - see Appendix A for areas included; (2) Rank ranges from 1 to 319
Source: The U.S. Conference of Mayors, Metro Economies Report, July 2003

INCOME

Per Capita/Median/Average Income

Area	Per Capita ($)	Median Household ($)	Average Household ($)
City	25,060	44,429	58,817
MSA[1]	25,996	49,740	65,664
U.S.	24,078	46,868	63,207

Note: Figures are 2003 estimates; (1) Metropolitan Statistical Area - see Appendix A for areas included
Source: Claritas, Inc.

Household Income Distribution

Area	Percent of Households Earning							
	Under $15,000	$15,000 -24,999	$25,000 -34,999	$35,000 -49,999	$50,000 -74,999	$75,000 -99,000	$100,000 -149,999	$150,000 and up
City	14.1	11.6	13.2	17.6	19.6	10.4	8.7	4.7
MSA[1]	11.9	10.2	11.6	16.6	21.0	12.2	10.6	6.0
U.S.	14.1	11.5	11.7	16.0	19.2	11.3	10.2	6.0

Note: Figures are 2003 estimates; (1) Metropolitan Statistical Area - see Appendix A for areas included
Source: Claritas, Inc.

Poverty Rates by Age

Area	All Ages	Under 5 Years Old	5 to 17 Years Old	18 to 64 Years Old	65 Years and Over
City	13.3	1.5	3.0	7.6	1.2
MSA[1]	10.1	1.1	2.3	5.7	1.0
U.S.	12.4	1.2	3.0	6.9	1.2

Note: Figures are percent of population with income in 1999 below poverty level and only include population for whom poverty status is determined; (1) Metropolitan Statistical Area - see Appendix A for areas included
Source: Census 2000, Summary File 3

Personal Bankruptcy Filing Rate

Area	2002	2003
Davidson County	8.85	9.07
U.S.	5.34	5.58

Note: Numbers are per 1,000 population and include Chapter 7 and Chapter 13 filings
Source: Federal Deposit Insurance Corporation (FDIC), Regional Economic Conditions (RECON), 2/25/2004

EMPLOYMENT

Labor Force and Employment

Area	Civilian Labor Force			Workers Employed		
	Dec. 2002	Dec. 2003	% Chg.	Dec. 2002	Dec. 2003	% Chg.
City	320,968	318,349	-0.8	309,755	305,361	-1.4
MSA[1]	697,522	691,455	-0.9	673,550	663,996	-1.4
U.S.	144,807,000	146,501,000	1.2	136,599,000	138,556,000	1.4

Note: Data is not seasonally adjusted and covers workers 16 years of age and older;
(1) Metropolitan Statistical Area - see Appendix A for areas included
Source: Bureau of Labor Statistics, http://stats.bls.gov

Unemployment Rate

Area	2003											
	Jan.	Feb.	Mar.	Apr.	May	Jun.	Jul.	Aug.	Sep.	Oct.	Nov.	Dec.
City	3.8	3.6	3.6	3.6	3.6	4.3	3.8	3.9	4.0	4.2	4.7	4.1
MSA[1]	3.9	3.7	3.6	3.6	3.5	4.2	3.8	3.9	3.9	4.2	4.5	4.0
U.S.	6.5	6.4	6.2	5.8	5.8	6.5	6.3	6.0	5.8	5.6	5.6	5.4

Note: Data is not seasonally adjusted and covers workers 16 years of age and older; All figures are percentages; (1) Metropolitan Statistical Area - see Appendix A for areas included
Source: Bureau of Labor Statistics, http://stats.bls.gov

Employment by Occupation

Occupation Classification	City (%)	MSA[1] (%)	U.S. (%)
Sales and Office	28.6	28.3	26.7
Professional and Related	21.9	19.8	20.2
Service	14.1	12.7	14.9
Production, Transportation, and Material Moving	12.1	14.4	14.6
Management, Business, and Financial	14.7	14.8	13.5
Construction, Extraction, and Maintenance	8.5	9.6	9.4
Farming, Forestry, and Fishing	0.1	0.3	0.7

Note: Figures cover employed civilians 16 years of age and older;
(1) Metropolitan Statistical Area - see Appendix A for areas included
Source: Census 2000, Summary File 3

Employment by Industry

Sector	MSA[1]		U.S.
	Number of Employees	Percent of Total	Percent of Total
Government	91,900	13.3	16.7
Education and Health Services	94,400	13.6	12.9
Professional and Business Services	82,500	11.9	12.3
Retail Trade	82,100	11.9	11.8
Manufacturing	78,700	11.4	11.0
Leisure and Hospitality	72,000	10.4	9.1
Finance Activities	44,700	6.5	6.1
Construction	n/a	n/a	5.1
Wholesale Trade	35,100	5.1	4.3
Other Services	30,200	4.4	4.1
Transportation and Utilities	27,000	3.9	3.7
Information	19,300	2.8	2.4
Natural Resources and Mining	n/a	n/a	0.4

Note: Figures cover non-farm employment as of December 2003 and are not seasonally adjusted;
(1) Metropolitan Statistical Area - see Appendix A for areas included; n/a not available
Source: Bureau of Labor Statistics, http://stats.bls.gov

Average Wages

Occupation	$/Hr.	Occupation	$/Hr.
Accountants and Auditors	22.98	Maids and Housekeeping Cleaners	7.70
Automotive Mechanics	16.20	Maintenance and Repair Workers	15.38
Bookkeepers	13.50	Marketing Managers	31.19
Carpenters	14.56	Nuclear Medicine Technologists	22.22
Cashiers	8.15	Nurses, Licensed Practical	15.83
Clerks, General Office	11.29	Nurses, Registered	26.10
Clerks, Receptionists/Information	10.68	Nursing Aides/Orderlies/Attendants	9.45
Clerks, Shipping/Receiving	11.88	Packers and Packagers, Hand	8.72
Computer Programmers	27.87	Physical Therapists	26.83
Computer Support Specialists	18.94	Postal Service Mail Carriers	18.62
Computer Systems Analysts	26.20	Real Estate Brokers	45.94
Cooks, Restaurant	9.73	Retail Salespersons	11.32
Dentists	28.68	Sales Reps., Exc. Tech./Scientific	29.19
Electrical Engineers	30.02	Sales Reps., Tech./Scientific	24.08
Electricians	18.28	Secretaries, Exc. Legal/Med./Exec.	12.22
Financial Managers	31.60	Security Guards	11.61
First-Line Supervisors/Mgrs., Sales	16.89	Surgeons	86.17
Food Preparation Workers	8.39	Teacher Assistants	7.00
General and Operations Managers	36.11	Teachers, Elementary School	16.40
Hairdressers/Cosmetologists	11.98	Teachers, Secondary School	17.30
Internists	81.30	Telemarketers	12.19
Janitors and Cleaners	9.28	Truck Drivers, Heavy/Tractor-Trailer	17.63
Landscaping/Groundskeeping Workers	9.35	Truck Drivers, Light/Delivery Svcs.	13.99
Lawyers	58.23	Waiters and Waitresses	6.90

Note: Wage data is for 2002 and covers the Metropolitan Statistical Area (see Appendix A for areas included).
Hourly wages for elementary/secondary school teachers and teacher assistants were calculated by the editors
from annual wage data assuming a 40 hour work week; n/a not available.
Source: Bureau of Labor Statistics, 2002 Metro Area Occupational Employment and Wage Estimates

Occupational Employment Projections: 1996 - 2006

Occupations Expected to Have the Largest Job Growth (ranked by numerical growth)	Fast-Growing Occupations[1] (ranked by percent growth)
1. Salespersons, retail	1. Personal and home care aides
2. Truck drivers, light	2. Systems analysts
3. Cashiers	3. Paralegals
4. General managers & top executives	4. Respiratory therapists
5. Janitors/cleaners/maids, ex. priv. hshld.	5. Home health aides
6. Food service workers	6. Directors, religious activities & educ.
7. Child care workers, private household	7. Computer engineers
8. Cooks, fast food and short order	8. Child care workers, private household
9. Registered nurses	9. Corrections officers & jailers
10. Waiters & waitresses	10. Emergency medical technicians

Note: Projections cover Tennessee; (1) Excludes occupations with total job growth less than 300
Source: U.S. Department of Labor, Employment and Training Administration, America's Labor Market Information System (ALMIS)

TAXES

State Corporate Income Tax Rates

State	Rate (%)	Number of Brackets	Low Bracket (Under $)	High Bracket (Over $)
Tennessee	6.5	1	na	na

Note: Tax rates as of December 31, 2003; na not applicable
Source: Tax Foundation, www.taxfoundation.org

State Individual Income Tax Rates

State	Federal Deductibility	Marginal Rate (%)	Number of Brackets	Low Bracket (Under $)	High Bracket (Over $)
Tennessee	No	6.0 (h)	na	na	na

Note: Tax rates as of December 31, 2003; Brackets apply to single taxpayers and married people filing separately; na not applicable; (h) Applies to interest and dividend income only.
Source: Tax Foundation, www.taxfoundation.org

Various State and Local Tax Rates

State Sales and Use (%)	Total Sales and Use (%)	Gasoline (cents/gal.)	Cigarette (cents/pack)	Spirits ($/gal.)	Table Wine ($/gal.)	Beer ($/gal.)
7.0 (l)	9.25	20	20	4.40	1.21	0.14

Note: Tax rates as of December 31, 2003.(l) Rate rose from 6% to 7% on July 1, 2002, but the rate on food remained 6%.
Source: Tax Foundation, www.taxfoundation.org

State Tax Burdens

Area	Combined State and Local Tax Burden		Combined Federal, State and Local Tax Burden	
	Percent	Rank	Percent	Rank
Tennessee	7.7	48	26.3	48
U.S. Average	9.7	-	30.0	-

Note: Figures are for 2003
Source: Tax Foundation, www.taxfoundation.org

Internal Revenue Service Tax Audits

IRS District	Percent of Returns Audited				
	1996	1997	1998	1999	2000
Kentucky-Tennessee	0.40	0.48	0.36	0.22	0.13
U.S.	0.66	0.61	0.46	0.31	0.20

Note: Figures cover IRS district audits of federal income tax returns filed by individuals. Geographic data on district audits for 2001 and 2002 are being withheld by the IRS. TRAC is challenging this policy.
Source: Syracuse University, Transactional Records Access Clearinghouse (TRAC), "Odds of IRS District Tax Audit 2000"

RESIDENTIAL REAL ESTATE

Building Permits

Area	Single-Family			Multi-Family			Total		
	2001	2002	Pct. Chg.	2001	2002	Pct. Chg.	2001	2002	Pct. Chg.
City	2,869	2,757	-3.9	547	588	7.5	3,416	3,345	-2.1
U.S.	1,235,600	1,332,600	7.9	401,100	415,100	3.5	1,636,700	1,747,700	6.8

Note: Figures represent new, privately-owned housing units authorized (unadjusted data)
Source: U.S. Census Bureau, Manufacturing, Mining, and Construction Statistics

Homeownership and Housing Vacancies

Area	Homeownership Rate[2] (%)			Rental Vacancy Rate[3] (%)			Homeowner Vacancy Rate[4] (%)		
	2001	2002[a]	2003	2001	2002[a]	2003	2001	2002[a]	2003
MSA[1]	67.7	69.6	68.9	7.5	7.1	7.8	2.3	2.0	2.5
U.S.	67.8	67.9	68.3	8.4	8.9	9.8	1.8	1.7	1.8

Note: (1) Metropolitan Statistical Area - see Appendix A for areas included; (2) The proportion of households that are owners; (3) The proportion of the rental inventory that is vacant for rent; (4) The proportion of the homeowner inventory that is vacant for sale; (a) 2002 figures have been revised; n/a not available
Source: U.S. Census Bureau, Housing Vacancies and Homeownership Annual Statistics: 2003

COMMERCIAL REAL ESTATE

Industrial/Office Markets

Type/Market Area	Inventory (sq. ft.)	Vacant (sq. ft.)	Vacancy Rate (%)	Under Construction (sq. ft.)	Net Absorption (sq. ft.)
Industrial Space Nashville	173,417,633	15,072,057	8.69	602,000	-1,620,177
Office Space Nashville	26,082,269	4,186,564	16.05	364,641	69,350

Note: Data as of 4th Quarter, 2003; n/a not available
Source: Society of Industrial and Office Realtors, 2004 Comparative Statistics of Industrial and Office Real Estate Markets

COMMERCIAL UTILITIES

Typical Monthly Electric Bills

Area	Commercial Service ($/month)		Industrial Service ($/month)	
	3 kW demand 1,000 kWh	40 kW demand 14,000 kWh	1,000 kW demand 200,000 kWh	50,000 kW demand 15,000,000 kWh
City	n/a	n/a	n/a	n/a
Average[1]	100	1,134	17,850	1,045,117

Note: Based on rates in effect July 1, 2003; (1) average based on 197 utilities; n/a not available
Source: Edison Electric Institute, Typical Bills and Average Rates Report, Summer 2003

TRANSPORTATION

Means of Transportation to Work

Area	Car/Truck/Van		Public Transportation			Bicycle	Walked	Other Means	Worked at Home
	Drove Alone	Car-pooled	Bus	Subway	Railroad				
City	78.5	13.5	1.7	0.0	0.0	0.1	2.4	0.8	3.0
MSA[1]	80.7	12.8	0.9	0.0	0.0	0.1	1.5	0.8	3.2
U.S.	75.7	12.2	2.5	1.5	0.5	0.4	2.9	1.0	3.3

Note: Figures shown are percentages and cover workers 16 years of age and older;
(1) Metropolitan Statistical Area - see Appendix A for areas included
Source: Census 2000, Summary File 3

Travel Time to Work

Area	Less Than 15 Minutes	15 to 29 Minutes	30 to 44 Minutes	45 to 59 Minutes	60 Minutes or More
City	24.2	46.1	21.1	4.6	3.9
MSA[1]	23.9	38.6	23.0	8.8	5.7
U.S.	29.4	36.1	19.1	7.4	8.0

Note: Figures are percentages and include workers 16 years old and over; (1) Metropolitan Statistical Area - see Appendix A for areas included
Source: Census 2000, Summary File 3

Roadway Congestion Index

Area	1982	1990	1996	2000	2001
City	0.83	0.85	0.93	0.98	1.03
Average[1]	0.82	1.01	1.08	1.16	1.17

Note: Values greater than 1.00 indicate undesirable mobility levels; (1) average of 75 urban areas
Source: Texas Transportation Institute, The 2003 Annual Urban Mobility Report

Transportation Statistics

Interstate highways (2004)	I-24; I-40; I-65
Public transportation (2002)	Metropolitan Transit Authority (MTA)
Buses	
Average fleet age in years	10.8
No. operated in max. service	109
Demand response	
Average fleet age in years	3.2
No. operated in max. service	28
Passenger air service	
Airport	Nashville International
Airlines (2003)	14
Boardings (2002)	4,009,959
Amtrak service (2004)	Bus connection
Major waterways/ports	Cumberland River; Port of Nashville

Source: Federal Transit Administration, National Transit Database, 2002; Editor & Publisher Market Guide, 2004; Bureau of Transportation Statistics, Airport Enplanement Activity for CY2002; www.amtrak.com

BUSINESSES

Major Business Headquarters

Company Name	2003 Rankings	
	Fortune 500	Forbes 500
Ardent Healthcare Systems	-	195
HCA	90	-
Ingram Industries	-	74
Vanguard Health Systems	-	189

Note: Companies listed are located in the city; dashes indicate no ranking
Fortune 500: Companies that produce a 10-K are ranked 1 to 500 based on 2002 revenue
Forbes 500: Private companies are ranked 1 to 281 based on 2002 revenue
Source: Fortune, April 14, 2003; www.forbes.com, November 6, 2003

Best Companies to Work For

Amsurg, headquartered in Nashville, is among the "200 Best Small Companies in 2003." Criteria: 3,500 companies whose latest 12-month sales were $5 million to $600 million were screened. Those with a net margin or five-year average ROE below 5% were cut. Banks, utilities, real estate investment trusts and limited partnerships whose financial structures are too different from most operating companies were also excluded. Shares had to be trading above $5 by the end of September 2003. Financial statement footnotes were examined for major issues. For the final ranking, equal weight was given to growth in sales, earnings and ROE for the past five years and the latest 12 months. *www.forbes.com, October 27, 2003*

Fast-Growing Businesses

According to *Inc.,* Nashville is home to two of America's 500 fastest-growing private companies: **Automated License Systems; Beacon Technologies.** Criteria: must be an independent, privately-held, U.S. corporation, proprietorship or partnership; sales of at least $200,000 in 1998; five-year operating/sales history; increase in 2002 sales over 2001 sales; holding companies, regulated banks, and utilities were excluded. *Inc. 500, America's Fastest-Growing Private Companies, October 15, 2003*

Nashville is home to four of *Business Week's* "hot growth" companies: **American Healthways; Amsurg; Renal Care Group; Tractor Supply**. Criteria: increase in sales and profits, return on capital and stock price. *Business Week, June 9, 2003*

According to *Fortune*, Nashville is home to two of America's 100 fastest-growing companies: **AmSurg; American Healthways**. Companies were ranked based on earnings-per-share growth, revenue growth and total return over the previous three years. Criteria for inclusion: public companies with sales of at least $50 million. Companies that lost money in the most recent quarter, or ended in the red for the past four quarters as a whole, were not eligible. Limited partnerships and REITs were also not considered. *Fortune, "America's Fastest-Growing Companies," September 1, 2003*

Women-Owned Firms: Number, Employment and Sales

Area	Number of Firms	Employ-ment	Sales ($000)	Rank[2]
MSA[1]	32,829	52,705	5,773,128	43

Note: (1) Metropolitan Statistical Area - see Appendix A for areas included;
(2) Calculated on an averaging of the number of businesses, employment, and sales
Source: The National Foundation for Women Business Owners, Women-Owned Businesses in the Top 50 Metropolitan Areas, 2002: A Fact Sheet

Women-Owned Firms: Growth

Area	Percent Change from 1997 to 2002			Rank[2]
	Number of Firms	Employ-ment	Sales	
MSA[1]	20.7	38.1	64.1	7
Top 50 MSAs	14.0	31.4	42.6	-

Note: (1) Metropolitan Statistical Area - see Appendix A for areas included; (2) Calculated on an averaging of the percent growth of number of businesses, employment, and sales
Source: The National Foundation for Women Business Owners, Women-Owned Businesses in the Top 50 Metropolitan Areas, 2002: A Fact Sheet

Minority and Women-Owned Businesses

Ownership	All Firms		Firms with Paid Employees			
	Firms	Sales ($000)	Firms	Sales ($000)	Employees	Payroll ($000)
Black	3,942	346,402	753	291,178	3,216	79,729
Hispanic	577	86,373	154	(a)	500 - 999	(a)
Women	12,322	1,939,824	2,163	1,714,167	21,783	424,444

Note: Figures cover firms located in the city; (a) Withheld to avoid disclosure
Source: 1997 Economic Census, Minority and Women-Owned Businesses

HOTELS

Hotels/Motels

Area	Hotels/Motels	Average Minimum Rates ($)		
		Tourist	First-Class	Deluxe
City	131	67	100	217

Source: OAG Travel Planner Online, Spring 2004

EVENT SITES

Major Event Sites, Meeting Places and Convention Centers

Name	Guest Rooms	Exhibit/ Meeting Space (sq. ft.)	Largest Meeting Room Capacity
Gentry Complex Tennessee State University	n/a	n/a	10,500
Grand Ole Opry House	n/a	n/a	4,424
Greer Stadium	n/a	n/a	17,500
Nashville Arena	n/a	n/a	20,000
Nashville Convention Center	n/a	n/a	9,000
Nashville Municipal Auditorium	n/a	n/a	9,900
Opryland Hotel Convention Center	2,883	600,000	7,574
Tennessee State Fairgrounds	n/a	n/a	n/a
Tennessee State University	n/a	n/a	10,000

Note: n/a not available
Source: Original research

Living Environment

COST OF LIVING

Cost of Living Index

Year	Composite Index	Groceries	Housing	Utilities	Trans-portation	Health Care	Misc. Goods/ Services
2001	92.7	97.4	87.6	80.4	97.3	81.1	98.0
2002	90.4	96.8	81.3	78.1	90.6	81.2	99.2
2003	97.3	105.9	84.1	93.8	117.5	84.7	101.7

Note: U.S. = 100; Figures are for Nashville-Franklin
Source: ACCRA, Cost of Living Index, 2001, 2002 and 2003 4-Quarter Averages

HOUSING

House Price Index (HPI)

Area	National Ranking[2]	Quarterly Change (%)	One-Year Change (%)	Five-Year Change (%)
MSA[1]	183	1.58	3.59	18.49
U.S.[3]	-	3.67	7.97	41.81

Note: The HPI is a weighted repeat sales index. It measures average price changes in repeat sales or refinancings on the same properties. This information is obtained by reviewing repeat mortgage transactions on single-family properties whose mortgages have been purchased or securitized by Fannie Mae of Freddie Mac in January 1975; (1) Metropolitan Statistical Area - see Appendix A for areas included; (2) Rankings are based on annual percentage change, for all MSAs containing at least 15,000 transactions over the last 10 years and ranges from 1 to 220; (3) figures based on a weighted division average; all figures are for the period ended December 31, 2003
Source: Office of Federal Housing Enterprise Oversight, House Price Index, March 1, 2004

Housing: Year Structure Built

Area	1990 -2000	1980 -1989	1970 -1979	1960 -1969	1950 -1959	1940 -1949	Before 1940	Median Year
City	16.0	19.2	19.7	16.8	13.7	6.8	7.8	1973
MSA[1]	25.8	20.1	19.1	13.8	9.8	4.9	6.6	1978
U.S.	17.0	15.8	18.5	13.7	12.7	7.3	15.0	1971

Note: Figures are percentages; (1) Metropolitan Statistical Area - see Appendix A for areas included
Source: Census 2000, Summary File 3

Average New Home Price

Area	2001	2002	2003
City[1]	180,103	187,251	200,133
U.S.	212,643	236,567	248,193

Note: Figures, in dollars, are based on a new home with 2,400 sq. ft. of living area on an 8,000 sq. ft. lot; (1) Nashville-Franklin
Source: ACCRA, Cost of Living Index, 2001, 2002 and 2003 4-Quarter Averages

Average Apartment Rent

Area	2001	2002	2003
City[1]	695	717	715
U.S.	674	708	721

Note: Figures, in dollars per month, are based on an unfurnished two bedroom, 1-1/2 or 2 bath apartment, approximately 950 sq. ft. in size, excluding all utilities except water; (1) Nashville-Franklin
Source: ACCRA, Cost of Living Index, 2001, 2002 and 2003 4-Quarter Averages

RESIDENTIAL UTILITIES

Average Residential Utility Costs

Area	All Electric ($/mth)	Part Electric ($/mth)	Other Energy ($/mth)	Phone ($/mth)
City[1]	–	49.70	46.35	29.24
U.S.	116.46	65.82	62.68	23.90

Note: (1) Nashville-Franklin
Source: ACCRA, Cost of Living Index, 2003 4-Quarter Average

HEALTH CARE

Average Health Care Costs

Area	Hospital ($/day)	Doctor ($/visit)	Dentist ($/visit)
City[1]	390.67	62.22	71.64
U.S.	678.35	67.91	83.90

Note: Hospital—based on a semi-private room; Doctor—based on a general practitioner's routine exam of an established patient; Dentist—based on adult teeth cleaning and periodic oral exam; (1) Nashville-Franklin
Source: ACCRA, Cost of Living Index, 2003 4-Quarter Average

Distribution of Non-Federal, Office-Based Physicians

Area	Total	Family/ General Practice	Medical	Surgical	Other
MSA[1] (number)	2,865	212	1,051	755	847
MSA[1] (rate per 10,000 pop.)	23.3	1.7	8.5	6.1	6.9
Metro Average[2] (rate per 10,000 pop.)	33.1	2.2	7.7	4.8	5.6

Note: Data as of December 31, 2001; (1) Metropolitan Statistical Area - see Appendix A for areas included; (2) Average of 81 MSAs and CMSAs in this book
Source: American Medical Association, Physician Characteristics & Distribution in the U.S., 2003-2004

Hospitals

Nashville has the following hospitals: 8 general medical and surgical; 2 psychiatric; 1 rehabilitation; 1 long-term acute care.
AHA Guide to the Healthcare Field, 2003-2004

According to *U.S. News,* Nashville has one of the best hospitals in the U.S.: **Vanderbilt University Hospital and Clinic**; *U.S. News Online, "America's Best Hospitals 2003"*

PRESIDENTIAL ELECTION

2000 Presidential Election Results

Area	Gore	Bush	Nader	Buchanan	Other
Davidson County	58.1	40.0	1.4	0.1	0.4
U.S.	48.4	47.9	2.7	0.4	0.6

Note: Results are percentages and may not add to 100% due to rounding
Source: www.cbsnews.com; www.uselectionatlas.org

EDUCATION

Public School District Statistics

District Name	Schls.	Enrollment	Classroom Teachers	Pupil/ Teacher Ratio	Minority Pupils[1] (%)	Current Expend.[2] ($/pupil)
Nashville-Davidson County SD	123	67,689	4,700	14.4	n/a	6,333

Note: Data covers the 2001-02 school year unless otherwise noted; (1) Fall 2000; (2) FY2000; n/a not available
Source: U.S. Department of Education, National Center for Education Statistics, Common Core of Data, Local Education Agency (School District) Universe Survey: School Year 2001-2002; U.S. Department of Education, National Center for Education Statistics, Digest of Education Statistics 2002

Educational Quality

School District	Education Quotient[1]	Graduate Outcome[2]	Community Index[3]	Resource Index[4]
Nashville-Davidson Co.	13	11	49	52

Note: Scores are national percentile rankings and range from 1 (worst) to 99 (best); (1) Combination of the Graduate Outcome, Community and Resource indexes weighted to reflect the greater importance of the Graduate Outcome and Resource Index; (2) Based on graduation rates and college board scores (SAT/ACT); (3) Based on the surrounding community's level of affluence and adult education; (4) Based on teacher salaries, per-pupil expenditures and student-teacher ratios.
Source: Expansion Management, December 2003

Educational Attainment by Race

Area	High School Graduate (%)					Bachelor's Degree (%)				
	Total	White	Black	Asian	Hisp.[2]	Total	White	Black	Asian	Hisp.[2]
City	81.1	84.2	75.1	80.9	53.2	29.7	32.9	20.1	49.9	14.3
MSA[1]	81.4	83.2	74.4	81.1	54.5	26.9	28.2	18.9	46.1	14.2
U.S.	80.4	83.6	72.3	80.4	52.4	24.4	26.1	14.3	44.1	10.4

Note: Figures shown cover persons 25 years old and over; (1) Metropolitan Statistical Area - see Appendix A for areas included; (2) people of Hispanic origin can be of any race
Source: Census 2000, Summary File 3

School Enrollment by Type

Area	Grades KG to 8				Grades 9 to 12			
	Public		Private		Public		Private	
	Enrollment	%	Enrollment	%	Enrollment	%	Enrollment	%
City	50,605	83.9	9,685	16.1	21,680	83.5	4,271	16.5
MSA[1]	136,243	86.5	21,347	13.5	56,641	85.6	9,515	14.4
U.S.	33,526,011	88.7	4,285,121	11.3	14,848,628	90.6	1,532,323	9.4

Note: Figures shown cover persons 3 years old and over; (1) Metropolitan Statistical Area - see Appendix A for areas included
Source: Census 2000, Summary File 3

School Enrollment by Race

Area	Grades KG to 8 (%)				Grades 9 to 12 (%)			
	White	Black	Asian	Hisp.[1]	White	Black	Asian	Hisp.[1]
City	52.8	38.8	2.2	4.9	52.6	39.8	2.4	4.2
MSA[2]	74.7	19.8	1.4	3.3	74.4	20.7	1.5	2.6
U.S.	68.5	15.5	3.3	16.8	68.8	15.5	3.8	15.7

Note: Figures shown cover persons 3 years old and over; (1) people of Hispanic origin can be of any race; (2) Metropolitan Statistical Area - see Appendix A for areas included
Source: Census 2000, Summary File 3

Classroom Teacher Salaries in Public Schools

District	B.A. Degree		M.A. Degree		Maximum	
	Min. ($)	Rank[1]	Max. ($)	Rank[1]	Max. ($)	Rank[1]
Nashville	27,734	87	48,881	76	57,687	57
DOD Average[2]	31,567	-	53,248	-	59,356	-

Note: Salaries are for 2001-2002; (1) Rank ranges from 1 to 100; (2) As per the U.S. Department of Defense Wage Fixing Authority
Source: American Federation of Teachers, Survey & Analysis of Teacher Salary Trends 2002

Higher Education

Four-Year Colleges			Two-Year Colleges			Medical Schools	Law Schools	Voc/Tech
Public	Private Non-profit	Private For-profit	Public	Private Non-profit	Private For-profit			
1	12	2	2	1	3	2	1	8

Note: Figures cover institutions located within the city limits.
Source: National Center for Education Statistics, The Integrated Postsecondary Education System (IPEDS) Peer Analysis System, 2002; usnews.com, America's Best Graduate Schools 2004, Medical School Directory; The College Blue Book, Occupational Education, 2003; Barron's Guide to Law Schools, 2003; Medical School Admission Requirements U.S. & Canada, 2003-2004

**MAJOR
EMPLOYERS**

Major Employers

Company Name	Industry	Type
American Home Patients	Home health care services	Single
Baptist Hospital	General medical and surgical hospitals	Headquarters
Columbia Summit Medical Center	General medical and surgical hospitals	Branch
Compucom Systems Inc	Computer integrated systems design	Branch
County of Sumner	Executive offices	Headquarters
Gaylord Entertainment Company	Hotels and motels	Headquarters
HCA Inc	General medical and surgical hospitals	Branch
Ingram Book Group Inc	Books, periodicals, and newspapers	Headquarters
Insource Electronics Inc	Electrical repair shops	Single
ITS	Employment agencies	Single
Mazda America Credit	Personal credit institutions	Headquarters
Opryland Hotel	Hotels and motels	Branch
Phillips Bookstore	Colleges and universities	Headquarters
Psychiatric Solutions Inc	Offices and clinics of medical doctors	Headquarters
State Industries Inc	Household appliances, nec	Headquarters
UPS	Courier services, except by air	Branch
Vanderbilt University Med Ctr	Colleges and universities	Headquarters

Note: Companies shown are located in the metropolitan area and have 1,500 or more employees.
Source: www.zapdata.com, March 2004

PUBLIC SAFETY

Crime Rate

Area	All Crimes	Violent Crimes				Property Crimes		
		Murder	Forcible Rape	Robbery	Aggrav. Assault	Burglary	Larceny -Theft	Motor Vehicle Theft
City	8,208.8	10.9	71.9	371.2	1,094.9	1,332.2	4,474.2	853.6
Suburbs[1]	3,421.5	2.7	35.3	41.6	345.2	600.2	2,182.6	213.8
MSA[2]	5,560.4	6.4	51.6	188.9	680.2	927.2	3,206.5	499.6
U.S.	4,118.8	5.6	33.0	145.9	310.1	746.2	2,445.8	432.1

Note: Figures are crimes per 100,000 population; (1) All areas within the MSA that are located outside the city limits; (2) Metropolitan Statistical Area - see Appendix A for areas included
Source: FBI Uniform Crime Reports, 2002

RECREATION

Culture and Recreation

Museums	Orchestras	Opera Companies	Dance Companies	Professional Theatres	Zoos	Pro Sports Teams[1]
13	1	1	2	6	1	2

Note: (1) Covers the Metropolitan Statistical Area - see Appendix A for areas included.
Source: The Grey House Performing Arts Directory, 2002; Official Museum Directory, 2004;
www.sportsvenues.com

Library System

The Nashville Public Library has 23 branches, holdings of 1,380,652 volumes, and a budget of $14,185,070 (2000-2001).
American Library Directory, 2003-2004

MEDIA

Newspapers

Name	Type	Freq.	Distribution	Circulation
Belle Meade News	General	1x/wk	Local	23,487
Green Hills News	General	1x/wk	Area	23,487
The Nashville Pride	General	1x/wk	Area	30,000
Nashville Scene	Alternative	1x/wk	Area	55,000
Nashville Today	General	1x/wk	Local	23,487
National Baptist Union Review	Black/Relig	1x/mth	United States	15,000
Observer	Jewish	2x/mth	State	3,300
Out & About Nashville	Gay/Lesbian	1x/mth	n/a	12,000
The Tennessean	General	7x/wk	Area	190,000
West Meade News	General	1x/wk	Local	20,000
West Side News	General	1x/wk	Local	23,487
Westview	General	1x/wk	Area	5,000

Note: Includes newspapers whose offices are located in the city and whose circulations are 1,000 or more; n/a not available
Source: Burrelle's Media Directory, 2003

Television Stations

Name	Ch.	Affiliation	Type	Owner
WKRN	2	ABCT	Commercial	Young Broadcasting Inc.
WSMV	4	NBCT	Commercial	Meredith Communications LLC
WTVF	5	CBST	Commercial	Landmark Television of Tennessee Inc.
WNPT	8	n/a	Public	n/a
WZTV	17	FBC	Commercial	Sinclair Broadcast Group
WNPX	28	PAXTV	Commercial	Paxson Communications Corporation
WUXP	30	UPN	Commercial	Sinclair Broadcast Group
WHTN	39	n/a	Commercial	Christian Television Network
WNAB	58	WB	n/a	Lambert Television

Note: Stations included broadcast from the Nashville metro area; n/a not available
Source: Burrelle's Media Directory, 2003

AM Radio Stations

Call Letters	Freq. (kHz)	Target Audience	Station Format	Music Format
WSM	650	General	M/N/S	Country
WENO	760	Religious	M/T	Christian
WMDB	880	General	M/N	Adult Contemporary
WYFN	980	G/R	M	Christian
WAMB	1160	General	M/N/S	Big Band
WNSG	1240	Religious	M	Gospel
WNQM	1300	H/R	N	n/a
WNAH	1360	Religious	M/N/S/T	Gospel
WKDA	1430	General	N	n/a
WVOL	1470	General	M	Adult Contemporary
WLAC	1510	General	M/N/T	Alternative
WCTZ	1550	Religious	M/T	Gospel

Note: Stations included broadcast from the Nashville metro area; n/a not available
The following abbreviations may be used:
Target Audience: A=Asian; B=Black; C=Christian; E=Ethnic; F=French; G=General; H=Hispanic;
M=Men; N=Native American; R=Religious; S=Senior Citizen; W=Women; Y=Young Adult; Z=Children
Station Format: E=Educational; M=Music; N=News; S=Sports; T=Talk
Music Format: AOR=Album Oriented Rock; MOR=Middle of the Road
Source: Burrelle's Media Directory, 2003

FM Radio Stations

Call Letters	Freq. (mHz)	Target Audience	Station Format	Music Format
WFSK	88.1	B/R	E/M/N/T	Adult Standards
WNAZ	89.1	Religious	M/T	Christian
WPLN	90.3	General	M/N	Classical
WRVU	91.1	General	M/N/S	Adult Standards
WHRS	91.7	General	M	Classical
WQQK	92.1	General	M	Adult Contemporary
WJXA	92.9	General	M/N	Adult Contemporary
WYYB	93.7	General	M	Christian
WRLG	94.1	General	M	Christian
WSM	95.5	General	M/N/S/T	Country
WMAK	96.3	General	M/N	Oldies
WSIX	97.9	General	M	Country
WAMB	98.7	General	M/N/S	Big Band
WWTN	99.7	Men	M/N/S/T	Jazz
WRLT	100.1	General	M	Alternative
WUBT	101.1	General	M/N/T	Urban Contemporary
WQZQ	102.5	General	M	Adult Contemporary
WBUZ	102.9	General	M/N/T	Modern Rock
WKDF	103.3	General	M/N/S	Country
WGFX	104.5	General	M/N/S/T	80's
WVRY	105.1	Christian	M/N/S	Christian
WNRQ	105.9	General	M	Classic Rock
WNPL	106.7	General	M	Urban Contemporary
WRVW	107.5	General	M	Top 40

Note: Stations included broadcast from the Nashville metro area
The following abbreviations may be used:
Target Audience: A=Asian; B=Black; C=Christian; E=Ethnic; F=French; G=General; H=Hispanic;
M=Men; N=Native American; R=Religious; S=Senior Citizen; W=Women; Y=Young Adult; Z=Children
Station Format: E=Educational; M=Music; N=News; S=Sports; T=Talk
Music Format: AOR=Album Oriented Rock; MOR=Middle of the Road
Source: Burrelle's Media Directory, 2003

CLIMATE

Average and Extreme Temperatures

Temperature	Jan	Feb	Mar	Apr	May	Jun	Jul	Aug	Sep	Oct	Nov	Dec	Yr.
Extreme High (°F)	78	84	86	91	95	106	107	104	105	94	84	79	107
Average High (°F)	47	51	60	71	79	87	90	89	83	72	60	50	70
Average Temp. (°F)	38	41	50	60	68	76	80	79	72	61	49	41	60
Average Low (°F)	28	31	39	48	57	65	69	68	61	48	39	31	49
Extreme Low (°F)	-17	-13	2	23	34	42	54	49	36	26	-1	-10	-17

Note: Figures cover the years 1948-1990
Source: National Climatic Data Center, International Station Meteorological Climate Summary, 9/96

Average Precipitation/Snowfall/Humidity

Precip./Humidity	Jan	Feb	Mar	Apr	May	Jun	Jul	Aug	Sep	Oct	Nov	Dec	Yr.
Avg. Precip. (in.)	4.4	4.2	5.0	4.1	4.6	3.7	3.8	3.3	3.2	2.6	3.9	4.6	47.4
Avg. Snowfall (in.)	4	3	1	Tr	0	0	0	0	0	Tr	1	1	11
Avg. Rel. Hum. 6am (%)	81	81	80	81	86	86	88	90	90	87	83	82	85
Avg. Rel. Hum. 3pm (%)	61	57	51	48	52	52	54	53	52	49	55	59	54

Note: Figures cover the years 1948-1990; Tr = Trace amounts (<0.05 in. of rain; <0.5 in. of snow)
Source: National Climatic Data Center, International Station Meteorological Climate Summary, 9/96

Weather Conditions

Temperature			Daytime Sky			Precipitation		
10°F & below	32°F & below	90°F & above	Clear	Partly cloudy	Cloudy	0.01 inch or more precip.	0.1 inch or more snow/ice	Thunder-storms
5	76	51	98	135	132	119	8	54

Note: Figures are average number of days per year and covers the years 1948-1990
Source: National Climatic Data Center, International Station Meteorological Climate Summary, 9/96

**HAZARDOUS
WASTE**

Superfund Sites

Nashville has no sites on the EPA's Superfund National Priorities List.
U.S. Environmental Protection Agency, National Priorities List, March 15, 2004

**AIR & WATER
QUALITY**

Maximum Pollutant Concentrations

	Particulate Matter (ug/m³)	Carbon Monoxide (ppm)	Sulfur Dioxide (ppm)	Nitrogen Dioxide (ppm)	Ozone 1-hour (ppm)	Ozone 8-hour (ppm)	Lead (ug/m³)
MSA[1] Level	52	5	0.018	0.016	0.11	0.09	1.24a
NAAQS[2]	150	9	0.140	0.053	0.12	0.08	1.50
Met NAAQS[2]	Yes	Yes	Yes	Yes	Yes	No	Yes

Note: (1) Metropolitan Statistical Area - see Appendix A for areas included; (2) National Ambient Air Quality Standards; n/a not available; (a) Localized impact from an industrial source in Williamson County
Units: ppm = parts per million; ug/m³ = micrograms per cubic meter
Source: EPA, Latest Findings on National Air Quality: 2002 Status and Trends, August 2003

Air Quality Index

In the Nashville MSA (see Appendix A for areas included), the Air Quality Index (AQI) exceeded 100 on 21 days in 2002. An AQI value greater than 100 indicates that air quality would have been in the unhealthful range on that day.
EPA, Latest Findings on National Air Quality: 2002 Status and Trends, August 2003

Watershed Health

The U.S. Environmental Protection Agency monitors the health of the aquatic resources for the nation's 2,000+ watersheds. **The Lower Cumberland-Sycamore watershed serves the Nashville area and received an overall Index of Watershed Indicators (IWI) score of 3 (less serious problems - low vulnerability).** The IWI score is based on seven condition and nine vulnerability indicators. The overall IWI score ranges from 1 (best health) to 6 (worst health). The Condition Indicators include: designated use attainment, fish and wildlife consumption advisories, source water condition, contaminated sediments, ambient water quality, and wetlands loss index. The Vulnerability Indicators include: aquatic species at risk, conventional and toxic loads over permitted limits, urban and agricultural runoff potential, population change, hydrologic modification, estuarine pollution susceptibility, and air deposition. *EPA, Index of Watershed Indicators, October 26, 2001*

Drinking Water

Water System Name	Pop. Served	Primary Water Source Type	Number of Violations January 2002-February 2004		
			Health Based	Significant Monitoring	Monitoring
Nashville Water Dept. #1	351,040	Surface	None	None	1

Note: Data as of February 19, 2004
Source: EPA, Office of Ground Water and Drinking Water, Safe Drinking Water Information System

Nashville tap water is alkaline, soft.
Editor & Publisher Market Guide, 2004

New Orleans, Louisiana

Background

Many people agree that New Orleans, the largest city in Louisiana, is on a par with San Francisco and New York City as one of the most colorful cities in the United States. The city is rich in unique local history, colorful "debauched" areas, and most importantly, an individual character that separates her from any city in the world.

New Orleans was founded on behalf of France by the brothers Le Moyne, Sieurs d'Iberville, and de Bienville, in 1718. Despite early obstacles such as disease, starvation, and an unwilling working class, New Orleans nevertheless emerged as a genteel antebellum slave society, fashioning itself after the rigid social hierarchy of Versailles. Even after New Orleans fell into Spanish hands, this unequal, however gracious, lifestyle continued.

The transfer of control from Spain to the United States in the Louisiana Purchase changed New Orleans's Old World isolation. American settlers introduced aggressive business acumen to the area, as well as the idea of respect for the self-made man. As trade opened up with countries around the world, this made for a very happy union. New Orleans became "Queen City of the South," growing prosperous from adventurous riverboat traders and speculators.

The highly popular musical form, Dixieland jazz, was born in New Orleans, and during the city's popular Mardi Gras festival, Dixieland musicians parade through the streets in joyous rhythm.

Today, despite a changing skyline, much of the city's Old World charm remains, resulting from a polyglot of Southern, Cajun, African-American, and European cultures. With its fantastic and numerous restaurants, indigenous music, and sultry, pleasing atmosphere, the city draws approximately eight million annual visitors. The city's Ernest N. Morial Convention Center hosts numerous convention-goers each year, who fill the city's 33,000-plus hotel rooms.

"Crescent City" also pays attention to its musical and literary heritage. The annual New Orleans Jazz & Heritage Festival and the Tennessee Williams/New Orleans Literary Festival are two major draws among numerous others.

The Louisiana Superdome, home to the New Orleans Saints, also plays host to the annual Nokia Sugar Bowl, as well as the occasional Super Bowl, NCAA tournament rounds, and other notable events.

New to the city's treasure trove of attractions is the Ogden Museum of Southern Art, affiliated with the University of New Orleans. The museum's collection includes works from the eighteenth through twenty-first centuries, gathered from throughout the south. A second phase of the project is expected to open in 2004.

Located upriver from the mouth of the Mississippi, New Orleans has long been a port town. In recent years, $400 million has been invested in new facilities at the port.

The New Orleans metro area is virtually surrounded by water, which influences its climate. Between mid-June and September, temperatures are kept down by near-daily sporadic thunderstorms. Cold spells sometimes reach the area in winter but seldom last. Frequent and sometimes heavy rains are typical. Tornadoes are extremely rare, although waterspouts are more common. Hurricanes have been known to cause destruction in the area.

Rankings

- New Orleans was ranked #139 out of 331 metro areas in *Cities Ranked & Rated*. Criteria: cost of living; climate; crime; transportation; economy and jobs; education; arts and culture; health and healthcare; leisure. *Cities Ranked & Rated, 1st Edition, 2004*

- *Ladies Home Journal* ranked America's 200 largest cities based on the qualities women surveyed care about most. New Orleans ranked #57 out of 57 in the big city category (population over 300,000). Criteria: crime; lifestyle; education; jobs; health; child care; politics; and the economy. *Ladies Home Journal Online, "The Best Cities for Women 2002"*

- New Orleans was selected as one of "The Top Ten Cities that Rock." The city was ranked #8. Criteria: overall music scene; retail music stores; live music venues. *Esquire, March 2004*

- New Orleans was selected as one of "America's Pet Healthiest Cities" by Purina. The city ranked #48 out of 50. Criteria: veterinary services; environment; and legislation. *Purina Pet Institute, "America's Pet Healthiest Cities," August 14, 2001*

- New Orleans was selected as one of the "Best Cities for Black Families." The city ranked #13 out of 20. For six months, bet.com compiled data on African Americans in those U.S. cities with the largest Black populations. The data, for African Americans specifically, involved the following: infant mortality; high school graduation; median income; homeownership; unemployment; business ownership; poverty rates; AIDS infection rates; percentage of children in single parent, typically fatherless, households; teen pregnancy; economic segregation index; violent and property crime. *www.bet.com, October 1, 2002*

- *Forbes* ranked the 40 most populous metro areas in the U.S. in terms of the best places to be single. The New Orleans metro area was ranked #23. Criteria: number of other singles; cost of living alone; nightlife; culture; job growth; coolness. *Forbes, June 5, 2003*

- *Forbes* ranked the 150 most populous metro areas in the U.S. in terms of the "Best Places for Business and Careers." The New Orleans metro area was ranked #136. Criteria: income and job growth; cost-of-doing-business; qualifications of the available pool of labor; crime rates; housing costs; net migration. *Forbes, May 9, 2003*

- New Orleans was selected as one of "America's Healthiest Cities" by *Natural Health* magazine. The city was ranked #16 out of the 50 largest urban areas in the U.S. Twenty-six criteria in the following four categories were examined: whether the city boasts natural offerings; how well the city promotes its resident's physical health; whether the city offers a healthy environment; how well the city fosters a sense of community. *Natural Health, April 2003*

- *Men's Health* ranked 101 U.S. cities in terms of the quality of their tap water. New Orleans received a grade of A. Criteria: levels of bacteria, arsenic, lead, trihalomethanes, and haloacetic acids were compared with the National Academy of Science's guidelines as well as with the EPA's more stringent maximum contaminant level goals. *Men's Health, March 2004*

- Sperling's BestPlaces ranked 331 metro areas and identified the most and least stressful U.S. cities. The New Orleans metro area ranked #3 out of the 100 largest metro areas (#1 = most stressful). Criteria: divorce rate; unemployment rate; violent and property crime; suicide rate; commute time; mental health; alcohol consumption; cloudy days. *www.BestPlaces.net, February 26, 2004*

- Sperling's BestPlaces in partnership with Pep Boys ranked 77 metro areas and identified "America's Most Drivable Cities." The New Orleans metro area ranked #17. Criteria: climate; road roughness; urban mobility; gas prices. *Pep Boys, "America's Most Drivable Cities," April 9, 2003*

- New Orleans was ranked #109 out of America's 200 largest metro areas in *SELF Magazine's* ranking of "America's Healthiest Cities for Women." Criteria: safety; air/water quality; cancer rates; and 21 other factors relating to health. *SELF Magazine, November 2003*

- New Orleans was identified as one of the most dangerous large metro areas for pedestrians in the U.S. The area ranked #26 out of the nations 49 largest metro areas. Criteria: average yearly pedestrian fatalities per capita (for the years 2000 and 2001) adjusted for the number of walkers. *Surface Transportation Policy Project, "Mean Streets 2002"*

- New Orleans was selected as one of the 25 fattest cities in America by *Men's Fitness Online*. It ranked #11 out of America's 50 largest cities. Criteria: gyms/sporting goods; nutrition; exercise/sports; overweight/sedentary; junk food; alcohol; smoking; television; air and water quality; climate; geography; commute time; parks/open space; recreation facilities; and health care. *Men's Fitness Online, America's Fittest/Fattest Cities 2003*

- New Orleans was ranked #46 out of 100 cities surveyed in *Child* magazine's ranking of the "Best Cities for Families." Criteria: number of pediatricians per capita; proximity to a children's hospital; immunization rates; infant mortality rate; air quality; water quality; school spending; pupil-teacher ratio; availability of parks/green space; nearby recreational opportunities; average commute time; number of sunny days; average cost of a 3-bedroom home; unemployment rate; future job growth; crime rate; percentage of children under 5; mandated minimum child care ratios. *Child, April 2001*

- *Zero Population Growth* ranked 239 cities in terms of children's health, safety, and economic well-being. New Orleans was ranked #108 out of 140 independent cities (cities with populations greater than 100,000 which were neither major cities nor suburbs/outer cities) and was given a grade of C+. Criteria: total population and population growth; percent of population under 18 years of age; number of children's museums; health improvement grade; percent of births to teens; percent of low birthweight infants; infant mortality rate; number of Title X-funded clinics; average SAT/ACT scores; average elementary and secondary class size; crime rate; unemployment rate; percent of affordable homes; number of bad air days; park acres per 1000 persons; library circulation per child; and children's program attendance counts. *Zero Population Growth, Kid Friendly Cities Report Card 2001*

- New Orleans was selected as one of America's 32 most livable cities by the non-profit group, Partners for Livable Communities. Criteria: environmental quality; parkland; ability to train new workers; job market; education; and use of the arts for economic development. *www.Livable.com, March 3, 2003*

- *Ladies Home Journal* ranked America's 200 largest cities in terms of safety. New Orleans ranked #141 out of 200. Criteria: violent crimes; crimes against property; and rape. *Ladies Home Journal Online, "The Best Cities for Women 2002"*

- New Orleans appeared on *Travel & Leisure's* list of the ten best cities in the U.S. and Canada. The city was ranked #6. Criteria: activities/attractions; culture/arts; restaurants/food; people; and value. *Travel & Leisure, "The World's Best Awards 2003"*

- *Condé Nast Traveler* polled over 32,000 readers for travel satisfaction. American cities were ranked based on the following criteria: friendliness; ambiance; culture/sites; restaurants; lodging and shopping. New Orleans appeared in the top 10, ranking #6. *Condé Nast Traveler, Readers' Choice Awards 2003*

- New Orleans was ranked #83 out of 268 metro areas in terms of its Creativity Index. The Creativity Index is a mix of four equally weighted factors: the Creative Class (scientists, engineers, architects, designers, writers, artists, musicians, or any profession where creativity is a key factor) share of the workforce; innovation, measured as patents per capita; high-tech industry, using the Milken Institute's Tech Pole Index; and diversity, measured by the Gay Index (a reasonable proxy for an areas' openness to different kinds of people and ideas). *The Rise of the Creative Class, 2002*

- New Orleans was ranked #70 out of 125 regions worldwide in terms of its "Knowledge Competitiveness Index." The index attempts to measure the knowledge-based development taking place throughout the world and is based on 17 measures of economic performance that indicate a region's ability to translate its knowledge capacity into economic value. *Robert Huggins Associates, "2003-2004 World Knowledge Competitiveness Index"*

- The New Orleans metro area was selected by *Yahoo! Internet Life* as one of "America's Most Wired Cities...and Towns." The area ranked #49 out of 87. Criteria: home and work net use; user sophistication; domain density; and available content. *Yahoo! Internet Life, April 2001*

- The New Orleans metro area was selected by Cranium as one of the "Top 50 Fun Cities" in America. The area ranked #50. Criteria includes: number of sports teams, restaurants, and dance performances; number of toy stores; city budget spent on recreation. *Cranium, November 4, 2003*

■ New Orleans was identified as one of the 100 "Most Unwired Cities" in the U.S. The area ranked #84. Criteria: number of public and commercial wireless access points; cell phone coverage offering wide area network Internet access; Internet penetration. *Intel, "Most Unwired Cities," March 4, 2003*

■ Scarborough Research measured the percentage of households who subscribe to cellular services among adults ages 18 and over in 75 U.S. markets. The New Orleans DMA (Designated Market Area) was ranked #18 out of 75. *Scarborough Research, Scarborough USA+ 2003 Release 1*

■ New Orleans was selected as one of "America's Most Literate Cities." The city ranked #40 out of the 64 largest U.S. cities. Criteria: booksellers; library support, holdings, and utilization; educational attainment; periodicals published; newspaper circulation. *University of Wisconsin-Whitewater, "America's Most Literate Cities," Summer 2003*

■ New Orleans was ranked #66 in *Prevention* magazine's survey of the "Best Walking Cities in the U.S." The magazine, in conjunction with the American Podiatric Medical Association, surveyed 125 of the most populated cities and then tabulated and weighed 20 criteria of interest to pedestrians. *Prevention, April, 2004*

■ New Orleans was selected as one of "America's Top 25 Arts Destinations." The area ranked #11 out of 25. Criteria: readers' top choices for arts travel destinations based on the richness and variety of visual arts sites, activities and events. *American Style, Winter 2002-2003*

■ The New Orleans metro area was cited as one of "The Best Places in the U.S. to Locate a Company." The area ranked #125 out of 329. Criteria: education (with emphasis on college board test results and high school graduation rates); availability of quality healthcare services and the cost to employers; quality of life; logistics workforce and companies; transportation infrastructure; quality and quantity of highly educated technical workers; business climate. *Expansion Management, July 2003*

■ The New Orleans metro area was selected as one of the "Top 40 Hottest Real Estate Markets" for expanding or relocating businesses." Criteria: rental costs; purchase prices; and vacancy rates of office and warehouse space. *Expansion Management, August 2003*

■ The New Orleans metro area appeared on *Forbes/Milken Institute* list of "Best Places for Business and Career." Rank: #168 out of 200 metro areas. Criteria: salary growth; job growth; number of technology clusters; overall concentration of technology activity relative to national average; and technology output growth. *www.forbes.com, Forbes/Milken Institute Best Places 2002*

■ The New Orleans metro area appeared on the "Milken Institute Best Performing Cities" index. Rank: #163 out of 200 large metro areas. Criteria: job growth; wage and salary growth; high-tech output growth. *Milken Institute, June 25, 2003*

■ The New Orleans metro area appeared on *Entrepreneur* magazine's list of the "Best Cities for Entrepreneurs" in 2003. The area ranked #32 out of 61 in the large city category. Criteria: entrepreneurial activity; small-business growth; economic growth; and risk. *www.Entrepreneur.com*

■ The New Orleans metro area was selected as one of the "Top 25 Cities for Doing Business in America." *Inc.* measured current-year employment growth in 277 regions as well as current trends in the annual average growth over the past three years, and compared employment expansion between the first and second halves of the last decade. Job growth factors account for two-thirds, and balance among industries accounts for one third of the final score for each city.The New Orleans metro area ranked #18 among large metro areas. *Inc. Magazine, March 2004*

■ The New Orleans metro area appeared on *IndustryWeek's* fourth annual World-Class Communities list. It ranked #132 out of 315 metro areas. Criteria: MSA Gross Metropolitan Product (GMP) per manufacturing employee; and MSA percent share of U.S. manufacturing Gross Domestic Product (GDP). *IndustryWeek, April 16, 2001*

- ING Group ranked the 125 largest metro areas according to the general financial security of residents. The New Orleans metro area was ranked #115 out of 125. Criteria: Earnings and Wealth Potential (household income, education, net assets, cost of living); Safety Net (health insurance, retirement savings, life insurance, income support programs); Personal Threats (unemployment rate, low-income households, crime rate); Community Economic Vitality (cost of community services, job quality, job creation, housing costs). *ING Group, "The Best Cities to Earn and Save Money: A Ranking of the Largest 125 U.S. Cities," 2001 Edition*

Business Environment

CITY FINANCES

City Government Finances

Component	2000-2001 ($000)	2000-2001 ($ per capita)
Total Revenues	974,083	2,010
Total Expenditures	890,082	1,836
Debt Outstanding	1,124,034	2,319
Cash and Securities	1,420,586	2,931

Source: U.S Census Bureau, Government Finances 2000-2001, August 2003

City Government Revenue by Source

Source	2000-2001 ($000)	2000-2001 ($ per capita)
General Revenue		
From Federal Government	60,402	125
From State Government	131,018	270
From Local Governments	0	0
Taxes		
Property	154,856	320
Sales	209,868	433
Personal Income	0	0
License	3,340	7
Charges	193,152	399
Liquor Store	0	0
Utility	55,217	114
Employee Retirement	33,130	68
Other	133,100	275

Source: U.S Census Bureau, Government Finances 2000-2001, August 2003

City Government Expenditures by Function

Function	2000-2001 ($000)	2000-2001 ($ per capita)	2000-2001 (%)
General Expenditures			
Airports	63,288	131	7.1
Corrections	25,590	53	2.9
Education	0	0	0.0
Fire Protection	57,361	118	6.4
Governmental Administration	99,042	204	11.1
Health	11,561	24	1.3
Highways	34,913	72	3.9
Hospitals	0	0	0.0
Housing and Community Development	82,947	171	9.3
Interest on General Debt	67,811	140	7.6
Libraries	6,943	14	0.8
Parking	8,075	17	0.9
Parks and Recreation	20,124	42	2.3
Police Protection	111,029	229	12.5
Public Welfare	2,567	5	0.3
Sewerage	68,767	142	7.7
Solid Waste Management	31,194	64	3.5
Liquor Store	0	0	0.0
Utility	87,551	181	9.8
Employee Retirement	37,005	76	4.2
Other	74,314	153	8.3

Source: U.S Census Bureau, Government Finances 2000-2001, August 2003

Municipal Bond Ratings

Area	Moody's
City	Aaa

Source: Mergent Bond Record, February 2004

DEMOGRAPHICS

Population Growth

Area	1990 Census	2000 Census	2003 Estimate	2008 Projection	Population Growth (%)	
					1990-2000	2000-2008
City	496,938	484,674	477,410	465,271	-2.5	-4.0
MSA[1]	1,285,270	1,337,726	1,335,236	1,333,393	4.1	-0.3
U.S.	248,709,873	281,421,906	290,647,163	305,918,071	13.2	8.7

Note: (1) Metropolitan Statistical Area - see Appendix A for areas included
Source: Claritas, Inc.

Number of Households and Average Household Size

Area	1990 Census	2000 Census	2003 Estimate	2008 Projection	2003 Average Household Size
City	188,235	188,251	186,857	184,468	2.6
MSA[1]	469,823	505,579	510,045	518,535	2.6
U.S.	91,947,410	105,480,101	109,440,059	116,034,472	2.7

Note: (1) Metropolitan Statistical Area - see Appendix A for areas included
Source: Claritas, Inc.

Race and Ethnicity

Area	White Non-Hispanic	Black Non-Hispanic	Asian Non-Hispanic	Other Race Non-Hispanic	Hispanic
City	27.3	67.8	2.4	2.5	3.0
MSA[1]	56.7	37.9	2.2	3.2	4.4
U.S.	74.5	12.4	3.8	9.3	13.2

Note: Figures are 2003 estimates; (1) Metropolitan Statistical Area - see Appendix A for areas included
Source: Claritas, Inc.

Segregation

City		MSA[1]	
Index[2]	Rank[3]	Index[2]	Rank[4]
70.6	23	74.7	29

Note: Figures are based on an analysis of Census 2000 data; (1) Metropolitan Statistical Area - see Appendix A for areas included; (2) Dissimilarity Index—the most commonly used measure of segregation between two groups, reflecting their relative distributions across neighborhoods within a city or metropolitan area. It can range in value from 0, indicating complete integration, to 100, indicating complete segregation; (3) Ranges from 1 (most segregated) to 100 (least segregated) and includes all the cities in this book; (4) Ranges from 1 (most segregated) to 318 (least segregated) and includes 318 metropolitan areas.
Source: www.CensusScope.org

Ancestry

Area	German	Irish[2]	English	American	Italian	Polish	French[3]	Scottish
City	5.4	4.7	3.4	2.0	3.2	0.6	5.6	0.7
MSA[1]	10.4	8.2	4.9	4.9	8.2	0.6	14.3	0.9
U.S.	15.2	10.9	8.7	7.3	5.6	3.2	3.0	1.7

Note: Figures include multiple ancestry (e.g. if a person reported being Irish and Italian, they were included in both columns); (1) Metropolitan Statistical Area - see Appendix A for areas included; (2) Includes Celtic; (3) Includes Alsatian but excludes Basque
Source: Census 2000, Summary File 3

Foreign-Born Population

Area	Percent of Population Born in:							
	Any Foreign Country	Europe	Asia	Africa	Oceania[2]	Canada	Mexico	Latin America[3]
City	4.3	0.7	1.6	0.2	0.0	0.1	0.1	1.7
MSA[1]	4.8	0.6	1.6	0.1	0.0	0.1	0.2	2.1
U.S.	11.1	1.7	2.9	0.3	0.1	0.3	3.3	2.5

Note: (1) Metropolitan Statistical Area - see Appendix A for areas included; (2) Includes Australia, New Zealand subregion, Melanesia, Micronesia, Polynesia, and Oceania n.e.c; (3) Includes Central America (excluding Mexico), South America, and the Caribbean.
Source: Census 2000, Summary File 3

Religion

Area	Catholic	Southern Baptist	United Methodist	ELCA[1]	LDS[2]	Presbyterian Church USA	Jewish Est.	Muslim Est.
County	28.1	5.7	2.3	0.2	0.1	0.7	1.8	0.8
U.S.	22.0	7.1	3.7	1.8	1.5	1.1	2.2	0.6

Note: Figures shown are the number of adherents as a percentage of the total population; Adherents are defined as all members, including full members, their children and the estimated number of other participants who are not considered members (e.g. the baptized, those not confirmed, those not eligible for communion, those regularly attending services, etc.); (1) Evangelical Lutheran Church in America; (2) The Church of Jesus Christ of Latter Day Saints
Source: Reprinted with permission from Religious Congregations and Membership in the United States 2000 (Nashville, Glenmary Research Center, 2002) Copyright Association of Statisticians of American Religious Bodies. All rights reserved.

Age Distribution

Area	Percent of Population						
	Under Age 5	Age 5 to 17	Age 18 to 34	Age 35 to 49	Age 50 to 64	Age 65 to 79	80 Years and Over
City	6.8	19.9	25.7	22.3	13.7	8.6	3.1
MSA[1]	6.8	19.9	23.3	23.8	14.8	8.7	2.7
U.S.	6.8	18.9	23.7	23.5	14.8	9.2	3.2

Note: (1) Metropolitan Statistical Area - see Appendix A for areas included
Source: Census 2000, Summary File 3

Marriage Status

Area	Never Married	Now Married Except Separated	Separated	Widowed	Divorced
City	40.9	35.5	3.6	8.1	11.8
MSA[1]	31.5	47.3	2.7	7.3	11.2
U.S.	27.1	54.4	2.2	6.6	9.7

Note: Figures cover population 15 years of age and older; (1) Metropolitan Statistical Area - see Appendix A for areas included
Source: Census 2000, Summary File 3

Male/Female Ratio

Area	Males	Females	Males per 100 Females
City	224,155	253,255	88.5
MSA[1]	639,471	695,765	91.9
U.S.	142,511,883	148,135,280	96.2

Note: Figures are 2003 estimates; (1) Metropolitan Statistical Area - see Appendix A for areas included
Source: Claritas, Inc.

ECONOMY

Gross Metropolitan Product

Area	1999	2000	2001	2002	2002 Rank[2]
MSA[1]	41.2	43.5	44.8	45.6	56

Note: Figures are in billions of dollars; (1) Metropolitan Statistical Area - see Appendix A for areas included; (2) Rank ranges from 1 to 319
Source: The U.S. Conference of Mayors, Metro Economies Report, July 2003

INCOME

Per Capita/Median/Average Income

Area	Per Capita ($)	Median Household ($)	Average Household ($)
City	18,925	30,357	47,208
MSA[1]	21,113	39,379	54,651
U.S.	24,078	46,868	63,207

Note: Figures are 2003 estimates; (1) Metropolitan Statistical Area - see Appendix A for areas included
Source: Claritas, Inc.

Household Income Distribution

Area	Percent of Households Earning							
	Under $15,000	$15,000 -24,999	$25,000 -34,999	$35,000 -49,999	$50,000 -74,999	$75,000 -99,000	$100,000 -149,999	$150,000 and up
City	27.9	15.1	13.0	14.5	13.2	6.6	5.4	4.2
MSA[1]	19.7	13.2	12.5	15.7	17.1	9.5	7.9	4.4
U.S.	14.1	11.5	11.7	16.0	19.2	11.3	10.2	6.0

Note: Figures are 2003 estimates; (1) Metropolitan Statistical Area - see Appendix A for areas included
Source: Claritas, Inc.

Poverty Rates by Age

Area	All Ages	Under 5 Years Old	5 to 17 Years Old	18 to 64 Years Old	65 Years and Over
City	27.9	3.0	8.1	14.7	2.2
MSA[1]	18.4	1.9	5.1	9.8	1.6
U.S.	12.4	1.2	3.0	6.9	1.2

Note: Figures are percent of population with income in 1999 below poverty level and only include population for whom poverty status is determined; (1) Metropolitan Statistical Area - see Appendix A for areas included
Source: Census 2000, Summary File 3

Personal Bankruptcy Filing Rate

Area	2002	2003
Orleans Parish	6.22	6.24
U.S.	5.34	5.58

Note: Numbers are per 1,000 population and include Chapter 7 and Chapter 13 filings
Source: Federal Deposit Insurance Corporation (FDIC), Regional Economic Conditions (RECON), 2/25/2004

EMPLOYMENT

Labor Force and Employment

Area	Civilian Labor Force			Workers Employed		
	Dec. 2002	Dec. 2003	% Chg.	Dec. 2002	Dec. 2003	% Chg.
City	188,988	196,951	4.2	177,642	185,369	4.3
MSA[1]	583,960	607,748	4.1	552,538	576,571	4.3
U.S.	144,807,000	146,501,000	1.2	136,599,000	138,556,000	1.4

Note: Data is not seasonally adjusted and covers workers 16 years of age and older;
(1) Metropolitan Statistical Area - see Appendix A for areas included
Source: Bureau of Labor Statistics, http://stats.bls.gov

Unemployment Rate

Area	2003											
	Jan.	Feb.	Mar.	Apr.	May	Jun.	Jul.	Aug.	Sep.	Oct.	Nov.	Dec.
City	5.9	5.4	5.5	5.2	5.5	7.5	7.5	7.8	6.5	6.0	5.8	5.9
MSA[1]	5.4	4.9	5.1	4.7	4.9	6.7	6.7	6.6	5.6	5.1	5.0	5.1
U.S.	6.5	6.4	6.2	5.8	5.8	6.5	6.3	6.0	5.8	5.6	5.6	5.4

Note: Data is not seasonally adjusted and covers workers 16 years of age and older; All figures are percentages; (1) Metropolitan Statistical Area - see Appendix A for areas included
Source: Bureau of Labor Statistics, http://stats.bls.gov

Employment by Occupation

Occupation Classification	City (%)	MSA[1] (%)	U.S. (%)
Sales and Office	25.8	28.0	26.7
Professional and Related	23.9	20.9	20.2
Service	22.1	17.3	14.9
Production, Transportation, and Material Moving	10.4	11.5	14.6
Management, Business, and Financial	10.8	12.0	13.5
Construction, Extraction, and Maintenance	6.8	10.0	9.4
Farming, Forestry, and Fishing	0.2	0.4	0.7

Note: Figures cover employed civilians 16 years of age and older;
(1) Metropolitan Statistical Area - see Appendix A for areas included
Source: Census 2000, Summary File 3

Employment by Industry

Sector	MSA[1]		U.S.
	Number of Employees	Percent of Total	Percent of Total
Government	105,200	17.1	16.7
Education and Health Services	85,400	13.9	12.9
Professional and Business Services	71,200	11.6	12.3
Retail Trade	68,700	11.2	11.8
Manufacturing	40,800	6.6	11.0
Leisure and Hospitality	80,800	13.1	9.1
Finance Activities	35,600	5.8	6.1
Construction	31,100	5.1	5.1
Wholesale Trade	26,500	4.3	4.3
Other Services	22,700	3.7	4.1
Transportation and Utilities	28,600	4.6	3.7
Information	9,500	1.5	2.4
Natural Resources and Mining	9,000	1.5	0.4

Note: Figures cover non-farm employment as of December 2003 and are not seasonally adjusted;
(1) Metropolitan Statistical Area - see Appendix A for areas included
Source: Bureau of Labor Statistics, http://stats.bls.gov

Average Wages

Occupation	$/Hr.	Occupation	$/Hr.
Accountants and Auditors	22.19	Maids and Housekeeping Cleaners	6.80
Automotive Mechanics	14.92	Maintenance and Repair Workers	14.42
Bookkeepers	12.64	Marketing Managers	31.23
Carpenters	13.32	Nuclear Medicine Technologists	22.83
Cashiers	6.89	Nurses, Licensed Practical	14.16
Clerks, General Office	9.95	Nurses, Registered	23.46
Clerks, Receptionists/Information	9.24	Nursing Aides/Orderlies/Attendants	7.50
Clerks, Shipping/Receiving	11.49	Packers and Packagers, Hand	8.17
Computer Programmers	26.53	Physical Therapists	30.18
Computer Support Specialists	18.92	Postal Service Mail Carriers	19.25
Computer Systems Analysts	27.80	Real Estate Brokers	16.43
Cooks, Restaurant	9.08	Retail Salespersons	9.64
Dentists	54.38	Sales Reps., Exc. Tech./Scientific	20.50
Electrical Engineers	34.07	Sales Reps., Tech./Scientific	25.70
Electricians	17.03	Secretaries, Exc. Legal/Med./Exec.	10.96
Financial Managers	29.12	Security Guards	8.61
First-Line Supervisors/Mgrs., Sales	15.22	Surgeons	93.13
Food Preparation Workers	6.92	Teacher Assistants	6.80
General and Operations Managers	35.96	Teachers, Elementary School	17.50
Hairdressers/Cosmetologists	9.74	Teachers, Secondary School	17.20
Internists	98.79	Telemarketers	19.65
Janitors and Cleaners	7.55	Truck Drivers, Heavy/Tractor-Trailer	13.95
Landscaping/Groundskeeping Workers	8.76	Truck Drivers, Light/Delivery Svcs.	12.91
Lawyers	57.42	Waiters and Waitresses	7.19

Note: Wage data is for 2002 and covers the Metropolitan Statistical Area (see Appendix A for areas included).
Hourly wages for elementary/secondary school teachers and teacher assistants were calculated by the editors
from annual wage data assuming a 40 hour work week; n/a not available.
Source: Bureau of Labor Statistics, 2002 Metro Area Occupational Employment and Wage Estimates

Occupational Employment Projections: 1996 - 2006

Occupations Expected to Have the Largest Job Growth (ranked by numerical growth)	Fast-Growing Occupations[1] (ranked by percent growth)
1. Cashiers	1. Database administrators
2. Salespersons, retail	2. Systems analysts
3. Registered nurses	3. Physical therapy assistants and aides
4. Truck drivers, light	4. Home health aides
5. General managers & top executives	5. Emergency medical technicians
6. Cooks, fast food and short order	6. Computer engineers
7. Home health aides	7. Medical assistants
8. Marketing & sales, supervisors	8. Engineering/science/computer sys. mgrs.
9. Maintenance repairers, general utility	9. Data processing equipment repairers
10. Nursing aides/orderlies/attendants	10. Physical therapists

Note: Projections cover Louisiana; (1) Excludes occupations with total job growth less than 300
Source: U.S. Department of Labor, Employment and Training Administration, America's Labor Market
Information System (ALMIS)

TAXES

State Corporate Income Tax Rates

State	Rate (%)	Number of Brackets	Low Bracket (Under $)	High Bracket (Over $)
Louisiana	4.0-8.0	5	0	200,000

Note: Tax rates as of December 31, 2003; na not applicable; Federal deductability.
Source: Tax Foundation, www.taxfoundation.org

State Individual Income Tax Rates

State	Federal Deductibility	Marginal Rate (%)	Number of Brackets	Low Bracket (Under $)	High Bracket (Over $)
Louisiana	Yes	2.0-6.0	3	0	50,000

Note: Tax rates as of December 31, 2003; Brackets apply to single taxpayers and married people filing
separately; na not applicable
Source: Tax Foundation, www.taxfoundation.org

Various State and Local Tax Rates

State Sales and Use (%)	Total Sales and Use (%)	Gasoline (cents/gal.)	Cigarette (cents/pack)	Spirits ($/gal.)	Table Wine ($/gal.)	Beer ($/gal.)
4.0	8.75	20	36	2.50	0.11	0.32

Note: Tax rates as of December 31, 2003
Source: Tax Foundation, www.taxfoundation.org

State Tax Burdens

Area	Combined State and Local Tax Burden		Combined Federal, State and Local Tax Burden	
	Percent	Rank	Percent	Rank
Louisiana	9.5	29	26.7	45
U.S. Average	9.7	-	30.0	-

Note: Figures are for 2003
Source: Tax Foundation, www.taxfoundation.org

Internal Revenue Service Tax Audits

IRS District	Percent of Returns Audited				
	1996	1997	1998	1999	2000
Gulf Coast	0.83	0.74	0.50	0.41	0.20
U.S.	0.66	0.61	0.46	0.31	0.20

Note: Figures cover IRS district audits of federal income tax returns filed by individuals. Geographic data on
district audits for 2001 and 2002 are being withheld by the IRS. TRAC is challenging this policy.
Source: Syracuse University, Transactional Records Access Clearinghouse (TRAC), "Odds of IRS District Tax
Audit 2000"

RESIDENTIAL REAL ESTATE

Building Permits

Area	Single-Family			Multi-Family			Total		
	2001	2002	Pct. Chg.	2001	2002	Pct. Chg.	2001	2002	Pct. Chg.
City	455	438	-3.7	172	178	3.5	627	616	-1.8
U.S.	1,235,600	1,332,600	7.9	401,100	415,100	3.5	1,636,700	1,747,700	6.8

Note: Figures represent new, privately-owned housing units authorized (unadjusted data)
Source: U.S. Census Bureau, Manufacturing, Mining, and Construction Statistics

Homeownership and Housing Vacancies

Area	Homeownership Rate[2] (%)			Rental Vacancy Rate[3] (%)			Homeowner Vacancy Rate[4] (%)		
	2001	2002[a]	2003	2001	2002[a]	2003	2001	2002[a]	2003
MSA[1]	62.0	60.1	61.5	8.2	8.1	7.6	1.8	0.8	0.7
U.S.	67.8	67.9	68.3	8.4	8.9	9.8	1.8	1.7	1.8

Note: (1) Metropolitan Statistical Area - see Appendix A for areas included; (2) The proportion of households that are owners; (3) The proportion of the rental inventory that is vacant for rent; (4) The proportion of the homeowner inventory that is vacant for sale; (a) 2002 figures have been revised; n/a not available
Source: U.S. Census Bureau, Housing Vacancies and Homeownership Annual Statistics: 2003

COMMERCIAL REAL ESTATE

Industrial/Office Markets

Type/Market Area	Inventory (sq. ft.)	Vacant (sq. ft.)	Vacancy Rate (%)	Under Construction (sq. ft.)	Net Absorption (sq. ft.)
Industrial Space					
New Orleans	54,595,524	4,313,150	7.90	250,000	462,800
Office Space					
New Orleans	14,943,050	2,059,947	13.79	0	-42,537

Note: Data as of 4th Quarter, 2003; n/a not available
Source: Society of Industrial and Office Realtors, 2004 Comparative Statistics of Industrial and Office Real Estate Markets

COMMERCIAL UTILITIES

Typical Monthly Electric Bills

Area	Commercial Service ($/month)		Industrial Service ($/month)	
	3 kW demand 1,000 kWh	40 kW demand 14,000 kWh	1,000 kW demand 200,000 kWh	50,000 kW demand 15,000,000 kWh
City	95	1,119	17,580	1,145,275
Average[1]	100	1,134	17,850	1,045,117

Note: Based on rates in effect July 1, 2003; (1) average based on 197 utilities
Source: Edison Electric Institute, Typical Bills and Average Rates Report, Summer 2003

TRANSPORTATION

Means of Transportation to Work

Area	Car/Truck/Van		Public Transportation			Bicycle	Walked	Other Means	Worked at Home
	Drove Alone	Car-pooled	Bus	Subway	Railroad				
City	60.3	16.1	12.4	0.0	0.0	1.2	5.2	2.1	2.7
MSA[1]	73.0	14.6	5.0	0.0	0.0	0.6	2.7	1.6	2.4
U.S.	75.7	12.2	2.5	1.5	0.5	0.4	2.9	1.0	3.3

Note: Figures shown are percentages and cover workers 16 years of age and older;
(1) Metropolitan Statistical Area - see Appendix A for areas included
Source: Census 2000, Summary File 3

Travel Time to Work

Area	Less Than 15 Minutes	15 to 29 Minutes	30 to 44 Minutes	45 to 59 Minutes	60 Minutes or More
City	23.2	43.2	20.3	6.1	7.2
MSA[1]	24.5	38.1	21.1	8.5	7.9
U.S.	29.4	36.1	19.1	7.4	8.0

Note: Figures are percentages and include workers 16 years old and over; (1) Metropolitan Statistical Area - see Appendix A for areas included
Source: Census 2000, Summary File 3

Roadway Congestion Index

Area	1982	1990	1996	2000	2001
City	0.92	0.94	0.96	0.97	0.97
Average[1]	0.82	1.01	1.08	1.16	1.17

Note: Values greater than 1.00 indicate undesirable mobility levels; (1) average of 75 urban areas
Source: Texas Transportation Institute, The 2003 Annual Urban Mobility Report

Transportation Statistics

Interstate highways (2004)	I-10; I-59
Public transportation (2002)	Regional Transit Authority of Orleans and Jefferson (NORTA)
Buses	
Average fleet age in years	5.3
No. operated in max. service	364
Light rail	
Average fleet age in years	65.2
No. operated in max. service	43
Demand response	
Average fleet age in years	1.4
No. operated in max. service	68
Passenger air service	
Airport	New Orleans International
Airlines (2003)	19
Boardings (2002)	4,598,838
Amtrak service (2004)	Yes
Major waterways/ports	Port of New Orleans; Mississippi River

Source: Federal Transit Administration, National Transit Database, 2002; Editor & Publisher Market Guide, 2004; Bureau of Transportation Statistics, Airport Enplanement Activity for CY2002; www.amtrak.com

BUSINESSES

Major Business Headquarters

Company Name	2003 Rankings	
	Fortune 500	Forbes 500
Entergy	224	-

Note: Companies listed are located in the city; dashes indicate no ranking
Fortune 500: Companies that produce a 10-K are ranked 1 to 500 based on 2002 revenue
Forbes 500: Private companies are ranked 1 to 281 based on 2002 revenue
Source: Fortune, April 14, 2003; www.forbes.com, November 6, 2003

Women-Owned Firms: Number, Employment and Sales

Area	Number of Firms	Employment	Sales ($000)	Rank[2]
MSA[1]	28,426	47,972	4,484,703	50

Note: (1) Metropolitan Statistical Area - see Appendix A for areas included;
(2) Calculated on an averaging of the number of businesses, employment, and sales
Source: The National Foundation for Women Business Owners, Women-Owned Businesses in the Top 50 Metropolitan Areas, 2002: A Fact Sheet

Women-Owned Firms: Growth

Area	Percent Change from 1997 to 2002			Rank[2]
	Number of Firms	Employ-ment	Sales	
MSA[1]	14.8	n/a	n/a	42
Top 50 MSAs	14.0	31.4	42.6	-

Note: (1) Metropolitan Statistical Area - see Appendix A for areas included; (2) Calculated on an averaging of the percent growth of number of businesses, employment, and sales
Source: The National Foundation for Women Business Owners, Women-Owned Businesses in the Top 50 Metropolitan Areas, 2002: A Fact Sheet

Minority and Women-Owned Businesses

Ownership	All Firms		Firms with Paid Employees			
	Firms	Sales ($000)	Firms	Sales ($000)	Employees	Payroll ($000)
Black	6,425	644,365	906	521,779	10,348	200,378
Hispanic	939	246,879	208	228,767	1,754	34,182
Women	8,039	1,256,807	1,250	1,102,488	14,396	275,371

Note: Figures cover firms located in the city
Source: 1997 Economic Census, Minority and Women-Owned Businesses

Minority Business Opportunity

New Orleans is home to one company which is on the Black Enterprise Industrial/Service 100 list (100 largest companies based on gross sales): **Lundy Enterprises L.L.C.**. Criteria: operational in previous calendar year; at least 51% black-owns and manufactures/owns the product it sells or provides industrial or consumer services. Brokerages, real estate firms and firms that provide professional services are not eligible. *Black Enterprise, www.blackenterprise.com, B.E. 100s, 2003 Report*

New Orleans is home to two companies which are on the Black Enterprise Bank 25 list (25 largest banks based on total assets, capital, deposits and loans, including mortgage-backed securities for the calendar year): **Liberty Bank & Trust Company**; **Dryades Savings Bank FSB**. Criteria: commercial banks or savings and loans that are classified by the Federal Reserve as black institutions and have been fully operational for the previous calendar year. *Black Enterprise, www.blackenterprise.com, B.E. 100s, 2003 Report*

HOTELS

Hotels/Motels

Area	Hotels/Motels	Average Minimum Rates ($)		
		Tourist	First-Class	Deluxe
City	157	72	108	173

Source: OAG Travel Planner Online, Spring 2004

New Orleans is home to two of the top 100 hotels in the U.S. and Canada according to *Travel & Leisure*: **Windsor Court** (#27); **Ritz-Carlton** (#47). Criteria: value, rooms/ambience, location, facilities/activities and service. *Travel & Leisure, "The World's Best Hotels 2003"*

EVENT SITES

Major Event Sites, Meeting Places and Convention Centers

Name	Guest Rooms	Exhibit/ Meeting Space (sq. ft.)	Largest Meeting Room Capacity
Ernest N. Morial Convention Center	n/a	1,100,000	n/a
Hilton New Orleans Riverside	1,600	130,000	3,640
Hyatt Regency New Orleans	1,184	115,000	20,520
Kiefer UNO Lakefront Arena	n/a	n/a	10,000
Louisiana Superdome	n/a	n/a	76,000
New Orleans Cultural Center	n/a	n/a	8,500
New Orleans Marriott	1,344	80,000	3,500
Radisson Hotel New Orleans	759	65,000	1,960
Sheraton New Orleans Hotel	1,100	90,000	2,700
Tad Gormley Stadium/Alerion Field	n/a	n/a	43,500
The Conference Auditorium at the Morial Center-New Orleans	n/a	232,000	4,000
The Fairmont Hotel New Orleans	700	70,000	2,600

Note: n/a not available
Source: Original research

Living Environment

COST OF LIVING

Cost of Living Index

Year	Composite Index	Groceries	Housing	Utilities	Trans-portation	Health Care	Misc. Goods/ Services
2001	99.7	103.2	92.7	115.8	104.6	102.4	98.0
2002	102.0	98.6	102.3	111.3	104.7	93.7	101.6
2003	100.2	93.3	102.2	108.9	101.4	88.6	99.6

Note: U.S. = 100
Source: ACCRA, Cost of Living Index, 2001, 2002 and 2003 4-Quarter Averages

HOUSING

House Price Index (HPI)

Area	National Ranking[2]	Quarterly Change (%)	One-Year Change (%)	Five-Year Change (%)
MSA[1]	97	3.06	6.84	29.44
U.S.[3]	-	3.67	7.97	41.81

Note: The HPI is a weighted repeat sales index. It measures average price changes in repeat sales or refinancings on the same properties. This information is obtained by reviewing repeat mortgage transactions on single-family properties whose mortgages have been purchased or securitized by Fannie Mae of Freddie Mac in January 1975; (1) Metropolitan Statistical Area - see Appendix A for areas included; (2) Rankings are based on annual percentage change, for all MSAs containing at least 15,000 transactions over the last 10 years and ranges from 1 to 220; (3) figures based on a weighted division average; all figures are for the period ended December 31, 2003
Source: Office of Federal Housing Enterprise Oversight, House Price Index, March 1, 2004

Housing: Year Structure Built

Area	1990 -2000	1980 -1989	1970 -1979	1960 -1969	1950 -1959	1940 -1949	Before 1940	Median Year
City	3.0	8.2	13.6	15.1	16.9	13.6	29.7	1954
MSA[1]	9.9	15.7	21.7	17.6	13.4	8.0	13.7	1968
U.S.	17.0	15.8	18.5	13.7	12.7	7.3	15.0	1971

Note: Figures are percentages; (1) Metropolitan Statistical Area - see Appendix A for areas included
Source: Census 2000, Summary File 3

Average New Home Price

Area	2001	2002	2003
City	186,469	243,131	251,359
U.S.	212,643	236,567	248,193

Note: Figures, in dollars, are based on a new home with 2,400 sq. ft. of living area on an 8,000 sq. ft. lot.
Source: ACCRA, Cost of Living Index, 2001, 2002 and 2003 4-Quarter Averages

Average Apartment Rent

Area	2001	2002	2003
City	790	804	777
U.S.	674	708	721

Note: Figures, in dollars per month, are based on an unfurnished two bedroom, 1-1/2 or 2 bath apartment, approximately 950 sq. ft. in size, excluding all utilities except water
Source: ACCRA, Cost of Living Index, 2001, 2002 and 2003 4-Quarter Averages

RESIDENTIAL UTILITIES

Average Residential Utility Costs

Area	All Electric ($/mth)	Part Electric ($/mth)	Other Energy ($/mth)	Phone ($/mth)
City	136.24	–	–	26.06
U.S.	116.46	65.82	62.68	23.90

Source: ACCRA, Cost of Living Index, 2003 4-Quarter Average

HEALTH CARE

Average Health Care Costs

Area	Hospital ($/day)	Doctor ($/visit)	Dentist ($/visit)
City	564.50	58.90	74.50
U.S.	678.35	67.91	83.90

Note: Hospital—based on a semi-private room; Doctor—based on a general practitioner's routine exam of an established patient; Dentist—based on adult teeth cleaning and periodic oral exam.
Source: ACCRA, Cost of Living Index, 2003 4-Quarter Average

Distribution of Non-Federal, Office-Based Physicians

Area	Total	Family/ General Practice	Specialties Medical	Specialties Surgical	Specialties Other
MSA[1] (number)	3,382	192	1,245	907	1,038
MSA[1] (rate per 10,000 pop.)	25.3	1.4	9.3	6.8	7.8
Metro Average[2] (rate per 10,000 pop.)	33.1	2.2	7.7	4.8	5.6

Note: Data as of December 31, 2001; (1) Metropolitan Statistical Area - see Appendix A for areas included; (2) Average of 81 MSAs and CMSAs in this book
Source: American Medical Association, Physician Characteristics & Distribution in the U.S., 2003-2004

Hospitals

New Orleans has the following hospitals: 11 general medical and surgical; 2 psychiatric; 1 chronic disease; 1 children's general; 1 children's psychiatric.
AHA Guide to the Healthcare Field, 2003-2004

PRESIDENTIAL ELECTION

2000 Presidential Election Results

Area	Gore	Bush	Nader	Buchanan	Other
Orleans Parish	75.9	21.8	1.7	0.4	0.3
U.S.	48.4	47.9	2.7	0.4	0.6

Note: Results are percentages and may not add to 100% due to rounding
Source: www.cbsnews.com; www.uselectionatlas.org

EDUCATION

Public School District Statistics

District Name	Schls.	Enroll- ment	Classroom Teachers	Pupil/ Teacher Ratio	Minority Pupils[1] (%)	Current Expend.[2] ($/pupil)
Orleans Parish School Board	130	73,185	4,552	16.1	96.1	5,587

Note: Data covers the 2001-02 school year unless otherwise noted; (1) Fall 2000; (2) FY2000; n/a not available
Source: U.S. Department of Education, National Center for Education Statistics, Common Core of Data, Local Education Agency (School District) Universe Survey: School Year 2001-2002; U.S. Department of Education, National Center for Education Statistics, Digest of Education Statistics 2002

Educational Quality

School District	Education Quotient[1]	Graduate Outcome[2]	Community Index[3]	Resource Index[4]
Orleans Parish School Board	1	1	18	35

Note: Scores are national percentile rankings and range from 1 (worst) to 99 (best); (1) Combination of the Graduate Outcome, Community and Resource indexes weighted to reflect the greater importance of the Graduate Outcome and Resource Index; (2) Based on graduation rates and college board scores (SAT/ACT); (3) Based on the surrounding community's level of affluence and adult education; (4) Based on teacher salaries, per-pupil expenditures and student-teacher ratios.
Source: Expansion Management, December 2003

Educational Attainment by Race

Area	High School Graduate (%)					Bachelor's Degree (%)				
	Total	White	Black	Asian	Hisp.[2]	Total	White	Black	Asian	Hisp.[2]
City	74.7	88.6	67.4	58.1	70.5	25.8	46.9	13.4	31.7	27.1
MSA[1]	77.7	83.6	67.6	64.8	71.0	22.6	27.4	12.7	33.5	20.8
U.S.	80.4	83.6	72.3	80.4	52.4	24.4	26.1	14.3	44.1	10.4

Note: Figures shown cover persons 25 years old and over; (1) Metropolitan Statistical Area - see Appendix A for areas included; (2) people of Hispanic origin can be of any race
Source: Census 2000, Summary File 3

School Enrollment by Type

Area	Grades KG to 8				Grades 9 to 12			
	Public		Private		Public		Private	
	Enrollment	%	Enrollment	%	Enrollment	%	Enrollment	%
City	56,336	81.5	12,783	18.5	25,536	82.7	5,343	17.3
MSA[1]	141,576	74.6	48,197	25.4	64,327	76.5	19,770	23.5
U.S.	33,526,011	88.7	4,285,121	11.3	14,848,628	90.6	1,532,323	9.4

Note: Figures shown cover persons 3 years old and over; (1) Metropolitan Statistical Area - see Appendix A for areas included
Source: Census 2000, Summary File 3

School Enrollment by Race

Area	Grades KG to 8 (%)				Grades 9 to 12 (%)			
	White	Black	Asian	Hisp.[1]	White	Black	Asian	Hisp.[1]
City	13.6	81.5	2.3	2.4	14.6	80.2	2.5	2.6
MSA[2]	46.8	47.2	2.2	4.2	47.3	46.8	2.4	4.1
U.S.	68.5	15.5	3.3	16.8	68.8	15.5	3.8	15.7

Note: Figures shown cover persons 3 years old and over; (1) people of Hispanic origin can be of any race; (2) Metropolitan Statistical Area - see Appendix A for areas included
Source: Census 2000, Summary File 3

Classroom Teacher Salaries in Public Schools

District	B.A. Degree		M.A. Degree		Maximum	
	Min. ($)	Rank[1]	Max. ($)	Rank[1]	Max. ($)	Rank[1]
New Orleans	28,249	80	44,288	86	45,875	94
DOD Average[2]	31,567	-	53,248	-	59,356	-

Note: Salaries are for 2001-2002; (1) Rank ranges from 1 to 100; (2) As per the U.S. Department of Defense Wage Fixing Authority
Source: American Federation of Teachers, Survey & Analysis of Teacher Salary Trends 2002

Higher Education

Four-Year Colleges			Two-Year Colleges			Medical Schools	Law Schools	Voc/ Tech
Public	Private Non-profit	Private For-profit	Public	Private Non-profit	Private For-profit			
3	10	1	2	0	3	2	2	12

Note: Figures cover institutions located within the city limits.
Source: National Center for Education Statistics, The Integrated Postsecondary Education System (IPEDS) Peer Analysis System, 2002; usnews.com, America's Best Graduate Schools 2004, Medical School Directory; The College Blue Book, Occupational Education, 2003; Barron's Guide to Law Schools, 2003; Medical School Admission Requirements U.S. & Canada, 2003-2004

**MAJOR
EMPLOYERS**

Major Employers

Company Name	Industry	Type
Builders Central LLC	Lumber and other building materials	Single
Charity Hospital	General medical and surgical hospitals	Headquarters
Comm Nav Surf Resfor	National security	Branch
East Jefferson Hospital	General medical and surgical hospitals	Headquarters
Harrahs Casino	Hotels and motels	Single
Jefferson Parish Sheriff Dept	Public order and safety, nec	Branch
Keenan Staffing Inc	Employment agencies	Headquarters
Lockheed Martin	Fabricated plate work (boiler shop)	Branch
Medi Lend Nursing Services Inc	Employment agencies	Single
New Orleans V A Medical Center	Administration of veterans' affairs	Branch
Northrop Grumman Avondale Ops	Shipbuilding and repairing	Single
Ochsner Foundation Hospital	General medical and surgical hospitals	Headquarters
Sewage & Water Board New Orleans	Refuse systems	Branch
Telecheck International	Functions related to depository banking	Headquarters
Tulane Medical Center Ltd	General medical and surgical hospitals	Single
Tulane Univ Hosp & Clinic	General medical and surgical hospitals	Headquarters
Tulane University	Colleges and universities	Headquarters
US Post Office	U.s. postal service	Branch
USDA National Finance Center	Regulation of agricultural marketing	Branch
West Jefferson Medical Center	General medical and surgical hospitals	Headquarters

Note: Companies shown are located in the metropolitan area and have 1,500 or more employees.
Source: www.zapdata.com, March 2004

PUBLIC SAFETY

Crime Rate

Area	All Crimes	Violent Crimes				Property Crimes		
		Murder	Forcible Rape	Robbery	Aggrav. Assault	Burglary	Larceny -Theft	Motor Vehicle Theft
City	6,418.9	53.1	33.3	410.2	440.6	978.9	2,946.6	1,556.3
Suburbs[1]	4,476.8	8.1	27.0	125.8	392.6	708.1	2,806.6	408.7
MSA[2]	5,180.4	24.4	29.3	228.8	410.0	806.2	2,857.3	824.5
U.S.	4,118.8	5.6	33.0	145.9	310.1	746.2	2,445.8	432.1

Note: Figures are crimes per 100,000 population; (1) All areas within the MSA that are located outside the city limits; (2) Metropolitan Statistical Area - see Appendix A for areas included
Source: FBI Uniform Crime Reports, 2002

RECREATION

Culture and Recreation

Museums	Orchestras	Opera Companies	Dance Companies	Professional Theatres	Zoos	Pro Sports Teams[1]
14	1	1	2	2	1	1

Note: (1) Covers the Metropolitan Statistical Area - see Appendix A for areas included.
Source: The Grey House Performing Arts Directory, 2002; Official Museum Directory, 2004; www.sportsvenues.com

Library System

The New Orleans Public Library has 14 branches, holdings of 794,830 volumes, and a budget of $7,266,792 (2003).
American Library Directory, 2003-2004

MEDIA

Newspapers

Name	Type	Freq.	Distribution	Circulation
Clarion Herald	Catholic	2x/mth	Regional	75,200
Gambit Weekly	Alternative	1x/wk	Local	50,000
Jewish Civic Press	Religious	1x/mth	Regional	15,000
Louisiana Weekly	Black	1x/wk	State	10,000
New Orleans Data Newsweekly	Black	1x/wk	Local	20,000
New Orleans Tribune	General	1x/mth	Local	25,000
The Times-Picayune	General	7x/wk	Area	275,000

Note: Includes newspapers whose offices are located in the city and whose circulations are 1,000 or more
Source: Burrelle's Media Directory, 2003

Television Stations

Name	Ch.	Affiliation	Type	Owner
WWL	4	CBST	Commercial	Belo Corporation
WDSU	6	NBCT	Commercial	Hearst-Argyle Broadcasting
WVUE	8	FBC	Commercial	Emmis Communications Corporation
WYES	12	PBS	Public	Greater New Orleans Educational TV Foundation
WHNO	20	n/a	Commercial	Lesea Broadcasting Corporation
WGNO	26	ABCT	Commercial	Tribune Broadcasting Company
WLAE	32	PBS	Public	Educational Broadcasting Foundation
WNOL	38	WB	Commercial	Tribune Broadcasting Company

Note: Stations included broadcast from the New Orleans metro area; n/a not available
Source: Burrelle's Media Directory, 2003

AM Radio Stations

Call Letters	Freq. (kHz)	Target Audience	Station Format	Music Format
WVOG	600	Religious	M/T	Christian
WLDC	640	General	M/N/S/T	Alternative
WTIX	690	General	M/N/S/T	Christian
WSHO	800	Religious	M/N/S/T	Christian
WWL	870	General	N/S/T	n/a
WYLD	940	Religious	M/N/S	Gospel
WBOK	1230	Religious	M	Gospel
WODT	1280	General	M/N	Blues
WSMB	1350	General	T	n/a
WBYU	1450	General	T	n/a

Note: Stations included broadcast from the New Orleans metro area; n/a not available
The following abbreviations may be used:
Target Audience: A=Asian; B=Black; C=Christian; E=Ethnic; F=French; G=General; H=Hispanic;
M=Men; N=Native American; R=Religious; S=Senior Citizen; W=Women; Y=Young Adult; Z=Children
Station Format: E=Educational; M=Music; N=News; S=Sports; T=Talk
Music Format: AOR=Album Oriented Rock; MOR=Middle of the Road
Source: Burrelle's Media Directory, 2003

FM Radio Stations

Call Letters	Freq. (mHz)	Target Audience	Station Format	Music Format
WRBH	88.3	General	N/T	n/a
WBSN	89.1	Religious	M	Adult Contemporary
WWNO	89.9	General	M/N	Adult Standards
KTLN	90.5	General	M/N	Adult Standards
WWOZ	90.7	General	E/M	Adult Standards
WTUL	91.5	General	M	Adult Standards
WQUE	93.3	General	M/N	Urban Contemporary
WTKL	95.7	General	M	Oldies
WYLD	98.5	General	M/N/T	Adult Contemporary
WRNO	99.5	General	M/T	Classic Rock
WNOE	101.1	General	M	Country
WLMG	101.9	General	M/N/T	Adult Contemporary
KMEZ	102.9	General	M	Adult Contemporary
KFXN	104.1	Women	M	Adult Top 40
KKND	106.7	General	M	Alternative

Note: Stations included broadcast from the New Orleans metro area; n/a not available
The following abbreviations may be used:
Target Audience: A=Asian; B=Black; C=Christian; E=Ethnic; F=French; G=General; H=Hispanic;
M=Men; N=Native American; R=Religious; S=Senior Citizen; W=Women; Y=Young Adult; Z=Children
Station Format: E=Educational; M=Music; N=News; S=Sports; T=Talk
Source: Burrelle's Media Directory, 2003

CLIMATE

Average and Extreme Temperatures

Temperature	Jan	Feb	Mar	Apr	May	Jun	Jul	Aug	Sep	Oct	Nov	Dec	Yr.
Extreme High (°F)	83	85	89	92	96	100	101	102	101	92	87	84	102
Average High (°F)	62	65	71	78	85	89	91	90	87	80	71	64	78
Average Temp. (°F)	53	56	62	69	75	81	82	82	79	70	61	55	69
Average Low (°F)	43	46	52	59	66	71	73	73	70	59	51	45	59
Extreme Low (°F)	14	19	25	32	41	50	60	60	42	35	24	11	11

Note: Figures cover the years 1948-1990
Source: National Climatic Data Center, International Station Meteorological Climate Summary, 9/96

Average Precipitation/Snowfall/Humidity

Precip./Humidity	Jan	Feb	Mar	Apr	May	Jun	Jul	Aug	Sep	Oct	Nov	Dec	Yr.
Avg. Precip. (in.)	4.7	5.6	5.2	4.7	4.4	5.4	6.4	5.9	5.5	2.8	4.4	5.5	60.6
Avg. Snowfall (in.)	Tr	Tr	Tr	0	0	0	0	0	0	0	0	Tr	Tr
Avg. Rel. Hum. 6am (%)	85	84	84	88	89	89	91	91	89	87	86	85	88
Avg. Rel. Hum. 3pm (%)	62	59	57	57	58	61	66	65	63	56	59	62	60

Note: Figures cover the years 1948-1990; Tr = Trace amounts (<0.05 in. of rain; <0.5 in. of snow)
Source: National Climatic Data Center, International Station Meteorological Climate Summary, 9/96

Weather Conditions

Temperature			Daytime Sky			Precipitation		
10°F & below	32°F & below	90°F & above	Clear	Partly cloudy	Cloudy	0.01 inch or more precip.	0.1 inch or more snow/ice	Thunder-storms
0	13	70	90	169	106	114	1	69

Note: Figures are average number of days per year and covers the years 1948-1990
Source: National Climatic Data Center, International Station Meteorological Climate Summary, 9/96

HAZARDOUS WASTE

Superfund Sites

New Orleans has one hazardous waste site on the EPA's Superfund National Priorities List: **Agriculture Street Landfill**. *U.S. Environmental Protection Agency, National Priorities List, March 15, 2004*

AIR & WATER
QUALITY

Maximum Pollutant Concentrations

	Particulate Matter (ug/m^3)	Carbon Monoxide (ppm)	Sulfur Dioxide (ppm)	Nitrogen Dioxide (ppm)	Ozone 1-hour (ppm)	Ozone 8-hour (ppm)	Lead (ug/m^3)
MSA[1] Level	74	4	0.016	0.017	0.11	0.08	0.12
NAAQS[2]	150	9	0.140	0.053	0.12	0.08	1.50
Met NAAQS[2]	Yes	Yes	Yes	Yes	Yes	Yes	Yes

Note: (1) Metropolitan Statistical Area - see Appendix A for areas included; (2) National Ambient Air Quality Standards; n/a not available
Units: ppm = parts per million; ug/m^3 = micrograms per cubic meter
Source: EPA, Latest Findings on National Air Quality: 2002 Status and Trends, August 2003

Air Quality Index

In the New Orleans MSA (see Appendix A for areas included), the Air Quality Index (AQI) exceeded 100 on 2 days in 2002. An AQI value greater than 100 indicates that air quality would have been in the unhealthful range on that day.
EPA, Latest Findings on National Air Quality: 2002 Status and Trends, August 2003

Watershed Health

The U.S. Environmental Protection Agency monitors the health of the aquatic resources for the nation's 2,000+ watersheds. **The Eastern Louisiana Coastal watershed serves the New Orleans area and received an overall Index of Watershed Indicators (IWI) score of 3 (less serious problems - low vulnerability).** The IWI score is based on seven condition and nine vulnerability indicators. The overall IWI score ranges from 1 (best health) to 6 (worst health). The Condition Indicators include: designated use attainment, fish and wildlife consumption advisories, source water condition, contaminated sediments, ambient water quality, and wetlands loss index. The Vulnerability Indicators include: aquatic species at risk, conventional and toxic loads over permitted limits, urban and agricultural runoff potential, population change, hydrologic modification, estuarine pollution susceptibility, and air deposition. *EPA, Index of Watershed Indicators, October 26, 2001*

Drinking Water

Water System Name	Pop. Served	Primary Water Source Type	Number of Violations January 2002-February 2004		
			Health Based	Significant Monitoring	Monitoring
New Orleans-Carrolton WW	428,000	Surface	None	None	None

Note: Data as of February 19, 2004
Source: EPA, Office of Ground Water and Drinking Water, Safe Drinking Water Information System

New Orleans tap water is alkaline, soft and fluoridated.
Editor & Publisher Market Guide, 2004

Orlando, Florida

Background

The city of Orlando can hold the viewer aghast with its rampant tourism. Not only is it home to the worldwide tourist attractions of Disney World, Epcot Center, and Sea World, but Orlando and its surrounding area also host such institutions as Medieval Times Dinner Tournament, Tupperware Exhibit and Museum, Wet-N-Wild, Watermania, and Sleuth's Mystery Dinner Theatre, as well as thousands of T-shirt, citrus, and shell vendor shacks.

Orlando has its own high-tech corridor called "Laser Lane" because of the University of Central Florida Center for Research and Education in Optics and Lasers. Manufacturing, government, business service, health care, and tourism supply significant numbers of jobs.

Aside from the glitz that pumps most of the money into its economy, Orlando is also called "The City Beautiful." The warm climate and abundant rains produce a variety of lush flora and fauna, which provide an attractive setting for the many young people who settle in the area, spending their nights in the numerous jazz clubs, restaurants, and pubs along Orange Avenue and Church Street. Stereotypically the land of orange juice and sunshine, Orlando may be the up-and-coming city for young job seekers and professionals.

This genteel setting is a far cry from Orlando's rough-and-tumble origins. The city started out as a makeshift campsite in the middle of a cotton plantation. The Civil War and devastating rains brought an end to the cotton trade, and its settlers turned to raising livestock. The transition to a new livelihood did not insure any peace and serenity. Rustling, chaotic brawls, and senseless shootings were everyday occurrences. Martial law had to be imposed by a few large ranch families.

The greatest impetus toward modernity came from the installation of Cape Canaveral, 50 miles away, which brought missile assembly and electronic component production to the area, and Walt Disney World, created out of 27,000 acres of unexplored swampland, which set the tone for Orlando as a tourist-oriented economy.

Orlando is also a major film production site. Nickelodeon, the world's largest teleproduction studio dedicated to children's television programming, is headquartered there, as are the Gold Channel, America's Health Network, and an increasing number of other cable networks.

The city is also home to a variety of arts and entertainment facilities, including the TD Waterhouse Centre and the NBA's Orlando Magic and other teams.

Orlando is surrounded by many lakes. Its relative humidity remains high year-round, though in winter the humidity may drop. June through September is the rainy season, during which time, scattered afternoon thunderstorms are an almost daily occurrence. During the winter months rainfall is light and the afternoons are most pleasant. Hurricanes are not usually considered a threat to the area.

Rankings

- Orlando was ranked #134 out of 331 metro areas in *Cities Ranked & Rated*. Criteria: cost of living; climate; crime; transportation; economy and jobs; education; arts and culture; health and healthcare; leisure. *Cities Ranked & Rated, 1st Edition, 2004*

- *Ladies Home Journal* ranked America's 200 largest cities based on the qualities women surveyed care about most. Orlando ranked #114 out of 143 in the smaller city category (population under 300,000). Criteria: crime; lifestyle; education; jobs; health; child care; politics; and the economy. *Ladies Home Journal Online, "The Best Cities for Women 2002"*

- Orlando was selected as one of "America's Top Ten Vegetarian-Friendly Cities." The city was ranked #8. Criteria: number of vegetarian restaurants; number of health food stores; number of vegetarian groups. *www.peta.org, February 26, 2004*

- Orlando was selected as one of "America's Pet Healthiest Cities" by Purina. The city ranked #27 out of 50. Criteria: veterinary services; environment; and legislation. *Purina Pet Institute, "America's Pet Healthiest Cities," August 14, 2001*

- *Forbes* ranked the 40 most populous metro areas in the U.S. in terms of the best places to be single. The Orlando metro area was ranked #20. Criteria: number of other singles; cost of living alone; nightlife; culture; job growth; coolness. *Forbes, June 5, 2003*

- *Forbes* ranked the 150 most populous metro areas in the U.S. in terms of the "Best Places for Business and Careers." The Orlando metro area was ranked #56. Criteria: income and job growth; cost-of-doing-business; qualifications of the available pool of labor; crime rates; housing costs; net migration. *Forbes, May 9, 2003*

- *Men's Health* ranked 101 U.S. cities in terms of the quality of their tap water. Orlando received a grade of. Criteria: levels of bacteria, arsenic, lead, trihalomethanes, and haloacetic acids were compared with the National Academy of Science's guidelines as well as with the EPA's more stringent maximum contaminant level goals. *Men's Health, March 2004*

- Sperling's BestPlaces ranked 331 metro areas and identified the most and least stressful U.S. cities. The Orlando metro area ranked #21 out of the 100 largest metro areas (#1 = most stressful). Criteria: divorce rate; unemployment rate; violent and property crime; suicide rate; commute time; mental health; alcohol consumption; cloudy days. *www.BestPlaces.net, February 26, 2004*

- Sperling's BestPlaces in partnership with Pep Boys ranked 77 metro areas and identified "America's Most Drivable Cities." The Orlando metro area ranked #19. Criteria: climate; road roughness; urban mobility; gas prices. *Pep Boys, "America's Most Drivable Cities," April 9, 2003*

- Orlando was ranked #178 out of America's 200 largest metro areas in *SELF Magazine's* ranking of "America's Healthiest Cities for Women." Criteria: safety; air/water quality; cancer rates; and 21 other factors relating to health. *SELF Magazine, November 2003*

- Orlando was identified as one of the most dangerous large metro areas for pedestrians in the U.S. The area ranked #1 out of the nations 49 largest metro areas. Criteria: average yearly pedestrian fatalities per capita (for the years 2000 and 2001) adjusted for the number of walkers. *Surface Transportation Policy Project, "Mean Streets 2002"*

- Orlando was selected as one of "The 10 Best Cities for Families" by *Child* magazine. It ranked #5 out of 100 cities surveyed. Criteria: number of pediatricians per capita; proximity to a children's hospital; immunization rates; infant mortality rate; air quality; water quality; school spending; pupil-teacher ratio; availability of parks/green space; nearby recreational opportunities; average commute time; number of sunny days; average cost of a 3-bedroom home; unemployment rate; future job growth; crime rate; percentage of children under 5; mandated minimum child care ratios. *Child, April 2001*

- *Zero Population Growth* ranked 239 cities in terms of children's health, safety, and economic well-being. Orlando was ranked #130 out of 140 independent cities (cities with populations greater than 100,000 which were neither major cities nor suburbs/outer cities) and was given a grade of C-. Criteria: total population and population growth; percent of population under 18 years of age; number of children's museums; health improvement grade; percent of births to teens; percent of low birthweight infants; infant mortality rate; number of Title X-funded clinics; average SAT/ACT scores; average elementary and secondary class size; crime rate; unemployment rate; percent of affordable homes; number of bad air days; park acres per 1000 persons; library circulation per child; and children's program attendance counts. *Zero Population Growth, Kid Friendly Cities Report Card 2001*

- Orlando was selected as one of America's 32 most livable cities by the non-profit group, Partners for Livable Communities. Criteria: environmental quality; parkland; ability to train new workers; job market; education; and use of the arts for economic development. *www.Livable.com, March 3, 2003*

- *Ladies Home Journal* ranked America's 200 largest cities in terms of safety. Orlando ranked #195 out of 200. Criteria: violent crimes; crimes against property; and rape. *Ladies Home Journal Online, "The Best Cities for Women 2002"*

- Orlando was ranked #49 out of 268 metro areas in terms of its Creativity Index. The Creativity Index is a mix of four equally weighted factors: the Creative Class (scientists, engineers, architects, designers, writers, artists, musicians, or any profession where creativity is a key factor) share of the workforce; innovation, measured as patents per capita; high-tech industry, using the Milken Institute's Tech Pole Index; and diversity, measured by the Gay Index (a reasonable proxy for an areas' openness to different kinds of people and ideas). *The Rise of the Creative Class, 2002*

- Orlando was ranked #40 out of 125 regions worldwide in terms of its "Knowledge Competitiveness Index." The index attempts to measure the knowledge-based development taking place throughout the world and is based on 17 measures of economic performance that indicate a region's ability to translate its knowledge capacity into economic value. *Robert Huggins Associates, "2003-2004 World Knowledge Competitiveness Index"*

- The Orlando metro area was selected by *Yahoo! Internet Life* as one of "America's Most Wired Cities...and Towns." The area ranked #30 out of 87. Criteria: home and work net use; user sophistication; domain density; and available content. *Yahoo! Internet Life, April 2001*

- The Orlando metro area was selected by Cranium as one of the "Top 50 Fun Cities" in America. The area ranked #36. Criteria includes: number of sports teams, restaurants, and dance performances; number of toy stores; city budget spent on recreation. *Cranium, November 4, 2003*

- Orlando was identified as one of the 100 "Most Unwired Cities" in the U.S. The area ranked #28. Criteria: number of public and commercial wireless access points; cell phone coverage offering wide area network Internet access; Internet penetration. *Intel, "Most Unwired Cities," March 4, 2003*

- Scarborough Research measured the percentage of households who subscribe to cellular services among adults ages 18 and over in 75 U.S. markets. The Orlando DMA (Designated Market Area) was ranked #41 out of 75. *Scarborough Research, Scarborough USA+ 2003 Release 1*

- Orlando was ranked #103 in *Prevention* magazine's survey of the "Best Walking Cities in the U.S." The magazine, in conjunction with the American Podiatric Medical Association, surveyed 125 of the most populated cities and then tabulated and weighed 20 criteria of interest to pedestrians. *Prevention, April, 2004*

- The Orlando metro area was selected as one of "America's 50 Hottest Cities for Business Relocations and Expansions." The area ranked #18. Criteria: 70 of the industry's most prominent site selection consultants were asked which cities their clients found the most attractive when it came to selecting an expansion or relocation site in 2003. *Expansion Management, January 2004*

- Orlando was selected as a "High-Tech Market to Watch" by *Site Selection*. Five emerging U.S. markets which show corporate growth developing in technology clusters were highlighted. *Site Selection, July 2001*

- The Orlando metro area was selected as one of the "Top 60 CyberCities in America" by *Site Selection*. CyberCities are magnets for growing high-tech companies. Criteria: total employment; average wages; total payroll; number of companies; R&D spending and venture capital in the 45 Standard Industrial Classification (SIC) codes that define the high-technology industry. *Site Selection, March 2002*

- The Orlando metro area was cited as one of "The Best Places in the U.S. to Locate a Company." The area ranked #188 out of 329. Criteria: education (with emphasis on college board test results and high school graduation rates); availability of quality healthcare services and the cost to employers; quality of life; logistics workforce and companies; transportation infrastructure; quality and quantity of highly educated technical workers; business climate. *Expansion Management, July 2003*

- The Orlando metro area was selected as one of the "Top 40 Hottest Real Estate Markets" for expanding or relocating businesses." Criteria: rental costs; purchase prices; and vacancy rates of office and warehouse space. *Expansion Management, August 2003*

- The Orlando metro area appeared on *Forbes/Milken Institute* list of "Best Places for Business and Career." Rank: #35 out of 200 metro areas. Criteria: salary growth; job growth; number of technology clusters; overall concentration of technology activity relative to national average; and technology output growth. *www.forbes.com, Forbes/Milken Institute Best Places 2002*

- The Orlando metro area appeared on the "Milken Institute Best Performing Cities" index. Rank: #45 out of 200 large metro areas. Criteria: job growth; wage and salary growth; high-tech output growth. *Milken Institute, June 25, 2003*

- The Orlando metro area appeared on *Entrepreneur* magazine's list of the "Best Cities for Entrepreneurs" in 2003. The area ranked #10 out of 61 in the large city category. Criteria: entrepreneurial activity; small-business growth; economic growth; and risk. *www.Entrepreneur.com*

- The Orlando metro area was selected as one of the "Top 25 Cities for Doing Business in America." *Inc.* measured current-year employment growth in 277 regions as well as current trends in the annual average growth over the past three years, and compared employment expansion between the first and second halves of the last decade. Job growth factors account for two-thirds, and balance among industries accounts for one third of the final score for each city.The Orlando metro area ranked #11 among large metro areas. *Inc. Magazine, March 2004*

- The Orlando metro area appeared on *IndustryWeek's* fourth annual World-Class Communities list. It ranked #161 out of 315 metro areas. Criteria: MSA Gross Metropolitan Product (GMP) per manufacturing employee; and MSA percent share of U.S. manufacturing Gross Domestic Product (GDP). *IndustryWeek, April 16, 2001*

- The Orlando metro area was selected as a "2001 Choice City" by *Business Development Outlook* magazine. Twenty-five cities were selected, based on data from the Bureau of Labor Statistics, Census Bureau, Federal Reserve, The Conference Board, and the U.S. Conference of Mayors, as being the most desirable into which a business can relocate or expand. *Business Development Outlook, 2001 Choice Cities*

- ING Group ranked the 125 largest metro areas according to the general financial security of residents. The Orlando metro area was ranked #75 out of 125. Criteria: Earnings and Wealth Potential (household income, education, net assets, cost of living); Safety Net (health insurance, retirement savings, life insurance, income support programs); Personal Threats (unemployment rate, low-income households, crime rate); Community Economic Vitality (cost of community services, job quality, job creation, housing costs). *ING Group, "The Best Cities to Earn and Save Money: A Ranking of the Largest 125 U.S. Cities," 2001 Edition*

Business Environment

CITY FINANCES

City Government Finances

Component	2000-2001 ($000)	2000-2001 ($ per capita)
Total Revenues	408,015	2,194
Total Expenditures	414,978	2,232
Debt Outstanding	382,365	2,056
Cash and Securities	950,745	5,113

Source: U.S Census Bureau, Government Finances 2000-2001, August 2003

City Government Revenue by Source

Source	2000-2001 ($000)	2000-2001 ($ per capita)
General Revenue		
From Federal Government	9,239	50
From State Government	38,159	205
From Local Governments	37,517	202
Taxes		
Property	57,589	310
Sales	61,913	333
Personal Income	0	0
License	0	0
Charges	104,166	560
Liquor Store	0	0
Utility	0	0
Employee Retirement	18,774	101
Other	80,658	434

Source: U.S Census Bureau, Government Finances 2000-2001, August 2003

City Government Expenditures by Function

Function	2000-2001 ($000)	2000-2001 ($ per capita)	2000-2001 (%)
General Expenditures			
Airports	0	0	0.0
Corrections	0	0	0.0
Education	0	0	0.0
Fire Protection	32,545	175	7.8
Governmental Administration	31,695	170	7.6
Health	0	0	0.0
Highways	49,394	266	11.9
Hospitals	0	0	0.0
Housing and Community Development	20,702	111	5.0
Interest on General Debt	23,804	128	5.7
Libraries	0	0	0.0
Parking	7,527	40	1.8
Parks and Recreation	58,289	313	14.0
Police Protection	64,070	345	15.4
Public Welfare	2,496	13	0.6
Sewerage	33,944	183	8.2
Solid Waste Management	20,548	111	5.0
Liquor Store	0	0	0.0
Utility	0	0	0.0
Employee Retirement	15,389	83	3.7
Other	54,575	293	13.2

Source: U.S Census Bureau, Government Finances 2000-2001, August 2003

Municipal Bond Ratings

Area	Moody's
City	Aa2

Source: Mergent Bond Record, February 2004

DEMOGRAPHICS

Population Growth

Area	1990 Census	2000 Census	2003 Estimate	2008 Projection	Population Growth (%) 1990-2000	Population Growth (%) 2000-2008
City	161,172	185,951	195,864	212,941	15.4	14.5
MSA[1]	1,224,852	1,644,561	1,801,123	2,057,952	34.3	25.1
U.S.	248,709,873	281,421,906	290,647,163	305,918,071	13.2	8.7

Note: (1) Metropolitan Statistical Area - see Appendix A for areas included
Source: Claritas, Inc.

Number of Households and Average Household Size

Area	1990 Census	2000 Census	2003 Estimate	2008 Projection	2003 Average Household Size
City	67,745	80,883	85,847	94,292	2.3
MSA[1]	465,275	625,248	684,189	780,191	2.6
U.S.	91,947,410	105,480,101	109,440,059	116,034,472	2.7

Note: (1) Metropolitan Statistical Area - see Appendix A for areas included
Source: Claritas, Inc.

Race and Ethnicity

Area	White Non-Hispanic	Black Non-Hispanic	Asian Non-Hispanic	Other Race Non-Hispanic	Hispanic
City	60.0	27.0	2.9	10.0	18.7
MSA[1]	74.0	14.2	2.9	9.0	17.6
U.S.	74.5	12.4	3.8	9.3	13.2

Note: Figures are 2003 estimates; (1) Metropolitan Statistical Area - see Appendix A for areas included
Source: Claritas, Inc.

Segregation

City Index[2]	City Rank[3]	MSA[1] Index[2]	MSA[1] Rank[4]
71.8	18	60.0	146

Note: Figures are based on an analysis of Census 2000 data; (1) Metropolitan Statistical Area - see Appendix A for areas included; (2) Dissimilarity Index—the most commonly used measure of segregation between two groups, reflecting their relative distributions across neighborhoods within a city or metropolitan area. It can range in value from 0, indicating complete integration, to 100, indicating complete segregation; (3) Ranges from 1 (most segregated) to 100 (least segregated) and includes all the cities in this book; (4) Ranges from 1 (most segregated) to 318 (least segregated) and includes 318 metropolitan areas.
Source: www.CensusScope.org

Ancestry

Area	German	Irish[2]	English	American	Italian	Polish	French[3]	Scottish
City	9.8	8.7	7.9	6.7	4.6	1.8	2.3	1.7
MSA[1]	13.2	10.9	10.1	7.7	6.0	2.5	2.9	2.1
U.S.	15.2	10.9	8.7	7.3	5.6	3.2	3.0	1.7

Note: Figures include multiple ancestry (e.g. if a person reported being Irish and Italian, they were included in both columns); (1) Metropolitan Statistical Area - see Appendix A for areas included; (2) Includes Celtic; (3) Includes Alsatian but excludes Basque
Source: Census 2000, Summary File 3

Foreign-Born Population

Area	Percent of Population Born in: Any Foreign Country	Europe	Asia	Africa	Oceania[2]	Canada	Mexico	Latin America[3]
City	14.4	1.4	2.4	0.5	0.0	0.5	0.6	8.9
MSA[1]	12.0	1.6	2.2	0.4	0.0	0.5	1.0	6.3
U.S.	11.1	1.7	2.9	0.3	0.1	0.3	3.3	2.5

Note: (1) Metropolitan Statistical Area - see Appendix A for areas included; (2) Includes Australia, New Zealand subregion, Melanesia, Micronesia, Polynesia, and Oceania n.e.c; (3) Includes Central America (excluding Mexico), South America, and the Caribbean.
Source: Census 2000, Summary File 3

Religion

Area	Catholic	Southern Baptist	United Meth-odist	ELCA[1]	LDS[2]	Presby-terian Church USA	Jewish Est.	Muslim Est.
County	13.3	8.2	3.3	0.6	0.6	1.7	1.2	0.2
U.S.	22.0	7.1	3.7	1.8	1.5	1.1	2.2	0.6

Note: Figures shown are the number of adherents as a percentage of the total population; Adherents are defined as all members, including full members, their children and the estimated number of other participants who are not considered members (e.g. the baptized, those not confirmed, those not eligible for communion, those regularly attending services, etc.); (1) Evangelical Lutheran Church in America; (2) The Church of Jesus Christ of Latter Day Saints
Source: Reprinted with permission from Religious Congregations and Membership in the United States 2000 (Nashville, Glenmary Research Center, 2002) Copyright Association of Statisticians of American Religious Bodies. All rights reserved.

Age Distribution

Area	Percent of Population						
	Under Age 5	Age 5 to 17	Age 18 to 34	Age 35 to 49	Age 50 to 64	Age 65 to 79	80 Years and Over
City	6.5	15.5	31.2	23.3	12.1	8.3	3.1
MSA[1]	6.5	18.2	24.4	24.2	14.4	9.5	2.9
U.S.	6.8	18.9	23.7	23.5	14.8	9.2	3.2

Note: (1) Metropolitan Statistical Area - see Appendix A for areas included
Source: Census 2000, Summary File 3

Marriage Status

Area	Never Married	Now Married Except Separated	Separated	Widowed	Divorced
City	35.8	40.5	3.7	6.1	13.8
MSA[1]	26.6	54.0	2.4	6.0	11.0
U.S.	27.1	54.4	2.2	6.6	9.7

Note: Figures cover population 15 years of age and older; (1) Metropolitan Statistical Area - see Appendix A for areas included
Source: Census 2000, Summary File 3

Male/Female Ratio

Area	Males	Females	Males per 100 Females
City	94,922	100,942	94.0
MSA[1]	885,394	915,729	96.7
U.S.	142,511,883	148,135,280	96.2

Note: Figures are 2003 estimates; (1) Metropolitan Statistical Area - see Appendix A for areas included
Source: Claritas, Inc.

ECONOMY

Gross Metropolitan Product

Area	1999	2000	2001	2002	2002 Rank[2]
MSA[1]	54.7	58.2	60.6	62.1	41

Note: Figures are in billions of dollars; (1) Metropolitan Statistical Area - see Appendix A for areas included; (2) Rank ranges from 1 to 319
Source: The U.S. Conference of Mayors, Metro Economies Report, July 2003

INCOME

Per Capita/Median/Average Income

Area	Per Capita ($)	Median Household ($)	Average Household ($)
City	23,492	40,071	53,143
MSA[1]	23,614	46,460	61,691
U.S.	24,078	46,868	63,207

Note: Figures are 2003 estimates; (1) Metropolitan Statistical Area - see Appendix A for areas included
Source: Claritas, Inc.

Household Income Distribution

Area	Percent of Households Earning							
	Under $15,000	$15,000 -24,999	$25,000 -34,999	$35,000 -49,999	$50,000 -74,999	$75,000 -99,000	$100,000 -149,999	$150,000 and up
City	15.0	13.7	14.7	19.6	17.9	8.9	6.6	3.7
MSA[1]	11.5	11.7	12.9	18.2	20.2	11.0	9.4	5.2
U.S.	14.1	11.5	11.7	16.0	19.2	11.3	10.2	6.0

Note: Figures are 2003 estimates; (1) Metropolitan Statistical Area - see Appendix A for areas included
Source: Claritas, Inc.

Poverty Rates by Age

Area	All Ages	Under 5 Years Old	5 to 17 Years Old	18 to 64 Years Old	65 Years and Over
City	15.9	2.0	4.1	8.5	1.3
MSA[1]	10.7	1.0	2.6	6.1	1.0
U.S.	12.4	1.2	3.0	6.9	1.2

Note: Figures are percent of population with income in 1999 below poverty level and only include population for whom poverty status is determined; (1) Metropolitan Statistical Area - see Appendix A for areas included
Source: Census 2000, Summary File 3

Personal Bankruptcy Filing Rate

Area	2002	2003
Orange County	6.02	6.05
U.S.	5.34	5.58

Note: Numbers are per 1,000 population and include Chapter 7 and Chapter 13 filings
Source: Federal Deposit Insurance Corporation (FDIC), Regional Economic Conditions (RECON), 2/25/2004

EMPLOYMENT

Labor Force and Employment

Area	Civilian Labor Force			Workers Employed		
	Dec. 2002	Dec. 2003	% Chg.	Dec. 2002	Dec. 2003	% Chg.
City	125,458	126,358	0.7	119,200	120,657	1.2
MSA[1]	949,823	956,906	0.7	905,446	916,509	1.2
U.S.	144,807,000	146,501,000	1.2	136,599,000	138,556,000	1.4

Note: Data is not seasonally adjusted and covers workers 16 years of age and older;
(1) Metropolitan Statistical Area - see Appendix A for areas included
Source: Bureau of Labor Statistics, http://stats.bls.gov

Unemployment Rate

Area	2003											
	Jan.	Feb.	Mar.	Apr.	May	Jun.	Jul.	Aug.	Sep.	Oct.	Nov.	Dec.
City	5.7	5.4	5.3	5.5	5.3	5.8	5.5	5.6	5.5	5.1	5.1	4.5
MSA[1]	5.4	5.1	5.0	5.1	4.9	5.4	5.1	5.2	5.1	4.8	4.8	4.2
U.S.	6.5	6.4	6.2	5.8	5.8	6.5	6.3	6.0	5.8	5.6	5.6	5.4

Note: Data is not seasonally adjusted and covers workers 16 years of age and older; All figures are percentages; (1) Metropolitan Statistical Area - see Appendix A for areas included
Source: Bureau of Labor Statistics, http://stats.bls.gov

Employment by Occupation

Occupation Classification	City (%)	MSA[1] (%)	U.S. (%)
Sales and Office	30.0	29.8	26.7
Professional and Related	18.9	18.4	20.2
Service	19.2	17.3	14.9
Production, Transportation, and Material Moving	9.8	10.2	14.6
Management, Business, and Financial	14.4	14.2	13.5
Construction, Extraction, and Maintenance	7.5	9.5	9.4
Farming, Forestry, and Fishing	0.2	0.5	0.7

Note: Figures cover employed civilians 16 years of age and older;
(1) Metropolitan Statistical Area - see Appendix A for areas included
Source: Census 2000, Summary File 3

Employment by Industry

Sector	MSA[1]		U.S.
	Number of Employees	Percent of Total	Percent of Total
Government	106,300	11.2	16.7
Education and Health Services	95,200	10.1	12.9
Professional and Business Services	156,900	16.6	12.3
Retail Trade	111,600	11.8	11.8
Manufacturing	41,100	4.3	11.0
Leisure and Hospitality	172,200	18.2	9.1
Finance Activities	58,100	6.1	6.1
Construction	63,000	6.7	5.1
Wholesale Trade	42,300	4.5	4.3
Other Services	46,600	4.9	4.1
Transportation and Utilities	27,100	2.9	3.7
Information	24,900	2.6	2.4
Natural Resources and Mining	500	0.1	0.4

Note: Figures cover non-farm employment as of December 2003 and are not seasonally adjusted;
(1) Metropolitan Statistical Area - see Appendix A for areas included
Source: Bureau of Labor Statistics, http://stats.bls.gov

Average Wages

Occupation	$/Hr.	Occupation	$/Hr.
Accountants and Auditors	22.66	Maids and Housekeeping Cleaners	7.72
Automotive Mechanics	15.50	Maintenance and Repair Workers	12.94
Bookkeepers	12.06	Marketing Managers	40.82
Carpenters	15.07	Nuclear Medicine Technologists	21.92
Cashiers	7.73	Nurses, Licensed Practical	15.10
Clerks, General Office	10.32	Nurses, Registered	21.65
Clerks, Receptionists/Information	9.85	Nursing Aides/Orderlies/Attendants	9.26
Clerks, Shipping/Receiving	11.26	Packers and Packagers, Hand	8.01
Computer Programmers	29.08	Physical Therapists	28.12
Computer Support Specialists	13.94	Postal Service Mail Carriers	19.04
Computer Systems Analysts	28.27	Real Estate Brokers	30.99
Cooks, Restaurant	10.69	Retail Salespersons	9.52
Dentists	69.01	Sales Reps., Exc. Tech./Scientific	24.46
Electrical Engineers	29.80	Sales Reps., Tech./Scientific	30.28
Electricians	16.04	Secretaries, Exc. Legal/Med./Exec.	12.60
Financial Managers	37.75	Security Guards	8.89
First-Line Supervisors/Mgrs., Sales	17.89	Surgeons	96.15
Food Preparation Workers	8.67	Teacher Assistants	8.60
General and Operations Managers	36.92	Teachers, Elementary School	18.30
Hairdressers/Cosmetologists	12.77	Teachers, Secondary School	19.70
Internists	90.62	Telemarketers	11.26
Janitors and Cleaners	8.30	Truck Drivers, Heavy/Tractor-Trailer	16.54
Landscaping/Groundskeeping Workers	10.08	Truck Drivers, Light/Delivery Svcs.	12.74
Lawyers	52.69	Waiters and Waitresses	6.63

Note: Wage data is for 2002 and covers the Metropolitan Statistical Area (see Appendix A for areas included).
Hourly wages for elementary/secondary school teachers and teacher assistants were calculated by the editors
from annual wage data assuming a 40 hour work week; n/a not available.
Source: Bureau of Labor Statistics, 2002 Metro Area Occupational Employment and Wage Estimates

Occupational Employment Projections: 1996 - 2006

Occupations Expected to Have the Largest Job Growth (ranked by numerical growth)	Fast-Growing Occupations[1] (ranked by percent growth)
1. Cashiers	1. Systems analysts
2. Salespersons, retail	2. Physical therapy assistants and aides
3. General managers & top executives	3. Desktop publishers
4. Registered nurses	4. Home health aides
5. Waiters & waitresses	5. Computer engineers
6. Marketing & sales, supervisors	6. Medical assistants
7. Janitors/cleaners/maids, ex. priv. hshld.	7. Physical therapists
8. General office clerks	8. Paralegals
9. Food preparation workers	9. Emergency medical technicians
10. Hand packers & packagers	10. Occupational therapists

Note: Projections cover Florida; (1) Excludes occupations with total job growth less than 300
Source: U.S. Department of Labor, Employment and Training Administration, America's Labor Market Information System (ALMIS)

TAXES

State Corporate Income Tax Rates

State	Rate (%)	Number of Brackets	Low Bracket (Under $)	High Bracket (Over $)
Florida	5.5	1	na	na

Note: Tax rates as of December 31, 2003; na not applicable; 3.3% alternative minimum rate.
Source: Tax Foundation, www.taxfoundation.org

State Individual Income Tax Rates

State	Federal Deductibility	Marginal Rate (%)	Number of Brackets	Low Bracket (Under $)	High Bracket (Over $)
Florida	No	None	na	na	na

Note: Tax rates as of December 31, 2003; Brackets apply to single taxpayers and married people filing separately; na not applicable
Source: Tax Foundation, www.taxfoundation.org

Various State and Local Tax Rates

State Sales and Use (%)	Total Sales and Use (%)	Gasoline (cents/gal.)	Cigarette (cents/pack)	Spirits ($/gal.)	Table Wine ($/gal.)	Beer ($/gal.)
6.0	6.5	13.9	33.9	6.50	2.25	0.48

Note: Tax rates as of December 31, 2003
Source: Tax Foundation, www.taxfoundation.org

State Tax Burdens

Area	Combined State and Local Tax Burden		Combined Federal, State and Local Tax Burden	
	Percent	Rank	Percent	Rank
Florida	8.4	45	29.0	23
U.S. Average	9.7	-	30.0	-

Note: Figures are for 2003
Source: Tax Foundation, www.taxfoundation.org

Internal Revenue Service Tax Audits

IRS District	Percent of Returns Audited				
	1996	1997	1998	1999	2000
North Florida	0.52	0.45	0.29	0.24	0.14
U.S.	0.66	0.61	0.46	0.31	0.20

Note: Figures cover IRS district audits of federal income tax returns filed by individuals. Geographic data on district audits for 2001 and 2002 are being withheld by the IRS. TRAC is challenging this policy.
Source: Syracuse University, Transactional Records Access Clearinghouse (TRAC), "Odds of IRS District Tax Audit 2000"

**RESIDENTIAL
REAL ESTATE**

Building Permits

Area	Single-Family			Multi-Family			Total		
	2001	2002	Pct. Chg.	2001	2002	Pct. Chg.	2001	2002	Pct. Chg.
City	447	699	56.4	1,059	2,833	167.5	1,506	3,532	134.5
U.S.	1,235,600	1,332,600	7.9	401,100	415,100	3.5	1,636,700	1,747,700	6.8

Note: Figures represent new, privately-owned housing units authorized (unadjusted data)
Source: U.S. Census Bureau, Manufacturing, Mining, and Construction Statistics

Homeownership and Housing Vacancies

Area	Homeownership Rate[2] (%)			Rental Vacancy Rate[3] (%)			Homeowner Vacancy Rate[4] (%)		
	2001	2002[a]	2003	2001	2002[a]	2003	2001	2002[a]	2003
MSA[1]	63.0	65.5	66.6	9.2	9.7	14.6	1.1	1.4	2.2
U.S.	67.8	67.9	68.3	8.4	8.9	9.8	1.8	1.7	1.8

Note: (1) Metropolitan Statistical Area - see Appendix A for areas included; (2) The proportion of households that are owners; (3) The proportion of the rental inventory that is vacant for rent; (4) The proportion of the homeowner inventory that is vacant for sale; (a) 2002 figures have been revised; n/a not available
Source: U.S. Census Bureau, Housing Vacancies and Homeownership Annual Statistics: 2003

**COMMERCIAL
REAL ESTATE**

Industrial/Office Markets

Type/Market Area	Inventory (sq. ft.)	Vacant (sq. ft.)	Vacancy Rate (%)	Under Construction (sq. ft.)	Net Absorption (sq. ft.)
Industrial Space					
Orlando	87,508,248	9,436,158	10.78	1,827,814	4,074,427
Office Space					
Orlando	22,933,135	3,237,695	14.12	455,000	488,972

Note: Data as of 4th Quarter, 2003; n/a not available
Source: Society of Industrial and Office Realtors, 2004 Comparative Statistics of Industrial and Office Real Estate Markets

**COMMERCIAL
UTILITIES**

Typical Monthly Electric Bills

Area	Commercial Service ($/month)		Industrial Service ($/month)	
	3 kW demand 1,000 kWh	40 kW demand 14,000 kWh	1,000 kW demand 200,000 kWh	50,000 kW demand 15,000,000 kWh
City	88	952	17,273	1,081,336
Average[1]	100	1,134	17,850	1,045,117

Note: Based on rates in effect July 1, 2003; (1) average based on 197 utilities
Source: Edison Electric Institute, Typical Bills and Average Rates Report, Summer 2003

TRANSPORTATION

Means of Transportation to Work

Area	Car/Truck/Van		Public Transportation			Bicycle	Walked	Other Means	Worked at Home
	Drove Alone	Car-pooled	Bus	Subway	Railroad				
City	78.9	11.2	3.9	0.0	0.0	0.6	1.9	1.3	2.2
MSA[1]	80.6	12.1	1.6	0.0	0.0	0.4	1.3	1.2	2.9
U.S.	75.7	12.2	2.5	1.5	0.5	0.4	2.9	1.0	3.3

Note: Figures shown are percentages and cover workers 16 years of age and older;
(1) Metropolitan Statistical Area - see Appendix A for areas included
Source: Census 2000, Summary File 3

Travel Time to Work

Area	Less Than 15 Minutes	15 to 29 Minutes	30 to 44 Minutes	45 to 59 Minutes	60 Minutes or More
City	21.7	43.7	23.6	5.9	5.1
MSA[1]	21.1	38.1	25.8	8.8	6.2
U.S.	29.4	36.1	19.1	7.4	8.0

*Note: Figures are percentages and include workers 16 years old and over; (1) Metropolitan Statistical Area -
see Appendix A for areas included*
Source: Census 2000, Summary File 3

Roadway Congestion Index

Area	1982	1990	1996	2000	2001
City	0.82	0.95	1.00	1.11	1.14
Average[1]	0.82	1.01	1.08	1.16	1.17

Note: Values greater than 1.00 indicate undesirable mobility levels; (1) average of 75 urban areas
Source: Texas Transportation Institute, The 2003 Annual Urban Mobility Report

Transportation Statistics

Interstate highways (2004)	I-4
Public transportation (2002)	Central Florida Regional Transportation Authority (Lynx)
Buses	
Average fleet age in years	5.6
No. operated in max. service	201
Demand response	
Average fleet age in years	1.5
No. operated in max. service	199
Passenger air service	
Airport	Orlando International
Airlines (2003)	38
Boardings (2002)	12,921,480
Amtrak service (2004)	Yes
Major waterways/ports	None

*Source: Federal Transit Administration, National Transit Database, 2002; Editor & Publisher Market Guide,
2004; Bureau of Transportation Statistics, Airport Enplanement Activity for CY2002; www.amtrak.com*

BUSINESSES

Major Business Headquarters

Company Name	2003 Rankings	
	Fortune 500	Forbes 500
Darden Restaurants	372	-
Hughes Supply	487	-

Note: Companies listed are located in the city; dashes indicate no ranking
Fortune 500: Companies that produce a 10-K are ranked 1 to 500 based on 2002 revenue
Forbes 500: Private companies are ranked 1 to 281 based on 2002 revenue
Source: Fortune, April 14, 2003; www.forbes.com, November 6, 2003

Best Companies to Work For

Darden Restaurants, headquartered in Orlando, is among the "50 Best Companies for
Minorities." Criteria: 1,200 of the largest U.S employers were surveyed—141 responded.
Those companies were analyzed on 15 quantitative and qualitative measures—from how well
minorities are paid to how many are in management. *Fortune, July 7, 2003*

Fast-Growing Businesses

According to *Inc.*, Orlando is home to three of America's 500 fastest-growing private
companies: **Co-Advantage Resources; Quality Assured Services; Restaurant Partners**.
Criteria: must be an independent, privately-held, U.S. corporation, proprietorship or
partnership; sales of at least $200,000 in 1998; five-year operating/sales history; increase in
2002 sales over 2001 sales; holding companies, regulated banks, and utilities were excluded.
Inc. 500, America's Fastest-Growing Private Companies, October 15, 2003

According to Deloitte & Touche LLP, Orlando is home to two of North America's 500 fastest-growing high-technology companies: **Coalescent Technologies Corporation; Riptide Software, Inc**. Companies are ranked by percentage growth in revenue over a five-year period. Criteria for inclusion: must be a U.S. or Canadian company developing and/or providing technology products or services; company must have been in business for five years with 1998 operating revenues of at least $50,000 USD or $75,000 CD and 2002 operating revenues of at least $1 million USD/CD. *Deloitte & Touche LLP, 2003 Technology Fast 500*

Women-Owned Firms: Number, Employment and Sales

Area	Number of Firms	Employ-ment	Sales ($000)	Rank[2]
MSA[1]	42,096	46,792	10,456,538	33

Note: (1) Metropolitan Statistical Area - see Appendix A for areas included;
(2) Calculated on an averaging of the number of businesses, employment, and sales
Source: The National Foundation for Women Business Owners, Women-Owned Businesses in the Top 50 Metropolitan Areas, 2002: A Fact Sheet

Women-Owned Firms: Growth

Area	Percent Change from 1997 to 2002			Rank[2]
	Number of Firms	Employ-ment	Sales	
MSA[1]	22.7	26.6	55.4	13
Top 50 MSAs	14.0	31.4	42.6	-

Note: (1) Metropolitan Statistical Area - see Appendix A for areas included; (2) Calculated on an averaging of the percent growth of number of businesses, employment, and sales
Source: The National Foundation for Women Business Owners, Women-Owned Businesses in the Top 50 Metropolitan Areas, 2002: A Fact Sheet

Minority and Women-Owned Businesses

Ownership	All Firms		Firms with Paid Employees			
	Firms	Sales ($000)	Firms	Sales ($000)	Employees	Payroll ($000)
Black	1,593	242,477	210	194,348	1,517	35,068
Hispanic	1,937	230,616	501	204,653	2,328	88,611
Women	4,915	1,268,892	1,410	1,119,783	10,105	239,629

Note: Figures cover firms located in the city
Source: 1997 Economic Census, Minority and Women-Owned Businesses

Minority Business Opportunity

Orlando is home to one company which is on the Black Enterprise Auto Dealer 100 list (100 largest dealers based on gross sales): **Tropical Ford Inc.**. Criteria: company must be operational in previous calendar year and at least 51% black-owned. *Black Enterprise, www.blackenterprise.com, B.E. 100s, 2003 Report*

Four of the 500 largest Hispanic-owned companies in the U.S. are located in Orlando. *Hispanic Business, June 2003*

Orlando is home to one company which is on the Hispanic Business Fastest-Growing 100 list (greatest sales growth over the past five years): **Jardon & Howard Technologies Inc.**. *Hispanic Business, July/August 2003*

HOTELS

Hotels/Motels

Area	Hotels/Motels	Average Minimum Rates ($)		
		Tourist	First-Class	Deluxe
City	222	65	89	205

Source: OAG Travel Planner Online, Spring 2004

EVENT SITES

Major Event Sites, Meeting Places and Convention Centers

Name	Guest Rooms	Exhibit/ Meeting Space (sq. ft.)	Largest Meeting Room Capacity
Marriott's Orlando World Center Resort	2,111	214,000	5,200
Orange County Convention Center	n/a	313,140	18,000
Orlando Centroplex	n/a	n/a	70,000
Renaissance Orlando Resort at Sea World	842	185,000	6,000
Rosen Centre Hotel	1,334	106,000	4,347
U.C.F. Arena University of Central Florida	n/a	31,000	5,322
Walt Disney World Swan and Dolphin	2,267	329,000	6,831

Note: n/a not available
Source: Original research

Living Environment

COST OF LIVING

Cost of Living Index

Year	Composite Index	Groceries	Housing	Utilities	Trans-portation	Health Care	Misc. Goods/Services
2001	98.8	102.4	90.9	105.3	96.2	105.9	102.0
2002	99.4	103.9	88.9	103.6	94.2	100.3	106.6
2003	98.4	101.8	91.3	101.7	95.8	96.7	103.3

Note: U.S. = 100
Source: ACCRA, Cost of Living Index, 2001, 2002 and 2003 4-Quarter Averages

HOUSING

House Price Index (HPI)

Area	National Ranking[2]	Quarterly Change (%)	One-Year Change (%)	Five-Year Change (%)
MSA[1]	81	3.68	8.26	42.88
U.S.[3]	-	3.67	7.97	41.81

Note: The HPI is a weighted repeat sales index. It measures average price changes in repeat sales or refinancings on the same properties. This information is obtained by reviewing repeat mortgage transactions on single-family properties whose mortgages have been purchased or securitized by Fannie Mae of Freddie Mac in January 1975; (1) Metropolitan Statistical Area - see Appendix A for areas included; (2) Rankings are based on annual percentage change, for all MSAs containing at least 15,000 transactions over the last 10 years and ranges from 1 to 220; (3) figures based on a weighted division average; all figures are for the period ended December 31, 2003
Source: Office of Federal Housing Enterprise Oversight, House Price Index, March 1, 2004

Housing: Year Structure Built

Area	1990-2000	1980-1989	1970-1979	1960-1969	1950-1959	1940-1949	Before 1940	Median Year
City	23.5	22.4	17.7	12.2	13.7	5.3	5.1	1978
MSA[1]	31.0	28.1	18.7	9.7	7.7	2.3	2.4	1983
U.S.	17.0	15.8	18.5	13.7	12.7	7.3	15.0	1971

Note: Figures are percentages; (1) Metropolitan Statistical Area - see Appendix A for areas included
Source: Census 2000, Summary File 3

Average New Home Price

Area	2001	2002	2003
City	190,483	204,048	216,369
U.S.	212,643	236,567	248,193

Note: Figures, in dollars, are based on a new home with 2,400 sq. ft. of living area on an 8,000 sq. ft. lot.
Source: ACCRA, Cost of Living Index, 2001, 2002 and 2003 4-Quarter Averages

Average Apartment Rent

Area	2001	2002	2003
City	669	726	797
U.S.	674	708	721

Note: Figures, in dollars per month, are based on an unfurnished two bedroom, 1-1/2 or 2 bath apartment, approximately 950 sq. ft. in size, excluding all utilities except water
Source: ACCRA, Cost of Living Index, 2001, 2002 and 2003 4-Quarter Averages

RESIDENTIAL UTILITIES

Average Residential Utility Costs

Area	All Electric ($/mth)	Part Electric ($/mth)	Other Energy ($/mth)	Phone ($/mth)
City	126.11	–	–	24.63
U.S.	116.46	65.82	62.68	23.90

Source: ACCRA, Cost of Living Index, 2003 4-Quarter Average

HEALTH CARE

Average Health Care Costs

Area	Hospital ($/day)	Doctor ($/visit)	Dentist ($/visit)
City	755.02	60.85	79.53
U.S.	678.35	67.91	83.90

Note: Hospital—based on a semi-private room; Doctor—based on a general practitioner's routine exam of an established patient; Dentist—based on adult teeth cleaning and periodic oral exam.
Source: ACCRA, Cost of Living Index, 2003 4-Quarter Average

Distribution of Non-Federal, Office-Based Physicians

Area	Total	Family/ General Practice	Specialties		
			Medical	Surgical	Other
MSA[1] (number)	2,703	389	957	697	660
MSA[1] (rate per 10,000 pop.)	16.4	2.4	5.8	4.2	4.0
Metro Average[2] (rate per 10,000 pop.)	33.1	2.2	7.7	4.8	5.6

Note: Data as of December 31, 2001; (1) Metropolitan Statistical Area - see Appendix A for areas included; (2) Average of 81 MSAs and CMSAs in this book
Source: American Medical Association, Physician Characteristics & Distribution in the U.S., 2003-2004

Hospitals

Orlando has the following hospitals: 3 general medical and surgical; 1 psychiatric.
AHA Guide to the Healthcare Field, 2003-2004

According to *U.S. News*, Orlando has one of the best hospitals in the U.S.: **Florida Hospital**; *U.S. News Online, "America's Best Hospitals 2003"*

PRESIDENTIAL ELECTION

2000 Presidential Election Results

Area	Gore	Bush	Nader	Buchanan	Other
Orange County	50.1	48.0	1.4	0.2	0.4
U.S.	48.4	47.9	2.7	0.4	0.6

Note: Results are percentages and may not add to 100% due to rounding
Source: www.cbsnews.com; www.uselectionatlas.org

EDUCATION

Public School District Statistics

District Name	Schls.	Enroll-ment	Classroom Teachers	Pupil/ Teacher Ratio	Minority Pupils[1] (%)	Current Expend.[2] ($/pupil)
Orange County SD	184	157,433	8,946	17.6	55.9	5,485

Note: Data covers the 2001-02 school year unless otherwise noted; (1) Fall 2000; (2) FY2000; n/a not available
Source: U.S. Department of Education, National Center for Education Statistics, Common Core of Data, Local Education Agency (School District) Universe Survey: School Year 2001-2002; U.S. Department of Education, National Center for Education Statistics, Digest of Education Statistics 2002

Educational Quality

School District	Education Quotient[1]	Graduate Outcome[2]	Community Index[3]	Resource Index[4]
Orange County	37	39	51	29

Note: Scores are national percentile rankings and range from 1 (worst) to 99 (best); (1) Combination of the Graduate Outcome, Community and Resource indexes weighted to reflect the greater importance of the Graduate Outcome and Resource Index; (2) Based on graduation rates and college board scores (SAT/ACT); (3) Based on the surrounding community's level of affluence and adult education; (4) Based on teacher salaries, per-pupil expenditures and student-teacher ratios.
Source: Expansion Management, December 2003

Educational Attainment by Race

Area	High School Graduate (%)					Bachelor's Degree (%)				
	Total	White	Black	Asian	Hisp.[2]	Total	White	Black	Asian	Hisp.[2]
City	82.2	88.9	63.5	86.0	73.8	28.2	34.0	12.4	41.9	18.7
MSA[1]	82.8	85.7	69.3	82.2	71.6	24.8	26.5	14.6	42.3	17.0
U.S.	80.4	83.6	72.3	80.4	52.4	24.4	26.1	14.3	44.1	10.4

Note: Figures shown cover persons 25 years old and over; (1) Metropolitan Statistical Area - see Appendix A for areas included; (2) people of Hispanic origin can be of any race
Source: Census 2000, Summary File 3

School Enrollment by Type

Area	Grades KG to 8				Grades 9 to 12			
	Public		Private		Public		Private	
	Enrollment	%	Enrollment	%	Enrollment	%	Enrollment	%
City	18,420	88.8	2,333	11.2	8,123	92.1	697	7.9
MSA[1]	186,352	87.2	27,385	12.8	83,562	92.0	7,301	8.0
U.S.	33,526,011	88.7	4,285,121	11.3	14,848,628	90.6	1,532,323	9.4

Note: Figures shown cover persons 3 years old and over; (1) Metropolitan Statistical Area - see Appendix A for areas included
Source: Census 2000, Summary File 3

School Enrollment by Race

Area	Grades KG to 8 (%)				Grades 9 to 12 (%)			
	White	Black	Asian	Hisp.[1]	White	Black	Asian	Hisp.[1]
City	44.2	42.9	1.6	21.3	44.0	40.0	2.8	21.8
MSA[2]	67.1	19.4	2.3	20.1	65.6	20.0	2.9	20.0
U.S.	68.5	15.5	3.3	16.8	68.8	15.5	3.8	15.7

Note: Figures shown cover persons 3 years old and over; (1) people of Hispanic origin can be of any race; (2) Metropolitan Statistical Area - see Appendix A for areas included
Source: Census 2000, Summary File 3

Classroom Teacher Salaries in Public Schools

District	B.A. Degree		M.A. Degree		Maximum	
	Min. ($)	Rank[1]	Max. ($)	Rank[1]	Max. ($)	Rank[1]
City	n/a	n/a	n/a	n/a	n/a	n/a
DOD Average[2]	31,567	-	53,248	-	59,356	-

Note: Salaries are for 2001-2002; (1) Rank ranges from 1 to 100; (2) As per the U.S. Department of Defense Wage Fixing Authority
Source: American Federation of Teachers, Survey & Analysis of Teacher Salary Trends 2002

Higher Education

Four-Year Colleges			Two-Year Colleges			Medical Schools	Law Schools	Voc/Tech
Public	Private Non-profit	Private For-profit	Public	Private Non-profit	Private For-profit			
1	5	6	2	1	5	0	1	14

Note: Figures cover institutions located within the city limits.
Source: National Center for Education Statistics, The Integrated Postsecondary Education System (IPEDS) Peer Analysis System, 2002; usnews.com, America's Best Graduate Schools 2004, Medical School Directory; The College Blue Book, Occupational Education, 2003; Barron's Guide to Law Schools, 2003; Medical School Admission Requirements U.S. & Canada, 2003-2004

**MAJOR
EMPLOYERS**

Major Employers

Company Name	Industry	Type
Convergys	Direct mail advertising services	Branch
Delta Management Group	Business services, nec	Single
Enertnment Dept Inventory Ctrl	Entertainers and entertainment groups	Branch
Epcot Center	Amusement parks	Headquarters
Lockheed Martin	Search and navigation equipment	Branch
Marriott	Hotels and motels	Branch
Morale Welfare & Recreation	National security	Branch
Neighborhood Service Officials	Civic and social associations	Branch
New Tribes Bible Institute	Religious organizations	Headquarters
Orlando Regional Medical Ctr	General medical and surgical hospitals	Headquarters
Sea World of Florida Inc	Amusement parks	Headquarters
Siemens Westinghouse Pwr Corp	Turbines and turbine generator sets	Headquarters
Stream International Inc	Prepackaged software	Branch
U C F	Colleges and universities	Headquarters
Universal Orlando	Amusement parks	Single
USPS Accounting	U.S. postal service	Branch
Walt Disney World Co	Eating places	Branch

Note: Companies shown are located in the metropolitan area and have 2,000 or more employees.
Source: www.zapdata.com, March 2004

PUBLIC SAFETY

Crime Rate

Area	All Crimes	Violent Crimes				Property Crimes		
		Murder	Forcible Rape	Robbery	Aggrav. Assault	Burglary	Larceny -Theft	Motor Vehicle Theft
City	10,867.9	7.7	62.2	531.7	1,259.4	1,907.9	5,966.4	1,132.4
Suburbs[1]	5,052.3	4.1	36.9	152.6	489.9	1,078.4	2,785.2	505.1
MSA[2]	5,709.9	4.5	39.8	195.5	576.9	1,172.2	3,144.9	576.1
U.S.	4,118.8	5.6	33.0	145.9	310.1	746.2	2,445.8	432.1

Note: Figures are crimes per 100,000 population; (1) All areas within the MSA that are located outside the city limits; (2) Metropolitan Statistical Area - see Appendix A for areas included
Source: FBI Uniform Crime Reports, 2002

RECREATION

Culture and Recreation

Museums	Orchestras	Opera Companies	Dance Companies	Professional Theatres	Zoos	Pro Sports Teams[1]
3	2	1	1	3	0	1

Note: (1) Covers the Metropolitan Statistical Area - see Appendix A for areas included.
Source: The Grey House Performing Arts Directory, 2002; Official Museum Directory, 2004; www.sportsvenues.com

Library System

The Orange County Library System has 14 branches, holdings of 2,100,000 volumes, and a budget of $25,021,312 (2001-2002).
American Library Directory, 2003-2004

MEDIA

Newspapers

Name	Type	Freq.	Distribution	Circulation
Central Florida Advocate	Black	1x/wk	Local	15,000
Latino International - Orlando Edition	Hispanic	1x/wk	State	45,000
The Orlando Sentinel	General	7x/wk	Regional	257,429
Orlando Sun Review	General	1x/wk	Local	16,000
Orlando Times	Black	1x/wk	United States	10,000
Orlando Weekly	Alternative	1x/wk	Local	50,000

Note: Includes newspapers whose offices are located in the city and whose circulations are 1,000 or more
Source: Burrelle's Media Directory, 2003

Television Stations

Name	Ch.	Affiliation	Type	Owner
WESH	2	NBCT	Commercial	Hearst-Argyle Broadcasting
WKMG	6	CBST	Commercial	Post-Newsweek Stations Inc.
WFTV	9	ABCT	Commercial	n/a
WMFE	24	PBS	Public	Community Communications Inc.
WRDQ	27	n/a	n/a	Cox Enterprises Inc.
WTGL	52	n/a	Non-comm.	n/a
WACX	55	n/a	Commercial	Associated Christian Television System
WOPX	56	PAXTV	Commercial	Paxson Communications Corporation
WRBW	65	UPN	Commercial	Rainbow Broadcasting Ltd.

Note: Stations included broadcast from the Orlando metro area; n/a not available
Source: Burrelle's Media Directory, 2003

AM Radio Stations

Call Letters	Freq. (kHz)	Target Audience	Station Format	Music Format
WFLF	540	General	N/S/T	n/a
WDBO	580	General	M/N/S/T	Adult Contemporary
WQTM	740	Men	S	n/a
WDYZ	990	Children	E/M/N	Top 40
WONQ	1030	Hispanic	M/N/S	Adult Contemporary
WIXL	1190	G/R	M/N/T	Christian
WRLZ	1270	H/R	M/T	Christian
WPRD	1440	A/H/R	N/T	n/a
WUNA	1480	Hispanic	M/T	Latin
WOKB	1600	Religious	M/T	Christian
WTIR	1680	General	M/N/T	Modern Rock

Note: Stations included broadcast from the Orlando metro area; n/a not available
The following abbreviations may be used:
Target Audience: A=Asian; B=Black; C=Christian; E=Ethnic; F=French; G=General; H=Hispanic; M=Men; N=Native American; R=Religious; S=Senior Citizen; W=Women; Y=Young Adult; Z=Children
Station Format: E=Educational; M=Music; N=News; S=Sports; T=Talk
Source: Burrelle's Media Directory, 2003

FM Radio Stations

Call Letters	Freq. (mHz)	Target Audience	Station Format	Music Format
WLAZ	88.7	Hispanic	E/M	Latin
WUCF	89.9	General	M/N	Jazz
WMFE	90.7	General	E/M/N	Classical
WPRK	91.5	General	E/M	Alternative
WWKA	92.3	General	M/N/S	Country
WCFB	94.5	General	M/N/S	Adult Contemporary
WPYO	95.3	General	M	Adult Top 40
WHTQ	96.5	General	M/N/S	Classic Rock
WMMO	98.9	General	M	Adult Contemporary
WSHE	100.3	General	M	Oldies
WJHM	101.9	B/G/H	M	Rhythm & Blues
WLOQ	103.1	General	M	Jazz
WTKS	104.1	General	M/T	Alternative
WOMX	105.1	General	M/N/T	Adult Contemporary
WOCL	105.9	General	M	Alternative
WXXL	106.7	General	M/N/T	Top 40
WMGF	107.7	General	M/N	Adult Contemporary

Note: Stations included broadcast from the Orlando metro area
The following abbreviations may be used:
Target Audience: A=Asian; B=Black; C=Christian; E=Ethnic; F=French; G=General; H=Hispanic; M=Men; N=Native American; R=Religious; S=Senior Citizen; W=Women; Y=Young Adult; Z=Children
Station Format: E=Educational; M=Music; N=News; S=Sports; T=Talk
Source: Burrelle's Media Directory, 2003

CLIMATE

Average and Extreme Temperatures

Temperature	Jan	Feb	Mar	Apr	May	Jun	Jul	Aug	Sep	Oct	Nov	Dec	Yr.
Extreme High (°F)	86	89	90	95	100	100	99	100	98	95	89	90	100
Average High (°F)	70	72	77	82	87	90	91	91	89	83	78	72	82
Average Temp. (°F)	59	62	67	72	77	81	82	82	81	75	68	62	72
Average Low (°F)	48	51	56	60	66	71	73	74	72	66	58	51	62
Extreme Low (°F)	19	29	25	38	51	53	64	65	57	44	32	20	19

Note: Figures cover the years 1952-1990
Source: National Climatic Data Center, International Station Meteorological Climate Summary, 9/96

Average Precipitation/Snowfall/Humidity

Precip./Humidity	Jan	Feb	Mar	Apr	May	Jun	Jul	Aug	Sep	Oct	Nov	Dec	Yr.
Avg. Precip. (in.)	2.3	2.8	3.4	2.0	3.2	7.0	7.2	5.8	5.8	2.7	3.5	2.0	47.7
Avg. Snowfall (in.)	Tr	0	0	0	0	0	0	0	0	0	0	0	Tr
Avg. Rel. Hum. 7am (%)	87	87	88	87	88	89	90	92	92	89	89	87	89
Avg. Rel. Hum. 4pm (%)	53	51	49	47	51	61	65	66	66	59	56	55	57

Note: Figures cover the years 1952-1990; Tr = Trace amounts (<0.05 in. of rain; <0.5 in. of snow)
Source: National Climatic Data Center, International Station Meteorological Climate Summary, 9/96

Weather Conditions

Temperature			Daytime Sky			Precipitation		
32°F & below	45°F & below	90°F & above	Clear	Partly cloudy	Cloudy	0.01 inch or more precip.	0.1 inch or more snow/ice	Thunder-storms
3	35	90	76	208	81	115	0	80

Note: Figures are average number of days per year and covers the years 1952-1990
Source: National Climatic Data Center, International Station Meteorological Climate Summary, 9/96

HAZARDOUS WASTE

Superfund Sites

Orlando has two hazardous waste sites on the EPA's Superfund National Priorities List: **Chevron Chemical Co. (Ortho Division); City Industries, Inc.**. *U.S. Environmental Protection Agency, National Priorities List, March 15, 2004*

AIR & WATER QUALITY

Maximum Pollutant Concentrations

	Particulate Matter (ug/m³)	Carbon Monoxide (ppm)	Sulfur Dioxide (ppm)	Nitrogen Dioxide (ppm)	Ozone 1-hour (ppm)	Ozone 8-hour (ppm)	Lead (ug/m³)
MSA[1] Level	38	3	0.005	0.011	0.1	0.08	n/a
NAAQS[2]	150	9	0.140	0.053	0.12	0.08	1.50
Met NAAQS[2]	Yes	Yes	Yes	Yes	Yes	Yes	n/a

Note: (1) Metropolitan Statistical Area - see Appendix A for areas included; (2) National Ambient Air Quality Standards; n/a not available
Units: ppm = parts per million; ug/m³ = micrograms per cubic meter
Source: EPA, Latest Findings on National Air Quality: 2002 Status and Trends, August 2003

Air Quality Index

In the Orlando MSA (see Appendix A for areas included), the Air Quality Index (AQI) exceeded 100 on 1 day in 2002. An AQI value greater than 100 indicates that air quality would have been in the unhealthful range on that day.
EPA, Latest Findings on National Air Quality: 2002 Status and Trends, August 2003

Watershed Health

The U.S. Environmental Protection Agency monitors the health of the aquatic resources for the nation's 2,000+ watersheds. **The Kissimmee watershed serves the Orlando area and received an overall Index of Watershed Indicators (IWI) score of 3 (less serious problems - low vulnerability).** The IWI score is based on seven condition and nine vulnerability indicators. The overall IWI score ranges from 1 (best health) to 6 (worst health). The

Condition Indicators include: designated use attainment, fish and wildlife consumption advisories, source water condition, contaminated sediments, ambient water quality, and wetlands loss index. The Vulnerability Indicators include: aquatic species at risk, conventional and toxic loads over permitted limits, urban and agricultural runoff potential, population change, hydrologic modification, estuarine pollution susceptibility, and air deposition. *EPA, Index of Watershed Indicators, October 26, 2001*

Drinking Water

Water System Name	Pop. Served	Primary Water Source Type	Number of Violations January 2002-February 2004		
			Health Based	Significant Monitoring	Monitoring
Orlando Utilities Commission	356,041	Ground	None	None	None

Note: Data as of February 19, 2004
Source: EPA, Office of Ground Water and Drinking Water, Safe Drinking Water Information System

Orlando tap water is alkaline, hard and fluoridated.
Editor & Publisher Market Guide, 2004

Plano, Texas

Background

Plano, just 20 miles north of downtown Dallas, is the largest city in Collin County. Its location, and the performance of its municipal government and local economy, help to explain why Plano proudly presents itself as a superb choice for families and businesses of all types.

The city was first settled in the 1840s during the era of the Republic of Texas, mostly by migrants from Kentucky and Tennessee who were seeking new hunting and grazing areas. In 1846, William Foreman, an early entrepreneur, established a sawmill and gristmill at the site, and later a store and cotton gin. Such improvements began to attract new settlers and, by 1850, residents decided they needed an official post office. Their first application requesting the name Filmore to the federal government, in honor of the president of the United States, was rejected, and in its place, Foreman's name was proposed. This alternative, however, was also rejected, and finally, the descriptive Plano—Spanish for plain—was suggested and adopted.

Cattle and other livestock were the mainstay of Plano's early economy, but gradually farmers began to exploit the rich, black soil of the area. Population and economic growth was slow and steady until the Civil War, but afterwards, with the growth of railroads and the adjacent towns, Plano began to assume its modern form. In 1872, with the completion of the Houston and Texas Railroad, Plano's economy took off, and the city was incorporated in 1873. Although for much its early life, Plano had been dependent on agriculture, all manner of building and business flourished toward the end of the nineteenth century, and it was said locally that virtually anything could be bought, sold, or traded in the city. By the mid-twentieth century, Plano had almost completed its conversion from farming to trading, and by the 1960s, the expansion of Dallas had exerted a significant effect.

With the historic shift of manufacturing and labor from the North to the South, Plano achieved its present-day economic maturity and strength. Today, Plano is the international headquarters of several large companies, such as EDS, Alcatel, Frito Lay, J.C. Penney, and Dr. Pepper/7 UP.

The Plano Independent School District (PISD) serves the City of Plano, portions of Dallas and Richardson, the City of Parker, and portions of Allen and Murphy. Twenty-one PISD schools have been named National Blue Ribbon Schools of Excellence, and average SAT scores are well above state and national averages. In 1999, Plano schools were selected by School Match, a national educational research firm, as an Award-Winning School System.

There are many institutions of higher learning in and around Plano, including Austin College, Collin County Community College, Plano Dallas Baptist University, Plano Richland College, Dallas Southern Methodist University, Irving University of North Texas, Denton University of Texas at Dallas, and Richardson University of Texas Southwestern Medical School.

Plano can be hot in the summer. The good news, though, is that there is plenty of sunshine. Winters are generally mild, and cold snaps are infrequent and short-lived. Rainfall is relatively plentiful and usually falls more often at night than during daytime.

Rankings

- Plano was selected as one of "America's Hottest Towns." *Money* screened a decade's worth of data for communities with above-average population growth, above-average income and above average home prices. Towns more than 60 miles from a major city and those with limited cultural or recreational offerings were cut. Local real estate prices were then compared with local median income to see where people are most willing to devote a high multiple of their annual income towards housing. 25 cities with populations above 100,000 made the final cut. Plano ranked #1 in the Western Region. *Money, January 2004*

- Dallas-Plano was ranked #95 out of 331 metro areas in *Cities Ranked & Rated*. Criteria: cost of living; climate; crime; transportation; economy and jobs; education; arts and culture; health and healthcare; leisure. *Cities Ranked & Rated, 1st Edition, 2004*

- *Ladies Home Journal* ranked America's 200 largest cities based on the qualities women surveyed care about most. Plano ranked #9 out of 143 in the smaller city category (population under 300,000). Criteria: crime; lifestyle; education; jobs; health; child care; politics; and the economy. *Ladies Home Journal Online, "The Best Cities for Women 2002"*

- Plano was selected as one of "America's Pet Healthiest Cities" by Purina. The city ranked #36 out of 50. Criteria: veterinary services; environment; and legislation. *Purina Pet Institute, "America's Pet Healthiest Cities," August 14, 2001*

- *Forbes* ranked the 40 most populous metro areas in the U.S. in terms of the best places to be single. The Dallas-Plano metro area was ranked #10. Criteria: number of other singles; cost of living alone; nightlife; culture; job growth; coolness. *Forbes, June 5, 2003*

- *Forbes* ranked the 150 most populous metro areas in the U.S. in terms of the "Best Places for Business and Careers." The Dallas-Plano metro area was ranked #9. Criteria: income and job growth; cost-of-doing-business; qualifications of the available pool of labor; crime rates; housing costs; net migration. *Forbes, May 9, 2003*

- *Men's Health* ranked 101 U.S. cities in terms of the quality of their tap water. Plano received a grade of C. Criteria: levels of bacteria, arsenic, lead, trihalomethanes, and haloacetic acids were compared with the National Academy of Science's guidelines as well as with the EPA's more stringent maximum contaminant level goals. *Men's Health, March 2004*

- Sperling's BestPlaces ranked 331 metro areas and identified the most and least stressful U.S. cities. The Dallas-Plano metro area ranked #10 out of the 100 largest metro areas (#1 = most stressful). Criteria: divorce rate; unemployment rate; violent and property crime; suicide rate; commute time; mental health; alcohol consumption; cloudy days. *www.BestPlaces.net, February 26, 2004*

- Sperling's BestPlaces in partnership with Pep Boys ranked 77 metro areas and identified "America's Most Drivable Cities." The Dallas-Plano metro area ranked #40. Criteria: climate; road roughness; urban mobility; gas prices. *Pep Boys, "America's Most Drivable Cities," April 9, 2003*

- Plano was selected as a 2003 Digital Cities Survey winner. The city ranked #4 in the mid-sized city category. The survey examined and assessed how city governments are utilizing information technology to operate and deliver quality service to their customers and citizens. *Center for Digital Government, "2003 Digital Cities Survey"*

- Dallas-Plano was ranked #173 out of America's 200 largest metro areas in *SELF Magazine's* ranking of "America's Healthiest Cities for Women." Criteria: safety; air/water quality; cancer rates; and 21 other factors relating to health. *SELF Magazine, November 2003*

- Dallas-Plano was identified as an asthma "hot spot" where high prevalence makes the condition a key issue and environmental "triggers" and other factors can make living with asthma a particular challenge. The area ranked #17 out of the nations 100 largest metro areas. Criteria: local asthma prevalence and mortality data; pollen scores; air pollution; asthma prescriptions; smoking laws; number of asthma specialists. *GlaxoSmithKline, October 29, 2002*

- *Zero Population Growth* ranked 239 cities in terms of children's health, safety, and economic well-being. Plano was ranked #5 out of 74 suburbs and outer cities (incorporated areas of more than 100,000 within the MSA of a major city) and was given a grade of A+. Criteria: total population and population growth; percent of population under 18 years of age; number of children's museums; health improvement grade; percent of births to teens; percent of low birthweight infants; infant mortality rate; number of Title X-funded clinics; average SAT/ACT scores; average elementary and secondary class size; crime rate; unemployment rate; percent of affordable homes; number of bad air days; park acres per 1000 persons; library circulation per child; and children's program attendance counts. *Zero Population Growth, Kid Friendly Cities Report Card 2001*

- *Ladies Home Journal* ranked America's 200 largest cities in terms of safety. Plano ranked #12 out of 200. Criteria: violent crimes; crimes against property; and rape. *Ladies Home Journal Online, "The Best Cities for Women 2002"*

- Dallas-Plano was ranked #11 out of 268 metro areas in terms of its Creativity Index. The Creativity Index is a mix of four equally weighted factors: the Creative Class (scientists, engineers, architects, designers, writers, artists, musicians, or any profession where creativity is a key factor) share of the workforce; innovation, measured as patents per capita; high-tech industry, using the Milken Institute's Tech Pole Index; and diversity, measured by the Gay Index (a reasonable proxy for an areas' openness to different kinds of people and ideas). *The Rise of the Creative Class, 2002*

- Dallas-Plano was ranked #13 out of 125 regions worldwide in terms of its "Knowledge Competitiveness Index." The index attempts to measure the knowledge-based development taking place throughout the world and is based on 17 measures of economic performance that indicate a region's ability to translate its knowledge capacity into economic value. *Robert Huggins Associates, "2003-2004 World Knowledge Competitiveness Index"*

- The Dallas-Plano metro area was selected by *Yahoo! Internet Life* as one of "America's Most Wired Cities...and Towns." The area ranked #17 out of 87. Criteria: home and work net use; user sophistication; domain density; and available content. *Yahoo! Internet Life, April 2001*

- The Dallas-Plano metro area was selected by Cranium as one of the "Top 50 Fun Cities" in America. The area ranked #34. Criteria includes: number of sports teams, restaurants, and dance performances; number of toy stores; city budget spent on recreation. *Cranium, November 4, 2003*

- Of the 25 largest U.S. markets, the Dallas-Plano DMA (designated market area) ranked #5 in terms of online shopping. Criteria: telephone surveys of nearly 50,000 U.S. households between July 2000 and June 2001 conducted by market research firm Centris. *American Demographics, February 2002*

- Dallas-Plano was identified as one of the 100 "Most Unwired Cities" in the U.S. The area ranked #16. Criteria: number of public and commercial wireless access points; cell phone coverage offering wide area network Internet access; Internet penetration. *Intel, "Most Unwired Cities," March 4, 2003*

- Scarborough Research measured the percentage of households who subscribe to cellular services among adults ages 18 and over in 75 U.S. markets. The Dallas-Plano DMA (Designated Market Area) was ranked #6 out of 75. *Scarborough Research, Scarborough USA+ 2003 Release 1*

- The Dallas-Plano metro area was selected as one of "America's 50 Hottest Cities for Business Relocations and Expansions." The area ranked #17. Criteria: 70 of the industry's most prominent site selection consultants were asked which cities their clients found the most attractive when it came to selecting an expansion or relocation site in 2003. *Expansion Management, January 2004*

- The Dallas-Plano metro area was selected as one of the "Top 60 CyberCities in America" by *Site Selection.* CyberCities are magnets for growing high-tech companies. Criteria: total employment; average wages; total payroll; number of companies; R&D spending and venture capital in the 45 Standard Industrial Classification (SIC) codes that define the high-technology industry. *Site Selection, March 2002*

- The Dallas-Plano metro area was cited as one of America's "Top 50 Metros" in terms of the availability of highly skilled, highly educated workers. The area ranked #36 out of 50. Criteria: degree holders (bachelors, masters, professional, and Ph.D.) as a percent of the workforce; science and engineering workers as a percent of the workforce; number of patents issued; number and type of colleges in each metro area. *Expansion Management, March 2004*

- The Dallas-Plano metro area was cited as one of "The Best Places in the U.S. to Locate a Company." The area ranked #12 out of 329. Criteria: education (with emphasis on college board test results and high school graduation rates); availability of quality healthcare services and the cost to employers; quality of life; logistics workforce and companies; transportation infrastructure; quality and quantity of highly educated technical workers; business climate. *Expansion Management, July 2003*

- The Dallas-Plano metro area was cited as one of America's "Most Picture Perfect Metros" by *Plant Sites and Parks* magazine. Each year *PSP* readers rank the metro areas they consider best bets for their companies to relocate or expand to in the coming year. The area ranked #1 out of 10. *Plant Sites and Parks, March 2004*

- The Dallas-Plano metro area was selected as one of the "Top 40 Hottest Real Estate Markets" for expanding or relocating businesses." Criteria: rental costs; purchase prices; and vacancy rates of office and warehouse space. *Expansion Management, August 2003*

- The Dallas-Plano metro area appeared on *Forbes/Milken Institute* list of "Best Places for Business and Career." Rank: #14 out of 200 metro areas. Criteria: salary growth; job growth; number of technology clusters; overall concentration of technology activity relative to national average; and technology output growth. *www.forbes.com, Forbes/Milken Institute Best Places 2002*

- The Dallas-Plano metro area appeared on the "Milken Institute Best Performing Cities" index. Rank: #78 out of 200 large metro areas. Criteria: job growth; wage and salary growth; high-tech output growth. *Milken Institute, June 25, 2003*

- The Dallas-Plano metro area appeared on *Entrepreneur* magazine's list of the "Best Cities for Entrepreneurs" in 2003. The area ranked #24 out of 61 in the large city category. Criteria: entrepreneurial activity; small-business growth; economic growth; and risk. *www.Entrepreneur.com*

- The Dallas-Plano metro area was selected as one of "The Top 20 Boom Towns in America." *Business 2.0* magazine and econometric research firm Global Insight compared 319 metropolitan areas in the U.S. and ranked the 61 with populations over 1 million. Criteria: a weighted formula that includes forecast growth rates in sectors that contain the economy's 10 most skilled occupational clusters; the prevalence of college degrees in the local workforce; median salary. The area ranked #18 among large metro areas. *Business 2.0 Magazine, March 2004*

- The Dallas-Plano metro area appeared on *IndustryWeek's* fourth annual World-Class Communities list. It ranked #5 out of 315 metro areas. Criteria: MSA Gross Metropolitan Product (GMP) per manufacturing employee; and MSA percent share of U.S. manufacturing Gross Domestic Product (GDP). *IndustryWeek, April 16, 2001*

- ING Group ranked the 125 largest metro areas according to the general financial security of residents. The Dallas-Plano metro area was ranked #35 out of 125. Criteria: Earnings and Wealth Potential (household income, education, net assets, cost of living); Safety Net (health insurance, retirement savings, life insurance, income support programs); Personal Threats (unemployment rate, low-income households, crime rate); Community Economic Vitality (cost of community services, job quality, job creation, housing costs). *ING Group, "The Best Cities to Earn and Save Money: A Ranking of the Largest 125 U.S. Cities," 2001 Edition*

Business Environment

CITY FINANCES

City Government Finances

Component	2000-2001 ($000)	2000-2001 ($ per capita)
Total Revenues	247,427	1,114
Total Expenditures	248,270	1,118
Debt Outstanding	275,955	1,243
Cash and Securities	144,359	650

Source: U.S Census Bureau, Government Finances 2000-2001, August 2003

City Government Revenue by Source

Source	2000-2001 ($000)	2000-2001 ($ per capita)
General Revenue		
From Federal Government	1,146	5
From State Government	24	0
From Local Governments	876	4
Taxes		
Property	71,055	320
Sales	65,654	296
Personal Income	0	0
License	0	0
Charges	57,628	260
Liquor Store	0	0
Utility	30,919	139
Employee Retirement	0	0
Other	20,125	91

Source: U.S Census Bureau, Government Finances 2000-2001, August 2003

City Government Expenditures by Function

Function	2000-2001 ($000)	2000-2001 ($ per capita)	2000-2001 (%)
General Expenditures			
Airports	0	0	0.0
Corrections	0	0	0.0
Education	0	0	0.0
Fire Protection	22,620	102	9.1
Governmental Administration	21,746	98	8.8
Health	1,812	8	0.7
Highways	21,857	98	8.8
Hospitals	0	0	0.0
Housing and Community Development	1,861	8	0.7
Interest on General Debt	11,330	51	4.6
Libraries	8,186	37	3.3
Parking	0	0	0.0
Parks and Recreation	25,568	115	10.3
Police Protection	30,737	138	12.4
Public Welfare	0	0	0.0
Sewerage	16,060	72	6.5
Solid Waste Management	13,404	60	5.4
Liquor Store	0	0	0.0
Utility	26,315	119	10.6
Employee Retirement	0	0	0.0
Other	46,774	211	18.8

Source: U.S Census Bureau, Government Finances 2000-2001, August 2003

Municipal Bond Ratings

Area	Moody's
City	Aaa

Source: Mergent Bond Record, February 2004

DEMOGRAPHICS

Population Growth

Area	1990 Census	2000 Census	2003 Estimate	2008 Projection	Population Growth (%) 1990-2000	2000-2008
City	128,507	222,030	254,312	306,757	72.8	38.2
MSA[1]	2,676,248	3,519,176	3,800,863	4,265,338	31.5	21.2
U.S.	248,709,873	281,421,906	290,647,163	305,918,071	13.2	8.7

Note: (1) Metropolitan Statistical Area - see Appendix A for areas included
Source: Claritas, Inc.

Number of Households and Average Household Size

Area	1990 Census	2000 Census	2003 Estimate	2008 Projection	2003 Average Household Size
City	44,273	80,875	94,051	116,212	2.7
MSA[1]	1,001,750	1,281,957	1,376,504	1,531,019	2.8
U.S.	91,947,410	105,480,101	109,440,059	116,034,472	2.7

Note: (1) Metropolitan Statistical Area - see Appendix A for areas included
Source: Claritas, Inc.

Race and Ethnicity

Area	White Non-Hispanic	Black Non-Hispanic	Asian Non-Hispanic	Other Race Non-Hispanic	Hispanic
City	77.4	5.2	10.8	6.6	10.3
MSA[1]	66.9	14.8	4.3	14.0	23.8
U.S.	74.5	12.4	3.8	9.3	13.2

Note: Figures are 2003 estimates; (1) Metropolitan Statistical Area - see Appendix A for areas included
Source: Claritas, Inc.

Segregation

City		MSA[1]	
Index[2]	Rank[3]	Index[2]	Rank[4]
28.2	99	64.4	110

Note: Figures are based on an analysis of Census 2000 data; (1) Metropolitan Statistical Area - see Appendix A for areas included; (2) Dissimilarity Index—the most commonly used measure of segregation between two groups, reflecting their relative distributions across neighborhoods within a city or metropolitan area. It can range in value from 0, indicating complete integration, to 100, indicating complete segregation; (3) Ranges from 1 (most segregated) to 100 (least segregated) and includes all the cities in this book; (4) Ranges from 1 (most segregated) to 318 (least segregated) and includes 318 metropolitan areas.
Source: www.CensusScope.org

Ancestry

Area	German	Irish[2]	English	American	Italian	Polish	French[3]	Scottish
City	16.3	10.8	11.9	6.8	4.1	2.5	3.0	2.6
MSA[1]	10.0	8.1	8.2	7.8	2.1	1.2	2.1	1.7
U.S.	15.2	10.9	8.7	7.3	5.6	3.2	3.0	1.7

Note: Figures include multiple ancestry (e.g. if a person reported being Irish and Italian, they were included in both columns); (1) Metropolitan Statistical Area - see Appendix A for areas included; (2) Includes Celtic; (3) Includes Alsatian but excludes Basque
Source: Census 2000, Summary File 3

Foreign-Born Population

Area	Any Foreign Country	Percent of Population Born in: Europe	Asia	Africa	Oceania[2]	Canada	Mexico	Latin America[3]
City	17.1	2.1	8.4	0.6	0.1	0.8	3.7	1.4
MSA[1]	16.8	0.9	3.4	0.6	0.0	0.3	9.8	1.8
U.S.	11.1	1.7	2.9	0.3	0.1	0.3	3.3	2.5

Note: (1) Metropolitan Statistical Area - see Appendix A for areas included; (2) Includes Australia, New Zealand subregion, Melanesia, Micronesia, Polynesia, and Oceania n.e.c; (3) Includes Central America (excluding Mexico), South America, and the Caribbean.
Source: Census 2000, Summary File 3

Religion

Area	Catholic	Southern Baptist	United Methodist	ELCA[1]	LDS[2]	Presbyterian Church USA	Jewish Est.	Muslim Est.
County	18.3	16.0	6.1	0.6	1.3	0.7	1.4	1.2
U.S.	22.0	7.1	3.7	1.8	1.5	1.1	2.2	0.6

Note: Figures shown are the number of adherents as a percentage of the total population; Adherents are defined as all members, including full members, their children and the estimated number of other participants who are not considered members (e.g. the baptized, those not confirmed, those not eligible for communion, those regularly attending services, etc.); (1) Evangelical Lutheran Church in America; (2) The Church of Jesus Christ of Latter Day Saints
Source: Reprinted with permission from Religious Congregations and Membership in the United States 2000 (Nashville, Glenmary Research Center, 2002) Copyright Association of Statisticians of American Religious Bodies. All rights reserved.

Age Distribution

Area	Percent of Population						
	Under Age 5	Age 5 to 17	Age 18 to 34	Age 35 to 49	Age 50 to 64	Age 65 to 79	80 Years and Over
City	8.2	20.3	22.7	29.5	14.5	3.7	1.1
MSA[1]	8.1	19.9	27.3	24.4	12.7	5.8	1.8
U.S.	6.8	18.9	23.7	23.5	14.8	9.2	3.2

Note: (1) Metropolitan Statistical Area - see Appendix A for areas included
Source: Census 2000, Summary File 3

Marriage Status

Area	Never Married	Now Married Except Separated	Separated	Widowed	Divorced
City	21.1	66.5	1.3	2.7	8.4
MSA[1]	27.2	55.6	2.5	4.6	10.1
U.S.	27.1	54.4	2.2	6.6	9.7

Note: Figures cover population 15 years of age and older; (1) Metropolitan Statistical Area - see Appendix A for areas included
Source: Census 2000, Summary File 3

Male/Female Ratio

Area	Males	Females	Males per 100 Females
City	126,586	127,726	99.1
MSA[1]	1,894,408	1,906,455	99.4
U.S.	142,511,883	148,135,280	96.2

Note: Figures are 2003 estimates; (1) Metropolitan Statistical Area - see Appendix A for areas included
Source: Claritas, Inc.

ECONOMY

Gross Metropolitan Product

Area	1999	2000	2001	2002	2002 Rank[2]
MSA[1]	148.3	159.9	164.7	166.9	9

Note: Figures are in billions of dollars; (1) Metropolitan Statistical Area - see Appendix A for areas included; (2) Rank ranges from 1 to 319
Source: The U.S. Conference of Mayors, Metro Economies Report, July 2003

INCOME

Per Capita/Median/Average Income

Area	Per Capita ($)	Median Household ($)	Average Household ($)
City	42,486	89,281	114,684
MSA[1]	27,294	55,076	74,939
U.S.	24,078	46,868	63,207

Note: Figures are 2003 estimates; (1) Metropolitan Statistical Area - see Appendix A for areas included
Source: Claritas, Inc.

Household Income Distribution

Area	Percent of Households Earning							
	Under $15,000	$15,000 -24,999	$25,000 -34,999	$35,000 -49,999	$50,000 -74,999	$75,000 -99,000	$100,000 -149,999	$150,000 and up
City	3.7	4.1	5.7	10.5	17.1	15.7	22.8	20.4
MSA[1]	10.2	9.2	10.9	15.8	19.4	12.7	13.0	8.9
U.S.	14.1	11.5	11.7	16.0	19.2	11.3	10.2	6.0

Note: Figures are 2003 estimates; (1) Metropolitan Statistical Area - see Appendix A for areas included
Source: Claritas, Inc.

Poverty Rates by Age

Area	All Ages	Under 5 Years Old	5 to 17 Years Old	18 to 64 Years Old	65 Years and Over
City	4.3	0.4	1.0	2.5	0.4
MSA[1]	11.1	1.3	2.8	6.3	0.7
U.S.	12.4	1.2	3.0	6.9	1.2

Note: Figures are percent of population with income in 1999 below poverty level and only include population for whom poverty status is determined; (1) Metropolitan Statistical Area - see Appendix A for areas included
Source: Census 2000, Summary File 3

Personal Bankruptcy Filing Rate

Area	2002	2003
Collin County	6.29	7.26
U.S.	5.34	5.58

Note: Numbers are per 1,000 population and include Chapter 7 and Chapter 13 filings
Source: Federal Deposit Insurance Corporation (FDIC), Regional Economic Conditions (RECON), 2/25/2004

EMPLOYMENT

Labor Force and Employment

Area	Civilian Labor Force			Workers Employed		
	Dec. 2002	Dec. 2003	% Chg.	Dec. 2002	Dec. 2003	% Chg.
City	155,194	156,134	0.6	147,455	149,667	1.5
MSA[1]	2,030,240	2,051,670	1.1	1,900,545	1,929,052	1.5
U.S.	144,807,000	146,501,000	1.2	136,599,000	138,556,000	1.4

Note: Data is not seasonally adjusted and covers workers 16 years of age and older;
(1) Metropolitan Statistical Area - see Appendix A for areas included
Source: Bureau of Labor Statistics, http://stats.bls.gov

Unemployment Rate

Area	2003											
	Jan.	Feb.	Mar.	Apr.	May	Jun.	Jul.	Aug.	Sep.	Oct.	Nov.	Dec.
City	5.7	5.7	5.6	5.3	5.5	6.1	5.7	5.3	5.1	4.7	4.5	4.1
MSA[1]	7.3	7.2	7.0	6.7	7.1	8.0	7.4	7.1	7.0	6.4	6.3	6.0
U.S.	6.5	6.4	6.2	5.8	5.8	6.5	6.3	6.0	5.8	5.6	5.6	5.4

Note: Data is not seasonally adjusted and covers workers 16 years of age and older; All figures are percentages; (1) Metropolitan Statistical Area - see Appendix A for areas included
Source: Bureau of Labor Statistics, http://stats.bls.gov

Employment by Occupation

Occupation Classification	City (%)	MSA[1] (%)	U.S. (%)
Sales and Office	27.3	28.7	26.7
Professional and Related	29.4	20.4	20.2
Service	8.0	12.3	14.9
Production, Transportation, and Material Moving	4.5	11.8	14.6
Management, Business, and Financial	26.2	16.8	13.5
Construction, Extraction, and Maintenance	4.6	9.9	9.4
Farming, Forestry, and Fishing	0.0	0.2	0.7

Note: Figures cover employed civilians 16 years of age and older;
(1) Metropolitan Statistical Area - see Appendix A for areas included
Source: Census 2000, Summary File 3

Employment by Industry

Sector	MSA[1]		U.S.
	Number of Employees	Percent of Total	Percent of Total
Government	241,000	12.6	16.7
Education and Health Services	191,600	10.0	12.9
Professional and Business Services	271,700	14.2	12.3
Retail Trade	222,800	11.6	11.8
Manufacturing	198,400	10.3	11.0
Leisure and Hospitality	170,700	8.9	9.1
Finance Activities	170,000	8.9	6.1
Construction	95,700	5.0	5.1
Wholesale Trade	123,400	6.4	4.3
Other Services	72,400	3.8	4.1
Transportation and Utilities	75,700	3.9	3.7
Information	77,800	4.1	2.4
Natural Resources and Mining	6,500	0.3	0.4

Note: Figures cover non-farm employment as of December 2003 and are not seasonally adjusted;
(1) Metropolitan Statistical Area - see Appendix A for areas included
Source: Bureau of Labor Statistics, http://stats.bls.gov

Average Wages

Occupation	$/Hr.	Occupation	$/Hr.
Accountants and Auditors	27.10	Maids and Housekeeping Cleaners	7.77
Automotive Mechanics	15.52	Maintenance and Repair Workers	13.28
Bookkeepers	14.98	Marketing Managers	42.93
Carpenters	13.66	Nuclear Medicine Technologists	26.90
Cashiers	8.22	Nurses, Licensed Practical	18.26
Clerks, General Office	11.70	Nurses, Registered	23.12
Clerks, Receptionists/Information	11.39	Nursing Aides/Orderlies/Attendants	9.16
Clerks, Shipping/Receiving	11.68	Packers and Packagers, Hand	8.85
Computer Programmers	35.10	Physical Therapists	31.68
Computer Support Specialists	23.53	Postal Service Mail Carriers	18.77
Computer Systems Analysts	31.49	Real Estate Brokers	29.72
Cooks, Restaurant	8.59	Retail Salespersons	10.86
Dentists	61.06	Sales Reps., Exc. Tech./Scientific	25.29
Electrical Engineers	38.29	Sales Reps., Tech./Scientific	30.77
Electricians	17.75	Secretaries, Exc. Legal/Med./Exec.	13.02
Financial Managers	43.37	Security Guards	10.18
First-Line Supervisors/Mgrs., Sales	18.46	Surgeons	71.39
Food Preparation Workers	7.92	Teacher Assistants	8.40
General and Operations Managers	41.74	Teachers, Elementary School	20.40
Hairdressers/Cosmetologists	11.04	Teachers, Secondary School	21.60
Internists	n/a	Telemarketers	11.82
Janitors and Cleaners	8.67	Truck Drivers, Heavy/Tractor-Trailer	16.40
Landscaping/Groundskeeping Workers	9.36	Truck Drivers, Light/Delivery Svcs.	13.50
Lawyers	56.67	Waiters and Waitresses	7.53

Note: Wage data is for 2002 and covers the Metropolitan Statistical Area (see Appendix A for areas included).
Hourly wages for elementary/secondary school teachers and teacher assistants were calculated by the editors
from annual wage data assuming a 40 hour work week; n/a not available.
Source: Bureau of Labor Statistics, 2002 Metro Area Occupational Employment and Wage Estimates

Occupational Employment Projections: 1996 - 2006

Occupations Expected to Have the Largest Job Growth (ranked by numerical growth)	Fast-Growing Occupations[1] (ranked by percent growth)
1. Cashiers	1. Desktop publishers
2. Salespersons, retail	2. Systems analysts
3. General managers & top executives	3. Customer service representatives
4. Truck drivers, light	4. Physical therapy assistants and aides
5. Child care workers, private household	5. Computer engineers
6. General office clerks	6. Emergency medical technicians
7. Systems analysts	7. Medical assistants
8. Food preparation workers	8. Respiratory therapists
9. Food service workers	9. Telephone & cable TV line install & repair
10. Registered nurses	10. Physical therapists

Note: Projections cover Texas; (1) Excludes occupations with total job growth less than 300
Source: U.S. Department of Labor, Employment and Training Administration, America's Labor Market Information System (ALMIS)

TAXES

State Corporate Income Tax Rates

State	Rate (%)	Number of Brackets	Low Bracket (Under $)	High Bracket (Over $)
Texas	None	na	na	na

Note: Tax rates as of December 31, 2003; na not applicable
Source: Tax Foundation, www.taxfoundation.org

State Individual Income Tax Rates

State	Federal Deductibility	Marginal Rate (%)	Number of Brackets	Low Bracket (Under $)	High Bracket (Over $)
Texas	No	None	na	na	na

Note: Tax rates as of December 31, 2003; Brackets apply to single taxpayers and married people filing separately; na not applicable
Source: Tax Foundation, www.taxfoundation.org

Various State and Local Tax Rates

State Sales and Use (%)	Total Sales and Use (%)	Gasoline (cents/gal.)	Cigarette (cents/pack)	Spirits ($/gal.)	Table Wine ($/gal.)	Beer ($/gal.)
6.25	8.25	20	41	2.40	0.20	0.20

Note: Tax rates as of December 31, 2003
Source: Tax Foundation, www.taxfoundation.org

State Tax Burdens

Area	Combined State and Local Tax Burden Percent	Rank	Combined Federal, State and Local Tax Burden Percent	Rank
Texas	8.3	47	28.4	31
U.S. Average	9.7	-	30.0	-

Note: Figures are for 2003
Source: Tax Foundation, www.taxfoundation.org

Internal Revenue Service Tax Audits

IRS District	Percent of Returns Audited 1996	1997	1998	1999	2000
North Texas	0.95	0.82	0.50	0.35	0.19
U.S.	0.66	0.61	0.46	0.31	0.20

Note: Figures cover IRS district audits of federal income tax returns filed by individuals. Geographic data on district audits for 2001 and 2002 are being withheld by the IRS. TRAC is challenging this policy.
Source: Syracuse University, Transactional Records Access Clearinghouse (TRAC), "Odds of IRS District Tax Audit 2000"

RESIDENTIAL REAL ESTATE

Building Permits

Area	Single-Family			Multi-Family			Total		
	2001	2002	Pct. Chg.	2001	2002	Pct. Chg.	2001	2002	Pct. Chg.
City	1,692	1,090	-35.6	0	0	-	1,692	1,090	-35.6
U.S.	1,235,600	1,332,600	7.9	401,100	415,100	3.5	1,636,700	1,747,700	6.8

Note: Figures represent new, privately-owned housing units authorized (unadjusted data)
Source: U.S. Census Bureau, Manufacturing, Mining, and Construction Statistics

Homeownership and Housing Vacancies

Area	Homeownership Rate[2] (%)			Rental Vacancy Rate[3] (%)			Homeowner Vacancy Rate[4] (%)		
	2001	2002[a]	2003	2001	2002[a]	2003	2001	2002[a]	2003
MSA[1]	62.8	61.1	63.1	6.5	11.6	12.4	2.0	1.4	2.0
U.S.	67.8	67.9	68.3	8.4	8.9	9.8	1.8	1.7	1.8

Note: (1) Metropolitan Statistical Area - see Appendix A for areas included; (2) The proportion of households that are owners; (3) The proportion of the rental inventory that is vacant for rent; (4) The proportion of the homeowner inventory that is vacant for sale; (a) 2002 figures have been revised; n/a not available
Source: U.S. Census Bureau, Housing Vacancies and Homeownership Annual Statistics: 2003

COMMERCIAL REAL ESTATE

Industrial/Office Markets

Type/Market Area	Inventory (sq. ft.)	Vacant (sq. ft.)	Vacancy Rate (%)	Under Construction (sq. ft.)	Net Absorption (sq. ft.)
Industrial Space					
Dallas	467,000,000	56,040,000	12.00	5,250,000	-1,455,000
Office Space					
Dallas	208,546,421	45,696,679	21.91	2,047,328	-3,916,225

Note: Data as of 4th Quarter, 2003; n/a not available
Source: Society of Industrial and Office Realtors, 2004 Comparative Statistics of Industrial and Office Real Estate Markets

COMMERCIAL UTILITIES

Typical Monthly Electric Bills

Area	Commercial Service ($/month)		Industrial Service ($/month)	
	3 kW demand 1,000 kWh	40 kW demand 14,000 kWh	1,000 kW demand 200,000 kWh	50,000 kW demand 15,000,000 kWh
City	114	1,271	n/a	n/a
Average[1]	100	1,134	17,850	1,045,117

Note: Based on rates in effect July 1, 2003; (1) average based on 197 utilities; n/a not available
Source: Edison Electric Institute, Typical Bills and Average Rates Report, Summer 2003

TRANSPORTATION

Means of Transportation to Work

Area	Car/Truck/Van		Public Transportation			Bicycle	Walked	Other Means	Worked at Home
	Drove Alone	Car-pooled	Bus	Subway	Railroad				
City	83.1	8.9	1.0	0.0	0.0	0.1	1.2	0.9	4.7
MSA[1]	77.6	14.3	2.1	0.1	0.1	0.1	1.5	1.0	3.1
U.S.	75.7	12.2	2.5	1.5	0.5	0.4	2.9	1.0	3.3

Note: Figures shown are percentages and cover workers 16 years of age and older;
(1) Metropolitan Statistical Area - see Appendix A for areas included
Source: Census 2000, Summary File 3

Travel Time to Work

Area	Less Than 15 Minutes	15 to 29 Minutes	30 to 44 Minutes	45 to 59 Minutes	60 Minutes or More
City	21.1	36.0	25.3	10.4	7.2
MSA[1]	22.0	35.0	24.7	10.4	7.9
U.S.	29.4	36.1	19.1	7.4	8.0

Note: Figures are percentages and include workers 16 years old and over; (1) Metropolitan Statistical Area - see Appendix A for areas included
Source: Census 2000, Summary File 3

Roadway Congestion Index

Area	1982	1990	1996	2000	2001
City	0.73	0.96	0.98	1.11	1.12
Average[1]	0.82	1.01	1.08	1.16	1.17

Note: Values greater than 1.00 indicate undesirable mobility levels; (1) average of 75 urban areas
Source: Texas Transportation Institute, The 2003 Annual Urban Mobility Report

Transportation Statistics

Interstate highways (2004)	I-20; I-30; I-35E; I-45
Public transportation (2002)	Dallas Area Rapid Transit (DART); First Transit Inc; Vancom
Buses	
Average fleet age in years	4.8; 7.2
No. operated in max. service	452; 265
Light rail	
Average fleet age in years	4.6; 13.9 (commuter rail)
No. operated in max. service	56; 17 (commuter rail)
Demand response	
Average fleet age in years	2.8 (2001)
No. operated in max. service	255 (2001)
Passenger air service	
Airport	Dallas-Ft. Worth International; Love Field
Airlines (2003)	37 (both airports)
Boardings (2002)	24,761,105; 2,815,907
Amtrak service (2004)	No
Major waterways/ports	None

Source: Federal Transit Administration, National Transit Database, 2002; Editor & Publisher Market Guide, 2004; Bureau of Transportation Statistics, Airport Enplanement Activity for CY2002; www.amtrak.com

BUSINESSES

Major Business Headquarters

Company Name	2003 Rankings	
	Fortune 500	Forbes 500
Electronic Data Systems	80	-
J.C. Penney	42	-

Note: Companies listed are located in the city; dashes indicate no ranking
Fortune 500: Companies that produce a 10-K are ranked 1 to 500 based on 2002 revenue
Forbes 500: Private companies are ranked 1 to 281 based on 2002 revenue
Source: Fortune, April 14, 2003; www.forbes.com, November 6, 2003

Fast-Growing Businesses

According to *Fortune*, Plano is home to one of America's 100 fastest-growing companies: **Denbury Resources**. Companies were ranked based on earnings-per-share growth, revenue growth and total return over the previous three years. Criteria for inclusion: public companies with sales of at least $50 million. Companies that lost money in the most recent quarter, or ended in the red for the past four quarters as a whole, were not eligible. Limited partnerships and REITs were also not considered. *Fortune, "America's Fastest-Growing Companies," September 1, 2003*

According to Deloitte & Touche LLP, Plano is home to two of North America's 500 fast-growing high-technology companies: **TECSys Development; True Automation Inc.** Companies are ranked by percentage growth in revenue over a five-year period. Criteria for inclusion: must be a U.S. or Canadian company developing and/or providing technology products or services; company must have been in business for five years with 1998 operating revenues of at least $50,000 USD or $75,000 CD and 2002 operating revenues of at least $1 million USD/CD. *Deloitte & Touche LLP, 2003 Technology Fast 500*

Women-Owned Firms: Number, Employment and Sales

Area	Number of Firms	Employ-ment	Sales ($000)	Rank[2]
MSA[1]	86,918	144,458	19,932,483	8

Note: (1) Metropolitan Statistical Area - see Appendix A for areas included;
(2) Calculated on an averaging of the number of businesses, employment, and sales
Source: The National Foundation for Women Business Owners, Women-Owned Businesses in the Top 50 Metropolitan Areas, 2002: A Fact Sheet

Women-Owned Firms: Growth

Area	Percent Change from 1997 to 2002			Rank[2]
	Number of Firms	Employ-ment	Sales	
MSA[1]	13.8	43.7	62.5	8
Top 50 MSAs	14.0	31.4	42.6	-

Note: (1) Metropolitan Statistical Area - see Appendix A for areas included; (2) Calculated on an averaging of the percent growth of number of businesses, employment, and sales
Source: The National Foundation for Women Business Owners, Women-Owned Businesses in the Top 50 Metropolitan Areas, 2002: A Fact Sheet

Minority and Women-Owned Businesses

Ownership	All Firms		Firms with Paid Employees			
	Firms	Sales ($000)	Firms	Sales ($000)	Employees	Payroll ($000)
Black	617	25,778	31	17,790	169	4,604
Hispanic	1,195	90,892	168	58,871	1,222	18,563
Women	5,229	344,813	449	242,598	3,075	51,835

Note: Figures cover firms located in the city
Source: 1997 Economic Census, Minority and Women-Owned Businesses

Minority Business Opportunity

Plano is home to one company which is on the Black Enterprise Auto Dealer 100 list (100 largest dealers based on gross sales): **Stephens Automotive Group**. Criteria: company must be operational in previous calendar year and at least 51% black-owned. *Black Enterprise, www.blackenterprise.com, B.E. 100s, 2003 Report*

Two of the 500 largest Hispanic-owned companies in the U.S. are located in Plano. *Hispanic Business, June 2003*

HOTELS

Hotels/Motels

Area	Hotels/Motels	Average Minimum Rates ($)		
		Tourist	First-Class	Deluxe
City	27	62	64	n/a

Note: n/a not available
Source: OAG Travel Planner Online, Spring 2004

EVENT SITES

Major Event Sites, Meeting Places and Convention Centers

Name	Guest Rooms	Exhibit/ Meeting Space (sq. ft.)	Largest Meeting Room Capacity
Doubletree Hotel & Conf. Ctr.	404	24,108	1,900
Harvey Hotel Plano	279	5,252	700
Holiday Inn Dallas Plano	160	7,000	600
Plano Centre	n/a	n/a	n/a

Note: n/a not available
Source: Original research

Living Environment

COST OF LIVING

Cost of Living Index

Year	Composite Index	Groceries	Housing	Utilities	Trans-portation	Health Care	Misc. Goods/Services
2001	102.3	99.6	103.1	103.9	111.4	114.1	98.0
2002	97.0	96.2	91.8	93.3	112.0	109.5	96.2
2003	97.6	89.9	91.1	102.3	109.3	105.3	100.8

Note: U.S. = 100
Source: ACCRA, Cost of Living Index, 2001, 2002 and 2003 4-Quarter Averages

HOUSING

House Price Index (HPI)

Area	National Ranking[2]	Quarterly Change (%)	One-Year Change (%)	Five-Year Change (%)
MSA[1]	212	0.67	2.10	26.76
U.S.[3]	-	3.67	7.97	41.81

Note: The HPI is a weighted repeat sales index. It measures average price changes in repeat sales or refinancings on the same properties. This information is obtained by reviewing repeat mortgage transactions on single-family properties whose mortgages have been purchased or securitized by Fannie Mae of Freddie Mac in January 1975; (1) Metropolitan Statistical Area - see Appendix A for areas included; (2) Rankings are based on annual percentage change, for all MSAs containing at least 15,000 transactions over the last 10 years and ranges from 1 to 220; (3) figures based on a weighted division average; all figures are for the period ended December 31, 2003
Source: Office of Federal Housing Enterprise Oversight, House Price Index, March 1, 2004

Housing: Year Structure Built

Area	1990-2000	1980-1989	1970-1979	1960-1969	1950-1959	1940-1949	Before 1940	Median Year
City	47.2	27.6	19.7	4.2	0.7	0.3	0.2	1989
MSA[1]	23.9	24.7	20.2	13.7	9.8	4.0	3.7	1979
U.S.	17.0	15.8	18.5	13.7	12.7	7.3	15.0	1971

Note: Figures are percentages; (1) Metropolitan Statistical Area - see Appendix A for areas included
Source: Census 2000, Summary File 3

Average New Home Price

Area	2001	2002	2003
City	197,163	195,125	196,636
U.S.	212,643	236,567	248,193

Note: Figures, in dollars, are based on a new home with 2,400 sq. ft. of living area on an 8,000 sq. ft. lot.
Source: ACCRA, Cost of Living Index, 2001, 2002 and 2003 4-Quarter Averages

Average Apartment Rent

Area	2001	2002	2003
City	979	926	963
U.S.	674	708	721

Note: Figures, in dollars per month, are based on an unfurnished two bedroom, 1-1/2 or 2 bath apartment, approximately 950 sq. ft. in size, excluding all utilities except water
Source: ACCRA, Cost of Living Index, 2001, 2002 and 2003 4-Quarter Averages

RESIDENTIAL UTILITIES

Average Residential Utility Costs

Area	All Electric ($/mth)	Part Electric ($/mth)	Other Energy ($/mth)	Phone ($/mth)
City	–	92.58	32.46	25.32
U.S.	116.46	65.82	62.68	23.90

Source: ACCRA, Cost of Living Index, 2003 4-Quarter Average

HEALTH CARE

Average Health Care Costs

Area	Hospital ($/day)	Doctor ($/visit)	Dentist ($/visit)
City	604.50	79.85	89.00
U.S.	678.35	67.91	83.90

Note: Hospital—based on a semi-private room; Doctor—based on a general practitioner's routine exam of an established patient; Dentist—based on adult teeth cleaning and periodic oral exam.
Source: ACCRA, Cost of Living Index, 2003 4-Quarter Average

Distribution of Non-Federal, Office-Based Physicians

Area	Total	Family/ General Practice	Specialties		
			Medical	Surgical	Other
CMSA[3] (number)	7,867	989	2,601	2,050	2,227
CMSA[3] (rate per 10,000 pop.)	15.1	1.9	5.0	3.9	4.3
Metro Average[2] (rate per 10,000 pop.)	33.1	2.2	7.7	4.8	5.6

Note: Data as of December 31, 2001; (1) Metropolitan Statistical Area - see Appendix A for areas included; (2) Average of 81 MSAs and CMSAs in this book; (3) Dallas-Fort Worth, TX Consolidated Metropolitan Statistical Area includes the following counties: Collin; Dallas; Denton; Ellis; Henderson; Hood; Hunt; Johnson; Kaufman; Parker; Rockwall; Tarrant
Source: American Medical Association, Physician Characteristics & Distribution in the U.S., 2003-2004

Hospitals

Plano has the following hospitals: 2 general medical and surgical; 1 rehabilitation.
AHA Guide to the Healthcare Field, 2003-2004

PRESIDENTIAL ELECTION

2000 Presidential Election Results

Area	Gore	Bush	Nader	Buchanan	Other
Collin County	24.4	73.1	1.8	0.2	0.5
U.S.	48.4	47.9	2.7	0.4	0.6

Note: Results are percentages and may not add to 100% due to rounding
Source: www.cbsnews.com; www.uselectionatlas.org

EDUCATION

Public School District Statistics

District Name	Schls.	Enroll- ment	Classroom Teachers	Pupil/ Teacher Ratio	Minority Pupils[1] (%)	Current Expend.[2] ($/pupil)
Plano ISD	64	49,091	3,528	13.9	30.8	6,395

Note: Data covers the 2001-02 school year unless otherwise noted; (1) Fall 2000; (2) FY2000; n/a not available
Source: U.S. Department of Education, National Center for Education Statistics, Common Core of Data, Local Education Agency (School District) Universe Survey; School Year 2001-2002; U.S. Department of Education, National Center for Education Statistics, Digest of Education Statistics 2002

Educational Quality

School District	Education Quotient[1]	Graduate Outcome[2]	Community Index[3]	Resource Index[4]
Plano ISD	94	92	94	64

Note: Scores are national percentile rankings and range from 1 (worst) to 99 (best); (1) Combination of the Graduate Outcome, Community and Resource indexes weighted to reflect the greater importance of the Graduate Outcome and Resource Index; (2) Based on graduation rates and college board scores (SAT/ACT); (3) Based on the surrounding community's level of affluence and adult education; (4) Based on teacher salaries, per-pupil expenditures and student-teacher ratios.
Source: Expansion Management, December 2003

Educational Attainment by Race

Area	High School Graduate (%)					Bachelor's Degree (%)				
	Total	White	Black	Asian	Hisp.[2]	Total	White	Black	Asian	Hisp.[2]
City	93.9	95.7	92.8	94.3	63.3	53.3	53.0	46.1	72.6	24.7
MSA[1]	79.4	84.4	78.9	83.4	41.5	30.0	34.0	18.5	52.2	8.7
U.S.	80.4	83.6	72.3	80.4	52.4	24.4	26.1	14.3	44.1	10.4

Note: Figures shown cover persons 25 years old and over; (1) Metropolitan Statistical Area - see Appendix A for areas included; (2) people of Hispanic origin can be of any race
Source: Census 2000, Summary File 3

School Enrollment by Type

Area	Grades KG to 8				Grades 9 to 12			
	Public		Private		Public		Private	
	Enrollment	%	Enrollment	%	Enrollment	%	Enrollment	%
City	28,544	88.8	3,606	11.2	11,760	93.6	799	6.4
MSA[1]	456,971	90.7	46,953	9.3	181,249	92.2	15,405	7.8
U.S.	33,526,011	88.7	4,285,121	11.3	14,848,628	90.6	1,532,323	9.4

Note: Figures shown cover persons 3 years old and over; (1) Metropolitan Statistical Area - see Appendix A for areas included
Source: Census 2000, Summary File 3

School Enrollment by Race

Area	Grades KG to 8 (%)				Grades 9 to 12 (%)			
	White	Black	Asian	Hisp.[1]	White	Black	Asian	Hisp.[1]
City	75.6	5.6	11.0	11.1	77.2	5.9	9.7	10.7
MSA[2]	60.7	18.0	3.6	28.9	61.2	18.7	4.0	25.8
U.S.	68.5	15.5	3.3	16.8	68.8	15.5	3.8	15.7

Note: Figures shown cover persons 3 years old and over; (1) people of Hispanic origin can be of any race; (2) Metropolitan Statistical Area - see Appendix A for areas included
Source: Census 2000, Summary File 3

Classroom Teacher Salaries in Public Schools

District	B.A. Degree		M.A. Degree		Maximum	
	Min. ($)	Rank[1]	Max. ($)	Rank[1]	Max. ($)	Rank[1]
City	n/a	n/a	n/a	n/a	n/a	n/a
DOD Average[2]	31,567	-	53,248	-	59,356	-

Note: Salaries are for 2001-2002; (1) Rank ranges from 1 to 100; (2) As per the U.S. Department of Defense Wage Fixing Authority
Source: American Federation of Teachers, Survey & Analysis of Teacher Salary Trends 2002

Higher Education

Four-Year Colleges			Two-Year Colleges			Medical Schools	Law Schools	Voc/Tech
Public	Private Non-profit	Private For-profit	Public	Private Non-profit	Private For-profit			
0	0	0	0	0	0	0	0	2

Note: Figures cover institutions located within the city limits.
Source: National Center for Education Statistics, The Integrated Postsecondary Education System (IPEDS) Peer Analysis System, 2002; usnews.com, America's Best Graduate Schools 2004, Medical School Directory; The College Blue Book, Occupational Education, 2003; Barron's Guide to Law Schools, 2003; Medical School Admission Requirements U.S. & Canada, 2003-2004

**MAJOR
EMPLOYERS**

Major Employers

Company Name	Industry	Type
A M R Corporation	Air transportation, scheduled	Headquarters
Accountemps	Employment agencies	Branch
Alcatel USA Inc	Telephone and telegraph apparatus	Branch
Bank of America	National commercial banks	Branch
Baylor University Medical Ctr	General medical and surgical hospitals	Headquarters
EDS	Data processing and preparation	Headquarters
GTE	Business services, nec	Single
JCP Publications Corp	Miscellaneous publishing	Headquarters
National Elec Contrs Assn	Insurance agents, brokers, and service	Headquarters
Nortel Networks Inc	General warehousing and storage	Branch
Parkland Health & Hospital Sys	General medical and surgical hospitals	Headquarters
Pcj Realty Two Inc	Real estate agents and managers	Single
Raytheon	Search and navigation equipment	Branch
Southwestern Medical School	Colleges and universities	Headquarters
Texas A & M Univ - Commerce	Public relations services	Branch
Texas Instruments	Semiconductors and related devices	Headquarters
UT Sothwstern Mdcal- Trnsplnts	Offices and clinics of medical doctors	Branch
Worldcom	Telephone communication, except radio	Branch

Note: Companies shown are located in the metropolitan area and have 3,500 or more employees.
Source: www.zapdata.com, March 2004

PUBLIC SAFETY

Crime Rate

Area	All Crimes	Violent Crimes				Property Crimes		
		Murder	Forcible Rape	Robbery	Aggrav. Assault	Burglary	Larceny -Theft	Motor Vehicle Theft
City	3,889.4	2.6	17.2	62.5	206.1	571.8	2,804.9	224.2
Suburbs[1]	6,013.3	8.1	38.7	286.8	375.4	1,129.0	3,387.9	787.4
MSA[2]	5,879.3	7.8	37.4	272.6	364.7	1,093.9	3,351.1	751.9
U.S.	4,118.8	5.6	33.0	145.9	310.1	746.2	2,445.8	432.1

Note: Figures are crimes per 100,000 population; (1) All areas within the MSA that are located outside the city limits; (2) Metropolitan Statistical Area - see Appendix A for areas included
Source: FBI Uniform Crime Reports, 2002

RECREATION

Culture and Recreation

Museums	Orchestras	Opera Companies	Dance Companies	Professional Theatres	Zoos	Pro Sports Teams[1]
1	0	0	0	0	0	3

Note: (1) Covers the Metropolitan Statistical Area - see Appendix A for areas included.
Source: The Grey House Performing Arts Directory, 2002; Official Museum Directory, 2004; www.sportsvenues.com

Library System

The Plano Public Library System has six branches, holdings of 612,451 volumes, and a budget of $10,124,852 (2001-2002).
American Library Directory, 2003-2004

MEDIA

Newspapers

Name	Type	Freq.	Distribution	Circulation
Plano Star Courier	Hispanic	5x/wk	State	12,909

Note: Includes newspapers whose offices are located in the city and whose circulations are 500 or more
Source: Burrelle's Media Directory, 2003

Television Stations

Name	Ch.	Affiliation	Type	Owner
KDTN	2	PBS	Non-comm.	North Texas Public Broadcasting Inc.
KDFW	4	FBC	Commercial	Fox Television Stations Inc.
WFAA	8	ABCT	Commercial	Belo Corporation
KTVT	11	CBST	Commercial	CBS
KERA	13	PBS	Public	North Texas Public Broadcasting Inc.
KUVN	23	UNIN	Commercial	Perenchio Television Inc.
KDFI	27	FBC	Commercial	Fox Television Stations Inc.
KDAF	33	WB	Commercial	Tribune Broadcasting Company
KXTX	39	TMUN	Commercial	Telemundo Group Inc.
KSTR	49	UNIN	Commercial	Univision Television Group

Note: Stations included broadcast from the Dallas metro area; n/a not available
Source: Burrelle's Media Directory, 2003

AM Radio Stations

Call Letters	Freq. (kHz)	Target Audience	Station Format	Music Format
KLIF	570	Men	N/T	n/a
KMKI	620	General	M	Oldies
KKLF	950	General	N/T	n/a
KHVN	970	Christian	M	Christian
KBIS	1150	Hispanic	M/N/T	Latin
KESS	1270	Hispanic	M/N/T	Latin
KTCK	1310	General	M/S/T	Top 40
KAHZ	1360	Hispanic	E/M/N/S/T	80's
KDXX	1480	Hispanic	M/N/T	Latin
KZMP	1540	Hispanic	M	Adult Contemporary
KRVA	1600	Hispanic	M/N/T	Latin
KTBK	1700	General	M/S	Classic Rock

Note: Stations included broadcast from the Dallas metro area; n/a not available
The following abbreviations may be used:
Target Audience: A=Asian; B=Black; C=Christian; E=Ethnic; F=French; G=General; H=Hispanic; M=Men; N=Native American; R=Religious; S=Senior Citizen; W=Women; Y=Young Adult; Z=Children
Station Format: E=Educational; M=Music; N=News; S=Sports; T=Talk
Source: Burrelle's Media Directory, 2003

FM Radio Stations

Call Letters	Freq. (mHz)	Target Audience	Station Format	Music Format
KMQX	89.1	General	E/M/T	Christian
KNON	89.3	B/H	E/M/N/T	Adult Standards
KTPW	89.7	Christian	M	Christian
KERA	90.1	General	M/N/T	Alternative
KVTT	91.7	Religious	E/M/T	Christian
KDBN	93.3	General	M/N/T	Classic Rock
KLNO	94.1	Hispanic	M	Latin
KSOC	94.5	General	M/N/T	Adult Contemporary
KHYI	95.3	General	M/S	Country
KEGL	97.1	General	M/N/S/T	Modern Rock
KBFB	97.9	General	M	Rhythm & Blues
KLUV	98.7	General	M/N/T	Oldies
KHCK	99.1	Hispanic	M	Latin
KPLX	99.5	General	M	Country
KRBV	100.3	General	M	Top 40
WRR	101.1	General	M/N/T	Classical
KZMP	101.7	Hispanic	M	Adult Contemporary
KDMX	102.9	Women	M/N/T	Adult Contemporary
KVIL	103.7	General	M	Adult Contemporary
KTCY	104.9	H/R	M/N/T	Christian
KYNG	105.3	General	M/T	80's
KHKS	106.1	General	M/N/T	Top 40
KDXT	106.7	Hispanic	M/N	Latin
KRVA	106.9	Hispanic	M/N/T	Latin
KRVF	107.1	Hispanic	M/N/S	Latin
KOAI	107.5	General	M/T	Adult Standards
KDXX	107.9	Hispanic	M/N/T	Latin

Note: Stations included broadcast from the Dallas metro area
The following abbreviations may be used:
Target Audience: A=Asian; B=Black; C=Christian; E=Ethnic; F=French; G=General; H=Hispanic;
M=Men; N=Native American; R=Religious; S=Senior Citizen; W=Women; Y=Young Adult; Z=Children
Station Format: E=Educational; M=Music; N=News; S=Sports; T=Talk
Music Format: AOR=Album Oriented Rock; MOR=Middle of the Road
Source: Burrelle's Media Directory, 2003

CLIMATE

Average and Extreme Temperatures

Temperature	Jan	Feb	Mar	Apr	May	Jun	Jul	Aug	Sep	Oct	Nov	Dec	Yr.
Extreme High (°F)	85	90	100	100	101	112	111	109	107	101	91	87	112
Average High (°F)	55	60	68	76	84	92	96	96	89	79	67	58	77
Average Temp. (°F)	45	50	57	66	74	82	86	86	79	68	56	48	67
Average Low (°F)	35	39	47	56	64	72	76	75	68	57	46	38	56
Extreme Low (°F)	-2	9	12	30	39	53	58	58	42	24	16	0	-2

Note: Figures cover the years 1945-1993
Source: National Climatic Data Center, International Station Meteorological Climate Summary, 9/96

Average Precipitation/Snowfall/Humidity

Precip./Humidity	Jan	Feb	Mar	Apr	May	Jun	Jul	Aug	Sep	Oct	Nov	Dec	Yr.
Avg. Precip. (in.)	1.9	2.3	2.6	3.8	4.9	3.4	2.1	2.3	2.9	3.3	2.3	2.1	33.9
Avg. Snowfall (in.)	1	1	Tr	Tr	0	0	0	0	0	Tr	Tr	Tr	3
Avg. Rel. Hum. 6am (%)	78	77	75	77	82	81	77	76	80	79	78	77	78
Avg. Rel. Hum. 3pm (%)	53	51	47	49	51	48	43	41	46	46	48	51	48

Note: Figures cover the years 1945-1993; Tr = Trace amounts (<0.05 in. of rain; <0.5 in. of snow)
Source: National Climatic Data Center, International Station Meteorological Climate Summary, 9/96

Weather Conditions

Temperature			Daytime Sky			Precipitation		
10°F & below	32°F & below	90°F & above	Clear	Partly cloudy	Cloudy	0.01 inch or more precip.	0.1 inch or more snow/ice	Thunder-storms
1	34	102	108	160	97	78	2	49

Note: Figures are average number of days per year and covers the years 1945-1993
Source: National Climatic Data Center, International Station Meteorological Climate Summary, 9/96

HAZARDOUS WASTE

Superfund Sites

Plano has no sites on the EPA's Superfund National Priorities List.
U.S. Environmental Protection Agency, National Priorities List, March 15, 2004

AIR & WATER QUALITY

Maximum Pollutant Concentrations

	Particulate Matter (ug/m^3)	Carbon Monoxide (ppm)	Sulfur Dioxide (ppm)	Nitrogen Dioxide (ppm)	Ozone 1-hour (ppm)	Ozone 8-hour (ppm)	Lead (ug/m^3)
MSA[1] Level	62	2	0.016	0.018	0.13	0.1	0.48a
NAAQS[2]	150	9	0.140	0.053	0.12	0.08	1.50
Met NAAQS[2]	Yes	Yes	Yes	Yes	No	No	Yes

Note: (1) Metropolitan Statistical Area - see Appendix A for areas included; (2) National Ambient Air Quality Standards; n/a not available; (a) Localized impact from an industrial source in Dallas. Concentration from highest nonpoint source site is 0.11 ug/m^3 in Collin County)
Units: ppm = parts per million; ug/m^3 = micrograms per cubic meter
Source: EPA, Latest Findings on National Air Quality: 2002 Status and Trends, August 2003

Air Quality Index

In the Dallas MSA (see Appendix A for areas included), the Air Quality Index (AQI) exceeded 100 on 22 days in 2002. An AQI value greater than 100 indicates that air quality would have been in the unhealthful range on that day.
EPA, Latest Findings on National Air Quality: 2002 Status and Trends, August 2003

Watershed Health

The U.S. Environmental Protection Agency monitors the health of the aquatic resources for the nation's 2,000+ watersheds. **The Upper Trinity watershed serves the Plano area and received an overall Index of Watershed Indicators (IWI) score of 5 (more serious problems - low vulnerability).** The IWI score is based on seven condition and nine vulnerability indicators. The overall IWI score ranges from 1 (best health) to 6 (worst health). The Condition Indicators include: designated use attainment, fish and wildlife consumption advisories, source water condition, contaminated sediments, ambient water quality, and wetlands loss index. The Vulnerability Indicators include: aquatic species at risk, conventional and toxic loads over permitted limits, urban and agricultural runoff potential, population change, hydrologic modification, estuarine pollution susceptibility, and air deposition. *EPA, Index of Watershed Indicators, October 26, 2001*

Drinking Water

Water System Name	Pop. Served	Primary Water Source Type	Number of Violations January 2002-February 2004		
			Health Based	Significant Monitoring	Monitoring
City of Plano	237,000	Purchased surface	None	None	None

Note: Data as of February 19, 2004
Source: EPA, Office of Ground Water and Drinking Water, Safe Drinking Water Information System

Plano tap water is alkaline, soft and fluoridated.
Editor & Publisher Market Guide, 2004

Saint Petersburg, Florida

Background

St. Petersburg, located in Pinellas County in western Florida, is the state's fourth-largest city, offering Gulf beaches, a vibrant economy, major league baseball, and a host of year-round recreational resources. The city is also a regional economic power with a thriving business environment built on retailing, high-tech manufacturing, finance, and insurance. Major employers in the area include the Pinellas County School District and Pinellas County Government, the City of St. Petersburg, and the Home Shopping Club. Recently, the professional Women's Tennis Association's world headquarters was consolidated in the city, while numerous residential projects are underway.

During the age of exploration in the sixteenth-century, St. Petersburg was visited by a distinguished group of Spanish adventurers and colonialists, including Juan Ponce de Leon in 1521, who thought the mythical Fountain of Youth might be nearby. Panfilo de Narvaez, a Spanish governor of Florida (1528), also visited, as did the energetic Hernando de Soto (1539).

Actual European settlements, however, were not established until much later. In 1843, Antonio Maximo set up a fishing village at what is now called Maximo Point, and the first house was built in 1856 by the rancher James Hay in what are now the St. Petersburg city limits. Settlement accelerated rapidly after this time, and even more so after 1881, when Hamilton Disston sparked St. Pete's first real-estate explosion by purchasing four million acres of land from the state of Florida. Disston built the first hotel and went to great lengths to popularize the town up and down the Eastern seaboard. The same was done by the railroad magnate Peter Demens, born Piotr Alexeitch Dementieff in St. Petersburg, Russia, who gave the city its present name.

Tourist excursions began in 1890, when the Orange Belt Railroad opened a link to St. Petersburg, carrying great stores of mackerel and snapper to Eastern cities. By the end of the century, millions of pounds of fish were being shipped annually. Since 1914, when the city was chosen by the St. Louis Browns as a spring training site, St. Petersburg has gone from strength to strength as a major U.S. sports capital. It is home to the Tampa Bay Devil Rays baseball team, the Tampa Bay Buccaneers, the Tampa Bay Mutiny, the Tampa Bay Lightning, and the Tampa Bay Storm.

Tropicana Field recently underwent a $62 million renovation for the inaugural season of the Tampa Bay Devil Rays, the pro baseball team. The domed facility has a 44,000-seat capacity and offers 65 luxury skyboxes. Florida Power Park, Home of Al Lang Field, is the Devil Rays' spring training facility and added 200 seats, a new rotunda entrance and concession stands.

The city has also hosted the X-Games, is the site of the annual St. Anthony's Triathlon, attended by athletes from all over the world, and manages the First America Running Festival.

Other sporting opportunities are available at 40 local golf courses, at marinas where deep-sea fishing trips originate daily, and at horse and greyhound tracks. The city parks are spread over 2,400 acres, including the seven-mile preserved downtown waterfront, and St. Petersburg boasts the longest urban hiking/biking trail in the Eastern U.S.—47 miles. There are five beaches, eight Public pools, and many tennis, racquetball and handball courts.

Cultural life is vibrant in the area, with the Florida International Museum a premier venue for world-class exhibitions, and the Salvador Dali Museum featuring the world's largest collection of the artist's works. The Museum of Fine Arts offers many works by Cezanne, Monet, Gauguin, Renoir, Rodin, George Wesley Bellows, and Georgia O'Keeffe.

Great Explorations, which has been called by the Miami Herald the most "user-friendly museum of its kind in the country," offers ever-changing arts and science exhibits. At the St. Petersburg Museum of History, one can see a splendid exhibit that explains the beginnings of commercial aviation, which began in this city in 1914. Finally, the Florida Holocaust Museum presents important exhibits from around the world.

The weather is subtropical, with only four days a year on average without sunshine. Daytime temperatures are quite pleasant and mild.

Rankings

- Tampa-St. Petersburg was ranked #48 out of 331 metro areas in *Cities Ranked & Rated.* Criteria: cost of living; climate; crime; transportation; economy and jobs; education; arts and culture; health and healthcare; leisure. *Cities Ranked & Rated, 1st Edition, 2004*

- *Ladies Home Journal* ranked America's 200 largest cities based on the qualities women surveyed care about most. Saint Petersburg ranked #129 out of 143 in the smaller city category (population under 300,000). Criteria: crime; lifestyle; education; jobs; health; child care; politics; and the economy. *Ladies Home Journal Online, "The Best Cities for Women 2002"*

- Saint Petersburg was selected as one of "America's Pet Healthiest Cities" by Purina. The city ranked #24 out of 50. Criteria: veterinary services; environment; and legislation. *Purina Pet Institute, "America's Pet Healthiest Cities," August 14, 2001*

- *Forbes* ranked the 40 most populous metro areas in the U.S. in terms of the best places to be single. The Tampa-St. Petersburg metro area was ranked #27. Criteria: number of other singles; cost of living alone; nightlife; culture; job growth; coolness. *Forbes, June 5, 2003*

- *Forbes* ranked the 150 most populous metro areas in the U.S. in terms of the "Best Places for Business and Careers." The Tampa-St. Petersburg metro area was ranked #91. Criteria: income and job growth; cost-of-doing-business; qualifications of the available pool of labor; crime rates; housing costs; net migration. *Forbes, May 9, 2003*

- *Men's Health* ranked 101 U.S. cities in terms of the quality of their tap water. Saint Petersburg received a grade of B. Criteria: levels of bacteria, arsenic, lead, trihalomethanes, and haloacetic acids were compared with the National Academy of Science's guidelines as well as with the EPA's more stringent maximum contaminant level goals. *Men's Health, March 2004*

- Sperling's BestPlaces ranked 331 metro areas and identified the most and least stressful U.S. cities. The Tampa-St. Petersburg metro area ranked #27 out of the 100 largest metro areas (#1 = most stressful). Criteria: divorce rate; unemployment rate; violent and property crime; suicide rate; commute time; mental health; alcohol consumption; cloudy days. *www.BestPlaces.net, February 26, 2004*

- Sperling's BestPlaces in partnership with Pep Boys ranked 77 metro areas and identified "America's Most Drivable Cities." The Tampa-St. Petersburg metro area ranked #21. Criteria: climate; road roughness; urban mobility; gas prices. *Pep Boys, "America's Most Drivable Cities," April 9, 2003*

- Tampa-St. Petersburg was ranked #149 out of America's 200 largest metro areas in *SELF Magazine's* ranking of "America's Healthiest Cities for Women." Criteria: safety; air/water quality; cancer rates; and 21 other factors relating to health. *SELF Magazine, November 2003*

- Tampa-St. Petersburg was identified as an asthma "hot spot" where high prevalence makes the condition a key issue and environmental "triggers" and other factors can make living with asthma a particular challenge. The area ranked #22 out of the nations 100 largest metro areas. Criteria: local asthma prevalence and mortality data; pollen scores; air pollution; asthma prescriptions; smoking laws; number of asthma specialists. *GlaxoSmithKline, October 29, 2002*

- Tampa-St. Petersburg was identified as one of the most dangerous large metro areas for pedestrians in the U.S. The area ranked #2 out of the nations 49 largest metro areas. Criteria: average yearly pedestrian fatalities per capita (for the years 2000 and 2001) adjusted for the number of walkers. *Surface Transportation Policy Project, "Mean Streets 2002"*

- Saint Petersburg was ranked #19 out of 100 cities surveyed in *Child* magazine's ranking of the "Best Cities for Families." Criteria: number of pediatricians per capita; proximity to a children's hospital; immunization rates; infant mortality rate; air quality; water quality; school spending; pupil-teacher ratio; availability of parks/green space; nearby recreational opportunities; average commute time; number of sunny days; average cost of a 3-bedroom home; unemployment rate; future job growth; crime rate; percentage of children under 5; mandated minimum child care ratios. *Child, April 2001*

- *Zero Population Growth* ranked 239 cities in terms of children's health, safety, and economic well-being. Saint Petersburg was ranked #132 out of 140 independent cities (cities with populations greater than 100,000 which were neither major cities nor suburbs/outer cities) and was given a grade of C-. Criteria: total population and population growth; percent of population under 18 years of age; number of children's museums; health improvement grade; percent of births to teens; percent of low birthweight infants; infant mortality rate; number of Title X-funded clinics; average SAT/ACT scores; average elementary and secondary class size; crime rate; unemployment rate; percent of affordable homes; number of bad air days; park acres per 1000 persons; library circulation per child; and children's program attendance counts. *Zero Population Growth, Kid Friendly Cities Report Card 2001*

- *Ladies Home Journal* ranked America's 200 largest cities in terms of safety. Saint Petersburg ranked #183 out of 200. Criteria: violent crimes; crimes against property; and rape. *Ladies Home Journal Online, "The Best Cities for Women 2002"*

- Tampa-St. Petersburg was ranked #38 out of 268 metro areas in terms of its Creativity Index. The Creativity Index is a mix of four equally weighted factors: the Creative Class (scientists, engineers, architects, designers, writers, artists, musicians, or any profession where creativity is a key factor) share of the workforce; innovation, measured as patents per capita; high-tech industry, using the Milken Institute's Tech Pole Index; and diversity, measured by the Gay Index (a reasonable proxy for an areas' openness to different kinds of people and ideas). *The Rise of the Creative Class, 2002*

- Tampa-St. Petersburg was ranked #45 out of 125 regions worldwide in terms of its "Knowledge Competitiveness Index." The index attempts to measure the knowledge-based development taking place throughout the world and is based on 17 measures of economic performance that indicate a region's ability to translate its knowledge capacity into economic value. *Robert Huggins Associates, "2003-2004 World Knowledge Competitiveness Index"*

- The Tampa-St. Petersburg metro area was selected by *Yahoo! Internet Life* as one of "America's Most Wired Cities...and Towns." The area ranked #37 out of 87. Criteria: home and work net use; user sophistication; domain density; and available content. *Yahoo! Internet Life, April 2001*

- Tampa-St. Petersburg was identified as one of the 100 "Most Unwired Cities" in the U.S. The area ranked #55. Criteria: number of public and commercial wireless access points; cell phone coverage offering wide area network Internet access; Internet penetration. *Intel, "Most Unwired Cities," March 4, 2003*

- Scarborough Research measured the percentage of households who subscribe to cellular services among adults ages 18 and over in 75 U.S. markets. The Tampa-St. Petersburg DMA (Designated Market Area) was ranked #46 out of 75. *Scarborough Research, Scarborough USA+ 2003 Release 1*

- The Tampa-St. Petersburg metro area was selected as one of "America's 50 Hottest Cities for Business Relocations and Expansions." The area ranked #26. Criteria: 70 of the industry's most prominent site selection consultants were asked which cities their clients found the most attractive when it came to selecting an expansion or relocation site in 2003. *Expansion Management, January 2004*

- The Tampa-St. Petersburg metro area was selected as one of the "Top 60 CyberCities in America" by *Site Selection*. CyberCities are magnets for growing high-tech companies. Criteria: total employment; average wages; total payroll; number of companies; R&D spending and venture capital in the 45 Standard Industrial Classification (SIC) codes that define the high-technology industry. *Site Selection, March 2002*

- The Tampa-St. Petersburg metro area was cited as one of "The Best Places in the U.S. to Locate a Company." The area ranked #99 out of 329. Criteria: education (with emphasis on college board test results and high school graduation rates); availability of quality healthcare services and the cost to employers; quality of life; logistics workforce and companies; transportation infrastructure; quality and quantity of highly educated technical workers; business climate. *Expansion Management, July 2003*

- The Tampa-St. Petersburg metro area was selected as one of the "Top 40 Hottest Real Estate Markets" for expanding or relocating businesses." Criteria: rental costs; purchase prices; and vacancy rates of office and warehouse space. *Expansion Management, August 2003*

- The Tampa-St. Petersburg metro area appeared on *Forbes/Milken Institute* list of "Best Places for Business and Career." Rank: #25 out of 200 metro areas. Criteria: salary growth; job growth; number of technology clusters; overall concentration of technology activity relative to national average; and technology output growth. *www.forbes.com, Forbes/Milken Institute Best Places 2002*

- The Tampa-St. Petersburg metro area appeared on the "Milken Institute Best Performing Cities" index. Rank: #27 out of 200 large metro areas. Criteria: job growth; wage and salary growth; high-tech output growth. *Milken Institute, June 25, 2003*

- The Tampa-St. Petersburg metro area appeared on *Entrepreneur* magazine's list of the "Best Cities for Entrepreneurs" in 2003. The area ranked #25 out of 61 in the large city category. Criteria: entrepreneurial activity; small-business growth; economic growth; and risk. *www.Entrepreneur.com*

- The Tampa-St. Petersburg metro area was selected as one of the "Top 25 Cities for Doing Business in America." *Inc.* measured current-year employment growth in 277 regions as well as current trends in the annual average growth over the past three years, and compared employment expansion between the first and second halves of the last decade. Job growth factors account for two-thirds, and balance among industries accounts for one third of the final score for each city.The Tampa-St. Petersburg metro area ranked #14 among large metro areas. *Inc. Magazine, March 2004*

- The Tampa-St. Petersburg metro area appeared on *IndustryWeek's* fourth annual World-Class Communities list. It ranked #220 out of 315 metro areas. Criteria: MSA Gross Metropolitan Product (GMP) per manufacturing employee; and MSA percent share of U.S. manufacturing Gross Domestic Product (GDP). *IndustryWeek, April 16, 2001*

- ING Group ranked the 125 largest metro areas according to the general financial security of residents. The Tampa-St. Petersburg metro area was ranked #80 out of 125. Criteria: Earnings and Wealth Potential (household income, education, net assets, cost of living); Safety Net (health insurance, retirement savings, life insurance, income support programs); Personal Threats (unemployment rate, low-income households, crime rate); Community Economic Vitality (cost of community services, job quality, job creation, housing costs). *ING Group, "The Best Cities to Earn and Save Money: A Ranking of the Largest 125 U.S. Cities," 2001 Edition*

Business Environment

CITY FINANCES

City Government Finances

Component	2000-2001 ($000)	2000-2001 ($ per capita)
Total Revenues	432,219	1,741
Total Expenditures	369,758	1,490
Debt Outstanding	535,025	2,155
Cash and Securities	1,106,274	4,457

Source: U.S Census Bureau, Government Finances 2000-2001, August 2003

City Government Revenue by Source

Source	2000-2001 ($000)	2000-2001 ($ per capita)
General Revenue		
From Federal Government	1,827	7
From State Government	28,040	113
From Local Governments	31,598	127
Taxes		
Property	56,552	228
Sales	46,747	188
Personal Income	0	0
License	0	0
Charges	112,036	451
Liquor Store	0	0
Utility	28,331	114
Employee Retirement	69,374	279
Other	57,714	233

Source: U.S Census Bureau, Government Finances 2000-2001, August 2003

City Government Expenditures by Function

Function	2000-2001 ($000)	2000-2001 ($ per capita)	2000-2001 (%)
General Expenditures			
Airports	2,506	10	0.7
Corrections	0	0	0.0
Education	0	0	0.0
Fire Protection	22,822	92	6.2
Governmental Administration	12,370	50	3.3
Health	5,714	23	1.5
Highways	34,894	141	9.4
Hospitals	0	0	0.0
Housing and Community Development	4,137	17	1.1
Interest on General Debt	28,167	113	7.6
Libraries	3,999	16	1.1
Parking	1,701	7	0.5
Parks and Recreation	36,099	145	9.8
Police Protection	53,680	216	14.5
Public Welfare	2,506	10	0.7
Sewerage	50,522	204	13.7
Solid Waste Management	32,596	131	8.8
Liquor Store	0	0	0.0
Utility	33,154	134	9.0
Employee Retirement	26,648	107	7.2
Other	18,243	73	4.9

Source: U.S Census Bureau, Government Finances 2000-2001, August 2003

Municipal Bond Ratings

Area	Moody's
City	n/a

Source: Mergent Bond Record, February 2004

DEMOGRAPHICS

Population Growth

Area	1990 Census	2000 Census	2003 Estimate	2008 Projection	Population Growth (%) 1990-2000	Population Growth (%) 2000-2008
City	238,846	248,232	252,265	259,782	3.9	4.7
MSA[1]	2,067,959	2,395,997	2,519,486	2,724,271	15.9	13.7
U.S.	248,709,873	281,421,906	290,647,163	305,918,071	13.2	8.7

Note: (1) Metropolitan Statistical Area - see Appendix A for areas included
Source: Claritas, Inc.

Number of Households and Average Household Size

Area	1990 Census	2000 Census	2003 Estimate	2008 Projection	2003 Average Household Size
City	105,847	109,663	111,353	114,479	2.3
MSA[1]	869,481	1,009,316	1,061,614	1,148,538	2.4
U.S.	91,947,410	105,480,101	109,440,059	116,034,472	2.7

Note: (1) Metropolitan Statistical Area - see Appendix A for areas included
Source: Claritas, Inc.

Race and Ethnicity

Area	White Non-Hispanic	Black Non-Hispanic	Asian Non-Hispanic	Other Race Non-Hispanic	Hispanic
City	70.6	22.8	2.9	3.8	4.5
MSA[1]	82.2	10.4	2.0	5.3	11.0
U.S.	74.5	12.4	3.8	9.3	13.2

Note: Figures are 2003 estimates; (1) Metropolitan Statistical Area - see Appendix A for areas included
Source: Claritas, Inc.

Segregation

City Index[2]	City Rank[3]	MSA[1] Index[2]	MSA[1] Rank[4]
76.7	9	68.4	72

Note: Figures are based on an analysis of Census 2000 data; (1) Metropolitan Statistical Area - see Appendix A for areas included; (2) Dissimilarity Index—the most commonly used measure of segregation between two groups, reflecting their relative distributions across neighborhoods within a city or metropolitan area. It can range in value from 0, indicating complete integration, to 100, indicating complete segregation; (3) Ranges from 1 (most segregated) to 100 (least segregated) and includes all the cities in this book; (4) Ranges from 1 (most segregated) to 318 (least segregated) and includes 318 metropolitan areas.
Source: www.CensusScope.org

Ancestry

Area	German	Irish[2]	English	American	Italian	Polish	French[3]	Scottish
City	14.7	12.4	11.1	5.7	6.8	3.0	3.8	2.5
MSA[1]	15.6	13.1	11.3	7.5	8.3	3.4	3.6	2.3
U.S.	15.2	10.9	8.7	7.3	5.6	3.2	3.0	1.7

Note: Figures include multiple ancestry (e.g. if a person reported being Irish and Italian, they were included in both columns); (1) Metropolitan Statistical Area - see Appendix A for areas included; (2) Includes Celtic; (3) Includes Alsatian but excludes Basque
Source: Census 2000, Summary File 3

Foreign-Born Population

Area	Any Foreign Country	Percent of Population Born in: Europe	Asia	Africa	Oceania[2]	Canada	Mexico	Latin America[3]
City	9.1	3.3	2.3	0.2	0.1	0.7	0.2	2.3
MSA[1]	9.8	2.6	1.7	0.2	0.0	0.8	1.1	3.3
U.S.	11.1	1.7	2.9	0.3	0.1	0.3	3.3	2.5

Note: (1) Metropolitan Statistical Area - see Appendix A for areas included; (2) Includes Australia, New Zealand subregion, Melanesia, Micronesia, Polynesia, and Oceania n.e.c.; (3) Includes Central America (excluding Mexico), South America, and the Caribbean.
Source: Census 2000, Summary File 3

Religion

Area	Catholic	Southern Baptist	United Meth-odist	ELCA[1]	LDS[2]	Presby-terian Church USA	Jewish Est.	Muslim Est.
County	12.2	3.9	4.4	0.9	0.2	1.3	2.6	0.5
U.S.	22.0	7.1	3.7	1.8	1.5	1.1	2.2	0.6

Note: Figures shown are the number of adherents as a percentage of the total population; Adherents are defined as all members, including full members, their children and the estimated number of other participants who are not considered members (e.g. the baptized, those not confirmed, those not eligible for communion, those regularly attending services, etc.); (1) Evangelical Lutheran Church in America; (2) The Church of Jesus Christ of Latter Day Saints
Source: Reprinted with permission from Religious Congregations and Membership in the United States 2000 (Nashville, Glenmary Research Center, 2002) Copyright Association of Statisticians of American Religious Bodies. All rights reserved.

Age Distribution

Area	Percent of Population						
	Under Age 5	Age 5 to 17	Age 18 to 34	Age 35 to 49	Age 50 to 64	Age 65 to 79	80 Years and Over
City	5.6	15.9	21.1	24.5	15.4	12.1	5.4
MSA[1]	5.7	16.1	20.1	22.8	16.1	13.9	5.4
U.S.	6.8	18.9	23.7	23.5	14.8	9.2	3.2

Note: (1) Metropolitan Statistical Area - see Appendix A for areas included
Source: Census 2000, Summary File 3

Marriage Status

Area	Never Married	Now Married Except Separated	Separated	Widowed	Divorced
City	27.8	45.5	2.8	9.0	14.9
MSA[1]	22.6	53.7	2.3	8.9	12.5
U.S.	27.1	54.4	2.2	6.6	9.7

Note: Figures cover population 15 years of age and older; (1) Metropolitan Statistical Area - see Appendix A for areas included
Source: Census 2000, Summary File 3

Male/Female Ratio

Area	Males	Females	Males per 100 Females
City	120,397	131,868	91.3
MSA[1]	1,213,693	1,305,793	92.9
U.S.	142,511,883	148,135,280	96.2

Note: Figures are 2003 estimates; (1) Metropolitan Statistical Area - see Appendix A for areas included
Source: Claritas, Inc.

ECONOMY

Gross Metropolitan Product

Area	1999	2000	2001	2002	2002 Rank[2]
MSA[1]	74.6	81.0	84.0	87.5	25

Note: Figures are in billions of dollars; (1) Metropolitan Statistical Area - see Appendix A for areas included; (2) Rank ranges from 1 to 319
Source: The U.S. Conference of Mayors, Metro Economies Report, July 2003

INCOME

Per Capita/Median/Average Income

Area	Per Capita ($)	Median Household ($)	Average Household ($)
City	23,564	39,026	52,666
MSA[1]	24,514	42,509	57,599
U.S.	24,078	46,868	63,207

Note: Figures are 2003 estimates; (1) Metropolitan Statistical Area - see Appendix A for areas included
Source: Claritas, Inc.

Household Income Distribution

Area	Percent of Households Earning							
	Under $15,000	$15,000 -24,999	$25,000 -34,999	$35,000 -49,999	$50,000 -74,999	$75,000 -99,000	$100,000 -149,999	$150,000 and up
City	16.5	14.2	14.7	17.5	17.7	8.9	6.8	3.7
MSA[1]	14.0	13.4	13.8	17.6	18.7	9.7	8.1	4.7
U.S.	14.1	11.5	11.7	16.0	19.2	11.3	10.2	6.0

Note: Figures are 2003 estimates; (1) Metropolitan Statistical Area - see Appendix A for areas included
Source: Claritas, Inc.

Poverty Rates by Age

Area	All Ages	Under 5 Years Old	5 to 17 Years Old	18 to 64 Years Old	65 Years and Over
City	13.3	1.1	3.1	7.2	1.8
MSA[1]	11.2	1.0	2.5	6.0	1.6
U.S.	12.4	1.2	3.0	6.9	1.2

Note: Figures are percent of population with income in 1999 below poverty level and only include population for whom poverty status is determined; (1) Metropolitan Statistical Area - see Appendix A for areas included
Source: Census 2000, Summary File 3

Personal Bankruptcy Filing Rate

Area	2002	2003
Pinellas County	5.72	5.89
U.S.	5.34	5.58

Note: Numbers are per 1,000 population and include Chapter 7 and Chapter 13 filings
Source: Federal Deposit Insurance Corporation (FDIC), Regional Economic Conditions (RECON), 2/25/2004

EMPLOYMENT

Labor Force and Employment

Area	Civilian Labor Force			Workers Employed		
	Dec. 2002	Dec. 2003	% Chg.	Dec. 2002	Dec. 2003	% Chg.
City	144,666	143,397	-0.9	137,369	137,277	-0.1
MSA[1]	1,316,323	1,307,890	-0.6	1,259,744	1,258,896	-0.1
U.S.	144,807,000	146,501,000	1.2	136,599,000	138,556,000	1.4

Note: Data is not seasonally adjusted and covers workers 16 years of age and older;
(1) Metropolitan Statistical Area - see Appendix A for areas included
Source: Bureau of Labor Statistics, http://stats.bls.gov

Unemployment Rate

Area	2003											
	Jan.	Feb.	Mar.	Apr.	May	Jun.	Jul.	Aug.	Sep.	Oct.	Nov.	Dec.
City	5.7	5.3	5.2	5.2	5.0	5.5	5.3	5.2	5.1	4.8	4.8	4.3
MSA[1]	4.9	4.5	4.4	4.4	4.3	4.7	4.5	4.6	4.6	4.2	4.1	3.7
U.S.	6.5	6.4	6.2	5.8	5.8	6.5	6.3	6.0	5.8	5.6	5.6	5.4

Note: Data is not seasonally adjusted and covers workers 16 years of age and older; All figures are percentages; (1) Metropolitan Statistical Area - see Appendix A for areas included
Source: Bureau of Labor Statistics, http://stats.bls.gov

Employment by Occupation

Occupation Classification	City (%)	MSA[1] (%)	U.S. (%)
Sales and Office	28.3	31.1	26.7
Professional and Related	20.8	19.1	20.2
Service	16.7	15.2	14.9
Production, Transportation, and Material Moving	12.7	11.2	14.6
Management, Business, and Financial	13.2	13.7	13.5
Construction, Extraction, and Maintenance	8.2	9.1	9.4
Farming, Forestry, and Fishing	0.1	0.5	0.7

Note: Figures cover employed civilians 16 years of age and older;
(1) Metropolitan Statistical Area - see Appendix A for areas included
Source: Census 2000, Summary File 3

Employment by Industry

Sector	MSA[1]		U.S.
	Number of Employees	Percent of Total	Percent of Total
Government	151,800	12.2	16.7
Education and Health Services	144,900	11.7	12.9
Professional and Business Services	296,800	23.9	12.3
Retail Trade	145,800	11.7	11.8
Manufacturing	70,600	5.7	11.0
Leisure and Hospitality	109,100	8.8	9.1
Finance Activities	94,200	7.6	6.1
Construction	69,200	5.6	5.1
Wholesale Trade	48,300	3.9	4.3
Other Services	49,000	3.9	4.1
Transportation and Utilities	29,400	2.4	3.7
Information	33,700	2.7	2.4
Natural Resources and Mining	500	<0.1	0.4

Note: Figures cover non-farm employment as of December 2003 and are not seasonally adjusted;
(1) Metropolitan Statistical Area - see Appendix A for areas included
Source: Bureau of Labor Statistics, http://stats.bls.gov

Average Wages

Occupation	$/Hr.	Occupation	$/Hr.
Accountants and Auditors	29.66	Maids and Housekeeping Cleaners	7.61
Automotive Mechanics	15.85	Maintenance and Repair Workers	12.33
Bookkeepers	12.46	Marketing Managers	40.93
Carpenters	13.58	Nuclear Medicine Technologists	22.73
Cashiers	7.51	Nurses, Licensed Practical	15.32
Clerks, General Office	10.35	Nurses, Registered	22.48
Clerks, Receptionists/Information	9.77	Nursing Aides/Orderlies/Attendants	10.04
Clerks, Shipping/Receiving	11.37	Packers and Packagers, Hand	7.38
Computer Programmers	27.87	Physical Therapists	29.54
Computer Support Specialists	19.43	Postal Service Mail Carriers	19.07
Computer Systems Analysts	31.04	Real Estate Brokers	28.33
Cooks, Restaurant	9.32	Retail Salespersons	10.83
Dentists	38.03	Sales Reps., Exc. Tech./Scientific	22.73
Electrical Engineers	32.25	Sales Reps., Tech./Scientific	31.28
Electricians	15.36	Secretaries, Exc. Legal/Med./Exec.	12.11
Financial Managers	37.30	Security Guards	8.85
First-Line Supervisors/Mgrs., Sales	17.62	Surgeons	95.68
Food Preparation Workers	7.98	Teacher Assistants	8.50
General and Operations Managers	39.13	Teachers, Elementary School	20.10
Hairdressers/Cosmetologists	10.79	Teachers, Secondary School	21.60
Internists	92.65	Telemarketers	12.45
Janitors and Cleaners	7.99	Truck Drivers, Heavy/Tractor-Trailer	14.41
Landscaping/Groundskeeping Workers	9.17	Truck Drivers, Light/Delivery Svcs.	11.87
Lawyers	50.77	Waiters and Waitresses	7.66

Note: Wage data is for 2002 and covers the Metropolitan Statistical Area (see Appendix A for areas included).
Hourly wages for elementary/secondary school teachers and teacher assistants were calculated by the editors
from annual wage data assuming a 40 hour work week; n/a not available.
Source: Bureau of Labor Statistics, 2002 Metro Area Occupational Employment and Wage Estimates

Occupational Employment Projections: 1996 - 2006

Occupations Expected to Have the Largest Job Growth (ranked by numerical growth)	Fast-Growing Occupations[1] (ranked by percent growth)
1. Cashiers	1. Systems analysts
2. Salespersons, retail	2. Physical therapy assistants and aides
3. General managers & top executives	3. Desktop publishers
4. Registered nurses	4. Home health aides
5. Waiters & waitresses	5. Computer engineers
6. Marketing & sales, supervisors	6. Medical assistants
7. Janitors/cleaners/maids, ex. priv. hshld.	7. Physical therapists
8. General office clerks	8. Paralegals
9. Food preparation workers	9. Emergency medical technicians
10. Hand packers & packagers	10. Occupational therapists

Note: Projections cover Florida; (1) Excludes occupations with total job growth less than 300
Source: U.S. Department of Labor, Employment and Training Administration, America's Labor Market Information System (ALMIS)

TAXES

State Corporate Income Tax Rates

State	Rate (%)	Number of Brackets	Low Bracket (Under $)	High Bracket (Over $)
Florida	5.5	1	na	na

Note: Tax rates as of December 31, 2003; na not applicable; 3.3% alternative minimum rate.
Source: Tax Foundation, www.taxfoundation.org

State Individual Income Tax Rates

State	Federal Deductibility	Marginal Rate (%)	Number of Brackets	Low Bracket (Under $)	High Bracket (Over $)
Florida	No	None	na	na	na

Note: Tax rates as of December 31, 2003; Brackets apply to single taxpayers and married people filing separately; na not applicable
Source: Tax Foundation, www.taxfoundation.org

Various State and Local Tax Rates

State Sales and Use (%)	Total Sales and Use (%)	Gasoline (cents/gal.)	Cigarette (cents/pack)	Spirits ($/gal.)	Table Wine ($/gal.)	Beer ($/gal.)
6.0	7.0	13.9	33.9	6.50	2.25	0.48

Note: Tax rates as of December 31, 2003
Source: Tax Foundation, www.taxfoundation.org

State Tax Burdens

Area	Combined State and Local Tax Burden Percent	Combined State and Local Tax Burden Rank	Combined Federal, State and Local Tax Burden Percent	Combined Federal, State and Local Tax Burden Rank
Florida	8.4	45	29.0	23
U.S. Average	9.7	-	30.0	-

Note: Figures are for 2003
Source: Tax Foundation, www.taxfoundation.org

Internal Revenue Service Tax Audits

IRS District	1996	1997	1998	1999	2000
North Florida	0.52	0.45	0.29	0.24	0.14
U.S.	0.66	0.61	0.46	0.31	0.20

Percent of Returns Audited

Note: Figures cover IRS district audits of federal income tax returns filed by individuals. Geographic data on district audits for 2001 and 2002 are being withheld by the IRS. TRAC is challenging this policy.
Source: Syracuse University, Transactional Records Access Clearinghouse (TRAC), "Odds of IRS District Tax Audit 2000"

RESIDENTIAL REAL ESTATE

Building Permits

Area	Single-Family			Multi-Family			Total		
	2001	2002	Pct. Chg.	2001	2002	Pct. Chg.	2001	2002	Pct. Chg.
City	334	291	-12.9	1,157	22	-98.1	1,491	313	-79.0
U.S.	1,235,600	1,332,600	7.9	401,100	415,100	3.5	1,636,700	1,747,700	6.8

Note: Figures represent new, privately-owned housing units authorized (unadjusted data)
Source: U.S. Census Bureau, Manufacturing, Mining, and Construction Statistics

Homeownership and Housing Vacancies

Area	Homeownership Rate[2] (%)			Rental Vacancy Rate[3] (%)			Homeowner Vacancy Rate[4] (%)		
	2001	2002[a]	2003	2001	2002[a]	2003	2001	2002[a]	2003
MSA[1]	70.7	70.5	69.8	12.0	11.1	9.9	2.0	1.9	1.8
U.S.	67.8	67.9	68.3	8.4	8.9	9.8	1.8	1.7	1.8

Note: (1) Metropolitan Statistical Area - see Appendix A for areas included; (2) The proportion of households that are owners; (3) The proportion of the rental inventory that is vacant for rent; (4) The proportion of the homeowner inventory that is vacant for sale; (a) 2002 figures have been revised; n/a not available
Source: U.S. Census Bureau, Housing Vacancies and Homeownership Annual Statistics: 2003

COMMERCIAL REAL ESTATE

Industrial/Office Markets

Type/Market Area	Inventory (sq. ft.)	Vacant (sq. ft.)	Vacancy Rate (%)	Under Construction (sq. ft.)	Net Absorption (sq. ft.)
Industrial Space					
Tampa	130,663,454	10,191,749	7.80	161,500	-574,131
Office Space					
Tampa	42,612,481	7,354,452	17.26	432,000	-412,228

Note: Data as of 4th Quarter, 2003; n/a not available
Source: Society of Industrial and Office Realtors, 2004 Comparative Statistics of Industrial and Office Real Estate Markets

COMMERCIAL UTILITIES

Typical Monthly Electric Bills

Area	Commercial Service ($/month)		Industrial Service ($/month)	
	3 kW demand 1,000 kWh	40 kW demand 14,000 kWh	1,000 kW demand 200,000 kWh	50,000 kW demand 15,000,000 kWh
City	87	885	13,732	938,964
Average[1]	100	1,134	17,850	1,045,117

Note: Based on rates in effect July 1, 2003; (1) average based on 197 utilities
Source: Edison Electric Institute, Typical Bills and Average Rates Report, Summer 2003

TRANSPORTATION

Means of Transportation to Work

Area	Car/Truck/Van		Public Transportation			Bicycle	Walked	Other Means	Worked at Home
	Drove Alone	Car-pooled	Bus	Subway	Railroad				
City	78.1	11.8	2.5	0.0	0.0	0.9	2.2	1.4	3.1
MSA[1]	79.7	12.4	1.2	0.0	0.0	0.6	1.7	1.2	3.1
U.S.	75.7	12.2	2.5	1.5	0.5	0.4	2.9	1.0	3.3

Note: Figures shown are percentages and cover workers 16 years of age and older;
(1) Metropolitan Statistical Area - see Appendix A for areas included
Source: Census 2000, Summary File 3

Travel Time to Work

Area	Less Than 15 Minutes	15 to 29 Minutes	30 to 44 Minutes	45 to 59 Minutes	60 Minutes or More
City	30.8	41.1	17.9	5.7	4.5
MSA[1]	26.4	37.8	21.3	8.1	6.5
U.S.	29.4	36.1	19.1	7.4	8.0

Note: Figures are percentages and include workers 16 years old and over; (1) Metropolitan Statistical Area - see Appendix A for areas included
Source: Census 2000, Summary File 3

Roadway Congestion Index

Area	1982	1990	1996	2000	2001
City	1.07	1.10	1.14	1.13	1.16
Average[1]	0.82	1.01	1.08	1.16	1.17

Note: Values greater than 1.00 indicate undesirable mobility levels; (1) average of 75 urban areas
Source: Texas Transportation Institute, The 2003 Annual Urban Mobility Report

Transportation Statistics

Interstate highways (2004)	I-275 connecting to I-75 and I-4
Public transportation (2002)	Pinellas Suncoast Transit Authority (PSTA)
Buses	
Average fleet age in years	5.6
No. operated in max. service	136
Demand response	
Average fleet age in years	0.0
No. operated in max. service	93
Passenger air service	
Airport	Tampa International; St. Petersburg-Clearwater International
Airlines (2003)	n/a
Boardings (2002)	7,726,576; 310,650
Amtrak service (2004)	Bus connection
Major waterways/ports	Gulf of Mexico; Tampa Bay

Source: Federal Transit Administration, National Transit Database, 2002; Editor & Publisher Market Guide, 2004; Bureau of Transportation Statistics, Airport Enplanement Activity for CY2002; www.amtrak.com

BUSINESSES

Major Business Headquarters

Company Name	2003 Rankings	
	Fortune 500	Forbes 500
Jabil Circuit	441	-

Note: Companies listed are located in the city; dashes indicate no ranking
Fortune 500: Companies that produce a 10-K are ranked 1 to 500 based on 2002 revenue
Forbes 500: Private companies are ranked 1 to 281 based on 2002 revenue
Source: Fortune, April 14, 2003; www.forbes.com, November 6, 2003

Fast-Growing Businesses

According to *Inc.*, Saint Petersburg is home to one of America's 500 fastest-growing private companies: **Omega Insurance Services**. Criteria: must be an independent, privately-held, U.S. corporation, proprietorship or partnership; sales of at least $200,000 in 1998; five-year operating/sales history; increase in 2002 sales over 2001 sales; holding companies, regulated banks, and utilities were excluded. *Inc. 500, America's Fastest-Growing Private Companies, October 15, 2003*

Women-Owned Firms: Number, Employment and Sales

Area	Number of Firms	Employ-ment	Sales ($000)	Rank[2]
MSA[1]	59,186	65,280	12,225,284	24

Note: (1) Metropolitan Statistical Area - see Appendix A for areas included;
(2) Calculated on an averaging of the number of businesses, employment, and sales
Source: The National Foundation for Women Business Owners, Women-Owned Businesses in the Top 50 Metropolitan Areas, 2002: A Fact Sheet

Women-Owned Firms: Growth

Area	Percent Change from 1997 to 2002			Rank[2]
	Number of Firms	Employ-ment	Sales	
MSA[1]	22.7	26.6	55.4	13
Top 50 MSAs	14.0	31.4	42.6	-

Note: (1) Metropolitan Statistical Area - see Appendix A for areas included; (2) Calculated on an averaging of the percent growth of number of businesses, employment, and sales
Source: The National Foundation for Women Business Owners, Women-Owned Businesses in the Top 50 Metropolitan Areas, 2002: A Fact Sheet

Minority and Women-Owned Businesses

Ownership	All Firms		Firms with Paid Employees			
	Firms	Sales ($000)	Firms	Sales ($000)	Employees	Payroll ($000)
Black	1,160	42,047	63	26,095	523	11,699
Hispanic	1,171	326,062	748	318,002	3,422	94,529
Women	6,106	347,965	1,169	271,408	3,484	82,992

Note: Figures cover firms located in the city
Source: 1997 Economic Census, Minority and Women-Owned Businesses

HOTELS

Hotels/Motels

Area	Hotels/Motels	Average Minimum Rates ($)		
		Tourist	First-Class	Deluxe
City	30	61	79	165

Source: OAG Travel Planner Online, Spring 2004

Saint Petersburg is home to one of the top 100 hotels in the U.S. and Canada according to *Travel & Leisure*: **Renaissance Vinoy Resort & Golf Club** (#73). Criteria: value, rooms/ambience, location, facilities/activities and service. *Travel & Leisure, "The World's Best Hotels 2003"*

EVENT SITES

Major Event Sites, Meeting Places and Convention Centers

Name	Guest Rooms	Exhibit/ Meeting Space (sq. ft.)	Largest Meeting Room Capacity
Bayfront Center/Mahaffey Theatre	n/a	23,500	8,400
Hilton St. Petersburg	333	33,000	1,200
Renaissance Vinoy Resort	380	28,000	600
Don CeSar Beach Resort	277	38,305	650
Suncoast Executive Inn & Conf. Ctr.	144	18,000	300
The Coliseum	n/a	17,500	2,000
Tropicana Field	n/a	n/a	45,000

Note: n/a not available
Source: Original research

Living Environment

COST OF LIVING

Cost of Living Index

Year	Composite Index	Groceries	Housing	Utilities	Trans-portation	Health Care	Misc. Goods/ Services
2001	95.8	99.6	91.1	114.8	96.2	89.6	94.1
2002	92.1	93.9	85.5	105.7	102.0	85.6	91.7
2003	91.1	95.7	83.3	96.0	103.0	85.0	91.7

Note: U.S. = 100; Figures are for St. Petersburg-Clearwater
Source: ACCRA, Cost of Living Index, 2001, 2002 and 2003 4-Quarter Averages

HOUSING

House Price Index (HPI)

Area	National Ranking[2]	Quarterly Change (%)	One-Year Change (%)	Five-Year Change (%)
MSA[1]	65	4.32	10.02	53.30
U.S.[3]	-	3.67	7.97	41.81

Note: The HPI is a weighted repeat sales index. It measures average price changes in repeat sales or refinancings on the same properties. This information is obtained by reviewing repeat mortgage transactions on single-family properties whose mortgages have been purchased or securitized by Fannie Mae of Freddie Mac in January 1975; (1) Metropolitan Statistical Area - see Appendix A for areas included; (2) Rankings are based on annual percentage change, for all MSAs containing at least 15,000 transactions over the last 10 years and ranges from 1 to 220; (3) figures based on a weighted division average; all figures are for the period ended December 31, 2003
Source: Office of Federal Housing Enterprise Oversight, House Price Index, March 1, 2004

Housing: Year Structure Built

Area	1990 -2000	1980 -1989	1970 -1979	1960 -1969	1950 -1959	1940 -1949	Before 1940	Median Year
City	5.3	10.5	20.2	19.9	26.2	7.6	10.2	1963
MSA[1]	17.2	25.9	25.4	13.6	11.0	3.3	3.5	1977
U.S.	17.0	15.8	18.5	13.7	12.7	7.3	15.0	1971

Note: Figures are percentages; (1) Metropolitan Statistical Area - see Appendix A for areas included
Source: Census 2000, Summary File 3

Average New Home Price

Area	2001	2002	2003
City[1]	189,368	190,735	199,335
U.S.	212,643	236,567	248,193

Note: Figures, in dollars, are based on a new home with 2,400 sq. ft. of living area on an 8,000 sq. ft. lot; (1) St. Petersburg-Clearwater
Source: ACCRA, Cost of Living Index, 2001, 2002 and 2003 4-Quarter Averages

Average Apartment Rent

Area	2001	2002	2003
City[1]	714	725	704
U.S.	674	708	721

Note: Figures, in dollars per month, are based on an unfurnished two bedroom, 1-1/2 or 2 bath apartment, approximately 950 sq. ft. in size, excluding all utilities except water; (1) St. Petersburg-Clearwater
Source: ACCRA, Cost of Living Index, 2001, 2002 and 2003 4-Quarter Averages

RESIDENTIAL UTILITIES

Average Residential Utility Costs

Area	All Electric ($/mth)	Part Electric ($/mth)	Other Energy ($/mth)	Phone ($/mth)
City[1]	124.70	–	–	21.62
U.S.	116.46	65.82	62.68	23.90

Note: (1) St. Petersburg-Clearwater
Source: ACCRA, Cost of Living Index, 2003 4-Quarter Average

HEALTH CARE

Average Health Care Costs

Area	Hospital ($/day)	Doctor ($/visit)	Dentist ($/visit)
City[1]	707.72	60.23	63.71
U.S.	678.35	67.91	83.90

Note: Hospital—based on a semi-private room; Doctor—based on a general practitioner's routine exam of an established patient; Dentist—based on adult teeth cleaning and periodic oral exam;
(1) St. Petersburg-Clearwater
Source: ACCRA, Cost of Living Index, 2003 4-Quarter Average

Distribution of Non-Federal, Office-Based Physicians

Area	Total	Family/ General Practice	Specialties Medical	Specialties Surgical	Specialties Other
MSA[1] (number)	4,519	494	1,785	1,081	1,159
MSA[1] (rate per 10,000 pop.)	18.9	2.1	7.4	4.5	4.8
Metro Average[2] (rate per 10,000 pop.)	33.1	2.2	7.7	4.8	5.6

Note: Data as of December 31, 2001; (1) Metropolitan Statistical Area - see Appendix A for areas included; (2) Average of 81 MSAs and CMSAs in this book
Source: American Medical Association, Physician Characteristics & Distribution in the U.S., 2003-2004

Hospitals

Saint Petersburg has the following hospitals: 7 general medical and surgical; 1 children's other specialty.
AHA Guide to the Healthcare Field, 2003-2004

PRESIDENTIAL ELECTION

2000 Presidential Election Results

Area	Gore	Bush	Nader	Buchanan	Other
Pinellas County	50.4	46.4	2.5	0.3	0.5
U.S.	48.4	47.9	2.7	0.4	0.6

Note: Results are percentages and may not add to 100% due to rounding
Source: www.cbsnews.com; www.uselectionatlas.org

EDUCATION

Public School District Statistics

District Name	Schls.	Enrollment	Classroom Teachers	Pupil/ Teacher Ratio	Minority Pupils[1] (%)	Current Expend.[2] ($/pupil)
Pinellas County SD	169	114,583	6,480	17.7	27.3	5,666

Note: Data covers the 2001-02 school year unless otherwise noted; (1) Fall 2000; (2) FY2000; n/a not available
Source: U.S. Department of Education, National Center for Education Statistics, Common Core of Data, Local Education Agency (School District) Universe Survey: School Year 2001-2002; U.S. Department of Education, National Center for Education Statistics, Digest of Education Statistics 2002

Educational Quality

School District	Education Quotient[1]	Graduate Outcome[2]	Community Index[3]	Resource Index[4]
Pinellas County	n/a	n/a	n/a	n/a

Note: Scores are national percentile rankings and range from 1 (worst) to 99 (best); (1) Combination of the Graduate Outcome, Community and Resource indexes weighted to reflect the greater importance of the Graduate Outcome and Resource Index; (2) Based on graduation rates and college board scores (SAT/ACT); (3) Based on the surrounding community's level of affluence and adult education; (4) Based on teacher salaries, per-pupil expenditures and student-teacher ratios.
Source: Expansion Management, December 2003

Educational Attainment by Race

Area	High School Graduate (%)					Bachelor's Degree (%)				
	Total	White	Black	Asian	Hisp.[2]	Total	White	Black	Asian	Hisp.[2]
City	81.9	85.8	67.8	67.0	77.2	22.8	26.0	10.1	24.7	20.2
MSA[1]	81.5	83.1	71.0	78.4	65.8	21.7	22.4	13.0	39.2	16.2
U.S.	80.4	83.6	72.3	80.4	52.4	24.4	26.1	14.3	44.1	10.4

Note: Figures shown cover persons 25 years old and over; (1) Metropolitan Statistical Area - see Appendix A for areas included; (2) people of Hispanic origin can be of any race
Source: Census 2000, Summary File 3

School Enrollment by Type

Area	Grades KG to 8				Grades 9 to 12			
	Public		Private		Public		Private	
	Enrollment	%	Enrollment	%	Enrollment	%	Enrollment	%
City	23,502	83.5	4,648	16.5	10,943	89.8	1,239	10.2
MSA[1]	239,025	86.3	38,069	13.7	103,629	90.5	10,836	9.5
U.S.	33,526,011	88.7	4,285,121	11.3	14,848,628	90.6	1,532,323	9.4

Note: Figures shown cover persons 3 years old and over; (1) Metropolitan Statistical Area - see Appendix A for areas included
Source: Census 2000, Summary File 3

School Enrollment by Race

Area	Grades KG to 8 (%)				Grades 9 to 12 (%)			
	White	Black	Asian	Hisp.[1]	White	Black	Asian	Hisp.[1]
City	56.1	35.5	3.1	4.7	53.9	36.0	4.9	4.8
MSA[2]	73.7	16.6	2.0	14.0	74.3	15.8	2.8	13.6
U.S.	68.5	15.5	3.3	16.8	68.8	15.5	3.8	15.7

Note: Figures shown cover persons 3 years old and over; (1) people of Hispanic origin can be of any race; (2) Metropolitan Statistical Area - see Appendix A for areas included
Source: Census 2000, Summary File 3

Classroom Teacher Salaries in Public Schools

District	B.A. Degree		M.A. Degree		Maximum	
	Min. ($)	Rank[1]	Max. ($)	Rank[1]	Max. ($)	Rank[1]
Saint Petersburg	29,400	64	49,600	71	51,800	80
DOD Average[2]	31,567	-	53,248	-	59,356	-

Note: Salaries are for 2001-2002; (1) Rank ranges from 1 to 100; (2) As per the U.S. Department of Defense Wage Fixing Authority
Source: American Federation of Teachers, Survey & Analysis of Teacher Salary Trends 2002

Higher Education

Four-Year Colleges			Two-Year Colleges			Medical Schools	Law Schools	Voc/ Tech
Public	Private Non-profit	Private For-profit	Public	Private Non-profit	Private For-profit			
0	2	0	1	0	1	0	1	10

Note: Figures cover institutions located within the city limits.
Source: National Center for Education Statistics, The Integrated Postsecondary Education System (IPEDS) Peer Analysis System, 2002; usnews.com, America's Best Graduate Schools 2004, Medical School Directory; The College Blue Book, Occupational Education, 2003; Barron's Guide to Law Schools, 2003; Medical School Admission Requirements U.S. & Canada, 2003-2004

MAJOR EMPLOYERS

Major Employers

Company Name	Industry	Type
AT&T Global Network Svcs LLC	Business consulting, nec	Headquarters
Bay Pines VAMC	Administration of veterans' affairs	Branch
Chase Manhattan	National commercial banks	Branch
Eckerd	General warehousing and storage	Branch
Honeywell	Aircraft engines and engine parts	Branch
Honeywell	Search and navigation equipment	Branch
HSN	Television broadcasting stations	Headquarters
Modern Business Associates	Help supply services	Single
Morton Plant Hospital	General medical and surgical hospitals	Headquarters
Professonal Employer Plans Inc	Employment agencies	Single
Sheriffs Office	Police protection	Branch
St Josephs Womens Hospital	General medical and surgical hospitals	Headquarters
Sykes Enterprises Incorporated	Custom computer programming services	Headquarters
Tampa General Healthcare	General medical and surgical hospitals	Headquarters
Tampa Pndc	U.s. postal service	Branch
Tech Data Corporation	Computers, peripherals, and software	Headquarters
Time Inc	Books, periodicals, and newspapers	Branch
University Book Store	Colleges and universities	Headquarters
University Community Health	General medical and surgical hospitals	Headquarters
US Post Office	U.s. postal service	Branch
Usani Sub LLC	Television broadcasting stations	Single
Verizon	Business services, nec	Branch
Verizon	Data processing and preparation	Headquarters

Note: Companies shown are located in the metropolitan area and have 2,000 or more employees.
Source: www.zapdata.com, March 2004

PUBLIC SAFETY

Crime Rate

Area	All Crimes	Violent Crimes				Property Crimes		
		Murder	Forcible Rape	Robbery	Aggrav. Assault	Burglary	Larceny -Theft	Motor Vehicle Theft
City	8,056.8	8.9	47.8	395.6	1,251.6	1,397.6	4,064.2	891.0
Suburbs[1]	5,649.9	4.9	45.0	205.3	538.7	1,105.4	3,100.0	650.6
MSA[2]	5,899.3	5.3	45.3	225.0	612.6	1,135.7	3,199.9	675.5
U.S.	4,118.8	5.6	33.0	145.9	310.1	746.2	2,445.8	432.1

Note: Figures are crimes per 100,000 population; (1) All areas within the MSA that are located outside the city limits; (2) Metropolitan Statistical Area - see Appendix A for areas included
Source: FBI Uniform Crime Reports, 2002

RECREATION

Culture and Recreation

Museums	Orchestras	Opera Companies	Dance Companies	Professional Theatres	Zoos	Pro Sports Teams[1]
6	0	0	1	2	0	3

Note: (1) Covers the Metropolitan Statistical Area - see Appendix A for areas included.
Source: The Grey House Performing Arts Directory, 2002; Official Museum Directory, 2004; www.sportsvenues.com

Library System

The Saint Petersburg Public Library has five branches and holdings of 435,634 volumes.
American Library Directory, 2003-2004

MEDIA

Newspapers

Name	Type	Freq.	Distribution	Circulation
Pinellas News	General	1x/wk	Local	2,800
St. Petersburg Times	General	7x/wk	Area	331,905
Weekly Challenger	Black	1x/wk	Local	35,500

Note: Includes newspapers whose offices are located in the city and whose circulations are 1,000 or more
Source: Burrelle's Media Directory, 2003

Television Stations

Name	Ch.	Affiliation	Type	Owner
WEDU	3	PBS	Public	Florida West Coast Public Broadcasting
WFLA	8	NBCT	Commercial	Media General Inc.
WTSP	10	CBST	Commercial	Gannett Broadcasting
WTVT	13	FBC	Commercial	Fox Television Stations Inc.
WUSF	16	PBS	Public	University of South Florida
WCLF	22	n/a	Commercial	Christian Television Network
WFTS	28	ABCT	Commercial	Scripps Howard Broadcasting
WMOR	32	n/a	Commercial	Hearst Corporation
WTTA	38	WB	Commercial	Sinclair Broadcast Group
WTOG	44	UPN	Commercial	Viacom International Inc.
WRMD	57	TMUN	Commercial	Telemundo Group Inc.
WVEA	62	UNIN	Commercial	Entravision Communications
WXPX	66	WB	n/a	Paxson Communications Corporation

Note: Stations included broadcast from the Tampa metro area; n/a not available
Source: Burrelle's Media Directory, 2003

AM Radio Stations

Call Letters	Freq. (kHz)	Target Audience	Station Format	Music Format
WHNZ	570	General	M/N/T	Country
WDAE	620	General	M/S/T	Adult Contemporary
WRMD	680	Hispanic	M	Latin
WLCC	760	Hispanic	M/N/S/T	Latin
WMGG	820	Hispanic	M/N	Latin
WGUL	860	General	M	Adult Standards
WTWD	910	Religious	M/T	Christian
WFLA	970	General	M/N/T	Big Band
WQYK	1010	General	M/S	Adult Contemporary
WWBA	1040	Religious	M/T	Jazz
WTIS	1110	Religious	T	n/a
WTMP	1150	Black	M/N/S/T	Adult Contemporary
WQBN	1300	Hispanic	M/N	Latin
WTAN	1340	General	N/S/T	n/a
WWMI	1380	Children	E/M	Oldies
WBRD	1420	Religious	M	Christian
WLVU	1470	General	T	n/a
WPSO	1500	Z/R	M/N/S/T	World Music
WXYB	1520	Ethnic	M/N/S/T	International
WAMA	1550	Hispanic	M	Adult Contemporary
WINV	1560	General	M	Country
WRXB	1590	General	M	Adult Standards

Note: Stations included broadcast from the Tampa metro area; n/a not available
The following abbreviations may be used:
Target Audience: A=Asian; B=Black; C=Christian; E=Ethnic; F=French; G=General; H=Hispanic;
M=Men; N=Native American; R=Religious; S=Senior Citizen; W=Women; Y=Young Adult; Z=Children
Station Format: E=Educational; M=Music; N=News; S=Sports; T=Talk
Music Format: AOR=Album Oriented Rock; MOR=Middle of the Road
Source: Burrelle's Media Directory, 2003

FM Radio Stations

Call Letters	Freq. (mHz)	Target Audience	Station Format	Music Format
WLMS	88.3	Religious	M/T	Christian
WMNF	88.5	General	M/N	Adult Contemporary
WUSF	89.7	General	M/N	Adult Standards
WBVM	90.5	Religious	M/N/T	Christian
WKES	91.1	Christian	M	Christian
WFTI	91.7	Religious	E/M/T	Christian
WYUU	92.5	General	M	Country
WFLZ	93.3	General	M/N/T	Top 40
WSJT	94.1	General	M	Jazz
WWRM	94.9	General	M/N/T	Adult Contemporary
WSSR	95.7	General	M/N/T	Adult Contemporary
WMGG	96.1	Hispanic	M/N/S	Latin
WXTB	97.9	General	M/N/S/T	AOR
WLLD	98.7	General	M	Top 40
WQYK	99.5	General	M/N	Country
WMTX	100.7	General	M/N	Adult Contemporary
WPOI	101.5	General	M/N/S	80's
WHPT	102.5	General	M	Classic Rock
WTBT	103.5	General	M/N/T	Classic Rock
WKZM	104.3	Religious	E/M/N/S/T	Christian
WRBQ	104.7	General	M/N/T	Oldies
WDUV	105.5	General	M	Easy Listening
WGUL	106.3	General	M	Adult Standards
WBBY	107.3	General	M	Adult Contemporary

Note: Stations included broadcast from the Tampa metro area
The following abbreviations may be used:
Target Audience: A=Asian; B=Black; C=Christian; E=Ethnic; F=French; G=General; H=Hispanic;
M=Men; N=Native American; R=Religious; S=Senior Citizen; W=Women; Y=Young Adult; Z=Children
Station Format: E=Educational; M=Music; N=News; S=Sports; T=Talk
Music Format: AOR=Album Oriented Rock; MOR=Middle of the Road
Source: Burrelle's Media Directory, 2003

CLIMATE

Average and Extreme Temperatures

Temperature	Jan	Feb	Mar	Apr	May	Jun	Jul	Aug	Sep	Oct	Nov	Dec	Yr.
Extreme High (°F)	85	88	91	93	98	99	97	98	96	94	90	86	99
Average High (°F)	70	72	76	82	87	90	90	90	89	84	77	72	82
Average Temp. (°F)	60	62	67	72	78	81	82	83	81	75	68	62	73
Average Low (°F)	50	52	56	61	67	73	74	74	73	66	57	52	63
Extreme Low (°F)	21	24	29	40	49	53	63	67	57	40	23	18	18

Note: Figures cover the years 1948-1990
Source: National Climatic Data Center, International Station Meteorological Climate Summary, 9/96

Average Precipitation/Snowfall/Humidity

Precip./Humidity	Jan	Feb	Mar	Apr	May	Jun	Jul	Aug	Sep	Oct	Nov	Dec	Yr.
Avg. Precip. (in.)	2.1	2.8	3.5	1.8	3.0	5.6	7.3	7.9	6.5	2.3	1.8	2.1	46.7
Avg. Snowfall (in.)	Tr	Tr	Tr	0	0	0	0	0	0	0	0	Tr	Tr
Avg. Rel. Hum. 7am (%)	87	87	86	86	85	86	88	90	91	89	88	87	88
Avg. Rel. Hum. 4pm (%)	56	55	54	51	52	60	65	66	64	57	56	57	58

Note: Figures cover the years 1948-1990; Tr = Trace amounts (<0.05 in. of rain; <0.5 in. of snow)
Source: National Climatic Data Center, International Station Meteorological Climate Summary, 9/96

Weather Conditions

Temperature			Daytime Sky			Precipitation		
32°F & below	45°F & below	90°F & above	Clear	Partly cloudy	Cloudy	0.01 inch or more precip.	0.1 inch or more snow/ice	Thunder-storms
3	35	85	81	204	80	107	< 1	87

Note: Figures are average number of days per year and covers the years 1948-1990
Source: National Climatic Data Center, International Station Meteorological Climate Summary, 9/96

HAZARDOUS WASTE

Superfund Sites

Saint Petersburg has no sites on the EPA's Superfund National Priorities List.
U.S. Environmental Protection Agency, National Priorities List, March 15, 2004

AIR & WATER QUALITY

Maximum Pollutant Concentrations

	Particulate Matter (ug/m³)	Carbon Monoxide (ppm)	Sulfur Dioxide (ppm)	Nitrogen Dioxide (ppm)	Ozone 1-hour (ppm)	Ozone 8-hour (ppm)	Lead (ug/m³)
MSA[1] Level	56	4	0.047	0.011	0.09	0.07	1.27a
NAAQS[2]	150	9	0.140	0.053	0.12	0.08	1.50
Met NAAQS[2]	Yes	Yes	Yes	Yes	Yes	Yes	Yes

Note: (1) Metropolitan Statistical Area - see Appendix A for areas included; (2) National Ambient Air Quality Standards; n/a not available; (a) Localized impact from an industrial source in Tampa. Concentration from highest nonpoint source site in metro area is 0.01 ug/m³ in Pinellas, FL
Units: ppm = parts per million; ug/m³ = micrograms per cubic meter
Source: EPA, Latest Findings on National Air Quality: 2002 Status and Trends, August 2003

Air Quality Index

In the Tampa MSA (see Appendix A for areas included), the Air Quality Index (AQI) exceeded 100 on 0 days in 2002. An AQI value greater than 100 indicates that air quality would have been in the unhealthful range on that day.
EPA, Latest Findings on National Air Quality: 2002 Status and Trends, August 2003

Watershed Health

The U.S. Environmental Protection Agency monitors the health of the aquatic resources for the nation's 2,000+ watersheds. **The Tampa watershed serves the Saint Petersburg area and received an overall Index of Watershed Indicators (IWI) score of 4 (less serious problems - high vulnerability).** The IWI score is based on seven condition and nine vulnerability indicators. The overall IWI score ranges from 1 (best health) to 6 (worst health). The Condition Indicators include: designated use attainment, fish and wildlife consumption advisories, source water condition, contaminated sediments, ambient water quality, and wetlands loss index. The Vulnerability Indicators include: aquatic species at risk, conventional and toxic loads over permitted limits, urban and agricultural runoff potential, population change, hydrologic modification, estuarine pollution susceptibility, and air deposition. *EPA, Index of Watershed Indicators, October 26, 2001*

Drinking Water

Water System Name	Pop. Served	Primary Water Source Type	Number of Violations January 2002-February 2004		
			Health Based	Significant Monitoring	Monitoring
City of St. Petersburg	322,437	Ground	None	None	None

Note: Data as of February 19, 2004
Source: EPA, Office of Ground Water and Drinking Water, Safe Drinking Water Information System

Saint Petersburg tap water is slightly alkaline, hard and not fluoridated.
Editor & Publisher Market Guide, 2004

San Antonio, Texas

Background

San Antonio is a charming preservation of its Mexican-Spanish heritage. Walking along its famous Paseo Del Rio at night, with cream-colored stucco structures, sea shell ornamented facades, and gently illuminating tiny lights is very romantic.

Emotional intensity is nothing new to San Antonio. The city began in the early eighteenth century as a cohesion of different Spanish missions, whose zealous aim was to convert the Coahuiltecan natives to Christianity and European ways of farming. A debilitating epidemic, however, killed most of the natives, as well as the missions' goal, causing the city to be abandoned.

In 1836, San Antonio became the site of interest again, when a small band of American soldiers were unable to successfully defend themselves against an army of 4,000 Mexican soldiers, led by General Antonio de Lopez Santa Anna. Fighting desperately from within the walls of the Mission San Antonio de Valero, or The Alamo, all 183 men were killed. This inspired the cry "Remember the Alamo" from the throats of every American soldier led by General Sam Houston, who was determined to wrest Texas territory and independence from Mexico.

Despite the Anglo victory over the Mexicans more than 150 years ago, the Mexican culture and its influence remain strong. We see evidence of this in the architecture, the Franciscan educational system, the variety of Spanish-language media, and the racial composition of the population, in which over half the city's residents are Latino.

This picturesque and practical blend of old and new makes San Antonio unique among American cities.

The city continues to draw tourists who come to visit not just the Alamo, but the nearby theme parks like Six Flags Fiesta Texas and SeaWorld, or to take in the famed River Walk, the charming promenade of shops, restaurants, and pubs. In addition, the city has used ingenuity to diversify its traditional economy. For instance, Kelly Air Force Base, which was decommissioned in 2001, is now a successful, nearly 5,000-acre business park, called Kelly USA. In 2004, Gore Design Completions announced plans to build a $12.5 million hangar in the park and add 350 employees in 2004.

Also, in 2003 plans for a new Toyota plant in San Antonio were announced. The $800 million plant will produce the Tundra truck and draw 2,000 new jobs to the state.

San Antonio's location on the edge of the Gulf Coastal Plains exposes it to a modified subtropical climate. Summers are hot, although extremely high temperatures are rare. Winters are mild. Since the city is only 140 miles from the Gulf of Mexico, tropical storms occasionally occur, bringing strong winds and heavy rains. Relative humidity is high in the morning, but tends to drop by late afternoon.

Rankings

- San Antonio was ranked #93 out of 331 metro areas in *Cities Ranked & Rated*. Criteria: cost of living; climate; crime; transportation; economy and jobs; education; arts and culture; health and healthcare; leisure. *Cities Ranked & Rated, 1st Edition, 2004*

- *Ladies Home Journal* ranked America's 200 largest cities based on the qualities women surveyed care about most. San Antonio ranked #38 out of 57 in the big city category (population over 300,000). Criteria: crime; lifestyle; education; jobs; health; child care; politics; and the economy. *Ladies Home Journal Online, "The Best Cities for Women 2002"*

- San Antonio was selected as one of "America's Pet Healthiest Cities" by Purina. The city ranked #37 out of 50. Criteria: veterinary services; environment; and legislation. *Purina Pet Institute, "America's Pet Healthiest Cities," August 14, 2001*

- San Antonio was selected as one of the "Top 10 Cities for Hispanics." The city was ranked #4. The cities were selected based on data from the following sources: *Forbes* magazine; CNN; *Money* magazine; local newspapers; U.S. Census; experts; natives and residents; www.bestplaces.net; www.findyourspot.com. *Hispanic Magazine, July/August 2002*

- *Forbes* ranked the 40 most populous metro areas in the U.S. in terms of the best places to be single. The San Antonio metro area was ranked #29. Criteria: number of other singles; cost of living alone; nightlife; culture; job growth; coolness. *Forbes, June 5, 2003*

- *Forbes* ranked the 150 most populous metro areas in the U.S. in terms of the "Best Places for Business and Careers." The San Antonio metro area was ranked #63. Criteria: income and job growth; cost-of-doing-business; qualifications of the available pool of labor; crime rates; housing costs; net migration. *Forbes, May 9, 2003*

- San Antonio was selected as one of "America's Healthiest Cities" by *Natural Health* magazine. The city was ranked #48 out of the 50 largest urban areas in the U.S. Twenty-six criteria in the following four categories were examined: whether the city boasts natural offerings; how well the city promotes its resident's physical health; whether the city offers a healthy environment; how well the city fosters a sense of community. *Natural Health, April 2003*

- *Men's Health* ranked 101 U.S. cities in terms of the quality of their tap water. San Antonio received a grade of B. Criteria: levels of bacteria, arsenic, lead, trihalomethanes, and haloacetic acids were compared with the National Academy of Science's guidelines as well as with the EPA's more stringent maximum contaminant level goals. *Men's Health, March 2004*

- Sperling's BestPlaces ranked 331 metro areas and identified the most and least stressful U.S. cities. The San Antonio metro area ranked #28 out of the 100 largest metro areas (#1 = most stressful). Criteria: divorce rate; unemployment rate; violent and property crime; suicide rate; commute time; mental health; alcohol consumption; cloudy days. *www.BestPlaces.net, February 26, 2004*

- Sperling's BestPlaces in partnership with Pep Boys ranked 77 metro areas and identified "America's Most Drivable Cities." The San Antonio metro area ranked #13. Criteria: climate; road roughness; urban mobility; gas prices. *Pep Boys, "America's Most Drivable Cities," April 9, 2003*

- San Antonio was ranked #121 out of America's 200 largest metro areas in *SELF Magazine's* ranking of "America's Healthiest Cities for Women." Criteria: safety; air/water quality; cancer rates; and 21 other factors relating to health. *SELF Magazine, November 2003*

- San Antonio was identified as one of the most dangerous large metro areas for pedestrians in the U.S. The area ranked #22 out of the nations 49 largest metro areas. Criteria: average yearly pedestrian fatalities per capita (for the years 2000 and 2001) adjusted for the number of walkers. *Surface Transportation Policy Project, "Mean Streets 2002"*

- San Antonio was selected as one of the 25 fattest cities in America by *Men's Fitness Online*. It ranked #13 out of America's 50 largest cities. Criteria: gyms/sporting goods; nutrition; exercise/sports; overweight/sedentary; junk food; alcohol; smoking; television; air and water quality; climate; geography; commute time; parks/open space; recreation facilities; and health care. *Men's Fitness Online, America's Fittest/Fattest Cities 2003*

- San Antonio was ranked #31 out of 100 cities surveyed in *Child* magazine's ranking of the "Best Cities for Families." Criteria: number of pediatricians per capita; proximity to a children's hospital; immunization rates; infant mortality rate; air quality; water quality; school spending; pupil-teacher ratio; availability of parks/green space; nearby recreational opportunities; average commute time; number of sunny days; average cost of a 3-bedroom home; unemployment rate; future job growth; crime rate; percentage of children under 5; mandated minimum child care ratios. *Child, April 2001*

- *Zero Population Growth* ranked 239 cities in terms of children's health, safety, and economic well-being. San Antonio was ranked #58 out of 140 independent cities (cities with populations greater than 100,000 which were neither major cities nor suburbs/outer cities) and was given a grade of B. Criteria: total population and population growth; percent of population under 18 years of age; number of children's museums; health improvement grade; percent of births to teens; percent of low birthweight infants; infant mortality rate; number of Title X-funded clinics; average SAT/ACT scores; average elementary and secondary class size; crime rate; unemployment rate; percent of affordable homes; number of bad air days; park acres per 1000 persons; library circulation per child; and children's program attendance counts. *Zero Population Growth, Kid Friendly Cities Report Card 2001*

- The San Antonio area was selected as one of "The 50 Most Alive Places to Live" in the U.S. Criteria: ethnic diversity; recreational options; cultural vitality; crime rate; opportunities for lifelong learning; quality of hospitals and restaurants; public transportation; walking accessibility; civic activities; and the kitsch factor. The area was ranked #9 out of 10 in the "Big City" category. *Modern Maturity, May-June 2000*

- San Antonio was selected as one of "The 15 Best Places to Live the Good Life." Criteria: availability of jobs; affordable housing; culture and entertainment; access to outdoor recreation; safety; colleges and universities; sense of community; proximity to comprehensive, well-regarded health care facilities; good public high schools; ease of getting around. *AARP The Magazine, May/June 2003*

- San Antonio was selected as one of America's best places to retire. Criteria: safety; climate; access to shopping, fun, games and entertainment; community; health care; and transportation. *America's 100 Best Places to Retire, 2000*

- San Antonio was selected as one of America's 32 most livable cities by the non-profit group, Partners for Livable Communities. Criteria: environmental quality; parkland; ability to train new workers; job market; education; and use of the arts for economic development. *www.Livable.com, March 3, 2003*

- San Antonio was identified as one of the safest large cities in America by Morgan Quitno. All cities with populations of 500,000 or more that reported crime rates in 2002 for murder, rape, robbery, aggravated assault, burglary, and motor vehicle thefts were ranked. The city ranked #7 out of the top 10. *www.morganquitno.com, 10th Annual America's Safest (and Most Dangerous) Cities Awards*

- *Ladies Home Journal* ranked America's 200 largest cities in terms of safety. San Antonio ranked #90 out of 200. Criteria: violent crimes; crimes against property; and rape. *Ladies Home Journal Online, "The Best Cities for Women 2002"*

- San Antonio was ranked #55 out of 268 metro areas in terms of its Creativity Index. The Creativity Index is a mix of four equally weighted factors: the Creative Class (scientists, engineers, architects, designers, writers, artists, musicians, or any profession where creativity is a key factor) share of the workforce; innovation, measured as patents per capita; high-tech industry, using the Milken Institute's Tech Pole Index; and diversity, measured by the Gay Index (a reasonable proxy for an areas' openness to different kinds of people and ideas). *The Rise of the Creative Class, 2002*

- San Antonio was ranked #43 out of 125 regions worldwide in terms of its "Knowledge Competitiveness Index." The index attempts to measure the knowledge-based development taking place throughout the world and is based on 17 measures of economic performance that indicate a region's ability to translate its knowledge capacity into economic value. *Robert Huggins Associates, "2003-2004 World Knowledge Competitiveness Index"*

- The San Antonio metro area was selected by *Yahoo! Internet Life* as one of "America's Most Wired Cities...and Towns." The area ranked #67 out of 87. Criteria: home and work net use; user sophistication; domain density; and available content. *Yahoo! Internet Life, April 2001*

- San Antonio was identified as one of the 100 "Most Unwired Cities" in the U.S. The area ranked #37. Criteria: number of public and commercial wireless access points; cell phone coverage offering wide area network Internet access; Internet penetration. *Intel, "Most Unwired Cities," March 4, 2003*

- Scarborough Research measured the percentage of households who subscribe to cellular services among adults ages 18 and over in 75 U.S. markets. The San Antonio DMA (Designated Market Area) was ranked #36 out of 75. *Scarborough Research, Scarborough USA+ 2003 Release 1*

- San Antonio was selected as one of "America's Most Literate Cities." The city ranked #60 out of the 64 largest U.S. cities. Criteria: booksellers; library support, holdings, and utilization; educational attainment; periodicals published; newspaper circulation. *University of Wisconsin-Whitewater, "America's Most Literate Cities," Summer 2003*

- San Antonio was ranked #15 in *Prevention* magazine's survey of the "Best Walking Cities in the U.S." The magazine, in conjunction with the American Podiatric Medical Association, surveyed 125 of the most populated cities and then tabulated and weighed 20 criteria of interest to pedestrians. *Prevention, April, 2004*

- San Antonio was selected as one of "America's Top 25 Arts Destinations." The area ranked #23 out of 25. Criteria: readers' top choices for arts travel destinations based on the richness and variety of visual arts sites, activities and events. *American Style, Winter 2002-2003*

- The San Antonio metro area was selected as one of "America's 50 Hottest Cities for Business Relocations and Expansions." The area ranked #8. Criteria: 70 of the industry's most prominent site selection consultants were asked which cities their clients found the most attractive when it came to selecting an expansion or relocation site in 2003. *Expansion Management, January 2004*

- The San Antonio metro area was selected as one of the "Top 60 CyberCities in America" by *Site Selection*. CyberCities are magnets for growing high-tech companies. Criteria: total employment; average wages; total payroll; number of companies; R&D spending and venture capital in the 45 Standard Industrial Classification (SIC) codes that define the high-technology industry. *Site Selection, March 2002*

- The San Antonio metro area was cited as one of "The Best Places in the U.S. to Locate a Company." The area ranked #67 out of 329. Criteria: education (with emphasis on college board test results and high school graduation rates); availability of quality healthcare services and the cost to employers; quality of life; logistics workforce and companies; transportation infrastructure; quality and quantity of highly educated technical workers; business climate. *Expansion Management, July 2003*

- The San Antonio metro area was selected as one of the "Top 40 Hottest Real Estate Markets" for expanding or relocating businesses." Criteria: rental costs; purchase prices; and vacancy rates of office and warehouse space. *Expansion Management, August 2003*

- The San Antonio metro area appeared on *Forbes/Milken Institute* list of "Best Places for Business and Career." Rank: #36 out of 200 metro areas. Criteria: salary growth; job growth; number of technology clusters; overall concentration of technology activity relative to national average; and technology output growth. *www.forbes.com, Forbes/Milken Institute Best Places 2002*

- The San Antonio metro area appeared on the "Milken Institute Best Performing Cities" index. Rank: #18 out of 200 large metro areas. Criteria: job growth; wage and salary growth; high-tech output growth. *Milken Institute, June 25, 2003*

- The San Antonio metro area appeared on *Entrepreneur* magazine's list of the "Best Cities for Entrepreneurs" in 2003. The area ranked #18 out of 61 in the large city category. Criteria: entrepreneurial activity; small-business growth; economic growth; and risk. *www.Entrepreneur.com*

- The San Antonio metro area was selected as one of the "Top 25 Cities for Doing Business in America." *Inc.* measured current-year employment growth in 277 regions as well as current trends in the annual average growth over the past three years, and compared employment expansion between the first and second halves of the last decade. Job growth factors account for two-thirds, and balance among industries accounts for one third of the final score for each city.The San Antonio metro area ranked #4 among large metro areas. *Inc. Magazine, March 2004*

- The San Antonio metro area appeared on *IndustryWeek's* fourth annual World-Class Communities list. It ranked #198 out of 315 metro areas. Criteria: MSA Gross Metropolitan Product (GMP) per manufacturing employee; and MSA percent share of U.S. manufacturing Gross Domestic Product (GDP). *IndustryWeek, April 16, 2001*

- The San Antonio metro area was selected as a "2001 Choice City" by *Business Development Outlook* magazine. Twenty-five cities were selected, based on data from the Bureau of Labor Statistics, Census Bureau, Federal Reserve, The Conference Board, and the U.S. Conference of Mayors, as being the most desirable into which a business can relocate or expand. *Business Development Outlook, 2001 Choice Cities*

- ING Group ranked the 125 largest metro areas according to the general financial security of residents. The San Antonio metro area was ranked #105 out of 125. Criteria: Earnings and Wealth Potential (household income, education, net assets, cost of living); Safety Net (health insurance, retirement savings, life insurance, income support programs); Personal Threats (unemployment rate, low-income households, crime rate); Community Economic Vitality (cost of community services, job quality, job creation, housing costs). *ING Group, "The Best Cities to Earn and Save Money: A Ranking of the Largest 125 U.S. Cities," 2001 Edition*

Business Environment

CITY FINANCES

City Government Finances

Component	2000-2001 ($000)	2000-2001 ($ per capita)
Total Revenues	2,463,094	2,152
Total Expenditures	2,387,516	2,086
Debt Outstanding	4,528,086	3,956
Cash and Securities	2,750,572	2,403

Source: U.S Census Bureau, Government Finances 2000-2001, August 2003

City Government Revenue by Source

Source	2000-2001 ($000)	2000-2001 ($ per capita)
General Revenue		
From Federal Government	40,584	35
From State Government	100,216	88
From Local Governments	7,629	7
Taxes		
Property	195,352	171
Sales	199,472	174
Personal Income	0	0
License	0	0
Charges	255,231	223
Liquor Store	0	0
Utility	1,425,815	1,246
Employee Retirement	52,798	46
Other	185,997	162

Source: U.S Census Bureau, Government Finances 2000-2001, August 2003

City Government Expenditures by Function

Function	2000-2001 ($000)	2000-2001 ($ per capita)	2000-2001 (%)
General Expenditures			
Airports	31,728	28	1.3
Corrections	665	1	0.0
Education	38,953	34	1.6
Fire Protection	111,664	98	4.7
Governmental Administration	45,449	40	1.9
Health	38,788	34	1.6
Highways	117,009	102	4.9
Hospitals	0	0	0.0
Housing and Community Development	11,216	10	0.5
Interest on General Debt	61,751	54	2.6
Libraries	18,282	16	0.8
Parking	9,549	8	0.4
Parks and Recreation	119,785	105	5.0
Police Protection	184,879	162	7.7
Public Welfare	46,011	40	1.9
Sewerage	102,365	89	4.3
Solid Waste Management	44,187	39	1.9
Liquor Store	0	0	0.0
Utility	1,252,194	1,094	52.4
Employee Retirement	47,299	41	2.0
Other	105,742	92	4.4

Source: U.S Census Bureau, Government Finances 2000-2001, August 2003

Municipal Bond Ratings

Area	Moody's
City	n/a

Source: Mergent Bond Record, February 2004

DEMOGRAPHICS

Population Growth

Area	1990 Census	2000 Census	2003 Estimate	2008 Projection	Population Growth (%) 1990-2000	2000-2008
City	997,258	1,144,646	1,189,891	1,266,854	14.8	10.7
MSA[1]	1,324,749	1,592,383	1,676,159	1,816,324	20.2	14.1
U.S.	248,709,873	281,421,906	290,647,163	305,918,071	13.2	8.7

Note: (1) Metropolitan Statistical Area - see Appendix A for areas included
Source: Claritas, Inc.

Number of Households and Average Household Size

Area	1990 Census	2000 Census	2003 Estimate	2008 Projection	2003 Average Household Size
City	345,912	405,474	424,480	457,107	2.8
MSA[1]	458,502	559,946	592,913	648,715	2.8
U.S.	91,947,410	105,480,101	109,440,059	116,034,472	2.7

Note: (1) Metropolitan Statistical Area - see Appendix A for areas included
Source: Claritas, Inc.

Race and Ethnicity

Area	White Non-Hispanic	Black Non-Hispanic	Asian Non-Hispanic	Other Race Non-Hispanic	Hispanic
City	67.2	6.9	1.7	24.2	59.1
MSA[1]	70.2	6.7	1.6	21.5	51.5
U.S.	74.5	12.4	3.8	9.3	13.2

Note: Figures are 2003 estimates; (1) Metropolitan Statistical Area - see Appendix A for areas included
Source: Claritas, Inc.

Segregation

City		MSA[1]	
Index[2]	Rank[3]	Index[2]	Rank[4]
53.5	65	55.5	191

Note: Figures are based on an analysis of Census 2000 data; (1) Metropolitan Statistical Area - see Appendix A for areas included; (2) Dissimilarity Index—the most commonly used measure of segregation between two groups, reflecting their relative distributions across neighborhoods within a city or metropolitan area. It can range in value from 0, indicating complete integration, to 100, indicating complete segregation; (3) Ranges from 1 (most segregated) to 100 (least segregated) and includes all the cities in this book; (4) Ranges from 1 (most segregated) to 318 (least segregated) and includes 318 metropolitan areas.
Source: www.CensusScope.org

Ancestry

Area	German	Irish[2]	English	American	Italian	Polish	French[3]	Scottish
City	9.0	5.2	5.0	3.2	1.9	1.3	1.8	1.0
MSA[1]	11.7	6.2	5.9	3.8	2.0	1.7	2.0	1.2
U.S.	15.2	10.9	8.7	7.3	5.6	3.2	3.0	1.7

Note: Figures include multiple ancestry (e.g. if a person reported being Irish and Italian, they were included in both columns); (1) Metropolitan Statistical Area - see Appendix A for areas included; (2) Includes Celtic; (3) Includes Alsatian but excludes Basque
Source: Census 2000, Summary File 3

Foreign-Born Population

Area	Any Foreign Country	Percent of Population Born in: Europe	Asia	Africa	Oceania[2]	Canada	Mexico	Latin America[3]
City	11.7	0.7	1.4	0.1	0.0	0.2	8.5	0.8
MSA[1]	10.2	0.8	1.3	0.1	0.0	0.2	7.1	0.7
U.S.	11.1	1.7	2.9	0.3	0.1	0.3	3.3	2.5

Note: (1) Metropolitan Statistical Area - see Appendix A for areas included; (2) Includes Australia, New Zealand subregion, Melanesia, Micronesia, Polynesia, and Oceania n.e.c; (3) Includes Central America (excluding Mexico), South America, and the Caribbean.
Source: Census 2000, Summary File 3

Religion

Area	Catholic	Southern Baptist	United Methodist	ELCA[1]	LDS[2]	Presbyterian Church USA	Jewish Est.	Muslim Est.
County	41.2	8.6	3.0	1.0	0.7	0.8	0.8	0.2
U.S.	22.0	7.1	3.7	1.8	1.5	1.1	2.2	0.6

Note: Figures shown are the number of adherents as a percentage of the total population; Adherents are defined as all members, including full members, their children and the estimated number of other participants who are not considered members (e.g. the baptized, those not confirmed, those not eligible for communion, those regularly attending services, etc.); (1) Evangelical Lutheran Church in America; (2) The Church of Jesus Christ of Latter Day Saints
Source: Reprinted with permission from Religious Congregations and Membership in the United States 2000 (Nashville, Glenmary Research Center, 2002) Copyright Association of Statisticians of American Religious Bodies. All rights reserved.

Age Distribution

Area	Percent of Population						
	Under Age 5	Age 5 to 17	Age 18 to 34	Age 35 to 49	Age 50 to 64	Age 65 to 79	80 Years and Over
City	8.0	20.4	26.1	22.3	12.7	7.9	2.5
MSA[1]	7.7	20.6	24.8	22.9	13.4	8.1	2.6
U.S.	6.8	18.9	23.7	23.5	14.8	9.2	3.2

Note: (1) Metropolitan Statistical Area - see Appendix A for areas included
Source: Census 2000, Summary File 3

Marriage Status

Area	Never Married	Now Married Except Separated	Separated	Widowed	Divorced
City	28.7	50.5	3.0	6.0	11.8
MSA[1]	26.9	53.6	2.6	5.9	11.1
U.S.	27.1	54.4	2.2	6.6	9.7

Note: Figures cover population 15 years of age and older; (1) Metropolitan Statistical Area - see Appendix A for areas included
Source: Census 2000, Summary File 3

Male/Female Ratio

Area	Males	Females	Males per 100 Females
City	575,191	614,700	93.6
MSA[1]	815,864	860,295	94.8
U.S.	142,511,883	148,135,280	96.2

Note: Figures are 2003 estimates; (1) Metropolitan Statistical Area - see Appendix A for areas included
Source: Claritas, Inc.

ECONOMY

Gross Metropolitan Product

Area	1999	2000	2001	2002	2002 Rank[2]
MSA[1]	50.6	54.3	56.3	58.1	44

Note: Figures are in billions of dollars; (1) Metropolitan Statistical Area - see Appendix A for areas included; (2) Rank ranges from 1 to 319
Source: The U.S. Conference of Mayors, Metro Economies Report, July 2003

INCOME

Per Capita/Median/Average Income

Area	Per Capita ($)	Median Household ($)	Average Household ($)
City	19,700	41,233	54,417
MSA[1]	20,890	44,312	58,236
U.S.	24,078	46,868	63,207

Note: Figures are 2003 estimates; (1) Metropolitan Statistical Area - see Appendix A for areas included
Source: Claritas, Inc.

Household Income Distribution

Area	Percent of Households Earning							
	Under $15,000	$15,000 -24,999	$25,000 -34,999	$35,000 -49,999	$50,000 -74,999	$75,000 -99,000	$100,000 -149,999	$150,000 and up
City	16.1	13.3	13.4	17.3	18.5	9.5	8.0	3.9
MSA[1]	14.3	12.3	12.7	17.3	19.5	10.4	9.0	4.5
U.S.	14.1	11.5	11.7	16.0	19.2	11.3	10.2	6.0

Note: Figures are 2003 estimates; (1) Metropolitan Statistical Area - see Appendix A for areas included
Source: Claritas, Inc.

Poverty Rates by Age

Area	All Ages	Under 5 Years Old	5 to 17 Years Old	18 to 64 Years Old	65 Years and Over
City	17.3	2.2	4.9	8.8	1.4
MSA[1]	15.1	1.8	4.3	7.7	1.2
U.S.	12.4	1.2	3.0	6.9	1.2

Note: Figures are percent of population with income in 1999 below poverty level and only include population for whom poverty status is determined; (1) Metropolitan Statistical Area - see Appendix A for areas included
Source: Census 2000, Summary File 3

Personal Bankruptcy Filing Rate

Area	2002	2003
Bexar County	3.36	3.80
U.S.	5.34	5.58

Note: Numbers are per 1,000 population and include Chapter 7 and Chapter 13 filings
Source: Federal Deposit Insurance Corporation (FDIC), Regional Economic Conditions (RECON), 2/25/2004

EMPLOYMENT

Labor Force and Employment

Area	Civilian Labor Force			Workers Employed		
	Dec. 2002	Dec. 2003	% Chg.	Dec. 2002	Dec. 2003	% Chg.
City	555,282	575,385	3.6	525,735	544,548	3.6
MSA[1]	815,164	843,304	3.5	775,430	803,178	3.6
U.S.	144,807,000	146,501,000	1.2	136,599,000	138,556,000	1.4

Note: Data is not seasonally adjusted and covers workers 16 years of age and older;
(1) Metropolitan Statistical Area - see Appendix A for areas included
Source: Bureau of Labor Statistics, http://stats.bls.gov

Unemployment Rate

Area	2003											
	Jan.	Feb.	Mar.	Apr.	May	Jun.	Jul.	Aug.	Sep.	Oct.	Nov.	Dec.
City	6.0	5.8	5.6	5.3	5.7	6.9	6.7	6.3	6.1	5.8	5.7	5.4
MSA[1]	5.4	5.2	5.1	4.8	5.1	6.2	6.0	5.7	5.5	5.1	5.1	4.8
U.S.	6.5	6.4	6.2	5.8	5.8	6.5	6.3	6.0	5.8	5.6	5.6	5.4

Note: Data is not seasonally adjusted and covers workers 16 years of age and older; All figures are percentages; (1) Metropolitan Statistical Area - see Appendix A for areas included
Source: Bureau of Labor Statistics, http://stats.bls.gov

Employment by Occupation

Occupation Classification	City (%)	MSA[1] (%)	U.S. (%)
Sales and Office	30.0	29.5	26.7
Professional and Related	19.6	19.7	20.2
Service	16.7	15.7	14.9
Production, Transportation, and Material Moving	10.7	11.2	14.6
Management, Business, and Financial	12.5	13.1	13.5
Construction, Extraction, and Maintenance	10.4	10.6	9.4
Farming, Forestry, and Fishing	0.1	0.2	0.7

Note: Figures cover employed civilians 16 years of age and older;
(1) Metropolitan Statistical Area - see Appendix A for areas included
Source: Census 2000, Summary File 3

Employment by Industry

| Sector | MSA[1] | | U.S. |
	Number of Employees	Percent of Total	Percent of Total
Government	136,500	18.8	16.7
Education and Health Services	97,700	13.4	12.9
Professional and Business Services	86,000	11.8	12.3
Retail Trade	88,100	12.1	11.8
Manufacturing	44,400	6.1	11.0
Leisure and Hospitality	77,100	10.6	9.1
Finance Activities	59,800	8.2	6.1
Construction	39,800	5.5	5.1
Wholesale Trade	26,800	3.7	4.3
Other Services	26,900	3.7	4.1
Transportation and Utilities	18,600	2.6	3.7
Information	24,000	3.3	2.4
Natural Resources and Mining	2,200	0.3	0.4

Note: Figures cover non-farm employment as of December 2003 and are not seasonally adjusted;
(1) Metropolitan Statistical Area - see Appendix A for areas included
Source: Bureau of Labor Statistics, http://stats.bls.gov

Average Wages

Occupation	$/Hr.	Occupation	$/Hr.
Accountants and Auditors	22.98	Maids and Housekeeping Cleaners	7.28
Automotive Mechanics	14.17	Maintenance and Repair Workers	12.33
Bookkeepers	12.84	Marketing Managers	32.95
Carpenters	13.55	Nuclear Medicine Technologists	22.50
Cashiers	7.80	Nurses, Licensed Practical	14.98
Clerks, General Office	10.42	Nurses, Registered	22.15
Clerks, Receptionists/Information	9.49	Nursing Aides/Orderlies/Attendants	7.95
Clerks, Shipping/Receiving	9.72	Packers and Packagers, Hand	7.90
Computer Programmers	23.80	Physical Therapists	26.03
Computer Support Specialists	15.66	Postal Service Mail Carriers	18.91
Computer Systems Analysts	20.94	Real Estate Brokers	22.67
Cooks, Restaurant	8.94	Retail Salespersons	9.91
Dentists	53.96	Sales Reps., Exc. Tech./Scientific	18.00
Electrical Engineers	32.99	Sales Reps., Tech./Scientific	27.06
Electricians	17.00	Secretaries, Exc. Legal/Med./Exec.	11.33
Financial Managers	33.61	Security Guards	9.03
First-Line Supervisors/Mgrs., Sales	16.30	Surgeons	99.29
Food Preparation Workers	7.79	Teacher Assistants	8.00
General and Operations Managers	36.13	Teachers, Elementary School	20.60
Hairdressers/Cosmetologists	11.58	Teachers, Secondary School	22.70
Internists	96.30	Telemarketers	9.01
Janitors and Cleaners	8.20	Truck Drivers, Heavy/Tractor-Trailer	14.09
Landscaping/Groundskeeping Workers	8.97	Truck Drivers, Light/Delivery Svcs.	10.97
Lawyers	46.41	Waiters and Waitresses	8.07

Note: Wage data is for 2002 and covers the Metropolitan Statistical Area (see Appendix A for areas included).
Hourly wages for elementary/secondary school teachers and teacher assistants were calculated by the editors
from annual wage data assuming a 40 hour work week; n/a not available.
Source: Bureau of Labor Statistics, 2002 Metro Area Occupational Employment and Wage Estimates

Occupational Employment Projections: 1996 - 2006

Occupations Expected to Have the Largest Job Growth (ranked by numerical growth)	Fast-Growing Occupations[1] (ranked by percent growth)
1. Cashiers	1. Desktop publishers
2. Salespersons, retail	2. Systems analysts
3. General managers & top executives	3. Customer service representatives
4. Truck drivers, light	4. Physical therapy assistants and aides
5. Child care workers, private household	5. Computer engineers
6. General office clerks	6. Emergency medical technicians
7. Systems analysts	7. Medical assistants
8. Food preparation workers	8. Respiratory therapists
9. Food service workers	9. Telephone & cable TV line install & repair
10. Registered nurses	10. Physical therapists

Note: Projections cover Texas; (1) Excludes occupations with total job growth less than 300
Source: U.S. Department of Labor, Employment and Training Administration, America's Labor Market Information System (ALMIS)

TAXES

State Corporate Income Tax Rates

State	Rate (%)	Number of Brackets	Low Bracket (Under $)	High Bracket (Over $)
Texas	None	na	na	na

Note: Tax rates as of December 31, 2003; na not applicable
Source: Tax Foundation, www.taxfoundation.org

State Individual Income Tax Rates

State	Federal Deductibility	Marginal Rate (%)	Number of Brackets	Low Bracket (Under $)	High Bracket (Over $)
Texas	No	None	na	na	na

Note: Tax rates as of December 31, 2003; Brackets apply to single taxpayers and married people filing separately; na not applicable
Source: Tax Foundation, www.taxfoundation.org

Various State and Local Tax Rates

State Sales and Use (%)	Total Sales and Use (%)	Gasoline (cents/gal.)	Cigarette (cents/pack)	Spirits ($/gal.)	Table Wine ($/gal.)	Beer ($/gal.)
6.25	7.875	20	41	2.40	0.20	0.20

Note: Tax rates as of December 31, 2003
Source: Tax Foundation, www.taxfoundation.org

State Tax Burdens

Area	Combined State and Local Tax Burden Percent	Rank	Combined Federal, State and Local Tax Burden Percent	Rank
Texas	8.3	47	28.4	31
U.S. Average	9.7	-	30.0	-

Note: Figures are for 2003
Source: Tax Foundation, www.taxfoundation.org

Internal Revenue Service Tax Audits

IRS District	1996	1997	1998	1999	2000
South Texas	0.55	0.50	0.50	0.31	0.17
U.S.	0.66	0.61	0.46	0.31	0.20

Percent of Returns Audited

Note: Figures cover IRS district audits of federal income tax returns filed by individuals. Geographic data on district audits for 2001 and 2002 are being withheld by the IRS. TRAC is challenging this policy.
Source: Syracuse University, Transactional Records Access Clearinghouse (TRAC), "Odds of IRS District Tax Audit 2000"

RESIDENTIAL
REAL ESTATE

Building Permits

Area	Single-Family 2001	Single-Family 2002	Pct. Chg.	Multi-Family 2001	Multi-Family 2002	Pct. Chg.	Total 2001	Total 2002	Pct. Chg.
City	6,281	6,454	2.8	3,443	2,552	-25.9	9,724	9,006	-7.4
U.S.	1,235,600	1,332,600	7.9	401,100	415,100	3.5	1,636,700	1,747,700	6.8

Note: Figures represent new, privately-owned housing units authorized (unadjusted data)
Source: U.S. Census Bureau, Manufacturing, Mining, and Construction Statistics

Homeownership and Housing Vacancies

Area	Homeownership Rate[2] (%) 2001	2002[a]	2003	Rental Vacancy Rate[3] (%) 2001	2002[a]	2003	Homeowner Vacancy Rate[4] (%) 2001	2002[a]	2003
MSA[1]	67.4	68.3	69.9	12.2	14.7	13.9	1.0	0.8	1.4
U.S.	67.8	67.9	68.3	8.4	8.9	9.8	1.8	1.7	1.8

Note: (1) Metropolitan Statistical Area - see Appendix A for areas included; (2) The proportion of households that are owners; (3) The proportion of the rental inventory that is vacant for rent; (4) The proportion of the homeowner inventory that is vacant for sale; (a) 2002 figures have been revised; n/a not available
Source: U.S. Census Bureau, Housing Vacancies and Homeownership Annual Statistics: 2003

COMMERCIAL
REAL ESTATE

Industrial/Office Markets

Type/Market Area	Inventory (sq. ft.)	Vacant (sq. ft.)	Vacancy Rate (%)	Under Construction (sq. ft.)	Net Absorption (sq. ft.)
Industrial Space					
San Antonio	143,584,396	14,663,564	10.21	702,846	1,466,388
Office Space					
San Antonio	18,447,211	3,122,814	16.93	75,700	-98,570

Note: Data as of 4th Quarter, 2003; n/a not available
Source: Society of Industrial and Office Realtors, 2004 Comparative Statistics of Industrial and Office Real Estate Markets

COMMERCIAL
UTILITIES

Typical Monthly Electric Bills

Area	Commercial Service ($/month) 3 kW demand 1,000 kWh	40 kW demand 14,000 kWh	Industrial Service ($/month) 1,000 kW demand 200,000 kWh	50,000 kW demand 15,000,000 kWh
City	n/a	n/a	n/a	n/a
Average[1]	100	1,134	17,850	1,045,117

Note: Based on rates in effect July 1, 2003; (1) average based on 197 utilities; n/a not available
Source: Edison Electric Institute, Typical Bills and Average Rates Report, Summer 2003

TRANSPORTATION

Means of Transportation to Work

Area	Car/Truck/Van Drove Alone	Car-pooled	Public Transportation Bus	Subway	Railroad	Bicycle	Walked	Other Means	Worked at Home
City	75.6	15.2	3.7	0.0	0.0	0.2	2.2	1.0	2.2
MSA[1]	76.2	14.7	2.8	0.0	0.0	0.1	2.4	1.2	2.6
U.S.	75.7	12.2	2.5	1.5	0.5	0.4	2.9	1.0	3.3

Note: Figures shown are percentages and cover workers 16 years of age and older;
(1) Metropolitan Statistical Area - see Appendix A for areas included
Source: Census 2000, Summary File 3

Travel Time to Work

Area	Less Than 15 Minutes	15 to 29 Minutes	30 to 44 Minutes	45 to 59 Minutes	60 Minutes or More
City	23.2	46.0	21.7	4.5	4.5
MSA[1]	23.9	43.2	22.2	5.7	5.0
U.S.	29.4	36.1	19.1	7.4	8.0

Note: Figures are percentages and include workers 16 years old and over; (1) Metropolitan Statistical Area - see Appendix A for areas included
Source: Census 2000, Summary File 3

Roadway Congestion Index

Area	1982	1990	1996	2000	2001
City	0.69	0.74	0.89	1.05	1.04
Average[1]	0.82	1.01	1.08	1.16	1.17

Note: Values greater than 1.00 indicate undesirable mobility levels; (1) average of 75 urban areas
Source: Texas Transportation Institute, The 2003 Annual Urban Mobility Report

Transportation Statistics

Interstate highways (2004)	I-10; I-35; I-37
Public transportation (2002)	VIA Metropolitan Transit (VIA)
Buses	
Average fleet age in years	7.3
No. operated in max. service	402
Demand response	
Average fleet age in years	4.5
No. operated in max. service	180
Passenger air service	
Airport	San Antonio International
Airlines (2003)	14
Boardings (2002)	3,224,764
Amtrak service (2004)	Yes
Major waterways/ports	None

Source: Federal Transit Administration, National Transit Database, 2002; Editor & Publisher Market Guide, 2004; Bureau of Transportation Statistics, Airport Enplanement Activity for CY2002; www.amtrak.com

BUSINESSES

Major Business Headquarters

Company Name	2003 Rankings	
	Fortune 500	Forbes 500
Clear Channel Communications	219	-
HE Butt Grocery	-	10
SBC Communications	27	-
Tesoro Petroleum	263	-
USAA	199	-
Valero Energy	55	-
Zachry Construction	-	136

Note: Companies listed are located in the city; dashes indicate no ranking
Fortune 500: Companies that produce a 10-K are ranked 1 to 500 based on 2002 revenue
Forbes 500: Private companies are ranked 1 to 281 based on 2002 revenue
Source: Fortune, April 14, 2003; www.forbes.com, November 6, 2003

Best Companies to Work For

Valero Energy, headquartered in San Antonio, is among the "100 Best Companies to Work for in 2004." Criteria: trust in management, pride in work/company, camaraderie, company responses to the Hewitt People Practices Inventory, and employee responses to their Great Place to Work survey. The companies also had to be at least 10 years old and have a minimum of 500 employees. *Fortune, January 12, 2004*

USAA, headquartered in San Antonio, is among the "100 Best Companies for Working Mothers." Criteria: fair wages, opportunities for women to advance, support for child care, flexible work schedules, family-friendly benefits, and work/life supports. *Working Mother, October 2003*

SBC Communications, headquartered in San Antonio, is among the "50 Best Companies for Minorities." Criteria: 1,200 of the largest U.S employers were surveyed—141 responded. Those companies were analyzed on 15 quantitative and qualitative measures—from how well minorities are paid to how many are in management. *Fortune, July 7, 2003*

USAA, headquartered in San Antonio, is among the "100 Best Places to Work in IT 2003." Criteria: compensation, turnover and training. *www.computerworld.com, 3/15/2004*

Fast-Growing Businesses

According to *Inc.*, San Antonio is home to one of America's 500 fastest-growing private companies: **SecureInfo**. Criteria: must be an independent, privately-held, U.S. corporation, proprietorship or partnership; sales of at least $200,000 in 1998; five-year operating/sales history; increase in 2002 sales over 2001 sales; holding companies, regulated banks, and utilities were excluded. *Inc. 500, America's Fastest-Growing Private Companies, October 15, 2003*

Women-Owned Firms: Number, Employment and Sales

Area	Number of Firms	Employ-ment	Sales ($000)	Rank[2]
MSA[1]	29,898	65,049	8,775,646	34

Note: (1) Metropolitan Statistical Area - see Appendix A for areas included;
(2) Calculated on an averaging of the number of businesses, employment, and sales
Source: The National Foundation for Women Business Owners, Women-Owned Businesses in the Top 50 Metropolitan Areas, 2002: A Fact Sheet

Women-Owned Firms: Growth

Area	Percent Change from 1997 to 2002			Rank[2]
	Number of Firms	Employ-ment	Sales	
MSA[1]	13.8	43.7	62.5	8
Top 50 MSAs	14.0	31.4	42.6	-

Note: (1) Metropolitan Statistical Area - see Appendix A for areas included; (2) Calculated on an averaging of the percent growth of number of businesses, employment, and sales
Source: The National Foundation for Women Business Owners, Women-Owned Businesses in the Top 50 Metropolitan Areas, 2002: A Fact Sheet

Minority and Women-Owned Businesses

Ownership	All Firms		Firms with Paid Employees			
	Firms	Sales ($000)	Firms	Sales ($000)	Employees	Payroll ($000)
Black	1,614	116,043	159	90,636	1,587	25,906
Hispanic	28,459	4,281,603	6,569	3,673,030	46,187	784,811
Women	18,496	4,001,123	3,944	3,703,116	31,952	701,460

Note: Figures cover firms located in the city
Source: 1997 Economic Census, Minority and Women-Owned Businesses

Minority Business Opportunity

10 of the 500 largest Hispanic-owned companies in the U.S. are located in San Antonio. *Hispanic Business, June 2003*

San Antonio is home to five companies which are on the Hispanic Business Fastest-Growing 100 list (greatest sales growth over the past five years): **Sphinx Consultants & Associates**; **The Alamo Travel Group**; **Professional Performance Devel. Group**; **Maldonado Nursery & Landscaping Inc.**; **Barrett Holdings Inc.**. *Hispanic Business, July/August 2003*

HOTELS

Hotels/Motels

Area	Hotels/Motels	Average Minimum Rates ($)		
		Tourist	First-Class	Deluxe
City	206	60	93	134

Source: OAG Travel Planner Online, Spring 2004

EVENT SITES

Major Event Sites, Meeting Places and Convention Centers

Name	Guest Rooms	Exhibit/ Meeting Space (sq. ft.)	Largest Meeting Room Capacity
Alamodome	n/a	n/a	73,000
Freeman Coliseum	n/a	n/a	12,000
Hyatt Regency San Antonio on the Riverwalk	632	39,000	4,205
Municipal Auditorium/San Antonio Convention Facilities	n/a	n/a	4,924
Nelson W. Wolff Municipal Stadium	n/a	n/a	6,200
San Antonio Convention Facilities	n/a	n/a	2,524
San Antonio Marriott Rivercenter/Riverwalk	1,087	65,000	6,400
Selma Musical Starplex	n/a	n/a	23,500
The St. Anthony A. Wyndham Grand Heritage Hotel	352	220,000	1,000

Note: n/a not available
Source: Original research

Living Environment

COST OF LIVING

Cost of Living Index

Year	Composite Index	Groceries	Housing	Utilities	Trans-portation	Health Care	Misc. Goods/ Services
2001	91.4	88.0	88.9	80.7	85.0	92.6	99.6
2002	88.2	81.9	84.3	80.1	83.1	95.1	97.0
2003	92.6	78.7	91.0	88.2	86.1	96.9	102.7

Note: U.S. = 100
Source: ACCRA, Cost of Living Index, 2001, 2002 and 2003 4-Quarter Averages

HOUSING

House Price Index (HPI)

Area	National Ranking[2]	Quarterly Change (%)	One-Year Change (%)	Five-Year Change (%)
MSA[1]	117	2.79	5.50	24.24
U.S.[3]	-	3.67	7.97	41.81

Note: The HPI is a weighted repeat sales index. It measures average price changes in repeat sales or refinancings on the same properties. This information is obtained by reviewing repeat mortgage transactions on single-family properties whose mortgages have been purchased or securitized by Fannie Mae of Freddie Mac in January 1975; (1) Metropolitan Statistical Area - see Appendix A for areas included; (2) Rankings are based on annual percentage change, for all MSAs containing at least 15,000 transactions over the last 10 years and ranges from 1 to 220; (3) figures based on a weighted division average; all figures are for the period ended December 31, 2003
Source: Office of Federal Housing Enterprise Oversight, House Price Index, March 1, 2004

Housing: Year Structure Built

Area	1990 -2000	1980 -1989	1970 -1979	1960 -1969	1950 -1959	1940 -1949	Before 1940	Median Year
City	16.4	22.0	19.9	14.9	13.2	6.9	6.6	1974
MSA[1]	20.1	22.5	20.1	13.6	11.3	6.1	6.2	1976
U.S.	17.0	15.8	18.5	13.7	12.7	7.3	15.0	1971

Note: Figures are percentages; (1) Metropolitan Statistical Area - see Appendix A for areas included
Source: Census 2000, Summary File 3

Average New Home Price

Area	2001	2002	2003
City	188,211	189,670	221,836
U.S.	212,643	236,567	248,193

Note: Figures, in dollars, are based on a new home with 2,400 sq. ft. of living area on an 8,000 sq. ft. lot.
Source: ACCRA, Cost of Living Index, 2001, 2002 and 2003 4-Quarter Averages

Average Apartment Rent

Area	2001	2002	2003
City	637	668	735
U.S.	674	708	721

Note: Figures, in dollars per month, are based on an unfurnished two bedroom, 1-1/2 or 2 bath apartment, approximately 950 sq. ft. in size, excluding all utilities except water
Source: ACCRA, Cost of Living Index, 2001, 2002 and 2003 4-Quarter Averages

RESIDENTIAL UTILITIES

Average Residential Utility Costs

Area	All Electric ($/mth)	Part Electric ($/mth)	Other Energy ($/mth)	Phone ($/mth)
City	–	75.15	36.80	20.52
U.S.	116.46	65.82	62.68	23.90

Source: ACCRA, Cost of Living Index, 2003 4-Quarter Average

HEALTH CARE

Average Health Care Costs

Area	Hospital ($/day)	Doctor ($/visit)	Dentist ($/visit)
City	610.01	66.63	85.80
U.S.	678.35	67.91	83.90

Note: Hospital—based on a semi-private room; Doctor—based on a general practitioner's routine exam of an established patient; Dentist—based on adult teeth cleaning and periodic oral exam.
Source: ACCRA, Cost of Living Index, 2003 4-Quarter Average

Distribution of Non-Federal, Office-Based Physicians

Area	Total	Family/ General Practice	Specialties		
			Medical	Surgical	Other
MSA[1] (number)	3,123	410	994	766	953
MSA[1] (rate per 10,000 pop.)	19.6	2.6	6.2	4.8	6.0
Metro Average[2] (rate per 10,000 pop.)	33.1	2.2	7.7	4.8	5.6

Note: Data as of December 31, 2001; (1) Metropolitan Statistical Area - see Appendix A for areas included; (2) Average of 81 MSAs and CMSAs in this book
Source: American Medical Association, Physician Characteristics & Distribution in the U.S., 2003-2004

Hospitals

San Antonio has the following hospitals: 15 general medical and surgical; 2 psychiatric; 1 tuberculosis and other respiratory disease; 2 rehabilitation; 2 long-term acute care; 1 other specialty; 1 children's psychiatric.
AHA Guide to the Healthcare Field, 2003-2004

According to *U.S. News*, San Antonio has one of the best hospitals in the U.S.: **University Health System**; *U.S. News Online, "America's Best Hospitals 2003"*

PRESIDENTIAL ELECTION

2000 Presidential Election Results

Area	Gore	Bush	Nader	Buchanan	Other
Bexar County	44.9	52.2	2.4	0.2	0.3
U.S.	48.4	47.9	2.7	0.4	0.6

Note: Results are percentages and may not add to 100% due to rounding
Source: www.cbsnews.com; www.uselectionatlas.org

EDUCATION

Public School District Statistics

District Name	Schls.	Enroll- ment	Classroom Teachers	Pupil/ Teacher Ratio	Minority Pupils[1] (%)	Current Expend.[2] ($/pupil)
Alamo Heights ISD	6	4,507	324	13.9	n/a	n/a
East Central ISD	12	7,891	505	15.6	n/a	n/a
Edgewood ISD	25	13,439	826	16.3	n/a	n/a
Fort Sam Houston ISD	2	1,232	115	10.7	n/a	n/a
Harlandale ISD	28	14,652	992	14.8	n/a	n/a
Judson ISD	21	17,160	1,178	14.6	n/a	5,922
Lackland ISD	2	1,052	90	11.6	n/a	n/a
New Frontiers Charter School	1	643	25	24.8	n/a	n/a
North East ISD	67	53,218	3,548	15.0	50.9	6,201
Northside ISD	85	66,000	4,351	15.2	63.3	5,824
San Antonio ISD	104	57,462	3,658	15.7	95.8	6,496
School of Excellence in Ed.	3	1,094	65	16.7	n/a	n/a
South San Antonio ISD	19	9,984	682	14.6	n/a	n/a
Southside ISD	7	4,652	309	15.0	n/a	n/a
Southwest ISD	15	9,445	656	14.4	n/a	n/a

Note: Data covers the 2001-02 school year unless otherwise noted; (1) Fall 2000; (2) FY2000; n/a not available
Source: U.S. Department of Education, National Center for Education Statistics, Common Core of Data, Local Education Agency (School District) Universe Survey: School Year 2001-2002; U.S. Department of Education, National Center for Education Statistics, Digest of Education Statistics 2002

Educational Quality

School District	Education Quotient[1]	Graduate Outcome[2]	Community Index[3]	Resource Index[4]
San Antonio ISD	12	11	2	56

Note: Scores are national percentile rankings and range from 1 (worst) to 99 (best); (1) Combination of the Graduate Outcome, Community and Resource indexes weighted to reflect the greater importance of the Graduate Outcome and Resource Index; (2) Based on graduation rates and college board scores (SAT/ACT); (3) Based on the surrounding community's level of affluence and adult education; (4) Based on teacher salaries, per-pupil expenditures and student-teacher ratios.
Source: Expansion Management, December 2003

Educational Attainment by Race

Area	High School Graduate (%)					Bachelor's Degree (%)				
	Total	White	Black	Asian	Hisp.[2]	Total	White	Black	Asian	Hisp.[2]
City	75.1	77.9	82.1	82.3	61.8	21.6	25.0	17.0	41.4	10.5
MSA[1]	77.3	80.2	83.2	81.4	62.3	22.4	25.5	18.0	38.4	10.6
U.S.	80.4	83.6	72.3	80.4	52.4	24.4	26.1	14.3	44.1	10.4

Note: Figures shown cover persons 25 years old and over; (1) Metropolitan Statistical Area - see Appendix A for areas included; (2) people of Hispanic origin can be of any race
Source: Census 2000, Summary File 3

School Enrollment by Type

Area	Grades KG to 8				Grades 9 to 12			
	Public		Private		Public		Private	
	Enrollment	%	Enrollment	%	Enrollment	%	Enrollment	%
City	153,162	90.8	15,589	9.2	66,419	92.3	5,523	7.7
MSA[1]	212,457	90.6	22,110	9.4	93,622	92.5	7,639	7.5
U.S.	33,526,011	88.7	4,285,121	11.3	14,848,628	90.6	1,532,323	9.4

Note: Figures shown cover persons 3 years old and over; (1) Metropolitan Statistical Area - see Appendix A for areas included
Source: Census 2000, Summary File 3

School Enrollment by Race

Area	Grades KG to 8 (%)				Grades 9 to 12 (%)			
	White	Black	Asian	Hisp.[1]	White	Black	Asian	Hisp.[1]
City	62.1	6.8	1.1	67.9	63.3	7.3	1.3	67.0
MSA[2]	65.0	6.8	1.1	60.4	66.3	7.4	1.3	58.9
U.S.	68.5	15.5	3.3	16.8	68.8	15.5	3.8	15.7

Note: Figures shown cover persons 3 years old and over; (1) people of Hispanic origin can be of any race; (2) Metropolitan Statistical Area - see Appendix A for areas included
Source: Census 2000, Summary File 3

Classroom Teacher Salaries in Public Schools

District	B.A. Degree		M.A. Degree		Maximum	
	Min. ($)	Rank[1]	Max. ($)	Rank[1]	Max. ($)	Rank[1]
San Antonio	34,000	28	55,699	32	55,699	68
DOD Average[2]	31,567	-	53,248	-	59,356	-

Note: Salaries are for 2001-2002; (1) Rank ranges from 1 to 100; (2) As per the U.S. Department of Defense Wage Fixing Authority
Source: American Federation of Teachers, Survey & Analysis of Teacher Salary Trends 2002

Higher Education

Four-Year Colleges			Two-Year Colleges			Medical Schools	Law Schools	Voc/ Tech
Public	Private Non-profit	Private For-profit	Public	Private Non-profit	Private For-profit			
2	6	0	4	1	2	1	1	20

Note: Figures cover institutions located within the city limits.
Source: National Center for Education Statistics, The Integrated Postsecondary Education System (IPEDS) Peer Analysis System, 2002; usnews.com, America's Best Graduate Schools 2004, Medical School Directory; The College Blue Book, Occupational Education, 2003; Barron's Guide to Law Schools, 2003; Medical School Admission Requirements U.S. & Canada, 2003-2004

**MAJOR
EMPLOYERS**

Major Employers

Company Name	Industry	Type
Air Education Training Command	National security	Branch
Air Force 37th Training Wing	National security	Branch
AT&T	Telephone communication, except radio	Branch
Baptist Medical Center	General medical and surgical hospitals	Branch
BASC	Vocational schools, nec	Branch
Boeing Company	Air transportation, scheduled	Branch
Christus Santa Rosa Health Care	General medical and surgical hospitals	Single
Cingular Wireless Llc	Radiotelephone communication	Branch
Methodist Healthcare System	General medical and surgical hospitals	Branch
Northeast Baptist Hospital	General medical and surgical hospitals	Headquarters
Pacific Telesis Group	Telephone communication, except radio	Headquarters
Prime Source Management	Help supply services	Single
Santa Rosa Childrens Hospital	Offices and clinics of medical doctors	Branch
South Texas Veterans	Administration of veterans' affairs	Branch
Southwest Research Institute	Commercial physical research	Headquarters
Takata-Petri LLC	Fabricated textile products, nec	Single
Univ TX Health Science Ctr	Colleges and universities	Headquarters
University Hospital	General medical and surgical hospitals	Headquarters
University Txas At San Antonio	Colleges and universities	Headquarters
USAA P & C Agency	Fire, marine, and casualty insurance	Headquarters
USAF Medical Center	Offices and clinics of medical doctors	Branch
West Teleservices	Business services, nec	Headquarters
Wilford Hall Medical Center	National security	Branch

Note: Companies shown are located in the metropolitan area and have 2,000 or more employees.
Source: www.zapdata.com, March 2004

PUBLIC SAFETY

Crime Rate

Area	All Crimes	Violent Crimes				Property Crimes		
		Murder	Forcible Rape	Robbery	Aggrav. Assault	Burglary	Larceny -Theft	Motor Vehicle Theft
City	7,873.3	8.4	38.8	176.8	593.1	1,118.1	5,457.6	480.4
Suburbs[1]	3,968.4	4.5	31.2	44.7	238.2	733.0	2,721.4	195.4
MSA[2]	6,775.3	7.3	36.7	139.7	493.3	1,009.8	4,688.3	400.3
U.S.	4,118.8	5.6	33.0	145.9	310.1	746.2	2,445.8	432.1

Note: Figures are crimes per 100,000 population; (1) All areas within the MSA that are located outside the city limits; (2) Metropolitan Statistical Area - see Appendix A for areas included
Source: FBI Uniform Crime Reports, 2002

RECREATION

Culture and Recreation

Museums	Orchestras	Opera Companies	Dance Companies	Professional Theatres	Zoos	Pro Sports Teams[1]
11	2	0	4	4	1	1

Note: (1) Covers the Metropolitan Statistical Area - see Appendix A for areas included.
Source: The Grey House Performing Arts Directory, 2002; Official Museum Directory, 2004; www.sportsvenues.com

Library System

The San Antonio Public Library has 28 branches, holdings of 1,982,577 volumes, and a budget of $20,453,148 (2001-2002).
American Library Directory, 2003-2004

MEDIA

Newspapers

Name	Type	Freq.	Distribution	Circulation
Kelly Observer	General	1x/wk	Local	18,500
Lackland Talespinner	General	1x/wk	Local	20,000
La Prensa de San Antonio	Hispanic	2x/wk	Regional	162,000
Metrocom Herald	General	1x/wk	Local	39,600
North San Antonio Times	General	1x/wk	Local	90,700
Northwest Recorder	General	1x/wk	Local	90,600
San Antonio Current	Alternative	1x/wk	Local	41,000
San Antonio Express-News	General	7x/wk	Regional	228,995
Southside Reporter	General	1x/wk	Local	68,000
Southside Sun	General	1x/wk	Local	31,000
Today's Catholic	Catholic	Hispanic 2x/mth		United States
Westside Sun	General	1x/wk	Local	50,000

Note: Includes newspapers whose offices are located in the city and whose circulations are 10,000 or more
Source: Burrelle's Media Directory, 2003

Television Stations

Name	Ch.	Affiliation	Type	Owner
WOAI	4	NBCT	Commercial	Clear Channel Broadcasting Inc.
KENS	5	CBST	Commercial	Belo Corporation
KLRN	9	PBS	Public	Alamo Public Telecommunications Council
KSAT	12	ABCT	Commercial	Post-Newsweek Business Information Inc.
KHCE	23	n/a	Non-comm.	Trinity Broadcasting Network
KPXL	26	PAXTV	Commercial	Paxson Communications Corporation
KABB	29	FBC	Commercial	Sinclair Broadcast Group
KRRT	35	WB	Commercial	Sinclair Broadcast Group
KWEX	41	UNIN	Commercial	Univision Television Group
KVDA	60	TMUN	Commercial	Telemundo Group Inc.

Note: Stations included broadcast from the San Antonio metro area; n/a not available
Source: Burrelle's Media Directory, 2003

AM Radio Stations

Call Letters	Freq. (kHz)	Target Audience	Station Format	Music Format
KTSA	550	General	M/N/T	Adult Contemporary
KSLR	630	G/R	E/M/N/T	Oldies
KKYX	680	General	M/N/S	Country
KSAH	720	Hispanic	M/N/S	Latin
KTKR	760	G/M	M/S	Adult Contemporary
KONO	860	General	M/N	Oldies
KLUP	930	General	M/T	Adult Standards
KBIB	1000	H/R	M	Christian
KDRY	1100	Religious	E/M/T	Christian
KENS	1160	General	M/N/T	Alternative
WOAI	1200	General	M/N/S/T	Latin
KZDC	1250	General	M/N/S/T	Latin
KCOR	1350	Hispanic	M/N/S	Latin
KEDA	1540	Hispanic	M/S	Latin

Note: Stations included broadcast from the San Antonio metro area
The following abbreviations may be used:
Target Audience: A=Asian; B=Black; C=Christian; E=Ethnic; F=French; G=General; H=Hispanic;
M=Men; N=Native American; R=Religious; S=Senior Citizen; W=Women; Y=Young Adult; Z=Children
Station Format: E=Educational; M=Music; N=News; S=Sports; T=Talk
Source: Burrelle's Media Directory, 2003

FM Radio Stations

Call Letters	Freq. (mHz)	Target Audience	Station Format	Music Format
KPAC	88.3	General	E/M	Classical
KSTX	89.1	General	E/M/N/T	Alternative
KTXI	90.1	General	E/M/N	Classical
KRTU	91.7	General	M	Adult Standards
KROM	92.9	Hispanic	M/N	Latin
KLEY	94.1	Hispanic	M/N/S	Latin
KCOR	95.1	Hispanic	M	Adult Contemporary
KBUC	95.7	General	M	Country
KXXM	96.1	General	M/N/T	Top 40
KAJA	97.3	General	M/N/S	Country
KISS	99.5	General	M/N/S	Modern Rock
KCYY	100.3	General	M/N	Country
KONO	101.1	General	M/N/S	Oldies
KQXT	101.9	General	M/N/T	Adult Contemporary
KTFM	102.7	General	M	Adult Contemporary
KZEP	104.5	General	M	Classic Rock
KSMG	105.3	General	M/N	80's
KCJZ	106.7	General	M/N/T	Adult Contemporary
KXTN	107.5	Hispanic	M	Country

Note: Stations included broadcast from the San Antonio metro area
The following abbreviations may be used:
Target Audience: A=Asian; B=Black; C=Christian; E=Ethnic; F=French; G=General; H=Hispanic;
M=Men; N=Native American; R=Religious; S=Senior Citizen; W=Women; Y=Young Adult; Z=Children
Station Format: E=Educational; M=Music; N=News; S=Sports; T=Talk
Source: Burrelle's Media Directory, 2003

CLIMATE

Average and Extreme Temperatures

Temperature	Jan	Feb	Mar	Apr	May	Jun	Jul	Aug	Sep	Oct	Nov	Dec	Yr.
Extreme High (°F)	89	97	100	100	103	105	106	108	103	98	94	90	108
Average High (°F)	62	66	74	80	86	92	95	95	90	82	71	64	80
Average Temp. (°F)	51	55	62	70	76	82	85	85	80	71	60	53	69
Average Low (°F)	39	43	50	58	66	72	74	74	69	59	49	41	58
Extreme Low (°F)	0	6	19	31	43	53	62	61	46	33	21	6	0

Note: Figures cover the years 1948-1990
Source: National Climatic Data Center, International Station Meteorological Climate Summary, 9/96

Average Precipitation/Snowfall/Humidity

Precip./Humidity	Jan	Feb	Mar	Apr	May	Jun	Jul	Aug	Sep	Oct	Nov	Dec	Yr.
Avg. Precip. (in.)	1.5	1.8	1.5	2.6	3.8	3.6	2.0	2.5	3.3	3.2	2.3	1.4	29.6
Avg. Snowfall (in.)	1	Tr	Tr	0	0	0	0	0	0	0	Tr	Tr	1
Avg. Rel. Hum. 6am (%)	79	80	79	82	87	87	87	86	85	83	81	79	83
Avg. Rel. Hum. 3pm (%)	51	48	45	48	51	48	43	42	47	46	48	49	47

Note: Figures cover the years 1948-1990; Tr = Trace amounts (<0.05 in. of rain; <0.5 in. of snow)
Source: National Climatic Data Center, International Station Meteorological Climate Summary, 9/96

Weather Conditions

Temperature			Daytime Sky			Precipitation		
32°F & below	45°F & below	90°F & above	Clear	Partly cloudy	Cloudy	0.01 inch or more precip.	0.1 inch or more snow/ice	Thunder-storms
23	91	112	97	153	115	81	1	36

Note: Figures are average number of days per year and covers the years 1948-1990
Source: National Climatic Data Center, International Station Meteorological Climate Summary, 9/96

HAZARDOUS WASTE

Superfund Sites

San Antonio has no sites on the EPA's Superfund National Priorities List.
U.S. Environmental Protection Agency, National Priorities List, March 15, 2004

**AIR & WATER
QUALITY**

Maximum Pollutant Concentrations

	Particulate Matter (ug/m³)	Carbon Monoxide (ppm)	Sulfur Dioxide (ppm)	Nitrogen Dioxide (ppm)	Ozone 1-hour (ppm)	Ozone 8-hour (ppm)	Lead (ug/m³)
MSA[1] Level	67	3	n/a	0.017	0.13	0.1	n/a
NAAQS[2]	150	9	0.140	0.053	0.12	0.08	1.50
Met NAAQS[2]	Yes	Yes	n/a	Yes	No	No	n/a

Note: (1) Metropolitan Statistical Area - see Appendix A for areas included; (2) National Ambient Air Quality Standards; n/a not available
Units: ppm = parts per million; ug/m³ = micrograms per cubic meter
Source: EPA, Latest Findings on National Air Quality: 2002 Status and Trends, August 2003

Air Quality Index

In the San Antonio MSA (see Appendix A for areas included), the Air Quality Index (AQI) exceeded 100 on 17 days in 2002. An AQI value greater than 100 indicates that air quality would have been in the unhealthful range on that day.
EPA, Latest Findings on National Air Quality: 2002 Status and Trends, August 2003

Watershed Health

The U.S. Environmental Protection Agency monitors the health of the aquatic resources for the nation's 2,000+ watersheds. **The Upper San Antonio watershed serves the San Antonio area and received an overall Index of Watershed Indicators (IWI) score of 3 (less serious problems - low vulnerability).** The IWI score is based on seven condition and nine vulnerability indicators. The overall IWI score ranges from 1 (best health) to 6 (worst health). The Condition Indicators include: designated use attainment, fish and wildlife consumption advisories, source water condition, contaminated sediments, ambient water quality, and wetlands loss index. The Vulnerability Indicators include: aquatic species at risk, conventional and toxic loads over permitted limits, urban and agricultural runoff potential, population change, hydrologic modification, estuarine pollution susceptibility, and air deposition. *EPA, Index of Watershed Indicators, October 26, 2001*

Drinking Water

Water System Name	Pop. Served	Primary Water Source Type	Number of Violations January 2002-February 2004		
			Health Based	Significant Monitoring	Monitoring
San Antonio Water System	1,219,113	Ground	None	None	None

Note: Data as of February 19, 2004
Source: EPA, Office of Ground Water and Drinking Water, Safe Drinking Water Information System

San Antonio tap water is not fluoridated and has moderate mineral content, chiefly sodium bicarbonate.
Editor & Publisher Market Guide, 2004

Savannah, Georgia

Background

Savannah, at the mouth of the Savannah River on the border between Georgia and South Carolina, is Georgia's second-fastest-growing city. It was established in 1733 when General James Oglethorpe landed with a group of settlers in the sailing vessel Anne, after a voyage of more than three months. City Hall now stands at the spot where Oglethorpe and his followers first camped at a small bluff overlooking the river.

Savannah is unique among American cities in that it was extensively planned while Oglethorpe was still in England. Each new settler was given a package of property, including a town lot, a garden space, and an outlying farm area. The town was planned in quadrants—the north and south for residences, and the east and west for public buildings.

The quadrant design was inspired in part by considerations of public defense, given the unsettled character of relations with Native Americans, but in fact an early treaty between the settlers and the Creek Indian Chief Tomochichi allowed Savannah to develop quite peacefully, with little of the hostility between Europeans and Indians that marred much of the development elsewhere in the colonies.

Savannah was taken by the British during the American Revolution, and in the patriotic siege that followed, many lives were lost. Count Pulaski, among other Revolutionary heroes, lost his life during the battle, but Savannah was eventually retaken in 1782 by the American Generals Nathaniel Greene and Anthony Wayne.

In the post-Revolutionary period, Savannah grew dramatically, its economic strength being driven in large part by Eli Whitney's cotton gin. As the world's leader in the cotton trade, Savannah also hosted a great development in export activity, and the first American steamboat built in the United States to cross the Atlantic was launched in its busy port.

Savannah's physical structure had been saved from the worst ravages of war, but the destruction of the area's infrastructure slowed its further development for an extended period, and "sleepy" became a common adjective applied to the once-vibrant economic center. In the long period of slow recovery that followed, one of the great Savannah success stories was the establishment of the Girl Scouts in 1912 by Juliette Gordon Low.

In 1954, an extensive fire destroyed a large portion of the historic City Market, and the area was bulldozed to make room for a parking garage. The Historic Savannah Foundation has worked unceasingly since then to maintain and improve Savannah's considerable architectural charms.

As a result, Savannah's Historic District was designated a Registered National Historic Landmark. Savannah has also been one of the favored sites for movie makers for decades. More than forty major movies have been filmed in Savannah including *Roots* (1976), *East of Eden* (1980), *Forrest Gump* (1993), *Midnight in the Garden of Good and Evil* (1997) and *The Legend of Bagger Vance* (1999), directed by Robert Redford.

Tourism, military services, port operations, and retail industries are major employers in the city. Savannah's port facilities, operated by the Georgia Port Authority, have seen notable growth in container tonnage in recent years. Military installations in the area include Hunter Army Airfield and Fort Stewart military bases, employing a combined 42,000 people.

In addition, the city's beauty draws not just tourists, but conventioneers. The Savannah International Trade & Convention Center is a state-of-the-art facility with 100,000 square feet of exhibition space, accommodating nearly 10,000 people.

Colleges and universities in the city include the Savannah College of Art and Design.

Savannah's climate is subtropical, with hot summers and mild winters, making the city an ideal locale for all-year outside activities.

Rankings

- Savannah was ranked #156 out of 331 metro areas in *Cities Ranked & Rated*. Criteria: cost of living; climate; crime; transportation; economy and jobs; education; arts and culture; health and healthcare; leisure. *Cities Ranked & Rated, 1st Edition, 2004*

- *Ladies Home Journal* ranked America's 200 largest cities based on the qualities women surveyed care about most. Savannah ranked #141 out of 143 in the smaller city category (population under 300,000). Criteria: crime; lifestyle; education; jobs; health; child care; politics; and the economy. *Ladies Home Journal Online, "The Best Cities for Women 2002"*

- *Forbes* ranked 168 smaller metro areas in the U.S. in terms of the "Best Places for Business and Careers." The Savannah metro area was ranked #50. Criteria: income and job growth; cost-of-doing-business; qualifications of the available pool of labor; crime rates; housing costs; net migration. *Forbes, May 9, 2003*

- *Men's Health* ranked 101 U.S. cities in terms of the quality of their tap water. Savannah received a grade of. Criteria: levels of bacteria, arsenic, lead, trihalomethanes, and haloacetic acids were compared with the National Academy of Science's guidelines as well as with the EPA's more stringent maximum contaminant level goals. *Men's Health, March 2004*

- Sperling's BestPlaces ranked 331 metro areas and identified the most and least stressful U.S. cities. The Savannah metro area ranked #44 out of 114 mid-size metro areas (#1 = most stressful). Criteria: divorce rate; unemployment rate; violent and property crime; suicide rate; commute time; mental health; alcohol consumption; cloudy days. *www.BestPlaces.net, February 26, 2004*

- Savannah was ranked #126 out of America's 200 largest metro areas in *SELF Magazine's* ranking of "America's Healthiest Cities for Women." Criteria: safety; air/water quality; cancer rates; and 21 other factors relating to health. *SELF Magazine, November 2003*

- *Zero Population Growth* ranked 239 cities in terms of children's health, safety, and economic well-being. Savannah was ranked #115 out of 140 independent cities (cities with populations greater than 100,000 which were neither major cities nor suburbs/outer cities) and was given a grade of C. Criteria: total population and population growth; percent of population under 18 years of age; number of children's museums; health improvement grade; percent of births to teens; percent of low birthweight infants; infant mortality rate; number of Title X-funded clinics; average SAT/ACT scores; average elementary and secondary class size; crime rate; unemployment rate; percent of affordable homes; number of bad air days; park acres per 1000 persons; library circulation per child; and children's program attendance counts. *Zero Population Growth, Kid Friendly Cities Report Card 2001*

- Savannah was selected as one of the "Best Places to Retire" in *Money* magazine's most recent survey of the best places to retire in America. Criteria: cities were ranked on a wide variety of quality-of-life factors important to retirees. *Money, July 2003*

- *Ladies Home Journal* ranked America's 200 largest cities in terms of safety. Savannah ranked #158 out of 200. Criteria: violent crimes; crimes against property; and rape. *Ladies Home Journal Online, "The Best Cities for Women 2002"*

- *Condé Nast Traveler* polled over 32,000 readers for travel satisfaction. American cities were ranked based on the following criteria: friendliness; ambiance; culture/sites; restaurants; lodging and shopping. Savannah appeared in the top 10, ranking #10. *Condé Nast Traveler, Readers' Choice Awards 2003*

- The Savannah metro area was cited as one of "The Best Places in the U.S. to Locate a Company." The area ranked #159 out of 329. Criteria: education (with emphasis on college board test results and high school graduation rates); availability of quality healthcare services and the cost to employers; quality of life; logistics workforce and companies; transportation infrastructure; quality and quantity of highly educated technical workers; business climate. *Expansion Management, July 2003*

- The Savannah metro area appeared on *Forbes/Milken Institute* list of "Best Places for Business and Career." Rank: #156 out of 200 metro areas. Criteria: salary growth; job growth; number of technology clusters; overall concentration of technology activity relative to national average; and technology output growth. *www.forbes.com, Forbes/Milken Institute Best Places 2002*

- The Savannah metro area appeared on the "Milken Institute Best Performing Cities" index. Rank: #75 out of 200 large metro areas. Criteria: job growth; wage and salary growth; high-tech output growth. *Milken Institute, June 25, 2003*

- The Savannah metro area appeared on *IndustryWeek's* fourth annual World-Class Communities list. It ranked #68 out of 315 metro areas. Criteria: MSA Gross Metropolitan Product (GMP) per manufacturing employee; and MSA percent share of U.S. manufacturing Gross Domestic Product (GDP). *IndustryWeek, April 16, 2001*

Business Environment

CITY FINANCES

City Government Finances

Component	2000-2001 ($000)	2000-2001 ($ per capita)
Total Revenues	279,709	2,127
Total Expenditures	230,661	1,754
Debt Outstanding	214,226	1,629
Cash and Securities	369,916	2,813

Source: U.S Census Bureau, Government Finances 2000-2001, August 2003

City Government Revenue by Source

Source	2000-2001 ($000)	2000-2001 ($ per capita)
General Revenue		
From Federal Government	23,097	176
From State Government	11,301	86
From Local Governments	31,733	241
Taxes		
Property	36,218	275
Sales	40,290	306
Personal Income	0	0
License	0	0
Charges	76,037	578
Liquor Store	0	0
Utility	24,187	184
Employee Retirement	4,715	36
Other	32,131	244

Source: U.S Census Bureau, Government Finances 2000-2001, August 2003

City Government Expenditures by Function

Function	2000-2001 ($000)	2000-2001 ($ per capita)	2000-2001 (%)
General Expenditures			
Airports	7,777	59	3.4
Corrections	224	2	0.1
Education	0	0	0.0
Fire Protection	12,256	93	5.3
Governmental Administration	11,306	86	4.9
Health	0	0	0.0
Highways	7,415	56	3.2
Hospitals	0	0	0.0
Housing and Community Development	16,977	129	7.4
Interest on General Debt	7,192	55	3.1
Libraries	0	0	0.0
Parking	2,347	18	1.0
Parks and Recreation	15,059	115	6.5
Police Protection	26,115	199	11.3
Public Welfare	916	7	0.4
Sewerage	30,189	230	13.1
Solid Waste Management	20,347	155	8.8
Liquor Store	0	0	0.0
Utility	28,437	216	12.3
Employee Retirement	6,777	52	2.9
Other	37,327	284	16.2

Source: U.S Census Bureau, Government Finances 2000-2001, August 2003

Municipal Bond Ratings

Area	Moody's
City	Aa3

Source: Mergent Bond Record, February 2004

DEMOGRAPHICS

Population Growth

Area	1990 Census	2000 Census	2003 Estimate	2008 Projection	Population Growth (%)	
					1990-2000	2000-2008
City	138,038	131,510	129,941	127,574	-4.7	-3.0
MSA[1]	258,060	293,000	301,712	316,118	13.5	7.9
U.S.	248,709,873	281,421,906	290,647,163	305,918,071	13.2	8.7

Note: (1) Metropolitan Statistical Area - see Appendix A for areas included
Source: Claritas, Inc.

Number of Households and Average Household Size

Area	1990 Census	2000 Census	2003 Estimate	2008 Projection	2003 Average Household Size
City	52,072	51,375	51,328	51,338	2.5
MSA[1]	94,940	111,105	115,609	123,302	2.6
U.S.	91,947,410	105,480,101	109,440,059	116,034,472	2.7

Note: (1) Metropolitan Statistical Area - see Appendix A for areas included
Source: Claritas, Inc.

Race and Ethnicity

Area	White Non-Hispanic	Black Non-Hispanic	Asian Non-Hispanic	Other Race Non-Hispanic	Hispanic
City	37.4	58.3	1.6	2.7	2.3
MSA[1]	61.0	34.9	1.6	2.5	2.3
U.S.	74.5	12.4	3.8	9.3	13.2

Note: Figures are 2003 estimates; (1) Metropolitan Statistical Area - see Appendix A for areas included
Source: Claritas, Inc.

Segregation

City		MSA[1]	
Index[2]	Rank[3]	Index[2]	Rank[4]
60.3	49	64.6	103

Note: Figures are based on an analysis of Census 2000 data; (1) Metropolitan Statistical Area - see Appendix A for areas included; (2) Dissimilarity Index—the most commonly used measure of segregation between two groups, reflecting their relative distributions across neighborhoods within a city or metropolitan area. It can range in value from 0, indicating complete integration, to 100, indicating complete segregation; (3) Ranges from 1 (most segregated) to 100 (least segregated) and includes all the cities in this book; (4) Ranges from 1 (most segregated) to 318 (least segregated) and includes 318 metropolitan areas.
Source: www.CensusScope.org

Ancestry

Area	German	Irish[2]	English	American	Italian	Polish	French[3]	Scottish
City	5.2	5.9	5.9	5.1	1.6	0.8	1.3	1.9
MSA[1]	8.6	8.6	8.3	10.5	2.2	1.1	1.9	2.3
U.S.	15.2	10.9	8.7	7.3	5.6	3.2	3.0	1.7

Note: Figures include multiple ancestry (e.g. if a person reported being Irish and Italian, they were included in both columns); (1) Metropolitan Statistical Area - see Appendix A for areas included; (2) Includes Celtic; (3) Includes Alsatian but excludes Basque
Source: Census 2000, Summary File 3

Foreign-Born Population

Area	Percent of Population Born in:							
	Any Foreign Country	Europe	Asia	Africa	Oceania[2]	Canada	Mexico	Latin America[3]
City	3.9	0.9	1.3	0.2	0.1	0.2	0.6	0.7
MSA[1]	3.5	0.8	1.3	0.2	0.0	0.2	0.4	0.6
U.S.	11.1	1.7	2.9	0.3	0.1	0.3	3.3	2.5

Note: (1) Metropolitan Statistical Area - see Appendix A for areas included; (2) Includes Australia, New Zealand subregion, Melanesia, Micronesia, Polynesia, and Oceania n.e.c; (3) Includes Central America (excluding Mexico), South America, and the Caribbean.
Source: Census 2000, Summary File 3

Religion

Area	Catholic	Southern Baptist	United Methodist	ELCA[1]	LDS[2]	Presbyterian Church USA	Jewish Est.	Muslim Est.
County	9.0	14.9	6.7	1.5	0.3	1.4	1.3	0.3
U.S.	22.0	7.1	3.7	1.8	1.5	1.1	2.2	0.6

Note: Figures shown are the number of adherents as a percentage of the total population; Adherents are defined as all members, including full members, their children and the estimated number of other participants who are not considered members (e.g. the baptized, those not confirmed, those not eligible for communion, those regularly attending services, etc.); (1) Evangelical Lutheran Church in America; (2) The Church of Jesus Christ of Latter Day Saints
Source: Reprinted with permission from Religious Congregations and Membership in the United States 2000 (Nashville, Glenmary Research Center, 2002) Copyright Association of Statisticians of American Religious Bodies. All rights reserved.

Age Distribution

Area	Percent of Population						
	Under Age 5	Age 5 to 17	Age 18 to 34	Age 35 to 49	Age 50 to 64	Age 65 to 79	80 Years and Over
City	7.0	18.6	27.7	20.1	13.2	9.4	4.0
MSA[1]	6.8	19.3	24.7	22.9	14.4	8.9	3.0
U.S.	6.8	18.9	23.7	23.5	14.8	9.2	3.2

Note: (1) Metropolitan Statistical Area - see Appendix A for areas included
Source: Census 2000, Summary File 3

Marriage Status

Area	Never Married	Now Married Except Separated	Separated	Widowed	Divorced
City	35.6	40.2	3.5	8.8	11.9
MSA[1]	27.7	51.8	2.4	7.0	11.1
U.S.	27.1	54.4	2.2	6.6	9.7

Note: Figures cover population 15 years of age and older; (1) Metropolitan Statistical Area - see Appendix A for areas included
Source: Census 2000, Summary File 3

Male/Female Ratio

Area	Males	Females	Males per 100 Females
City	61,334	68,607	89.4
MSA[1]	146,303	155,409	94.1
U.S.	142,511,883	148,135,280	96.2

Note: Figures are 2003 estimates; (1) Metropolitan Statistical Area - see Appendix A for areas included
Source: Claritas, Inc.

ECONOMY

Gross Metropolitan Product

Area	1999	2000	2001	2002	2002 Rank[2]
MSA[1]	9.7	10.5	10.8	11.3	154

Note: Figures are in billions of dollars; (1) Metropolitan Statistical Area - see Appendix A for areas included; (2) Rank ranges from 1 to 319
Source: The U.S. Conference of Mayors, Metro Economies Report, July 2003

INCOME

Per Capita/Median/Average Income

Area	Per Capita ($)	Median Household ($)	Average Household ($)
City	18,779	32,949	46,570
MSA[1]	23,849	45,054	61,541
U.S.	24,078	46,868	63,207

Note: Figures are 2003 estimates; (1) Metropolitan Statistical Area - see Appendix A for areas included
Source: Claritas, Inc.

Household Income Distribution

Area	Percent of Households Earning							
	Under $15,000	$15,000 -24,999	$25,000 -34,999	$35,000 -49,999	$50,000 -74,999	$75,000 -99,000	$100,000 -149,999	$150,000 and up
City	23.5	15.5	13.8	15.6	15.7	7.6	5.5	2.8
MSA[1]	15.9	11.9	12.0	15.3	18.7	11.3	9.6	5.4
U.S.	14.1	11.5	11.7	16.0	19.2	11.3	10.2	6.0

Note: Figures are 2003 estimates; (1) Metropolitan Statistical Area - see Appendix A for areas included
Source: Claritas, Inc.

Poverty Rates by Age

Area	All Ages	Under 5 Years Old	5 to 17 Years Old	18 to 64 Years Old	65 Years and Over
City	21.8	2.4	5.8	11.5	2.1
MSA[1]	14.5	1.5	3.8	7.8	1.4
U.S.	12.4	1.2	3.0	6.9	1.2

Note: Figures are percent of population with income in 1999 below poverty level and only include population for whom poverty status is determined; (1) Metropolitan Statistical Area - see Appendix A for areas included
Source: Census 2000, Summary File 3

Personal Bankruptcy Filing Rate

Area	2002	2003
Chatham County	10.74	10.68
U.S.	5.34	5.58

Note: Numbers are per 1,000 population and include Chapter 7 and Chapter 13 filings
Source: Federal Deposit Insurance Corporation (FDIC), Regional Economic Conditions (RECON), 2/25/2004

EMPLOYMENT

Labor Force and Employment

Area	Civilian Labor Force			Workers Employed		
	Dec. 2002	Dec. 2003	% Chg.	Dec. 2002	Dec. 2003	% Chg.
City	67,604	68,673	1.6	64,327	65,717	2.2
MSA[1]	144,262	146,603	1.6	138,529	141,524	2.2
U.S.	144,807,000	146,501,000	1.2	136,599,000	138,556,000	1.4

Note: Data is not seasonally adjusted and covers workers 16 years of age and older;
(1) Metropolitan Statistical Area - see Appendix A for areas included
Source: Bureau of Labor Statistics, http://stats.bls.gov

Unemployment Rate

Area	2003											
	Jan.	Feb.	Mar.	Apr.	May	Jun.	Jul.	Aug.	Sep.	Oct.	Nov.	Dec.
City	4.1	4.2	4.2	4.1	4.7	6.1	6.7	5.2	5.0	4.5	4.2	4.3
MSA[1]	3.4	3.5	3.5	3.4	3.8	4.9	5.7	4.1	4.1	3.7	3.4	3.5
U.S.	6.5	6.4	6.2	5.8	5.8	6.5	6.3	6.0	5.8	5.6	5.6	5.4

Note: Data is not seasonally adjusted and covers workers 16 years of age and older; All figures are percentages; (1) Metropolitan Statistical Area - see Appendix A for areas included
Source: Bureau of Labor Statistics, http://stats.bls.gov

Employment by Occupation

Occupation Classification	City (%)	MSA[1] (%)	U.S. (%)
Sales and Office	27.1	26.8	26.7
Professional and Related	19.1	19.9	20.2
Service	20.7	16.1	14.9
Production, Transportation, and Material Moving	14.0	13.9	14.6
Management, Business, and Financial	9.5	11.3	13.5
Construction, Extraction, and Maintenance	9.5	11.7	9.4
Farming, Forestry, and Fishing	0.1	0.3	0.7

Note: Figures cover employed civilians 16 years of age and older;
(1) Metropolitan Statistical Area - see Appendix A for areas included
Source: Census 2000, Summary File 3

Employment by Industry

Sector	MSA[1]		U.S.
	Number of Employees	Percent of Total	Percent of Total
Government	21,400	15.0	16.7
Education and Health Services	19,500	13.6	12.9
Professional and Business Services	15,800	11.1	12.3
Retail Trade	18,000	12.6	11.8
Manufacturing	13,500	9.4	11.0
Leisure and Hospitality	17,900	12.5	9.1
Finance Activities	6,500	4.5	6.1
Construction	n/a	n/a	5.1
Wholesale Trade	5,000	3.5	4.3
Other Services	7,000	4.9	4.1
Transportation and Utilities	8,000	5.6	3.7
Information	1,900	1.3	2.4
Natural Resources and Mining	n/a	n/a	0.4

Note: Figures cover non-farm employment as of December 2003 and are not seasonally adjusted;
(1) Metropolitan Statistical Area - see Appendix A for areas included; n/a not available
Source: Bureau of Labor Statistics, http://stats.bls.gov

Average Wages

Occupation	$/Hr.	Occupation	$/Hr.
Accountants and Auditors	20.15	Maids and Housekeeping Cleaners	6.93
Automotive Mechanics	13.79	Maintenance and Repair Workers	13.89
Bookkeepers	12.56	Marketing Managers	36.44
Carpenters	14.84	Nuclear Medicine Technologists	n/a
Cashiers	7.00	Nurses, Licensed Practical	13.06
Clerks, General Office	10.00	Nurses, Registered	23.22
Clerks, Receptionists/Information	9.51	Nursing Aides/Orderlies/Attendants	8.12
Clerks, Shipping/Receiving	11.56	Packers and Packagers, Hand	8.21
Computer Programmers	24.07	Physical Therapists	27.76
Computer Support Specialists	16.68	Postal Service Mail Carriers	18.71
Computer Systems Analysts	27.25	Real Estate Brokers	n/a
Cooks, Restaurant	8.17	Retail Salespersons	9.28
Dentists	77.71	Sales Reps., Exc. Tech./Scientific	20.66
Electrical Engineers	30.64	Sales Reps., Tech./Scientific	30.52
Electricians	15.95	Secretaries, Exc. Legal/Med./Exec.	11.30
Financial Managers	32.45	Security Guards	9.09
First-Line Supervisors/Mgrs., Sales	13.65	Surgeons	98.80
Food Preparation Workers	7.41	Teacher Assistants	7.40
General and Operations Managers	32.69	Teachers, Elementary School	21.20
Hairdressers/Cosmetologists	8.74	Teachers, Secondary School	21.50
Internists	76.80	Telemarketers	n/a
Janitors and Cleaners	7.59	Truck Drivers, Heavy/Tractor-Trailer	16.01
Landscaping/Groundskeeping Workers	9.31	Truck Drivers, Light/Delivery Svcs.	11.31
Lawyers	33.45	Waiters and Waitresses	7.07

Note: Wage data is for 2002 and covers the Metropolitan Statistical Area (see Appendix A for areas included).
Hourly wages for elementary/secondary school teachers and teacher assistants were calculated by the editors
from annual wage data assuming a 40 hour work week; n/a not available.
Source: Bureau of Labor Statistics, 2002 Metro Area Occupational Employment and Wage Estimates

Occupational Employment Projections: 1996 - 2006

Occupations Expected to Have the Largest Job Growth (ranked by numerical growth)	Fast-Growing Occupations[1] (ranked by percent growth)
1. General managers & top executives	1. Medical assistants
2. Cashiers	2. Physical therapy assistants and aides
3. Salespersons, retail	3. Occupational therapists
4. Child care workers, private household	4. Home health aides
5. Truck drivers, light	5. Occupational therapy assistants
6. General office clerks	6. Personal and home care aides
7. Systems analysts	7. Paralegals
8. Registered nurses	8. Respiratory therapists
9. Marketing & sales, supervisors	9. Customer service representatives
10. Receptionists and information clerks	10. Child care workers, private household

Note: Projections cover Georgia; (1) Excludes occupations with total job growth less than 300
Source: U.S. Department of Labor, Employment and Training Administration, America's Labor Market Information System (ALMIS)

TAXES

State Corporate Income Tax Rates

State	Rate (%)	Number of Brackets	Low Bracket (Under $)	High Bracket (Over $)
Georgia	6.0	1	na	na

Note: Tax rates as of December 31, 2003; na not applicable
Source: Tax Foundation, www.taxfoundation.org

State Individual Income Tax Rates

State	Federal Deductibility	Marginal Rate (%)	Number of Brackets	Low Bracket (Under $)	High Bracket (Over $)
Georgia	No	1.0-6.0	6	0	7,000

Note: Tax rates as of December 31, 2003; Brackets apply to single taxpayers and married people filing separately; na not applicable
Source: Tax Foundation, www.taxfoundation.org

Various State and Local Tax Rates

State Sales and Use (%)	Total Sales and Use (%)	Gasoline (cents/gal.)	Cigarette (cents/pack)	Spirits ($/gal.)	Table Wine ($/gal.)	Beer ($/gal.)
4.0	6.0	7.5	12	3.79	1.51	0.48

Note: Tax rates as of December 31, 2003
Source: Tax Foundation, www.taxfoundation.org

State Tax Burdens

Area	Combined State and Local Tax Burden		Combined Federal, State and Local Tax Burden	
	Percent	Rank	Percent	Rank
Georgia	9.9	16	29.2	20
U.S. Average	9.7	-	30.0	-

Note: Figures are for 2003
Source: Tax Foundation, www.taxfoundation.org

Internal Revenue Service Tax Audits

IRS District	Percent of Returns Audited				
	1996	1997	1998	1999	2000
Georgia	0.78	0.64	0.48	0.31	0.11
U.S.	0.66	0.61	0.46	0.31	0.20

Note: Figures cover IRS district audits of federal income tax returns filed by individuals. Geographic data on district audits for 2001 and 2002 are being withheld by the IRS. TRAC is challenging this policy.
Source: Syracuse University, Transactional Records Access Clearinghouse (TRAC), "Odds of IRS District Tax Audit 2000"

RESIDENTIAL REAL ESTATE

Building Permits

Area	Single-Family			Multi-Family			Total		
	2001	2002	Pct. Chg.	2001	2002	Pct. Chg.	2001	2002	Pct. Chg.
City	127	139	9.4	40	55	37.5	167	194	16.2
U.S.	1,235,600	1,332,600	7.9	401,100	415,100	3.5	1,636,700	1,747,700	6.8

Note: Figures represent new, privately-owned housing units authorized (unadjusted data)
Source: U.S. Census Bureau, Manufacturing, Mining, and Construction Statistics

Homeownership and Housing Vacancies

Area	Homeownership Rate[2] (%)			Rental Vacancy Rate[3] (%)			Homeowner Vacancy Rate[4] (%)		
	2001	2002[a]	2003	2001	2002[a]	2003	2001	2002[a]	2003
MSA[1]	n/a	n/a	n/a	n/a	n/a	n/a	n/a	n/a	n/a
U.S.	67.8	67.9	68.3	8.4	8.9	9.8	1.8	1.7	1.8

Note: (1) Metropolitan Statistical Area - see Appendix A for areas included; (2) The proportion of households that are owners; (3) The proportion of the rental inventory that is vacant for rent; (4) The proportion of the homeowner inventory that is vacant for sale; (a) 2002 figures have been revised; n/a not available
Source: U.S. Census Bureau, Housing Vacancies and Homeownership Annual Statistics: 2003

COMMERCIAL REAL ESTATE

Industrial/Office Markets

Type/Market Area	Inventory (sq. ft.)	Vacant (sq. ft.)	Vacancy Rate (%)	Under Construction (sq. ft.)	Net Absorption (sq. ft.)
Industrial Space					
Savannah	17,544,350	1,880,705	10.72	150,000	883,565
Office Space					
Savannah	1,549,957	250,753	16.18	25,000	-32,629

Note: Data as of 4th Quarter, 2003; n/a not available
Source: Society of Industrial and Office Realtors, 2004 Comparative Statistics of Industrial and Office Real Estate Markets

COMMERCIAL UTILITIES

Typical Monthly Electric Bills

Area	Commercial Service ($/month)		Industrial Service ($/month)	
	3 kW demand 1,000 kWh	40 kW demand 14,000 kWh	1,000 kW demand 200,000 kWh	50,000 kW demand 15,000,000 kWh
City	n/a	n/a	n/a	n/a
Average[1]	100	1,134	17,850	1,045,117

Note: Based on rates in effect July 1, 2003; (1) average based on 197 utilities; n/a not available
Source: Edison Electric Institute, Typical Bills and Average Rates Report, Summer 2003

TRANSPORTATION

Means of Transportation to Work

Area	Car/Truck/Van		Public Transportation			Bicycle	Walked	Other Means	Worked at Home
	Drove Alone	Car-pooled	Bus	Subway	Railroad				
City	70.8	15.3	4.5	0.0	0.0	1.1	4.3	1.6	2.4
MSA[1]	77.8	13.4	2.3	0.0	0.0	0.5	2.4	1.1	2.4
U.S.	75.7	12.2	2.5	1.5	0.5	0.4	2.9	1.0	3.3

Note: Figures shown are percentages and cover workers 16 years of age and older;
(1) Metropolitan Statistical Area - see Appendix A for areas included
Source: Census 2000, Summary File 3

Travel Time to Work

Area	Less Than 15 Minutes	15 to 29 Minutes	30 to 44 Minutes	45 to 59 Minutes	60 Minutes or More
City	34.2	41.9	15.3	4.0	4.6
MSA[1]	26.2	41.1	21.6	6.1	5.0
U.S.	29.4	36.1	19.1	7.4	8.0

Note: Figures are percentages and include workers 16 years old and over; (1) Metropolitan Statistical Area - see Appendix A for areas included
Source: Census 2000, Summary File 3

Transportation Statistics

Interstate highways (2004)	I-16; I-95
Public transportation (2002)	Chatham Area Transit Authority (CAT)
Buses	
Average fleet age in years	11.4
No. operated in max. service	52
Demand response	
Average fleet age in years	3.8
No. operated in max. service	16
Passenger air service	
Airport	Savannah International
Airlines (2003)	6
Boardings (2002)	846,683
Amtrak service (2004)	Yes
Major waterways/ports	Savannah River (Atlantic Ocean)

Source: Federal Transit Administration, National Transit Database, 2002; Editor & Publisher Market Guide, 2004; Bureau of Transportation Statistics, Airport Enplanement Activity for CY2002; www.amtrak.com

BUSINESSES

Major Business Headquarters

Company Name	2003 Rankings	
	Fortune 500	Forbes 500
Colonial Group	-	160

Note: Companies listed are located in the city; dashes indicate no ranking
Fortune 500: Companies that produce a 10-K are ranked 1 to 500 based on 2002 revenue
Forbes 500: Private companies are ranked 1 to 281 based on 2002 revenue
Source: Fortune, April 14, 2003; www.forbes.com, November 6, 2003

Best Companies to Work For

Memorial Health, headquartered in Savannah, is among the "100 Best Companies to Work for in 2004." Criteria: trust in management, pride in work/company, camaraderie, company responses to the Hewitt People Practices Inventory, and employee responses to their Great Place to Work survey. The companies also had to be at least 10 years old and have a minimum of 500 employees. *Fortune, January 12, 2004*

Minority and Women-Owned Businesses

Ownership	All Firms		Firms with Paid Employees			
	Firms	Sales ($000)	Firms	Sales ($000)	Employees	Payroll ($000)
Black	1,550	74,560	282	55,561	714	13,878
Hispanic	n/a	n/a	n/a	n/a	n/a	n/a
Women	2,310	345,322	584	302,255	3,504	59,359

Note: Figures cover firms located in the city; n/a not available
Source: 1997 Economic Census, Minority and Women-Owned Businesses

Minority Business Opportunity

Savannah is home to one company which is on the Black Enterprise Industrial/Service 100 list (100 largest companies based on gross sales): **Vanguard Holdings Inc.**. Criteria: operational in previous calendar year; at least 51% black-owned and manufactures/owns the product it sells or provides industrial or consumer services. Brokerages, real estate firms and firms that provide professional services are not eligible. *Black Enterprise, www.blackenterprise.com, B.E. 100s, 2003 Report*

HOTELS

Hotels/Motels

Area	Hotels/Motels	Average Minimum Rates ($)		
		Tourist	First-Class	Deluxe
City	86	66	128	189

Source: OAG Travel Planner Online, Spring 2004

EVENT SITES

Major Event Sites, Meeting Places and Convention Centers

Name	Guest Rooms	Exhibit/ Meeting Space (sq. ft.)	Largest Meeting Room Capacity

None listed in city

Source: Original research

Living Environment

COST OF LIVING

Cost of Living Index

Year	Composite Index	Groceries	Housing	Utilities	Trans-portation	Health Care	Misc. Goods/ Services
2001	102.9	103.0	107.2	98.3	95.2	95.6	103.7
2002	100.4	97.9	99.5	106.3	90.8	96.0	104.6
2003	98.0	94.8	98.6	100.5	94.2	91.8	100.0

Note: U.S. = 100
Source: ACCRA, Cost of Living Index, 2001, 2002 and 2003 4-Quarter Averages

HOUSING

House Price Index (HPI)

Area	National Ranking[2]	Quarterly Change (%)	One-Year Change (%)	Five-Year Change (%)
MSA[1]	112	1.90	5.84	34.51
U.S.[3]	-	3.67	7.97	41.81

Note: The HPI is a weighted repeat sales index. It measures average price changes in repeat sales or refinancings on the same properties. This information is obtained by reviewing repeat mortgage transactions on single-family properties whose mortgages have been purchased or securitized by Fannie Mae of Freddie Mac in January 1975; (1) Metropolitan Statistical Area - see Appendix A for areas included; (2) Rankings are based on annual percentage change, for all MSAs containing at least 15,000 transactions over the last 10 years and ranges from 1 to 220; (3) figures based on a weighted division average; all figures are for the period ended December 31, 2003
Source: Office of Federal Housing Enterprise Oversight, House Price Index, March 1, 2004

Housing: Year Structure Built

Area	1990 -2000	1980 -1989	1970 -1979	1960 -1969	1950 -1959	1940 -1949	Before 1940	Median Year
City	6.9	12.6	17.0	16.3	19.5	11.4	16.4	1962
MSA[1]	22.6	18.4	16.9	12.2	12.7	7.4	9.9	1975
U.S.	17.0	15.8	18.5	13.7	12.7	7.3	15.0	1971

Note: Figures are percentages; (1) Metropolitan Statistical Area - see Appendix A for areas included
Source: Census 2000, Summary File 3

Average New Home Price

Area	2001	2002	2003
City	234,978	239,675	248,804
U.S.	212,643	236,567	248,193

Note: Figures, in dollars, are based on a new home with 2,400 sq. ft. of living area on an 8,000 sq. ft. lot.
Source: ACCRA, Cost of Living Index, 2001, 2002 and 2003 4-Quarter Averages

Average Apartment Rent

Area	2001	2002	2003
City	641	698	694
U.S.	674	708	721

Note: Figures, in dollars per month, are based on an unfurnished two bedroom, 1-1/2 or 2 bath apartment, approximately 950 sq. ft. in size, excluding all utilities except water
Source: ACCRA, Cost of Living Index, 2001, 2002 and 2003 4-Quarter Averages

RESIDENTIAL UTILITIES

Average Residential Utility Costs

Area	All Electric ($/mth)	Part Electric ($/mth)	Other Energy ($/mth)	Phone ($/mth)
City	119.11	–	–	25.72
U.S.	116.46	65.82	62.68	23.90

Source: ACCRA, Cost of Living Index, 2003 4-Quarter Average

HEALTH CARE

Average Health Care Costs

Area	Hospital ($/day)	Doctor ($/visit)	Dentist ($/visit)
City	521.12	69.00	75.62
U.S.	678.35	67.91	83.90

Note: Hospital—based on a semi-private room; Doctor—based on a general practitioner's routine exam of an established patient; Dentist—based on adult teeth cleaning and periodic oral exam.
Source: ACCRA, Cost of Living Index, 2003 4-Quarter Average

Distribution of Non-Federal, Office-Based Physicians

Area	Total	Family/ General Practice	Specialties Medical	Specialties Surgical	Specialties Other
MSA[1] (number)	540	56	186	166	132
MSA[1] (rate per 10,000 pop.)	18.4	1.9	6.3	5.7	4.5
Metro Average[2] (rate per 10,000 pop.)	33.1	2.2	7.7	4.8	5.6

Note: Data as of December 31, 2001; (1) Metropolitan Statistical Area - see Appendix A for areas included; (2) Average of 81 MSAs and CMSAs in this book
Source: American Medical Association, Physician Characteristics & Distribution in the U.S., 2003-2004

Hospitals

Savannah has the following hospitals: 3 general medical and surgical; 2 psychiatric.
AHA Guide to the Healthcare Field, 2003-2004

PRESIDENTIAL ELECTION

2000 Presidential Election Results

Area	Gore	Bush	Nader	Buchanan	Other
Chatham County	49.5	49.9	0.0	0.2	0.4
U.S.	48.4	47.9	2.7	0.4	0.6

Note: Results are percentages and may not add to 100% due to rounding
Source: www.cbsnews.com; www.uselectionatlas.org

EDUCATION

Public School District Statistics

District Name	Schls.	Enroll-ment	Classroom Teachers	Pupil/ Teacher Ratio	Minority Pupils[1] (%)	Current Expend.[2] ($/pupil)
Chatham County	49	34,681	2,163	16.0	n/a	6,154

Note: Data covers the 2001-02 school year unless otherwise noted; (1) Fall 2000; (2) FY2000; n/a not available
Source: U.S. Department of Education, National Center for Education Statistics, Common Core of Data, Local Education Agency (School District) Universe Survey: School Year 2001-2002; U.S. Department of Education, National Center for Education Statistics, Digest of Education Statistics 2002

Educational Quality

School District	Education Quotient[1]	Graduate Outcome[2]	Community Index[3]	Resource Index[4]
Chatham County	11	9	40	48

Note: Scores are national percentile rankings and range from 1 (worst) to 99 (best); (1) Combination of the Graduate Outcome, Community and Resource indexes weighted to reflect the greater importance of the Graduate Outcome and Resource Index; (2) Based on graduation rates and college board scores (SAT/ACT); (3) Based on the surrounding community's level of affluence and adult education; (4) Based on teacher salaries, per-pupil expenditures and student-teacher ratios.
Source: Expansion Management, December 2003

Educational Attainment by Race

Area	High School Graduate (%)					Bachelor's Degree (%)				
	Total	White	Black	Asian	Hisp.[2]	Total	White	Black	Asian	Hisp.[2]
City	76.1	85.6	68.2	73.9	67.2	20.2	30.2	11.1	35.2	22.5
MSA[1]	79.9	85.3	69.5	72.5	69.5	23.2	27.9	12.4	37.0	24.2
U.S.	80.4	83.6	72.3	80.4	52.4	24.4	26.1	14.3	44.1	10.4

Note: Figures shown cover persons 25 years old and over; (1) Metropolitan Statistical Area - see Appendix A for areas included; (2) people of Hispanic origin can be of any race
Source: Census 2000, Summary File 3

School Enrollment by Type

Area	Grades KG to 8				Grades 9 to 12			
	Public		Private		Public		Private	
	Enrollment	%	Enrollment	%	Enrollment	%	Enrollment	%
City	15,838	89.9	1,787	10.1	7,278	90.2	792	9.8
MSA[1]	35,191	85.9	5,780	14.1	14,841	85.9	2,431	14.1
U.S.	33,526,011	88.7	4,285,121	11.3	14,848,628	90.6	1,532,323	9.4

Note: Figures shown cover persons 3 years old and over; (1) Metropolitan Statistical Area - see Appendix A for areas included
Source: Census 2000, Summary File 3

School Enrollment by Race

Area	Grades KG to 8 (%)				Grades 9 to 12 (%)			
	White	Black	Asian	Hisp.[1]	White	Black	Asian	Hisp.[1]
City	21.4	74.6	1.3	2.2	21.6	74.5	1.8	1.3
MSA[2]	51.2	44.0	1.5	2.2	49.0	47.2	1.5	1.7
U.S.	68.5	15.5	3.3	16.8	68.8	15.5	3.8	15.7

Note: Figures shown cover persons 3 years old and over; (1) people of Hispanic origin can be of any race; (2) Metropolitan Statistical Area - see Appendix A for areas included
Source: Census 2000, Summary File 3

Classroom Teacher Salaries in Public Schools

District	B.A. Degree		M.A. Degree		Maximum	
	Min. ($)	Rank[1]	Max. ($)	Rank[1]	Max. ($)	Rank[1]
City	n/a	n/a	n/a	n/a	n/a	n/a
DOD Average[2]	31,567	-	53,248	-	59,356	-

Note: Salaries are for 2001-2002; (1) Rank ranges from 1 to 100; (2) As per the U.S. Department of Defense Wage Fixing Authority
Source: American Federation of Teachers, Survey & Analysis of Teacher Salary Trends 2002

Higher Education

Four-Year Colleges			Two-Year Colleges			Medical Schools	Law Schools	Voc/ Tech
Public	Private Non-profit	Private For-profit	Public	Private Non-profit	Private For-profit			
2	1	1	1	0	0	0	0	0

Note: Figures cover institutions located within the city limits.
Source: National Center for Education Statistics, The Integrated Postsecondary Education System (IPEDS) Peer Analysis System, 2002; usnews.com, America's Best Graduate Schools 2004, Medical School Directory; The College Blue Book, Occupational Education, 2003; Barron's Guide to Law Schools, 2003; Medical School Admission Requirements U.S. & Canada, 2003-2004

MAJOR EMPLOYERS

Major Employers

Company Name	Industry	Type
Armstrong Atlantic State Univ	Colleges and universities	Headquarters
Candler Hospital Inc	General medical and surgical hospitals	Headquarters
Care One Home Health	General medical and surgical hospitals	Headquarters
City of Savannah	Executive offices	Headquarters
Foundation School	Colleges and universities	Branch
Georgia-Pacific	Paper mills	Branch
Great Dane Trailers	Truck trailers	Branch
Gulfstream Aerospace Corp Del	Aircraft	Headquarters
Kanter Hall International	Colleges and universities	Branch
Kerr McGee Pigments	Inorganic pigments	Single
Ne Trade Del Authority	Railroads, line-haul operating	Branch
Police Department	Elementary and secondary schools	Branch
Regional Hospital	Administration of public health programs	Branch
Stone Container Corporation	Paperboard mills	Branch
Sullivan Group	Employment agencies	Single
Telephone Service Observing	Radio broadcasting stations	Branch
Tidelands Comm Mental Hlth Ctr	Administration of public health programs	Branch

Note: Companies shown are located in the metropolitan area and have 450 or more employees.
Source: www.zapdata.com, March 2004

PUBLIC SAFETY

Crime Rate

Area	All Crimes	Violent Crimes				Property Crimes		
		Murder	Forcible Rape	Robbery	Aggrav. Assault	Burglary	Larceny -Theft	Motor Vehicle Theft
City	8,431.7	23.3	42.2	472.7	326.5	1,443.5	5,006.0	1,117.7
Suburbs[1]	3,945.2	5.9	16.6	104.2	292.5	838.0	2,367.0	321.0
MSA[2]	5,958.9	13.7	28.1	269.6	307.8	1,109.7	3,551.5	678.6
U.S.	4,118.8	5.6	33.0	145.9	310.1	746.2	2,445.8	432.1

Note: Figures are crimes per 100,000 population; (1) All areas within the MSA that are located outside the city limits; (2) Metropolitan Statistical Area - see Appendix A for areas included
Source: FBI Uniform Crime Reports, 2002

RECREATION

Culture and Recreation

Museums	Orchestras	Opera Companies	Dance Companies	Professional Theatres	Zoos	Pro Sports Teams[1]
9	0	0	0	0	0	0

Note: (1) Covers the Metropolitan Statistical Area - see Appendix A for areas included.
Source: The Grey House Performing Arts Directory, 2002; Official Museum Directory, 2004; www.sportsvenues.com

Library System

The Live Oak Public Libraries has 19 branches, holdings of 725,702 volumes, and a budget of $7,502,032 (2001-2002).
American Library Directory, 2003-2004

MEDIA

Newspapers

Name	Type	Freq.	Distribution	Circulation
Connect Savannah	General	1x/wk	Local	65,000
Freedom Journal	Black/Gen	1x/mth	Local	10,000
The Herald of Savannah	Black	1x/wk	Local	8,000
Savannah Morning News	General	7x/wk	Local	62,715
The Savannah Pennysaver	General	1x/wk	Area	82,000
The Savannah Tribune	Black	1x/wk	Local	8,000
The Statesboro Sun	General	1x/mth	Area	10,000

Note: Includes newspapers whose offices are located in the city and whose circulations are 500 or more
Source: Burrelle's Media Directory, 2003

Television Stations

Name	Ch.	Affiliation	Type	Owner
WSAV	3	NBCT	Commercial	Media General Inc.
WVAN	9	PBS	Public	Georgia Public Broadcasting
WTOC	11	CBST	Commercial	Raycom Media Inc.
WJCL	22	ABCT	Commercial	Gocom Communications
WTGS	28	FBC	Commercial	Brissette Broadcasting
WGSA	50	UPN/WB	Commercial	Southern T.V. Corporation

Note: Stations included broadcast from the Savannah metro area; n/a not available
Source: Burrelle's Media Directory, 2003

AM Radio Stations

Call Letters	Freq. (kHz)	Target Audience	Station Format	Music Format
WBMQ	630	General	N/T	n/a
WJLG	900	General	M/N/S/T	Gospel
WTKS	1290	Children	N/S/T	n/a
WHGM	1400	General	M	Gospel

Note: Stations included broadcast from the Savannah metro area; n/a not available
The following abbreviations may be used:
Target Audience: A=Asian; B=Black; C=Christian; E=Ethnic; F=French; G=General; H=Hispanic;
M=Men; N=Native American; R=Religious; S=Senior Citizen; W=Women; Y=Young Adult; Z=Children
Station Format: E=Educational; M=Music; N=News; S=Sports; T=Talk
Source: Burrelle's Media Directory, 2003

FM Radio Stations

Call Letters	Freq. (mHz)	Target Audience	Station Format	Music Format
WWIO	89.1	General	M/N/T	Classical
WYFS	89.5	Religious	E/M/N/S/T	Christian
WHCJ	90.3	General	E/M/N	Gospel
WSVH	91.1	General	M/N/T	Classical
WEAS	93.1	General	M/N/S	Urban Contemporary
WSCA	94.1	General	M	Urban Contemporary
WIXV	95.5	General	M	AOR
WJCL	96.5	General	M	Country
WAEV	97.3	General	M	Adult Contemporary
WYKZ	98.7	General	M/N	Adult Contemporary
WLVH	101.1	Black	M/N/T	Urban Contemporary
WZAT	102.1	Men	M/N/S/T	Top 40
WSIS	103.9	Black	M/N/S	Oldies
WRHQ	105.3	Religious	Young Adult	M

Note: Stations included broadcast from the Savannah metro area
The following abbreviations may be used:
Target Audience: A=Asian; B=Black; C=Christian; E=Ethnic; F=French; G=General; H=Hispanic;
M=Men; N=Native American; R=Religious; S=Senior Citizen; W=Women; Y=Young Adult; Z=Children
Station Format: E=Educational; M=Music; N=News; S=Sports; T=Talk
Music Format: AOR=Album Oriented Rock; MOR=Middle of the Road
Source: Burrelle's Media Directory, 2003

CLIMATE

Average and Extreme Temperatures

Temperature	Jan	Feb	Mar	Apr	May	Jun	Jul	Aug	Sep	Oct	Nov	Dec	Yr.
Extreme High (°F)	84	86	91	95	100	104	105	104	98	97	89	83	105
Average High (°F)	60	64	70	78	84	89	92	90	86	78	70	62	77
Average Temp. (°F)	49	53	59	66	74	79	82	81	77	68	59	52	67
Average Low (°F)	38	41	48	54	62	69	72	72	68	57	47	40	56
Extreme Low (°F)	3	14	20	32	39	51	61	57	43	28	15	9	3

Note: Figures cover the years 1950-1995
Source: National Climatic Data Center, International Station Meteorological Climate Summary, 9/96

Average Precipitation/Snowfall/Humidity

Precip./Humidity	Jan	Feb	Mar	Apr	May	Jun	Jul	Aug	Sep	Oct	Nov	Dec	Yr.
Avg. Precip. (in.)	3.5	3.1	3.9	3.2	4.2	5.6	6.8	7.2	5.0	2.9	2.2	2.7	50.3
Avg. Snowfall (in.)	Tr	Tr	Tr	0	0	0	0	0	0	0	Tr	Tr	Tr
Avg. Rel. Hum. 7am (%)	83	82	83	84	85	87	88	91	91	88	86	83	86
Avg. Rel. Hum. 4pm (%)	53	50	49	48	52	58	61	63	62	55	53	54	55

Note: Figures cover the years 1950-1995; Tr = Trace amounts (<0.05 in. of rain; <0.5 in. of snow)
Source: National Climatic Data Center, International Station Meteorological Climate Summary, 9/96

Weather Conditions

Temperature			Daytime Sky			Precipitation		
10°F & below	32°F & below	90°F & above	Clear	Partly cloudy	Cloudy	0.01 inch or more precip.	0.1 inch or more snow/ice	Thunderstorms
< 1	29	70	97	155	113	111	< 1	63

Note: Figures are average number of days per year and covers the years 1950-1995
Source: National Climatic Data Center, International Station Meteorological Climate Summary, 9/96

HAZARDOUS WASTE

Superfund Sites

Savannah has no sites on the EPA's Superfund National Priorities List.
U.S. Environmental Protection Agency, National Priorities List, March 15, 2004

AIR & WATER QUALITY

Maximum Pollutant Concentrations

	Particulate Matter (ug/m³)	Carbon Monoxide (ppm)	Sulfur Dioxide (ppm)	Nitrogen Dioxide (ppm)	Ozone 1-hour (ppm)	Ozone 8-hour (ppm)	Lead (ug/m³)
MSA[1] Level	49	n/a	0.022	n/a	0.08	0.07	n/a
NAAQS[2]	150	9	0.140	0.053	0.12	0.08	1.50
Met NAAQS[2]	Yes	n/a	Yes	n/a	Yes	Yes	n/a

Note: (1) Metropolitan Statistical Area - see Appendix A for areas included; (2) National Ambient Air Quality Standards; n/a not available
Units: ppm = parts per million; ug/m³ = micrograms per cubic meter
Source: EPA, Latest Findings on National Air Quality: 2002 Status and Trends, August 2003

Air Quality Index

Data not available.

Watershed Health

The U.S. Environmental Protection Agency monitors the health of the aquatic resources for the nation's 2,000+ watersheds. **The Lower Savannah watershed serves the Savannah area and received an overall Index of Watershed Indicators (IWI) score of 5 (more serious problems - low vulnerability).** The IWI score is based on seven condition and nine vulnerability indicators. The overall IWI score ranges from 1 (best health) to 6 (worst health).
EPA, Index of Watershed Indicators, October 26, 2001

Drinking Water

Water System Name	Pop. Served	Primary Water Source Type	Number of Violations January 2002-February 2004		
			Health Based	Significant Monitoring	Monitoring
Savannah-Main	163,688	Ground	None	None	2

Note: Data as of February 19, 2004
Source: EPA, Office of Ground Water and Drinking Water, Safe Drinking Water Information System

Savannah tap water is alkaline, hard and fluoridated.
Editor & Publisher Market Guide, 2004

Tampa, Florida

Background

Although Tampa was visited by Spanish explorers, such as Ponce de Leon and Hernando de Soto as early as 1521, this city, located on the mouth of the Hillsborough River on Tampa Bay, did not see significant growth until the mid-nineteenth century.

Like many cities in northern Florida such as Jacksonville, Tampa was a fort during the Seminole War, and during the Civil War it was captured by the Union Army. Later, Tampa enjoyed prosperity and development when the railroad transported tourists from up north to enjoy the warmth and sunshine of Florida.

Two historical events in the late nineteenth century set Tampa apart from other Florida cities. First, Tampa played a significant role during the Spanish-American War in 1898 as a chief port of embarkation for American troops to Cuba. During that time, Colonel Theodore Roosevelt occupied a Tampa hotel as his military headquarters. Second, a cigar factory in nearby Ybor City, named after owner Vicente Martinez Ybor, was the site where Jose Marti—the George Washington of Cuba—exhorted workers to take up arms against the tyranny of Spanish rule in the late 1800s.

Today, Tampa enjoys its role as a U.S. port. Major industries in and around Tampa include services, retail trade, government and finance, insurance and real estate. Significant employers include the Hillsborough County School District, Verizon Communications, the university of South Florida, Hillsborough County Government, and MacDill Air Force Base

The city is home to the NFL's Tampa Bay Buccaneers, Florida's Latin Quarter known as Ybor City (a National Historic Landmark District), Busch Gardens, and a Museum of Science and Industry.

Winters are mild, while summers are long, warm, and humid. Freezing temperatures occur on one or two mornings per year during December, January, and February. A dramatic feature of the Tampa climate is the summer thunderstorm season. Most occur during the late afternoon, sometimes causing temperatures to drop dramatically. The area is vulnerable to tidal surges, as the land has an elevation of less than 15 feet above sea level.

Rankings

- Tampa-St. Petersburg was ranked #48 out of 331 metro areas in *Cities Ranked & Rated*. Criteria: cost of living; climate; crime; transportation; economy and jobs; education; arts and culture; health and healthcare; leisure. *Cities Ranked & Rated, 1st Edition, 2004*

- *Ladies Home Journal* ranked America's 200 largest cities based on the qualities women surveyed care about most. Tampa ranked #32 out of 57 in the big city category (population over 300,000). Criteria: crime; lifestyle; education; jobs; health; child care; politics; and the economy. *Ladies Home Journal Online, "The Best Cities for Women 2002"*

- The Tampa-St. Petersburg metro area was selected as one of "America's Best Places to Live and Work 2003" by *Employment Review*. The area ranked #12 out of 20. Criteria: unemployment rate; projected job growth; cost of living; and industry specific data. *Employment Review, www.bestjobsusa.com*

- Tampa was selected as one of "America's Pet Healthiest Cities" by Purina. The city ranked #24 out of 50. Criteria: veterinary services; environment; and legislation. *Purina Pet Institute, "America's Pet Healthiest Cities," August 14, 2001*

- *Forbes* ranked the 40 most populous metro areas in the U.S. in terms of the best places to be single. The Tampa-St. Petersburg metro area was ranked #27. Criteria: number of other singles; cost of living alone; nightlife; culture; job growth; coolness. *Forbes, June 5, 2003*

- *Forbes* ranked the 150 most populous metro areas in the U.S. in terms of the "Best Places for Business and Careers." The Tampa-St. Petersburg metro area was ranked #91. Criteria: income and job growth; cost-of-doing-business; qualifications of the available pool of labor; crime rates; housing costs; net migration. *Forbes, May 9, 2003*

- *Men's Health* ranked 101 U.S. cities in terms of the quality of their tap water. Tampa received a grade of B. Criteria: levels of bacteria, arsenic, lead, trihalomethanes, and haloacetic acids were compared with the National Academy of Science's guidelines as well as with the EPA's more stringent maximum contaminant level goals. *Men's Health, March 2004*

- Sperling's BestPlaces ranked 331 metro areas and identified the most and least stressful U.S. cities. The Tampa-St. Petersburg metro area ranked #27 out of the 100 largest metro areas (#1 = most stressful). Criteria: divorce rate; unemployment rate; violent and property crime; suicide rate; commute time; mental health; alcohol consumption; cloudy days. *www.BestPlaces.net, February 26, 2004*

- Sperling's BestPlaces in partnership with Pep Boys ranked 77 metro areas and identified "America's Most Drivable Cities." The Tampa-St. Petersburg metro area ranked #21. Criteria: climate; road roughness; urban mobility; gas prices. *Pep Boys, "America's Most Drivable Cities," April 9, 2003*

- Tampa was selected as a 2003 Digital Cities Survey winner. The city ranked #1 in the large city category. The survey examined and assessed how city governments are utilizing information technology to operate and deliver quality service to their customers and citizens. *Center for Digital Government, "2003 Digital Cities Survey"*

- Tampa-St. Petersburg was ranked #149 out of America's 200 largest metro areas in *SELF Magazine's* ranking of "America's Healthiest Cities for Women." Criteria: safety; air/water quality; cancer rates; and 21 other factors relating to health. *SELF Magazine, November 2003*

- Tampa-St. Petersburg was identified as an asthma "hot spot" where high prevalence makes the condition a key issue and environmental "triggers" and other factors can make living with asthma a particular challenge. The area ranked #22 out of the nations 100 largest metro areas. Criteria: local asthma prevalence and mortality data; pollen scores; air pollution; asthma prescriptions; smoking laws; number of asthma specialists. *GlaxoSmithKline, October 29, 2002*

- Tampa-St. Petersburg was identified as one of the most dangerous large metro areas for pedestrians in the U.S. The area ranked #2 out of the nations 49 largest metro areas. Criteria: average yearly pedestrian fatalities per capita (for the years 2000 and 2001) adjusted for the number of walkers. *Surface Transportation Policy Project, "Mean Streets 2002"*

- Tampa was ranked #23 out of 100 cities surveyed in *Child* magazine's ranking of the "Best Cities for Families." Criteria: number of pediatricians per capita; proximity to a children's hospital; immunization rates; infant mortality rate; air quality; water quality; school spending; pupil-teacher ratio; availability of parks/green space; nearby recreational opportunities; average commute time; number of sunny days; average cost of a 3-bedroom home; unemployment rate; future job growth; crime rate; percentage of children under 5; mandated minimum child care ratios. *Child, April 2001*

- *Zero Population Growth* ranked 239 cities in terms of children's health, safety, and economic well-being. Tampa was ranked #21 out of 25 major cities (main city in a metro area with population of greater than 2 million) and was given a grade of C. Criteria: total population and population growth; percent of population under 18 years of age; number of children's museums; health improvement grade; percent of births to teens; percent of low birthweight infants; infant mortality rate; number of Title X-funded clinics; average SAT/ACT scores; average elementary and secondary class size; crime rate; unemployment rate; percent of affordable homes; number of bad air days; park acres per 1000 persons; library circulation per child; and children's program attendance counts. *Zero Population Growth, Kid Friendly Cities Report Card 2001*

- Tampa was selected as one of America's 32 most livable cities by the non-profit group, Partners for Livable Communities. Criteria: environmental quality; parkland; ability to train new workers; job market; education; and use of the arts for economic development. *www.Livable.com, March 3, 2003*

- *Ladies Home Journal* ranked America's 200 largest cities in terms of safety. Tampa ranked #196 out of 200. Criteria: violent crimes; crimes against property; and rape. *Ladies Home Journal Online, "The Best Cities for Women 2002"*

- Tampa-St. Petersburg was ranked #38 out of 268 metro areas in terms of its Creativity Index. The Creativity Index is a mix of four equally weighted factors: the Creative Class (scientists, engineers, architects, designers, writers, artists, musicians, or any profession where creativity is a key factor) share of the workforce; innovation, measured as patents per capita; high-tech industry, using the Milken Institute's Tech Pole Index; and diversity, measured by the Gay Index (a reasonable proxy for an areas' openness to different kinds of people and ideas). *The Rise of the Creative Class, 2002*

- Tampa-St. Petersburg was ranked #45 out of 125 regions worldwide in terms of its "Knowledge Competitiveness Index." The index attempts to measure the knowledge-based development taking place throughout the world and is based on 17 measures of economic performance that indicate a region's ability to translate its knowledge capacity into economic value. *Robert Huggins Associates, "2003-2004 World Knowledge Competitiveness Index"*

- The Tampa-St. Petersburg metro area was selected by *Yahoo! Internet Life* as one of "America's Most Wired Cities...and Towns." The area ranked #37 out of 87. Criteria: home and work net use; user sophistication; domain density; and available content. *Yahoo! Internet Life, April 2001*

- Tampa-St. Petersburg was identified as one of the 100 "Most Unwired Cities" in the U.S. The area ranked #55. Criteria: number of public and commercial wireless access points; cell phone coverage offering wide area network Internet access; Internet penetration. *Intel, "Most Unwired Cities," March 4, 2003*

- Scarborough Research measured the percentage of households who subscribe to cellular services among adults ages 18 and over in 75 U.S. markets. The Tampa-St. Petersburg DMA (Designated Market Area) was ranked #46 out of 75. *Scarborough Research, Scarborough USA+ 2003 Release 1*

- Tampa was selected as one of "America's Most Literate Cities." The city ranked #16 out of the 64 largest U.S. cities. Criteria: booksellers; library support, holdings, and utilization; educational attainment; periodicals published; newspaper circulation. *University of Wisconsin-Whitewater, "America's Most Literate Cities," Summer 2003*

- Tampa was chosen as one of America's ten best cities for running. The city was ranked #10. Criteria: nominations from *Runner's World* readers; input from longtime runners and frequent travelers Jeff Galloway, John Bingham, Hal Higdon, Doug Rennie, and Burt Yasso; key statistical data concerning the cities' trail networks, weather, air quality, street safety, and the number of local running clubs and road races. *www.runnersworld.com, December 16, 2002*

- Tampa was ranked #67 in *Prevention* magazine's survey of the "Best Walking Cities in the U.S." The magazine, in conjunction with the American Podiatric Medical Association, surveyed 125 of the most populated cities and then tabulated and weighed 20 criteria of interest to pedestrians. *Prevention, April, 2004*

- The Tampa-St. Petersburg metro area was selected as one of "America's 50 Hottest Cities for Business Relocations and Expansions." The area ranked #26. Criteria: 70 of the industry's most prominent site selection consultants were asked which cities their clients found the most attractive when it came to selecting an expansion or relocation site in 2003. *Expansion Management, January 2004*

- Tampa was selected as a "High-Tech Market to Watch" by *Site Selection*. Five emerging U.S. markets which show corporate growth developing in technology clusters were highlighted. *Site Selection, July 2001*

- The Tampa-St. Petersburg metro area was selected as one of the "Top 60 CyberCities in America" by *Site Selection*. CyberCities are magnets for growing high-tech companies. Criteria: total employment; average wages; total payroll; number of companies; R&D spending and venture capital in the 45 Standard Industrial Classification (SIC) codes that define the high-technology industry. *Site Selection, March 2002*

- The Tampa-St. Petersburg metro area was cited as one of "The Best Places in the U.S. to Locate a Company." The area ranked #99 out of 329. Criteria: education (with emphasis on college board test results and high school graduation rates); availability of quality healthcare services and the cost to employers; quality of life; logistics workforce and companies; transportation infrastructure; quality and quantity of highly educated technical workers; business climate. *Expansion Management, July 2003*

- The Tampa-St. Petersburg metro area was selected as one of the "Top 40 Hottest Real Estate Markets" for expanding or relocating businesses." Criteria: rental costs; purchase prices; and vacancy rates of office and warehouse space. *Expansion Management, August 2003*

- The Tampa-St. Petersburg metro area appeared on *Forbes/Milken Institute* list of "Best Places for Business and Career." Rank: #25 out of 200 metro areas. Criteria: salary growth; job growth; number of technology clusters; overall concentration of technology activity relative to national average; and technology output growth. *www.forbes.com, Forbes/Milken Institute Best Places 2002*

- The Tampa-St. Petersburg metro area appeared on the "Milken Institute Best Performing Cities" index. Rank: #27 out of 200 large metro areas. Criteria: job growth; wage and salary growth; high-tech output growth. *Milken Institute, June 25, 2003*

- The Tampa-St. Petersburg metro area appeared on *Entrepreneur* magazine's list of the "Best Cities for Entrepreneurs" in 2003. The area ranked #25 out of 61 in the large city category. Criteria: entrepreneurial activity; small-business growth; economic growth; and risk. *www.Entrepreneur.com*

- The Tampa-St. Petersburg metro area was selected as one of the "Top 25 Cities for Doing Business in America." *Inc.* measured current-year employment growth in 277 regions as well as current trends in the annual average growth over the past three years, and compared employment expansion between the first and second halves of the last decade. Job growth factors account for two-thirds, and balance among industries accounts for one third of the final score for each city.The Tampa-St. Petersburg metro area ranked #14 among large metro areas. *Inc. Magazine, March 2004*

- The Tampa-St. Petersburg metro area appeared on *IndustryWeek's* fourth annual World-Class Communities list. It ranked #220 out of 315 metro areas. Criteria: MSA Gross Metropolitan Product (GMP) per manufacturing employee; and MSA percent share of U.S. manufacturing Gross Domestic Product (GDP). *IndustryWeek, April 16, 2001*

■ ING Group ranked the 125 largest metro areas according to the general financial security of residents. The Tampa-St. Petersburg metro area was ranked #80 out of 125. Criteria: Earnings and Wealth Potential (household income, education, net assets, cost of living); Safety Net (health insurance, retirement savings, life insurance, income support programs); Personal Threats (unemployment rate, low-income households, crime rate); Community Economic Vitality (cost of community services, job quality, job creation, housing costs). *ING Group, "The Best Cities to Earn and Save Money: A Ranking of the Largest 125 U.S. Cities," 2001 Edition*

Business Environment

CITY FINANCES

City Government Finances

Component	2000-2001 ($000)	2000-2001 ($ per capita)
Total Revenues	709,966	2,340
Total Expenditures	589,115	1,941
Debt Outstanding	1,004,863	3,311
Cash and Securities	1,665,355	5,488

Source: U.S Census Bureau, Government Finances 2000-2001, August 2003

City Government Revenue by Source

Source	2000-2001 ($000)	2000-2001 ($ per capita)
General Revenue		
From Federal Government	15,872	52
From State Government	43,968	145
From Local Governments	3,693	12
Taxes		
Property	78,690	259
Sales	91,358	301
Personal Income	0	0
License	0	0
Charges	147,061	485
Liquor Store	0	0
Utility	46,494	153
Employee Retirement	218,843	721
Other	63,987	211

Source: U.S Census Bureau, Government Finances 2000-2001, August 2003

City Government Expenditures by Function

Function	2000-2001 ($000)	2000-2001 ($ per capita)	2000-2001 (%)
General Expenditures			
Airports	0	0	0.0
Corrections	0	0	0.0
Education	0	0	0.0
Fire Protection	36,987	122	6.3
Governmental Administration	18,251	60	3.1
Health	0	0	0.0
Highways	18,144	60	3.1
Hospitals	0	0	0.0
Housing and Community Development	6,403	21	1.1
Interest on General Debt	45,450	150	7.7
Libraries	0	0	0.0
Parking	33,577	111	5.7
Parks and Recreation	34,460	114	5.8
Police Protection	96,193	317	16.3
Public Welfare	13,822	46	2.3
Sewerage	67,028	221	11.4
Solid Waste Management	80,141	264	13.6
Liquor Store	0	0	0.0
Utility	65,496	216	11.1
Employee Retirement	45,604	150	7.7
Other	27,559	91	4.7

Source: U.S Census Bureau, Government Finances 2000-2001, August 2003

Municipal Bond Ratings

Area	Moody's
City	Aa3

Source: Mergent Bond Record, February 2004

DEMOGRAPHICS

Population Growth

Area	1990 Census	2000 Census	2003 Estimate	2008 Projection	Population Growth (%) 1990-2000	Population Growth (%) 2000-2008
City	279,960	303,447	317,155	339,991	8.4	12.0
MSA[1]	2,067,959	2,395,997	2,519,486	2,724,271	15.9	13.7
U.S.	248,709,873	281,421,906	290,647,163	305,918,071	13.2	8.7

Note: (1) Metropolitan Statistical Area - see Appendix A for areas included
Source: Claritas, Inc.

Number of Households and Average Household Size

Area	1990 Census	2000 Census	2003 Estimate	2008 Projection	2003 Average Household Size
City	114,771	124,758	130,439	139,795	2.4
MSA[1]	869,481	1,009,316	1,061,614	1,148,538	2.4
U.S.	91,947,410	105,480,101	109,440,059	116,034,472	2.7

Note: (1) Metropolitan Statistical Area - see Appendix A for areas included
Source: Claritas, Inc.

Race and Ethnicity

Area	White Non-Hispanic	Black Non-Hispanic	Asian Non-Hispanic	Other Race Non-Hispanic	Hispanic
City	63.5	26.2	2.3	8.0	19.9
MSA[1]	82.2	10.4	2.0	5.3	11.0
U.S.	74.5	12.4	3.8	9.3	13.2

Note: Figures are 2003 estimates; (1) Metropolitan Statistical Area - see Appendix A for areas included
Source: Claritas, Inc.

Segregation

City Index[2]	City Rank[3]	MSA[1] Index[2]	MSA[1] Rank[4]
65.4	33	68.4	72

Note: Figures are based on an analysis of Census 2000 data; (1) Metropolitan Statistical Area - see Appendix A for areas included; (2) Dissimilarity Index—the most commonly used measure of segregation between two groups, reflecting their relative distributions across neighborhoods within a city or metropolitan area. It can range in value from 0, indicating complete integration, to 100, indicating complete segregation; (3) Ranges from 1 (most segregated) to 100 (least segregated) and includes all the cities in this book; (4) Ranges from 1 (most segregated) to 318 (least segregated) and includes 318 metropolitan areas.
Source: www.CensusScope.org

Ancestry

Area	German	Irish[2]	English	American	Italian	Polish	French[3]	Scottish
City	9.2	8.4	7.7	6.2	5.6	1.7	2.4	1.8
MSA[1]	15.6	13.1	11.3	7.5	8.3	3.4	3.6	2.3
U.S.	15.2	10.9	8.7	7.3	5.6	3.2	3.0	1.7

Note: Figures include multiple ancestry (e.g. if a person reported being Irish and Italian, they were included in both columns); (1) Metropolitan Statistical Area - see Appendix A for areas included; (2) Includes Celtic; (3) Includes Alsatian but excludes Basque
Source: Census 2000, Summary File 3

Foreign-Born Population

Area	Any Foreign Country	Percent of Population Born in: Europe	Asia	Africa	Oceania[2]	Canada	Mexico	Latin America[3]
City	12.2	1.3	1.9	0.2	0.0	0.3	1.3	7.1
MSA[1]	9.8	2.6	1.7	0.2	0.0	0.8	1.1	3.3
U.S.	11.1	1.7	2.9	0.3	0.1	0.3	3.3	2.5

Note: (1) Metropolitan Statistical Area - see Appendix A for areas included; (2) Includes Australia, New Zealand subregion, Melanesia, Micronesia, Polynesia, and Oceania n.e.c; (3) Includes Central America (excluding Mexico), South America, and the Caribbean.
Source: Census 2000, Summary File 3

Religion

Area	Catholic	Southern Baptist	United Meth-odist	ELCA[1]	LDS[2]	Presby-terian Church USA	Jewish Est.	Muslim Est.
County	16.6	10.3	3.3	0.7	0.4	1.0	2.0	0.5
U.S.	22.0	7.1	3.7	1.8	1.5	1.1	2.2	0.6

Note: Figures shown are the number of adherents as a percentage of the total population; Adherents are defined as all members, including full members, their children and the estimated number of other participants who are not considered members (e.g. the baptized, those not confirmed, those not eligible for communion, those regularly attending services, etc.); (1) Evangelical Lutheran Church in America; (2) The Church of Jesus Christ of Latter Day Saints
Source: Reprinted with permission from Religious Congregations and Membership in the United States 2000 (Nashville, Glenmary Research Center, 2002) Copyright Association of Statisticians of American Religious Bodies. All rights reserved.

Age Distribution

Area	Percent of Population						
	Under Age 5	Age 5 to 17	Age 18 to 34	Age 35 to 49	Age 50 to 64	Age 65 to 79	80 Years and Over
City	6.7	17.9	25.8	23.4	13.6	9.1	3.4
MSA[1]	5.7	16.1	20.1	22.8	16.1	13.9	5.4
U.S.	6.8	18.9	23.7	23.5	14.8	9.2	3.2

Note: (1) Metropolitan Statistical Area - see Appendix A for areas included
Source: Census 2000, Summary File 3

Marriage Status

Area	Never Married	Now Married Except Separated	Separated	Widowed	Divorced
City	31.0	43.8	3.6	7.6	14.0
MSA[1]	22.6	53.7	2.3	8.9	12.5
U.S.	27.1	54.4	2.2	6.6	9.7

Note: Figures cover population 15 years of age and older; (1) Metropolitan Statistical Area - see Appendix A for areas included
Source: Census 2000, Summary File 3

Male/Female Ratio

Area	Males	Females	Males per 100 Females
City	154,865	162,290	95.4
MSA[1]	1,213,693	1,305,793	92.9
U.S.	142,511,883	148,135,280	96.2

Note: Figures are 2003 estimates; (1) Metropolitan Statistical Area - see Appendix A for areas included
Source: Claritas, Inc.

ECONOMY

Gross Metropolitan Product

Area	1999	2000	2001	2002	2002 Rank[2]
MSA[1]	74.6	81.0	84.0	87.5	25

Note: Figures are in billions of dollars; (1) Metropolitan Statistical Area - see Appendix A for areas included; (2) Rank ranges from 1 to 319
Source: The U.S. Conference of Mayors, Metro Economies Report, July 2003

INCOME

Per Capita/Median/Average Income

Area	Per Capita ($)	Median Household ($)	Average Household ($)
City	24,509	39,191	58,780
MSA[1]	24,514	42,509	57,599
U.S.	24,078	46,868	63,207

Note: Figures are 2003 estimates; (1) Metropolitan Statistical Area - see Appendix A for areas included
Source: Claritas, Inc.

Household Income Distribution

Area	Percent of Households Earning							
	Under $15,000	$15,000 -24,999	$25,000 -34,999	$35,000 -49,999	$50,000 -74,999	$75,000 -99,000	$100,000 -149,999	$150,000 and up
City	18.7	13.4	13.2	16.7	16.2	8.3	7.2	6.4
MSA[1]	14.0	13.4	13.8	17.6	18.7	9.7	8.1	4.7
U.S.	14.1	11.5	11.7	16.0	19.2	11.3	10.2	6.0

Note: Figures are 2003 estimates; (1) Metropolitan Statistical Area - see Appendix A for areas included
Source: Claritas, Inc.

Poverty Rates by Age

Area	All Ages	Under 5 Years Old	5 to 17 Years Old	18 to 64 Years Old	65 Years and Over
City	18.1	1.9	4.8	9.4	1.9
MSA[1]	11.2	1.0	2.5	6.0	1.6
U.S.	12.4	1.2	3.0	6.9	1.2

Note: Figures are percent of population with income in 1999 below poverty level and only include population for whom poverty status is determined; (1) Metropolitan Statistical Area - see Appendix A for areas included
Source: Census 2000, Summary File 3

Personal Bankruptcy Filing Rate

Area	2002	2003
Hillsborough County	6.35	6.51
U.S.	5.34	5.58

Note: Numbers are per 1,000 population and include Chapter 7 and Chapter 13 filings
Source: Federal Deposit Insurance Corporation (FDIC), Regional Economic Conditions (RECON), 2/25/2004

EMPLOYMENT

Labor Force and Employment

Area	Civilian Labor Force			Workers Employed		
	Dec. 2002	Dec. 2003	% Chg.	Dec. 2002	Dec. 2003	% Chg.
City	194,567	192,949	-0.8	184,641	184,517	-0.1
MSA[1]	1,316,323	1,307,890	-0.6	1,259,744	1,258,896	-0.1
U.S.	144,807,000	146,501,000	1.2	136,599,000	138,556,000	1.4

Note: Data is not seasonally adjusted and covers workers 16 years of age and older;
(1) Metropolitan Statistical Area - see Appendix A for areas included
Source: Bureau of Labor Statistics, http://stats.bls.gov

Unemployment Rate

Area	2003											
	Jan.	Feb.	Mar.	Apr.	May	Jun.	Jul.	Aug.	Sep.	Oct.	Nov.	Dec.
City	5.7	5.3	5.2	5.2	5.0	5.6	5.3	5.6	5.5	5.0	4.8	4.4
MSA[1]	4.9	4.5	4.4	4.4	4.3	4.7	4.5	4.6	4.6	4.2	4.1	3.7
U.S.	6.5	6.4	6.2	5.8	5.8	6.5	6.3	6.0	5.8	5.6	5.6	5.4

Note: Data is not seasonally adjusted and covers workers 16 years of age and older; All figures are percentages; (1) Metropolitan Statistical Area - see Appendix A for areas included
Source: Bureau of Labor Statistics, http://stats.bls.gov

Employment by Occupation

Occupation Classification	City (%)	MSA[1] (%)	U.S. (%)
Sales and Office	30.1	31.1	26.7
Professional and Related	20.2	19.1	20.2
Service	16.3	15.2	14.9
Production, Transportation, and Material Moving	10.9	11.2	14.6
Management, Business, and Financial	13.8	13.7	13.5
Construction, Extraction, and Maintenance	8.6	9.1	9.4
Farming, Forestry, and Fishing	0.2	0.5	0.7

Note: Figures cover employed civilians 16 years of age and older;
(1) Metropolitan Statistical Area - see Appendix A for areas included
Source: Census 2000, Summary File 3

Employment by Industry

Sector	MSA[1]		U.S.
	Number of Employees	Percent of Total	Percent of Total
Government	151,800	12.2	16.7
Education and Health Services	144,900	11.7	12.9
Professional and Business Services	296,800	23.9	12.3
Retail Trade	145,800	11.7	11.8
Manufacturing	70,600	5.7	11.0
Leisure and Hospitality	109,100	8.8	9.1
Finance Activities	94,200	7.6	6.1
Construction	69,200	5.6	5.1
Wholesale Trade	48,300	3.9	4.3
Other Services	49,000	3.9	4.1
Transportation and Utilities	29,400	2.4	3.7
Information	33,700	2.7	2.4
Natural Resources and Mining	500	<0.1	0.4

Note: Figures cover non-farm employment as of December 2003 and are not seasonally adjusted;
(1) Metropolitan Statistical Area - see Appendix A for areas included
Source: Bureau of Labor Statistics, http://stats.bls.gov

Average Wages

Occupation	$/Hr.	Occupation	$/Hr.
Accountants and Auditors	29.66	Maids and Housekeeping Cleaners	7.61
Automotive Mechanics	15.85	Maintenance and Repair Workers	12.33
Bookkeepers	12.46	Marketing Managers	40.93
Carpenters	13.58	Nuclear Medicine Technologists	22.73
Cashiers	7.51	Nurses, Licensed Practical	15.32
Clerks, General Office	10.35	Nurses, Registered	22.48
Clerks, Receptionists/Information	9.77	Nursing Aides/Orderlies/Attendants	10.04
Clerks, Shipping/Receiving	11.37	Packers and Packagers, Hand	7.38
Computer Programmers	27.87	Physical Therapists	29.54
Computer Support Specialists	19.43	Postal Service Mail Carriers	19.07
Computer Systems Analysts	31.04	Real Estate Brokers	28.33
Cooks, Restaurant	9.32	Retail Salespersons	10.83
Dentists	38.03	Sales Reps., Exc. Tech./Scientific	22.73
Electrical Engineers	32.25	Sales Reps., Tech./Scientific	31.28
Electricians	15.36	Secretaries, Exc. Legal/Med./Exec.	12.11
Financial Managers	37.30	Security Guards	8.85
First-Line Supervisors/Mgrs., Sales	17.62	Surgeons	95.68
Food Preparation Workers	7.98	Teacher Assistants	8.50
General and Operations Managers	39.13	Teachers, Elementary School	20.10
Hairdressers/Cosmetologists	10.79	Teachers, Secondary School	21.60
Internists	92.65	Telemarketers	12.45
Janitors and Cleaners	7.99	Truck Drivers, Heavy/Tractor-Trailer	14.41
Landscaping/Groundskeeping Workers	9.17	Truck Drivers, Light/Delivery Svcs.	11.87
Lawyers	50.77	Waiters and Waitresses	7.66

Note: Wage data is for 2002 and covers the Metropolitan Statistical Area (see Appendix A for areas included).
Hourly wages for elementary/secondary school teachers and teacher assistants were calculated by the editors
from annual wage data assuming a 40 hour work week; n/a not available.
Source: Bureau of Labor Statistics, 2002 Metro Area Occupational Employment and Wage Estimates

Occupational Employment Projections: 1996 - 2006

Occupations Expected to Have the Largest Job Growth (ranked by numerical growth)	Fast-Growing Occupations[1] (ranked by percent growth)
1. Cashiers	1. Systems analysts
2. Salespersons, retail	2. Physical therapy assistants and aides
3. General managers & top executives	3. Desktop publishers
4. Registered nurses	4. Home health aides
5. Waiters & waitresses	5. Computer engineers
6. Marketing & sales, supervisors	6. Medical assistants
7. Janitors/cleaners/maids, ex. priv. hshld.	7. Physical therapists
8. General office clerks	8. Paralegals
9. Food preparation workers	9. Emergency medical technicians
10. Hand packers & packagers	10. Occupational therapists

Note: Projections cover Florida; (1) Excludes occupations with total job growth less than 300
Source: U.S. Department of Labor, Employment and Training Administration, America's Labor Market Information System (ALMIS)

TAXES

State Corporate Income Tax Rates

State	Rate (%)	Number of Brackets	Low Bracket (Under $)	High Bracket (Over $)
Florida	5.5	1	na	na

Note: Tax rates as of December 31, 2003; na not applicable; 3.3% alternative minimum rate.
Source: Tax Foundation, www.taxfoundation.org

State Individual Income Tax Rates

State	Federal Deductibility	Marginal Rate (%)	Number of Brackets	Low Bracket (Under $)	High Bracket (Over $)
Florida	No	None	na	na	na

Note: Tax rates as of December 31, 2003; Brackets apply to single taxpayers and married people filing separately; na not applicable
Source: Tax Foundation, www.taxfoundation.org

Various State and Local Tax Rates

State Sales and Use (%)	Total Sales and Use (%)	Gasoline (cents/gal.)	Cigarette (cents/pack)	Spirits ($/gal.)	Table Wine ($/gal.)	Beer ($/gal.)
6.0	7.0	13.9	33.9	6.50	2.25	0.48

Note: Tax rates as of December 31, 2003
Source: Tax Foundation, www.taxfoundation.org

State Tax Burdens

Area	Combined State and Local Tax Burden		Combined Federal, State and Local Tax Burden	
	Percent	Rank	Percent	Rank
Florida	8.4	45	29.0	23
U.S. Average	9.7	-	30.0	-

Note: Figures are for 2003
Source: Tax Foundation, www.taxfoundation.org

Internal Revenue Service Tax Audits

IRS District	Percent of Returns Audited				
	1996	1997	1998	1999	2000
North Florida	0.52	0.45	0.29	0.24	0.14
U.S.	0.66	0.61	0.46	0.31	0.20

Note: Figures cover IRS district audits of federal income tax returns filed by individuals. Geographic data on district audits for 2001 and 2002 are being withheld by the IRS. TRAC is challenging this policy.
Source: Syracuse University, Transactional Records Access Clearinghouse (TRAC), "Odds of IRS District Tax Audit 2000"

RESIDENTIAL REAL ESTATE

Building Permits

Area	Single-Family			Multi-Family			Total		
	2001	2002	Pct. Chg.	2001	2002	Pct. Chg.	2001	2002	Pct. Chg.
City	1,736	1,675	-3.5	1,359	1,070	-21.3	3,095	2,745	-11.3
U.S.	1,235,600	1,332,600	7.9	401,100	415,100	3.5	1,636,700	1,747,700	6.8

Note: Figures represent new, privately-owned housing units authorized (unadjusted data)
Source: U.S. Census Bureau, Manufacturing, Mining, and Construction Statistics

Homeownership and Housing Vacancies

Area	Homeownership Rate[2] (%)			Rental Vacancy Rate[3] (%)			Homeowner Vacancy Rate[4] (%)		
	2001	2002[a]	2003	2001	2002[a]	2003	2001	2002[a]	2003
MSA[1]	70.7	70.5	69.8	12.0	11.1	9.9	2.0	1.9	1.8
U.S.	67.8	67.9	68.3	8.4	8.9	9.8	1.8	1.7	1.8

Note: (1) Metropolitan Statistical Area - see Appendix A for areas included; (2) The proportion of households that are owners; (3) The proportion of the rental inventory that is vacant for rent; (4) The proportion of the homeowner inventory that is vacant for sale; (a) 2002 figures have been revised; n/a not available
Source: U.S. Census Bureau, Housing Vacancies and Homeownership Annual Statistics: 2003

COMMERCIAL REAL ESTATE

Industrial/Office Markets

Type/Market Area	Inventory (sq. ft.)	Vacant (sq. ft.)	Vacancy Rate (%)	Under Construction (sq. ft.)	Net Absorption (sq. ft.)
Industrial Space					
Tampa	130,663,454	10,191,749	7.80	161,500	-574,131
Office Space					
Tampa	42,612,481	7,354,452	17.26	432,000	-412,228

Note: Data as of 4th Quarter, 2003; n/a not available
Source: Society of Industrial and Office Realtors, 2004 Comparative Statistics of Industrial and Office Real Estate Markets

COMMERCIAL UTILITIES

Typical Monthly Electric Bills

Area	Commercial Service ($/month)		Industrial Service ($/month)	
	3 kW demand 1,000 kWh	40 kW demand 14,000 kWh	1,000 kW demand 200,000 kWh	50,000 kW demand 15,000,000 kWh
City	94	1,200	18,424	1,176,518
Average[1]	100	1,134	17,850	1,045,117

Note: Based on rates in effect July 1, 2003; (1) average based on 197 utilities
Source: Edison Electric Institute, Typical Bills and Average Rates Report, Summer 2003

TRANSPORTATION

Means of Transportation to Work

Area	Car/Truck/Van		Public Transportation			Bicycle	Walked	Other Means	Worked at Home
	Drove Alone	Car-pooled	Bus	Subway	Railroad				
City	76.6	13.7	2.6	0.0	0.0	0.9	2.3	1.3	2.6
MSA[1]	79.7	12.4	1.2	0.0	0.0	0.6	1.7	1.2	3.1
U.S.	75.7	12.2	2.5	1.5	0.5	0.4	2.9	1.0	3.3

Note: Figures shown are percentages and cover workers 16 years of age and older;
(1) Metropolitan Statistical Area - see Appendix A for areas included
Source: Census 2000, Summary File 3

Travel Time to Work

Area	Less Than 15 Minutes	15 to 29 Minutes	30 to 44 Minutes	45 to 59 Minutes	60 Minutes or More
City	30.1	41.6	18.5	4.9	4.9
MSA[1]	26.4	37.8	21.3	8.1	6.5
U.S.	29.4	36.1	19.1	7.4	8.0

*Note: Figures are percentages and include workers 16 years old and over; (1) Metropolitan Statistical Area -
see Appendix A for areas included*
Source: Census 2000, Summary File 3

Roadway Congestion Index

Area	1982	1990	1996	2000	2001
City	1.07	1.10	1.14	1.13	1.16
Average[1]	0.82	1.01	1.08	1.16	1.17

Note: Values greater than 1.00 indicate undesirable mobility levels; (1) average of 75 urban areas
Source: Texas Transportation Institute, The 2003 Annual Urban Mobility Report

Transportation Statistics

Interstate highways (2004)	I-4; I-75
Public transportation (2002)	Hillsborough Area Regional Transit Authority (HART)
Buses	
Average fleet age in years	7.1
No. operated in max. service	171
Demand response	
Average fleet age in years	2.4
No. operated in max. service	24
Passenger air service	
Airport	Tampa International
Airlines (2003)	21
Boardings (2002)	7,726,576
Amtrak service (2004)	Yes
Major waterways/ports	Port of Tampa

*Source: Federal Transit Administration, National Transit Database, 2002; Editor & Publisher Market Guide,
2004; Bureau of Transportation Statistics, Airport Enplanement Activity for CY2002; www.amtrak.com*

BUSINESSES

Major Business Headquarters

Company Name	2003 Rankings	
	Fortune 500	Forbes 500
No companies listed	-	-

Note: Companies listed are located in the city; dashes indicate no ranking
Fortune 500: Companies that produce a 10-K are ranked 1 to 500 based on 2002 revenue
Forbes 500: Private companies are ranked 1 to 281 based on 2002 revenue
Source: Fortune, April 14, 2003; www.forbes.com, November 6, 2003

Best Companies to Work For

Maritrans, headquartered in Tampa, is among the "200 Best Small Companies in 2003."
Criteria: 3,500 companies whose latest 12-month sales were $5 million to $600 million were
screened. Those with a net margin or five-year average ROE below 5% were cut. Banks,
utilities, real estate investment trusts and limited partnerships whose financial structures are
too different from most operating companies were also excluded. Shares had to be trading
above $5 by the end of September 2003. Financial statement footnotes were examined for
major issues. For the final ranking, equal weight was given to growth in sales, earnings and
ROE for the past five years and the latest 12 months. *www.forbes.com, October 27, 2003*

Fast-Growing Businesses

According to *Inc.*, Tampa is home to one of America's 500 fastest-growing private companies:
For Any Occasion. Criteria: must be an independent, privately-held, U.S. corporation,
proprietorship or partnership; sales of at least $200,000 in 1998; five-year operating/sales
history; increase in 2002 sales over 2001 sales; holding companies, regulated banks, and

utilities were excluded. *Inc. 500, America's Fastest-Growing Private Companies, October 15, 2003*

According to Deloitte & Touche LLP, Tampa is home to one of North America's 500 fastest-growing high-technology companies: **Z-Tel Technologies, Inc**. Companies are ranked by percentage growth in revenue over a five-year period. Criteria for inclusion: must be a U.S. or Canadian company developing and/or providing technology products or services; company must have been in business for five years with 1998 operating revenues of at least $50,000 USD or $75,000 CD and 2002 operating revenues of at least $1 million USD/CD. *Deloitte & Touche LLP, 2003 Technology Fast 500*

Women-Owned Firms: Number, Employment and Sales

Area	Number of Firms	Employ- ment	Sales ($000)	Rank[2]
MSA[1]	59,186	65,280	12,225,284	24

Note: (1) Metropolitan Statistical Area - see Appendix A for areas included;
(2) Calculated on an averaging of the number of businesses, employment, and sales
Source: The National Foundation for Women Business Owners, Women-Owned Businesses in the Top 50 Metropolitan Areas, 2002: A Fact Sheet

Women-Owned Firms: Growth

Area	Percent Change from 1997 to 2002			Rank[2]
	Number of Firms	Employ- ment	Sales	
MSA[1]	22.7	26.6	55.4	13
Top 50 MSAs	14.0	31.4	42.6	-

Note: (1) Metropolitan Statistical Area - see Appendix A for areas included; (2) Calculated on an averaging of the percent growth of number of businesses, employment, and sales
Source: The National Foundation for Women Business Owners, Women-Owned Businesses in the Top 50 Metropolitan Areas, 2002: A Fact Sheet

Minority and Women-Owned Businesses

Ownership	All Firms		Firms with Paid Employees			
	Firms	Sales ($000)	Firms	Sales ($000)	Employees	Payroll ($000)
Black	1,747	160,444	110	142,207	857	34,444
Hispanic	4,391	967,154	1,954	880,870	11,794	298,687
Women	6,157	2,100,982	1,218	1,986,849	7,507	183,330

Note: Figures cover firms located in the city
Source: 1997 Economic Census, Minority and Women-Owned Businesses

Minority Business Opportunity

Tampa is home to one company which is on the Black Enterprise Industrial/Service 100 list (100 largest companies based on gross sales): **Sun State International Trucks L.L.C.**. Criteria: operational in previous calendar year; at least 51% black-owned and manufactures/owns the product it sells or provides industrial or consumer services. Brokerages, real estate firms and firms that provide professional services are not eligible. *Black Enterprise, www.blackenterprise.com, B.E. 100s, 2003 Report*

Tampa is home to one company which is on the Black Enterprise Auto Dealer 100 list (100 largest dealers based on gross sales): **S. Woods Enterprises Inc.**. Criteria: company must be operational in previous calendar year and at least 51% black-owned. *Black Enterprise, www.blackenterprise.com, B.E. 100s, 2003 Report*

Six of the 500 largest Hispanic-owned companies in the U.S. are located in Tampa. *Hispanic Business, June 2003*

Tampa is home to one company which is on the Hispanic Business Fastest-Growing 100 list (greatest sales growth over the past five years): **J.J. Sosa & Assoc. Inc.**. *Hispanic Business, July/August 2003*

HOTELS

Hotels/Motels

Area	Hotels/Motels	Average Minimum Rates ($)		
		Tourist	First-Class	Deluxe
City	99	73	114	119

Source: OAG Travel Planner Online, Spring 2004

EVENT SITES

Major Event Sites, Meeting Places and Convention Centers

Name	Guest Rooms	Exhibit/ Meeting Space (sq. ft.)	Largest Meeting Room Capacity
Florida State Fairgrounds	n/a	n/a	14,500
Houlihan's Stadium	n/a	n/a	74,301
Ice Palace	n/a	n/a	21,500
Legends Field	n/a	n/a	8,000
Plant City Stadium	n/a	n/a	6,500
Saddlebrook Resort-Tampa	800	82,000	2,000
Tampa Convention Center	n/a	600,000	4,060
Tampa Marriott Waterside Hotel	717	50,000	2,100

Note: n/a not available
Source: Original research

Living Environment

COST OF LIVING

Cost of Living Index

Year	Composite Index	Groceries	Housing	Utilities	Trans-portation	Health Care	Misc. Goods/ Services
2001	99.1	101.1	97.5	94.1	102.7	101.5	99.1
2002	97.5	96.8	94.8	96.9	106.5	102.0	96.7
2003	96.8	96.3	95.0	96.9	98.6	101.5	97.4

Note: U.S. = 100
Source: ACCRA, Cost of Living Index, 2001, 2002 and 2003 4-Quarter Averages

HOUSING

House Price Index (HPI)

Area	National Ranking[2]	Quarterly Change (%)	One-Year Change (%)	Five-Year Change (%)
MSA[1]	65	4.32	10.02	53.30
U.S.[3]	-	3.67	7.97	41.81

Note: The HPI is a weighted repeat sales index. It measures average price changes in repeat sales or refinancings on the same properties. This information is obtained by reviewing repeat mortgage transactions on single-family properties whose mortgages have been purchased or securitized by Fannie Mae of Freddie Mac in January 1975; (1) Metropolitan Statistical Area - see Appendix A for areas included; (2) Rankings are based on annual percentage change, for all MSAs containing at least 15,000 transactions over the last 10 years and ranges from 1 to 220; (3) figures based on a weighted division average; all figures are for the period ended December 31, 2003
Source: Office of Federal Housing Enterprise Oversight, House Price Index, March 1, 2004

Housing: Year Structure Built

Area	1990 -2000	1980 -1989	1970 -1979	1960 -1969	1950 -1959	1940 -1949	Before 1940	Median Year
City	13.5	14.9	15.5	16.0	20.2	9.2	10.8	1966
MSA[1]	17.2	25.9	25.4	13.6	11.0	3.3	3.5	1977
U.S.	17.0	15.8	18.5	13.7	12.7	7.3	15.0	1971

Note: Figures are percentages; (1) Metropolitan Statistical Area - see Appendix A for areas included
Source: Census 2000, Summary File 3

Average New Home Price

Area	2001	2002	2003
City	191,595	207,321	216,715
U.S.	212,643	236,567	248,193

Note: Figures, in dollars, are based on a new home with 2,400 sq. ft. of living area on an 8,000 sq. ft. lot.
Source: ACCRA, Cost of Living Index, 2001, 2002 and 2003 4-Quarter Averages

Average Apartment Rent

Area	2001	2002	2003
City	863	885	918
U.S.	674	708	721

Note: Figures, in dollars per month, are based on an unfurnished two bedroom, 1-1/2 or 2 bath apartment, approximately 950 sq. ft. in size, excluding all utilities except water
Source: ACCRA, Cost of Living Index, 2001, 2002 and 2003 4-Quarter Averages

RESIDENTIAL UTILITIES

Average Residential Utility Costs

Area	All Electric ($/mth)	Part Electric ($/mth)	Other Energy ($/mth)	Phone ($/mth)
City	128.24	–	–	21.16
U.S.	116.46	65.82	62.68	23.90

Source: ACCRA, Cost of Living Index, 2003 4-Quarter Average

HEALTH CARE

Average Health Care Costs

Area	Hospital ($/day)	Doctor ($/visit)	Dentist ($/visit)
City	699.88	66.02	87.91
U.S.	678.35	67.91	83.90

Note: Hospital—based on a semi-private room; Doctor—based on a general practitioner's routine exam of an established patient; Dentist—based on adult teeth cleaning and periodic oral exam.
Source: ACCRA, Cost of Living Index, 2003 4-Quarter Average

Distribution of Non-Federal, Office-Based Physicians

Area	Total	Family/ General Practice	Medical	Surgical	Other
MSA[1] (number)	4,519	494	1,785	1,081	1,159
MSA[1] (rate per 10,000 pop.)	18.9	2.1	7.4	4.5	4.8
Metro Average[2] (rate per 10,000 pop.)	33.1	2.2	7.7	4.8	5.6

Note: Data as of December 31, 2001; (1) Metropolitan Statistical Area - see Appendix A for areas included; (2) Average of 81 MSAs and CMSAs in this book
Source: American Medical Association, Physician Characteristics & Distribution in the U.S., 2003-2004

Hospitals

Tampa has the following hospitals: 7 general medical and surgical; 1 cancer; 2 other specialty; 1 children's orthopedic.
AHA Guide to the Healthcare Field, 2003-2004

According to *U.S. News*, Tampa has three of the best hospitals in the U.S.: **H. Lee Moffitt Cancer Center**; **St. Joseph's Hospital**; **Tampa General Hospital**; *U.S. News Online, "America's Best Hospitals 2003"*

PRESIDENTIAL ELECTION

2000 Presidential Election Results

Area	Gore	Bush	Nader	Buchanan	Other
Hillsborough County	47.1	50.2	2.1	0.2	0.5
U.S.	48.4	47.9	2.7	0.4	0.6

Note: Results are percentages and may not add to 100% due to rounding
Source: www.cbsnews.com; www.uselectionatlas.org

EDUCATION

Public School District Statistics

District Name	Schls.	Enroll- ment	Classroom Teachers	Pupil/ Teacher Ratio	Minority Pupils[1] (%)	Current Expend.[2] ($/pupil)
Hillsborough County SD	219	169,789	9,975	17.0	48.2	5,811

Note: Data covers the 2001-02 school year unless otherwise noted; (1) Fall 2000; (2) FY2000; n/a not available
Source: U.S. Department of Education, National Center for Education Statistics, Common Core of Data, Local Education Agency (School District) Universe Survey: School Year 2001-2002; U.S. Department of Education, National Center for Education Statistics, Digest of Education Statistics 2002

Educational Quality

School District	Education Quotient[1]	Graduate Outcome[2]	Community Index[3]	Resource Index[4]
Hillsborough County	72	76	46	31

Note: Scores are national percentile rankings and range from 1 (worst) to 99 (best); (1) Combination of the Graduate Outcome, Community and Resource indexes weighted to reflect the greater importance of the Graduate Outcome and Resource Index; (2) Based on graduation rates and college board scores (SAT/ACT); (3) Based on the surrounding community's level of affluence and adult education; (4) Based on teacher salaries, per-pupil expenditures and student-teacher ratios.
Source: Expansion Management, December 2003

Educational Attainment by Race

Area	High School Graduate (%)					Bachelor's Degree (%)				
	Total	White	Black	Asian	Hisp.[2]	Total	White	Black	Asian	Hisp.[2]
City	77.1	81.5	65.9	79.5	60.8	25.4	30.8	9.9	38.8	14.7
MSA[1]	81.5	83.1	71.0	78.4	65.8	21.7	22.4	13.0	39.2	16.2
U.S.	80.4	83.6	72.3	80.4	52.4	24.4	26.1	14.3	44.1	10.4

Note: Figures shown cover persons 25 years old and over; (1) Metropolitan Statistical Area - see Appendix A for areas included; (2) people of Hispanic origin can be of any race
Source: Census 2000, Summary File 3

School Enrollment by Type

Area	Grades KG to 8				Grades 9 to 12			
	Public		Private		Public		Private	
	Enrollment	%	Enrollment	%	Enrollment	%	Enrollment	%
City	34,437	87.0	5,154	13.0	14,603	90.2	1,585	9.8
MSA[1]	239,025	86.3	38,069	13.7	103,629	90.5	10,836	9.5
U.S.	33,526,011	88.7	4,285,121	11.3	14,848,628	90.6	1,532,323	9.4

Note: Figures shown cover persons 3 years old and over; (1) Metropolitan Statistical Area - see Appendix A for areas included
Source: Census 2000, Summary File 3

School Enrollment by Race

Area	Grades KG to 8 (%)				Grades 9 to 12 (%)			
	White	Black	Asian	Hisp.[1]	White	Black	Asian	Hisp.[1]
City	49.9	37.9	1.4	21.2	49.2	38.2	2.5	20.5
MSA[2]	73.7	16.6	2.0	14.0	74.3	15.8	2.8	13.6
U.S.	68.5	15.5	3.3	16.8	68.8	15.5	3.8	15.7

Note: Figures shown cover persons 3 years old and over; (1) people of Hispanic origin can be of any race; (2) Metropolitan Statistical Area - see Appendix A for areas included
Source: Census 2000, Summary File 3

Classroom Teacher Salaries in Public Schools

District	B.A. Degree		M.A. Degree		Maximum	
	Min. ($)	Rank[1]	Max. ($)	Rank[1]	Max. ($)	Rank[1]
Tampa	30,001	57	53,452	45	56,366	64
DOD Average[2]	31,567	-	53,248	-	59,356	-

Note: Salaries are for 2001-2002; (1) Rank ranges from 1 to 100; (2) As per the U.S. Department of Defense Wage Fixing Authority
Source: American Federation of Teachers, Survey & Analysis of Teacher Salary Trends 2002

Higher Education

Four-Year Colleges			Two-Year Colleges			Medical Schools	Law Schools	Voc/ Tech
Public	Private Non-profit	Private For-profit	Public	Private Non-profit	Private For-profit			
1	3	8	3	0	2	1	0	13

Note: Figures cover institutions located within the city limits.
Source: National Center for Education Statistics, The Integrated Postsecondary Education System (IPEDS) Peer Analysis System, 2002; usnews.com, America's Best Graduate Schools 2004, Medical School Directory; The College Blue Book, Occupational Education, 2003; Barron's Guide to Law Schools, 2003; Medical School Admission Requirements U.S. & Canada, 2003-2004

MAJOR EMPLOYERS

Major Employers

Company Name	Industry	Type
AT&T Global Network Svcs LLC	Business consulting, nec	Headquarters
Bay Pines VAMC	Administration of veterans' affairs	Branch
Chase Manhattan	National commercial banks	Branch
Eckerd	General warehousing and storage	Branch
Honeywell	Aircraft engines and engine parts	Branch
Honeywell	Search and navigation equipment	Branch
HSN	Television broadcasting stations	Headquarters
Modern Business Associates	Help supply services	Single
Morton Plant Hospital	General medical and surgical hospitals	Headquarters
Professonal Employer Plans Inc	Employment agencies	Single
Sheriffs Office	Police protection	Branch
St Josephs Womens Hospital	General medical and surgical hospitals	Headquarters
Sykes Enterprises Incorporated	Custom computer programming services	Headquarters
Tampa General Healthcare	General medical and surgical hospitals	Headquarters
Tampa Pndc	U.s. postal service	Branch
Tech Data Corporation	Computers, peripherals, and software	Headquarters
Time Inc	Books, periodicals, and newspapers	Branch
University Book Store	Colleges and universities	Headquarters
University Community Health	General medical and surgical hospitals	Headquarters
US Post Office	U.s. postal service	Branch
Usani Sub LLC	Television broadcasting stations	Single
Verizon	Business services, nec	Branch
Verizon	Data processing and preparation	Headquarters

Note: Companies shown are located in the metropolitan area and have 2,000 or more employees.
Source: www.zapdata.com, March 2004

PUBLIC SAFETY

Crime Rate

Area	All Crimes	Violent Crimes				Property Crimes		
		Murder	Forcible Rape	Robbery	Aggrav. Assault	Burglary	Larceny -Theft	Motor Vehicle Theft
City	11,149.6	11.7	64.3	735.5	1,170.4	1,980.0	5,069.9	2,117.7
Suburbs[1]	5,137.9	4.4	42.5	151.0	531.7	1,013.2	2,928.7	466.4
MSA[2]	5,899.3	5.3	45.3	225.0	612.6	1,135.7	3,199.9	675.5
U.S.	4,118.8	5.6	33.0	145.9	310.1	746.2	2,445.8	432.1

Note: Figures are crimes per 100,000 population; (1) All areas within the MSA that are located outside the city limits; (2) Metropolitan Statistical Area - see Appendix A for areas included
Source: FBI Uniform Crime Reports, 2002

RECREATION

Culture and Recreation

Museums	Orchestras	Opera Companies	Dance Companies	Professional Theatres	Zoos	Pro Sports Teams[1]
8	1	0	1	3	1	3

Note: (1) Covers the Metropolitan Statistical Area - see Appendix A for areas included.
Source: The Grey House Performing Arts Directory, 2002; Official Museum Directory, 2004; www.sportsvenues.com

Library System

The Tampa-Hillsborough County Public Library System has 22 branches, holdings of 2,126,111 volumes, and a budget of $24,731,820 (2003-2004).
American Library Directory, 2003-2004

MEDIA

Newspapers

Name	Type	Freq.	Distribution	Circulation
Brandon/Valrico Community News	General	1x/mth	Local	20,000
Carrollwood News	General	1x/wk	Local	47,000
Carrollwood/Northdale/Cheval	General	1x/mth	Local	26,000
The Florida Dollar Stretcher	Black	1x/wk	State	8,300
Florida Sentinel-Bulletin	Black/Gen	2x/wk	Local	23,000
The Free Press	General	1x/wk	Area	1,500
La Gaceta	Hispanic	1x/wk	Local	18,000
The Laker	General	1x/wk	Local	15,000
Nuevo Siglo	Hispanic	1x/wk	Area	22,000
Pennysaver Weekly News	General	1x/wk	Local	8,000
Riverview/Fishhawk/Apollo Beach Community News	General	1x/mth	Local	12,000
Tampa Tribune	General	7x/wk	Area	224,585
Temple Terrace Beacon	General	1x/wk	Local	22,000
Town 'n Country News	General	1x/wk	Area	23,700

Note: Includes newspapers whose offices are located in the city and whose circulations are 1,000 or more
Source: Burrelle's Media Directory, 2003

Television Stations

Name	Ch.	Affiliation	Type	Owner
WEDU	3	PBS	Public	Florida West Coast Public Broadcasting
WFLA	8	NBCT	Commercial	Media General Inc.
WTVT	13	FBC	Commercial	Fox Television Stations Inc.
WUSF	16	PBS	Public	University of South Florida
WFTS	28	ABCT	Commercial	Scripps Howard Broadcasting
WMOR	32	n/a	Commercial	Hearst Corporation
WTTA	38	WB	Commercial	Sinclair Broadcast Group
WBHS	50	n/a	Commercial	U.S. Broadcast Group
WRMD	57	TMUN	Commercial	Telemundo Group Inc.
WVEA	62	UNIN	Commercial	Entravision Communications
WXPX	66	WB	n/a	Paxson Communications Corporation

Note: Stations included broadcast from the Tampa metro area; n/a not available
Source: Burrelle's Media Directory, 2003

AM Radio Stations

Call Letters	Freq. (kHz)	Target Audience	Station Format	Music Format
WHNZ	570	General	M/N/T	Country
WDAE	620	General	M/S/T	Adult Contemporary
WRMD	680	Hispanic	M	Latin
WLCC	760	Hispanic	M/N/S/T	Latin
WMGG	820	Hispanic	M/N	Latin
WTWD	910	Religious	M/T	Christian
WFLA	970	General	M/N/T	Big Band
WQYK	1010	General	M/S	Adult Contemporary
WWBA	1040	Religious	M/T	Jazz
WTMP	1150	Black	M/N/S/T	Adult Contemporary
WQBN	1300	Hispanic	M/N	Latin
WLVU	1470	General	T	n/a
WAMA	1550	Hispanic	M	Adult Contemporary

Note: Stations included broadcast from the Tampa metro area; n/a not available
The following abbreviations may be used:
Target Audience: A=Asian; B=Black; C=Christian; E=Ethnic; F=French; G=General; H=Hispanic;
M=Men; N=Native American; R=Religious; S=Senior Citizen; W=Women; Y=Young Adult; Z=Children
Station Format: E=Educational; M=Music; N=News; S=Sports; T=Talk
Source: Burrelle's Media Directory, 2003

FM Radio Stations

Call Letters	Freq. (mHz)	Target Audience	Station Format	Music Format
WLMS	88.3	Religious	M/T	Christian
WMNF	88.5	General	M/N	Adult Contemporary
WUSF	89.7	General	M/N	Adult Standards
WBVM	90.5	Religious	M/N/T	Christian
WYUU	92.5	General	M	Country
WFLZ	93.3	General	M/N/T	Top 40
WSSR	95.7	General	M/N/T	Adult Contemporary
WMGG	96.1	Hispanic	M/N/S	Latin
WXTB	97.9	General	M/N/S/T	AOR
WQYK	99.5	General	M/N	Country
WMTX	100.7	General	M/N	Adult Contemporary
WTBT	103.5	General	M/N/T	Classic Rock
WRBQ	104.7	General	M/N/T	Oldies
WDUV	105.5	General	M	Easy Listening

Note: Stations included broadcast from the Tampa metro area
The following abbreviations may be used:
Target Audience: A=Asian; B=Black; C=Christian; E=Ethnic; F=French; G=General; H=Hispanic;
M=Men; N=Native American; R=Religious; S=Senior Citizen; W=Women; Y=Young Adult; Z=Children
Station Format: E=Educational; M=Music; N=News; S=Sports; T=Talk
Music Format: AOR=Album Oriented Rock; MOR=Middle of the Road
Source: Burrelle's Media Directory, 2003

CLIMATE

Average and Extreme Temperatures

Temperature	Jan	Feb	Mar	Apr	May	Jun	Jul	Aug	Sep	Oct	Nov	Dec	Yr.
Extreme High (°F)	85	88	91	93	98	99	97	98	96	94	90	86	99
Average High (°F)	70	72	76	82	87	90	90	90	89	84	77	72	82
Average Temp. (°F)	60	62	67	72	78	81	82	83	81	75	68	62	73
Average Low (°F)	50	52	56	61	67	73	74	74	73	66	57	52	63
Extreme Low (°F)	21	24	29	40	49	53	63	67	57	40	23	18	18

Note: Figures cover the years 1948-1990
Source: National Climatic Data Center, International Station Meteorological Climate Summary, 9/96

Average Precipitation/Snowfall/Humidity

Precip./Humidity	Jan	Feb	Mar	Apr	May	Jun	Jul	Aug	Sep	Oct	Nov	Dec	Yr.
Avg. Precip. (in.)	2.1	2.8	3.5	1.8	3.0	5.6	7.3	7.9	6.5	2.3	1.8	2.1	46.7
Avg. Snowfall (in.)	Tr	Tr	Tr	0	0	0	0	0	0	0	0	Tr	Tr
Avg. Rel. Hum. 7am (%)	87	87	86	86	85	86	88	90	91	89	88	87	88
Avg. Rel. Hum. 4pm (%)	56	55	54	51	52	60	65	66	64	57	56	57	58

Note: Figures cover the years 1948-1990; Tr = Trace amounts (<0.05 in. of rain; <0.5 in. of snow)
Source: National Climatic Data Center, International Station Meteorological Climate Summary, 9/96

Weather Conditions

Temperature			Daytime Sky			Precipitation		
32°F & below	45°F & below	90°F & above	Clear	Partly cloudy	Cloudy	0.01 inch or more precip.	0.1 inch or more snow/ice	Thunder-storms
3	35	85	81	204	80	107	< 1	87

Note: Figures are average number of days per year and covers the years 1948-1990
Source: National Climatic Data Center, International Station Meteorological Climate Summary, 9/96

HAZARDOUS WASTE

Superfund Sites

Tampa has seven hazardous waste sites on the EPA's Superfund National Priorities List: **Alaric Area GW Plume; Helena Chemical Co. (Tampa Plant); MRI Corp (Tampa); Peak Oil Co./Bay Drum Co.; Reeves Southeastern Galvanizing Corp.; Southern Solvents, Inc.; Stauffer Chemical Co (Tampa)**. *U.S. Environmental Protection Agency, National Priorities List, March 15, 2004*

AIR & WATER QUALITY

Maximum Pollutant Concentrations

	Particulate Matter (ug/m^3)	Carbon Monoxide (ppm)	Sulfur Dioxide (ppm)	Nitrogen Dioxide (ppm)	Ozone 1-hour (ppm)	Ozone 8-hour (ppm)	Lead (ug/m^3)
MSA[1] Level	56	4	0.047	0.011	0.09	0.07	1.27a
NAAQS[2]	150	9	0.140	0.053	0.12	0.08	1.50
Met NAAQS[2]	Yes	Yes	Yes	Yes	Yes	Yes	Yes

Note: (1) Metropolitan Statistical Area - see Appendix A for areas included; (2) National Ambient Air Quality Standards; n/a not available; (a) Localized impact from an industrial source in Tampa. Concentration from highest nonpoint source site in metro area is 0.01 ug/m^3 in Pinellas, FL
Units: ppm = parts per million; ug/m^3 = micrograms per cubic meter
Source: EPA, Latest Findings on National Air Quality: 2002 Status and Trends, August 2003

Air Quality Index

In the Tampa MSA (see Appendix A for areas included), the Air Quality Index (AQI) exceeded 100 on 0 days in 2002. An AQI value greater than 100 indicates that air quality would have been in the unhealthful range on that day.
EPA, Latest Findings on National Air Quality: 2002 Status and Trends, August 2003

Watershed Health

The U.S. Environmental Protection Agency monitors the health of the aquatic resources for the nation's 2,000+ watersheds. **The Hillsborough watershed serves the Tampa area and received an overall Index of Watershed Indicators (IWI) score of 6 (more serious problems - high vulnerability).** The IWI score is based on seven condition and nine vulnerability indicators. The overall IWI score ranges from 1 (best health) to 6 (worst health). The Condition Indicators include: designated use attainment, fish and wildlife consumption advisories, source water condition, contaminated sediments, ambient water quality, and wetlands loss index. The Vulnerability Indicators include: aquatic species at risk, conventional and toxic loads over permitted limits, urban and agricultural runoff potential, population change, hydrologic modification, estuarine pollution susceptibility, and air deposition. *EPA, Index of Watershed Indicators, October 26, 2001*

Drinking Water

Water System Name	Pop. Served	Primary Water Source Type	Number of Violations January 2002-February 2004		
			Health Based	Significant Monitoring	Monitoring
City of Tampa-Water Dept.	500,000	Surface	None	None	None

Note: Data as of February 19, 2004
Source: EPA, Office of Ground Water and Drinking Water, Safe Drinking Water Information System

Tampa tap water is alkaline, moderately hard and not fluoridated.
Editor & Publisher Market Guide, 2004

Appendix A: Metropolitan Statistical Areas

Atlanta, GA

Barrow, Bartow, Carroll, Cherokee, Clayton, Cobb, Coweta, DeKalb, Douglas, Fayette, Forsyth, Fulton, Gwinnett, Henry, Newton, Paulding, Pickens, Rockdale, Spalding, and Walton Counties (as of 6/30/93)

Barrow, Butts, Cherokee, Clayton, Cobb, Coweta, DeKalb, Douglas, Fayette, Forsyth, Fulton, Gwinnett, Henry, Newton, Paulding, Rockdale, Spalding, and Walton Counties (prior to 6/30/93)

Austin-San Marcos, TX

Bastrop, Caldwell, Hays, Travis and Williamson Counties (as of 6/30/93)

Hays, Travis and Williamson Counties (prior to 6/30/93)

Baton Rouge, LA

Ascension, East Baton Rouge, Livingston, and West Baton Rouge Parish

Birmingham, AL

Blount, Jefferson, St. Clair, and Shelby Counties (as of 6/30/93)

Blount, Jefferson, St. Clair, Shelby, and Walker Counties (prior to 6/30/93)

Charleston-North Charleston, SC

Berkeley, Charleston, and Dorchester Counties

Chattanooga, TN-GA

Catoosa, Dade and Walker County, GA; Hamilton and Marion County, TN (as of 6/30/93)

Catoosa, Dade and Walker County, GA; Hamilton, Marion and Sequatchie County, TN (prior to 6/30/93)

Columbia, SC

Lexington and Richland Counties

Dallas, TX

Collin, Dallas, Denton, Ellis, Henderson, Hunt, Kaufman and Rockwall Counties (as of 6/30/93)

Collin, Dallas, Denton, Ellis, Kaufman and Rockwall Counties(prior to 6/30/93)

El Paso, TX

El Paso County

Fort Lauderdale, FL

Broward County

Fort Worth-Arlington, TX

Hood, Johnson, Parker and Tarrant Counties (as of 6/30/93)

Johnson, Parker and Tarrant Counties (prior to 6/30/93)

Houston, TX

Chambers, Fort Bend, Harris, Liberty, Montgomery and Waller Counties(as of 6/30/93)

Fort Bend, Harris, Liberty, Montgomery and Waller Counties (prior to 6/30/93)

Huntsville, AL

Limestone and Madison Counties(as of 6/30/93)

Madison County (prior to 6/30/93)

Jacksonville, FL

Clay, Duval, Nassau and St. Johns Counties

Knoxville, TN

Anderson, Blount, Knox, Loudon, Sevier and Union Counties(as of 6/30/93)

Anderson, Blount, Grainger, Jefferson, Knox, Sevier and Union Counties(prior to 6/30/93)

Memphis, TN-AR-MS

Fayette, Shelby, and Tipton Counties, TN; Crittenden County, AR; DeSoto County, MS (as of 6/30/93)

Shelby and Tipton Counties, TN; Crittenden County, AR; DeSoto County, MS (prior to 6/30/93)

Miami, FL

Miami-Dade County

Nashville, TN

Cheatham, Davidson, Dickson, Robertson, Rutherford, Sumner, Williamson and Wilson Counties

New Orleans, LA

Jefferson, Orleans, Plaquemines, St. Bernard, St. Charles, St. James, St. John the Baptist and St. Tammany Parishes (as of 6/30/93)

Jefferson, Orleans, St. Bernard, St. Charles, St. John the Baptist and St. Tammany Parishes (prior to 6/30/93)

Orlando, FL

Lake, Orange, Osceola and Seminole Counties (as of 6/30/93)

Orange, Osceola and Seminole Counties (prior to 6/30/93)

Plano, TX

See Dallas, TX

San Antonio, TX

Bexar, Comal, Guadalupe and Wilson Counties (as of 6/30/93)

Bexar, Comal and Guadalupe Counties (prior to 6/30/93)

Savannah, GA

Bryan, Chatham, and Effingham Counties (as of 6/30/93)

Chatham and Effingham Counties (prior to 6/30/93)

St. Petersburg, FL

See Tampa-St. Petersburg-Clearwater, FL

Tampa-St. Petersburg-Clearwater, FL

Hernando, Hillsborough, Pasco and Pinellas Counties

APPENDIX B
Comparative Statistics

Population Growth: City

City	1990 Census	2000 Census	2003 Estimate	2008 Projection	Population Growth (%) 1990-2000	2000-2008
Albuquerque	388,375	448,607	457,910	474,664	15.5	5.8
Alexandria	111,526	128,283	135,053	145,974	15.0	13.8
Anchorage	226,338	260,283	270,680	288,967	15.0	11.0
Ann Arbor	111,018	114,024	115,428	117,674	2.7	3.2
Atlanta	394,092	416,474	420,964	430,764	5.7	3.4
Austin	499,053	656,562	704,618	786,193	31.6	19.7
Baltimore	736,014	651,154	641,455	624,724	-11.5	-4.1
Baton Rouge	223,299	227,818	225,958	223,972	2.0	-1.7
Bellevue	99,057	109,569	112,229	116,454	10.6	6.3
Birmingham	266,532	242,820	234,546	221,211	-8.9	-8.9
Boise City	144,317	185,787	194,156	208,411	28.7	12.2
Boston	574,283	589,141	593,745	600,654	2.6	2.0
Boulder	87,737	94,673	94,905	95,939	7.9	1.3
Buffalo	328,123	292,648	284,481	271,081	-10.8	-7.4
Cedar Rapids	110,829	120,758	122,516	125,474	9.0	3.9
Charleston	96,102	96,650	97,153	97,990	0.6	1.4
Charlotte	428,283	540,828	573,556	627,617	26.3	16.0
Chattanooga	152,695	155,554	154,883	153,872	1.9	-1.1
Chicago	2,783,726	2,896,016	2,913,275	2,944,582	4.0	1.7
Cincinnati	363,974	331,285	322,419	308,216	-9.0	-7.0
Cleveland	505,333	478,403	466,822	448,887	-5.3	-6.2
Colorado Spgs.	283,798	360,890	380,436	411,812	27.2	14.1
Columbia	115,475	116,278	115,539	114,575	0.7	-1.5
Columbus	648,656	711,470	728,856	757,489	9.7	6.5
Dallas	1,006,971	1,188,580	1,235,129	1,317,220	18.0	10.8
Denver	467,153	554,636	566,637	588,600	18.7	6.1
Des Moines	193,569	198,682	199,148	200,324	2.6	0.8
Detroit	1,027,974	951,270	924,670	880,816	-7.5	-7.4
Durham	151,737	187,035	194,840	207,766	23.3	11.1
El Paso	515,541	563,662	581,541	611,827	9.3	8.5
Eugene	118,073	137,893	141,991	148,912	16.8	8.0
Ft. Collins	89,555	118,652	125,741	137,154	32.5	15.6
Ft. Lauderdale	149,908	152,397	154,143	158,586	1.7	4.1
Ft. Wayne	205,671	205,727	204,861	203,424	0.0	-1.1
Ft. Worth	448,311	534,694	564,479	614,113	19.3	14.9
Grand Rapids	189,145	197,800	200,237	204,644	4.6	3.5
Green Bay	96,466	102,313	103,280	105,143	6.1	2.8
Greensboro	193,389	223,891	229,967	240,599	15.8	7.5
Honolulu	376,465	371,657	377,019	387,460	-1.3	4.3
Houston	1,697,610	1,953,631	2,026,976	2,154,705	15.1	10.3
Huntsville	161,842	158,216	156,323	153,460	-2.2	-3.0
Indianapolis	730,993	781,870	787,992	797,978	7.0	2.1
Irvine	111,754	143,072	152,446	168,017	28.0	17.4
Jacksonville	635,221	735,617	776,321	843,311	15.8	14.6
Kansas City	434,967	441,545	444,220	449,232	1.5	1.7
Knoxville	173,288	173,890	172,155	169,563	0.3	-2.5
Las Vegas	261,374	478,434	543,957	649,991	83.0	35.9
Lexington	225,366	260,512	266,875	278,028	15.6	6.7
Lincoln	193,629	225,581	232,650	244,560	16.5	8.4
Los Angeles	3,487,671	3,694,820	3,829,236	4,040,906	5.9	9.4
Louisville	269,160	256,231	253,485	248,930	-4.8	-2.8
Madison	193,451	208,054	212,745	220,695	7.5	6.1
Manchester	99,567	107,006	110,056	115,333	7.5	7.8

Population Growth: City *continued*

City	1990 Census	2000 Census	2003 Estimate	2008 Projection	Population Growth (%)	
					1990-2000	2000-2008
Memphis	660,536	650,100	640,811	627,176	-1.6	-3.5
Miami	358,843	362,470	367,581	377,654	1.0	4.2
Milwaukee	628,095	596,974	587,788	572,208	-5.0	-4.1
Minneapolis	368,383	382,618	381,676	380,149	3.9	-0.6
Naperville	90,506	128,358	138,120	153,978	41.8	20.0
Nashville	488,364	545,524	550,914	560,627	11.7	2.8
New Orleans	496,938	484,674	477,410	465,271	-2.5	-4.0
New York	7,322,552	8,008,278	8,140,877	8,370,954	9.4	4.5
Norfolk	261,229	234,403	234,718	234,497	-10.3	0.0
Oklahoma City	445,065	506,132	517,849	538,125	13.7	6.3
Omaha	371,972	390,007	391,898	395,920	4.8	1.5
Orlando	161,172	185,951	195,864	212,941	15.4	14.5
Overland Park	111,803	149,080	159,422	176,092	33.3	18.1
Philadelphia	1,585,577	1,517,550	1,493,134	1,452,965	-4.3	-4.3
Phoenix	989,873	1,321,045	1,413,559	1,572,182	33.5	19.0
Pittsburgh	369,785	334,563	326,091	312,715	-9.5	-6.5
Plano	128,507	222,030	254,312	306,757	72.8	38.2
Portland	485,833	529,121	540,328	558,948	8.9	5.6
Providence	160,734	173,618	179,847	189,995	8.0	9.4
Provo	87,148	105,166	110,076	118,335	20.7	12.5
Raleigh	226,841	276,093	287,122	307,031	21.7	11.2
Reno	139,950	180,480	191,236	209,238	29.0	15.9
Richmond	202,783	197,790	196,099	193,481	-2.5	-2.2
Rochester	231,642	219,773	218,034	214,928	-5.1	-2.2
Sacramento	368,923	407,018	427,109	460,312	10.3	13.1
St. Louis	396,685	348,189	339,794	324,526	-12.2	-6.8
St. Paul	272,235	287,151	288,790	290,994	5.5	1.3
St. Petersburg	238,846	248,232	252,265	259,782	3.9	4.7
Salt Lake City	159,796	181,743	185,545	192,332	13.7	5.8
San Antonio	997,258	1,144,646	1,189,891	1,266,854	14.8	10.7
San Diego	1,111,048	1,223,400	1,278,299	1,367,679	10.1	11.8
San Francisco	723,959	776,733	800,749	840,774	7.3	8.2
San Jose	784,324	894,943	928,776	987,073	14.1	10.3
Savannah	138,038	131,510	129,941	127,574	-4.7	-3.0
Scottsdale	130,300	202,705	223,805	258,864	55.6	27.7
Seattle	516,262	563,374	576,042	596,391	9.1	5.9
Sioux Falls	102,262	123,975	129,631	138,741	21.2	11.9
Springfield (IL)	108,997	111,454	111,230	111,003	2.3	-0.4
Springfield (MO)	142,557	151,580	152,442	154,382	6.3	1.8
Stamford	108,087	117,083	120,440	126,200	8.3	7.8
Syracuse	163,860	147,306	143,960	138,277	-10.1	-6.1
Tampa	279,960	303,447	317,155	339,991	8.4	12.0
Tucson	417,942	486,699	511,610	553,170	16.5	13.7
Tulsa	367,241	393,049	395,729	401,687	7.0	2.2
Virginia Beach	393,069	425,257	432,423	445,865	8.2	4.8
Washington	606,900	572,059	570,447	567,789	-5.7	-0.7
Wichita	313,693	344,284	346,505	351,262	9.8	2.0
U.S.	248,709,873	281,421,906	290,647,163	305,918,071	13.2	8.7

Source: Claritas, Inc.

Population Growth: Metro Area

Metro Area	1990 Census	2000 Census	2003 Estimate	2008 Projection	Population Growth (%)	
					1990-2000	2000-2008
Albuquerque	589,131	712,738	734,041	772,371	21.0	8.4
Alexandria	4,223,485	4,923,153	5,188,024	5,623,755	16.6	14.2
Anchorage	226,338	260,283	270,680	288,967	15.0	11.0
Ann Arbor	490,058	578,736	604,757	646,738	18.1	11.8
Atlanta	2,959,936	4,112,198	4,456,928	5,019,805	38.9	22.1
Austin	846,217	1,249,763	1,398,133	1,638,145	47.7	31.1
Baltimore	2,382,172	2,552,994	2,635,417	2,773,228	7.2	8.6
Baton Rouge	528,264	602,894	616,014	639,011	14.1	6.0
Bellevue	2,033,149	2,414,616	2,509,275	2,661,858	18.8	10.2
Birmingham	840,140	921,106	933,112	952,310	9.6	3.4
Boise City	295,851	432,345	468,652	527,133	46.1	21.9
Boston	5,686,021	6,057,826	6,178,337	6,368,401	6.5	5.1
Boulder	225,339	291,288	306,514	331,760	29.3	13.9
Buffalo	1,189,288	1,170,111	1,161,268	1,145,277	-1.6	-2.1
Cedar Rapids	168,767	191,701	196,350	204,019	13.6	6.4
Charleston	506,875	549,033	564,037	587,443	8.3	7.0
Charlotte	1,161,781	1,499,293	1,599,675	1,761,210	29.1	17.5
Chattanooga	424,303	465,161	472,948	485,306	9.6	4.3
Chicago	7,410,858	8,272,768	8,489,528	8,850,277	11.6	7.0
Cincinnati	1,526,092	1,646,395	1,675,427	1,722,601	7.9	4.6
Cleveland	2,202,040	2,250,871	2,246,381	2,240,650	2.2	-0.5
Colorado Spgs.	397,014	516,929	550,167	603,389	30.2	16.7
Columbia	453,181	536,691	553,888	583,847	18.4	8.8
Columbus	1,345,458	1,540,157	1,597,389	1,690,768	14.5	9.8
Dallas	2,676,248	3,519,176	3,800,863	4,265,338	31.5	21.2
Denver	1,622,980	2,109,282	2,237,576	2,444,242	30.0	15.9
Des Moines	392,928	456,022	469,011	490,766	16.1	7.6
Detroit	4,266,654	4,441,551	4,468,186	4,509,436	4.1	1.5
Durham	855,547	1,187,941	1,272,078	1,412,108	38.9	18.9
El Paso	591,610	679,622	707,569	754,535	14.9	11.0
Eugene	282,912	322,959	331,383	345,844	14.2	7.1
Ft. Collins	186,136	251,494	269,667	298,783	35.1	18.8
Ft. Lauderdale	1,255,488	1,623,018	1,710,917	1,869,055	29.3	15.2
Ft. Wayne	456,291	502,141	511,640	526,809	10.0	4.9
Ft. Worth	1,361,034	1,702,625	1,820,026	2,012,839	25.1	18.2
Grand Rapids	937,891	1,088,514	1,124,211	1,183,566	16.1	8.7
Green Bay	194,594	226,778	233,561	245,070	16.5	8.1
Greensboro	1,050,304	1,251,509	1,298,965	1,377,268	19.2	10.0
Honolulu	836,231	876,156	899,864	941,692	4.8	7.5
Houston	3,322,025	4,177,646	4,440,137	4,880,084	25.8	16.8
Huntsville	293,047	342,376	350,652	364,618	16.8	6.5
Indianapolis	1,380,491	1,607,486	1,665,679	1,758,822	16.4	9.4
Irvine	2,410,592	2,846,289	2,984,743	3,220,768	18.1	13.2
Jacksonville	906,727	1,100,491	1,170,545	1,287,102	21.4	17.0
Kansas City	1,582,875	1,776,062	1,821,109	1,895,496	12.2	6.7
Knoxville	585,970	687,249	704,383	733,195	17.3	6.7
Las Vegas	852,737	1,563,282	1,774,948	2,124,462	83.3	35.9
Lexington	405,936	479,198	495,124	522,114	18.0	9.0
Lincoln	213,641	250,291	258,538	272,427	17.2	8.8
Los Angeles	8,863,128	9,519,338	9,911,519	10,529,200	7.4	10.6
Louisville	948,829	1,025,598	1,043,162	1,070,668	8.1	4.4
Madison	367,085	426,526	441,942	467,473	16.2	9.6
Manchester	5,686,021	6,057,826	6,178,337	6,368,401	6.5	5.1

Population Growth: Metro Area *continued*

Metro Area	1990 Census	2000 Census	2003 Estimate	2008 Projection	Population Growth (%) 1990-2000	2000-2008
Memphis	1,007,306	1,135,614	1,160,656	1,201,191	12.7	5.8
Miami	1,937,094	2,253,362	2,354,447	2,526,221	16.3	12.1
Milwaukee	1,432,149	1,500,741	1,512,416	1,531,776	4.8	2.1
Minneapolis	2,538,834	2,968,806	3,069,297	3,232,074	16.9	8.9
Naperville	7,410,858	8,272,768	8,489,528	8,850,277	11.6	7.0
Nashville	985,028	1,231,311	1,281,020	1,363,394	25.0	10.7
New Orleans	1,285,270	1,337,726	1,335,236	1,333,393	4.1	-0.3
New York	8,546,878	9,314,235	9,468,596	9,734,181	9.0	4.5
Norfolk	1,443,244	1,569,541	1,609,109	1,676,810	8.8	6.8
Oklahoma City	958,839	1,083,346	1,109,380	1,154,359	13.0	6.6
Omaha	639,580	716,998	733,080	759,980	12.1	6.0
Orlando	1,224,852	1,644,561	1,801,123	2,057,952	34.3	25.1
Overland Park	1,582,875	1,776,062	1,821,109	1,895,496	12.2	6.7
Philadelphia	4,922,177	5,100,931	5,150,898	5,234,144	3.6	2.6
Phoenix	2,238,480	3,251,876	3,552,664	4,055,684	45.3	24.7
Pittsburgh	2,394,811	2,358,695	2,339,719	2,309,282	-1.5	-2.1
Plano	2,676,248	3,519,176	3,800,863	4,265,338	31.5	21.2
Portland	1,515,452	1,918,009	2,013,062	2,173,732	26.6	13.3
Providence	916,270	962,886	989,779	1,034,963	5.1	7.5
Provo	263,590	368,536	397,180	443,600	39.8	20.4
Raleigh	855,547	1,187,941	1,272,078	1,412,108	38.9	18.9
Reno	254,667	339,486	363,845	404,107	33.3	19.0
Richmond	865,640	996,512	1,032,197	1,093,227	15.1	9.7
Rochester	1,062,470	1,098,201	1,105,159	1,115,554	3.4	1.6
Sacramento	1,340,010	1,628,197	1,748,351	1,942,426	21.5	19.3
St. Louis	2,492,525	2,603,607	2,632,142	2,676,617	4.5	2.8
St. Paul	2,538,834	2,968,806	3,069,297	3,232,074	16.9	8.9
St. Petersburg	2,067,959	2,395,997	2,519,486	2,724,271	15.9	13.7
Salt Lake City	1,072,227	1,333,914	1,385,494	1,472,272	24.4	10.4
San Antonio	1,324,749	1,592,383	1,676,159	1,816,324	20.2	14.1
San Diego	2,498,016	2,813,833	2,960,132	3,196,716	12.6	13.6
San Francisco	1,603,678	1,731,183	1,777,529	1,857,268	8.0	7.3
San Jose	1,497,583	1,682,585	1,741,667	1,844,158	12.4	9.6
Savannah	258,060	293,000	301,712	316,118	13.5	7.9
Scottsdale	2,238,480	3,251,876	3,552,664	4,055,684	45.3	24.7
Seattle	2,033,149	2,414,616	2,509,275	2,661,858	18.8	10.2
Sioux Falls	139,236	172,412	181,250	195,450	23.8	13.4
Springfield (IL)	189,550	201,437	202,742	205,300	6.3	1.9
Springfield (MO)	264,346	325,721	339,760	363,527	23.2	11.6
Stamford	1,631,864	1,706,575	1,742,859	1,805,142	4.6	5.8
Syracuse	742,177	732,117	732,434	731,193	-1.4	-0.1
Tampa	2,067,959	2,395,997	2,519,486	2,724,271	15.9	13.7
Tucson	666,880	843,746	901,844	997,107	26.5	18.2
Tulsa	708,954	803,235	823,902	859,509	13.3	7.0
Virginia Beach	1,443,244	1,569,541	1,609,109	1,676,810	8.8	6.8
Washington	4,223,485	4,923,153	5,188,024	5,623,755	16.6	14.2
Wichita	485,270	545,220	552,597	566,506	12.4	3.9
U.S.	248,709,873	281,421,906	290,647,163	305,918,071	13.2	8.7

Note: Figures cover the Metropolitan Statistical Area (MSA) except for Boston, Manchester, Providence, and Stamford which are New England County Metropolitan Areas (NECMA) - see Appendix A for areas included
Source: Claritas, Inc.

Number of Households and Average Household Size: City

City	1990 Census	2000 Census	2003 Estimate	2008 Projection	2003 Average Household Size
Albuquerque	155,138	183,236	188,781	198,780	2.4
Alexandria	53,382	61,889	65,195	70,527	2.1
Anchorage	82,702	94,822	98,758	105,686	2.7
Ann Arbor	42,185	45,693	47,042	49,260	2.5
Atlanta	155,770	168,147	171,208	177,141	2.5
Austin	204,916	265,649	284,258	315,323	2.5
Baltimore	276,484	257,996	258,518	258,540	2.5
Baton Rouge	84,586	88,973	89,185	89,990	2.5
Bellevue	40,416	45,836	47,341	49,786	2.4
Birmingham	105,634	98,782	96,180	91,882	2.4
Boise City	56,950	74,438	78,535	85,529	2.5
Boston	228,464	239,528	242,987	248,466	2.4
Boulder	36,548	39,596	39,923	40,646	2.4
Buffalo	136,436	122,720	119,933	115,295	2.4
Cedar Rapids	44,382	49,820	51,078	53,249	2.4
Charleston	36,669	40,791	41,888	43,637	2.3
Charlotte	169,703	215,449	229,139	251,840	2.5
Chattanooga	62,275	65,499	65,880	66,594	2.4
Chicago	1,025,174	1,061,928	1,067,823	1,078,637	2.7
Cincinnati	154,298	148,095	146,272	143,331	2.2
Cleveland	199,669	190,638	186,997	181,437	2.5
Colorado Spgs.	111,843	141,516	149,343	161,878	2.5
Columbia	40,144	42,245	42,781	43,789	2.7
Columbus	262,528	301,534	312,728	331,702	2.3
Dallas	402,081	451,833	465,725	490,883	2.7
Denver	210,717	239,235	241,325	245,526	2.3
Des Moines	78,588	80,504	80,729	81,263	2.5
Detroit	374,057	336,428	325,824	308,746	2.8
Durham	61,424	74,981	78,114	83,335	2.5
El Paso	160,622	182,063	189,640	202,639	3.1
Eugene	48,233	58,110	60,418	64,418	2.4
Ft. Collins	34,328	45,882	48,917	53,839	2.6
Ft. Lauderdale	66,672	68,468	69,305	71,085	2.2
Ft. Wayne	80,823	83,333	84,025	85,190	2.4
Ft. Worth	168,516	195,078	204,867	221,001	2.8
Grand Rapids	69,036	73,217	74,531	76,913	2.7
Green Bay	38,383	41,591	42,430	43,939	2.4
Greensboro	78,710	92,394	95,438	100,754	2.4
Honolulu	137,631	140,337	143,833	150,386	2.6
Houston	641,561	717,945	740,360	779,391	2.7
Huntsville	63,838	66,742	67,373	68,611	2.3
Indianapolis	291,819	320,107	325,478	334,557	2.4
Irvine	40,827	51,199	54,239	58,968	2.8
Jacksonville	241,379	284,499	301,422	329,500	2.6
Kansas City	177,531	183,981	186,386	190,804	2.4
Knoxville	73,148	76,650	76,870	77,354	2.2
Las Vegas	100,809	176,750	198,455	232,629	2.7
Lexington	89,529	108,288	112,387	119,690	2.4
Lincoln	75,877	90,485	94,013	100,050	2.5
Los Angeles	1,218,134	1,275,412	1,317,121	1,380,698	2.9
Louisville	113,225	111,414	111,474	111,504	2.3
Madison	78,052	89,019	92,457	98,392	2.3
Manchester	40,338	44,247	45,820	48,543	2.4

Number of Households and Average Household Size: City *continued*

City	1990 Census	2000 Census	2003 Estimate	2008 Projection	2003 Average Household Size
Memphis	251,013	250,721	248,203	244,576	2.6
Miami	130,371	134,198	136,783	141,107	2.7
Milwaukee	240,543	232,188	229,813	225,646	2.6
Minneapolis	160,682	162,352	161,882	161,216	2.4
Naperville	30,567	43,751	47,152	52,713	2.9
Nashville	198,581	227,403	231,568	238,993	2.4
New Orleans	188,235	188,251	186,857	184,468	2.6
New York	2,819,401	3,021,588	3,055,735	3,115,460	2.7
Norfolk	89,478	86,210	87,404	89,147	2.7
Oklahoma City	178,768	204,434	210,127	220,128	2.5
Omaha	146,502	156,738	158,647	162,190	2.5
Orlando	67,745	80,883	85,847	94,292	2.3
Overland Park	44,938	59,703	63,902	70,737	2.5
Philadelphia	603,075	590,071	585,574	578,106	2.5
Phoenix	371,986	465,834	492,533	538,193	2.9
Pittsburgh	153,440	143,739	141,859	138,929	2.3
Plano	44,273	80,875	94,051	116,212	2.7
Portland	205,829	223,737	228,528	236,307	2.4
Providence	58,907	62,389	64,648	68,402	2.8
Provo	23,892	29,192	30,810	33,475	3.6
Raleigh	92,960	112,608	117,359	125,757	2.4
Reno	59,324	73,904	77,794	84,125	2.5
Richmond	85,224	84,549	84,249	83,832	2.3
Rochester	93,612	88,999	88,415	87,377	2.5
Sacramento	144,288	154,581	161,284	172,274	2.6
St. Louis	164,931	147,076	144,251	138,904	2.4
St. Paul	110,249	112,109	112,144	112,110	2.6
St. Petersburg	105,847	109,663	111,353	114,479	2.3
Salt Lake City	66,605	71,461	72,385	74,121	2.6
San Antonio	345,912	405,474	424,480	457,107	2.8
San Diego	406,303	450,691	471,149	504,081	2.7
San Francisco	305,584	329,700	339,810	356,615	2.4
San Jose	250,981	276,598	284,423	297,932	3.3
Savannah	52,072	51,375	51,328	51,338	2.5
Scottsdale	57,675	90,669	99,775	114,317	2.2
Seattle	236,705	258,499	264,947	275,067	2.2
Sioux Falls	40,274	49,731	52,342	56,644	2.5
Springfield (IL)	46,442	48,621	48,999	49,717	2.3
Springfield (MO)	58,065	64,691	66,105	68,765	2.3
Stamford	41,954	45,399	46,687	48,864	2.6
Syracuse	64,945	59,482	58,425	56,585	2.5
Tampa	114,771	124,758	130,439	139,795	2.4
Tucson	167,264	192,891	203,229	220,484	2.5
Tulsa	155,417	165,743	166,953	169,577	2.4
Virginia Beach	135,566	154,455	159,079	167,622	2.7
Washington	249,634	248,338	251,172	256,096	2.3
Wichita	126,674	139,087	140,140	142,344	2.5
U.S.	91,947,410	105,480,101	109,440,059	116,034,472	2.7

Source: Claritas, Inc.

Number of Households and Average Household Size: Metro Area

Metro Area	1990 Census	2000 Census	2003 Estimate	2008 Projection	2003 Average Household Size
Albuquerque	221,619	275,028	286,006	305,867	2.6
Alexandria	1,566,134	1,848,064	1,954,108	2,130,691	2.7
Anchorage	82,702	94,822	98,758	105,686	2.7
Ann Arbor	175,050	216,641	229,756	251,754	2.6
Atlanta	1,102,573	1,504,871	1,625,870	1,822,027	2.7
Austin	325,992	471,855	525,004	609,817	2.7
Baltimore	880,145	974,071	1,016,170	1,087,404	2.6
Baton Rouge	188,377	223,349	231,137	245,072	2.7
Bellevue	809,289	963,552	1,003,302	1,067,765	2.5
Birmingham	319,774	361,304	369,866	384,282	2.5
Boise City	108,759	158,426	171,788	193,263	2.7
Boston	2,111,448	2,313,452	2,380,278	2,489,949	2.6
Boulder	88,402	114,680	120,635	130,460	2.5
Buffalo	461,803	468,719	470,431	472,840	2.5
Cedar Rapids	65,501	76,753	79,463	84,069	2.5
Charleston	177,668	207,957	217,790	233,540	2.6
Charlotte	440,533	575,293	616,483	683,454	2.6
Chattanooga	163,101	185,144	190,378	199,089	2.5
Chicago	2,671,540	2,971,690	3,047,396	3,173,616	2.8
Cincinnati	574,602	645,048	664,410	697,084	2.5
Cleveland	845,178	892,562	900,601	915,092	2.5
Colorado Spgs.	146,965	192,409	204,887	224,783	2.7
Columbia	163,167	203,341	213,375	231,271	2.6
Columbus	513,501	610,757	640,367	690,296	2.5
Dallas	1,001,750	1,281,957	1,376,504	1,531,019	2.8
Denver	649,404	825,291	870,042	942,067	2.6
Des Moines	153,100	179,404	185,091	194,690	2.5
Detroit	1,580,063	1,695,331	1,722,895	1,768,961	2.6
Durham	334,506	461,097	492,945	545,432	2.6
El Paso	178,366	210,022	220,367	238,064	3.2
Eugene	110,799	130,453	135,051	143,065	2.5
Ft. Collins	70,472	97,164	104,804	117,203	2.6
Ft. Lauderdale	528,442	654,445	681,636	730,063	2.5
Ft. Wayne	168,809	192,052	197,833	207,471	2.6
Ft. Worth	506,281	624,807	666,045	733,150	2.7
Grand Rapids	333,911	396,047	412,309	439,929	2.7
Green Bay	72,280	87,295	91,212	98,066	2.6
Greensboro	414,793	498,751	519,572	554,252	2.5
Honolulu	265,304	286,450	296,681	314,879	3.0
Houston	1,193,305	1,462,665	1,545,709	1,683,473	2.9
Huntsville	110,893	134,643	139,782	148,726	2.5
Indianapolis	529,814	629,655	657,160	702,489	2.5
Irvine	827,076	935,287	969,033	1,025,601	3.1
Jacksonville	343,526	425,584	455,145	504,849	2.6
Kansas City	608,459	694,468	715,620	751,154	2.5
Knoxville	231,258	281,472	291,800	309,677	2.4
Las Vegas	330,490	588,371	662,231	780,942	2.7
Lexington	154,089	191,006	200,085	215,870	2.5
Lincoln	82,759	99,187	103,158	109,932	2.5
Los Angeles	2,989,542	3,133,774	3,240,855	3,404,589	3.1
Louisville	366,364	412,050	424,654	445,521	2.5
Madison	142,786	173,484	182,199	197,141	2.4
Manchester	2,111,448	2,313,452	2,380,278	2,489,949	2.6

Number of Households and Average Household Size: Metro Area *continued*

Metro Area	1990 Census	2000 Census	2003 Estimate	2008 Projection	2003 Average Household Size
Memphis	365,450	424,202	436,859	457,995	2.7
Miami	692,355	776,774	804,566	850,859	2.9
Milwaukee	537,722	587,657	599,676	619,754	2.5
Minneapolis	960,170	1,136,615	1,181,440	1,256,040	2.6
Naperville	2,671,540	2,971,690	3,047,396	3,173,616	2.8
Nashville	375,832	479,569	502,533	541,519	2.5
New Orleans	469,823	505,579	510,045	518,535	2.6
New York	3,252,415	3,484,108	3,525,574	3,597,284	2.7
Norfolk	511,136	577,659	599,313	637,127	2.7
Oklahoma City	367,775	424,764	438,494	462,571	2.5
Omaha	240,149	275,565	283,953	298,248	2.6
Orlando	465,275	625,248	684,189	780,191	2.6
Overland Park	608,459	694,468	715,620	751,154	2.5
Philadelphia	1,801,160	1,914,246	1,950,521	2,012,611	2.6
Phoenix	846,714	1,194,250	1,296,054	1,462,992	2.7
Pittsburgh	947,248	966,500	970,778	978,634	2.4
Plano	1,001,750	1,281,957	1,376,504	1,531,019	2.8
Portland	589,441	741,776	778,175	839,568	2.6
Providence	345,290	373,196	387,407	411,837	2.6
Provo	70,168	99,937	108,219	121,759	3.7
Raleigh	334,506	461,097	492,945	545,432	2.6
Reno	102,294	132,084	140,138	153,043	2.6
Richmond	331,824	387,721	404,241	432,851	2.6
Rochester	396,089	420,073	426,890	438,046	2.6
Sacramento	505,476	605,923	648,839	717,491	2.7
St. Louis	942,119	1,012,419	1,033,655	1,068,848	2.5
St. Paul	960,170	1,136,615	1,181,440	1,256,040	2.6
St. Petersburg	869,481	1,009,316	1,061,614	1,148,538	2.4
Salt Lake City	347,531	432,040	449,166	478,169	3.1
San Antonio	458,502	559,946	592,913	648,715	2.8
San Diego	887,403	994,677	1,043,746	1,121,993	2.8
San Francisco	642,504	684,453	699,900	726,341	2.5
San Jose	520,182	565,863	579,640	603,467	3.0
Savannah	94,940	111,105	115,609	123,302	2.6
Scottsdale	846,714	1,194,250	1,296,054	1,462,992	2.7
Seattle	809,289	963,552	1,003,302	1,067,765	2.5
Sioux Falls	53,142	66,778	70,585	76,812	2.6
Springfield (IL)	76,345	83,595	84,958	87,456	2.4
Springfield (MO)	101,791	129,357	136,373	148,548	2.5
Stamford	609,741	643,272	659,354	687,083	2.6
Syracuse	272,974	282,601	286,430	292,171	2.6
Tampa	869,481	1,009,316	1,061,614	1,148,538	2.4
Tucson	261,792	332,350	356,492	396,293	2.5
Tulsa	277,202	315,532	324,189	339,247	2.5
Virginia Beach	511,136	577,659	599,313	637,127	2.7
Washington	1,566,134	1,848,064	1,954,108	2,130,691	2.7
Wichita	186,640	210,552	213,730	219,682	2.6
U.S.	91,947,410	105,480,101	109,440,059	116,034,472	2.7

Note: Figures cover the Metropolitan Statistical Area (MSA) except for Boston, Manchester, Providence, and Stamford which are New England County Metropolitan Areas (NECMA) - see Appendix A for areas included
Source: Claritas, Inc.

Race and Ethnicity: City

City	White Non-Hispanic	Black Non-Hispanic	Asian Non-Hispanic	Other Race Non-Hispanic	Hispanic
Albuquerque	70.9	3.2	2.4	23.6	40.6
Alexandria	58.4	22.9	6.0	12.7	15.6
Anchorage	71.2	5.9	5.9	17.0	5.9
Ann Arbor	73.5	9.1	12.7	4.7	3.5
Atlanta	33.6	60.7	2.0	3.7	4.9
Austin	64.7	9.9	5.0	20.4	31.6
Baltimore	30.5	65.1	1.7	2.7	1.9
Baton Rouge	44.8	50.6	2.8	1.7	1.8
Bellevue	72.5	2.0	18.8	6.7	5.8
Birmingham	23.0	74.3	0.8	1.8	1.8
Boise City	91.7	0.8	2.2	5.2	4.8
Boston	53.3	25.5	7.8	13.4	15.2
Boulder	88.2	1.2	3.8	6.7	8.7
Buffalo	53.4	37.7	1.5	7.3	8.1
Cedar Rapids	91.4	3.9	1.9	2.8	1.8
Charleston	63.9	33.0	1.3	1.8	1.7
Charlotte	57.4	32.9	3.6	6.1	8.1
Chattanooga	59.1	36.3	1.6	2.9	2.4
Chicago	41.8	36.3	4.5	17.4	27.1
Cincinnati	52.1	43.6	1.6	2.7	1.4
Cleveland	40.3	51.7	1.4	6.6	7.8
Colorado Spgs.	80.2	6.6	3.0	10.3	12.4
Columbia	49.5	45.5	1.7	3.2	3.3
Columbus	67.1	24.9	3.7	4.4	2.7
Dallas	50.5	25.4	2.9	21.3	37.4
Denver	64.3	11.2	3.0	21.5	32.6
Des Moines	81.3	8.3	3.7	6.7	7.3
Detroit	11.5	81.8	1.0	5.7	5.6
Durham	44.6	43.9	3.8	7.6	9.5
El Paso	72.8	3.2	1.2	22.8	77.8
Eugene	87.7	1.3	3.7	7.3	5.3
Ft. Collins	89.3	1.0	2.6	7.1	9.0
Ft. Lauderdale	63.6	29.1	1.1	6.2	9.9
Ft. Wayne	74.4	17.9	1.7	6.0	6.4
Ft. Worth	59.4	20.1	2.8	17.7	30.9
Grand Rapids	66.1	20.8	1.7	11.4	14.4
Green Bay	84.5	1.6	4.0	9.9	8.2
Greensboro	54.4	38.0	3.0	4.6	4.8
Honolulu	19.3	1.7	56.0	23.0	4.3
Houston	48.8	25.0	5.5	20.6	38.9
Huntsville	62.8	31.7	2.3	3.3	2.2
Indianapolis	68.1	26.0	1.5	4.3	4.4
Irvine	59.1	1.4	31.6	7.9	7.4
Jacksonville	63.4	29.8	2.9	3.9	4.4
Kansas City	60.0	31.5	2.0	6.5	7.4
Knoxville	78.9	16.8	1.5	2.8	1.7
Las Vegas	69.4	10.3	5.0	15.4	24.5
Lexington	80.8	13.5	2.5	3.2	3.6
Lincoln	88.4	3.4	3.4	4.8	3.9
Los Angeles	46.3	11.0	10.1	32.6	47.6
Louisville	61.8	33.8	1.6	2.8	2.1
Madison	83.0	6.2	6.1	4.6	4.4
Manchester	91.1	2.3	2.5	4.1	5.0

Race and Ethnicity: City *continued*

City	White Non-Hispanic	Black Non-Hispanic	Asian Non-Hispanic	Other Race Non-Hispanic	Hispanic
Memphis	32.9	62.6	1.6	3.0	3.4
Miami	67.3	21.4	0.7	10.6	66.3
Milwaukee	48.1	38.3	3.2	10.4	13.0
Minneapolis	63.4	18.7	6.5	11.4	8.5
Naperville	84.3	3.3	10.2	2.2	3.4
Nashville	64.9	27.2	2.5	5.4	5.3
New Orleans	27.3	67.8	2.4	2.5	3.0
New York	43.7	26.5	10.4	19.5	27.4
Norfolk	47.1	45.0	2.9	4.9	4.0
Oklahoma City	67.8	15.3	3.7	13.2	10.9
Omaha	77.4	13.6	1.9	7.1	8.3
Orlando	60.0	27.0	2.9	10.0	18.7
Overland Park	90.2	2.7	4.1	3.1	4.0
Philadelphia	44.1	43.5	4.8	7.7	9.1
Phoenix	70.0	5.2	2.1	22.8	35.6
Pittsburgh	66.8	27.5	3.0	2.7	1.4
Plano	77.4	5.2	10.8	6.6	10.3
Portland	76.9	6.7	6.7	9.7	7.4
Providence	52.4	14.7	6.1	26.8	32.5
Provo	87.8	0.5	1.9	9.8	11.5
Raleigh	62.5	28.1	3.5	5.9	7.6
Reno	76.5	2.6	5.4	15.4	20.2
Richmond	37.7	57.5	1.3	3.6	2.9
Rochester	46.4	39.8	2.4	11.4	13.6
Sacramento	46.9	15.7	17.1	20.3	22.5
St. Louis	43.3	51.3	2.2	3.2	2.2
St. Paul	64.6	12.7	13.3	9.4	8.6
St. Petersburg	70.6	22.8	2.9	3.8	4.5
Salt Lake City	78.2	2.0	3.7	16.2	20.3
San Antonio	67.2	6.9	1.7	24.2	59.1
San Diego	59.4	7.8	14.2	18.7	26.1
San Francisco	49.2	7.6	31.3	11.9	14.1
San Jose	45.4	3.4	28.1	23.0	30.8
Savannah	37.4	58.3	1.6	2.7	2.3
Scottsdale	91.9	1.3	2.1	4.7	7.1
Seattle	69.5	8.3	13.5	8.7	5.6
Sioux Falls	91.2	2.0	1.3	5.5	2.8
Springfield (IL)	80.1	16.0	1.6	2.3	1.3
Springfield (MO)	91.2	3.4	1.5	3.9	2.5
Stamford	68.8	15.2	5.4	10.5	17.9
Syracuse	63.0	26.0	3.6	7.4	5.7
Tampa	63.5	26.2	2.3	8.0	19.9
Tucson	69.6	4.5	2.5	23.4	36.6
Tulsa	68.9	15.9	1.9	13.2	7.9
Virginia Beach	69.9	20.0	5.1	5.0	4.4
Washington	31.1	59.1	2.8	6.9	8.3
Wichita	74.1	11.6	4.3	10.0	10.4
U.S.	74.5	12.4	3.8	9.3	13.2

Note: Figures are 2003 estimates
Source: Claritas, Inc.

Race and Ethnicity: Metro Area

Metro Area	White Non-Hispanic	Black Non-Hispanic	Asian Non-Hispanic	Other Race Non-Hispanic	Hispanic
Albuquerque	69.0	2.6	1.8	26.7	42.0
Alexandria	59.4	26.1	7.0	7.5	9.2
Anchorage	71.2	5.9	5.9	17.0	5.9
Ann Arbor	84.8	7.6	3.9	3.7	3.2
Atlanta	62.4	29.1	3.5	5.1	7.0
Austin	72.4	7.8	3.7	16.1	26.6
Baltimore	66.9	27.6	2.9	2.7	2.1
Baton Rouge	64.8	31.9	1.6	1.7	1.8
Bellevue	77.6	4.5	9.9	8.1	5.6
Birmingham	67.4	29.8	0.9	1.9	2.0
Boise City	89.5	0.6	1.5	8.4	9.1
Boston	84.7	5.2	4.1	6.1	6.3
Boulder	88.2	0.9	3.1	7.8	10.9
Buffalo	83.4	11.9	1.4	3.4	3.1
Cedar Rapids	93.6	2.7	1.5	2.2	1.5
Charleston	64.8	30.9	1.4	2.9	2.6
Charlotte	73.1	20.6	2.0	4.2	5.7
Chattanooga	82.6	14.3	1.0	2.1	1.7
Chicago	65.3	18.7	4.8	11.1	17.9
Cincinnati	84.0	12.9	1.3	1.8	1.2
Cleveland	76.6	18.6	1.4	3.3	3.5
Colorado Spgs.	80.9	6.5	2.6	10.0	11.6
Columbia	63.7	32.1	1.5	2.7	2.6
Columbus	80.8	13.6	2.5	3.1	2.0
Dallas	66.9	14.8	4.3	14.0	23.8
Denver	78.9	5.6	3.1	12.4	19.2
Des Moines	89.4	4.1	2.4	4.2	4.5
Detroit	71.0	22.7	2.5	3.7	3.1
Durham	69.1	22.5	3.0	5.4	6.6
El Paso	73.6	3.1	1.0	22.3	79.4
Eugene	90.2	0.8	2.1	6.9	4.9
Ft. Collins	91.2	0.7	1.6	6.5	8.5
Ft. Lauderdale	69.4	21.1	2.4	7.1	17.9
Ft. Wayne	87.8	7.7	1.1	3.5	3.6
Ft. Worth	73.7	11.3	3.3	11.7	19.0
Grand Rapids	85.1	7.4	1.7	5.8	6.9
Green Bay	90.5	1.3	2.3	5.9	4.3
Greensboro	73.9	20.3	1.5	4.4	5.6
Honolulu	20.8	2.4	46.3	30.5	6.7
Houston	60.7	17.3	5.5	16.5	30.9
Huntsville	73.5	21.6	1.6	3.3	2.2
Indianapolis	81.8	14.0	1.3	3.0	2.9
Irvine	63.3	1.7	14.2	20.9	31.6
Jacksonville	72.0	22.1	2.4	3.5	4.0
Kansas City	80.4	12.8	1.7	5.0	5.6
Knoxville	91.1	5.8	1.0	2.0	1.4
Las Vegas	73.1	8.1	5.0	13.8	21.4
Lexington	86.3	9.5	1.6	2.7	2.7
Lincoln	89.3	3.1	3.1	4.5	3.6
Los Angeles	47.7	9.7	12.3	30.3	45.7
Louisville	82.3	14.2	1.2	2.3	1.8
Madison	88.3	4.3	3.6	3.8	3.6
Manchester	84.7	5.2	4.1	6.1	6.3

Race and Ethnicity: Metro Area *continued*

Metro Area	White Non-Hispanic	Black Non-Hispanic	Asian Non-Hispanic	Other Race Non-Hispanic	Hispanic
Memphis	52.9	43.1	1.5	2.5	2.7
Miami	69.6	20.2	1.5	8.8	58.6
Milwaukee	76.5	15.8	2.2	5.4	6.7
Minneapolis	85.4	5.6	4.4	4.6	3.6
Naperville	65.3	18.7	4.8	11.1	17.9
Nashville	79.2	15.5	1.7	3.6	3.6
New Orleans	56.7	37.9	2.2	3.2	4.4
New York	47.8	24.6	9.5	18.1	25.6
Norfolk	61.6	31.6	2.8	4.0	3.3
Oklahoma City	75.2	10.6	2.6	11.5	7.2
Omaha	84.7	8.4	1.6	5.3	6.0
Orlando	74.0	14.2	2.9	9.0	17.6
Overland Park	80.4	12.8	1.7	5.0	5.6
Philadelphia	71.7	20.2	3.6	4.5	5.4
Phoenix	76.3	3.8	2.2	17.7	25.9
Pittsburgh	89.1	8.3	1.2	1.4	0.8
Plano	66.9	14.8	4.3	14.0	23.8
Portland	83.7	2.7	4.8	8.7	8.0
Providence	83.4	4.8	2.5	9.3	10.0
Provo	92.0	0.3	1.1	6.6	7.5
Raleigh	69.1	22.5	3.0	5.4	6.6
Reno	79.7	2.1	4.4	13.8	17.4
Richmond	64.6	30.2	2.2	3.0	2.5
Rochester	83.3	10.6	1.9	4.1	4.6
Sacramento	69.3	7.8	9.3	13.6	14.9
St. Louis	78.0	18.4	1.5	2.1	1.6
St. Paul	85.4	5.6	4.4	4.6	3.6
St. Petersburg	82.2	10.4	2.0	5.3	11.0
Salt Lake City	86.9	1.2	2.3	9.7	11.6
San Antonio	70.2	6.7	1.6	21.5	51.5
San Diego	65.6	5.8	9.2	19.4	27.6
San Francisco	57.5	5.3	23.3	14.0	17.2
San Jose	51.7	2.8	27.0	18.5	24.6
Savannah	61.0	34.9	1.6	2.5	2.3
Scottsdale	76.3	3.8	2.2	17.7	25.9
Seattle	77.6	4.5	9.9	8.1	5.6
Sioux Falls	93.1	1.5	1.0	4.4	2.1
Springfield (IL)	87.6	9.5	1.1	1.8	1.1
Springfield (MO)	94.2	1.9	1.0	3.0	1.8
Stamford	78.5	10.9	3.0	7.6	11.6
Syracuse	88.4	6.8	1.6	3.2	2.2
Tampa	82.2	10.4	2.0	5.3	11.0
Tucson	74.8	3.1	2.1	20.0	29.9
Tulsa	75.3	9.0	1.3	14.4	5.2
Virginia Beach	61.6	31.6	2.8	4.0	3.3
Washington	59.4	26.1	7.0	7.5	9.2
Wichita	81.0	8.0	3.1	7.9	7.9
U.S.	74.5	12.4	3.8	9.3	13.2

Note: Figures are 2003 estimates and cover the Metropolitan Statistical Area (MSA) except for Boston, Manchester, Providence, and Stamford which are New England County Metropolitan Areas (NECMA) - see Appendix A for areas included
Source: Claritas, Inc.

Age Distribution: City

Area	Percent of Population						
	Under Age 5	Age 5 to 17	Age 18 to 34	Age 35 to 49	Age 50 to 64	Age 65 to 79	80 Years and Over
Albuquerque	6.9	17.5	25.4	23.9	14.4	8.7	3.2
Alexandria	6.2	10.5	34.3	25.4	14.6	6.2	2.7
Anchorage	7.6	21.5	24.9	27.2	13.5	4.3	1.0
Ann Arbor	5.1	11.5	45.2	19.2	11.1	5.8	2.1
Atlanta	6.4	15.9	32.8	22.3	12.7	7.0	2.9
Austin	7.1	15.4	37.5	22.9	10.5	4.9	1.7
Baltimore	6.4	18.3	25.2	22.6	14.2	9.8	3.4
Baton Rouge	6.8	17.6	31.1	20.2	12.8	8.5	3.0
Bellevue	5.6	15.5	23.4	24.6	17.4	10.2	3.3
Birmingham	6.8	18.3	25.9	22.6	12.9	9.9	3.7
Boise City	7.0	18.2	27.8	23.9	13.0	6.9	3.2
Boston	5.4	14.3	37.2	20.8	11.8	7.5	2.9
Boulder	3.9	10.7	45.5	20.4	11.5	5.3	2.6
Buffalo	7.1	19.2	25.4	22.1	12.6	9.8	3.7
Cedar Rapids	6.9	17.5	25.6	22.7	14.2	9.3	3.8
Charleston	5.6	14.4	32.1	20.4	13.8	9.6	4.1
Charlotte	7.1	17.6	29.4	24.3	12.9	6.6	2.1
Chattanooga	5.9	16.4	24.8	21.9	15.7	11.2	4.1
Chicago	7.5	18.6	29.4	21.5	12.6	7.7	2.6
Cincinnati	7.2	17.3	29.6	21.6	12.0	8.7	3.7
Cleveland	8.1	20.4	24.5	22.1	12.4	9.3	3.3
Colorado Spgs.	7.5	19.0	25.6	24.9	13.5	7.1	2.5
Columbia	5.4	14.7	39.3	19.5	10.8	7.4	2.8
Columbus	7.4	16.7	33.5	22.0	11.5	6.6	2.2
Dallas	8.3	18.2	31.5	22.0	11.4	6.3	2.3
Denver	6.7	15.1	31.2	22.9	12.9	8.1	3.2
Des Moines	7.6	17.0	27.1	22.4	13.5	8.8	3.6
Detroit	8.0	23.1	24.7	21.3	12.5	8.0	2.5
Durham	7.1	15.8	34.1	22.2	11.5	6.7	2.7
El Paso	8.3	22.6	24.1	21.6	12.7	8.5	2.2
Eugene	5.3	15.3	31.9	21.6	13.8	8.2	3.9
Ft. Collins	6.0	15.3	39.0	21.6	10.2	5.5	2.3
Ft. Lauderdale	5.1	14.1	22.6	26.1	16.7	11.1	4.3
Ft. Wayne	7.9	19.2	26.1	21.6	12.9	8.7	3.7
Ft. Worth	8.4	19.7	28.1	22.4	11.8	7.0	2.6
Grand Rapids	8.1	18.9	29.9	21.0	10.5	7.7	3.9
Green Bay	7.2	18.2	27.3	23.0	12.5	7.9	3.8
Greensboro	6.2	16.1	30.5	21.9	13.4	8.8	3.1
Honolulu	5.0	14.1	23.3	23.1	16.5	13.0	5.0
Houston	8.2	19.2	29.2	22.7	12.4	6.4	1.9
Huntsville	6.1	17.0	23.9	23.2	16.6	10.3	3.0
Indianapolis	7.4	18.2	26.7	23.6	13.1	8.2	2.8
Irvine	5.6	17.8	29.2	25.7	14.5	5.4	1.8
Jacksonville	7.3	19.4	25.1	24.2	13.8	7.8	2.4
Kansas City	7.1	18.2	26.0	23.4	13.6	8.7	3.0
Knoxville	5.8	13.8	32.4	20.4	13.2	10.3	4.1
Las Vegas	7.6	18.1	25.1	22.7	15.0	9.5	2.0
Lexington	6.2	15.1	31.6	23.5	13.7	7.4	2.6
Lincoln	6.7	16.3	32.1	22.0	12.5	7.6	2.9
Los Angeles	7.6	18.9	29.1	22.7	12.1	7.2	2.5
Louisville	6.6	17.1	24.8	23.3	13.6	10.4	4.3
Madison	5.1	12.4	39.4	21.3	12.5	6.7	2.6
Manchester	6.8	17.0	26.2	23.5	13.6	9.0	4.0

Age Distribution: City *continued*

Area	Percent of Population						
	Under Age 5	Age 5 to 17	Age 18 to 34	Age 35 to 49	Age 50 to 64	Age 65 to 79	80 Years and Over
Memphis	7.7	20.1	26.4	22.1	12.7	8.1	2.8
Miami	5.9	15.8	23.6	22.3	15.3	12.4	4.6
Milwaukee	7.9	20.8	27.8	21.0	11.7	7.9	3.0
Minneapolis	6.4	15.5	35.0	23.1	10.9	5.9	3.1
Naperville	8.3	23.7	19.2	29.4	13.1	4.6	1.7
Nashville	6.6	15.5	29.6	23.8	13.6	8.1	2.9
New Orleans	6.8	19.9	25.7	22.3	13.7	8.6	3.1
New York	6.7	17.5	26.8	22.9	14.4	8.6	3.1
Norfolk	7.1	16.9	33.6	20.5	11.0	8.1	2.8
Oklahoma City	7.3	18.2	25.6	23.0	14.4	8.6	2.9
Omaha	7.2	18.4	26.4	22.6	13.6	8.6	3.2
Orlando	6.5	15.5	31.2	23.3	12.1	8.3	3.1
Overland Park	7.1	18.5	21.7	26.1	15.0	8.2	3.3
Philadelphia	6.4	18.8	25.7	21.3	13.7	10.2	3.9
Phoenix	8.6	20.3	28.0	22.9	12.2	6.1	1.9
Pittsburgh	5.3	14.5	29.2	20.8	13.7	11.7	4.8
Plano	8.2	20.3	22.7	29.5	14.5	3.7	1.1
Portland	6.0	15.0	28.5	24.9	14.0	8.0	3.6
Providence	6.9	19.1	34.2	18.7	10.5	7.2	3.3
Provo	8.6	13.5	56.5	10.0	5.7	4.0	1.7
Raleigh	6.3	14.5	36.6	22.6	11.7	6.2	2.1
Reno	6.7	16.5	27.3	23.3	14.9	8.6	2.7
Richmond	6.3	15.6	29.7	22.1	12.9	9.5	3.9
Rochester	7.8	20.3	28.5	21.5	12.0	6.6	3.3
Sacramento	7.0	20.2	25.6	22.8	13.0	8.2	3.2
St. Louis	6.7	19.0	26.0	22.3	12.3	9.6	4.1
St. Paul	7.5	19.5	29.2	22.2	11.1	6.9	3.5
St. Petersburg	5.6	15.9	21.1	24.5	15.4	12.1	5.4
Salt Lake City	7.8	15.6	35.0	20.4	10.1	7.4	3.7
San Antonio	8.0	20.4	26.1	22.3	12.7	7.9	2.5
San Diego	6.7	17.2	30.0	23.3	12.4	7.8	2.6
San Francisco	4.0	10.4	32.1	25.0	14.6	10.0	3.8
San Jose	7.6	18.8	27.8	24.5	13.3	6.3	1.8
Savannah	7.0	18.6	27.7	20.1	13.2	9.4	4.0
Scottsdale	5.0	14.2	20.9	23.6	19.4	13.0	3.9
Seattle	4.6	10.9	33.5	25.1	13.8	8.1	4.0
Sioux Falls	7.3	17.9	27.8	23.3	12.7	7.9	3.1
Springfield (IL)	6.4	17.6	23.0	23.6	14.9	10.2	4.3
Springfield (MO)	5.9	14.0	31.8	20.1	13.2	10.3	4.7
Stamford	6.7	15.3	24.7	24.6	14.8	10.0	3.9
Syracuse	6.9	18.0	31.2	19.7	11.3	8.7	4.2
Tampa	6.7	17.9	25.8	23.4	13.6	9.1	3.4
Tucson	7.1	17.3	29.4	21.7	12.5	8.7	3.3
Tulsa	7.2	17.4	25.9	22.6	14.1	9.4	3.5
Virginia Beach	7.1	20.3	26.2	25.2	12.8	6.6	1.8
Washington	5.7	14.3	30.5	22.4	14.9	9.0	3.2
Wichita	7.9	19.1	25.0	23.0	13.1	8.8	3.1
U.S.	6.8	18.9	23.7	23.5	14.8	9.2	3.2

Source: Census 2000, Summary File 3

Age Distribution: Metro Area

Metro Area	Percent of Population						
	Under Age 5	Age 5 to 17	Age 18 to 34	Age 35 to 49	Age 50 to 64	Age 65 to 79	80 Years and Over
Albuquerque	7.0	19.2	23.6	24.3	14.6	8.4	2.8
Alexandria	6.9	18.3	24.6	25.8	15.3	6.8	2.2
Anchorage	7.6	21.5	24.9	27.2	13.5	4.3	1.0
Ann Arbor	6.5	18.0	27.7	24.4	14.6	6.7	2.2
Atlanta	7.5	19.1	27.0	25.4	13.5	5.8	1.8
Austin	7.4	17.9	31.5	24.4	11.7	5.4	1.8
Baltimore	6.5	18.8	22.3	24.9	15.5	9.0	3.0
Baton Rouge	7.2	20.0	26.9	22.9	13.6	7.3	2.2
Bellevue	6.3	17.4	25.2	26.1	14.7	7.4	2.9
Birmingham	6.7	18.4	23.5	23.7	15.0	9.5	3.2
Boise City	8.1	20.2	25.8	23.1	13.1	6.9	2.8
Boston	6.2	16.2	25.2	24.4	14.9	9.4	3.7
Boulder	6.0	16.8	29.5	26.0	13.8	5.7	2.1
Buffalo	6.0	18.3	20.9	23.5	15.3	11.6	4.3
Cedar Rapids	6.9	18.3	24.3	23.3	14.9	8.8	3.4
Charleston	6.7	19.0	25.6	23.6	14.8	8.0	2.4
Charlotte	7.1	18.3	25.7	24.4	14.5	7.8	2.4
Chattanooga	6.1	17.6	22.8	23.3	16.7	10.2	3.3
Chicago	7.4	19.4	24.9	23.6	13.9	7.9	2.8
Cincinnati	7.1	19.5	23.1	24.1	14.3	8.9	3.0
Cleveland	6.6	18.8	20.9	23.8	15.4	10.6	3.9
Colorado Spgs.	7.5	19.9	25.5	25.0	13.3	6.6	2.0
Columbia	6.5	18.5	26.5	24.2	14.5	7.6	2.3
Columbus	7.1	18.3	26.7	23.9	14.0	7.7	2.4
Dallas	8.1	19.9	27.3	24.4	12.7	5.8	1.8
Denver	7.1	18.6	25.6	25.6	14.1	6.8	2.2
Des Moines	7.5	18.4	24.6	23.9	14.4	8.1	3.0
Detroit	7.0	19.5	22.6	24.1	14.8	9.0	3.1
Durham	6.9	17.3	29.0	24.9	13.3	6.5	2.1
El Paso	8.6	23.3	24.8	21.4	12.1	7.8	2.0
Eugene	5.7	17.1	24.9	22.9	16.1	9.7	3.6
Ft. Collins	6.0	17.6	28.5	24.4	13.9	7.1	2.5
Ft. Lauderdale	6.3	17.2	21.3	24.8	14.4	10.7	5.4
Ft. Wayne	7.5	20.3	22.8	23.2	14.2	8.6	3.4
Ft. Worth	7.7	20.2	25.2	24.6	13.5	6.7	2.0
Grand Rapids	7.5	20.8	24.2	23.6	13.1	7.8	3.0
Green Bay	6.9	19.1	25.2	24.5	13.6	7.5	3.2
Greensboro	6.6	17.4	24.3	23.6	15.6	9.5	3.0
Honolulu	6.4	17.3	24.8	23.1	14.9	10.2	3.3
Houston	8.1	21.1	26.0	24.6	12.9	5.8	1.6
Huntsville	6.8	18.6	23.1	25.0	15.6	8.6	2.3
Indianapolis	7.4	19.1	24.0	24.3	14.2	8.1	2.8
Irvine	7.5	19.4	25.6	24.0	13.7	7.3	2.5
Jacksonville	6.8	19.3	23.3	24.6	15.0	8.5	2.6
Kansas City	7.2	19.3	23.0	24.5	14.6	8.4	3.0
Knoxville	6.0	16.6	23.8	23.5	16.7	10.2	3.3
Las Vegas	7.3	17.9	24.2	22.7	16.1	9.7	2.1
Lexington	6.4	16.3	29.7	23.3	14.2	7.6	2.6
Lincoln	6.6	16.9	30.5	22.5	13.0	7.6	2.8
Los Angeles	7.7	20.3	26.7	23.0	12.6	7.3	2.4
Louisville	6.7	18.0	22.7	24.5	15.5	9.5	3.1
Madison	6.0	16.5	30.3	24.3	13.6	6.7	2.7
Manchester	6.8	19.0	23.2	25.8	14.3	7.9	3.1

Age Distribution: Metro Area *continued*

Metro Area	Percent of Population						
	Under Age 5	Age 5 to 17	Age 18 to 34	Age 35 to 49	Age 50 to 64	Age 65 to 79	80 Years and Over
Memphis	7.6	20.7	24.1	23.7	13.9	7.6	2.4
Miami	6.4	18.3	23.9	23.2	14.9	9.9	3.4
Milwaukee	6.9	19.5	22.8	23.9	14.3	9.1	3.4
Minneapolis	7.1	19.6	24.5	25.5	13.7	6.9	2.7
Naperville	7.4	19.4	24.9	23.6	13.9	7.9	2.8
Nashville	6.9	17.9	25.9	24.8	14.5	7.6	2.5
New Orleans .	6.8	19.9	23.3	23.8	14.8	8.7	2.7
New York	6.7	17.6	25.9	23.2	14.7	8.8	3.2
Norfolk	6.9	19.4	25.7	24.2	13.6	7.9	2.4
Oklahoma City	6.9	18.6	25.4	23.1	14.6	8.5	2.8
Omaha	7.3	19.8	24.6	23.7	13.9	7.9	2.8
Orlando	6.5	18.2	24.4	24.2	14.4	9.5	2.9
Overland Park	7.2	19.3	23.0	24.5	14.6	8.4	3.0
Philadelphia	6.4	18.9	22.2	23.9	14.9	10.0	3.6
Phoenix	7.7	19.0	25.8	22.0	13.5	9.0	3.0
Pittsburgh	5.5	16.7	20.2	23.7	16.1	12.9	4.9
Plano	8.1	19.9	27.3	24.4	12.7	5.8	1.8
Portland	7.0	18.4	24.8	24.7	14.7	7.4	3.0
Providence	6.0	17.8	23.2	23.5	14.9	10.4	4.3
Provo	10.9	23.0	36.0	15.4	8.2	4.8	1.7
Raleigh	6.9	17.3	29.0	24.9	13.3	6.5	2.1
Reno	6.8	18.0	24.1	24.8	15.9	8.3	2.3
Richmond	6.5	18.7	23.2	25.3	15.1	8.5	2.8
Rochester	6.2	19.4	22.1	24.0	15.4	9.1	3.8
Sacramento	6.9	20.3	22.4	24.4	14.4	8.7	2.9
St. Louis	6.7	19.6	22.0	24.2	14.7	9.5	3.4
St. Paul	7.1	19.6	24.5	25.5	13.7	6.9	2.7
St. Petersburg	5.7	16.1	20.1	22.8	16.1	13.9	5.4
Salt Lake City	9.1	22.2	28.1	20.9	11.4	6.2	2.1
San Antonio	7.7	20.6	24.8	22.9	13.4	8.1	2.6
San Diego	7.0	18.6	26.9	23.5	12.8	8.3	2.9
San Francisco	5.1	13.5	26.7	25.6	15.8	9.6	3.6
San Jose	7.0	17.7	26.9	25.0	13.9	7.2	2.3
Savannah	6.8	19.3	24.7	22.9	14.4	8.9	3.0
Scottsdale	7.7	19.0	25.8	22.0	13.5	9.0	3.0
Seattle	6.3	17.4	25.2	26.1	14.7	7.4	2.9
Sioux Falls	7.4	19.2	25.6	24.0	12.9	7.8	3.1
Springfield (IL)	6.3	18.7	21.0	24.6	15.7	9.9	3.8
Springfield (MO)	6.5	17.3	26.2	22.4	14.7	9.3	3.6
Stamford	7.2	17.7	19.1	26.0	16.3	10.0	3.7
Syracuse	6.3	19.5	22.4	23.7	14.8	9.8	3.6
Tampa	5.7	16.1	20.1	22.8	16.1	13.9	5.4
Tucson	6.5	18.0	24.2	22.3	14.8	10.6	3.6
Tulsa	7.1	19.5	23.1	23.5	15.1	8.9	2.9
Virginia Beach	6.9	19.4	25.7	24.2	13.6	7.9	2.4
Washington	6.9	18.3	24.6	25.8	15.3	6.8	2.2
Wichita	7.6	20.4	23.0	23.7	13.4	8.8	3.0
U.S.	6.8	18.9	23.7	23.5	14.8	9.2	3.2

Note: Figures cover the Metropolitan Statistical Area (MSA) - see Appendix A for areas included
Source: Census 2000, Summary File 3

Segregation

Area	City		MSA[1]	
	Index[2]	Rank[3]	Index[2]	Rank[4]
Albuquerque	39.5	86	40.0	301
Alexandria	46.0	72	66.2	88
Anchorage	41.4	82	41.4	295
Ann Arbor	38.7	87	67.5	76
Atlanta	83.5	3	68.8	67
Austin	60.9	47	57.1	179
Baltimore	75.2	12	71.8	44
Baton Rouge	75.1	13	73.1	33
Bellevue	33.5	95	57.9	172
Birmingham	66.3	32	77.4	15
Boise City	32.9	96	37.1	310
Boston	75.8	10	68.8	68
Boulder	34.2	94	36.7	312
Buffalo	73.9	15	80.4	8
Cedar Rapids	45.9	73	51.8	219
Charleston	63.8	35	54.1	205
Charlotte	61.1	45	61.1	135
Chattanooga	66.9	31	73.1	34
Chicago	87.3	1	83.6	5
Cincinnati	63.0	40	78.0	14
Cleveland	79.4	8	79.7	9
Colorado Spgs.	46.1	71	46.5	261
Columbia	63.8	36	58.9	160
Columbus	61.0	46	66.9	78
Dallas	71.5	19	64.4	110
Denver	67.4	30	66.2	86
Des Moines	55.3	63	61.0	137
Detroit	63.3	39	86.7	2
Durham	57.8	57	52.7	214
El Paso	39.5	85	41.1	296
Eugene	25.5	100	37.9	308
Ft. Collins	37.0	90	42.5	286
Ft. Lauderdale	80.5	6	64.8	101
Ft. Wayne	68.8	25	75.4	26
Ft. Worth	62.5	41	64.5	106
Grand Rapids	58.6	54	71.9	41
Green Bay	38.5	88	53.1	211
Greensboro	62.3	42	64.5	108
Honolulu	49.4	69	44.0	281
Houston	75.5	11	71.8	45
Huntsville	67.9	28	60.5	141
Indianapolis	67.4	29	75.5	24
Irvine	37.3	89	43.8	282
Jacksonville	55.8	62	59.3	154
Kansas City	70.7	22	72.7	37
Knoxville	59.6	50	63.2	119
Las Vegas	42.4	78	47.4	254
Lexington	50.2	68	51.7	220
Lincoln	44.3	75	46.6	260
Los Angeles	74.0	14	70.5	53
Louisville	73.8	16	68.6	69
Madison	43.3	77	53.0	213
Manchester	40.8	83	68.8	68

Segregation *continued*

Area	City		MSA[1]	
	Index[2]	Rank[3]	Index[2]	Rank[4]
Memphis	68.6	26	72.2	40
Miami	80.3	7	75.8	22
Milwaukee	71.4	20	84.4	3
Minneapolis	61.3	44	64.5	107
Naperville	35.6	92	83.6	5
Nashville	57.6	58	61.7	128
New Orleans	70.6	23	74.7	29
New York	85.3	2	84.3	4
Norfolk	57.5	59	53.0	212
Oklahoma City	59.0	53	60.5	142
Omaha	70.2	24	69.8	57
Orlando	71.8	18	60.0	146
Overland Park	30.9	97	72.7	37
Philadelphia	80.6	5	76.9	18
Phoenix	54.4	64	49.1	244
Pittsburgh	71.3	21	72.5	38
Plano	28.2	99	64.4	110
Portland	57.0	60	55.8	189
Providence	50.8	67	65.5	95
Provo	36.9	91	46.0	263
Raleigh	56.2	61	52.7	214
Reno	41.6	79	44.1	279
Richmond	68.3	27	62.9	122
Rochester	58.0	56	71.1	50
Sacramento	49.1	70	59.6	150
St. Louis	72.4	17	78.0	13
St. Paul	52.6	66	64.5	107
St. Petersburg	76.7	9	68.4	72
Salt Lake City	44.7	74	47.8	252
San Antonio	53.5	65	55.5	191
San Diego	63.6	37	58.2	171
San Francisco	62.2	43	65.6	94
San Jose	44.0	76	45.9	264
Savannah	60.3	49	64.6	103
Scottsdale	28.8	98	49.1	244
Seattle	64.2	34	57.9	172
Sioux Falls	40.1	84	48.2	249
Springfield (IL)	58.4	55	65.5	98
Springfield (MO)	41.4	80	55.0	201
Stamford	63.4	38	71.1	51
Syracuse	59.5	51	73.6	32
Tampa	65.4	33	68.4	72
Tucson	35.0	93	44.2	277
Tulsa	60.3	48	64.1	113
Virginia Beach	41.4	81	53.0	212
Washington	81.5	4	66.2	88
Wichita	59.4	52	63.4	117

Note: Figures are based on an analysis of Census 2000 data; (1) Metropolitan Statistical Area - see Appendix A for areas included; (2) Dissimilarity Index—the most commonly used measure of segregation between two groups, reflecting their relative distributions across neighborhoods within a city or metropolitan area. It can range in value from 0, indicating complete integration, to 100, indicating complete segregation; (3) Ranges from 1 (most segregated) to 100 (least segregated) and includes all the cities in this book; (4) Ranges from 1 (most segregated) to 318 (least segregated) and includes 318 metropolitan areas.
Source: www.CensusScope.org

Religion

City	County	Catholic	Southern Baptist	United Meth-odist	ELCA[1]	LDS[2]	Presby-terian Church USA	Jewish Est.	Muslim Est.
Albuquerque	Bernalillo	34.4	4.0	2.0	1.4	1.5	0.9	1.4	0.3
Alexandria	Alexandria City	18.8	3.9	3.0	0.0	0.6	3.6	4.2	3.0
Anchorage	Anchorage	8.8	4.6	0.9	1.8	3.2	0.8	0.9	0.5
Ann Arbor	Washtenaw	12.9	0.7	2.2	1.7	0.5	1.4	2.2	1.5
Atlanta	Fulton	8.8	10.0	9.2	0.8	0.3	3.7	8.1	2.7
Austin	Travis	20.4	9.5	2.7	1.5	0.6	1.3	1.7	0.4
Baltimore	Baltimore City	12.5	0.8	2.7	1.8	0.1	1.5	8.7	1.6
Baton Rouge	East Baton Rouge	23.2	13.7	5.7	0.2	0.4	1.0	0.2	0.4
Bellevue	King	16.2	0.7	1.1	2.0	2.3	1.6	1.9	0.5
Birmingham	Jefferson	6.7	29.7	8.0	0.2	0.3	1.5	0.8	0.3
Boise City	Ada	12.3	1.0	2.0	1.0	15.2	0.7	0.3	0.1
Boston	Suffolk	45.0	0.6	0.2	0.1	0.1	0.1	3.6	2.0
Boulder	Boulder	20.2	1.0	1.8	3.0	1.6	1.8	4.5	1.4
Buffalo	Erie	57.3	0.2	2.0	2.0	0.2	1.3	2.1	0.6
Cedar Rapids	Linn	23.3	0.6	7.5	5.7	0.7	2.9	0.2	1.2
Charleston	Charleston	7.7	11.6	5.7	1.9	0.5	3.9	1.6	0.7
Charlotte	Mecklenburg	8.5	10.8	6.7	1.2	0.5	6.0	1.2	1.1
Chattanooga	Hamilton	3.2	21.6	8.0	0.3	0.2	1.3	0.5	0.7
Chicago	Cook	39.9	1.2	0.8	1.2	0.2	0.7	4.4	1.8
Cincinnati	Hamilton	26.8	1.8	3.6	0.7	0.4	2.3	2.7	0.1
Cleveland	Cuyahoga	34.9	0.3	2.2	1.4	0.2	1.1	5.7	1.5
Colorado Spgs.	El Paso	11.3	4.0	2.0	1.6	2.2	1.7	0.3	0.1
Columbia	Richland	4.0	13.5	7.0	2.7	0.3	3.1	0.9	0.4
Columbus	Franklin	13.7	2.1	4.1	2.8	0.4	1.5	1.5	0.6
Dallas	Dallas	21.7	12.7	4.8	0.5	0.5	1.3	1.7	1.0
Denver	Denver	28.7	1.3	1.6	0.9	0.6	1.1	6.9	1.1
Des Moines	Polk	15.5	0.2	5.3	6.3	0.5	1.9	0.6	0.3
Detroit	Wayne	21.9	0.5	1.0	1.0	0.2	1.0	0.4	2.3
Durham	Durham	4.4	12.8	5.6	0.5	0.8	2.0	1.8	0.9
El Paso	El Paso	51.5	3.6	1.3	0.2	0.8	0.4	0.7	0.1
Eugene	Lane	4.8	1.3	1.0	1.3	2.6	0.5	1.0	0.2
Ft. Collins	Larimer	12.8	0.9	2.1	2.1	2.5	1.8	0.4	0.5
Ft. Lauderdale	Broward	21.1	3.6	1.2	0.3	0.3	0.4	13.1	0.4
Ft. Wayne	Allen	17.4	1.1	4.5	3.8	0.3	1.0	0.3	0.2
Ft. Worth	Tarrant	11.5	18.7	6.8	0.6	0.8	0.8	0.4	1.0
Grand Rapids	Kent	20.0	0.1	1.8	1.3	0.4	0.8	0.3	1.2
Green Bay	Brown	52.4	0.3	2.0	6.2	0.3	0.7	0.2	0.0
Greensboro	Guilford	5.1	12.8	10.5	1.1	0.4	3.9	0.6	0.9
Honolulu	Honolulu	17.6	1.9	0.8	0.3	3.3	0.0	0.7	0.1
Houston	Harris	18.2	14.3	5.0	0.5	0.7	1.1	1.1	1.4
Huntsville	Madison	5.8	22.4	7.7	0.7	0.8	1.6	0.3	0.4
Indianapolis	Marion	12.7	1.7	3.7	0.7	0.3	1.8	1.2	0.3
Irvine	Orange	27.4	1.2	0.6	0.8	1.7	0.9	2.1	1.4
Jacksonville	Duval	8.3	18.4	3.7	0.5	0.7	1.7	0.8	0.3
Kansas City	Jackson	15.5	11.5	4.2	0.4	0.9	1.8	1.1	1.0
Knoxville	Knox	4.0	31.5	8.4	0.7	0.4	2.6	0.5	0.9
Las Vegas	Clark	17.2	1.9	0.4	0.6	6.0	0.3	5.5	0.1
Lexington	Fayette	10.0	14.1	6.1	0.5	0.7	1.8	0.8	0.4
Lincoln	Lancaster	10.5	0.9	6.3	5.1	0.9	2.3	0.3	0.5
Los Angeles	Los Angeles	40.0	1.2	0.6	0.3	1.0	0.6	5.9	1.0
Louisville	Jefferson	22.6	15.6	2.9	0.5	0.4	1.5	1.3	0.3
Madison	Dane	28.0	0.1	2.0	11.6	0.3	1.0	1.1	0.3
Manchester	Hillsborough	45.5	0.2	1.0	0.4	0.5	0.4	1.6	0.0

Religion *continued*

City	County	Catholic	Southern Baptist	United Methodist	ELCA[1]	LDS[2]	Presbyterian Church USA	Jewish Est.	Muslim Est.
Memphis	Shelby	5.7	16.9	5.4	0.2	0.3	1.2	1.0	0.4
Miami	Dade	24.1	3.6	0.8	0.3	0.3	0.2	5.5	0.3
Milwaukee	Milwaukee	27.8	1.0	1.0	3.0	0.2	0.5	1.8	0.3
Minneapolis	Hennepin	23.4	0.2	2.1	13.7	0.4	1.6	2.8	0.7
Naperville	DuPage	38.7	0.2	2.2	3.0	0.3	1.1	0.2	1.7
Nashville	Davidson	0.0	0.0	0.0	0.0	0.0	0.0	0.0	0.0
New Orleans	Orleans	28.1	5.7	2.3	0.2	0.1	0.7	1.8	0.8
New York	New York	36.7	0.1	0.8	0.3	0.3	0.7	20.5	2.4
Norfolk	Norfolk City	4.7	10.5	3.3	0.7	0.3	2.2	3.2	0.4
Oklahoma City	Oklahoma	6.5	26.4	9.4	0.6	0.7	1.3	0.4	0.4
Omaha	Douglas	27.7	1.7	2.8	5.4	1.0	2.3	1.4	0.4
Orlando	Orange	13.3	8.2	3.3	0.6	0.6	1.7	1.2	0.2
Overland Park	Johnson	21.3	3.1	4.5	1.8	0.8	3.5	2.7	0.0
Philadelphia	Philadelphia	32.4	1.2	1.3	1.0	0.1	0.7	5.7	2.8
Phoenix	Maricopa	17.3	2.5	1.1	1.7	5.0	0.6	2.0	0.3
Pittsburgh	Allegheny	49.4	0.2	3.7	2.5	0.2	4.7	2.7	0.6
Plano	Collin	18.3	16.0	6.1	0.6	1.3	0.7	1.4	1.2
Portland	Multnomah	22.7	0.7	0.9	1.2	1.6	1.6	2.9	0.6
Providence	Providence	52.1	0.0	0.6	0.3	0.2	0.1	1.7	0.3
Provo	Utah	1.0	0.1	0.0	0.0	88.1	0.1	0.0	0.0
Raleigh	Wake	9.5	12.6	7.4	0.9	0.6	2.7	1.0	0.5
Reno	Washoe	16.2	1.1	0.8	0.6	3.5	0.5	0.6	0.2
Richmond	Richmond City	5.1	12.5	5.8	0.3	0.0	0.4	7.6	0.4
Rochester	Monroe	35.7	0.1	2.0	1.4	0.4	1.9	3.1	0.6
Sacramento	Sacramento	18.3	1.7	0.6	0.7	2.5	0.9	1.4	0.5
St. Louis	Saint Louis City	20.3	4.4	1.4	1.4	0.1	0.8	1.3	1.2
St. Paul	Ramsey	31.2	0.1	1.6	12.2	0.4	1.2	1.6	0.5
St. Petersburg	Pinellas	12.2	3.9	4.4	0.9	0.2	1.3	2.6	0.5
Salt Lake City	Salt Lake	6.0	0.6	0.5	0.4	56.0	0.4	0.5	0.4
San Antonio	Bexar	41.2	8.6	3.0	1.0	0.7	0.8	0.8	0.2
San Diego	San Diego	29.5	1.0	0.7	0.6	1.6	0.9	2.5	0.3
San Francisco	San Francisco	23.3	0.4	1.7	0.2	0.2	0.5	6.4	2.9
San Jose	Santa Clara	28.7	1.0	0.9	0.6	1.2	0.6	3.2	1.1
Savannah	Chatham	9.0	14.9	6.7	1.5	0.3	1.4	1.3	0.3
Scottsdale	Maricopa	17.3	2.5	1.1	1.7	5.0	0.6	2.0	0.3
Seattle	King	16.2	0.7	1.1	2.0	2.3	1.6	1.9	0.5
Sioux Falls	Minnehaha	22.4	0.4	4.1	21.2	0.6	1.6	0.1	0.0
Springfield (IL)	Sangamon	19.5	2.6	6.1	1.8	0.5	3.1	0.6	0.2
Springfield (MO)	Greene	6.0	21.7	5.4	0.5	0.9	1.9	0.1	0.3
Stamford	Fairfield	49.2	0.2	1.7	0.8	0.3	0.7	4.4	1.7
Syracuse	Onondaga	32.1	0.2	5.2	1.7	0.3	1.3	2.0	0.7
Tampa	Hillsborough	16.6	10.3	3.3	0.7	0.4	1.0	2.0	0.5
Tucson	Pima	26.7	2.7	1.1	1.3	2.0	1.1	2.4	0.1
Tulsa	Tulsa	7.3	19.5	11.7	0.6	0.8	1.8	0.5	0.4
Virginia Beach	Virginia Beach City	9.6	4.7	4.6	0.5	0.5	1.4	1.8	0.0
Washington	District of Columbia	28.0	6.8	2.7	0.7	0.1	1.5	4.5	10.6
Wichita	Sedgwick	13.8	7.0	6.0	0.7	0.8	1.6	0.3	0.4
U.S.		22.0	7.1	3.7	1.8	1.5	1.1	2.2	0.6

Note: Figures shown are the number of adherents as a percentage of the total population; Adherents are defined as all members, including full members, their children and the estimated number of other participants who are not considered members (e.g. the baptized, those not confirmed, those not eligible for communion, those regularly attending services, etc.); (1) Evangelical Lutheran Church in America; (2) The Church of Jesus Christ of Latter Day Saints
Source: Reprinted with permission from Religious Congregations and Membership in the United States 2000 (Nashville, Glenmary Research Center, 2002) Copyright Association of Statisticians of American Religious Bodies. All rights reserved.

Ancestry: City

Area	German	Irish[1]	English	American	Italian	Polish	French[2]	Scottish
Albuquerque	12.6	9.2	9.0	4.1	3.7	1.7	2.6	2.2
Alexandria	11.2	11.4	10.5	3.0	4.6	2.4	2.2	2.5
Anchorage	17.6	11.6	10.0	6.0	3.2	2.3	3.4	2.7
Ann Arbor	19.8	11.1	11.8	2.6	4.7	6.4	3.6	3.3
Atlanta	4.5	4.5	5.9	3.0	1.6	0.8	1.2	1.6
Austin	12.9	8.4	8.8	4.3	2.5	1.4	2.7	2.3
Baltimore	7.4	6.0	3.2	2.5	2.8	2.8	0.7	0.7
Baton Rouge	6.2	5.7	6.3	4.2	3.9	0.5	8.9	1.1
Bellevue	15.8	10.3	12.8	3.4	3.3	2.1	3.5	3.1
Birmingham	2.3	2.8	3.2	3.9	0.8	0.3	0.6	0.8
Boise City	20.6	12.5	17.2	7.1	3.1	1.5	3.6	3.9
Boston	4.1	15.8	4.5	3.3	8.3	2.3	1.9	1.2
Boulder	20.9	13.9	15.1	2.9	5.6	3.7	3.3	4.2
Buffalo	13.6	12.2	4.0	1.6	11.7	11.7	1.8	0.9
Cedar Rapids	35.5	17.1	9.4	5.5	1.9	1.5	2.9	1.9
Charleston	10.7	9.2	10.9	6.2	3.2	1.6	2.8	3.3
Charlotte	10.1	7.8	8.5	6.7	3.3	1.5	1.8	2.4
Chattanooga	6.4	7.5	7.9	12.3	1.1	0.5	1.5	1.9
Chicago	6.5	6.6	2.0	1.3	3.5	7.3	0.8	0.5
Cincinnati	19.9	10.4	5.4	4.8	3.3	1.1	1.7	1.2
Cleveland	9.2	8.2	2.8	2.7	4.6	4.8	0.9	0.5
Colorado Spgs.	22.0	12.5	12.4	5.5	4.6	2.5	3.4	2.9
Columbia	8.3	6.2	7.7	5.2	2.1	0.9	1.9	2.2
Columbus	19.4	11.7	7.9	7.2	5.0	2.0	1.9	1.7
Dallas	6.1	5.0	5.8	4.1	1.4	0.8	1.5	1.2
Denver	13.8	9.6	8.3	3.4	3.5	2.0	2.5	2.0
Des Moines	21.5	12.7	9.3	6.8	3.9	0.9	2.4	1.6
Detroit	1.8	1.5	0.8	1.2	0.8	2.0	0.5	0.2
Durham	7.2	5.7	8.1	5.0	2.1	1.3	1.3	1.8
El Paso	4.6	2.9	2.8	2.7	1.2	0.5	1.0	0.6
Eugene	20.3	13.1	14.8	4.8	3.7	2.0	4.1	3.8
Ft. Collins	28.7	14.2	14.2	4.0	5.4	2.9	4.1	3.6
Ft. Lauderdale	10.4	10.3	8.2	5.9	7.6	2.9	2.7	1.8
Ft. Wayne	27.5	10.5	7.6	7.0	2.3	2.0	3.8	1.7
Ft. Worth	7.4	6.2	6.5	6.5	1.4	0.8	1.8	1.5
Grand Rapids	13.8	8.6	6.9	3.0	2.1	7.8	2.6	1.2
Green Bay	35.0	9.4	4.6	3.6	1.7	9.8	6.0	0.7
Greensboro	8.8	6.5	9.8	7.3	2.6	1.2	1.7	2.3
Honolulu	4.6	3.4	3.8	1.2	1.5	0.7	1.3	0.9
Houston	6.1	4.3	5.0	3.7	1.6	1.0	1.9	1.0
Huntsville	9.0	8.2	10.8	11.5	1.8	1.1	1.9	2.1
Indianapolis	16.6	10.2	7.7	9.3	2.2	1.4	2.0	1.7
Irvine	11.6	8.2	10.3	3.2	4.7	2.4	2.4	2.1
Jacksonville	9.6	9.0	8.5	9.3	3.5	1.4	2.2	1.8
Kansas City	15.4	10.4	8.1	5.8	3.6	1.4	2.1	1.5
Knoxville	10.0	9.9	10.2	13.3	1.9	0.9	1.7	2.5
Las Vegas	12.2	9.8	8.4	4.5	6.7	2.5	2.8	1.7
Lexington	13.5	12.0	12.4	11.7	2.6	1.3	2.0	2.4
Lincoln	39.8	12.7	11.0	3.9	1.8	2.4	2.8	1.6
Los Angeles	4.5	3.8	3.5	2.6	2.6	1.5	1.3	0.8
Louisville	15.2	11.2	7.8	8.7	1.7	0.7	1.7	1.4
Madison	35.9	14.6	9.8	2.7	3.8	5.4	3.1	1.8
Manchester	6.3	18.1	10.0	4.8	6.2	4.8	18.0	2.9

Ancestry: City *continued*

Area	German	Irish[1]	English	American	Italian	Polish	French[2]	Scottish
Memphis	4.2	4.9	5.2	4.5	1.6	0.5	1.1	1.2
Miami	1.2	1.0	1.1	3.1	1.4	0.4	0.8	0.3
Milwaukee	20.9	6.3	2.6	1.9	2.9	9.6	2.0	0.5
Minneapolis	21.5	10.1	6.1	1.6	2.2	4.1	3.3	1.7
Naperville	27.0	18.5	9.9	2.5	10.6	10.9	2.8	1.7
Nashville	8.8	8.9	9.0	10.9	1.9	0.9	1.8	2.0
New Orleans	5.4	4.7	3.4	2.0	3.2	0.6	5.6	0.7
New York	3.2	5.3	1.6	3.0	8.7	2.7	0.7	0.4
Norfolk	8.6	8.1	6.9	5.2	3.5	1.6	2.0	1.7
Oklahoma City	11.7	9.2	8.5	9.0	1.4	0.8	2.2	1.6
Omaha	28.7	16.0	8.5	3.5	4.8	4.7	2.5	1.3
Orlando	9.8	8.7	7.9	6.7	4.6	1.8	2.3	1.7
Overland Park	27.7	16.1	14.4	5.5	4.1	2.9	3.5	3.0
Philadelphia	8.1	13.6	2.9	1.8	9.2	4.3	0.7	0.5
Phoenix	13.7	9.4	8.0	4.0	4.4	2.4	2.4	1.6
Pittsburgh	19.7	15.8	4.6	2.2	11.8	8.4	1.4	1.3
Plano	16.3	10.8	11.9	6.8	4.1	2.5	3.0	2.6
Portland	18.8	12.2	11.7	3.8	3.7	1.9	3.5	3.2
Providence	3.4	9.7	4.9	2.5	13.8	2.4	3.8	1.0
Provo	11.5	4.7	30.4	4.6	2.4	0.6	2.3	4.9
Raleigh	10.0	8.4	11.9	6.2	3.5	1.9	2.1	2.9
Reno	15.9	12.7	11.4	4.5	6.6	1.7	3.5	2.6
Richmond	6.1	5.4	8.5	3.8	1.9	0.9	1.3	2.0
Rochester	10.9	9.6	5.8	2.2	10.0	2.7	2.1	1.2
Sacramento	8.4	6.8	6.3	3.1	3.8	0.8	2.1	1.3
St. Louis	14.5	8.6	3.9	3.1	3.6	1.5	2.4	0.7
St. Paul	25.5	12.8	5.3	1.8	3.2	3.8	3.8	1.2
St. Petersburg	14.7	12.4	11.1	5.7	6.8	3.0	3.8	2.5
Salt Lake City	10.8	6.7	20.9	4.3	2.8	1.0	2.4	4.3
San Antonio	9.0	5.2	5.0	3.2	1.9	1.3	1.8	1.0
San Diego	10.8	8.7	8.0	3.2	4.6	2.1	2.4	1.8
San Francisco	7.7	8.9	6.1	1.6	5.0	1.8	2.3	1.8
San Jose	7.6	6.1	5.6	1.9	4.8	1.2	1.8	1.2
Savannah	5.2	5.9	5.9	5.1	1.6	0.8	1.3	1.9
Scottsdale	20.6	14.1	13.4	4.5	8.5	4.4	3.7	2.9
Seattle	15.2	11.9	11.3	2.5	3.9	2.2	3.3	3.5
Sioux Falls	40.7	12.1	6.6	3.4	1.0	1.6	3.2	0.9
Springfield (IL)	24.4	15.6	11.8	7.1	6.0	2.0	2.7	2.0
Springfield (MO)	18.7	12.8	10.9	11.4	2.3	1.3	3.1	2.1
Stamford	6.6	10.5	5.2	3.0	17.0	5.6	1.7	1.1
Syracuse	12.2	15.9	7.6	2.4	14.1	5.0	4.2	1.4
Tampa	9.2	8.4	7.7	6.2	5.6	1.7	2.4	1.8
Tucson	14.4	9.7	8.3	3.7	4.0	2.3	2.7	1.9
Tulsa	13.2	10.4	10.1	8.0	1.8	1.0	2.7	2.0
Virginia Beach	13.7	12.4	11.8	7.3	5.6	2.5	2.9	2.6
Washington	4.8	4.9	4.4	1.7	2.2	1.4	1.2	1.1
Wichita	20.7	9.8	9.8	8.5	1.7	1.1	2.8	1.7
U.S.	15.2	10.9	8.7	7.3	5.6	3.2	3.0	1.7

Note: Figures include multiple ancestry (e.g. if a person reported being Irish and Italian, they were included in both columns); (1) Includes Celtic; (2) Includes Alsatian but excludes Basque
Source: Census 2000, Summary File 3

Ancestry: Metro Area

Metro Area	German	Irish[1]	English	American	Italian	Polish	French[2]	Scottish
Albuquerque	11.8	8.5	8.5	4.3	3.5	1.6	2.4	1.9
Alexandria	12.0	10.5	9.2	5.4	4.4	2.4	2.0	2.0
Anchorage	17.6	11.6	10.0	6.0	3.2	2.3	3.4	2.7
Ann Arbor	23.9	12.8	12.7	5.3	4.5	7.5	4.6	3.1
Atlanta	8.3	8.5	8.8	10.4	2.7	1.4	1.8	2.0
Austin	15.3	9.3	9.7	5.3	2.5	1.5	2.9	2.4
Baltimore	18.7	13.4	9.2	5.1	6.2	4.8	1.9	1.7
Baton Rouge	7.1	7.8	6.6	8.9	4.7	0.5	13.0	1.1
Bellevue	17.6	11.5	12.3	4.3	3.6	2.0	3.6	3.3
Birmingham	6.0	7.7	9.0	12.8	1.9	0.6	1.5	2.0
Boise City	19.3	11.1	16.0	7.7	2.8	1.2	3.1	3.4
Boston	5.9	24.3	10.9	3.9	15.4	3.5	4.7	2.6
Boulder	24.1	13.9	14.9	4.0	5.3	3.4	3.5	3.9
Buffalo	26.8	16.6	8.5	2.5	16.2	17.9	3.1	1.7
Cedar Rapids	36.8	16.7	10.1	5.8	1.8	1.4	2.9	1.8
Charleston	10.7	9.0	9.5	9.4	3.1	1.3	2.7	2.4
Charlotte	11.7	8.1	8.4	12.4	2.7	1.3	1.7	2.2
Chattanooga	8.0	9.8	9.6	18.7	1.3	0.6	1.6	2.0
Chicago	16.1	12.1	4.9	2.4	7.2	10.1	1.7	1.0
Cincinnati	30.6	14.4	9.5	9.8	3.8	1.3	2.5	1.6
Cleveland	20.1	13.8	8.1	4.0	9.6	8.3	1.7	1.6
Colorado Spgs.	22.4	12.4	12.0	5.9	4.5	2.5	3.4	2.8
Columbia	11.2	7.7	8.5	10.7	2.1	1.0	1.8	2.0
Columbus	23.4	13.1	10.0	9.3	5.0	2.2	2.2	2.0
Dallas	10.0	8.1	8.2	7.8	2.1	1.2	2.1	1.7
Denver	21.3	12.5	11.5	4.5	4.9	2.5	3.4	2.5
Des Moines	27.5	13.7	11.0	7.0	3.2	1.2	2.6	1.8
Detroit	17.0	10.4	8.0	3.8	6.4	10.8	4.4	2.3
Durham	10.4	8.6	11.8	9.9	3.5	1.8	2.1	2.7
El Paso	4.2	2.7	2.5	2.6	1.1	0.5	0.9	0.5
Eugene	20.8	12.8	14.3	6.2	3.4	1.8	4.1	3.5
Ft. Collins	29.7	14.0	14.4	4.9	4.5	2.6	3.9	3.2
Ft. Lauderdale	9.1	9.0	5.7	6.5	9.5	3.7	2.2	1.2
Ft. Wayne	31.5	9.7	8.1	9.2	2.0	1.9	3.8	1.6
Ft. Worth	11.4	9.2	9.1	9.7	2.0	1.2	2.4	1.9
Grand Rapids	19.7	10.1	9.8	5.0	2.5	6.7	3.9	1.6
Green Bay	38.4	10.4	4.5	3.7	2.2	11.0	6.4	0.8
Greensboro	10.5	7.0	9.7	14.8	2.0	1.0	1.5	2.0
Honolulu	5.3	4.0	3.8	1.4	1.7	0.8	1.3	0.9
Houston	9.2	6.6	6.6	5.9	2.2	1.4	2.6	1.3
Huntsville	9.0	9.3	10.1	15.8	1.7	1.0	1.9	2.0
Indianapolis	20.0	11.2	9.8	12.1	2.2	1.6	2.2	2.0
Irvine	11.7	8.7	8.9	3.5	4.7	1.9	2.6	1.9
Jacksonville	11.0	10.5	10.2	10.3	4.1	1.8	2.7	2.1
Kansas City	21.8	13.2	11.2	8.1	3.2	1.7	2.8	2.0
Knoxville	11.2	10.9	11.4	17.4	1.8	1.0	2.0	2.5
Las Vegas	13.4	10.5	9.3	5.0	6.6	2.6	3.0	1.7
Lexington	12.4	11.5	12.5	16.0	2.1	1.1	1.9	2.2
Lincoln	40.6	12.5	11.0	4.0	1.7	2.3	2.7	1.6
Los Angeles	5.8	4.6	4.4	2.5	2.8	1.3	1.5	1.0
Louisville	19.4	12.9	9.9	13.2	2.1	1.0	2.3	1.7
Madison	40.4	14.3	9.7	3.1	3.3	5.0	3.3	1.7
Manchester	7.8	19.8	12.7	5.2	8.1	5.0	16.3	3.0

Ancestry: Metro Area *continued*

Metro Area	German	Irish[1]	English	American	Italian	Polish	French[2]	Scottish
Memphis	6.3	7.5	7.2	8.6	2.2	0.7	1.6	1.5
Miami	2.6	2.3	2.0	4.0	2.3	1.0	1.0	0.4
Milwaukee	37.7	10.0	5.1	2.7	4.4	12.7	3.1	0.9
Minneapolis	34.4	12.8	6.8	2.7	2.8	5.0	4.4	1.4
Naperville	16.1	12.1	4.9	2.4	7.2	10.1	1.7	1.0
Nashville	9.8	10.2	10.4	15.4	2.1	1.1	2.1	2.2
New Orleans	10.4	8.2	4.9	4.9	8.2	0.6	14.3	0.9
New York	3.9	6.7	2.0	3.1	10.4	2.9	0.8	0.5
Norfolk	10.8	9.5	10.5	8.1	4.0	1.9	2.3	2.1
Oklahoma City	13.4	10.3	9.4	10.2	1.6	1.0	2.5	1.8
Omaha	32.3	16.3	9.6	4.2	4.5	4.5	2.8	1.4
Orlando	13.2	10.9	10.1	7.7	6.0	2.5	2.9	2.1
Overland Park	21.8	13.2	11.2	8.1	3.2	1.7	2.8	2.0
Philadelphia	17.1	20.6	8.3	3.2	14.4	5.7	1.6	1.4
Phoenix	16.2	10.5	10.3	4.6	4.9	2.7	2.9	1.9
Pittsburgh	26.5	17.1	8.5	3.8	15.2	8.9	1.8	1.9
Plano	10.0	8.1	8.2	7.8	2.1	1.2	2.1	1.7
Portland	20.8	11.8	12.7	5.5	3.5	1.8	3.7	3.1
Providence	4.6	17.6	11.7	3.0	16.9	4.1	11.9	1.8
Provo	10.8	4.7	33.5	6.9	2.1	0.5	2.2	4.8
Raleigh	10.4	8.6	11.8	9.9	3.5	1.8	2.1	2.7
Reno	17.1	13.8	12.6	4.6	6.8	1.9	3.9	2.6
Richmond	10.1	8.6	12.3	10.5	3.2	1.4	2.0	2.2
Rochester	22.4	16.7	13.9	4.4	16.7	5.4	3.5	2.2
Sacramento	14.4	10.7	10.7	4.6	5.4	1.4	3.3	2.2
St. Louis	29.6	13.9	8.5	6.2	4.5	2.6	4.4	1.3
St. Paul	34.4	12.8	6.8	2.7	2.8	5.0	4.4	1.4
St. Petersburg	15.6	13.1	11.3	7.5	8.3	3.4	3.6	2.3
Salt Lake City	12.0	6.2	27.4	6.4	2.8	0.8	2.3	4.3
San Antonio	11.7	6.2	5.9	3.8	2.0	1.7	2.0	1.2
San Diego	12.6	9.6	9.0	3.8	4.7	2.0	2.8	2.0
San Francisco	9.7	10.1	7.8	2.1	6.8	1.9	2.7	2.1
San Jose	9.2	7.1	7.2	2.3	5.2	1.5	2.2	1.6
Savannah	8.6	8.6	8.3	10.5	2.2	1.1	1.9	2.3
Scottsdale	16.2	10.5	10.3	4.6	4.9	2.7	2.9	1.9
Seattle	17.6	11.5	12.3	4.3	3.6	2.0	3.6	3.3
Sioux Falls	42.3	11.7	6.5	3.5	1.0	1.5	3.1	0.9
Springfield (IL)	26.6	15.5	12.8	7.6	5.6	1.9	2.8	2.2
Springfield (MO)	19.0	12.3	11.5	13.8	2.2	1.2	3.1	1.9
Stamford	10.1	15.4	10.4	3.9	17.3	5.3	2.5	2.3
Syracuse	17.7	20.2	14.6	4.7	15.7	6.8	6.0	2.0
Tampa	15.6	13.1	11.3	7.5	8.3	3.4	3.6	2.3
Tucson	16.2	10.6	10.3	4.1	4.4	2.5	3.1	2.3
Tulsa	13.6	11.1	9.4	10.3	1.7	0.9	2.6	1.8
Virginia Beach	10.8	9.5	10.5	8.1	4.0	1.9	2.3	2.1
Washington	12.0	10.5	9.2	5.4	4.4	2.4	2.0	2.0
Wichita	23.5	10.2	10.2	9.3	1.7	1.1	3.0	1.8
U.S.	15.2	10.9	8.7	7.3	5.6	3.2	3.0	1.7

Note: Figures cover the Metropolitan Statistical Area (MSA) - see Appendix A for areas included; Figures include multiple ancestry (e.g. if a person reported being Irish and Italian, they were included in both columns); (1) Includes Celtic; (2) Includes Alsatian but excludes Basque

Source: Census 2000, Summary File 3

Foreign-Born Population: City

City	Percent of Population Born in:						
	Any Foreign Country	Europe	Asia	Africa	Oceania[1]	Canada	Mexico	Latin America[2]
Albuquerque	8.9	1.1	1.6	0.1	0.1	0.3	4.9	0.8
Alexandria	25.4	2.2	6.3	6.0	0.1	0.4	0.9	9.7
Anchorage	8.2	1.6	4.1	0.1	0.2	0.5	0.6	1.1
Ann Arbor	16.6	3.7	9.6	0.8	0.1	0.9	0.3	1.2
Atlanta	6.6	0.9	1.4	0.7	0.0	0.2	2.1	1.1
Austin	16.6	1.1	3.8	0.3	0.1	0.3	9.4	1.6
Baltimore	4.6	1.1	1.2	0.6	0.0	0.1	0.2	1.4
Baton Rouge	4.4	0.7	2.2	0.4	0.0	0.1	0.2	0.8
Bellevue	24.5	5.3	13.6	0.6	0.3	1.6	2.2	0.9
Birmingham	2.1	0.3	0.6	0.2	0.0	0.1	0.7	0.3
Boise City	4.8	2.0	1.4	0.1	0.0	0.3	0.7	0.2
Boston	25.8	4.5	6.2	2.3	0.1	0.4	0.3	12.0
Boulder	11.5	2.8	3.3	0.4	0.2	0.6	3.5	0.7
Buffalo	4.4	1.6	1.3	0.4	0.0	0.3	0.1	0.7
Cedar Rapids	3.3	0.7	1.7	0.2	0.0	0.1	0.4	0.2
Charleston	3.6	1.4	1.1	0.2	0.0	0.2	0.2	0.4
Charlotte	11.0	1.4	2.9	0.9	0.1	0.3	3.1	2.5
Chattanooga	3.4	0.6	1.5	0.1	0.0	0.1	0.5	0.6
Chicago	21.7	5.0	3.9	0.4	0.0	0.1	10.1	2.1
Cincinnati	3.8	1.2	1.3	0.5	0.0	0.1	0.2	0.5
Cleveland	4.5	1.8	1.3	0.2	0.0	0.1	0.1	0.9
Colorado Spgs.	7.0	2.1	2.2	0.1	0.1	0.4	1.5	0.6
Columbia	4.1	0.9	1.5	0.2	0.0	0.2	0.6	0.7
Columbus	6.7	1.0	3.1	1.3	0.0	0.2	0.6	0.5
Dallas	24.4	0.9	2.6	0.9	0.0	0.2	17.6	2.3
Denver	17.4	1.8	2.3	0.6	0.1	0.3	11.4	0.9
Des Moines	7.9	1.6	2.6	0.5	0.0	0.1	2.3	0.7
Detroit	4.8	0.6	1.6	0.3	0.0	0.2	1.6	0.5
Durham	12.0	1.0	2.9	1.0	0.1	0.4	4.8	1.9
El Paso	26.1	1.0	1.0	0.1	0.0	0.1	23.4	0.5
Eugene	6.6	1.3	2.7	0.2	0.1	0.7	1.2	0.4
Ft. Collins	5.3	1.4	1.9	0.3	0.1	0.3	1.0	0.4
Ft. Lauderdale	21.7	3.8	1.3	0.4	0.1	1.1	0.5	14.5
Ft. Wayne	5.0	1.0	1.4	0.2	0.0	0.2	1.7	0.5
Ft. Worth	16.3	0.8	2.2	0.2	0.1	0.1	12.0	0.9
Grand Rapids	10.5	1.7	1.6	0.4	0.0	0.4	4.6	1.9
Green Bay	6.8	0.4	2.2	0.0	0.0	0.1	3.7	0.4
Greensboro	8.1	1.1	2.2	1.3	0.0	0.3	2.2	0.9
Honolulu	25.3	1.1	21.7	0.1	1.5	0.3	0.1	0.4
Houston	26.4	1.2	4.7	0.9	0.1	0.2	14.0	5.4
Huntsville	4.9	1.3	1.7	0.4	0.0	0.3	0.5	0.8
Indianapolis	4.6	0.8	1.2	0.3	0.0	0.1	1.6	0.6
Irvine	32.1	3.1	24.3	1.1	0.2	0.9	1.1	1.3
Jacksonville	5.9	1.5	2.4	0.2	0.0	0.2	0.2	1.5
Kansas City	5.8	0.7	1.7	0.5	0.0	0.1	2.0	0.8
Knoxville	3.0	0.9	1.2	0.1	0.0	0.1	0.4	0.3
Las Vegas	18.9	1.9	3.6	0.2	0.1	0.6	10.0	2.6
Lexington	5.9	1.1	2.2	0.3	0.0	0.2	1.7	0.5
Lincoln	5.9	1.2	3.0	0.3	0.1	0.1	0.8	0.5
Los Angeles	40.9	2.7	10.2	0.6	0.1	0.4	16.9	10.1
Louisville	3.8	1.0	1.3	0.3	0.0	0.1	0.2	0.9
Madison	9.1	1.4	4.7	0.5	0.1	0.3	1.3	0.8
Manchester	9.4	2.9	2.2	0.5	0.0	1.8	0.5	1.5

Foreign-Born Population: City *continued*

City	Percent of Population Born in:							
	Any Foreign Country	Europe	Asia	Africa	Oceania[1]	Canada	Mexico	Latin America[2]
Memphis	4.0	0.4	1.4	0.3	0.0	0.1	1.5	0.4
Miami	59.5	1.2	0.6	0.1	0.0	0.1	0.6	56.8
Milwaukee	7.7	1.3	2.0	0.2	0.0	0.1	3.5	0.6
Minneapolis	14.5	1.4	4.5	3.3	0.1	0.3	3.5	1.4
Naperville	11.7	2.6	6.9	0.2	0.1	0.7	0.6	0.6
Nashville	7.1	0.9	2.3	0.8	0.0	0.2	1.9	1.0
New Orleans	4.3	0.7	1.6	0.2	0.0	0.1	0.1	1.7
New York	35.9	7.0	8.6	1.2	0.1	0.2	1.5	17.3
Norfolk	5.0	0.9	2.5	0.3	0.0	0.1	0.2	1.0
Oklahoma City	8.5	0.5	3.0	0.3	0.0	0.1	4.0	0.6
Omaha	6.6	0.9	1.6	0.4	0.0	0.1	2.9	0.7
Orlando	14.4	1.4	2.4	0.5	0.0	0.5	0.6	8.9
Overland Park	7.4	1.5	3.6	0.2	0.1	0.3	1.0	0.8
Philadelphia	9.0	2.7	3.5	0.6	0.0	0.1	0.2	1.9
Phoenix	19.5	1.6	1.7	0.2	0.1	0.4	14.4	1.1
Pittsburgh	5.6	2.2	2.4	0.3	0.1	0.2	0.1	0.5
Plano	17.1	2.1	8.4	0.6	0.1	0.8	3.7	1.4
Portland	13.0	3.3	5.0	0.5	0.3	0.6	2.5	0.9
Providence	25.3	3.0	4.5	1.8	0.1	0.3	0.6	15.0
Provo	9.6	0.9	1.5	0.2	0.3	0.7	3.8	2.2
Raleigh	11.7	1.4	3.2	1.3	0.0	0.5	3.6	1.8
Reno	17.3	1.6	4.2	0.2	0.3	0.5	8.3	2.2
Richmond	3.9	0.7	1.0	0.3	0.0	0.1	0.4	1.4
Rochester	7.3	2.1	2.1	0.5	0.0	0.3	0.1	2.2
Sacramento	20.3	2.0	9.9	0.3	1.0	0.2	6.0	0.9
St. Louis	5.6	2.5	1.9	0.4	0.0	0.1	0.5	0.3
St. Paul	14.3	1.1	8.1	1.6	0.1	0.2	2.1	1.1
St. Petersburg	9.1	3.3	2.3	0.2	0.1	0.7	0.2	2.3
Salt Lake City	18.3	3.1	3.0	0.7	1.0	0.4	8.5	1.7
San Antonio	11.7	0.7	1.4	0.1	0.0	0.2	8.5	0.8
San Diego	25.7	2.4	10.5	0.8	0.2	0.5	10.1	1.2
San Francisco	36.8	5.1	22.6	0.4	0.4	0.5	3.0	4.9
San Jose	36.9	2.5	20.4	0.6	0.2	0.4	11.1	1.7
Savannah	3.9	0.9	1.3	0.2	0.1	0.2	0.6	0.7
Scottsdale	9.5	2.9	2.1	0.3	0.1	1.4	2.2	0.6
Seattle	16.9	2.7	9.4	1.3	0.3	0.9	1.4	0.8
Sioux Falls	4.6	1.4	1.1	1.1	0.0	0.1	0.5	0.4
Springfield (IL)	2.3	0.6	1.1	0.2	0.0	0.1	0.1	0.2
Springfield (MO)	2.4	0.6	0.9	0.2	0.1	0.1	0.4	0.2
Stamford	29.6	8.1	4.2	0.4	0.1	0.4	0.7	15.8
Syracuse	7.6	2.5	3.3	0.4	0.0	0.4	0.1	1.1
Tampa	12.2	1.3	1.9	0.2	0.0	0.3	1.3	7.1
Tucson	14.3	1.4	2.0	0.2	0.1	0.3	9.6	0.7
Tulsa	6.5	0.7	1.7	0.2	0.0	0.2	3.1	0.7
Virginia Beach	6.7	1.5	3.6	0.2	0.0	0.2	0.2	0.9
Washington	12.9	2.3	2.2	1.6	0.1	0.2	0.4	6.1
Wichita	8.1	0.6	3.2	0.3	0.1	0.2	3.4	0.5
U.S.	11.1	1.7	2.9	0.3	0.1	0.3	3.3	2.5

Note: (1) Includes Australia, New Zealand subregion, Melanesia, Micronesia, Polynesia, and Oceania n.e.c.;
(2) Includes Central America (excluding Mexico), South America, and the Caribbean.
Source: Census 2000, Summary File 3

Foreign-Born Population: Metro Area

Metro Area	Percent of Population Born in:							
	Any Foreign Country	Europe	Asia	Africa	Oceania[1]	Canada	Mexico	Latin America[2]
Albuquerque	7.9	1.0	1.2	0.1	0.0	0.3	4.7	0.6
Alexandria	16.9	2.1	6.1	1.9	0.1	0.2	0.7	5.9
Anchorage	8.2	1.6	4.1	0.1	0.2	0.5	0.6	1.1
Ann Arbor	6.8	1.8	3.2	0.3	0.0	0.7	0.3	0.6
Atlanta	10.3	1.3	2.8	0.9	0.0	0.2	2.9	2.1
Austin	12.2	1.0	2.9	0.3	0.0	0.2	6.7	1.1
Baltimore	5.7	1.5	2.2	0.5	0.0	0.2	0.2	1.1
Baton Rouge	3.0	0.5	1.3	0.2	0.0	0.1	0.3	0.6
Bellevue	13.8	2.8	6.9	0.7	0.2	1.0	1.5	0.6
Birmingham	2.3	0.4	0.7	0.1	0.0	0.1	0.7	0.3
Boise City	5.6	1.3	1.0	0.1	0.0	0.3	2.6	0.3
Boston	14.9	4.3	4.2	0.9	0.1	0.7	0.2	4.7
Boulder	9.4	2.1	2.5	0.2	0.1	0.5	3.5	0.5
Buffalo	4.4	2.0	1.1	0.2	0.0	0.7	0.0	0.4
Cedar Rapids	2.6	0.6	1.3	0.1	0.0	0.1	0.3	0.1
Charleston	3.3	1.0	1.0	0.1	0.1	0.2	0.6	0.4
Charlotte	6.7	0.9	1.5	0.4	0.0	0.2	2.3	1.4
Chattanooga	2.4	0.6	0.9	0.1	0.0	0.1	0.3	0.4
Chicago	17.2	4.4	3.9	0.3	0.0	0.2	7.1	1.3
Cincinnati	2.6	0.8	1.0	0.2	0.0	0.1	0.2	0.2
Cleveland	5.1	2.8	1.4	0.2	0.0	0.2	0.2	0.4
Colorado Spgs.	6.4	2.1	2.0	0.1	0.1	0.4	1.3	0.5
Columbia	3.5	0.9	1.2	0.1	0.0	0.2	0.6	0.6
Columbus	4.6	0.9	2.1	0.7	0.0	0.2	0.4	0.3
Dallas	16.8	0.9	3.4	0.6	0.0	0.3	9.8	1.8
Denver	11.1	1.7	2.3	0.4	0.1	0.4	5.5	0.7
Des Moines	5.3	1.3	1.7	0.3	0.0	0.1	1.3	0.6
Detroit	7.5	2.4	3.3	0.2	0.0	0.7	0.6	0.3
Durham	9.2	1.2	2.5	0.7	0.1	0.4	3.2	1.3
El Paso	27.4	0.9	0.9	0.1	0.0	0.1	25.0	0.5
Eugene	4.9	1.1	1.6	0.1	0.1	0.5	1.3	0.3
Ft. Collins	4.3	1.0	1.2	0.1	0.0	0.3	1.3	0.3
Ft. Lauderdale	25.3	3.6	1.9	0.4	0.0	1.3	0.7	17.5
Ft. Wayne	3.0	0.7	0.8	0.1	0.0	0.2	0.8	0.3
Ft. Worth	11.4	0.8	2.6	0.4	0.1	0.2	6.5	0.8
Grand Rapids	5.2	1.1	1.3	0.1	0.0	0.3	1.7	0.6
Green Bay	3.9	0.4	1.4	0.0	0.0	0.1	1.8	0.3
Greensboro	5.7	0.7	1.1	0.3	0.0	0.2	2.8	0.7
Honolulu	19.2	0.8	16.4	0.1	1.2	0.3	0.2	0.4
Houston	20.5	1.1	4.3	0.6	0.0	0.2	10.4	3.8
Huntsville	3.5	0.8	1.3	0.2	0.0	0.2	0.5	0.5
Indianapolis	3.4	0.7	1.0	0.2	0.0	0.1	1.0	0.4
Irvine	29.9	2.0	10.9	0.4	0.2	0.6	13.7	2.1
Jacksonville	5.4	1.5	2.0	0.2	0.0	0.3	0.2	1.3
Kansas City	4.5	0.7	1.4	0.2	0.0	0.2	1.5	0.5
Knoxville	2.1	0.6	0.8	0.1	0.0	0.1	0.3	0.2
Las Vegas	16.5	1.7	3.8	0.3	0.1	0.6	7.9	2.2
Lexington	4.0	0.7	1.4	0.2	0.0	0.2	1.2	0.3
Lincoln	5.4	1.2	2.7	0.3	0.1	0.1	0.7	0.4
Los Angeles	36.2	2.0	10.7	0.5	0.1	0.4	16.0	6.5
Louisville	2.7	0.8	1.0	0.2	0.0	0.1	0.3	0.4
Madison	6.3	1.1	2.8	0.3	0.0	0.3	1.2	0.6
Manchester	6.6	2.0	1.4	0.4	0.0	1.6	0.3	0.9

Foreign-Born Population: Metro Area *continued*

Metro Area	Any Foreign Country	Europe	Asia	Africa	Oceania[1]	Canada	Mexico	Latin America[2]
Memphis	3.3	0.5	1.2	0.2	0.0	0.1	1.0	0.3
Miami	50.9	2.0	1.3	0.2	0.0	0.2	0.9	46.3
Milwaukee	5.4	1.6	1.5	0.2	0.0	0.1	1.6	0.4
Minneapolis	7.1	1.1	3.0	1.0	0.0	0.3	1.0	0.6
Naperville	17.2	4.4	3.9	0.3	0.0	0.2	7.1	1.3
Nashville	4.7	0.7	1.5	0.4	0.0	0.2	1.3	0.6
New Orleans	4.8	0.6	1.6	0.1	0.0	0.1	0.2	2.1
New York	33.7	6.8	7.9	1.1	0.1	0.2	1.5	16.1
Norfolk	4.5	1.1	2.1	0.2	0.0	0.2	0.1	0.7
Oklahoma City	5.7	0.5	2.2	0.3	0.0	0.1	2.2	0.4
Omaha	4.8	0.8	1.3	0.3	0.0	0.1	1.8	0.5
Orlando	12.0	1.6	2.2	0.4	0.0	0.5	1.0	6.3
Overland Park	4.5	0.7	1.4	0.2	0.0	0.2	1.5	0.5
Philadelphia	7.0	2.3	2.8	0.4	0.0	0.2	0.3	1.1
Phoenix	14.1	1.5	1.8	0.2	0.1	0.6	9.2	0.8
Pittsburgh	2.6	1.3	0.9	0.1	0.0	0.1	0.0	0.2
Plano	16.8	0.9	3.4	0.6	0.0	0.3	9.8	1.8
Portland	10.9	2.5	3.6	0.2	0.2	0.6	3.1	0.6
Providence	12.0	4.8	1.9	1.0	0.0	0.4	0.2	3.6
Provo	6.3	0.7	0.9	0.1	0.2	0.6	2.5	1.4
Raleigh	9.2	1.2	2.5	0.7	0.1	0.4	3.2	1.3
Reno	14.1	1.4	3.4	0.1	0.3	0.5	6.7	1.7
Richmond	4.5	1.0	1.7	0.3	0.0	0.2	0.3	1.0
Rochester	5.7	2.4	1.7	0.2	0.0	0.5	0.1	0.9
Sacramento	13.9	2.7	5.9	0.2	0.4	0.4	3.6	0.7
St. Louis	3.1	1.1	1.2	0.2	0.0	0.1	0.3	0.2
St. Paul	7.1	1.1	3.0	1.0	0.0	0.3	1.0	0.6
St. Petersburg	9.8	2.6	1.7	0.2	0.0	0.8	1.1	3.3
Salt Lake City	8.6	1.5	1.7	0.2	0.4	0.3	3.5	1.1
San Antonio	10.2	0.8	1.3	0.1	0.0	0.2	7.1	0.7
San Diego	21.6	2.0	7.0	0.4	0.1	0.5	10.4	1.0
San Francisco	32.1	4.6	16.6	0.4	0.7	0.6	4.7	4.6
San Jose	34.1	3.4	19.5	0.5	0.2	0.6	8.3	1.5
Savannah	3.5	0.8	1.3	0.2	0.0	0.2	0.4	0.6
Scottsdale	14.1	1.5	1.8	0.2	0.1	0.6	9.2	0.8
Seattle	13.8	2.8	6.9	0.7	0.2	1.0	1.5	0.6
Sioux Falls	3.7	1.1	0.9	0.8	0.0	0.1	0.4	0.3
Springfield (IL)	1.8	0.6	0.8	0.1	0.0	0.1	0.1	0.2
Springfield (MO)	1.6	0.5	0.6	0.1	0.0	0.1	0.2	0.1
Stamford	20.4	6.5	3.4	0.4	0.1	0.6	0.8	8.6
Syracuse	4.3	1.8	1.5	0.1	0.0	0.4	0.0	0.5
Tampa	9.8	2.6	1.7	0.2	0.0	0.8	1.1	3.3
Tucson	11.9	1.5	1.7	0.2	0.1	0.5	7.4	0.6
Tulsa	4.1	0.6	1.1	0.1	0.0	0.2	1.7	0.4
Virginia Beach	4.5	1.1	2.1	0.2	0.0	0.2	0.1	0.7
Washington	16.9	2.1	6.1	1.9	0.1	0.2	0.7	5.9
Wichita	5.9	0.5	2.3	0.2	0.0	0.2	2.4	0.3
U.S.	11.1	1.7	2.9	0.3	0.1	0.3	3.3	2.5

Note: Figures cover the Metropolitan Statistical Area - see Appendix A for areas included; (1) Includes Australia, New Zealand subregion, Melanesia, Micronesia, Polynesia, and Oceania n.e.c.; (2) Includes Central America (excluding Mexico), South America, and the Caribbean.
Source: Census 2000, Summary File 3

Marriage Status: City

Area	Never Married	Now Married Except Separated	Separated	Widowed	Divorced
Albuquerque	30.2	48.7	1.7	5.7	13.7
Alexandria	39.0	43.1	2.8	4.6	10.5
Anchorage	28.4	53.7	2.1	3.2	12.5
Ann Arbor	50.3	38.5	0.9	3.2	7.1
Atlanta	45.5	31.4	4.1	7.7	11.3
Austin	39.4	43.9	2.0	3.7	11.0
Baltimore	42.5	32.0	5.6	9.3	10.5
Baton Rouge	39.3	40.6	2.8	7.2	10.1
Bellevue	25.3	58.5	1.0	5.1	10.1
Birmingham	35.2	38.0	4.0	9.5	13.3
Boise City	27.0	53.3	1.1	4.9	13.6
Boston	50.5	33.6	3.0	5.7	7.1
Boulder	49.1	37.5	1.1	3.5	8.8
Buffalo	40.0	36.2	4.3	9.1	10.4
Cedar Rapids	27.6	53.9	1.2	6.4	10.8
Charleston	40.2	40.0	3.2	7.9	8.8
Charlotte	32.7	49.6	3.0	5.2	9.4
Chattanooga	28.3	46.1	2.6	9.4	13.6
Chicago	40.9	39.9	3.4	7.0	8.8
Cincinnati	42.4	34.3	3.6	7.6	12.1
Cleveland	38.9	34.9	3.3	9.0	13.9
Colorado Spgs.	25.0	56.5	1.9	4.9	11.8
Columbia	41.6	40.5	3.3	6.5	8.2
Columbus	38.3	41.8	2.2	5.4	12.4
Dallas	34.4	45.8	3.5	5.4	10.8
Denver	35.9	43.2	2.3	5.8	12.7
Des Moines	28.2	51.0	1.7	6.5	12.7
Detroit	43.6	31.2	4.2	8.3	12.7
Durham	37.4	44.4	3.1	5.9	9.1
El Paso	26.8	54.3	3.2	6.1	9.7
Eugene	36.2	44.8	1.5	5.6	12.0
Ft. Collins	40.3	46.1	0.9	3.9	8.9
Ft. Lauderdale	35.3	40.0	3.3	7.3	14.0
Ft. Wayne	30.3	47.6	1.9	7.3	12.9
Ft. Worth	28.5	50.8	3.1	5.9	11.8
Grand Rapids	36.7	44.2	1.8	6.6	10.6
Green Bay	31.3	49.4	1.4	6.3	11.6
Greensboro	34.3	46.2	3.0	6.6	9.8
Honolulu	31.6	49.7	1.7	7.2	9.7
Houston	32.2	48.9	3.6	5.4	10.0
Huntsville	26.5	52.4	2.4	6.7	12.0
Indianapolis	31.8	46.6	2.1	6.4	13.1
Irvine	33.3	53.2	1.2	3.6	8.7
Jacksonville	26.5	50.9	3.0	6.3	13.3
Kansas City	32.5	45.1	2.7	6.6	13.1
Knoxville	34.6	41.6	2.2	8.4	13.3
Las Vegas	25.7	52.1	2.7	5.6	13.9
Lexington	32.2	49.4	2.0	5.5	11.0
Lincoln	33.4	50.6	1.1	5.1	9.8
Los Angeles	37.1	45.5	3.5	5.4	8.4
Louisville	35.2	38.5	3.1	8.9	14.3
Madison	44.3	41.7	1.1	3.8	9.1
Manchester	31.0	47.7	1.8	7.0	12.4

Marriage Status: City *continued*

Area	Never Married	Now Married Except Separated	Separated	Widowed	Divorced
Memphis	36.1	39.2	4.8	7.9	12.0
Miami	32.2	42.0	4.7	8.3	12.8
Milwaukee	41.4	38.3	2.7	6.6	11.1
Minneapolis	46.2	35.9	2.0	5.1	10.7
Naperville	22.2	67.7	0.7	3.5	6.0
Nashville	32.6	45.5	2.3	6.4	13.2
New Orleans	40.9	35.5	3.6	8.1	11.8
New York	37.6	43.4	4.3	7.0	7.7
Norfolk	37.0	40.6	5.3	6.8	10.3
Oklahoma City	26.4	51.3	2.4	6.4	13.6
Omaha	31.6	48.6	1.7	6.4	11.7
Orlando	35.8	40.5	3.7	6.1	13.8
Overland Park	23.1	61.2	0.9	5.6	9.3
Philadelphia	40.8	36.8	4.4	9.4	8.6
Phoenix	29.9	51.0	2.4	4.8	11.9
Pittsburgh	40.3	38.4	2.7	9.6	9.1
Plano	21.1	66.5	1.3	2.7	8.4
Portland	34.6	44.1	2.0	5.9	13.3
Providence	46.3	35.1	3.6	6.0	9.0
Provo	47.2	45.9	0.6	2.4	3.9
Raleigh	37.5	46.0	2.9	4.4	9.2
Reno	29.1	46.6	2.5	5.9	15.9
Richmond	40.9	34.7	4.2	8.6	11.5
Rochester	43.7	32.6	5.6	7.0	11.1
Sacramento	33.4	44.5	3.1	6.8	12.2
St. Louis	41.5	32.7	4.4	9.2	12.3
St. Paul	39.7	41.9	2.0	5.8	10.6
St. Petersburg	27.8	45.5	2.8	9.0	14.9
Salt Lake City	34.7	46.9	1.9	5.7	10.8
San Antonio	28.7	50.5	3.0	6.0	11.8
San Diego	35.0	47.5	2.4	4.9	10.2
San Francisco	44.8	38.6	1.9	6.1	8.6
San Jose	31.2	54.0	2.0	4.4	8.4
Savannah	35.6	40.2	3.5	8.8	11.9
Scottsdale	23.7	56.0	1.3	6.6	12.5
Seattle	41.8	39.9	1.6	5.4	11.4
Sioux Falls	30.0	52.5	1.3	5.8	10.4
Springfield (IL)	29.1	48.1	1.7	8.0	13.1
Springfield (MO)	31.4	46.0	1.8	7.1	13.7
Stamford	30.5	52.3	1.9	7.0	8.1
Syracuse	45.4	33.3	3.8	7.8	9.6
Tampa	31.0	43.8	3.6	7.6	14.0
Tucson	33.0	45.3	2.0	6.5	13.2
Tulsa	27.2	50.3	2.1	6.7	13.7
Virginia Beach	25.5	57.1	3.2	4.7	9.5
Washington	48.4	29.9	4.2	7.8	9.7
Wichita	25.5	53.6	1.7	6.4	12.8
U.S.	27.1	54.4	2.2	6.6	9.7

Note: Figures cover population 15 years of age and older
Source: Census 2000, Summary File 3

Marriage Status: Metro Area

Metro Area	Never Married	Now Married Except Separated	Separated	Widowed	Divorced
Albuquerque	28.6	51.5	1.6	5.6	12.6
Alexandria	30.9	52.7	2.8	5.1	8.5
Anchorage	28.4	53.7	2.1	3.2	12.5
Ann Arbor	31.3	54.5	0.9	4.5	8.7
Atlanta	29.1	53.8	2.1	4.8	10.2
Austin	32.2	51.7	1.8	3.8	10.4
Baltimore	29.4	50.9	3.3	7.1	9.1
Baton Rouge	30.8	51.1	2.2	6.0	10.0
Bellevue	29.2	53.2	1.5	4.8	11.3
Birmingham	25.1	54.5	2.1	7.6	10.8
Boise City	23.4	58.9	1.2	4.7	11.7
Boston	33.4	50.6	1.8	6.6	7.5
Boulder	32.9	52.1	1.2	3.7	10.1
Buffalo	28.4	52.1	2.2	8.6	8.7
Cedar Rapids	26.1	57.0	1.1	5.9	10.1
Charleston	29.5	51.6	3.3	6.3	9.3
Charlotte	25.5	57.0	2.7	5.8	8.9
Chattanooga	22.0	57.0	1.7	7.7	11.7
Chicago	31.2	52.1	2.0	6.4	8.3
Cincinnati	27.1	54.2	1.8	6.7	10.3
Cleveland	27.8	51.9	1.7	8.0	10.7
Colorado Spgs.	24.6	58.2	1.8	4.4	10.9
Columbia	28.7	53.3	2.9	5.9	9.3
Columbus	29.6	52.1	1.7	5.5	11.1
Dallas	27.2	55.6	2.5	4.6	10.1
Denver	27.8	54.2	1.7	4.6	11.7
Des Moines	25.0	57.6	1.3	5.5	10.7
Detroit	29.2	51.5	1.7	7.1	10.6
Durham	30.0	54.2	2.5	4.9	8.4
El Paso	26.8	55.3	3.1	5.7	9.1
Eugene	28.1	52.2	1.6	5.9	12.1
Ft. Collins	30.3	55.0	1.0	4.2	9.6
Ft. Lauderdale	25.9	51.3	2.6	8.4	11.8
Ft. Wayne	24.6	57.3	1.3	6.3	10.4
Ft. Worth	24.3	57.5	2.3	4.9	11.0
Grand Rapids	27.2	56.8	1.2	5.4	9.4
Green Bay	27.7	56.5	1.1	5.5	9.3
Greensboro	24.3	56.6	2.9	6.7	9.5
Honolulu	30.7	53.4	1.6	5.9	8.4
Houston	27.4	55.6	2.8	4.8	9.5
Huntsville	22.6	58.7	1.9	5.9	10.9
Indianapolis	25.8	55.0	1.6	6.0	11.6
Irvine	28.4	55.4	2.1	5.1	9.1
Jacksonville	24.4	54.1	2.5	6.2	12.6
Kansas City	25.1	55.6	1.8	6.0	11.4
Knoxville	22.7	57.5	1.5	7.0	11.4
Las Vegas	24.7	53.3	2.5	5.8	13.7
Lexington	28.6	53.2	1.9	5.6	10.7
Lincoln	32.1	52.4	1.0	5.0	9.5
Los Angeles	34.1	48.8	3.1	5.5	8.5
Louisville	25.4	53.5	1.9	7.0	12.2
Madison	34.8	51.0	1.1	4.0	9.1
Manchester	27.0	55.1	1.4	5.9	10.5

Marriage Status: Metro Area *continued*

Metro Area	Never Married	Now Married Except Separated	Separated	Widowed	Divorced
Memphis	29.8	49.1	3.6	6.7	10.7
Miami	28.7	49.2	3.6	6.9	11.5
Milwaukee	30.4	52.3	1.5	6.5	9.3
Minneapolis	29.7	55.1	1.1	4.8	9.2
Naperville	31.2	52.1	2.0	6.4	8.3
Nashville	26.3	54.8	1.8	5.6	11.5
New Orleans	31.5	47.3	2.7	7.3	11.2
New York	36.2	45.3	4.0	7.0	7.6
Norfolk	27.1	53.5	3.9	6.1	9.4
Oklahoma City	25.2	54.4	1.8	6.2	12.4
Omaha	27.6	54.8	1.4	5.7	10.5
Orlando	26.6	54.0	2.4	6.0	11.0
Overland Park	25.1	55.6	1.8	6.0	11.4
Philadelphia	30.6	51.3	2.7	7.6	7.8
Phoenix	26.5	55.0	1.9	5.6	11.0
Pittsburgh	26.2	54.5	1.9	9.2	8.3
Plano	27.2	55.6	2.5	4.6	10.1
Portland	26.8	54.6	1.7	5.3	11.6
Providence	29.2	52.0	1.9	7.7	9.2
Provo	32.6	58.6	0.8	3.0	4.9
Raleigh	30.0	54.2	2.5	4.9	8.4
Reno	25.7	52.1	1.9	5.4	14.9
Richmond	27.5	53.2	3.0	6.6	9.8
Rochester	28.8	52.6	2.8	6.9	8.9
Sacramento	26.8	53.1	2.4	5.9	11.8
St. Louis	27.3	53.3	1.9	7.1	10.3
St. Paul	29.7	55.1	1.1	4.8	9.2
St. Petersburg	22.6	53.7	2.3	8.9	12.5
Salt Lake City	27.6	57.6	1.4	4.1	9.3
San Antonio	26.9	53.6	2.6	5.9	11.1
San Diego	30.2	52.0	2.3	5.3	10.2
San Francisco	35.8	47.1	1.8	6.1	9.3
San Jose	30.2	54.8	1.8	4.7	8.5
Savannah	27.7	51.8	2.4	7.0	11.1
Scottsdale	26.5	55.0	1.9	5.6	11.0
Seattle	29.2	53.2	1.5	4.8	11.3
Sioux Falls	27.5	56.4	1.1	5.5	9.5
Springfield (IL)	25.4	54.0	1.5	7.1	12.0
Springfield (MO)	24.2	56.8	1.5	6.1	11.5
Stamford	25.7	58.6	1.5	6.5	7.7
Syracuse	29.1	52.3	2.8	7.1	8.7
Tampa	22.6	53.7	2.3	8.9	12.5
Tucson	27.8	52.0	1.6	6.6	12.0
Tulsa	22.7	57.5	1.7	6.1	12.1
Virginia Beach	27.1	53.5	3.9	6.1	9.4
Washington	30.9	52.7	2.8	5.1	8.5
Wichita	23.5	57.6	1.4	6.1	11.5
U.S.	27.1	54.4	2.2	6.6	9.7

Note: Figures cover population 15 years of age and older in the Metropolitan Statistical Area - see Appendix A for areas included
Source: Census 2000, Summary File 3

Male/Female Ratio: City

City	Males	Females	Males per 100 Females
Albuquerque	222,071	235,839	94.2
Alexandria	65,323	69,730	93.7
Anchorage	136,738	133,942	102.1
Ann Arbor	57,029	58,399	97.7
Atlanta	209,665	211,299	99.2
Austin	361,818	342,800	105.5
Baltimore	299,700	341,755	87.7
Baton Rouge	107,551	118,407	90.8
Bellevue	55,648	56,581	98.4
Birmingham	108,682	125,864	86.3
Boise City	96,254	97,902	98.3
Boston	286,288	307,457	93.1
Boulder	48,916	45,989	106.4
Buffalo	133,852	150,629	88.9
Cedar Rapids	59,613	62,903	94.8
Charleston	46,016	51,137	90.0
Charlotte	281,692	291,864	96.5
Chattanooga	73,226	81,657	89.7
Chicago	1,415,119	1,498,156	94.5
Cincinnati	152,638	169,781	89.9
Cleveland	221,467	245,355	90.3
Colorado Spgs.	188,087	192,349	97.8
Columbia	56,728	58,811	96.5
Columbus	354,563	374,293	94.7
Dallas	622,614	612,515	101.6
Denver	286,283	280,354	102.1
Des Moines	96,447	102,701	93.9
Detroit	436,754	487,916	89.5
Durham	93,991	100,849	93.2
El Paso	276,321	305,220	90.5
Eugene	69,326	72,665	95.4
Ft. Collins	63,045	62,696	100.6
Ft. Lauderdale	80,556	73,587	109.5
Ft. Wayne	99,316	105,545	94.1
Ft. Worth	278,756	285,723	97.6
Grand Rapids	98,160	102,077	96.2
Green Bay	51,111	52,169	98.0
Greensboro	108,537	121,430	89.4
Honolulu	185,023	191,996	96.4
Houston	1,012,395	1,014,581	99.8
Huntsville	75,124	81,199	92.5
Indianapolis	381,963	406,029	94.1
Irvine	73,675	78,771	93.5
Jacksonville	376,017	400,304	93.9
Kansas City	214,687	229,533	93.5
Knoxville	81,851	90,304	90.6
Las Vegas	275,142	268,815	102.4
Lexington	131,142	135,733	96.6
Lincoln	115,716	116,934	99.0
Los Angeles	1,907,421	1,921,815	99.3
Louisville	120,097	133,388	90.0
Madison	104,357	108,388	96.3
Manchester	53,966	56,090	96.2

Male/Female Ratio: City *continued*

City	Males	Females	Males per 100 Females
Memphis	304,021	336,790	90.3
Miami	182,308	185,273	98.4
Milwaukee	280,872	306,916	91.5
Minneapolis	191,929	189,747	101.1
Naperville	67,589	70,531	95.8
Nashville	267,034	283,880	94.1
New Orleans	224,155	253,255	88.5
New York	3,865,293	4,275,584	90.4
Norfolk	120,079	114,639	104.7
Oklahoma City	252,974	264,875	95.5
Omaha	190,984	200,914	95.1
Orlando	94,922	100,942	94.0
Overland Park	77,259	82,163	94.0
Philadelphia	694,622	798,512	87.0
Phoenix	717,923	695,636	103.2
Pittsburgh	155,460	170,631	91.1
Plano	126,586	127,726	99.1
Portland	267,227	273,101	97.8
Providence	85,972	93,875	91.6
Provo	53,107	56,969	93.2
Raleigh	142,196	144,926	98.1
Reno	97,326	93,910	103.6
Richmond	91,262	104,837	87.1
Rochester	104,373	113,661	91.8
Sacramento	207,749	219,360	94.7
St. Louis	160,095	179,699	89.1
St. Paul	140,253	148,537	94.4
St. Petersburg	120,397	131,868	91.3
Salt Lake City	94,086	91,459	102.9
San Antonio	575,191	614,700	93.6
San Diego	643,115	635,184	101.2
San Francisco	407,293	393,456	103.5
San Jose	471,317	457,459	103.0
Savannah	61,334	68,607	89.4
Scottsdale	107,737	116,068	92.8
Seattle	287,688	288,354	99.8
Sioux Falls	63,751	65,880	96.8
Springfield (IL)	52,249	58,981	88.6
Springfield (MO)	73,366	79,076	92.8
Stamford	58,250	62,190	93.7
Syracuse	67,967	75,993	89.4
Tampa	154,865	162,290	95.4
Tucson	250,392	261,218	95.9
Tulsa	191,395	204,334	93.7
Virginia Beach	213,725	218,698	97.7
Washington	269,453	300,994	89.5
Wichita	170,742	175,763	97.1
U.S.	142,511,883	148,135,280	96.2

Note: Figures are 2003 estimates
Source: Claritas, Inc.

Male/Female Ratio: Metro Area

Metro Area	Males	Females	Males per 100 Females
Albuquerque	358,693	375,348	95.6
Alexandria	2,524,890	2,663,134	94.8
Anchorage	136,738	133,942	102.1
Ann Arbor	301,990	302,767	99.7
Atlanta	2,200,527	2,256,401	97.5
Austin	708,670	689,463	102.8
Baltimore	1,267,843	1,367,574	92.7
Baton Rouge	298,537	317,477	94.0
Bellevue	1,249,469	1,259,806	99.2
Birmingham	447,063	486,049	92.0
Boise City	234,207	234,445	99.9
Boston	2,987,501	3,190,836	93.6
Boulder	154,729	151,785	101.9
Buffalo	556,204	605,064	91.9
Cedar Rapids	96,185	100,165	96.0
Charleston	276,599	287,438	96.2
Charlotte	785,761	813,914	96.5
Chattanooga	227,718	245,230	92.9
Chicago	4,154,448	4,335,080	95.8
Cincinnati	812,377	863,050	94.1
Cleveland	1,075,213	1,171,168	91.8
Colorado Spgs.	275,967	274,200	100.6
Columbia	267,919	285,969	93.7
Columbus	783,848	813,541	96.4
Dallas	1,894,408	1,906,455	99.4
Denver	1,118,365	1,119,211	99.9
Des Moines	227,796	241,215	94.4
Detroit	2,170,889	2,297,297	94.5
Durham	625,244	646,834	96.7
El Paso	341,357	366,212	93.2
Eugene	162,561	168,822	96.3
Ft. Collins	134,486	135,181	99.5
Ft. Lauderdale	824,485	886,432	93.0
Ft. Wayne	251,098	260,542	96.4
Ft. Worth	902,285	917,741	98.3
Grand Rapids	554,442	569,769	97.3
Green Bay	116,249	117,312	99.1
Greensboro	627,652	671,313	93.5
Honolulu	451,716	448,148	100.8
Houston	2,208,890	2,231,247	99.0
Huntsville	172,258	178,394	96.6
Indianapolis	813,420	852,259	95.4
Irvine	1,482,180	1,502,563	98.6
Jacksonville	569,303	601,242	94.7
Kansas City	888,666	932,443	95.3
Knoxville	340,800	363,583	93.7
Las Vegas	897,168	877,780	102.2
Lexington	242,109	253,015	95.7
Lincoln	128,980	129,558	99.6
Los Angeles	4,893,848	5,017,671	97.5
Louisville	504,824	538,338	93.8
Madison	218,336	223,606	97.6
Manchester	2,987,501	3,190,836	93.6

Male/Female Ratio: Metro Area *continued*

Metro Area	Males	Females	Males per 100 Females
Memphis	558,663	601,993	92.8
Miami	1,136,735	1,217,712	93.4
Milwaukee	732,304	780,112	93.9
Minneapolis	1,515,372	1,553,925	97.5
Naperville	4,154,448	4,335,080	95.8
Nashville	627,564	653,456	96.0
New Orleans	639,471	695,765	91.9
New York	4,504,825	4,963,771	90.8
Norfolk	791,547	817,562	96.8
Oklahoma City	542,843	566,537	95.8
Omaha	359,637	373,443	96.3
Orlando	885,394	915,729	96.7
Overland Park	888,666	932,443	95.3
Philadelphia	2,469,861	2,681,037	92.1
Phoenix	1,779,570	1,773,094	100.4
Pittsburgh	1,115,981	1,223,738	91.2
Plano	1,894,408	1,906,455	99.4
Portland	998,698	1,014,364	98.5
Providence	474,626	515,153	92.1
Provo	197,048	200,132	98.5
Raleigh	625,244	646,834	96.7
Reno	183,725	180,120	102.0
Richmond	496,088	536,109	92.5
Rochester	536,645	568,514	94.4
Sacramento	857,220	891,131	96.2
St. Louis	1,263,764	1,368,378	92.4
St. Paul	1,515,372	1,553,925	97.5
St. Petersburg	1,213,693	1,305,793	92.9
Salt Lake City	697,440	688,054	101.4
San Antonio	815,864	860,295	94.8
San Diego	1,485,367	1,474,765	100.7
San Francisco	890,145	887,384	100.3
San Jose	881,213	860,454	102.4
Savannah	146,303	155,409	94.1
Scottsdale	1,779,570	1,773,094	100.4
Seattle	1,249,469	1,259,806	99.2
Sioux Falls	89,677	91,573	97.9
Springfield (IL)	96,888	105,854	91.5
Springfield (MO)	165,167	174,593	94.6
Stamford	838,681	904,178	92.8
Syracuse	355,351	377,083	94.2
Tampa	1,213,693	1,305,793	92.9
Tucson	440,369	461,475	95.4
Tulsa	401,796	422,106	95.2
Virginia Beach	791,547	817,562	96.8
Washington	2,524,890	2,663,134	94.8
Wichita	273,075	279,522	97.7
U.S.	142,511,883	148,135,280	96.2

Note: Figures are 2003 estimates and cover the Metropolitan Statistical Area (MSA) except for Boston, Manchester, Providence, and Stamford which are New England County Metropolitan Areas (NECMA) - see Appendix A for areas included
Source: Claritas, Inc.

Gross Metropolitan Product

MSA[1]	1999	2000	2001	2002	2002 Rank[2]
Albuquerque	23.4	25.6	26.7	27.2	77
Alexandria	197.8	215.1	227.8	236.5	5
Anchorage	11.5	12.3	13.4	13.5	128
Ann Arbor	17.9	18.7	20.1	20.5	93
Atlanta	155.1	166.8	174.0	177.9	8
Austin	42.7	47.3	48.6	49.2	51
Baltimore	89.2	95.2	99.8	102.6	20
Baton Rouge	18.3	19.5	20.0	20.7	92
Bellevue	111.6	117.1	119.9	120.9	15
Birmingham	30.5	31.9	33.1	34.3	65
Boise City	13.3	15.0	15.2	15.4	118
Boston	228.0	248.7	258.7	266.9	4
Boulder	11.1	12.8	13.8	14.3	124
Buffalo	44.5	46.9	48.5	50.9	48
Cedar Rapids	7.3	7.8	7.8	7.8	193
Charleston	13.8	14.8	15.8	16.3	112
Charlotte	59.4	65.3	69.5	73.6	31
Chattanooga	16.7	17.7	18.2	19.1	100
Chicago	315.3	332.9	342.1	349.5	3
Cincinnati	56.2	59.0	60.9	63.1	38
Cleveland	76.6	79.8	81.2	82.3	27
Colorado Springs	17.6	19.2	20.4	21.5	89
Columbia	18.5	19.2	21.1	21.4	90
Columbus	56.4	60.0	62.4	64.0	37
Dallas	148.3	159.9	164.7	166.9	9
Denver	84.1	92.9	97.7	100.9	21
Des Moines	18.2	19.1	19.5	20.0	94
Detroit	149.9	156.6	159.6	161.7	10
Durham	41.7	44.7	46.9	48.7	52
El Paso	17.7	18.7	19.1	19.9	95
Eugene	9.7	10.3	10.7	11.2	155
Fort Collins	7.2	8.0	8.5	9.1	178
Fort Lauderdale	42.4	45.8	48.6	50.7	49
Fort Wayne	17.7	18.4	18.7	19.2	99
Fort Worth	56.8	61.7	64.1	66.2	36
Grand Rapids	40.3	42.3	43.9	45.0	57
Green Bay	9.4	10.1	10.3	10.7	162
Greensboro	45.1	48.7	49.9	51.8	46
Honolulu	31.3	32.7	33.4	34.3	64
Houston	156.8	170.5	179.4	185.4	7
Huntsville	10.4	10.9	11.3	11.8	148
Indianapolis	54.6	57.8	59.9	61.3	42
Irvine	122.7	135.0	143.7	150.7	11
Jacksonville	40.2	42.9	44.4	45.9	55
Kansas City	61.6	65.3	66.1	67.1	35
Knoxville	20.1	21.1	22.0	23.5	80
Las Vegas	50.0	54.1	58.0	60.9	43
Lexington	16.2	17.0	16.8	17.4	106
Lincoln	8.7	9.2	9.7	10.0	171
Los Angeles	347.6	375.8	395.0	411.0	2
Louisville	35.5	37.9	38.4	39.3	60
Madison	17.1	18.1	19.0	19.8	96
Manchester	27.4	30.3	31.3	32.1	68

Gross Metropolitan Product *continued*

MSA[1]	1999	2000	2001	2002	2002 Rank[2]
Memphis	37.6	39.2	40.4	41.8	58
Miami	66.6	70.6	73.5	75.7	30
Milwaukee	52.0	54.0	54.7	55.4	45
Minneapolis	113.8	122.9	126.3	128.9	12
Naperville	315.3	332.9	342.1	349.5	3
Nashville	42.7	44.6	45.9	48.0	53
New Orleans	41.2	43.5	44.8	45.6	56
New York	409.1	438.4	445.5	448.9	1
Norfolk	52.1	55.8	60.0	62.9	40
Oklahoma City	30.0	32.0	33.2	34.2	66
Omaha	24.9	26.1	27.3	28.0	76
Orlando	54.7	58.2	60.6	62.1	41
Overland Park	61.6	65.3	66.1	67.1	35
Philadelphia	169.8	180.4	187.5	192.3	6
Phoenix	104.5	112.9	119.0	124.9	14
Pittsburgh	75.4	79.4	82.4	84.0	26
Plano	148.3	159.9	164.7	166.9	9
Portland	67.4	72.7	75.4	76.9	29
Providence	29.8	33.8	35.4	36.5	62
Provo	7.6	8.3	8.7	9.1	179
Raleigh	41.7	44.7	46.9	48.7	52
Reno	13.6	14.5	15.0	15.8	115
Richmond	40.4	43.5	47.6	49.5	50
Rochester	41.9	44.4	45.8	46.6	54
Sacramento	58.5	63.5	67.8	71.9	32
Saint Louis	84.3	88.5	90.1	92.2	23
Saint Paul	113.8	122.9	126.3	128.9	12
Saint Petersburg	74.6	81.0	84.0	87.5	25
Salt Lake City	43.2	47.4	49.7	51.4	47
San Antonio	50.6	54.3	56.3	58.1	44
San Diego	102.0	111.9	118.5	125.0	13
San Francisco	100.8	110.2	113.1	110.6	17
San Jose	79.0	89.2	91.8	88.3	24
Savannah	9.7	10.5	10.8	11.3	154
Scottsdale	104.5	112.9	119.0	124.9	14
Seattle	111.6	117.1	119.9	120.9	15
Sioux Falls	7.0	7.5	7.7	8.0	191
Springfield	10.5	10.6	10.7	11.2	156
Springfield	10.3	11.0	11.1	11.4	153
Stamford	71.0	75.7	78.1	80.6	28
Syracuse	28.0	29.4	30.4	31.4	70
Tampa	74.6	81.0	84.0	87.5	25
Tucson	20.6	22.5	23.3	24.4	79
Tulsa	23.5	25.1	26.0	26.7	78
Virginia Beach	52.1	55.8	60.0	62.9	40
Washington	197.8	215.1	227.8	236.5	5
Wichita	16.9	17.5	18.1	18.1	102

Note: Figures are in billions of dollars; (1) Metropolitan Statistical Area - see Appendix A for areas included; (2) Rank ranges from 1 to 319
Source: The U.S. Conference of Mayors, Metro Economies Report, July 2003

Per Capita/Median/Average Income: City

City	Per Capita ($)	Median Household ($)	Average Household ($)
Albuquerque	23,530	43,139	56,455
Alexandria	42,289	63,334	86,449
Anchorage	27,490	60,275	74,289
Ann Arbor	30,690	52,262	73,997
Atlanta	28,822	40,606	69,545
Austin	27,963	49,984	68,594
Baltimore	18,572	32,472	45,483
Baton Rouge	20,671	33,715	51,759
Bellevue	41,530	73,193	98,093
Birmingham	17,107	29,968	40,519
Boise City	25,773	48,264	63,119
Boston	26,052	43,999	62,379
Boulder	30,768	50,208	71,771
Buffalo	16,374	26,939	38,086
Cedar Rapids	25,488	48,790	60,421
Charleston	25,538	39,766	58,373
Charlotte	30,566	53,951	75,882
Chattanooga	21,983	36,560	50,990
Chicago	22,414	43,605	60,574
Cincinnati	22,193	32,910	47,956
Cleveland	15,510	28,820	38,112
Colorado Spgs.	26,020	51,545	65,662
Columbia	21,306	34,829	53,702
Columbus	23,119	43,069	53,447
Dallas	23,942	42,295	62,952
Denver	27,349	45,834	63,714
Des Moines	21,642	42,578	52,538
Detroit	16,090	33,170	45,143
Durham	25,259	46,884	62,176
El Paso	16,122	36,076	49,108
Eugene	24,105	40,529	55,880
Ft. Collins	26,082	51,085	66,077
Ft. Lauderdale	30,206	42,335	66,164
Ft. Wayne	20,392	40,084	49,131
Ft. Worth	20,396	41,811	55,090
Grand Rapids	19,757	41,708	51,833
Green Bay	21,724	42,721	52,117
Greensboro	25,456	43,642	60,476
Honolulu	26,403	48,184	68,095
Houston	21,792	40,970	59,131
Huntsville	27,117	45,391	62,235
Indianapolis	24,322	44,640	58,272
Irvine	35,809	79,046	99,680
Jacksonville	22,858	44,875	58,231
Kansas City	23,234	42,013	54,911
Knoxville	19,971	30,976	43,541
Las Vegas	23,604	48,303	63,884
Lexington	26,380	44,701	61,600
Lincoln	23,807	45,782	57,883
Los Angeles	21,600	40,146	61,960
Louisville	20,398	32,493	45,556
Madison	26,756	47,439	60,419
Manchester	23,102	44,442	54,673

Per Capita/Median/Average Income: City *continued*

City	Per Capita ($)	Median Household ($)	Average Household ($)
Memphis	19,770	36,771	50,342
Miami	16,584	25,824	43,367
Milwaukee	17,893	35,856	45,159
Minneapolis	25,356	43,051	58,708
Naperville	41,094	100,104	119,839
Nashville	25,060	44,429	58,817
New Orleans	18,925	30,357	47,208
New York	23,925	42,232	63,149
Norfolk	19,161	34,933	47,495
Oklahoma City	21,409	39,045	52,186
Omaha	24,469	45,455	59,933
Orlando	23,492	40,071	53,143
Overland Park	36,995	71,316	91,653
Philadelphia	18,006	33,243	45,144
Phoenix	21,988	46,409	62,531
Pittsburgh	20,573	31,536	45,899
Plano	42,486	89,281	114,684
Portland	25,796	45,615	60,279
Providence	16,705	29,012	45,186
Provo	14,813	38,767	51,498
Raleigh	28,434	52,679	68,524
Reno	24,677	45,142	59,852
Richmond	22,447	34,487	50,940
Rochester	16,305	29,055	39,430
Sacramento	20,333	40,992	53,129
St. Louis	17,929	30,477	41,630
St. Paul	22,306	43,377	56,304
St. Petersburg	23,564	39,026	52,666
Salt Lake City	23,061	41,736	58,479
San Antonio	19,700	41,233	54,417
San Diego	25,929	50,324	69,126
San Francisco	39,553	65,692	92,360
San Jose	30,527	80,527	99,071
Savannah	18,779	32,949	46,570
Scottsdale	43,888	66,961	97,951
Seattle	34,017	52,601	72,727
Sioux Falls	23,849	46,009	58,377
Springfield (IL)	26,453	44,444	59,641
Springfield (MO)	19,951	32,671	44,688
Stamford	37,673	66,354	96,433
Syracuse	16,282	27,077	38,903
Tampa	24,509	39,191	58,780
Tucson	18,044	34,549	44,561
Tulsa	23,869	39,285	56,011
Virginia Beach	24,942	53,569	67,090
Washington	31,487	44,718	70,076
Wichita	22,646	43,786	55,502
U.S.	24,078	46,868	63,207

Note: Figures are 2003 estimates
Source: Claritas, Inc.

Per Capita/Median/Average Income: Metro Area

Metro Area	Per Capita ($)	Median Household ($)	Average Household ($)
Albuquerque	22,665	43,834	57,645
Alexandria	33,779	69,270	89,026
Anchorage	27,490	60,275	74,289
Ann Arbor	30,416	62,799	79,025
Atlanta	28,257	59,395	76,895
Austin	28,467	58,013	75,230
Baltimore	27,323	54,800	70,148
Baton Rouge	21,500	43,167	56,892
Bellevue	31,329	60,860	77,670
Birmingham	24,503	44,759	61,272
Boise City	22,859	47,950	61,678
Boston	29,866	58,764	76,730
Boulder	33,606	65,178	84,735
Buffalo	22,681	42,833	55,367
Cedar Rapids	26,053	51,936	63,746
Charleston	22,786	44,364	58,219
Charlotte	26,714	52,274	68,806
Chattanooga	22,626	42,449	55,764
Chicago	27,998	58,826	77,423
Cincinnati	26,528	49,925	66,398
Cleveland	25,263	47,371	62,478
Colorado Spgs.	25,471	53,972	67,413
Columbia	23,834	46,665	60,761
Columbus	26,183	49,831	64,796
Dallas	27,294	55,076	74,939
Denver	30,060	59,688	76,882
Des Moines	26,544	52,557	66,498
Detroit	27,815	55,756	71,743
Durham	28,146	55,835	71,990
El Paso	14,907	34,389	47,147
Eugene	22,248	41,648	54,077
Ft. Collins	27,764	56,674	70,798
Ft. Lauderdale	25,557	46,403	63,742
Ft. Wayne	22,981	47,414	58,984
Ft. Worth	24,731	51,391	66,968
Grand Rapids	23,657	51,287	63,714
Green Bay	24,951	52,009	63,062
Greensboro	23,843	45,337	59,084
Honolulu	24,043	56,414	71,256
Houston	24,199	49,676	69,099
Huntsville	24,935	47,917	62,008
Indianapolis	26,362	50,894	66,181
Irvine	27,883	64,590	84,984
Jacksonville	24,688	47,784	62,889
Kansas City	26,497	52,119	66,808
Knoxville	23,235	41,624	55,515
Las Vegas	22,859	46,771	60,705
Lexington	24,272	44,370	59,157
Lincoln	24,230	47,275	59,740
Los Angeles	21,848	46,105	66,128
Louisville	25,066	46,308	61,014
Madison	28,822	55,732	69,088
Manchester	29,866	58,764	76,730

Per Capita/Median/Average Income: Metro Area *continued*

Metro Area	Per Capita ($)	Median Household ($)	Average Household ($)
Memphis	23,258	45,698	61,289
Miami	20,063	39,947	58,022
Milwaukee	26,469	51,422	66,188
Minneapolis	30,052	61,961	77,427
Naperville	27,998	58,826	77,423
Nashville	25,996	49,740	65,664
New Orleans	21,113	39,379	54,651
New York	25,746	45,207	68,522
Norfolk	22,801	47,158	59,520
Oklahoma City	21,624	41,140	53,997
Omaha	25,351	51,137	65,000
Orlando	23,614	46,460	61,691
Overland Park	26,497	52,119	66,808
Philadelphia	26,741	52,346	69,756
Phoenix	24,526	50,130	66,687
Pittsburgh	23,610	41,827	56,182
Plano	27,294	55,076	74,939
Portland	26,521	53,510	68,038
Providence	23,470	45,356	59,247
Provo	18,027	52,816	65,624
Raleigh	28,146	55,835	71,990
Reno	26,432	51,381	67,920
Richmond	26,614	51,970	67,041
Rochester	23,708	47,572	60,536
Sacramento	25,133	51,870	67,058
St. Louis	25,678	49,512	64,784
St. Paul	30,052	61,961	77,427
St. Petersburg	24,514	42,509	57,599
Salt Lake City	22,411	55,285	68,573
San Antonio	20,890	44,312	58,236
San Diego	25,173	52,110	70,052
San Francisco	40,996	73,531	103,196
San Jose	37,234	86,127	111,019
Savannah	23,849	45,054	61,541
Scottsdale	24,526	50,130	66,687
Seattle	31,329	60,860	77,670
Sioux Falls	23,259	48,074	59,086
Springfield (IL)	26,262	48,649	62,305
Springfield (MO)	20,902	38,735	51,189
Stamford	33,928	61,914	89,006
Syracuse	22,207	43,556	56,045
Tampa	24,514	42,509	57,599
Tucson	22,411	41,819	56,078
Tulsa	22,354	42,760	56,316
Virginia Beach	22,801	47,158	59,520
Washington	33,779	69,270	89,026
Wichita	22,902	47,182	58,618
U.S.	24,078	46,868	63,207

Note: Figures are 2003 estimates and cover the Metropolitan Statistical Area (MSA) except for Boston, Manchester, Providence, and Stamford which are New England County Metropolitan Areas (NECMA) - see Appendix A for areas included
Source: Claritas, Inc.

Household Income Distribution: City

City	Percent of Households Earning							
	Under $15,000	$15,000 -24,999	$25,000 -34,999	$35,000 -49,999	$50,000 -74,999	$75,000 -99,000	$100,000 -149,999	$150,000 and up
Albuquerque	14.6	12.9	13.1	17.3	18.5	10.5	9.0	4.1
Alexandria	7.7	6.5	8.8	16.0	20.4	13.7	14.5	12.2
Anchorage	7.3	8.5	10.1	15.1	21.7	14.7	14.9	7.6
Ann Arbor	14.2	10.1	9.6	14.6	17.1	11.7	13.3	9.5
Atlanta	21.6	12.3	11.2	13.3	14.4	8.6	9.1	9.7
Austin	12.4	9.9	11.5	16.1	19.3	11.7	11.5	7.4
Baltimore	25.5	14.7	13.1	15.8	15.2	7.4	5.3	3.0
Baton Rouge	24.2	14.9	12.6	14.3	14.0	8.2	7.1	4.7
Bellevue	6.2	5.6	7.5	12.6	19.6	14.9	18.4	15.3
Birmingham	26.8	16.1	14.2	16.6	14.1	6.1	4.1	2.0
Boise City	10.3	11.8	12.3	17.7	20.7	11.9	10.0	5.3
Boston	20.3	10.5	10.5	14.5	16.9	10.7	10.1	6.6
Boulder	14.7	10.2	10.7	14.3	16.7	11.1	13.0	9.3
Buffalo	29.8	17.5	13.7	14.5	13.0	5.9	3.8	1.7
Cedar Rapids	10.7	10.9	12.2	17.6	23.0	12.6	9.2	3.8
Charleston	20.6	12.5	12.1	15.0	16.3	9.1	8.4	5.9
Charlotte	9.9	9.1	11.5	16.3	20.1	12.2	11.7	9.1
Chattanooga	20.3	14.6	13.3	16.5	16.7	8.3	6.1	4.1
Chicago	18.4	11.3	11.2	15.8	17.8	10.1	9.4	5.9
Cincinnati	24.1	15.0	13.8	15.7	14.5	7.3	5.8	3.8
Cleveland	28.1	16.4	14.4	15.8	14.3	6.0	3.6	1.4
Colorado Spgs.	9.8	10.2	12.0	16.7	21.6	12.8	11.3	5.6
Columbia	22.6	14.6	13.0	15.9	14.7	7.2	6.5	5.6
Columbus	15.1	12.1	13.2	17.8	20.2	10.7	7.9	2.9
Dallas	14.9	12.7	13.8	17.7	16.9	8.9	8.1	6.9
Denver	14.0	11.1	12.6	17.0	18.7	10.5	9.8	6.3
Des Moines	13.7	12.7	14.2	18.6	21.4	10.3	6.6	2.5
Detroit	24.9	14.4	13.0	15.1	15.5	8.1	6.5	2.4
Durham	14.9	10.7	11.8	15.9	19.2	11.5	10.5	5.5
El Paso	19.9	14.9	13.9	16.8	16.9	8.1	6.3	3.1
Eugene	18.7	12.8	12.3	16.6	17.5	9.1	8.1	4.8
Ft. Collins	12.3	10.9	10.7	15.3	19.4	12.9	12.7	5.9
Ft. Lauderdale	16.9	13.0	12.3	15.8	16.7	8.6	8.2	8.4
Ft. Wayne	14.7	14.4	14.3	19.5	19.8	9.2	6.1	2.0
Ft. Worth	15.4	13.1	13.4	17.8	18.4	10.0	8.0	3.9
Grand Rapids	15.6	13.0	13.2	18.3	19.6	10.5	7.1	2.8
Green Bay	14.0	13.3	13.3	18.3	22.0	9.9	6.6	2.7
Greensboro	13.6	12.6	13.8	17.5	19.0	9.7	8.2	5.7
Honolulu	14.2	10.4	11.5	15.9	17.4	11.0	11.5	8.1
Houston	16.6	13.1	13.5	17.0	16.6	8.9	8.4	5.9
Huntsville	15.6	12.3	11.7	15.0	18.0	10.8	10.4	6.2
Indianapolis	13.3	12.4	13.1	17.6	19.7	10.9	8.8	4.3
Irvine	8.7	5.3	5.8	10.3	17.5	15.2	20.0	17.2
Jacksonville	13.7	11.7	12.8	17.9	20.2	10.8	8.6	4.2
Kansas City	16.0	12.4	13.5	17.3	19.0	10.1	8.1	3.7
Knoxville	25.3	16.4	14.0	16.1	14.2	6.6	4.9	2.7
Las Vegas	11.8	11.1	11.9	17.0	20.4	12.0	10.2	5.5
Lexington	15.1	12.6	12.3	15.5	18.6	10.8	9.5	5.7
Lincoln	11.9	12.2	13.1	17.9	21.0	11.5	8.7	3.8
Los Angeles	19.4	13.3	12.3	14.7	15.7	9.0	8.6	7.1
Louisville	23.9	15.5	14.2	16.2	15.0	6.9	5.4	2.9
Madison	13.7	10.6	11.3	17.3	20.4	11.8	10.2	4.7
Manchester	13.8	12.2	12.6	18.1	21.7	11.3	7.2	3.0

Household Income Distribution: City *continued*

City	Percent of Households Earning							
	Under $15,000	$15,000 -24,999	$25,000 -34,999	$35,000 -49,999	$50,000 -74,999	$75,000 -99,000	$100,000 -149,999	$150,000 and up
Memphis	20.1	14.0	13.9	17.1	17.1	8.1	6.2	3.5
Miami	32.6	16.4	12.6	13.2	11.4	5.4	4.7	3.8
Milwaukee	19.9	14.8	14.3	17.8	17.7	8.5	5.2	1.8
Minneapolis	15.6	12.4	12.9	17.0	18.2	10.1	8.8	5.0
Naperville	3.2	3.7	4.6	7.7	15.2	15.6	26.4	23.7
Nashville	14.1	11.6	13.2	17.6	19.6	10.4	8.7	4.7
New Orleans	27.9	15.1	13.0	14.5	13.2	6.6	5.4	4.2
New York	21.5	11.1	10.6	14.1	16.4	9.7	9.4	7.2
Norfolk	20.0	15.2	14.9	17.6	16.9	7.1	5.1	3.1
Oklahoma City	17.2	14.3	13.9	17.2	17.7	9.1	7.2	3.5
Omaha	12.7	12.1	13.0	17.5	19.7	11.2	9.2	4.6
Orlando	15.0	13.7	14.7	19.6	17.9	8.9	6.6	3.7
Overland Park	4.7	5.7	8.1	14.0	20.5	15.7	18.3	13.0
Philadelphia	25.2	14.2	12.8	15.7	15.7	8.0	5.8	2.6
Phoenix	12.2	11.8	12.7	17.5	19.5	10.9	9.8	5.6
Pittsburgh	25.3	16.1	13.2	15.1	14.7	7.0	5.3	3.4
Plano	3.7	4.1	5.7	10.5	17.1	15.7	22.8	20.4
Portland	14.1	11.5	12.3	17.1	19.8	11.0	9.2	5.0
Providence	29.7	15.4	12.4	13.9	13.5	6.7	4.7	3.7
Provo	13.8	15.9	15.4	19.5	17.1	8.0	7.1	3.2
Raleigh	10.2	9.5	11.4	16.8	20.3	12.6	12.7	6.6
Reno	13.0	12.3	13.1	17.2	19.8	10.9	8.9	4.8
Richmond	22.0	14.8	14.0	16.1	15.3	7.4	6.1	4.4
Rochester	27.5	17.0	13.6	15.5	14.2	6.4	4.1	1.7
Sacramento	17.7	12.9	12.6	17.2	18.6	9.4	8.0	3.6
St. Louis	26.0	16.3	14.0	16.1	14.2	6.6	4.6	2.2
St. Paul	15.0	12.2	13.3	17.0	19.6	10.4	8.5	4.1
St. Petersburg	16.5	14.2	14.7	17.5	17.7	8.9	6.8	3.7
Salt Lake City	15.8	13.6	13.3	16.3	18.2	9.6	7.9	5.3
San Antonio	16.1	13.3	13.4	17.3	18.5	9.5	8.0	3.9
San Diego	12.6	10.8	11.1	15.2	18.7	12.0	11.9	7.6
San Francisco	12.6	7.6	7.5	11.9	16.7	12.5	15.9	15.4
San Jose	6.8	5.5	6.1	10.5	17.7	15.3	21.1	16.9
Savannah	23.5	15.5	13.8	15.6	15.7	7.6	5.5	2.8
Scottsdale	7.5	7.5	8.7	13.6	18.7	12.5	15.0	16.5
Seattle	12.4	9.6	10.5	15.5	18.6	12.2	12.6	8.5
Sioux Falls	10.8	11.9	13.6	18.7	21.7	10.7	8.5	4.2
Springfield (IL)	13.5	12.5	12.7	17.8	18.7	10.8	9.1	4.8
Springfield (MO)	19.7	18.1	15.9	18.9	14.1	6.2	4.4	2.7
Stamford	10.6	7.8	7.8	12.5	17.2	12.6	15.1	16.4
Syracuse	29.9	17.3	13.5	14.4	12.5	6.2	4.5	1.9
Tampa	18.7	13.4	13.2	16.7	16.2	8.3	7.2	6.4
Tucson	19.1	16.1	15.6	18.1	16.6	7.4	5.1	2.0
Tulsa	16.4	14.7	13.9	17.4	16.6	8.7	7.3	5.0
Virginia Beach	7.0	8.6	12.0	18.9	24.0	13.4	10.8	5.2
Washington	19.1	10.2	11.1	14.8	15.6	9.6	10.1	9.6
Wichita	13.7	12.7	13.3	17.5	20.5	10.9	8.0	3.4
U.S.	14.1	11.5	11.7	16.0	19.2	11.3	10.2	6.0

Note: Figures are 2003 estimates
Source: Claritas, Inc.

Household Income Distribution: Metro Area

Metro Area	Percent of Households Earning							
	Under $15,000	$15,000 -24,999	$25,000 -34,999	$35,000 -49,999	$50,000 -74,999	$75,000 -99,000	$100,000 -149,999	$150,000 and up
Albuquerque	14.1	12.8	12.8	17.4	18.9	10.6	9.0	4.4
Alexandria	7.6	6.2	7.8	13.2	19.6	15.1	17.5	12.9
Anchorage	7.3	8.5	10.1	15.1	21.7	14.7	14.9	7.6
Ann Arbor	9.1	8.1	9.0	13.7	19.6	14.6	16.6	9.2
Atlanta	9.3	8.0	9.6	15.2	21.0	14.0	14.1	8.9
Austin	10.2	8.4	9.9	15.1	20.2	13.7	14.0	8.6
Baltimore	11.9	9.4	10.1	14.8	20.1	13.5	13.0	7.2
Baton Rouge	17.3	12.4	11.8	15.6	18.1	11.2	9.3	4.2
Bellevue	8.8	7.9	9.5	14.8	20.9	14.7	14.8	8.7
Birmingham	16.0	11.7	11.8	16.2	18.4	10.8	9.5	5.7
Boise City	10.4	11.6	12.6	17.8	21.1	12.0	9.8	4.7
Boston	12.0	8.9	8.9	13.4	19.3	13.7	14.4	9.4
Boulder	9.1	7.4	8.6	13.4	18.9	14.0	16.7	11.8
Buffalo	16.3	13.2	12.3	15.7	19.0	10.9	8.9	3.7
Cedar Rapids	9.2	10.4	11.5	17.1	23.0	13.8	10.6	4.3
Charleston	15.2	11.9	12.4	16.9	19.5	10.8	8.9	4.4
Charlotte	10.8	9.5	11.3	16.5	21.2	12.7	11.4	6.6
Chattanooga	15.8	12.7	12.9	17.2	19.6	10.0	7.7	4.1
Chicago	10.9	8.5	9.3	14.4	19.8	13.7	14.2	9.3
Cincinnati	12.5	10.6	11.2	15.8	20.1	12.3	11.1	6.4
Cleveland	13.6	11.4	11.7	16.1	19.8	11.9	10.2	5.3
Colorado Spgs.	8.8	9.5	11.5	16.7	22.4	13.3	12.1	5.9
Columbia	13.2	11.5	12.2	16.9	20.1	11.7	9.6	4.8
Columbus	11.8	10.3	11.6	16.5	20.6	12.5	11.1	5.6
Dallas	10.2	9.2	10.9	15.8	19.4	12.7	13.0	8.9
Denver	8.5	7.9	10.0	15.5	21.0	14.2	14.4	8.6
Des Moines	9.6	9.9	11.5	16.8	22.1	13.6	11.2	5.4
Detroit	11.7	9.5	10.1	14.3	19.3	13.5	14.0	7.6
Durham	11.0	9.0	10.3	15.1	20.0	13.2	13.6	7.9
El Paso	20.4	16.1	14.4	16.8	16.1	7.6	5.7	2.8
Eugene	16.2	13.2	12.8	17.8	19.3	9.7	7.4	3.7
Ft. Collins	9.4	9.5	10.1	15.3	21.5	13.9	13.7	6.6
Ft. Lauderdale	13.8	11.9	12.0	16.2	18.6	11.1	10.3	6.2
Ft. Wayne	10.9	11.6	12.6	18.0	22.2	12.0	9.1	3.6
Ft. Worth	10.6	10.0	11.5	16.8	20.5	12.7	11.8	6.1
Grand Rapids	10.2	10.4	11.2	17.1	22.7	13.3	10.5	4.7
Green Bay	9.7	10.4	11.4	16.6	23.4	13.8	10.3	4.3
Greensboro	13.4	11.9	12.7	17.3	20.5	10.9	8.6	4.6
Honolulu	10.7	8.9	10.3	15.0	19.9	13.7	14.1	7.4
Houston	12.6	10.5	11.4	15.8	18.4	11.7	11.9	7.6
Huntsville	13.7	11.5	11.4	15.6	19.3	12.1	11.2	5.2
Indianapolis	10.8	10.7	11.5	16.3	20.6	12.8	11.5	5.8
Irvine	7.9	7.8	8.9	14.0	19.7	14.2	15.9	11.7
Jacksonville	12.2	11.0	12.2	17.2	20.7	11.6	9.9	5.3
Kansas City	10.6	9.7	11.4	16.5	21.1	13.2	11.6	5.9
Knoxville	16.4	13.1	13.0	16.8	18.6	9.8	8.0	4.2
Las Vegas	11.8	11.7	12.6	17.8	20.6	11.6	9.3	4.7
Lexington	15.4	12.4	12.2	15.9	19.0	11.0	9.2	4.8
Lincoln	11.3	11.7	12.6	17.7	21.4	12.0	9.3	4.2
Los Angeles	15.7	11.8	11.5	14.9	17.6	10.8	10.4	7.4
Louisville	13.8	11.6	12.2	16.5	19.8	11.3	9.7	5.1
Madison	9.7	9.0	10.3	16.0	22.1	14.4	12.6	6.0
Manchester	12.0	8.9	8.9	13.4	19.3	13.7	14.4	9.4

Household Income Distribution: Metro Area *continued*

Metro Area	Percent of Households Earning							
	Under $15,000	$15,000 -24,999	$25,000 -34,999	$35,000 -49,999	$50,000 -74,999	$75,000 -99,000	$100,000 -149,999	$150,000 and up
Memphis	15.5	11.3	11.7	16.1	19.1	11.3	9.6	5.3
Miami	19.5	13.1	12.3	15.6	16.7	9.1	8.0	5.7
Milwaukee	11.6	10.4	11.0	15.8	20.6	13.2	11.6	5.8
Minneapolis	7.9	7.8	9.3	14.6	21.6	15.4	15.1	8.2
Naperville	10.9	8.5	9.3	14.4	19.8	13.7	14.2	9.3
Nashville	11.9	10.2	11.6	16.6	21.0	12.2	10.6	6.0
New Orleans .	19.7	13.2	12.5	15.7	17.1	9.5	7.9	4.4
New York	20.0	10.6	10.2	13.7	16.4	10.1	10.4	8.7
Norfolk	12.1	11.0	12.5	17.6	21.4	11.8	9.3	4.1
Oklahoma City	15.8	13.5	13.5	17.5	18.7	9.8	7.5	3.6
Omaha	10.1	10.4	11.8	16.7	21.6	13.1	11.2	5.1
Orlando	11.5	11.7	12.9	18.2	20.2	11.0	9.4	5.2
Overland Park	10.6	9.7	11.4	16.5	21.1	13.2	11.6	5.9
Philadelphia	13.6	9.9	10.2	14.5	19.0	12.7	12.5	7.6
Phoenix	10.6	10.6	11.7	16.9	20.5	12.2	11.1	6.2
Pittsburgh	16.1	13.8	12.7	16.2	18.5	10.2	8.2	4.3
Plano	10.2	9.2	10.9	15.8	19.4	12.7	13.0	8.9
Portland	10.1	9.6	10.9	16.5	21.5	13.3	12.1	6.2
Providence	16.6	11.9	11.1	15.2	19.4	11.5	9.7	4.8
Provo	8.2	10.0	11.3	17.9	22.9	13.1	11.6	5.0
Raleigh	11.0	9.0	10.3	15.1	20.0	13.2	13.6	7.9
Reno	10.4	10.3	11.7	16.5	21.0	12.6	11.2	6.3
Richmond	11.1	9.8	11.4	16.1	20.8	13.1	11.6	6.1
Rochester	13.1	11.7	11.6	16.2	20.4	12.3	10.1	4.6
Sacramento	11.4	10.1	10.9	16.1	20.2	12.8	12.3	6.3
St. Louis	12.2	10.7	11.4	16.2	20.4	12.5	10.8	5.7
St. Paul	7.9	7.8	9.3	14.6	21.6	15.4	15.1	8.2
St. Petersburg	14.0	13.4	13.8	17.6	18.7	9.7	8.1	4.7
Salt Lake City	8.3	9.0	10.6	17.2	22.9	14.0	12.2	5.7
San Antonio	14.3	12.3	12.7	17.3	19.5	10.4	9.0	4.5
San Diego	11.1	10.5	11.2	15.6	19.5	12.4	12.2	7.5
San Francisco	9.3	6.6	6.8	11.4	16.8	13.4	17.5	18.2
San Jose	6.3	5.1	5.7	9.8	16.6	14.6	20.8	21.1
Savannah	15.9	11.9	12.0	15.3	18.7	11.3	9.6	5.4
Scottsdale	10.6	10.6	11.7	16.9	20.5	12.2	11.1	6.2
Seattle	8.8	7.9	9.5	14.8	20.9	14.7	14.8	8.7
Sioux Falls	10.0	11.0	13.0	18.4	23.5	11.6	8.7	3.8
Springfield (IL)	11.2	11.3	11.7	17.3	21.1	12.4	10.2	4.7
Springfield (MO)	15.4	15.1	14.8	18.7	18.1	8.5	6.0	3.3
Stamford	11.2	8.7	8.6	13.0	17.9	13.0	14.2	13.4
Syracuse	15.6	12.7	12.2	16.6	19.2	10.9	8.8	3.9
Tampa	14.0	13.4	13.8	17.6	18.7	9.7	8.1	4.7
Tucson	15.1	13.4	13.5	17.4	18.4	9.7	8.0	4.4
Tulsa	14.6	13.1	13.2	17.5	19.1	10.3	8.1	4.1
Virginia Beach	12.1	11.0	12.5	17.6	21.4	11.8	9.3	4.1
Washington	7.6	6.2	7.8	13.2	19.6	15.1	17.5	12.9
Wichita	12.0	11.5	12.5	17.4	21.7	12.3	9.1	3.6
U.S.	14.1	11.5	11.7	16.0	19.2	11.3	10.2	6.0

Note: Figures are 2003 estimates and cover the Metropolitan Statistical Area (MSA) except for Boston, Manchester, Providence, and Stamford which are New England County Metropolitan Areas (NECMA) - see Appendix A for areas included
Source: Claritas, Inc.

Poverty Rates by Age: City

City	All Ages	Under 5 Years Old	5 to 17 Years Old	18 to 64 Years Old	65 Years and Over
Albuquerque	13.5	1.4	3.0	8.2	1.0
Alexandria	8.9	0.8	1.6	5.8	0.7
Anchorage	7.3	0.8	1.9	4.3	0.3
Ann Arbor	16.6	0.5	1.0	14.7	0.4
Atlanta	24.4	2.7	6.4	13.2	2.1
Austin	14.4	1.3	2.6	10.0	0.6
Baltimore	22.9	2.3	5.5	12.8	2.4
Baton Rouge	24.0	2.5	5.5	14.3	1.6
Bellevue	5.7	0.3	1.0	3.6	0.8
Birmingham	24.7	2.6	6.4	13.3	2.4
Boise City	8.4	0.9	1.7	5.3	0.6
Boston	19.5	1.4	3.9	12.4	1.9
Boulder	17.4	0.6	1.2	15.1	0.5
Buffalo	26.6	3.2	7.1	14.4	1.8
Cedar Rapids	7.5	0.8	1.5	4.4	0.9
Charleston	19.1	1.6	3.5	12.1	1.9
Charlotte	10.6	1.0	2.5	6.3	0.8
Chattanooga	17.9	1.8	4.4	9.6	2.1
Chicago	19.6	2.2	5.3	10.6	1.6
Cincinnati	21.9	2.6	5.5	12.0	1.8
Cleveland	26.3	3.4	7.5	13.3	2.1
Colorado Spgs.	8.7	0.9	2.1	5.0	0.7
Columbia	22.1	2.1	4.9	13.0	2.0
Columbus	14.8	1.5	3.1	9.2	0.9
Dallas	17.8	2.2	4.6	9.9	1.1
Denver	14.3	1.4	3.1	8.7	1.1
Des Moines	11.4	1.4	2.5	6.5	0.9
Detroit	26.1	2.9	7.8	13.4	1.9
Durham	15.0	1.6	3.0	9.1	1.2
El Paso	22.2	2.6	6.7	11.1	1.9
Eugene	17.1	1.1	2.1	13.0	0.9
Ft. Collins	14.0	0.7	1.2	11.6	0.5
Ft. Lauderdale	17.7	1.6	4.1	10.3	1.7
Ft. Wayne	12.5	1.7	3.2	6.7	0.9
Ft. Worth	15.9	2.0	4.2	8.6	1.1
Grand Rapids	15.7	1.7	3.9	9.0	1.1
Green Bay	10.5	1.1	2.3	6.1	1.0
Greensboro	12.3	1.2	2.5	7.3	1.2
Honolulu	11.8	0.8	2.1	7.3	1.5
Houston	19.2	2.3	5.0	10.8	1.2
Huntsville	12.8	1.4	3.0	7.2	1.2
Indianapolis	11.9	1.4	2.9	6.7	0.9
Irvine	9.1	0.4	1.2	7.1	0.4
Jacksonville	12.2	1.3	3.2	6.4	1.2
Kansas City	14.3	1.6	3.6	7.9	1.2
Knoxville	20.8	1.9	3.5	13.7	1.7
Las Vegas	11.9	1.3	2.8	6.9	0.9
Lexington	12.9	1.1	2.2	8.8	0.9
Lincoln	10.1	0.9	1.8	6.8	0.6
Los Angeles	22.1	2.4	5.7	12.8	1.2
Louisville	21.6	2.6	5.5	11.6	1.9
Madison	15.0	0.7	1.4	12.5	0.4
Manchester	10.6	1.2	2.3	5.6	1.5

Poverty Rates by Age: City *continued*

City	All Ages	Under 5 Years Old	5 to 17 Years Old	18 to 64 Years Old	65 Years and Over
Memphis	20.6	2.7	5.8	10.4	1.6
Miami	28.5	2.2	6.2	15.0	5.0
Milwaukee	21.3	2.7	6.5	11.0	1.2
Minneapolis	16.9	1.6	4.0	10.4	0.9
Naperville	2.2	0.2	0.6	1.2	0.3
Nashville	13.3	1.5	3.0	7.6	1.2
New Orleans	27.9	3.0	8.1	14.7	2.2
New York	21.2	2.0	5.3	11.9	2.0
Norfolk	19.4	2.2	5.2	10.5	1.5
Oklahoma City	16.0	2.0	4.1	9.0	1.0
Omaha	11.3	1.2	2.9	6.4	0.8
Orlando	15.9	2.0	4.1	8.5	1.3
Overland Park	3.2	0.3	0.6	2.0	0.4
Philadelphia	22.9	2.1	5.9	12.5	2.4
Phoenix	15.8	2.1	4.1	8.8	0.8
Pittsburgh	20.4	1.8	4.0	12.3	2.2
Plano	4.3	0.4	1.0	2.5	0.4
Portland	13.1	1.0	2.4	8.4	1.2
Providence	29.1	3.1	8.2	15.8	2.0
Provo	26.8	1.5	2.0	23.0	0.3
Raleigh	11.5	1.0	2.1	7.6	0.8
Reno	12.6	1.5	2.4	7.8	0.8
Richmond	21.4	2.2	5.3	11.8	2.1
Rochester	25.9	3.1	7.7	13.6	1.4
Sacramento	20.0	2.1	6.0	10.9	1.0
St. Louis	24.6	2.6	6.9	12.7	2.3
St. Paul	15.6	1.7	4.8	8.1	1.0
St. Petersburg	13.3	1.1	3.1	7.2	1.8
Salt Lake City	15.3	1.5	3.0	9.9	0.9
San Antonio	17.3	2.2	4.9	8.8	1.4
San Diego	14.6	1.4	3.5	8.9	0.8
San Francisco	11.3	0.5	1.5	7.9	1.4
San Jose	8.8	0.8	2.1	5.4	0.6
Savannah	21.8	2.4	5.8	11.5	2.1
Scottsdale	5.8	0.3	0.8	3.7	1.0
Seattle	11.8	0.6	1.7	8.3	1.2
Sioux Falls	8.4	1.0	1.7	4.9	0.8
Springfield (IL)	11.7	1.3	3.0	6.3	1.1
Springfield (MO)	15.9	1.4	2.6	10.7	1.2
Stamford	7.9	0.6	1.3	4.7	1.3
Syracuse	27.3	3.1	6.2	16.4	1.6
Tampa	18.1	1.9	4.8	9.4	1.9
Tucson	18.4	1.9	4.1	11.1	1.3
Tulsa	14.1	1.8	3.4	7.9	1.0
Virginia Beach	6.5	0.7	1.8	3.7	0.4
Washington	20.2	1.9	4.6	11.7	2.0
Wichita	11.2	1.3	2.7	6.3	0.9
U.S.	12.4	1.2	3.0	6.9	1.2

Note: Figures are percent of population with income in 1999 below poverty level and only include population for whom poverty status is determined
Source: Census 2000, Summary File 3

Poverty Rates by Age: Metro Area

MSA[1]	All Ages	Under 5 Years Old	5 to 17 Years Old	18 to 64 Years Old	65 Years and Over
Albuquerque	13.8	1.5	3.4	7.9	1.0
Alexandria	7.4	0.7	1.7	4.4	0.7
Anchorage	7.3	0.8	1.9	4.3	0.3
Ann Arbor	8.2	0.6	1.2	5.8	0.6
Atlanta	9.4	1.0	2.3	5.4	0.7
Austin	11.1	1.0	2.1	7.4	0.6
Baltimore	9.8	0.9	2.3	5.5	1.1
Baton Rouge	16.2	1.6	3.9	9.5	1.2
Bellevue	7.9	0.6	1.6	5.0	0.7
Birmingham	13.1	1.3	3.2	7.1	1.6
Boise City	9.0	1.1	2.2	5.0	0.7
Boston	8.6	0.6	1.7	5.1	1.1
Boulder	9.5	0.6	1.3	7.1	0.5
Buffalo	11.9	1.3	2.9	6.5	1.2
Cedar Rapids	6.5	0.7	1.4	3.7	0.8
Charleston	14.0	1.4	3.6	7.7	1.3
Charlotte	9.3	0.9	2.2	5.3	1.0
Chattanooga	11.9	1.1	2.8	6.4	1.5
Chicago	10.5	1.1	2.7	5.8	0.9
Cincinnati	9.7	1.1	2.4	5.2	0.9
Cleveland	10.8	1.2	2.8	5.6	1.2
Colorado Spgs.	8.0	0.9	2.0	4.5	0.6
Columbia	11.7	1.1	2.7	6.8	1.1
Columbus	10.1	1.1	2.2	6.0	0.8
Dallas	11.1	1.3	2.8	6.3	0.7
Denver	8.1	0.8	1.8	4.8	0.6
Des Moines	7.5	0.9	1.6	4.3	0.7
Detroit	10.7	1.1	2.9	5.7	1.0
Durham	10.2	1.0	1.9	6.4	1.0
El Paso	23.8	2.8	7.4	11.8	1.8
Eugene	14.4	1.2	2.6	9.6	1.0
Ft. Collins	9.2	0.5	1.2	7.1	0.4
Ft. Lauderdale	11.5	1.0	2.7	6.2	1.6
Ft. Wayne	8.2	1.0	2.1	4.3	0.8
Ft. Worth	10.3	1.2	2.6	5.7	0.8
Grand Rapids	8.4	0.9	2.0	4.8	0.7
Green Bay	6.9	0.7	1.5	3.9	0.8
Greensboro	10.4	1.1	2.3	5.7	1.4
Honolulu	9.9	0.9	2.2	5.8	1.0
Houston	13.9	1.6	3.7	7.7	0.9
Huntsville	10.9	1.2	2.6	5.9	1.2
Indianapolis	8.6	0.9	2.0	4.8	0.8
Irvine	10.3	1.0	2.6	6.1	0.6
Jacksonville	10.7	1.1	2.8	5.7	1.1
Kansas City	8.5	0.9	2.1	4.7	0.8
Knoxville	12.0	1.1	2.4	7.3	1.3
Las Vegas	11.1	1.2	2.6	6.4	0.9
Lexington	12.6	1.2	2.3	8.0	1.1
Lincoln	9.5	0.8	1.8	6.3	0.6
Los Angeles	17.9	1.9	4.9	10.1	1.0
Louisville	10.9	1.3	2.7	5.9	1.0
Madison	9.4	0.5	1.2	7.3	0.4
Manchester	7.1	0.7	1.5	3.7	1.1

Poverty Rates by Age: Metro Area *continued*

MSA[1]	All Ages	Under 5 Years Old	5 to 17 Years Old	18 to 64 Years Old	65 Years and Over
Memphis	15.3	1.9	4.3	7.7	1.3
Miami	18.0	1.5	4.3	9.7	2.5
Milwaukee	10.6	1.3	3.0	5.5	0.8
Minneapolis	6.7	0.6	1.7	3.8	0.6
Naperville	10.5	1.1	2.7	5.8	0.9
Nashville	10.1	1.1	2.3	5.7	1.0
New Orleans	18.4	1.9	5.1	9.8	1.6
New York	19.5	1.8	4.9	10.9	1.9
Norfolk	10.6	1.2	2.9	5.7	0.9
Oklahoma City	13.5	1.5	3.3	7.8	0.9
Omaha	8.4	0.9	2.2	4.7	0.7
Orlando	10.7	1.0	2.6	6.1	1.0
Overland Park	8.5	0.9	2.1	4.7	0.8
Philadelphia	11.1	1.0	2.8	6.1	1.3
Phoenix	12.0	1.4	3.0	6.7	0.9
Pittsburgh	10.8	0.9	2.4	5.9	1.6
Plano	11.1	1.3	2.8	6.3	0.7
Portland	9.5	0.9	2.0	5.7	0.7
Providence	11.8	1.1	2.9	6.2	1.6
Provo	12.0	1.1	1.9	8.6	0.3
Raleigh	10.2	1.0	1.9	6.4	1.0
Reno	10.0	1.1	2.1	6.1	0.6
Richmond	9.3	0.9	2.3	5.1	0.9
Rochester	10.3	1.0	2.7	5.7	0.9
Sacramento	12.2	1.2	3.5	6.8	0.7
St. Louis	9.9	1.0	2.7	5.2	1.0
St. Paul	6.7	0.6	1.7	3.8	0.6
St. Petersburg	11.2	1.0	2.5	6.0	1.6
Salt Lake City	7.7	1.0	1.9	4.4	0.4
San Antonio	15.1	1.8	4.3	7.7	1.2
San Diego	12.4	1.2	3.2	7.3	0.8
San Francisco	8.4	0.5	1.3	5.7	1.0
San Jose	7.5	0.6	1.6	4.7	0.6
Savannah	14.5	1.5	3.8	7.8	1.4
Scottsdale	12.0	1.4	3.0	6.7	0.9
Seattle	7.9	0.6	1.6	5.0	0.7
Sioux Falls	7.1	0.8	1.5	4.0	0.8
Springfield (IL)	9.3	1.0	2.3	5.0	1.0
Springfield (MO)	11.8	1.1	2.5	7.2	1.0
Stamford	5.7	0.4	1.1	3.3	0.8
Syracuse	12.1	1.3	2.8	7.0	1.0
Tampa	11.2	1.0	2.5	6.0	1.6
Tucson	14.7	1.4	3.5	8.6	1.2
Tulsa	11.4	1.3	2.8	6.2	1.1
Virginia Beach	10.6	1.2	2.9	5.7	0.9
Washington	7.4	0.7	1.7	4.4	0.7
Wichita	9.1	1.1	2.2	5.0	0.8
U.S.	12.4	1.2	3.0	6.9	1.2

Note: Figures are percent of population with income in 1999 below poverty level and only include population for whom poverty status is determined; (1) Metropolitan Statistical Area - see Appendix A for areas included
Source: Census 2000, Summary File 3

Internal Revenue Service Tax Audits

City	IRS District	Percent of Returns Audited				
		1996	1997	1998	1999	2000
Albuquerque	Southwest	0.80	0.81	0.61	0.36	0.29
Alexandria	Virginia-West Virginia	0.42	0.39	0.29	0.22	0.13
Anchorage	Pacific Northwest	0.63	0.51	0.37	0.24	0.15
Ann Arbor	Michigan	0.44	0.36	0.29	0.19	0.11
Atlanta	Georgia	0.78	0.64	0.48	0.31	0.11
Austin	South Texas	0.55	0.50	0.50	0.31	0.17
Baltimore	Delaware-Maryland	0.53	0.53	0.42	0.25	0.13
Baton Rouge	Gulf Coast	0.83	0.74	0.50	0.41	0.20
Bellevue	Pacific Northwest	0.63	0.51	0.37	0.24	0.15
Birmingham	Gulf Coast	0.83	0.74	0.50	0.41	0.20
Boise City	Rocky Mountain	0.73	0.67	0.49	0.28	0.20
Boston	New England	0.46	0.37	0.30	0.21	0.16
Boulder	Rocky Mountain	0.73	0.67	0.49	0.28	0.20
Buffalo	Upstate New York	0.36	0.37	0.31	0.18	0.14
Cedar Rapids	Midwest	0.53	0.52	0.41	0.26	0.19
Charleston	North-South Carolina	0.48	0.34	0.28	0.21	0.16
Charlotte	North-South Carolina	0.48	0.34	0.28	0.21	0.16
Chattanooga	Kentucky-Tennessee	0.40	0.48	0.36	0.22	0.13
Chicago	Illinois	0.47	0.53	0.46	0.20	0.14
Cincinnati	Ohio	0.34	0.32	0.22	0.16	0.10
Cleveland	Ohio	0.34	0.32	0.22	0.16	0.10
Colorado Springs	Rocky Mountain	0.73	0.67	0.49	0.28	0.20
Columbia	North-South Carolina	0.48	0.34	0.28	0.21	0.16
Columbus	Ohio	0.34	0.32	0.22	0.16	0.10
Dallas	North Texas	0.95	0.82	0.50	0.35	0.19
Denver	Rocky Mountain	0.73	0.67	0.49	0.28	0.20
Des Moines	Midwest	0.53	0.52	0.41	0.26	0.19
Detroit	Michigan	0.44	0.36	0.29	0.19	0.11
Durham	North-South Carolina	0.48	0.34	0.28	0.21	0.16
El Paso	South Texas	0.55	0.50	0.50	0.31	0.17
Eugene	Pacific Northwest	0.63	0.51	0.37	0.24	0.15
Fort Collins	Rocky Mountain	0.73	0.67	0.49	0.28	0.20
Fort Lauderdale	South Florida	0.71	0.68	0.50	0.42	0.23
Fort Wayne	Indiana	0.51	0.43	0.30	0.22	0.14
Fort Worth	North Texas	0.95	0.82	0.50	0.35	0.19
Grand Rapids	Michigan	0.44	0.36	0.29	0.19	0.11
Green Bay	Midwest	0.53	0.52	0.41	0.26	0.19
Greensboro	North-South Carolina	0.48	0.34	0.28	0.21	0.16
Honolulu	Pacific Northwest	0.63	0.51	0.37	0.24	0.15
Houston	Houston	0.76	0.64	0.53	0.44	0.22
Huntsville	Gulf Coast	0.83	0.74	0.50	0.41	0.20
Indianapolis	Indiana	0.51	0.43	0.30	0.22	0.14
Irvine	Southern California	1.62	1.34	0.88	0.69	0.47
Jackson	Gulf Coast	0.83	0.74	0.50	0.41	0.20
Jacksonville	North Florida	0.52	0.45	0.29	0.24	0.14
Kansas City	Kansas-Missouri	0.51	0.45	0.38	0.30	0.16
Knoxville	Kentucky-Tennessee	0.40	0.48	0.36	0.22	0.13
Las Vegas	Southwest	0.80	0.81	0.61	0.36	0.29
Lexington	Kentucky-Tennessee	0.40	0.48	0.36	0.22	0.13
Lincoln	Midwest	0.53	0.52	0.41	0.26	0.19
Los Angeles	Los Angeles	1.59	1.54	0.98	0.67	0.48
Louisville	Kentucky-Tennessee	0.40	0.48	0.36	0.22	0.13
Madison	Midwest	0.53	0.52	0.41	0.26	0.19
Manchester	New England	0.46	0.37	0.30	0.21	0.16

Internal Revenue Service Tax Audits *continued*

City	IRS District	Percent of Returns Audited				
		1996	1997	1998	1999	2000
Memphis	Kentucky-Tennessee	0.40	0.48	0.36	0.22	0.13
Miami	South Florida	0.71	0.68	0.50	0.42	0.23
Milwaukee	Midwest	0.53	0.52	0.41	0.26	0.19
Minneapolis	North Central	0.68	0.76	0.59	0.50	0.47
Naperville	Illinois	0.47	0.53	0.46	0.20	0.14
Nashville	Kentucky-Tennessee	0.40	0.48	0.36	0.22	0.13
New Orleans	Gulf Coast	0.83	0.74	0.50	0.41	0.20
New York	Manhattan	0.75	0.77	0.61	0.44	0.37
Norfolk	Virginia-West Virginia	0.42	0.39	0.29	0.22	0.13
Oakland	Northern California	1.24	1.34	1.08	0.60	0.41
Oklahoma City	Arkansas-Oklahoma	0.72	0.63	0.58	0.35	0.21
Omaha	Midwest	0.53	0.52	0.41	0.26	0.19
Orlando	North Florida	0.52	0.45	0.29	0.24	0.14
Overland Park	Kansas-Missouri	0.51	0.45	0.38	0.30	0.16
Philadelphia	Pennsylvania	0.36	0.41	0.31	0.23	0.13
Phoenix	Southwest	0.80	0.81	0.61	0.36	0.29
Pittsburgh	Pennsylvania	0.36	0.41	0.31	0.23	0.13
Plano	North Texas	0.95	0.82	0.50	0.35	0.19
Portland	Pacific Northwest	0.63	0.51	0.37	0.24	0.15
Providence	Connecticut-Rhode Island	0.60	0.45	0.36	0.28	0.18
Provo	Rocky Mountain	0.73	0.67	0.49	0.28	0.20
Raleigh	North-South Carolina	0.48	0.34	0.28	0.21	0.16
Reno	Southwest	0.80	0.81	0.61	0.36	0.29
Richmond	Virginia-West Virginia	0.42	0.39	0.29	0.22	0.13
Rochester	Upstate New York	0.36	0.37	0.31	0.18	0.14
Sacramento	Northern California	1.24	1.34	1.08	0.60	0.41
Saint Louis	Kansas-Missouri	0.51	0.45	0.38	0.30	0.16
Saint Paul	North Central	0.68	0.76	0.59	0.50	0.47
Saint Petersburg	North Florida	0.52	0.45	0.29	0.24	0.14
Salt Lake City	Rocky Mountain	0.73	0.67	0.49	0.28	0.20
San Antonio	South Texas	0.55	0.50	0.50	0.31	0.17
San Diego	Southern California	1.62	1.34	0.88	0.69	0.47
San Francisco	Northern California	1.24	1.34	1.08	0.60	0.41
San Jose	Central California	1.17	0.91	0.71	0.56	0.29
Savannah	Georgia	0.78	0.64	0.48	0.31	0.11
Scottsdale	Southwest	0.80	0.81	0.61	0.36	0.29
Seattle	Pacific Northwest	0.63	0.51	0.37	0.24	0.15
Sioux Falls	North Central	0.68	0.76	0.59	0.50	0.47
Springfield	Illinois	0.47	0.53	0.46	0.20	0.14
Springfield	Kansas-Missouri	0.51	0.45	0.38	0.30	0.16
Stamford	Connecticut-Rhode Island	0.60	0.45	0.36	0.28	0.18
Syracuse	Upstate New York	0.36	0.37	0.31	0.18	0.14
Tampa	North Florida	0.52	0.45	0.29	0.24	0.14
Tucson	Southwest	0.80	0.81	0.61	0.36	0.29
Tulsa	Arkansas-Oklahoma	0.72	0.63	0.58	0.35	0.21
Virginia Beach	Virginia-West Virginia	0.42	0.39	0.29	0.22	0.13
Washington	Delaware-Maryland	0.53	0.53	0.42	0.25	0.13
Wichita	Kansas-Missouri	0.51	0.45	0.38	0.30	0.16
U.S.	U.S.	0.66	0.61	0.46	0.31	0.20

Note: Figures cover IRS district audits of federal income tax returns filed by individuals. Geographic data on district audits for 2001 and 2002 is being withheld by the IRS, TRAC is challenging this policy.
Source: Syracuse University, Transactional Records Access Clearinghouse (TRAC), "Odds of IRS District Tax Audit 2000"

Personal Bankruptcy Filing Rate

City	Area Covered	2002	2003
Albuquerque	Bernalillo County	5.35	5.58
Alexandria	City of Alexandria	3.28	3.08
Anchorage	Anchorage Borough	2.70	2.58
Ann Arbor	Washtenaw County	3.29	3.81
Atlanta	Fulton County	6.02	6.43
Austin	Travis County	3.23	3.86
Baltimore	City of Baltimore	9.03	9.46
Baton Rouge	East Baton Rouge Parish	5.26	5.66
Bellevue	King County	4.45	4.72
Birmingham	Jefferson County	12.48	13.47
Boise City	Ada County	7.22	7.57
Boston	Suffolk County	2.30	2.44
Boulder	Boulder County	2.85	3.30
Buffalo	Erie County	5.14	6.08
Cedar Rapids	Linn County	4.20	4.23
Charleston	Charleston County	2.82	2.89
Charlotte	Mecklenburg County	3.16	3.72
Chattanooga	Hamilton County	10.34	9.94
Chicago	Cook County	6.99	7.00
Cincinnati	Hamilton County	6.66	6.75
Cleveland	Cuyahoga County	7.91	9.10
Colorado Springs	El Paso County	5.78	6.65
Columbia	Richland County	4.44	4.85
Columbus	Franklin County	8.13	9.35
Dallas	Dallas County	4.12	4.53
Denver	Denver County	4.59	5.31
Des Moines	Polk County	5.11	5.41
Detroit	Wayne County	7.88	8.83
Durham	Durham County	5.43	5.72
El Paso	El Paso County	4.28	4.52
Eugene	Lane County	6.49	6.95
Fort Collins	Larimer County	4.43	5.09
Fort Lauderdale	Broward County	5.91	5.56
Fort Wayne	Allen County	7.47	8.27
Fort Worth	Tarrant County	4.99	6.28
Grand Rapids	Kent County	4.63	4.77
Green Bay	Brown County	3.91	4.51
Greensboro	Guilford County	4.49	4.67
Honolulu	Honolulu County	3.66	2.98
Houston	Harris County	3.06	3.67
Huntsville	Madison County	6.68	6.92
Indianapolis	Marion County	12.02	12.50
Irvine	Orange County	3.26	3.07
Jacksonville	Duval County	6.90	7.19
Kansas City	Jackson County	7.20	7.80
Knoxville	Knox County	6.48	6.71
Las Vegas	Clark County	9.89	10.41
Lexington	Fayette County	4.75	5.11
Lincoln	Lancaster County	4.27	4.96
Los Angeles	Los Angeles County	4.77	4.24
Louisville	Jefferson County	8.32	9.08
Madison	Dane County	3.44	3.87
Manchester	Hillsborough County	2.99	3.26

Personal Bankruptcy Filing Rate *continued*

City	Area Covered	2002	2003
Memphis	Shelby County	19.99	20.22
Miami	Miami-Dade County	6.53	6.42
Milwaukee	Milwaukee County	7.80	8.69
Minneapolis	Hennepin County	3.97	4.29
Naperville	DuPage County	3.44	3.57
Nashville	Davidson County	8.85	9.07
New Orleans	Orleans Parish	6.22	6.24
New York	Bronx County	3.76	4.36
New York	Kings County	3.07	3.24
New York	New York County	2.59	2.95
New York	Queens County	3.38	3.57
New York	Richmond County	3.08	2.91
Norfolk	City of Norfolk	7.52	7.74
Oklahoma City	Oklahoma County	8.62	9.47
Omaha	Douglas County	5.76	6.08
Orlando	Orange County	6.02	6.05
Overland Park	Johnson County	4.22	4.59
Philadelphia	Philadelphia County	6.35	6.57
Phoenix	Maricopa County	5.93	6.33
Pittsburgh	Allegheny County	4.84	5.35
Plano	Collin County	6.29	7.26
Portland	Multnomah County	6.80	6.76
Providence	Providence County	4.96	4.64
Provo	Utah County	6.84	7.23
Raleigh	Wake County	4.08	4.68
Reno	Washoe County	6.94	6.84
Richmond	City of Richmond	9.10	9.63
Rochester	Monroe County	4.14	4.27
Sacramento	Sacramento County	5.02	4.71
Saint Louis	City of Saint Louis	9.35	9.41
Saint Paul	Ramsey County	3.87	4.10
Saint Petersburg	Pinellas County	5.72	5.89
Salt Lake City	Salt Lake County	11.26	10.90
San Antonio	Bexar County	3.36	3.80
San Diego	San Diego County	4.14	3.73
San Francisco	San Francisco County	2.37	2.56
San Jose	Santa Clara County	2.47	2.87
Savannah	Chatham County	10.74	10.68
Scottsdale	Maricopa County	5.93	6.33
Seattle	King County	4.45	4.72
Sioux Falls	Minnehaha County	5.42	5.86
Springfield	Sangamon County	7.43	7.87
Springfield	Greene County	5.59	5.61
Stamford	Fairfield County	2.10	2.30
Syracuse	Onondaga County	5.56	6.28
Tampa	Hillsborough County	6.35	6.51
Tucson	Pima County	4.85	5.06
Tulsa	Tulsa County	6.70	7.85
Virginia Beach	City of Virginia Beach	7.53	7.37
Washington	District of Columbia	n/a	n/a
Wichita	Sedgwick County	6.76	6.94
U.S.	U.S.	5.34	5.58

Note: Numbers are per 1,000 population and include Chapter 7 and Chapter 13 filings; n/a not available
Source: Federal Deposit Insurance Corporation (FDIC),Regional Economic Conditions (RECON), 2/25/2004

Building Permits

City	Single-Family			Multi-Family			Total		
	2001	2002	Pct. Chg	2001	2002	Pct. Chg	2001	2002	Pct. Chg
Albuquerque	3,671	4,217	14.9	670	1,212	80.9	4,341	5,429	25.1
Alexandria	401	380	-5.2	928	864	-6.9	1,329	1,244	-6.4
Anchorage	1,055	923	-12.5	910	1,065	17.0	1,965	1,988	1.2
Ann Arbor	126	315	150.0	226	6	-97.3	352	321	-8.8
Atlanta	781	759	-2.8	6,013	5,890	-2.0	6,794	6,649	-2.1
Austin	2,119	2,431	14.7	4,603	3,943	-14.3	6,722	6,374	-5.2
Baltimore	115	181	57.4	80	112	40.0	195	293	50.3
Baton Rouge	215	260	20.9	134	445	232.1	349	705	102.0
Bellevue	147	150	2.0	359	268	-25.3	506	418	-17.4
Birmingham	108	188	74.1	24	76	216.7	132	264	100.0
Boise City	797	718	-9.9	995	675	-32.2	1,792	1,393	-22.3
Boston	78	71	-9.0	805	701	-12.9	883	772	-12.6
Boulder	51	74	45.1	163	219	34.4	214	293	36.9
Buffalo	59	123	108.5	206	16	-92.2	265	139	-47.5
Cedar Rapids	363	380	4.7	470	249	-47.0	833	629	-24.5
Charleston	782	1,053	34.7	144	380	163.9	926	1,433	54.8
Charlotte[1]	8,345	8,357	0.1	4,292	2,249	-47.6	12,637	10,606	-16.1
Chattanooga	533	549	3.0	360	159	-55.8	893	708	-20.7
Chicago	883	754	-14.6	5,786	7,774	34.4	6,669	8,528	27.9
Cincinnati	104	125	20.2	232	633	172.8	336	758	125.6
Cleveland	328	345	5.2	61	94	54.1	389	439	12.9
Colorado Springs[2]	5,254	4,999	-4.9	1,862	1,828	-1.8	7,116	6,827	-4.1
Columbia	443	398	-10.2	0	258	-	443	656	48.1
Columbus	3,058	3,196	4.5	3,815	4,716	23.6	6,873	7,912	15.1
Dallas	1,913	2,024	5.8	3,237	4,054	25.2	5,150	6,078	18.0
Denver	1,011	1,641	62.3	3,447	2,985	-13.4	4,458	4,626	3.8
Des Moines	283	342	20.8	86	154	79.1	369	496	34.4
Detroit	56	184	228.6	81	373	360.5	137	557	306.6
Durham	1,633	1,590	-2.6	1,565	1,110	-29.1	3,198	2,700	-15.6
El Paso	2,964	3,180	7.3	121	171	41.3	3,085	3,351	8.6
Eugene	633	673	6.3	127	155	22.0	760	828	8.9
Fort Collins	1,116	1,210	8.4	735	310	-57.8	1,851	1,520	-17.9
Fort Lauderdale	189	232	22.8	286	2,691	840.9	475	2,923	515.4
Fort Wayne	265	312	17.7	331	85	-74.3	596	397	-33.4
Fort Worth	5,026	6,649	32.3	832	1,460	75.5	5,858	8,109	38.4
Grand Rapids	225	197	-12.4	16	452	2,725.0	241	649	169.3
Green Bay	213	197	-7.5	182	262	44.0	395	459	16.2
Greensboro	1,349	1,339	-0.7	958	905	-5.5	2,307	2,244	-2.7
Honolulu[3]	1,673	1,964	17.4	302	709	134.8	1,975	2,673	35.3
Houston	4,366	4,547	4.1	5,521	6,673	20.9	9,887	11,220	13.5
Huntsville	400	514	28.5	558	172	-69.2	958	686	-28.4
Indianapolis	4,765	3,532	-25.9	1,108	1,731	56.2	5,873	5,263	-10.4
Irvine	1,338	1,006	-24.8	709	2,439	244.0	2,047	3,445	68.3
Jacksonville	4,832	5,397	11.7	1,765	2,612	48.0	6,597	8,009	21.4
Kansas City	1,208	1,507	24.8	973	1,146	17.8	2,181	2,653	21.6
Knoxville	336	327	-2.7	208	337	62.0	544	664	22.1
Las Vegas	4,295	4,454	3.7	880	1,110	26.1	5,175	5,564	7.5
Lexington	1,649	2,142	29.9	109	179	64.2	1,758	2,321	32.0
Lincoln	1,305	1,407	7.8	331	366	10.6	1,636	1,773	8.4
Los Angeles	1,596	1,215	-23.9	5,599	4,458	-20.4	7,195	5,673	-21.2
Louisville	277	146	-47.3	213	172	-19.2	490	318	-35.1
Madison	843	998	18.4	1,649	1,001	-39.3	2,492	1,999	-19.8
Manchester	105	180	71.4	171	539	215.2	276	719	160.5

Building Permits *continued*

City	Single-Family			Multi-Family			Total		
	2001	2002	Pct. Chg	2001	2002	Pct. Chg	2001	2002	Pct. Chg
Memphis[4]	3,450	4,147	20.2	1,310	1,189	-9.2	4,760	5,336	12.1
Miami	79	112	41.8	2,754	2,962	7.6	2,833	3,074	8.5
Milwaukee	154	150	-2.6	406	574	41.4	560	724	29.3
Minneapolis	226	237	4.9	519	1,652	218.3	745	1,889	153.6
Naperville	764	671	-12.2	298	396	32.9	1,062	1,067	0.5
Nashville	2,869	2,757	-3.9	547	588	7.5	3,416	3,345	-2.1
New Orleans	455	438	-3.7	172	178	3.5	627	616	-1.8
New York	1,701	1,337	-21.4	15,155	17,163	13.2	16,856	18,500	9.8
Norfolk	227	276	21.6	181	341	88.4	408	617	51.2
Oklahoma City	2,373	2,997	26.3	828	254	-69.3	3,201	3,251	1.6
Omaha	2,175	2,282	4.9	515	829	61.0	2,690	3,111	15.7
Orlando	447	699	56.4	1,059	2,833	167.5	1,506	3,532	134.5
Overland Park	927	793	-14.5	1,466	42	-97.1	2,393	835	-65.1
Philadelphia	104	147	41.3	668	407	-39.1	772	554	-28.2
Phoenix	5,501	7,116	29.4	4,132	2,159	-47.7	9,633	9,275	-3.7
Pittsburgh	86	145	68.6	65	496	663.1	151	641	324.5
Plano	1,692	1,090	-35.6	0	0	0.0	1,692	1,090	-35.6
Portland	1,040	1,088	4.6	632	1,246	97.2	1,672	2,334	39.6
Providence	36	35	-2.8	13	24	84.6	49	59	20.4
Provo	188	281	49.5	379	300	-20.8	567	581	2.5
Raleigh	3,648	3,807	4.4	2,665	569	-78.6	6,313	4,376	-30.7
Reno	1,453	1,425	-1.9	461	594	28.9	1,914	2,019	5.5
Richmond	179	161	-10.1	104	355	241.3	283	516	82.3
Rochester	40	38	-5.0	13	34	161.5	53	72	35.8
Sacramento	2,739	3,242	18.4	853	1,491	74.8	3,592	4,733	31.8
Saint Louis	126	150	19.0	52	141	171.2	178	291	63.5
Saint Paul	116	129	11.2	477	501	5.0	593	630	6.2
Saint Petersburg	334	291	-12.9	1,157	22	-98.1	1,491	313	-79.0
Salt Lake City	212	144	-32.1	501	330	-34.1	713	474	-33.5
San Antonio	6,281	6,454	2.8	3,443	2,552	-25.9	9,724	9,006	-7.4
San Diego	2,209	2,588	17.2	3,948	3,683	-6.7	6,157	6,271	1.9
San Francisco	94	82	-12.8	1,097	1,161	5.8	1,191	1,243	4.4
San Jose	540	620	14.8	2,835	1,845	-34.9	3,375	2,465	-27.0
Savannah	127	139	9.4	40	55	37.5	167	194	16.2
Scottsdale	1,672	1,328	-20.6	969	595	-38.6	2,641	1,923	-27.2
Seattle	484	886	83.1	3,162	2,884	-8.8	3,646	3,770	3.4
Sioux Falls	1,116	1,085	-2.8	683	364	-46.7	1,799	1,449	-19.5
Springfield	304	316	3.9	101	200	98.0	405	516	27.4
Springfield	404	486	20.3	129	530	310.9	533	1,016	90.6
Stamford	46	82	78.3	348	137	-60.6	394	219	-44.4
Syracuse	17	16	-5.9	5	0	-100.0	22	16	-27.3
Tampa	1,736	1,675	-3.5	1,359	1,070	-21.3	3,095	2,745	-11.3
Tucson	2,564	2,407	-6.1	692	791	14.3	3,256	3,198	-1.8
Tulsa	590	444	-24.7	93	372	300.0	683	816	19.5
Virginia Beach	1,636	1,896	15.9	203	440	116.7	1,839	2,336	27.0
Washington	131	383	192.4	765	1,208	57.9	896	1,591	77.6
Wichita	1,257	1,420	13.0	142	185	30.3	1,399	1,605	14.7
U.S.	1,235,600	1,332,600	7.9	401,100	415,100	3.5	1,636,700	1,747,700	6.8

Note: Figures represent new, privately-owned housing units authorized (unadjusted data); Figures are for the city except where noted;
(1) Mecklenburg County; (2) El Paso County; (3) Honolulu County; (4) Shelby County
Source: U.S. Census Bureau, Manufacturing, Mining, and Construction Statistics

Homeownership and Housing Vacancies

MSA[1]	Homeownership Rate[2] (%)			Rental Vacancy Rate[3] (%)			Homeowner Vacancy Rate[4] (%)		
	2001	2002[a]	2003	2001	2002[a]	2003	2001	2002[a]	2003
Alexandria	69.5	68.8	69.6	6.9	8.3	9.6	1.4	1.5	2.5
Atlanta	66.6	69.0	67.9	11.9	15.0	16.8	2.0	1.9	3.4
Austin	57.7	56.0	59.1	8.8	12.0	14.8	1.1	1.9	1.4
Baltimore	68.0	71.8	70.4	9.9	8.5	8.8	2.7	1.4	1.1
Bellevue	66.0	64.3	62.9	8.6	8.9	12.7	0.9	1.4	1.5
Birmingham	70.8	68.7	71.3	17.6	12.3	15.4	2.3	2.2	1.4
Boston	59.0	59.7	59.9	2.9	4.3	5.9	0.7	0.3	0.6
Buffalo	75.1	72.8	69.1	19.8	13.2	8.1	1.7	0.5	2.5
Charlotte	73.6	73.1	74.0	9.5	11.6	14.5	2.7	3.2	2.5
Chicago	67.8	67.6	68.6	9.1	11.4	13.7	1.7	2.0	1.6
Cincinnati	71.6	72.0	73.0	11.5	10.1	10.6	1.8	1.5	1.7
Cleveland	72.8	73.1	72.4	12.2	15.5	15.8	1.0	1.4	1.7
Columbus	64.7	67.8	68.1	11.0	12.7	15.4	2.2	2.1	1.5
Dallas	62.8	61.1	63.1	6.5	11.6	12.4	2.0	1.4	2.0
Denver	67.7	69.0	71.9	6.0	8.7	12.9	1.8	2.4	1.8
Detroit	76.1	75.6	75.3	9.9	12.1	11.8	1.5	1.9	1.6
Durham	62.9	63.6	66.0	13.0	13.2	18.1	5.9	2.9	1.3
Fort Lauderdale	76.1	73.7	74.0	7.1	6.0	8.1	2.4	2.4	1.5
Fort Worth	62.3	61.3	65.1	8.1	11.2	14.0	0.7	1.5	1.4
Grand Rapids	78.9	72.5	70.5	12.9	8.8	9.9	1.3	0.6	1.0
Greensboro	70.4	70.5	70.4	8.8	12.1	12.4	2.3	2.2	2.3
Honolulu	55.4	57.0	56.9	8.0	5.5	7.0	0.6	1.0	0.9
Houston	55.9	56.5	56.6	11.1	12.9	15.8	1.3	1.1	1.9
Indianapolis	70.9	74.5	72.9	9.1	11.1	12.4	2.4	3.0	2.2
Irvine	65.8	65.5	63.4	3.9	5.1	5.9	1.3	0.9	0.5
Jacksonville	68.4	66.1	67.2	4.6	7.3	9.7	0.6	0.8	4.8
Kansas City	75.0	75.1	76.9	9.2	11.3	11.0	2.0	1.3	2.4
Las Vegas	62.1	62.2	62.9	13.2	10.9	11.4	2.0	2.1	2.2
Los Angeles	50.1	50.2	50.0	3.4	3.9	3.2	1.2	0.8	0.8
Louisville	75.7	73.4	70.3	10.8	7.2	8.5	1.1	1.8	0.7
Memphis	66.4	66.1	65.8	8.8	12.2	12.2	2.6	2.1	1.5
Miami	58.8	55.1	55.9	8.3	7.9	8.8	1.6	1.5	1.9
Milwaukee	66.4	67.8	70.0	5.3	7.6	11.8	1.0	1.4	0.8
Minneapolis	73.5	74.1	75.2	5.1	6.1	8.1	0.5	0.7	1.3
Naperville	67.8	67.6	68.6	9.1	11.4	13.7	1.7	2.0	1.6
Nashville	67.7	69.6	68.9	7.5	7.1	7.8	2.3	2.0	2.5
New Orleans	62.0	60.1	61.5	8.2	8.1	7.6	1.8	0.8	0.7
New York	33.4	34.6	35.9	3.6	4.6	4.4	1.5	2.3	1.4
Norfolk	71.5	74.9	79.6	7.0	3.5	10.3	2.0	1.4	1.3
Oklahoma City	69.1	68.7	67.4	9.7	11.9	13.2	1.9	2.3	1.5
Omaha	67.6	67.8	68.2	10.0	12.1	10.0	1.4	0.8	0.9
Orlando	63.0	65.5	66.6	9.2	9.7	14.6	1.1	1.4	2.2
Overland Park	75.0	75.1	76.9	9.2	11.3	11.0	2.0	1.3	2.4
Philadelphia	73.6	73.7	73.2	9.5	8.6	10.9	1.1	1.6	1.4
Phoenix	69.2	68.9	69.4	10.0	13.2	12.0	2.4	2.3	2.0
Pittsburgh	71.8	71.8	71.4	5.8	9.1	10.5	1.0	1.5	1.6
Plano	62.8	61.1	63.1	6.5	11.6	12.4	2.0	1.4	2.0
Portland	65.3	65.9	66.1	7.1	9.3	10.8	3.6	1.9	2.2
Providence	59.6	59.4	59.0	4.9	4.9	5.6	0.7	0.5	1.0
Raleigh	62.9	63.6	66.0	13.0	13.2	18.1	5.9	2.9	1.3
Richmond	76.2	70.7	69.6	10.0	8.7	12.3	0.6	1.0	1.3
Rochester	63.8	65.0	65.6	7.9	8.4	9.1	3.0	1.1	0.9

Homeownership and Housing Vacancies *continued*

MSA[1]	Homeownership Rate[2] (%)			Rental Vacancy Rate[3] (%)			Homeowner Vacancy Rate[4] (%)		
	2001	2002[a]	2003	2001	2002[a]	2003	2001	2002[a]	2003
Sacramento	66.4	65.1	65.3	8.6	6.6	7.2	1.1	1.1	1.7
Saint Louis	70.9	73.0	73.3	17.8	6.2	8.4	1.6	1.7	2.2
Saint Paul	73.5	74.1	75.2	5.1	6.1	8.1	0.5	0.7	1.3
Saint Petersburg	70.7	70.5	69.8	12.0	11.1	9.9	2.0	1.9	1.8
Salt Lake City	72.9	75.3	74.7	7.0	7.4	9.4	1.9	1.5	3.0
San Antonio	67.4	68.3	69.9	12.2	14.7	13.9	1.0	0.8	1.4
San Diego	64.0	63.2	62.7	4.5	7.8	6.0	0.7	2.1	1.3
San Francisco	48.6	46.0	50.8	3.4	5.4	7.8	0.2	1.1	1.2
San Jose	63.0	56.9	59.4	5.2	6.6	9.5	1.2	0.9	2.3
Scottsdale	69.2	68.9	69.4	10.0	13.2	12.0	2.4	2.3	2.0
Seattle	66.0	64.3	62.9	8.6	8.9	12.7	0.9	1.4	1.5
Syracuse	59.2	59.2	60.2	13.9	12.6	18.1	3.4	2.1	0.8
Tampa	70.7	70.5	69.8	12.0	11.1	9.9	2.0	1.9	1.8
Tucson	64.4	60.5	61.1	13.1	10.6	11.8	0.9	1.4	1.9
Tulsa	66.1	62.1	62.5	7.1	13.1	10.5	1.7	3.0	3.3
Virginia Beach	71.5	74.9	79.6	7.0	3.5	10.3	2.0	1.4	1.3
Washington	69.5	68.8	69.6	6.9	8.3	9.6	1.4	1.5	2.5
U.S.	67.8	67.9	68.3	8.4	8.9	9.8	1.8	1.7	1.8

Note: (1) Metropolitan Statistical Area - see Appendix A for areas included; (2) The proportion of households that are owners; (3) The proportion of the rental inventory that is vacant for rent; (4) The proportion of the homeowner inventory that is vacant for sale; (a) 2002 figures have been revised; n/a not available
Source: U.S. Census Bureau, Housing Vacancies and Homeownership Annual Statistics: 2003

Employment by Industry

MSA[1]	(2)	(3)	(4)	(5)	(6)	(7)	(8)	(9)	(10)	(11)	(12)	(13)	(14)
Albuquerque	20.1	12.0	15.8	12.0	6.3	9.6	5.2	n/a	3.5	3.2	2.9	2.8	n/a
Alexandria	22.3	10.6	20.8	9.6	2.5	8.4	5.6	n/a	2.4	5.6	2.3	3.8	n/a
Anchorage	21.4	12.6	10.9	12.7	1.2	10.2	6.1	5.5	3.1	3.9	7.5	3.3	1.5
Ann Arbor	27.8	10.5	12.9	10.8	14.1	7.4	3.8	n/a	2.6	2.9	1.6	1.8	n/a
Atlanta	13.4	9.9	15.7	11.5	7.7	9.3	6.7	5.4	6.3	4.3	5.3	4.5	0.1
Austin	22.2	10.1	13.0	10.9	8.7	9.7	6.1	5.3	5.2	3.8	1.6	3.1	0.2
Baltimore	17.5	16.3	13.7	11.9	6.2	8.5	6.5	n/a	4.2	4.5	3.3	1.6	n/a
Baton Rouge	19.5	11.2	11.6	11.8	6.9	9.3	5.5	10.5	4.1	3.6	3.6	1.8	0.4
Bellevue	15.2	10.2	13.5	11.2	10.8	8.7	6.8	5.6	5.1	3.6	3.7	5.4	0.1
Birmingham	15.5	11.3	12.5	12.4	8.2	8.0	8.2	n/a	6.0	4.7	3.6	2.9	n/a
Boise City	15.6	12.7	14.1	12.3	12.7	8.7	5.4	n/a	4.2	2.9	3.0	1.7	n/a
Boston	11.9	19.0	16.0	10.5	8.2	8.4	8.5	4.1	4.2	3.5	2.5	3.2	<0.1
Boulder	18.6	10.1	16.1	10.5	12.7	9.3	4.8	n/a	3.2	3.1	1.3	6.2	n/a
Buffalo	17.5	15.4	11.4	11.9	12.2	8.4	6.2	n/a	4.0	4.2	3.5	1.8	n/a
Cedar Rapids	10.7	14.1	9.4	12.4	14.9	7.5	7.8	n/a	3.6	3.9	6.2	4.7	n/a
Charleston	19.9	11.1	12.8	12.8	7.9	11.6	4.2	n/a	3.1	2.9	4.6	1.3	n/a
Charlotte	13.2	8.6	14.3	11.1	12.3	8.3	8.4	6.1	5.7	4.3	4.6	3.0	0.1
Chattanooga	15.3	9.8	10.9	11.6	14.8	8.1	7.6	n/a	3.8	4.5	8.7	1.2	n/a
Chicago	12.6	12.0	15.5	10.9	11.2	8.2	7.7	4.9	5.7	4.3	4.5	2.3	<0.1
Cincinnati	12.4	12.8	14.9	11.6	12.2	9.8	6.4	n/a	5.3	4.1	4.2	1.7	n/a
Cleveland	13.6	15.5	11.9	11.2	14.4	8.5	7.3	n/a	4.8	3.9	3.0	1.9	n/a
Colorado Spgs.	17.3	9.7	14.0	12.0	8.6	10.9	7.3	n/a	2.3	5.7	1.8	4.3	n/a
Columbia	24.5	11.1	11.0	11.9	7.7	8.9	8.4	n/a	3.9	3.0	2.4	1.9	n/a
Columbus	16.8	11.1	13.7	13.0	8.1	9.3	8.7	n/a	4.3	4.1	4.0	2.3	n/a
Dallas	12.6	10.0	14.2	11.6	10.3	8.9	8.9	5.0	6.4	3.8	3.9	4.1	0.3
Denver	14.3	10.1	15.1	10.9	6.1	9.3	8.9	6.7	5.4	3.8	4.3	4.7	0.4
Des Moines	13.1	12.7	10.5	12.8	6.2	7.6	15.7	5.0	5.6	4.0	3.5	3.3	0.1
Detroit	11.7	12.2	17.1	11.4	15.6	8.8	5.7	n/a	4.7	3.7	3.3	1.8	n/a
Durham	19.8	12.2	14.9	11.1	9.9	8.2	4.6	5.5	4.0	4.5	1.9	3.2	0.2
El Paso	23.8	11.2	9.8	13.4	9.9	9.1	4.6	n/a	3.8	2.8	4.8	2.1	n/a
Eugene	18.9	13.0	10.5	13.6	12.9	9.4	5.3	4.5	3.6	3.5	1.9	2.4	0.6
Ft. Collins	n/a	n/a	n/a	n/a	n/a	n/a	n/a	n/a	n/a	n/a	n/a	n/a	n/a
Ft. Lauderdale	13.7	11.1	17.9	13.8	4.2	10.3	7.9	n/a	5.4	4.2	2.6	2.6	n/a
Ft. Wayne	9.6	13.2	8.3	11.6	21.8	9.0	5.4	n/a	5.2	4.8	4.2	1.6	n/a
Ft. Worth	14.1	10.8	10.7	12.2	12.3	9.6	5.8	5.4	4.7	4.1	7.4	2.3	0.5
Grand Rapids	10.6	13.4	11.3	11.7	22.4	8.4	4.0	4.7	5.3	4.1	2.5	1.5	0.1
Green Bay	11.7	12.2	8.7	11.0	18.1	9.4	7.2	n/a	3.9	4.1	6.9	1.7	n/a
Greensboro	11.7	13.7	11.3	11.1	18.4	8.5	5.5	4.7	4.7	4.2	4.6	1.6	0.1
Honolulu	22.7	12.5	13.4	10.9	2.7	13.9	5.1	n/a	3.3	4.5	4.6	1.9	n/a
Houston	14.2	11.3	13.7	10.9	8.9	8.4	6.0	7.4	5.4	4.0	5.0	1.7	3.0
Huntsville	21.8	6.6	19.3	11.9	15.9	8.3	3.0	n/a	2.8	3.9	1.4	1.2	n/a
Indianapolis	13.2	11.7	12.6	11.5	12.0	9.9	7.5	5.8	5.3	3.5	5.2	1.8	0.1
Irvine	10.7	8.7	17.8	11.4	12.5	11.0	8.6	5.9	5.8	3.3	1.9	2.3	<0.1
Jacksonville	12.7	11.4	14.8	12.7	5.7	9.2	10.2	6.4	4.9	4.6	5.1	2.2	0.1
Kansas City	14.6	11.5	12.8	11.6	8.7	9.4	7.4	n/a	5.0	4.4	4.6	4.9	n/a
Knoxville	16.7	10.7	11.0	14.1	11.6	12.5	5.1	n/a	4.5	4.2	3.0	1.7	n/a
Las Vegas	11.1	6.9	11.2	12.0	3.1	29.6	5.6	10.0	2.7	2.7	3.7	1.4	0.2
Lexington	20.3	12.4	10.0	11.8	14.4	9.8	3.9	n/a	3.7	3.8	2.7	2.1	n/a
Lincoln	23.0	12.6	9.5	10.8	9.7	9.8	6.9	n/a	2.5	4.0	4.2	2.1	n/a
Los Angeles	14.8	11.7	14.4	10.5	12.2	9.1	6.0	3.3	5.3	3.6	4.0	4.9	0.1
Louisville	12.5	12.6	11.3	11.3	12.8	9.4	6.7	n/a	4.7	5.3	6.4	1.9	n/a
Madison	24.7	9.9	10.3	11.6	9.0	7.9	8.6	n/a	3.6	4.9	2.4	2.3	n/a
Manchester	11.4	14.8	12.8	14.1	10.3	7.8	7.8	n/a	5.5	3.8	3.3	2.8	n/a

Employment by Industry *continued*

MSA[1]	(2)	(3)	(4)	(5)	(6)	(7)	(8)	(9)	(10)	(11)	(12)	(13)	(14)
Memphis	14.8	11.6	12.3	11.9	8.4	8.7	5.4	n/a	6.3	4.0	10.6	1.6	n/a
Miami	15.1	13.0	14.4	12.0	5.1	9.2	6.7	4.1	6.9	4.2	6.4	2.7	<0.1
Milwaukee	11.2	16.1	12.0	10.1	16.1	7.6	7.4	3.7	4.8	4.8	3.7	2.3	<0.1
Minneapolis	13.6	12.6	13.8	11.1	11.8	8.8	8.0	4.6	4.9	4.5	3.8	2.6	<0.1
Naperville	12.6	12.0	15.5	10.9	11.2	8.2	7.7	4.9	5.7	4.3	4.5	2.3	<0.1
Nashville	13.3	13.6	11.9	11.9	11.4	10.4	6.5	n/a	5.1	4.4	3.9	2.8	n/a
New Orleans	17.1	13.9	11.6	11.2	6.6	13.1	5.8	5.1	4.3	3.7	4.6	1.5	1.5
New York	15.7	18.8	14.7	8.7	3.7	7.4	11.3	n/a	4.2	4.1	3.3	4.5	n/a
Norfolk	20.4	10.6	13.6	12.9	8.0	9.9	5.0	n/a	3.1	4.6	3.5	2.2	n/a
Oklahoma City	20.4	12.8	12.4	11.9	7.0	9.7	6.3	4.1	3.8	5.1	2.7	2.4	1.3
Omaha	12.7	13.8	13.8	12.5	7.5	9.0	8.6	n/a	4.4	3.5	5.7	3.2	n/a
Orlando	11.2	10.1	16.6	11.8	4.3	18.2	6.1	6.7	4.5	4.9	2.9	2.6	0.1
Overland Park	14.6	11.5	12.8	11.6	8.7	9.4	7.4	n/a	5.0	4.4	4.6	4.9	n/a
Philadelphia	12.8	18.5	13.6	11.9	9.0	7.3	7.4	n/a	4.8	4.6	3.5	2.5	n/a
Phoenix	13.7	10.1	15.8	12.3	7.8	9.6	8.2	8.2	4.7	3.7	3.6	2.2	0.1
Pittsburgh	11.6	18.9	11.6	12.7	9.4	8.9	6.2	n/a	4.0	5.1	4.2	2.2	n/a
Plano	12.6	10.0	14.2	11.6	10.3	8.9	8.9	5.0	6.4	3.8	3.9	4.1	0.3
Portland	14.1	12.3	12.6	11.0	12.6	8.8	7.3	5.2	5.8	3.7	4.0	2.5	0.2
Providence	13.0	18.6	9.8	12.5	13.5	9.2	6.5	4.4	3.5	4.7	2.4	2.0	<0.1
Provo	14.6	21.9	11.5	13.1	10.4	7.6	3.9	n/a	2.3	2.5	1.2	4.2	n/a
Raleigh	19.8	12.2	14.9	11.1	9.9	8.2	4.6	5.5	4.0	4.5	1.9	3.2	0.2
Reno	13.4	9.3	11.6	11.3	6.6	18.8	5.3	8.5	5.2	3.2	5.1	1.6	0.1
Richmond	18.7	10.8	14.5	11.8	7.8	7.5	8.2	n/a	4.5	4.4	3.2	2.0	n/a
Rochester	16.7	18.8	10.6	11.7	15.4	7.5	4.2	3.4	3.5	3.7	1.8	2.6	0.1
Sacramento	25.1	10.0	11.8	12.1	5.1	9.5	7.5	8.1	2.7	3.4	1.9	2.7	0.1
Salt Lake City	17.7	9.6	13.5	12.3	9.9	8.4	7.3	n/a	4.6	3.2	4.6	2.8	n/a
San Antonio	18.8	13.4	11.8	12.1	6.1	10.6	8.2	5.5	3.7	3.7	2.6	3.3	0.3
San Diego	17.5	9.9	16.2	11.6	8.3	11.1	6.5	6.5	3.3	3.8	2.2	2.9	<0.1
San Francisco	13.6	10.5	18.6	10.3	4.8	11.7	9.5	4.6	2.9	4.0	4.8	4.8	<0.1
San Jose	11.0	11.1	19.2	9.9	20.2	7.8	4.1	4.4	3.9	2.9	1.6	3.6	<0.1
Savannah	15.0	13.6	11.1	12.6	9.4	12.5	4.5	n/a	3.5	4.9	5.6	1.3	n/a
Scottsdale	13.7	10.1	15.8	12.3	7.8	9.6	8.2	8.2	4.7	3.7	3.6	2.2	0.1
Seattle	15.2	10.2	13.5	11.2	10.8	8.7	6.8	5.6	5.1	3.6	3.7	5.4	0.1
Sioux Falls	8.9	18.0	7.2	13.8	10.2	9.6	12.5	n/a	4.9	4.2	3.6	2.1	n/a
Springfield (IL)	27.1	14.5	9.6	11.3	3.2	9.0	6.8	n/a	3.5	5.7	1.9	2.9	n/a
Springfield (MO)	12.3	17.5	8.2	13.9	9.9	9.1	6.1	n/a	5.4	4.6	5.6	2.9	n/a
St. Louis	12.7	15.0	13.8	11.6	11.1	9.9	6.0	n/a	4.2	4.3	3.4	2.2	n/a
St. Paul	13.6	12.6	13.8	11.1	11.8	8.8	8.0	4.6	4.9	4.5	3.8	2.6	<0.1
St. Petersburg	12.2	11.7	23.9	11.7	5.7	8.8	7.6	5.6	3.9	3.9	2.4	2.7	<0.1
Stamford	9.5	11.5	22.6	12.1	5.3	8.1	13.9	n/a	3.7	4.5	2.3	3.3	n/a
Syracuse	18.6	16.7	10.0	11.9	10.9	7.9	5.1	n/a	4.7	4.1	4.4	2.1	n/a
Tampa	12.2	11.7	23.9	11.7	5.7	8.8	7.6	5.6	3.9	3.9	2.4	2.7	<0.1
Tucson	22.7	13.3	12.0	11.9	8.1	10.4	4.3	6.6	2.0	4.1	2.2	2.2	0.3
Tulsa	11.9	13.4	12.2	11.9	11.9	8.5	6.3	4.7	4.3	5.4	5.5	3.0	1.0
Virginia Beach	20.4	10.6	13.6	12.9	8.0	9.9	5.0	n/a	3.1	4.6	3.5	2.2	n/a
Washington	22.3	10.6	20.8	9.6	2.5	8.4	5.6	n/a	2.4	5.6	2.3	3.8	n/a
Wichita	13.8	13.4	9.5	11.2	20.7	8.8	4.4	5.4	4.0	4.2	2.2	2.1	0.3
U.S.	16.7	12.9	12.3	11.8	11.0	9.1	6.1	5.1	4.3	4.1	3.7	2.4	0.4

Note: All figures are percentages covering non-farm employment as of December 2003 and are not seasonally adjusted;
(1) Metropolitan Statistical Area - see Appendix A for areas included; (2) Government; (3) Education and Health Services;
(4) Professional and Business Services; (5) Retail Trade; (6) Manufacturing; (7) Leisure and Hospitality; (8) Finance Activities;
(9) Construction; (10) Wholesale Trade; (11) Other Services; (12) Transportation and Utilities; (13) Information;
(14) Natural Resources and Mining; n/a not available
Source: Bureau of Labor Statistics, http://stats.bls.gov

Labor Force, Employment and Job Growth: City

City	Civilian Labor Force			Workers Employed		
	Dec. 2002	Dec. 2003	% Chg.	Dec. 2002	Dec. 2003	% Chg.
Albuquerque	257,363	259,965	1.0	247,009	248,955	0.8
Alexandria	81,722	83,443	2.1	79,562	81,662	2.6
Anchorage	149,932	159,948	6.7	141,240	151,551	7.3
Ann Arbor	69,418	70,486	1.5	68,008	68,758	1.1
Atlanta	241,484	245,196	1.5	221,503	229,519	3.6
Austin	410,034	420,005	2.4	387,900	399,355	3.0
Baltimore	289,437	293,285	1.3	267,875	270,524	1.0
Baton Rouge	115,576	119,821	3.7	108,658	112,854	3.9
Bellevue	62,174	61,769	-0.7	59,431	59,170	-0.4
Birmingham	128,078	133,278	4.1	119,550	124,258	3.9
Boise City	113,497	111,205	-2.0	107,873	107,112	-0.7
Boston	313,250	308,074	-1.7	296,500	292,102	-1.5
Boulder	76,054	71,930	-5.4	71,726	68,230	-4.9
Buffalo	144,341	145,352	0.7	130,231	130,307	0.1
Cedar Rapids	77,482	76,008	-1.9	73,796	72,527	-1.7
Charleston	44,952	53,409	18.8	43,130	51,443	19.3
Charlotte	316,321	320,165	1.2	296,941	302,063	1.7
Chattanooga	80,303	79,318	-1.2	77,085	75,831	-1.6
Chicago	1,324,143	1,343,839	1.5	1,219,450	1,245,657	2.1
Cincinnati	171,760	175,319	2.1	161,215	164,046	1.8
Cleveland	203,047	205,731	1.3	180,319	181,799	0.8
Colorado Spgs.	209,285	206,017	-1.6	196,018	193,757	-1.2
Columbia	48,589	48,196	-0.8	46,060	45,461	-1.3
Columbus	408,078	411,538	0.8	388,571	392,239	0.9
Dallas	697,119	703,480	0.9	640,249	649,853	1.5
Denver	298,573	306,913	2.8	278,124	285,553	2.7
Des Moines	131,579	132,306	0.6	125,448	126,259	0.6
Detroit	374,830	389,501	3.9	332,413	338,297	1.8
Durham	92,947	93,049	0.1	87,113	88,571	1.7
El Paso	266,666	272,278	2.1	245,780	251,167	2.2
Eugene	71,700	71,772	0.1	67,729	67,553	-0.3
Ft. Collins	75,394	79,004	4.8	71,169	74,640	4.9
Ft. Lauderdale	105,616	104,678	-0.9	98,392	98,523	0.1
Ft. Wayne	102,401	105,990	3.5	96,210	99,417	3.3
Ft. Worth	291,840	294,724	1.0	270,240	273,911	1.4
Grand Rapids	114,971	119,214	3.7	105,671	107,815	2.0
Green Bay	64,247	66,123	2.9	59,355	61,834	4.2
Greensboro	122,315	122,961	0.5	114,573	116,020	1.3
Honolulu	414,418	431,529	4.1	400,898	416,527	3.9
Houston	1,081,601	1,114,017	3.0	1,008,041	1,033,619	2.5
Huntsville	98,254	100,001	1.8	94,296	94,939	0.7
Indianapolis	427,076	430,105	0.7	404,682	407,034	0.6
Irvine	74,216	75,554	1.8	72,221	73,863	2.3
Jacksonville	385,615	385,451	-0.0	365,490	365,658	0.0
Kansas City	264,537	264,571	0.0	245,560	247,918	1.0
Knoxville	99,236	98,441	-0.8	96,228	94,921	-1.4
Las Vegas	277,751	275,058	-1.0	263,995	263,234	-0.3
Lexington	140,615	141,837	0.9	136,173	137,603	1.1
Lincoln	140,589	142,160	1.1	136,204	137,002	0.6
Los Angeles	1,891,030	1,907,112	0.9	1,759,381	1,774,256	0.8
Louisville	126,165	132,241	4.8	120,124	123,207	2.6
Madison	138,220	144,381	4.5	134,675	141,154	4.8
Manchester	61,610	63,175	2.5	58,632	60,579	3.3

Labor Force, Employment and Job Growth: City *continued*

City	Civilian Labor Force			Workers Employed		
	Dec. 2002	Dec. 2003	% Chg.	Dec. 2002	Dec. 2003	% Chg.
Memphis	325,454	324,558	-0.3	306,656	301,316	-1.7
Miami	193,371	189,850	-1.8	173,873	173,194	-0.4
Milwaukee	269,738	269,873	0.1	245,656	248,522	1.2
Minneapolis	217,523	217,063	-0.2	208,789	207,300	-0.7
Naperville	70,031	71,342	1.9	66,491	67,920	2.1
Nashville	320,968	318,349	-0.8	309,755	305,361	-1.4
New Orleans	188,988	196,951	4.2	177,642	185,369	4.3
New York	3,752,118	3,668,848	-2.2	3,440,284	3,376,365	-1.9
Norfolk	89,560	91,078	1.7	84,358	85,868	1.8
Oklahoma City	266,601	262,853	-1.4	254,636	250,429	-1.7
Omaha	220,304	222,396	0.9	210,769	212,699	0.9
Orlando	125,458	126,358	0.7	119,200	120,657	1.2
Overland Park	88,504	91,455	3.3	85,386	88,226	3.3
Philadelphia	681,278	672,075	-1.4	632,172	628,525	-0.6
Phoenix	828,175	823,052	-0.6	780,348	786,307	0.8
Pittsburgh	166,289	162,784	-2.1	158,291	155,927	-1.5
Plano	155,194	156,134	0.6	147,455	149,667	1.5
Portland	280,720	274,299	-2.3	257,903	253,083	-1.9
Providence	76,006	75,858	-0.2	71,017	71,467	0.6
Provo	66,022	68,249	3.4	62,586	65,688	5.0
Raleigh	188,601	189,317	0.4	177,599	180,572	1.7
Reno	104,922	103,820	-1.1	100,581	99,557	-1.0
Richmond	97,411	98,334	0.9	91,866	93,168	1.4
Rochester	117,346	115,907	-1.2	106,068	105,236	-0.8
Sacramento	219,006	221,872	1.3	204,678	207,642	1.4
Salt Lake City	117,003	120,415	2.9	109,618	114,531	4.5
San Antonio	555,282	575,385	3.6	525,735	544,548	3.6
San Diego	678,126	688,615	1.5	648,924	663,177	2.2
San Francisco	415,150	416,979	0.4	387,611	395,030	1.9
San Jose	481,257	462,806	-3.8	434,641	427,930	-1.5
Savannah	67,604	68,673	1.6	64,327	65,717	2.2
Scottsdale	118,540	118,367	-0.1	114,033	114,904	0.8
Seattle	364,313	361,474	-0.8	338,573	337,082	-0.4
Sioux Falls	79,930	78,767	-1.5	77,913	76,281	-2.1
Springfield (IL)	62,106	62,470	0.6	58,644	58,579	-0.1
Springfield (MO)	86,453	88,779	2.7	82,757	85,527	3.3
St. Louis	159,226	159,840	0.4	144,759	146,558	1.2
St. Paul	147,960	148,029	0.0	141,554	140,545	-0.7
St. Petersburg	144,666	143,397	-0.9	137,369	137,277	-0.1
Stamford	64,827	64,067	-1.2	62,599	61,863	-1.2
Syracuse	76,793	77,149	0.5	70,951	71,008	0.1
Tampa	194,567	192,949	-0.8	184,641	184,517	-0.1
Tucson	269,519	267,086	-0.9	255,843	256,627	0.3
Tulsa	224,353	218,801	-2.5	211,633	206,388	-2.5
Virginia Beach	214,218	218,014	1.8	207,511	211,224	1.8
Washington	299,493	303,914	1.5	280,951	285,023	1.4
Wichita	183,575	186,653	1.7	171,131	175,232	2.4
U.S.	144,807,000	146,501,000	1.2	136,599,000	138,556,000	1.4

Note: Data is not seasonally adjusted and covers workers 16 years of age and older
Source: Bureau of Labor Statistics, http://stats.bls.gov

Labor Force, Employment and Job Growth: Metro Area

MSA[1]	Civilian Labor Force			Workers Employed		
	Dec. 2002	Dec. 2003	% Chg.	Dec. 2002	Dec. 2003	% Chg.
Albuquerque	389,840	393,603	1.0	373,063	376,001	0.8
Alexandria	2,801,448	2,843,367	1.5	2,712,003	2,758,987	1.7
Anchorage	149,932	159,948	6.7	141,240	151,551	7.3
Ann Arbor	308,789	314,061	1.7	298,955	302,254	1.1
Atlanta	2,398,382	2,453,778	2.3	2,273,161	2,355,417	3.6
Austin	772,810	792,089	2.5	734,363	756,049	3.0
Baltimore	1,330,877	1,346,670	1.2	1,272,595	1,285,181	1.0
Baton Rouge	297,985	309,240	3.8	281,068	291,921	3.9
Bellevue	1,415,598	1,407,484	-0.6	1,327,167	1,321,323	-0.4
Birmingham	470,689	488,736	3.8	450,674	468,420	3.9
Boise City	249,992	245,424	-1.8	235,753	234,091	-0.7
Boston	1,926,700	1,897,468	-1.5	1,838,784	1,811,618	-1.5
Boulder	197,696	173,701	-12.1	187,244	165,255	-11.7
Buffalo	576,480	579,030	0.4	541,010	541,326	0.1
Cedar Rapids	120,584	118,306	-1.9	115,225	113,245	-1.7
Charleston	277,025	329,336	18.9	266,379	317,722	19.3
Charlotte	850,471	868,713	2.1	800,249	814,621	1.8
Chattanooga	239,084	236,945	-0.9	230,578	228,677	-0.8
Chicago	4,264,180	4,345,278	1.9	3,984,025	4,069,643	2.1
Cincinnati	860,285	879,803	2.3	825,634	840,549	1.8
Cleveland	1,102,773	1,114,558	1.1	1,037,046	1,045,556	0.8
Colorado Spgs.	281,675	277,282	-1.6	263,891	260,848	-1.2
Columbia	283,060	280,004	-1.1	273,357	269,802	-1.3
Columbus	875,194	883,163	0.9	838,889	846,809	0.9
Dallas	2,030,240	2,051,670	1.1	1,900,545	1,929,052	1.5
Denver	1,211,118	1,258,865	3.9	1,140,157	1,184,381	3.9
Des Moines	278,936	280,457	0.5	268,822	270,560	0.6
Detroit	2,180,310	2,242,315	2.8	2,056,667	2,093,073	1.8
Durham	693,273	697,282	0.6	659,066	670,102	1.7
El Paso	296,759	302,993	2.1	272,516	278,489	2.2
Eugene	171,275	171,515	0.1	160,728	160,311	-0.3
Ft. Collins	156,380	163,876	4.8	148,171	155,396	4.9
Ft. Lauderdale	858,512	852,633	-0.7	811,482	812,562	0.1
Ft. Wayne	271,023	280,765	3.6	257,617	266,206	3.3
Ft. Worth	960,267	970,256	1.0	906,339	918,653	1.4
Grand Rapids	601,730	618,086	2.7	565,255	576,723	2.0
Green Bay	141,796	146,782	3.5	134,992	140,630	4.2
Greensboro	670,936	677,677	1.0	631,504	639,480	1.3
Honolulu	414,418	431,529	4.1	400,898	416,527	3.9
Houston	2,279,494	2,347,043	3.0	2,152,882	2,207,509	2.5
Huntsville	175,600	178,231	1.5	168,389	169,537	0.7
Indianapolis	881,762	888,212	0.7	842,266	847,161	0.6
Irvine	1,573,005	1,598,133	1.6	1,512,216	1,546,609	2.3
Jacksonville	582,804	582,231	-0.1	555,153	555,410	0.0
Kansas City	1,000,309	1,014,737	1.4	944,636	962,518	1.9
Knoxville	379,630	376,118	-0.9	368,178	363,179	-1.4
Las Vegas	877,321	871,121	-0.7	833,223	833,133	-0.0
Lexington	252,753	255,188	1.0	243,805	246,365	1.1
Lincoln	155,424	157,124	1.1	150,794	151,677	0.6
Los Angeles	4,787,568	4,769,815	-0.4	4,492,388	4,464,324	-0.6
Louisville	556,919	568,819	2.1	529,612	543,140	2.6
Madison	281,366	294,169	4.6	274,302	287,498	4.8
Manchester	113,819	116,676	2.5	108,474	112,076	3.3

Labor Force, Employment and Job Growth: Metro Area *continued*

MSA[1]	Civilian Labor Force			Workers Employed		
	Dec. 2002	Dec. 2003	% Chg.	Dec. 2002	Dec. 2003	% Chg.
Memphis	577,101	576,375	-0.1	549,381	543,521	-1.1
Miami	1,113,155	1,097,776	-1.4	1,035,374	1,031,331	-0.4
Milwaukee	806,723	811,706	0.6	761,820	770,706	1.2
Minneapolis	1,820,503	1,814,910	-0.3	1,751,709	1,740,701	-0.6
Naperville	4,264,180	4,345,278	1.9	3,984,025	4,069,643	2.1
Nashville	697,522	691,455	-0.9	673,550	663,996	-1.4
New Orleans	583,960	607,748	4.1	552,538	576,571	4.3
New York	4,476,427	4,395,211	-1.8	4,135,894	4,080,091	-1.3
Norfolk	771,730	785,451	1.8	742,728	756,111	1.8
Oklahoma City	581,574	573,416	-1.4	558,308	549,083	-1.7
Omaha	419,401	422,945	0.8	404,270	406,706	0.6
Orlando	949,823	956,906	0.7	905,446	916,509	1.2
Overland Park	1,000,309	1,014,737	1.4	944,636	962,518	1.9
Philadelphia	2,653,797	2,645,028	-0.3	2,515,387	2,519,849	0.2
Phoenix	1,798,021	1,789,007	-0.5	1,702,656	1,715,659	0.8
Pittsburgh	1,206,477	1,177,624	-2.4	1,140,292	1,123,266	-1.5
Plano	2,030,240	2,051,670	1.1	1,900,545	1,929,052	1.5
Portland	1,086,023	1,065,431	-1.9	1,008,772	990,710	-1.8
Providence	640,371	642,432	0.3	606,088	608,757	0.4
Provo	182,412	188,873	3.5	173,937	182,556	5.0
Raleigh	693,273	697,282	0.6	659,066	670,102	1.7
Reno	197,678	195,609	-1.0	190,134	188,200	-1.0
Richmond	536,009	542,709	1.2	516,483	523,805	1.4
Rochester	578,457	572,921	-1.0	543,989	539,722	-0.8
Sacramento	871,339	883,110	1.4	826,203	838,170	1.4
Salt Lake City	742,156	766,101	3.2	701,721	733,172	4.5
San Antonio	815,164	843,304	3.5	775,430	803,178	3.6
San Diego	1,478,563	1,501,604	1.6	1,416,030	1,447,131	2.2
San Francisco	925,559	932,774	0.8	874,557	891,296	1.9
San Jose	937,735	904,855	-3.5	859,897	846,620	-1.5
Savannah	144,262	146,603	1.6	138,529	141,524	2.2
Scottsdale	1,798,021	1,789,007	-0.5	1,702,656	1,715,659	0.8
Seattle	1,415,598	1,407,484	-0.6	1,327,167	1,321,323	-0.4
Sioux Falls	112,113	110,394	-1.5	109,502	107,208	-2.1
Springfield (IL)	107,231	107,876	0.6	102,335	102,221	-0.1
Springfield (MO)	175,665	180,253	2.6	168,418	174,054	3.3
St. Louis	1,372,061	1,387,566	1.1	1,295,981	1,315,218	1.5
St. Paul	1,820,503	1,814,910	-0.3	1,751,709	1,740,701	-0.6
St. Petersburg	1,316,323	1,307,890	-0.6	1,259,744	1,258,896	-0.1
Stamford	189,454	187,328	-1.1	183,865	181,703	-1.2
Syracuse	375,934	377,659	0.5	354,833	355,120	0.1
Tampa	1,316,323	1,307,890	-0.6	1,259,744	1,258,896	-0.1
Tucson	432,844	429,432	-0.8	412,958	414,223	0.3
Tulsa	427,929	418,063	-2.3	405,216	395,172	-2.5
Virginia Beach	771,730	785,451	1.8	742,728	756,111	1.8
Washington	2,801,448	2,843,367	1.5	2,712,003	2,758,987	1.7
Wichita	289,277	294,410	1.8	271,549	278,056	2.4
U.S.	144,807,000	146,501,000	1.2	136,599,000	138,556,000	1.4

Note: Data is not seasonally adjusted and covers workers 16 years of age and older;
(1) Metropolitan Statistical Area - see Appendix A for areas included
Source: Bureau of Labor Statistics, http://stats.bls.gov

Unemployment Rate: City

City	2003											
	Jan.	Feb.	Mar.	Apr.	May	Jun.	Jul.	Aug.	Sep.	Oct.	Nov.	Dec.
Albuquerque	4.7	4.4	4.5	4.4	4.7	5.6	5.3	5.0	5.0	4.9	4.8	4.2
Alexandria	3.0	3.2	2.9	2.6	2.6	2.7	2.4	2.5	2.6	2.3	2.3	2.1
Anchorage	5.7	5.9	5.3	5.2	5.0	5.4	5.2	5.1	5.2	4.9	5.0	5.2
Ann Arbor	2.5	2.5	2.6	2.4	2.4	2.8	2.9	2.8	2.9	2.7	2.5	2.5
Atlanta	7.4	7.4	7.4	7.1	7.6	8.9	8.4	7.9	7.8	7.2	6.6	6.4
Austin	6.2	6.0	6.2	5.7	6.0	6.8	6.4	6.1	6.0	5.4	5.3	4.9
Baltimore	8.1	7.9	7.5	7.4	7.7	8.6	9.0	8.5	8.2	7.9	8.0	7.8
Baton Rouge	6.2	5.5	5.7	5.3	5.7	7.9	7.7	7.4	6.3	5.7	5.6	5.8
Bellevue	4.6	4.8	4.7	4.7	4.9	5.2	5.1	4.8	4.9	4.5	4.4	4.2
Birmingham	6.7	6.7	6.5	6.5	6.5	7.7	7.0	7.4	6.9	7.3	7.2	6.8
Boise City	5.0	4.9	5.2	5.1	4.5	4.5	4.7	4.6	4.4	4.1	3.9	3.7
Boston	5.7	5.4	5.9	5.5	5.8	6.4	6.4	6.6	6.5	5.8	5.4	5.2
Boulder	5.9	5.8	6.0	6.0	5.5	6.2	5.8	5.6	5.3	5.0	5.2	5.1
Buffalo	10.7	10.1	9.4	9.2	9.7	9.9	10.6	10.1	10.0	9.8	10.5	10.4
Cedar Rapids	5.5	5.3	5.3	4.6	4.5	4.8	4.4	4.6	4.6	4.2	4.3	4.6
Charleston	4.5	4.5	3.7	3.7	4.1	5.0	5.3	4.7	4.3	4.8	4.4	3.7
Charlotte	6.1	5.9	5.9	5.9	6.1	7.0	6.5	6.4	6.0	5.8	6.2	5.7
Chattanooga	4.4	4.2	4.0	4.2	3.9	4.9	4.6	4.7	4.4	4.5	4.8	4.4
Chicago	8.1	8.1	8.1	7.5	7.4	8.1	8.1	8.2	8.5	7.7	7.9	7.3
Cincinnati	7.0	7.2	7.2	6.7	7.0	8.1	7.2	6.9	7.2	6.6	6.7	6.4
Cleveland	12.7	13.1	13.0	12.6	12.4	13.4	12.4	11.6	12.0	11.3	11.4	11.6
Colorado Spgs.	6.4	6.2	6.4	6.3	5.7	6.5	6.2	5.9	5.8	5.5	5.8	6.0
Columbia	6.1	6.0	5.5	5.2	6.1	6.3	6.4	6.0	6.0	6.5	5.8	5.7
Columbus	5.6	5.8	5.9	5.6	5.8	6.4	5.6	5.3	5.4	4.9	4.9	4.7
Dallas	9.3	9.1	8.8	8.4	8.9	10.0	9.3	9.0	8.8	8.2	8.0	7.6
Denver	7.0	6.9	7.1	7.0	6.5	7.1	6.9	6.8	6.5	6.4	6.7	7.0
Des Moines	5.3	5.3	5.4	4.8	4.6	4.7	4.4	4.6	4.7	4.2	4.2	4.6
Detroit	13.3	13.7	14.0	12.9	13.4	15.4	16.1	14.5	14.9	14.3	13.2	13.1
Durham	6.1	5.9	5.8	5.9	5.9	6.4	6.1	6.0	5.4	5.3	5.4	4.8
El Paso	9.4	9.0	8.6	8.0	8.8	10.2	9.5	9.5	9.4	8.6	8.2	7.8
Eugene	6.8	6.9	6.7	7.4	6.7	7.2	7.0	6.6	6.5	6.0	6.0	5.9
Ft. Collins	6.1	5.9	6.0	5.7	5.3	5.8	5.5	5.4	5.3	5.0	5.4	5.5
Ft. Lauderdale	7.7	7.2	7.0	7.2	7.0	7.6	7.3	7.5	7.3	6.8	6.6	5.9
Ft. Wayne	6.4	6.6	6.5	6.6	6.4	6.3	7.1	6.7	6.5	6.3	6.1	6.2
Ft. Worth	8.4	8.2	8.1	7.9	8.3	9.4	8.9	8.5	8.3	7.6	7.4	7.1
Grand Rapids	9.9	9.9	10.2	11.1	9.8	11.2	11.7	10.5	10.4	10.4	9.9	9.6
Green Bay	8.7	8.9	8.8	7.8	7.1	8.1	7.7	7.6	6.8	6.4	6.2	6.5
Greensboro	6.2	6.0	5.9	6.0	6.1	7.1	7.0	6.6	6.1	6.4	6.1	5.6
Honolulu	3.4	2.7	3.0	3.3	3.4	3.8	3.8	4.0	4.0	3.9	3.9	3.5
Houston	7.9	7.8	7.7	7.7	8.2	9.3	8.8	8.5	8.4	7.7	7.7	7.2
Huntsville	4.3	4.2	4.0	4.0	4.0	4.7	4.8	4.7	4.6	4.9	4.9	5.1
Indianapolis	5.5	5.6	5.4	5.5	5.3	5.0	5.4	5.6	5.7	5.5	5.4	5.4
Irvine	2.8	2.8	2.7	2.7	2.6	2.8	2.8	2.7	2.6	2.6	2.5	2.2
Jacksonville	5.9	5.5	5.4	5.6	5.5	6.8	6.4	6.1	6.1	5.7	5.6	5.1
Kansas City	6.9	6.1	6.1	6.3	6.6	7.7	7.7	7.9	7.4	6.8	6.5	6.3
Knoxville	3.5	3.5	3.2	3.2	3.4	4.1	3.8	3.8	3.6	3.8	4.0	3.6
Las Vegas	5.5	5.2	5.4	5.5	5.0	5.6	5.6	5.2	5.2	4.9	4.5	4.3
Lexington	3.8	3.9	3.6	3.7	3.5	3.6	3.6	3.7	3.8	3.4	3.0	3.0
Lincoln	3.8	3.9	3.8	3.7	4.0	4.4	4.4	3.8	3.9	3.8	3.5	3.6
Los Angeles	7.7	7.6	7.3	7.4	7.4	8.1	8.7	8.2	7.9	8.0	7.6	7.0
Louisville	5.1	5.3	5.2	5.0	5.4	6.1	5.9	5.8	6.0	6.2	5.9	6.8
Madison	2.9	2.9	3.0	2.7	2.7	3.2	3.1	3.1	2.8	2.4	2.3	2.2
Manchester	5.4	4.6	4.8	4.4	4.1	4.2	4.3	4.5	4.4	4.1	4.4	4.1

Unemployment Rate: City *continued*

City	2003											
	Jan.	Feb.	Mar.	Apr.	May	Jun.	Jul.	Aug.	Sep.	Oct.	Nov.	Dec.
Memphis	6.5	6.1	6.1	6.0	6.2	7.8	7.1	7.1	7.1	7.6	8.1	7.2
Miami	11.2	10.7	10.3	10.7	10.3	11.2	10.7	10.9	10.5	9.9	9.7	8.8
Milwaukee	9.5	9.5	9.7	9.2	9.3	10.5	10.5	10.7	9.7	9.0	8.3	7.9
Minneapolis	4.7	4.4	4.5	4.5	4.6	5.8	5.3	5.1	5.8	5.2	4.9	4.5
Naperville	5.2	5.1	5.1	4.9	5.0	5.5	5.7	5.7	5.9	5.7	5.5	4.8
Nashville	3.8	3.6	3.6	3.6	3.6	4.3	3.8	3.9	4.0	4.2	4.7	4.1
New Orleans	5.9	5.4	5.5	5.2	5.5	7.5	7.5	7.8	6.5	6.0	5.8	5.9
New York	9.1	9.0	8.7	8.1	7.9	7.9	8.4	8.4	8.4	8.4	8.1	8.0
Norfolk	6.9	6.7	6.3	6.0	6.5	7.3	6.8	6.5	6.4	5.7	5.6	5.7
Oklahoma City	5.2	5.4	5.0	4.8	6.2	6.1	5.3	5.1	4.8	5.3	4.9	4.7
Omaha	4.8	4.9	5.0	4.8	5.0	5.5	5.2	4.6	4.7	4.5	4.2	4.4
Orlando	5.7	5.4	5.3	5.5	5.3	5.8	5.5	5.6	5.5	5.1	5.1	4.5
Overland Park	3.8	3.7	3.6	3.8	3.6	3.7	3.5	3.5	3.6	3.8	3.8	3.5
Philadelphia	8.3	8.4	7.6	7.3	7.8	8.0	7.9	7.3	7.6	7.8	7.4	6.5
Phoenix	5.6	5.6	5.6	5.6	5.6	5.8	6.0	6.0	5.6	4.9	4.5	4.5
Pittsburgh	5.9	6.0	5.3	4.8	5.3	5.4	5.4	5.0	4.9	4.9	4.7	4.2
Plano	5.7	5.7	5.6	5.3	5.5	6.1	5.7	5.3	5.1	4.7	4.5	4.1
Portland	9.6	9.6	9.6	9.1	9.1	9.8	9.4	8.9	8.9	8.4	8.0	7.7
Providence	7.5	7.5	6.8	6.6	7.4	7.8	7.8	7.1	6.0	5.5	5.8	5.8
Provo	5.3	5.5	5.7	4.8	4.9	5.4	4.9	4.8	4.3	3.9	4.0	3.8
Raleigh	5.9	5.7	5.6	5.5	5.4	6.1	5.8	5.5	5.1	4.9	5.1	4.6
Reno	5.9	5.3	5.3	5.1	4.5	4.7	4.5	4.2	4.2	4.1	4.0	4.1
Richmond	6.5	6.4	6.2	5.7	6.1	6.8	6.2	6.4	6.5	5.8	5.6	5.3
Rochester	10.3	9.6	9.0	9.2	10.0	10.1	10.5	9.8	10.4	9.9	9.9	9.2
Sacramento	7.1	6.9	6.6	6.5	6.4	7.1	7.3	7.1	6.8	7.1	6.9	6.4
Salt Lake City	6.3	6.7	6.9	6.1	6.6	7.0	6.5	6.4	5.8	5.3	5.3	4.9
San Antonio	6.0	5.8	5.6	5.3	5.7	6.9	6.7	6.3	6.1	5.8	5.7	5.4
San Diego	4.5	4.4	4.4	4.4	4.3	4.6	4.8	4.5	4.3	4.4	4.2	3.7
San Francisco	7.1	7.0	7.0	6.9	6.7	7.4	7.2	6.8	6.1	6.2	5.9	5.3
San Jose	10.2	10.0	9.9	9.9	9.5	10.1	9.9	9.4	8.8	8.9	8.5	7.5
Savannah	4.1	4.2	4.2	4.1	4.7	6.1	6.7	5.2	5.0	4.5	4.2	4.3
Scottsdale	3.7	3.7	3.7	3.7	3.7	3.8	4.0	3.9	3.7	3.2	2.9	2.9
Seattle	7.4	7.6	7.5	7.6	7.8	8.2	8.1	7.7	7.8	7.2	7.0	6.7
Sioux Falls	3.3	3.0	3.1	2.8	2.7	2.6	2.7	2.6	2.7	2.7	2.8	3.2
Springfield (IL)	6.5	6.5	6.2	5.3	5.2	6.5	6.6	6.8	6.6	5.9	6.5	6.2
Springfield (MO)	4.2	3.8	3.7	3.6	3.6	4.2	4.2	4.3	4.0	3.9	3.7	3.7
St. Louis	8.6	7.7	8.0	8.6	9.2	10.6	10.5	11.1	10.4	9.5	9.0	8.3
St. Paul	5.2	4.9	5.1	4.9	4.8	6.0	5.8	5.4	5.9	5.6	5.4	5.1
St. Petersburg	5.7	5.3	5.2	5.2	5.0	5.5	5.3	5.2	5.1	4.8	4.8	4.3
Stamford	4.3	4.3	4.1	4.0	3.9	3.9	4.1	3.8	3.4	3.4	3.4	3.4
Syracuse	8.3	7.7	7.1	7.2	7.6	7.6	7.7	7.4	8.0	7.7	8.1	8.0
Tampa	5.7	5.3	5.2	5.2	5.0	5.6	5.3	5.6	5.5	5.0	4.8	4.4
Tucson	4.8	4.8	4.9	4.7	4.7	5.1	5.5	5.2	4.8	4.3	4.0	3.9
Tulsa	6.7	6.9	6.5	6.2	6.6	7.3	6.8	6.3	6.1	6.4	6.0	5.7
Virginia Beach	3.5	3.6	3.6	3.4	3.7	4.0	3.9	3.7	3.7	3.3	3.3	3.1
Washington	6.5	7.1	6.3	6.5	6.1	7.3	7.0	7.3	6.0	6.7	6.6	6.2
Wichita	7.5	6.6	6.8	6.7	6.4	8.7	8.2	7.0	6.8	6.9	6.8	6.1
U.S.	6.5	6.4	6.2	5.8	5.8	6.5	6.3	6.0	5.8	5.6	5.6	5.4

Note: Data is not seasonally adjusted and covers workers 16 years of age and older; All figures are percentages
Source: Bureau of Labor Statistics, http://stats.bls.gov

Unemployment Rate: Metro Area

MSA[1]	2003											
	Jan.	Feb.	Mar.	Apr.	May	Jun.	Jul.	Aug.	Sep.	Oct.	Nov.	Dec.
Albuquerque	5.0	4.8	4.8	4.7	5.1	6.1	5.7	5.3	5.2	5.2	5.0	4.5
Alexandria	3.6	3.8	3.6	3.4	3.4	3.7	3.5	3.4	3.2	3.1	3.1	3.0
Anchorage	5.7	5.9	5.3	5.2	5.0	5.4	5.2	5.1	5.2	4.9	5.0	5.2
Ann Arbor	4.0	4.1	4.3	3.7	3.6	4.1	4.7	4.0	4.1	3.9	3.6	3.8
Atlanta	4.7	4.7	4.7	4.6	4.8	5.5	5.3	4.9	4.8	4.5	4.1	4.0
Austin	5.7	5.6	5.7	5.3	5.5	6.3	5.9	5.7	5.6	5.0	4.9	4.5
Baltimore	4.9	5.0	4.8	4.5	4.8	5.2	5.4	4.9	4.8	4.6	4.7	4.6
Baton Rouge	5.9	5.2	5.5	5.1	5.5	7.5	7.4	7.1	5.9	5.3	5.4	5.6
Bellevue	6.5	6.7	6.6	6.6	6.8	7.2	7.2	7.0	7.1	6.5	6.3	6.1
Birmingham	4.3	4.3	4.1	4.1	4.1	4.8	4.4	4.5	4.3	4.5	4.4	4.2
Boise City	5.8	5.9	5.8	5.7	4.9	4.9	5.2	5.1	4.9	4.7	4.7	4.6
Boston	5.1	4.9	5.3	4.7	4.9	5.3	5.2	5.3	5.4	4.9	4.6	4.5
Boulder	5.6	5.5	5.7	5.6	5.2	5.8	5.5	5.3	5.0	4.7	4.9	4.9
Buffalo	6.8	6.4	5.9	5.8	6.0	6.2	6.6	6.2	6.1	6.0	6.6	6.5
Cedar Rapids	5.2	5.0	5.0	4.3	4.2	4.5	4.2	4.3	4.3	3.9	4.1	4.3
Charleston	4.4	4.4	3.6	3.7	4.2	4.9	5.1	4.6	4.3	4.7	4.3	3.5
Charlotte	6.2	6.0	5.8	5.9	6.0	6.8	7.5	7.1	6.7	6.6	6.9	6.2
Chattanooga	3.5	3.5	3.4	3.3	3.3	4.0	3.8	3.7	3.5	3.7	3.7	3.5
Chicago	7.1	7.2	7.2	6.4	6.1	6.8	6.7	6.8	6.9	6.3	6.5	6.3
Cincinnati	5.1	5.4	5.2	4.7	4.8	5.5	5.1	4.7	4.8	4.6	4.6	4.5
Cleveland	7.0	7.3	7.2	6.7	6.4	7.0	6.6	6.0	6.2	5.7	5.9	6.2
Colorado Spgs.	6.4	6.1	6.4	6.3	5.7	6.5	6.2	5.8	5.8	5.5	5.8	5.9
Columbia	3.9	3.9	3.4	3.4	3.9	4.1	4.2	3.9	3.9	4.2	3.8	3.6
Columbus	5.0	5.2	5.2	4.9	4.9	5.5	4.9	4.5	4.6	4.2	4.2	4.1
Dallas	7.3	7.2	7.0	6.7	7.1	8.0	7.4	7.1	7.0	6.4	6.3	6.0
Denver	6.0	5.8	6.1	6.1	5.6	6.2	5.9	5.8	5.7	5.5	5.8	5.9
Des Moines	4.1	4.1	4.2	3.7	3.5	3.6	3.4	3.5	3.6	3.2	3.2	3.5
Detroit	6.9	7.0	7.2	6.4	6.6	7.6	8.3	7.1	7.2	7.1	6.6	6.7
Durham	5.0	4.7	4.6	4.6	4.6	5.1	4.8	4.6	4.3	4.1	4.3	3.9
El Paso	9.8	9.4	8.9	8.3	9.2	10.6	9.9	9.9	9.8	9.0	8.6	8.1
Eugene	7.5	7.6	7.4	8.2	7.5	8.0	7.7	7.3	7.2	6.7	6.6	6.5
Ft. Collins	5.7	5.5	5.6	5.4	4.9	5.4	5.1	5.0	5.0	4.7	5.0	5.2
Ft. Lauderdale	6.1	5.8	5.6	5.8	5.6	6.1	5.8	6.0	5.9	5.4	5.3	4.7
Ft. Wayne	5.2	5.4	5.2	5.2	5.0	4.8	6.1	5.3	5.1	5.1	5.1	5.2
Ft. Worth	6.4	6.2	6.2	5.9	6.3	7.1	6.7	6.4	6.3	5.7	5.6	5.3
Grand Rapids	7.4	7.4	7.6	7.3	6.9	8.1	8.5	7.4	7.3	7.2	6.8	6.7
Green Bay	5.6	5.8	5.7	5.0	4.5	5.2	4.9	4.8	4.3	4.1	4.0	4.2
Greensboro	6.1	5.9	5.7	5.8	6.0	6.7	6.8	6.3	5.8	5.8	6.1	5.6
Honolulu	3.4	2.7	3.0	3.3	3.4	3.8	3.8	4.0	4.0	3.9	3.9	3.5
Houston	6.5	6.4	6.4	6.3	6.7	7.7	7.2	7.0	6.9	6.3	6.3	5.9
Huntsville	4.4	4.3	4.3	4.5	4.0	4.7	4.9	4.6	4.6	4.8	4.9	4.9
Indianapolis	4.8	4.9	4.7	4.7	4.5	4.3	4.8	4.8	4.8	4.7	4.6	4.6
Irvine	4.0	4.0	3.9	3.8	3.7	4.0	4.1	3.9	3.7	3.8	3.7	3.2
Jacksonville	5.4	5.1	5.0	5.1	5.0	6.1	5.7	5.5	5.5	5.1	5.1	4.6
Kansas City	5.7	5.4	5.3	5.4	5.4	6.0	6.0	5.9	5.6	5.5	5.3	5.1
Knoxville	4.3	4.1	3.7	3.2	3.0	3.5	3.3	3.2	3.1	3.2	3.6	3.4
Las Vegas	5.6	5.2	5.5	5.5	5.0	5.6	5.7	5.3	5.3	5.0	4.6	4.4
Lexington	4.4	4.5	4.2	4.0	3.8	4.0	3.9	3.8	3.8	3.7	3.5	3.5
Lincoln	3.6	3.7	3.7	3.5	3.8	4.2	4.2	3.6	3.7	3.7	3.4	3.5
Los Angeles	7.0	6.8	6.6	6.8	6.8	7.3	8.0	7.5	7.3	7.2	6.8	6.4
Louisville	5.3	5.4	5.1	4.9	4.9	5.2	5.3	4.8	5.2	4.9	5.0	4.5
Madison	3.0	3.1	3.1	2.7	2.6	2.9	2.9	2.9	2.6	2.4	2.2	2.3
Manchester	5.2	4.3	4.5	4.2	3.9	4.1	4.2	4.5	4.4	4.0	4.3	3.9

Unemployment Rate: Metro Area *continued*

MSA[1]	2003											
	Jan.	Feb.	Mar.	Apr.	May	Jun.	Jul.	Aug.	Sep.	Oct.	Nov.	Dec.
Memphis	5.4	5.1	5.0	4.9	5.1	6.3	5.7	5.7	5.6	6.1	6.4	5.7
Miami	7.8	7.4	7.2	7.4	7.2	7.8	7.4	7.6	7.3	6.8	6.7	6.1
Milwaukee	6.2	6.2	6.3	5.9	5.8	6.6	6.5	6.5	6.0	5.5	5.2	5.1
Minneapolis	4.6	4.4	4.4	4.2	3.9	4.7	4.4	4.1	4.6	4.3	4.1	4.1
Naperville	7.1	7.2	7.2	6.4	6.1	6.8	6.7	6.8	6.9	6.3	6.5	6.3
Nashville	3.9	3.7	3.6	3.6	3.5	4.2	3.8	3.9	3.9	4.2	4.5	4.0
New Orleans	5.4	4.9	5.1	4.7	4.9	6.7	6.7	6.6	5.6	5.1	5.0	5.1
New York	8.3	8.4	7.9	7.3	7.1	7.1	7.5	7.4	7.9	7.6	7.2	7.2
Norfolk	4.5	4.4	4.2	3.9	4.3	4.8	4.5	4.3	4.3	3.9	3.8	3.7
Oklahoma City	4.7	4.8	4.5	4.3	5.5	5.5	4.8	4.6	4.3	4.7	4.4	4.2
Omaha	4.1	4.2	4.3	4.1	4.2	4.6	4.4	4.0	4.1	3.9	3.7	3.8
Orlando	5.4	5.1	5.0	5.1	4.9	5.4	5.1	5.2	5.1	4.8	4.8	4.2
Overland Park	5.7	5.4	5.3	5.4	5.4	6.0	6.0	5.9	5.6	5.5	5.3	5.1
Philadelphia	6.1	6.2	5.8	5.3	5.6	5.7	5.9	5.4	5.4	5.4	5.2	4.7
Phoenix	5.1	5.2	5.1	5.1	5.2	5.3	5.6	5.5	5.1	4.5	4.1	4.1
Pittsburgh	6.8	7.0	6.1	5.2	5.6	5.8	5.6	4.9	4.6	4.7	4.8	4.6
Plano	7.3	7.2	7.0	6.7	7.1	8.0	7.4	7.1	7.0	6.4	6.3	6.0
Portland	8.5	8.5	8.4	8.1	8.1	8.9	8.5	8.1	8.0	7.4	7.2	7.0
Providence	6.5	6.6	6.2	5.3	5.4	5.8	5.9	5.5	4.9	4.6	4.7	5.2
Provo	4.7	5.0	5.1	4.3	4.4	4.8	4.4	4.3	3.8	3.5	3.6	3.3
Raleigh	5.0	4.7	4.6	4.6	4.6	5.1	4.8	4.6	4.3	4.1	4.3	3.9
Reno	5.4	4.9	4.9	4.7	4.1	4.3	4.2	3.9	3.9	3.8	3.7	3.8
Richmond	4.3	4.3	4.1	3.8	4.0	4.5	4.1	4.2	4.2	3.7	3.6	3.5
Rochester	6.6	6.1	5.7	5.6	5.7	5.7	5.9	5.4	5.8	5.6	5.9	5.8
Sacramento	5.7	5.5	5.4	5.3	5.2	5.6	5.7	5.5	5.3	5.5	5.5	5.1
Salt Lake City	5.5	5.8	5.9	5.3	5.6	6.1	5.7	5.6	5.1	4.7	4.6	4.3
San Antonio	5.4	5.2	5.1	4.8	5.1	6.2	6.0	5.7	5.5	5.1	5.1	4.8
San Diego	4.5	4.3	4.4	4.3	4.2	4.5	4.7	4.4	4.2	4.3	4.1	3.6
San Francisco	5.9	5.8	5.8	5.8	5.6	6.1	6.0	5.7	5.2	5.3	5.0	4.4
San Jose	8.8	8.6	8.5	8.4	8.2	8.6	8.5	8.0	7.6	7.6	7.3	6.4
Savannah	3.4	3.5	3.5	3.4	3.8	4.9	5.7	4.1	4.1	3.7	3.4	3.5
Scottsdale	5.1	5.2	5.1	5.1	5.2	5.3	5.6	5.5	5.1	4.5	4.1	4.1
Seattle	6.5	6.7	6.6	6.6	6.8	7.2	7.2	7.0	7.1	6.5	6.3	6.1
Sioux Falls	3.1	2.8	2.9	2.6	2.4	2.4	2.5	2.3	2.5	2.4	2.5	2.9
Springfield (IL)	5.5	5.6	5.3	4.4	4.3	5.3	5.3	5.4	5.4	4.8	5.4	5.2
Springfield (MO)	4.2	3.8	3.5	3.5	3.3	3.9	4.0	4.0	3.7	3.5	3.4	3.4
St. Louis	5.7	5.3	5.2	5.1	5.3	6.3	6.2	6.2	5.8	5.4	5.4	5.2
St. Paul	4.6	4.4	4.4	4.2	3.9	4.7	4.4	4.1	4.6	4.3	4.1	4.1
St. Petersburg	4.9	4.5	4.4	4.4	4.3	4.7	4.5	4.6	4.6	4.2	4.1	3.7
Stamford	3.5	3.6	3.5	3.4	3.3	3.3	3.4	3.2	3.0	3.0	3.0	3.0
Syracuse	6.3	5.8	5.3	5.2	5.5	5.5	5.5	5.2	5.7	5.6	5.9	6.0
Tampa	4.9	4.5	4.4	4.4	4.3	4.7	4.5	4.6	4.6	4.2	4.1	3.7
Tucson	4.4	4.4	4.5	4.2	4.3	4.6	4.9	4.7	4.3	3.9	3.6	3.5
Tulsa	6.4	6.5	6.1	5.8	6.2	6.7	6.3	5.9	5.8	6.1	5.8	5.5
Virginia Beach	4.5	4.4	4.2	3.9	4.3	4.8	4.5	4.3	4.3	3.9	3.8	3.7
Washington	3.6	3.8	3.6	3.4	3.4	3.7	3.5	3.4	3.2	3.1	3.1	3.0
Wichita	6.8	5.9	6.1	6.0	5.7	7.7	7.3	6.4	6.1	6.2	6.1	5.6
U.S.	6.5	6.4	6.2	5.8	5.8	6.5	6.3	6.0	5.8	5.6	5.6	5.4

Note: Data is not seasonally adjusted and covers workers 16 years of age and older; All figures are percentages
(1) Metropolitan Statistical Area - see Appendix A for areas included
Source: Bureau of Labor Statistics, http://stats.bls.gov

Average Hourly Wages: Occupations A - C

MSA[1]	Accountants/ Auditors	Automotive Mechanics	Book- keepers	Carpenters	Cashiers	Clerks, Gen. Office	Clerks, Recep./Info.
Albuquerque	21.90	16.02	12.46	14.47	8.16	9.94	9.10
Alexandria	27.97	18.97	15.56	17.55	8.93	12.74	11.75
Anchorage	27.18	19.84	16.08	21.75	9.25	14.01	11.61
Ann Arbor	26.61	19.58	14.79	19.74	8.77	12.00	11.02
Atlanta	24.40	16.62	13.69	15.12	8.00	12.31	10.37
Austin	24.15	17.47	14.09	14.34	8.24	11.78	11.42
Baltimore	26.90	17.00	14.53	16.36	8.57	12.62	11.04
Baton Rouge	22.18	13.29	12.06	15.25	7.05	9.28	9.08
Bellevue	29.58	18.49	15.64	21.79	10.43	13.32	11.92
Birmingham	24.11	14.67	13.33	14.38	7.13	10.57	10.05
Boise City	22.49	14.57	12.36	14.22	8.18	10.91	10.71
Boston	26.21	17.55	16.34	22.58	8.65	13.47	12.47
Boulder	24.70	20.11	15.24	17.02	9.80	13.08	11.07
Buffalo	24.47	13.72	13.00	16.72	7.22	10.78	9.80
Cedar Rapids	23.59	14.39	13.52	16.70	7.61	10.55	10.00
Charleston	21.26	14.91	12.20	14.23	7.06	10.49	9.59
Charlotte	24.69	19.38	14.07	15.54	7.75	11.73	10.91
Chattanooga	21.30	13.23	12.73	15.53	7.50	9.98	9.80
Chicago	24.70	18.53	15.09	22.14	8.09	11.65	10.73
Cincinnati	24.99	15.54	14.01	17.57	7.92	11.02	10.55
Cleveland	24.97	16.17	13.56	19.78	7.49	11.49	10.06
Colorado Spgs.	23.09	17.82	14.16	16.00	8.72	12.01	11.08
Columbia	19.47	16.29	11.38	13.22	7.31	10.51	10.64
Columbus	25.19	16.93	13.90	15.86	8.04	11.41	10.14
Dallas	27.10	15.52	14.98	13.66	8.22	11.70	11.39
Denver	28.04	18.57	15.29	16.11	9.35	12.68	12.00
Des Moines	22.18	15.96	13.40	15.34	7.75	11.25	10.76
Detroit	28.17	18.91	14.79	21.53	8.45	13.20	11.57
Durham	24.52	17.86	13.92	15.21	8.02	11.76	10.82
El Paso	23.42	12.33	11.61	9.59	6.93	8.88	8.30
Eugene	25.16	16.06	13.42	15.91	9.10	11.54	11.47
Ft. Collins	22.98	16.97	13.92	14.26	8.63	11.16	11.32
Ft. Lauderdale	22.76	16.27	13.80	15.53	7.81	10.18	10.50
Ft. Wayne	23.02	15.40	12.47	15.91	7.60	10.10	10.21
Ft. Worth	25.79	16.23	13.56	13.91	7.93	11.27	11.06
Grand Rapids	25.15	18.36	13.68	15.91	8.02	11.63	10.67
Green Bay	25.24	15.87	13.28	18.02	7.85	11.51	10.54
Greensboro	21.69	16.55	13.59	13.50	7.70	11.00	10.55
Honolulu	23.64	16.23	13.95	25.63	9.87	11.53	11.42
Houston	25.39	16.59	14.60	14.42	7.51	10.77	10.87
Huntsville	22.61	14.09	12.21	13.79	7.10	10.39	9.83
Indianapolis	23.85	17.55	13.23	18.35	7.77	10.64	10.10
Irvine	28.09	17.31	16.13	21.56	9.79	12.65	10.92
Jacksonville	23.50	16.86	12.42	13.67	7.56	10.18	9.87
Kansas City	24.47	16.22	13.17	19.16	7.79	11.91	10.58
Knoxville	22.30	13.73	12.24	13.11	7.85	10.53	9.67
Las Vegas	23.49	17.39	13.46	19.15	8.74	11.02	11.13
Lexington	21.46	13.87	12.18	14.97	8.06	10.32	9.76
Lincoln	22.29	14.35	12.26	13.52	7.29	10.69	10.15
Los Angeles	29.04	15.25	15.26	20.86	9.86	12.38	11.10
Louisville	25.05	13.18	12.86	16.51	7.60	10.90	10.20
Madison	24.43	17.62	14.34	20.42	8.24	12.61	10.79
Manchester	22.15	18.07	14.02	18.15	8.19	12.04	10.37

Average Hourly Wages: Occupations A - C *continued*

MSA[1]	Accountants/ Auditors	Automotive Mechanics	Book- keepers	Carpenters	Cashiers	Clerks, Gen. Office	Clerks, Recep./Info.
Memphis	22.40	15.82	13.66	15.80	7.56	11.16	10.23
Miami	27.03	14.56	13.21	13.52	7.78	10.70	9.21
Milwaukee	27.98	16.74	13.83	20.47	7.89	11.60	10.79
Minneapolis	26.98	16.94	15.30	20.64	8.59	12.84	11.50
Naperville	24.70	18.53	15.09	22.14	8.09	11.65	10.73
Nashville	22.98	16.20	13.50	14.56	8.15	11.29	10.68
New Orleans	22.19	14.92	12.64	13.32	6.89	9.95	9.24
New York	32.73	15.23	17.17	23.62	8.13	12.59	13.02
Norfolk	22.60	15.54	12.36	14.46	7.07	10.28	8.83
Oklahoma City	21.50	13.92	12.24	12.54	7.18	9.76	10.40
Omaha	23.54	16.27	13.29	16.45	7.85	11.00	10.62
Orlando	22.66	15.50	12.06	15.07	7.73	10.32	9.85
Overland Park	24.47	16.22	13.17	19.16	7.79	11.91	10.58
Philadelphia	26.22	16.52	14.92	21.34	8.24	11.74	11.58
Phoenix	23.69	15.47	14.08	16.49	8.66	11.14	10.22
Pittsburgh	23.84	14.55	12.16	20.09	7.13	10.20	8.81
Plano	27.10	15.52	14.98	13.66	8.22	11.70	11.39
Portland	25.73	17.39	14.57	18.91	9.73	12.37	11.09
Providence	24.12	15.31	14.45	19.38	8.24	11.45	11.12
Provo	20.10	15.52	11.98	15.29	7.40	9.48	8.98
Raleigh	24.52	17.86	13.92	15.21	8.02	11.76	10.82
Reno	24.19	16.41	13.57	21.33	9.44	11.56	10.93
Richmond	25.12	18.07	13.66	15.10	7.76	11.54	9.74
Rochester	24.96	14.83	13.41	16.69	7.08	11.16	10.30
Sacramento	27.42	17.62	15.14	20.64	10.30	12.39	11.63
Salt Lake City	22.77	16.06	12.59	16.00	7.93	11.08	10.11
San Antonio	22.98	14.17	12.84	13.55	7.80	10.42	9.49
San Diego	24.90	17.87	15.02	19.24	9.53	11.55	11.14
San Francisco	31.98	21.33	18.53	25.59	10.80	13.54	14.90
San Jose	31.38	19.93	18.25	21.46	10.14	13.99	13.72
Savannah	20.15	13.79	12.56	14.84	7.00	10.00	9.51
Scottsdale	23.69	15.47	14.08	16.49	8.66	11.14	10.22
Seattle	29.58	18.49	15.64	21.79	10.43	13.32	11.92
Sioux Falls	20.81	14.36	11.39	13.71	7.39	9.22	9.37
Springfield (IL)	22.90	14.65	13.43	18.93	7.47	12.07	9.47
Springfield (MO)	20.80	15.22	11.05	14.15	7.40	9.86	9.07
St. Louis	23.67	16.54	13.80	22.32	7.81	11.45	10.28
St. Paul	26.98	16.94	15.30	20.64	8.59	12.84	11.50
St. Petersburg	29.66	15.85	12.46	13.58	7.51	10.35	9.77
Stamford	32.22	18.64	18.83	22.49	9.36	13.90	13.95
Syracuse	26.00	15.38	13.25	15.33	6.94	11.28	10.22
Tampa	29.66	15.85	12.46	13.58	7.51	10.35	9.77
Tucson	20.79	16.48	12.87	14.58	8.86	10.32	9.89
Tulsa	21.87	14.60	12.86	14.63	7.27	10.80	9.67
Virginia Beach	22.60	15.54	12.36	14.46	7.07	10.28	8.83
Washington	27.97	18.97	15.56	17.55	8.93	12.74	11.75
Wichita	23.71	15.02	12.56	15.77	7.43	10.06	9.89

Notes: Wage data is for 2002 and covers the Metropolitan Statistical Area - see Appendix A for areas included; n/a not available
Source: Bureau of Labor Statistics, 2002 Metro Area Occupational Employment and Wage Estimates

Average Hourly Wages: Occupations C - E

MSA[1]	Clerks, Ship./Rec.	Computer Program-mers	Computer Support Specialists	Computer Systems Analysts	Cooks, Restaurant	Dentists	Electrical Engineers
Albuquerque	11.42	27.19	18.11	28.29	8.71	61.01	36.74
Alexandria	12.94	31.88	23.21	34.60	10.39	80.32	36.15
Anchorage	13.58	28.69	21.54	33.14	11.55	n/a	36.57
Ann Arbor	13.15	28.66	18.68	30.15	10.39	n/a	33.68
Atlanta	12.14	28.85	19.86	35.36	9.51	60.16	31.80
Austin	12.14	34.02	22.79	28.91	9.19	82.17	38.45
Baltimore	12.80	26.97	20.60	32.66	9.40	52.89	33.33
Baton Rouge	11.40	24.18	18.95	25.34	8.22	64.43	36.74
Bellevue	14.46	40.21	23.52	32.69	11.37	37.93	36.91
Birmingham	11.24	27.63	20.24	28.62	8.20	86.46	30.86
Boise City	11.02	28.09	18.93	29.56	9.03	100.10	34.52
Boston	13.53	33.89	24.63	30.41	10.88	72.47	39.13
Boulder	12.57	33.55	20.95	n/a	10.52	n/a	33.09
Buffalo	12.05	25.25	20.19	26.49	8.59	45.90	30.94
Cedar Rapids	12.55	27.03	17.29	26.45	9.12	69.29	n/a
Charleston	10.66	22.36	16.46	22.35	9.23	77.41	25.59
Charlotte	12.17	30.74	24.99	n/a	10.24	42.52	n/a
Chattanooga	12.35	25.65	17.78	26.71	9.40	92.86	33.67
Chicago	12.81	30.14	21.47	33.17	9.61	39.79	32.34
Cincinnati	12.87	26.63	20.08	29.82	9.40	70.64	29.68
Cleveland	12.28	29.62	20.44	29.50	9.57	83.04	31.58
Colorado Spgs.	11.42	32.64	19.16	31.49	9.89	87.96	31.72
Columbia	11.28	24.78	16.26	24.12	8.28	60.17	29.30
Columbus	12.27	27.46	22.03	31.64	9.18	79.22	32.08
Dallas	11.68	35.10	23.53	31.49	8.59	61.06	38.29
Denver	12.76	32.75	23.75	34.05	10.30	82.21	33.02
Des Moines	12.21	25.93	18.08	28.81	9.87	80.08	29.60
Detroit	13.49	30.05	20.97	n/a	10.30	63.27	33.04
Durham	11.58	34.64	24.00	32.36	9.52	88.02	34.32
El Paso	9.61	n/a	16.15	25.23	7.46	96.87	28.30
Eugene	11.23	23.42	15.39	26.71	9.06	n/a	33.79
Ft. Collins	12.12	28.15	19.61	30.89	9.07	69.90	34.82
Ft. Lauderdale	11.23	30.14	18.06	30.40	9.36	75.78	31.20
Ft. Wayne	11.93	24.71	18.51	27.83	8.87	57.65	30.15
Ft. Worth	11.90	30.86	16.71	31.34	9.20	n/a	33.93
Grand Rapids	13.38	28.13	19.64	28.58	8.64	83.68	31.29
Green Bay	12.52	25.50	22.87	27.95	9.91	84.46	27.59
Greensboro	11.53	29.24	19.64	29.37	10.22	n/a	n/a
Honolulu	13.04	24.07	22.56	31.05	10.64	59.84	32.90
Houston	12.12	37.78	20.95	30.95	8.92	64.20	36.99
Huntsville	10.88	n/a	19.49	29.97	7.08	82.44	32.86
Indianapolis	11.90	27.25	18.87	28.13	10.08	70.86	29.01
Irvine	12.36	34.16	21.38	32.76	9.94	69.79	35.18
Jacksonville	11.52	42.08	19.10	30.68	9.64	80.07	32.28
Kansas City	11.97	28.94	20.53	29.54	9.74	63.84	30.74
Knoxville	11.36	25.89	16.49	27.16	9.34	72.33	32.04
Las Vegas	11.74	26.23	15.89	29.78	12.45	95.44	35.05
Lexington	11.65	n/a	17.42	29.40	9.38	50.05	29.95
Lincoln	11.12	25.06	16.88	24.54	8.94	62.88	29.42
Los Angeles	11.63	32.27	21.17	30.15	9.21	67.94	34.40
Louisville	11.66	26.24	18.24	28.64	9.57	55.20	31.33
Madison	12.06	27.94	20.01	26.22	9.83	57.38	35.95
Manchester	12.37	28.66	18.84	29.01	11.62	77.98	32.14

Average Hourly Wages: Occupations C - E *continued*

MSA[1]	Clerks, Ship./Rec.	Computer Program- mers	Computer Support Specialists	Computer Systems Analysts	Cooks, Restaurant	Dentists	Electrical Engineers
Memphis	11.25	29.21	16.96	27.53	8.43	84.77	31.12
Miami	10.56	27.14	18.98	28.93	9.45	85.76	35.13
Milwaukee	12.88	26.40	19.19	37.15	10.01	n/a	34.29
Minneapolis	13.53	28.83	20.23	31.30	10.21	65.65	35.02
Naperville	12.81	30.14	21.47	33.17	9.61	39.79	32.34
Nashville	11.88	27.87	18.94	26.20	9.73	28.68	30.02
New Orleans	11.49	26.53	18.92	27.80	9.08	54.38	34.07
New York	12.56	35.10	25.67	35.01	14.56	67.33	37.84
Norfolk	11.48	25.77	18.71	29.14	8.38	66.87	28.20
Oklahoma City	10.91	23.93	13.57	24.30	7.86	81.74	29.87
Omaha	11.30	26.70	19.11	26.05	10.15	67.05	31.24
Orlando	11.26	29.08	13.94	28.27	10.69	69.01	29.80
Overland Park	11.97	28.94	20.53	29.54	9.74	63.84	30.74
Philadelphia	12.91	30.36	21.08	32.06	9.94	75.31	32.70
Phoenix	10.81	28.00	20.80	31.79	9.86	71.39	36.19
Pittsburgh	11.34	26.86	18.20	29.12	8.95	37.83	32.72
Plano	11.68	35.10	23.53	31.49	8.59	61.06	38.29
Portland	12.98	26.89	17.78	30.28	9.60	n/a	33.95
Providence	11.82	27.95	19.43	30.05	10.23	72.33	31.01
Provo	10.37	25.27	n/a	25.15	8.60	n/a	30.56
Raleigh	11.58	34.64	24.00	32.36	9.52	88.02	34.32
Reno	11.81	26.25	17.43	31.06	10.38	101.09	32.48
Richmond	11.55	29.39	20.87	29.50	10.04	48.55	29.57
Rochester	11.92	29.51	19.86	29.43	10.43	55.14	32.98
Sacramento	13.38	33.10	20.10	29.87	10.19	75.93	37.82
Salt Lake City	11.90	28.85	14.59	28.16	9.47	64.40	34.14
San Antonio	9.72	23.80	15.66	20.94	8.94	53.96	32.99
San Diego	11.88	32.63	20.47	31.94	9.56	39.67	37.49
San Francisco	14.06	37.78	26.18	35.87	13.71	49.24	36.96
San Jose	14.53	37.35	28.83	35.34	10.99	78.75	42.44
Savannah	11.56	24.07	16.68	27.25	8.17	77.71	30.64
Scottsdale	10.81	28.00	20.80	31.79	9.86	71.39	36.19
Seattle	14.46	40.21	23.52	32.69	11.37	37.93	36.91
Sioux Falls	10.93	21.68	14.53	29.17	8.83	56.41	29.02
Springfield (IL)	11.54	23.72	20.18	28.37	8.53	28.19	n/a
Springfield (MO)	10.32	22.32	18.39	23.68	8.39	86.28	28.77
St. Louis	12.49	30.03	20.31	28.37	9.33	70.05	30.11
St. Paul	13.53	28.83	20.23	31.30	10.21	65.65	35.02
St. Petersburg	11.37	27.87	19.43	31.04	9.32	38.03	32.25
Stamford	15.00	34.76	22.50	33.51	12.23	59.76	34.90
Syracuse	11.66	25.86	17.34	28.81	9.80	n/a	32.95
Tampa	11.37	27.87	19.43	31.04	9.32	38.03	32.25
Tucson	9.94	26.70	17.66	26.73	10.49	63.94	34.25
Tulsa	11.18	29.34	15.89	28.25	7.51	n/a	31.08
Virginia Beach	11.48	25.77	18.71	29.14	8.38	66.87	28.20
Washington	12.94	31.88	23.21	34.60	10.39	80.32	36.15
Wichita	16.28	27.47	19.21	30.00	8.87	48.51	30.69

Notes: Wage data is for 2002 and covers the Metropolitan Statistical Area - see Appendix A for areas included; n/a not available
Source: Bureau of Labor Statistics, 2002 Metro Area Occupational Employment and Wage Estimates

Average Hourly Wages: Occupations E - I

MSA[1]	Electricians	Financial Managers	First-Line Supervisors/ Mgrs., Sales	Food Preparation Workers	General/ Oper. Mgrs.	Hairdressers/ Cosmetologists	Internists
Albuquerque	18.01	32.57	16.06	7.19	35.44	8.61	n/a
Alexandria	21.07	40.52	17.33	8.96	43.97	13.93	68.18
Anchorage	27.59	36.84	18.43	9.12	35.98	12.85	86.07
Ann Arbor	24.65	40.98	17.98	8.40	44.01	11.64	66.96
Atlanta	18.25	42.89	15.68	8.33	40.54	12.36	66.43
Austin	18.17	39.86	15.39	7.88	38.74	10.92	n/a
Baltimore	21.27	35.95	16.73	9.16	39.10	10.19	63.95
Baton Rouge	15.24	28.41	15.16	6.64	33.47	9.38	93.20
Bellevue	28.39	43.99	22.71	9.42	56.14	17.24	82.08
Birmingham	16.12	33.90	15.23	8.38	40.99	9.95	91.60
Boise City	19.00	33.96	14.97	8.50	31.52	8.32	n/a
Boston	24.84	49.59	18.07	9.69	49.58	12.11	64.78
Boulder	19.47	41.25	17.84	9.19	49.77	12.34	n/a
Buffalo	24.63	40.83	15.65	7.69	44.77	8.20	89.89
Cedar Rapids	23.54	33.78	15.79	7.89	38.46	10.40	n/a
Charleston	16.28	29.96	16.53	7.79	31.19	13.45	63.82
Charlotte	15.98	41.89	15.98	8.00	42.08	11.93	76.13
Chattanooga	19.74	27.32	15.34	7.99	33.05	10.84	99.33
Chicago	24.15	41.23	17.88	7.69	41.62	11.45	81.59
Cincinnati	19.42	35.12	15.73	8.62	39.89	12.36	n/a
Cleveland	23.40	40.62	16.28	8.20	41.45	8.98	65.07
Colorado Spgs.	20.26	38.38	17.60	8.53	40.95	10.53	n/a
Columbia	17.49	29.94	15.83	n/a	31.84	10.17	64.24
Columbus	19.48	41.43	16.10	8.53	39.09	11.77	93.39
Dallas	17.75	43.37	18.46	7.92	41.74	11.04	n/a
Denver	23.44	41.76	20.54	9.39	47.85	10.94	n/a
Des Moines	18.50	38.76	16.51	8.45	39.42	12.41	n/a
Detroit	27.63	47.62	18.26	9.87	50.75	10.46	89.95
Durham	18.58	38.41	16.39	8.69	39.67	11.46	80.35
El Paso	16.36	33.79	14.84	6.91	31.96	7.58	n/a
Eugene	23.37	35.37	18.26	8.37	39.21	10.86	n/a
Ft. Collins	17.86	36.23	17.72	8.32	38.36	11.63	n/a
Ft. Lauderdale	16.69	40.21	18.88	7.99	42.05	9.17	81.87
Ft. Wayne	23.23	33.49	15.18	7.96	36.31	11.40	62.56
Ft. Worth	17.76	37.48	17.06	8.05	35.45	10.30	81.24
Grand Rapids	21.21	40.57	17.68	9.01	46.66	10.63	61.49
Green Bay	22.43	37.50	18.26	8.34	40.24	11.52	92.34
Greensboro	16.30	37.94	16.05	7.29	37.78	13.05	66.53
Honolulu	25.79	35.98	17.16	10.51	40.60	14.40	57.78
Houston	18.16	42.03	16.94	7.86	39.11	12.11	n/a
Huntsville	19.69	30.67	14.86	7.99	36.73	8.70	74.00
Indianapolis	23.16	38.17	16.59	8.12	41.25	10.48	86.50
Irvine	23.54	45.95	20.06	9.06	52.60	9.76	72.63
Jacksonville	17.81	40.36	17.66	7.57	39.15	10.20	83.14
Kansas City	22.37	35.93	16.66	8.30	39.07	11.57	78.13
Knoxville	17.43	27.63	14.21	8.38	33.53	11.78	81.46
Las Vegas	21.49	37.70	16.01	9.53	42.38	9.08	99.22
Lexington	17.98	32.10	15.46	7.98	33.83	12.05	n/a
Lincoln	17.38	32.17	16.43	8.26	34.70	10.78	67.95
Los Angeles	19.70	46.68	18.94	8.90	52.66	9.81	78.23
Louisville	20.53	34.35	16.22	8.85	35.72	13.06	75.65
Madison	22.44	36.05	17.20	8.80	42.33	12.83	87.69
Manchester	18.69	36.47	16.99	9.46	39.73	11.11	81.03

Average Hourly Wages: Occupations E - I *continued*

MSA[1]	Electricians	Financial Managers	First-Line Supervisors/ Mgrs., Sales	Food Preparation Workers	General/ Oper. Mgrs.	Hairdressers/ Cosmetologists	Internists
Memphis	18.04	31.85	15.20	7.66	38.30	12.54	89.16
Miami	15.66	40.01	19.56	8.07	39.80	10.32	66.08
Milwaukee	24.12	37.79	19.02	8.53	44.34	11.18	79.28
Minneapolis	27.54	48.69	18.04	9.67	45.82	11.71	71.75
Naperville	24.15	41.23	17.88	7.69	41.62	11.45	81.59
Nashville	18.28	31.60	16.89	8.39	36.11	11.98	81.30
New Orleans	17.03	29.12	15.22	6.92	35.96	9.74	98.79
New York	29.38	61.39	19.87	9.67	62.01	11.72	77.75
Norfolk	16.42	36.07	15.40	7.50	36.74	11.49	84.87
Oklahoma City	17.07	30.89	14.96	6.84	32.47	8.87	63.39
Omaha	19.22	34.53	16.82	8.17	38.02	11.86	90.05
Orlando	16.04	37.75	17.89	8.67	36.92	12.77	90.62
Overland Park	22.37	35.93	16.66	8.30	39.07	11.57	78.13
Philadelphia	23.98	37.74	17.57	8.49	46.73	10.10	55.00
Phoenix	18.96	37.83	16.99	7.55	40.76	8.79	87.97
Pittsburgh	22.30	32.53	16.35	7.81	37.91	9.28	80.88
Plano	17.75	43.37	18.46	7.92	41.74	11.04	n/a
Portland	28.00	39.40	18.79	9.02	45.84	11.53	n/a
Providence	21.04	42.36	17.47	9.21	42.37	10.96	67.38
Provo	14.29	33.50	14.51	7.56	32.48	9.69	n/a
Raleigh	18.58	38.41	16.39	8.69	39.67	11.46	80.35
Reno	20.78	36.25	18.07	8.21	43.58	8.58	99.79
Richmond	19.04	40.43	15.98	8.03	40.04	11.37	n/a
Rochester	21.92	41.61	17.09	7.45	46.95	10.17	59.36
Sacramento	20.43	36.44	18.32	8.95	42.70	8.79	n/a
Salt Lake City	17.65	31.37	16.00	8.30	36.28	10.31	76.20
San Antonio	17.00	33.61	16.30	7.79	36.13	11.58	96.30
San Diego	20.85	42.10	18.77	8.68	48.83	11.17	88.59
San Francisco	30.80	53.71	20.02	9.34	54.81	15.82	93.37
San Jose	29.02	51.94	21.00	9.83	59.00	11.45	70.37
Savannah	15.95	32.45	13.65	7.41	32.69	8.74	76.80
Scottsdale	18.96	37.83	16.99	7.55	40.76	8.79	87.97
Seattle	28.39	43.99	22.71	9.42	56.14	17.24	82.08
Sioux Falls	15.57	37.91	16.48	8.19	44.29	12.95	n/a
Springfield (IL)	21.54	34.10	14.99	8.11	30.62	12.64	85.69
Springfield (MO)	16.91	29.17	14.93	7.54	30.91	9.41	88.24
St. Louis	27.79	35.80	16.38	7.92	37.40	10.34	77.58
St. Paul	27.54	48.69	18.04	9.67	45.82	11.71	71.75
St. Petersburg	15.36	37.30	17.62	7.98	39.13	10.79	92.65
Stamford	24.00	64.60	21.46	11.15	66.76	17.48	77.29
Syracuse	19.31	39.57	16.46	8.06	45.00	11.33	n/a
Tampa	15.36	37.30	17.62	7.98	39.13	10.79	92.65
Tucson	15.66	31.72	17.27	7.29	35.41	8.87	90.16
Tulsa	17.54	32.75	15.72	6.68	35.61	10.87	88.96
Virginia Beach	16.42	36.07	15.40	7.50	36.74	11.49	84.87
Washington	21.07	40.52	17.33	8.96	43.97	13.93	68.18
Wichita	19.30	33.34	15.79	7.71	34.96	10.98	65.71

Notes: Wage data is for 2002 and covers the Metropolitan Statistical Area - see Appendix A for areas included; n/a not available
Source: Bureau of Labor Statistics, 2002 Metro Area Occupational Employment and Wage Estimates

Average Hourly Wages: Occupations J - N

MSA[1]	Janitors/ Cleaners	Landscapers	Lawyers	Maids/ House- keepers	Main- tenance Repairers	Marketing Managers	Nuclear Medicine Technologists
Albuquerque	8.50	9.04	30.83	7.23	12.46	37.02	n/a
Alexandria	9.22	10.55	55.21	9.14	15.51	41.63	25.86
Anchorage	11.37	12.59	45.93	10.30	18.66	33.16	n/a
Ann Arbor	11.72	10.57	46.88	9.16	16.98	44.23	24.10
Atlanta	8.90	10.10	45.94	8.12	14.35	40.45	21.71
Austin	8.40	8.86	46.12	7.83	12.80	38.42	24.21
Baltimore	8.64	10.54	39.45	9.40	14.17	36.71	28.64
Baton Rouge	7.75	8.63	49.05	6.76	14.63	31.04	n/a
Bellevue	11.46	12.06	47.02	9.19	17.53	46.91	27.98
Birmingham	7.87	9.36	50.02	6.97	14.29	35.39	20.75
Boise City	8.45	9.19	38.66	7.69	13.88	33.98	n/a
Boston	11.52	13.28	49.79	9.70	16.52	48.97	24.56
Boulder	9.69	10.45	38.49	9.37	16.58	44.34	n/a
Buffalo	9.90	10.58	42.67	8.05	14.25	43.31	23.37
Cedar Rapids	10.75	10.81	36.89	8.16	14.98	32.85	n/a
Charleston	7.90	8.83	52.48	7.30	14.00	25.63	n/a
Charlotte	8.88	10.11	51.93	8.04	15.14	40.74	24.02
Chattanooga	8.77	9.88	48.26	7.62	14.79	31.72	n/a
Chicago	10.83	10.70	53.83	8.63	17.24	40.35	26.25
Cincinnati	9.88	11.26	50.56	8.70	15.48	37.65	22.89
Cleveland	9.99	10.69	52.96	8.26	15.12	37.54	22.65
Colorado Spgs.	9.39	10.28	49.30	8.12	14.04	38.58	n/a
Columbia	7.84	9.35	40.87	7.52	13.60	33.00	23.13
Columbus	10.16	10.69	38.69	8.34	15.07	40.64	n/a
Dallas	8.67	9.36	56.67	7.77	13.28	42.93	26.90
Denver	9.82	11.01	48.36	8.65	15.15	40.28	23.15
Des Moines	9.49	9.67	48.13	8.36	15.00	35.45	n/a
Detroit	11.63	10.72	41.05	9.08	18.14	47.12	23.18
Durham	8.38	11.92	46.37	8.41	15.25	48.68	21.44
El Paso	7.41	8.28	57.37	6.60	11.67	32.09	n/a
Eugene	9.68	11.20	40.11	8.25	13.88	33.85	n/a
Ft. Collins	9.48	10.28	41.68	7.93	15.09	40.22	n/a
Ft. Lauderdale	8.64	10.00	57.76	7.64	12.97	38.99	24.04
Ft. Wayne	10.15	9.96	40.88	7.67	15.43	33.33	20.89
Ft. Worth	9.44	9.21	44.07	7.74	14.00	38.86	24.56
Grand Rapids	10.60	11.13	51.99	8.45	15.54	53.96	21.65
Green Bay	9.98	11.07	52.43	8.28	15.62	40.57	n/a
Greensboro	8.36	9.47	53.60	8.08	14.64	44.46	n/a
Honolulu	9.42	11.55	43.76	11.08	14.90	43.50	n/a
Houston	7.65	8.86	65.87	7.35	13.60	39.67	24.82
Huntsville	8.18	10.00	45.45	6.92	15.24	39.10	n/a
Indianapolis	9.40	10.22	40.60	8.04	15.01	36.78	22.62
Irvine	9.82	9.95	57.86	8.41	16.21	45.74	26.26
Jacksonville	8.67	10.20	61.09	7.63	13.79	38.96	22.58
Kansas City	9.69	11.03	54.86	7.96	14.97	35.79	23.17
Knoxville	8.45	9.38	41.03	7.75	13.38	29.21	20.65
Las Vegas	10.50	10.09	42.03	10.09	16.55	39.44	22.01
Lexington	8.78	9.41	47.63	7.86	15.83	34.43	18.28
Lincoln	8.63	9.93	38.30	7.85	13.84	30.22	n/a
Los Angeles	10.51	10.84	56.42	8.80	16.19	44.66	28.26
Louisville	9.17	10.25	40.07	8.29	14.61	36.51	19.20
Madison	10.19	12.69	40.79	8.49	15.60	37.44	21.60
Manchester	10.10	12.32	53.33	9.04	15.73	39.18	n/a

Average Hourly Wages: Occupations J - N *continued*

MSA[1]	Janitors/ Cleaners	Landscapers	Lawyers	Maids/ House-keepers	Main-tenance Repairers	Marketing Managers	Nuclear Medicine Technologists
Memphis	8.15	10.13	42.15	7.36	14.86	37.19	20.16
Miami	8.09	9.32	51.54	7.32	11.97	39.54	25.59
Milwaukee	10.15	11.16	54.26	8.38	17.35	40.90	24.60
Minneapolis	10.38	12.33	50.76	9.54	17.05	53.12	25.23
Naperville	10.83	10.70	53.83	8.63	17.24	40.35	26.25
Nashville	9.28	9.35	58.23	7.70	15.38	31.19	22.22
New Orleans	7.55	8.76	57.42	6.80	14.42	31.23	22.83
New York	12.40	13.55	64.57	13.64	17.72	57.03	25.47
Norfolk	8.40	9.19	64.66	7.59	13.23	34.42	21.99
Oklahoma City	8.04	8.82	51.18	7.11	12.33	30.90	24.84
Omaha	9.58	10.46	49.77	8.25	13.31	40.38	23.20
Orlando	8.30	10.08	52.69	7.72	12.94	40.82	21.92
Overland Park	9.69	11.03	54.86	7.96	14.97	35.79	23.17
Philadelphia	10.64	10.89	49.79	9.22	16.18	41.42	23.83
Phoenix	8.56	8.87	43.28	7.54	13.45	35.42	24.46
Pittsburgh	9.84	10.03	50.94	7.96	14.86	36.51	20.66
Plano	8.67	9.36	56.67	7.77	13.28	42.93	26.90
Portland	10.37	11.45	42.27	8.75	16.10	42.26	25.48
Providence	10.58	10.87	38.82	9.36	15.73	38.03	25.15
Provo	8.33	11.04	45.74	7.92	12.55	34.96	n/a
Raleigh	8.38	11.92	46.37	8.41	15.25	48.68	21.44
Reno	8.94	10.22	55.82	8.28	15.84	37.07	23.46
Richmond	8.09	9.64	45.10	7.70	15.13	44.58	21.85
Rochester	9.64	10.24	48.09	7.79	18.19	43.19	22.88
Sacramento	10.02	10.82	50.91	8.71	15.33	38.43	28.86
Salt Lake City	8.70	9.60	65.19	7.86	14.17	39.17	n/a
San Antonio	8.20	8.97	46.41	7.28	12.33	32.95	22.50
San Diego	10.09	10.28	52.09	8.62	14.72	47.08	29.08
San Francisco	12.21	13.50	70.23	11.12	17.36	49.31	29.95
San Jose	10.99	12.33	72.59	8.90	19.07	59.91	28.30
Savannah	7.59	9.31	33.45	6.93	13.89	36.44	n/a
Scottsdale	8.56	8.87	43.28	7.54	13.45	35.42	24.46
Seattle	11.46	12.06	47.02	9.19	17.53	46.91	27.98
Sioux Falls	9.18	9.28	32.67	8.20	11.42	35.99	19.86
Springfield (IL)	11.09	11.77	41.64	7.76	13.53	30.45	n/a
Springfield (MO)	8.68	9.44	54.38	7.15	13.00	32.56	25.01
St. Louis	9.40	10.40	53.59	7.96	16.57	37.59	22.85
St. Paul	10.38	12.33	50.76	9.54	17.05	53.12	25.23
St. Petersburg	7.99	9.17	50.77	7.61	12.33	40.93	22.73
Stamford	11.24	13.21	62.70	9.82	18.10	57.31	n/a
Syracuse	9.58	11.30	42.48	7.25	14.89	49.01	23.05
Tampa	7.99	9.17	50.77	7.61	12.33	40.93	22.73
Tucson	8.29	8.66	37.13	7.24	12.11	33.23	23.21
Tulsa	8.16	9.54	30.59	7.27	13.59	33.26	23.79
Virginia Beach	8.40	9.19	64.66	7.59	13.23	34.42	21.99
Washington	9.22	10.55	55.21	9.14	15.51	41.63	25.86
Wichita	9.05	9.95	39.90	7.64	14.79	37.74	23.45

Notes: Wage data is for 2002 and covers the Metropolitan Statistical Area - see Appendix A for areas included; n/a not available
Source: Bureau of Labor Statistics, 2002 Metro Area Occupational Employment and Wage Estimates

Average Hourly Wages: Occupations N - R

MSA[1]	Nurses, Licensed Practical	Nurses, Registered	Nursing Aides/ Orderlies/ Attendants	Packers/ Packagers	Physical Therapists	Postal Mail Carriers	R.E. Brokers
Albuquerque	15.53	24.44	10.00	7.39	26.23	19.05	n/a
Alexandria	18.42	27.56	11.07	9.21	27.77	19.02	37.91
Anchorage	17.32	27.72	13.18	9.18	29.89	n/a	n/a
Ann Arbor	16.98	23.77	11.46	9.51	28.85	18.39	n/a
Atlanta	15.23	23.52	9.82	8.77	29.38	18.55	41.12
Austin	15.92	22.06	9.35	8.07	26.37	18.80	42.40
Baltimore	19.17	29.72	11.81	9.07	29.26	18.88	n/a
Baton Rouge	13.10	20.27	7.19	7.80	32.79	18.43	n/a
Bellevue	17.60	27.47	11.78	9.37	27.64	18.98	39.76
Birmingham	14.01	22.54	8.99	7.76	29.88	18.44	21.14
Boise City	15.41	23.51	9.22	n/a	41.36	n/a	n/a
Boston	19.34	27.71	11.94	9.41	28.29	19.07	52.45
Boulder	16.72	23.42	11.13	8.59	26.26	n/a	27.25
Buffalo	14.04	22.51	10.77	9.27	26.35	n/a	72.32
Cedar Rapids	13.78	18.89	10.14	8.74	26.73	n/a	n/a
Charleston	13.98	24.64	8.49	8.10	26.37	18.63	48.01
Charlotte	16.61	22.80	9.94	9.06	28.59	18.32	41.48
Chattanooga	14.35	20.90	9.13	8.63	29.34	18.58	n/a
Chicago	17.16	24.55	9.84	9.05	29.47	19.00	n/a
Cincinnati	17.90	22.66	10.68	8.83	28.49	18.94	n/a
Cleveland	16.58	24.07	9.91	9.80	29.48	19.13	24.21
Colorado Spgs.	15.89	21.31	10.16	9.15	25.67	n/a	n/a
Columbia	14.83	22.17	9.78	8.36	27.42	n/a	41.20
Columbus	17.31	23.39	10.66	8.99	25.85	18.79	31.28
Dallas	18.26	23.12	9.16	8.85	31.68	18.77	29.72
Denver	17.55	25.03	11.50	8.71	24.34	18.85	29.98
Des Moines	15.52	20.45	10.83	8.39	23.03	18.96	n/a
Detroit	17.09	25.60	10.75	8.40	31.72	18.95	75.90
Durham	15.25	23.00	9.69	9.37	28.90	18.31	20.26
El Paso	15.96	21.14	8.03	7.32	27.71	n/a	n/a
Eugene	n/a	n/a	11.05	10.29	n/a	n/a	n/a
Ft. Collins	16.64	22.51	9.93	7.69	25.40	n/a	30.48
Ft. Lauderdale	16.25	23.19	9.25	7.25	28.32	n/a	56.66
Ft. Wayne	15.59	20.15	9.97	9.94	25.93	18.96	n/a
Ft. Worth	15.95	23.96	9.38	8.13	29.92	18.77	n/a
Grand Rapids	15.73	23.15	10.54	8.81	25.67	18.67	n/a
Green Bay	14.82	21.83	10.49	12.04	26.43	n/a	n/a
Greensboro	15.77	22.29	9.18	8.90	31.65	18.69	18.98
Honolulu	16.09	28.26	11.24	9.16	27.82	n/a	47.88
Houston	17.57	24.60	8.59	7.99	30.64	19.12	25.98
Huntsville	12.18	n/a	7.95	n/a	22.70	n/a	n/a
Indianapolis	17.22	23.02	10.09	9.24	27.93	18.83	30.29
Irvine	18.84	27.74	10.69	8.66	34.54	n/a	37.05
Jacksonville	16.01	22.48	9.66	7.41	25.74	18.88	40.39
Kansas City	15.39	22.76	10.46	8.90	24.87	18.68	26.11
Knoxville	13.14	20.33	8.65	8.86	27.04	18.65	27.46
Las Vegas	16.81	25.59	10.70	7.72	32.99	18.82	21.85
Lexington	14.88	21.07	9.81	8.50	24.75	19.02	n/a
Lincoln	14.66	21.11	10.24	12.74	27.79	n/a	n/a
Los Angeles	17.90	28.25	9.92	8.38	32.83	n/a	55.95
Louisville	15.00	22.72	10.06	8.70	31.12	18.82	24.63
Madison	16.14	23.55	11.69	9.19	26.95	n/a	26.98
Manchester	16.40	23.09	11.64	8.32	28.71	19.01	22.69

Average Hourly Wages: Occupations N - R *continued*

MSA[1]	Nurses, Licensed Practical	Nurses, Registered	Nursing Aides/ Orderlies/ Attendants	Packers/ Packagers	Physical Therapists	Postal Mail Carriers	R.E. Brokers
Memphis	14.39	20.97	9.54	9.09	27.77	18.87	46.83
Miami	15.25	24.94	8.85	7.50	30.53	n/a	60.54
Milwaukee	17.82	24.38	10.38	9.05	27.77	18.85	n/a
Minneapolis	16.50	26.26	12.10	9.90	26.19	18.85	33.74
Naperville	17.16	24.55	9.84	9.05	29.47	19.00	n/a
Nashville	15.83	26.10	9.45	8.72	26.83	18.62	45.94
New Orleans	14.16	23.46	7.50	8.17	30.18	19.25	16.43
New York	17.34	30.68	13.46	8.88	31.26	18.66	n/a
Norfolk	13.40	21.98	8.74	7.82	26.35	19.03	35.83
Oklahoma City	13.60	20.61	8.46	7.82	28.52	18.92	n/a
Omaha	15.26	21.31	10.80	8.95	24.79	19.08	20.66
Orlando	15.10	21.65	9.26	8.01	28.12	19.04	30.99
Overland Park	15.39	22.76	10.46	8.90	24.87	18.68	26.11
Philadelphia	19.83	25.43	10.92	9.55	29.92	19.13	35.97
Phoenix	15.99	24.63	9.90	7.69	29.40	18.81	61.71
Pittsburgh	14.62	21.92	10.09	8.64	27.69	18.96	20.61
Plano	18.26	23.12	9.16	8.85	31.68	18.77	29.72
Portland	17.74	25.89	10.70	9.13	26.23	19.00	n/a
Providence	19.08	24.23	10.92	8.55	28.18	19.26	38.30
Provo	15.23	22.04	9.00	8.41	33.64	n/a	n/a
Raleigh	15.25	23.00	9.69	9.37	28.90	18.31	20.26
Reno	18.33	25.52	11.22	9.38	34.42	n/a	21.11
Richmond	16.32	22.77	9.88	7.92	28.69	18.97	21.85
Rochester	14.77	21.09	10.03	8.92	26.72	18.92	30.27
Sacramento	19.45	27.44	10.92	9.15	29.00	18.69	35.01
Salt Lake City	14.69	22.94	9.26	8.21	25.94	18.87	n/a
San Antonio	14.98	22.15	7.95	7.90	26.03	18.91	22.67
San Diego	17.34	27.73	10.68	8.37	31.59	n/a	41.01
San Francisco	21.05	34.64	13.56	9.54	32.25	19.15	56.48
San Jose	21.23	32.93	12.47	10.40	31.97	n/a	n/a
Savannah	13.06	23.22	8.12	8.21	27.76	18.71	n/a
Scottsdale	15.99	24.63	9.90	7.69	29.40	18.81	61.71
Seattle	17.60	27.47	11.78	9.37	27.64	18.98	39.76
Sioux Falls	13.11	20.31	9.57	8.98	25.06	n/a	n/a
Springfield (IL)	14.73	20.64	8.39	7.33	28.35	n/a	n/a
Springfield (MO)	12.18	19.45	8.58	8.28	24.81	18.54	n/a
St. Louis	15.42	21.87	9.40	8.47	25.07	18.89	38.62
St. Paul	16.50	26.26	12.10	9.90	26.19	18.85	33.74
St. Petersburg	15.32	22.48	10.04	7.38	29.54	19.07	28.33
Stamford	20.78	25.08	12.62	9.29	36.68	18.96	50.54
Syracuse	13.78	20.34	10.12	8.42	28.63	18.80	n/a
Tampa	15.32	22.48	10.04	7.38	29.54	19.07	28.33
Tucson	15.93	22.67	9.46	7.19	30.18	n/a	48.39
Tulsa	14.16	21.09	8.72	8.34	26.91	18.87	n/a
Virginia Beach	13.40	21.98	8.74	7.82	26.35	19.03	35.83
Washington	18.42	27.56	11.07	9.21	27.77	19.02	37.91
Wichita	15.03	19.12	9.89	8.56	28.98	18.75	n/a

Notes: Wage data is for 2002 and covers the Metropolitan Statistical Area - see Appendix A for areas included; n/a not available
Source: Bureau of Labor Statistics, 2002 Metro Area Occupational Employment and Wage Estimates

Average Hourly Wages: Occupations R - T

MSA[1]	Retail Salespersons	Sales Reps., Except Tech./Scien.	Sales Reps., Tech./Scien.	Secretaries, Exc. Leg./ Med./Exec.	Security Guards	Surgeons	Teacher Assistants
Albuquerque	10.00	21.62	27.63	11.37	8.86	77.21	6.80
Alexandria	10.84	25.33	35.46	15.08	11.90	68.44	9.20
Anchorage	12.94	22.49	20.25	13.82	12.24	n/a	n/a
Ann Arbor	11.33	27.43	38.34	13.72	10.06	95.22	10.90
Atlanta	10.90	24.37	31.29	12.69	9.43	88.61	8.50
Austin	11.46	21.39	32.20	12.32	10.01	97.57	9.60
Baltimore	10.25	23.13	42.44	12.68	11.26	93.68	10.00
Baton Rouge	9.51	20.56	28.64	10.94	9.41	99.42	7.80
Bellevue	13.05	23.74	30.35	15.40	11.67	74.01	11.70
Birmingham	10.91	25.16	32.20	11.49	8.82	101.06	7.80
Boise City	9.95	20.70	23.98	11.48	9.80	n/a	n/a
Boston	11.76	30.02	33.87	15.13	10.99	95.85	10.60
Boulder	10.97	30.89	31.06	14.17	10.71	99.17	9.00
Buffalo	8.80	21.97	25.11	12.36	9.10	89.87	9.30
Cedar Rapids	10.52	24.76	24.89	11.18	9.42	n/a	9.00
Charleston	10.23	18.49	25.84	11.38	8.77	82.95	7.70
Charlotte	10.82	25.89	26.11	12.28	11.03	94.76	9.50
Chattanooga	10.74	21.05	26.24	10.85	9.42	93.09	8.10
Chicago	10.84	25.19	28.77	15.07	10.69	84.53	10.40
Cincinnati	10.12	28.86	33.37	12.58	10.65	92.26	10.40
Cleveland	10.15	25.09	29.07	12.88	11.54	86.45	10.90
Colorado Spgs.	10.68	22.14	29.71	13.08	9.72	101.13	9.70
Columbia	10.49	22.23	24.32	11.36	8.70	n/a	7.50
Columbus	10.72	25.25	24.88	13.20	10.27	95.26	11.20
Dallas	10.86	25.29	30.77	13.02	10.18	71.39	8.40
Denver	11.95	26.57	34.83	14.51	11.35	97.50	10.00
Des Moines	12.34	26.44	25.58	12.65	10.00	101.04	8.20
Detroit	11.04	30.76	35.88	13.28	10.21	100.66	11.10
Durham	9.83	25.58	25.18	12.43	10.56	98.13	9.30
El Paso	9.39	19.45	36.55	9.77	8.27	n/a	7.50
Eugene	10.91	20.96	25.55	12.49	9.14	n/a	10.60
Ft. Collins	10.64	23.73	31.63	11.54	10.73	n/a	8.90
Ft. Lauderdale	10.66	26.73	25.60	12.00	9.49	63.11	n/a
Ft. Wayne	10.57	21.98	24.42	11.49	10.28	100.02	9.00
Ft. Worth	10.75	22.41	27.06	12.88	10.41	77.46	7.80
Grand Rapids	11.60	25.00	27.55	12.30	10.10	97.47	11.30
Green Bay	10.33	24.17	28.79	12.66	9.28	n/a	10.00
Greensboro	10.28	25.15	29.09	12.12	10.24	100.71	8.30
Honolulu	10.01	18.14	24.94	15.50	9.88	78.86	9.80
Houston	10.53	25.16	28.39	12.15	9.31	n/a	7.90
Huntsville	9.79	24.13	28.65	11.86	9.95	n/a	6.90
Indianapolis	10.89	26.00	31.03	12.26	10.06	89.41	9.50
Irvine	12.00	27.54	35.18	14.69	10.25	65.42	12.20
Jacksonville	10.25	21.95	21.42	11.77	8.95	93.54	9.80
Kansas City	10.77	26.21	35.67	12.55	11.81	99.20	8.60
Knoxville	10.75	23.76	21.99	10.37	9.25	95.08	7.10
Las Vegas	11.42	24.00	33.11	13.54	10.65	99.81	n/a
Lexington	9.90	21.36	35.06	11.67	9.63	92.20	n/a
Lincoln	9.76	21.14	26.31	11.30	10.14	99.31	8.00
Los Angeles	11.15	23.54	31.45	15.12	9.78	79.98	12.10
Louisville	10.82	22.78	30.24	11.64	10.18	99.02	n/a
Madison	10.31	25.89	24.83	13.57	9.65	n/a	10.40
Manchester	12.10	24.86	34.99	13.43	9.94	n/a	8.70

Average Hourly Wages: Occupations R - T *continued*

MSA[1]	Retail Salespersons	Sales Reps., Except Tech./Scien.	Sales Reps., Tech./Scien.	Secretaries, Exc. Leg./ Med./Exec.	Security Guards	Surgeons	Teacher Assistants
Memphis	11.39	21.53	37.20	11.79	9.63	100.39	6.80
Miami	10.23	21.44	27.99	11.46	8.53	98.53	7.50
Milwaukee	10.33	26.48	34.93	13.10	9.78	82.09	10.20
Minneapolis	10.95	30.78	36.53	14.79	11.09	97.84	10.90
Naperville	10.84	25.19	28.77	15.07	10.69	84.53	10.40
Nashville	11.32	29.19	24.08	12.22	11.61	86.17	7.00
New Orleans	9.64	20.50	25.70	10.96	8.61	93.13	6.80
New York	10.72	29.56	44.40	15.54	10.67	90.97	n/a
Norfolk	9.40	23.00	28.17	11.63	9.30	87.24	7.90
Oklahoma City	11.22	20.66	23.01	11.21	10.25	100.25	7.10
Omaha	10.54	22.28	24.39	11.99	10.75	94.03	8.30
Orlando	9.52	24.46	30.28	12.60	8.89	96.15	8.60
Overland Park	10.77	26.21	35.67	12.55	11.81	99.20	8.60
Philadelphia	10.43	25.96	32.77	13.78	9.78	75.29	8.60
Phoenix	11.17	21.69	24.26	12.54	10.38	87.55	8.80
Pittsburgh	9.39	22.06	30.80	11.07	8.42	n/a	9.10
Plano	10.86	25.29	30.77	13.02	10.18	71.39	8.40
Portland	11.62	26.01	30.24	13.63	10.34	n/a	11.70
Providence	10.50	22.51	30.02	12.96	10.21	82.10	10.20
Provo	9.48	21.05	32.45	10.97	10.24	100.00	8.40
Raleigh	9.83	25.58	25.18	12.43	10.56	98.13	9.30
Reno	11.64	21.02	28.74	14.04	9.83	n/a	n/a
Richmond	9.99	25.19	29.49	13.39	9.89	61.17	9.50
Rochester	9.57	23.76	32.35	12.61	10.68	86.12	9.00
Sacramento	11.54	23.58	32.90	13.72	9.69	86.67	10.50
Salt Lake City	10.37	23.60	29.65	12.05	11.24	94.90	9.10
San Antonio	9.91	18.00	27.06	11.33	9.03	99.29	8.00
San Diego	11.71	25.09	31.46	14.10	9.96	91.22	9.90
San Francisco	12.45	27.06	36.69	17.37	11.62	92.39	13.40
San Jose	12.08	31.88	42.07	17.22	12.85	n/a	11.50
Savannah	9.28	20.66	30.52	11.30	9.09	98.80	7.40
Scottsdale	11.17	21.69	24.26	12.54	10.38	87.55	8.80
Seattle	13.05	23.74	30.35	15.40	11.67	74.01	11.70
Sioux Falls	9.36	19.55	27.70	10.87	10.36	100.33	n/a
Springfield (IL)	9.57	23.00	26.12	12.94	11.20	n/a	9.00
Springfield (MO)	10.50	18.74	26.20	10.41	9.17	n/a	7.00
St. Louis	10.28	24.57	28.64	12.57	10.66	91.68	8.70
St. Paul	10.95	30.78	36.53	14.79	11.09	97.84	10.90
St. Petersburg	10.83	22.73	31.28	12.11	8.85	95.68	8.50
Stamford	14.33	39.47	37.56	15.79	10.67	90.66	11.80
Syracuse	8.54	23.05	27.75	11.88	10.75	95.09	9.50
Tampa	10.83	22.73	31.28	12.11	8.85	95.68	8.50
Tucson	10.30	18.23	25.88	11.47	9.39	100.13	8.80
Tulsa	10.37	21.02	27.56	11.36	9.80	100.50	7.50
Virginia Beach	9.40	23.00	28.17	11.63	9.30	87.24	7.90
Washington	10.84	25.33	35.46	15.08	11.90	68.44	9.20
Wichita	10.56	23.94	28.89	11.35	9.88	82.53	8.30

Notes: Wage data is for 2002 and covers the Metropolitan Statistical Area - see Appendix A for areas included; hourly wages for teacher assistants were calculated by the editors from annual wage data assuming a 40 hour work week; n/a not available
Source: Bureau of Labor Statistics, 2002 Metro Area Occupational Employment and Wage Estimates

Average Hourly Wages: Occupations T - Z

MSA[1]	Teachers, Elementary School	Teachers, Secondary School	Tele-marketers	Truck Driv., Heavy/ Trac. Trail.	Truck Drivers, Light	Waiters/ Waitresses
Albuquerque	n/a	n/a	9.50	14.86	12.50	6.91
Alexandria	21.50	22.40	12.35	17.19	13.45	7.97
Anchorage	n/a	n/a	9.57	19.22	14.19	7.23
Ann Arbor	24.30	24.00	11.38	17.84	13.11	7.17
Atlanta	21.80	21.90	12.11	18.58	12.72	7.59
Austin	19.50	20.20	11.44	14.72	13.19	7.61
Baltimore	23.60	23.40	10.44	16.17	14.37	7.25
Baton Rouge	17.10	n/a	n/a	15.12	12.26	6.35
Bellevue	20.70	21.40	12.11	18.11	14.08	9.59
Birmingham	18.70	20.60	8.49	17.00	12.76	6.57
Boise City	n/a	n/a	9.65	15.17	12.48	6.34
Boston	23.90	23.20	14.86	19.16	14.97	10.19
Boulder	n/a	21.10	11.43	15.65	13.04	8.00
Buffalo	24.00	23.30	10.50	16.96	12.06	6.55
Cedar Rapids	15.90	17.00	9.95	15.97	12.77	6.81
Charleston	17.60	16.80	9.68	15.96	11.18	6.43
Charlotte	19.10	19.60	n/a	17.09	13.30	6.99
Chattanooga	18.20	19.50	7.88	18.33	12.70	7.41
Chicago	21.60	26.90	11.17	19.09	15.37	7.56
Cincinnati	21.70	22.90	10.07	16.39	13.23	7.16
Cleveland	22.40	21.20	11.09	17.84	13.26	7.07
Colorado Spgs.	17.00	19.60	n/a	15.49	14.19	9.63
Columbia	17.30	19.20	n/a	16.57	12.10	6.91
Columbus	21.90	21.40	9.27	17.12	13.55	6.86
Dallas	20.40	21.60	11.82	16.40	13.50	7.53
Denver	19.80	22.30	11.03	17.16	13.78	9.68
Des Moines	17.10	19.30	9.43	17.40	13.46	6.70
Detroit	24.00	23.90	11.27	17.92	14.44	6.84
Durham	19.60	20.70	11.52	14.57	12.83	7.94
El Paso	19.00	19.40	n/a	12.84	11.29	6.68
Eugene	20.90	21.30	10.51	15.04	11.19	8.43
Ft. Collins	n/a	n/a	n/a	14.18	11.93	9.86
Ft. Lauderdale	n/a	n/a	10.22	14.07	11.57	7.65
Ft. Wayne	21.20	21.70	11.21	17.68	13.34	7.16
Ft. Worth	19.50	22.20	9.42	16.18	12.59	8.43
Grand Rapids	23.20	23.20	11.45	16.76	13.44	6.94
Green Bay	19.80	21.00	11.22	19.16	11.42	7.24
Greensboro	18.50	19.10	10.97	16.25	12.61	6.71
Honolulu	19.30	20.30	10.29	17.31	11.57	9.78
Houston	20.00	21.30	10.09	15.73	12.50	8.34
Huntsville	19.50	19.90	8.18	14.37	11.67	6.30
Indianapolis	21.40	23.40	10.17	17.64	14.34	6.97
Irvine	24.00	26.70	13.42	16.70	12.62	8.01
Jacksonville	20.60	20.70	11.06	16.90	14.10	7.45
Kansas City	16.80	18.30	11.20	17.57	13.02	7.21
Knoxville	18.80	19.80	n/a	16.94	10.84	6.59
Las Vegas	n/a	n/a	10.42	16.90	12.20	7.94
Lexington	18.80	20.00	11.64	18.81	11.99	7.41
Lincoln	17.40	18.20	9.58	16.85	13.15	6.30
Los Angeles	24.00	26.00	10.97	17.07	12.06	7.79
Louisville	22.60	23.20	10.11	16.35	n/a	6.73
Madison	18.80	19.50	8.97	16.74	11.22	7.06
Manchester	n/a	n/a	11.94	16.02	14.82	8.57

Average Hourly Wages: Occupations T - Z *continued*

MSA[1]	Teachers, Elementary School	Teachers, Secondary School	Tele-marketers	Truck Driv., Heavy/ Trac. Trail.	Truck Drivers, Light	Waiters/ Waitresses
Memphis	20.00	18.90	11.66	17.38	12.27	7.44
Miami	n/a	n/a	12.56	14.97	12.12	7.33
Milwaukee	21.80	23.20	11.56	18.16	11.26	7.38
Minneapolis	21.50	21.90	13.24	19.24	14.15	7.30
Naperville	21.60	26.90	11.17	19.09	15.37	7.56
Nashville	16.40	17.30	12.19	17.63	13.99	6.90
New Orleans	17.50	17.20	19.65	13.95	12.91	7.19
New York	n/a	n/a	12.23	20.05	14.99	10.97
Norfolk	20.40	21.50	9.63	14.67	10.65	7.19
Oklahoma City	15.60	15.70	7.90	16.17	9.85	6.97
Omaha	21.30	20.50	9.70	17.95	11.42	7.08
Orlando	18.30	19.70	11.26	16.54	12.74	6.63
Overland Park	16.80	18.30	11.20	17.57	13.02	7.21
Philadelphia	25.80	23.30	11.83	18.29	13.08	7.74
Phoenix	17.20	20.90	9.93	16.57	12.78	6.86
Pittsburgh	24.40	25.10	11.41	17.39	12.05	7.19
Plano	20.40	21.60	11.82	16.40	13.50	7.53
Portland	21.50	21.60	10.45	16.80	12.46	8.03
Providence	24.10	24.70	11.33	16.43	13.12	7.83
Provo	17.40	19.80	12.41	16.10	11.40	7.92
Raleigh	19.60	20.70	11.52	14.57	12.83	7.94
Reno	n/a	n/a	10.68	17.57	13.44	6.37
Richmond	20.50	21.50	15.20	17.67	10.88	6.90
Rochester	n/a	25.00	11.07	15.28	11.61	7.03
Sacramento	23.20	25.20	10.37	17.36	12.16	8.24
Salt Lake City	18.60	22.30	10.67	17.30	13.31	7.26
San Antonio	20.60	22.70	9.01	14.09	10.97	8.07
San Diego	23.30	24.90	11.01	16.52	11.96	8.52
San Francisco	22.80	24.70	13.11	17.78	13.72	9.46
San Jose	24.70	27.60	19.06	18.73	13.98	8.27
Savannah	21.20	21.50	n/a	16.01	11.31	7.07
Scottsdale	17.20	20.90	9.93	16.57	12.78	6.86
Seattle	20.70	21.40	12.11	18.11	14.08	9.59
Sioux Falls	n/a	16.40	10.39	16.31	11.66	6.35
Springfield (IL)	15.70	20.20	9.93	19.38	14.82	7.01
Springfield (MO)	15.40	15.80	9.34	16.12	12.70	8.04
St. Louis	19.40	19.70	10.78	18.64	13.42	7.65
St. Paul	21.50	21.90	13.24	19.24	14.15	7.30
St. Petersburg	20.10	21.60	12.45	14.41	11.87	7.66
Stamford	26.30	28.60	15.51	20.23	13.10	10.44
Syracuse	22.50	22.10	10.98	16.78	11.77	6.99
Tampa	20.10	21.60	12.45	14.41	11.87	7.66
Tucson	19.10	19.90	7.48	15.28	12.36	6.70
Tulsa	16.10	16.90	8.97	15.53	10.71	6.75
Virginia Beach	20.40	21.50	9.63	14.67	10.65	7.19
Washington	21.50	22.40	12.35	17.19	13.45	7.97
Wichita	17.90	16.90	8.75	14.96	9.17	7.15

Notes: Wage data is for 2002 and covers the Metropolitan Statistical Area - see Appendix A for areas included; hourly wages for elementary and secondary school teachers were calculated by the editors from annual wage data assuming a 40 hour work week; n/a not available
Source: Bureau of Labor Statistics, 2002 Metro Area Occupational Employment and Wage Estimates

Means of Transportation to Work: City

City	Car/Truck/Van		Public Transportation			Bicycle	Walked	Other Means	Worked at Home
	Drove Alone	Car-pooled	Bus	Subway	Railroad				
Albuquerque	77.7	12.5	1.6	0.0	0.0	1.1	2.7	0.7	3.6
Alexandria	62.8	13.2	6.4	9.3	0.1	0.5	3.0	1.2	3.5
Anchorage	74.4	14.6	1.8	0.0	0.0	0.5	2.7	2.3	3.7
Ann Arbor	62.6	7.9	6.3	0.0	0.0	2.3	15.8	0.7	4.4
Atlanta	64.0	12.4	11.5	3.0	0.2	0.3	3.5	1.3	3.8
Austin	73.6	13.9	4.3	0.0	0.0	0.9	2.5	1.3	3.4
Baltimore	54.7	15.2	16.2	1.4	0.8	0.3	7.1	1.9	2.3
Baton Rouge	77.6	12.4	2.2	0.0	0.0	0.8	3.8	0.8	2.4
Bellevue	74.0	10.6	6.6	0.0	0.0	0.4	2.6	0.6	5.1
Birmingham	76.9	15.8	2.4	0.0	0.0	0.1	2.4	1.1	1.2
Boise City	79.9	10.3	1.1	0.0	0.0	1.7	2.3	0.8	4.0
Boston	41.5	9.2	12.2	16.3	1.0	1.0	13.0	3.4	2.4
Boulder	59.8	8.7	8.3	0.0	0.0	6.9	9.0	0.8	6.5
Buffalo	65.4	14.4	11.3	0.6	0.0	0.4	5.3	0.9	1.7
Cedar Rapids	82.3	10.7	1.1	0.0	0.0	0.4	2.5	0.7	2.3
Charleston	73.5	11.6	2.7	0.0	0.0	1.2	6.6	1.6	2.7
Charlotte	77.8	13.4	3.0	0.0	0.0	0.1	1.5	1.0	3.2
Chattanooga	79.5	13.3	1.6	0.0	0.0	0.2	2.2	1.2	2.1
Chicago	50.1	14.5	13.7	9.7	1.7	0.5	5.7	1.8	2.4
Cincinnati	69.5	11.4	9.8	0.0	0.0	0.2	5.5	1.0	2.6
Cleveland	67.8	13.5	11.1	0.5	0.1	0.2	4.0	1.1	1.6
Colorado Spgs.	79.6	11.7	1.0	0.0	0.0	0.5	2.5	0.9	3.8
Columbia	65.4	11.3	3.7	0.0	0.0	0.4	13.4	3.1	2.7
Columbus	79.0	10.8	3.8	0.0	0.0	0.3	3.2	0.6	2.3
Dallas	70.8	17.8	5.0	0.2	0.2	0.1	1.9	1.2	2.8
Denver	68.3	13.5	8.0	0.1	0.1	1.0	4.3	1.1	3.7
Des Moines	78.9	12.5	2.3	0.0	0.0	0.2	2.9	0.7	2.3
Detroit	68.6	17.1	8.0	0.0	0.0	0.2	2.8	1.5	1.8
Durham	72.7	17.0	3.3	0.0	0.0	0.4	3.1	0.8	2.7
El Paso	76.5	15.8	2.2	0.0	0.0	0.1	2.0	1.1	2.2
Eugene	66.8	11.2	4.8	0.0	0.0	5.5	6.1	0.8	4.7
Ft. Collins	75.3	10.2	1.4	0.0	0.0	4.4	3.6	0.6	4.3
Ft. Lauderdale	75.2	11.3	4.4	0.0	0.2	1.1	2.4	1.7	3.8
Ft. Wayne	81.8	12.2	1.1	0.0	0.0	0.2	2.1	0.6	2.0
Ft. Worth	77.0	16.7	1.3	0.0	0.0	0.1	1.7	1.0	2.1
Grand Rapids	76.5	12.8	2.1	0.0	0.0	0.4	4.0	1.4	2.7
Green Bay	82.9	10.3	1.3	0.0	0.0	0.4	2.8	0.5	1.8
Greensboro	79.3	12.8	1.3	0.0	0.0	0.3	2.4	1.2	2.7
Honolulu	57.7	18.1	11.3	0.0	0.0	1.2	6.6	2.0	3.1
Houston	71.8	15.9	5.7	0.0	0.0	0.5	2.3	1.4	2.3
Huntsville	83.8	11.2	0.3	0.0	0.0	0.2	1.5	0.7	2.4
Indianapolis	80.0	12.3	2.3	0.0	0.0	0.2	2.0	0.7	2.5
Irvine	79.2	8.2	0.5	0.0	0.1	1.1	4.8	0.7	5.4
Jacksonville	79.2	13.4	1.7	0.0	0.0	0.4	1.8	1.5	1.9
Kansas City	78.7	11.8	3.6	0.0	0.0	0.1	2.3	0.8	2.6
Knoxville	80.5	10.5	1.3	0.0	0.0	0.3	4.2	0.8	2.3
Las Vegas	73.8	15.1	4.7	0.0	0.0	0.4	2.2	1.5	2.4
Lexington	79.9	11.2	1.2	0.0	0.0	0.6	4.0	0.6	2.5
Lincoln	80.7	10.1	1.2	0.0	0.0	1.0	3.4	0.8	2.9
Los Angeles	65.7	14.7	9.7	0.2	0.1	0.6	3.6	1.2	4.1
Louisville	73.5	12.6	6.7	0.0	0.0	0.4	4.1	0.8	1.8
Madison	65.7	9.6	6.9	0.0	0.0	3.2	10.7	0.8	3.1
Manchester	81.0	11.9	1.1	0.0	0.0	0.2	2.9	0.7	2.2

Means of Transportation to Work: City *continued*

| City | Car/Truck/Van | | Public Transportation | | | Bicycle | Walked | Other Means | Worked at Home |
	Drove Alone	Car-pooled	Bus	Subway	Railroad				
Memphis	76.6	15.7	2.8	0.0	0.0	0.1	1.9	1.1	1.7
Miami	64.5	16.3	10.0	0.7	0.3	0.6	3.7	1.9	2.1
Milwaukee	68.8	13.6	10.0	0.0	0.0	0.3	4.7	0.8	1.7
Minneapolis	61.6	11.3	14.4	0.0	0.0	1.9	6.6	0.8	3.4
Naperville	78.6	4.9	0.1	0.1	8.7	0.1	1.4	0.6	5.6
Nashville	78.5	13.5	1.7	0.0	0.0	0.1	2.4	0.8	3.0
New Orleans .	60.3	16.1	12.4	0.0	0.0	1.2	5.2	2.1	2.7
New York	24.9	8.0	11.4	37.6	1.6	0.5	10.4	2.8	2.9
Norfolk	66.8	14.2	4.2	0.0	0.0	0.5	6.8	3.7	3.8
Oklahoma City	80.4	13.1	0.7	0.0	0.0	0.1	1.6	1.3	2.7
Omaha	81.3	11.1	1.8	0.0	0.0	0.1	2.4	0.7	2.6
Orlando	78.9	11.2	3.9	0.0	0.0	0.6	1.9	1.3	2.2
Overland Park	86.8	6.5	0.4	0.0	0.0	0.1	0.7	0.5	5.1
Philadelphia	49.2	12.8	17.4	4.8	2.3	0.9	9.1	1.6	1.9
Phoenix	71.7	17.4	3.0	0.0	0.0	0.9	2.2	1.5	3.3
Pittsburgh	54.8	11.4	19.7	0.2	0.0	0.4	9.8	1.3	2.4
Plano	83.1	8.9	1.0	0.0	0.0	0.1	1.2	0.9	4.7
Portland	63.7	11.9	11.3	0.4	0.2	1.8	5.2	1.3	4.3
Providence	60.5	15.4	5.9	0.1	1.0	1.0	12.2	1.3	2.5
Provo	63.2	15.5	1.7	0.0	0.0	1.9	12.8	0.6	4.1
Raleigh	78.7	11.5	2.0	0.0	0.0	0.3	2.9	1.3	3.3
Reno	72.6	14.3	4.1	0.0	0.0	0.9	4.4	1.2	2.4
Richmond	70.6	12.6	8.1	0.0	0.0	1.1	4.4	0.9	2.3
Rochester	69.6	12.1	7.7	0.0	0.0	0.5	6.5	1.2	2.3
Sacramento	71.0	16.3	3.8	0.1	0.1	1.4	2.8	1.5	2.9
St. Louis	68.9	13.6	9.9	0.3	0.1	0.3	4.0	1.1	1.7
St. Paul	69.2	12.4	8.5	0.0	0.0	0.7	5.4	0.9	3.0
St. Petersburg	78.1	11.8	2.5	0.0	0.0	0.9	2.2	1.4	3.1
Salt Lake City	69.3	13.9	5.9	0.0	0.1	1.5	4.9	1.1	3.2
San Antonio	75.6	15.2	3.7	0.0	0.0	0.2	2.2	1.0	2.2
San Diego	74.0	12.2	3.8	0.0	0.0	0.7	3.6	1.5	4.0
San Francisco	40.5	10.8	21.4	6.0	0.6	2.0	9.4	4.8	4.6
San Jose	76.4	14.1	3.3	0.1	0.4	0.6	1.4	1.3	2.5
Savannah	70.8	15.3	4.5	0.0	0.0	1.1	4.3	1.6	2.4
Scottsdale	80.3	7.6	0.9	0.0	0.0	0.8	1.7	1.5	7.1
Seattle	56.5	11.2	17.3	0.0	0.0	1.9	7.4	1.1	4.6
Sioux Falls	84.3	9.2	0.7	0.0	0.0	0.2	2.3	0.6	2.7
Springfield (IL)	80.6	11.2	2.3	0.0	0.0	0.5	2.6	0.7	2.1
Springfield (MO)	80.1	11.0	1.0	0.0	0.0	0.6	3.6	1.1	2.6
Stamford	70.1	10.6	4.6	0.1	5.7	0.2	3.7	1.2	3.8
Syracuse	65.9	13.7	6.8	0.0	0.0	0.6	10.1	0.8	2.0
Tampa	76.6	13.7	2.6	0.0	0.0	0.9	2.3	1.3	2.6
Tucson	71.0	15.7	3.4	0.0	0.0	2.2	3.4	1.5	2.9
Tulsa	79.4	13.1	1.1	0.0	0.0	0.2	2.2	1.0	3.1
Virginia Beach	82.0	10.8	0.7	0.0	0.0	0.3	2.0	1.4	2.8
Washington	38.4	11.0	14.6	17.4	0.2	1.2	11.8	1.6	3.8
Wichita	84.4	10.2	0.7	0.0	0.0	0.2	1.4	0.8	2.3
U.S.	75.7	12.2	2.5	1.5	0.5	0.4	2.9	1.0	3.3

Note: Figures shown are percentages and cover workers 16 years of age and older
Source: Census 2000, Summary File 3

Means of Transportation to Work: Metro Area

MSA[1]	Car/Truck/Van		Public Transportation			Bicycle	Walked	Other Means	Worked at Home
	Drove Alone	Car-pooled	Bus	Subway	Railroad				
Albuquerque	77.7	13.3	1.2	0.0	0.0	0.8	2.3	0.9	3.9
Alexandria	67.8	13.4	4.0	6.5	0.4	0.3	3.0	0.9	3.7
Anchorage	74.4	14.6	1.8	0.0	0.0	0.5	2.7	2.3	3.7
Ann Arbor	80.1	8.5	1.8	0.0	0.0	0.6	4.9	0.6	3.4
Atlanta	77.0	13.6	2.4	1.0	0.1	0.1	1.3	1.1	3.5
Austin	76.5	13.7	2.5	0.0	0.0	0.6	2.1	1.1	3.6
Baltimore	75.5	11.5	4.3	0.9	0.6	0.2	2.9	1.0	3.2
Baton Rouge	82.0	11.7	1.0	0.0	0.0	0.3	2.0	0.8	2.2
Bellevue	70.4	12.6	7.8	0.0	0.0	0.7	3.2	0.9	4.4
Birmingham	83.5	11.7	0.7	0.0	0.0	0.1	1.2	0.7	2.2
Boise City	79.9	11.4	0.6	0.0	0.0	1.0	2.2	0.8	4.1
Boston	68.2	8.2	4.1	6.5	2.1	0.5	5.3	1.6	3.4
Boulder	70.8	10.4	4.8	0.0	0.0	2.8	4.1	0.7	6.4
Buffalo	81.7	9.4	3.1	0.2	0.0	0.2	2.7	0.6	2.1
Cedar Rapids	82.3	10.3	0.9	0.0	0.0	0.3	2.6	0.6	2.9
Charleston	78.1	13.0	1.1	0.0	0.0	0.5	3.5	1.6	2.2
Charlotte	80.9	12.9	1.3	0.0	0.0	0.1	1.2	0.8	2.8
Chattanooga	82.7	12.2	0.6	0.0	0.0	0.1	1.5	0.8	2.1
Chicago	69.3	11.0	5.0	3.6	3.5	0.3	3.2	1.1	3.0
Cincinnati	80.8	10.2	3.2	0.0	0.0	0.1	2.2	0.7	2.8
Cleveland	81.3	9.0	3.5	0.3	0.1	0.2	2.2	0.8	2.7
Colorado Spgs.	78.0	12.0	0.8	0.0	0.0	0.4	3.7	0.9	4.0
Columbia	79.3	11.9	1.1	0.0	0.0	0.1	3.7	1.3	2.5
Columbus	82.0	9.6	2.2	0.0	0.0	0.2	2.4	0.6	3.0
Dallas	77.6	14.3	2.1	0.1	0.1	0.1	1.5	1.0	3.1
Denver	76.1	11.6	4.4	0.1	0.0	0.4	2.1	0.8	4.5
Des Moines	81.8	10.7	1.5	0.0	0.0	0.2	2.1	0.5	3.3
Detroit	84.8	9.2	1.7	0.0	0.0	0.1	1.4	0.6	2.1
Durham	78.5	12.9	1.5	0.0	0.0	0.4	2.3	0.9	3.5
El Paso	75.9	16.2	2.2	0.0	0.0	0.1	2.2	1.3	2.1
Eugene	71.6	12.2	3.2	0.0	0.0	3.0	4.2	0.6	5.1
Ft. Collins	77.4	11.0	0.8	0.0	0.0	2.4	2.7	0.6	5.1
Ft. Lauderdale	80.0	12.0	1.9	0.0	0.1	0.5	1.3	1.1	2.9
Ft. Wayne	83.6	10.4	0.5	0.0	0.0	0.2	1.8	0.6	2.8
Ft. Worth	81.2	13.3	0.4	0.0	0.0	0.1	1.4	0.9	2.7
Grand Rapids	84.0	9.2	0.7	0.0	0.0	0.2	2.1	0.7	3.1
Green Bay	84.7	8.4	0.8	0.0	0.0	0.2	2.8	0.5	2.5
Greensboro	81.2	13.1	0.7	0.0	0.0	0.1	1.6	0.9	2.4
Honolulu	61.4	19.4	8.1	0.0	0.0	0.9	5.6	1.7	2.9
Houston	76.6	14.4	3.4	0.0	0.0	0.3	1.6	1.2	2.5
Huntsville	83.9	11.5	0.2	0.0	0.0	0.1	1.3	0.7	2.3
Indianapolis	82.8	10.5	1.2	0.0	0.0	0.2	1.7	0.7	2.9
Irvine	76.5	13.3	2.5	0.0	0.2	0.8	2.0	0.9	3.7
Jacksonville	80.3	12.6	1.3	0.0	0.0	0.5	1.7	1.4	2.3
Kansas City	82.8	10.4	1.2	0.0	0.0	0.1	1.4	0.7	3.4
Knoxville	84.2	10.0	0.4	0.0	0.0	0.1	1.9	0.6	2.7
Las Vegas	74.5	15.0	3.9	0.0	0.0	0.5	2.4	1.3	2.3
Lexington	79.8	11.9	0.7	0.0	0.0	0.4	3.9	0.6	2.7
Lincoln	80.6	10.2	1.1	0.0	0.0	0.9	3.2	0.7	3.2
Los Angeles	70.4	15.1	6.1	0.2	0.2	0.6	2.9	1.1	3.5
Louisville	82.0	10.9	2.1	0.0	0.0	0.2	1.7	0.7	2.4
Madison	74.1	9.5	4.0	0.0	0.0	1.7	6.2	0.6	3.8
Manchester	82.5	10.2	0.8	0.0	0.0	0.2	2.4	0.8	3.0

Means of Transportation to Work: Metro Area *continued*

MSA[1]	Car/Truck/Van		Public Transportation			Bicycle	Walked	Other Means	Worked at Home
	Drove Alone	Car-pooled	Bus	Subway	Railroad				
Memphis	80.9	13.0	1.6	0.0	0.0	0.1	1.3	0.9	2.2
Miami	73.8	14.6	4.3	0.6	0.2	0.5	2.2	1.2	2.7
Milwaukee	79.7	9.9	4.1	0.0	0.0	0.2	2.9	0.6	2.6
Minneapolis	78.3	10.0	4.4	0.0	0.0	0.4	2.4	0.6	3.8
Naperville	69.3	11.0	5.0	3.6	3.5	0.3	3.2	1.1	3.0
Nashville	80.7	12.8	0.9	0.0	0.0	0.1	1.5	0.8	3.2
New Orleans	73.0	14.6	5.0	0.0	0.0	0.6	2.7	1.6	2.4
New York	31.4	8.3	10.4	31.8	3.0	0.4	9.3	2.5	3.0
Norfolk	78.9	12.1	1.7	0.0	0.0	0.3	2.7	1.6	2.7
Oklahoma City	81.8	12.0	0.5	0.0	0.0	0.2	1.7	1.0	2.8
Omaha	82.9	10.5	1.1	0.0	0.0	0.1	1.9	0.6	2.9
Orlando	80.6	12.1	1.6	0.0	0.0	0.4	1.3	1.2	2.9
Overland Park	82.8	10.4	1.2	0.0	0.0	0.1	1.4	0.7	3.4
Philadelphia	72.3	10.1	5.5	1.8	2.1	0.3	4.1	0.9	2.9
Phoenix	74.6	15.3	1.8	0.0	0.0	0.9	2.1	1.4	3.7
Pittsburgh	77.4	9.7	5.6	0.1	0.0	0.1	3.6	1.0	2.4
Plano	77.6	14.3	2.1	0.1	0.1	0.1	1.5	1.0	3.1
Portland	73.1	11.5	5.3	0.4	0.2	0.8	3.0	1.1	4.6
Providence	80.7	10.6	1.7	0.0	0.6	0.2	3.3	0.8	2.1
Provo	72.5	14.9	1.3	0.0	0.0	0.8	4.9	0.5	5.0
Raleigh	78.5	12.9	1.5	0.0	0.0	0.4	2.3	0.9	3.5
Reno	75.3	13.8	3.0	0.0	0.0	0.7	3.2	1.2	2.9
Richmond	82.0	10.4	1.9	0.0	0.0	0.3	1.9	0.8	2.6
Rochester	81.8	9.1	1.9	0.0	0.0	0.2	3.5	0.6	2.9
Sacramento	76.2	13.6	2.0	0.1	0.2	0.7	2.0	1.2	4.1
St. Louis	82.6	9.9	2.1	0.2	0.0	0.1	1.6	0.7	2.8
St. Paul	78.3	10.0	4.4	0.0	0.0	0.4	2.4	0.6	3.8
St. Petersburg	79.7	12.4	1.2	0.0	0.0	0.6	1.7	1.2	3.1
Salt Lake City	77.2	13.1	2.5	0.1	0.2	0.4	1.8	0.9	3.8
San Antonio	76.2	14.7	2.8	0.0	0.0	0.1	2.4	1.2	2.6
San Diego	73.9	13.0	2.9	0.0	0.2	0.6	3.4	1.6	4.4
San Francisco	56.5	11.6	12.3	3.7	0.9	1.4	5.6	3.1	4.8
San Jose	77.3	12.2	2.6	0.1	0.6	1.2	1.8	1.0	3.1
Savannah	77.8	13.4	2.3	0.0	0.0	0.5	2.4	1.1	2.4
Scottsdale	74.6	15.3	1.8	0.0	0.0	0.9	2.1	1.4	3.7
Seattle	70.4	12.6	7.8	0.0	0.0	0.7	3.2	0.9	4.4
Sioux Falls	83.7	9.3	0.6	0.0	0.0	0.2	2.3	0.6	3.4
Springfield (IL)	81.8	11.1	1.4	0.0	0.0	0.3	2.1	0.6	2.7
Springfield (MO)	81.8	10.8	0.5	0.0	0.0	0.3	2.1	0.9	3.6
Stamford	69.1	8.4	2.6	0.2	9.9	0.1	2.9	0.9	5.9
Syracuse	80.0	10.2	1.8	0.0	0.0	0.2	4.1	0.6	3.0
Tampa	79.7	12.4	1.2	0.0	0.0	0.6	1.7	1.2	3.1
Tucson	73.8	14.7	2.4	0.0	0.0	1.4	2.6	1.4	3.6
Tulsa	81.1	12.6	0.6	0.0	0.0	0.1	1.6	0.8	3.1
Virginia Beach	78.9	12.1	1.7	0.0	0.0	0.3	2.7	1.6	2.7
Washington	67.8	13.4	4.0	6.5	0.4	0.3	3.0	0.9	3.7
Wichita	84.6	9.7	0.5	0.0	0.0	0.2	1.6	0.7	2.7
U.S.	75.7	12.2	2.5	1.5	0.5	0.4	2.9	1.0	3.3

Note: Figures shown are percentages and cover workers 16 years of age and older; (1) Metropolitan Statistical Area - see Appendix A for areas included
Source: Census 2000, Summary File 3

Travel Time to Work: City

City	Less Than 15 Minutes	15 to 29 Minutes	30 to 44 Minutes	45 to 59 Minutes	60 Minutes or More
Albuquerque	29.4	50.5	14.3	2.5	3.3
Alexandria	16.0	34.4	27.7	13.9	7.9
Anchorage	36.4	46.7	11.2	2.3	3.4
Ann Arbor	44.1	35.8	11.0	5.6	3.5
Atlanta	22.3	40.2	20.9	6.7	10.0
Austin	27.0	45.2	19.1	4.5	4.2
Baltimore	17.9	38.9	22.8	8.0	12.4
Baton Rouge	32.7	46.4	13.6	3.2	4.1
Bellevue	28.8	44.5	20.2	3.8	2.7
Birmingham	23.7	48.1	19.8	3.7	4.6
Boise City	38.4	48.2	9.3	1.6	2.4
Boston	17.6	34.7	28.6	10.7	8.3
Boulder	45.5	35.1	10.1	4.8	4.5
Buffalo	32.2	46.4	13.4	3.5	4.6
Cedar Rapids	49.2	39.3	7.2	1.8	2.4
Charleston	34.8	44.1	14.7	3.2	3.2
Charlotte	22.3	42.7	23.6	6.4	5.0
Chattanooga	33.4	48.0	13.1	2.4	3.2
Chicago	13.2	27.9	28.3	14.7	16.0
Cincinnati	26.0	46.5	18.3	4.7	4.6
Cleveland	22.0	45.0	20.7	5.6	6.7
Colorado Spgs.	31.4	48.0	13.7	2.8	4.1
Columbia	45.1	39.6	9.8	2.0	3.5
Columbus	26.1	49.1	17.7	3.6	3.4
Dallas	20.3	39.7	25.4	7.8	6.8
Denver	24.6	41.8	22.0	6.1	5.5
Des Moines	38.9	47.7	9.4	2.0	2.0
Detroit	17.2	43.2	24.3	7.2	8.1
Durham	30.9	46.3	15.7	3.9	3.2
El Paso	25.4	47.9	19.5	3.7	3.4
Eugene	48.2	40.4	6.4	1.8	3.2
Ft. Collins	45.6	38.9	7.8	2.8	4.9
Ft. Lauderdale	29.7	38.5	19.7	5.8	6.4
Ft. Wayne	32.7	48.9	12.3	2.7	3.3
Ft. Worth	24.6	42.7	19.9	6.5	6.2
Grand Rapids	36.1	47.1	10.7	2.7	3.3
Green Bay	45.4	42.9	6.4	2.5	2.8
Greensboro	34.3	45.6	13.3	2.8	3.9
Honolulu	26.2	42.2	21.6	5.4	4.6
Houston	20.8	37.3	26.1	8.3	7.5
Huntsville	38.0	47.4	10.4	1.9	2.3
Indianapolis	25.8	47.6	18.8	3.8	4.0
Irvine	29.9	44.5	14.1	5.0	6.5
Jacksonville	21.2	43.7	24.1	6.4	4.6
Kansas City	27.7	46.8	18.8	3.4	3.3
Knoxville	33.2	46.8	13.8	3.2	3.1
Las Vegas	19.7	45.9	24.5	4.6	5.3
Lexington	34.2	48.0	12.2	2.8	2.8
Lincoln	43.9	45.0	6.3	1.7	3.1
Los Angeles	18.9	35.6	25.7	9.3	10.6
Louisville	32.6	48.8	12.4	2.5	3.7
Madison	39.0	45.7	10.3	2.3	2.7
Manchester	39.2	37.2	13.0	4.0	6.6

Travel Time to Work: City *continued*

City	Less Than 15 Minutes	15 to 29 Minutes	30 to 44 Minutes	45 to 59 Minutes	60 Minutes or More
Memphis	24.0	48.2	20.0	3.9	3.9
Miami	20.0	38.9	24.8	6.6	9.6
Milwaukee	27.8	46.2	17.0	4.4	4.6
Minneapolis	26.1	50.0	17.0	3.3	3.7
Naperville	21.3	29.8	19.0	11.8	17.9
Nashville	24.2	46.1	21.1	4.6	3.9
New Orleans	23.2	43.2	20.3	6.1	7.2
New York	11.6	22.9	25.3	15.7	24.5
Norfolk	31.3	44.4	16.6	3.6	4.2
Oklahoma City	30.0	49.2	15.1	2.5	3.2
Omaha	36.0	50.3	9.9	1.4	2.5
Orlando	21.7	43.7	23.6	5.9	5.1
Overland Park	34.2	46.2	15.1	2.4	2.0
Philadelphia	17.2	32.2	26.2	11.7	12.7
Phoenix	22.5	38.4	25.1	7.9	6.1
Pittsburgh	27.1	43.5	19.6	5.1	4.8
Plano	21.1	36.0	25.3	10.4	7.2
Portland	25.5	45.6	19.2	4.9	4.8
Providence	40.6	38.7	11.6	3.8	5.3
Provo	55.7	32.3	5.6	3.1	3.3
Raleigh	29.2	44.5	18.1	4.3	3.9
Reno	41.4	45.8	7.0	2.4	3.4
Richmond	28.7	47.6	15.1	3.7	4.8
Rochester	36.7	46.3	10.6	2.3	4.0
Sacramento	27.5	45.6	17.3	4.4	5.3
St. Louis	25.0	43.8	19.4	5.7	6.1
St. Paul	30.0	46.8	16.0	3.9	3.2
St. Petersburg	30.8	41.1	17.9	5.7	4.5
Salt Lake City	38.1	43.7	12.2	2.8	3.2
San Antonio	23.2	46.0	21.7	4.5	4.5
San Diego	25.1	46.2	19.8	4.4	4.6
San Francisco	14.9	35.0	27.4	11.3	11.4
San Jose	16.8	39.9	26.4	9.3	7.5
Savannah	34.2	41.9	15.3	4.0	4.6
Scottsdale	26.9	39.4	22.6	7.1	4.1
Seattle	21.9	42.7	23.7	6.6	5.1
Sioux Falls	48.1	45.1	3.4	0.9	2.5
Springfield (IL)	41.6	47.6	6.1	1.7	3.0
Springfield (MO)	45.3	43.2	7.2	1.7	2.7
Stamford	33.9	39.2	13.1	3.7	10.0
Syracuse	47.6	39.5	7.0	2.3	3.7
Tampa	30.1	41.6	18.5	4.9	4.9
Tucson	30.2	45.5	16.9	3.4	4.0
Tulsa	36.1	49.5	9.8	1.8	2.8
Virginia Beach	23.1	46.6	21.5	5.0	3.8
Washington	15.7	36.6	28.5	10.0	9.2
Wichita	35.7	51.4	9.3	1.4	2.3
U.S.	29.4	36.1	19.1	7.4	8.0

Note: Figures are percentages and include workers 16 years old and over
Source: Census 2000, Summary File 3

Travel Time to Work: Metro Area

MSA[1]	Less Than 15 Minutes	15 to 29 Minutes	30 to 44 Minutes	45 to 59 Minutes	60 Minutes or More
Albuquerque	26.9	45.1	18.4	5.3	4.3
Alexandria	16.3	30.3	25.7	13.7	14.0
Anchorage	36.4	46.7	11.2	2.3	3.4
Ann Arbor	29.7	35.1	19.3	9.3	6.5
Atlanta	18.3	32.4	25.1	12.4	11.8
Austin	24.5	38.6	22.5	8.3	6.1
Baltimore	19.9	35.5	23.8	10.1	10.6
Baton Rouge	24.9	41.2	21.2	7.0	5.7
Bellevue	22.1	36.9	23.9	9.2	7.9
Birmingham	21.4	40.4	24.4	8.1	5.6
Boise City	33.1	45.9	15.3	3.1	2.7
Boston	23.3	31.4	24.3	11.0	10.1
Boulder	34.2	37.9	16.4	6.2	5.2
Buffalo	32.5	43.8	16.8	3.7	3.2
Cedar Rapids	43.6	42.0	9.9	2.1	2.5
Charleston	26.7	39.6	21.5	6.9	5.2
Charlotte	23.8	38.7	23.0	8.5	6.1
Chattanooga	25.4	44.3	20.6	5.6	4.1
Chicago	20.4	29.8	24.0	12.2	13.6
Cincinnati	24.9	41.4	22.0	6.8	4.8
Cleveland	26.3	40.5	21.8	6.7	4.7
Colorado Spgs.	30.4	44.9	16.0	3.9	4.8
Columbia	27.7	42.5	20.2	5.0	4.6
Columbus	26.6	44.1	19.6	5.5	4.2
Dallas	22.0	35.0	24.7	10.4	7.9
Denver	21.6	38.4	25.3	8.6	6.1
Des Moines	35.2	46.7	13.0	2.8	2.3
Detroit	23.4	38.4	23.3	8.5	6.4
Durham	24.7	40.4	22.3	7.4	5.2
El Paso	25.7	45.9	20.5	4.3	3.5
Eugene	39.8	41.1	11.6	3.0	4.5
Ft. Collins	38.7	37.7	12.8	4.7	6.0
Ft. Lauderdale	20.9	36.5	26.0	9.5	7.1
Ft. Wayne	34.5	43.3	14.8	3.9	3.5
Ft. Worth	23.4	37.8	22.6	8.8	7.5
Grand Rapids	34.9	42.9	14.8	4.1	3.3
Green Bay	43.0	44.2	7.7	2.3	2.7
Greensboro	30.0	44.3	16.9	4.6	4.3
Honolulu	23.5	34.3	23.8	9.5	8.9
Houston	20.3	33.8	25.5	11.1	9.3
Huntsville	28.7	44.5	19.1	4.6	3.0
Indianapolis	27.0	40.8	21.6	6.1	4.4
Irvine	22.1	37.6	23.8	8.0	8.5
Jacksonville	22.2	38.8	24.4	8.7	5.9
Kansas City	28.0	41.9	20.6	5.8	3.7
Knoxville	26.6	43.0	21.0	5.5	3.9
Las Vegas	24.4	45.2	20.9	4.2	5.2
Lexington	35.1	40.6	15.7	4.8	3.8
Lincoln	41.7	45.4	7.9	1.9	3.1
Los Angeles	20.7	34.6	24.1	9.7	10.9
Louisville	26.3	46.0	19.8	4.2	3.6
Madison	35.1	45.2	14.0	2.7	3.0
Manchester	31.3	38.0	16.5	5.7	8.5

Travel Time to Work: Metro Area *continued*

MSA[1]	Less Than 15 Minutes	15 to 29 Minutes	30 to 44 Minutes	45 to 59 Minutes	60 Minutes or More
Memphis	22.9	43.4	23.2	6.1	4.4
Miami	17.4	34.2	27.2	10.9	10.3
Milwaukee	29.7	43.7	18.3	4.6	3.7
Minneapolis	26.4	41.4	21.3	6.7	4.2
Naperville	20.4	29.8	24.0	12.2	13.6
Nashville	23.9	38.6	23.0	8.8	5.7
New Orleans	24.5	38.1	21.1	8.5	7.9
New York	13.3	24.0	24.4	14.9	23.5
Norfolk	26.0	42.9	20.3	5.9	4.9
Oklahoma City	30.2	43.4	18.3	4.4	3.7
Omaha	33.9	48.4	12.9	2.2	2.5
Orlando	21.1	38.1	25.8	8.8	6.2
Overland Park	28.0	41.9	20.6	5.8	3.7
Philadelphia	23.7	33.2	22.6	10.4	10.0
Phoenix	23.8	37.0	24.1	8.8	6.3
Pittsburgh	28.3	36.4	20.2	8.3	6.9
Plano	22.0	35.0	24.7	10.4	7.9
Portland	26.3	40.0	21.1	7.0	5.5
Providence	32.2	39.9	16.3	5.4	6.2
Provo	45.0	35.9	10.7	4.2	4.2
Raleigh	24.7	40.4	22.3	7.4	5.2
Reno	35.2	49.2	9.5	2.7	3.3
Richmond	24.0	44.3	21.4	5.8	4.5
Rochester	33.6	42.7	15.6	4.6	3.6
Sacramento	25.2	39.3	21.7	6.9	6.8
St. Louis	24.9	37.9	23.1	8.4	5.6
St. Paul	26.4	41.4	21.3	6.7	4.2
St. Petersburg	26.4	37.8	21.3	8.1	6.5
Salt Lake City	29.2	43.6	18.0	4.8	4.4
San Antonio	23.9	43.2	22.2	5.7	5.0
San Diego	24.7	40.7	21.6	6.7	6.4
San Francisco	19.1	34.5	25.0	10.8	10.6
San Jose	21.1	40.8	23.4	7.9	6.8
Savannah	26.2	41.1	21.6	6.1	5.0
Scottsdale	23.8	37.0	24.1	8.8	6.3
Seattle	22.1	36.9	23.9	9.2	7.9
Sioux Falls	42.6	46.3	7.1	1.3	2.7
Springfield (IL)	34.2	47.4	12.6	2.7	3.1
Springfield (MO)	33.5	43.7	15.5	3.7	3.6
Stamford	31.7	33.8	13.7	5.1	15.7
Syracuse	35.9	41.7	14.1	4.5	3.7
Tampa	26.4	37.8	21.3	8.1	6.5
Tucson	25.8	42.4	21.5	5.6	4.7
Tulsa	30.7	44.9	16.6	4.3	3.5
Virginia Beach	26.0	42.9	20.3	5.9	4.9
Washington	16.3	30.3	25.7	13.7	14.0
Wichita	34.8	47.3	13.2	2.4	2.3
U.S.	29.4	36.1	19.1	7.4	8.0

Note: Figures are percentages and include workers 16 years old and over; (1) Metropolitan Statistical Area - see Appendix A for areas included
Source: Census 2000, Summary File 3

2000 Presidential Election Results

City	Area Covered	Gore	Bush	Nader	Buchanan	Other
Albuquerque	Bernalillo County	48.7	46.6	4.0	0.2	0.5
Alexandria	Alexandria city	61.0	34.6	3.8	0.2	0.4
Anchorage	Alaska	27.9	59.0	9.9	1.8	1.4
Ann Arbor	Washtenaw County	59.8	36.2	3.3	0.0	0.6
Atlanta	Fulton County	58.0	40.0	0.0	0.2	1.7
Austin	Travis County	41.7	46.9	10.4	0.2	0.9
Baltimore	City of Baltimore	82.8	13.9	2.8	0.2	0.2
Baton Rouge	East Baton Rouge Parish	45.3	52.7	1.2	0.4	0.3
Bellevue	King County	60.0	34.4	4.7	0.2	0.7
Birmingham	Jefferson County	47.5	50.6	1.2	0.2	0.4
Boise City	Ada County	34.3	63.3	0.0	1.2	1.2
Boston	City of Boston	71.6	19.8	7.3	0.5	0.7
Boulder	Boulder County	50.1	36.4	11.8	0.3	1.3
Buffalo	Erie County	56.8	37.4	4.2	0.9	0.8
Cedar Rapids	Linn County	53.2	43.9	2.3	0.3	0.3
Charleston	Charleston County	44.4	52.2	2.4	0.1	0.8
Charlotte	Mecklenburg County	48.2	51.1	0.0	0.2	0.5
Chattanooga	Hamilton County	43.0	55.4	1.1	0.2	0.4
Chicago	Cook County	68.6	28.6	2.3	0.2	0.3
Cincinnati	Hamilton County	42.3	54.5	2.4	0.3	0.5
Cleveland	Cuyahoga County	62.2	33.6	3.0	0.5	0.7
Colorado Springs	El Paso County	30.8	63.9	3.5	0.7	1.0
Columbia	Richland County	54.3	43.1	1.9	0.1	0.5
Columbus	Franklin County	48.7	47.9	2.6	0.3	0.6
Dallas	Dallas County	44.9	52.6	1.9	0.1	0.4
Denver	Denver County	61.9	30.9	5.9	0.4	1.0
Des Moines	Polk County	51.6	45.9	1.9	0.2	0.3
Detroit	Wayne County	68.2	29.8	1.5	0.0	0.5
Durham	Durham County	63.4	35.5	0.0	0.5	0.6
El Paso	El Paso County	57.8	39.7	2.0	0.2	0.4
Eugene	Lane County	51.7	40.5	6.7	0.3	0.7
Fort Collins	Larimer County	38.9	52.7	6.9	0.5	1.1
Fort Lauderdale	Broward County	67.4	30.9	1.2	0.1	0.3
Fort Wayne	Allen County	36.6	61.9	0.0	0.8	0.7
Fort Worth	Tarrant County	36.8	60.7	1.9	0.2	0.4
Grand Rapids	Kent County	38.2	59.4	2.0	0.0	0.4
Green Bay	Brown County	45.6	50.4	3.1	0.6	0.3
Greensboro	Guilford County	48.5	50.9	0.0	0.3	0.3
Honolulu	Honolulu County	54.5	39.6	5.1	0.3	0.5
Houston	Harris County	42.9	54.3	2.4	0.2	0.3
Huntsville	Madison County	42.6	55.0	1.5	0.3	0.6
Indianapolis	Marion County	47.8	49.8	0.0	0.7	1.6
Irvine	Orange County	40.3	55.8	2.8	0.4	0.7
Jacksonville	Duval County	40.7	57.5	1.0	0.2	0.5
Kansas City	Jackson County	59.0	38.4	1.9	0.3	0.5
Knoxville	Knox County	40.5	57.7	1.2	0.2	0.5
Las Vegas	Clark County	51.3	44.7	2.1	0.8	1.1
Lexington	Fayette County	44.8	51.7	2.9	0.2	0.4
Lincoln	Lancaster County	41.7	51.9	5.7	0.3	0.5
Los Angeles	Los Angeles County	63.4	32.4	3.1	0.4	0.6
Louisville	Jefferson County	49.6	48.0	2.0	0.2	0.3
Madison	Dane County	61.2	32.6	5.6	0.1	0.5
Manchester	Hillsborough County	47.2	49.0	3.3	0.5	0.0

2000 Presidential Election Results *continued*

City	Area Covered	Gore	Bush	Nader	Buchanan	Other
Memphis	Shelby County	56.6	42.1	0.8	0.1	0.4
Miami	Dade County	52.6	46.3	0.9	0.1	0.2
Milwaukee	Milwaukee County	58.4	37.7	3.2	0.4	0.4
Minneapolis	Hennepin County	53.6	39.3	6.2	0.4	0.5
Naperville	Du Page County	41.9	55.2	2.4	0.2	0.3
Nashville	Davidson County	58.1	40.0	1.4	0.1	0.4
New Orleans	Orleans Parish	75.9	21.8	1.7	0.4	0.3
New York	New York City	77.1	18.8	3.3	0.4	0.5
Norfolk	Norfolk city	61.8	35.5	1.9	0.2	0.6
Oklahoma City	Oklahoma County	36.6	62.3	0.0	0.5	0.6
Omaha	Douglas County	39.8	55.3	4.0	0.4	0.6
Orlando	Orange County	50.1	48.0	1.4	0.2	0.4
Overland Park	Johnson County	36.4	59.8	3.0	0.3	0.6
Philadelphia	Philadelphia County	79.8	17.9	1.5	0.1	0.6
Phoenix	Maricopa County	43.3	53.0	2.5	0.8	0.4
Pittsburgh	Allegheny County	56.5	40.5	1.8	0.4	0.8
Plano	Collin County	24.4	73.1	1.8	0.2	0.5
Portland	Multnomah County	63.7	28.3	7.1	0.3	0.7
Providence	Providence County	73.7	17.7	7.7	0.5	0.4
Provo	Utah County	13.7	81.7	2.3	1.4	1.0
Raleigh	Wake County	45.7	53.5	0.0	0.2	0.7
Reno	Washoe County	42.6	52.0	3.4	0.6	1.4
Richmond	City of Richmond	64.8	30.8	3.7	0.1	0.6
Rochester	Monroe County	50.8	44.1	3.6	0.6	0.9
Sacramento	Sacramento County	49.2	45.5	4.1	0.5	0.8
Saint Louis	Saint Louis County	51.4	46.2	1.7	0.2	0.4
Saint Paul	Ramsey County	56.7	35.9	6.4	0.6	0.5
Saint Petersburg	Pinellas County	50.4	46.4	2.5	0.3	0.5
Salt Lake City	Salt Lake County	35.0	55.8	6.9	1.2	1.0
San Antonio	Bexar County	44.9	52.2	2.4	0.2	0.3
San Diego	San Diego County	45.6	49.6	3.5	0.4	0.7
San Francisco	San Francisco County	75.5	16.1	7.8	0.1	0.4
San Jose	Santa Clara County	60.7	34.4	3.5	0.3	1.1
Savannah	Chatham County	49.5	49.9	0.0	0.2	0.4
Scottsdale	Maricopa County	43.3	53.0	2.5	0.8	0.4
Seattle	King County	60.0	34.4	4.7	0.2	0.7
Sioux Falls	Minnehaha County	44.1	54.5	0.0	0.6	0.8
Springfield	Greene County	39.9	57.5	1.7	0.5	0.4
Springfield	Sangamon County	42.0	55.1	2.2	0.5	0.3
Stamford	Stamford County	62.0	34.3	2.6	0.2	0.9
Syracuse	Onondaga County	54.0	41.0	3.7	0.7	0.6
Tampa	Hillsborough County	47.1	50.2	2.1	0.2	0.5
Tucson	Pima County	51.5	43.2	4.3	0.6	0.4
Tulsa	Tulsa County	37.3	61.3	0.0	0.7	0.6
Virginia Beach	City of Virginia Beach	41.7	56.0	1.6	0.1	0.6
Washington	District of Columbia	85.4	9.0	5.2	0.0	0.4
Wichita	Sedgwick County	38.3	57.4	2.9	0.6	0.9
U.S.	U.S.	48.4	47.9	2.7	0.4	0.6

Note: Results are percentages and may not add to 100% due to rounding
Source: www.cbsnews.com; www.uselectionatlas.org

House Price Index (HPI)

MSA[1]	National Ranking[2]	Quarterly Change (%)	One-Year Change (%)	Five-Year Change (%)
Albuquerque	124	2.25	5.31	14.47
Alexandria	38	5.57	12.52	63.89
Anchorage	76	3.65	9.12	30.75
Ann Arbor	151	2.18	4.45	33.81
Atlanta	195	1.47	3.17	31.70
Austin	220	1.23	0.78	34.94
Baltimore	27	6.21	13.27	48.93
Baton Rouge	191	1.12	3.30	20.71
Bellevue	122	2.46	5.34	36.16
Birmingham	155	1.11	4.32	22.64
Boise City	166	1.66	4.09	23.00
Boston	73	4.37	9.27	77.39
Boulder	219	0.60	1.07	47.16
Buffalo	123	2.23	5.34	17.76
Cedar Rapids	175	1.42	3.82	19.23
Charleston	169	0.94	3.98	44.46
Charlotte	207	0.93	2.56	19.20
Chattanooga	137	1.95	4.93	24.92
Chicago	95	3.49	7.24	39.62
Cincinnati	163	1.78	4.16	24.14
Cleveland	170	1.60	3.95	21.30
Colorado Springs	208	1.07	2.53	30.65
Columbia	157	1.90	4.26	23.67
Columbus	153	1.96	4.41	23.21
Dallas	212	0.67	2.10	26.76
Denver	210	1.36	2.27	48.30
Des Moines	108	3.13	6.02	26.05
Detroit	181	1.51	3.62	31.25
Durham	206	1.17	2.56	18.70
El Paso	158	0.97	4.21	16.96
Eugene	104	3.22	6.49	18.60
Fort Collins	171	2.67	3.90	41.96
Fort Lauderdale	20	5.89	14.10	69.29
Fort Wayne	211	0.64	2.22	15.76
Fort Worth	197	0.79	2.99	25.12
Grand Rapids	162	1.78	4.16	27.82
Green Bay	121	2.75	5.40	24.66
Greensboro	198	1.59	2.94	18.70
Honolulu	42	5.16	11.99	32.43
Houston	186	1.54	3.53	32.00
Huntsville	203	0.42	2.73	16.45
Indianapolis	200	1.16	2.85	18.78
Irvine	12	6.83	15.70	77.22
Jacksonville	75	4.32	9.18	48.48
Kansas City	129	2.53	5.16	33.64
Knoxville	128	1.64	5.17	22.02
Las Vegas	37	6.00	12.52	35.82
Lexington	132	2.38	5.07	26.87
Lincoln	160	2.51	4.19	20.36
Los Angeles	8	7.25	16.60	69.56
Louisville	144	2.42	4.80	24.76
Madison	90	4.11	7.74	34.81
Manchester	62	4.75	10.29	77.67

House Price Index (HPI) *continued*

MSA[1]	National Ranking[2]	Quarterly Change (%)	One-Year Change (%)	Five-Year Change (%)
Memphis	205	1.32	2.66	16.68
Miami	18	5.72	14.25	64.07
Milwaukee	87	3.96	7.83	34.33
Minnepolis	71	4.43	9.41	62.31
Naperville	95	3.49	7.24	39.62
Nashville	183	1.58	3.59	18.49
New Orleans	97	3.06	6.84	29.44
New York	58	5.58	10.55	71.70
Norfolk	45	5.22	11.61	37.83
Oklahoma City	125	2.04	5.31	24.42
Omaha	145	2.43	4.74	22.63
Orlando	81	3.68	8.26	42.88
Overland Park	129	2.53	5.16	33.64
Philadelphia	47	5.08	11.41	46.92
Phoenix	105	3.32	6.45	35.65
Pittsburgh	114	2.45	5.61	25.81
Plano	212	0.67	2.10	26.76
Portland	109	3.11	5.96	22.45
Providence	10	6.66	16.02	79.05
Provo	216	0.50	1.65	10.37
Raleigh	206	1.17	2.56	18.70
Reno	31	6.42	13.06	37.53
Richmond	85	3.36	7.97	33.25
Rochester	147	1.86	4.68	16.62
Sacramento	17	6.24	14.33	80.19
Saint Louis	99	3.47	6.71	35.93
Saint Paul	71	4.43	9.41	62.31
Saint Petersburg	65	4.32	10.02	53.30
Salt Lake	215	0.49	1.66	10.18
San Antonio	117	2.79	5.50	24.24
San Diego	11	6.71	15.90	92.96
San Francisco	138	2.80	4.88	67.90
San Jose	218	1.50	1.28	57.02
Savannah	112	1.90	5.84	34.51
Scottsdale	105	3.32	6.45	35.65
Seattle	122	2.46	5.34	36.16
Sioux Falls	131	2.62	5.10	25.46
Springfield	193	1.95	3.23	11.28
Springfield	167	2.71	4.08	17.50
Stamford	100	2.34	6.69	59.98
Syracuse	113	3.13	5.81	24.85
Tampa	65	4.32	10.02	53.30
Tucson	78	4.43	8.70	34.23
Tulsa	196	1.19	3.04	23.96
Virginia Beach	45	5.22	11.61	37.83
Washington	38	5.57	12.52	63.89
Wichita	174	2.01	3.83	19.96
U.S.[3]	-	3.67	7.97	41.81

Note: The HPI is a weighted repeat sales index. It measures average price changes in repeat sales or refinancings on the same properties. This information is obtained by reviewing repeat mortgage transactions on single-family properties whose mortgages have been purchased or securitized by Fannie Mae of Freddie Mac in January 1975; (1) Metropolitan Statistical Area - see Appendix A for areas included; (2) Rankings are based on annual percentage change, for all MSAs containing at least 15,000 transactions over the last 10 years and ranges from 1 to 220; (3) figures based on a weighted division average; all figures are for the period ended December 31, 2003; n/a not available
Source: Office of Federal Housing Enterprise Oversight, House Price Index, March 1, 2004

Housing: Year Structure Built: City

City	1990 -2000	1980 -1989	1970 -1979	1960 -1969	1950 -1959	1940 -1949	Before 1940	Median Year
Albuquerque	20.1	18.4	23.5	13.8	14.6	5.9	3.6	1975
Alexandria	11.0	11.9	22.0	18.7	13.4	12.6	10.4	1967
Anchorage	12.6	28.2	34.7	13.8	7.9	2.1	0.6	1977
Ann Arbor	9.3	10.4	19.9	23.1	14.1	6.4	16.8	1966
Atlanta	11.2	9.2	13.8	20.6	17.8	10.7	16.8	1962
Austin	21.4	26.4	23.9	12.0	8.4	4.1	3.8	1979
Baltimore	2.7	4.5	7.7	11.3	18.9	18.0	36.8	1947
Baton Rouge	7.3	14.9	25.5	20.1	16.6	9.4	6.2	1969
Bellevue	17.2	18.9	25.7	23.6	11.8	1.5	1.2	1975
Birmingham	5.4	9.2	16.6	19.7	21.6	12.8	14.7	1960
Boise City	26.6	15.4	23.8	10.0	10.3	5.9	8.0	1977
Boston	3.4	5.8	8.3	9.9	9.7	9.5	53.5	1939
Boulder	12.3	16.9	26.7	21.3	11.7	2.8	8.3	1972
Buffalo	2.5	1.9	3.7	5.9	13.0	15.4	57.7	1939
Cedar Rapids	14.8	7.8	17.3	16.1	15.7	6.2	22.1	1964
Charleston	16.3	17.3	15.9	14.7	10.3	7.6	17.9	1970
Charlotte	26.9	20.7	17.0	15.3	11.1	5.0	4.0	1979
Chattanooga	10.4	12.5	17.3	19.3	16.9	10.2	13.4	1965
Chicago	4.5	4.0	8.5	13.6	17.1	14.3	38.0	1948
Cincinnati	2.8	4.0	9.7	14.8	16.0	12.7	40.0	1948
Cleveland	2.5	1.9	5.3	9.0	15.2	16.9	49.3	1940
Colorado Spgs.	20.1	22.5	24.3	13.4	9.2	2.8	7.7	1977
Columbia	13.5	10.5	15.1	18.3	19.3	11.0	12.3	1964
Columbus	18.5	14.6	17.6	15.3	12.7	7.2	14.1	1970
Dallas	12.5	20.2	20.1	18.5	16.0	7.0	5.7	1971
Denver	7.5	8.9	16.3	14.3	18.6	9.9	24.5	1958
Des Moines	7.3	7.7	13.6	12.0	17.4	11.4	30.6	1955
Detroit	1.7	2.1	5.0	9.8	25.2	26.3	29.9	1948
Durham	24.9	20.4	16.6	13.9	10.9	6.5	6.7	1977
El Paso	17.7	18.7	22.5	15.7	14.2	5.1	6.0	1974
Eugene	21.7	8.8	24.9	16.9	12.7	7.5	7.6	1972
Ft. Collins	30.4	20.2	25.0	10.2	5.2	2.3	6.6	1980
Ft. Lauderdale	4.6	6.9	24.9	29.0	25.1	6.2	3.2	1965
Ft. Wayne	7.6	10.0	17.6	19.4	15.7	9.5	20.1	1962
Ft. Worth	16.0	19.9	13.8	13.9	17.5	10.1	8.8	1970
Grand Rapids	6.4	7.0	8.6	12.6	16.6	12.3	36.5	1951
Green Bay	12.2	13.9	18.1	13.3	16.2	9.1	17.2	1966
Greensboro	20.7	17.9	18.4	16.1	13.4	6.4	7.1	1974
Honolulu	9.2	10.4	28.5	24.8	14.4	6.5	6.1	1969
Houston	11.1	17.8	27.8	18.6	13.4	6.1	5.2	1972
Huntsville	14.0	19.7	20.1	28.0	11.7	3.1	3.4	1972
Indianapolis	13.9	13.6	15.6	16.8	14.6	8.9	16.6	1966
Irvine	26.1	32.4	35.5	4.9	0.6	0.4	0.1	1983
Jacksonville	20.3	20.9	17.0	15.1	14.2	7.0	5.4	1975
Kansas City	10.2	9.9	13.7	16.2	17.1	10.3	22.6	1960
Knoxville	11.2	11.1	17.8	17.4	18.6	11.0	12.9	1964
Las Vegas	48.9	19.0	13.2	10.9	5.9	1.6	0.6	1989
Lexington	20.6	17.0	20.4	16.7	11.8	5.3	8.2	1974
Lincoln	20.0	12.8	19.2	12.9	14.4	4.9	15.9	1971
Los Angeles	6.2	11.1	15.0	17.5	20.5	13.0	16.7	1960
Louisville	4.5	4.1	9.2	14.1	19.2	15.9	32.9	1951
Madison	16.1	11.9	17.6	16.4	13.6	7.5	16.9	1967
Manchester	8.5	14.4	11.3	9.1	12.9	9.1	34.7	1955

Housing: Year Structure Built: City *continued*

City	1990 -2000	1980 -1989	1970 -1979	1960 -1969	1950 -1959	1940 -1949	Before 1940	Median Year
Memphis	7.6	12.8	20.4	21.2	19.4	9.4	9.0	1966
Miami	7.7	11.3	19.0	17.9	19.2	14.2	10.6	1963
Milwaukee	2.8	3.9	10.0	13.8	22.8	13.1	33.6	1951
Minneapolis	2.5	6.2	9.5	9.4	11.9	9.6	51.0	1939
Naperville	36.1	32.1	16.9	6.5	4.1	0.9	3.3	1986
Nashville	16.0	19.2	19.7	16.8	13.7	6.8	7.8	1973
New Orleans	3.0	8.2	13.6	15.1	16.9	13.6	29.7	1954
New York	4.1	4.9	8.6	15.2	15.8	15.3	36.0	1949
Norfolk	7.5	11.0	13.2	15.7	23.7	14.1	14.8	1959
Oklahoma City	12.4	18.9	19.7	16.4	15.0	8.3	9.3	1970
Omaha	9.2	9.8	19.2	18.2	14.0	7.6	21.9	1964
Orlando	23.5	22.4	17.7	12.2	13.7	5.3	5.1	1978
Overland Park	26.9	24.9	15.4	19.6	9.4	2.4	1.5	1981
Philadelphia	2.1	3.3	6.9	12.3	17.0	16.6	41.7	1945
Phoenix	20.0	22.9	25.1	13.4	12.5	3.6	2.5	1977
Pittsburgh	2.3	3.6	6.3	9.5	14.0	13.6	50.7	1939
Plano	47.2	27.6	19.7	4.2	0.7	0.3	0.2	1989
Portland	10.1	5.7	12.1	11.5	14.9	11.5	34.0	1953
Providence	4.8	6.6	9.7	8.8	11.5	11.6	47.0	1943
Provo	24.0	12.7	24.1	13.9	10.5	6.7	8.2	1974
Raleigh	26.3	26.6	17.6	12.9	7.7	4.1	4.9	1981
Reno	25.0	18.4	22.8	14.8	9.3	5.0	4.6	1977
Richmond	3.5	7.3	14.3	15.8	17.8	13.1	28.3	1955
Rochester	1.9	2.6	7.9	8.4	11.8	12.0	55.4	1939
Sacramento	9.0	18.4	18.4	15.2	15.5	10.6	13.0	1967
St. Louis	2.2	3.7	4.6	10.3	14.5	16.1	48.5	1941
St. Paul	2.2	6.5	10.8	11.1	14.9	9.4	45.1	1945
St. Petersburg	5.3	10.5	20.2	19.9	26.2	7.6	10.2	1963
Salt Lake City	7.3	7.6	13.6	11.1	15.2	13.4	31.7	1953
San Antonio	16.4	22.0	19.9	14.9	13.2	6.9	6.6	1974
San Diego	12.3	19.6	24.0	15.4	14.8	6.2	7.7	1972
San Francisco	4.1	4.9	7.0	9.4	11.4	13.2	49.9	1940
San Jose	12.3	14.8	28.5	23.6	11.9	3.8	5.2	1972
Savannah	6.9	12.6	17.0	16.3	19.5	11.4	16.4	1962
Scottsdale	37.7	23.8	19.1	12.4	6.1	0.4	0.3	1985
Seattle	9.9	9.0	9.9	12.2	14.0	12.5	32.4	1954
Sioux Falls	22.1	16.4	18.9	10.1	12.1	6.9	13.4	1974
Springfield (IL)	16.6	11.6	17.6	13.9	11.8	8.8	19.7	1967
Springfield (MO)	14.9	14.3	20.8	15.2	13.1	8.0	13.8	1970
Stamford	8.8	12.7	15.1	18.7	18.1	9.2	17.4	1963
Syracuse	2.4	3.7	8.4	10.9	14.6	12.0	48.0	1942
Tampa	13.5	14.9	15.5	16.0	20.2	9.2	10.8	1966
Tucson	15.6	19.1	25.4	14.4	15.5	5.7	4.3	1974
Tulsa	8.9	16.3	21.9	17.2	17.8	8.4	9.5	1968
Virginia Beach	17.3	32.5	24.9	14.5	7.7	1.8	1.3	1980
Washington	2.6	5.0	8.7	15.3	17.0	16.8	34.6	1949
Wichita	15.1	13.8	14.3	10.6	22.5	11.6	12.0	1964
U.S.	17.0	15.8	18.5	13.7	12.7	7.3	15.0	1971

Note: Figures are percentages
Source: Census 2000, Summary File 3

Housing: Year Structure Built: Metro Area

MSA[1]	1990 -2000	1980 -1989	1970 -1979	1960 -1969	1950 -1959	1940 -1949	Before 1940	Median Year
Albuquerque	24.3	20.3	22.0	12.5	12.0	5.1	3.7	1978
Alexandria	18.2	18.9	18.1	16.1	11.9	7.2	9.6	1973
Anchorage	12.6	28.2	34.7	13.8	7.9	2.1	0.6	1977
Ann Arbor	22.3	11.9	20.0	13.6	11.1	5.6	15.5	1972
Atlanta	30.8	24.6	18.0	12.0	7.1	3.2	4.2	1982
Austin	30.2	27.4	20.2	8.8	6.2	3.3	3.9	1983
Baltimore	15.2	14.9	15.6	13.3	15.0	9.9	16.0	1967
Baton Rouge	19.2	21.5	24.5	14.9	10.6	5.3	4.0	1976
Bellevue	19.8	18.4	17.7	14.7	10.3	6.4	12.5	1973
Birmingham	20.3	15.4	19.6	15.3	13.3	7.7	8.4	1973
Boise City	33.8	12.7	24.4	8.3	8.1	5.2	7.4	1979
Boston	7.0	9.3	11.6	11.8	13.2	8.5	38.6	1952
Boulder	24.6	17.7	26.4	14.4	7.7	2.5	6.9	1977
Buffalo	7.4	6.3	10.8	12.1	19.4	12.6	31.5	1953
Cedar Rapids	18.4	8.3	17.9	15.6	13.7	5.4	20.7	1967
Charleston	22.0	23.9	21.3	14.0	8.4	4.7	5.9	1978
Charlotte	30.3	19.1	16.3	12.7	10.0	5.5	6.1	1980
Chattanooga	18.1	15.8	20.0	15.9	13.4	8.0	8.9	1972
Chicago	12.4	9.8	15.9	15.3	16.1	9.2	21.3	1962
Cincinnati	16.4	11.2	14.8	13.9	14.5	8.3	20.9	1965
Cleveland	9.2	6.9	13.5	15.1	19.5	11.3	24.6	1957
Colorado Spgs.	22.0	22.2	23.6	13.1	9.2	2.6	7.2	1978
Columbia	24.8	20.1	22.1	14.4	9.9	4.2	4.6	1978
Columbus	20.7	13.5	17.5	15.0	12.8	6.3	14.2	1971
Dallas	23.9	24.7	20.2	13.7	9.8	4.0	3.7	1979
Denver	19.4	18.0	23.7	13.2	12.4	4.4	9.0	1975
Des Moines	18.8	11.9	17.8	12.1	12.4	7.2	19.9	1969
Detroit	12.2	9.2	15.4	14.9	21.9	12.5	13.9	1961
Durham	33.2	22.9	16.6	10.9	7.2	3.9	5.4	1983
El Paso	20.6	19.7	22.0	14.4	12.9	4.8	5.6	1976
Eugene	19.3	9.5	26.3	17.0	11.7	8.3	8.0	1972
Ft. Collins	29.5	17.7	26.9	10.3	5.2	2.6	8.0	1979
Ft. Lauderdale	19.5	21.2	29.8	17.2	9.5	1.7	1.0	1977
Ft. Wayne	16.8	11.6	16.3	14.2	12.0	7.1	22.1	1966
Ft. Worth	21.4	26.8	19.2	12.5	11.1	4.9	4.1	1979
Grand Rapids	20.1	13.7	15.7	12.2	12.7	7.9	17.6	1970
Green Bay	21.4	14.7	19.3	12.6	12.1	6.4	13.4	1973
Greensboro	23.3	17.8	18.1	14.3	12.3	6.3	7.8	1975
Honolulu	14.7	13.1	26.5	22.5	13.2	5.6	4.4	1972
Houston	19.8	23.0	26.6	13.6	9.4	4.3	3.4	1977
Huntsville	26.1	22.7	16.9	19.2	8.6	3.0	3.4	1979
Indianapolis	20.9	12.9	16.1	14.7	12.8	7.1	15.5	1970
Irvine	14.1	17.5	27.6	22.6	12.8	3.0	2.5	1973
Jacksonville	24.1	23.9	17.6	12.7	11.5	5.5	4.8	1979
Kansas City	17.2	15.0	18.1	15.5	14.1	7.1	12.9	1970
Knoxville	25.5	16.9	18.4	12.7	11.2	7.8	7.5	1976
Las Vegas	47.0	21.7	17.9	8.4	3.5	1.0	0.6	1989
Lexington	24.4	16.8	20.0	14.0	10.0	4.9	9.9	1976
Lincoln	20.4	12.6	19.6	12.7	13.5	4.7	16.4	1971
Los Angeles	6.9	12.3	15.6	17.8	22.3	12.2	12.9	1961
Louisville	16.6	10.3	18.6	16.6	15.6	8.4	13.8	1967
Madison	21.1	13.1	20.0	14.6	10.6	5.6	15.1	1972
Manchester	13.7	19.6	16.2	9.2	10.1	6.4	24.8	1969

Housing: Year Structure Built: Metro Area *continued*

MSA[1]	1990 -2000	1980 -1989	1970 -1979	1960 -1969	1950 -1959	1940 -1949	Before 1940	Median Year
Memphis	21.3	16.3	20.1	16.1	13.2	6.6	6.4	1974
Miami	15.2	18.2	22.5	16.8	16.5	6.7	4.2	1973
Milwaukee	12.6	8.2	14.8	13.7	18.6	9.2	22.9	1960
Minneapolis	17.6	16.8	18.1	12.8	12.3	5.3	17.1	1971
Naperville	12.4	9.8	15.9	15.3	16.1	9.2	21.3	1962
Nashville	25.8	20.1	19.1	13.8	9.8	4.9	6.6	1978
New Orleans	9.9	15.7	21.7	17.6	13.4	8.0	13.7	1968
New York	4.5	5.4	9.2	15.5	16.2	14.6	34.7	1950
Norfolk	18.4	22.1	18.9	15.2	12.5	6.4	6.4	1975
Oklahoma City	13.8	19.8	21.9	16.3	13.4	7.1	7.8	1972
Omaha	15.8	11.8	19.5	15.8	11.9	6.1	19.1	1968
Orlando	31.0	28.1	18.7	9.7	7.7	2.3	2.4	1983
Overland Park	17.2	15.0	18.1	15.5	14.1	7.1	12.9	1970
Philadelphia	9.4	10.0	13.0	13.9	17.3	11.1	25.3	1958
Phoenix	30.4	25.5	23.2	10.4	7.1	2.0	1.4	1982
Pittsburgh	7.8	7.5	12.7	12.3	17.2	11.9	30.5	1954
Plano	23.9	24.7	20.2	13.7	9.8	4.0	3.7	1979
Portland	24.6	13.0	20.9	11.3	9.1	6.5	14.7	1974
Providence	8.7	11.1	13.3	12.7	13.7	9.8	30.7	1957
Provo	33.9	12.7	22.8	9.1	8.4	5.4	7.8	1978
Raleigh	33.2	22.9	16.6	10.9	7.2	3.9	5.4	1983
Reno	27.3	20.6	25.0	13.0	7.3	3.5	3.3	1979
Richmond	18.6	19.7	19.2	13.8	12.2	6.5	10.0	1974
Rochester	9.6	10.4	14.8	14.7	12.6	7.2	30.8	1960
Sacramento	19.4	20.5	22.9	14.5	12.3	5.1	5.3	1976
St. Louis	14.0	13.4	15.6	16.0	15.2	8.8	17.0	1966
St. Paul	17.6	16.8	18.1	12.8	12.3	5.3	17.1	1971
St. Petersburg	17.2	25.9	25.4	13.6	11.0	3.3	3.5	1977
Salt Lake City	22.0	16.4	22.5	11.9	11.7	6.0	9.4	1975
San Antonio	20.1	22.5	20.1	13.6	11.3	6.1	6.2	1976
San Diego	13.9	21.9	26.3	15.0	12.9	4.9	5.1	1975
San Francisco	5.5	7.3	12.8	15.2	17.5	12.1	29.6	1955
San Jose	11.5	13.4	25.2	22.8	16.6	5.2	5.3	1970
Savannah	22.6	18.4	16.9	12.2	12.7	7.4	9.9	1975
Scottsdale	30.4	25.5	23.2	10.4	7.1	2.0	1.4	1982
Seattle	19.8	18.4	17.7	14.7	10.3	6.4	12.5	1973
Sioux Falls	23.0	14.7	19.0	9.7	10.8	6.3	16.4	1974
Springfield (IL)	17.2	11.5	18.9	13.3	12.2	8.6	18.4	1968
Springfield (MO)	25.8	16.7	20.0	11.9	8.9	5.5	11.2	1976
Stamford	7.4	11.4	12.9	17.1	20.2	9.2	21.9	1959
Syracuse	9.6	11.5	13.4	13.1	14.2	7.7	30.6	1958
Tampa	17.2	25.9	25.4	13.6	11.0	3.3	3.5	1977
Tucson	23.2	22.4	25.6	11.7	10.4	3.7	3.0	1978
Tulsa	15.2	19.1	23.4	14.1	13.2	6.5	8.5	1973
Virginia Beach	18.4	22.1	18.9	15.2	12.5	6.4	6.4	1975
Washington	18.2	18.9	18.1	16.1	11.9	7.2	9.6	1973
Wichita	17.6	14.1	15.3	10.1	20.9	9.5	12.6	1967
U.S.	17.0	15.8	18.5	13.7	12.7	7.3	15.0	1971

Note: Figures are percentages; (1) Metropolitan Statistical Area - see Appendix A for areas included
Source: Census 2000, Summary File 3

Educational Quality

City	School District	Education Quotient[1]	Graduate Outcome[2]	Community Index[3]	Resource Index[4]
Albuquerque	Albuquerque Public Schools	36	39	48	23
Alexandria	Alexandria City Public Schools	40	29	71	90
Anchorage	Anchorage	50	53	19	44
Ann Arbor	Ann Arbor Public Schools	77	75	62	65
Atlanta	Atlanta City	8	2	32	72
Austin	Austin ISD	73	75	27	54
Baltimore	Baltimore City Public School System	27	25	14	61
Baton Rouge	East Baton Rouge Parish	21	19	46	50
Bellevue	Bellevue	72	72	91	45
Birmingham	Birmingham City	12	16	15	25
Boise City	Boise City Independent 1	73	73	68	49
Boston	Boston	32	24	39	84
Boulder	Boulder Valley	81	81	88	45
Buffalo	Buffalo City	8	1	11	87
Cedar Rapids	Cedar Rapids Community	92	94	73	51
Charleston	Charleston County	28	25	45	54
Charlotte	Charlotte-Mecklenburg Schools	40	38	69	45
Chattanooga	Hamilton County	17	16	45	41
Chicago	City of Chicago 299	5	4	29	45
Cincinnati	Cincinnati City	59	55	26	83
Cleveland	Cleveland Municipal	8	1	5	83
Colorado Springs	Academy 20	79	82	96	26
Columbia	Richland School District 01	25	19	39	72
Columbus	Columbus City	8	2	31	74
Dallas	Dallas ISD	28	25	69	45
Denver	Denver County 1	2	1	45	38
Des Moines	Des Moines Ind. Community	77	76	52	62
Detroit	Detroit City	36	34	11	68
Durham	Durham Public Schools	36	32	55	58
El Paso	El Paso ISD	49	52	13	44
Eugene	Eugene 04J	54	54	66	40
Fort Collins	Poudre R-1	44	45	78	27
Fort Lauderdale	Broward County	13	14	50	27
Fort Wayne	Fort Wayne Community Schools	29	31	49	23
Fort Worth	Fort Worth ISD	19	16	66	47
Grand Rapids	Forest Hills Public Schools	90	92	58	55
Green Bay	Green Bay Area	44	38	57	72
Greensboro	Guilford County Schools	33	31	57	46
Honolulu	Hawaii Dept. of Education	58	54	61	67
Houston	Houston ISD	31	32	26	44
Huntsville	Huntsville City	38	40	57	29
Indianapolis	Indianapolis Public Schools	6	8	18	33
Irvine	Irvine Unified	89	91	92	36
Jacksonville	Duval County	31	34	47	22
Kansas City	Kansas City 33	9	4	20	73
Knoxville	Knox County	24	24	50	38
Las Vegas	Clark County	30	32	43	26
Lexington	Fayette County	45	41	59	58
Lincoln	Lincoln Public Schools	56	54	68	54
Los Angeles	Los Angeles Unified	5	4	23	49
Louisville	Jefferson County	32	30	46	53
Madison	Madison Metropolitan	89	87	52	73
Manchester	Manchester	52	51	49	47

Educational Quality *continued*

City	School District	Education Quotient[1]	Graduate Outcome[2]	Community Index[3]	Resource Index[4]
Memphis	Memphis City	2	1	24	41
Miami	Dade County	4	5	22	38
Milwaukee	Milwaukee	15	9	87	59
Minneapolis	Minneapolis	15	9	50	68
Naperville	Naperville CUD 203	95	97	97	49
Nashville	Nashville-Davidson Co.	13	11	49	52
New Orleans	Orleans Parish School Board	1	1	18	35
New York	New York City Public Schools	24	18	28	79
Norfolk	Norfolk City Public Schools	52	49	24	67
Oklahoma City	Oklahoma City	2	2	41	28
Omaha	Millard Public Schools	91	94	96	36
Orlando	Orange County	37	39	51	29
Overland Park	Blue Valley USD	98	96	98	78
Philadelphia	Philadelphia City	n/a	n/a	n/a	n/a
Phoenix	Paradise Valley Unified	73	76	81	30
Pittsburgh	Pittsburgh	16	6	27	92
Plano	Plano ISD	94	92	94	64
Portland	Portland 1J	42	41	62	50
Providence	Providence	29	27	12	59
Provo	Provo	48	54	61	11
Raleigh	Wake County Schools	83	85	79	38
Reno	Washoe County	42	46	57	22
Richmond	Henrico County Public Schools	79	78	72	53
Rochester	Rochester City	10	3	13	84
Sacramento	Sacramento City Unified	25	25	33	45
Saint Louis	St. Louis City	2	3	12	34
Saint Paul	Saint Paul	12	7	48	64
Saint Petersburg	Pinellas County	n/a	n/a	n/a	n/a
Salt Lake City	Salt Lake City	29	34	20	23
San Antonio	San Antonio ISD	12	11	2	56
San Diego	San Diego City Unified	22	19	49	53
San Francisco	San Francisco Unified	25	20	63	57
San Jose	San Jose Unified	80	79	61	57
Savannah	Chatham County	11	9	40	48
Scottsdale	Scottsdale Unified	83	86	87	32
Seattle	Seattle	67	66	71	55
Sioux Falls	Sioux Falls 49-5	86	94	66	18
Springfield	Springfield 186	21	17	47	58
Springfield	Springfield R-XII	67	70	44	42
Stamford	Stamford	34	27	71	67
Syracuse	Syracuse City	63	60	15	78
Tampa	Hillsborough County	72	76	46	31
Tucson	Tucson Unified	57	60	39	36
Tulsa	Tulsa	2	5	34	24
Virginia Beach	Virginia Beach City Public Schools	65	63	73	60
Washington	District of Columbia Public Schools	20	14	36	77
Wichita	Wichita USD	16	15	45	44

Note: Scores are national percentile rankings and range from 1 (worst) to 99 (best); (1) Combination of the Graduate Outcome, Community and Resource indexes weighted to reflect the greater importance of the Graduate Outcome and Resource Index; (2) Based on graduation rates and college board scores (SAT/ACT); (3) Based on the surrounding community's level of affluence and adult education; (4) Based on teacher salaries, per-pupil expenditures and student-teacher ratios.
Source: Expansion Management, December 2003

School Enrollment by Race: City

City	Grades KG to 8 (%)				Grades 9 to 12 (%)			
	White	Black	Asian	Hisp.[1]	White	Black	Asian	Hisp.[1]
Albuquerque	63.7	3.5	1.8	49.7	64.3	3.8	2.0	47.7
Alexandria	42.0	33.4	3.8	25.1	41.3	33.9	4.8	22.8
Anchorage	64.7	6.7	5.2	7.1	65.9	7.7	6.9	7.1
Ann Arbor	69.2	13.9	10.3	2.5	73.8	14.2	7.4	3.6
Atlanta	15.6	80.4	1.1	3.7	13.5	82.6	1.1	3.1
Austin	54.5	13.6	3.5	42.7	55.5	14.5	3.1	39.1
Baltimore	19.9	76.5	0.8	1.6	17.6	78.5	1.0	1.6
Baton Rouge	29.5	66.4	1.9	1.8	33.2	62.2	3.0	1.0
Bellevue	67.4	2.5	17.8	6.3	65.5	2.3	20.8	6.6
Birmingham	8.9	89.3	0.3	1.2	9.5	88.5	0.4	1.1
Boise City	90.6	0.9	1.4	6.0	90.5	1.2	1.8	4.3
Boston	30.2	41.7	6.7	24.2	28.9	42.2	7.7	21.4
Boulder	83.8	1.5	3.1	12.6	85.4	1.5	3.3	10.4
Buffalo	38.9	49.5	0.6	11.6	42.1	48.3	1.2	11.1
Cedar Rapids	87.6	5.3	1.9	2.7	88.2	5.1	2.7	1.8
Charleston	43.6	52.9	1.6	1.3	47.2	50.6	0.8	0.9
Charlotte	48.0	42.7	3.3	6.5	47.0	43.7	4.0	5.4
Chattanooga	43.3	51.4	1.5	2.3	42.8	52.5	2.2	1.0
Chicago	29.0	46.0	3.0	34.4	28.9	46.0	3.6	31.8
Cincinnati	34.8	61.3	0.6	1.0	35.8	59.7	0.6	1.3
Cleveland	30.2	61.3	0.8	9.2	29.6	61.8	0.9	8.8
Colorado Spgs.	76.6	7.4	2.1	14.6	75.7	8.3	3.4	14.1
Columbia	30.5	64.3	0.9	2.7	30.6	65.9	0.6	2.7
Columbus	56.5	34.6	2.5	2.7	55.9	35.3	2.9	2.8
Dallas	38.8	31.5	2.0	46.8	36.8	34.6	2.6	41.8
Denver	47.5	16.5	2.1	49.0	48.7	16.8	3.5	45.0
Des Moines	74.1	11.8	3.8	8.5	76.8	10.3	4.4	7.5
Detroit	7.1	86.3	0.9	5.1	7.4	86.4	1.0	4.7
Durham	31.2	59.1	2.2	7.1	35.2	57.9	2.3	4.5
El Paso	71.0	3.1	0.8	83.3	71.2	3.0	1.1	82.1
Eugene	83.8	1.7	2.8	8.7	85.5	1.6	2.9	5.6
Ft. Collins	87.4	1.0	1.9	10.0	88.5	1.2	1.3	11.0
Ft. Lauderdale	40.8	50.4	1.0	8.8	35.5	52.6	1.5	10.2
Ft. Wayne	65.5	24.6	1.4	6.4	66.6	25.1	2.3	5.9
Ft. Worth	51.1	23.2	2.3	39.7	47.8	27.5	2.8	35.1
Grand Rapids	51.3	31.1	1.8	17.1	54.0	29.9	2.6	16.3
Green Bay	76.5	2.5	8.4	9.6	79.2	1.2	8.3	7.6
Greensboro	44.4	46.4	3.6	4.8	48.4	43.3	4.1	3.4
Honolulu	12.2	1.7	46.0	7.2	10.7	1.8	54.7	5.4
Houston	41.3	29.3	3.9	46.6	40.3	29.7	5.3	43.3
Huntsville	55.6	37.8	1.2	2.8	57.1	34.8	2.7	3.1
Indianapolis	59.7	33.7	0.9	3.8	60.6	34.3	1.1	4.0
Irvine	60.3	1.4	27.3	8.6	60.0	1.3	27.9	9.1
Jacksonville	54.5	38.4	2.3	4.5	54.0	38.8	2.9	4.9
Kansas City	47.9	41.9	1.6	8.9	45.8	44.0	2.7	6.8
Knoxville	68.2	26.4	1.0	2.0	66.5	28.6	1.6	1.0
Las Vegas	62.3	13.1	3.4	32.3	63.0	13.3	4.5	29.8
Lexington	74.7	18.7	1.8	4.0	74.3	19.4	1.7	3.2
Lincoln	84.0	4.5	3.7	5.0	85.3	4.0	4.2	5.7
Los Angeles	39.1	11.7	6.5	62.8	36.8	11.9	8.0	61.5
Louisville	48.0	46.4	1.3	1.9	50.7	43.9	1.3	1.5
Madison	71.1	12.6	7.4	6.1	73.9	11.4	7.1	5.1
Manchester	88.0	4.2	1.8	6.6	87.9	4.6	2.1	5.9

School Enrollment by Race: City *continued*

City	Grades KG to 8 (%)				Grades 9 to 12 (%)			
	White	Black	Asian	Hisp.[1]	White	Black	Asian	Hisp.[1]
Memphis	20.0	76.1	1.1	2.6	21.6	74.8	1.1	2.1
Miami	56.2	32.0	0.3	54.1	52.1	33.2	0.4	57.2
Milwaukee	28.9	53.7	3.8	15.5	32.5	51.2	3.3	14.1
Minneapolis	38.2	31.9	12.0	10.0	38.2	33.9	12.3	8.9
Naperville	84.1	2.9	9.7	3.6	86.1	3.0	8.1	4.9
Nashville	52.8	38.8	2.2	4.9	52.6	39.8	2.4	4.2
New Orleans	13.6	81.5	2.3	2.4	14.6	80.2	2.5	2.6
New York	33.8	32.8	8.6	34.7	32.5	33.5	9.7	33.5
Norfolk	33.9	58.2	2.3	3.0	35.3	56.6	2.5	3.3
Oklahoma City	56.4	20.5	3.5	15.4	58.9	21.5	4.1	11.5
Omaha	69.6	19.2	1.4	10.1	72.5	18.4	1.7	6.8
Orlando	44.2	42.9	1.6	21.3	44.0	40.0	2.8	21.8
Overland Park	89.8	2.8	3.1	4.4	90.4	2.0	4.0	3.9
Philadelphia	31.4	54.1	3.7	12.3	33.2	52.7	4.5	10.6
Phoenix	62.9	5.8	1.6	45.6	64.9	6.2	2.1	40.5
Pittsburgh	50.1	44.7	1.2	1.3	55.1	39.1	1.0	1.4
Plano	75.6	5.6	11.0	11.1	77.2	5.9	9.7	10.7
Portland	68.0	9.7	7.1	9.9	68.3	11.0	8.0	8.0
Providence	36.6	20.1	7.0	43.8	33.4	19.0	8.7	44.4
Provo	83.7	0.7	0.8	18.1	90.3	0.2	1.1	11.9
Raleigh	51.6	38.0	3.2	7.2	54.1	36.1	3.6	6.6
Reno	69.5	2.4	4.7	29.5	68.0	3.3	6.0	28.9
Richmond	17.0	79.2	0.4	2.4	14.1	82.4	1.0	1.9
Rochester	27.6	53.4	1.4	19.3	27.2	53.6	2.4	17.5
Sacramento	32.7	21.1	19.3	28.5	34.1	18.5	23.4	24.6
St. Louis	26.6	68.0	1.5	2.0	29.1	65.3	1.8	1.9
St. Paul	44.1	17.0	24.4	10.2	47.2	15.5	24.4	10.2
St. Petersburg	56.1	35.5	3.1	4.7	53.9	36.0	4.9	4.8
Salt Lake City	68.8	3.2	3.0	29.5	72.1	3.9	3.2	22.0
San Antonio	62.1	6.8	1.1	67.9	63.3	7.3	1.3	67.0
San Diego	47.8	10.3	13.2	38.5	45.8	9.9	15.9	36.8
San Francisco	28.6	12.6	38.9	21.5	26.9	11.3	40.8	23.6
San Jose	41.2	3.4	25.1	39.9	39.4	3.4	27.0	39.0
Savannah	21.4	74.6	1.3	2.2	21.6	74.5	1.8	1.3
Scottsdale	89.0	1.2	1.9	10.3	89.1	1.6	2.7	9.3
Seattle	52.9	14.5	16.5	8.2	50.5	16.7	17.5	7.8
Sioux Falls	87.8	2.1	1.5	3.7	89.8	3.6	1.4	2.4
Springfield (IL)	68.7	25.7	1.8	0.8	74.2	22.1	0.9	1.8
Springfield (MO)	88.8	3.9	1.3	3.4	86.5	4.1	2.9	1.8
Stamford	58.5	23.3	4.1	20.5	54.6	27.0	3.6	23.1
Syracuse	44.5	41.2	1.9	9.2	48.6	37.5	3.2	6.5
Tampa	49.9	37.9	1.4	21.2	49.2	38.2	2.5	20.5
Tucson	59.4	5.2	1.6	51.2	58.9	5.5	1.7	51.4
Tulsa	58.5	22.2	1.5	9.1	60.5	22.6	2.9	7.4
Virginia Beach	64.5	24.6	4.0	5.2	65.9	22.5	5.7	5.0
Washington	13.0	78.3	1.1	8.9	12.6	77.7	1.8	9.9
Wichita	65.9	15.5	3.9	13.9	66.9	16.3	4.9	11.5
U.S.	68.5	15.5	3.3	16.8	68.8	15.5	3.8	15.7

Note: Figures shown cover persons 3 years old and over; (1) people of Hispanic origin can be of any race;
Source: Census 2000, Summary File 3

School Enrollment by Race: Metro Area

MSA[1]	Grades KG to 8 (%)				Grades 9 to 12 (%)			
	White	Black	Asian	Hisp.[2]	White	Black	Asian	Hisp.[2]
Albuquerque	61.5	2.6	1.2	50.4	62.9	2.5	1.5	49.0
Alexandria	54.3	30.4	5.8	9.9	53.1	30.9	6.6	10.2
Anchorage	64.7	6.7	5.2	7.1	65.9	7.7	6.9	7.1
Ann Arbor	84.0	8.3	2.6	3.5	85.5	8.1	2.3	4.0
Atlanta	56.5	35.2	3.0	6.2	56.3	35.5	3.6	5.3
Austin	66.6	9.5	2.7	34.2	67.3	10.3	2.5	31.0
Baltimore	61.1	32.7	2.4	2.3	60.1	33.3	3.0	2.3
Baton Rouge	56.8	40.0	1.2	1.8	58.4	38.0	1.9	1.6
Bellevue	73.2	5.5	9.2	6.6	73.1	5.4	10.5	5.8
Birmingham	60.1	37.1	0.6	2.0	59.8	38.0	0.6	1.3
Boise City	87.2	0.6	0.9	12.0	87.9	0.8	1.2	10.6
Boston	76.8	10.0	4.6	8.7	75.2	11.1	4.9	8.7
Boulder	85.0	0.7	3.0	15.5	87.0	0.8	2.6	12.7
Buffalo	77.2	16.4	0.9	4.5	79.7	14.7	1.5	4.0
Cedar Rapids	90.7	3.5	1.4	2.1	92.2	3.2	1.8	1.3
Charleston	54.5	40.7	1.0	2.6	53.4	42.0	1.5	2.5
Charlotte	67.2	26.1	1.8	5.0	67.2	27.1	2.2	3.8
Chattanooga	77.2	19.3	0.9	1.8	77.6	18.9	1.4	1.3
Chicago	58.6	23.4	3.9	22.2	58.7	23.2	4.6	20.2
Cincinnati	79.8	16.8	0.9	1.2	81.5	15.6	0.9	1.1
Cleveland	69.8	24.2	1.1	4.9	72.1	22.3	1.3	4.3
Colorado Spgs.	77.2	7.0	1.7	14.0	77.5	7.4	2.9	13.4
Columbia	56.0	40.0	1.0	2.7	54.2	41.6	1.4	2.2
Columbus	76.5	17.1	2.0	2.1	77.3	16.8	1.9	2.0
Dallas	60.7	18.0	3.6	28.9	61.2	18.7	4.0	25.8
Denver	73.1	6.9	2.7	24.9	74.5	6.6	3.4	21.9
Des Moines	86.3	5.3	2.2	5.5	87.0	5.0	2.5	4.7
Detroit	63.6	29.2	2.2	3.7	66.4	26.8	2.3	3.2
Durham	63.0	28.2	2.6	6.1	64.9	27.9	2.6	4.7
El Paso	72.4	2.8	0.7	85.0	71.9	2.8	1.0	83.9
Eugene	87.2	1.1	1.6	7.4	89.2	0.8	1.7	5.1
Ft. Collins	89.5	0.7	1.3	10.4	90.4	0.6	1.5	10.5
Ft. Lauderdale	59.2	30.1	2.2	19.3	55.9	32.4	2.4	19.4
Ft. Wayne	84.1	10.1	1.0	3.8	84.1	10.6	1.3	3.3
Ft. Worth	69.1	12.9	2.8	23.7	69.0	14.1	3.6	19.9
Grand Rapids	80.5	9.8	1.9	8.5	82.7	8.9	2.3	7.3
Green Bay	86.5	1.5	4.3	5.0	87.8	1.4	4.4	3.5
Greensboro	67.9	25.4	1.4	5.8	69.5	24.5	1.8	4.7
Honolulu	14.7	2.2	34.3	10.2	11.5	1.6	41.7	9.4
Houston	56.0	19.6	4.3	36.5	56.0	19.8	5.4	32.8
Huntsville	70.7	23.3	1.3	2.8	68.7	25.2	1.6	2.8
Indianapolis	77.4	17.7	1.0	2.6	77.7	18.0	1.1	2.7
Irvine	58.6	1.6	11.8	42.5	56.2	1.9	14.8	38.8
Jacksonville	64.6	29.0	1.9	4.4	64.2	28.7	2.5	5.0
Kansas City	75.5	16.1	1.3	6.4	75.6	16.7	1.9	5.5
Knoxville	88.4	8.0	0.9	1.3	88.5	8.2	1.0	1.1
Las Vegas	66.2	10.5	3.6	29.2	67.1	10.0	4.8	25.8
Lexington	83.1	11.8	1.4	2.6	82.8	12.4	1.3	2.0
Lincoln	85.6	4.0	3.3	4.4	86.9	3.5	3.7	5.0
Los Angeles	41.8	10.5	9.1	57.7	39.8	10.3	11.2	55.9
Louisville	77.1	18.5	0.9	1.7	78.3	17.6	0.8	1.6
Madison	84.2	6.6	3.5	4.3	85.2	6.2	3.7	3.5
Manchester	92.8	2.3	1.5	3.5	92.9	2.5	1.4	3.6

School Enrollment by Race: Metro Area *continued*

MSA[1]	Grades KG to 8 (%)				Grades 9 to 12 (%)			
	White	Black	Asian	Hisp.[2]	White	Black	Asian	Hisp.[2]
Memphis	43.1	53.1	1.2	2.2	44.0	52.4	1.3	1.9
Miami	62.1	27.4	1.1	49.4	57.8	29.7	1.2	52.5
Milwaukee	64.7	24.8	2.4	8.9	68.9	21.5	2.4	7.6
Minneapolis	79.3	7.7	6.0	4.4	80.8	7.1	6.3	3.8
Naperville	58.6	23.4	3.9	22.2	58.7	23.2	4.6	20.2
Nashville	74.7	19.8	1.4	3.3	74.4	20.7	1.5	2.6
New Orleans	46.8	47.2	2.2	4.2	47.3	46.8	2.4	4.1
New York	39.1	30.1	8.0	32.0	37.2	31.2	9.0	31.3
Norfolk	54.7	37.5	2.3	3.5	56.0	36.3	2.9	3.6
Oklahoma City	67.3	13.6	2.2	9.9	69.2	14.0	2.4	7.6
Omaha	80.5	11.0	1.2	7.2	82.0	10.7	1.4	5.6
Orlando	67.1	19.4	2.3	20.1	65.6	20.0	2.9	20.0
Overland Park	75.5	16.1	1.3	6.4	75.6	16.7	1.9	5.5
Philadelphia	65.6	24.9	3.1	7.0	64.8	25.6	3.7	6.4
Phoenix	68.7	4.4	1.7	35.6	70.9	4.6	2.0	31.5
Pittsburgh	84.8	11.9	1.0	0.9	87.2	9.9	0.9	1.0
Plano	60.7	18.0	3.6	28.9	61.2	18.7	4.0	25.8
Portland	80.1	3.1	4.4	9.9	81.9	3.4	4.8	7.7
Providence	79.3	5.8	2.7	12.8	79.8	5.6	3.6	11.5
Provo	91.8	0.5	0.6	7.5	93.6	0.2	0.6	6.1
Raleigh	63.0	28.2	2.6	6.1	64.9	27.9	2.6	4.7
Reno	74.2	2.0	3.8	25.1	74.0	3.0	4.4	22.4
Richmond	58.3	36.1	1.7	2.7	57.9	36.4	2.4	2.3
Rochester	76.9	14.5	1.7	6.7	79.0	13.5	2.3	5.3
Sacramento	61.7	9.9	9.5	19.4	63.2	9.0	11.1	17.1
St. Louis	71.8	24.1	1.1	1.8	73.7	22.5	1.3	1.8
St. Paul	79.3	7.7	6.0	4.4	80.8	7.1	6.3	3.8
St. Petersburg	73.7	16.6	2.0	14.0	74.3	15.8	2.8	13.6
Salt Lake City	85.4	1.1	1.7	12.7	87.1	1.0	2.1	10.6
San Antonio	65.0	6.8	1.1	60.4	66.3	7.4	1.3	58.9
San Diego	57.2	7.0	7.8	38.2	56.6	6.7	9.5	35.9
San Francisco	48.4	6.7	23.4	25.0	44.9	6.9	26.0	25.5
San Jose	47.3	2.6	24.3	32.8	45.3	3.1	25.2	33.5
Savannah	51.2	44.0	1.5	2.2	49.0	47.2	1.5	1.7
Scottsdale	68.7	4.4	1.7	35.6	70.9	4.6	2.0	31.5
Seattle	73.2	5.5	9.2	6.6	73.1	5.4	10.5	5.8
Sioux Falls	90.6	1.4	1.3	2.9	92.1	2.5	1.1	2.1
Springfield (IL)	81.6	14.5	1.1	1.0	85.0	11.8	0.6	1.1
Springfield (MO)	93.3	1.7	0.7	2.1	91.7	2.2	1.4	1.9
Stamford	76.6	11.9	4.0	11.6	73.0	14.2	3.5	14.8
Syracuse	84.3	9.3	1.3	3.1	86.5	7.9	1.5	2.1
Tampa	73.7	16.6	2.0	14.0	74.3	15.8	2.8	13.6
Tucson	65.5	3.4	1.5	42.8	65.7	3.6	1.9	40.6
Tulsa	68.0	11.5	1.2	6.0	69.6	11.3	1.8	5.2
Virginia Beach	54.7	37.5	2.3	3.5	56.0	36.3	2.9	3.6
Washington	54.3	30.4	5.8	9.9	53.1	30.9	6.6	10.2
Wichita	76.1	9.8	2.7	10.3	77.3	10.1	3.5	8.4
U.S.	68.5	15.5	3.3	16.8	68.8	15.5	3.8	15.7

*Note: Figures shown cover persons 3 years old and over; (1) Metropolitan Statistical Area -
see Appendix A for areas included; (2) people of Hispanic origin can be of any race*
Source: Census 2000, Summary File 3

School Enrollment by Type: City

City	Grades KG to 8				Grades 9 to 12			
	Public		Private		Public		Private	
	Enrollment	%	Enrollment	%	Enrollment	%	Enrollment	%
Albuquerque	47,609	87.4	6,870	12.6	22,015	89.4	2,624	10.6
Alexandria	8,227	83.2	1,664	16.8	3,573	84.2	671	15.8
Anchorage	36,289	91.6	3,329	8.4	14,603	93.1	1,075	6.9
Ann Arbor	7,740	82.9	1,602	17.1	3,508	91.5	324	8.5
Atlanta	44,189	90.4	4,700	9.6	18,138	88.8	2,282	11.2
Austin	66,530	92.0	5,793	8.0	26,233	93.4	1,863	6.6
Baltimore	73,446	84.0	14,015	16.0	32,879	86.3	5,206	13.7
Baton Rouge	22,342	77.9	6,338	22.1	10,183	81.1	2,369	18.9
Bellevue	10,116	86.7	1,558	13.3	4,678	90.8	473	9.2
Birmingham	29,131	89.8	3,301	10.2	12,815	92.3	1,073	7.7
Boise City	21,529	90.8	2,176	9.2	9,656	92.2	819	7.8
Boston	50,589	79.9	12,717	20.1	25,077	85.3	4,321	14.7
Boulder	6,276	88.9	787	11.1	2,815	90.5	296	9.5
Buffalo	34,925	84.6	6,361	15.4	14,330	86.7	2,189	13.3
Cedar Rapids	13,027	85.2	2,266	14.8	5,715	93.5	397	6.5
Charleston	8,108	80.5	1,962	19.5	3,422	79.0	908	21.0
Charlotte	59,671	85.3	10,257	14.7	23,929	88.0	3,270	12.0
Chattanooga	15,709	84.9	2,790	15.1	6,176	85.0	1,091	15.0
Chicago	329,687	83.5	65,116	16.5	132,701	82.7	27,737	17.3
Cincinnati	33,493	79.5	8,653	20.5	12,622	80.6	3,043	19.4
Cleveland	61,753	83.8	11,908	16.2	22,670	84.3	4,212	15.7
Colorado Spgs.	43,127	89.7	4,978	10.3	18,240	90.6	1,898	9.4
Columbia	10,338	87.7	1,454	12.3	4,994	87.1	741	12.9
Columbus	76,928	88.3	10,154	11.7	28,639	88.2	3,833	11.8
Dallas	141,212	89.6	16,443	10.4	54,733	89.9	6,166	10.1
Denver	53,202	87.7	7,484	12.3	20,810	89.6	2,412	10.4
Des Moines	21,715	90.5	2,270	9.5	9,273	91.6	852	8.4
Detroit	149,751	90.5	15,747	9.5	58,084	92.0	5,057	8.0
Durham	19,104	87.1	2,825	12.9	7,233	91.8	647	8.2
El Paso	86,000	93.3	6,128	6.7	39,565	94.1	2,469	5.9
Eugene	13,156	90.3	1,418	9.7	5,815	90.0	645	10.0
Ft. Collins	11,716	91.9	1,037	8.1	5,017	94.6	286	5.4
Ft. Lauderdale	12,934	82.4	2,769	17.6	6,278	84.6	1,141	15.4
Ft. Wayne	22,233	79.5	5,716	20.5	9,629	82.4	2,062	17.6
Ft. Worth	69,958	91.1	6,845	8.9	27,222	91.5	2,543	8.5
Grand Rapids	21,692	79.4	5,611	20.6	8,867	78.2	2,475	21.8
Green Bay	10,521	78.8	2,839	21.3	5,035	90.5	528	9.5
Greensboro	23,064	88.7	2,930	11.3	10,366	93.7	693	6.3
Honolulu	29,361	79.6	7,541	20.4	13,054	74.2	4,550	25.8
Houston	256,005	92.3	21,375	7.7	101,938	92.5	8,210	7.5
Huntsville	16,163	87.1	2,404	12.9	7,179	87.7	1,010	12.3
Indianapolis	83,767	82.2	18,091	17.8	34,219	86.1	5,520	13.9
Irvine	16,380	91.9	1,441	8.1	7,620	95.7	345	4.3
Jacksonville	88,145	85.4	15,094	14.6	35,819	86.6	5,563	13.4
Kansas City	49,028	85.0	8,649	15.0	20,065	85.3	3,465	14.7
Knoxville	15,184	88.4	1,990	11.6	6,409	89.2	776	10.8
Las Vegas	58,821	93.1	4,349	6.9	22,255	93.9	1,435	6.1
Lexington	24,534	85.4	4,202	14.6	9,857	86.3	1,563	13.7
Lincoln	20,876	82.5	4,438	17.5	10,055	85.9	1,653	14.1
Los Angeles	454,318	86.5	70,607	13.5	201,618	89.3	24,200	10.7
Louisville	27,065	84.1	5,098	15.9	11,516	84.9	2,042	15.1
Madison	15,810	87.7	2,221	12.3	8,024	93.3	580	6.7
Manchester	11,385	86.3	1,802	13.7	4,940	93.2	362	6.8

School Enrollment by Type: City *continued*

City	Grades KG to 8				Grades 9 to 12			
	Public		Private		Public		Private	
	Enrollment	%	Enrollment	%	Enrollment	%	Enrollment	%
Memphis	85,881	90.2	9,354	9.8	35,249	89.5	4,154	10.5
Miami	38,677	92.7	3,053	7.3	21,451	92.1	1,842	7.9
Milwaukee	77,113	81.2	17,815	18.8	30,746	84.8	5,525	15.2
Minneapolis	37,584	86.5	5,872	13.5	15,840	89.4	1,875	10.6
Naperville	20,099	91.4	1,887	8.6	7,436	89.8	844	10.2
Nashville	50,605	83.9	9,685	16.1	21,680	83.5	4,271	16.5
New Orleans	56,336	81.5	12,783	18.5	25,536	82.7	5,343	17.3
New York	821,776	80.7	196,006	19.3	390,758	82.0	85,562	18.0
Norfolk	26,349	89.8	2,984	10.2	10,488	91.1	1,029	8.9
Oklahoma City	59,290	90.6	6,153	9.4	24,860	91.1	2,438	8.9
Omaha	40,515	79.6	10,359	20.4	17,898	82.5	3,800	17.5
Orlando	18,420	88.8	2,333	11.2	8,123	92.1	697	7.9
Overland Park	16,589	84.5	3,042	15.5	6,945	86.9	1,044	13.1
Philadelphia	153,896	76.1	48,216	23.9	75,971	78.8	20,421	21.2
Phoenix	180,398	93.3	12,894	6.7	68,750	92.8	5,365	7.2
Pittsburgh	26,858	78.3	7,436	21.7	12,690	80.6	3,050	19.4
Plano	28,544	88.8	3,606	11.2	11,760	93.6	799	6.4
Portland	48,210	87.7	6,772	12.3	21,811	89.2	2,630	10.8
Providence	21,820	87.6	3,080	12.4	8,725	89.8	989	10.2
Provo	9,048	96.1	366	3.9	4,330	93.4	304	6.6
Raleigh	26,402	88.9	3,313	11.1	9,915	89.5	1,168	10.5
Reno	20,254	94.4	1,201	5.6	8,597	92.7	679	7.3
Richmond	19,801	87.2	2,901	12.8	7,775	88.1	1,047	11.9
Rochester	30,274	87.9	4,160	12.1	10,807	88.7	1,375	11.3
Sacramento	54,640	92.1	4,702	7.9	23,025	91.2	2,210	8.8
St. Louis	38,345	80.1	9,537	19.9	15,889	82.1	3,470	17.9
St. Paul	34,035	83.9	6,535	16.1	15,176	86.3	2,399	13.7
St. Petersburg	23,502	83.5	4,648	16.5	10,943	89.8	1,239	10.2
Salt Lake City	18,258	90.9	1,820	9.1	7,946	91.4	743	8.6
San Antonio	153,162	90.8	15,589	9.2	66,419	92.3	5,523	7.7
San Diego	139,884	91.0	13,786	9.0	59,532	93.0	4,489	7.0
San Francisco	42,881	72.8	16,049	27.2	24,540	83.1	4,991	16.9
San Jose	106,741	88.9	13,294	11.1	49,044	91.1	4,769	8.9
Savannah	15,838	89.9	1,787	10.1	7,278	90.2	792	9.8
Scottsdale	17,720	87.3	2,589	12.7	7,609	92.4	629	7.6
Seattle	34,022	78.1	9,538	21.9	16,241	80.5	3,925	19.5
Sioux Falls	13,213	86.9	1,987	13.1	6,279	89.1	769	10.9
Springfield (IL)	10,483	74.9	3,521	25.1	4,682	82.0	1,025	18.0
Springfield (MO)	13,701	92.2	1,155	7.8	5,634	91.5	525	8.5
Stamford	11,491	86.7	1,770	13.3	5,128	87.4	737	12.6
Syracuse	17,430	88.1	2,345	11.9	6,521	89.7	747	10.3
Tampa	34,437	87.0	5,154	13.0	14,603	90.2	1,585	9.8
Tucson	55,793	91.9	4,904	8.1	22,977	91.9	2,035	8.1
Tulsa	42,689	85.8	7,070	14.2	16,642	85.1	2,912	14.9
Virginia Beach	55,674	90.5	5,847	9.5	23,625	92.9	1,817	7.1
Washington	52,899	85.5	8,975	14.5	22,303	83.6	4,391	16.4
Wichita	39,908	84.6	7,241	15.4	16,815	87.2	2,474	12.8
U.S.	33,526,011	88.7	4,285,121	11.3	14,848,628	90.6	1,532,323	9.4

Note: Figures shown cover persons 3 years old and over
Source: Census 2000, Summary File 3

School Enrollment by Type: Metro Area

MSA[1]	Grades KG to 8				Grades 9 to 12			
	Public		Private		Public		Private	
	Enrollment	%	Enrollment	%	Enrollment	%	Enrollment	%
Albuquerque	84,412	88.0	11,536	12.0	37,748	89.6	4,358	10.4
Alexandria	556,504	85.7	92,990	14.3	239,684	88.0	32,576	12.0
Anchorage	36,289	91.6	3,329	8.4	14,603	93.1	1,075	6.9
Ann Arbor	66,568	89.7	7,641	10.3	29,523	93.9	1,913	6.1
Atlanta	511,746	90.2	55,562	9.8	207,156	91.5	19,214	8.5
Austin	147,604	92.3	12,299	7.7	60,104	94.4	3,576	5.6
Baltimore	286,618	83.7	55,822	16.3	126,427	85.6	21,257	14.4
Baton Rouge	66,397	78.6	18,036	21.4	31,093	82.9	6,425	17.1
Bellevue	260,622	88.3	34,672	11.7	116,866	91.1	11,446	8.9
Birmingham	108,002	88.8	13,686	11.2	46,620	91.2	4,503	8.8
Boise City	55,566	91.3	5,311	8.7	24,072	92.7	1,882	7.3
Boston	347,941	87.2	51,024	12.8	147,396	85.5	25,007	14.5
Boulder	30,621	88.7	3,890	11.3	13,101	92.0	1,146	8.0
Buffalo	128,746	84.5	23,691	15.5	58,792	88.9	7,351	11.1
Cedar Rapids	21,662	86.5	3,372	13.5	9,839	93.7	663	6.3
Charleston	65,879	86.6	10,174	13.4	27,841	87.9	3,845	12.1
Charlotte	176,153	88.3	23,233	11.7	71,217	91.1	6,951	8.9
Chattanooga	50,400	86.5	7,842	13.5	19,835	83.3	3,969	16.7
Chicago	980,199	85.2	169,831	14.8	411,578	87.3	59,611	12.7
Cincinnati	180,810	79.1	47,767	20.9	77,135	80.6	18,574	19.4
Cleveland	248,070	81.7	55,751	18.3	109,279	86.0	17,810	14.0
Colorado Spgs.	65,944	90.7	6,787	9.3	27,884	91.4	2,632	8.6
Columbia	64,099	91.7	5,837	8.3	28,539	92.5	2,319	7.5
Columbus	178,054	88.0	24,285	12.0	73,403	89.9	8,275	10.1
Dallas	456,971	90.7	46,953	9.3	181,249	92.2	15,405	7.8
Denver	250,673	90.0	27,814	10.0	104,095	91.3	9,939	8.7
Des Moines	53,644	90.8	5,417	9.2	23,513	92.7	1,860	7.3
Detroit	550,333	88.1	73,996	11.9	239,111	90.4	25,291	9.6
Durham	134,391	89.7	15,408	10.3	51,033	90.4	5,428	9.6
El Paso	107,817	94.1	6,804	5.9	49,887	94.5	2,915	5.5
Eugene	34,800	91.9	3,082	8.1	15,788	92.5	1,272	7.5
Ft. Collins	27,705	89.6	3,226	10.4	12,585	93.9	818	6.1
Ft. Lauderdale	175,895	86.9	26,604	13.1	77,084	87.7	10,767	12.3
Ft. Wayne	57,627	81.1	13,469	18.9	25,703	87.4	3,711	12.6
Ft. Worth	224,258	91.0	22,110	9.0	91,305	92.3	7,600	7.7
Grand Rapids	136,670	84.9	24,380	15.1	60,710	86.6	9,386	13.4
Green Bay	24,377	79.6	6,235	20.4	12,009	90.5	1,257	9.5
Greensboro	142,941	90.4	15,232	9.6	58,865	93.0	4,436	7.0
Honolulu	89,045	82.9	18,407	17.1	38,196	79.4	9,908	20.6
Houston	589,699	92.3	49,169	7.7	244,239	93.2	17,795	6.8
Huntsville	39,989	87.7	5,601	12.3	16,226	89.1	1,975	10.9
Indianapolis	187,223	86.2	29,909	13.8	76,997	89.2	9,345	10.8
Irvine	358,527	88.6	45,927	11.4	154,346	93.5	10,681	6.5
Jacksonville	131,666	86.5	20,471	13.5	55,375	88.2	7,379	11.8
Kansas City	212,067	87.5	30,212	12.5	90,420	89.1	11,050	10.9
Knoxville	72,586	90.0	8,074	10.0	31,473	91.8	2,809	8.2
Las Vegas	190,592	94.6	10,904	5.4	72,968	94.8	3,972	5.2
Lexington	48,932	86.9	7,363	13.1	20,298	89.2	2,451	10.8
Lincoln	24,001	83.0	4,912	17.0	11,765	86.3	1,865	13.7
Los Angeles	1,261,035	88.4	164,761	11.6	560,595	91.0	55,347	9.0
Louisville	104,712	80.1	25,959	19.9	47,494	83.5	9,408	16.5
Madison	44,489	89.8	5,034	10.2	20,659	94.4	1,235	5.6
Manchester	23,694	87.1	3,521	12.9	9,986	91.3	949	8.7

School Enrollment by Type: Metro Area *continued*

MSA[1]	Grades KG to 8				Grades 9 to 12			
	Public		Private		Public		Private	
	Enrollment	%	Enrollment	%	Enrollment	%	Enrollment	%
Memphis	149,569	88.4	19,693	11.6	61,138	87.4	8,828	12.6
Miami	257,812	87.1	38,141	12.9	130,916	88.5	16,983	11.5
Milwaukee	168,628	79.3	43,942	20.7	79,263	87.0	11,852	13.0
Minneapolis	360,354	87.5	51,396	12.5	163,520	92.1	13,991	7.9
Naperville	980,199	85.2	169,831	14.8	411,578	87.3	59,611	12.7
Nashville	136,243	86.5	21,347	13.5	56,641	85.6	9,515	14.4
New Orleans	141,576	74.6	48,197	25.4	64,327	76.5	19,770	23.5
New York	965,235	80.8	229,009	19.2	450,178	81.9	99,330	18.1
Norfolk	196,408	89.6	22,702	10.4	83,827	92.7	6,565	7.3
Oklahoma City	129,199	91.2	12,443	8.8	57,617	92.5	4,701	7.5
Omaha	82,606	83.0	16,937	17.0	37,494	86.1	6,066	13.9
Orlando	186,352	87.2	27,385	12.8	83,562	92.0	7,301	8.0
Overland Park	212,067	87.5	30,212	12.5	90,420	89.1	11,050	10.9
Philadelphia	544,674	79.7	138,763	20.3	248,356	81.5	56,489	18.5
Phoenix	414,735	93.4	29,200	6.6	163,065	93.8	10,740	6.2
Pittsburgh	237,516	86.3	37,647	13.7	114,399	91.8	10,230	8.2
Plano	456,971	90.7	46,953	9.3	181,249	92.2	15,405	7.8
Portland	219,761	88.8	27,653	11.2	95,236	91.4	8,906	8.6
Providence	131,803	87.2	19,325	12.8	57,810	87.9	7,987	12.1
Provo	56,391	96.9	1,786	3.1	24,610	96.2	976	3.8
Raleigh	134,391	89.7	15,408	10.3	51,033	90.4	5,428	9.6
Reno	41,138	94.0	2,646	6.0	17,229	93.4	1,216	6.6
Richmond	120,997	91.0	12,001	9.0	50,424	91.5	4,709	8.5
Rochester	137,259	89.9	15,386	10.1	59,420	91.9	5,236	8.1
Sacramento	213,241	90.3	22,784	9.7	93,412	92.7	7,388	7.3
St. Louis	288,749	80.5	70,107	19.5	129,252	83.7	25,180	16.3
St. Paul	360,354	87.5	51,396	12.5	163,520	92.1	13,991	7.9
St. Petersburg	239,025	86.3	38,069	13.7	103,629	90.5	10,836	9.5
Salt Lake City	189,691	94.4	11,196	5.6	93,135	95.6	4,302	4.4
San Antonio	212,457	90.6	22,110	9.4	93,622	92.5	7,639	7.5
San Diego	345,699	90.9	34,480	9.1	149,710	93.8	9,945	6.2
San Francisco	132,872	78.0	37,427	22.0	64,080	83.2	12,973	16.8
San Jose	184,435	86.6	28,642	13.4	83,075	89.8	9,411	10.2
Savannah	35,191	85.9	5,780	14.1	14,841	85.9	2,431	14.1
Scottsdale	414,735	93.4	29,200	6.6	163,065	93.8	10,740	6.2
Seattle	260,622	88.3	34,672	11.7	116,866	91.1	11,446	8.9
Sioux Falls	20,204	88.6	2,600	11.4	9,568	91.6	879	8.4
Springfield (IL)	21,617	82.2	4,679	17.8	9,747	86.8	1,480	13.2
Springfield (MO)	35,976	91.5	3,328	8.5	15,302	93.2	1,123	6.8
Stamford	39,768	84.9	7,049	15.1	14,756	83.9	2,827	16.1
Syracuse	93,216	92.1	8,025	7.9	40,699	94.7	2,300	5.3
Tampa	239,025	86.3	38,069	13.7	103,629	90.5	10,836	9.5
Tucson	98,857	91.6	9,092	8.4	42,008	91.8	3,736	8.2
Tulsa	100,102	89.6	11,603	10.4	42,559	90.5	4,446	9.5
Virginia Beach	196,408	89.6	22,702	10.4	83,827	92.7	6,565	7.3
Washington	556,504	85.7	92,990	14.3	239,684	88.0	32,576	12.0
Wichita	67,343	85.4	11,552	14.6	29,490	89.3	3,529	10.7
U.S.	33,526,011	88.7	4,285,121	11.3	14,848,628	90.6	1,532,323	9.4

Note: Figures shown cover persons 3 years old and over; (1) Metropolitan Statistical Area - see Appendix A for areas included
Source: Census 2000, Summary File 3

Educational Attainment by Race: City

City	High School Graduate (%)					Bachelor's Degree (%)				
	Total	White	Black	Asian	Hisp.[1]	Total	White	Black	Asian	Hisp.[1]
Albuquerque	85.9	88.6	86.3	81.1	72.4	31.8	35.8	23.7	40.3	15.2
Alexandria	86.8	93.3	79.9	86.9	51.5	54.3	66.9	28.3	55.9	21.3
Anchorage	90.3	93.6	87.9	73.2	76.4	28.9	32.6	15.5	24.0	16.3
Ann Arbor	95.7	97.0	84.3	96.9	89.6	69.3	70.9	38.7	87.4	60.4
Atlanta	76.9	92.4	66.8	79.2	53.6	34.6	66.1	12.7	54.0	20.8
Austin	83.4	90.2	79.1	90.7	55.7	40.4	47.6	19.0	67.0	15.5
Baltimore	68.4	73.3	65.3	77.8	62.2	19.1	33.0	10.0	52.3	24.6
Baton Rouge	80.1	91.9	67.2	74.1	77.6	31.7	45.1	15.6	47.8	34.5
Bellevue	94.3	95.9	93.4	92.8	65.9	54.1	54.2	39.1	63.0	28.7
Birmingham	75.5	81.0	73.1	88.3	56.2	18.5	30.7	12.8	66.8	15.7
Boise City	91.1	91.8	85.4	81.8	76.5	33.6	33.9	30.8	45.2	18.2
Boston	78.9	86.2	73.0	64.3	57.3	35.6	46.8	15.6	37.0	15.3
Boulder	94.7	96.1	92.7	92.1	54.4	66.9	68.1	48.8	78.6	29.3
Buffalo	74.6	77.4	71.3	73.2	59.5	18.3	22.7	10.2	40.5	13.0
Cedar Rapids	90.1	90.6	78.7	89.9	72.9	28.4	28.4	12.2	53.4	23.2
Charleston	83.7	93.3	64.5	86.3	77.3	37.5	48.8	14.7	57.2	26.3
Charlotte	84.9	90.9	77.8	76.8	48.4	36.4	45.9	18.9	39.6	13.0
Chattanooga	77.6	81.7	69.9	86.7	58.9	21.5	27.0	9.3	51.1	16.3
Chicago	71.8	78.4	70.7	79.7	46.6	25.5	36.3	13.5	48.2	8.5
Cincinnati	76.7	82.7	67.2	89.3	76.0	26.6	36.5	10.0	69.2	39.0
Cleveland	69.0	72.3	66.5	72.8	54.2	11.4	15.6	6.5	42.2	7.8
Colorado Spgs.	90.9	92.4	90.4	83.2	72.9	33.6	36.0	19.2	38.7	14.1
Columbia	82.3	91.5	70.5	96.6	77.9	35.7	52.8	13.9	63.6	25.2
Columbus	83.8	86.1	77.7	84.9	67.7	29.0	32.5	14.3	59.2	19.3
Dallas	70.4	78.3	73.9	78.5	33.4	27.7	38.5	13.5	50.5	6.5
Denver	78.9	85.1	79.7	77.0	46.1	34.5	42.0	17.8	40.7	7.8
Des Moines	83.0	85.4	78.8	61.0	49.4	21.8	23.2	14.2	17.2	8.9
Detroit	69.6	64.7	71.4	71.5	42.8	11.0	14.2	10.1	44.8	5.8
Durham	82.6	89.4	77.9	94.4	36.4	41.8	54.2	26.3	78.3	14.4
El Paso	68.6	69.6	89.6	83.4	59.9	18.3	20.0	21.7	42.7	12.0
Eugene	91.5	92.3	85.3	93.8	70.3	37.3	37.8	34.3	56.4	19.1
Ft. Collins	94.0	95.1	90.4	92.6	69.4	48.4	49.4	40.0	68.1	22.0
Ft. Lauderdale	79.0	88.9	50.3	72.9	68.3	27.9	35.4	5.2	30.3	22.7
Ft. Wayne	83.2	85.7	75.9	76.5	52.7	19.4	21.7	8.4	32.5	5.9
Ft. Worth	72.8	79.2	74.8	71.8	37.3	22.3	28.2	11.4	36.3	6.7
Grand Rapids	78.0	83.6	68.9	65.5	35.5	23.8	28.7	10.2	27.5	6.5
Green Bay	82.6	85.5	70.0	44.7	38.4	19.3	20.3	11.4	15.3	6.9
Greensboro	84.3	88.8	79.9	66.3	46.5	33.9	42.3	20.6	32.0	13.5
Honolulu	83.4	93.3	90.0	79.4	83.6	31.1	44.3	23.6	29.6	18.9
Houston	70.4	77.0	74.7	78.7	38.8	27.0	35.5	15.9	47.4	7.9
Huntsville	85.7	89.2	76.0	84.3	69.8	36.1	41.2	20.5	54.9	28.4
Indianapolis	81.3	83.8	74.9	85.8	54.1	25.4	28.9	13.3	57.8	13.9
Irvine	95.3	96.3	96.3	94.5	86.6	58.4	57.0	35.7	67.2	38.6
Jacksonville	82.3	85.4	74.2	81.5	79.0	21.1	23.7	13.2	34.7	21.9
Kansas City	82.5	87.3	74.5	72.8	58.3	25.7	31.9	11.9	36.7	10.8
Knoxville	78.4	79.4	73.3	88.1	69.6	24.6	26.0	13.5	63.2	26.4
Las Vegas	78.5	82.7	76.1	83.2	44.6	18.2	19.8	12.5	30.2	6.1
Lexington	85.8	87.5	76.2	91.6	54.5	35.6	38.3	14.5	68.0	14.6
Lincoln	90.2	91.8	81.3	67.6	64.3	33.3	34.2	17.7	35.8	19.5
Los Angeles	66.6	75.6	76.0	82.1	35.5	25.5	32.7	17.1	42.4	6.1
Louisville	76.1	78.9	69.2	74.4	53.8	21.3	26.5	8.2	43.7	15.5
Madison	92.4	94.1	77.5	86.8	72.0	48.2	49.3	20.0	67.1	34.1
Manchester	80.7	81.4	75.5	70.8	58.0	22.3	22.1	19.3	39.5	9.3

Educational Attainment by Race: City *continued*

City	High School Graduate (%)					Bachelor's Degree (%)				
	Total	White	Black	Asian	Hisp.[1]	Total	White	Black	Asian	Hisp.[1]
Memphis	76.4	86.1	69.8	75.8	46.1	20.9	32.9	11.3	49.5	12.6
Miami	52.7	54.4	49.6	81.4	47.2	16.2	19.5	6.5	44.6	13.4
Milwaukee	74.8	81.8	67.6	66.6	45.2	18.3	23.9	9.1	32.9	8.0
Minneapolis	85.0	90.7	75.0	63.1	48.7	37.4	44.7	14.0	32.2	13.3
Naperville	96.3	96.9	93.1	94.4	81.9	60.6	59.6	43.7	78.0	35.6
Nashville	81.1	84.2	75.1	80.9	53.2	29.7	32.9	20.1	49.9	14.3
New Orleans	74.7	88.6	67.4	58.1	70.5	25.8	46.9	13.4	31.7	27.1
New York	72.3	79.6	70.4	69.4	53.4	27.4	36.6	15.8	36.2	10.5
Norfolk	78.4	86.0	67.9	79.7	81.5	19.6	26.3	9.7	34.9	16.5
Oklahoma City	81.3	84.9	78.4	73.3	42.0	24.0	26.8	14.6	31.9	7.2
Omaha	86.0	89.0	76.2	88.0	46.2	28.7	31.4	11.4	57.5	9.9
Orlando	82.2	88.9	63.5	86.0	73.8	28.2	34.0	12.4	41.9	18.7
Overland Park	95.8	96.4	94.4	91.0	77.0	52.1	52.2	50.2	67.9	29.5
Philadelphia	71.2	76.1	68.4	62.9	49.5	17.9	23.7	10.3	32.7	9.2
Phoenix	76.6	82.5	77.5	80.1	43.1	22.7	26.1	15.2	42.1	6.1
Pittsburgh	81.3	83.0	75.2	92.0	76.7	26.2	29.1	12.2	76.6	40.3
Plano	93.9	95.7	92.8	94.3	63.3	53.3	53.0	46.1	72.6	24.7
Portland	85.7	88.8	78.4	68.5	59.5	32.6	35.5	15.3	26.7	14.5
Providence	65.8	72.0	67.6	59.5	45.3	24.4	31.8	15.0	29.0	6.6
Provo	89.4	92.1	75.4	88.5	62.4	35.7	37.3	25.4	51.7	15.5
Raleigh	88.5	93.6	81.0	87.7	45.0	44.9	53.7	24.2	60.7	13.6
Reno	82.4	86.4	82.6	83.7	42.6	25.0	26.9	15.2	34.6	6.6
Richmond	75.2	86.5	65.9	82.2	59.6	29.5	51.3	11.2	49.8	20.3
Rochester	73.0	80.4	64.8	68.5	53.4	20.1	28.5	8.2	33.5	8.2
Sacramento	77.3	84.1	80.6	65.6	57.2	23.9	29.6	13.6	25.6	10.3
St. Louis	71.3	77.7	64.7	66.8	61.8	19.1	28.1	8.8	33.2	16.6
St. Paul	83.8	89.2	79.1	52.6	56.7	32.0	37.0	16.3	17.2	12.9
St. Petersburg	81.9	85.8	67.8	67.0	77.2	22.8	26.0	10.1	24.7	20.2
Salt Lake City	83.4	87.7	76.5	77.2	47.5	34.9	38.0	16.2	45.5	9.4
San Antonio	75.1	77.9	82.1	82.3	61.8	21.6	25.0	17.0	41.4	10.5
San Diego	82.8	88.8	83.4	80.0	52.4	35.0	40.9	15.7	38.4	11.9
San Francisco	81.2	91.7	76.1	67.3	62.5	45.0	59.3	18.1	31.8	20.3
San Jose	78.3	84.8	88.0	79.7	52.1	31.6	33.9	28.0	40.7	8.9
Savannah	76.1	85.6	68.2	73.9	67.2	20.2	30.2	11.1	35.2	22.5
Scottsdale	93.5	94.3	92.6	92.6	69.8	44.1	44.6	41.6	58.1	21.3
Seattle	89.5	93.9	77.2	75.7	70.5	47.2	53.3	20.1	37.0	26.1
Sioux Falls	88.5	90.1	76.9	54.1	48.8	27.8	28.7	20.4	30.8	7.1
Springfield (IL)	87.4	89.0	76.1	91.3	84.1	30.6	32.3	15.4	62.9	30.9
Springfield (MO)	82.8	83.2	83.2	80.0	68.8	23.0	23.4	12.4	40.7	16.5
Stamford	82.2	86.6	69.6	91.0	58.8	39.6	44.5	17.0	70.0	11.8
Syracuse	76.2	80.3	66.1	70.4	54.6	23.2	26.6	8.9	53.4	14.7
Tampa	77.1	81.5	65.9	79.5	60.8	25.4	30.8	9.9	38.8	14.7
Tucson	80.4	84.6	80.8	77.0	60.5	22.9	25.9	14.7	40.0	9.8
Tulsa	84.4	87.1	79.4	77.7	48.3	28.3	31.9	14.2	40.3	9.6
Virginia Beach	90.4	92.0	85.9	84.2	87.2	28.1	30.4	18.1	33.4	19.1
Washington	77.8	94.4	70.4	81.9	47.8	39.1	77.3	17.5	58.2	24.8
Wichita	83.8	87.6	77.8	62.5	48.1	25.3	28.1	12.6	24.5	9.4
U.S.	80.4	83.6	72.3	80.4	52.4	24.4	26.1	14.3	44.1	10.4

Note: Figures shown cover persons 25 years old and over; (1) people of Hispanic origin can be of any race
Source: Census 2000, Summary File 3

Educational Attainment by Race: Metro Area

MSA[1]	High School Graduate (%)					Bachelor's Degree (%)				
	Total	White	Black	Asian	Hisp.[2]	Total	White	Black	Asian	Hisp.[2]
Albuquerque	83.9	87.3	85.3	81.1	70.4	28.4	32.8	22.5	39.4	13.2
Alexandria	86.7	91.1	81.3	85.4	57.7	41.8	49.2	24.1	53.9	21.0
Anchorage	90.3	93.6	87.9	73.2	76.4	28.9	32.6	15.5	24.0	16.3
Ann Arbor	90.1	90.7	83.0	94.1	75.4	36.9	36.4	24.1	80.5	28.9
Atlanta	84.0	86.8	81.0	80.0	51.7	32.0	36.1	21.9	46.4	16.1
Austin	84.8	89.7	80.0	88.5	58.6	36.7	41.1	20.1	62.2	14.7
Baltimore	81.9	85.1	72.9	84.4	75.1	29.2	33.0	16.1	53.2	28.7
Baton Rouge	81.9	87.1	69.6	75.9	77.9	24.9	27.9	16.4	50.0	30.0
Bellevue	90.1	92.3	82.4	82.2	67.8	35.9	37.0	21.1	40.9	19.0
Birmingham	80.6	83.2	74.2	87.6	57.9	24.7	28.3	14.6	65.5	17.3
Boise City	86.5	88.6	80.5	80.6	50.0	26.5	27.3	26.3	38.7	8.8
Boston	87.1	89.5	76.4	78.3	61.0	39.5	41.1	20.8	53.4	18.7
Boulder	92.8	94.6	91.5	90.1	57.6	52.4	53.8	45.0	65.2	18.2
Buffalo	83.0	84.7	70.7	83.9	61.9	23.2	24.3	11.1	63.4	15.6
Cedar Rapids	90.6	90.9	80.0	91.0	74.0	27.7	27.7	13.2	55.1	22.7
Charleston	81.3	87.4	67.3	79.3	67.5	25.0	30.9	10.7	38.0	16.5
Charlotte	80.5	83.0	74.7	76.4	48.6	26.5	29.1	16.5	37.8	11.9
Chattanooga	77.0	78.0	70.8	83.7	64.3	19.7	20.9	10.3	46.1	17.3
Chicago	81.0	85.8	74.3	86.9	47.8	30.1	34.1	15.6	57.5	8.9
Cincinnati	82.4	83.9	71.6	90.8	73.9	25.3	26.6	12.6	64.3	29.0
Cleveland	82.9	85.4	72.3	85.6	62.6	23.3	25.5	10.8	59.1	12.1
Colorado Spgs.	91.3	92.5	91.7	82.6	74.5	31.8	34.0	19.0	35.4	14.1
Columbia	84.3	87.6	77.2	84.6	70.2	29.2	34.1	17.3	50.7	21.1
Columbus	85.8	87.2	78.1	86.1	67.9	29.1	30.4	15.4	59.7	21.6
Dallas	79.4	84.4	78.9	83.4	41.5	30.0	34.0	18.5	52.2	8.7
Denver	86.4	89.6	83.6	79.8	55.9	34.2	37.3	21.0	40.6	10.6
Des Moines	88.6	90.1	80.3	67.9	54.6	28.7	29.7	16.3	28.7	11.7
Detroit	82.1	84.8	73.9	85.9	63.2	22.8	24.6	12.8	62.6	14.7
Durham	85.4	89.4	76.6	91.6	43.0	38.9	43.7	22.2	70.0	15.3
El Paso	65.8	66.5	88.1	83.2	57.0	16.6	18.0	21.1	42.7	10.6
Eugene	87.5	88.2	84.5	88.0	64.8	25.5	25.6	29.2	49.4	15.8
Ft. Collins	92.3	93.3	91.7	89.9	66.2	39.5	40.2	39.4	62.0	17.4
Ft. Lauderdale	82.0	85.5	69.2	81.0	75.7	24.5	26.8	14.7	38.8	23.0
Ft. Wayne	85.3	86.5	76.6	77.9	58.5	19.4	20.0	9.8	39.3	7.9
Ft. Worth	81.0	84.9	80.2	72.4	46.6	25.1	27.3	16.8	36.3	9.2
Grand Rapids	84.6	86.8	72.6	69.9	50.8	22.9	24.3	9.7	31.2	8.3
Green Bay	86.3	88.0	64.7	52.0	42.1	22.5	23.1	7.7	21.3	7.3
Greensboro	78.6	80.4	75.8	70.3	37.9	22.9	24.5	16.7	36.0	8.7
Honolulu	84.8	93.5	93.0	80.8	84.3	27.9	39.6	20.9	28.2	15.1
Houston	75.9	81.4	77.5	80.1	43.6	27.2	31.4	18.4	47.7	8.5
Huntsville	83.3	84.9	76.4	85.1	68.7	30.9	32.8	21.8	53.4	22.4
Indianapolis	84.0	85.5	75.6	86.7	58.9	25.8	27.4	13.8	57.3	16.7
Irvine	79.5	86.0	88.1	81.2	45.1	30.8	33.4	27.6	41.4	8.5
Jacksonville	83.6	86.2	74.0	81.5	79.5	22.9	25.0	13.2	35.2	21.4
Kansas City	86.7	88.8	77.4	80.9	61.4	28.5	30.6	14.6	46.6	13.3
Knoxville	79.6	79.8	76.0	88.9	71.4	23.5	23.6	15.6	60.9	23.6
Las Vegas	79.2	82.2	78.5	81.5	47.9	16.4	17.2	11.9	27.2	6.4
Lexington	82.1	82.9	75.1	91.2	52.8	28.7	29.7	13.5	66.5	13.9
Lincoln	90.5	92.0	81.5	67.8	64.1	32.6	33.3	17.7	36.0	19.3
Los Angeles	69.9	77.0	79.3	82.4	42.1	24.9	29.3	17.8	42.9	6.8
Louisville	81.3	82.3	74.6	84.7	64.4	22.2	23.4	11.8	51.0	17.2
Madison	92.2	93.3	77.6	87.0	67.8	40.6	41.0	19.2	65.5	27.2
Manchester	84.8	85.3	79.1	73.4	64.4	27.0	27.0	23.3	42.3	11.8

Educational Attainment by Race: Metro Area *continued*

MSA[1]	High School Graduate (%)					Bachelor's Degree (%)				
	Total	White	Black	Asian	Hisp.[1]	Total	White	Black	Asian	Hisp.[1]
Memphis	79.8	87.1	69.6	78.7	52.4	22.7	29.2	12.1	48.4	14.1
Miami	67.9	69.4	63.3	80.5	61.2	21.7	24.3	11.5	45.1	18.1
Milwaukee	84.5	88.2	68.3	77.2	52.4	27.0	29.7	10.3	46.6	10.7
Minneapolis	90.6	92.5	79.9	70.9	61.5	33.3	34.4	19.1	36.3	16.7
Naperville	81.0	85.8	74.3	86.9	47.8	30.1	34.1	15.6	57.5	8.9
Nashville	81.4	83.2	74.4	81.1	54.5	26.9	28.2	18.9	46.1	14.2
New Orleans	77.7	83.6	67.6	64.8	71.0	22.6	27.4	12.7	33.5	20.8
New York	74.0	81.2	70.8	70.9	53.9	29.2	37.9	16.3	38.1	11.0
Norfolk	84.7	88.7	75.1	82.7	84.9	23.8	27.6	14.2	35.2	19.8
Oklahoma City	83.6	85.7	80.7	76.8	50.1	24.4	26.1	15.6	37.3	9.6
Omaha	88.0	89.9	78.2	85.8	53.7	28.0	29.3	13.5	51.1	11.6
Orlando	82.8	85.7	69.3	82.2	71.6	24.8	26.5	14.6	42.3	17.0
Overland Park	86.7	88.8	77.4	80.9	61.4	28.5	30.6	14.6	46.6	13.3
Philadelphia	82.2	85.7	71.9	77.2	55.5	27.7	31.1	12.8	46.7	12.8
Phoenix	81.9	86.3	81.6	84.9	49.3	25.1	27.3	19.4	46.6	7.8
Pittsburgh	85.1	85.5	78.2	90.5	80.7	23.8	24.2	12.8	70.8	31.6
Plano	79.4	84.4	78.9	83.4	41.5	30.0	34.0	18.5	52.2	8.7
Portland	87.2	89.4	80.4	79.1	53.7	28.8	29.6	18.0	38.3	11.8
Providence	76.0	77.8	70.5	68.3	50.2	23.6	24.5	16.8	35.4	8.5
Provo	90.9	92.2	78.7	91.5	62.8	31.5	32.1	25.7	48.7	16.2
Raleigh	85.4	89.4	76.6	91.6	43.0	38.9	43.7	22.2	70.0	15.3
Reno	83.9	87.3	84.2	83.2	45.9	23.7	25.2	16.7	34.2	6.9
Richmond	82.6	87.0	72.7	78.7	68.8	29.2	34.5	15.4	47.0	20.2
Rochester	84.4	87.0	65.1	80.3	57.7	27.1	28.7	10.6	52.6	12.2
Sacramento	85.0	88.7	83.1	73.8	63.6	25.9	27.8	16.2	31.6	12.3
St. Louis	83.4	85.5	73.4	84.0	74.3	25.3	27.3	13.0	55.2	24.0
St. Paul	90.6	92.5	79.9	70.9	61.5	33.3	34.4	19.1	36.3	16.7
St. Petersburg	81.5	83.1	71.0	78.4	65.8	21.7	22.4	13.0	39.2	16.2
Salt Lake City	87.5	89.9	83.0	78.2	56.5	26.5	27.6	19.5	34.8	9.4
San Antonio	77.3	80.2	83.2	81.4	62.3	22.4	25.5	18.0	38.4	10.6
San Diego	82.6	87.7	86.1	81.3	53.5	29.5	33.1	16.3	37.2	10.7
San Francisco	84.2	91.3	75.9	75.6	59.2	43.6	51.3	18.5	38.9	16.2
San Jose	83.4	88.4	88.6	84.8	55.1	40.5	42.5	29.7	51.3	11.0
Savannah	79.9	85.3	69.5	72.5	69.5	23.2	27.9	12.4	37.0	24.2
Scottsdale	81.9	86.3	81.6	84.9	49.3	25.1	27.3	19.4	46.6	7.8
Seattle	90.1	92.3	82.4	82.2	67.8	35.9	37.0	21.1	40.9	19.0
Sioux Falls	88.6	89.7	78.0	54.3	52.0	25.9	26.5	20.4	29.5	8.2
Springfield (IL)	88.1	89.0	76.6	91.3	84.8	28.1	28.7	15.7	63.1	30.1
Springfield (MO)	84.0	84.3	82.2	80.5	71.0	22.4	22.6	13.9	40.9	15.1
Stamford	87.6	90.4	71.6	91.8	62.0	49.4	53.5	17.2	69.9	14.2
Syracuse	83.8	85.3	65.7	77.3	61.1	24.1	24.5	10.0	54.0	19.7
Tampa	81.5	83.1	71.0	78.4	65.8	21.7	22.4	13.0	39.2	16.2
Tucson	83.4	87.1	81.9	80.5	62.8	26.7	29.7	16.8	43.3	10.9
Tulsa	83.7	85.2	79.2	77.8	54.2	23.2	25.0	14.8	37.4	11.8
Virginia Beach	84.7	88.7	75.1	82.7	84.9	23.8	27.6	14.2	35.2	19.8
Washington	86.7	91.1	81.3	85.4	57.7	41.8	49.2	24.1	53.9	21.0
Wichita	85.3	88.1	78.0	62.4	51.5	24.7	26.5	13.0	23.7	9.6
U.S.	80.4	83.6	72.3	80.4	52.4	24.4	26.1	14.3	44.1	10.4

Note: Figures shown cover persons 25 years old and over; (1) Metropolitan Statistical Area - see Appendix A for areas included; (2) people of Hispanic origin can be of any race
Source: Census 2000, Summary File 3

Cost of Living Index

Area	Composite	Groceries	Housing	Utilities	Transp.	Health	Misc.
Albuquerque	102.6	99.3	106.2	105.7	103.5	113.9	98.3
Alexandria[1]	136.1	108.8	195.7	107.2	119.9	127.1	110.2
Anchorage	120.5	127.2	127.6	92.8	112.4	147.0	116.2
Ann Arbor	n/a	n/a	n/a	n/a	n/a	n/a	n/a
Atlanta	97.2	99.7	92.2	92.4	100.0	105.3	100.3
Austin	102.2	89.8	107.8	105.4	96.7	106.2	102.6
Baltimore	94.8	94.1	87.3	100.2	97.5	91.2	99.5
Baton Rouge	100.9	110.4	94.4	110.5	99.4	110.1	99.1
Bellevue[2]	127.9	114.2	154.9	114.3	117.9	149.9	114.6
Birmingham[1]	96.5	100.4	84.2	104.3	95.6	84.2	105.0
Boise City	96.8	89.0	91.1	94.2	103.6	108.5	102.3
Boston[1]	136.7	118.5	180.7	149.8	112.1	120.8	111.1
Boulder	117.8	112.1	160.5	76.2	108.2	123.7	97.4
Buffalo	100.8	108.4	94.2	135.8	104.7	97.3	92.0
Cedar Rapids	93.5	90.8	82.4	103.9	95.5	93.1	100.7
Charleston[1]	98.4	99.0	94.2	101.4	97.2	102.4	100.8
Charlotte	95.9	96.6	89.3	91.9	98.2	99.9	101.6
Chattanooga	93.0	94.3	83.9	89.6	100.6	101.6	98.3
Chicago	133.0	118.3	180.9	112.3	114.9	135.5	108.8
Cincinnati	95.4	94.8	85.4	111.5	97.1	98.4	98.5
Cleveland	103.3	110.1	98.7	113.3	107.9	109.0	99.4
Colorado Springs	98.3	102.8	99.3	87.4	101.7	113.2	95.8
Columbia	96.1	97.4	90.3	110.3	92.0	97.2	97.3
Columbus	106.4	105.5	113.1	113.9	105.1	96.6	101.2
Dallas[1]	96.7	95.3	92.1	91.3	100.1	100.6	101.4
Denver[1]	105.6	107.0	111.2	92.3	107.3	120.2	102.0
Des Moines	95.2	88.4	94.2	102.2	95.0	93.3	97.1
Detroit	108.3	104.7	116.1	114.8	106.8	118.9	100.2
Durham	95.6	100.9	88.4	101.1	98.5	102.9	96.3
El Paso	92.9	104.2	83.3	93.3	95.8	112.5	93.3
Eugene	108.9	105.4	118.6	101.3	107.6	121.3	103.0
Fort Collins	101.3	106.3	100.7	89.7	106.7	105.8	101.0
Fort Lauderdale	121.3	103.2	157.3	104.8	104.1	123.0	107.3
Fort Wayne[3]	91.3	92.3	85.0	99.7	95.2	83.8	93.7
Fort Worth	93.7	97.2	86.2	95.6	94.8	98.3	97.3
Grand Rapids	99.3	106.6	90.0	101.4	104.3	97.5	102.6
Green Bay	96.9	87.8	99.8	92.7	100.7	104.0	97.6
Greensboro[4]	92.7	94.0	87.9	90.4	92.2	84.0	98.2
Honolulu	154.3	151.7	219.1	148.7	129.3	119.1	112.0
Houston[1]	91.2	85.8	79.4	100.3	104.3	102.6	95.7
Huntsville	93.0	99.8	76.3	92.6	103.0	89.5	102.4
Indianapolis[5]	92.6	94.9	86.6	91.6	93.2	93.8	96.8
Irvine[6]	133.5	111.6	198.4	99.8	113.8	118.4	103.8
Jacksonville	91.2	102.9	82.3	89.3	95.1	79.9	94.8
Kansas City[1]	98.7	94.3	93.6	97.8	101.7	102.8	103.9
Knoxville	89.6	93.6	78.8	95.0	88.3	88.9	96.2
Las Vegas	103.4	108.7	98.2	92.0	110.7	124.3	104.5
Lexington[1]	95.2	99.3	92.4	102.0	94.3	91.7	94.5
Lincoln	97.9	90.1	101.4	95.1	97.8	91.9	99.7
Los Angeles[1]	145.4	117.9	220.7	133.2	116.8	108.5	107.7
Louisville	92.1	86.1	84.8	94.8	108.2	80.0	96.8
Madison	n/a	n/a	n/a	n/a	n/a	n/a	n/a
Manchester	104.8	105.6	120.1	111.4	99.2	80.5	93.7

Cost of Living Index *continued*

Area	Composite	Groceries	Housing	Utilities	Transp.	Health	Misc.
Memphis	90.3	92.0	79.4	86.9	95.8	95.5	97.7
Miami[7]	113.8	104.5	130.9	104.6	108.5	107.5	108.0
Milwaukee[1]	101.3	100.2	109.2	95.8	104.9	95.9	95.9
Minneapolis	110.8	100.8	118.4	113.4	110.9	127.2	105.6
Naperville[8]	107.0	112.2	105.8	116.9	107.1	114.6	101.8
Nashville[9]	97.3	105.9	84.1	93.8	117.5	84.7	101.7
New Orleans	100.2	93.3	102.2	108.9	101.4	88.6	99.6
New York[10]	218.8	142.0	409.3	147.5	124.6	177.7	139.2
Norfolk[11]	97.4	97.8	94.5	118.1	100.2	97.0	92.8
Oklahoma City	91.9	88.0	84.5	99.3	97.6	96.5	95.5
Omaha	92.5	89.8	84.2	110.0	100.9	96.8	92.6
Orlando	98.4	101.8	91.3	101.7	95.8	96.7	103.3
Overland Park[1]	98.7	94.3	93.6	97.8	101.7	102.8	103.9
Philadelphia	121.1	114.2	130.5	134.0	113.1	119.4	114.6
Phoenix	98.0	101.2	87.3	93.0	109.8	111.1	102.4
Pittsburgh	97.0	102.2	89.9	100.5	113.0	83.7	96.6
Plano	97.6	89.9	91.1	102.3	109.3	105.3	100.8
Portland[1]	113.4	110.4	116.9	104.5	112.4	130.9	112.5
Providence	n/a	n/a	n/a	n/a	n/a	n/a	n/a
Provo[12]	95.4	95.8	86.7	87.0	100.2	94.2	104.1
Raleigh	101.2	105.3	101.6	97.2	96.4	102.7	101.1
Reno[13]	103.4	101.7	101.0	104.3	117.0	101.6	102.2
Richmond	100.8	108.6	94.7	104.3	99.4	85.1	104.2
Rochester	n/a	n/a	n/a	n/a	n/a	n/a	n/a
Sacramento	122.2	126.7	129.1	131.3	114.3	146.6	110.7
Saint Louis[1]	103.6	113.6	98.7	95.9	99.4	98.7	107.9
Saint Paul	106.5	99.7	101.4	92.7	122.7	118.0	110.9
Saint Petersburg[14]	91.1	95.7	83.3	96.0	103.0	85.0	91.7
Salt Lake City	102.6	98.8	106.2	90.7	109.4	95.0	103.4
San Antonio	92.6	78.7	91.0	88.2	86.1	96.9	102.7
San Diego	139.2	124.2	204.3	90.3	126.0	136.6	107.6
San Francisco	178.7	123.5	322.6	109.4	127.9	149.4	115.6
San Jose	164.0	131.5	271.3	109.3	131.4	161.7	110.1
Savannah	98.0	94.8	98.6	100.5	94.2	91.8	100.0
Scottsdale	116.0	104.2	152.5	94.5	110.5	121.7	96.9
Seattle	127.9	114.2	154.9	114.3	117.9	149.9	114.6
Sioux Falls	95.2	89.5	85.9	117.1	96.0	95.7	98.8
Springfield	95.1	96.5	86.9	112.0	97.0	97.4	95.7
Springfield	88.1	98.7	78.7	73.9	91.7	98.1	93.8
Stamford	154.3	115.2	240.0	120.8	115.9	142.8	118.8
Syracuse	99.9	104.7	87.0	125.8	106.9	90.2	100.2
Tampa	96.8	96.3	95.0	96.9	98.6	101.5	97.4
Tucson	96.7	115.3	80.8	100.1	109.0	107.1	96.8
Tulsa	92.1	90.6	79.3	95.3	101.4	92.3	100.2
Virginia Beach[11]	97.4	97.8	94.5	118.1	100.2	97.0	92.8
Washington[1]	136.1	108.8	195.7	107.2	119.9	127.1	110.2
Wichita	94.8	95.0	80.1	109.3	101.3	96.7	101.2
U.S.	100.0	100.0	100.0	100.0	100.0	100.0	100.0

Note: (1) Metropolitan Statistical Area (MSA) - see Appendix A for areas included; All figures are 2003 4-quarter averages except for Anchorage, Raleigh, Sacramento and St. Paul which are 2001 4-quarter averages and Columbus and Scottsdale which are 2001 4-quarter averages; (2) Seattle (data for Bellevue was not available); (3) Fort Wayne-Allen County; (4) Winston-Salem (data for Greensboro was not available); (5) Indianpolis/Marion County; (6) Orange County; (7) Miami-Dade County; (8) Joliet/Will County, IL (located within the Chicago MSA); (9) Nashville-Franklin; (10) Manhattan; (11) Hampton Roads/SE Virginia area; (12) Provo-Orem; (13) Reno-Sparks; (14) St. Petersburg-Clearwater
Source: ACCRA, Cost of Living Index, 2003 4-Quarter Average unless noted otherwise

Average New Home Prices and Apartment Rent

Area	Price ($)	Rent ($/month)
Albuquerque	260,499	786
Alexandria[1]	451,103	1,806
Anchorage	295,435	947
Ann Arbor	n/a	n/a
Atlanta	224,132	736
Austin	255,261	931
Baltimore	214,144	693
Baton Rouge	241,149	610
Bellevue[2]	395,617	1,003
Birmingham[1]	206,856	650
Boise City	218,925	749
Boston[1]	436,069	1,448
Boulder	425,628	974
Buffalo	232,055	719
Cedar Rapids	205,535	603
Charleston[1]	233,846	722
Charlotte	225,495	606
Chattanooga	206,085	654
Chicago	442,322	1,361
Cincinnati	203,697	722
Cleveland	228,273	900
Colorado Springs	240,879	767
Columbia	217,136	752
Columbus	252,665	663
Dallas[1]	209,222	902
Denver[1]	278,762	810
Des Moines	242,003	590
Detroit	337,305	834
Durham	210,324	759
El Paso	201,646	660
Eugene	304,504	792
Fort Collins	245,267	801
Fort Lauderdale	387,300	1,178
Fort Wayne[3]	210,000	601
Fort Worth	205,387	748
Grand Rapids	219,900	664
Green Bay	257,129	573
Greensboro[4]	223,394	611
Honolulu	556,450	1,525
Houston[1]	184,831	767
Huntsville	187,354	585
Indianapolis[5]	208,862	703
Irvine[6]	485,779	1,404
Jacksonville	193,957	700
Kansas City[1]	227,614	744
Knoxville	194,357	593
Las Vegas	235,891	814
Lexington[1]	225,365	710
Lincoln	261,025	633
Los Angeles[1]	564,646	1,413
Louisville	203,570	689
Madison	n/a	n/a
Manchester	284,643	976

Average New Home Prices and Apartment Rent *continued*

Area	Price ($)	Rent ($/month)
Memphis	188,690	678
Miami[7]	308,295	1,163
Milwaukee[1]	270,869	745
Minneapolis	282,488	1,018
Naperville[8]	245,905	931
Nashville[9]	200,133	715
New Orleans	251,359	777
New York[10]	944,300	3,560
Norfolk[11]	226,197	753
Oklahoma City	208,770	617
Omaha	203,955	677
Orlando	216,369	797
Overland Park[1]	227,614	744
Philadelphia	297,678	1,210
Phoenix	214,010	670
Pittsburgh	223,546	642
Plano	196,636	963
Portland[1]	298,983	773
Providence	n/a	n/a
Provo[12]	208,309	701
Raleigh	232,358	689
Reno[13]	236,645	855
Richmond	228,701	750
Rochester	n/a	n/a
Sacramento	309,700	849
Saint Louis[1]	245,160	698
Saint Paul	230,587	837
Saint Petersburg[14]	199,335	704
Salt Lake City	259,728	837
San Antonio	221,836	735
San Diego	524,355	1,314
San Francisco	823,661	1,998
San Jose	687,787	1,708
Savannah	248,804	694
Scottsdale	353,317	761
Seattle	395,617	1,003
Sioux Falls	208,143	681
Springfield	213,032	625
Springfield	192,500	574
Stamford	600,752	1,715
Syracuse	216,424	618
Tampa	216,715	918
Tucson	188,311	733
Tulsa	200,256	497
Virginia Beach[11]	226,197	753
Washington[1]	451,103	1,806
Wichita	202,819	552
U.S.	248,193	721

Note: Figures are based on a new home with 2,400 sq. ft. of living area on an 8,000 sq. ft. lot; Figures are based on an unfurnished two bedroom, 1-1/2 or 2 bath apartment, approximately 950 sq. ft., excluding utilities except water; n/a not available; (1) Metropolitan Statistical Area (MSA) - see Appendix A for areas included; All figures are 2003 4-quarter averages except for Anchorage, Raleigh, Sacramento and St. Paul which are 2001 4-quarter averages and Columbus and Scottsdale which are 2001 4-quarter averages; (2) Seattle (data for Bellevue was not available); (3) Fort Wayne-Allen County; (4) Winston-Salem (data for Greensboro was not available); (5) Indianpolis/Marion County; (6) Orange County; (7) Miami-Dade County; (8) Joliet/Will County, IL (located within the Chicago MSA); (9) Nashville-Franklin; (10) Manhattan; (11) Hampton Roads/SE Virginia area; (12) Provo-Orem; (13) Reno-Sparks; (14) St. Petersburg-Clearwater
Source: ACCRA, Cost of Living Index, 2003 4-Quarter Average unless noted otherwise

Average Residential Utility Costs

Area	All Electric ($/mth)	Part Electric ($/mth)	Other Energy ($/mth)	Phone ($/mth)
Albuquerque	–	65.71	67.44	24.99
Alexandria[1]	–	64.07	70.16	25.61
Anchorage	–	56.58	52.49	21.44
Ann Arbor	n/a	n/a	n/a	n/a
Atlanta	105.80	–	–	24.90
Austin	–	94.75	39.47	24.14
Baltimore	–	73.36	57.20	22.48
Baton Rouge	149.41	–	–	23.19
Bellevue[2]	151.17	–	–	25.01
Birmingham[1]	–	67.63	63.91	24.62
Boise City	–	44.86	60.20	26.23
Boston[1]	–	108.24	109.97	26.96
Boulder	–	48.02	39.41	20.87
Buffalo	–	74.97	103.04	30.16
Cedar Rapids	–	81.97	67.79	19.14
Charleston[1]	134.18	–	–	22.17
Charlotte	114.82	–	–	22.02
Chattanooga	–	48.85	66.85	20.37
Chicago	–	59.03	77.77	27.95
Cincinnati	–	75.50	62.49	27.12
Cleveland	–	84.04	78.40	21.15
Colorado Springs	–	43.23	52.36	25.14
Columbia	146.19	–	–	24.03
Columbus	–	66.02	75.39	19.25
Dallas[1]	–	92.80	29.63	19.46
Denver[1]	–	53.99	54.22	24.18
Des Moines	–	65.48	78.30	19.85
Detroit	–	86.51	56.51	28.26
Durham	120.77	–	–	25.31
El Paso	–	76.51	34.98	23.80
Eugene	101.68	–	–	31.14
Fort Collins	–	36.35	53.57	27.89
Fort Lauderdale	144.82	–	–	21.44
Fort Wayne[3]	–	48.88	72.74	24.77
Fort Worth	–	93.25	33.43	20.67
Grand Rapids	–	54.25	61.19	27.54
Green Bay	–	53.42	74.19	18.79
Greensboro[4]	118.32	–	–	20.12
Honolulu	217.05	–	–	26.61
Houston[1]	–	98.55	35.03	21.67
Huntsville	96.98	–	–	27.58
Indianapolis[5]	–	47.94	73.94	20.61
Irvine[6]	–	102.92	45.30	17.87
Jacksonville	98.66	–	–	25.12
Kansas City[1]	–	56.62	66.86	23.07
Knoxville	–	52.60	64.51	23.20
Las Vegas	–	93.09	36.58	17.78
Lexington[1]	–	36.21	72.62	29.84
Lincoln	–	46.59	56.38	27.37
Los Angeles[1]	–	140.79	44.04	26.63
Louisville	–	37.62	63.57	27.67
Madison	n/a	n/a	n/a	n/a
Manchester	–	47.70	88.35	27.83

Average Residential Utility Costs *continued*

Area	All Electric ($/mth)	Part Electric ($/mth)	Other Energy ($/mth)	Phone ($/mth)
Memphis	–	55.47	42.66	23.85
Miami[7]	144.82	–	–	21.31
Milwaukee[1]	–	57.52	82.01	18.07
Minneapolis	–	53.54	67.21	33.23
Naperville[8]	–	60.22	68.77	32.93
Nashville[9]	–	49.70	46.35	29.24
New Orleans	136.24	–	–	26.06
New York[10]	–	115.22	107.34	24.29
Norfolk[11]	–	72.30	69.37	29.99
Oklahoma City	–	76.34	49.50	23.29
Omaha	–	52.84	52.93	35.50
Orlando	126.11	–	–	24.63
Overland Park[1]	–	56.62	66.86	23.07
Philadelphia	–	71.71	80.57	36.68
Phoenix	115.50	–	–	22.50
Pittsburgh	–	80.11	66.34	18.07
Plano	–	92.58	32.46	25.32
Portland[1]	–	66.41	64.90	25.37
Providence	n/a	n/a	n/a	n/a
Provo[12]	–	50.81	42.90	25.52
Raleigh	121.13	–	–	23.11
Reno[13]	–	68.58	83.44	18.74
Richmond	127.21	–	–	25.88
Rochester	n/a	n/a	n/a	n/a
Sacramento	–	136.79	28.84	16.99
Saint Louis[1]	–	64.54	62.22	21.00
Saint Paul	–	54.05	52.31	24.38
Saint Petersburg[14]	124.70	–	–	21.62
Salt Lake City	–	46.78	47.85	27.22
San Antonio	–	75.15	36.80	20.52
San Diego	–	54.82	60.01	21.06
San Francisco	–	72.57	80.33	21.51
San Jose	–	118.77	33.91	21.89
Savannah	119.11	–	–	25.72
Scottsdale	114.36	–	–	20.37
Seattle	151.17	–	–	25.01
Sioux Falls	–	58.95	83.39	29.20
Springfield	–	47.38	69.48	33.49
Springfield	–	42.36	48.19	18.25
Stamford	–	73.36	102.47	21.76
Syracuse	–	78.13	81.22	29.69
Tampa	128.24	–	–	21.16
Tucson	–	88.20	45.10	21.61
Tulsa	–	62.73	46.89	25.53
Virginia Beach[11]	–	72.30	69.37	29.99
Washington[1]	–	64.07	70.16	25.61
Wichita	–	63.99	66.99	28.37
U.S.	116.46	65.82	62.68	23.90

Note: (1) Metropolitan Statistical Area (MSA) - see Appendix A for areas included; All figures are 2003 4-quarter averages except for Anchorage, Raleigh, Sacramento and St. Paul which are 2001 4-quarter averages and Columbus and Scottsdale which are 2001 4-quarter averages; (2) Seattle (data for Bellevue was not available); (3) Fort Wayne-Allen County; (4) Winston-Salem (data for Greensboro was not available); (5) Indianpolis/Marion County; (6) Orange County; (7) Miami-Dade County; (8) Joliet/Will County, IL (located within the Chicago MSA); (9) Nashville-Franklin; (10) Manhattan; (11) Hampton Roads/SE Virginia area; (12) Provo-Orem; (13) Reno-Sparks; (14) St. Petersburg-Clearwater
Source: ACCRA, Cost of Living Index, 2003 4-Quarter Average unless noted otherwise

Average Health Care Costs

Area	Hospital ($/day)	Doctor ($/visit)	Dentist ($/visit)
Albuquerque	634.38	77.83	99.60
Alexandria[1]	1,104.25	85.68	102.14
Anchorage	827.72	92.46	140.82
Ann Arbor	n/a	n/a	n/a
Atlanta	560.69	75.15	93.04
Austin	568.81	80.87	91.53
Baltimore	664.35	61.88	74.50
Baton Rouge	434.41	80.63	98.02
Bellevue[2]	853.58	82.98	149.32
Birmingham[1]	574.30	59.84	66.22
Boise City	652.38	73.52	94.89
Boston[1]	916.34	87.97	97.72
Boulder	1,319.19	49.89	110.16
Buffalo	685.50	55.21	87.88
Cedar Rapids	489.50	67.13	79.63
Charleston[1]	614.92	77.36	83.69
Charlotte	526.67	69.91	90.03
Chattanooga	599.15	91.30	75.51
Chicago	1,309.70	83.35	108.36
Cincinnati	569.83	65.05	87.30
Cleveland	1,045.20	73.75	80.80
Colorado Springs	729.67	73.01	99.16
Columbia	445.44	67.50	87.50
Columbus	455.87	58.69	75.57
Dallas[1]	679.73	72.63	79.66
Denver[1]	824.88	75.89	107.33
Des Moines	642.50	63.50	79.46
Detroit	897.30	67.46	108.74
Durham	698.70	78.55	81.17
El Paso	923.31	71.39	91.44
Eugene	697.83	77.98	112.62
Fort Collins	793.25	74.40	85.32
Fort Lauderdale	625.40	91.74	108.68
Fort Wayne[3]	597.83	57.93	67.54
Fort Worth	568.40	65.81	87.45
Grand Rapids	478.44	60.63	90.47
Green Bay	636.81	79.48	86.05
Greensboro[4]	323.25	63.60	75.80
Honolulu	877.00	76.11	97.40
Houston[1]	617.69	72.75	87.08
Huntsville	645.13	57.70	73.55
Indianapolis[5]	540.43	69.51	77.22
Irvine[6]	1,130.03	82.38	86.38
Jacksonville	495.50	62.50	59.50
Kansas City[1]	791.02	71.55	82.44
Knoxville	555.93	66.25	73.15
Las Vegas	884.80	76.31	110.09
Lexington[1]	547.24	66.75	76.18
Lincoln	540.42	74.23	71.94
Los Angeles[1]	1,121.33	76.23	72.33
Louisville	491.50	63.04	66.13
Madison	n/a	n/a	n/a
Manchester	615.62	57.87	64.39

Average Health Care Costs *continued*

Area	Hospital ($/day)	Doctor ($/visit)	Dentist ($/visit)
Memphis	492.00	71.25	82.75
Miami[7]	911.21	78.18	81.48
Milwaukee[1]	466.53	73.13	82.96
Minneapolis	1,313.40	83.79	96.80
Naperville[8]	734.88	79.00	98.43
Nashville[9]	390.67	62.22	71.64
New Orleans	564.50	58.90	74.50
New York[10]	2,327.00	109.79	122.42
Norfolk[11]	453.58	58.37	92.76
Oklahoma City	465.73	62.36	87.68
Omaha	526.57	67.55	83.60
Orlando	755.02	60.85	79.53
Overland Park[1]	791.02	71.55	82.44
Philadelphia	1,457.30	70.52	84.03
Phoenix	795.23	68.52	98.00
Pittsburgh	653.15	59.50	61.95
Plano	604.50	79.85	89.00
Portland[1]	752.35	85.53	121.91
Providence	n/a	n/a	n/a
Provo[12]	732.91	56.26	78.87
Raleigh	409.46	78.27	85.17
Reno[13]	804.92	75.80	80.15
Richmond	499.06	61.45	69.10
Rochester	n/a	n/a	n/a
Sacramento	1,794.15	65.30	107.93
Saint Louis[1]	557.00	82.62	75.63
Saint Paul	1,113.23	75.61	79.61
Saint Petersburg[14]	707.72	60.23	63.71
Salt Lake City	503.93	69.41	80.97
San Antonio	610.01	66.63	85.80
San Diego	1,452.48	75.74	108.04
San Francisco	2,592.14	71.05	94.85
San Jose	2,151.46	98.05	116.60
Savannah	521.12	69.00	75.62
Scottsdale	821.96	66.26	94.71
Seattle	853.58	82.98	149.32
Sioux Falls	672.38	62.38	80.75
Springfield	678.54	72.19	77.25
Springfield	545.00	65.99	89.21
Stamford	1,006.83	92.32	128.50
Syracuse	815.88	61.02	67.76
Tampa	699.88	66.02	87.91
Tucson	938.83	66.00	87.32
Tulsa	494.27	69.42	77.69
Virginia Beach[11]	453.58	58.37	92.76
Washington[1]	1,104.25	85.68	102.14
Wichita	714.39	64.30	79.69
U.S.	678.35	67.91	83.90

Note: Hospital - based on a semi-private room. Doctor - based on a general practitioner's routine exam of an established patient. Dentist - based on adult teeth cleaning and periodic oral exam; n/a not available; (1) Metropolitan Statistical Area (MSA) - see Appendix A for areas included; All figures are 2003 4-quarter averages except for Anchorage, Raleigh, Sacramento and St. Paul which are 2001 4-quarter averages and Columbus and Scottsdale which are 2001 4-quarter averages; (2) Seattle (data for Bellevue was not available); (3) Fort Wayne-Allen County; (4) Winston-Salem (data for Greensboro was not available); (5) Indianpolis/Marion County; (6) Orange County; (7) Miami-Dade County; (8) Joliet/Will County, IL (located within the Chicago MSA); (9) Nashville-Franklin; (10) Manhattan; (11) Hampton Roads/SE Virginia area; (12) Provo-Orem; (13) Reno-Sparks; (14) St. Petersburg-Clearwater
Source: ACCRA, Cost of Living Index, 2003 4-Quarter Average unless noted otherwise

Distribution of Non-Federal, Office-Based Physicians

MSA[1]	Total	Family/ General Practice	Specialties		
			Medical	Surgical	Other
Albuquerque	21.2	3.1	7.5	4.2	6.4
Alexandria	23.8	1.9	9.6	5.6	6.7
Anchorage	21.8	3.8	6.0	6.0	6.0
Ann Arbor	18.0	1.7	7.2	4.1	5.0
Atlanta	17.0	1.5	6.4	4.4	4.6
Austin	17.4	2.8	5.4	4.3	4.9
Baltimore	23.8	1.9	9.6	5.6	6.7
Baton Rouge	17.1	2.3	6.0	4.6	4.1
Bellevue	21.5	3.8	6.7	4.6	6.3
Birmingham	24.2	2.0	9.3	6.5	6.5
Boise City	18.5	3.4	5.1	5.2	4.8
Boston	28.3	1.9	11.9	6.1	8.4
Boulder	20.3	2.7	7.1	4.6	5.9
Buffalo	18.9	1.8	7.6	5.0	4.5
Cedar Rapids	17.1	4.1	4.3	3.7	5.0
Charleston	25.4	2.6	8.4	6.4	8.1
Charlotte	17.4	2.4	6.1	4.8	4.0
Chattanooga	18.8	2.1	6.4	5.2	5.2
Chicago	19.4	2.1	7.7	4.3	5.2
Cincinnati	18.5	2.3	6.9	4.2	5.0
Cleveland	21.2	1.9	8.2	5.1	6.0
Colorado Springs	15.6	2.0	4.3	4.2	5.0
Columbia	21.7	3.0	6.5	5.5	6.7
Columbus	18.1	2.7	5.8	4.3	5.3
Dallas	15.1	1.9	5.0	3.9	4.3
Denver	20.3	2.7	7.1	4.6	5.9
Des Moines	14.2	1.8	4.4	3.8	4.1
Detroit	18.0	1.7	7.2	4.1	5.0
Durham	25.8	2.7	9.6	5.8	7.8
El Paso	12.0	1.2	4.1	3.1	3.5
Eugene	18.4	3.7	5.4	4.3	4.9
Fort Collins	17.7	4.6	4.3	4.5	4.3
Fort Lauderdale	21.6	2.5	8.7	5.1	5.4
Fort Wayne	13.5	2.1	3.9	3.7	3.8
Fort Worth	15.1	1.9	5.0	3.9	4.3
Grand Rapids	14.1	2.2	4.4	3.7	3.8
Green Bay	19.3	2.3	6.4	5.2	5.4
Greensboro	17.4	2.2	6.2	4.6	4.5
Honolulu	23.0	2.1	9.2	5.7	6.1
Houston	18.0	2.3	6.1	4.3	5.2
Huntsville	17.0	3.2	5.3	4.6	4.0
Indianapolis	20.9	2.9	6.9	4.9	6.3
Irvine	17.6	2.4	6.4	4.1	4.7
Jacksonville	18.7	2.8	6.3	4.6	5.1
Kansas City	17.6	2.2	6.1	4.4	4.8
Knoxville	23.2	3.4	8.0	5.7	6.0
Las Vegas	13.1	1.6	4.8	3.2	3.4
Lexington	24.0	2.0	8.2	5.8	8.0
Lincoln	19.8	3.3	6.0	4.9	5.7
Los Angeles	17.6	2.4	6.4	4.1	4.7
Louisville	22.5	2.5	7.9	5.6	6.5
Madison	31.2	4.7	10.4	6.3	9.8
Manchester	28.3	1.9	11.9	6.1	8.4

Distribution of Non-Federal, Office-Based Physicians *continued*

MSA[1]	Total	Family/ General Practice	Specialties		
			Medical	Surgical	Other
Memphis	18.3	1.8	7.0	4.8	4.8
Miami	21.6	2.5	8.7	5.1	5.4
Milwaukee	22.2	2.8	7.6	4.9	6.8
Minneapolis	18.7	3.8	6.2	4.1	4.6
Naperville	19.4	2.1	7.7	4.3	5.2
Nashville	23.3	1.7	8.5	6.1	6.9
New Orleans	25.3	1.4	9.3	6.8	7.8
New York	24.2	1.2	10.9	5.6	6.5
Norfolk	16.6	2.6	5.5	4.3	4.2
Oklahoma City	17.7	2.3	5.4	4.5	5.4
Omaha	21.8	3.4	7.1	5.4	5.9
Orlando	16.4	2.4	5.8	4.2	4.0
Overland Park	17.6	2.2	6.1	4.4	4.8
Philadelphia	21.5	1.9	8.4	5.0	6.3
Phoenix	15.3	2.1	5.1	3.8	4.2
Pittsburgh	22.8	2.6	8.3	5.4	6.4
Plano	15.1	1.9	5.0	3.9	4.3
Portland	19.3	2.5	6.9	4.5	5.4
Providence	19.1	1.3	8.4	4.7	4.6
Provo	11.5	2.5	3.0	3.3	2.8
Raleigh	25.8	2.7	9.6	5.8	7.8
Reno	21.7	3.2	6.1	5.8	6.6
Richmond	20.1	2.6	7.2	5.0	5.3
Rochester	20.0	1.5	8.9	4.4	5.2
Sacramento	18.8	2.9	6.2	4.3	5.4
Saint Louis	19.4	1.3	7.9	5.0	5.3
Saint Paul	18.7	3.8	6.2	4.1	4.6
Saint Petersburg	18.9	2.1	7.4	4.5	4.8
Salt Lake City	17.7	2.1	5.8	4.6	5.2
San Antonio	19.6	2.6	6.2	4.8	6.0
San Diego	19.8	2.6	6.8	4.7	5.8
San Francisco	23.5	2.4	9.1	5.2	6.9
San Jose	23.5	2.4	9.1	5.2	6.9
Savannah	18.4	1.9	6.3	5.7	4.5
Scottsdale	15.3	2.1	5.1	3.8	4.2
Seattle	21.5	3.8	6.7	4.6	6.3
Sioux Falls	27.7	4.2	8.9	7.2	7.4
Springfield	18.4	2.3	6.0	4.7	5.3
Springfield	29.9	2.7	10.8	7.3	9.1
Stamford	24.2	1.2	10.9	5.6	6.5
Syracuse	21.4	2.9	7.3	5.3	5.9
Tampa	18.9	2.1	7.4	4.5	4.8
Tucson	21.5	2.4	7.1	4.9	7.2
Tulsa	14.7	2.3	5.0	3.5	3.8
Virginia Beach	16.6	2.6	5.5	4.3	4.2
Washington	23.8	1.9	9.6	5.6	6.7
Wichita	15.1	3.3	4.4	3.5	3.9
Metro Average[2]	33.1	2.2	7.7	4.8	5.6

Note: Data as of December 31, 2001; (1) Figures cover the Metropolitan Statistical Area unless otherwise noted - see Appendix A for areas included; (2) Average of 81 MSAs and CMSAs in this book; (3) Boston-Worcester-Lawrence, MA-NH-ME-CT Consolidated Metropolitan Statistical Area includes parts of the following counties: Massachusetts (Bristol, Essex, Hampden, Middlesex, Norfolk, Plymouth, Suffolk, Worcester); New Hampshire (Hillsborough, Merrimack, Rockingham, Strafford); Maine (York); Connecticut (Windham); (4) Chicago-Gary-Kenosha, IL-IN-WI Consolidated Metropolitan Statistical Area includes the following counties: Illinois (Cook, DeKalb, DuPage, Grundy, Kankakee, Kane, Kendall, Lake, McHenry, Will); Indiana (Lake, Porter); Wisconsin (Kenosha); (5) Cincinnati-Hamilton, OH-KY-IN Consolidated Metropolitan Statistical Area includes the following counties: Indiana (Dearborn, Ohio); Kentucky (Boone, Campbell, Gallatin, Grant, Kenton, Pendleton); Ohio (Brown, Butler, Clermont, Hamilton, Warren);

(6) Cleveland-Akron, OH Consolidated Metropolitan Statistical Area includes the following counties: Ashtabula; Cuyahoga; Geauga; Lake; Lorain; Medina; Portage; Summit; (7) Dallas-Fort Worth, TX Consolidated Metropolitan Statistical Area includes the following counties: Collin; Dallas; Denton; Ellis; Henderson; Hood; Hunt; Johnson; Kaufman; Parker; Rockwall; Tarrant; (8) Denver-Boulder-Greeley, CO Consolidated Metropolitan Statistical Area includes the following counties: Adams; Arapahoe; Boulder; Denver; Douglas; Jefferson; Weld; (9) Detroit-Ann Arbor-Flint, MI Consolidated Metropolitan Statistical Area includes the following counties: Genesee; Lapeer; Lenawee; Livingston; Macomb; Monroe; Oakland; St. Clair; Washtenaw; Wayne; (10) Houston-Galveston-Brazoria, TX Consolidated Metropolitan Statistical Area includes the following counties: Brazoria; Chambers; Fort Bend; Galveston; Harris; Liberty; Montgomery; Waller; (11) Los Angeles-Riverside-Orange, CA Consolidated Metropolitan Statistical Area includes the following counties: Los Angeles; Orange; Riverside; San Bernardino; Ventura; (12) Miami-Fort Lauderdale, FL Consolidated Metropolitan Statistical Area includes the following counties: Broward; Miami-Dade; (13) Milwaukee-Racine, WI Consolidated Metropolitan Statistical Area includes the following counties: Milwaukee; Ozaukee; Washington; Waukesha; Racine; (14) New York-Northern New Jersey-Long Island, NY-NJ-CT-PA Consolidated Metropolitan Statistical Area includes the following counties: New Jersey (Bergen, Essex, Hudson, Hunterdon, Mercer, Middlesex, Monmouth, Morris, Ocean, Passaic, Somerset, Sussex, Union, Warren); Connecticut (parts of Fairfield, Litchfield, Middlesex, New Haven); New York (Dutchess, Nassau, Suffolk, Bronx, Kings, New York, Putnam, Queens, Richmond, Rockland, Westchester, Orange); Pennsylvania (Pike); (15) Philadelphia-Wilmington-Atlantic City, PA-NJ-DE-MD Consolidated Metropolitan Statistical Area includes the following counties: Pennsylvania (Bucks, Chester, Delaware, Montgomery, Philadelphia); New Jersey (Atlantic, Burlington, Camden, Cape May, Cumberland, Gloucester, Salem); Delaware (New Castle); Maryland (Cecil); (16) Portland-Salem, OR-WA Consolidated Metropolitan Statistical Area includes the following counties: Oregon (Clackamas, Columbia, Marion, Multnomah, Polk, Washington, Yamhill); Washington (Clark); (17) Sacramento-Yolo, CA Consolidated Metropolitan Statistical Area includes the following counties: El Dorado; Placer; Sacramento; Yolo; (18) San Francisco-Oakland-San Jose, CA Consolidated Metropolitan Statistical Area includes the following counties: Alameda; Contra Costa; Marin; Napa; San Francisco; San Mateo; Santa Clara; Santa Cruz; Solano; Sonoma; (19) Seattle-Tacoma-Bremerton, WA Consolidated Metropolitan Statistical Area includes the following counties: Island; King; Kitsap; Pierce; Snohomish; Thurston; (20) Washington-Baltimore, DC-MD-VA-WV Consolidated Metropolitan Statistical Area includes the following counties and the District of Columbia: Maryland (Anne Arundel, Baltimore, Baltimore City, Calvert, Carroll, Charles, Frederick, Harford, Howard, Montgomery, Prince George's, Queen Anne's, Washington); Virginia (Alexandria City, Arlington, Clarke, Culpeper, Fairfax, Fairfax City, Falls Church City, Fauquier, Fredericksburg City, King George, Loudoun, Manassas City, Manassas Park City, Prince William, Spotsylvania, Stafford, Warren); West Virginia (Berkeley, Jefferson)
Source: American Medical Association, Physician Characteristics & Distribution in the U.S., 2003-2004

This page intentionally left blank.

Crime Rate: City

City	All Crimes	Violent Crimes				Property Crimes		
		Murder	Forcible Rape	Robbery	Aggrav. Assault	Burglary	Larceny -Theft	Motor Vehicle Theft
Albuquerque	7,817.0	11.1	64.0	283.1	710.4	1,191.7	4,671.4	885.3
Alexandria	3,907.6	2.3	15.9	133.2	160.4	364.7	2,672.1	559.1
Anchorage	5,114.5	6.7	95.0	142.9	399.2	569.1	3,462.7	438.9
Ann Arbor	3,232.2	4.3	22.5	75.4	158.7	745.0	2,068.4	157.8
Atlanta	11,355.2	34.9	63.4	957.1	1,233.8	1,964.2	5,443.5	1,658.3
Austin	6,267.1	3.6	37.3	171.2	254.9	1,008.5	4,334.5	457.1
Baltimore	8,318.6	37.7	26.5	702.5	1,288.2	1,305.3	3,981.4	977.0
Baton Rouge	8,292.2	25.8	58.2	484.4	600.0	1,781.1	4,710.0	632.8
Bellevue	4,112.8	0.0	23.0	42.5	58.5	537.1	2,968.5	483.1
Birmingham	8,680.6	26.5	97.6	484.1	692.7	1,791.6	4,751.6	836.4
Boise City	4,543.0	3.1	47.8	43.6	258.1	684.5	3,224.4	281.5
Boston	5,986.5	10.1	61.9	424.7	669.6	642.1	2,988.4	1,189.7
Boulder	3,773.5	5.0	48.4	45.4	134.1	540.4	2,809.7	190.5
Buffalo	6,436.8	14.6	62.6	550.7	643.8	1,305.5	3,085.2	774.4
Cedar Rapids	5,968.4	1.7	47.0	85.8	220.3	916.7	4,445.1	251.7
Charleston	7,071.8	13.1	37.4	261.8	546.8	1,031.9	4,299.5	881.3
Charlotte	7,512.7	10.4	44.7	447.2	670.0	1,625.7	3,997.7	717.0
Chattanooga	10,010.3	15.1	70.7	394.3	1,033.4	1,623.9	5,969.5	903.4
Chicago	n/a	22.1	n/a	630.7	845.5	869.6	3,280.1	859.2
Cincinnati	8,763.1	19.2	116.4	723.7	398.8	1,938.7	4,358.6	1,207.7
Cleveland	6,900.2	16.6	128.6	678.0	499.1	1,682.2	2,753.1	1,142.6
Colorado Springs	5,770.0	6.6	72.7	131.4	326.6	1,074.5	3,738.8	419.2
Columbia	8,658.7	8.4	69.7	417.5	797.2	1,376.9	5,219.4	769.5
Columbus	9,257.7	11.3	94.0	489.4	313.2	2,244.7	5,038.6	1,066.5
Dallas	9,024.7	15.8	52.8	647.7	654.5	1,639.3	4,535.4	1,479.3
Denver	5,529.5	8.8	55.8	205.3	264.8	1,052.6	2,661.7	1,280.5
Des Moines	6,909.1	4.5	56.7	145.4	182.6	840.6	5,172.3	507.0
Detroit	8,839.5	41.8	73.6	653.6	1,303.8	1,496.8	2,790.0	2,480.0
Durham	7,480.0	15.5	38.8	487.3	394.7	1,597.3	4,387.9	558.6
El Paso	4,585.6	2.4	37.5	97.7	523.5	377.2	3,208.0	339.4
Eugene	6,558.3	1.4	39.5	109.2	180.4	851.8	4,808.1	567.9
Fort Collins	4,320.5	0.0	79.6	28.2	242.9	593.7	3,209.6	166.5
Fort Lauderdale	7,329.7	7.5	24.5	419.8	431.1	1,557.4	4,027.2	862.2
Fort Wayne	5,831.5	11.5	54.2	217.9	122.4	974.2	3,967.6	483.7
Fort Worth	8,021.7	9.5	57.5	295.1	397.7	1,743.4	4,813.5	705.0
Grand Rapids	5,645.2	4.0	37.5	254.0	793.9	1,154.3	3,061.6	340.0
Green Bay	3,624.6	1.0	60.7	70.3	242.8	611.8	2,377.9	260.1
Greensboro	6,536.9	12.1	44.5	303.3	348.3	1,273.0	4,058.4	497.4
Honolulu	6,360.4	2.0	33.8	119.1	134.0	992.0	4,136.9	942.7
Houston	7,313.9	12.5	43.7	549.5	617.4	1,318.5	3,599.2	1,173.1
Huntsville	6,369.6	3.1	51.4	197.3	350.2	1,073.8	4,208.8	484.9
Indianapolis	6,032.5	13.9	54.8	365.3	501.0	1,201.7	3,087.1	808.7
Irvine	2,443.2	0.7	13.5	41.8	52.6	584.5	1,576.9	173.3
Jacksonville	6,632.5	11.7	36.0	262.1	605.8	1,192.5	3,820.7	703.8
Kansas City	10,039.5	18.5	67.0	449.2	817.6	1,782.2	5,397.3	1,507.7
Knoxville	6,762.8	11.9	41.8	312.1	738.2	1,204.9	3,769.9	684.0
Las Vegas	4,924.8	11.9	42.8	327.3	396.5	965.4	2,098.2	1,082.7
Lexington	4,746.3	5.7	44.4	237.3	254.4	924.5	3,034.0	246.0
Lincoln	6,582.8	2.6	43.0	78.5	435.2	883.6	4,909.1	230.8
Los Angeles	4,986.0	17.1	36.9	448.9	846.6	662.4	2,083.6	890.5
Louisville	6,081.0	9.7	30.3	383.7	319.3	1,315.3	3,078.3	944.4
Madison	4,191.7	1.4	42.6	126.0	187.6	741.0	2,794.5	298.5
Manchester	3,210.9	0.0	39.9	105.1	74.3	558.8	2,210.9	221.9

Crime Rate: City *continued*

City	All Crimes	Violent Crimes				Property Crimes		
		Murder	Forcible Rape	Robbery	Aggrav. Assault	Burglary	Larceny -Theft	Motor Vehicle Theft
Memphis	9,939.9	22.8	78.0	640.1	836.0	2,466.6	4,504.7	1,391.7
Miami	8,957.3	17.1	25.3	713.9	1,150.5	1,572.9	4,191.1	1,286.4
Milwaukee	7,647.8	18.3	53.8	527.9	354.7	1,143.0	4,363.3	1,186.8
Minneapolis	6,820.9	12.0	92.7	459.5	491.8	1,135.5	3,750.1	879.3
Naperville	n/a	0.8	n/a	10.0	47.6	256.5	1,475.1	71.4
Nashville	8,208.8	10.9	71.9	371.2	1,094.9	1,332.2	4,474.2	853.6
New Orleans	6,418.9	53.1	33.3	410.2	440.6	978.9	2,946.6	1,556.3
New York	3,100.1	7.3	20.9	336.8	424.7	372.3	1,603.7	334.4
Norfolk	6,407.7	17.0	47.6	293.6	202.1	727.9	4,446.0	673.6
Oklahoma City	9,743.2	7.4	86.8	228.1	500.0	1,622.4	6,573.5	725.0
Omaha	7,303.2	6.6	43.9	253.2	414.1	817.1	4,691.8	1,076.4
Orlando	10,867.9	7.7	62.2	531.7	1,259.4	1,907.9	5,966.4	1,132.4
Overland Park	3,443.5	1.3	17.3	30.5	192.6	371.2	2,464.8	365.9
Philadelphia	5,471.1	18.9	67.9	581.9	647.2	737.7	2,544.8	872.7
Phoenix	7,823.5	12.6	29.2	290.0	395.8	1,199.7	4,072.4	1,823.9
Pittsburgh	5,762.1	13.7	43.2	471.8	578.9	962.8	2,951.0	740.7
Plano	3,889.4	2.6	17.2	62.5	206.1	571.8	2,804.9	224.2
Portland	7,955.7	3.7	65.0	237.6	522.2	1,047.0	5,129.0	951.1
Providence	7,825.6	13.0	61.5	310.5	350.0	1,233.9	4,241.9	1,614.9
Provo	3,352.6	0.0	33.9	21.1	96.3	471.2	2,556.9	173.3
Raleigh	6,248.8	6.7	37.1	244.2	400.9	1,344.2	3,746.5	469.2
Reno	5,922.4	4.6	64.2	229.2	458.0	656.1	3,946.9	563.4
Richmond	8,833.2	37.8	57.9	632.5	550.5	1,455.4	4,870.5	1,228.7
Rochester	7,622.0	18.9	48.2	438.1	299.7	1,111.9	4,440.9	1,264.2
Sacramento	7,294.3	11.1	43.8	410.9	374.7	1,189.4	3,684.6	1,579.7
Saint Louis	14,285.7	31.4	38.5	798.3	1,256.1	1,999.7	7,375.6	2,786.1
Saint Paul	6,076.1	4.4	65.5	332.1	403.1	1,103.1	3,426.9	741.0
Saint Petersburg	8,056.8	8.9	47.8	395.6	1,251.6	1,397.6	4,064.2	891.0
Salt Lake City	10,110.7	5.8	57.8	253.6	336.9	1,332.6	7,075.2	1,048.8
San Antonio	7,873.3	8.4	38.8	176.8	593.1	1,118.1	5,457.6	480.4
San Diego	3,951.9	3.7	26.0	128.3	409.1	602.3	1,937.7	844.8
San Francisco	5,299.0	8.4	26.1	398.4	319.5	738.5	3,038.5	769.6
San Jose	2,601.7	2.8	40.8	89.1	312.8	326.1	1,470.3	359.7
Savannah	8,431.7	23.3	42.2	472.7	326.5	1,443.5	5,006.0	1,117.7
Scottsdale	4,700.9	0.5	29.2	79.3	115.0	1,292.3	2,545.3	639.2
Seattle	8,004.3	4.5	26.2	271.7	403.0	1,256.7	4,610.0	1,432.2
Sioux Falls	3,351.3	0.8	92.0	41.6	182.4	521.6	2,356.9	156.0
Springfield	7,851.6	2.6	66.4	144.5	477.0	1,224.7	5,434.8	501.7
Springfield	n/a	4.4	n/a	302.4	748.1	1,535.2	5,389.9	308.6
Stamford	2,015.6	1.7	11.8	123.6	98.3	209.3	1,320.5	250.5
Syracuse	6,583.9	15.5	28.9	370.5	606.5	1,297.8	3,402.5	862.1
Tampa	11,149.6	11.7	64.3	735.5	1,170.4	1,980.0	5,069.9	2,117.7
Tucson	9,692.9	9.1	65.3	260.8	574.6	1,297.7	6,286.4	1,199.0
Tulsa	7,568.5	6.5	61.1	226.4	792.3	1,586.4	4,000.0	895.8
Virginia Beach	3,666.8	0.7	30.1	101.1	85.8	522.6	2,734.3	192.2
Washington	7,768.3	46.2	45.9	653.5	850.2	905.1	3,661.4	1,605.9
Wichita	6,930.4	5.8	59.8	228.9	386.4	1,282.1	4,463.2	504.3
U.S.	4,118.8	5.6	33.0	145.9	310.1	746.2	2,445.8	432.1

Note: Figures shown are crimes per 100,000 population; n/a not available; All figures are for 2002
Source: FBI Uniform Crime Reports 2002

Crime Rate: Suburbs

Suburbs[1]	All Crimes	Violent Crimes				Property Crimes		
		Murder	Forcible Rape	Robbery	Aggrav. Assault	Burglary	Larceny -Theft	Motor Vehicle Theft
Albuquerque	3,361.3	7.1	44.2	76.5	523.8	675.3	1,717.8	316.7
Alexandria	4,050.9	9.6	23.1	204.8	273.3	504.9	2,353.0	682.3
Anchorage	n/a	n/a	n/a	n/a	n/a	n/a	n/a	n/a
Ann Arbor	2,823.3	2.8	39.6	43.8	170.4	528.1	1,825.3	213.2
Atlanta	3,881.6	5.3	20.1	130.9	170.0	752.1	2,351.4	451.8
Austin	3,095.4	2.3	39.5	37.0	185.1	656.7	2,019.4	155.4
Baltimore	4,030.7	3.3	23.1	154.5	444.6	619.1	2,459.7	326.3
Baton Rouge	5,701.9	7.2	34.0	80.0	332.8	1,145.9	3,819.5	282.5
Bellevue	5,272.1	3.1	36.7	124.9	199.5	843.0	3,098.5	966.2
Birmingham	3,261.0	2.9	24.3	95.7	139.6	620.1	2,128.3	250.2
Boise City	3,813.8	2.3	57.5	23.9	212.1	704.8	2,532.6	280.6
Boston	2,278.1	1.1	15.3	63.7	223.4	349.9	1,391.6	233.0
Boulder	n/a	n/a	n/a	n/a	n/a	n/a	n/a	n/a
Buffalo	2,537.5	1.0	15.9	59.6	136.1	392.8	1,761.0	170.9
Cedar Rapids	1,696.7	0.0	12.6	9.8	66.0	418.6	1,088.5	101.1
Charleston	5,532.1	8.4	52.3	175.3	600.5	976.0	3,108.5	611.1
Charlotte	n/a	n/a	n/a	n/a	n/a	n/a	n/a	n/a
Chattanooga	3,264.3	4.4	17.6	32.0	256.2	685.1	2,050.9	218.2
Chicago	n/a	n/a	n/a	n/a	n/a	n/a	n/a	n/a
Cincinnati	3,480.4	1.4	28.7	61.4	132.6	526.5	2,519.7	210.2
Cleveland	n/a	n/a	n/a	n/a	n/a	n/a	n/a	n/a
Colorado Springs	2,269.9	8.6	17.7	34.9	165.2	518.1	1,356.1	169.4
Columbia	5,212.5	7.2	43.9	153.1	560.2	1,068.8	2,929.0	450.3
Columbus	3,637.0	2.6	34.7	72.7	57.0	767.8	2,479.2	223.0
Dallas	4,275.2	3.7	29.5	81.4	216.9	815.7	2,747.2	380.9
Denver	4,571.7	3.1	44.1	76.8	209.9	642.8	2,962.2	632.8
Des Moines	3,211.9	1.2	15.9	23.2	162.6	480.1	2,350.0	178.9
Detroit	3,060.0	2.5	34.3	65.0	230.4	490.4	1,868.6	368.9
Durham	4,384.5	4.1	20.5	117.4	223.3	1,013.0	2,728.2	278.0
El Paso	2,488.4	2.5	42.1	21.5	270.8	404.6	1,541.4	205.6
Eugene	3,863.4	2.1	21.5	34.6	124.4	670.4	2,642.8	367.5
Fort Collins	3,254.7	0.0	47.4	23.7	128.6	481.4	2,432.1	141.5
Fort Lauderdale	3,993.5	5.1	27.9	150.2	326.6	665.5	2,367.2	451.0
Fort Wayne	2,003.0	1.7	18.0	32.0	73.3	380.7	1,353.9	143.5
Fort Worth	4,729.9	3.0	32.1	99.3	223.5	825.7	3,188.8	357.6
Grand Rapids	3,342.0	1.7	53.5	35.1	214.5	622.8	2,187.1	227.4
Green Bay	2,290.4	2.4	14.3	10.3	28.5	344.5	1,799.4	91.1
Greensboro	4,587.8	5.0	25.9	114.1	247.4	1,065.1	2,859.6	270.8
Honolulu	n/a	n/a	n/a	n/a	n/a	n/a	n/a	n/a
Houston	3,916.7	4.7	29.8	122.3	298.3	799.6	2,280.2	381.9
Huntsville	2,417.8	4.8	18.8	37.1	97.4	544.2	1,545.8	169.5
Indianapolis	n/a	n/a	n/a	n/a	n/a	n/a	n/a	n/a
Irvine	2,806.5	2.7	15.3	97.3	171.8	442.0	1,698.8	378.7
Jacksonville	4,186.5	3.1	34.9	90.9	549.9	792.8	2,414.6	300.3
Kansas City	n/a	n/a	n/a	n/a	n/a	n/a	n/a	n/a
Knoxville	3,653.2	2.7	27.3	40.7	269.2	880.1	2,180.1	253.1
Las Vegas	4,569.7	5.7	34.4	138.3	288.7	1,085.1	2,358.0	659.4
Lexington	n/a	n/a	n/a	n/a	n/a	n/a	n/a	n/a
Lincoln	3,808.7	0.0	16.0	24.0	68.1	781.0	2,787.5	132.2
Los Angeles	3,371.7	8.4	24.5	211.9	373.9	607.5	1,518.5	626.9
Louisville	4,239.6	4.7	15.1	62.7	351.9	838.3	2,689.6	277.2
Madison	2,751.0	0.9	15.8	30.2	71.7	355.5	2,159.5	117.3
Manchester	1,544.4	0.0	30.8	17.0	66.8	228.1	1,076.6	125.2

Crime Rate: Suburbs *continued*

Suburbs[1]	All Crimes	Violent Crimes				Property Crimes		
		Murder	Forcible Rape	Robbery	Aggrav. Assault	Burglary	Larceny -Theft	Motor Vehicle Theft
Memphis	n/a	n/a	n/a	n/a	n/a	n/a	n/a	n/a
Miami	6,828.1	7.0	37.5	289.7	630.4	1,019.4	4,018.2	825.8
Milwaukee	n/a	n/a	n/a	n/a	n/a	n/a	n/a	n/a
Minneapolis	3,612.6	1.7	34.7	69.4	119.1	511.7	2,611.1	264.9
Naperville	n/a	n/a	n/a	n/a	n/a	n/a	n/a	n/a
Nashville	3,421.5	2.7	35.3	41.6	345.2	600.2	2,182.6	213.8
New Orleans	4,476.8	8.1	27.0	125.8	392.6	708.1	2,806.6	408.7
New York	2,196.6	2.7	8.5	99.4	162.2	292.9	1,447.3	183.5
Norfolk	4,140.1	4.2	32.6	151.9	257.3	642.9	2,713.9	337.2
Oklahoma City	3,593.5	2.2	36.1	41.9	218.5	871.3	2,203.2	220.2
Omaha	4,203.0	2.1	33.7	42.1	193.1	601.0	2,892.3	438.7
Orlando	5,052.3	4.1	36.9	152.6	489.9	1,078.4	2,785.2	505.1
Overland Park	n/a	n/a	n/a	n/a	n/a	n/a	n/a	n/a
Philadelphia	2,513.2	3.1	18.8	87.5	172.9	385.8	1,630.5	214.6
Phoenix	6,178.3	5.2	26.3	99.8	334.4	1,163.2	3,572.8	976.6
Pittsburgh	2,266.6	3.3	21.4	60.2	161.6	362.9	1,491.7	165.6
Plano	6,013.3	8.1	38.7	286.8	375.4	1,129.0	3,387.9	787.4
Portland	4,005.8	1.5	35.0	59.5	102.5	607.8	2,783.0	416.5
Providence	2,923.7	1.7	31.5	60.5	188.5	492.7	1,876.8	272.1
Provo	3,698.8	1.1	15.7	11.7	58.2	571.8	2,858.7	181.6
Raleigh	4,454.9	5.6	19.2	154.9	204.7	1,032.5	2,760.3	277.7
Reno	3,383.1	1.7	35.8	71.1	215.7	659.7	2,101.2	297.8
Richmond	3,487.2	4.6	19.3	84.6	130.7	477.9	2,538.2	231.8
Rochester	2,386.9	1.0	14.3	32.4	66.9	317.8	1,833.2	121.3
Sacramento	4,008.9	3.2	32.5	111.9	294.5	786.7	2,162.6	617.4
Saint Louis	n/a	n/a	n/a	n/a	n/a	n/a	n/a	n/a
Saint Paul	3,806.6	2.9	39.7	96.9	141.9	537.4	2,686.3	301.6
Saint Petersburg	5,649.9	4.9	45.0	205.3	538.7	1,105.4	3,100.0	650.6
Salt Lake City	4,637.3	1.7	44.6	47.1	154.1	671.6	3,355.5	362.7
San Antonio	3,968.4	4.5	31.2	44.7	238.2	733.0	2,721.4	195.4
San Diego	3,350.1	2.4	28.4	104.0	279.7	640.4	1,739.1	556.1
San Francisco	2,664.7	2.5	20.1	85.9	154.7	404.8	1,689.6	307.0
San Jose	2,695.1	1.3	20.1	57.7	177.8	375.7	1,855.4	207.1
Savannah	3,945.2	5.9	16.6	104.2	292.5	838.0	2,367.0	321.0
Scottsdale	6,989.3	8.7	27.4	183.6	375.6	1,170.4	3,857.6	1,366.1
Seattle	4,372.0	2.5	39.1	75.4	129.3	699.0	2,630.9	795.8
Sioux Falls	1,730.1	0.0	38.9	4.1	75.8	452.5	1,077.0	81.9
Springfield	2,318.9	1.1	9.1	9.6	252.6	489.9	1,405.3	151.2
Springfield	n/a	n/a	n/a	n/a	n/a	n/a	n/a	n/a
Stamford	1,825.7	0.8	7.9	50.4	96.6	254.3	1,264.3	151.5
Syracuse	2,377.1	1.7	16.6	31.3	100.8	420.6	1,734.9	71.1
Tampa	5,137.9	4.4	42.5	151.0	531.7	1,013.2	2,928.7	466.4
Tucson	4,612.3	6.8	26.1	54.5	165.1	730.5	2,971.4	657.8
Tulsa	2,800.4	3.6	28.7	27.4	213.6	592.3	1,701.2	233.6
Virginia Beach	4,780.5	8.1	36.6	199.8	309.7	705.0	3,061.1	460.0
Washington	3,572.9	4.7	19.9	145.5	196.4	449.7	2,195.7	560.9
Wichita	2,936.1	3.0	33.5	26.1	190.2	566.5	1,958.7	158.1
U.S.	4,118.8	5.6	33.0	145.9	310.1	746.2	2,445.8	432.1

Note: Figures shown are crimes per 100,000 population; n/a not available; All figures are for 2002; (1) All areas within the MSA that are located outside the city limits
Source: FBI Uniform Crime Reports 2002

Crime Rate: Metro Area

MSA[1]	All Crimes	Violent Crimes				Property Crimes		
		Murder	Forcible Rape	Robbery	Aggrav. Assault	Burglary	Larceny -Theft	Motor Vehicle Theft
Albuquerque	6,165.8	9.6	56.7	206.5	641.3	1,000.3	3,576.8	674.6
Alexandria	4,047.1	9.4	22.9	202.9	270.4	501.2	2,361.4	679.0
Anchorage	n/a	n/a	n/a	n/a	n/a	n/a	n/a	n/a
Ann Arbor	2,903.8	3.1	36.2	50.1	168.1	570.9	1,873.2	202.3
Atlanta	4,638.5	8.3	24.5	214.6	277.7	874.9	2,664.6	574.0
Austin	4,761.6	3.0	38.4	107.5	221.8	841.5	3,235.6	313.9
Baltimore	5,124.3	12.0	24.0	294.3	659.8	794.1	2,847.8	492.3
Baton Rouge	6,680.7	14.2	43.2	232.8	433.7	1,385.9	4,156.0	414.9
Bellevue	5,219.5	2.9	36.1	121.2	193.1	829.2	3,092.6	944.3
Birmingham	4,689.7	9.1	43.6	198.1	285.4	928.9	2,819.8	404.7
Boise City	4,127.1	2.7	53.3	32.4	231.9	696.0	2,829.9	281.0
Boston	2,919.5	2.6	23.4	126.2	300.5	400.5	1,667.8	398.5
Boulder	n/a	n/a	n/a	n/a	n/a	n/a	n/a	n/a
Buffalo	3,512.7	4.4	27.6	182.4	263.1	621.1	2,092.2	321.9
Cedar Rapids	4,387.6	1.0	34.3	57.7	163.2	732.4	3,203.0	196.0
Charleston	5,803.1	9.3	49.6	190.6	591.0	985.8	3,318.2	658.7
Charlotte	n/a	n/a	n/a	n/a	n/a	n/a	n/a	n/a
Chattanooga	5,503.9	8.0	35.2	152.3	514.2	996.8	3,351.8	445.7
Chicago	n/a	n/a	n/a	n/a	n/a	n/a	n/a	n/a
Cincinnati	4,541.6	4.9	46.3	194.4	186.1	810.1	2,889.1	410.6
Cleveland	n/a	n/a	n/a	n/a	n/a	n/a	n/a	n/a
Colorado Springs	4,713.4	7.2	56.1	102.3	277.9	906.6	3,019.6	343.8
Columbia	5,959.2	7.5	49.5	210.4	611.6	1,135.6	3,425.2	519.5
Columbus	6,233.5	6.6	62.1	265.2	175.4	1,450.0	3,661.5	612.6
Dallas	5,879.3	7.8	37.4	272.6	364.7	1,093.9	3,351.1	751.9
Denver	4,821.0	4.6	47.1	110.2	224.2	749.5	2,884.0	801.4
Des Moines	4,822.7	2.6	33.7	76.5	171.3	637.2	3,579.6	321.9
Detroit	4,297.8	10.9	42.7	191.1	460.3	705.9	2,065.9	821.0
Durham	4,871.8	5.9	23.4	175.7	250.3	1,105.0	2,989.5	322.2
El Paso	4,227.8	2.4	38.3	84.7	480.4	381.9	2,923.6	316.5
Eugene	5,014.0	1.8	29.2	66.5	148.3	747.9	3,567.3	453.1
Fort Collins	3,757.5	0.0	62.6	25.8	182.5	534.4	2,798.9	153.3
Fort Lauderdale	4,306.8	5.3	27.6	175.5	336.4	749.3	2,523.1	489.6
Fort Wayne	3,571.5	5.7	32.8	108.1	93.4	623.8	2,424.7	282.9
Fort Worth	5,763.6	5.0	40.1	160.8	278.2	1,113.9	3,699.0	466.7
Grand Rapids	3,760.5	2.1	50.6	74.9	319.8	719.4	2,346.0	247.8
Green Bay	2,892.4	1.7	35.2	37.4	125.2	465.1	2,060.4	167.4
Greensboro	4,936.5	6.3	29.2	148.0	265.5	1,102.3	3,074.0	311.3
Honolulu	n/a	n/a	n/a	n/a	n/a	n/a	n/a	n/a
Houston	5,505.4	8.4	36.3	322.1	447.5	1,042.2	2,897.0	751.9
Huntsville	4,243.9	4.1	33.9	111.2	214.2	788.9	2,776.4	315.3
Indianapolis	n/a	n/a	n/a	n/a	n/a	n/a	n/a	n/a
Irvine	2,788.2	2.6	15.2	94.5	165.8	449.1	1,692.7	368.3
Jacksonville	5,821.5	8.9	35.6	205.3	587.2	1,059.9	3,354.5	570.0
Kansas City	n/a	n/a	n/a	n/a	n/a	n/a	n/a	n/a
Knoxville	4,440.0	5.0	31.0	109.4	387.8	962.3	2,582.3	362.1
Las Vegas	4,811.1	9.9	40.1	266.8	362.0	1,003.7	2,181.4	947.2
Lexington	n/a	n/a	n/a	n/a	n/a	n/a	n/a	n/a
Lincoln	6,308.9	2.4	40.3	73.1	399.0	873.4	4,699.7	221.0
Los Angeles	3,998.3	11.8	29.3	303.9	557.4	628.8	1,737.9	729.2
Louisville	4,696.5	6.0	18.9	142.4	343.8	956.6	2,786.0	442.8
Madison	3,453.7	1.2	28.9	77.0	128.3	543.6	2,469.2	205.7
Manchester	2,443.3	0.0	35.7	64.5	70.8	406.5	1,688.5	177.3

Crime Rate: Metro Area *continued*

MSA[1]	All Crimes	Violent Crimes				Property Crimes		
		Murder	Forcible Rape	Robbery	Aggrav. Assault	Burglary	Larceny -Theft	Motor Vehicle Theft
Memphis	n/a	n/a	n/a	n/a	n/a	n/a	n/a	n/a
Miami	7,170.6	8.7	35.5	358.0	714.1	1,108.5	4,046.0	899.9
Milwaukee	n/a	n/a	n/a	n/a	n/a	n/a	n/a	n/a
Minneapolis	4,026.1	3.0	42.2	119.7	167.2	592.1	2,757.9	344.1
Naperville	n/a	n/a	n/a	n/a	n/a	n/a	n/a	n/a
Nashville	5,560.4	6.4	51.6	188.9	680.2	927.2	3,206.5	499.6
New Orleans	5,180.4	24.4	29.3	228.8	410.0	806.2	2,857.3	824.5
New York	2,973.4	6.6	19.2	303.5	387.9	361.2	1,581.8	313.2
Norfolk	4,478.8	6.1	34.9	173.1	249.1	655.6	2,972.6	387.4
Oklahoma City	6,466.6	4.6	59.8	128.9	350.0	1,222.2	4,245.0	456.0
Omaha	5,890.7	4.6	39.2	157.1	313.4	718.6	3,871.9	785.9
Orlando	5,709.9	4.5	39.8	195.5	576.9	1,172.2	3,144.9	576.1
Overland Park	n/a	n/a	n/a	n/a	n/a	n/a	n/a	n/a
Philadelphia	3,389.7	7.8	33.4	234.0	313.4	490.1	1,901.4	409.6
Phoenix	6,846.7	8.2	27.5	177.1	359.4	1,178.0	3,775.8	1,320.8
Pittsburgh	2,772.0	4.8	24.6	119.7	221.9	449.7	1,702.6	248.7
Plano	5,879.3	7.8	37.4	272.6	364.7	1,093.9	3,351.1	751.9
Portland	5,095.3	2.1	43.3	108.6	218.3	729.0	3,430.1	564.0
Providence	3,659.1	3.4	36.0	98.0	212.7	603.9	2,231.6	473.5
Provo	3,600.0	0.8	20.9	14.4	69.1	543.1	2,772.5	179.2
Raleigh	4,871.8	5.9	23.4	175.7	250.3	1,105.0	2,989.5	322.2
Reno	4,733.0	3.2	50.9	155.2	344.5	657.8	3,082.4	439.0
Richmond	4,548.3	11.2	27.0	193.3	214.1	671.9	3,001.1	429.7
Rochester	3,434.5	4.6	21.1	113.6	113.5	476.7	2,355.1	350.1
Sacramento	4,830.2	5.2	35.3	186.7	314.6	887.4	2,543.1	858.0
Saint Louis	n/a	n/a	n/a	n/a	n/a	n/a	n/a	n/a
Saint Paul	4,026.1	3.0	42.2	119.7	167.2	592.1	2,757.9	344.1
Saint Petersburg	5,899.3	5.3	45.3	225.0	612.6	1,135.7	3,199.9	675.5
Salt Lake City	5,383.0	2.2	46.4	75.2	179.0	761.7	3,862.3	456.2
San Antonio	6,775.3	7.3	36.7	139.7	493.3	1,009.8	4,688.3	400.3
San Diego	3,611.8	3.0	27.4	114.6	336.0	623.8	1,825.4	681.6
San Francisco	3,846.6	5.2	22.8	226.1	228.7	554.6	2,294.8	514.5
San Jose	2,645.4	2.1	31.1	74.4	249.6	349.3	1,650.6	288.2
Savannah	5,958.9	13.7	28.1	269.6	307.8	1,109.7	3,551.5	678.6
Scottsdale	6,846.7	8.2	27.5	177.1	359.4	1,178.0	3,775.8	1,320.8
Seattle	5,219.5	2.9	36.1	121.2	193.1	829.2	3,092.6	944.3
Sioux Falls	2,895.8	0.6	77.1	31.1	152.4	502.2	1,997.3	135.2
Springfield	4,893.6	1.8	35.7	72.4	357.0	831.9	3,280.5	314.3
Springfield	n/a	n/a	n/a	n/a	n/a	n/a	n/a	n/a
Stamford	1,888.6	1.1	9.2	74.6	97.1	239.4	1,282.9	184.3
Syracuse	3,223.5	4.5	19.1	99.6	202.5	597.1	2,070.5	230.3
Tampa	5,899.3	5.3	45.3	225.0	612.6	1,135.7	3,199.9	675.5
Tucson	7,542.9	8.1	48.7	173.5	401.3	1,057.7	4,883.6	970.0
Tulsa	5,133.6	5.0	44.5	124.8	496.8	1,078.7	2,826.0	557.6
Virginia Beach	4,478.8	6.1	34.9	173.1	249.1	655.6	2,972.6	387.4
Washington	4,047.1	9.4	22.9	202.9	270.4	501.2	2,361.4	679.0
Wichita	5,458.3	4.7	50.1	154.1	314.1	1,018.4	3,540.2	376.7
U.S.	4,118.8	5.6	33.0	145.9	310.1	746.2	2,445.8	432.1

Note: Figures shown are crimes per 100,000 population; n/a not available; All figures are for 2002;
(1) Metropolitan Statistical Area - see Appendix A for areas included
Source: FBI Uniform Crime Reports 2002

Temperature & Precipitation: Yearly Averages and Extremes

City	Extreme Low (°F)	Average Low (°F)	Average Temp. (°F)	Average High (°F)	Extreme High (°F)	Average Precip. (in.)	Average Snow (in.)
Albuquerque	-17	43	57	70	105	8.5	11
Alexandria	-5	49	58	67	104	39.5	18
Anchorage	-34	29	36	43	85	15.7	71
Ann Arbor	-21	39	49	58	104	32.4	41
Atlanta	-8	52	62	72	105	49.8	2
Austin	-2	58	69	79	109	31.1	1
Baltimore	-7	45	56	65	105	41.2	21
Baton Rouge	8	57	68	78	103	58.5	Trace
Bellevue	0	44	52	59	99	38.4	13
Birmingham	-6	51	63	74	106	53.5	2
Boise City	-25	39	51	63	111	11.8	22
Boston	-12	44	52	59	102	42.9	41
Boulder	-25	37	51	64	103	15.5	63
Buffalo	-20	40	48	56	99	38.1	90
Cedar Rapids	-34	36	47	57	105	34.4	33
Charleston	6	55	66	76	104	52.1	1
Charlotte	-5	50	61	71	104	42.8	6
Chattanooga	-10	49	60	71	106	53.3	4
Chicago	-27	40	49	59	104	35.4	39
Cincinnati	-25	44	54	64	103	40.9	23
Cleveland	-19	41	50	59	104	37.1	55
Colorado Spgs.	-24	36	49	62	99	17.0	48
Columbia	-1	51	64	75	107	48.3	2
Columbus	-19	42	52	62	104	37.9	28
Dallas	-2	56	67	77	112	33.9	3
Denver	-25	37	51	64	103	15.5	63
Des Moines	-24	40	50	60	108	31.8	33
Detroit	-21	39	49	58	104	32.4	41
Durham	-9	48	60	71	105	42.0	8
El Paso	-8	50	64	78	114	8.6	6
Eugene	-12	42	53	63	108	47.3	7
Ft. Collins[1]	-25	37	51	64	103	15.5	63
Ft. Lauderdale[2]	30	69	76	83	98	57.1	0
Ft. Wayne	-22	40	50	60	106	35.9	33
Ft. Worth	-1	55	66	76	113	32.3	3
Grand Rapids	-22	38	48	57	102	34.7	73
Green Bay	-31	34	44	54	99	28.3	46
Greensboro	-8	47	58	69	103	42.5	10
Honolulu	52	70	77	84	94	22.4	0
Houston	7	58	69	79	107	46.9	Trace
Huntsville	-11	50	61	71	104	56.8	4
Indianapolis	-23	42	53	62	104	40.2	25
Irvine	25	53	64	75	112	11.9	Trace
Jacksonville	7	58	69	79	103	52.0	0
Kansas City	-23	44	54	64	109	38.1	21
Knoxville	-24	48	59	69	103	46.7	13
Las Vegas	8	53	67	80	116	4.0	1
Lexington	-21	45	55	65	103	45.1	17
Lincoln	-33	39	51	62	108	29.1	27
Los Angeles	27	55	63	70	110	11.3	Trace
Louisville	-20	46	57	67	105	43.9	17
Madison	-37	35	46	57	104	31.1	42
Manchester	-33	34	46	57	102	36.9	63

Temperature & Precipitation: Yearly Averages and Extremes *continued*

City	Extreme Low (°F)	Average Low (°F)	Average Temp. (°F)	Average High (°F)	Extreme High (°F)	Average Precip. (in.)	Average Snow (in.)
Memphis	0	52	65	77	107	54.8	1
Miami	30	69	76	83	98	57.1	0
Milwaukee	-26	38	47	55	103	32.0	49
Minneapolis	-34	35	45	54	105	27.1	52
Naperville	-27	40	49	59	104	35.4	39
Nashville	-17	49	60	70	107	47.4	11
New Orleans	11	59	69	78	102	60.6	Trace
New York	-2	47	55	62	104	47.0	23
Norfolk	-3	51	60	68	104	45.0	8
Oklahoma City	-8	49	60	71	110	32.8	10
Omaha	-23	40	51	62	110	30.1	29
Orlando	19	62	72	82	100	47.7	Trace
Overland Park	-23	44	54	64	109	38.1	21
Philadelphia	-7	45	55	64	104	41.4	22
Phoenix	17	59	72	86	122	7.3	Trace
Pittsburgh	-18	41	51	60	103	37.1	43
Plano	-2	56	67	77	112	33.9	3
Portland	-3	45	54	62	107	37.5	7
Providence	-13	42	51	60	104	45.3	35
Provo	-22	40	52	64	107	15.6	63
Raleigh	-9	48	60	71	105	42.0	8
Reno	-16	33	50	67	105	7.2	24
Richmond	-8	48	58	69	105	43.0	13
Rochester	-19	39	48	57	100	31.8	92
Sacramento	18	48	61	73	115	17.3	Trace
Salt Lake City	-22	40	52	64	107	15.6	63
San Antonio	0	58	69	80	108	29.6	1
San Diego	29	57	64	71	111	9.5	Trace
San Francisco	24	49	57	65	106	19.3	Trace
San Jose	21	50	59	68	105	13.5	Trace
Savannah	3	56	67	77	105	50.3	Trace
Scottsdale	17	59	72	86	122	7.3	Trace
Seattle	0	44	52	59	99	38.4	13
Sioux Falls	-36	35	46	57	110	24.6	38
Springfield (IL)	-24	44	54	63	112	34.9	21
Springfield (MO)	-17	45	56	67	113	42.0	18
St. Louis	-18	46	56	66	115	36.8	20
St. Paul	-34	35	45	54	105	27.1	52
St. Petersburg	18	63	73	82	99	46.7	Trace
Stamford	-7	44	52	60	103	41.4	25
Syracuse	-26	38	48	57	98	38.5	107
Tampa	18	63	73	82	99	46.7	Trace
Tucson	16	55	69	82	117	11.6	2
Tulsa	-8	50	61	71	112	38.9	10
Virginia Beach	-3	51	60	69	104	44.8	8
Washington	-5	49	58	67	104	39.5	18
Wichita	-21	45	57	68	113	29.3	17

Note: (1) Data is for Denver, which is located 60 miles south of Ft. Collins;
(2) Data is for Miami, which is located 22 miles south of Ft. Lauderdale
Source: National Climatic Data Center, International Station Meteorological Climate Summary, 9/96

Weather Conditions

City	Temperature			Daytime Sky			Precipitation		
	10°F & below	32°F & below	90°F & above	Clear	Partly cloudy	Cloudy	.01 inch or more precip.	1.0 inch or more snow/ice	Thunder-storms
Albuquerque	4	114	65	140	161	64	60	9	38
Alexandria	2	71	34	84	144	137	112	9	30
Anchorage	n/a	194	n/a	50	115	200	113	49	2
Ann Arbor	n/a	136	12	74	134	157	135	38	32
Atlanta	1	49	38	98	147	120	116	3	48
Austin	< 1	20	111	105	148	112	83	1	41
Baltimore	6	97	31	91	143	131	113	13	27
Baton Rouge	< 1	21	86	99	150	116	113	< 1	73
Bellevue	n/a	38	3	57	121	187	157	8	8
Birmingham	1	57	59	91	161	113	119	1	57
Boise City	n/a	124	45	106	133	126	91	22	14
Boston	n/a	97	12	88	127	150	253	48	18
Boulder	24	155	33	99	177	89	90	38	39
Buffalo	n/a	131	4	47	144	174	169	65	30
Cedar Rapids	n/a	156	16	89	132	144	109	28	42
Charleston	< 1	33	53	89	162	114	114	1	59
Charlotte	1	65	44	98	142	125	113	3	41
Chattanooga	2	73	48	88	141	136	120	3	55
Chicago	n/a	132	17	83	136	146	125	31	38
Cincinnati	14	107	23	80	126	159	127	25	39
Cleveland	n/a	123	12	63	127	175	157	48	34
Colorado Spgs.	21	161	18	108	157	100	98	33	49
Columbia	< 1	58	77	97	149	119	110	1	53
Columbus	n/a	118	19	72	137	156	136	29	40
Dallas	1	34	102	108	160	97	78	2	49
Denver	24	155	33	99	177	89	90	38	39
Des Moines	n/a	137	26	99	129	137	106	25	46
Detroit	n/a	136	12	74	134	157	135	38	32
Durham	n/a	n/a	39	98	143	124	110	3	42
El Paso	1	59	106	147	164	54	49	3	35
Eugene	n/a	n/a	15	75	115	175	136	4	3
Ft. Collins[1]	24	155	33	99	177	89	90	38	39
Ft. Lauderdale[2]	n/a	n/a	55	48	263	54	128	0	74
Ft. Wayne	n/a	131	16	75	140	150	131	31	39
Ft. Worth	1	40	100	123	136	106	79	3	47
Grand Rapids	n/a	146	11	67	119	179	142	57	34
Green Bay	n/a	163	7	86	125	154	120	40	33
Greensboro	3	85	32	94	143	128	113	5	43
Honolulu	n/a	n/a	23	25	286	54	98	0	7
Houston	n/a	n/a	96	83	168	114	101	1	62
Huntsville	2	66	49	70	118	177	116	2	54
Indianapolis	19	119	19	83	128	154	127	24	43
Irvine	0	2	18	95	192	78	41	0	4
Jacksonville	< 1	16	83	86	181	98	114	1	65
Kansas City	22	110	39	112	134	119	103	17	51
Knoxville	3	73	33	85	142	138	125	8	47
Las Vegas	< 1	37	134	185	132	48	27	2	13
Lexington	11	96	22	86	136	143	129	17	44
Lincoln	n/a	145	40	108	135	122	94	19	46
Los Angeles	0	< 1	5	131	125	109	34	0	1
Louisville	8	90	35	82	143	140	125	15	45
Madison	n/a	161	14	88	119	158	118	38	40
Manchester	n/a	171	12	87	131	147	125	32	19

Weather Conditions *continued*

City	Temperature			Daytime Sky			Precipitation		
	10°F & below	32°F & below	90°F & above	Clear	Partly cloudy	Cloudy	.01 inch or more precip.	1.0 inch or more snow/ice	Thunder-storms
Memphis	1	53	86	101	152	112	104	2	59
Miami	n/a	n/a	55	48	263	54	128	0	74
Milwaukee	n/a	141	10	90	118	157	126	38	35
Minneapolis	n/a	156	16	93	125	147	113	41	37
Naperville	n/a	132	17	83	136	146	125	31	38
Nashville	5	76	51	98	135	132	119	8	54
New Orleans	0	13	70	90	169	106	114	1	69
New York	n/a	n/a	18	85	166	114	120	11	20
Norfolk	< 1	54	32	89	149	127	115	6	37
Oklahoma City	5	79	70	124	131	110	80	8	50
Omaha	n/a	139	35	100	142	123	97	20	46
Orlando	n/a	n/a	90	76	208	81	115	0	80
Overland Park	22	110	39	112	134	119	103	17	51
Philadelphia	5	94	23	81	146	138	117	14	27
Phoenix	0	10	167	186	125	54	37	< 1	23
Pittsburgh	n/a	121	8	62	137	166	154	42	35
Plano	1	34	102	108	160	97	78	2	49
Portland	n/a	37	11	67	116	182	152	4	7
Providence	n/a	117	9	85	134	146	123	21	21
Provo	n/a	128	56	94	152	119	92	38	38
Raleigh	n/a	n/a	39	98	143	124	110	3	42
Reno	14	178	50	143	139	83	50	17	14
Richmond	3	79	41	90	147	128	115	7	43
Rochester	n/a	135	11	58	137	170	157	65	27
Sacramento	0	21	73	175	111	79	58	< 1	2
Salt Lake City	n/a	128	56	94	152	119	92	38	38
San Antonio	n/a	n/a	112	97	153	115	81	1	36
San Diego	0	< 1	4	115	126	124	40	0	5
San Francisco	0	6	4	136	130	99	63	< 1	5
San Jose	0	5	5	106	180	79	57	< 1	6
Savannah	< 1	29	70	97	155	113	111	< 1	63
Scottsdale	0	10	167	186	125	54	37	< 1	23
Seattle	n/a	38	3	57	121	187	157	8	8
Sioux Falls	n/a	n/a	n/a	95	136	134	n/a	n/a	n/a
Springfield (IL)	19	111	34	96	126	143	111	18	49
Springfield (MO)	12	102	42	113	119	133	109	14	55
St. Louis	13	100	43	97	138	130	109	14	46
St. Paul	n/a	156	16	93	125	147	113	41	37
St. Petersburg	n/a	n/a	85	81	204	80	107	< 1	87
Stamford	n/a	n/a	7	80	146	139	118	17	22
Syracuse	n/a	136	9	56	135	174	170	67	27
Tampa	n/a	n/a	85	81	204	80	107	< 1	87
Tucson	0	18	140	177	119	69	54	2	42
Tulsa	6	78	74	117	141	107	88	8	50
Virginia Beach	< 1	53	33	89	149	127	115	5	38
Washington	2	71	34	84	144	137	112	9	30
Wichita	13	110	63	117	132	116	87	13	54

Note: Figures are average number of days per year; n/a not available; (1) Data is for Denver, which is located 60 miles south of Ft. Collins; (2) Data is for Miami, which is located 22 miles south of Ft. Lauderdale
Source: National Climatic Data Center, International Station Meteorological Climate Summary, 9/96

Watershed Health

City	Watershed	Index of Watershed Indicators Score (IWI definition)
Albuquerque	Rio Grande-Albuquerque	3 (less serious problems - low vulnerability)
Alexandria	Middle Potomac-Anacostia-Occoquan	4 (less serious problems - high vulnerability)
Anchorage	Anchorage	0 (insufficient data)
Ann Arbor	Huron	5 (more serious problems - low vulnerability)
Atlanta	Upper Ocmulgee	3 (less serious problems - low vulnerability)
Austin	Austin-Travis Lakes	3 (less serious problems - low vulnerability)
Baltimore	Gunpowder-Patapsco	4 (less serious problems - high vulnerability)
Baton Rouge	Amite	6 (more serious problems - high vulnerability)
Bellevue	Puget Sound	5 (more serious problems - low vulnerability)
Birmingham	Locust	3 (less serious problems - low vulnerability)
Boise City	Lower Boise	5 (more serious problems - low vulnerability)
Boston	Charles	6 (more serious problems - high vulnerability)
Buffalo	Buffalo-Eighteenmile	1 (better quality - low vulnerability)
Cedar Rapids	Lower Cedar	1 (better quality - low vulnerability)
Charlotte	Lower Catawba	4 (less serious problems - high vulnerability)
Chattanooga	Middle Tennessee-Chickamauga	3 (less serious problems - low vulnerability)
Chicago	Chicago	5 (more serious problems - low vulnerability)
Cincinnati	Middle Ohio-Laughery	6 (more serious problems - high vulnerability)
Cleveland	Cuyahoga	5 (more serious problems - low vulnerability)
Colorado Springs	Fountain	1 (better quality - low vulnerability)
Columbia	Congaree	3 (less serious problems - low vulnerability)
Columbus	Upper Scioto	4 (less serious problems - high vulnerability)
Dallas	Upper Trinity	5 (more serious problems - low vulnerability)
Denver	Middle South Platte-Cherry Creek	1 (better quality - low vulnerability)
Des Moines	Middle Des Moines	3 (less serious problems - low vulnerability)
Detroit	Detroit	5 (more serious problems - low vulnerability)
Durham	Upper Neuse	2 (better quality - high vulnerability)
El Paso	Rio Grande-Fort Quitman	1 (better quality - low vulnerability)
Eugene	Upper Willamette	3 (less serious problems - low vulnerability)
Fort Collins	Cache La Poudre	1 (better quality - low vulnerability)
Fort Lauderdale	Everglades	4 (less serious problems - high vulnerability)
Fort Wayne	St. Joseph	6 (more serious problems - high vulnerability)
Fort Worth	Lower West Fork Trinity	1 (better quality - low vulnerability)
Grand Rapids	Lower Grand	5 (more serious problems - low vulnerability)
Green Bay	Lower Fox	6 (more serious problems - high vulnerability)
Greensboro	Haw	2 (better quality - high vulnerability)
Honolulu	Oahu	3 (less serious problems - low vulnerability)
Houston	Buffalo-San Jacinto	5 (more serious problems - low vulnerability)
Huntsville	Wheeler Lake	6 (more serious problems - high vulnerability)
Indianapolis	Upper White	6 (more serious problems - high vulnerability)
Irvine	Newport Bay	5 (more serious problems - low vulnerability)
Jackson	Middle Pearl-Strong	4 (less serious problems - high vulnerability)
Jacksonville	Lower St. Johns	6 (more serious problems - high vulnerability)
Kansas City	Lower Missouri-Crooked	6 (more serious problems - high vulnerability)
Knoxville	Watts Bar Lake	5 (more serious problems - low vulnerability)
Las Vegas	Las Vegas Wash	3 (less serious problems - low vulnerability)
Lexington	Lower Kentucky	4 (less serious problems - high vulnerability)
Lincoln	Salt	3 (less serious problems - low vulnerability)
Los Angeles	Los Angeles	3 (less serious problems - low vulnerability)
Louisville	Silver-Little Kentucky	6 (more serious problems - high vulnerability)
Madison	Upper Rock	4 (less serious problems - high vulnerability)
Manchester	Merrimack	6 (more serious problems - high vulnerability)

Watershed Health *continued*

City	Watershed	Index of Watershed Indicators Score (IWI definition)
Memphis	Lower Mississippi-Memphis	1 (better quality - low vulnerability)
Miami	Everglades	4 (less serious problems - high vulnerability)
Milwaukee	Milwaukee	5 (more serious problems - low vulnerability)
Minneapolis	Twin Cities	6 (more serious problems - high vulnerability)
Naperville	Des Plaines	5 (more serious problems - low vulnerability)
Nashville	Lower Cumberland-Sycamore	3 (less serious problems - low vulnerability)
New Orleans	Eastern Louisiana Coastal	3 (less serious problems - low vulnerability)
New York	Lower Hudson	2 (better quality - high vulnerability)
Norfolk	Lynnhaven-Poquoson	3 (less serious problems - low vulnerability)
Oakland	San Francisco Bay	2 (better quality - high vulnerability)
Oklahoma City	Lower North Canadian	3 (less serious problems - low vulnerability)
Omaha	Big Papillion-Mosquito	1 (better quality - low vulnerability)
Orlando	Kissimmee	3 (less serious problems - low vulnerability)
Overland Park	Lower Missouri-Crooked	6 (more serious problems - high vulnerability)
Philadelphia	Schuylkill	6 (more serious problems - high vulnerability)
Phoenix	Lower Salt	2 (better quality - high vulnerability)
Pittsburgh	Lower Allegheny	3 (less serious problems - low vulnerability)
Plano	Upper Trinity	5 (more serious problems - low vulnerability)
Portland	Lower Willamette	5 (more serious problems - low vulnerability)
Providence	Narragansett	4 (less serious problems - high vulnerability)
Provo	Provo	3 (less serious problems - low vulnerability)
Raleigh	Upper Neuse	2 (better quality - high vulnerability)
Reno	Truckee	3 (less serious problems - low vulnerability)
Richmond	Middle James-Willis	n/a (insufficient data)
Rochester	Lower Genesee	3 (less serious problems - low vulnerability)
Sacramento	Lower Sacramento	3 (less serious problems - low vulnerability)
Saint Paul	Twin Cities	6 (more serious problems - high vulnerability)
Saint Petersburg	Tampa	4 (less serious problems - high vulnerability)
Salt Lake City	Jordan	3 (less serious problems - low vulnerability)
San Antonio	Upper San Antonio	3 (less serious problems - low vulnerability)
San Diego	San Diego	2 (better quality - high vulnerability)
San Francisco	San Francisco Bay	2 (better quality - high vulnerability)
San Jose	Coyote	5 (more serious problems - low vulnerability)
Savannah	Lower Savannah	5 (more serious problems - low vulnerability)
Scottsdale	Lower Salt	2 (better quality - high vulnerability)
Seattle	Puget Sound	5 (more serious problems - low vulnerability)
Sioux Falls	Lower Big Sioux	5 (more serious problems - low vulnerability)
Springfield	James	1 (better quality - low vulnerability)
Springfield	South Fork Sangamon	5 (more serious problems - low vulnerability)
St. Louis	Cahokia-Joachim	5 (more serious problems - low vulnerability)
Stamford	Saugatuck	5 (more serious problems - low vulnerability)
Syracuse	Seneca	4 (less serious problems - high vulnerability)
Tampa	Hillsborough	6 (more serious problems - high vulnerability)
Tucson	Upper Santa Cruz	3 (less serious problems - low vulnerability)
Tulsa	Polecat-Snake	3 (less serious problems - low vulnerability)
Virginia Beach	Lynnhaven-Poquoson	3 (less serious problems - low vulnerability)
Washington	Middle Potomac-Anacostia-Occoquan	4 (less serious problems - high vulnerability)
Wichita	Little Arkansas	3 (less serious problems - low vulnerability)

Note: Watersheds are holding areas for the nation's drinking water supply. The Index of Watershed Indicators (IWI) score is based on seven condition and nine vulnerability indicators. The overall IWI score ranges from 1 (best health) to 6 (worst health).
Source: U.S. Environmental Protection Agency, Index of Watershed Indicators, October 26, 2001

Tap Water Characteristics

City	Tap Water
Albuquerque	Alkaline, hard and fluoridated
Alexandria	Slightly alkaline and medium soft
Anchorage	Neutral, hard and fluoridated
Ann Arbor	Alkaline, soft and fluoridated
Atlanta	Neutral, soft
Austin	Alkaline, soft and fluoridated
Baltimore	Alkaline, very soft and fluoridated
Baton Rouge	Neutral, very soft and not fluoridated
Bellevue	Soft
Birmingham	Alkaline, soft
Boise City	Alkaline, soft
Boston	The Metropolitan Water District (combined sources, Quabbin Reservoir and Wachusett Reservoir) supplies municipal Boston and the ABC City Zone. Water is soft and slightly acid.
Boulder	Neutral, very soft and fluoridated
Buffalo	Alkaline, hard and fluoridated
Cedar Rapids	Alkaline, hard and fluoridated
Charleston	Alkaline, very soft and fluoridated
Charlotte	Alkaline, very soft and fluoridated
Chattanooga	Slightly alkaline, moderately hard and fluoridated
Chicago	Alkaline (Lake Michigan) and fluoridated
Cincinnati	Alkaline, hard and fluoridated
Cleveland	Alkaline, hard and fluoridated
Colorado Springs	From watershed on Pikes Peak and Continental Divide. It's pure, filtered and fluoridated
Columbia	Alkaline, very soft and fluoridated
Columbus	Slightly alkaline, moderately hard
Dallas	Moderately hard and fluoridated
Denver	Alkaline, 53% of supply hard, 47% of supply soft; West Slope, fluoridated. East Slope, not fluoridated
Des Moines	Alkaline, soft and fluoridated
Detroit	Alkaline, soft
Durham	Alkaline, soft and fluoridated
El Paso	Soft and fluoridated
Eugene	Neutral, very soft
Fort Collins	Alkaline, very soft
Fort Lauderdale	Alkaline, very soft and fluoridated
Fort Wayne	Alkaline, soft and fluoridated
Fort Worth	Alkaline, hard and fluoridated
Grand Rapids	Alkaline, hard and fluoridated
Green Bay	From Lake Michigan. It's alkaline, hard and fluoridated
Greensboro	Alkaline, soft
Honolulu	Alkaline, soft and not fluoridated
Houston	Alkaline, hard
Huntsville	Neutral, hard and fluoridated
Indianapolis	Alkaline, hard and fluoridated. Three separate systems with separate sources and purification plants
Irvine	Not available
Jacksonville	Alkaline, very hard and naturally fluoridated
Kansas City	Neutral, soft and fluoridated
Knoxville	Alkaline, hard and fluoridated
Las Vegas	Alkaline, hard
Lexington	Alkaline, medium and fluoridated
Lincoln	Alkaline, hard and fluoridated
Los Angeles	Hardness ranges from 4.2-15.1 gpg. The alkalinity also varies, ranging from 5.4-8.6 gpg. The Owens River Aqueduct accounts for approximately 70% of the water supply and is slightly alkaline and moderately soft with 4.2 gpg total hardness.
Louisville	Fluoridated
Madison	Alkaline, hard and fluoridated
Manchester	Slightly acid and very soft

Tap Water Characteristics *continued*

City	Tap Water
Memphis	Neutral, hardness 46ppm and fluoridated
Miami	Alkaline, soft and fluoridated
Milwaukee	Alkaline, medium hard and fluoridated
Minneapolis	Alkaline, soft and fluoridated. Water is hard in the suburbs.
Naperville	Alkaline (Lake Michigan) and fluoridated
Nashville	Alkaline, soft
New Orleans	Alkaline, soft and fluoridated
New York	There are three major sources: the Catskills & Delaware subsytems (neutral, soft, average pH 7.0) and Croton subsystem (alkaline, moderately hard, average pH 7.1). All three supplies are fluoridated and chlorinated.
Norfolk	Low alkalinity, slightly soft and fluoridated
Oklahoma City	Alkaline, soft and fluoridated
Omaha	Moderately alkaline, moderately soft, fluoridated
Orlando	Alkaline, hard and fluoridated
Overland Park	Neutral, soft and fluoridated
Philadelphia	Slightly acid, moderately hard (Schuykill River), moderately soft (Delaware River); fluoridated
Phoenix	Alkaline, approximately 11 grains of hardness per gallon and fluoridated
Pittsburgh	Alkaline, soft 9 months, hard 3 months (June, July, August); fluoridated
Plano	Alkaline, soft and fluoridated
Portland	Neutral, very soft and not fluoridated
Providence	Alkaline and very soft
Provo	Alkaline and hard
Raleigh	Neutral, soft and fluoridated
Reno	Alkaline, very soft and not fluoridated
Richmond	Alkaline, soft and fluoridated
Rochester	Neutral, soft
Sacramento	Varies, soft to hard and not fluoridated
Saint Louis	Alkaline, moderately hard and fluoridated
Saint Paul	Alkaline, soft and fluoridated
Saint Petersburg	Slightly alkaline, hard and not fluoridated
Salt Lake City	Alkaline, hard and not fluoridated
San Antonio	Not fluoridated and has moderate mineral content, chiefly sodium bicarbonate
San Diego	Hard and not fluoridated
San Francisco	Alkaline, very soft and fluoridated
San Jose	Alkaline, very hard and not fluoridated
Savannah	Alkaline, hard and fluoridated
Scottsdale	Alkaline and hard
Seattle	Alkaline, very soft
Sioux Falls	Alkaline, hard and fluoridated
Springfield	Alkaline, hard and fluoridated
Springfield	From Lake Springfield. It's neutral and soft
Stamford	Slightly acid, moderately soft and fluoridated
Syracuse	Slightly alkaline, moderately hard and fluoridated
Tampa	Alkaline, moderately hard and not fluoridated
Tucson	Alkaline and very hard from South Side Reservoir No. 1 and alkaline, soft and not fluoridated from North Side Reservoir No. 3
Tulsa	Alkaline, soft and fluoridated
Virginia Beach	Low alkalinity, slightly soft and fluoridated
Washington	Slightly alkaline and medium soft
Wichita	Soft

Source: Editor & Publisher Market Guide 2004

Air Quality

MSA[1]	AQI>100[2] (days)	Ozone 1-hour (ppm)	Ozone 8-hour (ppm)	Carbon Monoxide (ppm)	Sulfur Dioxide (ppm)	Nitrogen Dioxide (ppm)	Particulate Matter (ug/m^3)	Lead (ug/m^3)
Albuquerque	4	0.09	0.08	4	n/a	0.019	144	0.03
Alexandria	39	0.15	0.11	5	0.021	0.025	60	n/a
Anchorage	n/a	n/a	n/a	6	n/a	n/a	104	n/a
Ann Arbor	n/a	0.1	0.09	n/a	n/a	n/a	n/a	0.01
Atlanta	37	0.14	0.1	4	0.018	0.019	52	0.04
Austin	5	0.1	0.09	1	n/a	0.004	43	n/a
Baltimore	44	0.14	0.11	3	0.021	0.025	81	0.01
Baton Rouge	7	0.13	0.08	4	0.036	0.018	69	n/a
Bellevue	7	0.09	0.07	5	0.014	0.019	57	0.03
Birmingham	23	0.11	0.09	12	0.015	n/a	160	n/a
Boise City	n/a	0.1	0.08	3	n/a	n/a	136	n/a
Boston	26	0.15	0.11	2	0.021	0.025	49	0.01
Boulder	n/a	0.09	0.08	3	n/a	n/a	50	n/a
Buffalo	22	0.12	0.11	2	0.072	0.02	49	0.01
Cedar Rapids	n/a	0.09	0.07	1	0.031	n/a	45	n/a
Charleston	3	0.1	0.07	3	0.01	0.01	40	0.01
Charlotte	40	0.13	0.11	3	0.011	0.015	49	0.01
Chattanooga	n/a	0.11	0.1	n/a	n/a	n/a	50	n/a
Chicago	26	0.13	0.1	4	0.025	0.032	106	0.04
Cincinnati	32	0.13	0.1	3	0.043	0.021	59	n/a
Cleveland	33	0.13	0.12	2	0.041	0.022	113	0.12[a]
Colorado Springs	n/a	0.08	0.07	5	n/a	n/a	58	0.01
Columbia	n/a	0.12	0.09	3	0.018	0.012	111	0.01
Columbus	30	0.12	0.1	3	0.017	n/a	77	0.03[b]
Dallas	22	0.13	0.1	2	0.016	0.018	62	0.48[c]
Denver	8	0.11	0.09	4	0.023	0.035	126	0.13
Des Moines	n/a	0.07	0.06	3	n/a	0.012	69	n/a
Detroit	28	0.12	0.1	4	0.049	0.021	111	0.03
Durham	30	0.12	0.11	3	0.01	n/a	59	n/a
El Paso	18	0.13	0.09	7	0.006	0.021	534	1.02
Eugene	n/a	0.08	0.07	4	n/a	n/a	80	0
Fort Collins	n/a	0.1	0.09	3	n/a	n/a	46	n/a
Fort Lauderdale	3	0.1	0.07	4	0.011	0.009	35	n/a
Fort Wayne	n/a	0.11	0.1	3	n/a	n/a	103	n/a
Fort Worth	33	0.14	0.11	2	n/a	0.013	50	n/a
Grand Rapids	24	0.13	0.11	3	0.007	0.017	48	0.01
Green Bay	n/a	0.09	0.08	n/a	0.013	n/a	n/a	n/a
Greensboro	32	0.13	0.1	4	0.024	0.014	57	n/a
Honolulu	2	0.05	0.04	2	0.005	0.004	33	n/a
Houston	30	0.17	0.1	3	0.022	0.019	95	0.01
Huntsville	n/a	0.1	0.08	n/a	n/a	n/a	47	n/a
Indianapolis	26	0.13	0.11	5	0.024	0.018	54	0.04[d]
Irvine	21	0.13	0.08	5	0.009	0.025	64	n/a
Jacksonville	1	0.09	0.07	3	0.054	0.015	119	0.01
Kansas City	12	0.11	0.09	3	0.015	0.017	66	n/a
Knoxville	45	0.12	0.1	2	0.07	n/a	135	n/a
Las Vegas	14	0.1	0.09	6	0.006	0.023	185	n/a
Lexington	n/a	0.1	0.09	2	0.016	0.012	74	n/a
Lincoln	n/a	0.06	0.05	4	n/a	n/a	n/a	n/a
Los Angeles	108	0.16	0.13	9	0.007	0.04	118	0.04
Louisville	29	0.12	0.1	5	0.03	0.02	66	n/a
Madison	n/a	0.09	0.08	n/a	n/a	n/a	38	n/a
Manchester	n/a	0.11	0.09	3	0.046	0.013	59	n/a

Air Quality *continued*

MSA[1]	AQI>100[2] (days)	Ozone 1-hour (ppm)	Ozone 8-hour (ppm)	Carbon Monoxide (ppm)	Sulfur Dioxide (ppm)	Nitrogen Dioxide (ppm)	Particulate Matter (ug/m^3)	Lead (ug/m^3)
Memphis	17	0.13	0.1	4	0.03	0.022	56	0.01[e]
Miami	1	0.09	0.07	3	0.004	0.014	43	n/a
Milwaukee	12	0.12	0.1	3	0.024	n/a	50	n/a
Minneapolis	2	0.1	0.08	4	0.018	0.019	88	0.09[f]
Naperville	26	0.13	0.1	4	0.025	0.032	106	0.04
Nashville	21	0.11	0.09	5	0.018	0.016	52	1.24[g]
New Orleans	2	0.11	0.08	4	0.016	0.017	74	0.12
New York	34	0.13	0.1	3	0.039	0.038	51	0.01
Norfolk	15	0.13	0.1	4	0.031	0.018	38	n/a
Oklahoma City	4	0.11	0.08	3	0.006	0.014	50	n/a
Omaha	0	0.08	0.07	4	0.009	n/a	110	0.05[h]
Orlando	1	0.1	0.08	3	0.005	0.011	38	n/a
Overland Park	12	0.11	0.09	3	0.015	0.017	66	n/a
Philadelphia	39	0.14	0.11	3	0.028	0.03	71	0.04
Phoenix	22	0.12	0.09	6	0.01	0.035	174	n/a
Pittsburgh	55	0.12	0.11	3	0.075	0.02	108	0.11
Plano	22	0.13	0.1	2	0.016	0.018	62	0.48[c]
Portland	6	0.12	0.06	6	n/a	n/a	67	0.02
Providence	15	0.12	0.09	3	0.027	n/a	40	n/a
Provo	n/a	0.1	0.08	5	n/a	0.025	101	n/a
Raleigh	30	0.12	0.11	3	0.01	n/a	59	n/a
Reno	n/a	0.1	0.08	4	n/a	n/a	93	n/a
Richmond	25	0.14	0.11	2	0.021	0.02	37	n/a
Rochester	13	0.11	0.1	2	0.016	n/a	n/a	n/a
Sacramento	77	0.15	0.11	4	0.009	0.02	90	0
Saint Louis	36	0.13	0.1	7	0.05	0.023	224	2.24[i]
Saint Paul	2	0.1	0.08	4	0.018	0.019	88	0.09[f]
Saint Petersburg	0	0.09	0.07	4	0.047	0.011	56	1.27[j]
Salt Lake City	36	0.11	0.09	4	0.01	0.027	123	0.05
San Antonio	17	0.13	0.1	3	n/a	0.017	67	n/a
San Diego	20	0.12	0.1	4	0.01	0.022	112	0.02
San Francisco	17	0.08	0.05	3	n/a	n/a	n/a	0.01
San Jose	13	0.12	0.08	n/a	n/a	n/a	n/a	0.01
Savannah	n/a	0.08	0.07	n/a	0.022	n/a	49	n/a
Scottsdale	22	0.12	0.09	6	0.01	0.035	174	n/a
Seattle	7	0.09	0.07	5	0.014	0.019	57	0.03
Sioux Falls	n/a	0.07	0.06	n/a	n/a	n/a	91	n/a
Springfield	n/a	0.1	0.08	2	0.017	n/a	n/a	n/a
Springfield	n/a	0.09	0.08	3	0.041	0.011	43	n/a
Stamford	n/a	0.15	0.11	3	0.035	0.019	68	n/a
Syracuse	10	0.1	0.09	2	0.013	n/a	n/a	n/a
Tampa	0	0.09	0.07	4	0.047	0.011	56	1.27[j]
Tucson	3	0.09	0.08	3	0.004	0.017	192	n/a
Tulsa	6	0.11	0.08	3	0.032	0.011	51	n/a
Virginia Beach	15	0.13	0.1	4	0.031	0.018	38	n/a
Washington	39	0.15	0.11	5	0.021	0.025	60	n/a
Wichita	n/a	0.09	0.08	4	n/a	n/a	111	n/a
NAAQS[4]	n/a	0.12	0.08	9	0.140	0.053	150	1.50

Note: (1) Metropolitan Statistical Area - see Appendix A for areas included; (2) Number of days the Air Quality Index (AQI) exceeded 100 in 2002. An AQI value greater than 100 indicates that air quality would be in the unhealthful range on that day; (4) National Ambient Air Quality Standard; n/a not available; (a) Localized impact from an industrial source in Cleveland. Concentration from highest nonpoint source site in Cleveland (0.03 ug/m^3); (b) Localized impact from an industrial source in Columbus; (c) Localized impact from an industrial source in Dallas. Concentration from highest nonpoint source site is 0.11 ug/m^3 in Collin County); (d) Localized impact from an industrial source in Indianapolis; (e) Localized impact from an industrial source in Memphis; (f) Localized impact from an industrial source in Eagan, MN. Concentration from highest nonpoint source site in Minneapolis (0.01 ug/m^3); (g) Localized impact from an industrial source in Williamson County; (h) Localized impact from an industrial source in Omaha; (i)

Localized impact from an industrial source in Herculaneum, MO. Concentration from highest nonpoint source site in metro area is in Wood River, IL (0.04 ug/m^3); (j) Localized impact from an industrial source in Tampa. Concentration from highest nonpoint source site in metro area is in Pinellas, FL (0.01 ug/m^3);
Units: ppm = parts per million; ug/m^3 = micrograms per cubic meter
Source: EPA, Latest Findings on National Air Quality: 2002 Status and Trends, August 2003

Appendix C: Chambers of Commerce

Atlanta, GA

Metro Atlanta Chamber of
Commerce
235 Andrew Young International
Boulevard NW
Atlanta, GA 30303
Phone: (404) 880-9000
Fax: (404) 586-8497

Austin, TX

Greater Austin Chamber of
Commerce
210 Barton Springs Road
Suite 400
Austin, TX 78704
Phone: (512) 478-9383
Fax: (512) 478-6389

Baton Rouge, LA

Baton Rouge Chamber of
Commerce
564 Laurel Street
Baton Rouge, LA 70801
Phone: (225) 381-7125
Fax: (225) 336-4306

Economic Development
Corporation
1051 North 3rd Street
Room 156
Baton Rouge, LA 70802
Phone: (225) 342-5388
Fax: (225) 342-5389

Birmingham, AL

Birmingham Area Chamber of
Commerce
505 North 20th Street
Suite 200
Birmingham, AL 35203
Phone: (205) 324-2100
Fax: (205)324-2560

Chattanooga, TN

Chattanooga Chamber of Commerce
811 Broad Street
Chattanooga, TN 37402
Phone: (423) 756-2121
Fax: (423) 267-7242

Community Development
Department
100 East 11th Street
Room 104, City Hall Annex
Chattanooga, TN 37402
Phone: (423) 757-5133
Fax: (423) 425-6447

Charleston, SC

Central Midlands Council of
Government Research Data Center
236 Stoneridge Drive
Columbia, SC 29210
Phone: (803) 376-5390
Fax: (803) 376-5394

Columbia, SC

City of Columbia Office of
Economic Development
1201 Main Street
Suite 250
Columbia, SC 29201
Phone: (803) 734-2700
Fax: (803) 734-2702

Columbia Chamber of Commerce
930 Richland Street
Columbia, SC 29201
Phone: (803) 733-1110
Fax: (803) 733-1149

Dallas, TX

City of Dallas
Economic Development Department
1500 Marilla Street
Room 5C South
Dallas, TX 75201
Phone: (214) 670-1685
Fax: (214) 670-0158

Greater Dallas Chamber of
Commerce
700 North Pearl Street
Suite 1200
Dallas, TX 75201
Phone: (214) 746-6600
Fax: (214) 746-6799

El Paso, TX

City of El Paso Department
of Economic Development
2 Civic Center Plaza
El Paso, TX 79901
Phone: (915) 533-4284
Fax: (915) 541-1316

Greater El Paso Chamber of
Commerce
10 Civic Center Plaza
El Paso, TX 79901
Phone: (915) 534-0500
Fax: (915) 534-0510

Fort Lauderdale, FL

Fort Lauderdale Chamber of
Commerce
512 NE 3rd Avenue
Fort Lauderdale, FL 33301
Phone: (954) 462-6000
Fax: (954) 527-8766

Fort Worth, TX

City of Fort Worth
Economic Development
City Hall
900 Monroe Street
Suite 301
Fort Worth, TX 76102
Phone: (817) 871-6103
Fax: (817) 392-2431

Fort Worth Chamber of Commerce
777 Taylor Street
Suite 900
Fort Worth, TX 76102-4997
Phone: (817) 336-2491
Fax: (817) 877-4034

Houston, TX

Greater Houston Partnership
1200 Smith Street
Suite 700
Houston, TX 77002-4309
Phone: (713) 844-3600
Fax: (713) 844-0200

Huntsville, AL

Tennessee Valley Authority
Economic Development Corp.
4960 Corporate Drive
Suite 125F
Huntsville, AL 35805
Phone: (256) 430-4804
Fax: (256) 430-4801

Huntsville Chamber of Commerce
P.O. Box 408
Huntsville, AL 35804-0408
Phone: (256) 535-2000
Fax: (256) 535-2015

Jacksonville, FL

Jacksonville Chamber of Commerce
3 Independent Drive
Jacksonville, FL 32202
Phone: (904) 366-6600
Fax: (904) 632-0617

Knoxville, TN

Knoxville Chamber Partnership
601 West Summit Hill Drive
Suite 300
Knoxville, TN 37902-2021
Phone: (865) 637-4550
Fax: (865) 523-2071

Memphis, TN

Memphis Area Chamber of
Commerce
22 North Front Street
Suite 200
Memphis, TN 38103
Phone: (901) 543-3500
Fax: (901) 543-3510

Miami, FL

Greater Miami Chamber of
Commerce
Renaissance Hotel
1601 Biscayne Boulevard
Miami, FL 33132-1260
Phone: (305) 350-7700
Fax: (305) 374-6902

The Beacon Council
80 Southwest 8th Street
Suite 2400
Miami, FL 33130
Phone: (305) 579-1300
Fax: (305) 375-0271

Nashville, TN

Nashville Area Chamber of
Commerce
211 Commerce Street
Suite 100
Nashville, TN 37201
Phone: (615) 743-3000
Fax: (615) 256-3074

New Orleans, LA

New Orleans Regional Chamber of
Commerce
601 Poydras Street
Suite 1700
New Orleans, LA 70130
Phone: (504) 527-6900
Fax: (504) 527-6950

Orlando, FL

Metro Orlando Economic
Development Commission
of Mid-Florida
301 East Pine Street
Suite 900
Orlando, FL 32801
Phone: (407) 422-7159
Fax: (407) 843-9514

Orlando Regional Chamber of
Commerce
75 South Ivanhoe Boulevard
Orlando, FL 32804
Phone: (407) 425-1234
Fax: (407) 835-2500

Plano, TX

Plano Chamber of Commerce
1200 East 15th Street
Plano, TX 75074
Phone: (972) 424-7547
Fax: (972) 422-5182

Plano Economic Development
Board
4800 Preston Park Boulevard
Suite A-100
Plano, TX 75093
Phone: (972) 985-3700
Fax: (972) 985-3703

Saint Petersburg, FL

Saint Petersburg Area Chamber of
Commerce
100 2nd Avenue North
Suite 150
Saint Petersburg, FL 33701
Phone: (727) 821-4715
Fax: (727) 895-6326

San Antonio, TX

Greater San Antonio Chamber of
Commerce
P.O. Box 1628
San Antonio, TX 78296
Phone: (210) 229-2100
Fax: (210) 229-1600

San Antonio Economic
Development Department
P.O. Box 839966
San Antonio, TX 78283-3966
Phone: (210) 207-8080
Fax: (210) 207-8151

Savannah, GA

Economic Development Authority
P.O. Box 128
Savannah, GA 31402
Phone: (912) 447-8450
Fax: (912) 447-8455

Savannah Chamber of Commerce
P.O. Box 1628
Savannah, GA 31402-1628
Phone: (912) 644-6400
Fax: (912) 644-6498

Tampa, FL

Greater Tampa Chamber of
Commerce
P.O. Box 420
Tampa, FL 33601-0420
Phone: (813) 228-7777
Fax: (813) 223-7899

Appendix D: State Departments of Labor

Alabama

Department of Industrial Relations
649 Monroe Street
Mongomery, AL 36131
Phone: (334) 242-8055
Fax: (334) 242-3960

Florida

Florida Agency for Workforce
Innovation
107 East Madison Street
Suite 100
Tallahassee, FL 32399
Phone: (850) 488-7228
Fax: (850) 921-3223

Georgia

Georgia Department of Labor
Commisioner's Office
148 Andrew Young International
Boulevard, Northeast

Suite 600
Atlanta, GA 30303-1751
Phone: (404) 656-3011
Fax: (404) 656-2683

Louisiana

Louisiana Department of
Employment & Training
Research & Statistics
PO Box 94094
Baton Rouge, LA 70804-9094
Phone: (225) 342-3141
Fax: (225) 342-9192

South Carolina

South Carolina Department of Labor
Employment Security Commission
631 Hampton Street
Columbia, SC 29201
Phone: (803) 737-2660
Fax: (803) 737-2838

Tennessee

Tennesee Department of
Employment Security
Research and Statistics Division
500 James Robertson Parkway
11th Floor
Nashville, TN 37245-1000
Phone: (615) 741-2116
Fax: (615) 532-9434

Texas

Texas Labor Market
Information Department
and Workforce Commission
9001 IH-35 N
Suite 103-A
Austin, TX 78753
Phone: (512) 491-4800
Fax: (512) 491-4904

Universal Reference Publications
Statistical & Demographic Reference Books

Profiles of America: Facts, Figures & Statistics for Every Populated Place in the United States

Profiles of America is the only source that pulls together, in one place, statistical, historical and descriptive information about every place in the United States in an easy-to-use format. This award winning reference set, now in its second edition, compiles statistics and data from over 20 different sources – the latest census information has been included along with more than nine brand new statistical topics. This Four-Volume Set details over 40,000 places, from the biggest metropolis to the smallest unincorporated hamlet, and provides statistical details and information on over 50 different topics including Geography, Climate, Population, Vital Statistics, Economy, Income, Taxes, Education, Housing, Health & Environment, Public Safety, Newspapers, Transportation, Presidential Election Results and Information Contacts or Chambers of Commerce. Profiles are arranged, for ease-of-use, by state and then by county. Each county begins with a County-Wide Overview and is followed by information for each Community in that particular county. The Community Profiles within the county are arranged alphabetically. *Profiles of America* is a virtual snapshot of America at your fingertips and a unique compilation of information that will be widely used in any reference collection.

A Library Journal Best Reference Book *"An outstanding compilation."* –Library Journal

10,000 pages; Four Volume Set; Softcover ISBN 1-891482-80-7, $595.00

America's Top-Rated Smaller Cities, 2004

A perfect companion to *America's Top-Rated Cities*, *America's Top-Rated Smaller Cities* provides current, comprehensive business and living profiles of smaller cities (population 25,000-99,999) that have been cited as the best for business and living in the United States. Sixty cities make up this 2004 edition of *America's Top-Rated Smaller Cities*, all are top-ranked by Population Growth, Median Income, Unemployment Rate and Crime Rate. City reports reflect the most current data available on a wide-range of statistics, including Employment & Earnings, Household Income, Unemployment Rate, Population Characteristics, Taxes, Cost of Living, Education, Health Care, Public Safety, Recreation, Media, Air & Water Quality and much more. Plus, each city report contains a Background of the City, and an Overview of the State Finances. *America's Top-Rated Smaller Cities* offers a reliable, one-stop source for statistical data that, before now, could only be found scattered in hundreds of sources. This volume is designed for a wide range of readers: individuals considering relocating a residence or business; professionals considering expanding their business or changing careers; general and market researchers; real estate consultants; human resource personnel; urban planners and investors.

"Provides current, comprehensive statistical information in one easy-to-use source...
Recommended for public and academic libraries and specialized collections." –Library Journal

1,100 pages; Softcover ISBN 1-59237-043-8, $160.00

Crime in America's Top-Rated Cities, 2000

This volume includes over 20 years of crime statistics in all major crime categories: violent crimes, property crimes and total crime. *Crime in America's Top-Rated Cities* is conveniently arranged by city and covers 76 top-rated cities. *Crime in America's Top-Rated Cities* offers details that compare the number of crimes and crime rates for the city, suburbs and metro area along with national crime trends for violent, property and total crimes. Also, this handbook contains important information and statistics on Anti-Crime Programs, Crime Risk, Hate Crimes, Illegal Drugs, Law Enforcement, Correctional Facilities, Death Penalty Laws and much more. A much-needed resource for people who are relocating, business professionals, general researchers, the press, law enforcement officials and students of criminal justice.

"Data is easy to access and will save hours of searching." –Global Enforcement Review

832 pages; Softcover ISBN 1-891482-84-X, $155.00

The American Tally, 2003/04 Statistics & Comparative Rankings for U.S. Cities with Populations over 10,000

This important statistical handbook compiles, all in one place, comparative statistics on all U.S. cities and towns with a 10,000+ population. *The American Tally* provides statistical details on over 4,000 cities and towns and profiles how they compare with one another in Population Characteristics, Education, Language & Immigration, Income & Employment and Housing. Each section begins with an alphabetical listing of cities by state, allowing for quick access to both the statistics and relative rankings of any city. Next, the highest and lowest cities are listed in each statistic. These important, informative lists provide quick reference to which cities are at both extremes of the spectrum for each statistic. Unlike any other reference, *The American Tally* provides quick, easy access to comparative statistics – a must-have for any reference collection.

"A solid library reference." -Bookwatch

500 pages; Softcover ISBN 1-930956-29-0, $125.00

To preview any of our Directories Risk-Free for 30 days, call (800) 562-2139 or fax to (518) 789-0556

The Comparative Guide to American Suburbs, 2004

The Comparative Guide to American Suburbs is a one-stop source for Statistics on the 2,000+ suburban communities surrounding the 50 largest metropolitan areas – their population characteristics, income levels, economy, school system and important data on how they compare to one another. Organized into 50 Metropolitan Area chapters, each chapter contains an overview of the Metropolitan Area, a detailed Map followed by a comprehensive Statistical Profile of each Suburban Community, including Contact Information, Physical Characteristics, Population Characteristics, Income, Economy, Unemployment Rate, Cost of Living, Education, Chambers of Commerce and more. Next, statistical data is sorted into Ranking Tables that rank the suburbs by twenty different criteria, including Population, Per Capita Income, Unemployment Rate, Crime Rate, Cost of Living and more. *The Comparative Guide to American Suburbs* is the best source for locating data on suburbs. Those looking to relocate, as well as those doing preliminary market research, will find this an invaluable timesaving resource.

"Public and academic libraries will find this compilation useful...The work draws together figures from many sources and will be especially helpful for job relocation decisions." – Booklist

1,700 pages; Softcover ISBN 1-59237-004-7, $130.00

The Hispanic Databook: Statistics for all US Counties & Cities with Over 10,000 Population

The Hispanic Databook brings together a wide range of data relating to the Hispanic population for over 10,000 cities and counties. This second edition has been completely updated with figures from the latest census and has been broadly expanded to include dozens of new data elements. The Hispanic population in the United States has increased over 42% in the last 10 years. Persons of Hispanic origin account for 12.5% of the total population of the United States. These 35 million people are represented across the country, in every state. For ease of use, *The Hispanic Databook* is arranged alphabetically by state, then alphabetically by place name. More than 20 statistical data points are reported for each place, including Total Population, Percent Hispanic, Percent who Speak Spanish, Percent who Speak Only Spanish, Hispanic and Overall Per Capita Income, Hispanic and Overall Percent High School Graduates and Percent of Hispanic Population by Ancestry. A useful resource for those searching for demographics data, career search and relocation information and also for market research. With data ranging from Ancestry to Education, *The Hispanic Databook* presents a useful compilation of information that will be a much-needed resource in the reference collection of any public or academic library along with the marketing collection of any company whose primary focus in on the Hispanic population.

1,000 pages; Softcover ISBN 1-59237-008-X, $150.00

Ancestry in America: A Comparative Guide to Over 200 Ethnic Backgrounds

This brand new reference work pulls together thousands of comparative statistics on the Ethnic Backgrounds of all populated places in the United States with populations over 10,000. Never before has this kind of information been reported in a single volume. *Ancestry in America* is divided into two sections: Statistics by Place and Comparative Rankings. Section One, Statistics by Place, is made up of a list of over 200 ancestry and race categories arranged alphabetically by each of the 5,000 different places with populations over 10,000. The population number of the ancestry group in that city or town is provided along with the percent that group represents of the total population. This informative city-by-city section allows the user to quickly and easily explore the ethnic makeup of all major population bases in the United States. Section Two, Comparative Rankings, contains three tables for each ethnicity and race. In the first table, the top 150 populated places are ranked by population number for that particular ancestry group, regardless of population. In the second table, the top 150 populated places are ranked by the percent of the total population for that ancestry group. In the third table, those top 150 populated places with 10,000 population are ranked by population number for each ancestry group. These easy-to-navigate tables allow users to see ancestry population patterns and make city-by-city comparisons as well. Plus, as an added bonus with the purchase of *Ancestry in America*, a free companion CD-ROM is available that lists statistics and rankings for all of the 35,000 populated places in the United States. This brand new, information-packed resource will serve a wide-range or research requests for demographics, population characteristics, relocation information and much more. *Ancestry in America: A Comparative Guide to Over 200 Ethnic Backgrounds* will be an important acquisition to all reference collections.

1,500 pages; Softcover ISBN 1-59237-029-2, $225.00

The Value of a Dollar – Millennium Edition

A guide to practical economy, *The Value of a Dollar* records the actual prices of thousands of items that consumers purchased from the Civil War to the present, along with facts about investment options and income opportunities. The first edition, published by Gale Research in 1994, covered the period of 1860 to 1989. This second edition has been completely redesigned and revised and now contains two new chapters, 1990-1994 and 1995-1999. Each 5-year chapter includes a Historical Snapshot, Consumer Expenditures, Investments, Selected Income, Income/Standard Jobs, Food Basket, Standard Prices and Miscellany. This interesting and useful publication will be widely used in any reference collection.

"Recommended for high school, college and public libraries." –ARBA

493 pages; Hardcover ISBN 1-891482-49-1, $135.00

To preview any of our Directories Risk-Free for 30 days, call (800) 562-2139 or fax to (518) 789-0556

Working Americans 1880-1999
Volume I: The Working Class, Volume II: The Middle Class, Volume III: The Upper Class

Each of the volumes in the *Working Americans 1880-1999* series focuses on a particular class of Americans, The Working Class, The Middle Class and The Upper Class over the last 120 years. Chapters in each volume focus on one decade and profile three to five families. Family Profiles include real data on Income & Job Descriptions, Selected Prices of the Times, Annual Income, Annual Budgets, Family Finances, Life at Work, Life at Home, Life in the Community, Working Conditions, Cost of Living, Amusements and much more. Each chapter also contains an Economic Profile with Average Wages of other Professions, a selection of Typical Pricing, Key Events & Inventions, News Profiles, Articles from Local Media and Illustrations. The *Working Americans* series captures the lifestyles of each of the classes from the last twelve decades, covers a vast array of occupations and ethnic backgrounds and travels the entire nation. These interesting and useful compilations of portraits of the American Working, Middle and Upper Classes during the last 120 years will be an important addition to any high school, public or academic library reference collection.

"These interesting, unique compilations of economic and social facts, figures and graphs will support multiple research needs. They will engage and enlighten patrons in high school, public and academic library collections." —Booklist (on Volumes I and II)

Volume I: The Working Class ◆ 558 pages; Hardcover ISBN 1-891482-81-5, $145.00
Volume II: The Middle Class ◆ 591 pages; Hardcover ISBN 1-891482-72-6; $145.00
Volume III: The Upper Class ◆ 567 pages; Hardcover ISBN 1-930956-38-X, $145.00

Working Americans 1880-1999 Volume IV: Their Children

This Fourth Volume in the highly successful *Working Americans 1880-1999* series focuses on American children, decade by decade from 1880 to 1999. This interesting and useful volume introduces the reader to three children in each decade, one from each of the Working, Middle and Upper classes. Like the first three volumes in the series, the individual profiles are created from interviews, diaries, statistical studies, biographies and news reports. Profiles cover a broad range of ethnic backgrounds, geographic area and lifestyles – everything from an orphan in Memphis in 1882, following the Yellow Fever epidemic of 1878 to an eleven-year-old nephew of a beer baron and owner of the New York Yankees in New York City in 1921. Chapters also contain important supplementary materials including News Features as well as information on everything from Schools to Parks, Infectious Diseases to Childhood Fears along with Entertainment, Family Life and much more to provide an informative overview of the lifestyles of children from each decade. This interesting account of what life was like for Children in the Working, Middle and Upper Classes will be a welcome addition to the reference collection of any high school, public or academic library.

600 pages; Hardcover ISBN 1-930956-35-5, $145.00
Four Volume Set (Volumes I-IV), Hardcover ISBN 1-59237-017-9, $540.00

Working Americans 1880-2003 Volume V: Americans At War

Working Americans 1880-2003 Volume V: Americans At War is divided into 11 chapters, each covering a decade from 1880-2003 and examines the lives of Americans during the time of war, including declared conflicts, one-time military actions, protests, and preparations for war. Each decade includes several personal profiles, whether on the battlefield or on the homefront, that tell the stories of civilians, soldiers, and officers during the decade. The profiles examine: Life at Home; Life at Work; and Life in the Community. Each decade also includes an Economic Profile with statistical comparisons, a Historical Snapshot, News Profiles, local News Articles, and Illustrations that provide a solid historical background to the decade being examined. Profiles range widely not only geographically, but also emotionally, from that of a girl whose leg was torn off in a blast during WWI, to the boredom of being stationed in the Dakotas as the Indian Wars were drawing to a close. As in previous volumes of the *Working Americans* series, information is presented in narrative form, but hard facts and real-life situations back up each story. The basis of the profiles come from diaries, private print books, personal interviews, family histories, estate documents and magazine articles. For easy reference, *Working Americans 1880-2003 Volume V: Americans At War* includes an in-depth Subject Index. The *Working Americans* series has become an important reference for public libraries, academic libraries and high school libraries. This fifth volume will be a welcome addition to all of these types of reference collections.

600 pages; Hardcover ISBN 1-59237-024-1; $145.00
Five Volume Set (Volumes I-V), Hardcover ISBN 1-59237-034-9, $675.00

To preview any of our Directories Risk-Free for 30 days, call (800) 562-2139 or fax to (518) 789-0556

The Comparative Guide to American Elementary & Secondary Schools, 2004/05

The only guide of its kind, this award winning compilation offers a snapshot profile of every public school district in the United States serving 1,500 or more students – more than 5,900 districts are covered. Organized alphabetically by district within state, each chapter begins with a Statistical Overview of the state. Each district listing includes contact information (name, address, phone number and web site) plus Grades Served, the Numbers of Students and Teachers and the Number of Regular, Special Education, Alternative and Vocational Schools in the district along with statistics on Student/Classroom Teacher Ratios, Drop Out Rates, Ethnicity, the Numbers of Librarians and Guidance Counselors and District Expenditures per student. As an added bonus, *The Comparative Guide to American Elementary and Secondary Schools* provides important ranking tables, both by state and nationally, for each data element. For easy navigation through this wealth of information, this handbook contains a useful City Index that lists all districts that operate schools within a city. These important comparative statistics are necessary for anyone considering relocation or doing comparative research on their own district and would be a perfect acquisition for any public library or school district library.

"This straightforward guide is an easy way to find general information. Valuable for academic and large public library collections." –ARBA

2,400 pages; Softcover ISBN 1-59237-047-0, $125.00

The Environmental Resource Handbook, 2004

The Environmental Resource Handbook, now in its second edition, is the most up-to-date and comprehensive source for Environmental Resources and Statistics. Section I: Resources provides detailed contact information for thousands of information sources, including Associations & Organizations, Awards & Honors, Conferences, Foundations & Grants, Environmental Health, Government Agencies, National Parks & Wildlife Refuges, Publications, Research Centers, Educational Programs, Green Product Catalogs, Consultants and much more. Section II: Statistics, provides statistics and rankings on hundreds of important topics, including Children's Environmental Index, Municipal Finances, Toxic Chemicals, Recycling, Climate, Air & Water Quality and more. This kind of up-to-date environmental data, all in one place, is not available anywhere else on the market place today. This vast compilation of resources and statistics is a must-have for all public and academic libraries as well as any organization with a primary focus on the environment.

"...the intrinsic value of the information make it worth consideration by libraries with environmental collections and environmentally concerned users." –Booklist

1,000 pages; Softcover ISBN 1-59237-030-6, $155.00 ◆ Online Database $300.00

Weather America, A Thirty-Year Summary of Statistical Weather Data and Rankings, 2001

This valuable resource provides extensive climatological data for over 4,000 National and Cooperative Weather Stations throughout the United States. *Weather America* begins with a new Major Storms section that details major storm events of the nation and a National Rankings section that details rankings for several data elements, such as Maximum Temperature and Precipitation. The main body of *Weather America* is organized into 50 state sections. Each section provides a Data Table on each Weather Station, organized alphabetically, that provides statistics on Maximum and Minimum Temperatures, Precipitation, Snowfall, Extreme Temperatures, Foggy Days, Humidity and more. State sections contain two brand new features in this edition – a City Index and a narrative Description of the climatic conditions of the state. Each section also includes a revised Map of the State that includes not only weather stations, but cities and towns.

"Best Reference Book of the Year." –Library Journal

2,013 pages; Softcover ISBN 1-891482-29-7, $175.00

Education Directories

Educators Resource Directory, 2003/04

Educators Resource Directory is a comprehensive resource that provides the educational professional with thousands of resources and statistical data for professional development. This directory saves hours of research time by providing immediate access to Associations & Organizations, Conferences & Trade Shows, Educational Research Centers, Employment Opportunities & Teaching Abroad, School Library Services, Scholarships, Financial Resources, Professional Consultants, Computer Software & Testing Resources and much more. Plus, this comprehensive directory also includes a section on Statistics and Rankings with over 100 tables, including statistics on Average Teacher Salaries, SAT/ACT scores, Revenues & Expenditures and more. These important statistics will allow the user to see how their school rates among others, make relocation decisions and so much more. In addition to the Entry & Publisher Index, Geographic Index and Web Sites Index, our editors have added a Subject & Grade Index to this 2003/04 edition – so now it's even quicker and easier to locate information. *Educators Resource Directory* will be a well-used addition to the reference collection of any school district, education department or public library.

"Recommended for all collections that serve elementary and secondary school professionals." –Choice

1,000 pages; Softcover ISBN 1-59237-002-0, $145.00 ◆ Online Database $195.00 ◆ Online Database & Directory Combo $280.00

To preview any of our Directories Risk-Free for 30 days, call (800) 562-2139 or fax to (518) 789-0556

Sedgwick Press
Health Directories

The Complete Mental Health Directory, 2004

This is the most comprehensive resource covering the field of behavioral health, with critical information for both the layman and the mental health professional. For the layman, this directory offers understandable descriptions of 25 Mental Health Disorders as well as detailed information on Associations, Media, Support Groups and Mental Health Facilities. For the professional, *The Complete Mental Health Directory* offers critical and comprehensive information on Managed Care Organizations, Information Systems, Government Agencies and Provider Organizations. This comprehensive volume of needed information will be widely used in any reference collection.

"... the strength of this directory is that it consolidates widely dispersed information into a single volume." –Booklist

800 pages; Softcover ISBN 1-59237-046-2, $165.00 ♦ Online Database $215.00 ♦ Online & Directory Combo $300.00

The Complete Directory for People with Disabilities, 2004

A wealth of information, now in one comprehensive sourcebook. Completely updated for 2004, this edition contains more information than ever before, including thousands of new entries and enhancements to existing entries and thousands of additional web sites and e-mail addresses. This up-to-date directory is the most comprehensive resource available for people with disabilities, detailing Independent Living Centers, Rehabilitation Facilities, State & Federal Agencies, Associations, Support Groups, Periodicals & Books, Assistive Devices, Employment & Education Programs, Camps and Travel Groups. Each year, more libraries, schools, colleges, hospitals, rehabilitation centers and individuals add *The Complete Directory for People with Disabilities* to their collections, making sure that this information is readily available to the families, individuals and professionals who can benefit most from the amazing wealth of resources cataloged here.

"No other reference tool exists to meet the special needs of the disabled in one convenient resource for information." –Library Journal

1,200 pages; Softcover ISBN 1-59237-007-1, $165.00 ♦ Online Database $215.00 ♦ Online Database & Directory Combo $300.00

The Complete Directory for People with Chronic Illness, 2003/04

Thousands of hours of research have gone into this completely updated 2003/04 edition – several new chapters have been added along with thousands of new entries and enhancements to existing entries. Plus, each chronic illness chapter has been reviewed by an medical expert in the field. This widely-hailed directory is structured around the 90 most prevalent chronic illnesses – from Asthma to Cancer to Wilson's Disease – and provides a comprehensive overview of the support services and information resources available for people diagnosed with a chronic illness. Each chronic illness has its own chapter and contains a brief description in layman's language, followed by important resources for National & Local Organizations, State Agencies, Newsletters, Books & Periodicals, Libraries & Research Centers, Support Groups & Hotlines, Web Sites and much more. This directory is an important resource for health care professionals, the collections of hospital and health care libraries, as well as an invaluable tool for people with a chronic illness and their support network.

"A must purchase for all hospital and health care libraries and is strongly recommended for all public library reference departments." –ARBA

1,200 pages; Softcover ISBN 1-930956-83-5, $165.00 ♦ Online Database $215.00 ♦ Online Database & Directory Combo $300.00

The Complete Learning Disabilities Directory, 2003/04

The Complete Learning Disabilities Directory is the most comprehensive database of Programs, Services, Curriculum Materials, Professional Meetings & Resources, Camps, Newsletters and Support Groups for teachers, students and families concerned with learning disabilities. This information-packed directory includes information about Associations & Organizations, Schools, Colleges, Testing Materials, Government Agencies, Legal Resources and much more. For quick, easy access to information, this directory contains four indexes: Entry Name Index, Subject Index and Geographic Index. With every passing year, the field of learning disabilities attracts more attention and the network of caring, committed and knowledgeable professionals grows every day. This directory is an invaluable research tool for these parents, students and professionals.

"Due to its wealth and depth of coverage, parents, teachers and others... should find this an invaluable resource." –Booklist

900 pages; Softcover ISBN 1-930956-79-7, $145.00 ♦ Online Database $195.00 ♦ Online Database & Directory Combo $280.00

To preview any of our Directories Risk-Free for 30 days, call (800) 562-2139 or fax to (518) 789-0556

The Directory of Drug & Alcohol Residential Rehabilitation Facilities, 2004

This brand new directory is the first-ever resource to bring together, all in one place, data on the thousands of drug and alcohol residential rehabilitation facilities in the United States. *The Directory of Drug & Alcohol Residential Rehabilitation Facilities* covers over 6,000 facilities, with detailed contact information for each one, including mailing address, phone and fax numbers, email addresses and web sites, mission statement, type of treatment programs, cost, average length of stay, numbers of residents and counselors, accreditation, insurance plans accepted, type of environment, religious affiliation, education components and much more. It also contains a helpful chapter on General Resources that provides contact information for Associations, Print & Electronic Media, Support Groups and Conferences. Multiple indexes allow the user to pinpoint the facilities that meet very specific criteria. This time-saving tool is what so many counselors, parents and medical professionals have been asking for. *The Directory of Drug & Alcohol Residential Rehabilitation Facilities* will be a helpful tool in locating the right source for treatment for a wide range of individuals. This comprehensive directory will be an important acquisition for all reference collections: public and academic libraries, case managers, social workers, state agencies and many more.

1,000 pages; Softcover ISBN 1-59237-031-4, $165.00

Older Americans Information Directory, 2004/05

Completely updated for 2004/05, this Fifth Edition has been completely revised and now contains 1,000 new listings, over 8,000 updates to existing listings and over 3,000 brand new e-mail addresses and web sites. You'll find important resources for Older Americans including National, Regional, State & Local Organizations, Government Agencies, Research Centers, Libraries & Information Centers, Legal Resources, Discount Travel Information, Continuing Education Programs, Disability Aids & Assistive Devices, Health, Print Media and Electronic Media. Three indexes: Entry Index, Subject Index and Geographic Index make it easy to find just the right source of information. This comprehensive guide to resources for Older Americans will be a welcome addition to any reference collection.

"Highly recommended for academic, public, health science and consumer libraries…" –Choice

1,200 pages; Softcover ISBN 1-59237-037-3, $165.00 ◆ Online Database $215.00 ◆ Online Database & Directory Combo $300.00

The Complete Directory for Pediatric Disorders, 2002/03

This important directory provides parents and caregivers with information about Pediatric Conditions, Disorders, Diseases and Disabilities, including Blood Disorders, Bone & Spinal Disorders, Brain Defects & Abnormalities, Chromosomal Disorders, Congenital Heart Defects, Movement Disorders, Neuromuscular Disorders and Pediatric Tumors & Cancers. This carefully written directory offers: understandable Descriptions of 15 major bodily systems; Descriptions of more than 200 Disorders and a Resources Section, detailing National Agencies & Associations, State Associations, Online Services, Libraries & Resource Centers, Research Centers, Support Groups & Hotlines, Camps, Books and Periodicals. This resource will provide immediate access to information crucial to families and caregivers when coping with children's illnesses.

"Recommended for public and consumer health libraries." –Library Journal

1,120 pages; Softcover ISBN 1-930956-61-4, $165.00 ◆ Online Database $215.00 ◆ Online Database & Directory Combo $300.00

The Complete Directory for People with Rare Disorders, 2002/03

This outstanding reference is produced in conjunction with the National Organization for Rare Disorders to provide comprehensive and needed access to important information on over 1,000 rare disorders, including Cancers and Muscular, Genetic and Blood Disorders. An informative Disorder Description is provided for each of the 1,100 disorders (rare Cancers and Muscular, Genetic and Blood Disorders) followed by information on National and State Organizations dealing with a particular disorder, Umbrella Organizations that cover a wide range of disorders, the Publications that can be useful when researching a disorder and the Government Agencies to contact. Detailed and up-to-date listings contain mailing address, phone and fax numbers, web sites and e-mail addresses along with a description. For quick, easy access to information, this directory contains two indexes: Entry Name Index and Acronym/Keyword Index along with an informative Guide for Rare Disorder Advocates. The Complete Directory for People with Rare Disorders will be an invaluable tool for the thousands of families that have been struck with a rare or "orphan" disease, who feel that they have no place to turn and will be a much-used addition to the reference collection of any public or academic library.

"Quick access to information… public libraries and hospital patient libraries will find this a useful resource in directing users to support groups or agencies dealing with a rare disorder." –Booklist

726 pages; Softcover ISBN 1-891482-18-1, $165.00

Sedgwick Press
Hospital & Health Plan Directories

The Directory of Hospital Personnel, 2004

The Directory of Hospital Personnel is the best resource you can have at your fingertips when researching or marketing a product or service to the hospital market. A "Who's Who" of the hospital universe, this directory puts you in touch with over 150,000 key decision-makers. With 100% verification of data you can rest assured that you will reach the right person with just one call. Every hospital in the U.S. is profiled, listed alphabetically by city within state. *The Directory of Hospital Personnel* is the only complete source for key hospital decision-makers by name. Whether you want to define or restructure sales territories... locate hospitals with the purchasing power to accept your proposals... keep track of important contacts or colleagues... or find information on which insurance plans are accepted, *The Directory of Hospital Personnel* gives you the information you need – easily, efficiently, effectively and accurately.

"Recommended for college, university and medical libraries." -ARBA

2,500 pages; Softcover ISBN 1-59237-026-8 $275.00 ♦ Online Database $545.00 ♦ Online Database & Directory Combo, $650.00

The Directory of Health Care Group Purchasing Organizations, 2004

This comprehensive directory provides the important data you need to get in touch with over 1,000 Group Purchasing Organizations. By providing in-depth information on this growing market and its members, *The Directory of Health Care Group Purchasing Organizations* fills a major need for the most accurate and comprehensive information on over 1,000 GPOs – Mailing Address, Phone & Fax Numbers, E-mail Addresses, Key Contacts, Purchasing Agents, Group Descriptions, Membership Categorization, Standard Vendor Proposal Requirements, Membership Fees & Terms, Expanded Services, Total Member Beds & Outpatient Visits represented and more. With its comprehensive and detailed information on each purchasing organization, *The Directory of Health Care Group Purchasing Organizations* is the go-to source for anyone looking to target this market.

"The information is clearly arranged and easy to access...recommended for those needing this very specialized information." –ARBA

1,000 pages; Softcover ISBN 1-59237-036-5, $325.00 ♦ Online Database, $650.00 ♦ Online Database & Directory Combo, $750.00

The HMO/PPO Directory, 2004

The HMO/PPO Directory is a comprehensive source that provides detailed information about Health Maintenance Organizations and Preferred Provider Organizations nationwide. This comprehensive directory details more information about more managed health care organizations than ever before. Over 1,100 HMOs, PPOs and affiliated companies are listed, arranged alphabetically by state. Detailed listings include Key Contact Information, Prescription Drug Benefits, Enrollment, Geographical Areas served, Affiliated Physicians & Hospitals, Federal Qualifications, Status, Year Founded, Managed Care Partners, Employer References, Fees & Payment Information and more. Plus, five years of historical information is included related to Revenues, Net Income, Medical Loss Ratios, Membership Enrollment and Number of Patient Complaints. *The HMO/PPO Directory* provides the most comprehensive information on the most companies available on the market place today.

"Helpful to individuals requesting certain HMO/PPO issues such as co-payment costs, subscription costs and patient complaints. Individuals concerned (or those with questions) about their insurance may find this text to be of use to them." -ARBA

600 pages; Softcover ISBN 1-59237-022-5, $250.00 ♦ Online Database, $495.00 ♦ Online Database & Directory Combo, $600.00

The Directory of Independent Ambulatory Care Centers, 2002/03

This first edition of *The Directory of Independent Ambulatory Care Centers* provides access to detailed information that, before now, could only be found scattered in hundreds of different sources. This comprehensive and up-to-date directory pulls together a vast array of contact information for over 7,200 Ambulatory Surgery Centers, Ambulatory General and Urgent Care Clinics, and Diagnostic Imaging Centers that are not affiliated with a hospital or major medical center. Detailed listings include Mailing Address, Phone & Fax Numbers, E-mail and Web Site addresses, Contact Name and Phone Numbers of the Medical Director and other Key Executives and Purchasing Agents, Specialties & Services Offered, Year Founded, Numbers of Employees and Surgeons, Number of Operating Rooms, Number of Cases seen per year, Overnight Options, Contracted Services and much more. Listings are arranged by State, by Center Category and then alphabetically by Organization Name. *The Directory of Independent Ambulatory Care Centers* is a must-have resource for anyone marketing a product or service to this important industry and will be an invaluable tool for those searching for a local care center that will meet their specific needs.

"Among the numerous hospital directories, no other provides information on independent ambulatory centers. A handy, well-organized resource that would be useful in medical center libraries and public libraries." –Choice

986 pages; Softcover ISBN 1-930956-90-8, $185.00 ♦ Online Database, $365.00 ♦ Online Database & Directory Combo, $450.00

To preview any of our Directories Risk-Free for 30 days, call (800) 562-2139 or fax to (518) 789-0556

Grey House Publishing
Business Directories

The Directory of Business Information Resources, 2003/04

With 100% verification, over 1,000 new listings and more than 12,000 updates, this 2003/04 edition of *The Directory of Business Information Resources* is the most up-to-date source for contacts in over 98 business areas – from advertising and agriculture to utilities and wholesalers. This carefully researched volume details: the Associations representing each industry; the Newsletters that keep members current; the Magazines and Journals - with their "Special Issues" - that are important to the trade, the Conventions that are "must attends," Databases, Directories and Industry Web Sites that provide access to must-have marketing resources. Includes contact names, phone & fax numbers, web sites and e-mail addresses. This one-volume resource is a gold mine of information and would be a welcome addition to any reference collection.

"This is a most useful and easy-to-use addition to any researcher's library." – The Information Professionals Institute

2,500 pages; Softcover ISBN 1-59237-000-4, $250.00 ♦ Online Database $495.00

Nations of the World, 2004 A Political, Economic and Business Handbook

This completely revised Third Edition covers all the nations of the world in an easy-to-use, single volume. Each nation is profiled in a single chapter that includes Key Facts, Political & Economic Issues, a Country Profile and Business Information. In this fast-changing world, it is extremely important to make sure that the most up-to-date information is included in your reference collection. This 2004 edition is just the answer. Each of the 200+ country chapters have been carefully reviewed by a political expert to make sure that the text reflects the most current information on Politics, Travel Advisories, Economics and more. You'll find such vital information as a Country Map, Population Characteristics, Inflation, Agricultural Production, Foreign Debt, Political History, Foreign Policy, Regional Insecurity, Economics, Trade & Tourism, Historical Profile, Political Systems, Ethnicity, Languages, Media, Climate, Hotels, Chambers of Commerce, Banking, Travel Information and more. Five Regional Chapters follow the main text and include a Regional Map, an Introductory Article, Key Indicators and Currencies for the Region. New for 2004, an all-inclusive CD-ROM is available as a companion to the printed text. Noted for its sophisticated, up-to-date and reliable compilation of political, economic and business information, this brand new edition will be an important acquisition to any public, academic or special library reference collection.

"A useful addition to both general reference collections and business collections." –RUSQ

1,700 pages; Print Version Only Softcover ISBN 1-59237-006-3, $145.00 ♦ Print Version and CD-ROM $180.00

International Business and Trade Directories, 2003/04

Completely updated, the Third Edition of *International Business and Trade Directories* now contains more than 10,000 entries, over 2,000 more than the last edition, making this directory the most comprehensive resource of the worlds business and trade directories. Entries include content descriptions, price, publisher's name and address, web site and e-mail addresses, phone and fax numbers and editorial staff. Organized by industry group, and then by region, this resource puts over 10,000 industry-specific business and trade directories at the reader's fingertips. Three indexes are included for quick access to information: Geographic Index, Publisher Index and Title Index. Public, college and corporate libraries, as well as individuals and corporations seeking critical market information will want to add this directory to their marketing collection.

1,800 pages; Softcover ISBN 1-930956-63-0, $225.00 ♦ Online Database (includes a free copy of the directory) $450.00

Sports Market Place Directory, 2004

For over 20 years, this comprehensive, up-to-date directory has offered direct access to the Who, What, When & Where of the Sports Industry. With over 20,000 updates and enhancements, this 2004 *Sports Market Place Directory* is the most detailed, comprehensive and current sports business reference source available. In 1,800 information-packed pages, *Sports Market Place Directory* profiles contact information and key executives for: Single Sport Organizations, Professional Leagues, Multi-Sport Organizations, Disabled Sports, High School & Youth Sports, Military Sports, Olympic Organizations, Media, Sponsors, Sponsorship & Marketing Event Agencies, Event & Meeting Calendars, Professional Services, College Sports, Manufacturers & Retailers, Facilities and much more. *The Sports Market Place Directory* provides organization's contact information with detailed descriptions including: Key Contacts, physical, mailing, email and web addresses plus phone and fax numbers. Plus, nine important indexes make sure that you can find the information you're looking for quickly and easily: Entry Index, Single Sport Index, Media Index, Sponsor Index, Agency Index, Manufacturers Index, Brand Name Index, Facilities Index and Executive/Geographic Index. For over twenty years, *The Sports Market Place Directory* has assisted thousands of individuals in their pursuit of a career in the sports industry.

1,800 pages; Softcover ISBN 1-59237-048-9, $225.00 ♦ CD-ROM $479.00 ♦ Online Database $479.00

To preview any of our Directories Risk-Free for 30 days, call (800) 562-2139 or fax to (518) 789-0556

The Directory of Venture Capital Firms, 2004

This edition has been extensively updated and broadly expanded to offer direct access to over 2,800 Domestic and International Venture Capital Firms, including address, phone & fax numbers, e-mail addresses and web sites for both primary and branch locations. Entries include details on the firm's Mission Statement, Industry Group Preferences, Geographic Preferences, Average and Minimum Investments and Investment Criteria. You'll also find details that are available nowhere else, including the Firm's Portfolio Companies and extensive information on each of the firm's Managing Partners, such as Education, Professional Background and Directorships held, along with the Partner's E-mail Address. *The Directory of Venture Capital Firms* offers five important indexes: Geographic Index, Executive Name Index, Portfolio Company Index, Industry Preference Index and College & University Index. With its comprehensive coverage and detailed, extensive information on each company, *The Directory of Venture Capital Firms* is an important addition to any finance collection.

> *"The sheer number of listings, the descriptive information provided and the outstanding indexing make this directory a better value than its principal competitor, Pratt's Guide to Venture Capital Sources. Recommended for business collections in large public, academic and business libraries." –Choice*

1,300 pages; Softcover ISBN 1-59237-025-X, $450.00 ♦ Online Database (includes a free copy of the directory) $889.00

The Directory of Mail Order Catalogs, 2004

Published since 1981, this Eighteenth Edition features 100% verification of data and is the premier source of information on the mail order catalog industry. Details over 12,000 consumer catalog companies with 44 different product chapters from Animals to Toys & Games. Contains detailed contact information including e-mail addresses and web sites along with important business details such as employee size, years in business, sales volume, catalog size, number of catalogs mailed and more. Four indexes provide quick access to information: Catalog & Company Name Index, Geographic Index, Product Index and Web Sites Index.

> *"This is a godsend for those looking for information." –Reference Book Review*
> *"The scope and arrangement make this directory useful. Certainly the broad coverage of subjects is not available elsewhere in a single-volume format." –Booklist*

1,700 pages; Softcover ISBN 1-59237-027-6, $250.00 ♦ Online Database (includes a free copy of the directory) $495.00

The Directory of Business to Business Catalogs, 2004

The completely updated 2004 *Directory of Business to Business Catalogs*, provides details on over 6,000 suppliers of everything from computers to laboratory supplies… office products to office design… marketing resources to safety equipment… landscaping to maintenance suppliers… building construction and much more. Detailed entries offer mailing address, phone & fax numbers, e-mail addresses, web sites, key contacts, sales volume, employee size, catalog printing information and more. Jut about every kind of product a business needs in its day-to-day operations is covered in this carefully-researched volume. Three indexes are provided for at-a-glance access to information: Catalog & Company Name Index, Geographic Index and Web Sites Index.

> *"Much smaller and easier to use than the Thomas Register or Sweet's Catalog, it is an excellent choice for libraries… wishing to supplement their business supplier resources." –Booklist*

800 pages; Softcover ISBN 1-59237-028-4, $165.00 ♦ Online Database (includes a free copy of the directory) $325.00

Thomas Food and Beverage Market Place, 2004

Thomas Food and Beverage Market Place is bigger and better than ever with thousands of new companies, thousands of updates to existing companies and two revised and enhanced product category indexes. This comprehensive directory profiles over 18,000 Food & Beverage Manufacturers, 12,000 Equipment & Supply Companies, 2,200 Transportation & Warehouse Companies, 2,000 Brokers & Wholesalers, 8,000 Importers & Exporters, 900 Industry Resources and hundreds of Mail Order Catalogs. Listings include detailed Contact Information, Sales Volumes, Key Contacts, Brand & Product Information, Packaging Details and much more. *Thomas Food and Beverage Market Place* is available as a three-volume printed set, a subscription-based Online Database via the Internet, on CD-ROM, as well as mailing lists and a licensable database.

> *"An essential purchase for those in the food industry but will also be useful in public libraries where needed. Much of the information will be difficult and time consuming to locate without this handy three-volume ready-reference source." –ARBA*

8,500 pages, 3 Volume Set; Softcover ISBN 1-59237-018-7, $495.00 ♦ CD-ROM $695.00 ♦
CD-ROM & 3 Volume Set Combo $895.00 ♦ Online Database $695.00 ♦ Online Database & 3 Volume Set Combo, $895.00

To preview any of our Directories Risk-Free for 30 days, call (800) 562-2139 or fax to (518) 789-0556

The Grey House Safety & Security Directory, 2004

The Grey House Safety & Security Directory is the most comprehensive reference tool and buyer's guide for the safety and security industry. Published continuously since 1943 as *Best's Safety & Security Directory*, Grey House acquired the title in 2002. Arranged by safety topic, each chapter begins with OSHA regulations for the topic, followed by Training Articles written by top professionals in the field and Self-Inspection Checklists. Next, each topic contains Buyer's Guide sections that feature related products and services. Topics include Administration, Insurance, Loss Control & Consulting, Protective Equipment & Apparel, Noise & Vibration, Facilities Monitoring & Maintenance, Employee Health Maintenance & Ergonomics, Retail Food Services, Machine Guards, Process Guidelines & Tool Handling, Ordinary Materials Handling, Hazardous Materials Handling, Workplace Preparation & Maintenance, Electrical Lighting & Safety, Fire & Rescue and Security. The Buyer's Guide sections are carefully indexed within each topic area to ensure that you can find the supplies needed to meet OSHA's regulations. Six important indexes make finding information and product manufacturers quick and easy: Geographical Index of Manufacturers and Distributors, Company Profile Index, Brand Name Index, Product Index, Index of Web Sites and Index of Advertisers. This comprehensive, up-to-date reference will provide every tool necessary to make sure a business is in compliance with OSHA regulations and locate the products and services needed to meet those regulations.

1,500 pages, 2 Volume Set; Softcover ISBN 1-59237-033-0, $225.00

The Grey House Homeland Security Directory, 2004

This brand new directory features the latest contact information for government and private organizations involved with Homeland Security along with the latest product information and provides detailed profiles of nearly 1,000 Federal & State Organizations & Agencies and over 3,000 Officials and Key Executives involved with Homeland Security. These listings are incredibly detailed and include Mailing Address, Phone & Fax Numbers, Email Addresses & Web Sites, a complete Description of the Agency and a complete list of the Officials and Key Executives associated with the Agency. Next, *The Grey House Homeland Security Directory* provides the go-to source for Homeland Security Products & Services. This section features over 2,000 Companies that provide Consulting, Products or Services. With this Buyer's Guide at their fingertips, users can locate suppliers of everything from Training Materials to Access Controls, from Perimeter Security to BioTerrorism Countermeasures and everything in between – complete with contact information and product descriptions. A handy Product Locator Index is provided to quickly and easily locate suppliers of a particular product. Lastly, an Information Resources Section provides immediate access to contact information for hundreds of Associations, Newsletters, Magazines, Trade Shows, Databases and Directories that focus on Homeland Security. This comprehensive, information-packed resource will be a welcome tool for any company or agency that is in need of Homeland Security information and will be a necessary acquisition for the reference collection of all public libraries and large school districts.

800 pages; Softcover ISBN 1-59237-035-7, $195.00 ◆ Online Database (includes a free copy of the directory) $385.00

The Grey House Performing Arts Directory, 2004

The Grey House Performing Arts Directory is the most comprehensive resource covering the Performing Arts. This important directory provides current information on over 8,500 Dance Companies, Instrumental Music Programs, Opera Companies, Choral Groups, Theater Companies, Performing Arts Series and Performing Arts Facilities. Plus, this edition now contains a brand new section on Artist Management Groups. In addition to mailing address, phone & fax numbers, e-mail addresses and web sites, dozens of other fields of available information include mission statement, key contacts, facilities, seating capacity, season, attendance and more. *The Grey House Performing Arts Directory* pulls together thousands of Performing Arts Organizations, Facilities and Information Resources into an easy-to-use source – this kind of comprehensiveness and extensive detail is not available in any resource on the market place today.

"An immensely useful and user-friendly new reference tool... recommended for public, academic and certain special library reference collections." –Booklist

1,500 pages; Softcover ISBN 1-59237-023-3, $170.00 ◆ Online Database $335.00

Research Services Directory, 2003/04 Commercial & Corporate Research Centers

This Ninth Edition provides access to well over 8,000 independent Commercial Research Firms, Corporate Research Centers and Laboratories offering contract services for hands-on, basic or applied research. *Research Services Directory* covers the thousands of types of research companies, including Biotechnology & Pharmaceutical Developers, Consumer Product Research, Defense Contractors, Electronics & Software Engineers, Think Tanks, Forensic Investigators, Independent Commercial Laboratories, Information Brokers, Market & Survey Research Companies, Medical Diagnostic Facilities, Product Research & Development Firms and more. Each entry provides the company's name, mailing address, phone & fax numbers, key contacts, web site, e-mail address, as well as a company description and research and technical fields served. Four indexes provide immediate access to this wealth of information: Research Firms Index, Geographic Index, Personnel Name Index and Subject Index.

"An important source for organizations in need of information about laboratories, individuals and other facilities." –ARBA

1,400 pages; Softcover ISBN 1-59237-003-9, $395.00 ◆ Online Database (includes a free copy of the directory) $850.00

To preview any of our Directories Risk-Free for 30 days, call (800) 562-2139 or fax to (518) 789-0556